Red Hat® Linux®
System
Administration

Thomas Schenk, et al.

SAMS

Unleashed

Red Hat® Linux® System Administration Unleashed

Copyright © 2000 by Sams Publishing

International Standard Book Number: 0-672-31755-9

Library of Congress Catalog Card Number: 99-64103

Printed in the United States of America

First Printing: June 2000

02 01 00   4 3 2 1

This publication was produced using the Advent 3B2 Publishing System.

Trademarks

Warning and Disclaimer

ASSOCIATE PUBLISHER
Michael Stephens

EXECUTIVE EDITOR
Rosemarie Graham

DEVELOPMENT EDITOR
Jeff Durham

MANAGING EDITOR
Matt Purcell

PROJECT EDITOR
George E. Nedeff

COPY EDITOR
Kim Cofer

INDEXER
Heather McNeill

PROOFREADERS
Julie Cook
Tony Reitz

TECHNICAL EDITORS
Jason Carlyle
Rick Crelia
Max Kupiak

TEAM COORDINATOR
Pamalee Nelson

MEDIA DEVELOPER
Dan Scherf

INTERIOR DESIGN
Gary Adair

COVER DESIGN
Aren Howell

COPYWRITER
Eric Borgert

3B2 DESIGN
Daniela Radersdorf

3B2 PRODUCTION
Brandon Allen
Susan Geiselman
Cheryl Lynch

Contents at a Glance

Introduction   **1**

PART I   Introduction to Linux System Administration   5

1   What Is a Systems Administrator?   **7**

2   Essential Tools for System Administrators   **17**

PART II   Linux Essentials   47

3   Installation Strategies   **49**

4   Where Do I Find...?   **81**

5   Starting Up and Shutting Down   **111**

6   System Failure Diagnosis and Recovery   **141**

PART III   Filesystem and Disk Management   171

7   Filesystems   **173**

8   Adding or Replacing Disks   **211**

9   Linux and RAID   **227**

10   Removable Media Devices   **271**

PART IV   Backup and Recovery   297

11   What to Backup and How   **299**

12   Media Selection and Storage   **333**

13   Recovery from Data Loss   **345**

PART V   Networking   369

14   TCP/IP and Ethernet   **371**

15   Sharing Resources (Print and File Services)   **409**

16   Network Monitoring   **435**

17   Integrating with Windows NT Networks   *461*

18   Integrating with Other Network Operating Systems   **493**

PART VI   Internet Services   527

19   Setting Up Internet Services   **529**

20   Electronic Mail   **553**

21   FTP and Anonymous FTP   **609**

22   Web Serving   **637**

23   News Services   **671**

24   Internet Telephony and Conferencing   **713**

25   Security Principles   **739**

PART VII   Security and Firewalls   783

26   Firewall Strategies   **785**

27   The Security Administrator's Toolbox   **819**

28   I've Been Hacked: What Now?   **841**

PART VIII   User Management and Interaction   859

29   Users and Groups   **861**

30   Helping Users   **895**

PART IX   Shells, Scripting, and Automation   923

31   Shells   **925**

32   Shell Scripting   **967**

33   Automation   **1017**

PART X   System Tuning and Kernel Building   1045

34   Tuning Your Linux System   **1047**

35   Customizing the Linux Kernel   **1081**

36   Centennial School District, Portland, Oregon   **1135**

Index   1165

Contents

PART I   Introduction to Linux System Administration   5

1   What Is a Systems Administrator?   7

The Linux Systems Administrator 8

    A Simple Definition 8

    The SAGE Definition 9

Required Background and Skills 11

    The Linux Guy 11

    Customer Service Orientation 12

    Thrives on Challenge 12

Systems Administrator Duties and Responsibilities 13

    User Management 13

    Hardware and Software Maintenance 14

    Network Administration 14

    Summary 15

2   Essential Tools for System Administrators   17

Power Tools for Super Users 18

    UNIX Commands for Power Users 18

    Linuxconf, The Control-Panel, and Configuration Utilities 31

Web Resources for Administrators 36

    The Linux Documentation Project 36

    Linux Kernel Archives and Kernelnotes 37

    Linuxcare 39

    Linux Today 40

    Other Web Sites of Interest 41

Other Sources of Information 41

    Mailing Lists 42

    FTP Archives 43

    Newsgroups 43

    Summary 45

PART II   Linux Essentials   47

3   Installation Strategies   49

Default Installation Versus Customized Approaches 50

    Individual Installations 50

    Scalability Issues 55

Cloning Installations 56
   A Homegrown Approach 56
   Using Kickstart Files and RPM 68
A Template-Based Approach 69
   Establishing an Install Template 69
   Class-Based Customization 75
   An Implementation Example 77
Summary 79

4   Where Do I Find...?   81
Hand Me That Map Please 82
   The Filesystem Hierarchy Standard 82
   The Red Hat Filesystem Layout 89
Examining Processes 90
   The proc Filesystem 91
   Process Status Tools 98
   Checking Devices... 101
Device Naming Scheme 107
   Assigned Major and Minor Numbers 107
   An Alternative Device Management Scheme 108
Summary 109

5   Starting Up and Shutting Down   111
Linux Boot Loaders... 112
   Boot Loader Overview 112
   LILO, The Linux Loader 113
   LILO Tips and Tricks 122
   Alternatives to LILO 127
The Linux Boot Process and System Initialization Scripts............. 128
   Kernel Startup and Device Initialization..................... 128
   /etc/inittab and rc Scripts 130
   More About Runlevels 134
Shutting Down 137
   Changing Runlevels... 138
   The shutdown Commands 139
Summary 140

6   System Failure Diagnosis and Recovery   141
Kernel Oops.. 142
   Kernel Panic 143
Hardware Errors 144
   Identifying Hardware Errors at Startup 144
   BIOS Problems... 145

Plug-and-Play (PnP) Devices 145

PCI Devices 146

Diagnostic Tools 147

Using /proc for Diagnosis 147

The isapnp Program 148

Network Interface Card (NIC) Diagnostics...................... 149

DOS Diagnostics.. 151

Building and Using Rescue Disks................................ 152

Building a Rescue Disk...................................... 153

Starting a Rescue Session 154

Rescue Disk Toolkit 155

Rebuilding LILO 155

Rewriting Configuration Files 156

Repairing a Partition.. 156

Emergency File Copying..................................... 157

Recovering Deleted Files..................................... 160

Analysis of System Logs....................................... 160

Interpreting Log Messages 161

Locating the Source of Kernel Errors............................ 163

Decoding Kernel Errors...................................... 165

Using the System.map File 168

Seeking Assistance 169

Summary.. 169

PART III   Filesystem and Disk Management   171

7   Filesystems   173

The Physical Realm of Disks and Partitions......................... 174

Single Versus Multiple Disks 174

Partitioning Strategies....................................... 175

Partitioning Using fdisk..................................... 177

Partitioning with cfdisk 181

Partitioning with sfdisk 182

Disk Druid 185

Filesystem Creation and Management 187

Filesystem Tools 187

Filesystem Repair and Maintenance Using fsck.................. 188

Accessing Filesystems with mount 194

Space Allocation Strategies and Estimating Growth............... 196

Filesystem Types 197
 The Minix Filesystem 197
 The Extended 2 Filesystem 198
 Other Filesystem Types... 198
Space Management and Quotas 198
 Monitoring Space Usage... 199
 Local Versus Shared Filesystems 204
 Establishing Filesystem Quotas................................ 205
Summary 209

8   Adding or Replacing Disks   211

IDE Device Naming 212
 IDE Disk Device Interface..................................... 212
Managing the /etc/fstab File.................................. 214
 /etc/fstab File Format.. 214
 Dissecting a Filesystem Configuration File (/etc/fstab)........ 215
SCSI Concerns 217
 Why Choose SCSI?.. 217
 SCSI Chains 217
 Selecting a Controller 218
 Supported SCSI Devices.. 219
 Cabling Requirements.. 221
 Device Termination and SCSI IDs.............................. 222
 SCSI Device Naming 223
Other Devices 225
Summary 225

9   Linux and RAID   227

The History of Linux RAID Support 228
RAID Overview 228
 Objectives of RAID.. 228
 RAID Levels 230
Linux Software RAID... 234
 RAID Tools 235
 Supported RAID Levels 239
 Implementing Software RAID.................................... 244
Hardware RAID and Linux 266
 RAID Controller Drivers 267
 External RAID Devices 268
Other Sources of Information 269
Summary 269

10   Removable Media Devices   271

Removable Media Devices 272
    Floppy Drives... 272
    CD-ROM Drives 273
    CD-R and CD-RW Drives.................................... 274
Parallel Port Storage Devices.................................... 285
    Adding Support to Your Kernel.............................. 286
    Zip Drives... 287
    Parallel Port ATAPI/IDE Devices 288
Granting Access to Users 289
    The mtools Package 289
    Giving Users the Power to Mount 292
    Automatic Mounting of Removable Media.................... 294
    A Hybrid Approach 296
Summary.. 296

PART IV   Backup and Recovery   297

11   What to Back Up and How   299

Filesystem Contents 301
    System Configuration Files.................................. 301
    User Files 301
    Task-Oriented Files... 302
Finding New Files.. 303
    Files Added Since the Install 303
    Determining Available Back-Up Devices 304
Backup Strategies 305
    Full Backups as a Strategy 306
Partial Backups 309
    General Guidelines for Partial Backups....................... 309
Bringing a New Red Hat Linux Box Online 310
    Backup the Original Operating System 310
    Backup After the Applications are Installed.................... 311
    Backup Daily Operations.................................... 312
Types of Backups 313
    Full Backups.. 313
    Partial Backups 314
    Incremental Backups.. 314
Developing a Rotation Schedule 315
    Casual Home User 315
    A Typical Workstation 318
    A Backup Case Study 321

Writable CD-ROM Usage 321
Other Media Options.. 322
Developing Backup Scripts 323
Using `tar` for Backups 323
Implementing Full Backups and Restoring with `dump` and `restore` . 324
Quick Archiving with `cpio` 326
Possible Backup Problems and Alternatives 327
Dedicated Backup Software.................................... 327
Summary 331

12   Media Selection and Storage   333
Backup Media.. 334
Sources of Information for Tape Backups 334
Device Selection Criteria 334
The Autoloader Question 335
Media Selection Criteria...................................... 336
Tape Driver Interfaces.. 339
Floppy Tape Devices.. 339
ATAPI Tape Drives 340
SCSI Tape Devices 340
Storage Issues 341
Onsite Storage... 341
Offsite Storage 342
Multiple Copies 342
Tape Escrow Services 342
Summary 343

13   Recovery from Data Loss   345
Some Data Loss Scenarios....................................... 346
User Errors.. 347
Simple Prevention Measures to Avoid User Errors 349
Viruses and Other Destructive Software......................... 354
Preventative Measures Against Destructive Software 355
System Crackers and Malcontents 357
Preventative Measures Against Destructive People 358
Hardware Failure 359
Prevention and Recovery Methods............................. 359
Other Disaster Scenarios...................................... 361
The Cost Of Data Recovery 362
Direct Costs... 362
Indirect Costs 362

Disaster Recovery Planning 364
   Plan Development 364
   Plan Maintenance 367
Summary 368

PART V   Networking   369

14   TCP/IP and Ethernet   371

Network Layers 372
   Network Access Layer 373
   Internet Layer 373
   Transport Layer 374
   Application Layer 375
IP Addresses 375
   Address Classes 375
   Classless IP Addresses 376
   Subnetting 377
Running TCP/IP over Ethernet 377
   Ethernet Cards and Cables 378
   Ethernet Hubs 379
   Switches 379
   Using Switches 380
   Choosing Ethernet Media 380
Adding an Ethernet Interface 382
   Kernel Level Configuration 382
   Software Level Configuration 383
Routing 383
   Routing Gateways 384
   Configuring Routing 384
   The Routing Table 385
   Dynamic Routing 390
Name Services 397
   Historical Background 397
   DNS 398
   Name Services on UNIX and Linux Systems 399
   Network Information Service 405
Summary 408

15   Sharing Resources (Print and File Services)   409

Networking Is About Sharing 410
   Sharing with Linux/UNIX Hosts 410
   Sharing with Other Operating Systems 410

Setting Up Print Queues...411
   Setting Up a Local Printer.....................................411
   Granting Access to Others......................................416
   Setting Up a Remote Printer....................................416
Network File Services..418
   NFS Server Configuration.......................................418
   The /etc/exports File..421
   NFS Client Configuration.......................................424
   AFS and Coda...426
The Automount Daemon and Autofs....................................427
   The BSD Automount Daemon.......................................427
   Linux Autofs...431
Summary..432

16   Network Monitoring   435
   Why Monitor?...436
   Monitoring Systems...437
   Sniffers...444
      Uses for Sniffers...448
      Dangers of Sniffers...450
   Traffic Analyzers..451
      Determining Network Bottlenecks.............................457
      Analyzing Types of Traffic..................................458
   Summary..460

17   Integrating with Windows NT Networks   461
   Networking the Windows Way.....................................462
      Speaking the Lingo..462
      A Simple NT Network...463
   Linux and Samba in an NT Environment...........................464
      Samba Overview..465
      Analyzing the Samba Configuration File......................476
      Linux and Samba as a Client OS..............................484
      Linux and Samba as a Server OS..............................487
      Sources of Samba Help.......................................491
   Summary..492

18   Integrating with Other Network Operating Systems   493
   Getting Along with Your Neighbors..............................494
      Using the Right Tool for the Job............................494
   Linux in a NetWare Environment.................................495
      NetWare Interoperability Options............................495
      Adding IPX Protocol Support to Your Kernel..................496
      NetWare Networking Concepts.................................496

Linux as NetWare Client.......................................497
Linux as NetWare Server......................................498
Starting the mars-nwe Server 512
Linux in an AppleTalk Environment 513
Configuring Kernel AppleTalk Support..........................514
Configuring AppleTalk Services on Linux 514
Starting the Netatalk Server 525
Summary...525

PART VI   Internet Services   527

19   Setting Up Internet Services   529
Choosing Services to Offer....................................530
Low-Level Services 530
Internet Services 531
Remote Login Service 531
Other Internet Services.....................................531
The Internet Server inetd.....................................531
The /etc/inetd.conf File....................................532
Using TCP-Wrappers 534
Logging 535
Access Control..535
Configuration 536
Testing tcpd Configuration 538
xinetd as an Alternative to inetd 538
Configuring xinetd 539
Standard Services: Remote Login, Execution, and File-Copy 541
Telnet 541
The R-Commands..543
SSH, the Secure Shell Service 547
Summary...552

20   Electronic Mail   553
MTAs, MUAs, and MDAs 554
SMTP Services 555
SMTP's Original Use...555
POP and IMAP Services...556
Post Office Protocol (POP)..................................556
Interactive Mail Access Protocol (IMAP) 556
Configuring Mail Collection...................................556
Dealing with Spam 557

Choosing an MTA 558
    Generational MTAs 558
sendmail 559
    sendmail Features and Options 559
    Setting Up sendmail for Various Configuration............... 560
Clever Bits... 563
    Multiple Domains.. 563
    Declaring the Virtual User Table 564
    Testing and Running sendmail.............................. 565
Smail... 566
    Smail Transports, Directors, and Routers.................. 566
    Smail Configuration 567
    Workstation Configuration 568
    Configuration Files....................................... 568
    Director Files.. 569
    Router Files 573
    Running smail 575
Qmail... 575
    Qmail Delivery Options 575
    Qmail Message Handling 576
    Qmail User Ids and Configuration Files.................... 576
Exim.. 577
    Exim Configuration 577
    Exim Workstations 578
    Mail Hub 578
    Spam Protection 578
Ancillary Programs for
    Mail Handling... 579
Fetchmail 579
    Running Fetchmail... 580
Supporting Multiple Email Clients............................. 581
    Spool Access.. 582
    Locking Issues 582
Popular Linux Email Clients................................... 583
    Mail/mailx.. 583
    Elm/Pine.. 584
    Xfmail.. 585
Aliases... 585
    Managing Aliases.. 585
    Alias Master File Locations............................... 586
    Structuring Aliases....................................... 586

Mandatory Aliases... 587
Aliases Versus Mailing Lists 587
Distributed Management of Aliases 588
Mailing Lists with `majordomo` 588
Moderated Versus Unmoderated Lists 589
Open Versus Closed Lists 590
Privacy and Security.. 590
To Archive or Not to Archive 590
Archiving and FTP 591
Configuring a Digest-Only List 591
References.. 605
Choosing and Installing an MTA 606
Particular MTAs.. 606
Anti-spam Measures 607
Summary 607

21   FTP and Anonymous FTP   609
Allowing FTP to Your Servers.................................... 611
Configuring Anonymous FTP with WU-FTPD 618
Alternative FTP Servers.. 619
Security and Legal Issues 621
Protecting Your FTP Servers 621
Dealing with Warez D00dz.................................... 631
Summary 636

22   Web Serving   637
Introduction to Web Serving..................................... 638
Apache... 638
About the Apache Project 638
Installing Apache... 640
Starting and Stopping Apache 640
Configuring Apache 641
Various Configuration Techniques............................. 649
Apache Security Tips 653
Apache Modules 654
Configuring Virtual Hosts 657
Comanche 662
Apache Add-ons 663
Squid 665
Features of Squid 665
Starting Squid.. 666
Configuring Squid.. 666

Other Web Servers 667
        Roxen Challenger 667
        Boa 668
        dhttpd 669
        fhttpd 669
        ghttpd 669
        thttpd 669
        WN 670
    Summary 670

23   News Services   671
    So You Want to Run a News Server? 672
        Capacity Planning 672
        Running a News Server 674
        Outsourcing News Services 675
    INN and Friends 676
        Installing INN 676
        Configuring INN 681
        Spam Filtering Options with INN 701
        Diablo 701
        Using nntpcache 702
    News Clients 705
        Text Clients 705
        Graphical Clients 707
        Alternatives for Reading News 711
    Places to Ask Questions and Find Answers 711
    Summary 712

24   Internet Telephony and Conferencing   713
    An Introduction to Internet Telephony 714
        ICQ 714
        The Problems That Hinder Widespread
            Usage of Internet Telephony 715
        Hardware Requirements 717
        The Multicast Backbone (mbone) 719
    Internet Relay Chat (IRC) 721
        How IRC Works 721
        ircII 722
        Obtaining ircII 723
        Installing ircII 723
        Running ircII 724
        Zircon, an X-Windows Program for IRC 725

X-Chat 726

BitchX 727

ICQ and Clones 728

ICQ, IP-Masquerading and Firewalls 728

JavaICQ from Mirabilis 729

licq 731

micq 732

Multimedia Conferencing Tools 733

Speak Freely 734

QSeeMe 735

CU-SeeMe 736

Summary 737

25   Security Principles   739

Determining Your Security Needs 740

Types of Attacks 741

Securing Your Red Hat Server 743

Passwords 743

System Files 750

Physical Security—Minimizing the Physical Risks 767

Securing Services 768

Filesystem Security 770

Security Monitoring 772

Check Your Log Files 772

Checking Network Interfaces 773

Check for New setuid/setgid Files 773

Check /var/spool/cron 773

Check /var/spool/atjobs 773

Check for Altered System Files 774

Be Aware of the Latest Threats 774

Keep Your Software Up-to-Date 775

Developing Security Policies 775

Setup Policies 776

Maintenance Policies 777

Reaction Policies 777

Making the Rules 777

Enforcing Strict Compliance 778

Dealing with Infractions 779

Summary 781

PART VII   Security and Firewalls   783

26   Firewall Strategies   785

Types of Firewalls 787
    Bastion Host System 787
Firewall Options 789
Linux Proxy Services 790
    Proxy Software 791
Linux Kernel Configuration 792
    Transproxy 793
SOCKS Proxy Server 795
    Setting Up SOCKS 795
    Tuning SOCKS Configuration Files 796
Squid 2 798
    Squid Configuration and Installation 798
TIS FireWall ToolKit 800
    Obtaining FWTK 801
    Configuring FWTK 801
    Configuring the Telnet Proxy 803
Setting Up a Firewall 805
    Packet Filtering 805
Setting Up a Firewall with ipchains 810
    Installing ipchains 810
    Understanding Packet Filtering 811
    Examples of Firewalls 814
Debugging Firewalls 817
    Using DNS Servers Outside the Firewall 817
Summary 817

27   The Security Administrator's Toolbox   819

Building Your Security Administrator's Toolbox 820
    Granting Privileges with sudo 820
    Additional Security Tools 829
    Sources of Security Tools 832
Security Resources on the Web 834
    The USENIX Web Site 834
    Red Hat Security Information 834
    Linux Portal Sites 835
Sources of Information Other than the Web 836
    comp.security.announce and Other USENET Newsgroups 836
    Security Mailing Lists 837
    Miscellaneous Lists 839
Summary 840

28   I've Been Hacked: What Now? 841

Intruder Alert! 842
    Rules of Engagement 842
    Gathering Evidence of Intrusion 843
Determining the Extent of Intrusion 844
    Analyzing System Logs...................................... 845
    Intrusion Detection Tools 846
    Trinux as a Security Tool 848
    Cleaning Up After the Unwanted Visitor 854
Reinstalling the Operating System from Scratch.................... 855
    When to Throw in the Towel................................. 855
    Trusting Your Backups...................................... 856
    Reinstallation from Media.................................. 856
Summary 857

PART VIII   User Management and Interaction   859

29   Users and Groups   861

Adding Users to the System..................................... 862
Granting Permissions to Users.................................. 862
Establishing Groups 862
    The Evils of Shared Accounts 863
System Files 864
    The /etc/passwd File 865
    The /etc/group File 866
    The /etc/shadow File 867
    The /etc/gshadow File 868
    The /etc/login.defs 869
    The /etc/skel Directory 869
Adding and Deleting User Accounts 869
    Adding a User Manually..................................... 870
    A Note on Editing /etc/passwd and /etc/group Manually 873
    Adding a User Using the Command-line Tools.................. 873
    Manipulating User Accounts in Batch Mode 881
    Disabling User Accounts.................................... 882
When to Delete a User Account 882
    userdel 883
Effective Use of Groups 884
    groupadd... 884
    groupdel... 884
    groupmod... 885
    grpck 885
    Adding a Group with the GUI Tools 886

Using Groups to Grant Permissions.................................887
The `newgrp` Command 888
    `newgrp`...888
Other System Commands Related to Users and Groups..............888
    `chage`..888
    `chfn`...889
    `chgrp`..889
    `chown`..890
    `chsh`...891
    `gpasswd` 891
    `groups`...891
    `passwd`...892
    `su` 892
    `usermod` 892
Summary 893

30 Helping Users 895

Users Are Not Lusers 896
    Establishing the Ground Rules 896
    Dealing with Interruptions 899
    Minimizing Interruptions Through Training......................901
    A Combination Approach to User Interaction.....................902
Developing a Help Desk...903
    Qualities of a Good Help Desk..................................903
    Help Desk Manning Strategies 905
    An Open Source Solution..906
    Setting Up a WREQ-Based Help Desk for Red Hat...............908
Learning How to Say No...918
    The Customer Isn't Always Right 918
    Dealing with Troublesome Users 919
    Grant No Exceptions..922
Summary 922

PART IX Shells, Scripting, and Automation 923

31 Shells 925

Getting Started with Shells 926
    Differences Between the Shells.................................926
    Selecting a Shell for Interactive Use..........................927
    Interactive and Non-Interactive Modes 928

bash, the Bourne Again Shell...................................... 928
    Features of bash.. 929
    Wildcards... 929
    Aliases 931
    Command-Line Completion 932
    Pipes... 932
    Input and Output Redirection................................ 933
    History... 934
    Command-Line Editing 936
    Job Control... 937
    Built-In Commands... 939
    Startup for Interactive Sessions 940
    Startup for Non-Interactive Sessions.......................... 941
    Quoting 942
    bash Variables 942
    Modifying the Command Prompt 944
    Advantages and Disadvantages of bash........................ 945
tcsh, the Enhanced C Shell...................................... 945
    Features of tcsh 945
    Wildcards... 946
    Aliases 947
    Command-Line Completion 948
    Spelling Correction 949
    Pipes... 950
    Input and Output Redirection................................ 950
    History... 951
    Job Control... 952
    Built-In Commands... 955
    Key Bindings 957
    Startup and Shutdown for Interactive Sessions 959
    Automatic, Periodic, and Timed Events........................ 960
    Variables 960
    Editing the Command Prompt 962
    Advantages and Disadvantages of tcsh 963
Other Shells 964
    The Z Shell... 964
    The Public Domain Korn Shell 964
Summary.. 965

32   Shell Scripting   967

Introduction to Shell Scripting................................... 968
    The Importance of Shell Scripting 968
    The Shell Script Defined.................................... 968

Interpreted Versus Compiled 969
Selecting Your Scripting Shell 970
Standardizing Scripts 972
Shell Scripting Using bash 972
bash Syntax 972
Creating and Using Variables 974
Expressions 978
Control Structures 983
Built-in Commands 990
Parsing Command-Line Parameters 999
Using Functions 1001
Some Sample bash Scripts 1003
Debugging Shell Scripts 1005
perl Scripting 1007
Features of perl 1007
Getting Started with perl 1008
perl Control Structures 1009
Additional perl Resources 1010
Other Languages 1010
Tcl/Tk 1010
Python 1012
Eiffel 1013
Programming Tools 1014
Make 1014
RCS 1015
CVS 1015
Summary 1016

33   Automation   1017
Managing Chaos 1018
Automating Tasks 1019
Automating Regular Tasks 1020
Using at for One-Time Tasks 1021
The at Utility 1022
Examples of Using at 1024
The batch Utility 1027
The atq Utility 1028
The atrm Utility 1028
The atrun Utility 1028
The at Daemon 1029
Specifying Which Users Can Use at 1030

Using cron.. 1031
    cron Startup 1031
    Using crontab Effectively 1033
    The Anatomy of a crontab Entry............................. 1034
    Global cron Files.. 1038
    Specifying Which Users Can Use cron 1038
    Examples of Using cron 1039
Debugging cron Jobs 1040
    Capturing Output.. 1040
    Using printf and echo as Debugging Tools.................. 1040
    Examining the Log Files 1042
Summary... 1042

PART X   System Tuning and Kernel Building   1045

34   Tuning Your Linux System   1047
General Areas of Tuning...................................... 1049
    Specific Tuning Aspects and Questions...................... 1049
Weighing Costs and Benefits 1052
    Hardware Costs 1053
    System Requirements and Needs............................. 1053
    Performance Enhancements.................................. 1054
Understanding Performance Measurement Techniques.............. 1055
    Console-Based Tools 1055
    Graphical Utilities....................................... 1062
    Real Time Versus Gathered Performance Data................. 1064
    Process Management 1065
Understanding Network Performance............................ 1067
    Benchmarking and Testing the Network 1067
Memory and Swap Space 1068
    Deciding How Much RAM Is Needed........................... 1068
    Figuring Actual RAM Requirements 1069
Swap Space Priorities.. 1071
    Calculating Swap Space.................................... 1071
    Assigning Swap Space...................................... 1072
Swap Partitions Versus Swap Files............................ 1074
    Swap Files.. 1074
    Swap Partitions 1075
Tunable Kernel Parameters in /proc 1075
    Why Alter the Kernel?..................................... 1075
    Understanding /proc 1076
Using echo to Alter System Behavior 1078
    Understanding the Anti-Ping Setting 1078
Summary... 1079

35 Customizing the Linux Kernel 1081

Use the Source 1082

Why Recompile? Reasons for Recompiling..................... 1082

Obtaining the Source...................................... 1084

Kernel Sources and Patches Provided by Red Hat.............. 1087

Kernel Source Code Layout................................. 1089

Patching the Kernel Source 1091

Official Versus Unofficial Patches 1092

Where to Obtain Patches 1093

Kernel Loadable Modules 1094

Advantages of Modular Kernels............................. 1095

Enabling Module Support................................... 1096

The Module Utilities 1097

When Not to Use Modules 1099

Kernel Building 1100

Configuring the Linux Kernel.............................. 1100

Tweaking the Makefile 1126

Handling Multiple Versions of the Kernel 1127

Custom Installation Scripts 1131

Running make 1132

Summary 1133

36 Centennial School District, Portland, Oregon 1135

Background on Centennial...................................... 1136

How Bynari Got Involved 1137

From Dallas to Portland 1137

Written Requirements from Connie 1138

Concerns of the Project Team 1138

Summarizing Centennial's Resources 1140

Organizational Initiatives 1141

Centennial Chooses Red Hat................................... 1141

The Challenge.. 1142

Enter Linux and Red Hat's 6.0................................. 1142

The Internet for Curriculum................................... 1143

Red Hat 6.0 Helps Centennial Meet Requirements 1143

Red Hat 6.0 and the Internet................................... 1144

Defining Other Requirements 1144

Constraints.. 1145

Technical Expertise and Knowledgeable Management 1145

Project Specifications 1145

Short- and Long-Term Objectives 1146

The Project Plan... 1146

Web Server.. 1147

Securing Access to the Applications............................ 1147
Network Authentication, Access, and User Administration
      with Samba.. 1148
Samba in Centennial's Heterogeneous Environment................ 1149
Training the Centennial Team 1149
Back to Samba... 1150
      Global Printing Services Using Samba 1151
      Using Samba to Access the Red Hat 6.0 System
            from a Windows PC................................... 1152
Networking Macintosh Computers in the Linux Environment........ 1152
Limited Administrative Control and Access to the Network 1153
Progress for Centennial 1154
Internet Access... 1155
Using IP Masquerading 1155
      Advantages of Using IP Masquerading 1155
Linux 2.2.x Kernels 1155
Distributing the Productivity Application 1156
Electronic Mail... 1156
Example: `sendmail.cf` File 1157
System Administration... 1158
Managing Users and Groups 1159
Different User Account Management Scenarios 1159
Content Management Using TCP Wrappers...................... 1161
Using an FTP Server to Download Files......................... 1162
Summary... 1163

Index   1165

About the Lead Author

Thomas Schenk is a Systems Engineer at VA Linux in its professional services division, where he serves as a consultant to VA Linux customers in the areas of system administration, tools programming, and managing large Linux installations. Prior to that he was a Senior System Administrator at Deja.com, where he oversaw the administration of one of the largest Linux-based Web sites on the Internet. His primary responsibilities at Deja.com included keeping track of new developments in the Linux community, maintaining the operating system template used on Deja.com servers, and helping to build relationships with Linux developers and vendors. He can often be found lurking on the Linux Kernel, Linux SMP, and Linux Net mailing lists and is always willing to lend a hand when he is able. Tom's involvement with Linux began in 1992, while working at Texas A&M, Corpus Christi, when he downloaded the version 0.12 boot and root floppies and used them to build his first Linux system on a 386SX-16 personal computer. In addition to Linux, he has administered most flavors of commercial UNIX from Sun, IBM, SGI, HP, DEC, and SCO and either runs or has experimented with most of the available free UNIX systems. In addition to being a systems admin, Tom enjoys programming in Perl and developing systems administration tools.

When not working or experimenting on his home network, Tom and his wife E.J. are kept busy raising their two children, Nicholas and Nia. Tom and E.J. are both active volunteers in school and extracurricular activities including the PTA, PIPs basketball, Austin Children's Choir, and dance classes, just to name a few. Tom's interests other than computing including listening to music of all types, reading science fiction and fantasy, primitive camping, and cooking (especially chili).

About the Contributing Authors

Derek Barber is a computer consultant living in Vancouver, Canada. He has worked as both a programmer and a system administrator for several companies. Derek discovered Linux four years ago and has been deeply involved with it and other free software projects ever since. He is currently employed full-time as the programming lead for an e-commerce company specializing in deploying Linux-based e-commerce solutions. Derek is the system administrator and a programmer for 32BitsOnline magazine as well, and is also is the editor for hex20, an online programming magazine. In addition to his computer training, Derek is also working on a music degree and is interested in developing music software.

Derek Murphy is the systems administrator for R.E. Gilmore Investments Corp. in Kanata, Ontario, Canada. He has been implementing mission-critical Linux servers and workstations in this production environment since 1996, on a network that currently numbers over 300 computers and moves an excess of three terabytes of data per week.

Elliot Turner is the founder of MimeStar, Inc., a security software development company based in Blacksburg, Virginia. He is the author of SecureNet PRO, an enterprise-scalable network intrusion detection and response system available for various UNIX platforms. His earlier activities include being contracted by Secure Networks, Inc., to work on the Ballista network security auditing system and being employed by VTLS, Inc., to assist in development of the Virtua library automation system. He has worked with the Glade (a Gtk GUI builder) project by submitting source code patches and bug reports. He is also the author of ThreeD, a multipurpose 3D graphics API for MS-DOS and various UNIX platforms. ThreeD supports over 45 different rasterization techniques, hierarchical 3D scene management, real-time 3D mesh morphing, and landscape generation and deformation. Elliot's other work includes an optical character recognition system that utilizes neural network technology, and KASIE, a context-independent expert system/ discovery engine. KASIE uses a general-purpose knowledge representation syntax so that it may engage in different types of simulation activities without any need for source code updates.

Neil Brown has worked as a UNIX (Solaris and HP/UX) and network administrator for Bell Atlantic and is currently working as a Senior Consultant for Aston Brooke Corporation, doing development work on client projects. Neil has been running Linux as his home platform of choice since the early days of the SoftLanding floppy distributions, and is an enthusiastic supporter of Linux in the workplace. In his spare time, he enjoys developing entertainment software in C++ and keeping his system on the bleeding edge of the supported hardware list.

Robert Haig has been using computers for more than 15 years. He started using UNIX 10 years ago and has been administering a UNIX box of some flavor or another for the last 8 years. He started running Linux in 1992 with a Slackware distribution, and he is currently running a small Web hosting service out of his house to pay for the bandwidth he needs. Robert has been running Usenet news servers for about 5 years. Three of those he spent running the news server for IBM that was (for a while) IBM's only link to the rest of Usenet. That server was listed as IBM US's preferred news server for reading clients to connect to. Currently he's the Usenet news administrator and a Linux administrator for Deja.com. Deja.com accepts about 40GB of news every day from all of our news feeds. Robert currently works for NowDocs, a pre-IPO company in Austin, Texas, where he does systems programming and administration.

Jaron Rubenstein co-founded Logicept Corporation in 1999 with Michael Cohn. As Executive Vice-President, Jaron manages Logicept's financial and technical operations. As Director of Technology, Jaron leads the research and development of new technologies and manages their implementation in customer projects. Jaron also directs Logicept's Linux Systems Integration services and administrates the corporation's internal systems. Jaron has held technical positions with Lockheed Martin Corporation and Reuters Information Technologies and has provided software and systems consulting services for National Public Radio, The New Piper Aircraft Company, Dell Manufacturing, Cadaret Grant, Porter Novelli, Hill & Knowlton, Worth Publishers, and many other organizations. Through these experiences, Jaron has mastered the design and implementation of mission-critical software that is both efficient and easy to use.

Aaron Crane has been a system administrator and has been programming professionally for seven years. In that time he has lived and computed in his native England (Manchester and London) as well as in Boulder, Colorado, and he is soon moving to Edinburgh to study for a Ph.D. in Computer Science. He is currently the System Manager for a company researching applications of phonology to automatic speech recognition.

Ido Dubrawsky started working with UNIX systems back in 1987 when he co-op'ed at IBM Federal Systems Division in Houston, Texas. At the time he was working on his bachelor's degree in Aerospace Engineering at the University of Texas at Austin. After finishing his master's in May of 1992, Ido was hired by the Navigation Systems Division of the Jet Propulsion Laboratory in Pasadena, California. Ido worked there as a maneuver analyst for the Galileo Project. Being one of the few users with knowledge of UNIX, he was assigned the task of assistant system administrator. After almost a year and a half at JPL, he returned to UT Austin to pursue a Ph.D. in Molecular Biology. While he was waiting for admission into the graduate program in Molecular Biology, he worked at the Center for Space Research as a system/network administrator. There, he ran a mixture of HP-UX, AIX, SunOS 4.1.3, Solaris 2.2, Linux, Ultrix, IRIX, and VMS systems. The hardware platform ranged from an RS/6000 to a SPARCstation 10 to an HP 9000/800 series server to a PC and a Macintosh. After 3 years, he left the Ph.D. program and was hired as the system administrator for the Physics department. This position required him to work with PCs running Red Hat Linux, Compaq Proliants running Solaris 2.5.1 for x86, and a Sun Enterprise 450 server as well. In April 1999, he was hired by Deja.com to work on system administration issues as well as infrastructure development. Ido currently works for Globeset, where he is the Manager for UNIX and Network Services.

Raphael Mankin has degrees in Math and Computer Science, and a Ph.D. in Engineering. He worked on the design of compilers and operating systems at Southampton. After leaving the university, he worked on compilers and translators for various languages, including a lot of source code conversion. Around 1980, he installed and maintained the first commercial UNIX system in Britain. Around 1982 he designed and wrote the first commercial RDBMS application in Britain. He spent the next years juggling operating systems, compilers, databases, and networks in a variety of jobs. Today, he is the Technical Director of a Web services company.

Jason Fink has been involved with technology since he was 12 years old when he smoked his first (of many to come) power supply in 1982 and went onto Vocational Electronics where he specialized in microprocessor architectures and assembly programming. After school, Jason enlisted in the U.S. Navy, where he worked on mainframe systems. In the navy Jason learned CMS-2Y programming, which he employed for diagnostic writing. It was during his enlistment that Jason was first exposed to UNIX, more specifically SUN and HP systems. Additionally, Jason also started what seems to be a lifelong endeavor, his pursuit of a college degree. After he left the Navy, Jason went to work for Lockheed Martin Technologies to support a Naval Test Facility at Wallop's Island, Virginia, where he began to work on UNIX systems almost exclusively. At Wallop's Island, Jason learned shell programming and the essentials of systems and network administration. It was during this time he became interested in Linux and got a hold of Slackware 1.0.13, and ever since the first time he logged on he has been using Linux at home and work. Jason currently is the head UNIX Systems Administrator for Ipsos-ASI, "The Market Research Company." He is still pursuing his degree and has opted for the B.S. to M.S. in Computer Sciences program at the American Institute for Computer Sciences (http://www.aics.edu/) so he can stay on the move and have a steady degree track. In his non-school/work time Jason maintains his own Web server at the Diverge.Org Domain (http://www.diverge.org/) and is the editor, designer, and lead author of the UNIX and LINUX Computing Journal (http://www.diverge.org/ulcj/). He has also contributed to the Linux Gazette (http://www.linuxgazette.com/) and Linux Today (http://www.linuxtoday.com/). Aside from administration, Jason has low-level programmed in a variety of languages such as C, C++, and Perl. His interests in Linux and UNIX lean more toward engineering and architectures (it is said the most dangerous thing to see at Ipsos-ASI is Jason Fink carrying a pile of Linux and GNU CD-ROMs, a bucket of hardware, and a screwdriver). When he isn't writing, researching, studying, or at work—which is rare—Jason can be found surfing the waves or spending quiet time at home.

Tom Adelstein is the co-founder of Bynari International, a global consultancy specializing in Linux. Tom's responsibilities include business development and identifying technical opportunities for the company. He began his career in technology as an EDP auditor and eventually rose to partner. In 1979, he started up an IT consulting department in a CPA firm where he experienced many achievements, including organizing the development group that built CAS, the first comprehensive accounting package for microprocessor-based systems, which he sold to Moore Business Systems. Tom's involvement in Linux began in 1994, when a friend told him about a "free" UNIX operating system. Bynari is Tom's fourth start-up. His prior ventures include an interactive stock brokerage firm purchased by HSN in 1987. In 1982, he started the investment banking division of Equity Management Corporation, where he automated due diligence and asset acquisition. Although Tom majored in business, his peers consider him able in functional, business, and technical areas. Tom enjoys rolling up his sleeves and getting hands-on in projects. His post-graduate studies have focused strictly on technology subjects. When he is not working or writing, Tom enjoys outdoor activities with his wife, Yvonne, a former collegiate track star and antique dealer. The couple like to go on long distance runs and can be found in the gym most evenings. They also study screenwriting together.

Gene Wilburn has been using UNIX systems since 1978. He has been a system/network administrator since 1981 and has been a frequent contributor to computer publications in Canada and the United States. He is currently Assistant Director of New Media Resources at the Royal Ontario Museum in Toronto, Canada, where he oversees a small farm of Linux and FreeBSD servers. When not administering UNIX systems and writing Perl scripts, he performs folk music on six- and twelve-string guitars and acoustic bass.

Dedication

To my wife, Eun Joung, and our children Nicholas and Nia.

—Tom

Acknowledgments

When I set out to write this book, I had no idea of the investment in time and research that would be required. As a novice author, I was unprepared, and I would like to thank the staff at Sams Publishing, especially my acquisitions editors, Don Roche and Rosemarie Graham, for their encouragement and patience with me throughout this process.

Much of the information presented here I learned under the guidance of senior systems administrators, and I would like to thank Rami El-Charif and Theo Krenek especially for taking me under their wings and helping me to get where I am today.

I would especially like to thank my wife E.J. for her patience with the entire process. I would also like to thank her for teaching me an important lesson. The potential to do a great thing coupled with encouragement to keep at it is the key to success. Thank you for providing the encouragement.

I would also like to thank Mr. James Seal, my high school calculus teacher, who initially inspired my interest in personal computers. It was in his class that I became hooked on computers.

And finally, I would like to thank Linus Torvalds and the rest of the Linux community for creating Linux. It was Linux that enabled me to learn about UNIX and gain the skills required to write this book. I hope that through this book I can give something useful back to that community.

—Tom

Tell Us What You Think!

As the reader of this book, *you* are our most important critic and commentator. We value your opinion and want to know what we're doing right, what we could do better, what areas you'd like to see us publish in, and any other words of wisdom you're willing to pass our way.

As a Publisher for Sams Publishing, I welcome your comments. You can fax, email, or write me directly to let me know what you did or didn't like about this book—as well as what we can do to make our books stronger.

Please note that I cannot help you with technical problems related to the topic of this book, and that due to the high volume of mail I receive, I might not be able to reply to every message.

When you write, please be sure to include this book's title and author as well as your name and phone or fax number. I will carefully review your comments and share them with the authors and editors who worked on the book.

Fax: 317-581-4770

Email: michael.stephens@macmillanusa.com

Mail: Michael Stephens
          Publisher
          Sams Publishing
          201 West 103rd Street
          Indianapolis, IN 46290 USA

So You Want to Be a Systems Administrator

If you are like many systems administrators, you did not choose this career, it was chosen for you. Unlike many other areas of the computer industry, like software engineering and integrated circuit design, there are few, if any, schools that offer UNIX systems administration as a degree choice. Many of the best administrators are self-taught. I have worked with systems administrators with degrees in Psychology, Economics, and Business Administration, as well as people without any degree at all. What is common among all of these people, and the reason why they were chosen to do this job, is a keen interest in systems and the ability to jump quickly from one emergency to the next. These are people who thrive on interrupts and have a higher than normal tolerance for stress. I think that this attitude is what separates systems administrators from others in the computer industry. A co-worker of mine once described the level of intensity at our place of work accurately when he said, "If I wanted a low-stress job, I'd become an air-traffic controller." So strap on your pagers, order some takeout Chinese food, and prepare yourself for a descent into the madness that is Linux systems administration.

Who Is This Book's Intended Audience?

This book is intended for intermediate to experienced computer users who have been tasked with the administration of a Linux system. It is not a beginner's book—it is intended to be most useful to people already serving as systems administrators of other network operating systems, such as UNIX, Windows NT, and Netware. If you are ready to take the next step in your knowledge of Linux, this book is for you.

What Do You Need to Know Prior to Reading This Book?

This book assumes that you have at least some familiarity with Linux or UNIX commands, that you are comfortable using a command shell, and that you have more than a basic knowledge of networks. It also assumes that even if you are not a Linux expert, you are familiar with the commands that you can use to get help, such as man.

What Will You Learn from This Book?

This book covers a wide variety of topics, ranging from user management to systems security. You will learn through examples how to integrate your Linux system into a TCP/IP network and how to set up Internet services. You will also learn how to use tools like Samba and netatalk to share resources with other operating systems on the network. This book is not just a technical reference, however; it also discusses approaches to user management and how to make your systems more useful to users.

What Software Will You Need?

This book assumes that you have access to a networked Linux system running Red Hat Linux. No other special software is required.

How This Book Is Organized

This book is divided into ten sections, each dealing with a different aspect of Linux administration. These sections may be read in any order you choose. The ten sections are

- **Part I: Introduction to Linux Systems Administration**—The two chapters in this section discuss the job of systems administrators, their duties and responsibilities, the tools of the trade, and where to look for information helpful in the performance of those duties.

- **Part II: Linux Essentials**—This section consists of four chapters covering information required by all Linux administrators. This includes information on installation strategies and a system roadmap covering the filesystem layout and how to look at processes and devices. Information on starting and stopping your Linux systems is also covered, as well as information on what to do in the event of a system crash.

- **Part III: Filesystem and Disk Management**—This section, comprised of four chapters, begins with a look at partitioning strategies, filesystem management, and space management issues. The discussion then continues with coverage of adding and replacing disks in your systems and related issues, such as device naming conventions and SCSI. Next, it delves into the topic of RAID, both software and hardware, and finishes off with a look at removable media devices, such as CD-ROM and Zip drives.

- **Part IV: Backup and Recovery**—The chapters in this section are devoted to determining what to back up, how to back it up, and recovery issues.

- **Part V: Networking**—This section begins with a discussion of TCP/IP networking essentials, including routing and name services. It continues with a discussion about sharing resources such as file and print services, focusing on sharing with other Linux/UNIX systems. Network analysis and tuning are also covered, and the section finishes up with coverage of how Samba, the NetWare emulator, and netatalk can be used to allow your Linux systems to share resources with and interact with Windows NT and other network operating systems.

- **Part VI: Internet Services**—Seven chapters make up this section. Coverage includes the basic services such as telnet, the R commands, and ssh. It continues with electronic mail and mailing lists. Next are the big three—FTP, Apache, and Usenet—followed by coverage of Internet telephony and conferencing tools. This section ends with a discussion of security principles and guidelines for developing a security policy.

- **Part VII: Security and Firewalls**—This is one of the most important sections of the book. It starts by covering firewall strategies and then turns to resources available to the security administrator, including sources of security tools and information. The section closes with a discussion about dealing with a system breach.

- **Part VIII: User Management and Interaction**—This section has two chapters on adding users and groups to a system, methods of delegating authority through the use of groups, and how to deal effectively with users. It includes a discussion of setting up a help desk to manage your interaction with users.

- **Part IX: Shells, Scripting, and Automation**—The three chapters in this section discuss using the command shells available with Linux, shell scripting, and how to make your job easier through automation.

- **Part X: System Tuning and Kernel Building**—This section delves into the black arts of system tuning and building customized kernels. It also includes a case study of how Linux was used at a school district in Portland, Oregon.

Conventions Used in This Book

The following typographic conventions are used in this book:

- Code lines, commands, statements, variables, and any text you type or see onscreen appears in a `mono` typeface. **`Bold mono`** typeface is often used to represent the user's input.

- Placeholders in syntax descriptions appear in an *italic mono* typeface. Replace the placeholder with the actual filename, parameter, or whatever element it represents.

- *Italics* highlight technical terms when they're being defined.

- The [➡] icon is used before a line of code that is really a continuation of the preceding line. Sometimes a line of code is too long to fit as a single line on the page. If you see [➡] before a line of code, remember that it's part of the line immediately above it.

- The book also contains Notes, Tips, and Cautions to help you spot important or useful information more quickly. Some of these are helpful shortcuts to help you work more efficiently.

Introduction to Linux System Administration

PART

I

IN THIS PART

1 What Is a System Administrator? *7*

2 Essential Tools for System Administrators *17*

CHAPTER 1

What Is a Systems Administrator?

IN THIS CHAPTER

- The Linux Systems Administrator   *8*
- Required Background and Skills   *11*
- Systems Administrator Duties and Responsibilities   *13*

Ask a group of Information Systems managers to define the role of a systems administrator and you will probably get a wide variety of answers that describe seemingly unrelated jobs. This is largely due to the fact that the role is defined by the nature of the systems that the systems administrator is tasked with maintaining.

For example, consider two systems administrators, Tom and Janet. Tom works at a small title company where the systems were installed by a systems integrator. Along with the operating system, the integrator installed a document management system and set up interoffice electronic mail. These are the only applications that the system runs and Tom is the only administrator. His responsibilities are to keep the systems up and running, to manage user accounts, and to backup the system. Janet, on the other hand, works for a software development company. They create products for a variety of UNIX platforms and do a significant part of their business on the Internet. Janet is a member of a systems administration team and her specialty is network administration. Her responsibilities include maintenance of the firewall, Web server, and FTP site. This is in addition to network planning and normal administration tasks on several different flavors of UNIX. As you can see, Tom and Janet require very different skill sets, however they are both systems administrators.

How then do you define the role of a Linux systems administrator? To answer this and other questions, this chapter looks at the definition of what a Linux systems administrator is. It also looks at the skills an administrator is likely to possess, and some common duties and responsibilities.

The Linux Systems Administrator

This book is specifically targeted at the Linux systems administrator for medium to large networks of computers running the Red Hat Linux operating system. Networks of this size are characterized by 50 or more client systems served by multiple servers. It is intended to cover topics that are unique to this environment, as opposed to the small site or single-user workstation. The following section starts with the definition of a Linux systems administrator.

A Simple Definition

A Linux systems administrator is the person responsible for the maintenance and proper operation of the Linux systems utilized within a company. This typically includes everything from selecting the hardware on which to install the system, the installation and initial configuration, to the ongoing maintenance of both the hardware and software that comprise the system. As you can see, this definition can be as broad or as narrow as the needs of the company demand. This is one reason for the wide range of salaries offered to

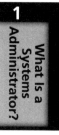

systems administrators as can be seen in the results of the InformationWeek Research 1999 National IT Salary Survey. According to this survey, a systems administrator can expect to make anywhere from $40,000 per year to $70,000 per year. Factors that determine the salary include

- Specialized skills, such as networking or security

- Years of experience

- The industry you work in

- Geographical location

For example, Tom, our systems administrator at the small title company will probably be paid a much lower salary than Janet, the systems administrator at the software development company. This disparity in the job functions of systems administrators led to the formation of the SAGE group of USENIX.

The SAGE Definition

To address the need for a more robust definition of a systems administrator, the *Systems Administration Guild* (SAGE) was formed as a task group of USENIX. This task force was set up to define the skills required to be a UNIX systems administrator. To this end, SAGE has published job descriptions for the levels of novice, junior, intermediate, and senior systems administrators. This section examines these levels and the skills required for each of them. As a flavor of UNIX, these definitions also apply to Linux.

> **Note**
>
> These job descriptions are just a sample of the information available through SAGE, which can be found at the USENIX Web site at http://www.usenix.org/sage. SAGE membership is useful in a number of ways, including full access to their publications on the Web as well as discounts when attending USENIX sponsored events, such the LISA conferences.

The novice administrator is the lowest level defined by SAGE. Their skill set includes good interpersonal skills and the ability to communicate well. This includes the ability to explain either verbally or in writing how to perform simple tasks and procedures. The novice administrator follows instructions well and is familiar with UNIX at a user level. This is the entry level for systems administration, and appropriate tasks for this level include first line support activities and systems maintenance under the direct supervision of more experienced systems administrators.

The next level defined by SAGE is the junior administrator. The administrator at this level has had between one and three years of experience as a systems administrator and possesses all of the skills of the novice administrator. In addition, the junior administrator is capable of training users and novice administrators and has highly developed UNIX skills. These skills include

- The ability to boot and shutdown systems

- Managing user accounts

- Backing up systems

- An understanding of UNIX concepts such as job control

- A working knowledge of filesystem semantics

- An understanding of the distinction between kernel processes and user processes

Desirable skills for a junior systems administrator also include the ability to write simple shell scripts and a familiarity with networking concepts. A junior administrator should have the skills necessary to maintain a site of one to ten systems alone or to assist with the maintenance of a larger site under the general supervision of a more senior administrator or systems manager.

At the three to five years of experience mark, SAGE defines the intermediate to advanced systems administrator. At this level, the UNIX skills of the administrator include an understanding of devices and device drivers, swapping and paging, security fundamentals, and installation and configuration issues. An intermediate administrator should be able to set up electronic mail systems, define printers, and build and install software packages. This person should also have a solid grasp on networking, which includes setting up NFS, NIS, and domain name services, as well as the ability to write scripts and do at least some basic debugging of C programs. At this level, the administrator is expected to show initiative and be a self-starter able to contribute to the management of a medium to large site with minimal supervision. It is also typical for administrators at this level to have some degree of influence in the purchasing process, usually through evaluating new products and recommending products for purchase.

The highest level defined by SAGE is the senior systems administrator. This level is usually reached when the systems administrator has more than five years of experience. The senior systems administrator has exceptional UNIX skills and understands all aspects of managing a large networked system. The senior administrator has the interpersonal skills required to interact with vendors and company management and the supervisory skills required to lead

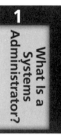

a team of less-experienced administrators. The senior administrator is able to take a task from the definition of a problem statement to the design and implementation of a solution. It is at this level that an administrator is usually granted purchasing authority and has the responsibility to justify these purchases.

In addition to these skills, some systems administrators become specialists in areas such as security, database administration, network administration, systems analysis and tuning, or programming. These specialists are often found at contracting firms and move from project to project wherever their skills are needed. One alternative to specialization is moving into management roles and taking on the responsibilities of managing teams of systems administrators. At the management level, it's not uncommon to be involved in the development of information technology strategies and policies.

Required Background and Skills

Not everyone who is familiar with Linux has what it takes to be a good systems administrator. This section looks at some of the specific skills and traits needed to be an effective Linux systems administrator. These traits fall into three basic areas:

- Strong Linux/UNIX skills

- A customer service mindset

- The ability to thrive in the midst of chaos

The Linux Guy

First and foremost, the effective systems administrator must have very strong Linux/UNIX skills. There is no greater measure of this than being known at your company as "the Linux guy." This is the person others come to when they have a Linux question, whether it concerns how to use a particular command to accomplish a task or how to configure a new device in their system. The Linux guy is the person who is not afraid to jump into the source code to see how something is done. Although the ability to hack the kernel is not a requirement, the Linux guy is usually at least passingly familiar with what is required to build a kernel from the source, how to install a custom built kernel, and where to look in the source tree for the various subsystems and drivers that make up the kernel. In addition to this, the Linux guy is often an evangelist and will gladly spend hours talking about the benefits of Linux over other operating systems. Specific skills that are characteristic of the Linux guy include the ability to effectively use the shell, including input and output redirection, shell metacharacters, and how to pipe multiple commands together to accomplish a task.

Customer Service Orientation

One key characteristic of any good systems administrator is a customer service orientation. This means knowing that users are not an annoyance to be dealt with, but the purpose of your existence. A good systems administrator is able to balance the needs and wants of the user base with the requirements of keeping the systems up and running and performing their assigned tasks. This customer service orientation does not mean giving customers everything that they ask for, but rather being willing to listen, and if users' requests are not possible to tell them so. On the other hand, if the request is possible, you should be able to determine if it is also feasible and in the best interests of the company. Only after all of these steps have been taken should user requests be granted.

Another aspect of customer service that applies to the systems administrator is that of documentation. Just as a customer service representative must keep a written record of their interaction with customers, a systems administrator should keep track of their interaction with systems. This may be as simple as keeping a systems diary, either on paper or electronically in which you record problems and solutions. This diary will not only allow you to keep track of what changes you make on systems, but will also help your team members or successors.

The other aspect of customer service that is applicable to being a good systems administrator is that of following up on issues and documenting system changes so that your fellow systems administrators can see what was done and when in the event that something goes wrong.

Thrives on Challenge

Another aspect of systems administration that challenges many people is the ability to thrive in an environment where interruptions and change are the rule instead of the exception. This characteristic separates the good systems administrator from the rest. The interrupt-driven aspect of systems administration is what turns many people off from the job because having to continually switch from one task to another can be quite stressful. As a fellow systems administrator once told me, "If I wanted a lower stress job, I would have become an air traffic controller." People who do not like to switch from task to task throughout the day will probably not be able to deal with the stress of being a systems administrator. In addition to user interrupts, the job of a systems administrator is often overlooked when systems are running smoothly. The only time people will know you exist is when there is a problem. Therefore, the systems administrator must be able to deal with the challenge of obscurity except in times of trouble.

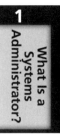

Systems Administrator Duties and Responsibilities

Systems administrator duties and responsibilities can be broken down into many categories, but three of them stand out as the ones that will consume the lion's share of your time. They are user management, hardware and software maintenance, and network administration. These, of course, can be further broken down into subcategories and that is what this book will do. But first, the following sections briefly discuss these three and give some examples of tasks that fall under them.

User Management

One of the most time-consuming tasks that faces any systems administrator is dealing with users. From the time that their accounts are created, they will be placing demands on you to do things to make their use of the systems easier. This sometimes leads to the view that users are a plague on your systems and should be treated as such. This is the wrong attitude, and with appropriate training and adequately defined communications channels, the management of users and their requests can become much easier.

There are many subcategories under user management, and the needs and concerns of users will influence your policy and decision-making processes in areas not normally thought of as related to user management. Here is a list of some of the tasks usually associated with the management of users on a Linux system:

- Adding and deleting user accounts
- Creating groups
- Training users
- Establishing acceptable use policies
- Setting up a help desk system to deal with user issues
- Setting filesystem quotas
- Creating email aliases

This is, of course, not a comprehensive list but it gives you an idea of some of the things you will learn as you go through this book. Most of these topics are covered in Chapter 29, "Users and Groups" and Chapter 30, "Helping Users." If user management is one of your primary duties, those chapters may be a good place to start.

Hardware and Software Maintenance

Another major duty of systems administrators is the maintenance of both hardware and software. The seasoned systems administrator will feel just as comfortable with a screwdriver as with a keyboard, and it is not unusual in many shops for hardware maintenance to be a major part of the systems administrator's responsibilities. Some of the tasks that fall under this category include the following:

- Installing and configuring the operating system

- Filesystem and disk management

- RAID management

- Kernel tuning and customization

- Device driver installation

- System failure diagnosis and recovery

- Adding and removing hardware on a system

This list could go on and on, but you get the idea. Again, each of these topics is covered later in the book and the issues associated with each of these areas are explored. Demonstrations of the various techniques and some possible solutions to the problems of managing hardware and software on a Linux system are also included.

Network Administration

One of the major duties of any systems administrator, especially in light of the explosion of the Internet in recent years, is the administration and management of networks. Since very early in its development, Linux has supported networking, not always well, but supported nonetheless. Networking tasks can be broken down into two major subcategories. The first of these has to do with setting up services for an intranet. Here is a sample of some of the tasks that might fall into this category:

- Installing and configuring network interface cards

- Connecting Linux hosts to hubs and switches

- Connecting Linux hosts to routers

- Configuring a Linux host as a router

- Setting up network printing and file sharing with NFS

- Establishing name services with NIS and DNS

- Integrating your Linux systems with other operating systems

Naturally, the other major subcategory has to do with services for the Internet. A systems administrator needs to know how to do this; however, it is not uncommon for these types of tasks to be outsourced to networking specialists. These specialists are normally employed to architect a system and help with the initial implementation, but the maintenance is then usually left to the local systems administration staff. Here are some sample tasks that are associated with this category:

- Setting up email servers and clients

- Installing and configuring Web servers

- Configuring and running a news server

- Setting up a firewall and establishing security policy

- Providing for remote access to your network

- Dealing with attempts to break into your system

These are just some of the tasks you will be faced with as a Linux systems administrator. Each of these is covered later in this book, with numerous examples to assist you in the mastery of each.

Summary

As you can see, the job of the Linux systems administrator is a complex one with a variety of required skills and personality traits. You must be able to balance the needs and wants of users with the stated goals of the organization for which you work. You must be able to juggle multiple, sometimes conflicting priorities. You will require a lot of specialized knowledge and will have to work hard to keep this knowledge current. The goal of this book is to provide a tool that will allow you to accomplish each of these goals. It should be a teaching tool for those who want to advance their knowledge and a reference for those who already possess the skills and knowledge to be called a Linux systems administrator.

CHAPTER 2

Essential Tools for System Administrators

IN THIS CHAPTER

- Power Tools for Super Users   *18*
- Web Resources for Administrators   *36*
- Other Sources of Information   *41*

As the administrator of Red Hat Linux systems, you are expected to have a grasp of Linux beyond that of normal Linux users. Your knowledge of Linux commands is extensive and you are the expert that everyone else comes to for answers to their Linux questions. This chapter serves as a review of those commands that are not part of the normal user's repertoire, but that are invaluable in carrying out your duties as a systems administrator. This chapter begins with a discussion of the commands and concepts that you should know as a superuser. The discussion then continues with coverage of the systems administration and configuration tools that are available on your Red Hat Linux system. This includes coverage of the control-panel, linuxconf, and the various configuration utilities such as sndconfig.

Power Tools for Super Users

Beyond the basic Linux command set, there are a plethora of tools available to power users that you as a systems administrator should know. This section covers a few of these, giving examples of their use. However, there are a few concepts that you must understand before you can utilize these tools to the fullest. Once these concepts have been covered, we will proceed with a discussion of the commands that separate the casual Linux user from the power user.

UNIX Commands for Power Users

Before beginning the discussion of those commands that should be a part of every system administrator's repertoire, there are a couple of concepts that you must understand to make full use of those commands. The first of these is the concept of *regular expressions,* which are used extensively by commands like awk, sed, and grep for pattern matching. They are also key to the mastery of scripting languages like perl and tcl. The other critical concept is that of *filename substitution*, or globbing, as performed by the various user shells. Failure to grasp both of these concepts will mean that you are not making the most of the commands available, which will limit your effectiveness as an administrator.

Regular Expressions

Regular expressions are a way of specifying a string to be matched. An example of this would be the grep command. Regular expressions are composed of pieces, which are strings of one or more characters to match. They may also contain special meta characters that act as wildcards, matching zero or more characters. There are also positional matching characters that can indicate the beginning or end of a string, and grouping characters that can be used to specify ranges or groups of characters to match or exclude. Table 2.1 shows the wildcard and positional characters and their meanings.

TABLE 2.1 Regular Expression Meta Characters

Meta Character	Meaning
.	Match any single character.
*	Match the previous character 0 or more times.
+	Match the previous character 1 or more times.
?	Match the previous character 0 or 1 times.
^	Start matching at the beginning of a string.
$	Match the end of a string.
|	The OR operator.

By using these wildcards along with some strings, you can construct some simple regular expressions. To demonstrate the use of regular expressions, we will start with a file containing the following lines:

```
tschenk:x:500:100:Thomas Schenk,Rm 164,502-2603,:/home/tschenk:/bin/bash
eunjoung:x:501:100:E.J. Schenk,Rm 503,503-1467,:/home/eunjoung:/bin/ash
nicholas:x:502:100:Nick Schenk,Rm 503,503-1465,:/home/nicholas:/bin/tcsh
nia:x:503:105:Nia Schenk,Rm 104,502-6514,:/home/nia:/bin/bash
bob:x:504:105:Robert Smith,Rm 504,503-1465,:/home/bob:/bin/ksh
bkreed:x:505:100:Bob Reed,Rm 504,503-1467,:/home/bkreed:/bin/bash
chuck:x:506:100:Charles Brown,Rm 104,502-4158,:/home/chuck:/bin/bash
chucky:x:507:105:Chuck Jones,Rm 504,503-1465,:/home/chucky:/bin/zsh
diane:x:508:100:Diane Wilson,Rm 104,502-4156,:/home/diane:/bin/bash
dwilson:x:509:100:Dwight Wilson,Rm 504,503-1466,:/home/dwilson:/bin/tcsh
ashley:x:510:105:Ashley Waters,Rm 504,503-1468,:/home/ashley:/bin/tcsh
bashton:x:511:100:Bill Ashton,Rm 100,502-6105,:/home/bashton:/bin/zsh
```

As you can see, this is part of a password file and for the purposes of our examples, we will refer to it as passwd. Using this file, we will attempt to use egrep with some simple regular expressions to find the answers to the following questions:

1. How many users in the passwd file have a last name of Schenk?

2. How many users have a first name of Bob or Robert?

3. What is the full name of the user chuck?

4. How many users use bash as their shell?

To answer the first question, we need to know the structure of the passwd file. In the passwd file, the last name is preceded by a space and followed by a comma. With this knowledge, we could issue the following command to find out how many people in the passwd file have a last name of Schenk.

```
egrep " Schenk," passwd
```

It could be argued that in this case, the comma and the space were not required to get the correct answer. However, it is good practice to describe the string you are searching for as much as possible. The regular expression as shown contains no special characters. It consists of a simple string of characters. The meaning of this regular expression is "a space followed by the word Schenk followed by a comma." Here is the output of the command as you would see it on the command line:

```
tschenk:x:500:100:Thomas Schenk,Rm 164,502-2603,:/home/tschenk:/bin/bash
eunjoung:x:501:100:E.J. Schenk,Rm 503,503-1467,:/home/eunjoung:/bin/ash
nicholas:x:502:100:Nick Schenk,Rm 503,503-1465,:/home/nicholas:/bin/tcsh
nia:x:503:105:Nia Schenk,Rm 104,502-6514,:/home/nia:/bin/bash
```

How many users have a first name of Bob or Robert? This second question is similar to the first. To answer this question, we could issue the following egrep command, which demonstrates the use of the | operator in a regular expression. The | is an OR operator and is used to specify that you are searching for either the string on the left-hand side of the | symbol or the string on the right-hand side. It also demonstrates one of the uses of parentheses in regular expressions.

```
egrep ":(Bob|Robert) " passwd
```

In this example, the regular expressions could be translated as "a colon, followed by either the string Bob or the string Robert, followed by a space." Note the parentheses surrounding the strings Bob and Robert. These are examples of the grouping operators. The output of this command would look like this:

```
bob:x:504:105:Robert Smith,Rm 504,503-1465,:/home/bob:/bin/ksh
bkreed:x:505:100:Bob Reed,Rm 504,503-1467,:/home/bkreed:/bin/bash
```

Our third question is, "What is the full name of the user chuck?" This requires use of one of the positional meta characters to get the single line containing the correct answer. It also requires that you know the format of the passwd file. Failure to take into account the structure of the passwd file could lead you to issue the following command:

```
egrep "chuck" passwd
```

This would result in the following output, which contains the correct line as well as an incorrect line for a user with an id of chucky. In addition, if the passwd file contained a user id of upchuck or woodchuck, these would also have been returned.

```
chuck:x:506:100:Charles Brown,Rm 104,502-4158,:/home/chuck:/bin/bash
chucky:x:507:105:Chuck Jones,Rm 504,503-1465,:/home/chucky:/bin/zsh
```

The most correct regular expression to use to answer this question would specify that the matching line begin with the string chuck followed by a colon. The egrep command using this regular expression would be as shown here:

```
egrep "^chuck:" passwd
```

This command would return the single line that begins with the word chuck followed by a colon and give us the answer to the third question: Charles Brown.

The final question, "How many users use bash as their shell?", requires the use of another of the positional meta characters to avoid getting extra data. At first glance, it would appear that a simple command such as the following would give the correct answer:

```
egrep "bash" passwd |wc -l
```

This would result in an answer of six, which is incorrect due to the inclusion of the userid bashton in the results. Again, knowledge of the structure of the passwd file is required to formulate the correct regular expression, demonstrated in this command, which returns the correct answer of five:

```
egrep "bash$" passwd | wc -l
```

In addition to the regular expression meta characters shown here, there are others that include ways to specify a range or set of characters, referred to as *bracket expressions*. Table 2.2 shows examples of bracket expressions and their meanings.

TABLE 2.2   Bracket Expressions

Regular Expression	Meaning
[A-Z]	Match all characters in the range A-Z in the current character set collating sequence.
[13579]	Match all characters specified between the brackets.
[^a-z]	Match all characters not in the range a-z in the current character set collating sequence.
[:alpha:]	Match all characters in the alpha class as defined in ctype(3).
[*.?+|]	Match the characters "*", ".", "?", "+", "|".

There are forms of regular expressions other than those covered here, but a full discussion of them is beyond the scope of this book. Many of the commands in the power user arsenal rely on knowledge of regular expressions, as do scripting languages like perl and tcl.

Filename Substitution

Filename substitution, or globbing, confuses many users because it uses many of the same meta characters as regular expressions, but they have different meanings. Table 2.3 shows the common globbing characters and their meanings. These apply to both the Bourne Again Shell (bash) and tcsh, an enhanced version of the Berkeley C-shell, the two most popular shells on Linux systems.

TABLE 2.3 Filename Substitution Meta Characters

Globbing Character	Meaning
?	Match any single character in a filename.
*	Match zero or more characters in a filename.
[...]	Match any of the characters between the brackets.
[^...]	Match any characters not specified in the brackets.
{aaa,bbb,ccc}	Expand to aaa, bbb, and ccc in order.
~	Expand to the current user's home directory if it is the first character in the pattern.

To better understand this concept of filename substitution, we will assume the following directory contents and demonstrate using various shell commands, such as `ls` and `echo`.

BUGS	config.h.in	interfaces.c	sudo.pod
CHANGES	config.log	interfaces.o	sudo_setenv.c
COPYING	config.status	lex.yy.c	sudo_setenv.o
FAQ	config.sub	lex.yy.o	sudoers
HISTORY	configure	logging.c	sudoers.cat
INSTALL	configure.in	logging.o	sudoers.man
INSTALL.configure	dce_pwent.c	lsearch.c	sudoers.pod
Makefile	emul	mkinstalldirs	testsudoers.c
Makefile.in	find_path.c	options.h	tgetpass.c
OPTIONS	find_path.o	parse.c	tgetpass.o
PORTING	fnmatch.3	parse.lex	utime.c
README	fnmatch.c	parse.o	version.h
RUNSON	getspwuid.c	parse.yacc	visudo*
TODO	getspwuid.o	pathnames.h	visudo.c
TROUBLESHOOTING	getwd.c	putenv.c	visudo.cat
acsite.m4	goodpath.c	sample.sudoers	visudo.man
aixcrypt.exp	goodpath.o	strdup.c	visudo.o
alloca.c	indent.pro	sudo	visudo.pod
check.c	ins_2001.h	sudo-lex.yy.c	y.tab.c
check.o	ins_classic.h	sudo.c	y.tab.h
compat.h	ins_csops.h	sudo.cat	y.tab.o
config.cache	ins_goons.h	sudo.h	

```
config.guess     install-sh     sudo.man
config.h         insults.h      sudo.o
```

This is a directory listing of the source code and object code generated for the `sudo` command. With this directory listing as our sample, we will answer the following questions using the `echo` and `ls` commands to generate the desired output.

1. Which of these files begin with the letter "I"?
2. Which files in the directory contain the character "y"?
3. How would you assign all filenames that end in ".c" or ".h" to a shell variable `FOO`?
4. How would you copy all files starting with "y." to your home directory?
5. How would you list all files starting with "visudo." except those ending with a ".c" or ".o" extension?
6. How can you list all files starting with the letter "s" and ending with a single character extension?

The first question asks us to list all files beginning with the letter "I". This example will demonstrate the use of the "*" globbing character. To answer this question, we would issue the following command, giving the output shown.

```
[tschenk@quicksilver sudo.v1.5.3]$ ls I*
INSTALL  INSTALL.configure
```

The next question also requires the use of the "*" globbing character. Remember that this character matches zero or more characters, thus the expression "*y*" used in the following command translates to "zero or more characters followed by the letter 'y' followed by zero or more characters." This means that the output will include files that start and end with the letter "y" as well as those that include "y" somewhere in the middle. Here is the command and its output:

```
[tschenk@quicksilver sudo.v1.5.3]$ ls *y*
aixcrypt.exp lex.yy.o    sudo-lex.yy.c  y.tab.h
lex.yy.c     parse.yacc  y.tab.c        y.tab.o
```

In the next example, we will use the `echo` command to assign all of the files ending with ".c" or ".h" to a shell environment variable `FOO`. This will demonstrate the use of the brackets in filename substitution.

```
[tschenk@quicksilver sudo.v1.5.3]$ FOO=`echo *.[ch]`
[tschenk@quicksilver sudo.v1.5.3]$ echo $FOO
alloca.c check.c compat.h config.h dce_pwent.c find_path.c fnmatch.c
getspwuid.c getwd.c goodpath.c ins_2001.h ins_classic.h ins_csops.h
ins_goons.h insults.h interfaces.c lex.yy.c logging.c lsearch.c options.h
parse.c pathnames.h putenv.c strdup.c sudo-lex.yy.c sudo.c sudo.h
```

```
sudo_setenv.c testsudoers.c tgetpass.c utime.c version.h visudo.c y.tab.c
y.tab.h
(newlines inserted to improve readability)
```

The next example asks us to copy all files starting with "y." to the current user's home directory. This will be accomplished using the "~", or tilde operator. Please note that this expansion will only occur if the "~" character is the first in a string and is followed by a "/" character or an alphanumeric character.

```
[tschenk@quicksilver sudo.v1.5.3]$ ls y.*
y.tab.c  y.tab.h  y.tab.o
[tschenk@quicksilver sudo.v1.5.3]$ cp y.* ~
[tschenk@quicksilver sudo.v1.5.3]$ ls ~/y.*
/home/tschenk/y.tab.c  /home/tschenk/y.tab.h  /home/tschenk/y.tab.o
```

Example number five asks us to list all files starting with "visudo." Except those ending with an extension of ".c" or ".o". This is actually trickier than it first appears. Take a look at the following listing and you will see that it actually takes a combination of brackets with the negation operator, the "*" operator, and curly brace expansion to accomplish the desired result.

```
[tschenk@quicksilver sudo.v1.5.3]$ ls visudo.*
visudo.c  visudo.cat  visudo.man  visudo.o  visudo.pod

[tschenk@quicksilver sudo.v1.5.3]$ ls visudo.[^co]
ls: visudo.[^co]: No such file or directory

[tschenk@quicksilver sudo.v1.5.3]$ ls visudo.[^co]*
visudo.man  visudo.pod

[tschenk@quicksilver sudo.v1.5.3]$ ls visudo.{[^co]*,cat}
visudo.cat  visudo.man  visudo.pod
```

The final example is a very simple one that demonstrates the use of the "?", or single character wildcard. Take a look at the following to see how we get the desired result of all files starting with the letter "s" and ending in a single character extension.

```
[tschenk@quicksilver sudo.v1.5.3]$ ls s*.?
strdup.c      sudo-lex.yy.c  sudo.c  sudo.h  sudo.o
sudo_setenv.c  sudo_setenv.o
```

Power Commands for Power Users

There are hundreds of commands available on Linux systems and the normal user will probably never learn all of them. In fact, most users will learn the minimal set of commands necessary to accomplish their job. This is what separates them from the power users, whose thirst for knowledge will lead them to learn the most effective ways to accomplish any task. The following set of commands allows the power user to perform tasks that may seem impossible to normal users. At the very least, it simplifies what otherwise is a complex combination of the few basic commands normal users know. This section covers the following commands and gives a few examples of their use:

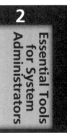

- `find`

- `awk`

- `sed`

You may look at the list above and think that these commands are not especially powerful. However, the following examples will show that these commands, when used with their plethora of options or in combination with each other, are quite powerful and will let you accomplish tasks that the normal user will marvel at. Let's start with a truly powerful command—the `find` command.

find

The `find` command, as its name implies, is used to find files in a filesystem. In general, the form of the `find` command is the command name, followed by a path to begin searching, followed by an expression made up of options, tests, and actions. In its simplest form, the `find` command starts with the current directory and performs the `-print` action. Here is an example showing this default action.

```
[nia@quicksilver nia]$ find
.
./.Xdefaults
./.bash_logout
./.bash_profile
./.bashrc
./.screenrc
./.bash_history
./.kde
./.kde/share
./.kde/share/applnk
./.kde/share/apps
./.kde/share/apps/kdehelp
./.kde/share/apps/kdisknav
```

```
./.kde/share/apps/kfm
./.kde/share/apps/kfm/bookmarks
./.kde/share/apps/kfm/desktop
./.kde/share/apps/kfm/tmp
./.kde/share/apps/kpanel
./.kde/share/apps/kpanel/applnk
./.kde/share/config
./.kde/share/config/desktop0rc
./.kde/share/config/kcmdisplayrc
./.kde/share/config/kfmrc
./.kde/share/config/kpanelrc
./.kde/share/config/kvtrc
./.kde/share/icons
./.kde/share/icons/mini
./.kde/share/mimelnk
./.kderc
./Desktop
./Desktop/.directory
./Desktop/Autostart
./Desktop/Printer.kdelnk
./Desktop/Templates
./Desktop/Templates/Device.kdelnk
./Desktop/Templates/Ftpurl.kdelnk
./Desktop/Templates/MimeType.kdelnk
./Desktop/Templates/Program.kdelnk
./Desktop/Templates/URL.kdelnk
./Desktop/Templates/WWWUrl.kdelnk
./Desktop/Trash
./Desktop/cdrom.kdelnk
./Desktop/floppy.kdelnk
./.xauth
```

Now if this were the only thing that the find command was capable of, it would not be very useful. Table 2.4 takes a look at some of the available options to the find command and what they mean.

TABLE 2.4 Command-Line Options of the find Command

Option	Meaning
-daystart	Calculate times from the start of the day instead of 24 hours ago. Used in conjunction with -atime, -ctime, and -mtime tests. For example, find /tmp -daystart -atime 1 -print will list all files in /tmp accessed since today began.

TABLE **2.4** continued

Option	Meaning
-depth	Process the files in a directory before you process the directory itself. This option is useful if the order of processing is important, such as if you were removing all files in a directory and then needed to remove the directory.
-follow	Process the file referenced by a symlink, not the symlink. This option might be useful if you were piping the output of the find command to a backup command like tar or afio, where you want to store the actual file and not the symbolic link.
-maxdepth N	Descend at most N directory levels below that specified in the path portion of the command line.
-mindepth N	Do not apply tests and actions to files at depths less than N.
-noleaf	This option turns off an optimization that tells find to assume that there are two fewer subdirectories than the hard link count. This option is needed when searching filesystems that do not adhere to Linux semantics, like MS-DOS filesystems.
-xdev, -mount	These two options are synonyms. They direct find to not descend directories on filesystems other than the one containing the starting directory. This is useful when searching by inode, or if you want to exclude network filesystems from your search.

2

Essential Tools
for System
Administrators

As you can see, with the appropriate options, the default behavior of find can be altered to provide more utility. In addition to the options listed in Table 2.4, you can specify any number of tests to the files found by the find command. These include tests to check the various times associated with a file, the permissions, owner, file type, and others. For a complete list of the available tests, refer to the find manual page. To see how some of these tests can be useful, let's look at a few examples.

For our first example, we want to find all of the executable files in a directory. To accomplish this, we will use the -maxdepth option to limit our search to the current directory. We'll also use the -perm and the -type tests to specify regular files with any of the executable bits set.

```
[tschenk@nomad ppp]$ ls -l
total 5
-rw-------  1 root    daemon         78 Apr  9 22:33 chap-secrets
-rwxr-xr-x  1 root    root          265 Sep 16  1997 ip-down*
-rwxr-xr-x  1 root    root          349 May  7  1998 ip-up*
-rw-r--r--  1 root    daemon          5 Apr  9 22:33 options
-rw-------  1 root    daemon         77 Apr  9 22:33 pap-secrets
[tschenk@nomad ppp]$ find . -perm -111 -type f
./ip-down
./ip-up
```

Now suppose we want to look through all of the files in the /usr/sbin directory tree and find any that have the setuid bit set and that are owned by root. To accomplish this, we issue the find command with the -owner and the -perm tests. But instead of the default -print action, we will specify the -ls option to get an ls type listing.

```
[tschenk@nomad /usr]$ find sbin -user root -perm -4000 -ls
143415    6 -rwsr-xr-x  1 root    root    5736 Apr 19 14:39   sbin/usernetctl
143500  293 -rwsr-sr-x  1 root    root  299364 Apr 19 15:38   sbin/sendmail
143537   17 -rwsr-xr-x  1 root    bin    16488 Mar 22 14:53   sbin/traceroute
143541   11 -rwsr-xr-x  1 root    root   10708 Apr 12 10:29   sbin/userhelper
143564   19 -rwsr-xr-x  1 root    root   18576 Apr  1 06:52      sbin/fping
```

In addition to simple actions like -print and -ls, there are other actions including the most powerful—the -exec action. With this action, you can specify that for each file found, an arbitrary action be performed. If you consider this for a moment, you can see how this can be an immensely powerful tool. Say, for example, that you want to run a daily script that did an md5sum on all of the setuid root programs on your system so that you can compare them with what you recorded on the previous day to detect changes. Such a script might look like this:

```
#!/bin/sh

# Start by running the find command to locate the setuid programs and
# execute the md5sum program against them.

if [ -f /var/local/setuid.log ]; then
    FIRSTTIME=false
    mv /var/local/setuid.log /var/local/setuid.log.OLD
else
    FIRSTTIME=true
fi

find / -perm -4000 -exec md5sum {} \; > /var/local/setuid.log

if [ "$FIRSTTIME" = "false" ]; then
    cd /var/local
    diff -u setuid.log.OLD setuid.log ¦ mail -s "Setuid Report" root
fi

exit 0
```

Caution

This is just a sample of what you can do with `find`, and with this power comes a couple of words of warning. First, always double- and triple-check your syntax before hitting the return key. This is especially important if you are using the `-exec` action and performing a destructive operation, such as removing files. Secondly, the `find` command can be quite resource intensive and should be used with care. This is true for a couple of reasons. The first is that by its nature, `find` must examine every file located under the specified starting directory and optionally perform some test upon it. The second is that with the `-exec` action, you can specify an arbitrary command or script to run against any files found. You must therefore take into consideration the resource usage of the command or script being run. There is nothing more dangerous than a malformed `find` command with a resource hogging action.

awk

Another command that you as a power user will find useful is the `awk` command. This command is actually a powerful scripting language whose primary function is the generation of reports. In fact, many of the report generation features of `awk` influenced similar features in perl. Many administrators find `awk` most useful in simple one-line commands or as parts of simple shell scripts. Take, for example, the following command line:

```
ps auwx | awk ' NR > 1 { print $1 }' | sort | uniq
```

This command line does the following:

- Takes the output of `ps`
- Skips the first line
- Chops off the user names
- Sorts the user names
- Runs `uniq` on the sorted list

This results in a list of all userids who currently have processes running on the system.

This is a very simple use of awk, but as stated, `awk` is primarily a text processing and report generation tool. The following command sequence demonstrates this capability. This command takes the GECOS information from field 5 of the `passwd` file and generates a report of the username, office number, and office telephone.

```
[tschenk@nomad redhat]$ awk -F ':' \
'BEGIN { printf "%-15.15s%-15.15s%-10.10s\n\n",
"FULL NAME", "OFFICE NO.", "PHONE" }
{ split($5 f,","); 
  printf "%-15.15s%-15.15s%-10.10s\n", f[1], f[2], f[3] }' passwd
FULL NAME       OFFICE NO.      PHONE

Thomas Schenk   Rm 164          502-2603
E.J. Schenk     Rm 503          503-1467
Nick Schenk     Rm 503          503-1465
Nia Schenk      Rm 104          502-6514
Robert Smith    Rm 504          503-1465
Bob Reed        Rm 504          503-1467
Charles Brown   Rm 104          502-4158
Chuck Jones     Rm 504          503-1465
Diane Wilson    Rm 104          502-4156
Dwight Wilson   Rm 504          503-1466
Ashley Waters   Rm 504          503-1468
Bill Ashton     Rm 100          502-6105
```

Now, you may be thinking that perl could do this much more easily. But consider this: Sometimes awk is the better choice because in cases like this one, it is a much lighter weight process, without the startup overhead of perl. This difference in overhead is one of the reasons why familiarity with awk is a useful skill. The awk scripting language allows you to generate reports, make calculations, and perform other tasks just like perl. On the other hand, perl is a more general-purpose scripting language. Due to its support of extension modules, perl can be used to build very complex systems that are beyond the capabilities of awk. However, even though perl is a more featureful scripting language, for small tasks awk may be the better choice. If you think of awk and perl as hammers, awk is a carpenter's claw hammer and perl is a five pound sledge; which one you use depends on the size of the nail.

sed

The next command we will cover is the stream editor sed. This command is useful primarily for quick search-and-replace options. And by writing simple script files for sed, you can perform multiple changes to a file. This capability is quite useful in script files.

Here is an example where sed is of use to save a lot of typing associated with a change in company name and logo.

This example utilizes the sed command along with the file locating capabilities of the find command. Combining the two allows you to do two things:

1. Replace the old company name.

2. Replace references to the old logo filename with a reference to the new logo filename.

```
[root@nomad html]# cat /tmp/sedscript
s/Widget Makers/Widget.com/g
s/widgetlogo.gif/widgetlogo2.gif/g
[root@nomad html]# cat /tmp/rename.sh
#!/bin/bash

FNAME=$1

mv ${FNAME} ${FNAME}.OLD

sed -f /tmp/sedscript ${FNAME}.OLD > ${FNAME}
[root@nomad html]# find . -name "*.html" -exec /tmp/rename.sh {} \;
```

This is just one of the many uses of sed, but as you can see, this simple script saved someone a lot of typing. Instead of having to visit each HTML file on the company Web site to change the company name and logo using an editor, the script does the work for us. This means that a task that might have taken a person several hours can be accomplished much quicker. For a more detailed description of the options available for the sed command, refer to the manual page.

The few commands that we've just covered are not the only commands that you will find useful in your role as Linux systems administrator, but with these three used in combination with your mastery of the shell of your choice, you can accomplish tasks that others cannot.

Linuxconf, The Control-Panel, and Configuration Utilities

In addition to tools like find, awk, and sed, which you can use to build other tools to make systems administration easier, the Red Hat Linux distribution comes with several tools to aid you as a systems administrator. Among these tools are Linuxconf, the control-panel program, and several configuration utilities for configuring things such sound support, network, and so on. This section briefly discusses each of these tools and describes how to start them. It also discusses some of their features, but does not go into any depth on their functionality because that is covered in other sections of this book.

The Linuxconf System

The Linuxconf system is a powerful administration tool that can be used in both text and graphical modes. It can be used to perform many configuration tasks on your Linux system. Some of these tasks include

- Network configuration

- User account management

- Filesystem management

- Boot loader management

In addition to these tasks, Linuxconf can also be used to archive configuration information, creating configuration profiles which you can then switch between. These profiles could be useful, for example on a laptop system, which must be capable of working on your work network, but that you also wish to have work on your home network. By storing a profile of the network configuration required to interact with each of the networks, you can easily move from one environment to another by changing profiles. It can also manage the mounting and unmounting of filesystems, shut down your Linux system, and control PPP, SLIP, and PLIP links. Figure 2.1 is a screenshot of the Linuxconf graphical version, showing the top level menu options.

FIGURE 2.1

Linuxconf in graphical mode.

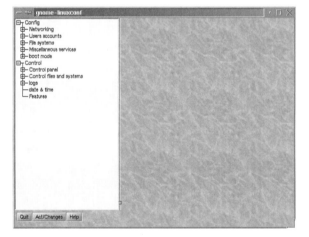

As mentioned, Linuxconf also has a non-graphical mode, which uses the same tree-based structure. Our discussion is limited to the graphical version of Linuxconf; however, the menu structure is identical and if you prefer to use the text version of Linuxconf, the following discussion applies just the same. As you can see, Linuxconf uses a tree structured menu system to group like tasks together. If you click on the block containing the plus sign next to the word Networking, you will see that this expands to three subheadings:

1. Client tasks
2. Server tasks
3. Misc.

If you click on the box next to Client tasks, you will see that it also expands into a multitude of tasks related to configuring a network on a client system. This includes managing the /etc/hosts file, specifying a name server to connect to, routing and gateway information, managing the host name search path (which edits the /etc/nsswitch.conf file), and several other options. If you expand all of the submenus, you will see that Linuxconf allows you to perform a large number of common administration tasks without ever having to touch the command line. In addition, one of the features of Linuxconf that differentiates it from some of the other system administration tools available for Linux is that not only can you change the configuration information, you can also immediately activate your changes.

Another tool provided by Red Hat Linux to assist administrators is the control-panel. The control-panel is provided as a simple launcher for other configuration utilities. By default, it includes buttons to allow you to do the following:

- Start the runlevel editor
- Set the system time and date
- Configure a printer
- Configure the network
- Configure a modem
- Manage kerneld and /etc/conf.modules
- Search online help
- Start Linuxconf

As you can see, there is some duplication between some of the control-panel modules and Linuxconf but this allows you to choose the tool that you prefer. The biggest example of this duplication is the network configuration module. In addition, some of the modules do very little, such as the modem configuration module, which asks you which COM port your modem is on and then creates a symbolic link from that device to /dev/modem. This is not to say that the control-panel is not useful.

For example, configuring PPP using the control-panel is normally quite simple and involves the following steps:

1. Configure your modem using the modem configuration tool.
2. Select the network configurator from the control-panel shown in Figure 2.2. This will bring up the dialog box shown in Figure 2.3.
3. Click on the Interfaces tab, and then click the Add button. This will present a dialog box that you would use to specify an interface type.
4. Select type PPP and click the OK button.
5. A final dialog box is presented that allows you to specify the phone number to dial, your PPP login name, the associated password, and whether to use PAP authentication. Enter the appropriate values.
6. If you want, you can also click the Customize button to set options such as whether to set up a default route, whether the interface should be started at boot time, whether the PPP connection should be restarted if it fails, customize the chat script for logging into your service provider, and so on.
7. Once you have saved the configuration information, click the Activate button to test, and you are all set.

FIGURE 2.2
The control-panel.

In addition to Linuxconf and the control-panel, Red Hat also provides some simple tools to configure specific functionality or devices. Table 2.5 lists a few of these tools and their purpose.

FIGURE 2.3
The Network Configurator dialog.

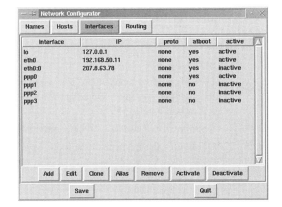

FIGURE 2.4
The Runlevel editor.

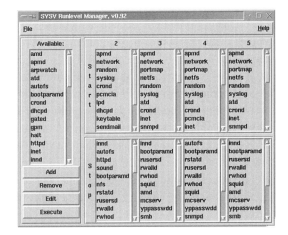

FIGURE 2.5
The Red Hat printer tool.

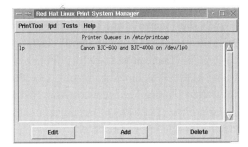

TABLE 2.5 Red Hat Linux Configuration Tools

Command	Function
authconfig	Allows you to specify the use of NIS, shadow, and/or MD5 passwords.
mouseconfig	Presents a list of mouse types for you to select from and creates the /dev/mouse link. Also called from the Xconfigurator to set the mouse type for X.
sndconfig	Configures and tests sound card settings.
kbdconfig	Configures the keyboard type to be used at system startup.
timeconfig	Allows you to specify the timezone in which you are located and whether your system clock is set to UTC.

Web Resources for Administrators

Linux was born on the Internet and it is because of the Internet that Linux has grown to the point it is at today. Examples of this growth can be found in just about every part of the Linux kernel and the various distributions. Without the medium of the Internet, there could not have been the wealth of code contributed by people from around the world. There also could not have been the collaboration required to build distributions and get them into the hands of the estimated 7 to 10 million Linux users in the world today. This being the case, there are abundant resources available on the Internet in general to assist Linux users, and specifically on the World Wide Web. This section takes a look at some of the resources that will be of immense assistance to systems administrators of Linux systems. The Web sites selected for inclusion here are just a sampling of those available. For more Linux resources on the Web, check your favorite search engine, or look for the links pages at the sites described here.

The Linux Documentation Project

One of the Web sites that all systems administrators should be familiar with is the Linux Documentation Project Web site located at the University of North Carolina at http://metalab.unc.edu/LDP/. The Linux Documentation Project, or LDP for short, is a project to produce Linux documentation that can be freely distributed over the Internet, just as Linux is freely distributed. The LDP has volunteers creating such documentation as the Linux Installation and Getting Started Guide, The Network Administrators Guide, The System Administrator's Guide, and a wealth of howto documentation on just about any subject imaginable. Everything from selecting compatible hardware to setting up PPP, or even setting up your system to display information in Chinese, is documented by people who have taken the time to learn the steps involved in a process. By doing so, others benefit from their experience. In addition, the LDP maintains the Linux manual pages, frequently asked questions lists, and the Linux Gazette.

FIGURE 2.6
The Linux Docu-mentation Project home page.

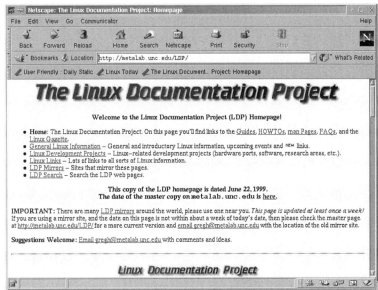

The majority of the documents you will find at the Linux Documentation Project site are available on the Red Hat installation media and by default are installed under /usr/doc/HOWTO and /usr/doc/LDP in a variety of formats, including HTML, PostScript, DVI, text, and SGML. Many of the documents have also been translated into languages other than English, including Spanish, German, Korean, Italian, and Japanese, just to name a few. Visit the LDP Web site to find updates to the HOWTOs and to look for new translations. These updates are announced on the comp.os.linux.announce newsgroup.

Linux Kernel Archives and Kernelnotes

Keeping abreast of changes to the Linux kernel can be a full-time job if you let it, but by utilizing the following two sites, you can stay on top of the changes as they occur and also have a useful starting place when looking for Linux information.

The definitive place on the Web to look for new kernel releases is the Linux Kernel Archives at http://www.kernel.org/ (see Figure 2.7). This is the official site where new releases of the kernel from Linus Torvalds are found. But kernel sources are not the limit of the information you will find here. You can also find links to the international cryptographic patches to the Linux kernel, a definition of what Linux is, and most importantly, a list of mirror sites for the Linux kernel sources. I say most importantly because when a new kernel release is made, it becomes next to impossible to connect to the Web site due to the high volume of traffic. Fortunately, there are mirrors galore for the Linux source code and if you are willing to wait a day or so, you can easily get the latest patch.

FIGURE 2.7
The Linux Kernel Archives.

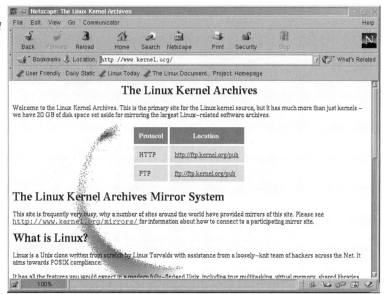

For more than kernel source, a favorite site among Linux users is Kernelnotes, formerly known as LinuxHQ. This site maintains a plethora of information related to the Linux kernel, including

- Source code browsers for the latest stable and development branches of the kernel

- Patch summaries describing what new and wonderful features are available

- Pointers to patch repositories for patches that haven't made it into the mainstream kernel yet

There are also lots of links to other sources of information including Alan Cox's home page as maintainer of the old stable source tree; a mirror of the Linux Documentation Project pages; and archives of the various Linux mailing lists, including linux-kernel, where all of the key kernel developers hang out. You can visit this wonderful Web site at `http://kernelnotes.com/` (see Figure 2.8).

FIGURE **2.8**
*The
Kernelnotes.org
site.*

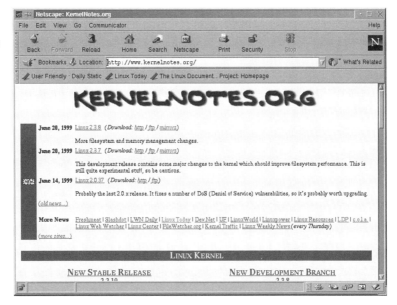

Linuxcare

Another invaluable resource to systems administrators of Linux systems is a relative
newcomer in the Linux world, but is backed by some long-time Linux supporters.
Linuxcare provides a range of services, including

- Technical support

- Education and training

- Consulting

- Open source development

In addition to these services, Linuxcare also maintains a searchable Linux knowledge base.
They will also provide problem tracking for your Open Source project, and provide Linux
forums in which you can participate. To top it off, Linuxcare is a Linux portal site
providing the latest Linux news and information. Finally, you can find information on
hardware that has been certified to run with Linux from major manufacturers such as Dell,
Compaq, and IBM. You will find them on the Web at `http://linuxcare.com/`
(see Figure 2.9).

FIGURE **2.9**
The Linuxcare home page.

Linux Today

One other Linux resource on the Web is the Linux Today site. This site does much of your Web surfing for you. It collects information from news sources all over the Web, including articles about Linux, security announcements, and new releases of the kernel. In addition to news postings, you can read original editorials from the Linux Today staff, as well as interact with the Linux community utilizing the feedback options. If you are looking for up-to-the-minute news about who is doing what with Linux, Linux Today is the place to look. In addition to the breaking headlines, Linux Today also provides a place to look for or post Linux-related jobs. Through its sister site, Linux PR, you can find press releases about Linux-related products or from companies that support Linux. Linux Today can be found on the Web at `http://linuxtoday.com` and Linux PR can be found at `http://linuxpr.com`. A sample of the type of information you can find at Linux Today can be seen in Figure 2.10, which shows their home page.

FIGURE **2.10**

The Linux Today home page.

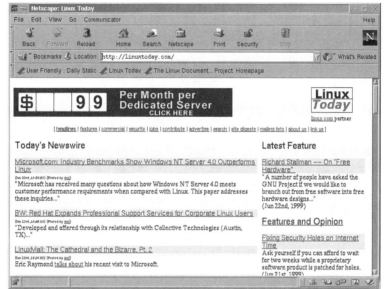

Other Web Sites of Interest

The sites already mentioned are but a sampling of those that might be of use to the systems administrator. There is a wealth of other sites, both general purpose and specific to a particular facet of Linux. These sites are too numerous to mention, but here are a few of my personal favorites:

- `http://www.slashdot.org/` Slashdot is where developers and systems administrators can come to discuss the technology news of the day.

- `http://www.linux.com/` This is a portal site and contains a section of particular interest to administrators on system tuning.

- `http://www.freshmeat.org/` Freshmeat is an excellent site at which to find the latest open source software and discuss it with the developer.

Other Sources of Information

In addition to the resources found on the Web, the Internet has much more to offer to the Linux community. Some of these resources include FTP sites that carry software for Linux, mailing lists where developers can interact with one another and develop the newest features for Linux, and newsgroups where anyone can ask questions about and share their enthusiasm for Linux. Following are just a few of these resources.

Mailing Lists

If you want to hobnob with the Linux development crowd, especially the kernel developers, the place to hang out is on the various mailing lists available to Linux users. Covering topics ranging from hard core kernel development to the promotion of Linux as a business solution, the Linux mailing lists are a subscription service that you can join or leave as the mood strikes you, provided you play by the list owner's rules. Unlike newsgroups and the Web, where everyone is able to participate as they see fit, mailing lists are a little bit more restrictive. This is done so that the signal-to-noise ratio stays high. A list owner or moderator may remove you from a list subscription at their discretion. The following table lists a few of the mailing lists and their submission addresses:

Mailing List	*Submission Address*
linux-kernel	`linux-kernel@vger.rutgers.edu`
linux-smp	`linux-smp@vget.rutgets.edu`
linux-net	`linux-net@vget.rutgets.edu`
linux-gcc	`linux-gcc@vget.rutgets.edu`
linux-raid	`linux-raid@vget.rutgets.edu`
linux-scsi	`linux-scsi@vget.rutgets.edu`

To subscribe to any of these lists, which are managed by Majordomo, send email to `<listname>-request@vget.rutgers.edu` with `subscribe` in the message body. For example, to subscribe to the linux-kernel mailing list, your could issue the following command:

```
echo subscribe | mail linux-kernel-request@vger.rutgers.edu
```

In addition to these, and the many other Linux lists managed via the mailing list server at Rutgers, there are mailing lists for most major projects and distributions. Red Hat Linux is no exception. You can subscribe to several lists at Red Hat, including the following:

Mailing List	*Submission Address*
redhat-announce-list	`redhat-announce-list@redhat.com`
redhat-devel-list	`redhat-devel-list@redhat.com`
redhat-list	`redhat-list@redhat.com`

To subscribe to any of the Red Hat lists, the format is slightly different than the ones managed from Rutgers. You must send email to `<listname>-request@redhat.com` with a subject of `"subscribe"` as shown in the following command line, which would subscribe the sender to the redhat-announce-list:

```
mail -s "subscribe" redhat-announce-list@redhat.com </dev/null
```

FTP Archives

As your systems grow, you will often find a need to locate software for your Linux system that is not provided on the Red Hat distribution media. This is where the FTP archives come in. Since the early days of Linux, there have been several repositories of Linux software available. Table 2.6 is a list of some of the biggest and most popular software archives for Linux users and a description of the software you will find there.

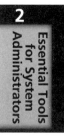

TABLE 2.6 Popular Linux FTP Archives

FTP Site	Description
tsx-11.mit.edu	One of the original Linux archive sites located at the Massachusetts Institute of Technology. A good source for new releases of XFree86 for Linux, the GNU C compiler, and many other software packages for a Linux system.
metalab.unc.edu	Formerly known as sunsite.unc.edu, this repository at the University of North Carolina is probably the best-known Linux archive in the world. If it is available for Linux, chances are that you can find a copy of it here.
ftp.*.kernel.org	A system of mirror sites for Linux kernel sources, you replace the asterisk with a country code, for example us for the United States.
ftp.redhat.com	The primary Red Hat FTP site, where you will find the latest official distributions.
updates.redhat.com	When updates are posted for the Red Hat distribution, they are uploaded to this site.
developer.redhat.com	The Red Hat developer community has a number of trusted developers who updated to this site as part of the Red Hat Contribution Network.
contrib.redhat.com	The site where anyone who can make an RPM is allowed to upload a packaged software product.

Newsgroups

In addition to the Web and mailing lists, there are a great many Usenet newsgroups devoted to the Linux operating system. Table 2.7 is a partial listing of some of the major newsgroups and their focus.

TABLE 2.7   Linux-Related USENET Newsgroups

Newsgroup Name	Description
comp.os.linux.advocacy	Devoted to the advocacy of the Linux operating system and to answering the question, "Why is Linux the greatest thing since sliced bread?"
comp.os.linux.announce	Announcements concerning applications for Linux, new distributions, and items of general interest to the Linux community are posted here after approval by the moderator.
comp.os.linux.answers	If you are looking for a FAQ or HOWTO for Linux, it will be posted here. A moderated newsgroup.
comp.os.linux.development.apps	A forum for people developing application software for the Linux operating system, this newsgroup is a good place to ask questions, enlist development help, or to look for beta testers.
comp.os.linux.development.system	This newsgroup is the place for systems programmers to discuss new features they would like to see added to the kernel and to post code that implements them.
comp.os.linux.hardware	If you need to find out if the Acme NetRocket network interface card works with Linux, this is the place to ask.
comp.os.linux.misc	When your question just doesn't seem to fit into any other category, this is the place to ask it.
comp.os.linux.networking	Discussions of Linux networking setup or network code development are the order of the day in this group.
comp.os.linux.portable	For those people who want to take Linux on the road, this newsgroup is a place to find out which PCMCIA devices work with Linux, how to get them working if it is possible, and which laptop systems to avoid.
comp.os.linux.security	Security of Linux systems, including discussions of how to implement firewalls, where to obtain security patches, and announcements of security problems with Linux are the topic of this newsgroup.
comp.os.linux.setup	If you are getting started and need assistance with setting up your Linux system, this is where to ask.

You can read these and many other newsgroups via your Internet service provider, but if your ISP doesn't carry newsgroups, do not despair. You can subscribe to these and many other newsgroups using your Web browser. Simply make a visit to Deja.com and register for My Deja.com. Not only are you able to read newsgroups, but Deja.com provides the largest archive of Usenet articles available on the Internet and a powerful search engine as well.

Summary

In your role as a systems administrator, you are expected to have skills beyond those of the regular user. This chapter has taken a look at some of the concepts and utilities that you as power user should know. It also examined the systems administration utilities provided with the Red Hat Linux distribution. Finally, you have learned some of the resources available to the Linux administrator on the Internet, including Web sites, mailing lists, FTP archives, and Usenet newsgroups. All of these tools are available to make your job easier. It is up to you to learn to use them and to take advantage of them.

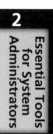

2

Essential Tools for System Administrators

Linux Essentials

PART

II

IN THIS PART

3 Installation Strategies   *49*

4 Where Do I Find...?   *81*

5 Starting Up and Shutting Down   *111*

6 System Failure Diagnosis and Recovery   *141*

Installation Strategies

IN THIS CHAPTER

- Default Installation Versus Customized Approaches **50**
- Cloning Installations **56**
- A Template-Based Approach **69**

At some point in your experience as a systems administrator, you have had to perform an installation of the Linux operating system. This chapter deals with the issues involved in doing installations on multiple computers. It does not cover the Red Hat installation procedure in detail, but instead deals with how to make installing systems as efficient and simple as possible. Although the Red Hat installation procedure has become quite simple for the experienced administrator, it can be time consuming. A lot of time that could be better spent is wasted if you use the default installation method provided by Red Hat.

Default Installation Versus Customized Approaches

Many users would question the need to use any installation method other than the default installation method provided by Red Hat. After all, Red Hat has invested significant amounts of time to make installation as simple as possible. If, however, you find that you are spending more time installing the operating system than you would like, this chapter will provide some alternative approaches to installation that may be of interest to you. This section discusses some of the pros and cons of using the default install versus some other method and shows some examples of installation strategies that you might select as alternatives.

Individual Installations

When dealing with individual installations, or if you install very few Linux systems, there is little incentive for developing or using an alternative installation method. Red Hat installation has become very simple and with a little advanced preparation, can go quite quickly. On a modern machine with a CD-ROM drive, an installation can take as little as 15 to 20 minutes from boot to completion, whereas other installation methods such as FTP or HTTP network installs can take considerably longer due to the overhead of transferring data across the network. In all, Red Hat Linux 6.1 provides five methods of installation. These methods are

- Local CD-ROM

- Hard drive

- NFS install

- FTP install

- HTTP install

This section examines these methods and discusses some of the advantages and disadvantages of each, along with some of the problems that you might encounter.

Local CD-ROM

By far the easiest method of installing Red Hat is from a local CD-ROM drive. This method has the advantage of being fast, requiring no network connectivity, and requiring no space on your hard drive. In addition, this method is supported by the boot floppy that comes with Red Hat unless your CD-ROM drive is attached to a PCMCIA card. In this case, you will require the PCMCIA boot floppy, which can be found on the install media in the images directory. To install via this method, you need a supported CD-ROM drive. This drive can be an ATAPI drive, a SCSI drive, or one of the supported proprietary drives. In addition, if your system supports booting from the CD-ROM drive, you don't even need a floppy drive to get started. To get started with an installation from a local CD-ROM, either boot from the Red Hat default boot floppy or directly from the CD-ROM drive. You will answer a couple of questions regarding which language to use and what type of keyboard you have, and then you will be presented with a dialog box that asks where to install from, as shown in Figure 3.1.

FIGURE 3.1

Selecting a CD-ROM install.

If required, the appropriate modules will be loaded to support your CD-ROM drive, you will be prompted to insert the CD into your drive, and installation will proceed as normal.

Hard Drive

Another fast installation method is the install from hard drive. To accomplish this installation, the installation files are copied to a hard drive partition that will not be installed to, such as an existing Windows or MS-DOS partition. This installation method has the advantage of not requiring connectivity to a network and also not requiring a supported CD-ROM. Like the CD-ROM install, it is supported by the boot floppy that comes in the boxed set. It is not very useful, however, if you want to dedicate the entire hard drive to Linux, although this does not preclude using this installation method if you do want the entire machine devoted to Linux. To use this installation method, you will require sufficient hard drive space to hold the contents of the Red Hat directory from an installation CD or FTP site. You will also need to create boot floppies from the boot.img file in the images directory on the installation CD or from the Red Hat FTP site. This installation method is selected as shown in Figure 3.2. Once you select this option, you will be required to specify the hard drive partition to install from and the directory containing the Red Hat installation files as shown in Figure 3.3.

FIGURE **3.2**

Selecting a hard drive install.

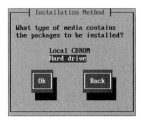

FIGURE **3.3**

The hard drive install options dialog box.

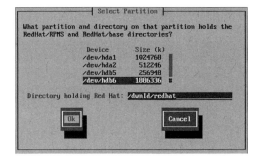

NFS Install

If you do not have a supported CD-ROM drive and have insufficient space to copy the installation files to a hard drive partition to do a hard drive installation, you can choose to do a network installation. One type of network installation is the NFS install. Of the network installation methods, the NFS install has the advantage of being the fastest because the files do not have to first be transferred to the local system before installing them. Like the other network install methods, it shares the disadvantage of requiring network connectivity.

To perform this type of install requires that you are connected to a network and that a server on that network contains an exported filesystem containing the Red Hat installation files. This network connectivity can be either a connection to a local area network or a connection to the Internet, such as a PPP connection over a modem. The easiest way to set this up if you are connected via a local area network is to mount the install CD on a machine and export the mount point for the CD. Another alternative is to copy the CD contents to a hard drive and export the appropriate partition. The speed of an NFS install is limited by the bandwidth of your network, and is only slightly slower than a hard drive install. In addition to the requirement that the Red Hat installation files be on an exported filesystem, this installation method also requires that you create a different boot disk from the `bootnet.img` file on the install CD. This boot floppy can be created with the following command on another Linux system:

```
[root@nomad images]# dd if=bootnet.img of=/dev/fd0 bs=512
2880+0 records in
2880+0 records out
```

If you do not have another Linux system available, you can create the network boot floppy under Windows using the `rawrite` utility, which is also found on the installation CD. This installation looks just like the normal install, except instead of presenting a dialog with options to install from a local CD-ROM or hard drive, you will be presented with a dialog box asking whether you want to install from an NFS image, an FTP site, or an HTTP install as shown in Figure 3.4. If you select this install method, you will then be presented with the dialog box shown in Figure 3.5, in which you specify the NFS server and the directory containing the Red Hat install files.

FIGURE 3.4

Selecting an NFS install.

FIGURE 3.5

The NFS install options dialog box.

If you frequently install Linux on machines that do not have CD-ROM drives, such as to a laptop, the NFS installation option may be a good one to consider.

FTP Install

The next network installation method is the FTP installation, which you select from the menu as shown in Figure 3.6. This installation method has the advantage of not requiring that you have an installation CD or an image of the installation files available on your network, but has the disadvantage of being slow. It can be especially slow if you install over the Internet using a Red Hat mirror site. However, if you do not have an FTP server or do not want to set one up, you can use the FTP install by mounting a CD-ROM on any machine with an FTP server running. In this case, you could use non-anonymous FTP and if you use this method on an isolated network segment with little traffic, this installation method is reasonably fast. The option to use non-anonymous FTP as well as the specification of the FTP server to use is shown in Figure 3.7. The FTP install even works if you have to go through a proxy to get to the FTP server.

FIGURE 3.6

Selecting the FTP install.

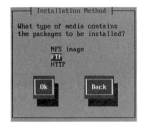

FIGURE 3.7

The FTP install options dialog box.

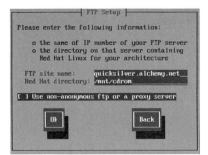

HTTP Install

A new installation method introduced with Red Hat Linux 6.0 is the HTTP install. This method is essentially the same as the FTP install, with the exception of the protocol used to retrieve the files. This option is provided to allow for installations in situations where other installation methods are not available, due to firewalls or other restrictions. This installation method has the same advantages and disadvantages as the FTP install. The selection of this install method is shown in Figure 3.8. Once you have selected this installation method, you will be presented with the dialog box shown in Figure 3.9. Here, you enter the name or IP address of the HTTP server to install from, the directory containing the Red Hat installation files, and whether or not to use a proxy server when connecting to the server.

FIGURE 3.8
Selecting the HTTP install.

FIGURE 3.9
The HTTP install options dialog box.

Scalability Issues

You may be wondering why anyone would think of creating another installation method, considering all the ones just described that are available for Red Hat. One possible answer to this is scalability. Any of the previous methods are fine if you do not frequently install systems; however, if you are installing multiple systems per week, the time spent waiting on any of these installation methods becomes significant. The next section looks at one alternative method for installing a Linux system.

Cloning Installations

To address the problem of scalability, it is often useful to create a standard installation image and to simply clone it to a new machine when required. Apart from the initial setup, this can result in significantly faster installs and less work required to maintain systems because they are all exactly the same. This section looks at a couple of approaches to cloning systems—one a custom-built solution and the other provided by Red Hat.

A Homegrown Approach

One simple approach to installing Linux systems is to install one how you want it, create an image of the installation, and then copy that image to new machines as they are needed. A simple method for creating this image is to use an archival utility such as `afio` or `cpio` to create a file containing the contents of each filesystem that you want to re-create on new systems. The approach outlined here uses this idea and shows how a system can be taken from an uninstalled state to a fully functional state by following these simple steps:

1. Boot the system to be installed using floppies.
2. Establish network connectivity.
3. Remotely partition the disk and make filesystems.
4. Install the OS image on the newly partitioned disk.
5. Make minimal customizations required.
6. Install boot loader and reboot.

This approach assumes that your systems are all basically the same, which for most companies is reasonable to expect, since you usually find a hardware vendor and stick with them for as long as they give you good service and reasonable prices. By basically the same, I mean that the systems to be installed are all based on the same family of processors and that they all use similar hardware. For example, most of the systems that I administer are Intel-based, dual-processor systems with large capacity SCSI or IDE hard drives, and one or more network cards. If your systems do not meet this criteria of being basically the same, you will probably not be well served by this installation method. Let's examine this approach step by step, showing the tools required and how to combine them to go from raw system to fully installed system with a minimal amount of work.

Boot the System from Floppies

In order for this approach to work, you must first create a set of floppies that will allow a system to be booted and connected to a network. A useful package to facilitate this is YARD, which stands for Yet Another Rescue Disk. YARD does not come with Red Hat, but a search of `http://freshmeat.net/` or `http://linuxapps.com/` will locate it for you.

This package helps you build boot and root floppies with which you can boot a system, and using a RAM disk, include enough tools to get a system connected to a network. What to include on the floppy set is your decision as long as the following files are present and working properly:

- `in.rshd`
- `in.rexecd`
- `in.rlogind`
- `sfdisk`
- `mke2fs`
- `mkswap`
- `afio`
- `gzip`
- `mount`
- `umount`
- `sync`
- `rm`
- `lilo`

Establish Network Connectivity

As part of the files installed on the boot and root floppies, one is a `.bashrc` file for root that contains the definition of a function called `setup`. This function prompts the user for a hostname to use for the machine to be installed and then performs the steps required to configure an ethernet interface with that name and associated IP address. Once this is completed, it establishes routing for the networks it needs to be able to see, and starts the `inetd` and `syslog` daemons. The definition of this function is network specific, so using the one that I use would do you no good, but by examining the steps taken by this function, you can easily modify it to work with your networks. The code in Listing 3.1 shows the contents of the `.bashrc` on my boot floppies, which implements the `setup` function.

LISTING 3.1   Implementation of the `Setup` Function in `/root/.bashrc`

```
\# defines the setup function used to establish network connectivity

setup () {
```

LISTING 3.1   continued

```
# Function to set up network connectivity for installation

# Prompt the user for the type of NIC to use
echo "Drivers are available for the following NICS:"
echo "    1 -- 3Com 509 10Mbit (3c509)"
echo "    2 -- Kingston KNE100TX or Digital DE500 (de4x5)"
echo "    3 -- Intel EtherExpress Pro/100+ (eepro100)"
echo -n "Enter the number for the appropriate driver to load  "
read nic

echo ""
case $nic in
    1)      echo -n "Loading 3c509 module..."
            /sbin/insmod 3c509
            LOADED=`/sbin/lsmod | grep 3c509`
            if [ "$LOADED" != "" ]; then
                echo "done."
            else
                echo "failed...aborting."
                return
            fi
            ;;
    2)      echo "Loading de4x5 module..."
            /sbin/insmod de4x5
            LOADED=`/sbin/lsmod | grep de4x5`
            if [ "$LOADED" != "" ]; then
                echo "done."
            else
                echo "failed...aborting."
                return
            fi
            ;;
    3)      echo "Loading eepro100 module..."
            /sbin/insmod eepro100
            LOADED=`/sbin/lsmod | grep eepro100`
            if [ "$LOADED" != "" ]; then
                echo "done."
            else
                echo "failed...aborting."
                return
            fi
```

LISTING 3.1   continued

```
            ;;
    *)      echo "Invalid response...exiting"
            return
            ;;
esac

DONE=N

while [ "$DONE" != "Y" ]; do
    # Now that the module is loaded, prompt for the hostname to use
    echo ""
    echo -n "Enter the fully qualified hostname to use:  "
    read hname

    HNAME=`echo $hname | cut -d. -f1`
    HIP=`grep " $HNAME" /etc/hosts | cut -f1`

    if [ "$HIP" = "" ]; then
        echo ""
        echo -n "$hname not found in /etc/hosts...use anyways (y/n)?  "
        read ans

        if [ "$ans" = "y" -o "$ans" = "Y" ]; then
            echo -n "Enter the IP address for $hname:  "
            read HIP
        fi
    else
        echo ""
        echo -n "$HIP found for $hname...is this correct (y/n)?  "
        read ans
    fi

    if [ "$ans" = "y" -o "$ans" = "Y" ]; then
        DONE=Y
    fi
done

# We now have a hostname and IP address.  Determine from them the
# appropriate routes to setup and start the inetd.
hostname $hname
echo $hname >>/etc/HOSTNAME
```

LISTING 3.1   continued

```
export HOSTNAME=$hname

DEV="192.168.50"

ATDEV=`echo $HIP | grep $DEV`

if [ "$ATDEV" != "" ]; then
    ifconfig eth0 $HIP broadcast 205.238.143.255 netmask 255.255.255.0
    route add -net 192.168.50.0 netmask 255.255.255.0 dev eth0
    route add default gw 192.168.50.2 metric 1 dev eth0
    echo ""
    echo "Verify network setup by pinging quicksilver."
    /usr/sbin/inetd
    return
fi

echo "Unfamiliar network...establish network connectivity manually"

}
```

This `setup` function has its own requirements for utilities that must be on your boot floppies. These required commands are

- `hostname`
- `cut`
- `grep`
- `insmod`
- `lsmod`
- `ifconfig`
- `route`
- `inetd`

These commands are used to load the appropriate module for the network card, figure out what the IP address for the machine is based on the hostname supplied by the user, and to configure the ethernet interface and prepare to receive connections via the network.

Partition Disks and Make Filesystems

Now that you are on the network, the remainder of the work can be done remotely. Because you have included sfdisk on your boot floppies and you are not currently using the hard drives, you can now partition the boot disk and make the filesystems and swap spaces you will need to proceed with the install. This is accomplished using the script in Listing 3.2, which connects to the machine you have booted from floppies, runs the sfdisk command to create partitions on the target host boot drive, and then runs mke2fs to create filesystems on the new partitions. In addition, if you have specified the creation of a swap partition, the script runs mkswap to initialize it.

LISTING 3.2 A Script for Remotely Partitioning a Hard Drive Using sfdisk

```perl
#!/usr/bin/perl

use Getopt::Std;
use Net::Ping;

$USAGE = "Usage: dprepare -t host -p pfile -b bdev [-c]\n"
    . "       or dprepare -h\n\n"
    . "    -t host   host to partition and create filesystems on\n"
    . "    -p pfile  name of file containing partition information\n"
    . "    -b bdev   device name of boot drive\n"
    . "    -c        check for badblocks when creating filesystems\n"
    . "    -h        print this usage statement\n";

# Parse the arguments
getopts('t:p:b:ch');

# Give the usage statement if the ask for it
if (defined $opt_h) {
    print $USAGE;
    exit 1;
}

# Print a usage statement if required arguments are missing
if ((!defined $opt_t) || (!defined $opt_p) || (!defined $opt_b)) {
    print "No target, partition file or boot device specified.\n";
    print $USAGE;
    exit 1;
}

# Check for the existence of the partition file
```

3

Installation
Strategies

LISTING 3.2   continued

```perl
if ( ! -f $opt_p ) {
    print "Partition file not found\n";
    print $USAGE;
    exit 1;
}

# Verify that we can reach the target host and if not abort.
if (! pingable($opt_t)) {
    print "Unable to ping target host $opt_t...aborting.\n";
    exit 1;
}

# Next check to see if the boot device exists on the target host.
if ($opt_b =~ /sd/) {
    $avail = `rsh $opt_t 'cat /proc/scsi/scsi/ | grep -A 2 \"Id: 00\"
    ➥| grep Direct-Access' `;
    chomp $avail;
} else {
    $avail = `rsh $opt_t "cat /proc/ide/$opt_b/media"`
    chomp $avail;
    if ($avail ne "disk") {
        $avail = "";
    }
}

if ( $avail eq "" ) {
    print "Unable to verify $opt_b on $opt_t...aborting.\n";
    exit 1;
}

# Now we open the partition definition file, read it one line at a time
# and for each line depending on the type, store the command we will use
# to create either a swap device or filesystem on the partition.
open(PFILE, "$opt_p");
open(SFILE, ">/tmp/sfdisk.in");
$i = 1;
while (<PFILE>) {
    ($dnum,$size,$type,$active,$mntpt,$mntorder) = split(/,/, $_);
    chomp $mntorder;

    $checkbad = (defined $opt_c) ? "-c" : undef;
```

LISTING 3.2   continued

```perl
    if (($type eq "L") || ($type eq "83")) {
        $device = "/dev/$opt_b" . "$dnum";
        $fscmd[$i] = "mke2fs $checkbad $device";
        $i++;
    } elsif (($type eq "S") or ($type eq "82")) {
        $device = "/dev/$opt_b" . "$dnum";
        $fscmd[$i] = "mkswap $checkbad $device";
        $i++;
    }

    print SFILE ",$size,$type,$active\n";


}
close(SFILE);
close(PFILE);

# We have the commands we need to create the desired filesystems and
# swap spaces, so now lets actually partition the disk, sync the disk,
# and then create them.
$pcmd = "cat /tmp/sfdisk.in | rsh $opt_t "
    . "'/sbin/sfdisk -uM /dev/$opt_b ; /bin/sync'";
system($pcmd);
$j = 1;
while ($j < $i) {
    if ($fscmd[$j] ne "") {
        print "Executing $fscmd[$j]\n";
        system($fscmd[$j]);
    }
    $j++;
}

exit 0;

################ SUBROUTINES ################

# Check to see if the target host is alive
sub pingable {
    my $target = shift;

    my $p = Net::Ping->new("icmp");
    return $p->ping($target);
}
```

3

Installation
Strategies

The syntax of the partition file is critical to the proper operation of this script. This file is used to build the input file to the sfdisk command. Each line consists of a device name, a start point, the size in megabytes for the partition, the partition type, a flag indicating whether the partition should be marked active or not, and finally, the eventual mount point and a sequence number indicating the order in which they should be mounted. Following is a sample partition file. Note that in this file, you specify a /dev/sda4 partition, but give it no values. This is required to satisfy the sfdisk command.

```
1,1024,L,*,/,1
2,128,S,-,
3,,E,-,
4,,,-,
5,1024,L,-/usr,2
6,,L,-/var,3
```

This sample file above creates a partition on /dev/sda1 of 1024 megabytes, with a type of L (for Linux native), and marks it active. It then creates a type S, or swap partition, of 128 megabytes on /dev/sda2. The next partition is of type E, or extended, and because no size was specified, takes up the remainder of the disk. Now you specify /dev/sda4, which has no values for size, start, or type. This partition does not really exist, but must be specified to satisfy sfdisk. The next real partition is /dev/sda5, which is a logical drive of type L that is 1024 megabytes in size. The final partition is /dev/sda6, which is also type L and takes up the remainder of the extended partition. Using this sample partition file and the script in Listing 3.2 generates the following output:

```
[root@quicksilver chapter3]# ./dprepare -t nomad -b hda -p partfile

Disk /dev/hda: 128 heads, 63 sectors, 785 cylinders
Old situation:
Units = megabytes of 1048576 bytes, blocks of 1024 bytes, counting from 0

   Device Boot Start    End    MB   #blocks   Id  System
/dev/sda1            0+  1535-  1536-  1572448+   b  Win95 FAT32
/dev/sda2      *  1535+  3027-  1493-  1528128   83  Linux
/dev/sda3         3027+  3090-    63     64512   82  Linux swap
/dev/sda4            0    -      0         0    0  Empty
New situation:
Units = megabytes of 1048576 bytes, blocks of 1024 bytes, counting from 0

   Device Boot Start    End    MB   #blocks   Id  System
/dev/sda1      *     0+  1027-  1028-  1052351+  83  Linux
/dev/sda2         1027+  1157-   130-   133056   82  Linux swap
/dev/sda3         1157+  3090-  1934-  1979712    5  Extended
```

```
/dev/sda4          0      -      0        0    0  Empty
/dev/sda5       1157+   2185-   1028-  1052351+  83  Linux
/dev/sda6       2185+   3090-    906-   927359+  83  Linux
Executing mke2fs  /dev/sda1
Executing mkswap  /dev/sda2
Executing mke2fs  /dev/sda5
Executing mke2fs  /dev/sda6
```

Install the OS Image

Now that you have some filesystems to work with, you mount them and using your install image previously created, transfer the operating system to the new system over the network. The image is an afio archive and the installation process merely unpacks the archive to standard output, which is piped to an `rsh` command, which writes the data to the prepared partitions on the remote system. The script, shown in Listing 3.3, uses the same partition file as the previous script and takes the same arguments.

LISTING 3.3   The `osinst` Installation Script

```perl
#!/usr/bin/perl

use Getopt::Std;
use Net::Ping;

# Parse the argument list.

$USAGE = "Usage: osinst -t host -p pfile -b bdev\n"
       . "    or osinst -h\n\n"
       . "    -t host   host to install the operating system on\n"
       . "    -p pfile  name of file containing partition information\n"
       . "    -b bdev   device name of boot drive\n"
       . "    -h        print this usage statement\n";

# Parse the arguments
getopts('t:p:b:h');

# Give the usage statement if the ask for it
if (defined $opt_h) {
    print $USAGE;
    exit 1;
}

# Print a usage statement if required arguments are missing
if ((!defined $opt_t) || (!defined $opt_p) || (!defined $opt_b)) {
```

3

Installation Strategies

LISTING 3.3   continued

```
    print "No target, partition file or boot device specified.\n";
    print $USAGE;
    exit 1;
}


# Check for the existence of the partition file
if ( ! -f $opt_p ) {
    print "Partition file not found\n";
    print $USAGE;
    exit 1;
}


# Verify that we can reach the target host and if not abort.
if (! pingable($opt_t)) {
    print "Unable to ping target host $opt_t...aborting.\n";
    exit 1;
}


# Next check to see if the boot device exists on the target host.
if ($opt_b =~ /sd/) {
    $avail = `rsh $opt_t 'cat /proc/scsi/scsi/ | grep -A 2 \"Id: 00\"
    ➥| grep Direct-Access' `;
    chomp $avail;
} else {
    $avail = `rsh $opt_t "cat /proc/ide/$opt_b/media"` ;
    chomp $avail;
    if ($avail ne "disk") {
        $avail = "";
    }
}


if ( $avail eq "" ) {
    print ''Unable to verify $opt_b on $opt_t...aborting.\n";
    exit 1;
}

# Now we open the partition definition file, read it one line at a time
# and for each line determine if a mount point is specified and if so,
# mount that partition on the remote system.
open(PFILE, "$opt_p");
while (<PFILE>) {
```

LISTING 3.3   continued

```
    ($dnum,$size,$type,$active,$mntpt,$mntorder) = split(/,/, $_);
    chomp $mntorder;

    if ($mntpt ne "") {
        $device = "/dev/$opt_b" . "$dnum";
        $rcmd[$mntorder] = "rsh $opt_t 'mkdir -p /inst" . "$mntpt; "
                        . "mount $device /inst" . "$mntpt; ";
    }

}
close(PFILE);

for ($i = 1; $i <= scalar @rcmd; $i++) {
    print "Executing $rcmd[$i]";
    system($rcmd[$i]);
}

# Now that the partitions are mounted in the correct order, we can copy
# our template to it.
$ostmplt = "/var/lib/OStemplate.afio.gz";
$instcmd = "cat $ostmplt ¦ rsh $opt_t 'cd /mnt ; gzip -dc "
        . "¦ afio -i -z /proc/self/fd/0";

system($instcmd);

exit 0;

################ SUBROUTINES ################

# Check to see if the target host is alive
sub pingable {
    my $target = shift;

    my $p = Net::Ping->new("icmp");
    return $p->ping($target);
}
```

This script could be enhanced to do things such as checking to ensure that there is sufficient space on the mounted partitions to hold the template. This is left as an exercise for the reader.

Make Host Specific Customizations to the Installed Image

Once the operating system image has been installed, a minimal amount of customization is required to make the system functional. This customization includes setting the proper network settings, specifically the IP address and the hostname. This can be accomplished easily using a script or by logging into the system and editing the files by hand. The amount of customization required depends on several factors, including the complexity of your network, whether or not you use dynamic IP address assignment, and other factors. How you customize is left to you.

Install Boot Loader

The final step for installing a system that will not be running the X Windows system is to install the boot loader. This is simply a matter of running lilo against the `lilo.conf` file that is part of the installed operating system image. Assuming that you have the installed image mounted as `/mnt`, this can easily be accomplished by issuing the following command:

```
/mnt/sbin/lilo -r /mnt -v -v
```

Once this is done, you are ready to reboot you newly installed system. Depending on the degree of automation you add to this process, you can make the installation of a new system a simple matter of booting from floppies, getting on the network, and issuing a script from the host containing your operating system template. I have used this method for some time with great success. The time to install a system once booted from floppies is under five minutes.

The homegrown approach described here is just one method. If you are not inclined to use it, there are alternatives including one from Red Hat, known as a kickstart.

Using Kickstart Files and RPM

If the previously described method of installation sounds like a lot of work, that's because it is. An alternative approach to installing multiple systems with minimal fuss is to use the kickstart capabilities provided by Red Hat. The kickstart method is accomplished by creating a file that specifies the answers to the questions asked by the installation program. This file can be copied to the boot floppy or can be made available on the network and the name is dependent on which of these two options you choose. Details on using the kickstart method are found in the installation guide that is included with your Red Hat Linux software. With kickstart files, you can eliminate the bulk of the interaction required by the install program and predefine a set of packages to be installed on a system. This method allows you to use any of the installation methods supported by Red Hat, but not have to answer all of the questions. The primary difference between this method and the homegrown approach just described is that even with kickstart files, there is no installation method available from Red Hat that uses a network push model.

A Template-Based Approach

The methods described thus far are useful if your machines are all basically the same, but if your network is composed of several classes of machines, it might be useful to consider the following approach to managing system installations. This approach relies on the fact that at some level, all systems must have a common core of software in order to function on the network. This core becomes your base template, which you can install to all machines as a first step to bringing a new machine online. For purposes of this discussion, we will assume that your network is divided into two parts. The first part is your administrative network, which is where the day-to-day work of the company is performed and where machines fall into four base categories. These are a development workstation, a development server, an administrative server, and an administrative workstation. The second part of the network is the production network, which consists of Web servers, database servers, and mail servers.

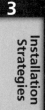

Establishing an Install Template

Based on the network described in the preceding section, you will begin by creating an install template. There will be two flavors of install templated—one minimalist template for the production network, and a second more featureful template for your administrative network. Let's start with a discussion of the production template.

The Production Template

Since the production servers are not intended for interactive use, the install template for them will not include several items that you might normally find on a Red Hat system. Some of the items that will be specifically excluded from the production template include the following:

- X Windows software
- Compilers
- Personal productivity software
- Office applications
- Documentation

- Games

- Word publishing software

In fact, the production template will include the bare minimum of software required to accomplish the following tasks:

- Boot the system

- Connect to the network

- Run scripts and programs

The first task is accomplished by installing the base Linux utilities found in /bin and /sbin along with the devices support in the /dev directory and configuration data found in /etc and /var. There is no need for most of the software normally found in /usr, with the exception of some of the utilities found in /usr/bin and support files in /usr/share and /usr/lib. An exact list of these files is not presented here because it would take up several pages, but a good starting point for determining which files are required can be found in the Filesystem Hierarchy Standard, which is described in Chapter 4, "Where Do I Find...?"

Next, you add the network connectivity support. These files are primarily the clients found in /usr/bin and the daemons found in /usr/sbin. This includes such items as the telnet daemons and clients, the daemons to support the remote commands such as rcp, rsh, and rlogin, and other network related files, such as /etc/services, /etc/protocols, and /etc/inetd.conf. It would also include those files required to protect your system, such as tcpd, ipchains, and proxy software if desired. The minimal set of files needed to establish network connectivity is the same as described in the discussion of creating boot floppies found earlier in this chapter.

Finally, there are the files required for program runtime support, such as shared libraries and files needed to support any scripting languages you will be using on the system, such as perl or tcl and their supporting files.

All of these files can be obtained from the Red Hat installation media, and with careful pruning can be made to fit in under 200 megabytes of disk space with some space for growth. This would naturally not include space for growth filesystems like /var or /tmp, but with judicious planning, you can have a thin server system base that you can customize to serve whatever purpose you like. Listing 3.4 specifies a list of packages that I use to meet the criteria specified here. This set of packages requires approximately 175 megabytes of hard drive space, but could be trimmed even further by the elimination of manual pages, info files, and other data not essential to the operation of a system.

LISTING 3.4 List of Packages for Thin Server Installation

```
setup
filesystem
basesystem
ldconfig
glibc
chkconfig
mktemp
termcap
libtermcap
bash
apmd
ncurses
info
fileutils
grep
ash
at
authconfig
bash2
bc
bdflush
bind
bind-utils
binutils
bzip2
caching-nameserver
sed
console-tools
e2fsprogs
rmt
cpio
cracklib
cracklib-dicts
crontabs
textutils
shadow-utils
dev
diffutils
ed
eject
emacs
emacs-nox
```

3

Installation
Strategies

LISTING 3.4 continued

```
etcskel
file
findutils
ftp
gawk
gd
gdb
gdbm
getty_ps
glib
gmp
gpm
groff
gzip
hdparm
initscripts
ipchains
isapnptools
ispell
joe
kbdconfig
kernel
kernel-pcmcia-cs
kernel-smp
ld.so
less
libc
libstdc++
lilo
pwdb
pam
sh-utils
redhat-release
linuxconf
logrotate
losetup
lsof
ltrace
mailcap
mailx
make
MAKEDEV
```

LISTING 3.4   continued

```
man
man-pages
mingetty
mkbootdisk
mkinitrd
mkkickstart
modutils
mount
mouseconfig
mt-st
mtools
nc
ncompress
net-tools
netkit-base
newt
ntsysv
passwd
perl
portmap
procmail
procps
psmisc
pump
quota
raidtools
rdist
readline
redhat-logos
rhs-hwdiag
rootfiles
rpm
rsh
rsync
sash
screen
sendmail
sendmail-cf
setconsole
setserial
setuptool
slang
```

3

Installation Strategies

LISTING 3.4   continued

```
slocate
ssh
ssh-clients
ssh-extras
ssh-server
stat
strace
sudo
sysklogd
SysVinit
tar
tcp_wrappers
tcpdump
tcsh
telnet
time
timeconfig
tmpwatch
traceroute
ucd-snmp
ucd-snmp-utils
unzip
utempter
util-linux
vim-common
vim-minimal
vixie-cron
wget
which
words
wu-ftpd
XFree86-libs
xntp3
zip
zlib
```

The Administrative Template

The requirements for the administrative template differ in several important ways. In a normal administrative network, you will usually have shared resources that you make available to all systems connected to your network via the network filesystem or NFS. In addition, these systems are used for interactive work on a daily basis and therefore require software to make time spent on the systems as productive as possible. To reduce the amount of work required to maintain these systems, it is often desirable to have software that requires frequent updates on shared filesystems. In this manner, you can install a package once and have it immediately available to all users of the network. Examples of software that you might want to install in this fashion include the X Windows software, TeX, compilers, graphical user interfaces like KDE or Gnome, and office suites. The base requirements for the administrative template build on those of the production template to include the following additional features:

- Software to access shared filesystems

- Personal productivity software

- Documentation

- Word publishing software

The shared resources on the network would likely include software to support the different functions of the four types of systems found there. For example, the administrative workstations would access network-capable versions of office suites and other software from the administrative servers. The development workstations and servers would share software such as compilers and interpreters. The primary difference between the workstations and servers in both cases is the computing power of the servers and the availability of resource-intensive applications, such as databases.

Class-Based Customization

The most difficult part of this installation strategy is developing the system by which machines are customized based on the class of machine to which they belong. In our example network, we have already identified four classes of systems on the administrative network and three on the production network. A method for achieving the customization required to make a generic system into one of the specific classes of systems is to maintain a class template, which can be installed on top of the base operating system. In addition, you could also have a function-based template, so that each function is a package that can be installed on top of the base system to add specific functionality. Let's take a look at each class and discuss how to convert a system containing the base template into a system capable of performing a specific function, starting with the administrative network.

3

Installation
Strategies

The Administrative Network

The administrative workstations on the network are systems used for the tasks normally associated with personnel working in office administration, finance and accounting, human resources, and management. They share a need to be able to access office suites, personal productivity software, such as calendars and email software, and administrative servers where these applications are usually installed. The customization of this type of system includes configuration of the client software required to access the shared administrative resources on the network. The formula for building the administrative workstation is base operating system template plus changes to fstab to mount shared filesystems on administrative servers.

The administrative server is the system on the network that contains the shared administrative resources accessed by the administrative workstations. Naturally, there can be more than one of these servers. The customization required to make a system with the base template installed into an administrative server is configuration of the network filesystem server software, configuration of services such as DNS, SMTP, and POP or IMAP. In addition, the administrative servers are likely to be where the company intranet servers are located, such as internal Web servers. The administrative servers are usually not the thin servers as described for the production network, but are more likely to contain multiple services on a single server. The formula for building an administrative server is base operating system template plus exported filesystems providing shared administrative resources plus some set of services, such as intranet Web server, mail server, or DNS server.

The development workstation, like the administrative workstation, requires little customization, except for the configuration of the client software required to access the shared development resources available on the network. The difference is in the types of resources that the workstation needs access to. The development workstation would require access to system documentation, development tools such as compilers and interpreters. Also, because development is usually driven by people working on the administrative side of the business, access to tools like office suites and personal productivity software would be required for them as well. The development workstation consists of the base template plus changes to fstab to access development servers plus changes to fstab to access administrative servers' shared software.

These servers contain the shared resources needed by the development workstations and run specific resource-intensive applications, such as development database servers, test harnesses, and similar processes. Like the administrative servers, development servers require configuration to share filesystems and other services and, again, are not likely to be the thin servers of the production network. The development server is made by first installing the base operating system template, adding exported filesystems for access by development workstations, and adding resource-intensive applications.

The Production Network

The idea behind the production network is the same as for the administrative network, except that the base template is thinner. This allows you to create the various thin servers for the production network with minimal work.

For example, the Web server becomes simply a matter of taking the basic template for production servers and adding Web serving software and the documents to be served. You could also add limitations to the configuration to restrict access to this class of machines to port 80 only.

The same holds true for the other classes on the production network, such as the database servers and the mail servers. By creating the class templates, you can mix and match services on top of the base operating system template, thus reducing installation time and making maintenance much easier.

An Implementation Example

To implement a class-based template scheme such as described is not as difficult as it may sound. Here are the steps needed to implement such a scheme:

1. Create the base template and installation method.
2. Create the class templates.
3. Create a distribution method for the class template.

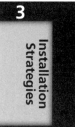

The first step of this plan could be implemented using the homegrown approach described earlier in this chapter. With this method in place, the battle is more than half won.

The second step is to create the class templates. One method of doing this is to create a directory hierarchy such as shown in Listing 3.5.

LISTING 3.5 Sample Directory Hierarchy for Class-based Template

```
.
|-- Db
|   |-- etc
|   |   |-- rc.d
|   |   |   |-- init.d
|   |   |   |   `-- database
|   |   |   `-- rc5.d
|   |   |       |-- K01database -> ../init.d/database
|   |   |       `-- S99database -> ../init.d/database
|   |   `-- services
|   |-- usr
|
```

LISTING 3.5   continued

```
¦   ¦   `-- local
¦   ¦         ¦-- bin
¦   ¦         ¦    `-- dbengine
¦   ¦          `-- data
¦   ¦               ¦-- table1.dat
¦   ¦                `-- table1.ndx
¦    `-- var
¦         `-- local
¦              `-- lib
¦                    ¦-- db.conf
¦                     `-- db.msg
¦-- Mail
¦   ¦-- etc
¦   ¦   ¦-- aliases
¦   ¦    `-- sendmail.cf
¦    `-- var
¦         `-- spool
¦               `-- mqueue
 `-- Web
     ¦-- etc
     ¦    `-- rc.d
     ¦         ¦-- init.d
     ¦         ¦    `-- httpd
     ¦          `-- rc5.d
     ¦               ¦-- K30httpd -> ../init.d/httpd
     ¦                `-- S70httpd -> ../init.d/httpd
     ¦-- usr
     ¦    ;-- sbin
     ¦         `-- apache
      `-- var
           `-- www
                ¦-- cgi-bin
                ¦-- conf
                ¦    ¦-- access.conf
                ¦    ¦-- httpd.conf
                ¦     `-- srm.conf
                ¦-- htdocs
                ¦    `-- index.html
```

LISTING **3.5**   continued

```
`·· logs
    ¦·· access_log
    ¦·· error_log
    ··· server_log
```

There are alternative approaches that could be used equally as well. One such approach is to maintain diffs between the base operating system template and the customized files required to turn the base systems into a specialized one. One problem with this approach is that it does not deal with binary files very well. Another approach, and one that I recommend, is to use software like `rdist` or `rsync` to install the files that are missing or that differ from the base template. The advantage of using either of these two software packages is that not only can they be used to initially install the files required to customize an installation, but they can also be used to keep the systems in synchronization once they are installed.

The final step then becomes to create a distribution file for each class that can be given to the `rdist` or `rsync` command, which would add the files contained within the class template to the base operating system to create a specialized system. This file can be created by hand, or if you prefer, you can create a program or script that creates this distribution file for you.

By utilizing the principles described in this section, you can create a system by which systems can be installed and maintained with a minimal amount of effort. What I have attempted to do is not to specify a specific product or set of products, but to describe the components of an installation system. How you implement each of these components is your decision. Whether you use a homegrown approach for installing the base operating system, or to use a system like kickstart is irrelevant. What is important is to get a base system installed that can then be customized to meet a particular need using the distribution method you select.

Summary

Although Red Hat Linux has several installation methods that allow you great flexibility, there are issues with how scalable the various installation methods are. This chapter discussed a couple of alternative approaches that can be built and used to great advantage by a systems administrator. These methods can be a great time saver. By using tools available on the installation media from Red Hat, a fast, easy to maintain system for installing large numbers of machines can be created. The homegrown approach described here also shows a network push method of installation that allows the systems administrator to remotely install systems once a simple network setup script has been run to connect new systems to a network.

CHAPTER 4

Where Do I Find...?

IN THIS CHAPTER

- Hand Me That Map Please   *82*
- Examining Processes   *90*
- Device Naming Scheme   *107*

Many of you reading this chapter are long-time users of Red Hat Linux and will find that you know everything covered here. If this is the case, you may want to skip reading it. If, on the other hand, you are coming to Linux from other UNIX flavors or from a background of using Windows, then read on. This chapter is designed to help the administrator who may be familiar with other flavors of Linux or UNIX to locate system files on your system. We'll also take a look at the device naming scheme used by Linux. In addition, we'll cover the Filesystem Hierarchy Standard, which is a proposed standard for Linux systems and other UNIX systems that specifies where files of various types should be located, along with a justification for the placement.

Hand Me That Map Please

If you are not familiar with Red Hat Linux, locating system files (especially configuration files) can be difficult. This is especially true if you are new to UNIX and Linux and are used to the Windows world. This section discusses the standard that Red Hat and other distributors of Linux use as the basis for the filesystem layout, and then speaks specifically about the Red Hat Linux distribution and where to look for files of various types.

The Filesystem Hierarchy Standard

The Filesystem Hierarchy Standard is the work of contributors from all over the Internet. It is designed to be a guide for distribution vendors, application developers, and others that specifies a standard location for the various parts of the operating system and associated software. Although primarily driven by people from the Linux community, this standard is also proposed by other operating systems including the commercial UNIX vendors and other freely available UNIX systems such as FreeBSD, OpenBSD, and NetBSD.

The work to standardize filesystems started as a project in the Linux community to help deal with the growing number of distributions. The idea was to provide some compatibility between different distributions. Doing this allows systems that adhere to the standard to profit from the work of others, and also allows developers to create one package that puts things into their proper place on all distributions.

Work began in the fall of 1993 and was called the *FileSystem Standard*, or FSSTND. The first public release of this standard was made in February 1994, on St. Valentine's Day. Development of this Linux-specific standard continued until early 1995, when the focus of the group was changed to include not only Linux, but other UNIX-like systems as well, such as FreeBSD. With the support of members of that community, an effort was made to expand the scope of the FSSTND to focus on issues that were applicable to all UNIX-like systems and at that time, the name was changed to the *Filesystem Hierarchy Standard* (FHS).

The purpose of the standard was to specify the directory layout and the location of files in that layout to be used by systems integrators, application developers, and others. Some of the goals of the standard are to ease the job of systems administrators who have to work with multiple operating systems, application developers, and documentation writers. By standardizing the location of system files across all compliant systems, the systems administrator can always look in the same place to find configuration files. The applications developer knows where to find systems files, such as `utmp` and mail spool directories, and documentation written for one compliant system can be easily adapted to another compliant system. These locations for files, commands, and devices are reached by consensus between the contributors to the standard. The discussions that lead to this consensus take place on the FHS mailing list, which can be subscribed to by sending email to `fhs-discuss@ucsd.edu` with the command "`ADD fhs-discuss`" in the body, as demonstrated by the following command.

```
echo "ADD fhs-discuss" | mail -s "" listserv@ucsd.edu
```

Before you jump onto the list and start making suggestions about how to change the standard, it is recommended that you do the following four things:

- Read the current standard and the justification which can be found at `http://www.pathname.com/fhs/`.

- Read the Frequently Asked Questions list.

- Read the archived postings to the list.

- Lurk on the list for a while to get an understanding of the list politics.

By following these guidelines, the signal-to-noise ratio of the list is kept high and you won't get flamed for bringing up redundant topics. Good examples that are sure to raise the ire of veteran list members are the location of the mail spool directory and integrating the X11R6 tree into the `/usr` hierarchy.

Now that you know how to get onto the list and how to contribute to the development of this standard, let's take a look at how the filesystem is defined, starting with some definitions.

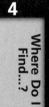

> **Implementation**—An *implementation* is a software package, operating system distribution, or set of data files.

> **Fully compliant**—An implementation is *fully compliant* if all files within the implementation are located as specified by the standard. The implementation must look for files specified by the standard primarily or exclusively in the place specified by the standard.

Partially compliant—Applicable to complete distribution only, *partially compliant* means that a significant subset of the files in the distribution are located as specified in the standard. Partially compliant systems should have a list available that defines where the implementation and the standard diverge. This list must be submitted to the FHS mailing list for reporting purposes.

Fully compatible—An implementation is *fully compatible* if all files within the implementation can be found in the location specified by the standard, even if this is not the true location of the file in this implementation. The fully compatible implementation must look for files specified by the standard in the location specified, but may also look elsewhere.

Partially compatible—This again applies only to full distributions and means that a significant portion of the files in the distribution are located as specified in the standard. Like the fully compatible implementation, this location does not have to be the true location of the files and the implementation is not restricted to looking for files specified in the standard in their standard location.

Now that these terms are defined, we can start looking at the layout specified by the standard.

The Root Directory

Because the standard is designed to be usable by systems of all descriptions, it recommends that you keep the root filesystem files to a minimum. There are a number of reasons for keeping the root filesystem small. One of these is to keep the boot sequence short. Another is that by limiting the root partition to files required to boot and restore backups, you can more easily recover from damage to other filesystems such as /usr. The following tree diagram shows the structure defined for the root filesystem and what each part is supposed to consist of.

```
/
¦-- bin    command binaries essential to system operation
¦-- boot   files used by the boot loader program
¦-- dev    device special files
¦-- etc    system configuration files specific to this host
¦-- home   home directories for system users
¦-- lib    essential shared libraries and kernel modules
¦-- mnt    mount point for temporarily mounted filesystems
¦-- opt    directory to hold system add-on applications
¦-- root   home directory for the systems administrator
¦-- sbin   system binaries essential to boot the system
```

```
¦-- tmp    temporary file space
¦-- usr    base of the secondary hierarchy
`-- var    variable system data including system logs
```

Some restrictions placed on the root directory are that no applications be allowed to create or require special files in the root directory, and that the contents of the root directory be kept to a minimum. This becomes clearer as we examine each of the directories found in the root filesystem.

The first directory in the preceding list is the /bin directory, which contains commands essential to system operation. The FHS contains a list of the files that should be found there. These commands fall into three categories:

- General commands
- Restoration commands
- Network commands

The first category includes commands such as ls, cp, mv, and rm. It also includes the Bourne and C-shells or their equivalents, such as ash, bash, or tcsh. Essential commands are those that system initialization scripts use and those required to access other filesystems, such as /usr and /var after the system has booted.

The second category of commands is loosely defined to be the minimal set required to restore other parts of the system, such as tar, gzip, or other commands used by your backup system.

The final category of commands are network commands and include hostname, domainname, netstat, and ping. Regardless of the category, these are commands that both root and normal users may need to run, as opposed to those intended for administrative use only, such as those found in /sbin. The next directory in the diagram is /boot, which contains files required by the boot loader program. Files may include map files, kernel images, and other data not normally edited by hand. The commands required to create boot loader maps should be located in /sbin, and configuration files for the boot loader should be kept in the /etc directory. There may be restrictions on where this directory is physically located, such as on some personal computers based on the Intel iX86 family of processors, which require that these files be located below cylinder 1024, or other restrictions as to the filesystem type on which these files are located. In such cases, the filenames can be altered to conform to the restrictions of the filesystem in question.

Unlike Windows and other popular operating systems, each device available on Linux and other UNIX systems is represented by a special file that you can access using normal file semantics. The /dev directory contains these device special files. In addition to these files, this directory may also contain a program or script called MAKEDEV that is used to create

4

Where Do I
Find...?

these device special files. There may also be a script or program call MAKEDEV.local to create locally required device files. Red Hat Linux contains the MAKEDEV script in /dev and you may use it to create standard device files in the event they become damaged or corrupted.

Configuration files specific to the local host are contained in the /etcdirectory. These files include such files as hostname files, X Windows configuration files, and any other files that are not sharable between systems. Examples of these files include lilo.conf, syslog.conf, motd, issue, passwd, ld.so.conf, and shells. Also found here are many network configuration files, such as hosts.equiv, hosts.allow, hosts.deny, printcap, resolv.conf, and others. X Windows configuration files are contained in a subdirectory called X11 and include such files as the XF86Config, system wide xinitrc files, and configuration files for the xdm program and related programs.

The /home directory contains user home directories and is usually either a mount point for a separate filesystem or a symbolic link to such a filesystem.

The next directory is /lib, which contains the shared libraries required by commands and systems binaries and also contains a subdirectory called modules, which contains loadable kernel modules. Another subdirectory of the root directory is /mnt, which is used to temporarily mount filesystems. Some systems create subdirectories in this directory that correspond to removable media devices, such as CD-ROM drives and floppy drives.

One of the major hierarchy mount points in the root directory is rooted at /opt. This directory is used to hold application add-on packages. These add-on packages typically are self-contained in a subdirectory that contains bin, lib, man, and others that mimic the subdirectories of the root directory. There are also subdirectories of /opt called bin, lib, man, and others that are reserved for use by the local administrator.

The home directory of the systems administrator or root user is called /root. This directory is separate from other home directories because the home directories for users are often located on a separate filesystem from the root filesystem that might not be available at boot time. By making the /root home directory a real directory on the root filesystem, it is available as long as the root filesystem remains undamaged. Applications often require a space to create temporary files during operation. The /tmp directory is designed to serve this purpose. Files created in this directory are strictly for temporary use and any expectations as to the lifetime of these files are not valid.

Systems binaries are contained in the /sbin directory. These systems binaries are broken down into four categories by function. These categories are

- General commands

- Shutdown commands

- Filesystem management commands

- Network commands

Specific examples of each of these categories are detailed in the FHS standard. The general category includes commands such as `getty`, `init`, `update`, and `clock`. The shutdown category includes `shutdown`, `halt`, and `reboot`. The filesystem management category includes `fdisk`, `fsck`, and `mkfs`, and the network category includes `ifconfig` and `route`.

The final two directories specified in the standard are `/usr` and `/var`, each of which contains a number of specialized subdirectories. First, let's take a look at the `/usr` hierarchy. This standard defines the following subdirectories for the `/usr` hierarchy.

```
/usr
¦-- X11R6    X Windows Version 11 Release 6 files
¦-- X386     X Windows Version 11 Release 5 files for iX86 systems
¦-- bin      the majority of available user commands
¦-- games    games and tutorials
¦-- include  system header files required by C and C++ compilers
¦-- lib      libraries
¦-- local    a local hierarchy
¦-- sbin     non-essential system binaries
¦-- share    architecture independent data, such as man pages
`-- src      source code, including the kernel source
```

The X11R6 and X386 hierarchies are defined by the XFree86 group and are incorporated wholesale. The only files related to these hierarchies that live outside of them are local configuration files, such as `XF86Config`, `xinitrc`, and `xdm`, which reside in `/etc/X11`.

The `/usr/bin` directory is where the majority of the user level commands for the system reside. These include all of the standard Linux utilities not found in `/bin`, such as `find`, `grep`, and any other non-essential commands.

The `/usr/games` directory, as the name implies, contains game executables. In addition to games, this directory may also contain tutorial programs.

The `/usr/include` directory contains header files used by the C and C++ compilers in the compilation of programs. Included in this directory are subdirectories or symbolic links that point to the kernel header files, X Windows header files, and C++ header files.

Libraries used to compile other programs, as well as libraries of routines for interpreted languages like tcl and perl, are found in the `/usr/lib` directory. This directory was traditionally the location of the `sendmail` binary, but because this binary has now been relocated to `/usr/sbin`, there may be a compatibility link to `sendmail`.

4

Where Do I
Find...?

The structure of the /usr/local hierarchy is a mirror of the /usr hierarchy with the exception of the local directory itself. After an initial installation of the distribution, this hierarchy should be empty and its use reserved for the local systems administrator.

Non-essential system binaries, such as network daemons, reside in /usr/sbin. Here you will find files such as in.telnetd, syslogd, sendmail, and the inetd program. The list of files included here depends on the services available on the system.

Another large hierarchy under /usr is found in /usr/share. This directory is reserved for architecture independent files, such as manual pages, dictionary files, documentation, terminfo definitions, national language support files, and time zone information files. The standard contains a more complete definition of this hierarchy.

The final directory in /usr defined in the standard is /usr/src, which contains source code, including source code for the kernel.

The last big hierarchy rooted at the top level is /var and contains variable data including state data for running applications. Here is the defined directory structure under /var:

```
/var
|--account  process accounting logs, if supported
|--cache    application cache data
|--crash    crash dumps generated by the system, if supported
|--games    variable game data, such as high score files
|--lock     device and application lock files
|--log      system log files
|--mail     user mail spool files
|--opt      variable data for packages in /opt
|--run      files relevant to running processes, such as pid files
|--spool    application spool data
|--state    variable state information
|--tmp      temporary files preserved between system reboots
`--yp       NIS database files
```

Many of these directories are self-explanatory. For a full description of their use, refer to the standards document. A few of them are worth noting here because they contain information that the systems administrator will use on a daily basis.

One of these is the /var/log directory, which contains system log files created by the syslogd and klogd daemons.

Another directory frequently used in the day-to-day operation of your system is the /var/run directory, which is primarily used to store pid files. These pid files are useful in determining the process id of system daemons. This information is required if you want to send signals to these daemons using the kill command.

Device and application lock files are stored in /var/lock and this is where you look if you need to remove a locked file that is inhibiting a program.

The next directory on our list of important directories is the user mail spool directory, /var/mail. This directory is one of the places to look to diagnose problems with a user's mail.

The final directory that we are concerned with under /var is the /var/yp directory, which is used to store database files for the network information system or NIS daemons.

The Red Hat Filesystem Layout

Red Hat Linux systems are partially compliant with the Filesystem Hierarchy Standard. The differences between the standard and the Red Hat filesystem layout are minimal. The most visible of the changes is the location of the user mail spool files, which on Red Hat Linux 6.0 systems are located in the /var/spool/mail directory. Another major area of divergence is the location of the manual pages and other systems documentation, which are in /usr/doc and /usr/man, instead of /usr/share/man as specified in the standard. The remainder of this section describes some of the directories of interest to an administrator of Red Hat Linux systems.

The /etc/sysconfig Directory

The bulk of the system configuration variables used by the initialization scripts in /etc/rc.d are defined in files contained in the /etc/sysconfig directory. Files found in this directory include files named init, mouse, keyboard, soundcard, and network. These define variables related to the configuration of these systems or devices. A major subdirectory on this one is the network-scripts directory, which contains the scripts required to bring up the various configured network interfaces. It contains scripts and more configuration files that actually bring the various interfaces up and down, using many of the configuration variables defined in the /etc/sysconfig directory.

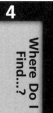

The /etc/rc.d Directory

Red Hat Linux uses a slightly modified System V style of system initialization scripts. For users of Solaris or HP/UX systems, this structure will seem quite natural. The major difference is that instead of the initialization script directory being located in /etc, it is located one level lower in /etc/rc.d along with the runlevel specific directories.

File for the Apache Web Server

Because the Apache Web server is considered an integral part of the Red Hat Linux operating system, Red Hat has chosen to store the configuration files for it in a subdirectory of /etc called httpd. This directory contains configuration files, such as the php3.ini file, and the files contained in the conf directory—access.conf, httpd.conf, and srm.conf. This is in keeping with the filesystem hierarchy standard. Also in keeping with the standard is the location for the log files, in /var/log/httpd, which contains access_log and error log. For those who are used to storing all Apache files in a single location, this may be somewhat confusing. To further confuse issues, the default htdocs tree is located in a subdirectory of /home/httpd called html, and the default cgi-bin directory is located there as well. If you want to make upgrading Apache from the official source distribution easier, you can remove the Apache package distributed by Red Hat and install all files under /usr/local/apache. Alternatively, you can use information from the source rpm for Apache to configure Apache in the same way Red Hat does.

Documentation

Documentation for the Red Hat Linux system is plentiful and if installed can be found in one of several places on your system. The following table describes the documentation available and where to look for it on your system.

Documentation Type	Format	Location
System manual pages	nroff	/usr/man/man*
GNU info pages	info	/usr/info
LDP HOWTO documents	text	/usr/doc/HOWTO
LDP manuals	html	/usr/doc/LDP/*
Red Hat Install Guide	html	/usr/doc/rhl-install-guide-en-6.0
Red Hat Getting Started	html	/usr/doc/rhl-getting-started-guide-en-6.0
Apache Manual	html	/home/httpd/html/manual
README files for rpms	text	/usr/doc/<package-name>

Examining Processes

This section takes a look at the methods available to run processes on your Red Hat Linux system. This includes the classic methods like ps and top, as well as direct examination of the files in the proc pseudo filesystem to determine the filesystem state. To get started, we will look at the tools provided with Red Hat Linux.

The `proc` Filesystem

One of the more interesting features of Linux that is shared by other modern UNIX implementations, such as Solaris, is the `proc` filesystem. This filesystem is not a filesystem in the sense that you can create filesystems of this type to store files. It is an abstraction mechanism that allows you to use simple tools such as `cat` to examine various parts of kernel memory, simply by looking at the contents of a file. Let's take a look at the types of information you can extract by examining the `proc`filesystem.

The Numbered Directories

In the `proc` filesystem, which is mounted at `/proc`, you can find a number of directories with numbers for names. These numbers are the process ids. In each of these numbered directories, you will find information about each process, including

- The current working directory

- The number of open file descriptors and the files or processes associated with each

- Shared memory areas

- The environment in which the process is running

- The command line with which it was invoked

Let's take a look at one of these directories and see the types of information that we can derive from it. Take a look at the following directory listing from the `proc` filesystem for a process running with process id 32233.

```
tschenk@quicksilver:/proc/32233 [1106]$ ls -l
total 0
-r--r--r--   1 tschenk  users          0 Jul  1 23:55 cmdline
lrwx------   1 tschenk  users          0 Jul  1 23:55 cwd ->
➥ /home/tschenk/
-r--------   1 tschenk  users          0 Jul  1 23:55 environ
lrwx------   1 tschenk  users          0 Jul  1 23:55 exe ->
➥/usr/lib/netscape/netscape-communicator*
dr-x------   2 tschenk  users          0 Jul  1 23:55 fd/
pr--r--r--   1 tschenk  users          0 Jul  1 23:55 maps¦
-rw-------   1 tschenk  users          0 Jul  1 23:55 mem
lrwx------   1 tschenk  users          0 Jul  1 23:55 root -> //
-r--r--r--   1 tschenk  users          0 Jul  1 23:55 stat
-r--r--r--   1 tschenk  users          0 Jul  1 23:55 statm
-r--r--r--   1 tschenk  users          0 Jul  1 23:55 status
```

From this simple directory list, we can already tell the following about the process that this directory describes:

- From the cwd symbolic link, we can determine that the process was invoked from the /home/tschenk directory.

- From the exe symbolic link, we can tell that the executable name was /usr/lib/netscape/netscape-communicator.

- From the root symbolic link, we can tell that we didn't chroot before executing this command.

This is quite a lot of information from a simple directory listing. Now let's take a look at some of the other information that we can obtain from this directory. Consider the following commands and their output.

```
tschenk@quicksilver:/proc/32233 [1110]$ more cmdline
(dns helper)
```

From this command, and from the name of the executable as shown by the exe symbolic link, we can see that this process was invoked as dns helper, which is a child process initiated by netscape-communicator to do name server lookups.

```
tschenk@quicksilver:/proc/32233 [1120]$ more environ ¦ tr '\000' '\n'
USERNAME=tschenk
HISTSIZE=1000
HOSTNAME=quicksilver.alchemy.net
LOGNAME=tschenk
HISTFILESIZE=1000
INIT_VERSION=sysvinit-2.74
VISUAL=/usr/local/bin/vi
MAIL=/var/spool/mail/tschenk
PAGER=less
WWW_HOME=http://www.deja.com
notify=1
TERM=linux
HOSTTYPE=i386
PATH=/home/tschenk/bin:/home/tschenk/Office50/bin:/opt/Corel/wpbin:
➥/bin:/usr/bin:/usr/bin/mh:/sbin:/usr/sbin:/usr/local/sbin:/usr/X11R6/bin:
➥/usr/openwin/bin:/usr/local/bin:/usr/local/bin/X11:/usr/games:
➥/usr/local/games
CONSOLE=/dev/console
KDEDIR=/usr
PRINTER=lp
HOME=/home/tschenk
```

```
MAILBOX=/var/spool/mail/tschenk
INPUTRC=/etc/inputrc
HOSTFILE=/etc/hosts
PREVLEVEL=N
RUNLEVEL=5
SHELL=/bin/bash
XAUTHORITY=/home/tschenk/.Xauthority
LOCALARCH=linux
PLATFORM=linux
HOSTCONTROL=ignoredups
MORE=-c
USER=tschenk
GDM_LANG=C
AUTOBOOT=YES
GROUP=users
LESS=-Ce
BOOT_IMAGE=RedHat6
DISPLAY=:0
OSTYPE=Linux
cdable_vars=1
NNTPSERVER=news.realtime.com
GDMSESSION=KDE
SHLVL=1
ORGANIZATION=Deja News, Inc., Austin, Texas, USA
LOCALHOST=quicksilver.alchemy.net
```

Here we have simulated the output of the printenv command, using the more command and tr to translate nulls into newline characters. Knowledge of this structure can be useful when writing shell scripts or if you are interested in writing your own utilities.

In these next two examples, we look at the file descriptor information and determine how many open file descriptors there are and the purpose of each.

```
tschenk@quicksilver:/proc/32233 [1148]$ ls -1 fd ¦ wc -l
     6

tschenk@quicksilver:/proc/32233 [1149]$ ls -l fd
total 0
lr-x------   1 tschenk  users           64 Jul  2 00:10 0 ->
➡pipe:[93306]
l-wx------   1 tschenk  users           64 Jul  2 00:10 1 ->
➡pipe:[93307]
l-wx------   1 tschenk  users           64 Jul  2 00:10 2 ->
```

```
➥/home/tschenk/.xsession-errors
lr-x------   1 tschenk  users          64 Jul  2 00:10 3 ->
➥pipe:[93306]
lrwx------   1 tschenk  users          64 Jul  2 00:10 4 ->
➥/dev/zero
l-wx------   1 tschenk  users          64 Jul  2 00:10 6 ->
➥pipe:[93307]
```

As shown in the following code, additional human-readable information about a process
can be obtained from the status file. Included is information about the process id, the parent
process id, who the program is running as, the current state, memory usage information,
and other information such as signals received and the capabilities information related to
the process.

```
tschenk@quicksilver:/proc/32233 [1152]$ cat status
Name:   netscape-commun
State:  S (sleeping)
Pid:    32233
PPid:   32223
Uid:    500     500     500     500
Gid:    100     100     100     100
FDSize: 32
Groups: 100
VmSize:    16712 kB
VmLck:         0 kB
VmRSS:      3644 kB
VmData:      560 kB
VmStk:        12 kB
VmExe:     10976 kB
VmLib:      2444 kB
SigPnd: 0000000000000000
SigBlk: 0000000000002000
SigIgn: 0000000000000a87
SigCgt: 0000000000000400
CapInh: 00000000fffffeff
CapPrm: 0000000000000000
CapEff: 0000000000000000
```

There is additional information in the numbered directories, such as the maps pipe that can
show you what shared libraries and other loadable modules a process has mapped in
memory. This is useful for programs like Apache that contain a loadable module scheme to
add functionality.

```
tschenk@quicksilver:/proc/642 [1007]$ cat maps
08048000-08070000 r-xp 00000000 08:02 143375
➥/usr/sbin/httpd
08070000-08071000 rw-p 00027000 08:02 143375
➥/usr/sbin/httpd
08071000-0808f000 rwxp 00000000 00:00 0
40000000-40012000 r-xp 00000000 08:02 30722
➥/lib/ld-2.1.1.so
40012000-40013000 rw-p 00011000 08:02 30722
➥/lib/ld-2.1.1.so
40013000-40014000 rwxp 00000000 00:00 0
40014000-40015000 rw-p 00000000 00:00 0
40015000-40016000 r-xp 00000000 08:02 178204
➥/usr/lib/apache/mod_env.so
40016000-40017000 rw-p 00000000 08:02 178204
➥/usr/lib/apache/mod_env.so
40017000-40018000 r-xp 00000000 08:02 178211
➥/usr/lib/apache/mod_log_agent.so
40018000-40019000 rw-p 00000000 08:02 178211
➥/usr/lib/apache/mod_log_agent.so
4001a000-40035000 r-xp 00000000 08:02 30740
➥/lib/libm-2.1.1.so
40035000-40036000 rw-p 0001a000 08:02 30740
➥/lib/libm-2.1.1.so
40036000-4003b000 r-xp 00000000 08:02 30731
➥/lib/libcrypt-2.1.1.so
4003b000-4003c000 rw-p 00004000 08:02 30731
➥/lib/libcrypt-2.1.1.so
4003c000-40063000 rw-p 00000000 00:00 0
40063000-4009b000 r-xp 00000000 08:02 30733
➥/lib/libdb-2.1.1.so
4009b000-4009d000 rw-p 00037000 08:02 30733
➥/lib/libdb-2.1.1.so
4009d000-4009f000 r-xp 00000000 08:02 30738
➥/lib/libdl-2.1.1.so
4009f000-400a0000 rw-p 00001000 08:02 30738
➥/lib/libdl-2.1.1.so
400a0000-400a1000 rw-p 00000000 00:00 0
400a1000-40187000 r-xp 00000000 08:02 30729
➥/lib/libc-2.1 (deleted)
40187000-4018c000 rw-p 000e5000 08:02 30729
➥/lib/libc-2.1 (deleted)
4018c000-4018f000 rw-p 00000000 00:00 0
```

```
4018f000-40191000 r-xp 00000000 08:02 178212
➥/usr/lib/apache/mod_log_config.so
40191000-40193000 rw-p 00001000 08:02 178212
➥/usr/lib/apache/mod_log_config.so
40193000-40194000 r-xp 00000000 08:02 178213
➥/usr/lib/apache/mod_log_referer.so
40194000-40195000 rw-p 00000000 08:02 178213
➥/usr/lib/apache/mod_log_referer.so
40195000-40197000 r-xp 00000000 08:02 178214
➥/usr/lib/apache/mod_mime.so
40197000-40198000 rw-p 00001000 08:02 178214
➥/usr/lib/apache/mod_mime.so
40198000-4019d000 r-xp 00000000 08:02 178217
➥/usr/lib/apache/mod_negotiation.so
4019d000-4019e000 rw-p 00004000 08:02 178217
➥/usr/lib/apache/mod_negotiation.so
4019e000-401a1000 r-xp 00000000 08:02 178221
➥/usr/lib/apache/mod_status.so
401a1000-401a2000 rw-p 00002000 08:02 178221
➥/usr/lib/apache/mod_status.so
401a2000-401a5000 r-xp 00000000 08:02 178210
➥/usr/lib/apache/mod_info.so
401a5000-401a6000 rw-p 00002000 08:02 178210
➥/usr/lib/apache/mod_info.so
401a6000-401ac000 r-xp 00000000 08:02 178209
➥/usr/lib/apache/mod_include.so
401ac000-401ad000 rw-p 00005000 08:02 178209
➥/usr/lib/apache/mod_include.so
401ad000-401b1000 r-xp 00000000 08:02 178198
➥/usr/lib/apache/mod_autoindex.so
401b1000-401b3000 rw-p 00003000 08:02 178198
➥/usr/lib/apache/mod_autoindex.so
401b3000-401b4000 r-xp 00000000 08:02 178203
➥/usr/lib/apache/mod_dir.so
401b4000-401b5000 rw-p 00000000 08:02 178203
➥/usr/lib/apache/mod_dir.so
401b5000-401b7000 r-xp 00000000 08:02 178201
➥/usr/lib/apache/mod_cgi.so
401b7000-401b8000 rw-p 00001000 08:02 178201
➥/usr/lib/apache/mod_cgi.so
401b8000-401b9000 r-xp 00000000 08:02 178194
➥/usr/lib/apache/mod_asis.so
401b9000-401ba000 rw-p 00000000 08:02 178194
```

➥/usr/lib/apache/mod_asis.so
401ba000-401bd000 r-xp 00000000 08:02 178208
➥/usr/lib/apache/mod_imap.so
401bd000-401be000 rw-p 00002000 08:02 178208
➥/usr/lib/apache/mod_imap.so
401be000-401bf000 r-xp 00000000 08:02 178192
➥/usr/lib/apache/mod_actions.so
401bf000-401c0000 rw-p 00000000 08:02 178192
➥/usr/lib/apache/mod_actions.so
401c0000-401c1000 r-xp 00000000 08:02 178223
➥/usr/lib/apache/mod_userdir.so
401c1000-401c2000 rw-p 00000000 08:02 178223
➥/usr/lib/apache/mod_userdir.so
401c2000-401d0000 r-xp 00000000 08:02 178190
➥/usr/lib/apache/libproxy.so
401d0000-401d1000 rw-p 0000d000 08:02 178190
➥/usr/lib/apache/libproxy.so
401d1000-401d3000 r-xp 00000000 08:02 178193
➥/usr/lib/apache/mod_alias.so
401d3000-401d4000 rw-p 00001000 08:02 178193
➥/usr/lib/apache/mod_alias.so
401d4000-401de000 r-xp 00000000 08:02 178218
➥/usr/lib/apache/mod_rewrite.so
401de000-401df000 rw-p 00009000 08:02 178218
➥/usr/lib/apache/mod_rewrite.so
401df000-401e0000 r-xp 00000000 08:02 178191
➥/usr/lib/apache/mod_access.so
401e0000-401e2000 rw-p 00000000 08:02 178191
➥/usr/lib/apache/mod_access.so
401e2000-401e4000 r-xp 00000000 08:02 178195
➥/usr/lib/apache/mod_auth.so
401e4000-401e5000 rw-p 00001000 08:02 178195
➥/usr/lib/apache/mod_auth.so
401e5000-401e6000 r-xp 00000000 08:02 178196
➥/usr/lib/apache/mod_auth_anon.so
401e6000-401e7000 rw-p 00000000 08:02 178196
➥/usr/lib/apache/mod_auth_anon.so
401e7000-401e8000 r-xp 00000000 08:02 178197
➥/usr/lib/apache/mod_auth_db.so
401e8000-401e9000 rw-p 00000000 08:02 178197
➥/usr/lib/apache/mod_auth_db.so
401e9000-401eb000 r-xp 00000000 08:02 178202
➥/usr/lib/apache/mod_digest.so

4

Where Do I
Find...?

```
401eb000-401ec000 rw-p 00001000 08:02 178202
➥/usr/lib/apache/mod_digest.so
401ec000-401ed000 r-xp 00000000 08:02 178206
➥/usr/lib/apache/mod_expires.so
401ed000-401ee000 rw-p 00000000 08:02 178206
➥/usr/lib/apache/mod_expires.so
401ee000-401ef000 r-xp 00000000 08:02 178207
➥/usr/lib/apache/mod_headers.so
401ef000-401f0000 rw-p 00000000 08:02 178207
➥/usr/lib/apache/mod_headers.so
401f0000-401f1000 r-xp 00000000 08:02 178224
➥/usr/lib/apache/mod_usertrack.so
401f1000-401f2000 rw-p 00000000 08:02 178224
➥/usr/lib/apache/mod_usertrack.so
401f2000-401f3000 r-xp 00000000 08:02 178219
➥/usr/lib/apache/mod_setenvif.so
401f3000-401f4000 rw-p 00000000 08:02 178219
➥/usr/lib/apache/mod_setenvif.so
401fa000-40202000 r-xp 00000000 08:02 30760
➥/lib/libnss_files-2.1.1.so
40202000-40203000 rw-p 00007000 08:02 30760
➥/lib/libnss_files-2.1.1.so
40203000-4020f000 rwxs 00000000 00:00 0
bfffb000-c0000000 rwxp ffffc000 00:00 0
```

As you can see, this output shows not only the modules and shared libraries being used by apache, but also where they are located. This information can be quite useful in debugging. Full details of the maps file may be found in the proc manual page, obtained with the command:

```
man 5 proc
```

Process Status Tools

The standard method of examining the state of your system is through use of the process status tools contained in the procps package. These tools include ps, top, vmstat, free, uptime, w, and others. Each one of them uses the proc pseudo filesystem to collect data on your Linux system, as opposed to the older method of using /dev/kmem or reading from kernel memory by mapping to it directly. This makes for much easier maintenance of these tools.

For those who prefer graphical utilities for monitoring system status, there are several tools that come with your Red Hat system. If you prefer the KDE desktop environment, you can use `ktop`, shown in Figure 4.1. On the other hand, if GNOME is more your style, `gtop`, shown in Figure 4.2, gives you similar capabilities. Each has slightly different features that make them easier to work with than the command-line version of `top`, and if you spend most of your time in the graphical environment both are worth getting to know.

FIGURE 4.1

Ktop—The KDE version of the Top utility.

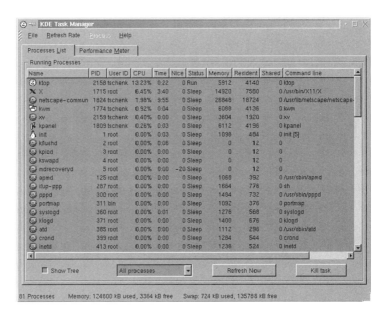

Another graphical tool written for the KDE environment is `kpm`, the KDE process manager, shown in Figure 4.3. It is very similar to `ktop`, but with a slightly different layout as shown here.

Another very useful command for examining the status of your system is `procinfo`, shown in Figure 4.4. This command can present summaries of information, such as memory utilization, uptime, interrupts, and load averages either as a one-time command or in full screen mode in a manner similar to the `top` command.

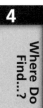

FIGURE 4.2
Gtop—*The GNOME version of the Top utility.*

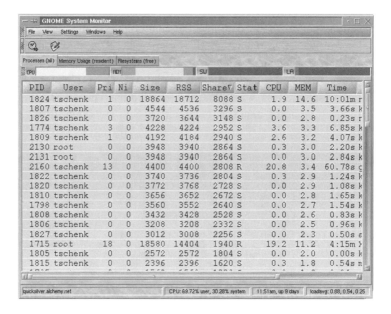

FIGURE 4.3
kpm—*The KDE Process Manager.*

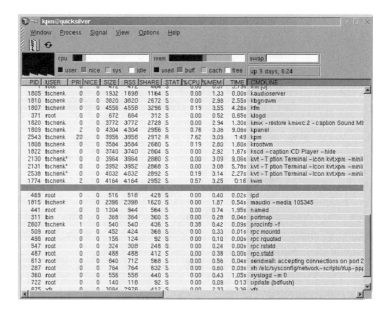

FIGURE **4.4**
procinfo *in Full
Screen Mode.*

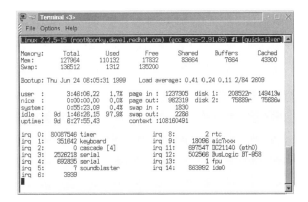

Checking Devices

The `proc` filesystem also provides mechanisms to query devices recognized by the Linux kernel. This information ranges from the IRQs used by various devices to the type and number of disk drives installed and much more. The following commands demonstrate the types of information available in the `proc` filesystem and how to examine it.

```
tschenk@quicksilver:~ [1040]$ cat /proc/cpuinfo
processor       : 0
vendor_id       : GenuineIntel
cpu family      : 5
model           : 2
model name      : Pentium 75 - 200
stepping        : 12
cpu MHz         : 167.047402
fdiv_bug        : no
hlt_bug         : no
sep_bug         : no
f00f_bug        : yes
fpu             : yes
fpu_exception   : yes
cpuid level     : 1
wp              : yes
flags           : fpu vme de pse tsc msr mce cx8
bogomips        : 66.56
```

To determine the type of processor that a Linux system has, you can do as shown here and examine the contents of the `/proc/cpuinfo` file. The preceding example shows that this system recognizes one Pentium 166MHz processor. It also shows that this is not an MMX processor and which of the various Pentium bugs that this processor is susceptible to. Unfortunately, unless the running kernel has been compiled with multiprocessor support,

there is no way to determine how many processors a system has. If you did include multiprocessor support in your kernel, this fact will be reflected in the /proc/cpuinfo file as well as the boot messages.

> **Note**
>
> Please note that you cannot infer from the following output whether this system is or is not a multiprocessor system. This output merely shows that the running kernel only recognizes one processor. If this were a multiprocessor system running a kernel compiled without SMP support, you would get output as shown in the preceding example.

```
tschenk@quicksilver:~ [1038]$ cat /proc/devices
Character devices:
  1 mem
  2 pty
  3 ttyp
  4 ttyS
  5 cua
  7 vcs
 10 misc
 14 sound
 29 fb
 36 netlink
128 ptm
136 pts

Block devices:
  1 ramdisk
  2 fd
  3 ide0
  7 loop
  8 sd
  9 md
 11 sr
```

The /proc/devices file is a good starting place to see which devices are supported by the Linux kernel. This file lists character and block devices for which drivers are available in the running kernel along with their major numbers.

```
tschenk@quicksilver:~ [1042]$ cat /proc/interrupts
          CPU0
  0:   80221572        XT-PIC  timer
  1:     358387        XT-PIC  keyboard
  2:          0        XT-PIC  cascade
  3:    2532364        XT-PIC  serial
  4:     692835        XT-PIC  serial
  5:          7        XT-PIC  soundblaster
  8:          2        XT-PIC  rtc
  9:      18096        XT-PIC  aic7xxx
 11:     697549        XT-PIC  DC21140 (eth0)
 12:     502952        XT-PIC  BusLogic BT-958
 13:          1        XT-PIC  fpu
 14:     868012        XT-PIC  ide0
NMI:          0
```

```
tschenk@quicksilver:~ [1043]$ cat /proc/dma
 1: SoundBlaster8
 4: cascade
 5: SoundBlaster16
```

```
tschenk@quicksilver:~ [1044]$ cat /proc/ioports
0000-001f : dma1
0020-003f : pic1
0040-005f : timer
0060-006f : keyboard
0070-007f : rtc
0080-008f : dma page reg
00a0-00bf : pic2
00c0-00df : dma2
00f0-00ff : fpu
01f0-01f7 : ide0
0220-022f : soundblaster
02f8-02ff : serial(auto)
0330-0333 : MPU-401 UART
03c0-03df : vga+
03e8-03ef : serial(auto)
03f6-03f6 : ide0
03f8-03ff : serial(auto)
0620-0623 : sound driver (AWE32)
0a20-0a23 : sound driver (AWE32)
0e20-0e23 : sound driver (AWE32)
6000-60be : aic7xxx
```

```
6400-6403 : BusLogic BT-958
6600-667f : DC21140 (eth0)
f000-f007 : ide0
f008-f00f : ide1
```

The preceding three commands show the IRQ, DMA, and I/O ranges for the various
devices in this system. For example, I can determine from the output that I have a
Soundblaster AWE 32 card in the system using IRQ 7, DMA channels 1 and 5, and several
I/O port ranges. I can also see how many interrupts each device has generated.

```
tschenk@quicksilver:~ [1052]$ cat /proc/pci
PCI devices found:
  Bus  0, device   0, function  0:
    Host bridge: Intel 82439HX Triton II (rev 3).
      Medium devsel.  Master Capable.  Latency=32.
  Bus  0, device   7, function  0:
    ISA bridge: Intel 82371SB PIIX3 ISA (rev 1).
      Medium devsel.  Fast back-to-back capable.   Master Capable.   No bursts.
  Bus  0, device   7, function  1:
    IDE interface: Intel 82371SB PIIX3 IDE (rev 0).
      Medium devsel.  Fast back-to-back capable.  Master Capable.   Latency=32.
      I/O at 0xf000 [0xf001].
  Bus  0, device  17, function  0:
    SCSI storage controller: BusLogic MultiMaster (rev 8).
      Fast devsel.   IRQ 12.  Master Capable.  Latency=32.  Min Gnt=8.Max Lat=8.
      I/O at 0x6400 [0x6401].
      Non-prefetchable 32 bit memory at 0xe1804000 [0xe1804000].
  Bus  0, device  18, function  0:
    VGA compatible controller: Matrox Millennium II (rev 0).
      Medium devsel.  Fast back-to-back capable.  IRQ 12.  Master      Capable.
➥    Latency=32.
      Prefetchable 32 bit memory at 0xe0000000 [0xe0000008].
      Non-prefetchable 32 bit memory at 0xe1800000 [0xe1800000].
      Non-prefetchable 32 bit memory at 0xe1000000 [0xe1000000].
  Bus  0, device  19, function  0:
    SCSI storage controller: Adaptec AIC-7850 (rev 1).
      Medium devsel.  Fast back-to-back capable.  IRQ 9.  Master      Capable.
➥    Latency=32.  Min Gnt=4.Max Lat=4.
      I/O at 0x6000 [0x6001].
      Non-prefetchable 32 bit memory at 0xe1805000 [0xe1805000].
  Bus  0, device  20, function  0:
    Ethernet controller: DEC DC21140 (rev 34).
      Medium devsel.  Fast back-to-back capable.  IRQ 11.  Master      Capable.
➥    Latency=96.  Min Gnt=20.Max Lat=40.
```

```
I/O at 0x6600 [0x6601].
Non-prefetchable 32 bit memory at 0xe1806000 [0xe1806000].
```

The /proc/pci file contains information about the various PCI devices in your system. For example, the preceding output shows that this system contains two SCSI controllers, one a BusLogic MultiMaster, and the other an Adaptec AIC-7850. It also shows that the video card is a Matrox Millennium II and that the ethernet controller is based on the DEC DC21140 chipset.

```
tschenk@quicksilver:~ [1055]$ ls /proc/ide
drivers  hda@  ide0/

tschenk@quicksilver:~ [1056]$ cat /proc/ide/drivers
ide-cdrom version 4.53
ide-disk version 1.08

tschenk@quicksilver:~ [1065]$ cat /proc/ide/hda/media
cdrom

tschenk@quicksilver:~ [1066]$ cat /proc/ide/hda/model
CD-ROM CDU311
```

The preceding three commands show that this system has a single IDE device attached to the primary IDE controller, that the kernel has drivers loaded or compiled in for IDE disks and CD-ROM drives, and that the attached IDE device is a Sony CDU311 CD-ROM drive.

```
tschenk@quicksilver:~ [1075]$ ls /proc/scsi
BusLogic/  aic7xxx/  scsi

tschenk@quicksilver:~ [1076]$ cat /proc/scsi/scsi
Attached devices:
Host: scsi0 Channel: 00 Id: 00 Lun: 00
  Vendor: SEAGATE  Model: ST34572W        Rev: 0876
  Type:   Direct-Access                   ANSI SCSI revision: 02
Host: scsi0 Channel: 00 Id: 01 Lun: 00
  Vendor: SEAGATE  Model: ST19171W        Rev: 0023
  Type:   Direct-Access                   ANSI SCSI revision: 02
Host: scsi1 Channel: 00 Id: 06 Lun: 00
  Vendor: NEC      Model: CD-ROM DRIVE:500 Rev: 1.0
  Type:   CD-ROM                          ANSI SCSI revision: 02
```

```
tschenk@quicksilver:~ [1085]$ ls /proc/scsi/BusLogic/
0

tschenk@quicksilver:~ [1086]$ ls /proc/scsi/aic7xxx/
1
```

As with the IDE devices, there is also information about the various SCSI devices attached to this system. The preceding commands show that there are three SCSI devices attached to the system, two SCSI disks and a CD-ROM drive, along with their manufacturer, SCSI id, and the controller to which they are attached. It also shows the device drivers used and which one is recognized as scsi0 and scsi1. Not shown, but also available by examining the contents of the files /proc/scsi/BusLogic/0 and /proc/scsi/aic7xxx/1 are details about driver versions and the configuration of the controllers.

```
tschenk@quicksilver:~ [1088]$ cat /proc/sound
OSS/Free:3.8s2++-971130
Load type: Driver loaded as a module
Kernel: Linux quicksilver.alchemy.net 2.2.5-15 #1 Mon Apr 19 22:21:09
➥                      EDT 1999 i586
Config options: 0

Installed drivers:

Card config:

Audio devices:
0: Sound Blaster 16 (4.13) (DUPLEX)

Synth devices:
0: AWE32-0.4.3 (RAM512k)

Midi devices:
0: Sound Blaster 16
1: AWE Midi Emu

Timers:
0: System clock

Mixers:
0: Sound Blaster
```

The contents of /proc/sound show the driver version, and also that sound support is loaded as a module and the various devices supported by the loaded driver. This is the same information that is available by examining /dev/sndstat.

Device Naming Scheme

The naming schemes for the various devices supported by the Linux kernel are documented in the devices.txt file included with the kernel source code. This file contains the names of the devices as well as their major and minor number assignments. Device driver authors should always consult this file before assigning their own device major and minor numbers to avoid conflicts with other devices, as well as follow the instructions contained therein to request the assignment of a permanent set of numbers.

Assigned Major and Minor Numbers

A complete list of the assigned major and minor device numbers is included with the Linux kernel source code in both ASCII text format and as LaTeX source. The files are /usr/src/linux/Documentation/devices.txt, which is the ASCII version, and /usr/src/linux/Documentation/devices.tex, which is the LaTeX source and the definitive list. This document is not included here in its entirety, but Table 4.1 shows the names, major numbers, and device types for some of the most common devices.

TABLE 4.1 Assigned Device Numbers and Names

Device Type	Major	Type	Device Name
First IDE controller devices	3	block	/dev/hd[a-b]* (1)
Second IDE controller devices	22	block	/dev/hd[c-d]* (1)
Third IDE controller devices	33	block	/dev/hd[e-f]* (1)
Fourth IDE controller devices	34	block	/dev/hd[g-h]* (1)
IDE tape devices	37	char	/dev/ht0 and /dev/nht0 (2)
SCSI disks	8	block	/dev/sd[a-p]* (3)
SCSI disks	65	block	/dev/sd[q-v]* (3)
SCSI disks	66	block	/dev/sda[g-v]* (3)
SCSI disks	67	block	/dev/sda[w-z]* and /dev/sdb[a-l]* (3)
SCSI CDROM drives	11	block	/dev/scd[0-7] (4)
SCSI tape devices	9	char	/dev/st[0-9]* and /dev/nst[0-9]* (2)
Floppy controller tape devices	27	char	/dev/*qft* & /dev/n*qft* (2)
Parallel port IDE disk devices	45	block	/dev/pd* (5)
Parallel port ATAPI CDROM devices	96	block	/dev/pcd*

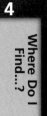

4

Where Do I Find...?

TABLE **4.1**   continued

Device Type	Major	Type	Device Name
Parallel port ATAPI disk devices	96	block	/dev/pf* (6)
Parallel port ATAPI tape devices	96	char	/dev/pt[0-9] and /dev/npt[0-9] (2)
Software RAID devices	9	block	/dev/md[0-9]*
Parallel printers	6	char	/dev/lp*
Virtual consoles	4	char	/dev/tty[0-9]*
Serial ports (call in)	4	char	/dev/ttyS*
Serial ports (call out)	5	char	/dev/cua* (7)

(1) IDE devices are allowed up to 4 primary partitions and 59 logical partitions per disk, corresponding to minor numbers 1-63 for the first device on the controller and 65-127 for the second. Minor numbers 0 applies to the whole first device and 64 to the whole second device.

(2) Tape device names beginning with n as /dev/nst0 refer to devices that do not rewind on device close.

(3) SCSI disk devices are limited to 16 partitions per disk with each partition referred to by a hexadecimal digit in the range 1-f with 0 reserved for the entire disk.

(4) SCSI CDROM devices sometimes use the naming scheme /dev/sr[0-9].

(5) Parallel port IDE drives are limited to 16 partitions just like SCSI drives.

(6) Parallel port ATAPI disk devices refer to floppy drives, not hard drives and follow a naming scheme similar to the regular floppy devices.

(7) Red Hat still includes the call out devices even though their use is deprecated by the 2.2.x kernel.

An Alternative Device Management Scheme

The current device naming and management scheme has several limitations, especially when it comes to handling SCSI and IDE drives. Specifically, the notion of assigning names to devices that are not immutable, but that change based on how many devices were detected before it, can lead to many problems. Consider the following example.

SCSI drives attached to a SCSI controller are assigned names that are related to the SCSI id assigned to them. As the SCSI controller scans the bus, it assigns the first disk name, /dev/sda, to the disk with the lowest SCSI id. This leads to problems when you change the id of SCSI drives, when you add or remove a disk from a system, or when a disk fails. Say that you have a system with two SCSI disks with SCSI ids set to 0 and 3. The first of these would be named /dev/sda and the second would be named /dev/sdb. If you decide to add a third disk to your system with its SCSI id set to 1, you would now have this new device recognized as /dev/sdb and the device with id 3 would now be recognized as /dev/sdc. The implications of this are that you would have to make sure that any configuration files, such as /etc/fstab, that reference the disk with SCSI id 3 as /dev/sdb would have to be changed to refer to `/dev/sdc` instead. Now suppose that the new disk fails. Until that disk is repaired or replaced, you would again have to refer to the device with SCSI id 3 as `/dev/sdb`. On a single system this may not seem like much of a problem, but when you start talking about a network of hundreds of systems, you can see that this could become a maintenance nightmare.

One proposed solution to this problem is to name devices using a scheme such that the names of a device never change as long as the ID of the device remains constant. This is similar to what other operating systems such as Solaris do. To implement this functionality under Linux, a patch called `devfs` is available on the Web site of its author, Richard Gooch, at `http://www.atnf.csiro.au/~rgooch/linux/kernel-patches.html`. In addition to solving naming issues with devices, this patch has other benefits, including dynamic device allocation based on which devices are detected by the kernel. This patch is slated for incorporation into a future kernel release, probably early in the 2.3.x development cycle.

Summary

As with other operating systems, a large part of being able to administer the system is knowing where to find configuration information and how to examine the state of the running system. This chapter covered where to look for the various types of files, both configuration files and executables, by looking at the standard and seeing how Red Hat diverges from that standard. Also covered were some of the tools needed to examine the state of a running Linux system and the source of this information in the `proc` filesystem. Finally, device naming was covered, both the standard scheme used by Red Hat and an alternative system that you can incorporate if you so choose. Hopefully, you can now find your way around your Linux system and are able to determine much of the configuration information that you will need to effectively administer it.

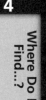

CHAPTER 5

Starting Up and Shutting Down

IN THIS CHAPTER

- Linux Boot Loaders   *112*
- The Linux Boot Process
  and System Initialization Scripts   *128*
- Shutting Down   *137*

Unlike other operating systems commonly in use today, the process of starting up and shutting down your Red Hat Linux system is not black magic to the systems administrator. The administrator has to make choices about which boot loaders to use and know how to configure the selected boot loader. The administrator also has to know where to look to modify and update system initialization scripts. And finally, he or she must know how to shut down the system correctly, and know the consequences of an improper shutdown.

This chapter looks at some of the available boot loaders for Linux, describes their operation, and demonstrates how to configure them. Once we have covered the process of booting your Linux system, we will move on to what happens during the kernel boot process, and take a look at the system initialization scripts. We will also look at how to customize them to meet the specific needs of the system. Lastly, we will cover the proper way to shut down your Linux system.

Linux Boot Loaders

To get started, let's take a look at what is involved in booting your Linux system. This process is architecture dependent, but instead of trying to cover all of the architectures for which Linux is available, we will concentrate our discussion on the Intel x86 platform. In addition, we will restrict our discussion to booting from a hard drive because it is unlikely that your Linux servers will be booting from a floppy.

Boot Loader Overview

Before we get into the details of boot loaders, it is useful to have an understanding of the layout of the hard drive. A sample hard drive layout is illustrated in Figure 5.1.

The preceding figure shows a disk that has been partitioned into two primary partitions and an extended partition containing four logical partitions. The start of each partition table contains a sector called the *boot sector*. The boot sector for the whole disk is known as the *master boot record*, or MBR.

The boot process begins with the master boot record, which is the first sector of the disk and contains the boot loader code. During the boot sequence, the following steps take place:

1. The boot loader code loads into memory.
2. Via a loader-dependent mechanism, the boot loader selects the partition to boot.
3. Once the partition is selected, the boot loader passes control to the boot sector of the partition, which loads the operating system.

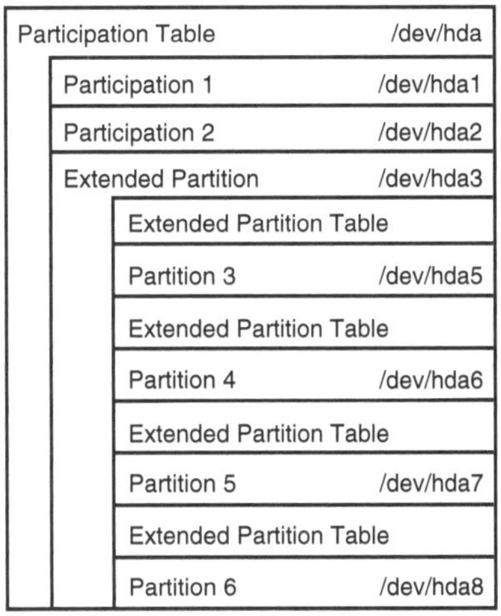

FIGURE 5.1

A sample hard drive layout containing six partitions.

Participation Table	/dev/hda
Participation 1	/dev/hda1
Participation 2	/dev/hda2
Extended Partition	/dev/hda3

Extended Partition Table	
Partition 3	/dev/hda5
Extended Partition Table	
Partition 4	/dev/hda6
Extended Partition Table	
Partition 5	/dev/hda7
Extended Partition Table	
Partition 6	/dev/hda8

This is of course a very simplified version of what happens, but it is sufficient for the purposes of this discussion. Now let's take a look at what code can be loaded into this master boot record.

If your system is running DOS or descendants such as Windows, the master boot record is most likely a DOS-style MBR. This type of MBR contains a loader that works by searching for a partition marked active in the partition table and passing control to the code contained in the boot sector of that active partition, which in turn loads the operating system. This is not the only possible method, but it is the default for most personal computers based on the x86 platform. Differences occur because there are any number of boot loader programs available for the x86 platform, including the one we are going to talk about next.

LILO, The Linux Loader

For those running pure Linux systems, the most popular boot loader is the Linux loader called LILO. This loader has an extensive feature set and can be installed in a many different ways. This section examines some sample setups and discusses the advantages and disadvantages of each.

Before covering these example setups, we must first differentiate between LILO the loader and /sbin/lilo, the map installer. LILO is the program written to the boot sector of a disk that loads operating systems and starts their execution. The map installer, /sbin/lilo, is a utility that parses the configuration file /etc/lilo.conf. It installs to this boot sector and creates the map file that contains the information required to accomplish this.

A Pure Linux System Example

For our first example, let's start with a system that runs Linux with only one possible kernel. For each example, we will use the hard drive layout presented in Figure 5.2. The hard drive has a total of five partitions. The first two are primary partitions and the other three are logical partitions contained within a single extended partition.

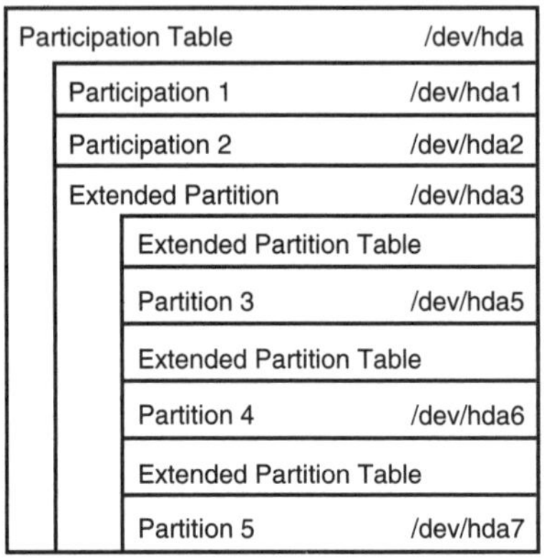

FIGURE 5.2

A sample hard drive layout prepared for Linux.

Participation Table	/dev/hda
Participation 1	/dev/hda1
Participation 2	/dev/hda2
Extended Partition	/dev/hda3
Extended Partition Table	
Partition 3	/dev/hda5
Extended Partition Table	
Partition 4	/dev/hda6
Extended Partition Table	
Partition 5	/dev/hda7

This system is set up in classic Linux style, as described here:

- The root partition is partition 1 on device /dev/hda1.

- The /usr partition is on partition 2, /dev/hda2.

- Partition 3 contains a swap partition, /dev/sda5.

- /home is on partition 4, /dev/sda6.

- /var is on partition 5, /dev/sda7.

The first question we must answer is where to install LILO. We have four choices given the setup just described. These four choices correspond to the Linux filesystem partitions. The only partition on which we could not install LILO is the Linux swap partition on /dev/sda5. Any of the other partitions could be used to install LILO on. This may seem contrary to what you have done in the past and it is subject to a couple of caveats, but nonetheless it is a true statement. That being said, it is customary to install LILO in one of two locations. The first of these is the boot sector of the partition containing the Linux root partition, which in our example is /dev/hda1. This boot sequence is shown in Figure 5.3, in which a DOS MBR is loaded, searches for the active partition (/dev/hda1), and the boot sector there loads the Linux kernel into memory and executes it.

FIGURE 5.3
The DOS MBR boot sequence.

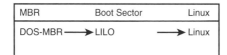

There are some advantages to this setup, as well as some drawbacks. One advantage is that if the machine is ever retasked to run another operating system, the only action required to get rid of LILO is to repartition the hard drive. On the other hand, there are a couple disadvantages to using this method. The first is that the system has to have been installed with Windows or DOS in order to get the DOS MBR onto the hard drive. Alternatively, you can use the DOS FDISK command with the /MBR switch to create the master boot record. Another minor disadvantage of this setup is that you must make the partition where LILO is installed active in order for the DOS MBR to find it.

Another option is to install LILO on the master boot record in place of the DOS MBR. This results in a boot sequence as illustrated in Figure 5.4. Since this is a pure Linux system, this is probably the more natural setup, but it has the disadvantage of requiring that you have a method to replace LILO on the MBR if you ever take Linux off of this system. It does not require that the disk be prepared first with DOS or Windows, and LILO does not use the active flag to determine which partition to boot.

FIGURE 5.4
The LILO MBR boot sequence.

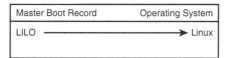

So how do you determine where LILO should be installed? If you install all of your systems using the Red Hat installation media, you will be given two choices:

- The master boot record
- The first Linux partition

If your system is Linux only and the boot disk has never been partitioned with DOS or Windows, you should select the master boot record. This is because there is no boot loader currently loaded in the master boot record to pass control to LILO. If your system originally contained DOS or Windows or your system will be dual boot, you may select either. Remember that if you select the first Linux partition, you must mark it active so that the loader in the master boot record can find it. Once you have made your selection, the installation program constructs the appropriate lilo.conf file for you and runs

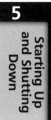

/sbin/lilo, the map installer. Naturally, you can also do this manually after your system is installed, by editing the lilo.conf file and running /sbin/lilo at the command prompt.

Note

Learning how to manipulate the lilo.conf file and use the map installer, /sbin/lilo, is highly recommended. There are a plethora of configuration options that you can choose from with LILO. The Red Hat installation program constructs only the most basic configuration file. Some of the more interesting options available are described later in this chapter in the section "LILO Tips and Tricks."

The following listing shows the lilo.conf file needed to install LILO on the Linux root partition.

```
#
# General section
#
boot = /dev/hda1
install = /boot/boot.b
verbose = 2
prompt

# After 5 seconds, boot the default image
timeout = 50

#
# Boot my Linux 2.2.5 kernel
#

image = /boot/vmlinuz-2.2.5
        label = linux
        root = /dev/hda1
        read-only
        initrd = /boot/initrd.gz
```

The primary line of interest in the preceding file is boot = /dev/hda1. This line tells LILO where to install itself. By changing this line as shown in the following file listing, LILO will instead load itself into the master boot record.

```
#
# General section
#
```

```
boot = /dev/hda
install = /boot/boot.b
verbose = 2
prompt

# After 5 seconds, boot the default image
timeout = 50

#
# Boot my Linux 2.2.5 kernel
#

image = /boot/vmlinuz-2.2.5
        label = linux
        root = /dev/hda1
        read-only
        initrd = /boot/initrd.gz
```

A System with Two Operating Systems

A slightly more involved example involves booting other operating systems. For example, if you have a system that you want to be dual boot between Windows and Linux, LILO can accomplish this as well. Going back to our defined partitions, let's assume that this time, Windows is installed on the first partition. Here's how we'll set it up:

- Windows—located on the first partition, `/dev/hda1`

- Linux root—located on the second partition, `/dev/hda2`

The remaining partitions are used by other Linux filesystems. In this case, we will be installing LILO in the master boot record, even though this means that if we decide to uninstall it, we have to go back and deal with recreating the master boot record. Consider the following `lilo.conf` file:

```
#
# General section
#
boot = /dev/hda
install = /boot/boot.b
verbose = 2
prompt

# After 5 seconds, boot the default image
timeout = 50
```

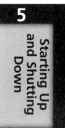

```
#
# Boot my Linux 2.2.5 kernel
#
image = /boot/vmlinuz-2.2.5
        label = linux
        root = /dev/hda2
        read-only
        initrd = /boot/initrd.gz


#
# Boot Windows on the first partition
#
other = /dev/hda1
    label = windows
    table = /dev/hda
```

In this file, we introduce the keyword other, which is used to specify the partitions containing other operating systems. We also see the first use of the table keyword, which specifies where the partition table information resides for this operating system. The boot sequence in this case is illustrated in Figure 5.5.

FIGURE 5.5

Dual boot with LILO as MBR.

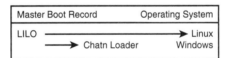

The /etc/lilo.conf File

To fully understand these examples you must understand the syntax of the LILO configuration file /etc/lilo.conf, so let's take a look at each of the available keywords and their meanings. There are two sections to a LILO configuration file. The first is the global keywords section. Specifying keywords is not required here, but is usually done to avoid unnecessary repetition. Table 5.1 shows the keywords for the global section and their meanings.

TABLE 5.1 LILO Global Section Keywords

Keyword Syntax	Description
backup=filename	When lilo is run, a backup of the boot sector being written to is copied to the named file.
boot=boot_dev	Names the partition to which lilo will write the boot loader code.

TABLE 5.1 continued

Keyword Syntax	Description
compact	Requests that optimizations be done that will reduce load time and make the map file smaller.
default=name	Specifies which image will be loaded by default. If this keyword is omitted, the first defined image is used.
delay=n	Waits for n/10 seconds before booting the default image. This option is useful if you want to give more time to interrupt the boot sequence.
fix-table	Allows LILO to adjust partition table entries so that the linear addresses of the first and last sector of the partition match the sector/head/cylinder addresses. Use with caution.
force-backup=filename	This works like backup, but will overwrite an existing file called filename, which backup will not.
ignore-table	Ignores corrupt partition tables and installs LILO as specified in the configuration file.
install=boot_sector	Specifies the file to use as the new boot sector. The default is /boot/boot.b.
linear	Uses linear addressing mode instead of addressing the disk using the sector/head/cylinder method. This may not work if compact is specified.
map=filename	Uses the named file as the map file. Defaults to /boot/map.
message=filename	Specifies a file to be presented to be displayed prior to the boot prompt. You can use this file to display messages or a list of available images to users.
prompt	Presents to boot prompt without any intervention by the user. Unattended reboots are not possible if this keyword is present and the timeout keyword is not.
timeout=n	If no user input is received in n/10 seconds, boots the default image.
verbose=level	level specifies the amount of information for lilo to print when run. Valid levels are negative numbers, which means only warnings and errors are displayed and numbers in the range 0-5, with each providing more information.

These are not all of the keywords, but they are the ones you'll most likely use. In addition to the global keywords, there are a number of per-image keywords available. Some of these per-image keywords can also be specified in the global section to serve as default values for all defined images. Table 5.2 defines some of the most common per-image keywords. An asterisk indicates those keywords that can be specified as either per-image keywords or as global keywords.

5

Starting Up and Shutting Down

TABLE 5.2 LILO Per-image Keywords

Keyword Syntax	Description
alias=name	Specifies a secondary name for the current image.
fallback=command_line *	If the current image is running and the system crashes, the command line specified is passed to LILO on the next boot.
label=name	Gives a name to the current image.
lock *	Allows you to reboot to the current image regardless of its position in the map. The current image becomes the default until it is overridden by user input.
password=password *	Prompts the user for a password before booting this image. If you use this option, you must ensure that the lilo.conf file is not readable by anyone other than the root user, since the password is not encrypted.
restricted	This option is only valid if the password option is used. It modifies the password behavior so that a password challenge is only made if the user specifies command-line parameters at the boot prompt.
single-key *	With this option set, you can have images activated with a single keystroke (no need to press Enter) if you have defined a single key alias or label.

The last set of keywords, described in Table 5.3, are those that apply only to the booting of Linux kernels.

TABLE 5.3 LILO Keywords for Linux Kernels

Keyword Syntax	Description
append=string	Adds the specified string to the kernel command line.
initrd=filename	Specifies the file that contains the image to be loaded into the initial ramdisk.
ramdisk=size	Specifies the size of the optional RAM disk with the default being read from the kernel image. Setting size to zero means that no ramdisk should be created.
read-only	When the kernel image is booted, the root filesystem will be mounted read-only so that it may be checked with fsck and then remounted.
read-write	The root filesystem will be mounted read-write.
root=device	The specified device contains the root filesystem.
vga=mode	The VGA text mode is set based on the mode specified, where mode is one of normal (80x25), extended (80x50), ask, or a number. Valid numbers can be determined by first specifying ask, which will give you a list of detected modes and then replacing ask with one of the numbers that were presented.

Command-Line Options for `/sbin/lilo`

In addition to all of the options available in the configuration file, there are a number of command-line options that can alter the behavior of LILO. Many of these result in behavior that mimics configuration file keywords. These options are shown in Table 5.4.

TABLE 5.4   LILO Command-Line Options

Command-Line Option	Configuration File Keyword
-b boot_dev	boot = boot_dev
-c	compact
-d N	delay = N
-D name	default = name
-i boot_sector	install = boot_sector
-l	linear
-m file	map = file
-P fix	fix-table
-P ignore	ignore-table
-s filename	backup = filename
-S filename	force-backup = filename
-v	verbose = level

Other options to `lilo` that may be used with the map installer include options to query the map file, stuff the command line for the next reboot, or to specify a different configuration file name. Table 5.5 shows these options and their meanings.

TABLE 5.5   More LILO Command-Line Options

Command-Line Option	Description
-C filename	Uses `filename` as the configuration file instead of the default `/etc/lilo.conf`.
-q	Queries the map file for a list of images.
-r directory	Before executing commands, chroot to directory. This is useful when booting from repair disks.
-R string	Stores this string in the map file to be used as the command line for the next reboot. This can be used to alter the default kernel temporarily while testing. This command line is removed from the map file once it is used.
-t	Test only mode. This performs all of the actions as specified on the command line and in the configuration file, but does not install the new map.
-u [device_name]	Restores a backup copy of the specified device boot sector. Validation is performed by checking a timestamp.
-U [device_name]	The same as `-u`, but no validation is performed.

LILO Tips and Tricks

Now that we have gotten our feet wet, let's take a look at a more complicated example. In this example, we have multiple operating systems installed and want LILO to boot all of them. The following list describes the data required to construct the `/etc/lilo.conf` file.

- The first partition, `/dev/hda1`, contains Windows

- Partition 2 contains Fred's Linux 0.5

- Partition 3 contains Red Hat Linux

- Partition 4 is a Linux swap partition

- Partition 5 contains FreeBSD

For various reasons, we want Fred's Linux and Red Hat to be totally independent of each other. In addition, this is a modern machine that does not suffer from the 1024 cylinder problem with large drives. Now that we have the parameters of the problem defined, please refer to Listing 5.1 to see what the `lilo.conf` file looks like.

LISTING 5.1   `/etc/lilo.conf`

```
#
# General section
#
boot = /dev/hda
compact
install = /boot/boot.b
message = /etc/lilo.msg
verbose = 2
lock


# After 10 seconds, boot the default image
prompt
timeout = 100


#
# Boot my Linux 2.2.5 kernel from /dev/hda5
# This kernel requires a password to boot if you specify any
# kernel command options.
#
image = /boot/vmlinuz-2.2.5
        label = Red Hat
```

LISTING 5.1   continued

```
        alias = 1
        root = /dev/hda5
        read-only
        password = s0l@r¦$
        restricted
        initrd = /boot/initrd.gz


#
# Boot my experimental Linux 2.3.8 kernel from /dev/hda5.
# This kernel requires a password to be specified.
#
image = /boot/vmlinuz-2.3.8
        label = Testing
        alias = 2
        root = /dev/hda5
        read-only
        password = d¦9¦+@1
        initrd = /boot/initrd-2.3.8.gz
        fallback = Red Hat


#
# Boot Windows from /dev/hda1.
#
other = /dev/hda1
    label = Windows
    alias = 3
        single-key
    table = /dev/hda


#
# Boot Fred's Linux from /dev/hda2.
#
other = /dev/hda2
    label = Fred
    alias = 4
        single-key
    table = /dev/hda


#
# Boot FreeBSD from /dev/hda7.
#
other = /dev/hda7
```

LISTING 5.1 continued

```
label = FreeBSD
alias = 5
    single-key
table = /dev/hda
```

Let's take this example apart and see what it does by examining the options used. You may be surprised at the level of control you are allowed and some of the interesting things you can do with LILO.

The global section comes first, and as you can see from the boot option, LILO will be installed in place of the master boot record. LILO is expected to optimize the loading process.

Next, we specify the file to be used as the boot sector. This line could be left out of this example because the value used is the default.

Now we come to the message option. In our example, this is set to /etc/lilo.msg. Here are the contents of that file, which as you can see, contain a simple menu and instructions to the user on what to do:

```
^L

              +----¦ Select The OS To Run ¦----+
              ¦                                 ¦
              ¦ 1.  Red Hat Linux 6.0           ¦
              ¦                                 ¦
              ¦ 2.  Experimental Kernel 2.3.8   ¦
              ¦        (Password Required)      ¦
              ¦                                 ¦
              ¦ 3.  Windows 95                  ¦
              ¦                                 ¦
              ¦ 4.  Fred's Linux                ¦
              ¦                                 ¦
              ¦ 5.  FreeBSD 3.0                 ¦
              ¦                                 ¦
              ¦   Defaults to system booted     ¦
              ¦ most recently after 10 seconds  ¦
              ¦                                 ¦
              ¦ Enter the number of the OS you  ¦
              ¦        wish to start.           ¦
              ¦                                 ¦
              +---------------------------------+
```

The file begins with a form feed character. This is generated using vi and typing Ctrl+V followed immediately by Ctrl+L. This character causes LILO to clear the screen before displaying the rest of the file, which contains no color and straight ASCII text only.

Tip

There are patches to LILO that allow you to create fancy color screens, and that include the line drawing characters available on the Web at
`http://www.stack.nl/~stilgar/lilocolors.html`.

The next keyword is set to display information about labels, aliases, and other diagnostic information when the `lilo` map installer is run. The level of messages can be adjusted using this keyword, and the value here of 2 is just my preference.

Next, you'll find a keyword that many people find useful, especially when testing a new kernel. By specifying the `lock` keyword, LILO remembers which image you last booted, and provided that the currently booted image doesn't have a fallback keyword specified and that you do not crash your system, LILO will keep booting that image until you explicitly request a different image.

The next two keywords are ones that I almost always include in `lilo.conf`. They are the `prompt` and `timeout` keywords. With `prompt` specified, LILO will wait for user input without requiring the user to interrupt the boot sequence with a keypress. The `timeout` keyword is a failsafe, so that if the user doesn't respond within the specified number of tenths of a second, the boot process will continue anyway, allowing for unattended reboots.

This covers the general keywords specified. Now we can take a look at each of the defined images and see some of the interesting things you can do with LILO keywords on a per-image basis.

LILO Per-Image Keywords

Our sample config file begins the per-image definitions with a definition for a Linux kernel image that uses the kernel file `/boot/vmlinuz-2.2.5`. Using the `label` and `alias` keywords, this kernel is given the names Red Hat and 1 in the map file. The root keyword specifies that the root filesystem for this kernel is `/dev/hda5`. When this kernel is booted, this filesystem will initially be mounted read-only and an initial ramdisk will be loaded from the image found in `/boot/initrd.gz`. Finally, the user will be prompted to enter a password if they attempt to pass anything on the kernel command line. This means that a password is required to boot into single user mode, and although this measure is not foolproof, it could deter some would-be crackers.

5

Starting Up and Shutting Down

Next, an image is defined that uses an experimental kernel contained in
`/boot/vmlinuz-2.3.8`, called `Testing`, with an alias of 2. The root filesystem is the same
as the previous kernel, and like the previous kernel definition, an initial ramdisk is specified
and the root filesystem is initially mounted read-only. Two differences between this kernel
and the preceding one are that this image always requires a password, and if the system
crashes while running, the system will reboot to the Red Hat kernel regardless of the
previously defined `lock` keyword.

The image defined next is used to boot the system into Windows. It is easy to determine
that we consider this a foreign operating system by the use of the `other` keyword. This
keyword defines where LILO should look for this operating system. In this case, the
foreign operating system resides on `/dev/hda1`, the first partition on the first IDE hard
drive. The keywords defined for this image give it a name of `Windows` with an alias of 3.
The user has only to type the number 3 to select this image and the partition table
information needed by this operating system can be found on `/dev/hda`. As you can see, it
is quite simple.

The next image is the most interesting one defined thus far because it appears that we have
not correctly defined it. You may be wondering why we didn't specify the kernel image file
and other normal kernel options. To answer these questions, we have only to look at the
definition of the problem that we specified. In it we stated that we wanted Fred's Linux to
be totally independent of the Red Hat installation. If we had specified the path to an image
boot file as was done for the other two kernel images, we would have been sharing a
partition where these images reside and thus violating the stated parameters of the problem.
To overcome this, Fred's Linux is treated like any other guest operating system. The only
problem with that is that we are still without a boot sector for the partition containing Fred's
Linux. This problem is solved by creating a simple `lilo.conf` file for Fred's Linux that
installs lilo into the boot sector where it resides and allowing it to boot only Fred's Linux.
This simple `lilo.conf` file would look something like this:

```
#
# General section
#
boot = /dev/hda2
install = /boot/boot.b
delay = 50
verbose = 2

#
# Boot my Linux 2.2.5 kernel
#
```

```
image = /boot/vmlinuz-2.3.8
        label = linux
        root = /dev/hda2
        read-only
        initrd = /boot/initrd.gz
```

As you can see, there are no prompt and timeout options specified, which results in Fred's Linux booting immediately unless interrupted by a user keystroke. The primary reason for including the delay is to allow for the passing of command-line options, such as `single` to boot into single user mode.

The final image defined is the same as the one that is used to boot Windows, except that it boots FreeBSD. The boot sequence given the preceding configuration is illustrated in Figure 5.6.

FIGURE 5.6
Multiple OS with LILO as MBR.

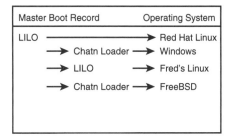

As you can plainly see, you can customize LILO in many different ways to suit your needs. The combinations are not quite endless, but with the available options, you can come up with some very complex arrangements.

Alternatives to LILO

Although LILO is the most popular boot loader for Linux, it is definitely not the only one available. There are many boot loaders, both commercial and non-commercial, that are capable of loading Linux. This section lists a few of these and where you can obtain them.

If you don't like the idea of altering the boot sectors on your system drives, one of the options for booting Linux is LOADLIN, which is a DOS program that is capable of loading and executing the Linux kernel. Recent additions to this software include support for bzImages and initial RAM disks. The software, which contains documentation, is available by FTP from the Linux archives at `ftp://metalabs.unc.edu/pub/linux/system/boot/dualboot/`.

Another boot loader that can be used to replace the master boot record and that presents a menu of available operating systems is the bootactv program. This program is included with the `pfdisk` package and is available by FTP from `ftp://ftp.funet.fi/pub/Linux/tools/`. This package works, but appears not to have been updated since 1992.

SYSLINUX is a boot loader for Linux that allows you to boot from DOS floppies and is used by some distributions as their installation floppies. This program is primarily used to create boot floppies and is not intended to be a general-purpose boot loader. SYSLINUX is available by FTP from `ftp://metalabs.unc.edu/pub/linux/system/boot/loaders/`.

Two other boot loaders available in the same place as SYSLINUX are GRUB and CHOS. Both of these are general-purpose boot loaders that present users with interactive menus allowing them to boot the operating system of their choice in a manner similar to the OS/2 boot manager.

System Commander® Deluxe is a commercial offering from V Communications that is capable of booting Linux. Much more than a boot loader, System Commander manages the entire installation process for new operating systems. It protects existing operating systems from the new ones being installed, resizes partitions to make room for new operating systems, and so on. The company Web site at `http://www.v-com.com` has complete information on features and pricing.

This is not an exhaustive list by any stretch of the imagination. If you are not happy with LILO, a simple Net search may yield a program more suitable to your needs.

The Linux Boot Process and System Initialization Scripts

Once the boot loader has loaded a Linux kernel, what next? This section discusses the process of loading the kernel, including device initialization, and the handoff to the `init` process, which starts the many processes required to actually make your Linux system useful.

Kernel Startup and Device Initialization

Starting the Linux kernel is much like starting any other operating system in that it all starts with the boot sector code. As discussed earlier, the boot sector code is responsible for loading the operating system kernel into memory and executing it. For Linux, this results in the following sequence of events:

- Loading and uncompressing the kernel

- Detecting and configuring devices

- Handing off to the `init` process

The first part of this process is where the boot loader is involved. LILO or another boot loader loads the Linux kernel into memory and starts it running. To get things going, Linux uncompresses itself and gathers some information from the system BIOS that it needs to run. Once all of the required information has been gathered, it discards the BIOS. Keep in mind that other than the information it has already gathered, none of the BIOS services are available.

Now the process of detecting hardware begins. The first thing the kernel detects are the type of processor available, the console settings, and the amount of memory available to the system. The memory detection is not always as simple as it sounds, which is why one of the most common pieces of information passed on by the boot loader is the amount of physical RAM installed in the system. This is less true of modern systems, but older systems almost always needed to know if you had more than 64 Megs of physical memory. As your system continues booting, the devices for which you have drivers available (either compiled into the system or available as modules loaded from an initial ramdisk) are detected, and various initialization messages are printed to the console. This information can be viewed using the command `dmesg` as soon as the system is ready. It is stored in the kernel's ring buffer, but as the name implies, this buffer does not grow indefinitely. If your system generates a large number of kernel messages, you can quickly lose the information regarding device initialization. To prevent this, Red Hat has added a line to the startup `rc.sysinit` script in `/etc/rc.d` to capture the message during startup:

```
dmesg > /var/log/dmesg
```

This will create a file in `/var/log` called `dmesg`, that contains the kernel boot messages and any kernel messages generated by the modules loaded in `rc.modules`. This information can be very useful in debugging problems and in determining which devices were detected and in what order. In addition to capturing the boot messages, the `dmesg` command can be used at any time to examine the contents of the kernel ring buffer. Full details of this command can be found in the `dmesg(8)` manual page.

Once all of the devices have been detected and the various kernel subsystems such as the VFS have been started, the root directory is mounted and control is passed to the `init` program. The `init` program is then responsible for starting up the rest of the system through the use of initialization scripts, normally found in `/etc/rc.d` and subdirectories.

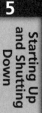

/etc/inittab and rc Scripts

The init process is the program that takes control from the kernel and starts up all of the required processes on the system, making it ready to use. On your Linux system, the init process always has process ID 1. init is responsible for keeping track of the current runlevel and managing the transitions between runlevels. There are two basic models that init can take to accomplish all of this.

The first of these is the model used by most flavors of UNIX based on the BSD distributions. This model uses a minimal number of startup files, called rc scripts, which are normally found in the /etc directory with names like rc, rc.local, and so on. Red Hat, and most other distributions of Linux, do not use this model. Instead, they opt to use the System V Release 4 style of initialization scripts. These scripts are stored in a directory typically called init.d, and for each defined runlevel, there is a directory called rcN.d where N is the runlevel that contains a series of symbolic links to the scripts in init.d. On System V-based systems such as HP/UX and Solaris, these directories are normally found in /etc; however, on your Red Hat Linux system, these directories are stored one level deeper in a directory called /etc/rc.d.

To understand the job of init, let's take a look at the configuration file it depends on: /etc/inittab. This file defines actions required of init based on runlevels. Following is a description of the lines found in the /etc/inittab from a Red Hat Linux system.

The first thing defined in this inittab is the default runlevel, which is set to 5. On Red Hat systems, 5 is defined as the level at which the X Windows system is the default interface and logins are performed via the gdm interface, which presents a graphical login screen to the user. This line looks like this:

```
id:5:initdefault:
```

Following the definition of the default runlevel is the definition of the startup scripts. Each definition consists of an id, followed by the runlevels at which this action is to be taken, followed by the action to be taken, and finally, the process to be executed. The action field determines the order in which these scripts are executed. Scripts with an action of sysinit are run first.

In this example, the first script to be run is a script called booterd. This script draws the fancy boot screen used by Red Hat. Next, the modules initialization script, rc.modules, is run with an argument of default. Following this, the rc.serial script runs to initialize the serial ports on our system. Once all scripts with an action of sysinit are run, init runs scripts with an action of boot or bootwait. The difference between these two actions is that for bootwait, init waits until the specified process has completed before continuing, whereas with boot it does not. Our example inittab file contains a single line with the sysinit action that executes the rc.boot script. Here is the line that performs these steps in the boot process:

```
si::sysinit:/etc/rc.d/rc.sysinit
```

To implement the desired System V style of startup, we require a line for each runlevel that defines how to get to that runlevel. These next nine lines from inittab do just that. At each level, the rc script is run with the runlevel as an argument.

```
l0:0:wait:/etc/rc.d/rc 0
l1:1:wait:/etc/rc.d/rc 1
l2:2:wait:/etc/rc.d/rc 2
l3:3:wait:/etc/rc.d/rc 3
l4:4:wait:/etc/rc.d/rc 4
l5:5:wait:/etc/rc.d/rc 5
l6:6:wait:/etc/rc.d/rc 6
```

Two things of interest about these lines are the rc script that is called, and the final line, which is provided as a failsafe mechanism in case the change to runlevel 6, which reboots the system, fails. The basic idea behind the rc script is to perform the following:

- Change directory to /etc/rc.d/rcN.d where N is the specified runlevel.

- Run all of the scripts starting with the letter K with an argument of stop. The order is determined by the filenames.

- Run all of the scripts that begin with the letter S with an argument of start.

There is, naturally, a little more to it than that, but that is the general idea.

Following these lines is a line that specifies a process that is run at every runlevel. This line runs the update utility once each time a runlevel transition is made.

```
ud::once:/sbin/update
```

The next line in our inittab file defines the process to run when the user presses Ctrl+Alt+Del. This line states that at any runlevel, pressing this key sequence will cause the system to reboot using the shutdown command.

```
ca::ctrlaltdel:/sbin/shutdown -t3 -r now
```

A relatively new feature of the init package is the ability to define a special key sequence that triggers an action by the init process. The default inittab file for Red Hat does not include an example of this, but by adding the following line, which does nothing more than echo a message to the console, you can implement this feature yourself. If you want to take advantage of this feature, refer to the manual page for inittab.

```
kb::kbrequest:/bin/echo "Keyboard Request--edit /etc/inittab to let this work."
```

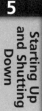

5

Starting Up
and Shutting
Down

The init program is also capable of interpreting signals from a smart UPS. This is typically implemented by having a daemon that monitors the UPS status and based on that status, sends signals to the initprocess. There are three actions that can be specified for these types of events:

- powerfail—A power failure has occurred and we are running off of battery power.

- powerfailnow—The power has failed and the battery is low.

- powerokwait—The power has been restored.

Our example inittab file shows the types of action that could be taken to deal with these events.

```
pf::powerfail:/sbin/shutdown -h +5 "Power Failure; System Shutting Down"
pr:12345:powerokwait:/sbin/shutdown -c "Power Restored; Shutdown Cancelled"
```

The next group of lines in our example inittab are responsible for managing the gettyprocesses on the virtual consoles. Similar entries would be used to run getty on serial devices, but our example does not include any lines of that nature.

```
1:12345:respawn:/sbin/mingetty tty1
2:2345:respawn:/sbin/mingetty tty2
3:2345:respawn:/sbin/mingetty tty3
4:2345:respawn:/sbin/mingetty tty4
5:2345:respawn:/sbin/mingetty tty5
6:2345:respawn:/sbin/mingetty tty6
```

The syntax of these getty lines are highly dependent on which of the available getty versions you choose to use on your system. Therefore, it's always necessary to refer to the manual page for the version of getty you run to determine the correct syntax. If you decode to change getty versions, it is also a good idea to keep at least one virtual console running under the old one until you are certain that the new one is working correctly.

The final line in our example inittab file is used to start the graphical login program for the X Windows system. There are several of these available. The traditional one that comes with the XFree86 distribution is xdm. In addition, the KDE desktop environment has its own version of this program called kdm and GNOME also has one called gdm. Since both KDE and GNOME are standard parts of a Red Hat installation, our sample includes an invocation of prefdm, which is a symbolic link to either kdm or gdm, depending on the system administrator preference.

```
x:5:respawn:/etc/X11/prefdm -nodaemon
```

Now, let's put it all together and add some comments for clarity. Here is the resulting /etc/inittab file for our Red Hat Linux system.

```
#
# inittab      This file describes how the INIT process should set up
#              the system in a certain run-level.
#
# Author:      Miquel van Smoorenburg, <miquels@drinkel.nl.mugnet.org>
#              Modified for RHS Linux by Marc Ewing and Donnie Barnes
#

# The runlevels used by COL are:
#   0 - halt (Do NOT set initdefault to this)
#   1 - Single user mode (including initialisation of network interfaces,
#       if you do have networking)
#   2 - Multiuser, (without NFS-Server und some such)
#       (basically the same as 3, if you do not have networking)
#   3 - Full multiuser mode
#   4 - unused
#       (should be equal to 3, for now)
#   5 - X11
#   6 - reboot (Do NOT set initdefault to this)

#
# Default runlevel.
id:5:initdefault:

# System initialization.
si::sysinit:/etc/rc.d/rc.sysinit

l0:0:wait:/etc/rc.d/rc 0
l1:1:wait:/etc/rc.d/rc 1
l2:2:wait:/etc/rc.d/rc 2
l3:3:wait:/etc/rc.d/rc 3
l4:4:wait:/etc/rc.d/rc 4
l5:5:wait:/etc/rc.d/rc 5
l6:6:wait:/etc/rc.d/rc 6

# Trap CTRL-ALT-DELETE
ca::ctrlaltdel:/sbin/shutdown -t3 -r now

# Action on special keypress (ALT-UpArrow).
kb::kbrequest:/bin/echo "Keyboard Request--edit /etc/inittab to let this work."

# When our UPS tells us power has failed, assume we have a few minutes
# of power left.  Schedule a shutdown for 2 minutes from now.
```

```
# This does, of course, assume you have powerd installed and your
# UPS connected and working correctly.
pf::powerfail:/sbin/shutdown -h +5 "Power Failure; System Shutting Down"

# If power was restored before the shutdown kicked in, cancel it.
po:12345:powerokwait:/sbin/shutdown -c "Power Restored; Shutdown Cancelled"


# Run gettys in standard runlevels
1:12345:respawn:/sbin/mingetty tty1
2:2345:respawn:/sbin/mingetty tty2
3:2345:respawn:/sbin/mingetty tty3
4:2345:respawn:/sbin/mingetty tty4
5:2345:respawn:/sbin/mingetty tty5
6:2345:respawn:/sbin/mingetty tty6

# Run kdm in runlevel 5
x:5:respawn:/etc/X11/prefdm -nodaemon
```

More About Runlevels

Now that you have an understanding of the `init` command, we can cover a topic we touched on briefly during our examination of the `inittab` file. We'll look at runlevels and managing the processes that run at each defined runlevel.

As stated earlier, Red Hat Linux uses a System V style of start scripts. This style differs from the BSD style in that each daemon or function to be started automatically by the system is controlled by a script that takes at least two possible arguments—`start` and `stop`.

For example, to start the Web server running on a system, a control script called `httpd`, `web`, or `apache` could be created that performs all of the actions required to start or stop the server depending on the argument given to the script. By separating each service or function into separate scripts, it becomes easier to define a runlevel. You simply have to decide which services and functions should be running at that runlevel and then start them using their control scripts. To do this, each runlevel has a directory in `/etc/rc.d` called `rcN.d`, where `N` is the runlevel, (`rc3.d` contains the collection of scripts that need to be run at this level). To further simplify matters, all of the scripts are collected into a central directory called `/etc/rc.d/init.d`.

Let's take a look at one of these directories to see how this works in practice. Following is a directory list of /etc/rc.d/rc1.d, which defines single user mode for our Red Hat system:

```
[root@quicksilver rc1.d]# ls -lo
total 0
lrwxrwxrwx   1 root     19 Jun 19 09:38 K00linuxconf ->../init.d/linuxconf*
lrwxrwxrwx   1 root     14 Jun 19 09:29 K05innd -> ../init.d/innd*
lrwxrwxrwx   1 root     18 Jun 19 09:14 K05keytable -> ../init.d/keytable*
lrwxrwxrwx   1 root     16 Jun 19 09:13 K08autofs -> ../init.d/autofs*
lrwxrwxrwx   1 root     13 Jun 19 09:15 K10xfs -> ../init.d/xfs*
lrwxrwxrwx   1 root     13 Jun 19 09:26 K15gpm -> ../init.d/gpm*
lrwxrwxrwx   1 root     15 Jun 19 09:13 K15httpd -> ../init.d/httpd*
lrwxrwxrwx   1 root     15 Jun 19 09:46 K15sound -> ../init.d/sound*
lrwxrwxrwx   1 root     20 Jun 19 09:13 K20bootparamd ->../init.d/bootparamd*
lrwxrwxrwx   1 root     13 Jun 19 09:36 K20nfs -> ../init.d/nfs*
lrwxrwxrwx   1 root     16 Jun 19 09:46 K20rstatd -> ../init.d/rstatd*
lrwxrwxrwx   1 root     17 Jun 19 09:46 K20rusersd -> ../init.d/rusersd*
lrwxrwxrwx   1 root     16 Jun 19 09:46 K20rwalld -> ../init.d/rwalld*
lrwxrwxrwx   1 root     15 Jun 19 09:46 K20rwhod -> ../init.d/rwhod*
lrwxrwxrwx   1 root     15 Jun 19 09:48 K25squid -> ../init.d/squid*
lrwxrwxrwx   1 root     13 Jun 19 09:12 K28amd -> ../init.d/amd*
lrwxrwxrwx   1 root     16 Jun 19 09:38 K30mcserv -> ../init.d/mcserv*
lrwxrwxrwx   1 root     18 Jun 19 09:47 K30sendmail -> ../init.d/sendmail*
lrwxrwxrwx   1 root     19 Jun 19 10:04 K34yppasswdd ->../init.d/yppasswdd*
lrwxrwxrwx   1 root     15 Jun 19 09:17 K35dhcpd -> ../init.d/dhcpd*
lrwxrwxrwx   1 root     15 Jun 19 09:13 K45named -> ../init.d/named*
lrwxrwxrwx   1 root     14 Jun 19 09:40 K50inet -> ../init.d/inet*
lrwxrwxrwx   1 root     15 Jun 19 09:56 K50snmpd -> ../init.d/snmpd*
lrwxrwxrwx   1 root     16 Jun 19 09:46 K55routed -> ../init.d/routed*
lrwxrwxrwx   1 root     13 Jun 19 09:13 K60atd -> ../init.d/atd*
lrwxrwxrwx   1 root     15 Jun 19 09:14 K60crond -> ../init.d/crond*
lrwxrwxrwx   1 root     13 Jun 19 09:38 K60lpd -> ../init.d/lpd*
lrwxrwxrwx   1 root     15 Jun 19 09:20 K75gated -> ../init.d/gated*
lrwxrwxrwx   1 root     14 Jun 19 09:42 K80nscd -> ../init.d/nscd*
lrwxrwxrwx   1 root     15 Jun 19 09:14 K85netfs -> ../init.d/netfs*
lrwxrwxrwx   1 root     16 Jun 19 10:04 K88ypserv -> ../init.d/ypserv*
lrwxrwxrwx   1 root     17 Jun 19 09:43 K89portmap -> ../init.d/portmap*
lrwxrwxrwx   1 root     17 Jun 19 09:14 K90network -> ../init.d/network*
lrwxrwxrwx   1 root     14 Jun 19 09:13 K92apmd -> ../init.d/apmd*
lrwxrwxrwx   1 root     16 Jun 19 09:34 K96pcmcia -> ../init.d/pcmcia*
lrwxrwxrwx   1 root     16 Jun 19 09:14 K99syslog -> ../init.d/syslog*
lrwxrwxrwx   1 root     16 Jun 19 09:14 S00single -> ../init.d/single*
lrwxrwxrwx   1 root     16 Jun 19 09:14 S20random -> ../init.d/random*
```

As you can see, all of the entries in this directory are symbolic links to scripts in the `/etc/rc.d/init.d` directory. Notice that the links are named using the convention K or S followed by a two-digit number, which is followed by the name of the script to which the link points.

For example, the symbolic link that points to the `nis-client` script in `/etc/rc.d/init.d` is named `K79nis-client`. This naming scheme is important because it determines which services to start and which to stop and also the order in which these actions should occur. As you recall, when you enter a runlevel, `init` causes the `/etc/rc.d/rc` script to be run with the runlevel as an argument. The `rc` script enters the runlevel directory—in this case, `rc1.d`—and first runs all of the files starting with the letter K with a `stop` argument and then runs all of the scripts starting with the letter S with a `start` argument.

You can now see that in order to transition from the default runlevel of 5 to single user mode or runlevel 1, you must shut down all network services and daemons, leaving only the essential hardware services active.

You may be thinking that managing this symlink farm is too complicated and difficult. Fortunately, Red Hat has provided a better way to manage this task. If you log in as root, you have access to the control-panel application shown in Figure 5.7, which includes a button to invoke the runlevel editor.

FIGURE 5.7
The control-panel.

This will bring up a utility that allows you to select the services and daemons you want automatically started at each runlevel. You can also invoke the runlevel editor utility directly, by running the following command:

```
wish /usr/X11R6/bin/tksysv
```

Figure 5.8 shows what this program looks like.

This utility takes all of the work out of maintaining the dozens of symbolic links in the `/etc/rc.d` hierarchy. This system still requires that you have an understanding of how to perform maintenance on the directories by hand, but it is much easier. If you did want to manage this by hand, here are the steps you would have to take.

FIGURE 5.8

The Runlevel editor.

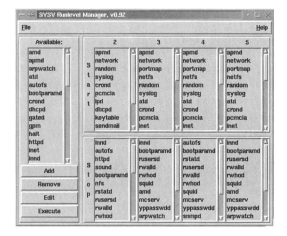

1. Determine which services or functions are required to support your new service, such as network support, access to NFS filesystems, or access to a name server.

2. Determine which runlevels you want your service to run at.

3. Create your control script and place it in `/etc/rc.d/init.d`. The easiest way to do this is to copy an existing script in that directory and modify it to work with your service.

4. Create the appropriate symbolic links to start your service at the appropriate runlevel and to shut it down as well.

Tip

If you choose to modify an existing script, please note that you should carefully examine any parameters specified at the beginning of the script. Some of these can be removed or modified for use in your script and you may need to add additional ones. The advantage of using this strategy is that your script will save you considerable time if you are adding services to your system.

Shutting Down

Shutting down your Linux system is not the trivial operation that shutting down a DOS system is. Due to the multiuser, multiprocessing nature of Linux systems, you should always be careful about how your system is shut down. Failure to do so can result in damage to filesystems and unexpected behavior.

Changing Runlevels

There are several runlevels defined under Linux. With Red Hat Linux, and the included System V `init` package, there are 10 defined runlevels. Two of these are reserved for shutting down the system. This section looks at each of these runlevels and their purpose.

Runlevels zero and six are used for shutting down the system. The difference between the two is that zero is used for a complete halt and power down and six is used for a system restart.

The lowest runlevel at which you can interact with the system is runlevel one, sometimes called single user mode. This runlevel is generally used by the systems administrator for maintenance tasks, such as checking filesystems for consistency or other maintenance tasks that would be impaired by having the system available to multiple users. An alias for this runlevel is runlevel S.

The next available runlevel is runlevel two, which allows access to multiple users and has networking services available, but may not include optional services like Web servers or NFS filesystems.

The default runlevel for systems that do not bring up the graphical interface at boot time is runlevel three. At this level, all services of the system are available and multiple users can access the system. For Red Hat systems, this runlevel is equivalent to runlevel four.

The default runlevel for systems that start up and immediately bring up the graphical interface is runlevel five. The only difference between this runlevel and runlevel three is that at this level, the xdm or equivalent graphical login program is started. On Red Hat systems with the KDE desktop installed, this equivalent is kdm, and with GNOME it is gdm.

In addition to these predefined runlevels, there are three user-defined runlevels available. These are defined as runlevel A, B, or C and what occurs at each runlevel is totally up to the local systems administrator.

To switch between runlevels you have two options with Red Hat Linux. The first of these is the `init` command itself, which you run by giving it an argument of the runlevel you want to change to. The other option is the `telinit` command, which differs from `init` in that you can specify the time interval between the sending of the SIGTERM and SIGKILL signals that normally occurs when you change runlevels.

The `shutdown` Commands

There are number of ways to ensure a proper shutdown of your Linux system. The most common is the `shutdown` command, whose use is reserved for the super user. The general form for the invocation of the `shutdown` command is as follows:

```
shutdown [-t secs] [options] time [message to users]
```

Direct invocation of the `shutdown` command is not the only way to shutdown a Linux system. However, before we cover the alternative methods of shutting down your system, let's take a look at the options to the `shutdown` command as shown in Table 5.6.

TABLE 5.6 `shutdown` **Command-Line Options**

Option	Description
-r	This option tells `init` to reboot the system once all processes have been shut down.
-h	Halts the system once all processes have been shut down.
-k	Does not really shut down, just sends the warning message to users.
-c	Cancels a running `shutdown` command.
-t secs	Tells `init` to delay the specified number of seconds between sending the `SIGTERM` signal and the `SIGKILL` signal.
-f	Skips the filesystem check on reboot.
-F	Forces a filesystem check on reboot.
time	Time to perform the shutdown. Time may be specified as an absolute time in hh:mm format or as +N where N is the number of minutes from the current time. You may also specify the time as "now," which is an alias for +0 minutes.
message	Optionally, you may send system users a message using the `wall` command.

Some of the alternative methods of shutting down your Red Hat Linux system include changing the runlevel to zero or six, depending on whether you want to halt or reboot your system. You can also shut down your system using the Ctrl+Alt+Del key sequence, provided you have included a line in your `/etc/inittab` such as shown in the earlier example.

Three alternative commands that can be used to shut down your system are `halt`, `reboot`, and `poweroff`. These commands actually invoke shutdown unless the runlevel is already zero or six, making them safe to use at any runlevel.

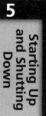

5

Starting Up
and Shutting
Down

Summary

In this chapter, we have covered the proper procedures for starting up and shutting down your Red Hat Linux system, including a discussion of boot loaders, the kernel boot process, and the different runlevels at which you can run your Linux systems. Special emphasis was given to the LILO boot loader and on the structure employed by Red Hat to start up all of the processes and services required to make your system a useful server.

System Failure Diagnosis and Recovery

In This Chapter

- Kernel Oops **142**
- Hardware Errors **144**
- Diagnostic Tools **147**
- Building and Using Rescue Disks **152**
- Analysis of System Logs **160**
- Locating the Source of Kernel Errors **163**
- Seeking Assistance **169**

CHAPTER 6

As stable as Linux is, it can occasionally experience a system failure. Compared with other operating systems, Linux is impressively reliable and a system failure is the exception rather than the rule, but when a failure occurs it is your task as system administrator to track down whatever is causing the system failure and resolve it.

Failures can result from a variety of causes, including hardware problems; a new kernel; an experimental, immature driver; a misconfigured initialization file; or a trashed executable. This chapter looks at some of the more common ways of diagnosing problems and investigates creating and using rescue disks.

There are very few graphical programs available for system diagnosis. This is one area where the traditional command-line utilities and services reign supreme. Almost all system failure diagnosis is done from the command line in a standard terminal session. Knowing your Linux text editors and knowing how to move around your Linux system and issue appropriate commands as needed is *de rigueur* for any system administrator.

Kernel Oops

At the most fundamental level, the Linux kernel communicates messages to the rest of the system via its `printk()` function. If a message is considered important, `printk()` will display the message on the system console as well as hand off a copy to the `klogd` daemon to be logged to disk. The reason for displaying these messages on the console as well as logging them is to allow for severe conditions, such as a disk failure, where the message may not be able to be logged to disk and would be lost.

The Linux kernel is programmed to throw an "oops" condition—a kind of "something not very good just happened and here's where it occurred" message when it detects a kernel error. A kernel oops, or protection fault, normally occurs when the kernel code is dereferencing a structure pointer that has a null value or invalid address. It will attempt, where possible, to log the condition and supply you with some information to help with debugging the problem.

A kernel oops is not commonly encountered on a production system (an important system set up for maximum stability). Oops conditions are more apt to show up when you set up a test system with an experimental kernel and experimental drivers, when you rebuild your kernel and misconfigure some aspect of it, or when there's a hardware problem.

On Red Hat systems, kernel oops messages are normally logged by `klogd` into `/var/messages` via the `syslogd` facility. Later, this chapter takes closer look at how to decode these messages and how to submit a bug report using them, in the section "Locating the Source of Kernel Errors."

System Failure Diagnosis and Recovery

CHAPTER 6

143

6

System Failure
Diagnosis and
Recovery

Kernel Panic

One of the more disconcerting things that can happen on a Linux system is to have the kernel detect something wrong and call a halt to the proceedings. This safety-valve feature is actually a normal part of the kernel communication process.

If the kernel encounters a fatal condition, such as attempting to use a memory address that is no longer available, it issues a "kernel panic." The kernel will halt operation and `printk()` will display the error message on the console, then wait for someone to come along, note the message, and reboot the system. For unattended systems, it is sometimes preferable to have the system log the message then reboot itself automatically, if possible. This can be achieved by adding the following line to the appropriate stanza in `/etc/lilo.conf`:

```
panic=30
```

This instructs the system to attempt to reboot itself thirty seconds after encountering an oops condition.

> **Tip**
>
> A LILO trick that is sometimes useful for troubleshooting is to raise the threshold of messages that the kernel `printk()` displays on the console. The default is to log anything greater than DEBUG level. If you add the `debug` option to `/etc/lilo.conf` (or manually boot the system as `linux debug` at the LILO prompt), it changes the console log level to DEBUG level, which displays all kernel messages on the console.

Some conditions are too severe for the system to be able to continue, such as when the boot process cannot find a Linux filesystem to mount. In this situation, `printk()` will display a kernel panic on the system console that will prompt you to further investigate the situation. In a worst-case scenario, the system might hang with no explanation. This is the most difficult type of problem to resolve. When severe problems occur, the first thing to look for is a hardware error.

Hardware Errors

With any Intel or Intel-compatible computer, hardware errors can be caused by a number of conditions, including hardware interrupt conflicts, faulty device drivers, BIOS problems on the system board, or hardware component failure. Diagnosing hardware errors follows a time-honored pattern: Look first for obvious problems and if that leads nowhere, look deeper for more subtle causes.

Start by checking all the obvious things such as internal and external cables, power supplies, power cables, network activity lights, powerbar switches, and UPS switches. A routine but careful examination of the physical environment can often save wasted effort. It's self-defeating to work hard at restoring a hard disk, only to find hours later that the problem was merely a loose connector.

There are two times when hardware problems are most likely to occur: 1) When you first build your Red Hat system on an Intel PC, and 2) When you add or change hardware. If your system has been running without problems and no changes have been made, it is possible that an existing hardware component has failed or that a driver has become corrupted.

Identifying Hardware Errors at Startup

Red Hat 6 provides a considerable amount of help in identifying hardware errors at startup. The startup messages identify hardware devices that have been probed successfully. If you're at the console, you can scroll backwards, using Ctrl+PageUp, to examine messages that have already scrolled by. On successfully probed ports, Red Hat 6 displays an OK message in green on a color monitor.

If it's too late to scroll back the console monitor, Red Hat offers two additional ways to view startup messages. You can replay these messages by typing /bin/dmesg (as shown in the previous chapter), and Red Hat supplies another file, /var/log/boot.log, that can be scanned for additional diagnostic messages:

```
[root@wallace /root]# less /var/log/boot.log

Aug 26 15:20:37 wallace fsck: /dev/hda4: clean, 64978/499712 files,
➥1061324/1992 060 blocks
Aug 26 15:20:37 wallace rc.sysinit: Checking root filesystem succeeded
Aug 26 15:20:37 wallace isapnp: Board 1 has Identity 61 10 00 4b
14 51 00 8c 0e:
  CTL0051 Serial No 268454676 [checksum 61]
Aug 26 15:20:37 wallace isapnp: CTL0051/268454676[0]{Audio
```

System Failure Diagnosis and Recovery
CHAPTER 6

145

6
System Failure
Diagnosis and
Recovery

```
      }: Port
s 0x220 0x330 0x388; IRQ5 DMA1 DMA5 --- Enabled OK
Aug 26 15:20:37 wallace isapnp: CTL0051/268454676[2]{Game
      }: Port
 0x200; --- Enabled OK
Aug 26 15:20:37 wallace rc.sysinit: Setting up ISA PNP devices succeeded
```

This file is a variant of /var/log/dmesg and it provides another place to look for information that might help diagnose hardware problems. It supplies information from processes such as isapnp, a program that attempts to set Plug-and-Play devices.

The classic condition to watch for when experiencing a hardware problem is "last change syndrome." The last piece of hardware you changed, or added, is likely to be the culprit. These changes can be subtle, such as substituting a 3Com 905B network card for a 3Com 905 card. Unless your device driver is current enough to support the 905B, the network card will stop working, and a failure to initialize the card will be displayed in the startup messages.

If you have added a second drive and you receive a "Kernel panic: VFS: Unable to mount root fs ..." message during a LILO boot, check the cabling. If you accidentally plugged your primary drive internal cable into the secondary controller, on an EIDE drive, your /dev/hda drive will be seen as /dev/hdc and Linux will not boot. Restoring the cable to its original system-board connector will resolve the problem.

BIOS Problems

Linux gets deployed on a wide range of Intel-compatible hardware and sometimes a particular system-board BIOS will cause problems. If you're experiencing quirky, intermittent hardware glitches, try switching off any special features in the system BIOS. You might also check with the manufacturer's Web site to see if there's an upgrade to the BIOS. Upgrades have been known to cure certain system board incompatibilities with Linux.

Plug-and-Play (PnP) Devices

Plug-and-Play is a specification that is designed to allocate four specific resources to drivers and hardware: I/O addresses, IRQs, DMA channels (ISA bus only), and memory regions. Some BIOSes do a good job of detecting and configuring PnP devices and some don't. If the BIOS doesn't adjust the device correctly, the device can be left in a disabled state.

If you're attempting to install an ISA PnP card that is not being detected by Linux, check to see if PnP can be disabled with a DOS utility. A PnP card usually includes a DOS utility diskette that can be used to adjust the card's settings. If the DOS utility has been misplaced or lost, the utility is often available from the manufacturer's Web site. It is often easier to configure a card manually than to get PnP to work when it's being stubborn. In certain cases, however, you might not want to do this. If you have a Linux/Windows dual-boot system, for instance, Windows may be depending on the card's PnP settings or you may not have access to the DOS utilities required to switch off PnP. Some cards are PnP only, offering no option for disabling this feature.

Alternatively, you can attempt to adjust the settings with the Linux `isapnp` utility. This is discussed in the section "Diagnostic Tools," later in the chapter.

PCI Devices

Occasionally, newer PCI devices will not be recognized and initialized correctly. If this happens you will see the following kernel message:

```
Warning : Unknown PCI device (8086:7100). Please read include/linux/pci.h
```

This can be caused by your system board chipset PCI-CPU bridge or PCI-ISA bridge. Your first step is to try to find which PCI device is causing the problem. Check `/proc/pci` for information to see if there are any obvious clues. The following listing shows how to display the contents of `/proc/pci`:

```
[root@wallace /root]# cat /proc/pci
PCI devices found:
  Bus  0, device   0, function  0:
    Host bridge: Intel 82439HX Triton II (rev 1).
      Medium devsel.  Master Capable.  Latency=32.
  Bus  0, device   7, function  0:
    ISA bridge: Intel 82371SB PIIX3 ISA (rev 0).
      Medium devsel.  Fast back-to-back capable.  Master Capable.  No bursts.
  Bus  0, device   7, function  1:
    IDE interface: Intel 82371SB PIIX3 IDE (rev 0).
      Medium devsel.  Fast back-to-back capable.  Master Capable.  Latency=32.
      I/O at 0xffa0 [0xffa1].
  Bus  0, device  17, function  0:
    VGA compatible controller: Matrox Millennium II (rev 0).
      Medium devsel.  Fast back-to-back capable.  IRQ 11.  Master Capable.
      ⮞Latency=32.
      Prefetchable 32 bit memory at 0xfd000000 [0xfd000008].
      Non-prefetchable 32 bit memory at 0xffafc000 [0xffafc000].
      Non-prefetchable 32 bit memory at 0xff000000 [0xff000000].
```

```
Bus  0, device  20, function  0:
  Ethernet controller: DEC DC21140 (rev 34).
    Medium devsel.  Fast back-to-back capable.  IRQ 3.  Master Capable.
    ➥Latency=32.  Min Gnt=20.Max Lat=40.
    I/O at 0xec80 [0xec81].
    Non-prefetchable 32 bit memory at 0xffafbf80 [0xffafbf80].
```

If you're unable to resolve the problem, you should send a description of the problem along to the Linux hardware information maintainers. Instructions on how to file a report can be found in the Linux Hardware Compatibility HOWTO located in /usr/doc/HOWTO. You may also need to search Internet resources for the location of a more up-to-date driver for the device.

The preceding listing (for /proc/pci) provides an example of how the Linux /proc filesystem can be used as a diagnostic tool. The next section explores additional uses of /proc.

Diagnostic Tools

Linux supplies a number of useful diagnostic tools to assist with troubleshooting. These include the /proc filesystem, isapnp, ifconfig, and network card diagnostic programs. This section looks at ways of using these tools to troubleshoot hardware problems.

Using /proc for Diagnosis

In addition to /var/log/dmesg and /var/log/boot.log, one of the most useful diagnostic tools in Linux is the /proc filesystem, outlined in Chapter 4, "Where Do I Find...?" As you have seen in the case of PCI information, it provides information that can be useful for diagnosing system problems.

Interrupt conflicts, for instance, can prevent hardware devices from working properly. You can check the status of interrupts by inspecting /proc/interrupts. To inspect this file, type cat /proc/interrupts, as in the following listing:

```
[root@wallace /root]# cat /proc/interrupts
          CPU0
  0:    518188        XT-PIC  timer
  1:     15017        XT-PIC  keyboard
  2:         0        XT-PIC  cascade
  3:    339652        XT-PIC  eth0
  4:     61197        XT-PIC  serial
```

```
   5:           1        XT-PIC  soundblaster
   8:           2        XT-PIC  rtc
  13:           1        XT-PIC  fpu
  14:       64601        XT-PIC  ide0
NMI:           0
```

In this example, a PCI network card has selected IRQ 3, which could lead to a potential conflict with an older fixed-IRQ ISA card.

Similarly, /proc can be used to see the state of ISA registered DMA channels, where sound cards and ISA SCSI cards have the potential to conflict. Type cat /proc/dma, as in the following listing, to inspect DMA channel assignments:

```
[root@wallace /root]# cat /proc/dma
 1: SoundBlaster8
 4: cascade
 5: SoundBlaster16
```

On the system in this example, for instance, an older, manually set ISA SCSI adapter would have to be adjusted to avoid DMA channels 1 and 5. In general, PCI devices no longer use DMA channels, so DMA conflicts tend to occur mainly with ISA cards.

With the increasing tendency to use loadable modules in Linux rather than compiling drivers into the Linux kernel, it is also useful to check /proc/modules to see if the modules you expect to see are in fact loaded:

```
[root@wallace /root]# cat /proc/modules
nfsd                150936   8 (autoclean)
lockd                30856   1 (autoclean) [nfsd]
sunrpc               52356   1 (autoclean) [nfsd lockd]
tulip                25252   1 (autoclean)
opl3                 11208   0
sb                   33204   0
uart401               5968   0 [sb]
sound                57208   0 [opl3 sb uart401]
soundlow               300   0 [sound]
soundcore             2372   6 [sb sound]
```

This listing shows the NIC driver (tulip) and the Sound Blaster driver (sb) loaded at boot time on this system. If an expected driver is not listed, it narrows down troubleshooting to a problem involving modular support for the device.

The isapnp Program

The isapnp program will carry out instructions in the /etc/isapnp.conf file to configure ISA PnP cards. This program checks to see if resources are available and generates a

System Failure Diagnosis and Recovery

CHAPTER 6

149

6

System Failure
Diagnosis and
Recovery

diagnostic message if there is a conflict. It uses a corresponding file, /etc/isapnp.gone, to track resources that are unavailable but not tracked as such by the /proc filesystem. Part of the isapnp toolset is the program pnpdump, which probes for ISA PnP cards and sends the results to standard output:

```
[root@wallace /root]# /sbin/pnpdump > /etc/isapnp.conf.new
```

An edited version of this output can be used to create the /etc/isapnp.conf file. By default, all the entries in the new file are commented out. You must remove the comments and adjust the settings for any devices you want to control.

The isapnp program is normally run at startup to configure ISA PnP devices. Adjusting the /etc/isapnp.conf file requires a solid understanding of PnP, which the isapnp toolset documentation does not provide. You will need to study the Linux Plug-and-Play HOWTO, located in /usr/doc/HOWTO, before attempting to configure this file.

Network Interface Card (NIC) Diagnostics

Linux supports a large number of network interface cards, or NICs. When a NIC does not appear to be functioning correctly, there are a number of ways to troubleshoot the problem, ranging from the ifconfig program to NIC-specific diagnostic programs.

ifconfig

When a server or workstation does not seem to be responding on a network, and the network driver appears to be loaded, you can give the setup a quick test with the ifconfig utility when logged in as root, as in the following listing:

```
[root@wallace /root]# /sbin/ifconfig
eth0      Link encap:Ethernet  HWaddr 00:E0:29:0C:6C:7F
          inet addr:192.168.168.100  Bcast:192.168.168.255 Mask:255.255.255.0
          UP BROADCAST RUNNING MULTICAST  MTU:1500  Metric:1
          RX packets:243311 errors:0 dropped:0 overruns:0 frame:0
          TX packets:228487 errors:0 dropped:0 overruns:0 carrier:0
          collisions:142 txqueuelen:100
          Interrupt:3 Base address:0xec80

lo        Link encap:Local Loopback
          inet addr:127.0.0.1  Mask:255.0.0.0
          UP LOOPBACK RUNNING  MTU:3924  Metric:1
          RX packets:48 errors:0 dropped:0 overruns:0 frame:0
          TX packets:48 errors:0 dropped:0 overruns:0 carrier:0
          collisions:0 txqueuelen:0
```

Repeating this command a few times on an active network should show RX (receive) packet and TX (transmit) packet numbers increasing steadily. If this isn't happening, replace the network cable just in case it's the cable that's faulty. If it still doesn't show an accretion of packet activity, look into both the hardware and the network configuration.

If a second network card in the same system, eth1, does not show up here, it didn't initialize properly. Check for interrupt conflicts and module configurations in either /etc/lilo.conf or /etc/conf.modules. Occasionally, a second NIC needs an explicit initialization in your /etc/lilo.conf boot stanza, for example:

```
append="ether=10,0x300,eth1"
```

If ifconfig reports an EAGAIN error, it indicates an interrupt conflict. The message means try again when the interrupt conflict is cleared. To resolve the problem, compare the interrupt request reported by ifconfig with the contents of /proc/interrupts to determine which devices conflict. The IRQ that a PCI device uses is also reported in /proc/pci.

If ifconfig reports an IRQ of 0 or 255 for a PCI NIC, it indicates the card has not yet been assigned an IRQ. This is caused when the BIOS does not have enough lines available for PCI devices (they're all assigned to ISA devices instead of PnP) or the BIOS has a "PnP OS" or "Windows 9x support" option that must be disabled.

If a PCI NIC is requesting a valid IRQ but that interrupt is already being used by another PCI device, the easiest solution is to put the conflicting device on another IRQ line via the system BIOS. PCI cards have no way of setting their own IRQ line. This is done at boot time by the PC BIOS.

NIC Diagnostic Programs

If your NIC device driver is loading and the IRQ is fine, but something is still not working right, you can download the source code for diagnostic utilities for many popular NICs from Donald Becker's "Linux at CESDIS" site: http://cesdis.gsfc.nasa.gov/linux/linux.html at NASA.

Compile the program that corresponds to your NIC with the directions supplied at the end of the source code and run them as root to get diagnostics. For the popular Digital DC21040 "tulip" series OEMed by many vendors, the diagnostic utility is called tulip-diag. A readout from the compiled program looks like this:

```
[root@wallace diag]# /usr/local/bin/diag/tulip-diag -m
tulip-diag.c:v1.12 7/31/99 Donald Becker (becker@cesdis.gsfc.nasa.gov)
Index #1: Found a Digital DS21140 Tulip adapter at 0xec80.
 Port selection is MII, half-duplex.
 Transmit started, Receive started, half-duplex.
```

```
The Rx process state is 'Waiting for packets'.
The Tx process state is 'Idle'.
The transmit threshold is 128.
MII PHY found at address 3, status 0x786d.
MII PHY #3 transceiver registers:
  3100 786d 2000 5c01 01e1 0021 0000 0000
  0000 0000 0000 0000 0000 0000 0000 0000
  0000 0000 0000 0000 0000 0000 0001 8060
  8020 0c63 0000 3000 a3b9 0080 e505 001b.
```

Another useful utility from the CESDIS site is the general-purpose `pci-config` program that displays readouts of all the PCI devices on your system. Running `pci-config` on the PCI device number for the preceding Digital Tulip NIC yields the following:

```
[root@wallace diag]# ./pci-config -# 4
pci-config.c:v1.06 7/24/99 Donald Becker (becker@cesdis.gsfc.nasa.gov)
Device #4 at bus 0 device/function 20/0.
  00091011 02800117 02000022 00002008 0000ec81 ffafbf80 00000000 00000000
  00000000 00000000 00000000 200110b8 ffa80000 00000000 00000000 28140103
  00000a00 00000000 00000000 00000000 00000000 00000000 00000000 00000000
  00000000 00000000 00000000 00000000 00000000 00000000 00000000 00000000
  00000000 00000000 00000000 00000000 00000000 00000000 00000000 00000000
  00000000 00000000 00000000 00000000 00000000 00000000 00000000 00000000
  00000000 00000000 00000000 00000000 00000000 00000000 00000000 00000000
  00000000 00000000 00000000 00000000 00000000 00000000 00000000 00000000
  Base Address 0: I/O at 0000ec80.
  Base Address 1: Memory at ffafbf80.
```

The `pci-config` utility can be used to put the device to sleep, wake the device, set it to Wake-on-LAN mode, or display the PCI registers, as in the preceding listing. The documentation for these utilities is in the source code.

DOS Diagnostics

Even on a dedicated Linux server, it can be useful to include a bootable DOS partition where DOS utilities can be stored and executed. Many brand-name PCs, such as Dell, Compaq, and IBM, include proprietary DOS-based diagnostic tools that make hardware troubleshooting easier. There are also a number of commercial DOS utility programs that do a particularly good job of testing hardware components and stress-testing memory chips.

Keeping a minimal installation of Windows 95 (or higher) in the DOS partition can also be useful. Its Control Panel, System, Devices readout is handy for checking on card settings, especially if a card works on the Windows side but not the Linux side. The readouts may yield clues that might be missed otherwise. A Windows 95 partition can also come in handy as emergency storage for Linux.

Diagnostic programs are useful for the initial configuration of hardware devices, but after a system has been running well and something unexpected occurs, such as a hardware component failure, your focus as system administrator changes from setup to emergency rescue. For this you will need some rescue tools.

Building and Using Rescue Disks

Although computer systems are becoming increasingly reliable, components sometimes fail. Hard disk drives, being mechanical devices, have a higher rate of failure than other components. When a hard drive experiences a total failure, few system administrators will attempt to recover any of the data on the drive. Unless you're using RAID, the normal procedure is to insert a new drive, build up the base operating system from scratch, and then restore all your important files and settings from backup.

The importance of good backup procedures for your Linux systems cannot be overemphasized. Backup is your ultimate safety net. Make sure your systems are being backed up regularly and that your backup tapes or other media are tested periodically by restoring randomly selected files from the backup media.

Many disk failures are not total, however. A hard drive may develop a bad spot. Linux attempts to watch for gradual problems by doing a fast integrity check of the filesystem on each partition with fsck at boot time, prior to mounting the partition. During every few reboots, fsck will perform a more thorough check on the filesystems.

When a bad spot occurs, it may trash some files, corrupting the file, directory structure, or inode number. This can affect an entire subtree, leaving it inaccessible. Even worse, it can result in a corrupted structure that spreads by normal file operations, trashing more data than was located in the original bad spot.

Not all file corruptions are created by faulty hardware. As system administrator, it is not uncommon to make a human error, such as accidentally erasing the system's password file, setting then forgetting the root password, installing a new kernel and forgetting to run lilo to create new boot information, or incorrectly editing /etc/fstab, resulting in a system that won't boot.

System Failure Diagnosis and Recovery

CHAPTER 6

153

6

System Failure
Diagnosis and
Recovery

When these things happen, it's time to reach into your doctor's bag for your Linux rescue disk set. A rescue system is a floppy disk or set of floppy disks that allow you to boot a very small version of the Linux operating system that resides in RAM. Once you're online in rescue mode, the rescue disks contain enough basic tools to allow you to attempt repairs to your Red Hat Linux system or, in a severely bad situation, recover as many files as possible.

Building a Rescue Disk

Obviously, it's more convenient to have a rescue disk on hand when you need it rather than having to learn how to create one in the midst of a crisis. A rescue disk should be one of the first things you create after setting up your system.

Red Hat has a pre-made rescue disk image available on its CD-ROM and its Web site. If you use the standard CD-ROM mount point for your Red Hat system, the rescue disk image will be found at /mnt/cdrom/images/rescue.img and you can transfer this to floppy disk.

To create a rescue disk from Linux, insert the Red Hat CD-ROM and mount it and insert a fresh 1.44Mb 3.5-inch blank floppy disk. Type the following commands as root (assuming that your 1.44Mb disk drive is /dev/fd0 and that it is a high-density 1.44Mb drive):

```
[root@wallace /root]# fdformat /dev/fd0H1440
Double-sided, 80 tracks, 18 sec/track. Total capacity 1440 kB.
Formatting ... done
Verifying ... done
[root@wallace /root]# mount /dev/cdrom /mnt/cdrom
[root@wallace /root]# cd /mnt/cdrom/images
[root@wallace images]# dd if=rescue.img of=/dev/fd0
2880+0 records in
2880+0 records out
```

You can also create a rescue disk from DOS. Insert a formatted DOS disk into your DOS A: drive and type the following (if your CD-ROM drive is not E:, substitute the letter for your CD-ROM drive):

```
C:\>cd e:
E:\>cd dosutils
E:\DOSUTILS>rawrite
The image file is ..\images\rescue.img
The destination is a:
```

This creates a Red Hat rescue disk. It is designed to work with the Red Hat boot disk. If you don't have a Red Hat boot disk, you can use the Red Hat mkbootdisk utility to create one.

To see if you have the `mkbootdisk` utility, type `rpm -q mkbootdisk`. You will also need to know your kernel version, which is fed as a parameter to `mkbootdisk`. You determine this with `uname -r`. Again, insert a fresh 1.44Mb 3.5-inch floppy disk and type these commands:

```
[root@wallace /root]# rpm -q mkbootdisk
mkbootdisk1.2-2
[root@wallace /root]# fdformat /dev/fd0H1440
Doublesided, 80 tracks, 18 sec/track. Total capacity 1440 kB.
Formatting ... done
Verifying ... done
[root@wallace /root]# mount /dev/cdrom /mnt/cdrom
[root@wallace /root]# cd /mnt/cdrom/images
[root@wallace images]# uname -r
2.2.5-15
[root@wallace images]# mkbootdisk --device /dev/fd0 2.2.5-15
Insert a disk in /dev/fd0. Any information on the disk will be lost.
Press <Enter> to continue or ^C to abort:
```

Starting a Rescue Session

To start a rescue session, insert your Red Hat boot disk and boot the system. When the LILO prompt appears type **rescue** and press Enter. When the system reaches the line "VFS: Insert root floppy disk to be loaded into RAM disk and press ENTER", insert your Red Hat rescue disk and press Enter.

You will see the following on the screen:

```
RAMDISK: Compressed image found at block 0
VFS: Mounted root (ext2 filesystem) readonly
change_root: old root has d_count=1
Trying to unmount old root ... okay
Freeing unused kernel memory: 60k freed

This is the Red Hat rescue disk. Most of the basic system commands are
in /bin

Type exit to halt the system.

#
```

System Failure Diagnosis and Recovery

CHAPTER 6

155

6

System Failure
Diagnosis and
Recovery

Rescue Disk Toolkit

The rescue disk provides a troubleshooting environment. You can perform simple or complex operations, depending on your needs and your knowledge of Linux. When you type ls at the # prompt, you will see a familiar directory structure:

```
# ls
bin          etc          lost+found   proc       tmp
dev          lib          mnt          sbin       usr
```

Of more interest are the tools listed in /bin:

```
# cd /bin
# ls
ash        df         init       modprobe   rm       tac
badblocks  e2fsck     insmod     mount      route    tail
cat        fdisk      ln         mt         rpm      tar
chmod      grep       ls         mv         sed      traceroute
chroot     gunzip     lsmod      open       sh       umount
cp         gzip       mkdir      pico       swapoff
cpio       head       mke2fs     ping       swapon
dd         ifconfig   mknod      ps         sync
#
```

There are just enough tools in this environment to undertake a number of repairs and adjustments. Note that the included editor is Pico, the small editor from the Pine mail reader. One of the critical utilities is e2fsck, the program that allows you to attempt to repair a damaged partition.

Rebuilding LILO

Let's consider a common problem. On a dual-boot system, you upgrade your Windows partition with a Windows reinstall or upgrade, and LILO disappears. This is because Windows overwrites the master boot record where LILO exists, even though it doesn't use the MBR itself.

To reinstall LILO you need to know which partition holds your Linux root filesystem. In the following rescue example, the root filesystem is located on /dev/hda4:

```
# mount -t ext2 /dev/hda4 /mnt/image
# chroot /mnt/image
bash# /sbin/lilo
Added linux *
Added dos
bash# exit
```

```
# cd /
# umount /mnt/image
```

There are simpler ways of doing this (for example, booting with your boot floppy, logging in as root and typing lilo) but solving this problem with a rescue disk is good practice for a more serious emergency session. In this simple example, we mounted the Linux filesystem on /mnt/image, then chroot'd to /mnt/image to make that directory our root directory. It also launched a bash shell. From there, simply executing the /sbin/lilo command rewrote LILO into the MBR.

This technique can also be used to fix another common problem: building a new kernel but forgetting to run /sbin/lilo to write the new boot information to the MBR. This condition will often prevent you from booting Linux at all, necessitating a rescue operation to restore use of the system.

Rewriting Configuration Files

Simple misconfigurations of configuration files are easily repaired in rescue mode. Let's say we inadvertently make a typo while editing /etc/fstab and can't get back into the system. We meant to write /dev/hda4 in the first line as our key partition to mount, but our keyboard bounced and we entered /dev/hda44 without noticing, and now Linux won't boot.

Return to rescue mode, mount /dev/hda4 as before, edit the /etc/fstab file, save it, and reboot, with relief:

```
# mount -t ext2 /dev/hda4 /mnt/image
# pico -w /mnt/image/etc/fstab
# umount /mnt/image
```

Repairing a Partition

While Linux is booting, fsck will attempt to fix any partitions that don't come up clean during an integrity check. This often happens after an abrupt shutdown where power is removed from the system before the shutdown procedure finishes, as can occur during a power outage or an inadvertent shutdown by accidentally turning off the computer.

The rescue disk set can be used to manually run e2fsck to check and attempt to repair disk damage.

```
# e2fsck -f /dev/hda4
e2fsck 1.14, 9-Jan-1999 for EXT2 FS 0.5b, 95/08/09
Pass 1: Checking inodes, blocks, and sizes
Pass 2: Checking directory structure
Pass 3: Checking directory connectivity
```

```
Pass 4: Checking reference counts
Pass 5: Checking group summary information
/dev/hda4: 68381/499712 files (0.7% noncontiguous), 1367942/1992060 blocks
#
```

Repairing a badly damaged filesystem may require you to run e2fsck several times in sequence before all the problems clear.

Emergency File Copying

If a hard disk is damaged beyond the ability of e2fsck to repair completely, but parts of it are still accessible, the rescue disk set can be used to try to copy off important files. If there is no separate Linux partition to mount and copy to, you can use floppy disks. The following is an example of an emergency file copy procedure in which a floppy disk is formatted and initialized with a Linux filesystem and selected configuration files from a damaged hard disk are copied to floppy:

```
# fdformat /dev/fd0H1440
# mke2fs /dev/fd0
mke2fs 1.14, 9-Jan-1999 for EXT2 FS 0.5b, 95/08/09
Linux ext2 filesystem format
Filesystem label=
360 inodes, 1440 blocks
72 blocks (5.00%) reserved for the super user
First data block=1
Block size=1024 (log=0)
Fragment size=1024 (log=0)
1 block group
8192 blocks per group, 8192 fragments per group
360 inodes per group

Writing inode tables: done
Writing superblocks and filesystem accounting information: done
# mount -t ext2 /dev/hda4 /mnt/image
# mount -t ext2 /dev/fd0 /mnt/floppy
# cd /mnt/floppy
# cp /mnt/image/etc/*.conf .
# cp /mnt/image/etc/conf.modules .
# ls
conf.modules    inetd.conf    logrotate.conf   nssswitch.conf   resolv.conf
dosemu.conf     isapnp.conf   lost+found       ntp.conf         smb.conf
gpmroot.conf    ld.so.conf    mtools.conf      pine.conf        syslog.conf
host.conf       lilo.conf     named.conf       pwdb.conf        yp.conf
# cd /mnt
```

```
# umount floppy
# umount image
#
```

This procedure can be repeated for passwd files, user files, httpd files—in short, any files that can still be recovered. Additional floppy disks can be initialized and mounted, repeating the process for all except large files.

Tip

As useful as the Red Hat rescue disk set is, it doesn't pack in as many tools as some of the "Linux on a floppy" distributions that can also be used for rescue missions. The Red Hat rescue set, for instance, does not have a `vi` or `emacs` emulator, nor does it supply file support for `vfat` and `fat32` DOS/Windows partitions.

One very popular single-disk Linux is `tomsrtbt`, available at http://www.toms.net/rb/. This extremely versatile tool packs an amazing number of programs and device drivers onto a single, compressed 1.7Mb 3.5-inch floppy. The following listing from the `tomsrtbt` Web site shows the included programs and drivers:
3) Contents

```
  Stuff (modules, manpages, scripts, binaries, kernel):


2.0.36 3c589_cs BusLogic CVF DEC_ELCP EEXPRESS EEXPRESS_PRO
EL2 EL3 EXT2 FAT FAT32 FD IDE IDECD IDEFLOPPY IDEPCMCIA
IDETAPE ISO9660 JOLIET LOOP MATH_EMULATION MINIX MSDOS
NE2000 NFS PROC RAM SD SERIAL SLIP SMC SR TR ULTRA VFAT
VORTEX WD80x3 ah152x_cs aha152x aha1542 aic7xxx ash awk
badblocks bdflush bzip2 cardbus cardmgr cat ce ce.help chattr
chgrp chmod chown chroot clear cmp cp cpio cut date dd ddate
debugfs df dirname dmesg dmsdos ds du dumpe2fs dutil e2fsck
eata echo egrep elvis emacs extend false fdflush fdformat
fdisk fdomain filesize find fmt fsck.ext2 fsck.msdos fstab
grep gzip halt head hexedit hostname i82365 ifconfig ifport
ile init inittab insmod kill killall5 ksyms length less
libc.so.5.4.13 lilo lilo.conf ln loadkeys login losetup ls
lsattr mawk memtest mingetty miterm mkdir mkdosfs mke2fs
mkfifo mkfs.minix mklost+found mknod mkswap mnsed more mount
mt mv nc ncr53c8xx nmclan_cs ntfs pax pcmcia pcmcia_core
pcnet_cs ping plip ppa printf ps pwd qlogic_cs qlogicfas
reboot reset rm rmdir rmmod route rsh rshd script scsi_info
seagate sed serial_cs setserial sh slattach sleep slip snarf
```

System Failure Diagnosis and Recovery

CHAPTER 6

159

6
System Failure
Diagnosis and
Recovery

```
sort split stty swapoff swapon sync tail tar tcic tee telnet
test touch tune2fs umount update vi vi.help wc
```

The disk even includes man pages. With `tomsrtbt` you can use your DOS/Windows partition, if you have one, to copy files to if you're rescuing files from a badly damaged Linux partition. This is much more efficient than copying critical files to floppy disks and it provides a handy place for copying files back into a new Linux setup if reformatting the Linux partitions becomes necessary. This is yet another reason to consider maintaining a modest-sized DOS partition on your Linux system.

Tip

A file rescue mission with a booted `tomsrtbt` looks like this:
```
# mkdir /mnt/image
# mkdir /mnt/dos
# mount -t ext2 /dev/hda4 /mnt/image
# mount -t vfat /dev/hda1 /mnt/dos
# mkdir /mnt/dos/rescuefiles
# cd /mnt/dos/rescuefiles
/mnt/dos/rescuefiles# cp /mnt/image/etc/*.conf .
/mnt/dos/rescuefiles# cp /mnt/image/etc/conf.modules .
/mnt/dos/rescuefiles# ls
dosemu.conf      isapnp.conf      mtools.conf      pine.conf      syslog.conf
gpm-root.conf    ld.so.conf       named.conf       pwdb.conf      yp.conf
host.conf        lilo.conf        nsswitch.conf    resolv.conf
inetd.conf       logrotate.conf   ntp.conf         smb.conf
/mnt/dos/rescuefiles# cd /mnt
/mnt# umount dos ; umount image
/mnt#
```

This session, in contrast to the Red Hat rescue session, displays files in color on a color monitor, displays pathnames at the prompt, and includes command-line history. As a system administrator, you will marvel at the versatility of `tomsrtbt` and will find many additional uses for this handy tool. Keep one in your toolkit. You can use it to turn almost any Intel PC into an instant, if limited, Linux computer.

Recovering Deleted Files

For most practical purposes, a deleted file in Linux is not recoverable—what's gone is gone. Upon deletion, the file's blocks on the hard disk are released and the next create file request may grab them for use. This is one of the reasons why backup is so vital, not to mention using extreme care with commands such as rm. A misplaced asterisk, as in "rm * ~" instead of "rm *~" to delete emacs backup files, can have dispiriting consequences, especially when performed by superuser in a critical system directory.

For the extremely determined, however, file recovery is sometimes possible. If the system is not too busy (that is, not creating a lot of new files), there is some chance the raw data has not been overwritten and that it may be recoverable. By using a utility called debugfs, you may be able to read off the raw file data and write it somewhere safe.

The debugfs program is part of the e2fsprogs utilities, downloadable from http://web.mit.edu/tytso/www/linux/e2fsprogs.html. Instructions for undertaking the arduous task of file recovery are outlined in the Linux Ext2fs Undeletion mini-HOWTO located in /usr/doc/HOWTO/mini. On the whole, it is far easier to restore from backup.

With luck, both rescue missions and hardware problem diagnoses should be occasional rather than regular activities. In contrast, analyzing Linux system log files is an on-going, long-term commitment. The next section introduces one of the most central aspects of system administration: examining and analyzing system log files.

Analysis of System Logs

The heart of Linux system administration lies in analyzing system logs. Whether for security purposes, compiling statistics of Web site visits, or diagnosing system problems, analyzing log files is one of the chief responsibilities of those who maintain Linux systems.

Linux, like the UNIX it is based on, logs information on nearly every aspect of its operation. The principal directory for this is /var/log. Messages are posted to /var/log/messages by the syslogd program, which uses /etc/syslog.conf as its initialization file. Kernel messages are picked up by kerneld and passed to syslogd for posting. A typical /var/log directory looks something like this:

```
[root@wallace log]# ls /var/log
boot.log    httpd      messages     secure       spooler.2  xferlog.1
cron        lastlog    messages.1   secure.1     spooler.3  xferlog.2
cron.1      lastlog.1  messages.2   secure.2     spooler.4  xferlog.3
cron.2      maillog    messages.3   secure.3     squid      xferlog.4
cron.3      maillog.1  messages.4   secure.4     uucp
cron.4      maillog.2  netconf.log  sendmail.st  wtmp
```

```
dmesg          maillog.3 netconf.log.1 spooler     wtmp.1
htmlaccess.log maillog.4 samba         spooler.1   xferlog
```

The extensions .1, .2, .3, and .4 come from the logrotate program that rotates the logs, normally on a weekly cycle, dropping off the previous .4 at each rotation. This rotation is important because without it, a disk could easily fill up with log files. Specialty application logs, such as the logs for Apache, Samba, or Squid, reside in directories below /var/log—for example, /var/log/httpd and /var/log/samba.

The log files that contain useful information for system failure diagnosis are boot.log, dmesg, cron, and messages. The boot.log and dmesg files contain startup and shutdown information and nothing else. They're useful for looking at the past several startups and shutdowns to see if anything amiss has been recorded.

The cron file is not normally directly associated with system diagnosis, but cron jobs can trigger hardware errors. Hence, cron file error messages are sometimes a useful alert of impending failure.

Interpreting Log Messages

The primary log file for inspection for system problems is the /var/log/messages file—a general catchall that includes, among other things, kernel messages. You can take a quick look at a sample of the normal kinds of kernel messages that are logged by typing grep kernel /var/log/messages as root:

```
[root@wallace log]# grep kernel /var/log/messages
Aug 31 17:50:27 wallace kernel: hdb: ATAPI 7X CDROM drive, 120kB Cache
Aug 31 17:50:27 wallace kernel: Uniform CDROM driver Revision: 2.54
Aug 31 17:50:27 wallace kernel: Floppy drive(s): fd0 is 1.44M
Aug 31 17:50:27 wallace kernel: FDC 0 is a post-1991 82077
Aug 31 17:50:27 wallace kernel: md driver 0.90.0 MAX_MD_DEVS=256, MAX_REAL=12
Aug 31 17:50:27 wallace kernel: raid5: measuring checksumming speed
Aug 31 17:50:27 wallace kernel:    8regs     :   168.402 MB/sec
Aug 31 17:50:27 wallace kernel:    32regs    :   148.209 MB/sec
Aug 31 17:50:27 wallace kernel: using fastest function: 8regs (168.402 MB/sec)
Aug 31 17:50:27 wallace kernel: scsi : 0 hosts.
Aug 31 17:50:27 wallace kernel: scsi : detected total.
Aug 31 17:50:27 wallace kernel: md.c: sizeof(mdp_super_t) = 4096
Aug 31 17:50:27 wallace kernel: Partition check:
Aug 31 17:50:27 wallace kernel:  hda: hda1 hda2 hda3 hda4
Aug 31 17:50:27 wallace kernel: autodetecting RAID arrays
Aug 31 17:50:27 wallace kernel: autorun ...
Aug 31 17:50:27 wallace kernel: ... autorun DONE.
Aug 31 17:50:27 wallace kernel: VFS: Mounted root (ext2 filesystem) readonly.
```

```
Aug 31 17:50:27 wallace kernel: Freeing unused kernel memory: 60k freed
Aug 31 17:50:27 wallace kernel: Adding Swap: 136548k swapspace (priority -1)
```

Note the file format. Each entry begins with date, then time, then host name, then the process that supplied the message, and finally, the message itself. Although this is all normal-looking information from the kernel, here is a partial readout from a system that is experiencing some intermittent SCSI problems (note particularly the aborting command lines in the listing):

```
[root@darwin /root]# grep kernel /var/log/messages ¦ more
Aug 31 02:30:22 darwin kernel: scsi : aborting command due to timeout :
➥pid 15077, sc
si0, channel 0, id 0, lun 0 Read (6) 04 6b 83 02 00
Aug 31 02:30:42 darwin kernel: scsi : aborting command due to timeout :
➥pid 15077, sc
si0, channel 0, id 0, lun 0 Read (6) 04 6b 83 02 00
Aug 31 02:30:42 darwin kernel: scsi : aborting command due to timeout :
➥pid 15078, sc
si0, channel 0, id 0, lun 0 Write (6) 06 70 0f 02 00
Aug 31 02:31:02 darwin kernel: scsi : aborting command due to timeout :
➥pid 15077, sc
si0, channel 0, id 0, lun 0 Read (6) 04 6b 83 02 00
Aug 31 02:31:02 darwin kernel: scsi : aborting command due to timeout :
➥pid 15078, sc
si0, channel 0, id 0, lun 0 Write (6) 06 70 0f 02 00
Aug 31 02:31:22 darwin kernel: scsi : aborting command due to timeout :
➥pid 15077, sc
si0, channel 0, id 0, lun 0 Read (6) 04 6b 83 02 00
```

As system administrator, you would want to take this system offline for some adapter diagnostics and tape device diagnostics as well as to check all SCSI cables and terminators. If the problem continues to show up in the logs, it might be time to consider replacing the SCSI adapter or the tape unit. Note the time of day—02:30. This error occurred during nightly tape backup. The backup procedure itself reported nothing amiss.

Scanning through kernel messages in /var/log/messages on a routine basis provides you with a certain amount of proactive system monitoring. In the previous example, for instance, though the backup is being completed, all is not well with the SCSI setup. Catching a problem like this as early as possible prevents more serious problems from occurring later.

System administrators use stable releases of the Linux kernel on production systems, and the system log messages generated on production systems tend to be routine. However, on experimental systems that use the latest kernel releases, system administrators can expect to encounter glitches in the Linux kernel itself. The next section explains how to deal with error messages reported by the kernel.

Locating the Source of Kernel Errors

The Linux kernel is being developed at a very fast pace and most system administrators will need to update their system kernel from time to time, either for security reasons or for added feature support. For anyone who lives on the edge of kernel development—kernel developers and those who contribute device drivers—upgrading kernels is a frequent activity.

The kernel supports such a wide variety of hardware, including new drivers for new devices, that kernel-level problems sometimes occur. Other than severe kernel problems, which can cause a kernel panic, other kernel problems that create a kernel oops get logged into /var/log/messages (and are often displayed on your console). Experimental versions of programs and drivers have been known to create a kernel oops condition.

The Linux kernel maintainers point out that genuine kernel oops are rare these days, though they sometimes happen. Most kernel oops messages are actually bugs in kernel software such as drivers. A bug is slightly different from a genuine oops, though the bug may trigger an oops message. The most important step when encountering an oops message is determining under which conditions the misbehavior can be triggered and whether it is reproducible.

When encountering a suspected oops condition, grep through /var/log/messages on "kernel" and look for a pattern like this:

```
Aug 29 09:51:01 blizard kernel: Unable to handle kernel paging request at
➥virtual address f15e97cc
Aug 29 09:51:01 blizard kernel: current->tss.cr3 = 0062d000, %cr3 = 0062d000
Aug 29 09:51:01 blizard kernel: *pde = 00000000
Aug 29 09:51:01 blizard kernel: Oops: 0002
Aug 29 09:51:01 blizard kernel: CPU:    0
Aug 29 09:51:01 blizard kernel: EIP:    0010:[oops:_oops+16/3868]
Aug 29 09:51:01 blizard kernel: EFLAGS: 00010212
Aug 29 09:51:01 blizard kernel: eax: 315e97cc   ebx: 003a6f80   ecx: 001be77b
➥edx: 00237c0c
```

```
Aug 29 09:51:01 blizard kernel: esi: 00000000   edi: bffffdb3   ebp: 00589f90
➡esp: 00589f8c
Aug 29 09:51:01 blizard kernel: ds: 0018   es: 0018   fs: 002b   gs: 002b
➡ss: 0018
Aug 29 09:51:01 blizard kernel: Process oops_test (pid: 3374, process nr: 21,
➡stackpage=00589000)
Aug 29 09:51:01 blizard kernel: Stack: 315e97cc 00589f98 0100b0b4 bffffed4
➡0012e38e 00240c64 003a6f80 00000001
Aug 29 09:51:01 blizard kernel:        00000000 00237810 bfffff00 0010a7fa
➡00000003 00000001 00000000 bfffff00
Aug 29 09:51:01 blizard kernel:        bffffdb3 bffffed4 ffffffda 0000002b
➡0007002b 0000002b 0000002b 00000036
Aug 29 09:51:01 blizard kernel: Call Trace: [oops:_oops_ioctl+48/80]
➡[_sys_ioctl+254/272] [_system_call+82/128]
Aug 29 09:51:01 blizard kernel: Code: c7 00 05 00 00 00 eb 08 90 90 90 90 90
➡90 90 90 89 ec 5d c3
```

This example is from the file oops-tracing.txt located in /usr/src/linux/
Documentation. This file is required reading for any system administrator dealing with
oops messages.

A kernel oops is essentially a protection fault, and oops messages were designed to help
kernel maintainers and device-driver authors locate the source of the problem. When an
oops condition occurs, the klogd daemon translates important memory addresses in the
kernel log messages to their symbolic equivalents. This translated message is then
forwarded from klogd to syslogd where, on Red Hat systems, it is logged by default to
/var/log/messages.

The klogd daemon provides the name of the module that created the oops condition, and it
provides as much symbolic information as possible. klogd performs two types of address
resolution: static and dynamic. The static translation uses the System.map file, located at
/boot/System.map on Red Hat systems.

Dynamic address translation is required for kernel loadable modules. Memory for these
modules is allocated from the kernel's dynamic memory pools, so there are no fixed
locations for the module or for its functions and symbols. For dynamic addresses, klogd
draws upon system calls to determine which modules are loaded and where they are located
in memory, building a symbol table that can be used to debug a protection fault in a
loadable kernel module.

Decoding Kernel Errors

For the most part, the only immediately useful information you can glean from an oops message, in its raw state, is identifying which program or driver is causing a problem. The Linux kernel maintainers have developed a system for decoding the results of oops messages and reporting them back to the maintainers. This includes running `ksymoops` to decode the oops message, saving the output to a report file, and filing a report, along with any system-specific information that might be useful.

ksymoops

The program used to decode oops messages is `ksymoops`, which gets loaded on a Red Hat 6 system if you select "Kernel development" during a custom install. To use `ksymoops`, you need to compile it, then copy the oops message from `/var/log/messages` to a separate file and run it through `ksymoops`.

Before you can use `ksymoops`, you need to compile it for your system:

```
[root@wallace /root]# cd /usr/src/linux/scripts/ksymoops
[root@wallace ksymoops]# make
```

The documentation for `ksymoops` is `/usr/src/linux/scripts/ksymoops/README`. It does not create a man page, but the essential options are

```
Usage:       ksymoops
             [-v vmlinux]  Where to read vmlinux
             [-V]          No vmlinux is available
             [-o object_dir]       Directory containing modules
             [-O]          No modules is available
             [-k ksyms]    Where to read ksyms
             [-K]          No ksyms is available
             [-l lsmod]    Where to read lsmod
             [-L]          No lsmod is available
             [-m system.map]       Where to read System.map
             [-M]          No System.map is available
             [-s save.map] Save consolidated map
             [-c code_bytes]       How many bytes in each unit of code
             [-1]          One shot toggle (exit after first Oops)
             [-d]          Increase debug level by 1
             [-h]          Print help text
```

The purpose of `ksymoops` is to provide trace information for debugging an oops. In the previous oops message, for instance, use a text editor to extract and copy the raw oops message from the log file to the file `/tmp/oops.txt`. You would then run it through `ksymoops` as follows:

```
[root@wallace /root]# cd /usr/src/linux/ksymoops/ksymoops
[root@wallace ksymoops]# ./ksymoops < /tmp/oops.txt > /tmp/ksymoops.rpt
```

A Sample `ksymoops` Report

Once a `ksymoops` report has been created, it can be examined for any immediately useful information. A typical `ksymoops` report will look similar to this example posted to the linux-kernel mailing list:

```
ksymoops -v /usr/src/linux-2.3.12/vmlinux -K -m
➥/usr/src/linux-2.3.12/System.map crash.txt
ksymoops 0.7c on i686 2.2.11.  Options used
  -v /usr/src/linux-2.3.12/vmlinux (specified)
  -K (specified)
  -l /proc/modules (default)
  -o /lib/modules/2.2.11/ (default)
  -m /usr/src/linux-2.3.12/System.map (specified)


No modules in ksyms, skipping objects
No ksyms, skipping lsmod
Oops: 0000
CPU:    0
EIP:    0010:[<c01c72cb>]
Using defaults from ksymoops -t elf32-i386 -a i386
EFLAGS: 00010202
eax: 048b2824  ebx: 00000000  ecx: 00000000  edx: df24fe4c
esi: c0081800  edi: 0001a000  ebp: c0081c80  esp: df24fdd8
ds: 0018  es: 0018  ss: 0018
Process ifconfig (pid: 235, stackpage=df24f000)
Stack: 00000000 00000005 e0004000 00000000 00002050 00000014 e0004000 c025bfa0
   c010b078 00000005 c025bfa0 df24fe4c 00000050 c0b6a920 00000005 df24fe44
   c01101fa 00000005 df24fe4c c0b6a920 df24fe4c 00000278 e0004000 c010b1e3
Call Trace: [<e0004000>] [<e0004000>] [<c010b078>] [<c01101fa>] [<e0004000>]
➥[<c010b1e3>]
[<c0109218>]
   [<e0004010>] [<e0004000>] [<e0004010>] [<e0000018>] [<c01c66da>]
   ➥[<c01c68f4>]
[<e0004000>] [<c016c30d>]
   [<c016cfa8>] [<c0186c16>] [<c016d51f>] [<c018838c>] [<c0168585>]
   ➥[<c0136c51>]
[<c010917c>]
Code: 8b 40 5c 01 86 bc 05 00 00 8b 14 2b f0 ff 4a 70 0f 94 c0 84
```

```
>>EIP; c01c72cb <speedo_interrupt+1e3/35c>  <=====
Trace; e0004000 <END_OF_CODE+1fd48df0/????>
Trace; e0004000 <END_OF_CODE+1fd48df0/????>
Trace; c010b078 <handle_IRQ_event+50/80>
Trace; c01101fa <do_level_ioapic_IRQ+62/a8>
Trace; e0004000 <END_OF_CODE+1fd48df0/????>
Trace; c010b1e3 <do_IRQ+3b/58>
Trace; c0109218 <ret_from_intr+0/20>
Trace; e0004010 <END_OF_CODE+1fd48e00/????>
Trace; e0004000 <END_OF_CODE+1fd48df0/????>
Trace; e0004010 <END_OF_CODE+1fd48e00/????>
Trace; e0000018 <END_OF_CODE+1fd44e08/????>
Trace; c01c66da <mdio_read+3e/5c>
Trace; c01c68f4 <speedo_open+19c/1a8>
Trace; e0004000 <END_OF_CODE+1fd48df0/????>
Trace; c016c30d <dev_open+25/7c>
Trace; c016cfa8 <dev_change_flags+54/110>
Trace; c0186c16 <devinet_ioctl+22e/510>
Trace; c016d51f <dev_ioctl+17b/2cc>
Trace; c018838c <inet_ioctl+138/17c>
Trace; c0168585 <sock_ioctl+1d/24>
Trace; c0136c51 <sys_ioctl+1e1/240>
Trace; c010917c <system_call+34/38>
Code;  c01c72cb <speedo_interrupt+1e3/35c>
00000000 <_EIP>:
Code;  c01c72cb <speedo_interrupt+1e3/35c>  <=====
 0:  8b 40 5c                 movl  0x5c(%eax),%eax  <=====
Code;  c01c72ce <speedo_interrupt+1e6/35c>
 3:  01 86 bc 05 00 00        addl  %eax,0x5bc(%esi)
Code;  c01c72d4 <speedo_interrupt+1ec/35c>
 9:  8b 14 2b                 movl  (%ebx,%ebp,1),%edx
Code;  c01c72d7 <speedo_interrupt+1ef/35c>
 c:  f0 ff 4a 70              lock decl 0x70(%edx)
Code;  c01c72db <speedo_interrupt+1f3/35c>
 10:  0f 94 c0                 sete  %al
Code;  c01c72de <speedo_interrupt+1f6/35c>
 13:  84 00                    testb %al,(%eax)


1.980u 0.130s 0:02.03 103.9%    0+0k 0+0io 700pf+0w
```

A kernel bug can be reported, along with this `ksymoops` report and other information about your setup, to `linux-kernel@vger.rutgers.edu`. Note however, that you should first check to see if yours is a known problem before firing off a report to the extremely busy linux-kernel mailing list. Check `/usr/src/linux/REPORTING-BUGS` for instructions on how to file a bug report.

Using the `System.map` File

When you compile a kernel (or install a fresh system), the process creates a kernel `System.map` usually located in `/boot/System.map`. Experimental kernels will, by default, have their map located in `/usr/src/linux/System.map`. The `System.map` is a symbol table of the static addresses for a particular version of the kernel. The ksymoops program attempts to match up memory addresses with information from `System.map` in its report. For this reason, kernel oops messages have to be decoded on the machine that created the oops condition, to get the correct matchup.

A typical `System.map` contains the following type of information:

```
c01be29c t cdrom_ioctl
c01bef30 T cdrom_sysctl_info
c01bf328 t cdrom_procfs_modcount
c01bf32c t cdrom_sysctl_register
c01bf364 T pci_find_slot
c01bf398 T pci_find_device
c01bf3d4 T pci_find_class
c01bf3f8 T pci_read_config_byte
c01bf424 T pci_read_config_word
c01bf450 T pci_read_config_dword
c01bf47c T pci_write_config_byte
c01bf4a8 T pci_write_config_word
c01bf4d8 T pci_write_config_dword
c01bf504 T pci_set_master
c01bf594 t proc_bus_pci_lseek
c01bf5f0 t proc_bus_pci_read
c01bf820 t proc_bus_pci_write
c01bfa1c T get_pci_dev_info
c01bfb38 T pci_proc_attach_device
c01bfbdc T pci_proc_detach_device
c01bfc18 t pci_lookup_dev
c01bfc74 t pci_strclass
c01c0130 t pci_strvendor
c01c0cec t pci_strdev
c01c0d10 t sprint_dev_config
```

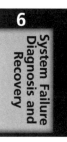

```
c01c11b8 T get_pci_list
c01c1260 T pcibios_find_class
c01c12b4 T pcibios_find_device
c01c131c t cursor_timer_handler
```

If you're accustomed to reading register and symbolic information, you can sometimes troubleshoot ksymoops output yourself by reading the output and correlating it to a particular part of your system.

Seeking Assistance

Without doubt, one of the best sources of information to assist you with system failure diagnosis and recovery is the documentation that comes with Linux itself. The Linux HOWTO guides (located in /usr/doc/HOWTO) are among the most accessible sources of information. The man pages for klogd and syslogd provide invaluable insights. Likewise, the README files and other text files (.txt) scattered throughout /usr/src/linux provide essential information.

There are a number of Internet services that can provide additional assistance. The linux-kernel mailing list FAQ is located at http://www.tux.org/lkml/ and helpful newsgroups includecomp.os.linux.hardware, comp.os.linux.admin, comp.os.linux.setup, and comp.os.linux.misc. Excellent Red Hat-specific assistance can be found in the Red Hat mailing list. See www.redhat.com/support/ for subscription information.

Summary

No part of system administration is more frustrating to deal with than system failure, but hardware component failure and occasional system errors are a fact of life with any computer system. Although Linux is a complex operating system, it provides a good set of tools for diagnosing and fixing problems, ranging from the /proc filesystem to emergency repair disks.

By learning how to use these tools you will be able to isolate the cause of problems and often be able to fix them quickly. By regularly scanning your system logs, you will become that jewel among computer professionals: the proactive, caring system administrator.

Filesystem and Disk Management

PART

III

IN THIS PART

7 Filesystems   *173*

8 Adding or Replacing Disks   *211*

9 Linux and RAID   *227*

10 Removable Media Devices   *271*

Filesystems

I**N** T**HIS** C**HAPTER**

- The Physical Realm of Disks and Partitions   *174*
- Filesystem Creation and Management   *187*
- Filesystem Types   *197*
- Space Management and Quotas   *198*

7

C**HAPTER**

One of the questions I often hear from people just starting out with Linux is how to allocate space and manage their filesystems. One reason for this is that unlike most Windows systems, in which all files are contained on a single drive partition called the C: drive, the Linux filesystem is typically spread across multiple partitions. Choosing the correct size for these partitions can be difficult. This chapter tries to answer that question. We will first take a look at the tools for disk partitioning, and when multiple disks can be an advantage over a single disk. Next, we will discuss the tools for creating and repairing filesystems. We will then take a look at the primary filesystem type used in Linux installations and discuss some of the advantages and disadvantages of each. Finally, we will look at managing disk space and using quotas. So let's get started.

The Physical Realm of Disks and Partitions

Before looking at the tools for creating and managing filesystems, we will look at the physical realm of disks and partitions, starting with some guidelines on when it is to your advantage to use multiple disks versus a single disk. After that, the tools provided by Red Hat for partitioning disks will be examined and some partitioning schemes will be compared and contrasted.

Single Versus Multiple Disks

With the size of disk drives ever increasing and their prices continuing to fall, it is not uncommon for systems today to be shipped with boot disks of ten gigabytes or more. This is in contrast to systems of just a few years ago, when disk drives over one gigabyte were rare. With this change in the availability of high capacity disks, it is no longer a requirement that you have multiple disks in order to install the operating system and still have room for growth filesystems like /home, /var, and /usr/local. This is especially true of personal workstations, where a single disk will in most cases be the norm. Single disks might also be appropriate in single-purpose servers like a DNS server or a small Web server, where the disk space requirements are small. This being the case, why would you want to have multiple disks in a system?

The first and most obvious reason for wanting multiple disks in a system is that you need more space than is available on a single disk. There are several factors to consider when analyzing the need for multiple disks to meet space requirements. Two of the these factors are physical space in the server case along with the power capacity and cooling capabilities. Failure to observe these precautions will result in avoidable server failures and reduced drive life. Another consideration is whether the space will be used for a shared filesystem.

Depending on the number and type of clients that will be sharing the resource, and the storage capacity required, it may be that your file storage requirements are better served by a dedicated file server. A final consideration that is often overlooked is whether your backup solution has the capacity to handle the amount of disk storage you are adding.

A second reason for using multiple disks is to increase performance. For example, if you have multiple swap partitions, spreading them across several disks can increase swap performance. This is not always true, however, due to limitations of personal computer hardware, such as IDE controllers. Due to the nature of IDE devices, if you have two drives connected to the same controller and put swap spaces on each of the drives, you will not see much of a performance advantage. If, however, you were to attach the drives to different controllers, you should get a performance enhancement. This consideration is not restricted to swap spaces. Another way in which having multiple disks in a system can be used to increase performance is by tuning the filesystems based on the nature of the applications that use them. This may be something as simple as mounting a mail spool directory with the noatime option. Or it could be more complicated, such as tuning the block size, bytes per inode, and sector read ahead to match the read and write behavior of the application that will be accessing the filesystem. This second type of tuning, of course, requires thorough analysis and an in-depth understanding of the uses to which the filesystem will be put. However, the performance enhancements achieved can be substantial.

Partitioning Strategies

Whether you use a single disk or multiple disks, you will need to create one or more partitions to contain the files that make up your Linux installation. The number and size of the partitions that you will need, however, is the subject of some debate. There are two basic schools of thought on this and each has its merits, so I will describe them here and let you decide which you think is best for your situation.

Separate Partitions for Each Filesystem

The classic school of thought usually prescribes separate partitions for the root filesystem, the /usr filesystem, the /home filesystem, /usr/local, /opt, /boot, /var, and sometimes /tmp. The primary argument for this arrangement is that corruption of a filesystem will have minimal impact on the other filesystems and filling up /home, /tmp, or /var will not have the same negative impact as filling up the root filesystem would have. Another reason for this division is that the root filesystem can be kept small and contain only those parts of the system required to boot the system, thus allowing you to make use of old small disks. For example, suppose you have a system that contains three disks, two 250 megabyte drives, /dev/hda and /dev/hdb, and a third disk, /dev/hdc, that is four gigabytes in size.

Using the strategy of giving each part of the system its own filesystem, you could create the following partitioning scheme.

For the first disk, /dev/hda, you could create the root filesystem and give it 175 megabytes of space, create an 11 megabyte /boot partition to hold your kernel images, and use the remaining 64 megabytes for a swap partition. For the second disk, you might set aside 125 megabytes for /var, 61 megabytes for /tmp, and a second swap partition of 64 megabytes. This leaves the four gigabyte disk to hold /usr, which for a full installation of Red Hat requires about one gigabyte, and allows you to divide the remaining three gigabytes between /home, /usr/local, and /opt. The size of each is determined by estimating the amount of local customization that you will be doing, the number of users on the system, and the number of commercial packages you are likely to be installing.

An advantage of this setup is that if you later decide to share any of these filesystems, they are individual entities that can be easily exported. This is not a great advantage, however, because Linux NFS can export not only filesystem mount points, but also subdirectories of those mount points. This is not true of all UNIX variants, and some people like to pretend that this functionality does not exist. A disadvantage of this setup is that if one of your filesystems runs out of space, you must add more disk space and split what was once a logical unit, such as /usr, into something less useful, such as /usr and /usr/X11R6. This makes exporting more complicated. Another disadvantage of the many partition schemes is that you end up with ordering dependencies for mounting them, which should be avoided if possible.

Keeping the Number of Partitions to a Minimum

An alternative strategy that has been gaining favor in recent years is to keep the number of partitions to a minimum. An example of this is the partitioning strategy I typically use on server systems. For a nine-gigabyte disk I normally create a total of six partitions, allocated as follows:

- A 1.5-gigabyte partition to hold the entire Red Hat installation.

- A 200-megabyte partition to hold a minimalist Red Hat install for emergency recovery.

- Two swap partitions of 128 megabytes each.

- Two partitions that are of equal size that take up the remaining space on the disk.

The actual layout used is two primary partitions, an extended partition, and four logical drives inside of the extended partition. The first partition contains the entire installation with the exception of the /var hierarchy, /home, /opt, /tmp, and /usr/local. Of these filesystem hierarchies, the ones that remain on the local system are /var and /tmp.

All others are shared resources that reside on a file server. The reasoning behind this strategy is that /var and /tmp are variable size filesystems and need to be segregated from the root filesystem, so as not to fill it up. The traditional separating of /usr from the root filesystem is not observed because it is not shared with other systems. In the event that you start adding software to /usr or some other subdirectory included on the large first partition, you can segregate it at that time by adding a disk to the system and moving some part of the system to the new disk. You could, for example, move /usr/X11R6 to a separate partition and mount that partition at the old /usr/X11R6 directory after it is cleaned. If however, you follow the standards outlined in the Filesystem Hierarchy Standard, you should never have to do this, since all software added locally will end up in either the /usr/local or /opt hierarchies.

An interesting facet of this partitioning scheme is the minimalist partition. This partition contains the minimal Red Hat installation plus networking support. This partition is a replacement root partition that allows the system to boot and that contains all of the tools required to recover any other part of the system. The beauty of this strategy is that the system initialization scripts can be written such that in the event of a root filesystem corruption, the system can be made to boot from the maintenance partition. This is especially useful if your systems are maintained remotely. The use of the maintenance root allows you to access the system via a network, and you can repair the remainder of the system from a distinct partition. It does not require manual intervention such as booting from rescue floppies or access to the console.

Partitioning Using fdisk

There are a number of different tools available with your Linux system to partition your hard drives. The oldest and still one of the most popular of these is the fdisk command, which lives in the /sbin directory. This is a command-line tool that works on just about any type of terminal. This fdisk program has very few command-line options because it is primarily intended for interactive use. Normal invocation requires that you specify the device to work on, with a default determined at compile time. The command-line options that are available are described in Table 7.1.

TABLE 7.1   fdisk Command-Line Options

Option	Description
-v	Prints the version number and exits.
-l [device]	Prints the partition table of the specified device. If no device is given, prints the partition tables of the first four IDE drives (/dev/hd[a-d]), the first eight SCSI drives (/dev/sd[a-h]), the first eight drives connected to the first channel of a DAC RAID controller (/dev/rd/c0d[0-7]), and the first eight drives connected to a Compac Smart2 Intelligent Disk Array controller (/dev/ida/c0d[0-7]).
-u	Displays sizes in sectors instead of cylinders.
-s partition	Displays the size of the specified partition in blocks.

The reason for the dearth of command-line options is that fdisk is intended primarily for interactive use as opposed to use in scripts. When you invoke fdisk with a device name as an argument, you will be presented with a prompt, at which you may enter commands to add, delete, print, or otherwise modify the partition table of that device. The following session transcript shows the available commands and demonstrates a couple of the nondestructive ones.

```
[root@madmax /root]# fdisk /dev/hda
Command (m for help): m
Command action
   a   toggle a bootable flag
   b   edit bsd disklabel
   c   toggle the dos compatibility flag
   d   delete a partition
   l   list known partition types
   m   print this menu
   n   add a new partition
   o   create a new empty DOS partition table
   p   print the partition table
   q   quit without saving changes
   s   create a new empty Sun disklabel
   t   change a partition's system id
   u   change display/entry units
   v   verify the partition table
   w   write table to disk and exit
   x   extra functionality (experts only)

Command (m for help): a
Partition number (1-4): 1
```

```
Command (m for help): p

Disk /dev/hda: 64 heads, 63 sectors, 1024 cylinders
Units = cylinders of 4032 * 512 bytes

    Device Boot    Start     End    Blocks   Id  System
/dev/hda1    *         1     991   1997824+  83  Linux
/dev/hda2             992    1024     66528  82  Linux swap

Command (m for help): a
Partition number (1-4): 1

Command (m for help): p

Disk /dev/hda: 64 heads, 63 sectors, 1024 cylinders
Units = cylinders of 4032 * 512 bytes

    Device Boot    Start     End    Blocks   Id  System
/dev/hda1              1     991   1997824+  83  Linux
/dev/hda2             992    1024     66528  82  Linux swap

Command (m for help): u
Changing display/entry units to sectors

Command (m for help): p

Disk /dev/hda: 64 heads, 63 sectors, 1024 cylinders
Units = sectors of 1 * 512 bytes

    Device Boot    Start       End    Blocks   Id  System
/dev/hda1             63   3995711   1997824+  83  Linux
/dev/hda2        3995712   4128767     66528  82  Linux swap

Command (m for help): u
Changing display/entry units to cylinders

Command (m for help): p

Disk /dev/hda: 64 heads, 63 sectors, 1024 cylinders
Units = cylinders of 4032 * 512 bytes

    Device Boot    Start     End    Blocks   Id  System
/dev/hda1              1     991   1997824+  83  Linux
```

7

Filesystems

```
/dev/hda2          992      1024     66528    82  Linux swap

Command (m for help): x

Expert command (m for help): m
Command action
   b   move beginning of data in a partition
   c   change number of cylinders
   d   print the raw data in the partition table
   e   list extended partitions
   g   create an IRIX partition table
   h   change number of heads
   m   print this menu
   p   print the partition table
   q   quit without saving changes
   r   return to main menu
   s   change number of sectors
   v   verify the partition table
   w   write table to disk and exit

Expert command (m for help): d
Device: /dev/hda
0x000: FA EB 6C 00 00 00 4C 49 4C 4F 01 00 14 00 5A 00
0x010: 00 00 00 00 24 DD 77 37 29 32 80 02 01 2A 32 80
0x020: 02 01 28 32 80 02 01 01 00 00 00 00 00 00 00 2C
0x030: 32 80 02 01 38 32 80 01 01 39 32 80 01 01 3A 32
0x040: 80 01 01 3B 32 80 01 01 3C 32 80 01 01 3D 32 80
0x050: 01 01 3E 32 80 01 01 3F 32 80 01 01 00 00 00 00
0x060: 00 00 00 00 00 00 00 00 00 00 00 00 00 00 00 B8
0x070: C0 07 8E D8 8C 06 6A 00 89 36 68 00 89 1E 6C 00
0x080: 88 16 6E 00 B8 00 9A 8E C0 B9 00 01 29 F6 29 FF
0x090: FC F3 A5 EA 98 00 00 9A FA 8E D8 8E C0 BC 00 B0
0x0A0: B8 00 90 8E D0 FB B0 0D E8 5B 00 B0 0A E8 56 00
0x0B0: B0 4C E8 51 00 BE 34 00 B8 00 0B 8E C0 31 DB FC
0x0C0: AD 89 C1 AD 89 C2 09 C8 74 20 46 E8 43 00 72 06
0x0D0: 81 C3 00 02 EB EA 50 B0 20 E8 2A 00 58 88 E0 E8
0x0E0: 12 00 31 C0 88 C2 CD 13 EB CB B0 49 E8 17 00 EA
0x0F0: 00 00 00 0B 50 C0 E8 04 E8 01 00 58 24 0F 04 30
0x100: 3C 3A 72 02 04 07 30 FF B4 0E CD 10 C3 5A 59 5B
0x110: C3 F6 C2 40 74 54 80 E2 BF 53 51 52 B4 08 CD 13
0x120: 72 EB 88 F0 5A 88 16 77 01 88 F2 30 F6 51 86 CD
0x130: D0 C5 D0 C5 80 E5 03 89 0E 75 01 59 83 E1 3F F6
0x140: E1 01 C8 93 58 F7 F3 92 F6 F1 FE C4 88 26 78 01
```

```
0x150: 92 88 D6 8A 16 77 01 3B 06 75 01 77 13 86 C4 D0
0x160: C8 D0 C8 0A 06 78 01 89 C1 5B B8 01 02 CD 13 C3
0x170: 5B 31 C0 F9 C3 00 00 00 00 00 00 00 00 00 00 00
0x180: 00 00 00 00 00 00 00 00 00 00 00 00 00 00 00 00
0x190: 00 00 00 00 00 00 00 00 00 00 00 00 00 00 00 00
0x1A0: 00 00 00 00 00 00 00 00 00 00 00 00 00 00 00 00
0x1B0: 00 00 00 00 00 00 00 00 00 00 00 00 00 00 00 01
0x1C0: 01 00 83 3F FF DE 3F 00 00 00 01 F8 3C 00 00 00
0x1D0: C1 DF 82 3F FF FF 40 F8 3C 00 C0 07 02 00 00 00
0x1E0: 00 00 00 00 00 00 00 00 00 00 00 00 00 00 00 00
0x1F0: 00 00 00 00 00 00 00 00 00 00 00 00 00 00 55 AA
```

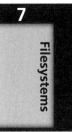

```
Expert command (m for help): r

Command (m for help): q
```

As you can see, fdisk is quite simple to use. If you require more information on the command menus than the brief descriptions provided by the m command, you should refer to the manual page.

Partitioning with cfdisk

If you prefer a screen-oriented partitioning tool, similar to the MS-DOS fdisk utility, try out cfdisk. This utility provides most of the same functionality as fdisk, but uses curses to display the information in a full screen display, as shown in Figure 7.1.

Interacting with cfdisk is very simple. You select the partition to work on using the up and down arrow keys, and select the action to perform on it using either the single letter commands, which you can display using the Help option, or by selecting one of the commands displayed at the bottom of the screen using the left and right arrow keys.

As you can see from Figure 7.1, cfdisk is an interactive command and therefore, like the fdisk utility, it has few command-line options. The command-line options that are available, however, are described in Table 7.2.

FIGURE 7.1

cfdisk Main Screen.

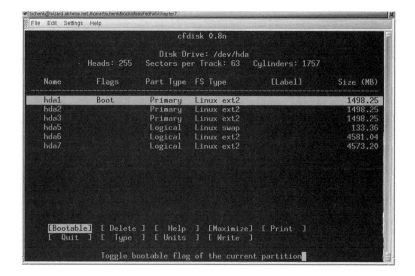

TABLE 7.2   cfdisk Command-Line Options

Option	Description
-a	Uses an arrow cursor to indicate the partition instead of the reverse video highlighting.
-z	Assumes that the user will be rewriting the entire partition table and skips reading the information from disk.
-v	Displays the cfdisk version and copyright and exit.
-c cylinders -h heads -s sectors	Specifies the number of cylinders, heads, and sectors instead of using the information supplied by the BIOS to the kernel at boot time. These three options must be used together and are very dangerous. Use with extreme caution.
-P opt	Displays information in the format specified by the opt argument, which may be r for raw data format, s for sector order format, or t for raw format. For a complete description of these formats, refer to the cfdisk manual page.

Partitioning with sfdisk

As you can see, both the fdisk and cfdisk utilities are easy to use interactively, but if you need the ability to partition a disk in a script, they are of little use. This is the reason for the existence of yet another partitioning utility, sfdisk. This tool, unlike the other two, has a wealth of command-line options as shown in Table 7.4 and takes its input from standard input, making it suitable as the target of a pipeline or for use with a here-document. It can be especially useful if you want to quickly create a single large partition on a number of disks. Take, for example, the following code sample. This simple for loop will create a single partition consisting of the entire disk on the four SCSI drives, /dev/sdb, /dev/sdc, /dev/sdd, and /dev/sde.

7

Filesystems

> **Note**
>
> A here-document refers to lines in a script that represent information that is normally received via standard input or from a file. A here-document begins with the I/O redirection operator << followed by a delimiter word. The here-document is terminated by a line containing only the delimiter word. In the following example, the here-document begins with <<EOF and ends with EOF.
>
> ```
> /bin/cat >foo.sh <<EOF
> #!/bin/sh
> echo ''This is a test''
> exit 0
> EOF
> ```
>
> This command creates a file foo.sh that contains everything in the here-document between <<EOF and EOF.

```
for f in sdb sdc sdd sde; do
    echo ",,,-" | /sbin/sfdisk /dev/$f
done
```

> **Caution**
>
> As with many other Linux utilities, with this power comes added risk. A simple typing mistake, for example, typing sda instead of sdd, would result in the partition table of your first SCSI drive being overwritten, which means you have destroyed your boot drive if you have a SCSI-only system.

The sfdisk utility reads from standard input to determine how to create partitions. The lines it reads contain the starting cylinder, the size in cylinders of the partition, the partition id (type), an active flag, and optionally, the cylinder, head, and sector for the start and end of the partition. These final two fields are rarely used and should be used with extreme caution. A description of these input fields, acceptable values, and the defaults are described in Table 7.3.

TABLE 7.3 sfdisk Input Fields

Field	Description
start_cylinder	The first cylinder of the partition. Defaults to the first available cylinder.
size	The size in cylinders for the partition. Defaults to the number of cylinders remaining on the disk.
id	The partition id or type. Acceptable values are the hex ID or the letters L, E, S, or X for Linux native (83), extended (5), Linux swap (82), or Linux extended (85).
active flag	This field is a flag that indicates whether to mark the partition active or not. Acceptable values are an asterisk (*) for active and a hyphen (-) for not.
c,h,s	The cylinder, head, and sector to start the partition at.
c,h,s	The cylinder, head, and sector to end the partition at.

Although this format takes a little more work to master than the interactive versions of fdisk, it is well worth the effort. This partitioning utility is the only one that can easily be used via rsh and, unlike the other partitioning tools already discussed, has many command-line options, as described in Table 7.4.

TABLE 7.4 sfdisk Command-Line Options

Option	Description
-v --version	Prints version number of sfdisk and exits immediately.
-? --help	Prints a usage message and exits immediately.
-T --list-types	Prints the recognized partition types.
-s --show-size	Lists the size of a partition.
-g --show-geometry	Lists the kernel's idea of the indicated disk geometry.
-l --list	Lists the partitions of a device.
-d	Dumps the partitions of a device in a format useful as input to sfdisk.
-V --verify	Tests whether partitions seem correct.
-i --increment	Starts numbering cylinders at 1 instead of 0.
-N number	Changes only the single partition indicated.
-Anumber	Makes the indicated partition(s) active, and all others inactive.
-c --id number [Id]	If no Id argument given: prints the partition Id of the indicated partition. If an Id argument is present: changes the type (Id) of the indicated partition to the given value.
-uS -uB -uC -uM	Accepts or reports in units of sectors (blocks, cylinders, megabytes, respectively). The default is cylinders, at least when the geometry is known.
-x --show-extended	Also lists non-primary extended partitions on output, and expects descriptors for them on input.

TABLE 7.4 continued

Option	Description
-C cylinders	Specifies the number of cylinders, possibly overriding what the kernel thinks.
-H heads	Specifies the number of heads, possibly overriding what the kernel thinks.
-S sectors	Specifies the number of sectors, possibly overriding what the kernel thinks.
-f --force	Does what I say, even if it is stupid.
-q --quiet	Suppresses warning messages.
-L --Linux	Does not complain about things irrelevant for Linux.
-D --DOS	For DOS-compatibility: wastes a little space.
--IBM --leave-last	Tells sfdisk that it should not allocate the last cylinder.
-n	Goes through all the motions, but does not actually write to disk.
-R	Only executes the BLKRRPART ioctl (to make the kernel re-read the partition table).
--no-reread	Suppresses the check for a mounted or in-use device.
-O file	Just before writing the new partition, outputs the sectors that are going to be overwritten to file.
-I file	Restores an old partition table using file, which must have been created using the -O option.

Disk Druid

During the installation of your Red Hat Linux distribution, you have one other option for partitioning your disk: Disk Druid. This program is a full-screen partition editor and filesystem manager that is available only during the installation procedure. It contains a number of features not normally found in a partition manager, such as the ability to add mount points for NFS filesystems. The Disk Druid main screen, shown in Figure 7.2, is divided into three main sections: the current partitions section, the drive summaries section, and the buttons/function key section that perform the various actions available. Many people do not like Disk Druid because it is somewhat inflexible. For example, Disk Druid will only create one primary Linux partition, and makes all other partitions you specify as logical drives within an extended partition. This can be severely limiting and you can run into trouble especially on dual-boot systems. For maximum flexibility, I recommend one of the other partitioning tools available, like fdisk.

FIGURE 7.2

The Disk Druid main screen.

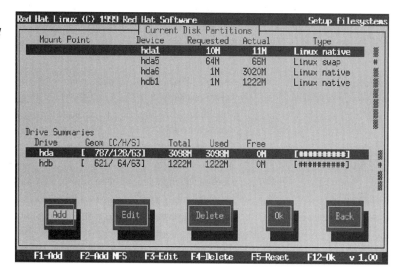

The first section is the current partitions screen, which lists the partitions on the disk and includes information on the mount point, the partition type, the amount of space requested for the partition, the amount of space actually available, and the device name for the partition. By selecting one of these partitions and pressing the Enter key, you bring up a dialog that allows you to edit this information.

The next section is the drive summaries section, which is purely an informational display that shows all of the drives recognized during the installation procedure. The information displayed includes the device name, the geometry in cylinder/head/sector format, the space currently allocated, the total space on the drive, the amount of free space, and a representation of amount of space used.

The bottom section of the Disk Druid screen is the buttons/function key section, which contains buttons to Add, Edit, and Delete partitions, with corresponding function keys. In addition, there is an Ok button to commit changes made and a Back button to return to the prior step in the installation procedure. Two function keys that have no button equivalents are the F5 reset function, and the F2 key for adding mount points for NFS filesystems.

If you need further information on the use of Disk Druid, you can refer to the Red Hat Linux Installation Guide that comes with your Linux distribution, either the book or the online version found in `/usr/doc/rhl-install-guide-en-6.0/manual`.

Filesystem Creation and Management

Now that we have taken a look at disks and partitioning, we can discuss the creation of filesystems and the tools required to maintain them. This section covers the filesystem creation and maintenance utilities, looks at a couple of strategies for allocating space for filesystems, and shows how to estimate growth as your user base expands and your systems grow.

Filesystem Tools

The standard tool for creating filesystems on Linux systems is the `mkfs` command. This utility is actually a front end for several filesystem-specific `mkfs` commands that are named `mkfs.<fstype>`, where `<fstype>` is the filesystem type as you would specify it for the `-t` option of the `mount` command.

mkfs Options Common to All Filesystem Types

There are a number of options that are common to all filesystems that may be created using the `mkfs` command. These options are specified in Table 7.5.

TABLE 7.5 mkfs Options Common to All Filesystems

Option	Description
`-V`	Produces verbose output. This option may be specified more than once, but if it is, it causes the command to display what would have happened, but not to do it.
`-v`	Produces verbose output.
`-t fstype`	Creates a filesystem of the specified type by spawning the `mkfs.<fstype>` command.
`-c`	Checks the device for bad blocks before creating the filesystem on it.
`-l filename`	Reads the list of bad blocks from `filename`.

All other options are passed to the filesystem-specific `mkfs` command. Your Red Hat system comes with three of these commands; one for the second extended filesystem (`mkfs.ext2`), one for the Minix filesystem (`mkfs.minix`), and one for the MS-DOS filesystem (`mkfs.msdos`), each of which has its own set of options.

If no filesystem type is specified to the `mkfs` command using the `-t` option, the default filesystem type is extended type 2, commonly referred to as ext2. There are a number of options for this command detailed in the manual page for `mkfs.ext2`, and the most commonly used options are described in Table 7.6.

TABLE 7.6 mkfs Options Specific to the Extended Type 2 Filesystem

Option	Description
`-b block_size`	Specifies the size of a block in bytes. Defaults to 1024.
`-i bytes_per_inode`	Specifies the bytes/inode ratio. Defaults to 4096.
`-m integer`	Specifies the percentage of the disk space to reserve for use by the root user. Defaults to 5 percent.
`-q`	Runs in quiet mode.
`-v`	Runs in verbose mode.

Balancing these options to get the best performance from your filesystems requires a great deal of thought as to the nature of applications that will be using them. Most often this tuning is a matter of adjusting the block size and the bytes to inode ratio, but may also include reducing the amount of space reserved for the superuser.

Filesystem Repair and Maintenance Using fsck

Once you have created your filesystems, you need to be able to maintain them and to repair them in the event of damage. For this purpose, you use the `fsck` utility. Like the `mkfs` command, `fsck` is a front end that runs filesystem-specific versions of `fsck` and runs them in parallel so as to reduce the amount of time required to bring a system up.

Just like the `mkfs` command, there are a number of command-line options that the front end accepts and the rest are passed to the filesystem-specific version of `fsck`. The options that are accepted by the `fsck` front end are described in Table 7.7.

TABLE 7.7 fsck Command-Line Options

Option	Description
`-A`	Checks all of the filesystems in `/etc/fstab`, starting with the root filesystem. Normally used at system startup.
`-R`	Used with the `-A` option, checks all filesystems except for the root filesystem.
`-T`	Does not display the title on startup.
`-N`	Does not execute, just displays what would have been done.
`-P`	Runs the filesystem check on the root partition in parallel with the other partitions instead of first. Used with the `-A` option.
`-s`	Serializes the filesystem checks instead of running the checks in parallel.
`-V`	Verbose output.

TABLE 7.7 continued

Option	Description
-t fstype	Specifies the filesystem type to check. The fstype you specify is appended to a prefix of "fsck." and the resulting command is executed.

There is an effort underway to standardize the options for the filesystem-specific `fsck` utilities; however, there are still disparities. The options in Table 7.8, however, are common to most of them.

TABLE 7.8 Common `fsck.<fstype>` Options

Option	Description
-a	Assumes a yes answer to all questions. Use with caution.
-r	Interactively repairs the filesystem.

The unified front end to the filesystem checker utility ensures consistent return codes from `fsck`, and this return code can be used in the system initialization scripts to automatically attempt recovery from `fsck` failures. Following is a code snippet from `/etc/rc.d/rc.sysinit` that shows return code handling for `fsck`.

```
if [ ! -f /fastboot ]; then
      STRING="Checking root filesystem"
      echo $STRING
      initlog -c "fsck  -T -a $fsckoptions /"
      rc=$?

      if [ "$rc" = "0" ]; then
            success "$STRING"
            echo
      elif [ "$rc" = "1" ]; then
            passed "$STRING"
            echo
      fi

      # A return of 2 or higher means there were serious problems.
      if [ $rc -gt 1 ]; then
            failure "$STRING"
            echo
            echo
            echo "*** An error occurred during the file system check."
            echo "*** Dropping you to a shell; the system will reboot"
            echo "*** when you leave the shell."
```

```
                    PS1="(Repair filesystem) \#"; export PS1
                    sulogin

                    echo "Unmounting file systems"
                    umount -a
                    mount -n -o remount,ro /
                    echo "Automatic reboot in progress."
                    reboot
            elif [ "$rc" = "1" ]; then
                    _RUN_QUOTACHECK=1
            fi
    fi
```

Interpreting fsck Return Codes

The possible return codes from fsck are broken down into three categories. The first of these is signified by a return code of 0, which means that no filesystem errors were found. The next result category is signified by a return code of 1, which means that filesystem errors were found and corrected. This return code is common if a system fails unexpectedly and the filesystems are not cleanly unmounted. The final result category is signified by a return code of 2 or greater. This level requires manual intervention by the systems administrator in the majority of cases. In the case of the preceding rc.sysinit code, the boot process is halted and the user is prompted to either enter the root password and perform maintenance by hand, or to continue by pressing Ctrl+D. Either way, this can be a bad thing to happen if you are not able to easily access the console. This is the situation that the maintenance root partition described above attempts to alleviate. By replacing the call to sulogin in the rc.sysinit snippet with the following code, the system will reboot itself to the maintenance root, which will give you the opportunity to login remotely and correct the regular root filesystem or any other part of the system that requires it.

```
        # A return of 2 or higher means there were serious problems.
        if [ $rc -gt 1 ]; then
                failure "$STRING"
                echo
                echo
                echo "*** An error occurred during the file system check."
                echo "*** The system will reboot to the maintenence root"
                echo "*** partition unless you press Ctrl-D within 5 sec."

                /sbin/pause 5
                $prc = $?

                if [ $prc -eq 0 ]; then
```

```
              /sbin/lilo -R maint
      else
              sulogin
      fi

      echo "Unmounting file systems"
      umount -a
      mount -n -o remount,ro /
      echo "Automatic reboot in progress."
      reboot
elif [ "$rc" = "1" ]; then
      _RUN_QUOTACHECK=1
fi
```

In this example, the user is given a timeout period during which he can press Ctrl+D to enter a sulogin session. If the user does nothing, lilo is called with an image name that corresponds to the maintenance partition and the system is rebooted. The -R option as well as many other options to lilo that make this type of script possible are covered in Chapter 5, "Starting Up and Shutting Down."

> **Note**
>
> The pause program called in the preceding code sample is a simple C program that takes a number of seconds as an argument and if the user does not press Enter or a control character within the given number of seconds, the program exits with a return code of zero. Pressing Enter or a control character within this given timeout causes the program to exit with a non-zero return code. The source code for the pause program is found in Listing 7.1.

LISTING 7.1   The pause Program (pause.c)

```c
#include <stdio.h>
#include <sys/types.h>
#include <sys/time.h>
#include <fcntl.h>
#include <termios.h>
#include <unistd.h>

int
main(int argc, char** argv)
{
```

LISTING 7.1   continued

```c
    fd_set rset;                    /* used for select() call          */
    struct timeval tv;              /* structure used to set the timeout */
    int retval = 0;                 /* the value returned by select()  */
    int timeout = 30;               /* the default timeout is seconds  */
    int count = 0;                  /* the number of characters pending */
    int val;                        /* FLAGS to set with fcntl         */
    char *buffer;                   /* buffer to hold characters read  */
    struct termios term;            /* used to set noecho mode         */
    struct termios termsave;        /* used to restore terminal state  */

    /* Zero the fd_set and then set a watch on STDIN */
    FD_ZERO(&rset);
    FD_SET(STDIN_FILENO, &rset);

    fprintf(stderr, "argc = %d\n", argc);
    switch (argc) {
        case 1: {
            break;
            }
        case 2: {
            if (isdigit(argv[1][0])) {
                timeout = atoi(argv[1]);
            } else {
                fprintf(stderr, "Usage:  %s [nnn]\n", argv[0]);
                fprintf(stderr, "  where nnn is the number of seconds\n");
                fprintf(stderr, "  to wait for input. (default is 30)\n");
                exit(-1);
            }
            break;
            }
        default: {
            fprintf(stderr, "Usage:  %s [-e] [nnn]\n", argv[0]);
            fprintf(stderr, "  where nnn is the number of seconds\n");
            fprintf(stderr, "  to wait for input. (default is 30)\n");
            exit(-1);
            }
    }


    /* set the timeout for the select call */
    tv.tv_sec = timeout;
    tv.tv_usec = 0;
```

LISTING 7.1   continued

```c
/*
 * Set nonblocking mode for STDIN, so that if the user types anything
 * other than a return or control character, the program won't pause
 * indefinitely.
 */
val = fcntl(STDIN_FILENO, F_GETFL, 0);
val |= O_NONBLOCK;
fcntl(STDIN_FILENO, F_SETFL, val);

/*
 * Set noecho mode for the terminal so that no characters are echoed
 * to the screen while we are waiting.
 */
tcgetattr(STDIN_FILENO, &term);
termsave = term;
term.c_lflag &= ~ECHO;
tcsetattr(STDIN_FILENO, TCSANOW, &term);

retval = select((STDIN_FILENO + 1), &rset, NULL, NULL, &tv);

/*
 * If the user typed a return or a control D character, retval will be
 * non-zero and we can read whatever they typed in to clear the input
 * buffer.  If not, simply flush the buffer.
 */
if (retval) {
    if ((ioctl(STDIN_FILENO, FIONREAD, &count) == 0)) {
        buffer = (char *)malloc(count + 1);
        read(STDIN_FILENO, buffer, count);

        if (buffer[count - 1] == '\n') {
            buffer[count - 1] = '\0';
        }

        /* free buffer before exiting if*/
        free(buffer);
    }
} else {
    tcflush(STDIN_FILENO, TCIOFLUSH);
}
```

LISTING 7.1   continued

```
/* reset the terminal state */
tcsetattr(STDIN_FILENO, TCSANOW, &termsave);

/* Exit with a 1 if retval was set, otherwise exit with a zero. */
exit(retval);
}
```

Accessing Filesystems with mount

We have covered how to partition drives and create filesystems on the created partitions. Now we will look at the utilities for adding and removing them from the filesystem hierarchy: mount and umount. The mount command for Linux is much like that of any other UNIX flavor, with one notable exception. This exception is the ability to allow normal users to mount and umount filesystems. This ability is often granted to allow access to removable media devices, such as floppy drives and CD-ROM drives. This ability is discussed in some detail in Chapter 10, "Managing Removable Media Devices."

The standard form of the mount command takes two arguments. The first of these is the device to mount, such as /dev/hda1, and the second is the directory on which to mount the filesystem. There are of course a number of available command-line options that can affect the behavior of the mount command. Table 7.8 shows the options to the mount command.

TABLE 7.8   mount Command-Line Options

Option	Description
-V	Displays version and exit.
-h	Prints a usage statement and exit.
-v	Executes in verbose mode.
-a	Mounts all filesystems (of the given types) mentioned in fstab.
-F	Forks off a new incarnation of mount for each device.
-f	Causes everything to be done except for the actual system call.
-n	Mounts without writing in /etc/mtab.
-s	Ignores mount options not supported by a filesystem type.
-r	Mounts the filesystem read-only. A synonym is -o ro.
-w	Mounts the filesystem read/write. This is the default. A synonym is -o rw.
-L label	Mounts the partition that has the specified label.
-U uuid	Mounts the partition that has the specified uuid.
-t vfstype	Mounts the filesystem as one of type vfstype. Requires support for that type of filesystem be available in the kernel.

TABLE 7.8 continued

Option	Description
-o	Options are specified with a -o flag followed by a comma-separated string of options. A complete list of available options are found in the mount manual page.

The complete list of options available to the mount command is quite extensive and in addition to the generic options that apply to all filesystem types, there are also numerous filesystem-specific options. Some of the more commonly used options and what they do are described in Table 7.9.

TABLE 7.9 mount Options

Option	Description
async	All I/O to the filesystem should be done asynchronously.
auto	Can be mounted with the -a option.
defaults	Uses default options: rw, suid, dev, exec, auto, nouser, and async.
dev	Interprets character or block special devices on the filesystem.
noatime	Does not update inode access times on this filesystem (for example, for faster access on the news spool to speed up news servers).
noauto	Can only be mounted explicitly (that is, the -a option will not cause the filesystem to be mounted).
nodev	Does not interpret character or block special devices on the filesystem.
noexec	Does not allow execution of any binaries on the mounted filesystem.
nosuid	Does not allow setuid or setgid bits to take effect.
remount	Attempts to remount an already-mounted filesystem.
ro	Mounts the filesystem read-only.
rw	Mounts the filesystem read-write.
sync	All I/O to the filesystem should be done synchronously.
user	Allows an ordinary user to mount the filesystem. This option implies the options noexec, nosuid, and nodev.

The complementary command to the mount command is, of course, the umount command. This command removes a filesystem from the filesystem hierarchy and is invoked with a single argument of either the device file to unmount or the mount point where it is mounted. It should be noted that the Linux umount command is missing one key option that is implemented on most other UNIX flavors. This is the -f option to force the unmounting of a device.

Space Allocation Strategies and Estimating Growth

Space allocation is a problem that all system administrators face and that has no easy answers. However, with planning, and knowledge of how various parts of the Linux filesystem are used, you can successfully allocate space for your filesystems. There are a number of factors to consider when allocating space for filesystems. Some of these factors include

- Does the filesystem contain growth files, such as logs or database files?

- Is the filesystem writable by users like the /home filesystem?

- Is the filesystem one intended for additions to the system like /opt or /usr/local?

- Is the filesystem unlikely to change in the near future?

Answering these questions will help you to identify the filesystems that are likely to require the most disk space. They will also help you to determine the correct strategy to pursue when assigning space to the various partitions that make up your system.

Space Allocation

Consider a typical Linux system connected to a network on which the /home, /usr/local, and /opt filesystems are shared resources that reside on an NFS server. This typical Linux system has a single nine-gigabyte disk drive and is used solely by a single user. In this particular case, since all of the growth filesystems except /var live on the NFS server, we are faced with a decision as to how much space to devote to /var versus the root filesystem and required swap space. The strategy I would employ would be as follows. First, since all of the locally customizable areas are on an NFS server, the data that must be installed on the workstation becomes generic. Therefore, it is of no use to segregate /usr and the root filesystems. I would create a large partition to contain these two hierarchies. For Red Hat Linux 6.1, this requires about one gigabyte, depending on how much extra software you install.

Configuration File Growth and System Package Upgrades

To allow for growth of configuration files and the upgrading of system packages, and to leave a little breathing room, we can give this filesystem half again as much space, for a total of 1.5 gigabytes. Out of the remaining 7.5 gigabytes, 256 megabytes will be allocated to swap space, and 0.75 gigabytes will be used for the /var hierarchy. In addition, /tmp will be removed and replaced with a symbolic link to /var/tmp, thus eliminating a potential problem area from the root filesystem. That still leaves 6.5 gigabytes of space unused. This space can remain unallocated and reserved for future growth; however, I usually like to give the workstation user a space on their home directory to write files. I could give all of the remaining 6.5 gigabytes to the local user, but I would more likely give the user half of the remaining space or about 3.25 gigabytes. This allocation of space allows the user to have a place to download files from the Internet, write his or her Netscape cache directories to, and generally just store junk without cluttering his or her home directories on the NFS servers. This leaves 3.25 gigabytes unallocated, which I would leave alone in the event that there is a need to expand in the future. This ends our discussion of space allocation. We are ready to move on to the filesystem types supported by Linux.

Filesystem Types

One of the primary reasons why Linux makes such a good glue operating system in heterogeneous network environments is that it supports many filesystem types. These include Linux native, such as the extended, extended 2, and xiafs; non-native, such as the MS-DOS, NTFS, and BSD filesystems; and network, such as NFS, SMB, and Coda filesystems. This section looks at some of the most common Linux-native filesystems and discusses when it is appropriate to use each of them.

The Minix Filesystem

The oldest filesystem type supported by Linux is the Minix filesystem. This filesystem is an independent implementation of the filesystem used by the Minix operating system and was chosen initially because Minix was required to bootstrap Linux. The Minix filesystem is still an option in the 2.2 kernels, but it is rarely used. There are a number of reasons for his, including a filename length limitation of 30 characters and a filesystem size limitation of 64 megabytes per filesystem. This is not to say that it is not useful, but with these limitations and other deficiencies, it is not generally used. Some of the places where the Minix filesystem is still useful is on bootable floppy sets, where space is at a premium. This filesystem is also useful if you are creating a temporary ramdisk or if you want to create a filesystem on an ordinary file and mount it via the loop device mechanism.

One of the advantages of using the Minix filesystem is that there is less overhead from the filesystem structures stored on the disk. Another advantage of the Minix filesystem is in speed. The Minix filesystem has less overhead and as a result, many filesystem operations are faster when run against it. The primary disadvantage of the Minix filesystem is the limited filename length.

When customizing your kernel as described in Chapter 35, "Customizing the Linux Kernel," it is usually a wise choice to include support for the Minix filesystem as a module and to use it as the filesystem type for RAM disks, boot floppies, and for your initrd.

The Extended 2 Filesystem

The primary Linux filesystem type used today is the extended 2 filesystem. The extended 2 filesystem is a Linux-native filesystem in that it was created specifically for Linux and was not ported from another operating system. This filesystem does not have the filename limitations or restrictions on filesystem size that the Minix filesystem does, although it does have its own limits. The extended 2 filesystem is a full-featured filesystem type that supports long filenames of up to 256 characters, filesystems sizes of up to two terabytes, and individual files up to two gigabytes. This last limitation is only on the 32-bit versions of Linux, such as the Intel platform, and can be exceeded by applying kernel patches. Naturally, this limit does not apply to the 64-bit version of Linux, such as the Alpha port.

Every kernel you build should include support for the extended 2 filesystem, and the utility of compiling it as a module is questionable. The only exception to this rule might be a kernel built for use only on a boot floppy set, in which case including the extended 2 filesystem as a module could be a space saver that is well worth it.

Other Filesystem Types

In addition to the Minix and extended 2 filesystem types, the Linux 2.0 kernel also included support for the original extended filesystem, and the xia filesystem type. Both of these filesystems are now considered obsolete and support for them was dropped from the 2.2 kernels such as the one that comes with Red Hat Linux 6.1. In addition to these Linux native types, there is also support for a number of other filesystem types. Some of these filesystems are required to support special devices like CD-ROM or DVD drives. Others are filesystems used by other operating systems, including MS-DOS, Windows, Windows NT, and BSD UNIX that you might want to access. There are also network filesystems like the SMB filesystem, NFS, and Coda. Finally, there are specialized filesystems like the proc filesystem and the /dev/pts filesystems required to support specific kernel features. As you can see, there is a wide variety of filesystems supported by Linux with more being added all the time. We are now ready to look at the related topics of space management and quotas.

Space Management and Quotas

One of the most annoying tasks facing a systems administrator is making sure that filesystems do not fill up and that individual users do not use more space than is reasonable in share filesystems such as user home directories. This is an important task for a number of reasons and there are different ways to tackle it, some easier than others and some more popular than others. This section examines this issue and looks at ways to help make the task less onerous by providing monitoring methods. It also examines how quotas can be used to manage filesystems and ensure that your users do not abuse their privileges by filling up filesystems.

Monitoring Space Usage

An easy method of monitoring space usage is with a script that runs df periodically and notifies you if space gets below a user-defined threshold. These scripts can be quite simple, or as the following example demonstrates, much more complex. Listing 7.2 contains a script that I use to monitor disk space usage on a number of systems that I maintain. The script is written in Perl and is intended to be run from a cron job once an hour, or more frequently if you so desire. It uses modules that are readily available with Red Hat Linux or from your local CPAN mirror.

7

Filesystems

LISTING 7.2   checkspace.pl

```perl
#!/usr/bin/perl
#
# $Id: 755907.txt,v 1.5 1999/09/17 11:43:34 tschenk Exp $
#
# checkspace.pl - perl script to check for filesystems that are nearing 100%
#                 utilization

use Sys::Hostname;
use Getopt::Std;
use POSIX;
use strict;
#use vars qw(%FSystemLevels %ENotify %PNotify);

########
# MAIN
########

# -*-perl-*-
# This hash contains the notification levels and is keyed by the hostname
# and filesystem to check.  The filesystems with default as the hostname
# are checked on every host that this script runs on.
my %FSystemLevels = (
    'nomad:/v/v10'    =>    'b:94:97:99',
    'nomad:/v/v12'    =>    'b:94:97:99',
    'quicksilver:/usr/local'    =>    'b:94:97:99',
    'quicksilver:/home'    =>    'b:94:97:99',
```

LISTING 7.2   continued

```perl
    'wizard:/opt'     =>    'i:94:97:99',
    'wizard:/usr/local'    =>    'i:94:97:99',
);


# The list of people to notify by e-mail at each level, separated by colons.
# There should be one entry here for each entry in the FSystemLevels hash
# with a matching key.
my %ENotify = (
    'nomad:/v/v10'    =>    'tschenk:siteops:siteops',
    'nomad:/v/v12'    =>    'tschenk:siteops:siteops',
    'quicksilver:/usr/local'    =>    'tschenk:siteops:siteops',
    'quicksilver:/home'    =>    'tschenk:siteops:siteops',
    'wizard:/opt'    =>    'tschenk:siteops:siteops',
    'wizard:/usr/local'    =>    'tschenk:siteops:siteops',
);


# The list of people to notify by pager at each level, separated by colons.
# There should be one entry here for each entry in the FSystemLevels hash
# with a matching key.
my %PNotify = (
    'nomad:/v/v10' => 'tschenk-page:meb-page:tschenk-page,bmcfarla-page',
    'nomad:/v/v12' => 'tschenk-page:meb-page:tschenk-page,bmcfarla-page',
    'quicksilver:/usr/local' => 'tschenk-page:meb-page:tschenk-page,bmcfarla-page',
    'quicksilver:/home' => 'tschenk-page:meb-page:tschenk-page,bmcfarla-page',
    'wizard:/opt' => 'tschenk-page:meb-page:tschenk-page,bmcfarla-page',
    'wizard:/usr/local' => 'tschenk-page:meb-page:tschenk-page,bmcfarla-page',
);


# Parse the command line options
my %options = &parse_cmd_line;


if (defined($options{Error})) {
    print STDERR "$options{Error}\n";
    &print_usage;
    exit(1);
}


# Perform the checks
my $hostname = hostname();
$hostname =~ s/\.alchemy\.net//;


foreach my $value (keys(%FSystemLevels)) {
```

LISTING 7.2 continued

```perl
    my ($host, $fsystem) = split(/:/, $value);

    if (($host eq $hostname) or ($host eq "default")) {
        &checkspace($hostname, $fsystem, $FSystemLevels{$value},
            $ENotify{$value}, $PNotify{$value});
    }

}

# Exit
exit(0);


##############
# SUBROUTINES
##############
sub print_usage {
    my $USAGE = "Usage: $0 [options]
    where options are:
        -n          Run the script, but don't actually send notifications
        -v          Be verbose in your reporting
        -h          Print this usage statement\n\n";

    print STDERR $USAGE;
}

sub parse_cmd_line {
    my %opts;

    getopts("nvh");

    $opts{Dryrun} = (defined($::opt_n)) ? $::opt_n : 0;
    $opts{Verbose} = (defined($::opt_v)) ? $::opt_v : 0;

    if ((scalar(@ARGV) > 0) || (defined($::opt_h))) {
        &print_usage;
        exit(1);
    }

    return %opts;
}

sub checkspace {
```

LISTING 7.2   continued

```perl
my $host = shift;
my $fs = shift;
my $levelstr = shift;
my $emailstr = shift;
my $pagestr = shift;

my @levels = split(/:/, $levelstr);
my $checktype = undef;
my @email = split(/:/, $emailstr);
my @pager = split(/:/, $pagestr);

$levels[0] == "i" ? $checktype = "-i" : $checktype = undef;
shift @levels;

my $level;
for ($level = (scalar(@levels) - 1); $level >= 0; $level--) {
    if ($options{Verbose}) {
        print "Checking space on $fs.\n";
    }

    my $used = `df $checktype $fs | tail -1 | awk '{print \$5}' |
        ➥sed -e 's/%//1'`;
    chomp $used;
    my $fsname = $fs;
    $fsname =~ tr/\///_/;
    my $lockfile = "/tmp/checkspace" . $fsname . "_" . $levels[$level]
        . ".lock";

    if (-f $lockfile) {
        if ($used < $levels[$level]) {
            if ($options{Dryrun}) {
                print "Removing lockfile $lockfile.\n";
            } else {
                unlink($lockfile);
            }
        } else {
            last;
        }
    } else {
        if ($used >= $levels[$level]) {
            open(LOCKFILE, ">$lockfile");
            print LOCKFILE $$;
```

LISTING 7.2 continued

```perl
                close(LOCKFILE);
                if ($email[$level] ne "none") {
                    &notify_email($hostname,$fs,$level,$used,$email[$level]);
                }
                if ($pager[$level] ne "none") {
                    &notify_pager($hostname,$fs,$level,$used,$pager[$level]);
                }
                last;
            }
        }
    }
}

sub notify_email {
    my $host = shift;
    my $fs = shift;
    my $level = shift;
    my $used = shift;
    my $recipients = shift;

    my @subjstr = ("[WARNING]", "[CRITICAL]", "[CRISIS]");

    my $msg = `df $fs`;

    if ($options{Verbose}) {
        print "Sending e-mail notification to $recipients.\n";
    }
    if (!$options{Dryrun}) {
        open(SENDMAIL, "|/usr/sbin/sendmail $recipients");
        print SENDMAIL <<EOF;
Subject: $subjstr[$level] $host:$fs $used\% full

Notification from checkspace.pl:

$msg

EOF
        close(SENDMAIL);
    } else {
        print "$msg\n";
    }
}
```

7

Filesystems

LISTING 7.2 continued

```perl
sub notify_pager {
    my $host = shift;
    my $fs = shift;
    my $level = shift;
    my $used = shift;
    my $recipients = shift;

    my @subjstr = ("[WARNING]", "[CRITICAL]", "[CRISIS]");

    if ($options{Verbose}) {
        print "Sending pager notification to $recipients.\n";
    }
    if (!$options{Dryrun}) {
        open(SENDMAIL, "¦/usr/sbin/sendmail $recipients");
        print SENDMAIL <<EOF;
Notification from checkspace.pl:  $subjstr[$level] $host:$fs $used\% full

EOF
        close(SENDMAIL);
    } else {
        print "$subjstr[$level] $host:$fs $used\% full\n";
    }
}
```

This script is quite flexible and contains provisions for two notification methods, paging and email, based on three levels of usage. In addition, you can have the script check for inode exhaustion instead of disk block consumption and by tweaking the configuration parameters, you can eliminate one of the notification methods.

Local Versus Shared Filesystems

Another facet of managing disk space is the decision on which filesystems to share on the network and which to keep local. The extreme case of this is the diskless workstation, in which all files are physically located on a network server and the workstation is booted from a floppy or bootrom. At the other extreme is the standalone workstation that is network connected, but that shares no filesystems at all. However, the most common situation is somewhere in between, in which filesystems such as /opt, /usr/local, and /usr/share are located on a network file server and shared between systems.

You may wonder what network filesystems have to do with managing space. The answer is that shared filesystems reduce the administrative overhead of managing disk space by reducing the number of systems on which you have to worry about filling up disks or having room to expand. For information on setting up shared filesystem resources, refer to Chapter 15, "Sharing Resources (Print and File Services)."

Establishing Filesystem Quotas

One method of managing disk space on your servers is through the use of filesystem quotas. Most users cringe at the thought of quotas because they feel that they are an unnecessary restriction designed to make their lives more difficult. On the other hand, many systems administrators feel that quotas are a necessary part of filesystem management. The inconvenience to users is a small price to pay for the peace of mind that you get knowing that no one user can hog all of the space on a filesystem.

Quotas come in two basic flavors under Linux: user level quotas and group level quotas. To use quotas on your Linux systems, you must first enable support for them in your kernel configuration and be aware that quotas only work for the extended 2 filesystem type. Therefore, you must answer yes to the quota support question when configuring your kernel and to the extended 2 filesystem. Red Hat Linux includes the tools required to take advantage of this kernel support, but if you want to build them yourself or see if a new version exists, you can retrieve the latest quota tools from ftp.funet.fi at `ftp://ftp.funet.fi/pub/Linux/PEOPLE/Linus/subsystems/quota/all.tar.gz`. This toolset consists of five utilities whose purpose is described in Table 7.10.

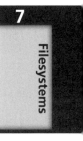

TABLE 7.10   Quota Utilities

Utility	Description
quotaon	Turns on quota accounting.
quotaoff	Turns off quota accounting.
quotacheck	Scans the filesystem for current disk usage and updates the `quota.user` and `quota.group` files with the most recent usage statistics.
repquota	Generates a formatted report of disk space usage.
edquota	Utility to alter user or group quotas.

Once you have enabled quota support in your kernel and made sure that you have the quota tools installed, you may now start setting up quotas. Before getting into the implementation details, the following sections review some concepts used when discussing quotas that need to be understood in order to effectively use them.

Understanding the Concept of Quotas

The first concept to understand is that of quotas themselves and what implementing quotas means. Filesystem quotas are a mechanism by which a user or a group of users is limited in the amount of space that they can use in a particular filesystem. Basically, the amount of space they use is monitored and if it exceeds their allocation, they are first given a warning. If they continue to exceed the quota, they are no longer permitted to add files to the filesystem.

Hard and Soft Limits

This brings us to the concept of limits. There are two types of limits concerning quotas. The first of these two types is a soft limit, which is the amount of disk space allocated to a user on a particular filesystem. If no grace period is allowed, this is an absolute limit and users are not allowed to exceed it. If you allow a grace period, which is a time period that users are allowed to exceed their quota, the soft limit becomes a borderline at which users are warned that they are exceeding their quota. They are allowed to exceed this quota for the grace period, with one caveat: the hard limit. The hard limit is the absolute limit that a user is cannot exceed if a grace period is defined. Finally, you should also remember that quotas can be set on either individual user accounts or on a group, and that the information on the user and group quotas are stored in files at the root of a filesystem called `quota.user` and `quota.group`.

Implementing Quotas

With these concepts in mind, let's take a look at implementing quotas on a system. This will involve a number of steps, starting with modifications to the system initialization scripts. Red Hat by default includes support for quotas, and the modifications to the system initialization scripts to support quotas are already in place. There are three parts of the `/etc/rc.d/rc.sysinit` script involved in checking quotas. The first stanza as shown following runs quotacheck against the root partition to update the quota.user and quota.group files.

```
# Update quotas if fsck was run on /.
if [ X"$_RUN_QUOTACHECK" = X1 -a -x /sbin/quotacheck ]; then
        action "Checking root filesystem quotas"  /sbin/quotacheck -v /
fi
```

This code checks only the root filesystem. Once this has been done, and after the other local filesystems have been mounted and checked for consistency, a similar command is run for the remaining filesystems as shown in this next code block.

```
        elif [ "$rc" = "1" -a -x /sbin/quotacheck ]; then
                action "Checking filesystem quotas" /sbin/quotacheck -v -R -a
        fi
```

In this code example, quotacheck is called with the -a and -R options, which signifies that the command should be run against all filesystems with quotas mentioned in the /etc/fstab file with the exception of the root filesystem. Once quotacheck has been run, it is time to turn on the quota accounting as shown in the following stanza from rc.sysinit.

```
if [ -x /sbin/quotaon ]; then
    action "Turning on user and group quotas for local filesystems" \
    /sbin/quotaon -a
fi
```

This invocation of quotaon indicates that it should be run against all filesystems with quotas as defined in the /etc/fstab. How do you define filesystems with quotas in /etc/fstab? Well, here is a sample that shows first a filesystem, /home, on which user level quotas are active, another, /v/00, on which group quotas are active, and a third, /usr/local, on which both user and group quotas are active.

```
/dev/hda3    /home        ext2    defaults,usrquota             1 1
/dev/hda5    /vol/00      ext2    defaults,grpquota             1 1
/dev/hda7    /usr/local   ext2    defaults,usrquota,grpquota    1 1
```

Having set up the /etc/fstab file, we are now ready to create the quota.user and quota.group files for each filesystem. Continuing the example as shown in the /etc/fstab file, we would need to issue the following commands as root in order to do this:

```
for f in /home /vol/00 /usr/local; do
    cd $f
    touch quota.user
    touch quota.group
    chmod 600 quota.{user,group}
    cd -
done
```

The next step is to reboot your system to test that the startup scripts do the correct thing. Once the system is back up and running again, you are ready to proceed with setting up the user and group limits as you desire.

The command used to set the limits for users is the edquota command. This command is found on your Red Hat system in /usr/sbin. There are not a lot of options to edquota, but the options and their uses are shown in Table 7.11.

TABLE 7.11   edquota Options

Options	Description
-u	Edits the user quota of the specified user.
-g	Edits the group quota of the specified group.
-p prototype_user	Uses the quotas of prototype_user as the default for specified users.
-t	Edits the soft limits for each filesystem. The default values for the soft limits are found in the quota.h file in /usr/include/ linux.

Some Option Examples

Although knowing the options is important, it is usually much more useful to see some examples. In the following example, we will continue the same example that we began earlier in the chapter and set up the quotas on /usr/local and /vol/00. In the first example, we will run the edquota command with the -g option against /vol/00 for the group cdwriter. This filesystem is one on which users are allowed to store anything that would be unreasonable to keep in their home directory, and on my systems is also a space where audio files can be stored until they are written to a CD-RW drive.

```
[root@wizard /root]# edquota -g cdwriter
```

This command results in the current disk usage being calculated for the user specified along with their quota limits being read from the file and displayed in an editor something like this:

```
Quotas for group cdwriter:
/dev/hda7: blocks in use: 497, limits (soft = 10000, hard = 15000)
        inodes in use: 1, limits (soft = 2500, hard = 3000)
/dev/hda2: blocks in use: 169569, limits (soft = 300000, hard = 305000)
        inodes in use: 31, limits (soft = 7500, hard = 8000)
```

As you can see from this example, the cdwriter group is limited to using 10,000 blocks on /dev/hda7 (/usr/local), of which it is currently using 497 blocks. In addition, on /dev/hda2 (/opt), members of this group are restricted to an additional 300,000 blocks. Now let's take a look at the grace periods that have been defined. This is done using the edquota command with the -g and -t options in combination. In this case, an edit session is started with the editor defined in the EDITOR environment variable.

```
Time units may be: days, hours, minutes, or seconds
Grace period before enforcing soft limits for users:
/dev/hda7: block grace period: 7 days, file grace period: 7 days
```

In each event, the quota information is retrieved from the kernel and then transformed into a readable format. To change the quota information, you simply edit the file, changing the numbers as desired. When you save the file, the information is parsed, translated back into the kernels format, and stored in the `quota.group` file at the root of the filesystem.

The final thing that you should do is to periodically run the quotacheck command to keep the quota information up to date. This can be accomplished by creating a cron job that runs the quotacheck, probably at least once per month. Something like the following would suffice:

```
0 2 * * *      /sbin/quotacheck -augv
```

This crontab entry is not included by Red Hat by default, even though they provide everything else you need to run quotas on your system. The important thing to remember when considering whether or not to implement quotas is to take your time and consider whether the administrative overhead of setting up quotas is more expensive than the time spent worrying about and managing filesystems that are filling up. As someone who was on the receiving end of pages regarding filesystems filling up at 3:00 a.m., you can guess where my vote would be cast.

Summary

In this chapter, we have looked at several topics, starting with partition schemes and the tools used to partition disks. We also discussed a couple of different strategies on how the disk should be partitioned. The creation and maintenance of filesystems was covered and finally, space management techniques were covered, including a discussion of filesystem quotas. A couple of additional sources of information related to these topics include the Filesystem Hierarchy Standard, which discusses space allocation issues and how they recommend that disks be partitioned to hold a Linux filesystem, and the Quota mini-howto. These documents can be found on the Internet at the following URLs:

Filesystem Hierarchy Standard: `http://www.pathname.com/fhs/2.0/fhs-toc.html`

Quota Mini-Howto: `http://linuxdoc.org/HOWTO/mini/Quota.html`

Adding or Replacing Disks

In This Chapter

- IDE Device Naming   *212*
- Managing the `/etc/fstab` File   *214*
- SCSI Concerns   *217*
- Other Devices   *225*

CHAPTER 8

Whether you are building a new server or upgrading an existing one, disk storage is likely to play a major role in the administration of your Linux server.

In the past decade, disk storage costs have dropped in price from dollars to pennies per megabyte. As storage has become more affordable, applications have begun to take advantage of larger amounts of storage for their program files and data. Linux server applications are no exception to this rule, and tend to use more storage resources than other applications because they typically service multiple users.

This chapter discusses the basics of adding or replacing hard disks on your Linux server system. It starts by describing the Integrated Drive Electronics (IDE) interface and its configuration under Linux. It then moves on to the more advanced Small Computer System Interface (SCSI) and discusses its complex hardware requirements and Linux configuration.

IDE Device Naming

IDE hard disk drives are among the most common hard disk drives available today. IDE disks are available with capacities in excess of 24 gigabytes (GB) and can provide the massive amounts of storage required for modern servers. In addition, their cost per megabyte of storage is extremely low as compared with competing non-linear storage technologies.

IDE Disk Device Interface

The interface to IDE disk devices takes the form of block device files, which are stored in the /dev directory. Red Hat Linux v6.0 comes with 136 IDE device files already created in the /dev directory. The filename of each device is made up of three parts—a prefix, a drive device specification, and an optional partition number (see Figure 8.1). IDE disk devices begin with the prefix hd. The next part of the device filename refers to the drive itself. IDE disk interfaces have the capability of supporting up to two disks (a Master and a Slave) per IDE channel. The IDE specification does not allow more than four IDE channels to be installed in a system, limiting the system to a maximum of eight IDE devices. Most modern motherboards have IDE controllers built onto them, usually with two channels, allowing up to four devices without adding any additional controller cards. Table 8.1 shows the standard naming conventions for IDE devices.

FIGURE 8.1
Linux IDE device interface file naming scheme.

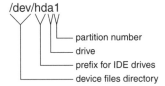

/dev/hda1

— partition number
— drive
— prefix for IDE drives
— device files directory

TABLE 8.1 Linux IDE Device Interface Filenames

IDE Controller Channel	Master/ Slave	IDE Device Name
1	Master	hda
1	Slave	hdb
2	Master	hdc
2	Slave	hdd
3	Master	hde
3	Slave	hdf
4	Master	hdg
4	Slave	hdh

These device names refer to the whole disk, or entire CD-ROM. Quite often it is necessary to specify a particular partition on the IDE device (for instance, when mounting that partition). IDE device partitions are specified by appending the partition name onto the disk device name. For example, the first partition on the Master IDE drive on the first controller would be named hda1. Refer to Table 8.2 for more examples of IDE device naming.

TABLE 8.2 Sample Device Interface Filenames for IDE Partitions

Device Name	Specified Device
hda1	First partition, Master IDE drive on IDE port 1
hdd3	Third partition, Slave IDE drive on IDE port 2
hdc2	Second Partition, Master IDE drive on IDE port 2
hdb16	Sixteenth Partition, Slave IDE drive on IDE port 1

The significance of the disk partition numbers varies based on the hardware architecture. On Intel hardware architectures, Linux partitions 1 through 4 are primary partitions and partition numbers of 5 and greater are logical partitions. In any case, it is generally necessary to specify the partition whenever your operation is applicable to only one of the partitions on the disk.

IDE hard disk drives, IDE CD-ROM drives, Iomega IDE Zip drives, and other IDE devices all share the same naming scheme under Linux. If you have a drive interface that uses older drive controller technologies such as MFM or RLL, drives connected to these controllers will use the same device file naming scheme as IDE drives.

8

Adding or Replacing Disks

If the device file you need doesn't exist in the /dev directory, refer to the information in Chapter 4, "Where Do I Find...?", on the Device Naming Scheme and the Major and Minor Numbers for devices to create your own IDE device files.

The next section discusses the system configuration of these IDE devices under Linux.

Managing the /etc/fstab File

The /etc/fstab file contains descriptive information about the filesystems available to the Linux system and the devices that each filesystem corresponds to. Each filesystem is described on a separate line in the file.

/etc/fstab File Format

Each line in the fstab file consists of six fields: file device name or remote filesystem, mount point, filesystem type, mount options, dump designation, and fsck pass number. The file device name is simply the name of the device file that the filesystem represents (for example, /dev/hda3). The mount point indicates the default location in the directory tree where the filesystem will be mounted (for example, /home). The filesystem type tells the mount utilities what filesystem is contained on the specified device (for example, ext2). The next field contains options that are used when the filesystem is mounted. These options, which form a comma-separated list, may include any valid mount(8) option. Refer to Table 8.3 for a list of the most commonly used mount options (additional mount options can be found by looking at the mount(8) man page). You should also note that certain filesystems have their own sets of unique options that can be applied at mount time. The dump designation field is used by the dump(8) command to determine whether the filesystem needs to be dumped (field is 1) or does not need to be dumped (field is 0).

The last field in the fstab file, thefsck pass number, is used by the fsck(8) command to determine the order in which filesystems will be checked at boot time. At boot, fsck is run by the system initialization scripts to check the filesystem(s) for errors. The pass number setting allows the administrator to specify that fsck should run on a particular filesystem first, in parallel, or not at all. Correctly specifying this parameter will ensure disk integrity while minimizing the time required to fsck the system at boot-time. The root filesystem should always be set to 1, which specifies that it should be checked first. Other important filesystems (/usr, /home, and so on) should have a setting of 2, which allows them to be checked in parallel by fsck, after the root filesystem has been checked. Filesystems that are removable (such as those on a CD-ROM or JAZ drive) should be set to 0, which ensures that they will not be checked by fsck at boot-time.

TABLE 8.3 Commonly Used `mount(8)` Options

Option	Description
async	Filesystem I/O should be performed asynchronously
auto	Automatically mounts this filesystem at boot
defaults	Default options: `async`, `auto`, `dev`, `exec`, `nouser`, and `rw`
dev	Interprets character or block devices on the system
noauto	Only mounts explicitly (does not mount at boot)
nouser	Does not allow users to mount/unmount this filesystem
ro	Read-only
rw	Read-write
noexec	Does not allow execution of any files on this filesystem
user	Allows users to mount/unmount this filesystem

Dissecting a Filesystem Configuration File (`/etc/fstab`)

One way to more fully understand the Filesystem Configuration File is to dissect a real `/etc/fstab` file line by line. The following is a sample `/etc/fstab` file and a line-by-line dissection of its contents. The line numbers are for reference only; they are not part of the file.

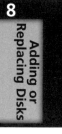

```
1:    /dev/hda1     /             ext2      defaults     1 1
2:    /dev/hda2     /usr          ext2      defaults     0 2
3:    /dev/hda3     /home         ext2      defaults     0 2
4:    /dev/hda4     swap          swap      defaults     0 0
5:    /dev/fd0      /mnt/floppy   ext2      noauto       0 0
6:    /dev/cdrom    /mnt/cdrom    iso9660   noauto,ro    0 0
7:    none          /proc         proc      defaults     0 0
```

Line 1: `/dev/hda1`

The first line of the file contains the designation for the root, or "/", mount point and specifies that `/dev/hda1` contains an `ext2` filesystem, is to be mounted with the default settings, needs to be dumped, and should be checked (via `fsck`) at boot.

Line 2: `/dev/hda2`

This line contains the designation for the `/usr` partition and specifies that `/dev/hda2` contains an `ext2` filesystem, is to be mounted with the default settings, does not need to be dumped, and does not need to be checked via `fsck` at boot.

Line 3: /dev/hda3

This line contains the same settings as Line 2, but specifies that the /dev/hda3 device be mounted at the /home mount point.

Line 4: /dev/hda4

This partition contains information about the swap filesystem and is enabled using the swapon(8) command rather than the mount(8) command. The swapon command is generally called by the system's initialization scripts and is not utilized by the system administrator. Most Linux servers have at least one swap partition.

Line 5: Floppy Disk

This line of the /etc/fstab file specifies that the floppy disk device (/dev/fd0) be mounted at /mnt/floppy and is of type ext2. It is common practice to change this filesystem specification, which is the default under Red Hat Linux, to type vfat. This will allow the mounting of Microsoft Windows (and DOS) disks by default. The noauto mount option on this line specifies that the disk should not be mounted automatically at boot time. Having the floppy drive mounted at boot time wouldn't make much sense because most of the time you probably won't have any disks inserted in the floppy drive at boot time. However, by making this entry in the fstab file, system administrators can mount a floppy with the abbreviated mount /mnt/floppy command (no additional options need to be specified).

Line 6: CD-ROM

This line serves a similar purpose to the Floppy Disk entry. The primary difference between these two entries is the filesystem type (iso9660 refers to the ISO 9660 CD-ROM filesystem specification) and the additional option ro. The ro option is short for read-only and designates that the filesystem should be mounted read-only, as you would expect for a CD-ROM. Note that the device specification, /dev/cdrom, is likely to be a symbolic link to the real CD-ROM device (typically an IDE device, such as /dev/hdb, or a SCSI device, such as /dev/scd0).

Line 7: Proc Filesystem

The final line of the fstab file doesn't specify a device at all, but rather a special kind of filesystem called the /proc filesystem. The /proc filesystem provides an interface to internal data structures in the kernel. This filesystem can be invaluable in writing scripts and applications that monitor (or analyze) kernel runtime data. Kernel data structures are generally viewable in a standard file format (although the structures are not files at all, but memory locations in kernel memory space).

With the basics of the /etc/fstab configuration out of the way, the next section begins to look into SCSI filesystems and their configuration.

SCSI Concerns

As a server's storage needs increase, the use of high-performance SCSI hard disk drives becomes more appealing. Generally speaking, SCSI (pronounced "scuzzy") disks are designed and manufactured for the server-class computing market. While more and more high-end desktops are being built with SCSI hard disks, SCSI still remains a predominantly server-class component. Hard disks using the SCSI interface are generally available in larger capacities than their IDE counterparts and generally have faster spindle speeds (the speed at which the hard disk platters themselves spin).

Why Choose SCSI?

There are a number of factors that make SCSI the ideal choice for servers. The SCSI interface allows disk access operations (reads, writes, and so on) to occur in parallel across all of the devices connected to the SCSI controller card making it the ideal choice for multitasking Linux server environments. When a server has multiple users (or multiple services) that need access to different parts of a disk, or different disks in the system, SCSI allows commands to be queued and executed in parallel. Most SCSI host adapters have on-board processors that offload storage processing from the system's CPU(s). This frees up the system to work on other things while the data is stored (or retrieved) from the storage devices. Most IDE controllers are on the motherboard and use the system's processor(s) to handle all of their data storage/retrieval operations. SCSI also permits a larger number of devices to be connected than IDE allows.

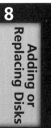

SCSI Chains

The set of devices attached to a particular SCSI controller is often referred to as the *SCSI chain* or *SCSI channel* (see Figure 8.2). Different SCSI technologies provide different capabilities. Narrow SCSI chains can contain up to seven devices (really eight devices, but the SCSI controller itself counts as a device). A newer version of SCSI, Wide SCSI, allows up to 15 devices (16 minus one for the controller) on a single SCSI chain. Currently available SCSI technologies offer disk transfer rates as high as 80MB/sec. Some modern SCSI host adapters are capable of supporting two or more SCSI channels, each with a seven or 15 device capacity.

FIGURE 8.2
Diagram of a SCSI chain.

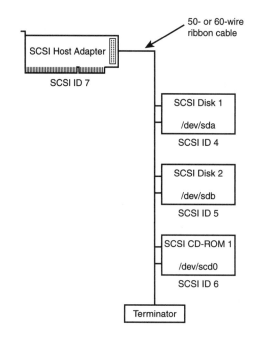

TABLE 8.4 SCSI Technologies and Capabilities

	SCSI 1	*SCSI 2*	*Ultra SCSI*	*Utra2 SCSI*
Bus Width	8-bit	8-bit (Fast) 16-bit (FastWide)	8-bit (Ultra) 16-bit (UltraWide)	16-bit
Data Transfer Rate	10MB/sec	10MB/sec (Fast) 20MB/sec (FastWide)	20MB/sec (Ultra) 40MB/sec (UltraWide)	80MB/sec
Number of Devices Per Channel	7	7 (Fast) 15 (FastWide)	7 (Ultra) 15 (UltraWide)	15

Selecting a Controller

The first hardware decision to make after deciding to use SCSI drives in your system is choosing the SCSI host adapter. The choice of which host adapter is best is almost as much of a religious war as the choice of the operating system itself. Although several controllers are used extensively in the Linux community, there are two particular brands that are most popular: Mylex and Adaptec. Mylex (BusLogic), now owned by IBM, was one of the first

SCSI hardware manufacturers to fully embrace Linux by providing fully supported Linux drivers for their cards. Because of the high quality of their cards and their reliable driver support, these cards are highly recommended for use under Linux. The second most popular brand of SCSI cards is Adaptec—not due to their official support of Linux (of which there was none until recently), but rather due to their popularity in the hardware market. Until recently, Adaptec refused to divulge the hardware information required to write drivers for their SCSI cards. Without this information, Linux developers reverse-engineered the devices and built some of the most stable drivers in the Linux kernel. Most Adaptec SCSI host adapters are now well supported under Linux.

Supported SCSI Devices

Red Hat groups hardware into four categories of support ranging from fully supported and reliable to incompatible. Table 8.5 lists those SCSI devices that are fully supported by Red Hat and are considered "Tier 1 Supported" devices. The controllers on this list have been tested by Red Hat for use with Red Hat Linux v6.0 and are fully compatible with the operating system. For an exhaustive list of the SCSI controllers officially supported by Red Hat Linux v6.0, refer to the "Red Hat Linux Hardware Compatibility List for Intel/6.0."

LISTING 8.5   Red Hat Tier 1 Supported SCSI Controllers

```
Mylex (a.k.a. BusLogic) MultiMaster and FlashPoint adapters

    FlashPoint Series PCI Host Adapters:
            FlashPoint LT (BT-930) Ultra SCSI-3,
            FlashPoint LT (BT-930R) Ultra SCSI-3
              with RAIDPlus,
            FlashPoint LT (BT-920) Ultra SCSI-3
              (BT-930 without BIOS),
            FlashPoint DL (BT-932) Dual Channel
              Ultra SCSI-3,
            FlashPoint DL (BT-932R) Dual Channel
              - Ultra SCSI-3 with RAIDPlus,
            FlashPoint LW (BT-950R) Wide Ultra
              SCSI-3 with RAIDPlus,
            FlashPoint DW (BT-952) Dual Channel
              Wide Ultra SCSI-3,
            FlashPoint DW (BT-952R) Dual Channel
              Wide Ultra-SCSI-3 with RAIDPlus;

    MultiMaster "W" Series Host Adapters:
            BT-948 PCI Ultra SCSI-3,
            BT-958 PCI Wide Ultra SCSI-3,
```

8

**Adding or
Replacing Disks**

LISTING 8.5   continued

```
                BT-958D PCI Wide Differential Ultra SCSI-3;

        MultiMaster "C" Series Host Adapters:
                BT-946C PCI Fast SCSI-2,
                BT-956C PCI Wide Fast SCSI-2,
                BT-956CD PCI Wide Differential Fast SCSI-2,
                BT-445C VLB Fast SCSI-2,
                BT-747C EISA Fast SCSI-2,
                BT-757C EISA Wide Fast SCSI-2,
                BT-757CD EISA Wide Differential Fast SCSI-2,
                BT-545C ISA Fast SCSI-2,
                BT-540CF ISA Fast SCSI-2;

        MultiMaster "S" Series Host Adapters:
                BT-445S VLB Fast SCSI-2,
                BT-747S EISA Fast SCSI-2,
                BT-747D EISA Differential Fast SCSI-2,
                BT-757S EISA Wide Fast SCSI-2,
                BT-757D EISA Wide Differential Fast SCSI-2,
                BT-545S ISA Fast SCSI-2,
                BT-542D ISA Differential Fast SCSI-2,
                BT-742A EISA SCSI-2 (742A revision H),
                BT-542B ISA SCSI-2 (542B revision H);

        MultiMaster "A" Series Host Adapters:
                BT-742A EISA SCSI-2 (742A revisions A - G),
                BT-542B ISA SCSI-2 (542B revisions A - G);
                some AMI FastDisk Host Adapters

Advansys
        ABP510, ABP5150, ABP5140, ABP5142,
        ABP902, ABP915, ABP920, ABP930, ABP930U,
        ABP930UA, ABP960, ABP960U, ABP542,
        ABP742, ABP842, ABP940, ABP940U,
        ABP940UA, ABP970, ABP970U, ABP940UW,
        ABP970UW, ABP752, ABP852, ABP950,
        ABP950UW, ABP980, ABP980U, ABP980UA

Adaptec
        AHA-274x - EISA,  AHA-284x - VLB,
        AHA-29xx - PCI,
        AHA-394x - PCI, AHA-398x - PCI RAID,
```

LISTING **8.5**   continued

```
    AHA-274x, AHA-274xT, AHA-2842,
    AHA-2910B, AHA-2920C, AHA-2930/U/U2,
    AHA-2940/W/U/UW/AU/U2W/U2/U2B/U2BOEM,
    AHA-2944D/WD/UD/UWD,
    AHA-2950U2/W/B,
    AHA-3940/U/W/UW/AUW/U2W/U2B,
    AHA-3950U2D, AHA-3985/U/W/UW,
    AIC-777x, AIC-785x,  AIC-786x,
    AIC-787x, AIC-788x , AIC-789x,
    AIC-3860

ICP Disk Array Controller
    GDT6111RP, GDT6121RP, GDT6511RP, GDT6521RP, GDT5117RP, GDT6127RP,
    GDT6517RP, GDT6527RP, GDT6537RP, GDT6557RP
```

Note

Many other SCSI adapters are supported as either Tier 2 or Tier 3 Support devices, or through third-party patches. Check the Red Hat Web site for updated hardware compatibility information.

Cabling Requirements

SCSI cabling problems are the number one cause of problems when installing SCSI systems. It is well worth the added expense of buying high-quality SCSI cables and ensuring that the SCSI specifications are followed when connecting cables. SCSI cabling requirements vary greatly among the different SCSI technologies. Consult the User's Manual for your SCSI adapter to ensure that your SCSI cable(s) are of sufficient quality and compliant with your card's requirements. These requirements include the maximum length of SCSI chain cabling, the maximum number of devices on a chain, and the type of termination required (see Table 8.6). The maximum length of the cabling becomes more important when connecting external SCSI devices to the chain.

TABLE 8.6   Maximum Cable Lengths for Various SCSI Technologies

Maximum Chain Length Technology	Speed	Passive Termination	Active Termination
SCSI 2	10MB/sec	3m	25m
Ultra	20MB/sec	1.5m	25m
Ultra2	40MB/sec	n/a	12m

Note

The Ultra2 SCSI standard specifies that only active termination be used for Ultra2 SCSI chains.

Device Termination and SCSI IDs

If cabling problems are the most likely cause of SCSI problems, SCSI device termination and ID settings are a close second. Taking the time to properly set the device numbering and terminate the SCSI bus correctly will eliminate the need for a large amount of troubleshooting down the road.

SCSI termination and SCSI device numbering are really quite simple. SCSI uses a bus architecture that runs through all of the SCSI devices and the host adapter. This bus was referred to earlier as the SCSI chain or SCSI channel. The bus usually consists of a single SCSI cable (or several, daisy-chained cables) that is terminated with a passive (or active) terminator on one end, connected to the SCSI host adapter on the other end, and connected to all the devices in between. Each SCSI device has a SCSI ID that distinguishes it from the other devices on the chain. Because the device ID is set on the device itself, the hardware technician must ensure that each device is set to a unique SCSI ID. Different devices have different methods of setting the SCSI ID, but the range of IDs is from 0 through 7 for Narrow SCSI and 0 through 15 for Wide SCSI. Generally, the SCSI controller itself is configured to SCSI ID 7, leaving the other IDs available for devices. The order of the SCSI IDs generally indicates the boot order of the devices, and the naming of the device files (for example, sda and so on).

Passive and Active SCSI Terminators

SCSI termination is required to prevent reflections at either end of the SCSI bus. A SCSI terminator can take one of two forms: passive or active. A passive terminator consists of a pair of resistors that serve to end the bus. An active terminator consists of a pair of resistors that are connected to a common regulated power supply. The differences in the allowable

SCSI bus lengths for different SCSI technologies in Table 8.6 show how the decision of which type of terminator to use affects the capabilities of the chain. Some devices may provide internal auto-termination capabilities, eliminating the need for external termination. Because this auto-termination varies from device to device, and may not be fully compatible with all SCSI host adapters, check your owner's manuals before enabling this feature.

Once the cabling requirements have been determined, the drives need to be connected to one another and to the host adapter to form the SCSI chain. Internal devices (devices within the main server cabinet) are generally connected with a long SCSI ribbon-cable with a terminator on one end and the host adapter on the other (refer to Figure 8.2). External devices may be a bit more confusing because they are generally connected in a daisy-chain fashion and terminated at the last SCSI device chassis (see Figure 8.3). Note that large-capacity SCSI device cabinets, especially hardware RAID cabinets, are generally terminated internally and do not require additional termination. Check your device cabinet owner's manual for the specific requirements of your hardware.

FIGURE 8.3

Daisy-chaining of external SCSI devices.

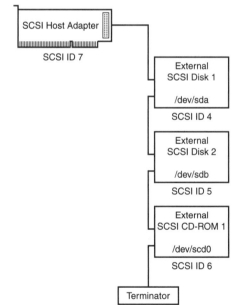

SCSI Device Naming

SCSI disk devices are named using a similar naming scheme to that of IDE disks. All SCSI disk devices begin with the prefix `sd` (SCSI disk) and are stored in the `/dev` directory.

Red Hat Linux v6.0 comes with 256 SCSI device files (the first 16 SCSI disks) already created in the /dev directory. The next part of the device name refers to the physical drive device that the device file refers to. For disk numbers greater then 26, two letters are used to designate the physical disk (sdaa, sdab, and so on through sddx). Generally, the first disk device on the SCSI chain is sda, the second is sdb, and so on. As with IDE devices, specific partitions of SCSI devices are specified by appending the partition number to the device file name (for example, /dev/sda4 is the fourth partition of the first SCSI disk). SCSI devices may have up to 15 partitions (numbered 1-15) per device.

Unlike IDE CD-ROM devices, SCSI CD-ROM devices follow a slightly different naming convention than SCSI hard disks. SCSI CD-ROMs are designated by the prefix scd, followed by the CD-ROM drive number (for example, /dev/scd0 is the first SCSI CD-ROM device). CD-ROM filesystems do not have partitions, so no partition number is appended to the device name. Note that on some older Linux systems, the device prefix for SCSI CD-ROMs is sr.

Because SCSI controllers may have multiple channels on each controller, and many SCSI controllers can be placed in a system, Linux supports up to 128 SCSI devices. If you require device files for more devices than are currently created in your /dev directory, follow Table 8.7 to determine the device major and minor numbers to create the devices. You can create these devices using the mknod(1) command (refer to Chapter 4 for more information). The device minor number for whole disk devices (that is, sda) is determined by the number listed in the table (for example, 0 for sda, 32 for sdc, and so on). The minor number for a device file specifying a partition (that is, sda1) is determined by adding the partition number (1-15) to the minor number for that disk (for example, sda1 would be 1, sdb1 would be 17).

TABLE 8.7 SCSI Disk Device Naming for Large Numbers of Disks

Disk Devices	Device Filenames	Device Major Number	Device Minor Number
0-15	sda-sdp	8	0, 16, 32, ... 240
16-31	sdq-sdaf	65	0, 16, 32, ... 240
32-47	sdaq-sdav	66	0, 16, 32, ... 240
48-63	sdaw-sdbl	67	0, 16, 32, ... 240
64-79	sdbm-sdcb	68	0, 16, 32, ... 240
80-95	sdcc-sdcr	69	0, 16, 32, ... 240
96-111	sdcs-sddh	70	0, 16, 32, ... 240
112-127	sddi-sddx	71	0, 16, 32, ... 240

Other types of SCSI devices (scanners, tape drives, media changers, RAID arrays, and so on) are also supported under Linux, but use different device naming conventions. Consult the kernel documentation or Red Hat's online help for more information. Other devices are discussed in the following section.

Other Devices

As time passes, your storage needs are likely to increase. Although SCSI is the current predominant technology for server storage, Fibre Channel is likely to be the technology that replaces SCSI in the long run. Fibre Channel storage, often deployed in Storage Area Networks (SANs), is a gigabit interconnect technology that offers storage capacities for very large-scale storage needs. Currently, Red Hat Linux does not officially support any Fibre Channel devices. However, there are several unsupported drivers for Fibre Channel host adapters available as a part of the GFS Project (`http://www.globalfilesystem.com`). As this technology becomes more prevalent in server-class hardware, support for these devices will increase.

There are also advancements in SCSI technology leading to the implementation of a card fulfilling the Ultra3 SCSI standard. Adaptec already has a Linux-supported offering that it calls Ultra160/m, which offers transfer rates of up to 160MB/sec and includes several advancements for ensuring reliability of SCSI data transfers.

Summary

This chapter discussed the details of managing storage on a Red Hat Linux system. The details of the IDE and SCSI interfaces and their configurations were covered. Keep in mind that storage needs will only increase over time—be sure to add disks with as much capacity as is affordable. By mastering the disk configuration information in this chapter, the addition (or replacement) of hard disk storage becomes a simple component of server maintenance.

Linux and RAID

IN THIS CHAPTER

- The History of Linux RAID Support **228**

- RAID Overview   **228**

- Linux Software RAID   **234**

- Hardware RAID and Linux   **266**

- Other Sources of Information   **269**

CHAPTER 9

One of the required features of any modern operating system to allow it to be used as a server is support for *Redundant Arrays of Inexpensive Disks,* or RAID. Red Hat Linux is no exception to this and RAID is supported under Linux via both software and hardware.

This chapter begins with an overview of RAID concepts. It then describes Linux software RAID, including coverage of the RAID tools and a section on using RAID on your root filesystem. Finally, it presents information regarding Linux support for hardware RAID controllers, including the configuration options required to add support for them to your kernel.

The History of Linux RAID Support

Support for software RAID was first incorporated into the Linux kernel in February, 1996 with the release of kernel version 1.3.69. This support was written by Marc Zyngier and at that time, the support was limited to linear mode md devices (commonly referred to as concatenated drives) and RAID level 0, or striping. Work to support additional levels of software RAID began shortly thereafter by Gadi Oxman, Ingo Molnar, Miguel de Icaza, and others, and in November, 1997, support for RAID levels 1, 4, and 5 were added to the 2.1.63 development kernel release. This support was finally backported to the 2.0.x stable release tree in July, 1998 when it was added to the 2.0.35 kernel release. Linux also supports hardware RAID in the form of support for RAID controllers and support for RAID devices that connect to a SCSI or IDE controller or even to the parallel port.

RAID Overview

Before discussing the details of Linux software and hardware RAID, it is essential to understand what RAID is, and why you would want to use it. RAID was first described in a paper titled "Case for Redundant Arrays of Inexpensive Disks (RAID)," published by Patterson, Garth, and Katz of The University of California at Berkeley in 1987. Since its introduction, RAID has been implemented in both hardware and software, or a combination of the two. There were three major objectives for RAID as described in the 1987 RAID paper. These were reduced cost for data storage, increased performance, and increased reliability. Let's examine each of these objectives and how they are achieved through RAID.

Objectives of RAID

The first objective was reduced cost for large amounts of storage space. It is important to remember that at the time the 1987 RAID paper was written, large filesystems were usually implemented using *single, large and expensive disks* (SLEDs) that were proprietary to each hardware manufacturer. By comparison, you could purchase an equivalent amount of storage in the form of commodity drives, such as those used in personal computers for a much lower cost. The objective of reduced cost was achieved by utilizing these inexpensive commodity drives in place of the SLEDs. Because the use of proprietary disk drive subsystems is no longer prevalent, especially in the PC market, the acronym RAID is now often defined as Redundant Array of Independent Disks, as opposed to Redundant Array of Inexpensive Disks. In addition, with the falling costs of hard drives and the fact that there is little difference in the cost per megabyte between large capacity drives and small capacity drives, cost is usually not an important consideration in deciding whether to implement a RAID storage solution.

Reliability, or more accurately, data availability, is another goal of RAID implementations. Reliability is achieved by maintaining multiple copies of data, parity information, or checksums stored with the data on the array, with the exact method determined by the RAID level being implemented. For example, redundancy is achieved in a RAID level 1 implementation through a mirroring scheme in which data is duplicated in multiple places on individual disks making up the RAID array. The storing of parity or checksum data on the RAID device that can be used to recreate lost data in case of a failure is used in the implementation of RAID levels 2, 3, 4, and 5. The requirement for data availability is usually a major factor in the decision to use a RAID storage array. Other aspects of reliability include the ability of RAID arrays to automatically correct themselves in the event of a disk failure, and features of RAID such as hot-swapping of failed disks. *Hot-swapping* refers to the ability to remove a disk from the array without having to shut down the system.

The final objective as described in the RAID paper is that of performance. By taking advantage of the increased number of spindles and read/write heads as well as the controller mechanisms of the independent drives in the array, better performance can be achieved. Other performance measures often found in RAID implementation include caching mechanisms or algorithms and input/output optimization to take advantage of the multiple controllers and read/write heads.

Take, for example, an implementation of RAID level 1. This RAID level achieves redundancy by writing all data to the array twice, once on the data disks and once on the mirror disks. Since the data is stored on two or more sets of physical devices, when it is time to read the data, the read heads on all of the physical devices can be used to read blocks of data simultaneously. Whether this is significant is dependent on how effectively the hardware or software implements it. Performance enhancements are not always achieved through the use of RAID, however, due to the overhead of calculating parity or checksum information or of the multiple writes used to achieve redundancy. In hardware RAID solutions, this is usually addressed by onboard cache memory and caching schemes, such as write-back caching. In software RAID, it is up to the driver author to optimize the input/output functions as much as possible to take advantage of the available mechanisms and operating system features. Other factors that can affect performance include stripe size, filesystem block size, and the read and write characteristics of the applications utilizing the RAID. Like reliability, RAID performance is usually an important factor to consider when deciding to implement a RAID storage solution.

RAID Levels

The choice of RAID level to use is dependent on how important each of the three objectives is to you. Each of these RAID levels has distinct advantages and disadvantages that you will have to consider when deciding which to use. This section describes how each level is characterized and the applications for which it might be appropriate. It also looks at some of the advantages and disadvantages of each RAID level.

The lowest level of true RAID defined in the 1987 RAID paper is RAID level 1, commonly referred to as *mirroring* (see Figure 9.1). In a mirroring scheme, two or more disk sets of equal storage capacity are required, making this level of RAID the most expensive in terms of disk hardware.

For example, if you wanted to have an 8Gb filesystem with one mirror (a total of two disk sets), you would need 16Gb of raw disk space. This is one of the disadvantages of RAID level 1. Another disadvantage is in write speed to the mirror. When a write occurs, the RAID subsystem causes the data to be written redundantly, so that the data is mirrored or copied on each disk set. This means that in a single-way mirror, each write by an application results in two writes by the RAID subsystem. In multi-way mirrors, each write by the application results in N writes by the RAID subsystem, where N is the number of mirrors plus one. Read operations, however, are usually improved due to the fact that multiple requests for data can be read from any of the disk sets, which means that read performance can be improved two times in a one-way mirror or N plus one times in an N-way mirror. This scheme also makes recovery in the event of a failure very simple because all that is required to recover is to copy the data from an undamaged disk set to the one that failed.

RAID level 1 is the simplest form of RAID to implement in software with the exception of the capability to do hot swaps of failed disks. The best implementations of this RAID level are done with hardware that is capable of doing parallel reads and writes and that includes a caching mechanism to reduce the write penalty. Mirrors are well suited to any application that requires very high availability, such as payroll, accounting, and other financial applications. Linux software RAID drivers support RAID level 1 and the majority of hardware RAID controllers also support this level of RAID. See Figure 9.1 for a conceptual diagram of a 1-way mirror.

Figure 9.1

A RAID level 1 array (aka 1-way mirror).

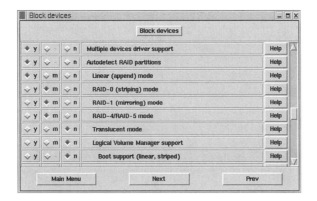

RAID level 2 utilizes parallel access and *error-correctingcode* (ECC), developed by R. W. Hamming in the 1950s, to achieve redundancy. The use of ECC, as opposed to parity, is what differentiates RAID level 2 from other RAID levels. As you can see in Figure 9.2, data is sent in parallel to all disks in the array. A checksum is calculated for the data and is stored on multiple check disks. The error-correcting algorithm used for RAID level 2 was first developed to correct errors in mainframe memory and was adapted for use with RAID. This RAID level is rarely implemented for several reasons, not the least of which is that most modern disks implement hardware level ECC, making RAID level 2 little safer than a filesystem with battery backup that is always shutdown cleanly. This RAID level is best suited to applications in which large amounts of data are accessed sequentially, such as scientific data analysis. There is no support for RAID level 2 in Linux software RAID. Support for RAID level 2 in hardware for Linux is dependent on the controller or external RAID device selected.

Figure 9.2

A RAID level 2 array.

A	A	A	ECC	ECC
B	B	B	ECC	ECC
C	C	C	ECC	ECC
D	D	D	ECC	ECC

ECC data for strip A is stored on multiple disks on corresponding stripe.

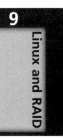

RAID level 3 is another level that is well suited to applications in which large amounts of data are accessed sequentially. In this scheme, which is illustrated in Figure 9.3, data is striped across multiple disks and parity information is calculated using an exclusive or function and stored on a separate disk. At first glance, you will see little difference between RAID level 3 and RAID level 4. The two major differences are that in RAID level 3, the smallest possible stripe size is used, which negates the advantage of multiple input/output operations and RAID level 3 requires that the drive spindles be synchronized. This last requirement is one of the reasons why this RAID level is rarely implemented. Modern drives lack spindle synchronization capabilities. Like RAID level 2, level 3 is best suited to applications such as scientific data analysis in which large quantities of data are accessed sequentially. Like RAID level 2, Linux software RAID does not implement RAID level 3 and hardware support for this RAID level is dependent on the hardware chosen.

FIGURE 9.3

A RAID level 3 or level 4 array.

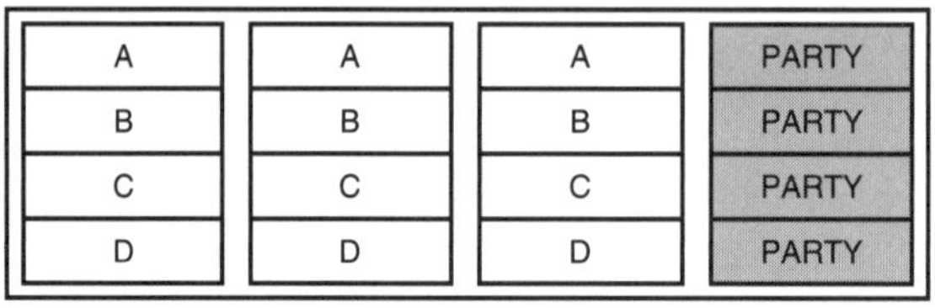

A	A	A	PARTY
B	B	B	PARTY
C	C	C	PARTY
D	D	D	PARTY

Data interleaved across stripes and redundancy information stored on another disk (indicated by the shaded area).

A RAID level 4 array consists of multiple data disks with a shared parity disk and is similar to RAID level 3. It differs from RAID level 3 in that drive spindles do not have to be synchronized and data access and can be done on multiple disks in the array simultaneously. Conceptually, a RAID level 4 array looks much like a RAID level 3 array as shown in Figure 9.3, the differences being stripe size and the lack of synchronization of the drives in RAID level 4. The obvious drawback to this system is that since all parity information is stored on a single disk, this disk can become a bottleneck in a write-intensive environment. Like RAID level 3, data is striped across multiple disks in the array and the parity information is calculated using an exclusive or function. To implement an array of this type in which you want *N* disks worth of storage space, you are required to have N+1 disks in the array. The reliability of RAID level 4 is comparable to mirroring, but due to the lesser hardware requirements it is preferred in many cases. RAID level 4 is best suited to data that is not updated frequently, but is read often, and is sometimes used in database environments that meet this criterion. RAID level 4 is supported by the RAID level 5 module of the Linux software RAID implementation.

One of the most flexible RAID levels is RAID level 5. As shown in Figure 9.4, RAID level 5 arrays store data across multiple disks like RAID level 4, but the parity information required to rebuild a failed array is spread across multiple disks, thus eliminating the single parity disk bottleneck. This RAID level is well suited to many different applications where reliability is of the utmost importance, but there is a penalty in speed and rebuilds can be very complicated. As with RAID level 1, a good implementation of RAID level 5 needs an efficient cache to offset the time required to write data to the array. Recommended uses of RAID level 5 include database servers, file and application servers, and Internet servers, such as news, email, and Web servers. Linux supports both software and hardware implementations of RAID level 5.

Figure 9.4

A RAID level 5 array.

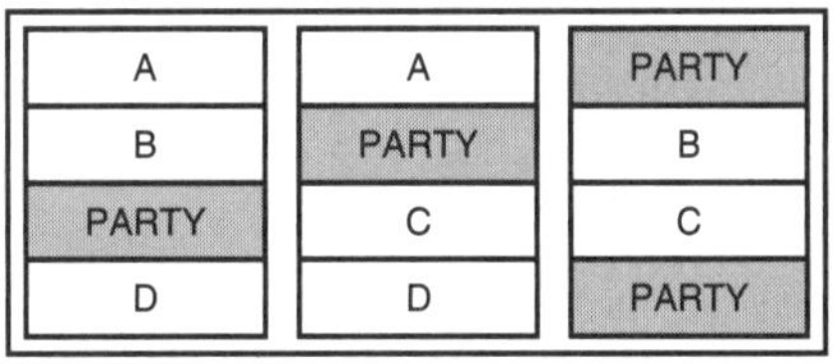

A	A	PARTY
B	PARTY	B
PARTY	C	C
D	D	PARTY

Data interleaved across multiple drives and party information stored on multiple disks to eliminate party read bottlenecks.

The idea of interleaving data across multiple drives, which forms the foundation of the other RAID levels, is referred to as RAID level 0, or striping. This is not truly RAID in that there is no redundancy. The primary purpose of striping is to increase performance. Disks in the array are divided up into chunks (as shown in Figure 9.5) and data is written so that contiguous blocks of data are stored on multiple disks. Reads and writes to the array are very fast because they can be performed in parallel, utilizing the multiple disks in the array simultaneously. This idea of striping data across multiple disks is one of the performance features of RAID and is the foundation of all other RAID levels, but in and of itself does nothing to improve reliability.

Figure 9.5

RAID level 0 (aka striping).

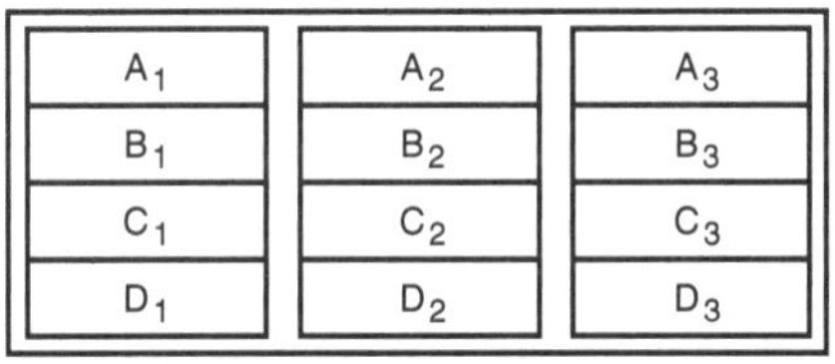

A_1	A_2	A_3
B_1	B_2	B_3
C_1	C_2	C_3
D_1	D_2	D_3

Data write order: A1, A2, A3, B1, B2, B3, C1, C2, C3

9

Linux and RAID

Because no parity or checksum data is stored for a RAID level 0 array, the loss of a disk in the array translates to a loss of all data on the array. RAID level 0 is therefore not recommended for any application that requires high availability of data. This is not to say that RAID level 0 is not useful, and in fact it can be highly effective in applications that achieve redundancy in other ways. Consider, for example, a cluster of database hosts, all of which contain the same data. RAID level 0 could be used on the filesystems containing the database tables to increase performance while redundancy is achieved via replication on each host in the cluster. Some common uses for RAID level 0 arrays are to capture streaming data or applications that require very high bandwidth like video editing and production or image manipulation. RAID level 0 was one of the first RAID levels implemented in Linux software RAID.

Other RAID levels not described in the Berkeley RAID paper are available, including support in hardware RAID for striping of mirror sets, sometimes referred to as RAID level 10, and support for mirroring of striped sets, also known as RAID 0/1. These combinations of RAID levels are non-standard, however, and naming conventions vary from vendor to vendor. Linux software RAID supports only one of these non-standard RAID levels, which is the mirroring of striped arrays. These combinations are useful to increase performance and reliability.

Linux Software RAID

Linux developers began working on implementing software RAID starting in 1994 with two independent projects. Both of these projects started with a simple desire to concatenate multiple physical devices into a single logical device. The one that survived was referred to as the *multiple devicesdriver,* or md driver. The md driver went through several revisions and was made a part of the development kernel source tree in February, 1996, with the release of kernel 1.3.69. At that time, there were two modes implemented: linear mode and true software RAID.

Linear mode allows for the concatenation of multiple physical drives into a single logical drive and offers no performance gains, since the disks are not accessed in parallel. The sole purpose of linear mode is to append multiple physical devices into a single logical device to allow for bigger filesystems. This release also implemented RAID level 0, or striping, which can greatly increase performance, but does nothing to increase reliability.

Some time thereafter, another group of developers began to implement true software RAID using the md driver as their starting point. Current Linux kernels from the stable kernel branch, 2.2, have support for software RAID levels 0, 1, 4, and 5 that can be built in to the kernel or loaded as dynamic modules. With the release of Red Hat 6.0, Linux has greatly improved RAID support, including the ability of the kernel to handle reconstruction of damaged arrays utilizing spare CPU cycles and spare disks added to RAID arrays when they are created. It also includes autodetection of RAID arrays by the kernel at boot time and the ability to add and remove physical devices from a running RAID array. This section describes the RAID tools required to create and manage software RAID arrays, and discusses how to implement each of the RAID levels supported by the Linux software RAID drivers.

RAID Tools

The RAID support available with Red Hat Linux 6.0 is not the support found in the stock kernel. Red Hat has upgraded the RAID software drivers and the RAID tools to a more recent set than is currently found in the original kernel source.

Note

To see the complete set of patches applied to the original Linux source tree, examine the source RPM for the kernel. To install this SRPM, look for `kernel-2.2.5-15.src.rpm` either on the Red Hat FTP site or on the SRPM CD-ROM that comes with the Red Hat distribution. Once you have installed this RPM, you can examine all of the kernel patches applied by looking in the `/usr/src/redhat/` SOURCES directory.

Red Hat Linux comes with version 0.90 of the RAID tools. These commands differ from their predecessors significantly and include features required to support the extra functionality provided by the updated RAID drivers supplied with the kernel sources. The RAID command set resides in the `/sbin` directory and consists of tools in Table 9.1.

TABLE 9.1 The RAID Commands and Their Functions

Command	Function
mkraid	Initializes RAID device arrays
raidstart	Configures RAID devices in the kernel and activates them
raidhotadd	Adds spare devices to a running RAID array
raidhotremove	Removes devices from a running RAID array
raidstop	Unconfigures a RAID device array

The first command to consider is the `mkraid` command. The `mkraid` command is used to initialize RAID devices and is applicable to all RAID levels supported by the Linux software RAID drivers. The `mkraid` command is similar in function to the `mkfs` command used to create a filesystem in that it is the first step in preparing the RAID array to receive data. In normal usage, the only time that this command is used is during the creation of a RAID array because like the `mkfs` command, this command is destructive to the data on the RAID array. It reads from a configuration file, either one that you specify with the `-c` command-line option or the default `/etc/raidtab`, to determine the specifics of each RAID device. The options for the `mkraid` command are described in the manual page and in Table 9.2.

9

Linux and RAID

TABLE 9.2 Command-Line Options for `mkraid`

Option	Description
`-v, --version`	Displays a short version statement, then exits.
`-h, --help`	Displays the usage statement.
`-c, --configfile file`	Uses `file` as the configuration file instead of the `/etc/raidtab`.
`-f, --force`	Initializes the array, even if it appears to be already initialized.
`-o, --update`	Instead of initializing each device in the array, this option causes `mkraid` to update the version information stored on the RAID array to the version of the current kernel and although it is non-destructive, it should be used with care.

Before describing the other commands of the RAID tool set, let us examine the RAID configuration file, `/etc/raidtab`. The `raidtab` stanzas include the RAID level, the number and names of the partitions that make up the array, and other required information that is dependent on the RAID level being implemented. A detailed explanation of the format of the `/etc/raidtab` file can be found later in this chapter along with examples for each RAID level supported by the software RAID drivers. You must create this configuration file according to a strict syntax that is described in the raidtab manual page and in Table 9.3.

TABLE 9.3 `/etc/raidtab` Keywords and Meanings

Keyword	Meaning
`raiddev device`	This line begins a stanza in the RAID configuration file and it specifies the device name to assign to the RAID.
`raid-level integer`	The integer value assigned to this keyword specifies the RAID level for the current `raiddev`. Available values are -1, 0, 1, 4, and 5, corresponding to linear, RAID-0, RAID-1, RAID-4, and RAID-5. Linear mode may also be specified with the word `linear` instead of the integer value.
`nr-raid-disks count`	The number of disk partitions in the array.
`nr-spare-disks count`	The number of spare disks in the array that can be used by the kernel in automatic reconstruction of a damaged array.
`device device file`	The name of the device file to be added to the array. There will be multiple device entries for each RAID array defined. The number of device entries must equal the number given to the `nr-raid-disks` parameter.
`raid-disk index`	The position in the active disk array of the most recently defined device starting at 0.
`spare-disk index`	The position in the spare disk array of the most recently defined device starting at 0.
`parity-disk index`	The position in the parity disk array of the most recently defined device starting at 0.

TABLE 9.3 continued

Keyword	Meaning
`parity-algorithm` which	The RAID level 5 parity algorithm to use for the current array. Possible values for this parameter are left-asymmetric, right-asymmetric, left-symmetric, or right-symmetric.
`chunk-size` size	The size in K bytes of a stripe.
`persistent-superblock` bool	If set to 1, a special superblock is written to each physical device in the array that is read by the kernel instead of the `/etc/raidtab` file to configure the RAID device. A value of 1 is required if you want to be able to boot from a RAID device.

Unlike earlier releases of the RAID tool set, the RAID tools included with Red Hat 6.0 do not include a `ckraid` command. This command was previously required to check and optionally correct discrepancies in RAID device arrays. This functionality is now handled by a kernel thread that uses spare CPU cycles to perform any required corrections to the configured RAID devices. The status of reconstruction is now determined by examining the `/proc/mdstat` file.

The next commands we will cover are collectively referred to as the RAID management utilities. These commands are applicable to all RAID levels, including linear mode and RAID level 0 arrays. These commands are `raidstart`, `raidhotadd`, `raidhotremove`, and `raidstop`. They are in actuality all the same command. `raidhotadd`, `raidhotremove`, and `raidstop` are just links to the `raidstart` command. By invoking this command with different names, different functionality is achieved.

Note

Creating RAID device arrays depends on two things. The first of these is RAID driver support in the kernel and the second is the appropriate device files in `/dev`. The major number for the md devices is 9 with minor numbers starting at 0 and incrementing by 1 for each RAID device. If there are no device entries in your `/dev` directory, here are the commands required to create the default four md devices supported by the md device driver:

```
/sbin/mknod b 9 0 /dev/md0
/sbin/mknod b 9 1 /dev/md1
/sbin/mknod b 9 2 /dev/md2
/sbin/mknod b 9 3 /dev/md3
```

9

Linux and RAID

Although you can configure any RAID devices you create to be autodetected by the kernel during the boot sequence, you may also manually start and stop them if you so desire. You might want to manually start your RAID arrays to shorten the time required to boot the system. In addition, you may need to ensure that the RAID is fully functional prior to starting some other system software. You may also want to be able to continue booting the system even if the RAID fails.

In order to manually start a RAID array, you would use the `raidstart`command. This command examines the RAID configuration file and if the `-a` option is supplied, it activates all of the RAID devices described therein. In the absence of the `-a` option, you are required to specify a device file corresponding to the array you want to start. This one command replaces the`raidadd` and`raidrun` commands from the older RAID tool set. You must execute the `raidstart` command before you can create a filesystem or swap device on the RAID array, mount an existing filesystem, or access the filesystem or swap device on the array in any fashion. The opposite command in the suite is the`raidstop` command, which deactivates the drives in the RAID array and unconfigures them in the kernel. You should run this command only after all open files on the array have been closed and the RAID device has been unmounted. Both of these commands read either the default configuration file, `/etc/raidtab`, or the configuration file specified with the `-c` option. The complete set of options available to these commands are described in the `raidstart` manual page and in Table 9.4.

TABLE **9.4** Command-Line Options for `raidstart`

Option	Description
`-a, --all`	Runs the command against all of the devices specified in the configuration file.
`-c, --configfile file`	Uses `file` as the configuration file. The default is `/etc/raidtab`.
`-h, --help`	Displays a brief usage statement and then exits.
`-V, --version`	Displays the version number of the RAID tools and then exits.

The other two commands in the RAID management command set are `raidhotadd`and`raidhotremove`. These commands are used to add or remove physical devices from running arrays. This allows for the addition of spare disks to an array and for the removal of dead disks from an array. As stated previously, these commands are really just links to the `raidstart` command and as such, read required information from the RAID configuration file.

Warning

Support for hot reconstruction of RAID arrays is a new feature and according to the authors is still not production level code. It is highly recommended that before utilizing any of these commands to create storage for critical data that you conduct your experiments to determine the stability of the arrays. And as always, keep good backups.

Now that the commands used to work with RAID arrays have been covered, we can begin to look at what it takes to create the various types of RAID arrays supported by the Linux kernel. We will start with linear md devices and RAID level 0 arrays and then proceed with the more complex RAID levels.

Supported RAID Levels

Creating a RAID array requires that your kernel support the md device driver and the appropriate RAID level driver. This support can be compiled into your kernel, or built as modules that can be loaded and unloaded as required. For purposes of this discussion, assume that you have compiled the md driver code into your kernel and built the various RAID level code as dynamically loadable kernel modules. This section shows samples of the appropriate entries in the RAID configuration file needed to create an array of each type.

Let's start with a linear md array. The first thing to consider when building a linear array is the partitions that will make up the array. The normal use for a linear array is to combine several small disks to create a storage space with enough space to be useful. This usually means that there will be a single partition on each of the drives that uses the entire disk or that you are combining several small partitions to create one larger one. In the following example, we are combining a small partition left over after creating other filesystems on the first SCSI drive in a system with two other small SCSI drives. Here is a sample entry from `/etc/raidtab`:

```
raiddev            /dev/md0
raid-level         linear
nr-raid-disks      3
nr-spare-disks     0
chunk-size         4
device             /dev/sda3
raid-disk          0
device             /dev/sdb1
raid-disk          1
```

9

Linux and RAID

```
device          /dev/sdc1
raid-disk       2
```

Linear devices are simply concatenations of multiple devices and are accessed sequentially. If you add the devices /dev/sda3, /dev/sdb1, and /dev/sdc1 to the array as in the example, that data will be written to /dev/sda3 until it fills up and then will continue writing to /dev/sdb1 until all of the data is written. There are some people who will claim a performance advantage to using linear arrays, but due to the nature of the extended 2 filesystem, which is designed to avoid fragmentation of files, these claims are dubious at best. The biggest drawback to using linear devices is that they actually increase the likelihood of data loss because the loss of any of the component disk drives will result in the loss of all data on the array. For this reason, it is usually not a good idea to use linear arrays to store critical data. One good use for linear arrays is to create the component parts of a mirrored array. For example, if you have two 100Mb disks and one 200Mb disk, you could combine the two 100Mb disks as a linear array and use the resulting device as a mirror for the 200Mb disk.

Note

You will notice in the sample entry for the linear md array that a chunk-size is specified. This is contrary to the documentation of the raid tools. However, failure to specify a chunk-size will result in failure to create the array.

The next example is of a RAID level 0 array. The raidtab entry for this type of array is very similar to the linear array. The only differences are that you must specify the raid-level as 0 instead of -1 and you must supply the chunk-size parameter. In a RAID level 0 array, the disk is divided into chunks of a user specified size and writes are interleaved across all of the disks in the array, thus giving a performance advantage. This performance advantage is due to the fact that the read/write heads of all of the drives in the array may be utilized in parallel. The amount of this performance advantage is dependent on many factors, including block size of the filesystem created on the array, the input/output characteristics of the applications reading and writing data to the array, and the chunk size selected.

Note

The performance advantage to RAID level 0 arrays will not be realized if the array is composed of multiple partitions of the same hard drive. The advantage comes from being able to simultaneously use the heads of multiple disk drives.

Here is a sample entry in /etc/raidtab for a RAID level 0 array, using three disk partitions:

```
raiddev                 /dev/md0
raid-level      0
nr-raid-disks       3
chunk-size      64
device          /dev/sdb1
raid-disk       0
device          /dev/sdc1
raid-disk       1
device          /dev/sdd1
raid-disk       2
```

Note

Due to the way in which striping is done, it is desirable to have the component parts of a RAID level 0 array be the same geometry. Failure to adhere to this rule can affect the performance of the array. Say, for example, that you create RAID level 0 array using a 100Mb partition on /dev/sda2 and a 150Mb partition on /dev/sdb1. In this case, all of the space would be would be divided up into the user specified stripe size and all access to the first 200Mb of the resulting 250Mb array would be interleaved across the two devices, thus increasing performance. Access to the final 50Mb of the array, which is physically located on a single disk, cannot ake advantage of multiple read/write heads of both devices and therefore is no faster than access to a single disk. It can even be slower due to the fact that access must now go through both the RAID code layer as well as the regular filesystem layer.

Linear devices and RAID level 0 arrays may be used for the root filesystem provided that support for this is compiled into your kernel.

RAID level 1 arrays are the lowest level of true RAID arrays supported by the Linux software RAID drivers. In order to create a mirrored array, or a RAID level 1 array, the entry is quite simple. In fact, it looks remarkably like the entry for a RAID level 0 device. The following is an example of a simple one-way mirror stanza from /etc/raidtab. In this example, there are two disks only. To create an N-way mirror, you could modify the entry and simply add to the number of raid disks and the number of device entries.

9

Linux and RAID

> **Note**
>
> The term N-way mirror refers to a mirror in which N copies of the data, not counting the original, are maintained. For example, a 4-way mirror means that the original data, plus 4 copies of the data are maintained.

The amount of usable space in an N-way mirror composed of N+1disks of size S is S. For example, if you create a two-way mirror using three 4Gb disks drives, the usable space will be 4Gb. This means that in terms of raw disk space requirements, RAID level 1 is the most expensive.

```
raiddev /dev/md0
raid-level       1
nr-raid-disks       2
chunk-size       64
device           /dev/sdc1
raid-disk        0
device           /dev/sdd1
raid-disk        1
```

> **Warning**
>
> The devices making up a mirror should all be the same size. Failure to adhere to this rule will not affect performance, however the difference in the sizes of the parts of the mirror will be wasted space.

RAID level 4 arrays are supported by the RAID level 5 module and the only difference between the /etc/raidtab entry for a RAID level 4 array and a RAID level 5 array is the absence of the parity-algorithm keyword. This keyword describes how the parity information will be stored on disk and the definition of the parity disk. The formula for determining the number of physical disks required for a RAID level 4 array of size S is $(S/N) + 1 = D$. In this formula, N refers to the size of the disk drives in the array, S refers to the amount of usable space desired, and D is the number of physical disks. Alternatively, to determine the amount of usable space in a RAID level 4 array composed of five 9Gb disks, you would use the formula $S = N(D-1)$. Substituting 9 for N, the size of each disk, and 5 for D, the number of physical disks, we find that S, the usable space, will be 9(5-1) or 36Gb. In the following example, if each of the devices specified were 2Gb in size, the total space available on the array would be 6Gb. This is a sample of a RAID level 4 array made up of 4 disks. In this configuration, three of the devices are striped and used for storing data and one is used to store parity information, which is calculated by applying an `exclusive or` function to the data in a stripe.

```
raiddev                 /dev/md0
raid-level      4
nr-raid-disks       4
nr-spare-disks       0
chunk-size      64
device              /dev/sda3
raid-disk       0
device              /dev/sdb1
raid-disk       1
device              /dev/sdc1
raid-disk       2
device              /dev/sdd1
parity-disk         0
```

The RAID level 5 array is similar to the RAID level 4 array, but the parity information is spread across all of the disks in the array and the formula for computing the physical device requirements is the same. To convert the previous entry into a RAID level 5 entry, three things must change. The first of these is the raid-level, which of course should be changed to 5. The next is the addition of the parity-algorithm keyword and value, and finally, removal of the parity-disk keyword. This would make the entry look like the following. If the partitions represented by /dev/sdb1, /dev/sdc1, and /dev/sdd1 were each 4Gb, the total size of this array would be 8Gb of usable storage.

```
raiddev                 /dev/md0
raid-level      5
nr-raid-disks       3
nr-spare-disks       0
parity-algorithm    left-symmetric
chunk-size      64
device              /dev/sdb1
raid-disk       0
device              /dev/sdc1
raid-disk       1
device              /dev/sdd1
raid-disk       2
```

9

Linux and RAID

The most complicated example is the one required to implement a mirror consisting of multiple striped arrays. In this example, four disks of equal size, S, will be used to create an array of 2 * S in size. Please note the order in which the arrays are declared in the /etc/raidtab file. Due to the manner in which the parser is designed, this ordering is essential.

```
raiddev             /dev/md0
raid-level      0
nr-raid-disks       2
chunk-size      64
device          /dev/sdb1
raid-disk       0
device          /dev/sdc1
raid-disk       1

raiddev             /dev/md1
raid-level      0
nr-raid-disks       2
chunk-size      64
device          /dev/sdd1
raid-disk       0
device          /dev/sde1
raid-disk       1

raiddev             /dev/md2
raid-level      1
nr-raid-disks       2
nr-spare-disks      0
chunk-size      64
device          /dev/md0
raid-disk       0
device          /dev/md1
raid-disk       1
```

Implementing Software RAID

Now that you have an understanding of the tools used to build and manage Linux software RAID, we can demonstrate their usage and actually build some RAID arrays. The following examples cover each step required to build Linux software RAID arrays. We will start with a coverage of the kernel modules and options required to support Linux software RAID. Once this kernel support is added, we will give a specific example of building arrays of each type that is supported. When you have mastered the individual commands, we will put them all together to construct a RAID building script.

To begin with, let us consider the steps to configuring any RAID array. These steps are fundamentally the same for each level of RAID. Once we have the steps defined, we will go over them in detail, demonstrating the specific commands required to build a RAID array. These steps are

1. Load the appropriate kernel modules to support the level of RAID desired.
2. Create an appropriate entry in the `/etc/raidtab` file.
3. Define the RAID devices to the kernel.
4. Activate the RAID array.
5. Create a filesystem on the array and mount it.

The first step is to load the appropriate kernel modules to support the level of RAID desired. This implies that support for RAID has been compiled into the kernel. If this is not the case, then read on. If your kernel already has the appropriate support, you can skip the next paragraph.

Change directory to the top level of the kernel source tree, usually `/usr/src/linux`. Invoke `make` using one of the kernel configuration make targets, such as `xconfig` or `menuconfig`, to begin configuration of the kernel. The RAID support options are located under the Block Devices option from the top-level menu. The supporting option required for RAID support is the Multiple Devices driver support, which cannot be compiled as a module. Once you have selected this option, you may then select which RAID levels to support. The available options are

- Linear (append) mode
- RAID-0 (striping) mode
- RAID-1 (mirroring) mode
- RAID-4/RAID-5 mode

All of these may be compiled as modules that can be loaded and unloaded as required. However, if you want to have a linear mode or RAID level 0 root partition, you must compile the one you want into the kernel and then select the Boot Support (linear, striped) option. Once you have compiled and installed your new kernel, you must load the appropriate RAID module prior to proceeding with the next steps (see Figure 9.6). For a more detailed description of how to customize your Linux kernel, refer to Chapter 34, "Tuning Your Linux System," which covers this topic in detail.

9

Linux and RAID

FIGURE 9.6

Software RAID options of kernel configuration using make xconfig.

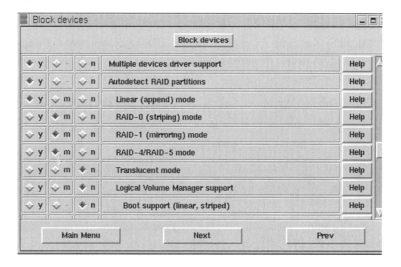

The next step is to create an appropriate entry for your RAID array in the raid configuration file. The default filename for this configuration file is /etc/raidtab, however, you can call this file whatever you choose. This file is only used in the creation of RAID arrays and if you have chosen to use the persistent-superblock option as recommended by the driver authors, it is no longer required. The exception to this rule is if you want to use the raidhotadd and raidhotremove commands. It is, however, recommended that you keep this file up to date and available in the event you need it to recover a damaged system or if you want to recreate the configuration on another system.

Before we proceed to the next step, let us define our test system. This test system is a server class system consisting of dual processors, 1Gb of RAM, and a SCSI controller with five 9Gb drives attached. The first SCSI drive is reserved for the operating system installation and the remaining four drives will be used to construct the RAID arrays.

For our first example, we are going to create a linear md device consisting of two of the 9Gb drives, /dev/sdb and /dev/sdc. Here is the raidtab entry required to implement this:

```
# Linear md device
raiddev                 /dev/md0
raid-level              linear
nr-raid-disks           2
persistent-superblock      1
chunk-size              4
device                  /dev/sdb1
raid-disk               0
device                  /dev/sdc1
raid-disk               1
```

Once this entry has been created, we can prepare the disks for autodetection and activation. Using the `fdisk` command, create a single large partition on `/dev/sdb` and `/dev/sdc`. Once these partitions are created, set the partition type to FD. Here is a sample session in which `fdisk` is used to perform this step on `/dev/sdb` and `sfdisk` is used to perform the same step with a single command on `/dev/sdc`:

```
[root@hqtest18 /root]# fdisk /dev/sdb


The number of cylinders for this disk is set to 1106.
There is nothing wrong with that, but this is larger than 1024,
and could in certain setups cause problems with:
1) software that runs at boot time (e.g., LILO)
2) booting and partitioning software from other OSs
   (e.g., DOS FDISK, OS/2 FDISK)


Command (m for help): p

Disk /dev/sdb: 255 heads, 63 sectors, 1106 cylinders
Units = cylinders of 16065 * 512 bytes

   Device Boot    Start      End    Blocks   Id  System
/dev/sdb1             1     1106   8883913+   83  Linux


Command (m for help): d
Partition number (1-4): 1


Command (m for help): n
Command action
   e   extended
   p   primary partition (1-4)
p
Partition number (1-4): 1
First cylinder (1-1106, default 1): 1
Last cylinder or +size or +sizeM or +sizeK (1-1106, default 1106): 1106


Command (m for help): p

Disk /dev/sdb: 255 heads, 63 sectors, 1106 cylinders
Units = cylinders of 16065 * 512 bytes

   Device Boot    Start      End    Blocks   Id  System
/dev/sdb1             1     1106   8883913+   83  Linux
```

9

Linux and RAID

```
Command (m for help): t
Partition number (1-4): 1
Hex code (type L to list codes): fd
Changed system type of partition 1 to fd (Unknown)


Command (m for help): p

Disk /dev/sdb: 255 heads, 63 sectors, 1106 cylinders
Units = cylinders of 16065 * 512 bytes

   Device Boot    Start     End    Blocks    Id  System
/dev/sdb1              1    1106  8883913+   fd  Unknown


Command (m for help): w
The partition table has been altered!

Calling ioctl() to re-read partition table.
Syncing disks.

WARNING: If you have created or modified any DOS 6.x
partitions, please see the fdisk manual page for additional
information.

[root@hqtest18 /root]# echo ",,fd,-" ¦ sfdisk /dev/sdc
Checking that no-one is using this disk right now ...
OK
Disk /dev/sdc: 255 heads, 63 sectors, 1106 cylinders
Old situation:
Units = cylinders of 8225280 bytes, blocks of 1024 bytes, counting from 0

   Device Boot Start     End   #cyls    #blocks   Id  System
/dev/sdc1           0+   1105   1106-  8883944+   fd  Unknown
/dev/sdc2           0       -      0         0     0  Empty
/dev/sdc3           0       -      0         0     0  Empty
/dev/sdc4           0       -      0         0     0  Empty
New situation:
Units = cylinders of 8225280 bytes, blocks of 1024 bytes, counting from 0

   Device Boot Start     End   #cyls    #blocks   Id  System
/dev/sdc1           0+   1105   1106-  8883944+   fd  Unknown
/dev/sdc2           0       -      0         0     0  Empty
/dev/sdc3           0       -      0         0     0  Empty
/dev/sdc4           0       -      0         0     0  Empty
```

```
Warning: no primary partition is marked bootable (active)
This does not matter for LILO, but the DOS MBR will not boot this disk.
Successfully wrote the new partition table

Re-reading the partition table ...

If you created or changed a DOS partition, /dev/foo7, say, then use dd(1)
to zero the first 512 bytes:  dd if=/dev/zero of=/dev/foo7 bs=512 count=1
(See fdisk(8).)
```

Now we can initialize the arrays using the mkraid command. For purposes of our example, we will create each device separately, but be aware that if multiple devices were defined in the /etc/raidtab file, they could all be created at one time by specifying the --all option to the mkraid command. The following session transcript shows the creation of the device defined by the /etc/raidtab entry above along with some commands to show the effect of each step.

```
[root@hqtest18 /root]# cat /proc/mdstat
Personalities : [raid0]
read_ahead not set
unused devices: <none>

[root@hqtest18 /root]# mkraid /dev/md0
handling MD device /dev/md0
analyzing super-block
disk 0: /dev/sdb1, 8883913kB, raid superblock at 8883840kB
disk 1: /dev/sdc1, 8883913kB, raid superblock at 8883840kB

[root@hqtest18 /root]# cat /proc/mdstat
Personalities : [linear] [raid0]
read_ahead 1024 sectors
md0 : active linear sdc1[1] sdb1[0] 17767680 blocks 32k rounding
unused devices: <none>

[root@hqtest18 /root]# mke2fs -b 4096 -i 262144 /dev/md0
mke2fs 1.14, 9-Jan-1999 for EXT2 FS 0.5b, 95/08/09
Linux ext2 filesystem format
Filesystem label=
69632 inodes, 4441920 blocks
222096 blocks (5.00%) reserved for the super user
First data block=0
Block size=4096 (log=2)
Fragment size=4096 (log=2)
136 block groups
```

9

Linux and RAID

```
32768 blocks per group, 32768 fragments per group
512 inodes per group
Superblock backups stored on blocks:
    32768, 65536, 98304, 131072, 163840, 196608, 229376, 262144,  294912,
    327680, 360448, 393216, 425984, 458752, 491520, 524288, 557056,
    589824,
    622592, 655360, 688128, 720896, 753664, 786432, 819200, 851968,
    884736,
    917504, 950272, 983040, 1015808, 1048576, 1081344, 1114112, 1146880,
    1179648, 1212416, 1245184, 1277952, 1310720, 1343488, 1376256,
    1409024,
    1441792, 1474560, 1507328, 1540096, 1572864, 1605632, 1638400,
    1671168,
    1703936, 1736704, 1769472, 1802240, 1835008, 1867776, 1900544,
    1933312,
    1966080, 1998848, 2031616, 2064384, 2097152, 2129920, 2162688,
    2195456,
    2228224, 2260992, 2293760, 2326528, 2359296, 2392064, 2424832,
    2457600,
    2490368, 2523136, 2555904, 2588672, 2621440, 2654208, 2686976,
    2719744,
    2752512, 2785280, 2818048, 2850816, 2883584, 2916352, 2949120,
    2981888,
    3014656, 3047424, 3080192, 3112960, 3145728, 3178496, 3211264,
    3244032,
    3276800, 3309568, 3342336, 3375104, 3407872, 3440640, 3473408,
    3506176,
    3538944, 3571712, 3604480, 3637248, 3670016, 3702784, 3735552,
    3768320,
    3801088, 3833856, 3866624, 3899392, 3932160, 3964928, 3997696,
    4030464,
    4063232, 4096000, 4128768, 4161536, 4194304, 4227072, 4259840,
    4292608,
    4325376, 4358144, 4390912, 4423680

Writing inode tables: done
Writing superblocks and filesystem accounting information: done

[root@hqtest18 /root]# mkdir -p /raid

[root@hqtest18 /root]# mount /dev/md0 /raid

[root@hqtest18 /root]# df
```

```
Filesystem          1k-blocks      Used Available Use% Mounted on
/dev/sda2            2035638     81695   1848718   4% /
/dev/sda7            6172033    974808   4877534  17% /usr
/dev/md0            17756256        52  16867820   0% /raid


[root@hqtest18 /root]# ls /raid
lost+found


[root@hqtest18 /root]# umount /raid
[root@hqtest18 /root]# raidstop /dev/md0
```

Now that we have seen how to create linear md devices, let's move on to a RAID level 0 array and a simple RAID level 1 mirror. We will be using the same set of disks for this example, so we must first modify /etc/raidtab and create the following entries:

```
# RAID-0 array example
raiddev             /dev/md0
raid-level          0
persistent-superblock    1
chunk-size          32
nr-raid-disks       2
nr-spare-disks      0
device              /dev/sdb1
raid-disk           0
device              /dev/sdc1
raid-disk           1


# RAID-1 array example
raiddev             /dev/md1
raid-level          1
persistent-superblock    1
chunk-size          32
nr-raid-disks       2
nr-spare-disks      0
device              /dev/sdd1
raid-disk           0
device              /dev/sde1
raid-disk           1
```

9

Linux and RAID

This entry will create a RAID level 0 array using /dev/sdb1 and /dev/sdc1, making the size of the array equal to the combined size of these two partitions. In our example, they are the same size. Again, to instantiate this RAID array, you simply run the mkraid command. Here is what this might look like:

```
[root@hqtest18 /root]# cat /proc/mdstat
Personalities : [linear] [raid0]
read_ahead 1024 sectors
unused devices: <none>


[root@hqtest18 /root]# mkraid /dev/md0
handling MD device /dev/md0
analyzing super-block
disk 0: /dev/sdb1, 8883913kB, raid superblock at 8883840kB
disk 1: /dev/sdc1, 8883913kB, raid superblock at 8883840kB


[root@hqtest18 /root]# cat /proc/mdstat
Personalities : [linear] [raid0]
read_ahead 1024 sectors
md0 : active raid0 sdc1[1] sdb1[0] 17767680 blocks 32k chunks
unused devices: <none>


[root@hqtest18 /root]# mkraid /dev/md1
handling MD device /dev/md1
analyzing super-block
disk 0: /dev/sdd1, 8883913kB, raid superblock at 8883840kB
disk 1: /dev/sde1, 8883913kB, raid superblock at 8883840kB


[root@hqtest18 /root]# cat /proc/mdstat
Personalities : [linear] [raid0] [raid1]
read_ahead 1024 sectors
md1 : active raid1 sde1[1] sdd1[0] 8883840 blocks [2/2] [UU]
resync=0% finish=21.6min
md0 : active raid0 sdc1[1] sdb1[0] 17767680 blocks 32k chunks
unused devices: <none>


[root@hqtest18 /root]# mkdir -p /raid1
[root@hqtest18 /root]# mkdir -p /raid2


[root@hqtest18 /root]# mke2fs -b 4096 -i 262144 /dev/md0
mke2fs 1.14, 9-Jan-1999 for EXT2 FS 0.5b, 95/08/09
Linux ext2 filesystem format
Filesystem label=
```

```
69632 inodes, 4441920 blocks
222096 blocks (5.00%) reserved for the super user
First data block=0
Block size=4096 (log=2)
Fragment size=4096 (log=2)
136 block groups
32768 blocks per group, 32768 fragments per group
512 inodes per group
Superblock backups stored on blocks:
    32768, 65536, 98304, 131072, 163840, 196608, 229376, 262144, 294912,
    327680, 360448, 393216, 425984, 458752, 491520, 524288, 557056,
    589824,
    622592, 655360, 688128, 720896, 753664, 786432, 819200, 851968,
    884736,
    917504, 950272, 983040, 1015808, 1048576, 1081344, 1114112, 1146880,
    1179648, 1212416, 1245184, 1277952, 1310720, 1343488, 1376256,
    1409024,
    1441792, 1474560, 1507328, 1540096, 1572864, 1605632, 1638400,
    1671168,
    1703936, 1736704, 1769472, 1802240, 1835008, 1867776, 1900544,
    1933312,
    1966080, 1998848, 2031616, 2064384, 2097152, 2129920, 2162688,
    2195456,
    2228224, 2260992, 2293760, 2326528, 2359296, 2392064, 2424832,
    2457600,
    2490368, 2523136, 2555904, 2588672, 2621440, 2654208, 2686976,
    2719744,
    2752512, 2785280, 2818048, 2850816, 2883584, 2916352, 2949120,
    2981888,
    3014656, 3047424, 3080192, 3112960, 3145728, 3178496, 3211264,
    3244032,
    3276800, 3309568, 3342336, 3375104, 3407872, 3440640, 3473408,
    3506176,
    3538944, 3571712, 3604480, 3637248, 3670016, 3702784, 3735552,
    3768320,
    3801088, 3833856, 3866624, 3899392, 3932160, 3964928, 3997696,
    4030464,
    4063232, 4096000, 4128768, 4161536, 4194304, 4227072, 4259840,
    4292608,
    4325376, 4358144, 4390912, 4423680

Writing inode tables:    done
```

9

Linux and RAID

```
Writing superblocks and filesystem accounting information: done


[root@hqtest18 /root]# mke2fs -b 4096 -i 262144 /dev/md1
mke2fs 1.14, 9-Jan-1999 for EXT2 FS 0.5b, 95/08/09
Linux ext2 filesystem format
Filesystem label=
34816 inodes, 2220960 blocks
111048 blocks (5.00%) reserved for the super user
First data block=0
Block size=4096 (log=2)
Fragment size=4096 (log=2)
68 block groups
32768 blocks per group, 32768 fragments per group
512 inodes per group
Superblock backups stored on blocks:
    32768, 65536, 98304, 131072, 163840, 196608, 229376, 262144, 294912,
    327680, 360448, 393216, 425984, 458752, 491520, 524288, 557056,
    589824,
    622592, 655360, 688128, 720896, 753664, 786432, 819200, 851968,
    884736,
    917504, 950272, 983040, 1015808, 1048576, 1081344, 1114112, 1146880,
    1179648, 1212416, 1245184, 1277952, 1310720, 1343488, 1376256,
    1409024,
    1441792, 1474560, 1507328, 1540096, 1572864, 1605632, 1638400,
    1671168,
    1703936, 1736704, 1769472, 1802240, 1835008, 1867776, 1900544,
    1933312,
    1966080, 1998848, 2031616, 2064384, 2097152, 2129920, 2162688,
    2195456


Writing inode tables:  done
Writing superblocks and filesystem accounting information: done


[root@hqtest18 /root]# mount /dev/md0 /raid1
[root@hqtest18 /root]# mount /dev/md1 /raid2


[root@hqtest18 /root]# df
Filesystem          1k-blocks      Used Available Use% Mounted on
/dev/sda2             2035638     81721   1848692   4% /
/dev/sda7             6172033    974808   4877534  17% /usr
/dev/md0             17756256        52  16867820   0% /raid1
/dev/md1              8878400        52   8434156   0% /raid2
```

```
[root@hqtest18 /root]# ls /raid1
lost+found

[root@hqtest18 /root]# ls /raid2
lost+found

[root@hqtest18 /root]# cat /proc/mdstat
Personalities : [linear] [raid0] [raid1]
read_ahead 1024 sectors
md1 : active raid1 sde1[1] sdd1[0] 8883840 blocks [2/2] [UU]
resync=9% finish=20.8min
md0 : active raid0 sdc1[1] sdb1[0] 17767680 blocks 32k chunks
unused devices: <none>


[root@hqtest18 /root]# umount /raid2
[root@hqtest18 /root]# umount /raid1
[root@hqtest18 /root]# raidstop /dev/md0
[root@hqtest18 /root]# raidstop /dev/md1
[root@hqtest18 /root]# cat /proc/mdstat
Personalities : [linear] [raid0] [raid1]
read_ahead 1024 sectors
unused devices: <none>
```

After we have unmounted the filesystem and have created and used `raidstop` to deactivate the array, we are ready to create a more complex mirror. In this example, we will create a mirror consisting of two RAID level 0 arrays. This will require three stanzas in `/etc/raidtab` and in this case, ordering of the entries is crucial. The `/etc/raidtab` file is parsed sequentially and therefore we must define the two RAID level 0 arrays first and then define the mirror. Here is what this looks like:

```
# Mirror consisting of two striped arrays
raiddev              /dev/md0
raid-level        0
persistent-superblock    0
chunk-size        32
nr-raid-disks        2
nr-spare-disks        0
device              /dev/sdb1
raid-disk         0
device              /dev/sdc1
raid-disk         1

raiddev              /dev/md1
raid-level        0
```

```
persistent-superblock     0
chunk-size        32
nr-raid-disks         2
nr-spare-disks        0
device               /dev/sdd1
raid-disk        0
device               /dev/sde1
raid-disk        1


raiddev              /dev/md2
raid-level        1
persistent-superblock     0
chunk-size        32
nr-raid-disks         2
nr-spare-disks        0
device               /dev/md0
raid-disk        0
device               /dev/md1
raid-disk        1
```

One of the advantages of this setup is that writes to the components of the mirror get the performance advantage of RAID level 0 in addition to the performance advantage of mirrors on read operations. This combination is mistakenly called RAID level 10 in some of the Linux RAID documentation found on the Web. It is in fact the exact opposite of RAID level 10, which is the creation of a RAID level 0 array consisting of two RAID level 1 arrays. Here is what creation of this configuration would look like:

```
[root@hqtest18 /root]# cat /proc/mdstat
Personalities : [linear] [raid0] [raid1]
read_ahead 1024 sectors
·unused devices: <none>


[root@hqtest18 /root]# mkraid /dev/md0
handling MD device /dev/md0
analyzing super-block
disk 0: /dev/sdb1, 8883913kB, raid superblock at 8883840kB
disk 1: /dev/sdc1, 8883913kB, raid superblock at 8883840kB


[root@hqtest18 /root]# mkraid /dev/md1
handling MD device /dev/md1
analyzing super-block
disk 0: /dev/sdd1, 8883913kB, raid superblock at 8883840kB
disk 1: /dev/sde1, 8883913kB, raid superblock at 8883840kB
```

```
[root@hqtest18 /root]# cat /proc/mdstat
Personalities : [linear] [raid0] [raid1]
read_ahead 1024 sectors
md1 : active raid0 sde1[1] sdd1[0] 17767808 blocks 32k chunks
md0 : active raid0 sdc1[1] sdb1[0] 17767808 blocks 32k chunks
unused devices: <none>


[root@hqtest18 /root]# mkraid /dev/md2
handling MD device /dev/md2
analyzing super-block
disk 0: /dev/md0, 17767808kB, raid superblock at 17767744kB
disk 1: /dev/md1, 17767808kB, raid superblock at 17767744kB


[root@hqtest18 /root]# cat /proc/mdstat
Personalities : [linear] [raid0] [raid1]
read_ahead 1024 sectors
md2 : active raid1 md1[1] md0[0] 17767808 blocks [2/2] [UU]
resync=0% finish=38.6min
md1 : active raid0 sde1[1] sdd1[0] 17767808 blocks 32k chunks
md0 : active raid0 sdc1[1] sdb1[0] 17767808 blocks 32k chunks
unused devices: <none>


[root@hqtest18 /root]# mke2fs -b 4096 -i 262144 /dev/md2
mke2fs 1.14, 9-Jan-1999 for EXT2 FS 0.5b, 95/08/09
Linux ext2 filesystem format
Filesystem label=
69632 inodes, 4441952 blocks
222097 blocks (5.00%) reserved for the super user
First data block=0
Block size=4096 (log=2)
Fragment size=4096 (log=2)
136 block groups
32768 blocks per group, 32768 fragments per group
512 inodes per group
Superblock backups stored on blocks:
    32768, 65536, 98304, 131072, 163840, 196608, 229376, 262144, 294912,
    327680, 360448, 393216, 425984, 458752, 491520, 524288, 557056,
 589824,
    622592, 655360, 688128, 720896, 753664, 786432, 819200, 851968,
 884736,
    917504, 950272, 983040, 1015808, 1048576, 1081344, 1114112, 1146880,
    1179648, 1212416, 1245184, 1277952, 1310720, 1343488, 1376256,
```

9

Linux and RAID

```
1409024,
   1441792, 1474560, 1507328, 1540096, 1572864, 1605632, 1638400,
1671168,
   1703936, 1736704, 1769472, 1802240, 1835008, 1867776, 1900544,
1933312,
   1966080, 1998848, 2031616, 2064384, 2097152, 2129920, 2162688,
2195456,
   2228224, 2260992, 2293760, 2326528, 2359296, 2392064, 2424832,
2457600,
   2490368, 2523136, 2555904, 2588672, 2621440, 2654208, 2686976,
2719744,
   2752512, 2785280, 2818048, 2850816, 2883584, 2916352, 2949120,
2981888,
   3014656, 3047424, 3080192, 3112960, 3145728, 3178496, 3211264,
3244032,
   3276800, 3309568, 3342336, 3375104, 3407872, 3440640, 3473408,
3506176,
   3538944, 3571712, 3604480, 3637248, 3670016, 3702784, 3735552,
3768320,
   3801088, 3833856, 3866624, 3899392, 3932160, 3964928, 3997696,
4030464,
   4063232, 4096000, 4128768, 4161536, 4194304, 4227072, 4259840,
4292608,
   4325376, 4358144, 4390912, 4423680

Writing inode tables:    done
Writing superblocks and filesystem accounting information: done

[root@hqtest18 /root]# mount /dev/md2 /raid

[root@hqtest18 /root]# df
Filesystem          1k-blocks      Used Available Use% Mounted on
/dev/sda2            2035638      81745   1848668   4% /
/dev/sda7            6172033     974808   4877534  17% /usr
/dev/md2            17756384         52  16867944   0% /raid

[root@hqtest18 /root]# ls /raid
lost+found

[root@hqtest18 /root]# umount /raid

[root@hqtest18 /root]# raidstop /dev/md2
```

```
[root@hqtest18 /root]# raidstop /dev/md1

[root@hqtest18 /root]# raidstop /dev/md0

[root@hqtest18 /root]# cat /proc/mdstat
Personalities : [linear] [raid0] [raid1]
read_ahead 1024 sectors
unused devices: <none>
```

Again, let us unmount the filesystem we created and use `raidstop` to deactivate the array. We are ready now to create the next type of RAID array, the RAID level 4 array. For this array, we will use three of the disks as data disks and the fourth disk as the parity disk with no spares. Here is the `/etc/raidtab` entry created for this example:

```
# RAID-4 array example
raiddev              /dev/md0
raid-level           4
persistent-superblock    0
chunk-size         32
nr-raid-disks        4
nr-spare-disks         0
device             /dev/sdb1
raid-disk          0
device             /dev/sdc1
raid-disk          1
device             /dev/sdd1
raid-disk          2
device             /dev/sde1
parity-disk          0
```

The following session transcript shows the creation of the array, the creation of a filesystem on the array, and the contents of the md status file in `/proc`. As you can see, it is possible to start using the array immediately after it is registered with the kernel, even though the array is not completely initialized. Although this is possible, it is recommended that you do not begin writing data to the array until the initialization is completed. You can determine when this happens by watching the process table and by checking `/proc/mdstat`.

```
[root@hqtest18 /root]# cat /proc/mdstat
Personalities : [linear] [raid0] [raid1]
read_ahead 1024 sectors
unused devices: <none>

[root@hqtest18 /root]# mkraid /dev/md0
handling MD device /dev/md0
```

9

Linux and RAID

```
analyzing super-block
disk 0: /dev/sdb1, 8883913kB, raid superblock at 8883840kB
disk 1: /dev/sdc1, 8883913kB, raid superblock at 8883840kB
disk 2: /dev/sdd1, 8883913kB, raid superblock at 8883840kB
disk 3: /dev/sde1, 8883913kB, raid superblock at 8883840kB


[root@hqtest18 /root]# cat /proc/mdstat
Personalities : [linear] [raid0] [raid1] [raid5]
read_ahead 1024 sectors
md0 : active raid5 sde1[3] sdd1[2] sdc1[1] sdb1[0] 26651712 blocks
level 4, 32k chunk, algorithm 0 [4/4] [UUUU] resync=0% finish=47.8min
unused devices: <none>


[root@hqtest18 /root]# mke2fs -b 4096 -i 262144 /dev/md0
mke2fs 1.14, 9-Jan-1999 for EXT2 FS 0.5b, 95/08/09
Linux ext2 filesystem format
Filesystem label=
104448 inodes, 6662928 blocks
333146 blocks (5.00%) reserved for the super user
First data block=0
Block size=4096 (log=2)
Fragment size=4096 (log=2)
204 block groups
32768 blocks per group, 32768 fragments per group
512 inodes per group
Superblock backups stored on blocks:
    32768, 65536, 98304, 131072, 163840, 196608, 229376, 262144, 294912,
    327680, 360448, 393216, 425984, 458752, 491520, 524288, 557056,
 589824,
    622592, 655360, 688128, 720896, 753664, 786432, 819200, 851968,
 884736,
    917504, 950272, 983040, 1015808, 1048576, 1081344, 1114112, 1146880,
    1179648, 1212416, 1245184, 1277952, 1310720, 1343488, 1376256,
 1409024,
    1441792, 1474560, 1507328, 1540096, 1572864, 1605632, 1638400,
 1671168,
    1703936, 1736704, 1769472, 1802240, 1835008, 1867776, 1900544,
 1933312,
    1966080, 1998848, 2031616, 2064384, 2097152, 2129920, 2162688,
 2195456,
    2228224, 2260992, 2293760, 2326528, 2359296, 2392064, 2424832,
 2457600,
    2490368, 2523136, 2555904, 2588672, 2621440, 2654208, 2686976,
```

```
2719744,
    2752512, 2785280, 2818048, 2850816, 2883584, 2916352, 2949120,
2981888,
    3014656, 3047424, 3080192, 3112960, 3145728, 3178496, 3211264,
3244032,
    3276800, 3309568, 3342336, 3375104, 3407872, 3440640, 3473408,
3506176,
    3538944, 3571712, 3604480, 3637248, 3670016, 3702784, 3735552,
3768320,
    3801088, 3833856, 3866624, 3899392, 3932160, 3964928, 3997696,
4030464,
    4063232, 4096000, 4128768, 4161536, 4194304, 4227072, 4259840,
4292608,
    4325376, 4358144, 4390912, 4423680, 4456448, 4489216, 4521984,
4554752,
    4587520, 4620288, 4653056, 4685824, 4718592, 4751360, 4784128,
4816896,
    4849664, 4882432, 4915200, 4947968, 4980736, 5013504, 5046272,
 5079040,
    5111808, 5144576, 5177344, 5210112, 5242880, 5275648, 5308416,
 5341184,
    5373952, 5406720, 5439488, 5472256, 5505024, 5537792, 5570560,
5603328,
    5636096, 5668864, 5701632, 5734400, 5767168, 5799936, 5832704,
 5865472,
    5898240, 5931008, 5963776, 5996544, 6029312, 6062080, 6094848,
 6127616,
    6160384, 6193152, 6225920, 6258688, 6291456, 6324224, 6356992,
 6389760,
    6422528, 6455296, 6488064, 6520832, 6553600, 6586368, 6619136,
 6651904

Writing inode tables:   done
Writing superblocks and filesystem accounting information: done

[root@hqtest18 /root]# mount /dev/md0 /raid

[root@hqtest18 /root]# df
Filesystem            1k-blocks     Used Available Use% Mounted on
/dev/sda2               2035638    81769   1848644   4% /
/dev/sda7               6172033   974808   4877534  17% /usr
/dev/md0               26634576       52  25301940   0% /raid
```

```
[root@hqtest18 /root]# ls /raid
lost+found

[root@hqtest18 /root]# umount /raid

[root@hqtest18 /root]# raidstop /dev/md0

[root@hqtest18 /root]# cat /proc/mdstat
Personalities : [linear] [raid0] [raid1] [raid5]
read_ahead 1024 sectors
unused devices: <none>
```

Our final example is the one that is most commonly used, a RAID level 5 array. This RAID level is often selected because it offers the redundancy advantages of RAID levels 1 and 4 without the write penalty of mirroring, and without the parity checking bottleneck of RAID level 4. Let's look at the /etc/raidtab entry for this example.

```
# RAID-5 array example with one spare
raiddev              /dev/md0
raid-level           5
persistent-superblock     0
chunk-size           32
parity-algorithm     left-symmetric
nr-raid-disks        3
#    nr-spare-disks          1
device               /dev/sdb1
raid-disk            0
device               /dev/sdc1
raid-disk            1
device               /dev/sdd1
raid-disk            2
#    device               /dev/sde1
#    spare-disk           0
```

You will note in the entry above the addition of a keyword, parity-algorithm. This entry controls the algorithm used to determine which disk in each slice will be used to store the parity data. You will also note that the entries for nr-spare-disks and the definition of /dev/sde1 as a spare are commented out, so that for the following session, this definition results in the creation of a filesystem that is 16Gb is size.

The formula for calculating the size of a RAID level 5 array is (N - 1) * S, where N is the value of nr-raid-disks and S is the size of the smallest device used in the creation of the array. In this example, using four identical disks of 9 Gb each, this is (3 - 1) * 9Gb or 18Gb of space for the filesystem created on the array.

```
[root@hqtest18 /root]# cat /proc/mdstat
Personalities : [linear] [raid0] [raid1] [raid5]
read_ahead 1024 sectors
unused devices: <none>


[root@hqtest18 /root]# mkraid /dev/md0
handling MD device /dev/md0
analyzing super-block
disk 0: /dev/sdb1, 8883913kB, raid superblock at 8883840kB
disk 1: /dev/sdc1, 8883913kB, raid superblock at 8883840kB
disk 2: /dev/sdd1, 8883913kB, raid superblock at 8883840kB


[root@hqtest18 /root]# mke2fs -b 4096 -i 262144 /dev/md0
mke2fs 1.14, 9-Jan-1999 for EXT2 FS 0.5b, 95/08/09
Linux ext2 filesystem format
Filesystem label=
69632 inodes, 4441952 blocks
222097 blocks (5.00%) reserved for the super user
First data block=0
Block size=4096 (log=2)
Fragment size=4096 (log=2)
136 block groups
32768 blocks per group, 32768 fragments per group
512 inodes per group
Superblock backups stored on blocks:
    32768, 65536, 98304, 131072, 163840, 196608, 229376, 262144, 294912,
    327680, 360448, 393216, 425984, 458752, 491520, 524288, 557056,
589824,
    622592, 655360, 688128, 720896, 753664, 786432, 819200, 851968,
884736,
    917504, 950272, 983040, 1015808, 1048576, 1081344, 1114112, 1146880,
    1179648, 1212416, 1245184, 1277952, 1310720, 1343488, 1376256,
1409024,
    1441792, 1474560, 1507328, 1540096, 1572864, 1605632, 1638400,
1671168,
    1703936, 1736704, 1769472, 1802240, 1835008, 1867776, 1900544,
1933312,
    1966080, 1998848, 2031616, 2064384, 2097152, 2129920, 2162688,
2195456,
    2228224, 2260992, 2293760, 2326528, 2359296, 2392064, 2424832,
2457600,
    2490368, 2523136, 2555904, 2588672, 2621440, 2654208, 2686976,
```

```
2719744,
    2752512, 2785280, 2818048, 2850816, 2883584, 2916352, 2949120,
2981888,
    3014656, 3047424, 3080192, 3112960, 3145728, 3178496, 3211264,
3244032,
    3276800, 3309568, 3342336, 3375104, 3407872, 3440640, 3473408,
3506176,
    3538944, 3571712, 3604480, 3637248, 3670016, 3702784, 3735552,
3768320,
    3801088, 3833856, 3866624, 3899392, 3932160, 3964928, 3997696,
4030464,
    4063232, 4096000, 4128768, 4161536, 4194304, 4227072, 4259840,
4292608,
    4325376, 4358144, 4390912, 4423680

Writing inode tables:    done
Writing superblocks and filesystem accounting information: done


[root@hqtest18 /root]# cat /proc/mdstat
Personalities : [linear] [raid0] [raid1] [raid5]
read_ahead 1024 sectors
md0 : active raid5 sdd1[2] sdc1[1] sdb1[0] 17767808 blocks level 5, 32k
chunk, algorithm 2 [3/3] [UUU] resync=0% finish=60.0min
unused devices: <none>


[root@hqtest18 /root]# mount /dev/md0 /raid


[root@hqtest18 /root]# df
Filesystem          1k-blocks       Used Available Use% Mounted on
/dev/sda2             2035638      81777   1848636   4% /
/dev/sda7             6172033     974808   4877534  17% /usr
/dev/md0             17756384         52  16867944   0% /raid

[root@hqtest18 /root]# ls /raid
lost+found
```

Now that we have a working RAID level 5 array, let's make it a little more robust by adding a spare disk that can be used to do hot reconstruction in the event of a disk failure. To do this, we must modify our /etc/raidtab entry by uncommenting the nr-spare-disks entry and the definition of /dev/sde1 as a spare disk, resulting in a raidtab entry that looks like this:

```
# RAID-5 array example with one spare
raiddev              /dev/md0
```

```
raid-level          5
persistent-superblock    0
chunk-size          32
parity-algorithm    left-symmetric
nr-raid-disks       3
nr-spare-disks       1
device              /dev/sdb1
raid-disk          0
device              /dev/sdc1
raid-disk          1
device              /dev/sdd1
raid-disk          2
device              /dev/sde1
spare-disk          0
```

Once these changes have been made, we run the `raidhotadd` command as shown here to add this spare disk to the array:

```
[root@hqtest18 /root]# raidhotadd /dev/md0 /dev/sde1

[root@hqtest18 /root]# cat /proc/mdstat
Personalities : [linear] [raid0] [raid1] [raid5]
read_ahead 1024 sectors
md0 : active raid5 sde1[3] sdd1[2] sdc1[1] sdb1[0] 17767808 blocks
 level 5, 32k chunk, algorithm 2 [3/3] [UUU] resync=3% finish=48.8min
unused devices: <none>
```

As you can see, the `sde1` device is now part of the RAID array and construction of the array is proceeding. This is an important new feature of software RAID for Linux that was lacking in previous releases.

One final topic concerning Linux software RAID is booting from a RAID device. With Red Hat 6.0, this procedure has become much easier, with the exception of installation. Red Hat boot images do not currently support installing to a RAID device, which means that you must first install on a normal partition and then copy the installation to the RAID array that you create.

There are actually multiple methods for booting from a RAID array. The original method is documented in a HOWTO document called the "Root RAID HOWTO cookbook," by Michael A. Robinton. This document can be found in the `/usr/doc/HOWTO` directory of your Red Hat installation, provided that you included this when you set up your system, in a file named `Root-RAID-HOWTO`. This method is very complex and with the 2.2 series kernels, totally unnecessary. Another method for booting from a RAID is documented very briefly in the kernel source tree, in the Documentation directory in `md.txt`. This method

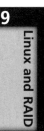

9

Linux and RAID

involves including support in your kernel for booting from RAID and passing the RAID configuration information to the kernel at boot time via LILO or Loadlin. The final and most recent method of booting from RAID is documented in `/usr/doc/raidtools-0.90/` `Software-RAID-Howto.txt`. This method allows you to set up a mirror and boot from it. Using the information presented here along with any of these documents will allow you to boot from RAID if you so desire.

Hardware RAID and Linux

In addition to support for software RAID, Linux also supports hardware RAID implementations. When deciding whether to choose hardware RAID or software RAID, there are three basic considerations. These considerations are cost, performance, and whether or not the Linux kernel supports it.

Let's start with cost. If you have ever priced RAID hardware, you are probably thinking that Linux software RAID wins in this category hands down. You may have to think again, however, when you factor in all of the costs associated with each solution. Some of the items you will have to factor into your cost calculations include the amount of time required to recover from a disk failure, the cost of training administrators to work with the hardware or software solution chosen, and other factors besides the cost of the hardware itself. With software RAID, for example, you may have to factor in the time required to monitor the mailing lists and Linux newsgroups so that you can stay abreast of developments by the RAID maintainers. You may also have to factor in the cost of recompiling your kernel to take advantage of a new feature in the drivers. With hardware solutions, you may have to factor in the time required to reboot the system to use the management tools for the device that are not yet available for Linux. Take the time to determine the complete costs before implementing a RAID solution.

Performance is another consideration. The performance of a RAID solution is dependent on many factors. Some of these include the optimization of driver code, the speed of the drives used, bus speeds, cache, and others. Hardware does not always win in this contest. If you have a poorly supported RAID controller or one that does not have enough cache on board, software RAID can sometimes outperform hardware RAID. Performing your own benchmarks is one of the few ways to gauge this.

Whether or not the Linux kernel supports a solution is another consideration. If you have a need for a RAID level 3 array, software RAID under Linux is impossible. There are hardware RAID solutions that implement this level that work with Linux. Support for a particular solution in Linux normally comes in one of two varieties. The first variety is support for devices that look like a supported device. An example of this is external RAID enclosures that connect to the Linux host via a SCSI controller. The other variety is driver support in the Linux kernel for a RAID controller.

RAID Controller Drivers

The Linux kernel shipped with Red Hat 6.0 has support for RAID controllers from several manufacturers. These manufacturers include Mylex, DPT, IBM, American Megatrends, IPC, and a plethora of clone manufacturers. This section looks at each of the drivers that can be compiled into the kernel and the controllers that they support. Some of the questions to ask yourself when looking at RAID controllers like those supported in the Linux kernel include the following:

- What RAID levels are implemented?

- Is configuration management software available in the controller firmware or natively under Linux?

- How many devices can be attached?

- How many SCSI channels does the controller have?

- How much cache is available?

- Is the cache memory upgradeable and does it require non-standard memory modules to do so?

- How stable is the driver support?

The first driver is the DAC960 driver, written by Leonard Zubkoff to support RAID controllers from Mylex. The configuration option you must select to include support for this controller is `CONFIG_BLK_DEV_DAC960`, which is accessed in the kernel config under the Block Devices section. Inclusion of this driver in your kernel gives you support for the eXtremeRAID 1100, AcceleRAID 150, 200, and 250, and a number of RAID controllers built around the Intel i960 RISC processor. One thing that differentiates this driver from other hardware RAID controllers is that there is no reliance on the kernel SCSI subsystem. This gives the DAC960 driver a performance advantage. Detailed documentation on this driver, including a list of supported models, driver features, and usage notes can be found in the kernel source tree under the `drivers/block` directory in the `README.DAC960` file.

9

Linux and RAID

Another driver that is available in the Linux kernel is the EATA/DMA driver, which supports the SmartRAID family of controllers from DPT. These controllers support RAID levels 0, 1, and 5. One of the drawbacks of this controller is the lack of management tools that work under Linux. To change parameters, rebuild damaged arrays, and to perform other maintenance tasks, you must reboot your system and use the software tools that come with the hardware. This can be problematic and should be taken into consideration when deciding whether to use this controller.

A recent addition to the kernel is support for the AMI MegaRAID controllers. These controllers are popular with OEMs like Dell, who use them in their PowerEdge family of servers. One factor in favor of these controllers is the announcement of support for Linux by AMI, including their management tools. Another factor is the integrated management features built in to the controller BIOS, which eliminates the need to boot into a different operation system to manage the array.

External RAID Devices

The types of RAID devices supported by Linux for the longest amount of time are external RAID devices. These devices normally come in their own cases, which contain all of the hardware and firmware necessary to implement RAID. Many of these devices are able to connect to a standard SCSI controller and appear to the operating system as a single device. These devices are usually quite costly, but when you factor in repair time, support requirements, and features of these devices such as hot swapping of drives, they can actually be very cost effective. Things to look for when considering the purchase of external raid devices include the following:

- Are any special drivers required to be loaded?

- Does the device support hot swapping of drives?

- Does the device have a single or multiple device channels?

- How does the device attach to the host system (SCSI, fiber channel)?

- What type of controller is required for the host system?

- Is this type of controller supported by the Linux kernel?

- What RAID levels are implemented?

- Is the drive capacity expandable?

- How is the device configured?

There are other considerations as well, but these questions are a good starting point. A good hardware solution will address each of these concerns as they arise.

Other Sources of Information

RAID support for Linux is constantly evolving and keeping up with it can become a full-time job. One of the most useful means of keeping up with developments is the `linux-raid` mailing list. Other adopters of RAID as well as the developers of the software RAID tools and driver authors for hardware RAID controllers frequent this list. Majordomo manages this list and the subscription address is `linux-raid-request@vger.rutgers.edu`. To subscribe, send a message with a body of `subscribe` to this address.

Summary

This chapter covered a lot of information on software and hardware RAID support under Linux. It looked at the specific implementation of software RAID included with Red Hat as well as the hardware support for RAID in the Linux kernel. Before moving on to other subjects, let's compare the two one last time.

Software RAID under Linux has matured to the point where it can be relied on to protect mission-critical data and offers the following advantages:

- It is easy to implement.

- It is inexpensive in terms of hardware.

- Hot reconstruction is available with the latest releases.

- It has support for most popular RAID levels.

On the other hand, there are a few disadvantages that you need to consider when deciding on whether to implement software RAID. A few of these are

- It is costly in terms of the training required to create and maintain.

- Performance is usually less than hardware implementations.

- Advanced features such as hot swapping and hot reconstruction are relatively young and untested.

Compare this with Linux hardware RAID support. In this area, some of the key advantages include

- Implementations of multiple RAID levels not included in the Linux kernel software RAID modules.

- Performance is usually better than software RAID, given sufficient cache memory and driver support.

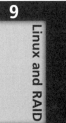
9
Linux and RAID

These advantages are balanced by a number of disadvantages associated with hardware RAID:

- Many hardware RAID drivers in the Linux kernel are immature.

- There is limited support from RAID vendors (although this is slowly changing).

- Expensive hardware is required.

As you can see, each of the solutions to the RAID question has advantages and disadvantages. What you as a systems administrator must do is weigh each of these carefully and be very cautious in your implementation decision. Hopefully, with its explanation of the different RAID levels and the examples of how to implement them in software and hardware, this chapter has prepared you to make this decision.

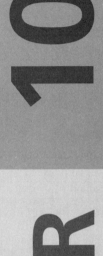

Managing Removable Media Devices

In This Chapter

- Removable Media Devices   *272*
- Parallel Port Storage Devices   *285*
- Granting Access to Users   *289*

CHAPTER 10

For users coming from the world of Microsoft operating systems, where the user has complete control over every device on the system, sitting down at a Linux system and not being able to use the floppy drive or CD-ROM drive can be quite a shock. This chapter looks at some of the removable media devices supported by Linux, including devices that connect to the parallel port such as Zip and Jaz drives. It covers the use of tools to create your own data and audio CDs using CD-R and CD-RW drives. It also looks at how to grant access to these devices for your users without giving away control of the systems in the process.

Removable Media Devices

This first section looks at the support under Linux for the standard removable media devices, starting with floppy drives, then moving on to CD-ROM drives, and next to writable and rewritable CD drives. It also looks at the current state of support for newer devices, such as DVD-ROM drives.

Floppy Drives

Linux supports up to four floppy drives on up to two floppy drive controllers for a total of eight drives, numbered 0-7. These drives may be standard 5.25" or 3.5" drives in a number of different capacities. The capacity of the floppy is determined by looking at the device used to access it. Table 10.1 lists the floppy device special files included in the Red Hat distribution and their capacities.

TABLE 10.1 Supported Floppy Drive Device Names

Device File	Description
/dev/fd0	Controller 1, drive 1 autodetect
/dev/fd0d360	5.25" 360K in a 360K drive
/dev/fd0h360	5.25" 360K in a 1200K drive
/dev/fd0h720	5.25" 720K in a 1200K drive
/dev/fd0h1200	5.25" 1200K in a 1200K drive
/dev/fd0D360	3.5" 360K Double Density
/dev/fd0H360	3.5" 360K Double Density
/dev/fd0D720	3.5" 720K Double Density
/dev/fd0H720	3.5" 720K Double Density
/dev/fd0H1440	3.5" 1440K High Density
/dev/fd1	Controller 1, drive 2 autodetect
/dev/fd1d360	5.25" 360K in a 360K drive
/dev/fd1h360	5.25" 360K in a 1200K drive
/dev/fd1h720	5.25" 720K in a 1200K drive

TABLE **10.1**   continued

Device File	Description
/dev/fd1h1200	5.25" 1200K in a 1200K drive
/dev/fd1D360	3.5" 360K Double Density
/dev/fd1H360	3.5" 360K Double Density
/dev/fd1D720	3.5" 720K Double Density
/dev/fd1H720	3.5" 720K Double Density
/dev/fd1H1440	3.5" 1440K High Density

There are other devices described in the devices.txt file; however, those in the table are those that are included with the Red Hat distribution.

> **Note**
>
> Red Hat uses the old format for the naming of floppy devices instead of the current naming scheme. The official naming scheme is described in /usr/src/linux/Documentation/devices.txt, which contains the following note:
>
> "NOTE: The letter in the device name (d, q, h or u) signifies the type of drive: 5.25" Double Density , 5.25" Quad Density (q), 5.25" High Density (h) or 3.5" (any model, u). The use of the capital letters D, H and E for the 3.5" models have been deprecated, since the drive type is insignificant for these devices."

The floppy driver can be included as a part of the kernel or as a module, and a plethora of options are available to get it to work on your system. These options are described in Chapter 35, "Customizing the Linux Kernel."

CD-ROM Drives

Another type of removable media device supported by the Linux kernel is the CD-ROM drive, which has become a standard part of most modern personal computers. With the explosive growth of software, the CD-ROM drive has become essential to minimize shipping costs of software packages. Consider, for example, an office suite such as Star Office. If this software were shipped only on 3.5" floppies, it would take approximately thirty-five of them to contain the package. If we assume that 3.5" floppies cost $0.08 each, that means it would cost $2.80 for the media alone, not to mention the added shipping costs for the extra weight. Contrast this with the cost of a CD-ROM at less than $1 each with a capacity of 650M, and you can see how using CD-ROM technology can make a substantial difference in software packaging and shipping costs.

Standard CD-ROM drives have long been supported by the Linux kernel, starting with the proprietary drives that first became available from manufacturers such as Sony, and continuing on through the introduction of the IDE and ATAPI drives found on modern personal computers. In addition, CD-ROM drives are also supported via the SCSI subsystem, and most recently, drives connected via the parallel port.

The support in the kernel for CD-ROM devices extends beyond the hardware. It includes the ISO9660 filesystem, which is the standard filesystem for CDs. This allows CDs created for DOS to be read by Linux. In addition, there is support for the Rock Ridge extensions to the ISO9660 filesystem, which allows for long filename support such as used by Linux. A recent addition is support for the Joliet filesystem, which is used by recent versions of Microsoft Windows NT. In addition to these CD native filesystems, you can also access CDs created with any of the other filesystems supported by the kernel, although CDs of this type are exceedingly rare.

CD-R and CD-RW Drives

In addition to the normal CD-ROM drives supported by Linux, the CD-ROM support also includes support for recordable CD drives, or CD-R, and rewritable CD drives, or CD-RW. Just as with normal CD-ROM drives, this support includes ATAPI/IDE, SCSI, and external devices connected to the parallel ports. One of the criteria to consider when selecting a drive of this type is the speed of the system to which you plan to attach it, and what other tasks that system will be running. The current generation of software used to write data to CD-R or CD-RW drives is sensitive to the rate at which it is written. Failure to feed the data at a constant rate can lead to buffer underruns, which can cause data corruption on the media. Another factor that can affect this is the size of the buffer on the drive itself, if any, and the interface to the drive. Although there is a cost premium, most heavy users of CD-R and CD-RW drives prefer those that connect to a SCSI controller and it is these drives that are the best supported.

Creating CDs with Linux Software

Although there are several packages that can be used to create CDs on your Red Hat Linux system, only part of what you need was included on the Red Hat 6.0 media. This part was the mkisofs command, which is used to create an ISO9660 filesystem image that can be written to the CD-R or CD-RW media. The command required to write this image to the media is what was missing. This deficiency was corrected, however, with the Red Hat Linux 6.1 release, which includes all of the software required to burn your own CDs. This section demonstrates how to create a data CD from a filesystem and also how to duplicate a CD on a system with a CD-ROM drive in addition to the recordable drive.

The first step in creating a CD is to create an ISO9660 image. This assumes, of course, that you want to create a CD that can be read on multiple operating systems. For purposes of this example, we will be creating a CD that contains the Linux source tree. This is a contrived example because the size of the unpacked source tree is much smaller than will fit on a CD, but for purposes of demonstrating the use of the mkisofs command, it will suffice. Before we start, however, we will take a look at some of the command-line options of the mkisofs command. This is only a subset of the command-line options, which are described in full in the manual page. These command-line options are described in Table 10.2.

TABLE **10.2** mkisofs Command-Line Options

Option	*Description*
`-b boot_image`	Uses `boot_image` as the boot image when making a bootable CD using the El Torito format.
`-C last_sess_start,` `next_sess_start`	Used when creating a multisession CD. This option takes the sector number of the last session and the sector number to start the next session at. Used with `-M`.
	The pair of numbers may be obtained by using cdrecord with the `-msinfo` option.
`-c boot_catalog`	Specifies the pathname of the boot catalog to be used when making an El Torito bootable CD relative to the source path.
`-f`	Follows symbolic links when generating the filesystem.
`-J`	Generates Joliet directory records in addition to regular ISO9660 filenames.
`-log-file log_file`	Redirects all error, warning, and informational messages to `log_file` instead of the standard error.
`-m glob`	Excludes glob from being written to CD-ROM.
`-M path or -M device`	Specifies path to existing ISO9660 image to be merged for a multisession CD image.
`-o filename`	Name of the output ISO9660 filesystem image.
`-R`	Generates SUSP and RR records using the Rock Ridge protocol to further describe the files on the ISO9660 filesystem.
`-r`	This is like the `-R` option, but uid and gid on files are set to zero and all read bits are set to true so that files and directories have world permission on the client. If any execute bit is set for a file or a directory, sets all of the execute bits, and all write bits are cleared. Also removes setuid or setgid bits.
`-T`	Generates a file `TRANS.TBL` in each directory on the CD-ROM, which can be used on non-Rock Ridge capable systems to help establish the correct filenames.
`-V volid`	Specifies the volume ID to be written into the master block.
`-v`	Verbose execution.

10

Managing
Removable
Media
Devices

A more detailed explanation of these options can be found in the manual page. However, for the purposes of our example this information is sufficient. The following session transcript demonstrates the creation of an ISO9660 filesystem image from the Red Hat kernel source tree using the mkisofs command.

```
[root@madmax src]# ls
linux  linux-2.2.5  redhat  typescript

[root@madmax src]# cd linux-2.2.5

[root@madmax linux-2.2.5]# mkisofs -r -m *.o -m *.a -m vmlinux -m System.map
 -m  zImage -m bzImage -m core -V "RedHat 6.0 Kernel Source" -o ../ksource.img ./
Using SEMAPHOR.000;1 for  ./include/asm-i386/semaphore.h (semaphore-helper.h)
Using UMSDOS_F.000;1 for  ./include/linux/umsdos_fs_i.h (umsdos_fs.h)
Using SYSV_FS_.000;1 for  ./include/linux/sysv_fs_sb.h (sysv_fs_i.h)
Using ROMFS_FS.000;1 for  ./include/linux/romfs_fs_sb.h (romfs_fs_i.h)
Using ROMFS_FS.001;1 for  ./include/linux/romfs_fs_i.h (romfs_fs.h)
Using QNX4_FS_.000;1 for  ./include/linux/qnx4_fs_sb.h (qnx4_fs_i.h)
Using NTFS_FS_.000;1 for  ./include/linux/ntfs_fs_sb.h (ntfs_fs_i.h)
Using MSDOS_FS.000;1 for  ./include/linux/msdos_fs_sb.h (msdos_fs_i.h)
Using MSDOS_FS.001;1 for  ./include/linux/msdos_fs_i.h (msdos_fs.h)
Using MINIX_FS.000;1 for  ./include/linux/minix_fs_sb.h (minix_fs_i.h)
Using MINIX_FS.001;1 for  ./include/linux/minix_fs_i.h (minix_fs.h)
Using HPFS_FS_.000;1 for  ./include/linux/hpfs_fs_sb.h (hpfs_fs_i.h)
Using EXT2_FS_.000;1 for  ./include/linux/ext2_fs_sb.h (ext2_fs_i.h)
Using AFFS_FS_.000;1 for  ./include/linux/affs_fs_sb.h (affs_fs_i.h)
Using ADFS_FS_.000;1 for  ./include/linux/adfs_fs_sb.h (adfs_fs_i.h)
Using PARPORT_.000;1 for  ./include/linux/modules/parport_probe.ver
➥(parport_init.ver)
Using PARPORT_.001;1 for  ./include/linux/modules/parport_probe.stamp
➥(parport_init.stamp)
Using IP_MASQ_.000;1 for  ./include/linux/modules/ip_masq_mod.ver
➥(ip_masq_app.ver)
Using IP_MASQ_.001;1 for  ./include/linux/modules/ip_masq_mod.stamp
➥(ip_masq_app.stamp)
Using FBCON-CF.000;1 for  ./include/linux/modules/fbcon-cfb8.ver
➥(fbcon-cfb32.ver)
Using FBCON-CF.001;1 for  ./include/linux/modules/fbcon-cfb8.stamp
➥(fbcon-cfb32.stamp)
Using FBCON-CF.002;1 for  ./include/linux/modules/fbcon-cfb32.ver
➥(fbcon-cfb24.ver)
Using FBCON-CF.003;1 for  ./include/linux/modules/fbcon-cfb32.stamp
➥(fbcon-cfb24.stamp)
```

```
Using FBCON-CF.004;1 for  ./include/linux/modules/fbcon-cfb24.ver
➡(fbcon-cfb16.ver)
Using FBCON-CF.005;1 for  ./include/linux/modules/fbcon-cfb24.stamp
➡(fbcon-cfb16.stamp)
Using W83977AF.000;1 for  ./include/net/irda/w83977af_ir.h (w83977af.h)
Using IRLPT_SE.000;1 for  ./include/net/irda/irlpt_server_fsm.h
➡(irlpt_server.h)
Using IRLPT_CL.000;1 for  ./include/net/irda/irlpt_cli_fsm.h (irlpt_cli.h)
Using FBCON-IP.000;1 for  ./include/video/fbcon-iplan2p8.h (fbcon-iplan2p4.h)
Using FBCON-IP.001;1 for  ./include/video/fbcon-iplan2p4.h (fbcon-iplan2p2.h)
Using FBCON-CF.000;1 for  ./include/video/fbcon-cfb8.h (fbcon-cfb4.h)
Using FBCON-CF.001;1 for  ./include/video/fbcon-cfb4.h (fbcon-cfb32.h)
Using FBCON-CF.002;1 for  ./include/video/fbcon-cfb32.h (fbcon-cfb24.h)
Using FBCON-CF.003;1 for  ./include/video/fbcon-cfb24.h (fbcon-cfb2.h)
Using FBCON-CF.004;1 for  ./include/video/fbcon-cfb2.h (fbcon-cfb16.h)
Using JOYSTICK.000;1 for  ./Documentation/joystick.txt (joystick-parport.txt)
Using JOYSTICK.001;1 for  ./Documentation/joystick-parport.txt
➡(joystick-api.txt)
Using SMP.000;1 for  ./Documentation/smp.txt (SMP.txt)
Using SYS_SPAR.000;1 for  ./arch/sparc64/kernel/sys_sparc32.c (sys_sparc.c)
Using README.000;1 for  ./drivers/char/README.cyclomY (README.cycladesZ)
Using ZFTAPE-R.000;1 for  ./drivers/char/ftape/zftape/zftape-rw.h
➡(zftape-read.h)
Using ZFTAPE-R.001;1 for  ./drivers/char/ftape/zftape/zftape-rw.c
➡(zftape-read.c)
Using PARPORT_.000;1 for  ./drivers/misc/parport_share.c (parport_procfs.c)
Using PARPORT_.001;1 for  ./drivers/misc/parport_procfs.c (parport_pc.c)
Using PARPORT_.002;1 for  ./drivers/misc/parport_pc.c (parport_init.c)
Using PARPORT_.003;1 for  ./drivers/misc/parport_init.c (parport_ieee1284.c)
Using PARPORT_.004;1 for  ./drivers/misc/parport_ieee1284.c (parport_ax.c)
Using PARPORT_.005;1 for  ./drivers/misc/parport_ax.c (parport_arc.c)
Using SMC-ULTR.000;1 for  ./drivers/net/smc-ultra32.c (smc-ultra.c)
Using BAYCOM_S.000;1 for  ./drivers/net/hamradio/baycom_ser_hdx.c
➡(baycom_ser_fdx.c)
Using SM_AFSK2.000;1 for  ./drivers/net/hamradio/soundmodem/sm_afsk2666.c
➡(sm_afsk2400_8.c)
```

```
Using SM_AFSK2.001;1 for  ./drivers/net/hamradio/soundmodem/sm_afsk2400_8.c
➥(sm_afsk2400_7.c)
Using QLOGICPT.000;1 for  ./drivers/scsi/qlogicpti_asm.c (qlogicpti.c)
Using QLOGICIS.000;1 for  ./drivers/scsi/qlogicisp_asm.c (qlogicisp.c)
Using QLOGICFC.000;1 for  ./drivers/scsi/qlogicfc_asm.c (qlogicfc.c)
Using EATA_PIO.000;1 for  ./drivers/scsi/eata_pio_proc.c (eata_pio.c)
Using EATA_DMA.000;1 for  ./drivers/scsi/eata_dma_proc.h (eata_dma.h)
Using EATA_DMA.001;1 for  ./drivers/scsi/eata_dma_proc.c (eata_dma.c)
Using CYBERSTO.000;1 for  ./drivers/scsi/cyberstormII.h (cyberstorm.h)
Using CYBERSTO.001;1 for  ./drivers/scsi/cyberstormII.c (cyberstorm.c)
Using AIC7XXX_.000;1 for  ./drivers/scsi/aic7xxx_seq.c (aic7xxx_proc.c)
Using README.000;1 for  ./drivers/scsi/README.qlogicisp (README.qlogicfas)
Using README.001;1 for  ./drivers/scsi/README.ncr53c8xx (README.ncr53c7xx)
Using SEQUENCE.000;1 for  ./drivers/sound/sequencer_syms.c (sequencer.c)
Using AWE_COMP.000;1 for  ./drivers/sound/lowlevel/awe_compat.h
➥(awe_compat-linux.h)
Using AWE_COMP.001;1 for  ./drivers/sound/lowlevel/awe_compat-linux.h
➥(awe_compat-fbsd.h)
Using FONT_SUN.000;1 for  ./drivers/video/font_sun8x16.c (font_sun12x22.c)
Using FBCON-IP.000;1 for  ./drivers/video/fbcon-iplan2p8.c (fbcon-iplan2p4.c)
Using FBCON-IP.001;1 for  ./drivers/video/fbcon-iplan2p4.c (fbcon-iplan2p2.c)
Using FBCON-CF.000;1 for  ./drivers/video/fbcon-cfb8.c (fbcon-cfb4.c)
Using FBCON-CF.001;1 for  ./drivers/video/fbcon-cfb4.c (fbcon-cfb32.c)
Using FBCON-CF.002;1 for  ./drivers/video/fbcon-cfb32.c (fbcon-cfb24.c)
Using FBCON-CF.003;1 for  ./drivers/video/fbcon-cfb24.c (fbcon-cfb2.c)
Using FBCON-CF.004;1 for  ./drivers/video/fbcon-cfb2.c (fbcon-cfb16.c)
Using BINFMT_E.000;1 for  ./fs/binfmt_em86.c (binfmt_elf.c)
Using NLS_ISO8.000;1 for  ./fs/nls/nls_iso8859-9.c (nls_iso8859-8.c)
Using NLS_ISO8.001;1 for  ./fs/nls/nls_iso8859-8.c (nls_iso8859-7.c)
Using NLS_ISO8.002;1 for  ./fs/nls/nls_iso8859-7.c (nls_iso8859-6.c)
Using NLS_ISO8.003;1 for  ./fs/nls/nls_iso8859-6.c (nls_iso8859-5.c)
Using NLS_ISO8.004;1 for  ./fs/nls/nls_iso8859-5.c (nls_iso8859-4.c)
Using NLS_ISO8.005;1 for  ./fs/nls/nls_iso8859-4.c (nls_iso8859-3.c)
Using NLS_ISO8.006;1 for  ./fs/nls/nls_iso8859-3.c (nls_iso8859-2.c)
Using NLS_ISO8.007;1 for  ./fs/nls/nls_iso8859-2.c (nls_iso8859-15.c)
Using NLS_ISO8.008;1 for  ./fs/nls/nls_iso8859-15.c (nls_iso8859-1.c)
Using NLS_CP86.000;1 for  ./fs/nls/nls_cp869.c (nls_cp866.c)
Using NLS_CP86.001;1 for  ./fs/nls/nls_cp866.c (nls_cp865.c)
Using NLS_CP86.002;1 for  ./fs/nls/nls_cp865.c (nls_cp864.c)
Using NLS_CP86.003;1 for  ./fs/nls/nls_cp864.c (nls_cp863.c)
Using NLS_CP86.004;1 for  ./fs/nls/nls_cp863.c (nls_cp862.c)
Using NLS_CP86.005;1 for  ./fs/nls/nls_cp862.c (nls_cp861.c)
Using NLS_CP86.006;1 for  ./fs/nls/nls_cp861.c (nls_cp860.c)
```

```
Using NLS_CP85.000;1 for  ./fs/nls/nls_cp857.c (nls_cp855.c)
Using NLS_CP85.001;1 for  ./fs/nls/nls_cp855.c (nls_cp852.c)
Using NLS_CP85.002;1 for  ./fs/nls/nls_cp852.c (nls_cp850.c)
Using AX25_STD.000;1 for  ./net/ax25/ax25_std_timer.c (ax25_std_subr.c)
Using AX25_STD.001;1 for  ./net/ax25/ax25_std_subr.c (ax25_std_in.c)
Using AX25_DS_.000;1 for  ./net/ax25/ax25_ds_timer.c (ax25_ds_subr.c)
Using AX25_DS_.001;1 for  ./net/ax25/ax25_ds_subr.c (ax25_ds_in.c)
Using IP_MASQ_.000;1 for  ./net/ipv4/ip_masq_vdolive.c (ip_masq_user.c)
Using IP_MASQ_.001;1 for  ./net/ipv4/ip_masq_user.c (ip_masq_raudio.c)
Using IP_MASQ_.002;1 for  ./net/ipv4/ip_masq_raudio.c (ip_masq_quake.c)
Using IP_MASQ_.003;1 for  ./net/ipv4/ip_masq_quake.c (ip_masq_portfw.c)
Using IP_MASQ_.004;1 for  ./net/ipv4/ip_masq_portfw.c (ip_masq_mod.c)
Using IP_MASQ_.005;1 for  ./net/ipv4/ip_masq_mod.c (ip_masq_mfw.c)
Using IP_MASQ_.006;1 for  ./net/ipv4/ip_masq_mfw.c (ip_masq_irc.c)
Using IP_MASQ_.007;1 for  ./net/ipv4/ip_masq_irc.c (ip_masq_ftp.c)
Using IP_MASQ_.008;1 for  ./net/ipv4/ip_masq_ftp.c (ip_masq_cuseeme.c)
Using IP_MASQ_.009;1 for  ./net/ipv4/ip_masq_cuseeme.c (ip_masq_autofw.c)
Using IP_MASQ_.00A;1 for  ./net/ipv4/ip_masq_autofw.c (ip_masq_app.c)
Using IRLAN_PR.000;1 for  ./net/irda/irlan/irlan_provider_event.c
➥(irlan_provider.c)
Using IRLAN_CL.000;1 for  ./net/irda/irlan/irlan_client_event.c
➥(irlan_client.c)
Using IRLPT_SR.000;1 for  ./net/irda/irlpt/irlpt_srvr_fsm.c (irlpt_srvr.c)
Using IRLPT_CL.000;1 for  ./net/irda/irlpt/irlpt_cli_fsm.c (irlpt_cli.c)
Using CLS_RSVP.000;1 for  ./net/sched/cls_rsvp6.c (cls_rsvp.c)
Using SERIAL_C.000;1 for  ./pcmcia-cs-3.0.9/clients/serial_cs.c (serial_cb.c)
Using MEMORY_C.000;1 for  ./pcmcia-cs-3.0.9/clients/memory_cs.c (memory_cb.c)
Using IFLASH2_.000;1 for  ./pcmcia-cs-3.0.9/clients/iflash2_mtd.c
➥(iflash2+_mtd.c)
Using DUMP_CIS.000;1 for  ./pcmcia-cs-3.0.9/debug-tools/dump_cisreg.c
➥(dump_cis.c)
Using MEMORY_C.000;1 for  ./pcmcia-cs-3.0.9/man/memory_cs.4 (memory_cb.4)
 18.51% done, estimate finish Sat Sep 25 11:48:35 1999
 36.96% done, estimate finish Sat Sep 25 11:48:40 1999
 55.46% done, estimate finish Sat Sep 25 11:48:38 1999
 73.91% done, estimate finish Sat Sep 25 11:48:36 1999
 92.41% done, estimate finish Sat Sep 25 11:48:43 1999
Total extents actually written = 27061
Total translation table size: 0
Total rockridge attributes bytes: 338222
Total directory bytes: 731136
Path table size(bytes): 2600
Max brk space used 18e000
```

10

Managing
Removable
Media
Devices

```
27061 extents written (52 Mb)

[root@madmax linux-2.2.5]# mount -t iso9660 -o loop=/dev/loop0,ro
../ksource.img /mnt/cdrom

[root@madmax linux-2.2.5]# cd /mnt/cdrom

[root@madmax cdrom]# ls -a
.              MAINTAINERS          Rules.make   include   mm
..             Makefile             arch         init      modules
COPYING        README               drivers      ipc       net
CREDITS        README.kernel-sources  fs         kernel    pcmcia-cs-3.0.9
Documentation  REPORTING-BUGS       ibcs         lib       scripts

[root@madmax cdrom]# cd

[root@madmax /root]# umount /mnt/cdrom
```

As you can see, the long filenames in the kernel source tree were converted to the 8.3 format specified by the ISO9660 standard. However, since we specified the `-r` option and Linux supports the Rock Ridge extensions to ISO9660, when the image is mounted the filenames show up just like in the original source tree. It is usually a good idea to mount the image you create to verify that the filesystem image is properly created. You can do this by using the loop device and the loop option to the mount command. Another interesting option was the multiple `-m` options used to exclude object files, library archives, and other files that would be present if you had built a kernel in the source tree.

Now that an image has been created, you can use either the cdwrite or cdrecord command to transfer the image to the CD-R or CD-RW media. Of these commands, only cdrecord is included on the Red Hat installation media. The decision on which of these two commands to use is up to you, and is dependent on support for hardware and other features that you may require. Please note that cdrecord is being actively maintained and that cdwrite is not. If there is not a specific feature that you need that is only supported in cdwrite, I recommend that you stick with cdrecord. These packages are available from the following FTP sites if you want to build them from the source, or from the Red Hat contrib mirrors if you prefer prebuilt binaries:

```
ftp://ftp.fokus.gmd.de/pub/unix/cdrecord/ (cdrecord)
     ftp://sunsite.unc.edu/pub/Linux/utils/disk-management/ (cdwrite)
```

Be sure to get the appropriate command to support your hardware. For purposes of our example, we will use the cdrecord command because it supports ATAPI as well as SCSI devices. The cdrecord command supports a large number of command-line options, and some of the most common are described in Table 10.3. The option type indicates where on the command line the options may appear. The general options must all be specified before any track options or track filenames.

TABLE 10.3 cdrecord Command-Line Options

Option	Type	Description
-version	General	Prints out the cdrecord version info and exits.
-v	General	the general verbosity level by 1.
-V	General	the SCSI command transport verbosity by 1.
-debug	General	Prints additional debugging messages.
-dummy	General	Goes through all steps of burning with the laser off.
-multi	General	Allows multisession CDs to be made. This option must be used for all sessions of the disk except the last.
-msinfo	General	Retrieves multisession info in a format suitable for the mkisofs command to use with the -C option.
-toc	General	Displays the table of contents or PMA info for a CD.
-fix	General	Fixates the disk only.
-nofix	General	Does not fixate a disk. Used to create an audio disk in steps.
speed=#	General	Sets the speed factor for the writing process to #.
blank=type	General	Blanks a CD-RW disk and exits or blanks the disk before writing. To obtain a list of blanking types, set type equal to help.
dev=target	General	Writes to device specified by target. The format of target is devicename:scsibus, scsiid,lun. This may be shortened to those parts required to uniquely identify the drive. (Example: dev=0,2,0 for Bus 0, ID 2, Lun 0)
-checkdrive	General	Checks if a driver for the current drive is present and exits. An exit status of 0 indicates success.
-scanbus	General	Displays the inquiry strings for all SCSI devices on the bus.
-inq	General	Displays the device inquiry info and exits.

10

Managing
Removable
Media
Devices

TABLE **10.3**   continued

Option	Type	Description
-prcap	General	Displays the drive capabilities for SCSI-3/mmc drives.
-audio	Track	All subsequent tracks are written to disk in CD-DA audio format.
-data	Track	All subsequent tracks are written to disk in CD-ROM mode 1 format.
-mode2, -xa1, -xa2, -cdi	Track	All subsequent tracks are written to disk in the specified format (CD-ROM mode 2, CD-ROM XA mode 1, CD-ROM XA mode 2, or CDI format).
-swab	Track	Assumes audio data is in byte-swapped (little-endian) order.
-isosize	Track	Uses the ISO9660 filesystem size as the size of the next track.

To continue our example, we will now write the image we created with mkisofs to a CD-R disk using cdrecord. It is a good idea to do this when the machine is relatively idle, due to the sensitivity of the burning process. This process requires a constant stream of data and if load on the device bus or system load interrupts this stream, a buffer underrun will occur. Then the disk being written will be useless, unless you happen to be creating a mobile or like-gold coasters. Following is a sample of the command to write our ISO9660 image to disk and then to mount and verify that the write was successful.

```
[root@wizard src]# cdrecord -scanbus
Cdrecord release 1.8a17 Copyright  1995-1998 Jrg Schilling
scsibus0:
        0) *
        1) *
        2) '           ' 'CD-R/RW RW7040S ' '1.10' Removable CD-ROM
        3) *
        4) *
        5) *
        6) *
        7) *


[root@wizard src]# cdrecord -dummy -v -isosize speed=4 dev=2,0 ksource.img
Cdrecord release 1.8a17 Copyright  1995-1998 Jrg Schilling
TOC Type: 1 = CD-ROM
scsidev: '2,0'
scsibus: 0 target: 2 lun: 0
atapi: 0
```

```
Device type    : Removable CD-ROM
Version        : 2
Response Format: 2
Capabilities   :
Vendor_info    : '          '
Identifikation : 'CD-R/RW RW7040S '
Revision       : '1.10'
Device seems to be: Generic mmc CD-RW.
Using generic SCSI-3/mmc CD-R driver (mmc_cdr).
Driver flags   : SWABAUDIO
Track 01: data    52 MB
Total size:       60 MB (06:00.84) = 27063 sectors
Lout start:       61 MB (06:02/63) = 27063 sectors
Current Secsize: 2048
ATIP info from disk:
  Indicated writing power: 4
  Is not unrestricted
  Is not erasable
  ATIP start of lead in:  232276 (151:39/01)
  ATIP start of lead out: 72226 (116:05/01)
Disk type unknown
Manufacturer unknown (not in table)
Blocks total: 333226 Blocks current: 333226 Blocks remaining: 306163
Starting to write CD/DVD at speed 4 in dummy mode for single session.
Last chance to quit, starting dummy write in 1 seconds.
Waiting for reader process to fill input-buffer ... input-buffer ready.
Starting new track at sector: 0
Track 01:   Track 01:  52 of  52 MB written (fifo 100%).
Track 01: Total bytes read/written: 55420928/55420928 (27061 sectors).
Writing  time:   93.369s
Fixating...
WARNING: Some drives don't like fixation in dummy mode.
Fixating time:    0.013s
cdrecord: fifo had 1692 puts and 1692 gets.
cdrecord: fifo was 0 times empty and 1530 times full, min fill was 96%.


[root@wizard src]# cdrecord -v -isosize speed=4 dev=2,0 ksource.img
Cdrecord release 1.8a17 Copyright  1995-1998 Jrg Schilling
TOC Type: 1 = CD-ROM
scsidev: '2,0'
scsibus: 0 target: 2 lun: 0
atapi: 0
Device type    : Removable CD-ROM
```

```
Version       : 2
Response Format: 2
Capabilities  :
Vendor_info   : '        '
Identifikation : 'CD-R/RW RW7040S '
Revision      : '1.10'
ATIP info from disk:
  Indicated writing power: 4
  Is not unrestricted
  Is not erasable
  ATIP start of lead in:  232276 (151:39/01)
  ATIP start of lead out: 72226 (116:05/01)
Disk type unknown
Manufacturer unknown (not in table)
Blocks total: 333226 Blocks current: 306013 Blocks remaining: 278950
Starting to write CD/DVD at speed 4 in write mode for single session.
Last chance to quit, starting real write in 1 seconds.
Waiting for reader process to fill input-buffer ... input-buffer ready.
Starting new track at sector: 0
Track 01:  52 of  52 MB written (fifo 100%).
Track 01: Total bytes read/written: 55420928/55420928 (27061 sectors).
Writing  time:   94.725s
Fixating...
Fixating time:   61.882s
cdrecord: fifo had 1692 puts and 1692 gets.
cdrecord: fifo was 0 times empty and 1473 times full, min fill was 94%.


[root@wizard src]# mount -t iso9660 /dev/scd0 /mnt/cdrom
mount: block device /dev/scd0 is write-protected, mounting read-only


[root@wizard src]# cd /mnt/cdrom


[root@wizard cdrom]# ls
COPYING        README               drivers  ipc    net
CREDITS        README.kernel-sources fs       kernel pcmcia-cs-3.0.9
Documentation  REPORTING-BUGS        ibcs     lib    scripts
MAINTAINERS    Rules.make            include  mm
Makefile       arch                  init     modules


[root@wizard src]# umount /mnt/cdrom


[root@wizard src]# eject scd0
```

In order to construct the appropriate command line, we first issued the cdrecord command with the -scanbus option. This gave us the appropriate device entry to use. We then indicated the speed at which to write the image to disk. In this case, the attached burner writes at 4x speeds, and therefore, we specified a speed of 4. If the machine is totally idle while burning the images, you can sometimes set the speed higher than the device specifies. However, you might want to use the -dummy option to try this out before actually burning a CD-R disk to see if it will work. The -dummy option goes through all the steps of burning the CD-R except for activating the laser. It is a very useful debugging tool that can save you from creating too many gold coasters. The other options specify that you want verbose output and to use the ISO9660 filesystem size as the size of the next track. Once the burning is complete, the next thing you should do is to verify that the write was successful. To do this, you simply mount the CD you created and attempt to read from it.

Now that you know how to write to CD-R and CD-RW drives under Linux, you can use this knowledge for any number of purposes. One such purpose could be to create backups of kernel or other software builds. Other uses include specialized backups; for example, log files from a Web site that you must keep but that are not large enough to warrant writing them to tape, or that you want quick access to. Another use that has become popular is to create images of software packages that you do not use regularly, but that you want quick access to in the event that they are needed. Now that we have covered the creation of CDs, we can move on to other removable media devices, starting with those that connect to the parallel port of your system.

Parallel Port Storage Devices

Other removable media devices that have become quite popular recently are storage devices that attach to your computer via the parallel port. These devices include drives from Iomega, such as Zip and Jaz drives, which utilize drivers that make them appear as SCSI devices to Linux, as well as a growing number of ATAPI/IDE devices from other manufacturers such as SyQuest and MicroSolutions. This section takes a look at what is required to add support to your kernel for these types of devices, and then looks at Zip drives in particular because they are one of the more popular of these devices. This discussion is concerned with Zip drives that connect to the parallel port only. If your Zip drive attaches to the IDE controller or the SCSI controller, it should appear to the system as just another SCSI or IDE device.

Adding Support to Your Kernel

The first step in adding support to your kernel for parallel port storage devices is to determine which driver you will require. There are basically three choices. The first of these is the ppa driver, which is suitable for the older parallel port Zip drives. For newer Zip drives, like the ZIP Plus and the 250 megabyte Zip drives, use the imm (Iomega MatchMaker) driver. Both of these drivers are part of the SCSI support for Linux and are configured as low-level SCSI drivers in the kernel configuration. For parallel port ATAPI or IDE devices, there is a driver known as the paride driver. This driver is useful for a number of external storage devices that connect via the parallel port, including the following:

- MicroSolutions backpack CD-ROM

- MicroSolutions backpack PD/CD

- MicroSolutions backpack hard-drives

- MicroSolutions backpack 8000t tape drive

- SyQuest EZ-135, EZ-230 & SparQ drives

- Avatar Shark

- Imation Superdisk LS-120

- Maxell Superdisk LS-120

- FreeCom Power CD

- Hewlett-Packard 5GB and 8GB tape drives

- Hewlett-Packard 7100 and 7200 CD-RW drives

The steps involved in adding support for the ppa or imm drivers are the same as for any other type of SCSI device. You must first select support for SCSI devices, then the specific types of SCSI devices (disks, CD, tape, and generic), and finally the specific low-level driver for your controller. It is at the low-level driver level that you select either the ppa or imm drivers. These options are clearly labeled for the type of Zip drive that they support and if you have further questions about which driver is appropriate, the kernel configuration help includes valuable information.

The paride support configuration options are located under the block devices portion of the kernel configuration. You must first answer the parallel port IDE device support question with either M to build as a module or Y to compile support into your kernel. You will then be prompted to select the types of devices to support, much like in the SCSI device configuration. Once you have done this, you will need to select one or more protocol modules based on the types of devices you want to support. Once again, the configuration help is your friend here and if you are unsure, you can enable all protocols as modules and let the driver figure it out for you.

Assuming that you are using the kernel provided with the Red Hat 6.1 distribution and are using the 2.2.12 kernel that came with it, you do not have to do any of the preceding steps. The kernel is already configured and supports the ppa, imm, and paride drivers and associated protocols as modules.

Zip Drives

Assuming that you are using the default Red Hat kernel or that you have successfully rebuilt your kernel to support the type of Zip drive that you have as described in Chapter 35, how do you actually use the drive? There are two basic steps involved:

1. Load the appropriate driver module.
2. Load a Zip disk and use it.

Loading the module is a matter of using insmod or modprobe with the correct driver. For purposes of this example, we will assume a modern ZIP Plus drive, using the imm driver. The command you would issue in this case and sample output are

```
[root@wizard root] modprobe -a imm
imm: Version 2.03 (for Linux 2.0.0)
imm: Found device at ID 6, Attempting to use EPP 32 bit
imm: Communication established with ID 6 using EPP 32 bit
scsi0 : Iomega VPI2 (imm) interface
scsi : 1 host.
 Vendor: IOMEGA    Model: ZIP 100       Rev: J.67
 Type:  Direct-Access  ANSI SCSI revision: 02 Detected scsi removable disk sda
      at scsi0, channel 0, id 6, lun 0
 SCSI device sda: hdwr sector= 512 bytes.  Sectors= 196608 [96 MB] [0.1 GB]
sda: Write Protect is off
sda: sda4
```

You may notice that the Zip disk in the drive is detected as /dev/sda and that it has a single partition sda4. The reason why the partition is numbered 4 is the subject of debate; however, the best explanation put forth thus far is that the Macintosh tools for Zip drives require it to be so and that all disks are partitioned in that manner for compatibility.

10

Managing Removable Media Devices

Now that the driver is loaded and the disk has been recognized, it is time to start actually using the disk. There are three scenarios here. The first is that you will be using Zip disks preformatted for Windows. In this case, you must create a mount point and then mount the disk and begin using it with the following commands:

```
mkdir /mnt/zip; mount -t vfat /dev/sda4 /mnt/zip
```

The filesystem on the disk is now mounted and you access it like any other mount vfat partition, with standard Linux commands such as ls, cp, mv, and rm. In the event that you prefer to have a Linux filesystem on the Zip disk, you can use the following commands to create a Linux partition and filesystem on the disk:

```
echo ",,,-" | /sbin/sfdisk /dev/sda ; mke2fs /dev/sda1
```

This has the effect of creating a single Linux partition, /dev/sda1, on the disk that takes up the entire disk and then creating a filesystem on it. Once this is done, you can mount the newly created extended type 2 filesystem and treat it as you would any other disk.

Parallel Port ATAPI/IDE Devices

Other devices that connect to the parallel port of your system, such as the Imation Superdisk LS-120 or any of the MicroSolutions backpack devices, are also supported. These devices make use of the paride drivers that are part of the Linux 2.2.x kernel. Just as with the Zip drive support, using these devices is just a matter of loading the appropriate modules and then accessing the devices via the appropriate device names, assuming that you have configured your kernel to support them. In this case, the modules to be loaded are broken into three categories:

- The paride module, which provides a registry and basic control of the parallel port.

- The protocol module for the devices you have attached.

- The high-level modules for the specific device types, such as disk drives, CD drives, or floppy drives.

For example, if you have a SyQuest EZ135A drive connected to your system, the modules you need are the paride module, the epat protocol module, and the pd disk module. In this case, the output resulting from installing these modules might look like this:

```
[root@wizard etc] insmod paride
paride: version 1.0 installed

[root@wizard etc] insmod epat
paride: epat registered as protocol 0

[root@wizard etc] insmod pd
```

```
pd: pd version 1.0, major 45, cluster 64, nice 0
pda: Sharing parport1 at 0x378
pda: epat 1.0, Shuttle EPAT chip c3 at 0x378, mode 5 (EPP-32), delay 1
pda: SyQuest EZ135A, 262144 blocks [128M], (512/16/32), removable media
 pda: pda1
```

In order to access this device, you must create the appropriate device special files in the /dev directory. These devices should already exist on your Red Hat system; however, if they do not, there is a script in the file /usr/src/linux/Documentation/paride.txt that will create them for you. Once these devices are created, they are accessed just like other ATAPI/IDE devices, with the exception of the device name. Now that we have taken a look at the various types of removable media devices available for Linux, let's move on to the topic of granting access to users.

Granting Access to Users

There are methods for allowing access to the removable media devices on your system without giving away root access. This section covers two of these options, one specifically for DOS filesystems, and the other a method for giving users the ability to mount removable media without compromising the security of the system. It also looks at using the automounter to mount removable media and some of the advantages and disadvantages of doing so. Please note that you probably do not want to give access to removable media devices to users on your server systems. The methods described here are most appropriate to workstations.

The mtools Package

One method available for granting access to removable devices under Linux is via the mtools package. This package contains a number of commands that correspond to DOS commands and that are used to access DOS filesystem types, such as FAT and VFAT. Table 10.4 shows a list of some of the most common mtool commands, their DOS counterparts (if one exists), and what they do.

TABLE 10.4   mtools Commands

Mtool Command	DOS Command	Description
mattrib	attrib	Sets the DOS file attributes on a file.
mbadblocks		Scans a disk for bad blocks and marks them.
mcd	cd	Changes directory on a DOS filesystem.

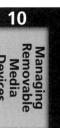

10

Managing
Removable
Media
Devices

TABLE 10.4 continued

Mtool Command	DOS Command	Description
mcopy	copy	Copies files to or from a DOS filesystem.
mdel	del	Deletes files from a DOS filesystem.
mdeltree	deltree	Deletes a directory and all files under it.
mdi	rdir	Displays a directory listing.
mdu		Shows the disk space usage of a DOS filesystem.
mformat	format	Does a minimal DOS format of the specified device.
mlabel	label	Sets the volume label on a DOS filesystem.
mmd	md	Creates a directory on a DOS filesystem.
mmove	move	Moves or renames a file or directory on a DOS filesystem.
mrd	rd	Removes a directory from a DOS filesystem.
mren	ren	Renames a file on a DOS filesystem.
mtype	type	Displays a text file on a DOS filesystem.
mzip		Issues Zip disk specific commands. Allows you to eject, write protect, remove write protection, and so on.

The ability of these commands to access various devices that may contain DOS filesystems is determined by the /etc/mtools.conf file. On a default Red Hat installation, this file looks like this:

```
/etc/mtools.conf


# Example mtools.conf files.  Uncomment the lines which correspond to
# your architecture and comment out the "SAMPLE FILE" line below

# Linux floppy drives
drive a: file="/dev/fd0" exclusive 1.44m
drive b: file="/dev/fd1" exclusive 1.44m

# First SCSI hard disk partition
#drive c: file="/dev/sda1"
```

```
# First IDE hard disk partition
#drive c: file="/dev/hda1"


# # dosemu floppy image
# drive m: file="/var/lib/dosemu/diskimage"


# dosemu hdimage
drive n: file="/var/lib/dosemu/hdimage" offset=8832


# # Atari ramdisk image
# drive o: file="/tmp/atari_rd" offset=136


# # ZIP disk for Solaris:
# Drive X is ZIP-100 at target 5
# drive X: file="/dev/rdsk/c0t5d0s2" partition=4 scsi=1 nodelay


# # ZIP disk for SunOS:
# # Zip drive is at target 5, which default kernel calls tape st1 !!
# drive Y: file="/dev/rsd5c" partition=4 scsi=1 nodelay


# # autoselect zip drive/floppy on HP-UX 9/10
#    drive a: file="/dev/rdsk/c201d5"       exclusive partition=4
#    drive a: file="/dev/rdsk/c201d5s0"     exclusive partition=4
#    drive a: file="/dev/rfloppy/c201d0s0" exclusive


#          A/UX target 5 on 1st scsi bus   jaz or zip
# drive X: file="/dev/rdsk/c105d0s31"       partition=4



# Some examples for BeOS.
# floppy drive. hardcoded in devices.c, so no real need to define it here
#drive a: file="/dev/floppy_disk" exclusive
# ZIP drive on SCSI ID 6
#drive z: file="/dev/scsi_disk_060" offset=16384 fat_bits=16


# SCO Unix 3.2v4
# # Floppy disk drives
#
# drive a: file="/dev/install" exclusive
# drive b: file="/dev/install1" exclusive
#
# # SCSI hard disk partitions
#
```

```
# drive c: file="/dev/dsk/0sC"
# drive d: file="/dev/dsk/0sD"
# drive e: file="/dev/dsk/0sE"
# drive f: file="/dev/dsk/0sF"
# drive g: file="/dev/dsk/0sG"
# drive h: file="/dev/dsk/0sH"

# # uncomment the following line to display all file names in lower
# # case by default
# mtools_lower_case=1
```

The comments in the file describe the purpose of each entry, and the manual page for mtools gives a more detailed description of how entries may be added to this file. In addition, the most detailed documentation of the mtools suite can be accessed on your Red Hat system by issuing the command

```
info mtools
```

or by looking up mtools using the info mode of Emacs.

The obvious drawback to the mtools suite is that it only works with DOS filesystems. Other than this, the mtools suite may be a simple solution to the problem of giving users access to removable devices. If their primary purpose is enabling "sneakernet" transfers of files, this may be enough.

Giving Users the Power to Mount

Another option available to systems administrators is to grant users the ability to mount removable devices like floppy and CD-ROM drives through a special option to the mount command. Modern mount versions all support this option and enabling it consists of two steps. The first is to create mount points for the removable media devices and the second is to modify /etc/fstab to set the appropriate mount options to allow users access. Giving users the ability to mount removable media like floppies or CD-ROM drives is not a decision to be made lightly. It can be useful, however, so that users may transfer files between systems that are not networked.

Creating Mount Points

Creating mount points may sound like a trivial exercise, but here are a few suggestions that may be helpful:

- Use a descriptive name for the mount points, such as `/mnt/dosa` for what would be the A drive in Windows or DOS.

- Create multiple mount points for different filesystem types so that users do not have to learn mount options.

By way of example, consider the following. User workstations all have a single floppy drive and an IDE CD-ROM drive accessible as `/dev/cdrom`. You want to allow users to mount floppies formatted for Linux (extended 2 filesystem) or DOS/Windows and data CDs. In this case, the mount points I would create would be:

- `/mnt/dosA` for DOS/Windows formatted floppies

- `/mnt/fd0` for Linux formatted floppies

- `/mnt/cdrom` for data CDs

If I were to later add a Zip drive to a system and wanted to allow the user to mount either DOS or Linux formatted disks on it, I would add additional mount points:

- `/mnt/zip` for Linux formatted Zip disks

- `/mnt/zipdos` for DOS/Windows formatted disks

Modifying `/etc/fstab`

To support user mounting of these types of drives, you must modify the filesystem table `/etc/fstab`. Here is a sample line from this file that demonstrates the two options you must specify in order to allow ordinary users to mount filesystems:

```
/etc/fstab Entry
```

```
/dev/fd0    /mnt/fd0    ext2    noauto,nosuid,user,rw    1    0
```

In this entry, we specify a number of options. The first of these is the `noauto` option, which indicates that this filesystem should not be mounted automatically (that is, with the mount -a option). This is important mostly at boot time, when you will most likely not have a floppy in the disk drive and you do not want to wait for the floppy device to timeout. The next option is the `nosuid` option, which is an important security consideration and disallows the execution of setuid and setgid programs from the floppy. The `user` option is the key to allowing users to mount this filesystem. This option, which may only be set in the `/etc/fstab` file, tells the `mount` program to disable the check that the current user is root. This means that normal users are now permitted to mount the floppy device on the mount point `/mnt/fd0` simply by issuing the command

```
mount /mnt/fd0
```

10

Managing Removable Media Devices

Once mounted in this fashion, only the user who mounted it or the superuser may unmount it.

To continue the previous example, here are the `/etc/fstab` entries required to support DOS floppies, Linux floppies, CDs, and Zip disks mountable by ordinary users:

```
# For mounting Linux formatted floppies
/dev/fd0    /mnt/fd0    ext2    noauto,nosuid,user,rw    1    0


# For mounting DOS/Windows formatted floppies
/dev/fd0    /mnt/dosA    vfat    noauto,nosuid,user,rw    1    0


# For mounting CD-ROM disks
/dev/cdrom    /mnt/cdrom    iso9660    noauto,nosuid,user,ro    1    0


# For mounting Linux formatted ZIP disks
/dev/sda1    /mnt/zip    ext2    noauto,nosuid,user,rw    1    0


# For mounting DOS/Windows formatted ZIP disks
/dev/sda4    /mnt/zipdos    vfat    noauto,nosuid,user,rw    1    0
```

Automatic Mounting of Removable Media

Yet another option for dealing with removable media is to configure the Linux autofs to support these devices without requiring the user to do anything more than insert the media and access the appropriate directory. By default, Red Hat Linux supports this functionality for the CD drive provided that you have installed the `autofs` support. Using this default setup, the user can access the CD drive by loading a CD into the drive and changing directory to `/misc/cd`. Once the user is finished with the CD, he simply changes directory to somewhere other than the CD filesystem and waits for the timeout of 60 seconds to expire before unloading the CD from the drive.

The configuration files required to set up this support are `/etc/auto.master`, the master `autofs` configuration file, and whatever file is specified by it that contains the entries for the removable media. To continue with the example from the previous section, here are the required configuration files that must be created to support automatic mounting:

```
 /etc/auto.master


# Sample auto.master file
# Format of this file:
# mountpoint map options
# For details of the format look at autofs(8).
```

```
# An entry for mountpoint /misc, which is used for mounting removable
# media devices as defined in the map file /etc/auto.misc.  These
# devices will be unmounted following an inactivity timeout of 30
# seconds.
/misc     /etc/auto.misc     --timeout 30



 /etc/auto.misc

# Allow the mounting of CD-ROM disks on /misc/cdrom
cdrom          -fstype=iso9660,ro     :/dev/cdrom

# For mounting Linux formatted floppies
fd0            -fstype=ext2,nosuid     :/dev/fd0

# For mounting DOS/Windows formatted floppies
dosA           -fstype=vfat,nosuid     :/dev/fd0

# For mounting Linux formatted ZIP disks
zip            -fstype=ext2,nosuid     :/dev/sda1

# For mounting DOS/Windows formatted ZIP disks
zipdos           -fstype=vfat,nosuid     :/dev/sda4
```

With these configuration files and with the `autofs` script in `/etc/rc.d/init.d` run at boot time, users will be able to access floppy drives, Zip disks, and CDs on the system. They can do so by changing directory to a directory under misc that corresponds to one of the keys in the `auto.misc` file.

There are a number of advantages to this method of allowing access. One of these is that the user does not need to learn any special commands in order to use them. Additionally, the `auto.master` and `auto.misc` files may be incorporated into NIS setups, eliminating the need to modify the `fstab` files on every host you want to grant access to. On the down side, the timeout parameter can be a problem, especially if your users are impatient. They may not like the idea of having to wait 30 seconds to remove the media.

For more information on configuring and using the `autofs` as well as information on using amd, the Berkeley automount daemon, see Chapter 15, "Sharing Resources (Print and File Services)," which describes their use in greater detail.

10

Managing Removable Media Devices

A Hybrid Approach

Yet another potential method for granting access to removable media is to take a hybrid approach. In this approach, you might configure mtools to allow access to DOS formatted floppies and zip disks, and use the autofs or user mount approach to allow access to Linux formatted filesystems and CD-ROM drives. This approach is a case of using the right tool for the job. Again, it should be noted that granting access to removable media devices to users should not be done arbitrarily and security concerns should be considered when making the decision.

Summary

This chapter looked at some of the removable media devices supported by Linux, including floppy drives, CD-ROM, CD-R, CD-RW, and devices that attach to the parallel port, such as Zip drives and portable ATAPI/IDE devices. It covered details of using CD-R and CD-RW drives to create your own CD data disks and some of the uses for these devices. It also gave a brief howto on connecting Zip drives to your system via the parallel port and information on using the paride driver to support some of the other types of devices available, like MicroSolutions backpack devices. Finally, this chapter covered a few methods for allowing users to access these removable devices, without giving them root access or compromising security. There are additional sources of information available with your Red Hat system in the following files:

- `/usr/src/linux/Documentation/paride.txt`

- `/usr/doc/HOWTO/mini/ZIP-Drive`

Backup and Recovery

PART

IV

IN THIS PART

11 What to Back Up and How   *299*

12 Media Selection and Storage   *333*

13 Recovery from Data Loss   *345*

What to Back Up and How

In This Chapter

- Filesystem Contents   *301*
- Finding New Files   *303*
- Backup Strategies   *305*
- Partial Backups   *309*
- Bringing a New Red Hat Linux Box Online   *310*
- Types of Backups   *313*
- Developing a Rotation Schedule   *315*
- Developing Backup Scripts   *323*

You've surely heard of Murphy's Law, which in its simplest form states, "Anything that can go wrong, will." I'm not the first person who has observed this particular phenomenon of nature, but I have observed it. Repeatedly. It's especially true when dealing with computers.

At some point in time, I promise, you will have a file or files that become totally unreadable for one reason or another. The reason may be hardware failure, fire, flood, earthquake, static electricity, user finger problems, or even sunspots (don't laugh—the year 2000 is going to be a banner year for sunspot activity, according to astronomers. Check out the Web page at NASA at `http://wwwssl.msfc.nasa.gov/newhome/headlines/ast19oct98_1.htm`. You have been warned!) Hard drives and floppy drives all have moving parts, and moving parts will eventually wear out.

If any of that happens, you and your users will *really* appreciate having backups. In this day and age of cheap storage media, not having backups is inexcusable. As a system administrator, your primary task is to keep the system up and running. Backups are second on that list. The short answer to the question, "What do I back up, and how do I do it?" is the single, most-popular answer to just about *any* computer question that a system administrator might be asked. That answer is, of course, "It depends." You are about to learn what it depends on, so that you can attack your particular requirements with the ultimate system administrator weapon—knowledge.

The knowledge you require for proper implementation of backups breaks down into four broad categories:

- What to back up (filesystem contents)

  Determining what needs to be backed up and what doesn't allows you to make the best use out of your resources, whatever they may be.

- Where to backup to (backup devices)

  Some backup devices are available on every computer. Other devices are beyond the reach of all but a select few.

- How to backup (backup commands)

  The variety of programs available to perform backups grows at an ever-increasing rate, but the "old stand-by" commands are still as useful as ever.

- When to backup (site policy)

  How often to back up and how thorough the backup should be are dictated by a number of concerns, including the value of your data versus the cost of backing up.

Filesystem Contents

This section describes the contents of the filesystem as fitting into one (or more) of three general categories. Those categories are system configuration files, user files, and task-oriented files.

System Configuration Files

The majority of system configuration files reside in /etc and its subdirectories, although there are others scattered all over the directory tree.

Some are configuration files for various processes that are always running on your computer, such as the daemon programs inetd, syslogd, klogd, and crond. Other files contain configuration information for the programs that are executed at system boot-up, such as whether you selected a graphical or text initial login screen. Still other files in this category inform the kernel as to which modules are to be loaded at boot time; which users have accounts on this machine; which ones of the many daemon processes are to be started during system initialization; and so on. Without these files, your Red Hat Linux system is not going to function at all.

Some of these files need to be changed often in order for your computer to function exactly the way that you want it to. Others, once configured, are rarely touched.

User Files

User files are the personal files of the people who use your system. Typically, these files reside in the user's home directory because most users do not have the ability to write anywhere else. When you create a new user, about 17 files are moved into the new home directory from /etc/skel. In addition to these files, the files /etc/passwd, /etc/shadow, and /etc/group are modified. A file for that username is created in /var/log/cron and /var/spool. Once the user logs in, more files will be created, deleted, and changed.

One of these users will be you, or should be. Good security practice dictates that, even if you are the only user of a system, you should never be logged in as the root user unless you have to be. A simple typographical error or a misplaced mouse click as root can destroy files and subdirectories almost instantly. The typical user account cannot harm the system because it does not have the necessary permissions to affect any of the system files. The root account does have this power.

Task-Oriented Files

Task-oriented files are the configuration and data files used by specific programs on the computer that are above and beyond the operating system. Typically, the computer concerned is used primarily for one or more specific purposes—perhaps a news server, mail server, database server, or whatever. All Linux computers have certain processes running, such as `init`, `inetd`, `syslogd`, and so on, in order to function. Most will have `sendmail` or another Mail Transport Agent (MTA) running in order to deliver mail. Indeed, the MTA could be considered as part of the system configuration because many processes mail errors to the `root` user, or the MTA on a particular machine may be heavily optimized to run a corporation's entire email system. Few will run the Internet News daemon `INN`. Those who do will find the configuration files in the directory `/etc/news`, and the data files (usually) located in `/var/spool/news/articles`. After successfully configuring `INN` for the first time, you seldom need to revisit those files. Other common tasks include databases such as `postgresql`, name servers such as `bind`, spreadsheet programs such as `Gnumeric`, and Web servers such as Apache. If the data or configuration files for these programs are destroyed or become corrupted, you will have to re-create them unless you are able to restore from the latest backup. Restoring from a backed-up copy is much easier.

Configuration files are usually tiny compared to the data files generated by programs. Typically, the configuration files for any given program will fit comfortably on a single floppy. Data files can be a totally different story. The data files used by `INN` for a full newsfeed grow at a rate that is measured in gigabytes per day. A news server that includes just the Linux groups will require in excess of 500 megabytes of disk storage within a week, and the files will number in the tens of thousands. Databases and spreadsheets can be any size, from thousands of bytes to thousands of megabytes, depending on the usage.

These data files may occupy an entire hard drive or a multi-gigabyte RAID storage device. The particular program may use only a single file or hundreds of files in one directory. They may be located on the local filesystem, or be NFS mounted from a machine across the room, down the hall, or on the other side of the planet. They could change on a minute-by-minute basis, change according to a human user's preferences, or stay the same indefinitely. As the system administrator, all you have to do is ensure that all of the existing data and configuration files, and any new ones that may have been created, are backed up, and that those backups are readily available when needed. Finding existing files is easy if you know their names; finding files that were modified after the install or that were not created by you directly presents slightly more of a challenge.

Finding New Files

Before you can find new files, you have to decide what constitutes old ones. One demarcation line that is easily observed is the installation date. Any files older than that are part of the distribution that has been copied with the timestamps intact. Any files newer than that must be files that have been added or modified.

Files Added Since the Install

In order to generate a listing of all those files that exist right after an installation and that are not part of the distribution, try the following command the first time your brand new system reboots after the installation completes. I've had to break this command line and others throughout this chapter in order to fit the page width of this book. The Linux command-line limit is *much* longer than will print here on one line, or on your screen, for that matter. A code continuation character (➡) is used to indicate a continuing line of code.

```
find / -path '/tmp' -prune -o -path '/proc' -prune -o -path '/var/lock'
➡-prune -o -path '/var/run' -prune -o -type f -mtime -1
```

These lines instruct the `find` command to search the entire filesystem, except the listed subdirectories, and print the names of only those files that are less than one day old. Depending on the speed of your hard drive and CPU, this may take quite a while to execute. To create an editable list, redirect the output of this command to a file by adding `> filename` to the end of the command.

This command line excludes the subdirectories `/tmp`, `/proc`, `/var/lock`, and `/var/run` for specific reasons. Files in `/tmp` are usually scratch files used by various programs. The exception to that rule is the file `/tmp/install.log`, which was created as you installed Red Hat Linux. You can't really "back up" the `/proc` subdirectory in the usual sense of the word. Although the contents of this directory appear to be files and subdirectories, they are not. These apparent file and subdirectory entries are really interfaces to internal data structures in the running kernel. For example, what appears to be a file named `kcore` is an image of all of memory. The remaining files and subdirectories are used by currently running processes. The details of the `/proc` system are documented in the file `proc.txt`, which you will find in the `/usr/src/linux/Documentation` directory.

Those same currently running processes created most of the files in `/var/run` and `/var/lock`. Backing them up is pointless (and in some cases impossible) because those running processes are the only things that have use for them, and they won't be running on the backup medium! I haven't excluded the log files in `/var/log`; however, you may want to do so.

There were 260 filenames listed as being less than 24 hours old that were found by this command when I ran it. Those files did not exist on the installation medium but were unique to my computer. They had been generated by my particular responses to the installation questions. This list included the files created for the `root` user to be able to use X (in my case, I installed all of the KDE, Gnome, FVWM, and Enlightenment window managers), as well as system configuration files for the daemons I wanted to run, my network information, and so on. I would not have wanted to try to find them individually—that would have been a dull, boring, repetitive task. Doing dull, boring, repetitive tasks is something computers excel at, so I used the computer to do the "grunt work" of finding files changed since the install completed.

Determining Available Back-Up Devices

Now you need to decide which device you will do your backups on, so that you know where you need to send the backup commands. Are you using the first floppy drive, `/dev/fd0`? Are you using a tape drive? If you are going to use the tape drive, do you know its real name?

If you are you using a tape drive, you need to be aware of the fact that each tape drive has two different device names associated with it. One device name is the "automatically rewinding" name. At the completion of any command sent to it, the device automatically rewinds the tape back to the beginning, ready for the next command. The other device name, the "non-rewinding device," doesn't rewind the tape automatically; you have to do it yourself, typically with the program `mt`. Using the non-rewinding version lets you store more than one backup session per tape, which is very handy for storing several small, incremental backups onto the same tape. With the rewinding device, positioning the tape is not an option. A non-rewinding device will just stop after the writing (or reading) is complete, waiting for further instructions.

The first SCSI tape drive can be referred to as `/dev/nst0` or `/dev/nrst0` for rewinding and non-rewinding, respectively. I doubt that the name stands for "non-rewinding scsi tape zero," but who knows? A tape drive on a floppy controller is referred to as `/dev/ftape` and `/dev/nftape` or `/dev/rft0` and `/dev/nrft0`. Again, probably not "non-rewinding floppy tape zero."

A writable CD-ROM is known by the drive's name: `/dev/sg0` is my SCSI CD-ROM writer. You will have to determine the appropriate device name for your particular backup device. This will have been part of that particular piece of hardware's installation.

The device you use for your backups will be dictated by availability—it's really difficult to back up files to a non-existent device!

Now that you have an idea of what you need to back up and where to back it up to, all you need to decide is how often to do backups, and how long to keep the backed-up files. This is what is meant by a backup strategy.

Backup Strategies

If you think about, you can come up with a plan that will make life much easier. As a system administrator, you are required by law to be lazy (the First Computer Law is "THINK!"—it is an effort to cancel out Murphy's Law). A good system administrator will think for two days to save three keystrokes—or at least that's my excuse!

Deciding on a backup strategy is actually quite easy, once you know what you need.

In the real world, there is no one correct way to implement backups, and thus no ideal backup strategy that works for everybody. The closest you can get to an ideal situation is to back up every file constantly, so that the difference between the original and the backup is a matter of seconds, or perhaps minutes. High-availability systems will need to implement this particular strategy at any cost. This usually is implemented by using hardware RAID 5 (Redundant Array of Independent Disks at level 5). To quote from the Software-RAID Mini-Howto (this document is available on your Red Hat Linux filesystem under `/usr/doc/HOWTO/mini`, if you installed the documentation):

> Q: What is RAID?
>
> A: RAID stands for "Redundant Array of Inexpensive Disks", and is meant to be a way of creating a fast and reliable disk-drive subsystem out of individual disks. In the PC world, "I" has come to stand for "Independent", where marketing forces continue to differentiate IDE and SCSI. In its original meaning, "I" meant "Inexpensive as compared to refrigerator-sized mainframe 3380 DASD", monster drives which made nice houses look cheap, and diamond rings look like trinkets.

Hardware RAID consists of a special hard drive controller and several hard drives. The data is placed on the hard drives independently of the operating system, using one of a number of scenarios that the system administrator has chosen. These are known as RAID levels. There are several RAID levels, each with its own advantages and disadvantages.

RAID-0 is striping—just using several hard drives as though they were one larger one.

RAID-1 is mirroring—two hard drives each have the exact same data on them.

Higher levels of RAID incorporate things such as parity drives and combinations of the lower-level features (striping, mirroring, parity, and so on). Software RAID works, but is not as fast or reliable as hardware-based RAID.

RAID-5 (or most any level of RAID) isn't really needed for the majority of users because of the costs of obtaining and configuring the equipment. For more information on high availability, point your favorite Web browser to `http://metalab.unc.edu` in the directory `/pub/Linux/ALPHA/linux-ha/` at the document named High-Availability-HOWTO.htm.

To determine what your backup strategy will be depends to a great extent on who you are (student, large-system system administrator, small business owner, and so on); what you're using this particular computer for (general usage, a specific server, corporate resource, and so on); and how valuable you consider the information on the computer to be. The more valuable the information, the more imperative to back it up and the more you should be willing to spend to protect it, both in time and money.

Full Backups as a Strategy

The simplest backup strategy is to copy every file on the hard drive to your favorite storage medium on a regular basis. This is also known as a *full backup*, because you backup the full system (see, some computer terms *do* make sense!). If something goes awry, all that is needed is that latest copy, and you are back to where you were when that copy was made. Red Hat Linux ships with several tools that will allow you to do this very thing, so we'll just take a quick look at them now.

The `dd` command:

```
dd if=/dev/hda2 of=/dev/nst0
```

This sample command writes an image of the second IDE hard drive partition to the non-rewinding streaming tape device attached to the local computer's floppy drive controller. For a SCSI tape drive, the output device would have been `/dev/nst0`. No matter the output device (`dd` will even create a file that can be mounted via the `loop` device!), everything is there, but only as one massive chunk of data that has to be restored as a single entity. There is no way to select only specific files or directories. It is an all-or-nothing procedure. At first glance this doesn't seem very useful, but consider this: If there were a hard drive failure, a boot disk with the `dd` command on it could restore the entire contents of this partition with the following single command:

```
dd if=/dev/nst0 of=/dev/hda2
```

If this particular tape was restored on any other computer's hard drive, it would then be an exact copy of the original, file for file.

The `dump` command:

```
/sbin/dump -0u -f /dev/nst0 /
```

This command has the same effect as the `dd` command—the entire root partition is saved. The advantage to using the `dump` command is that the corresponding `restore` is capable of selecting specific files and/or directories off of the tape. As an added bonus, `dump` can be used to back up individual subdirectories instead of entire disks, unlike `dd`, which only works with files.

The `tar` command:

```
tar cvf /dev/nst0 -X /proc/*' /
```

Full dumps should only be made when no other people or programs are modifying files in the filesystem. If files are modified while `tar` is making the backup, they may not be stored properly in the archive, in which case you won't be able to restore them when you want to. Also, you will want to specify that the `/proc` subdirectory should be skipped, or your `tar` process will never finish!

The `cpio` command:

```
find / -path '/proc' -prune -o -path /dev' -prune -o
➥-print ¦ cpio -ov > /dev/nst0
```

In addition to not being able to back up the `/proc` directory, the `cpio` program doesn't handle backing up the devices in the `/dev` subdirectory well. The default, when restoring, is for `cpio` to not create directories or over-write existing files.

Full Backup to a Remote Machine

These examples all show the backup being done on a local tape drive attached to the floppy tape controller, but they could just as easily be done on a tape drive or any other device on a remote computer. In order to back up onto a remote machine, the two machines involved must be configured to allow this, using the remote login programs. These "r-programs," as they are often called, are potentially a massive security risk when installed onto an Internet-connected machine, so you should consider using something along the lines of `ssh` (the home page is at `http://www.cs.hut.fi/ssh`), if your governmental regulations regarding encryption software permit it. Be that as it may, to enable one machine named *clarence* to back up files to the tape unit physically located on another machine named *felix,* you need to do the following, substituting the correct IP addresses and hostnames:

Each machine has an entry for the other in `/etc/hosts`. The two lines will look similar to

```
192.168.45.16    clarence.ntsc.ca clarence
192.168.45.5     felix.ntsc.ca felix
```

The tape-equipped machine *felix* has an entry for all of the hosts it allows backups to be done for in /etc/hosts.equiv.

```
clarence.ntsc.ca root
```

Backup host *felix* also has an entry in /root/.rhosts for all of those allowed hosts (actually, in my case, the filename is /root/.shosts because I got into the habit of using ssh several years ago).

```
clarence.ntsc.ca
```

The permissions on the file .rhosts (or .shosts!) must be set to 600 (read/write for the owner only) and the owner must be set to be root.

If you use ssh, the /etc/ssh_known_hosts file on *felix* must have an entry for *clarence*'s public key. (All of the names this machine is known by are prepended to the single-line value found in the file /etc/ssh_host_key.pub on *clarence*.)I've truncated the lengthy key value that starts with 1146605 on the following line:

```
clarence.ntsc.ca,clarence    1024 37 114660556[truncated]
```

The backup commands are the same local commands, except that the backup device name becomes prefixed with the name of the machine it is on, and a colon. For example, this command given on *clarence*

```
dd if=/dev/hda2 of=felix:/dev/nst0
```

causes an image of the second partition on *clarence*'s first hard drive to be backed up to the SCSI tape drive on *felix*. Similarly,

```
tar xvf felix:/dev/nftape *netscape-v202-export.i486-unknown-linux.tar.gz
```

causes a very old copy of a popular Web browser to be read off of the tape drive attached to *felix*'s floppy disk controller and placed into the current directory on *clarence*.

Full Backup Disadvantages

For most systems, doing a complete backup of the entire hard drive is not always practical because of the time involved and the amount of storage space needed. If the backup is being done across a network, bandwidth may also be impacted. Also, while the backup is being done, you will notice degraded performance on the machine being backed up, and perhaps also on the backup host.

Partial Backups

If you cannot always back up the whole system every time, it makes sense to back up only the most valuable information. The value of information may be measured in terms of dollars required to replace it, dollars not in revenue while the information is unavailable, or simple inconvenience if that information is not there. What price do you put on your Ph.D. thesis if it's gone the day before it's due to be presented? How much is your time worth while you replace missing data instead of doing something else?

In some cases, not having backups would be considered as merely a temporary setback. Other cases could cause bankruptcy.

You have to decide on what is important to you, and how valuable it is; I can only give you a few hints as to what to look for.

General Guidelines for Partial Backups

How do you decide what to do? There are a few general guidelines to help make the decision as to what your strategy might be, based in part on which category you feel that your computer belongs to.

In ancient times (before Linus Torvalds wrote Linux...), a UNIX computer was typically purchased, installed, and configured for a specific task. It might be the corporate database, a WAIS, GOPHER, or FTP server, a CAD station, or what have you. A system administrator would install the operating system (whichever one it might be) and then install and configure the application(s) needed. The final act, before turning the machine over to the tender mercy of the user, would be to perform a backup of the whole thing. This backup would probably be done on a tape unit, either on that machine or somewhere on the network. Daily backups would be done based on the system administrator's perceived need to protect that machine's users' local information, according to the set procedures for his organization as established at the management level.

This strategy is still a perfectly valid one, and is in use today in many sites around the world. It is, however, not the only possible one.

The backup requirements of a standalone computer that connects to a network only occasionally (for example, by using dial-up access to the Internet for email and Web browsing) are different from those of a computer that implements a corporate data repository or one that handles the dial-in access accounts of a number of users.

Bringing a New Red Hat Linux Box Online

The process of bringing a new Red Hat Linux box online can be thought of as consisting of three distinct phases; each one offers an opportunity to implement a slightly different backup strategy, depending on the projected final usage of the particular computer. These phases are covered in the following sections.

Backup the Original Operating System

Some people like to back up the entire operating system once it has booted up for the first time after the installation has completed. I don't, usually. My reasoning for this is that, if the entire drive goes down, I'll need to reinstall the operating system anyway, in order to be able to run the backup recovery tool itself. Plus, when I reinstall the O/S, it will probably be a newer version than the old one, and some configuration files may have changed their formats. Linux is, after all, a moving target, as are many of the applications that Red Hat ships with its distribution or that you may have obtained from over the Internet. The basic installation files are always available from the original media. The configuration files that are not on the installation media (networking configuration files spring most readily to the mind of a Network Systems Administrator, for no apparent reason) are easily re-created by reinstalling that particular package. At the point of the first reboot, there is nothing on the server/workstation that cannot be easily replaced. A full backup may take more time to complete than it would take to do a new installation, and I can usually live with the trade off.

That being said, I have had occasion to back up the entire basic install to tape (I like using the dump command for reasons that will become apparent), and then take that media and a boot disk to another computer with the same hardware, and restore an exact, out-of-the-box replica as fast as the restore can go. I have also created the tape at this point in time expressly because of the abuse the machine would be expected to take, perhaps multiple times during the course of a single day. Reinstalling onto the same hardware from a disk image can be very convenient. Just boot from a floppy, type in a single command, and walk away. The only instructions you need to give to the user are, "When the prompt appears again, remove the disk and the tape and press the reset button. Call me when you kill it the next time."

Another advantage to doing this is that you do not have to answer all of the installation questions again and again. Of course, the new machine is an exact copy of the original in every detail, including machine name and IP address. This can be very useful if you've upgraded a hard drive or you are configuring several machines at the same time. If you were running a computer lab for the purpose of teaching, restoring the machine to its original state this way at the start of each course would save considerable time over having to go through the installation procedure again.

Using the `tar` Command

Another opportunity presented at this time is to use the `tar` command to store all the subdirectories, except `/proc` and `/tmp`, of course. (Remember, the file named `/proc/kcore` is actually an image of all of memory, and cannot be backed up using `tar` or `cpio`. As for `/tmp`, there should be nothing there that you need to worry about.) This will give you a known-good base of all the files on a running system. Any of the files in the `tar` may be extracted any time you want, either individually or in bulk, should the need arise.

Backup After the Applications are Installed

Installing and configuring all of those applications that are required by this particular computer is the job of the system administrator. Installing a program in a system directory requires `root` access, and the system administrator is `root`. In order for the system to be fully usable, various programs require that their configuration files be changed in order to be the most efficient. For example, `INN` can be a bit difficult to get exactly right. `sendmail` is a personal favorite of mine that I like to configure exactly the way I want. I invariably install `ssh` on a new system right after building my own custom version of the kernel. If you have to configure a modem, it will have files containing telephone numbers, login IDs, modem initialization strings, and so on. These changes take time to implement. To re-create the same changes several months later may not be as convenient as restoring all of them at once with a single command.

If this machine is to be used for a single purpose (a task-oriented machine such as a News, Mail, firewall/gateway, or Web server), a full backup done after this point allows for restoring the entire filesystem (or any part of it) back to its original state as quickly as possible.

If this machine is to be a backup server upon which you have installed a third-party backup program (there are many available, as you will soon see), or if you have just configured one of the backup programs that were part of your Red Hat Linux distribution, when this phase is complete would be the perfect time to make a full backup of the entire system. A pleasant benefit is that you could also verify that all the hardware is working by restoring a file or two just for the sake of being able to do so.

Backup Daily Operations

Every time you or anyone else uses your computer, something will change, some-where—editor preferences, desktop colors, World Wide Web bookmarks, command history, something. Trying to discern and remember them all can be done, but it is time-consuming. I've never known a system administrator yet who wasn't short of time. So, you will want to have some sort of ongoing, regularly scheduled backup procedure happening. Unless, of course, you want to start over from square one every time a disaster happens...

Of these three phases, daily operation is the only one that doesn't have a limited timeframe, especially under the Linux operating system that can measure real uptimes in the hundreds of days. In addition to users creating, deleting, and modifying files in their home directories, there will probably be changes made at the system level by the system administrator upgrading system utilities—for example, a newer version of the kernel. Those changes are not on the installation media, nor are they on the First Boot backups. These new versions of system programs are being released all the time, as improvements are made at both system and user-space levels.

Changes Made Via Text Editor

Changes made by hand (using your favorite text editor, whether it be `emacs`, `vi`, `pico`, `gedit`, or something else) are easy to keep track of. Buy yourself a loose-leaf binder, and whenever you make changes to any file, record the filename on the back page. This will then become an instant back-up list. Once finished, copy the changed file(s) to your backup medium of choice, and you are done. A complete restore involves installing the operating system and adding those files you have changed. Of course, some files change more frequently than others; the `~/.bash_history` file changes every time you exit the login shell. The `/etc/passwd` file changes every time you add a user, while `/etc/shadow` changes every time anyone changes their password. You do insist that all of your users, including yourself, change their passwords periodically, don't you?

Changes Made Via Graphical Tools

Changes made using one of the graphical tools are a little harder to keep track of manually. The RPM query command will tell you where the documentation files to that particular program are, and the documentation files will tell you where the configuration files live. This is awkward to keep track of manually, but it can be done with some effort on the part of the system administrator. Luckily, there are ways to automate the whole procedure.

Deciding Site Strategy

Whether the tool is a sophisticated backup utility or a simple script, you can automate your backup strategy once you know what it is. Therefore, the first step is to decide what your site strategy will be. As long as what you need is where you can get it when you need it, there are no wrong answers. A site strategy is the list of backup procedures and rules to be followed for this particular site, whether it consists of one machine or 100.

Your backup strategy will consist of answering the following questions:

- Which files need to be backed up?

- How often do they change, and need re-backing up?

- How much storage space will they occupy?

- How much storage space is available?

- How important are having these files available?

- Can you live without these files for any given time period?

- How long will it take to go from nothing to usable?

Once you have answered these questions, as only you can do for your system, you will be ready to begin implementing a strategy that fits your needs. This strategy will be your guide to when, how, what, and where to back up your files.

Types of Backups

There are three basic types of backups, with enough possible variations to handle every contingency. There are full backups, where every file on the computer is saved off to the backup medium. There are partial backups, where only certain files are backed up, typically listed in a file somewhere. Last, but not least, there are incremental backups. Incremental backups deal with the files that have changed since the last backup was done. Each of these has its own advantages and disadvantages, as you will see.

Full Backups

Traditionally, the term "full backup" was used to describe the process whereby all of the files associated with a particular computer were saved, usually to tape. All that was needed was a full restore to bring the computer back to the state it was in when the full backup was done. The problem with doing a full backup is that it can take a long time, depending on the speed of the backup medium, and it can take up a lot of space on that backup medium. A full backup to a two-gigabyte storage device is not nearly as annoying as trying the same backup to floppy disks. A full backup of a default full install of a Red Hat i386 system is approximately 1.2 gigabytes, before compression. After compression, it will occupy about 560 megabytes, which is about the same amount of storage as the original CD-ROM used to install it.

Partial Backups

Partial backups involve specific files. The restoration process is very straightforward—just restore the file(s) from the latest backup medium, and you're done.

The problem with partial backups is that if you haven't backed up a file that you now need, it's not there. To completely restore a system may take much longer than is acceptable. Partial backups are especially susceptible to Murphy's Law. Be careful!

Incremental Backups

An incremental backup indicates that only some of the files are being saved—those that have changed since the last backup was done, either full or incremental, of the same or higher level. To get from nothing back to the state that you were in when the last incremental was done, you have to restore the last full backup, and then, in turn, apply all the incremental backups in the same order that they were made. Incrementals don't take nearly as long as full backups (most of the files on a Linux system don't change, unless you upgrade packages often), nor do they require as much space. The problem with incremental backups manifests itself when a total restore needs to be done—how many incremental backups have been done since the last full backup was done? Then, all you need do is to make any changes to the file(s) that were done since that last incremental backup, and everything is the way it was before you needed to start this procedure. (This is the short version. Just like everything else computer-related, this procedure can be altered in any of several ways.)

Incremental Backup Level

An incremental backup level is just a numeric value that is arbitrarily assigned by the system administrator. The values for these levels range from 0 to 9, with 0 (the highest priority) being a full backup, and 9 being the lowest priority. Every level-n incremental backs up all files changed since the previous backup at the same or a higher numbered level. This allows for a weekly level-2 backup to catch all files done since the monthly level-0, even if a level-7 was done every night. The use of levels is not required; the level number must be specifically assigned if you want one. If you don't specify a particular level, most software assumes level-0 as a default value. But, if you used the level-7/level-2 method referred to above, then that restore would only require all the level-2 tapes, then the level-7 tapes done since the last level-2 one, and the same manual final intervention. This could significantly reduce the number of restore media needed and the time to complete the restore itself.

If you made a full backup of the original install and have done nothing but incremental backups since, the restoration procedure could take a very long time. In order to minimize this time, you will want to set up a rotation schedule for your backups. Using different levels of backup in such a manner leads to the idea of a rotation schedule. Strangely enough, that's covered next.

Developing a Rotation Schedule

The term "rotation schedule" refers to the way that information is backed up (using varying levels of incremental backups, usually) and to the number, location, and re-use of your backup media. The backup medium may be tape, tape cartridge, (re)writable CD-ROM, Zip disk, Jaz drive, removable hard drive, floppy disk, or anything else that you want to use. Write-once media can be used for backups, but their reinsertion into the backup pool is not possible. The backup pool is the term used to describe the number of items available (tapes, disks, and so on) for backing up onto.

The purpose of having a rotation schedule is to enable the system administrator (you) to be able to recover specific files with a minimum of effort and wasted time. As an extra side benefit, your users will call you a hero when the deleted file(s) appear back on the system as if by magic. How you let them show their appreciation (read: bribe) is, of course, your concern—and theirs!

How do you decide upon a viable rotation schedule? That depends... are you beginning to hate that phrase? One of the basic criteria will be storage media budget. How much money are you willing to pay during any given time period to protect your data? This will then decide the type of backup medium and the size of your backup pool. How much data needs to be backed up? That data will occupy how many backup media during how long a time period? The following sections illustrate examples of rotation schedules.

Casual Home User

A simple home system that's used only for email and occasional Web browsing needs to be backed up less often than the system that contains all the financial records for a company. One possible rotation schedule for the typical home user who uses the computer mostly on weekends follows:

Monday: Full (level-0) backup

Tuesday-Friday: Incremental at level-3

Saturday: Incremental at level-2

Sunday: Incremental at level-2

The Backup Rationale

The full backup is done while everyone is at work/school. The entire backup would need to fit on a single storage device (disk or tape, for example) in order to run completely unattended. If two storage media are required, start the backup Sunday at bedtime, and change to the next one before you leave the house Monday. Yes, having to change the media is a nuisance. The only easy way out is to backup onto a medium that is capable of holding everything that the system could possibly contain. Another alternative is to consider the installation medium as being your level-0 backup, and do a level-1 backup on Monday. This will significantly reduce storage requirements.

Tuesday-Friday are shown as level-3 for the reason that the typical home user doesn't get a lot of use out of the computer during the week because of other commitments, such as school or work, but the system does get some usage.

Saturday and Sunday are typically heavier usage days. Those backups will be larger than those generated by the level-3 backup, and will include that data as well. If a restore is needed, either backup provides the needed files in a single restore session. These level-2 backups are done on both days because of an interesting observation of one of those things often attributed to Murphy's Law: Bad things tend to happen when you use the machine a lot.

Here's advice from someone who has been there, done that, got the t-shirt, and had his wife toss it into the trash when it wore out: *Never* use the same medium for a full backup and an incremental. *Always* keep at least one full backup around that you know is good. This means that the absolute minimum number of backup media is three: One for the level-0 that was made the last time, one for the intervening incremental backups, and one for the next level-0. Never overwrite a level-0 backup if you don't have at least one known-good level-0 in reserve. All of this assumes that all the information fits on one medium, of course.

If you want to use the original CD as your level-0 backup, then the rotation schedule needs to be modified somewhat, so that the Monday level-1 backup is of use to you. The backup software will have to be tricked into thinking that it has used the original installation files as part of a level-0 backup. Then, on Monday, don't perform a level-0 backup, which would back up the entire filesystem—use a level-1 instead. This instructs your software to include all files that have been modified since the last level-1 or greater backup was done and to ignore the level-0 files. The advantage here is that, after re-installing Linux, the files on the level-1 backup are all the files changed since a level-0 backup was done, no matter how long ago that was.

Configuring dump to Accept Installation as Level-0

To configure the program dump to do this, you basically have two choices.

As soon as the system is configured, execute the command

```
/sbin/dump -0u -f /dev/null -B 8192000 /
```

in order to create the entry in /etc/dumpdates that declares now as being the time of the last level-0 dump. (This is referred to as the *epoch*—the beginning of time.) This basically says to dump, "Create a level-0 backup (-0u) on device /dev/null (-f /dev/null) (which throws the resulting files away) of my entire 8-gigabyte hard drive (-B 8192000), starting at the root (/)."

If the system has been running for any length of time, you probably will have to avail yourself of the second choice, which is to manually edit the file /etc/dumpdates to reflect the time of installation. See the section "Developing Backup Scripts" later in the chapter for a hint or two on how to retroactively figure out when the date of installation was, if you don't remember. A line in /etc/dumpdates that looks like this:

```
/dev/hda2        0 Sat Jul 31 20:31:16 1999
```

creates an initial state for the dump program to start from. Subsequent incremental dumps add their information to the /etc/dumpdates file like this (I show a level-1, done immediately after users were added to the system):

```
/dev/hda2        1 Sat Jul 31 20:47:01 1999
```

and the program will never know that a real dump has never been done. Yes, we just lied to the computer, but don't worry about it. Real system administrators do that all the time in order to get things done. Real operating systems will let you lie to them, but you had better have a very good reason, and be right!

Immediately after the users have been added, Internet connectivity established, email and Web clients configured, and everything works to your satisfaction, everything that has been changed from the basic installation is backed up with a level-1 backup. To recover from a major disaster, install the operating system, then restore this level-1 backup, and you are back online. Add in the latest periodic level 2-9 incremental backups and you can be as current as you want to be, without needing to store hundreds (or possibly thousands) of megabytes of data.

Using this backup strategy allows me to use my old 40-megabytes-per-tape floppy-drive-controller-based tape drive to back up my 8-gigabyte Red Hat Linux hard drive with just a little ingenuity on my part. Actually, it allows me to back up all of my home network's machines on a regular basis with a minimum of hassle. Some of my machines now have enough changes that they require multiple tapes for the level-1 backup, but I'm too cheap to buy a new tape unit when the old one works just fine. If I do purchase a new, larger tape unit, this same strategy will work with no modification. As the information accumulates, however, I will just need to add more tapes to my pool.

A Typical Workstation

A workstation that contains data that cannot be replaced easily (perhaps it's the accounts payable) would more than likely implement a rotation schedule along different lines than the home user would use. There are probably more resources available for the backup procedure than are available to a home user. The basic tenets (Backup! Backup! Backup!) are the same, but the consequences of failing to do so are more than likely more severe. A sample backup scenario could be implemented this way:

Sunday:	Full (level-0) backup
Tuesday-Saturday:	Incremental at level-3

The Backup Rationale

A full backup is performed on Sunday, when the machine is least busy. Full backups take the longest amount of time and the most storage space, so it makes sense to do them when the machine is least busy. If this machine is in a production environment, it works for a living and cannot be unavailable for any extended amount of time during business hours. You will want to have a large enough storage device to handle a complete backup, if possible. Otherwise, schedule the backup for early Sunday and be prepared to drop by the office later in the day.

From Tuesday to Saturday, an incremental backup is performed. Only the files that have changed each day are saved. If there is a disaster on Sunday, restore the previous Sunday's full backup and apply the incrementals from Tuesday to Saturday in turn, and you're back in business. Depending on the storage capacity of your backup medium, the entire set of incremental backups could be on a single one. There are now tapes available that are capable of holding 30 gigabytes each. The drives they fit into cost less than $500. These prices will undoubtedly be lower by the time you read this.

No backup is scheduled for Monday because if the backups are running early in the morning (3:00 a.m. is a time I have seen often in back up scripts—I don't know why everyone picks 3:00 a.m., but I've seen several that do) nothing will have changed since the full backup Sunday.

Incremental Backups On the Same Tape as Full Backups

Never, never store incremental backups on the same tape as the full! Bad idea. One small defect or minor accident with the tape and it can be rendered entirely useless.

After the end of the first week, new media (we'll call them set-2) are introduced and the backup process is repeated. The third week, set-2 is replaced with set-3. Then, set-4 makes an appearance. You now have four complete sets of backups that cover the entire previous month. Every single file that was present on the system when the backups were done is right there, ready to be restored if needed. Some files are present only on the four full backups. Other files appear only once on one of the various incremental tapes.

Deciding On Set Capacity

You keep adding sets until you have enough. How many are enough? It depends on how much archival capacity you want to have. There's no such thing as too much if you can afford the costs of the media. Another factor to consider is the life expectancy of your data. From how far back in time are files going to be needed? Will anyone ever need last month's version of a particular file? Or the version of a file that changes daily as it existed last Tuesday? Or would last week's Sunday version be better? The number of sets (also known as the *pool*) will determine how far back in time your data can be retrieved.

Whenever you get to the point where you have a large enough archive saved, the original set-1 re-enters the writing process, and this cycle is then repeated for as many times as writing to any given tape is safe. When you decide that set-1 has reached its maximum number of writes limit, the retired set-1 then goes into the archives. If you need to maintain a complete, permanent archival copy, then no tape is ever recycled. Used tapes, after they are verified, of course, get moved to the archives when the cycle reaches them.

```
Sample WorkStation BackUp Medium Rotation Schedule
                Sun  Tue  Wed  Thu  Fri  Sat
week 1 set-1 full incr incr incr incr incr
week 2 set-2 full incr incr incr incr incr
week 3 set-3 full incr incr incr incr incr
week 4 set-4 full incr incr incr incr incr
    ¦    ¦    ¦    ¦    ¦    ¦    ¦    ¦    ¦
week X set-1 full incr incr incr incr incr
```

This strategy will give you a minimum of the past X weeks' (less one day) worth of files, depending on how many media (tapes) there are in your pool. The last three groups of media are often referred to as the Son (last version), Father (previous version to the Son), and Grandfather (previous version to the Father). If each day uses a separate medium, even with recycling at the start of week 5, you would be keeping almost an entire month's data handy. If you use one tape for the full and one tape for all the incrementals for any given week, the eight tapes needed for a five week cycle would allow for a complete archive of three full weeks. The number of media needed depends on the amount of data you need to keep.

According to the basic tenets of Murphy's Law, if you have the backups you'll never need them. You will only really need a backed up file after the tape that it was stored on has been recycled.

Restoring Individual Files

Restoring individual files off of these archives is a simple matter of inserting the correct medium and recovering that particular file. If the time of the last update of that file isn't known, then you will have to go back onto each previous day's backup until you find it. The worst case is that you will need to search backwards until you hit the last full backup tape, in this case a total of six tapes.

A complete restoration involves recovering the last full backup, and then each of the subsequent ones until the last is reached. Any changes made since the last backup are lost, and will have to be entered in manually.

The sample workstation backup medium rotation schedule in the preceding section shows the set-1 media being reused for week number X. You cannot normally reuse a CD-ROM, of course, but you can reuse any rewritable medium, by definition. The important question from the system administrator's point of view is, "How many times is it safe to reuse one of these?" Here's the Standard Computer Answer, (again!): It depends. It depends on the storage medium that you are using. It depends on how much of a risk you are willing to take with your data. It depends on how much money you can put into media.

Are you using tape? Some system administrators claim that any tape can be used up to a maximum of 10 times. Others claim that twenty is the magic number. Still others maintain that any given tape should be used only once, then placed in an archive. Some tape manufacturers print their own recommendations on the packaging of new tapes. Who do you believe? "Trust your feelings, Luke!" is as good an answer as any. Personally, I will use any particular tape for as many times as the data on it can be verified to be correct, unless the backup is of particular importance to me, in which case one is the magic number. Professionally, I use a tape just once, and the old ones are archived at an offsite location I have never been to in a fireproof vault I have never seen. I have also never needed to have one of those tapes returned to me for file retrieval, but we do keep more than a year's worth of old data on hand. Never reuse the tape with the only known-good version of a file you are currently backing up on it. If the tape reached its limit with the last write and fails while

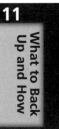

trying to write this backup, your only copy of the file is history. What you don't want is for the tape you've just used to be unreadable when the time comes that you need some of the data on it. Always verify backups yourself, manually. When the writing of data to a tape fails at all, junk that tape, obtain another one, and redo the backup.

A Backup Case Study

A True Backup Story: (I will not identify the "they" in the following story. It *could* have been me, but it *wasn't*. This time.)

They had been doing backups for 18 months, every night, faithfully. They kept an archive of everything, stored on many, many tapes, neatly labeled in the custom storage rack in the back room, safe, away from users with grubby little fingers, and possible magnetic paper clips in their pockets. Then, one dark and stormy night, they needed to restore a system file. Placing the previous night's tape in a drive, they found it unreadable. It appeared to be blank. They inserted the tape from the night before, and were presented with the same result. They Did Not Panic. They created a version of the missing file the hard way, by hand-modifying a file off of another server. Then, they went through the entire tape archive library, one tape at a time. I'm told that there were about 500 tapes in total and that it took a Seriously Long Time to check each and every one, but the system administrator is a very methodical type of guy. Persistent, too. They discovered that not a single tape had byte one stored on it. Subsequent investigation revealed that the tape unit had been defective from the beginning, right out of the box, and the Verify option to the backup software that they were using didn't catch the error because of this hardware defect. It also was revealed that this was the first time that anyone had ever tried to get a file back off of any of the tapes.

They use a different tape drive now. Part of the Junior System Administrator's duties each day is to restore any three files off of the previous night's tape before including it in the rotation, Just In Case. Funnily enough, they haven't needed to restore anything since, but if they ever do need a file back, they know that the restore will work.

Writable CD-ROM Usage

How many times can you use writable CD-ROM? Once is the usual answer, but you may have multi-session capabilities on your particular writer. In either event, you have a semi-permanent archival copy. I say semi-permanent because the actual life span of the CD-ROM media has yet to be determined. With proper storage (which simply means the traditional cool, dark place), a CD will undoubtedly last 50 years or so. This may far exceed your archival requirements, or it may not. The problem with writing a CD-ROM is that the amount of storage on one is limited to about 660 megabytes.

The newer, rewritable CD-ROM can be used multiple times, but again, how many before the medium deteriorates? Several, at least. Storage capacity of a rewritable CD-ROM at this point in time is also limited to about 660 megabytes, but they keep inventing new versions of the hardware.

Other Media Options

Do you use disks for your backups? Floppy diskettes, although tedious for large backups, are reusable several times. (Let's see: 500 megabytes of needed backup files divided by 1.44 megabytes per disk times a minute or so to fill each with data equals much longer than I want to sit there... but, if that's all you have, then use them! You will undoubtedly want to be very selective about what you back up, but do it! You might want to consider buying a tape drive, though. Types of storage media are discussed in Chapter 12, "Media Selection and Storage.") When diskettes go bad, though, they very rarely give a warning of impending failure. A spare hard drive is an option to consider, unless it gets zapped at the same time as the original.

Zip drives and Jaz disks hold about 100 and 1000 megabytes, respectively. These, and other removable-disk style media, are rewritable. They need to be stored properly, however, as in "Nowhere near electrical equipment such as computer monitors." The data they hold can be readily restored when needed. The parallel port versions are considerably slower than the IDE or SCSI-bus-based ones, but they have enough capacity to make backups feasible.

If all this sounds as though I am biased in favor of tape storage for backups, it's probably because I am. Sorry. Tape is reasonably inexpensive. The drive units themselves, while not extremely cheap, are reasonably priced, and are usually quite reliable. By the nature of tape software, it is usually a trivial process to insert another tape when the end of a particular tape is reached and continue on. This is not always the case with other types of storage media.

I have used the term tape a lot so far, and will continue to do so, but feel free to mentally substitute the medium of your choice. I have tried (and failed miserably) to not let my bias toward tape show, but at least I admit to having one. The main tape repository where I work holds 1.6 terabytes of data when it is full—80 twenty-gigabyte tapes. The backup software handles two units of 42 nine-gigabyte hard drives, each raided (in hardware) to level 5. One of those disk enclosures is a backup of the other, because of the need to always be running. There was no real alternative to tape backup storage for us, because of the sheer volume of data we have to consider. How long is a tape? Just keep adding volumes until it is long enough for your needs.

Now you have decided what you are going to back up. You know which device you will back up the data to. You have determined what your backup strategy and rotation schedule will be. So far, the focus has been on interactive backups—those that typically are run only once or whenever the need arises to have a backup done for a specific purpose. Next we'll look at automating the task, because all system administrators are always way too overworked to have to do this sort of thing manually every time. Or, maybe we're just too lazy to want to type all those commands in all the time? No, it must be overwork.

Developing Backup Scripts

The scripting possibilities for doing backups are, quite literally, infinite. No two scripts to do the same task will ever be exactly the same, simply because no two people writing them are exactly the same. So, take what I am about to show you and modify to your heart's content. Just make sure that what you end up with meets your requirements.

Using `tar` for Backups

It is quite possible to use the `tar` command as the only backup mechanism on a system, whether that system is a simple home system, an at-work workstation, or a full-time server. The mechanics of it can be quite simple. On a regular schedule, a full backup is done (this is often referred to as "level-0"), followed by subsequent, regularly scheduled incremental backups.

A Backup Scenario Using `tar`

Linux is installed, complete with networking, dial-up access to the local Internet service provider, accounts for users, email, and Web browsers. Everything is perfect. It has taken some time to get to this point because of other commitments. If there's a problem, you want the system to be restored with a minimum of down time because the users includes the operator—you.

To determine which files have changed since the original install, you just need to know when that original install was done. If you've forgotten, there are a number of clues you can use. If you look at the dates of the symbolic links in /bin and /sbin, you will notice that many of them have the timestamp of when you installed Red Hat Linux. The command

```
find /bin -type l -exec ls -l {} \;
```

will display a listing of all the links in the /bin directory. The oldest timestamps will have been created at installation time by the setup script. If you haven't modified your time zone since the install (that is, you got the correct answer at configuration time), you will find that one of the last things the Red Hat configuration did was to create the link /etc/localtime.

If you have not changed the X server since the install, the link /etc/X11/X (which points to the particular X server you use, such as XF86_Mach64 or XF86_FBDev) is one of the last symbolic links to have been created by the install. The link /usr/X11R6/bin/X, which points to Xwrapper, will be a few minutes older because it was created earlier in the installation. The timestamp on the file /boot/map is also a good candidate, unless, of course, you've recompiled your kernel.

One of the quickest and easiest methods to back up files with is the tar command. It exists on every Linux installation you will ever find (in case you need to restore a file from one machine on another), as well as every UNIX under the sun (including, he said with a straight face, SUN's) that I have ever seen. Variants other than GNU tar generally do not understand gzip compression, so be careful to not use the -z option on files you want to export to those.

The following command will back up all files changed within the last two days, except those in the subdirectories /dev, /var/lock, /var/spool, /tmp, and /proc into a file called changed.tar:

```
    find / -path '/dev' -prune -o -path '/var/lock' -prune -o
➥-path '/var/spool' -prune -o -path '/tmp' -prune -o
➥-path '/proc' -prune -o -type f -mtime 2
➥-print0 ¦ tar --null -cvf changed.tar --files-from=-
```

Alternatively, if you first issue the command

```
    touch -t 07120000 sentinel
```

to create a file called sentinel with the timestamp of July 12 at 00:00 hours (my test system was installed the evening of 11 July), you could use:

```
    find / -path '/var/log' -prune -o -path '/proc' -prune -o
➥-path '/tmp' -prune -o  -path '/dev' -prune -o
➥-type f -newer sentinel -print0
➥¦ tar --null -cvf changed.tar --files-from=-
```

Adding the -g SNAPSHOT-FILE-NAME option would create a file that allows incrementals (the -G option) to know which files were backed up at which level. This file contains the date the last backup was done, and information for each file backed up, one per line. It can get to be rather large.

Implementing Full Backups and Restoring with dump and restore

If entire filesystems (that is, the whole disk drive) or entire directories need to be backed up, the dump and restore programs are also available. The dump program has built-in support for "dump-levels." This "dump-level" is the same as that used by the `tar` program: Any dump-level backs up files that have been changed or added since the same or higher-numbered level was done. Level-0 is highest, level-9 lowest, so a level-1 includes levels 1 through 9, but not level-0.

This command creates a level-0 backup of one subdirectory:

```
/sbin/dump -0u -f /dev/nst0 /usr/src
```

All files are backed up, in this case to the tape unit attached to the floppy drive controller. An incremental may be given a dump-level arbitrarily from 1 to 9; if you always use the same value, you will get files modified since the last incremental at the same level or a higher numbered one.

The command

```
/sbin/dump -3u -f /dev/nst0 /usr/src
```

would only back up changed files from the `/usr/src` tree if they have been modified since the last level-3 or higher numbered backup was run.

To recover files, directories, or filesystems backed up with the `dump` command, the `restore` command is used. When used with the `-i` option (as in `restore -if /dev/nst0`), specific files or subdirectories may be recovered. For example, restoring the file `/etc/cron.daily/logrotate`, which I have modified, generates this for output:

```
[root@clarence /root]# /sbin/restore -if /dev/nst0
restore > ls
.:
dev/  etc/  root/  tmp/  usr/  var/

restore > cd etc
restore > ls
./etc:
cron.daily/ dumpdates

restore > add cron.daily
restore > ls cron.daily
./etc/cron.daily:
*logrotate

restore > extract
You have not read any tapes yet.
Unless you know which volume your file(s) are on you should start
with the last volume and work towards the first.
Specify next volume #: 1
```

```
set owner/mode for '.'? [yn] n
restore > quit
[root@clarence /root]# ls ./etc
cron.daily
[root@clarence /root]# ls ./etc/cron.daily/
logrotate
```

This particular implementation of `restore` dumps core if I just give the command `add etc/cron.daily/logrotate` without adding the `cron.daily` subdirectory first. I'm not exactly sure why, but since I have the source code, I could look through it and fix that particular bug. Or I could email the author a bug report. Or I could do what you see here, and work around it. The restore listing of the `etc/cron.daily` subdirectory has an asterisk in front of the name `logrotate` to indicate that it has been added to the extraction list. You will notice that the extraction restored the intervening `etc/` subdirectory relative to my current working directory. This allows me to restore system files that may be broken now, because of upgrades, and just copy over what I want. The line about "specify next volume" comes in handy if the dump occupies several tapes and you know where the specific file you want is located.

Quick Archiving with `cpio`

Another candidate for quick archiving is the `cpio` program, especially if you need to move from one kind of machine to another. The fact that `cpio`'s default is to not create directories or overwrite existing files is either good or bad, depending on your needs of the moment.

There are many variations possible; consult the `man` and `info` pages for `dump`, `find`, `tar`, and `cpio` (`info dump`, `info tar`, `info find`, `info cpio`, `man tar`, `man find`, `man cpio`) to see some more examples.

Any of these commands can be placed into a script file and executed via `cron`. It is always a really good idea to run the script from the command line first, so that you can see if there are any errors in the output before you just let it go. If your script generates output on STDOUT (that's system administrator-speak for "The script has an echo line in it somewhere") the owner of the `cron` job will be mailed what would have been printed to the screen—perhaps a final line reading something along the lines of:

```
echo The backup script completed on ·date·
```

so that you will know it is time to replace the tape.

Possible Backup Problems and Alternatives

There is a little problem with using one of these methods as your only backup method: How do you determine which tar file contains the specific file(s) you need? How do you know when a specific file was backed up? You need to keep track of what was backed up, when that happened, and where the file is. This file, or possibly these files, will constitute what is known as an index. The GNU `tar` program has the `-gfilename` option, which puts the date of the run into the file named `filename`. The option `-G` generates a list of the files that were backed up into the tar. Add a custom script or two (or seven), and you have a backup system that you know in every detail—if you have the time and ability to do all of this. If you do not, consider the alternatives.

Dedicated Backup Software

One alternative is to obtain specific software to do your backups with. Dedicated backup software is available from a number of sources. Some are released under the GNU Public License and are free; others are commercial, proprietary products. How do you find out what is available for your use under Linux? You check out the usual places, of course. A quick check with the Linux Applications and Utilities Page at `http://www.chariot.com/linapp2.html` revealed a list of five commercial products and six free ones. Checking with LinuxBerg at `http://www.linuxberg.com` revealed 18 console backup applications and three specifically written for X. The Linux Links site at `http://linuxlinks.com` held a listing of 34 entries in the backup section, but it also included a program to write CD-ROMs as a backup utility. By the time you read this, I suspect there will be more programs available from more places.

If you are using a particular software package to implement your backups, the author(s) will typically have their own implementation for keeping track of the tape contents. They may even have decided to store the information in a format that is only understood by their program. Other programs will use text-based index files and store the data in one of the standard formats, such as `tar` or `cpio`. Which do you choose? If you guessed that the answer is "It depends," then you are starting to catch on to this whole system administrator thing.

Before you commit yourself (and your entire organization) to using any backup program, you should very carefully evaluate it to see if it meets your needs, not the needs of the author or the needs of the company that is selling it. Your needs. If it doesn't do what you need, you will be very sorry at some point in time—usually while people are depending on the backups to save them from something unpleasant.

Evaluating Backup Software

Like everything else, there's no one way to decide if any particular backup software package is right for you until after you've used it for a while. Hopefully, if it isn't right for you for one reason or another, you won't lose any data. You don't want to have to tell someone that the files are safely backed up, but the only program in the world that can get the data back out again is not available because the only copy you have of that program is on the tape. Or, that when you tried to back up the files, the program destroyed the original data and then saved that corrupted version, so that's all you can give back.

There are some things that you should look for in backup software, though. Number one on the list is reliability. A backup program that periodically fails is worse than useless, because you don't have your backups when you think you do. If the buggy program corrupted the original data that you wanted to back up before any backup could be made, you will not be popular with anyone, including yourself. How do you tell if a backup program is reliable? The absolute best way is to use it for a period of time on data that you can afford to lose. For what period of time should you test backup software? If your data keeps growing at a great rate, that probation period may never end, although you should have a pretty good idea after the end of your second time through the rotation schedule. Another means of evaluating backup software is to talk to people who are currently using it, before you commit yourself.

If the software is proprietary, the salespeople should be able to put you in contact with whomever they think you should talk to—probably a happy customer. Find out if that customer has the same (or similar) needs as you in terms of numbers of files and storage requirements. The downside is that you will probably not get to talk to unhappy customers about what some of the drawbacks to the program are. Don't kid yourself, all software has some drawbacks. The trick is to pick drawbacks that you can live with, once you know what they are.

Open source software, on the other hand, typically has a mailing list that you can subscribe to before you commit. Some have separate mailing lists for users and developers; others have just one list. In either event, the authors are often active participants. Both the good and the bad are typical topics of discussion.

With a proprietary package, the chances are that you will never know who wrote it, or be able to ask technical questions about the program itself. Open source software allows anyone the opportunity to examine the code for potential problems.

The rest of the list of things to look for in backup software will vary from one person to the next. If you are trying to back up several hundred thousand files occupying hundreds of gigabytes every day, your needs will not be the same as if you were concerned with only tens or hundreds of files.

You should look at ease of use. Will this software require a highly skilled person to set it up? Can this software be run by existing staff right now, or will special training be required in order to get it to do what you want?

There may also be issues of compatibility with existing archives of backed up software. If you move from a `tar`-based system to a proprietary format, and then back again, what happens to the proprietary-format archives if you need to get at something inside?

How easily is the software obtained? If you use a specific program to back up your systems and you add a different operating system to your network, will that software support it? If it isn't supported directly, are you able to support it indirectly? For example, can you easily back up a non-local, NFS mounted directory? How would you restore those files?

A Backup Software Evaluation Sample

As an example of how I would evaluate backup software, let's consider the program `taper`. `taper` is distributed with Red Hat Linux, and was written by Yusuf Nagree. The home page is located at `http://www.lugos.si/delo/taper/index.html`. The installation program lists it under applications/backup. It installs quite easily. When run for the first time, it responds with a rather cryptic message:

```
[root@clarence /root]# /usr/sbin/taper
Set tape drive using -T option
```

A quick reading of the documentation located in `/usr/doc/taper-6.9` reveals a great deal of information. (As a system administrator, you will read a great deal of documentation. Or you will destroy your system often. The choice is yours. I highly recommend reading the docs. RTFMis a standard answer from a system administrator. It *could* stand for Read The FAQ and Manual. FAQ stands for Frequently Asked Questions. Mailing lists, Usenet groups, and application home pages often have a FAQ available where common answers for common questions are answered.)

The program is considered by the author to be Beta because he only knows that it works on his system. It worked just fine on the floppy-tape equipped machine that I tried it on.

It was written with a floppy-controller tape drive in mind because the author only has one of those. I suspect that using this program on a SCSI tape device would pose no problems, but I would need to test it before I was sure. I'm a system administrator—paranoia is a prerequisite!

The `-T` option is for specifying which kind of tape drive is attached to this computer. The list given includes SCSI as well as the floppy-controller devices, IDE drives, floppy disks, and files.

There is a limit of about 30,000 files unless you have a large amount of physical memory. Without looking at the sources, which are available, I'm not sure how much a large amount is. Backing up a complete Red Hat install would require in excess of 130,000 files.

Once a tape device (or a file) is specified, `taper` is controlled via text-based menus.

`taper` needs to know where the backups will be kept, and where to keep its index files. The first thing that you want to do is set up your preferences—things such as the storage medium (the program supports tape, file, disk, and networked media, according to the docs). You are able to specify the size of the backup devices, which is needed, for example, if you use 40Mb tapes and need to back up 50Mb of data. If you don't remember the keystroke needed for a particular operation, pressing the "?" key brings up a list of keystrokes. Then, select the files or subdirectories that you want backed up (with "s"), and when you are done, the "f" key starts things rolling. It's fast and it appears to be reliable. It will automatically skip the /proc subdirectory.

In order to restore files onto another computer, the index files as well as the program have to be moved there. There wasn't a man page installed, but the documentation in /usr/doc/taper-6.9 is very clear. It allows for unattended full and incremental backups (via cron), and the index is fully browseable within the program so that you can recover specific files.

A major drawback, from my point of view, is that the data appears to be stored in a format that is only understood by `taper`, and that this format has been changed from earlier versions. I have machines on my internal network that are never updated, for the reason that they accomplish their tasks quite adequately as they are. Because they are on an internal, private network, security is not an issue.

My conclusion: This is not the program of choice for me. I require portable backup files—they may be restored onto any of a number of machines. It may be the perfect backup program for you, or not. If not, then check out another—perhaps kdat is the backup program for you.

kdat

kdat is another backup program that also ships with Red Hat Linux (it would be installed if you installed the KDE window manager). It can be found under KDE menus, Utilities, Tape Backup Tool. It doesn't work with remote tape drives, which is one of my prerequisites. It does, however, use standard `tar` commands to save to tape. It has been designed to be a graphical front end to use the `tar` program and a local tape drive. It does not meet my requirements because I have several machines to back up onto the one tape unit, but it just may be the exact thing that you are looking for.

Summary

I have presented a lot of information in this chapter. I really hope that it has helped you in your quest to acquire more knowledge about backing up your system. The basic steps involve making the following decisions:

- What needs to be backed up? The entire hard drive? Specific subdirectories? Only certain files?

- How often does it need to be backed up? Daily? Monthly?

- Where will it be backed up to? Tape? CD-ROM? Disk? A local device, or a remote one?

- How will the actual backup be done? A specific program? A custom written script file?

- How much archival data needs to be kept around? Everything for the last week (or month, or quarter, or year)? Just everything as it was at the end of a specific time period?

Here are some URLs you might find useful:

The Linux Software-RAID How-To

`file:///usr/doc/HOWTO/mini/Software-RAID`

The Linux high Availability How-To

`http://metalab.unc.edu/pub/Linux/ALPHA/linux-ha/High-Availability-HOWTO.htm`

SSH—Secure Shell

`http://www.cs.hut.fi/ssh`

The Linux Applications and Utilities Page

`http://www.chariot.com/linapp2.html`

LinuxBerg

`http://www.linuxberg.com`

Linux Links

`http://linuxlinks.com`

12

CHAPTER

Media Selection and Storage

IN THIS CHAPTER

- Backup Media   *334*
- Tape Driver Interfaces   *339*
- Storage Issues   *341*

Backup Media

Once the decisions of what to back up and how to implement the backups have been made, the next decision focuses on the media to be used for the backups. In the past, the only choice of media for backups was tape. In today's market, however, the choice is no longer whether to use tapes, floppy, CD, or DVD, but what kind of tape or what kind of floppy. Over the past few years, backup media has become more varied than ever before. The media used to backup systems today include WORM drives, magneto-optical drives, SCSI tape devices, IDE tape devices, floppy tape devices, DVD drives, and CD recorders. While the choice of media available for use in backups vary greatly, this chapter focuses specifically on tape media. Device selection is covered first, followed by media selection, tape driver interfaces available, and finally, storage issues.

Sources of Information for Tape Backups

There are a large number of Web pages devoted to backups and to vendor-specific devices. Naturally, because the information on these pages is presented by a particular vendor, it is wise to remember to take information making wild claims about reliability or media life with a grain of salt. A couple of sites that focus specifically on backups and that may be of interest to you when making the decision about backups and backup media are

- Backup Central at `http://www.backupcentral.com`
- Exabyte Corporation at `http://www.exabyte.com`

In addition, there are a number of Usenet newsgroups that may be useful as well. For example, the newsgroup `comp.os.linux.hardware` might be a good place to start. You can use this newsgroup to query other Linux users about Linux compatible tape drives, their performance, reliability, and other information about the hardware aspects of selecting your backup media. Another group that may be of interest is `comp.periphs.scsi`, where you can find out about SCSI peripherals, including tape drives. If you are looking for specific information regarding a particular type of media or tape drive, you might conduct a search on Deja.com to see if anyone else is discussing that product.

Device Selection Criteria

There are a number of factors that you should consider when selecting the device to use in your backup system, not the least of which is cost. This includes not only the cost of the backup device, but also the cost of the media and the time you will have to spend configuring your system to support the selected device. Cost, however, should not be the primary factor in the equation. Some other criteria to consider include the following:

- Support by the Linux kernel for the device chosen

- Support for the device by the backup software you have chosen

- Data storage capacity of the media

- Data transfer rate of the backup device

Of these factors, the first one that I would consider is whether or not the device is supported natively by the Linux kernel. You may find a backup solution that is inexpensive, has sufficient data storage capacity to meet your needs, and find backup software, whether freeware, shareware, or commercial, that will work with the device, but if your version of the Linux kernel doesn't support the device, you are out of luck.

The next consideration is whether the backup software you have chosen is compatible with the device. For example, if your backup software is a custom package that you developed and it uses the dump command, using a recordable CD drive as the media is not an option.

The data storage capacity of the media is another factor that must be carefully considered. For example, in the early days of DOS, when a 20-megabyte hard drive was considered sufficient for a desktop system, it was not uncommon to use floppy disks to back up a system. In fact, this was one of the few backup media choices available. Now, however, when systems come with 8-, 10-, or 14-gigabyte drives, anyone who would consider backing up their system to floppy would probably be committed to a mental institution. It is therefore very important to take into account the data capacity of the media for the devices you are considering.

Finally, and what is arguably the most important factor in making your decision next to support by the Linux kernel, is the transfer rate for writing data to the device. You may find that there are several possible solutions that you could implement, but what good does it do to have a supported and inexpensive backup device capable of backing up your entire system if it takes a week to do so?

The Autoloader Question

Another aspect to consider when evaluating backup devices is whether to purchase one with an autoloading mechanism. As disks get bigger and bigger (and the data never seems to stop filling them up), the ability to back up a single machine onto a single tape has become harder. The solution is to have multiple tapes for a single machine. However, backing up one machine onto multiple tapes usually means that a human being has to be present to change tapes. Backing up large amounts of data is no mean feat with only a single tape drive. Using autoloaders, however, this task becomes trivial since the autoloader (coupled with the backup software) takes care of inserting new tapes into the tape drive when a tape gets full. Autoloaders provide the ability to do nightly, unattended backups once again.

Autoloading mechanisms can hold anywhere from six to several hundred tapes. This permits large sites to back up anywhere from several gigabytes of data to several terabytes. However, the most important feature of autoloaders is the fact that they restore the ability to do unattended backups.

A word of caution is again in order when considering autoloader mechanisms as part of your backup solution. That word of caution is support. Does the backup software you are considering support the autoloader mechanism? This is not as mundane a concern as you might think. If you want to implement your own backup software, you will need to determine if the device you are considering includes a mechanism for accessing the autoloader. A perfect example of this is the 14 cartridge DLT libraries available. Most of these libraries include two tape drives and connect to a SCSI controller, meaning that the Linux support is there. The problem arises in that finding the software required to activate the autoloader can be a problem.

Autoloader Controls

If you do decide to go with an autoloader, there are a couple of options for controlling it, should the need arise. One of these is to obtain the freeware mtx command from the Web site of Leonard Zubkoff at `http://www.dandelion.org/`. This program uses the SCSI generic driver to send commands to the autoloader. Unfortunately, if your library includes more than a single tape drive, the mtx command will do you no good. Another option in this case is to use the freeware SCSI changer device driver written by Gerd Knorr, available on his Web site at `http://www.in-berlin.de/User/kraxel/linux.html`. This option is a kernel patch that implements the SCSI-3 Medium Changer command set. It comes with the source code for the module as well as the code to a generic utility for loading, unloading, and otherwise manipulating the changer. With this device driver, your options increase to include a whole range of devices that all come with an autoloader robot.

Media Selection Criteria

Another aspect of developing a backup solution is the selection of the tape media to be used. There are a number of different types of tapes available. The most common formats of tapes today include 4mm DAT (also known as DDS), 8mm, and DLT. Other tape formats include the QIC formats, such as QIC 150, used on many older SCSI systems, and the QIC formats used by tape drives that connect to your Linux system via the floppy controller.

Some of these, such as the QIC 150, are slowly disappearing; however, QIC tape drives and tapes are still around. It should be noted that ever since Conner bought out Archive, production of the QIC 150 tape drives has stopped and so the market will eventually disappear altogether.

Deciding what media to use for backups depends mostly on how much data needs to be backed up and the cost of the media. For sites that have data in the terabyte range, DLT tapes provide the most versatile solution. For small sites, 8mm and 4mm provide adequate flexibility to any backup plan as well as offer low cost. The cost for 8mm tapes is around $4 per tape, whereas 4mm tapes usually cost between $3 and $14 per tape depending on the type of tape purchased (that is, DDS-2 or DDS-3). DLT tapes can cost $70-$80 each. The following sections discuss the various tape formats in a little more detail.

4mm DDS

The 4mm Digital Data Storage (DDS) tape drive originally came out of the digital audio tape format introduced in the early '90s to the stereo market. With the failure of this tape format to supplant the traditional cassette tape in the consumer market, tape manufacturers realized that this technology, due to its high fidelity, was ideally suited for the computer industry as a backup medium.

A typical 4mm DDS tape can hold anywhere from 2GB (DDS-1, 90m length) to 24GB (DDS-3, 125m length, with compression). Obviously, DDS-3 tapes and drives are more expensive than DDS-1 tapes and drives. However, like the QIC tape drive, DDS-1 drives are becoming harder and harder to find. Fortunately, the majority of DDS-3 tape drives available on the market today are backward compatible, so you can continue to use the DDS-1 media if it is most suitable to your backup needs. The cost per gigabyte of storage is dependent on the tape length, but at current market prices ranges from $1.06-$2.16, making the DDS format quite popular.

The 4mm tape drive has supplanted the QIC tape drive at the low end of the market and has made significant inroads against the 8mm format. Like its bigger brother, the 4mm drive is small and quiet. Also like the 8mm drives, these devices have comparatively short head life due to the fact that both formats use helical scan. Helical scan refers to the rotating head method of reading and writing tapes found in these tape drives and also is used in video cassette recorders. One problem with this media is that it is less reliable than the 8mm format.

8mm Exabyte

As already noted, 8mm tape drives use the exact same mechanism as a VCR. These drives were developed by Exabyte Corporation in 1987 and are one of the most common SCSI tape devices. The 8mm tape drives are reliable, quiet, and very convenient. The tapes themselves are inexpensive and easily stored. The main downside to the 8mm tape drive is the relatively short head and tape life. This is due to the high rate of relative motion across the tape heads. Because data is recorded on the tape using the helical scan method of VCRs, the heads are positioned approximately 6 degrees relative to the media. The tape is wrapped 3/4 of the way around the spool that holds the heads and this spool spins while the tape slides up and down over the spool. This motion results in a high density of data on the tape and closely packed tracks that angle across the length of the tape from one edge to the other.

Manufacturers of 8mm media produce a variety of 8mm tape grades. These grades can vary in composition, abrasiveness, thickness, and length. Videotapes are manufactured for a lower density of information than data grade tapes. This is because video recorders do not require the same accuracy as data recording. Also, videotapes are not designed for long term storage, which is exactly what a backup system is implemented for. Because of these issues, DO NOT use video grade tapes in an 8mm tape drive. It will shorten the life of the spool and tape heads and the reliability of the backup will be in serious question.

Data throughput for 8mm drives can range anywhere from 250-500 kb/s for older 8mm tape drive models (such as the Exabyte 8200) to 1-2 mb/s on newer drives (such as the Exabyte Eliant 820).

The 8mm tapes can store anywhere from 2.5-25GB of data. When considering that the 8mm tapes cost from $6-$90, the cost per gigabyte for the 8mm format is approximately $2.40-$3.72.

DLT

Digital Linear Tape (DLT) differs from 4mm and 8mm tape systems in that there is only one spool, the supply spool, located inside the data cartridge. The cartridge has a swinging gate, which is opened by the drive mechanism to extract the tape leader. The tape leader has an oval hole in it that the drive uses to "hook" the tape.

In DLT, the data is written in parallel to the tape motion with two tracks being written at once. This method results in a low level of relative motion between the tape and the heads, thereby resulting in longer head lifetime. It is not uncommon for DLT tape to stand up to over 100,000 read/write passes, making DLT not only one of the largest capacity tape media available, but also one of the most reliable.

Data throughput for DLT averages approximately 1.5MB/s-5MB/s sustained native (that is, uncompressed) transfer rates. The tape capacity can vary from 10-70GB per tape. The only disadvantage to DLT is the cost of the media. Tapes can cost $80 or more each. This might sound very expensive, however when you consider that a single cartridge can hold 35GB of uncompressed data (and 70GB of compressed data), the cost per gigabyte for a DLT tape is quite economical at around $1-$2/GB.

8mm/AIT

A newcomer in the tape market is the 8mm/AIT (Advanced Intelligent Tape). These tapes can store anywhere from 50GB (native) written at 6MB/s to 100GB (compressed) written at 12MB/s. These tape drives are the next generation of 8mm format tape drives that use the helical scan method of writing to the tape. These newer tapes are more expensive than their older 8mm brethren and the drives are significantly more expensive as well. If you need huge storage capacity, however, these are the only tape systems that are able to compare well with DLT.

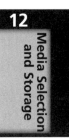

The cost of 8mm/AIT tapes is a little higher than regular 8mm tapes and comes out to be around $2.10/GB. These tapes have a shelf life of around 30,000 uses.

Tape Driver Interfaces

When most people think of tape drives, they think of either the floppy tape devices that were made popular by the PC explosion of the late 1980s, or of SCSI devices such as those available with most UNIX systems. This section takes a look at some of the ways that tape devices may be attached to your Linux host.

Floppy Tape Devices

Floppy tape drives are simply that—tape drives connected to the floppy drive controller located on the motherboard of the computer. Ftape itself is not a program, but a driver. Ftape supports a limited number of drives. The drives should conform to the QIC-117 and one of the QIC-40, QIC-80, QIC-3010, or QIC-3020 standards. Additionally, the ftape driver program also supports the Ditto 2GB, Ditto Max, and Colorado Tracker parallel port tape drives and parallel port tape drives based on the Micro Solutions Inc, Backpack interface. Ftape does not support ATAPI or SCSI drives. These are accessed respectively through the kernel IDE and SCSI drivers.

Some freeware/shareware backup software that support the ftape driver include amanda, tob, afbackup, taper, and KBackup 1.2.10. BRU and PerfectBACKUP+ are a couple of commercial backup programs that support the ftape driver.

In order to use any of these types of devices, you must ensure that your kernel supports them. This is accomplished by selecting from the various ftape driver options available in the kernel configuration scripts. For more information on the support in the Linux kernel for these types of devices, refer to the ftape.txt file in /usr/src/linux/Documentation and to the Ftape-HOWTO that comes with the Linux installation media.

ATAPI Tape Drives

ATAPI is an acronym that stands for AT Attachment Packet Interface. The original ATA interface was used in the old 286/386 computers. IDE is synonymous with ATA and stands for Integrated Drive Electronics.

ATAPI is a new protocol built on the ATA-2 (EIDE, Enhanced IDE) specifications and is similar to SCSI protocols. With ATA/IDE, each tape drive has a built-in controller. These types of drives are meant to attach almost directly to the ISA bus of a motherboard. Unlike SCSI, there is no single controller card to manage the throughput between the device and the CPU.

The main advantage of ATAPI tape drives is the cost. Typically, these are the lowest cost drives on the market. However, the drawback of these tape drives is that without a controller to manage the communication between these devices and the CPU, when they need attention, the CPU must service their request. Therefore, on a machine with ATAPI devices, a tape backup may take longer because of the fact that other ATAPI devices may interrupt the CPU while it is talking to the tape device.

Just as with the floppy tape devices, Linux includes kernel support for tape drives attached to the ATAPI interface. See Chapter 35, "Customizing the Linux Kernel," for details on how to recompile your kernel to include support for these types of devices.

SCSI Tape Devices

SCSI stands for Small Computer System Interface. It is a standard interface for connecting peripherals to a computer system. The SCSI interface definition provides for standard SCSI commands to be used for communication with the attached peripherals. The most common version of SCSI in use today is probably SCSI-2. SCSI-3 is slowly gaining on SCSI-2 in popularity, but still remains a bit of a novelty at the present time.

The IDE interface can accommodate only two drives per channel and two channels per system. This results in a total of four devices. SCSI, on the other hand can accommodate more than four devices. The number of devices on a SCSI bus can range from seven (narrow-SCSI) to 15 (wide-SCSI). Also, unlike ATAPI devices, SCSI devices communicate with the SCSI controller, which then communicates with the system CPU. This enhances throughput on the system from device to CPU and back. ATAPI devices tie up the CPU while transferring data. Finally, ATAPI really supports disk and CD-ROM. There is limited support for tape.

SCSI lends itself well to tape drives because of the throughput capabilities of the controller. The SCSI controller uses DMA to transfer data thus freeing the CPU for other tasks. Also, the highest performance devices are usually available in SCSI. So, the largest, fastest tape drives are more likely found in SCSI format. This is simply due to the fact that SCSI lends itself best to performance when it comes to backing up a single server or an entire network.

Kernel support for SCSI tape drives requires that you first include SCSI support in general and secondly that you select the SCSI tape support, which can be included in your kernel or built separately as a module. In addition, you may also have to include SCSI generic support if your tape device is equipped with an autoloader that you want to use in random access mode.

Once a backup device and media have been chosen, the next topic to consider is storage of the backup media.

Storage Issues

Once a backup plan has been chosen and implemented, the next step in securing data involves storing the backup media in a safe place. This may sound like it is the easiest step, but in this section, you will see that the decision may not be as cut-and-dry as you initially imagined.

Onsite Storage

Although very tempting, onsite storage is not the best way to ensure the survival of a company's backup tapes. Should a fire or any other disaster strike the building where the company is located and the backup tapes are stored there, the possibility exists that the backup tapes will also be lost.

It is possible, given the proper precautions, to store backup media onsite. Such a storage method would require the purchase of a fireproof, waterproof storage cabinet. Although such a cabinet would not ensure survival of the media given a different sort of disaster (earthquake, tornado, and so on) it would help insure against the more common threat of fire/water/smoke damage.

The main benefit of storing backup media onsite is the convenience of being able to grab a tape at a moment's notice and restore a file from it.

Offsite Storage

Offsite storage involves procuring a secure location where the backup media can be stored. The main problem with this is the inconvenience of having to travel out to the storage site. Also, a poorly chosen storage site may be subject to crime. Offsite storage should never be an employee's house or apartment. One good method of offsite storage would be to place the tapes in a safety deposit box in a bank. This provides not only for security from theft, vandalism, or fire, but also provides a controlled environment that could help extend the shelf life of the backup media.

Multiple Copies

Although the implication of backups involves making a copy of pertinent data, many times the assumption that the backup has run does not imply that the data is completely safe. Media errors are the most common problems that can plague the integrity of a backup. It is best, if possible, to repeat a backup on an additional tape—especially if the data in question is critical. This helps ensure that the backup was completed to a good tape. This doesn't mean that just by using an additional tape the chance of a media error ruining a backup is eliminated. If necessary, more than one additional tape can be used. The key concept here is that repeating the same backup to more than one tape reduces the possibility that a media error will ruin the backup. Also, repeating a backup to multiple tapes and then storing those tapes in different locations increases the possibility that recovery is likely should a disaster occur.

Another point to stress when dealing with backups is verification of a backup. All too often system administrators simply put tapes into tape drives, go home, come back the next day, take the tapes out of the tape drives, and put them back in their holders. Not once are the backups verified. This leads to a false sense of security. Without verifying that the tapes can be read, the backups do not ensure security.

One other advantage of creating multiple copies of a backup is that it now becomes safer to keep a copy onsite. Even if the original is damaged, you can still recover using the secondary copy.

Tape Escrow Services

One of the options employed by many companies today is the use of a tape escrow service. A tape escrow service provides for storage of backup media at a secure, climate-controlled, offsite facility. The convenience of this type of service comes when a particular tape is needed. Rather than having to trudge through a large number of tapes, the escrow service is contacted, provided with the information of which tape is needed and within a short period of time a courier brings the requested tape by.

The tape escrow service takes care of storage problems (environmental control, security, and so on). It also provides for pickup and delivery of tapes. In essence, the tape escrow service takes care of the management of backup tapes. For the end user, a tape escrow service is like a black hole—tapes go in and, (unlike a black hole) when requested, tapes come out.

The decision to use a tape escrow service is usually a safe one. However, be aware that these services may cost a significant amount of money and unless you are creating large volumes of tapes, it may be less expensive to simply store the tapes offsite yourself at the bank, as discussed earlier.

Summary

With all the choices available these days for the media to use in backups, the decision has become harder and harder. Fortunately, these media formats do not appear to be going the way of the dinosaurs anytime soon and so choosing one will ensure that backups made today will be usable in the future should the need arise.

This chapter took a look at some of the issues involved in selecting the appropriate media type and devices for use in your backup solution. It looked at drive types, different types of tape media, and also at some of the storage issues involved. Hopefully, with this information, you can now make an informed decision that will ensure that your company's valuable data is well protected now and into the future.

12
Media Selection and Storage

Recovery from Data Loss

In This Chapter

- Some Data Loss Scenarios **346**
- The Cost of Data Recovery **362**
- Disaster Recovery Planning **364**

Since the purpose of computers is to process data, loss of that data can be disastrous to a company. In almost every case, lost data translates at some level to lost revenue. This revenue loss can be direct, such as lost sales because an inventory database is lost, or indirect, such as time spent by users and system administrators recovering data instead of performing their normal job functions. Therefore, being aware of possible data loss scenarios and taking preventative measures to minimize the risk of data loss is almost always worth the time spent on these measures.

From the system administrator's point of view, there are few things that will ruin your day faster than having to recover lost data. This is largely due to the stress that your users will put on you to get the data back quickly. Few users realize the amount of work required to do this and the costs associated with data recovery. On top of this, the higher up the company ladder the person who lost the data is, the more pressure you will be under to drop everything and focus exclusively on the recovery.

This chapter looks at a number of topics related to lost data and how to recover it, including

- Common data loss scenarios

- Costs associated with data recovery

- Planning for disaster recovery

In addition, this chapter also covers some techniques that can be used to minimize the risk of data loss and make recovering lost data less of a chore.

Some Data Loss Scenarios

There are any number of ways in which data can be lost, but the bottom line is that you as system administrator must be prepared to deal with each of them. This section looks at some of the most common data loss scenarios, namely:

- User error

- Viruses and other destructive software

- System crackers and malcontents

- Hardware failure

There are other ways in which data can be lost, but these are a few of the most common. By being prepared for these scenarios, you can make the process of data recovery much less stressful. We'll begin by looking at data loss caused by user error.

User Errors

By far the most aggravating cause of data loss is errors made by your users. The only thing more aggravating than having to deal with this scenario is having to hear all of the excuses that they give you for their mistakes. I call this type of error the "my dog ate my home directory scenario." Listening to users explain how they lost their files makes me understand how school teachers must feel when they ask their students what happened to their homework. It is inevitable, however, and losing your temper will only make matters worse. So let's take a look at some of the most common errors made by users and steps you can take to minimize the chances of them occurring.

Mistyped Commands

I have lost count of the times that I have had to recover files lost to users who mistype a rm, cp, or mv command. Here is one of the most common mistakes:

```
$ rm foo *
```

The user, in attempting to remove all files beginning with *foo*, inadvertently puts a space between the match string and the wildcard character (the asterisk), which matches zero or more characters in a filename. This has the unwanted result of removing a file called *foo* if it exists along with all other files in the current directory. Consider the following sequence of commands. The user is attempting to clean up a directory containing some code he is working on and realizes his mistake when the rm command produces output as shown in Listing 13.1.

13

Recovery from
Data Loss

LISTING 13.1 Sample Showing the Results of a Misplaced Wildcard Character

```
[tschenk@marcanthony work]$ ls -l
total 96
-rw-r--r--   1 tschenk  staff       14849 Mar  9 00:18 Makefile
-rw-r--r--   1 tschenk  staff       35522 Mar  9 00:18 README
drwxr-xr-x   2 tschenk  staff        4096 Mar  9 00:18 docs
-rw-r--r--   1 tschenk  staff        1176 Mar  9 00:21 foobar
-rw-r--r--   1 tschenk  staff         870 Mar  9 00:21 foobar~
-rw-r--r--   1 tschenk  staff          82 Mar  9 00:19 foobaz
drwxr-xr-x   4 tschenk  staff        4096 Mar  9 00:22 lib
-rw-r--r--   1 tschenk  staff         866 Mar  9 00:19 line.c
-rw-r--r--   1 tschenk  staff        5956 Mar  9 00:20 main.c
-rw-r--r--   1 tschenk  staff        2230 Mar  9 00:20 page.c
-rw-r--r--   1 tschenk  staff        6371 Mar  9 00:20 parse.c
[tschenk@marcanthony work]$ rm foo *
rm: cannot remove `foo': No such file or directory
rm: docs: is a directory
```

LISTING **13.1**   continued

```
rm: lib: is a directory
[tschenk@marcanthony work]$ ls -l
total 8
drwxr-xr-x   2 tschenk   staff      4096 Mar  9 00:18 docs
drwxr-xr-x   4 tschenk   staff      4096 Mar  9 00:22 lib
```

The user now begins to panic and comes running to you for salvation. If the user is lucky, the files will not have been modified since the last backup. In this case, you retrieve the appropriate backup media and extract the files from it. If the user is unlucky, all of the files will have been created since the last backup or reside on a filesystem that is not backed up and they will have to be re-created by hand. A more common situation is that the files were modified since the most recent backup. In this case, you would restore the most recent copy of the file from the backup media and the user would be required to do the work to bring it up to date. Regardless of the situation, this means work for the system administrator or for the unlucky user.

Output Redirection and Piping Errors

Another way that users get into trouble is with output redirection and pipes. The output redirection character ">" is a means by which data that would have been printed on the terminal is redirected to a file or possibly a device. This is a very useful technique when employed correctly; however, it can also lead to disaster if used incorrectly. Piping, or stringing a series of commands together with the "|" operator, is another useful technique that can be misused. Listing 13.2 is a perfect example of how output redirection combined with a pipe can cause unexpected results.

LISTING **13.2**   Example of a Piping and Redirection Error

```
[tschenk@marcanthony foo]$ ls -l
total 4
-rw-r--r--   1 tschenk   staff       912 Mar 13 23:09 fstab
[tschenk@marcanthony foo]$ cat fstab
/dev/hda1          /              ext2    defaults      1 1
/dev/hda5          /home          ext2    defaults      1 2
/dev/cdrom         /mnt/cdrom     iso9660 noauto,owner,ro 0 0
/dev/hda11         /opt           ext2    defaults      1 2
/dev/hda9          /tmp           ext2    defaults      1 2
/dev/hda6          /usr           ext2    defaults      1 2
/dev/hda7          /usr/local     ext2    defaults      1 2
/dev/hda10         /var           ext2    defaults      1 2
/dev/hda8          swap           swap    defaults      0 0
```

LISTING **13.2** continued

```
/dev/fd0              /mnt/floppy            ext2    noauto,owner   0 0
none                  /proc                  proc    defaults       0 0
none                  /dev/pts               devpts  gid=5,mode=620 0 0
[tschenk@marcanthony foo]$ cat fstab ¦ sed s'/ext2/ext3/' > fstab
[tschenk@marcanthony foo]$ ls -l
total 0
-rw-r--r--   1 tschenk  staff          0 Mar 13 23:09 fstab
```

The user is attempting to replace all occurrences of ext2 in the fstab file with ext3 without creating a temporary file. However, as you can see, instead of the expected outcome of simply replacing occurrences of the string ext2 with ext3, it ended up destroying the contents of the file. This will not occur every time, but is dependent on how the scheduler handles the running of the two commands in the pipeline. Unlike Windows, in which commands in a pipeline are executed sequentially, commands in a pipeline under Linux are executed in parallel. In the preceding case, the sed command received the first time slice, causing the output file of the sed command, fstab, to be created before the original file was read by the cat command.

Users with Root Access

While these types of errors and the resulting data loss are bad, consider how much worse they could be if the user had root privileges like you do as the system administrator. In this case, the malformed rm command or bad pipe could have disastrous results. Consider, for example, the mistyped rm command in the previous discussion. If you were logged in as root at the time and the command was executed in /lib, this error could result in the system becoming unusable. This is also true with the malformed pipe. If the sed command were run against the /etc/passwd file and it was lost, you would have prevented all users from accessing the system. And if you do not have a backup, the situation could become even worse. It is therefore important to always double-check your commands before you hit the Enter key. In addition, you can put into place a few simple preventative measures to help avoid these errors.

Simple Prevention Measures to Avoid User Errors

Some of these user errors can be avoided. There are a few simple techniques that could have reduced the likelihood of this type of data loss. Some of these techniques include

- Using aliases to require verification of destructive commands.

- Using RCS to track changes to important files.

- Creating personal backup sets in a nightly cron job.

- Using sudo to limit user root access.

Let's take a look at how applying these simple prevention measures can help users to recover easily or avoid mistakes like those just discussed.

Using Aliases to Prevent Data Loss

One of the simplest techniques you can employ is to create aliases for some of the commands that cause users to lose data. Here is an example that is employed by default for the root user on Red Hat systems:

```
# .bashrc

# User specific aliases and functions

alias rm='rm -i'
alias cp='cp -i'
alias mv='mv -i'

# Source global definitions
if [ -f /etc/bashrc ]; then
        . /etc/bashrc
fi
```

Note the three aliases in the .bashrc file for rm, cp, and mv. The -i option to each of these commands requires confirmation by the user before performing a destructive action. In this case, a destructive action would be removing a file with rm or overwriting it with mv or cp. Listing 13.3 shows how the command-line session in Listing 13.1 would have looked if these aliases had been in effect.

LISTING 13.3   Sample Output Showing How rm Alias Can Prevent Data Loss

```
[tschenk@marcanthony work]$ ls -l
total 96
-rw-r--r--  1 tschenk  staff       14849 Mar  9 00:37 Makefile
-rw-r--r--  1 tschenk  staff       35522 Mar  9 00:37 README
drwxr-xr-x  2 tschenk  staff        4096 Mar  9 00:18 docs
-rw-r--r--  1 tschenk  staff        1176 Mar  9 00:37 foobar
-rw-r--r--  1 tschenk  staff         870 Mar  9 00:37 foobar~
-rw-r--r--  1 tschenk  staff          82 Mar  9 00:37 foobaz
drwxr-xr-x  4 tschenk  staff        4096 Mar  9 00:22 lib
-rw-r--r--  1 tschenk  staff         866 Mar  9 00:37 line.c
-rw-r--r--  1 tschenk  staff        5956 Mar  9 00:37 main.c
```

LISTING **13.3**   continued

```
-rw-r--r--  1 tschenk  staff       2230 Mar  9 00:37 page.c
-rw-r--r--  1 tschenk  staff       6371 Mar  9 00:37 parse.c
[tschenk@marcanthony work]$ rm foo *
rm: cannot remove `foo': No such file or directory
rm: remove ·Makefile'?
```

With the rm alias in effect, the user is prompted before the files are actually removed, allowing him to realize his mistake without having to suffer the loss of data. You are not interrupted and life is good. Unfortunately, many users find the prompts to remove files annoying and turn off these aliases. I always try to encourage users to keep these aliases, since I have myself been saved many times by this simple technique.

Using RCS to Track Files

Another technique that can be employed by users to protect important files is to use a revision control system such as RCS or CVS. Revision control systems allow users to track changes to files, usually by storing the original file and then tracking the changes using deltas. In Listing 13.4, you can see how using RCS could have allowed the user to recover from the loss of the fstab file that occurred in the piping and redirection example.

LISTING **13.4**   Simple Example Showing How RCS Can be Used to Prevent Data Loss

```
[tschenk@marcanthony foo]$ ls -l
total 4
-rw-r--r--  1 tschenk  staff        912 Mar 14 01:13 fstab
[tschenk@marcanthony foo]$ mkdir RCS
[tschenk@marcanthony foo]$ ci -u fstab
RCS/fstab,v  <-- fstab
enter description, terminated with single '.' or end of file:
NOTE: This is NOT the log message!
>> Filesystem table
>> .
initial revision: 1.1
done
[tschenk@marcanthony foo]$ ls -l
total 8
drwxr-xr-x  2 tschenk  staff       4096 Mar 14 01:14 RCS
-r--r--r--  1 tschenk  staff        912 Mar 14 01:15 fstab
[tschenk@marcanthony foo]$ co -u fstab
RCS/fstab,v  --> fstab
revision 1.1 (unlocked)
done
```

13

Recovery from
Data Loss

LISTING **13.4**   continued

```
[tschenk@marcanthony foo]$ ls -l
total 8
drwxr-xr-x   2 tschenk  staff        4096 Mar 14 01:14 RCS
-rw-r--r--   1 tschenk  staff         912 Mar 14 01:15 fstab
[tschenk@marcanthony foo]$ cat fstab | sed s'/ext2/ext3/' > fstab
[tschenk@marcanthony foo]$ ls -l
total 4
drwxr-xr-x   2 tschenk  staff        4096 Mar 14 01:14 RCS
-rw-r--r--   1 tschenk  staff           0 Mar 14 01:15 fstab
[tschenk@marcanthony foo]$ co -l fstab
RCS/fstab,v  -->  fstab
revision 1.1 (locked)
writable fstab exists; remove it? [ny](n): y
done
[tschenk@marcanthony foo]$ ls -l
total 8
drwxr-xr-x   2 tschenk  staff        4096 Mar 14 01:18 RCS
-rw-r--r--   1 tschenk  staff         912 Mar 14 01:18 fstab
```

In this example, the user creates a directory called RCS in the current directory, and using the ci command checks in the current version of the file. To then work on the file, the user uses the co command with the -l option to check out and lock the file. The user now runs the sed command as in Listing 13.2 with the same results. However, this time the user is able to recover the contents of the file by simply checking out the current revision from RCS again using the co -l command, and answering yes at the prompt. This restores the file to the original state and we can attempt the replacement again, using a temporary file this time to avoid the error. This may seem like a lot of work, but it has other advantages besides being able to recover lost files. By using RCS or CVS to keep important files and entering meaningful log messages when checking in files, the changes to a file can be easily determined by using another RCS command—rlog. Using RCS also makes it easy to determine if someone has changed a file improperly by providing the rcsdiff command to compare a file with the latest checked-in revision. This assumes that you always properly check out files to work on them and then check in the changes when you are done.

Creating Personal Backups

Another simple technique that users can employ to help prevent loss of their data due to mistakes like the ones we have been talking about is the creation of personal backups. These backups can be implemented using a simple shell script that creates a tar archive of the important files to be protected that is run from a nightly cron job. Listing 13.5 is a sample of such a script that creates a backup of any files in the user's home directory that have changed in the past 24 hours and stores them in a file in a user-defined directory.

LISTING 13.5 Simple Personal Backup Script Using `tar`

```
#!/bin/bash

# First create a basename for the tar file consisting of the username
# and the current date.
TODAY=` date +%Y%m%d `
ARCHNAME="${USER}_${TODAY}"

# Specify a list of directories under my home directory to backup.
BACKUPDIRS="Mail projects docs"
STORAGE=${HOME}/.archives

# Loop through our list of backup directories and for each one, create
# an incremental backup of all files modified within the last two days
# so that each file resides in at least two different backup files.
for DIR in ${BACKUPDIRS}; do
    ARCHNAME="${ARCHNAME}_${DIR}"

    /usr/bin/find $HOME/$DIR -mtime -2 -print \
        | /bin/tar cvzf ${STORAGE}/${ARCHNAME}.tar.gz -T -

done

exit 0
```

The user could use this script by simply modifying the definition of the `BACKUPDIRS` variable and the `STORAGE` variable to fit his needs and then creating a crontab entry to run it once a night. Using this method would allow the user to first attempt to recover files from his personal backups before coming to the system administrator for recovery from the system backups. This may or may not be a good option for your systems depending on workstation disk space or disk space on shared filesystems where the user might attempt to store the backup files.

Using `sudo` to Limit Root Access

These measures can be applied to normal users as well as to users with root access. However, one additional measure can also be taken: limit access to root privileges using sudo. For those cases where a user has a legitimate reason for accessing the system with root privileges, grant this access using sudo and limit the access to just those commands required for the user to do his or her job. It is rarely a good idea to give normal users root privileges on a system. However, by using sudo, you not only limit the access, but also gain the benefit of a log of the commands that the user is performing. You also get warnings when a user attempts to perform actions as root, which you have not granted him. More information regarding the use of sudo can be found in Chapter 27, "The Security Administrator's Toolbox."

Now that we have covered some of the common user errors that can result in data loss, we can move on to the next data loss scenario that we as system administrators must deal with: viruses, trojan horses, and other destructive software.

Viruses and Other Destructive Software

Although user error caused by mistyped commands and other causes can be a trial of your patience, software that destroys data either intentionally or because of logic errors can be even more troublesome. This section discusses some measures to prevent destructive software from destroying your data.

Viruses

Unlike Windows, in which users have complete control over the entire system, Linux systems have security features built in. This makes it much more difficult for malicious programs to propagate and this is one of the main reasons why there are so few viruses on Linux systems. A *virus* is a program that attaches itself to another executable and when executed, attempts to propagate itself to other executables. In addition to this behavior, the virus usually also performs some other action, ranging from benign, such as displaying a message, to destructive, such as scrambling the contents of your partition table.

Trojan Horses

Another type of malicious program is known as a trojan horse. A *trojan horse* is a program that masquerades as another program. The trojan horse may be designed to work like the program that it replaces and to do things such as capture passwords and mail them to the person who created the trojan horse. It could also do more destructive things like removing critical files or directories. The destructiveness of trojan horses depends on who executes the program.

Worms

A *worm* is a program that takes advantage of weaknesses in a system to propagate itself to other systems. Worms are typically designed to seek out weaknesses in networks and are usually not destructive. The problem with worms is that they may result in denials of service due to their attempts to move to other systems.

Other Destructive Software

In addition to software that is intentionally destructive, there are other programs that, due to defects in their design, can be just as or more destructive. The software development house has to be especially careful of this problem and be prepared for the fallout. For example, say that a software developer in your organization designs a program that, based on some aging algorithm, removes old files from a database directory. This program consults a configuration file that contains the file locations and how long the files should be kept. An error in the algorithm used to determine whether a file should be removed could result in lost data. In this case, the software is not intentionally destructive, but a programming error can still cause data loss. It is a wise precaution, therefore, to thoroughly test software of this nature before using it on critical systems.

Preventative Measures Against Destructive Software

Just as with the previous class of errors, there are steps that you as an administrator can take to minimize the risk of data loss due to viruses and other destructive software. Some of these measures include

- Virus scanning software

- Victim hosts for software testing and development

- Software to verify the integrity of installed software

- Environment settings to minimize risk

The following sections take a look at each of these measures briefly and discuss their merits in preventing data loss.

Virus Scanning Software

Although viruses are uncommon on Linux systems, there are still risks. In answer to these risks, virus scanning software has been developed and is available for your Linux system. Virus scanners examine executables on your system looking for known virus signatures and warn you if they are found. More advanced virus scanning software can also recognize patterns that are similar to known viruses and flag these files for examination as well. Even if you are not worried about virus infection on your Linux system, it may be a good idea to look into virus scanning software for your email systems, especially if you have Windows or Macintosh clients who receive their mail through your Linux host. Another instance where virus scanners should be employed is on filesystems exported to Windows or Macintosh clients. If you are running Samba or another system by which you share files with these types of clients, especially in an application server role, the use of a virus scanner can help to prevent the spread of infected programs.

Victim Hosts

Another measure you can take to protect your systems is to set up a number of victim hosts on which to test new software. A victim host is one that you expect to be damaged in the testing and development of software systems. These hosts should be isolated as much as possible from development servers and production hosts and are typically not backed up. They should also be relatively easy to rebuild from scratch if the files on the system become corrupted either intentionally or by malicious software. These hosts are particularly effective in preventing data loss due to unintentional errors in software. They are also a good place to test out new software from sources external to your organization prior to installing it on critical hosts.

Software Integrity Checkers

In addition to virus scanning software, another method of prevention that is good at detecting the presence of viruses and trojan horses is a class of software called integrity checkers. One of the most popular of these is Tripwire, which is available for evaluation at `http://www.tripwire.com/`. The integrity checker is a piece of software that records information about the files installed on a system in a database. It periodically checks to ensure that the files have not changed in any way and sets off an alarm if they have. This is especially effective in finding trojan horses and viruses, due to the fact that these types of software cause changes in system binaries. Integrity checkers can be purchased, as in the case of Tripwire, or can be written in house. On your Red Hat system, you can use the capabilities of the `rpm` utility to implement a simple integrity checker by running `rpm` with the `--verify` option and looking for anomalies in the output. An added benefit to integrity checkers is that they can tip you off to intruders on your systems.

Environment Settings

Unlike DOS and Windows systems, where the current directory is included in your path by default, on Linux systems you must explicitly include it if you so desire. This being said, however, it is more important to make sure that it is not. Trojan horses and viruses rely on the fact that many system administrators are lazy and would rather add the current directory to their path than type the path to a program to execute it. It is this laziness that can result in the execution of a program that destroys your system, so you have to choose. Would you rather spend a few extra seconds typing the path to a program you want to execute or spend hours recovering from the havoc created by a virus or trojan?

Now that we have covered destructive software, we are ready to move on to the next data loss scenario, destructive people.

System Crackers and Malcontents

Another possible cause of data loss is the actions of malicious people, either system crackers who break into your systems or people within your organization who have an axe to grind. This section takes a look at these two types of people and how to keep the risk of data loss through their actions to a minimum.

System Crackers

One of the worst fears of many system administrators is the fear that their systems will be broken into by outsiders. These system crackers break into systems for any number of reasons, ranging from curiosity to a desire to damage your system. I use the term cracker instead of the more common term hacker because cracker is the more correct term. A *hacker* is a person who programs or tinkers with computers for the love of computers and for the recognition of his peers. A *cracker*, on the other hand, is a person who through various means, many of which are illegal, attempts to gain access to computer systems belonging to others. Their motives for doing this are varied. Some do it for the thrill of defeating the security measures you may have put in place and once they have gained access, lose interest and move on to new systems. Unfortunately, the system crackers may have more malicious intentions and even if they do not destroy files, you may be forced to reinstall a system after such an intrusion in order to ensure that sensitive data on your systems is protected. The worst case, of course, is the cracker who takes a perverse pleasure in not only gaining access to your systems, but also in destroying data found there.

Malcontents

Another type of person you have to be careful of is who I like to call the malcontent. Malcontents are usually the most dangerous type of destructive user because they already have access to your systems. These people are the type who, to redress a slight, either real or imagined, will destroy data intentionally. These people most often show their colors on their way out of an organization, but this is not always the case. Naturally, the greater the level of access to your systems that the malcontent has, the greater the risk. There is no greater risk to your systems than a disgruntled system administrator.

Preventative Measures Against Destructive People

Dealing with malicious users and system crackers can be a difficult proposition. This is especially true of users who have legitimate access to your systems. There are, however, measures that can be taken to help prevent data loss due to their actions.

Keeping System Crackers Out

The key to preventing data loss caused by system crackers is to prevent them from accessing your system in the first place. This means developing and implementing an effective security strategy. The measures you take usually fall into one of two broad categories:

- Firewalls to protect your network from intrusion

- Physical security to protect direct access

An in-depth coverage of these topics is beyond the scope of this chapter due to the complexity of the subject. This material is, however, covered elsewhere in this book. Information on implementing firewalls is covered in Chapter 26, "Firewall Strategies," and physical security is covered in Chapter 25, "Security Principles." In addition, there is information on what to do if a system cracker does compromise your system and how to deal with the intrusion. This is covered in Chapter 28, "I've Been Hacked: What Now?"

Dealing with Malicious Users

The greatest risk when dealing with malicious users is that they will do something to destroy data using their legitimate access. The only fortunate aspect of dealing with these users is that they usually only attempt to damage your systems when they are leaving the organization. This means that you can take some preventative measures to try to stop them from succeeding. One such measure is to establish a policy of disabling access to a system during the exit interview and to escort employees off of the premises without allowing them any further access to systems on your network. Unfortunately, if these users are sophisticated and they are aware that they will be leaving, they can use facilities such as cron or at to take action even when they are not at their terminal. Two things you can to do help prevent this are to monitor cron and at jobs as they are entered and to only allow increased levels of access via sudo or some other method that logs the actions taken.

Having covered user errors, destructive software, and destructive users, we are now ready to cover one final data loss scenario: hardware failure.

Hardware Failure

If you operate a computer long enough, you are sure to have a hardware failure. The most common type of hardware failure is disk drive failure. There are, however, other types of hardware failure that can cause data loss. This section looks at some of the hardware failure modes and how to deal with them.

Hard Drive Failure

By far the most common type of hardware failure is failure of a hard drive. Fortunately, most failures of this type are usually preceded by kernel messages indicating problems accessing the data stored on the drives. For example, SCSI drives will often report read or write errors prior to a complete failure. It is therefore important to monitor system logs and be on the alert for such errors. This behavior is also true of IDE drives; however, the IDE driver is usually less verbose than the SCSI drivers.

Memory Errors

Another, less common failure is the failure of system memory. These failures can result in data loss when they cause system crashes or when data held in corrupted memory is flushed to disk. Unfortunately, there is almost never any warning prior to memory failure and the data corruption can be hard to spot unless you are looking for it. There is little you can do to prevent this type of error except to be prepared with good backups.

Prevention and Recovery Methods

Recovery from hardware failures can be a costly proposition. It is therefore important to try to catch impending hardware failure if at all possible. If caught early, the effects of hardware failure can be minimized. This section discusses some measures you can take to be alert to impending hardware failure and what you can do to recover data lost due to failures of this type.

Data Redundancy Measures

One of the common steps to avoid data loss due to hardware failure is the use of Redundant Arrays of Inexpensive Disks (RAID) technology. RAID by definition stores information that makes the data stored on the arrays recoverable, even in the face of hard drive failure. For example, in a RAID 5 array, for each block of data a checksum is stored that allows data to be recovered even if a disk is lost. A full description of the RAID options available on Linux systems can be found in Chapter 9, "Linux and RAID." This chapter covers not only how to implement RAID under Linux, but also defines the different RAID levels and how they protect your data from loss.

13

Recovery from
Data Loss

System Log Watchers

Since hard drive failure is the most common type of hardware failure, there are measures that you can take to be alerted to the signs of impending problems. One such method is to use a system log watcher. Log watchers watch system logs for patterns specified by the system administrator. Once a match occurs, a warning is sent and usually notification of the system administrator occurs, either by pager or email. One such system log watcher that you can implement is called Swatch. You can find this software through a search at `http://www.freshmeat.net/`. Swatch uses a configuration file to specify regular expressions to watch for and the action to take when a match occurs. Although Swatch was originally developed as a security tool, it is generic enough to watch for hardware errors reported in system logs as well. These actions include the ability to send email, which implies the ability to send a page through an email-to-pager gateway.

Recovery from Tape Backups

If a hard drive or memory failure occurs and you are forced to recover the data on the system, the best situation is to have a recent viable backup from which you can restore. Once the failed hardware has been replaced, you are now faced with the job of restoring from these backups. The exact procedure is of course dependent on the backup method that you employ, but typically involves the following steps:

- Restoration of the most recent full backup

- Application of incremental backups that were taken since the most recent full backup

If you are interested in learning more about backup strategies, refer to Chapter 11, "What to Back Up and How."

Data Recovery Using dd

If you are caught without good backups, all may not be lost. If you have lots of disk space available and time to devote to the recovery, you may be able to recover some data from a failed hard drive if it is still accessible by Linux. If this is the case, you can use the `dd` command to read raw blocks from the damaged drive and store the output in a file on another disk. For example, if you install the damaged disk drive as `/dev/hdb` in a system, you can use the following command to copy the contents of first partition of that drive to a file for analysis:

```
$ dd if=/dev/hdb1 of=hdimage bs=1024
```

Using this method, you may run into the maximum file size limit if the hard drive partition is very large. This command will read chunks of data from the disk in 1024-byte chunks and write it to a file called `hdimage`. Once you have read as much data as possible from the damaged disk, you have two options. The first option is to attempt to mount the file using the loop device. This will only work if you were able to get the entire partition into a single file using the dd command. The command to do this looks something like this:

```
$ mount -o loop=/dev/loop0,ro hdimage /mnt/recover
```

This command specifies that you want to mount the file hdimage read-only at the mount point /mnt/recover. If this is successful, you can then copy data from the hdimage to a good disk and may even be able to use tools like fsck to repair filesystem damage that may have occurred. If this is not successful, you have a second option: Use an editor to examine the hdimage and look for recognizable patterns to recover. The biggest drawback to this method is that it can be very time-consuming and relies on the disk drive being recognized by Linux.

Hard Drive Clean Room Recovery

In the event that you do not have a viable backup of the data on a hard drive and the drive is not accessible by the operating system, all is not necessarily lost. One option that you can use is to utilize a data recovery company. These companies specialize in recovering data from disks that are no longer readable via normal means. The typical method involves removing the platters from a hard drive in a clean room environment and reading all of the data from the disk that is recoverable and shipping it back to you. As you might expect, this is not cheap. The cost is dependent on the amount of data recovered and the level of effort required to recover it, and can range from $100 for recovery of the data on a floppy drive to $15,000 or more for the recovery of a large hard disk drive.

Other Disaster Scenarios

The data loss scenarios covered thus far are not the only ones that can cause you to lose data. However, they are some of the common ones. Others include loss through fire, flood, or other natural disasters. You can also lose data through theft or vandalism. The only recourse in these events is to replace the damaged or stolen systems and hope that your backup strategy has been successful in protecting your data.

Now that we have looked at some of the ways in which you can lose your data, let's take a look at the cost of recovery.

The Cost of Data Recovery

Whether the data loss is the result of user error, hardware failure, or natural disaster, there will be costs associated with the recovery. These costs can be divided into two basic categories: direct costs and indirect costs. This section examines some of these costs. It is important to ensure that the management of your organization is aware of these costs. If they understand the costs of recovery, it will make it easier for you as system administrator to justify preventative measures like those we have already discussed.

Direct Costs

The first category of costs associated with recovering lost data is direct costs. These are the costs that you can easily quantify by pointing to invoices and purchase orders. These include the cost of replacing failed hardware and the costs associated with your backup solution.

Hardware Replacement

The cost most commonly associated with recovery is the cost of replacing damaged or lost hardware. If a disk drive fails, there is a fixed cost to replace it. This is also true in the case of replacing lost or damaged systems. It is important to keep records of these types of costs and to periodically analyze the collected data so that realistic plans for data recovery can be made.

Backup Costs

Another direct cost is the cost of implementing your backup solution. This includes the cost of backup hardware, software, and storage media, as well as the cost of offsite storage of backups. These costs can often be quite expensive, but when compared to the other costs associated with lost data, they are well justified.

Indirect Costs

Other costs associated with data recovery are less quantifiable; however, they are equally as important to consider. Some of these indirect costs include

- Time spent by a system administrator doing the recovery.

- Delays to projects being worked on by the system administrator.

- System downtime, which can equate to lost revenue or lost revenue opportunities.

Although these can be hard to quantify, they are still important to consider when calculating the cost of data recovery.

Sysadmin Time

From the system administrator point of view, this is the heaviest cost associated with data recovery. If you are forced to go to your backup tapes, you must determine which backup tape to use, possibly retrieve it from an offsite storage location, and then wait for a typically slow tape device to restore the data to the system. This operation may take hours or even days, depending on the amount of data that needs to be recovered. Because time spent recovering data is time that could have been spent completing projects, it is important to weigh this when determining whether the cost is justified. For example, suppose a user error results in that user losing some email and the backup media containing that email has been sent to an offsite storage facility. It is up the system administrator and his management to determine if the time spent retrieving the backup media and restoring the files is justified. It is often easier to have the user request that the originators of the email resend it instead.

Project Delays

Another indirect cost directly related to the cost of system administrator time is the cost of delaying other projects on which the system administrator is working. If the system administrator is working on a high profile project that is critical to meeting organization goals, it may not be in the best interest of the organization to interrupt that work to recover some lost data. This again depends on the importance of the data being recovered and the impact of delaying the restoration so as not to interfere with project work. You can often determine the importance of having this data restored immediately by asking the requestor a few simple questions:

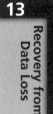

1. Is recovery of this data more important than the completion of the project I am working on?
2. Are you willing to justify this to my manager?
3. If this recovery is not more important, what would be an acceptable timeframe for the recovery?

If the user answers no to the first question, then the answer to the third question can be used to determine the priority of the recovery request. If the answer to the first question is yes, then only if the answer to the second question is also yes should the system administrator delay his project to fulfill the recovery request.

System Downtime

A final cost to consider is that of system downtime due to the loss of the data. Depending on the business of the organization and how critical the system affected is, system downtime can cost the company significantly. For example, if the affected system is the only database server backend to an e-commerce site, system downtime can mean lost revenue and is sometimes measured in thousands of dollars per hour or even per minute. In this case, it is critical to restore the data in question as fast as is humanly possible. If, on the other hand, the lost data is replicated on other systems, then redirecting queries to a backup database server may buy you time to do the restore at a more normal pace. This should normally be a call made by the management of the organization. In addition, systems like this should be covered in any disaster recovery planning that takes place and recovery procedures should be well defined.

Having taken a look at the cost of data recovery, both direct and indirect, we are ready now to move on to the topic of disaster recovery planning.

Disaster Recovery Planning

One of the keys to successful recovery from data loss scenarios like those covered in this chapter is to have a plan in place prior to the loss. Planning will ensure that the management of an organization is aware of possible data loss scenarios, the costs associated with them, and what preventative measures should be taken to minimize the risks. This section looks first at how to develop a disaster recovery plan and then at how to maintain that plan so that it doesn't become just another useless document sitting in a policy and procedures manual somewhere.

Plan Development

Developing a disaster recovery plan is a task that is often overlooked, especially in small organizations. Only when a data loss scenario occurs do people usually start to think about how to recover, and lacking a good plan, some are unable to recover. Just as with security, the importance of a plan to deal with data loss is essential because the question is not *if* you are going to lose critical data, the question is *when*. So let's take a look at the elements that should go into creating an effective disaster recovery plan. I will provide a sample that illustrates the type of information to include in each part. This sample is not intended to be a complete disaster recovery plan, but it should give you a general idea of how such a plan might be implemented.

Outline Data Loss Scenarios

One of the first things that your recovery plan should do is outline the data loss scenarios that the plan will cover. These include the ones covered at the beginning of this chapter as well as any others that you feel need to be covered. For example, if your organization is located near the San Andreas fault in California, you will probably have a section related to earthquake damage to your systems. On the other hand, if you are located on the Gulf Coast, you should probably include a section on loss due to hurricanes. As you develop this section, it is important to describe the risks associated with each scenario as much as possible in preparation for the next part of the plan: disaster recovery costs.

Sample of Data Loss Scenario

The following is a sample of the type of information you might include in this section of the plan. This sample plan is for a fictional company, TLS Enterprises, which maintains a large Web site consisting of multiple Web servers. The Web site is located at a co-location facility called Xunil, and the company has recently set up a small secondary site at another location.

Disaster Scenario: Fire at the Xunil Facility

A primary risk to the organization is a fire at the Xunil co-location facility. In this event, data may be lost due to hard drive failure and loss of systems. Additionally, the potential for lost revenue is severe, since the alternative site recently established is not currently capable of sustaining the current traffic levels.

Estimate the Cost of Recovery

Once you have determined the data loss scenarios that your plan will address, you should then try to estimate the costs associated with each. These cost estimates should address both direct and indirect costs such as

- Hardware replacement costs, if any

- Recovery time

- Potential revenue loss associated with the data loss

If there are multiple recovery methods available to deal with a particular data loss scenario, then each should be presented with their associated costs so that the organization management can determine the proper course of action to take in the event of disaster.

Sample of Disaster Recovery Cost Analysis

This section continues with the previous example and shows the cost analysis for the disaster scenario of a fire at the co-location facility.

Cost Analysis for Recovery from Fire at Xunil

Recovery from a fire at the Xunil co-location facility will include the following items:

1. Replacement of hardware systems. Replacing all current systems will cost a minimum of $1,350,000. This cost includes servers, network hardware, and other miscellaneous equipment (racks, tools, and cabling).

2. Downtime during repairs. The cost of downtime has been estimated at $25,000 per day of lost revenue due to the reduced amount of traffic that can be handled by the secondary site.

3. System admin time. The effort required to replace the lost servers, including installation and configuration, is estimated at 10 man days to increase the capacity of the secondary site to match that of the primary and 2 man months to re-create the primary site. These estimates are calculated from the date of delivery of the replacement equipment.

Outline Preventative Measures

If preventative measures have been implemented to minimize the risks of data loss, such as the use of RAID or offsite storage of backups, then these measures need to be spelled out in your plan as well. These measures need to be documented because they will affect how recovery will take place and the costs associated with that recovery.

Sample of Preventative Measures Section

This section shows the part of the document that outlines the preventative measures taken to minimize the risk of the disaster scenario we have been covering.

Fire at Xunil Facility Preventative Measures

In order to minimize the risk associated with this scenario, the following preventative measures have been implemented:

1. Data from critical servers is replicated from the primary Web site to the secondary Web site on an hourly basis. This is accomplished by means of a streaming process that sends transactions from the primary site to the secondary site that is run from a cron job. This means that at most, one hour of data would be lost.

2. All configuration data from production hosts is stored in a repository at the development headquarters, enabling any systems lost to a fire to be re-created quickly.

3. The Xunil co-location facility is equipped with a Halon fire suppression system.

4. A secondary site is available that can handle 60% of the capacity of the primary site in the event of an emergency.

Publish the Plan

Once you have covered the scenarios for data loss, the costs associated with recovery, and what measures have been taken to minimize the risks, the plan should be presented to management for approval. Once this approval has been given, the plan should be published so that it is available to others in the company. This leads us to the next topic: plan maintenance.

Plan Maintenance

So you have now developed a plan for data recovery and have published it. What now? The utility of your plan will now depend on how well it is maintained. A plan that is developed and then never looked at until it is needed is likely to be out of date and not very useful. Therefore, you should be prepared to maintain the plan, not only on a scheduled basis, but also when making changes to your systems that may impact the plan. Following are some guidelines for keeping your plan up-to-date so that it will be useful when disaster strikes.

Scheduled Plan Reviews

Whenever you as a system administrator create a plan, policy, or procedure, you should always create a schedule for review. This will ensure that the document stays current. How frequently you review the plan is up to you, but I recommend that reviews be scheduled at least twice per year. Reviews should address three things:

1. Are the data loss scenarios still relevant?
2. Have new preventative measures been implemented?
3. Are the cost estimates still valid?

By addressing these items, you can ensure that your plan is more than just a document gathering dust and will actually be useful if the situation arises in which you need it.

Updates to Reflect System Changes

In addition to scheduled reviews, you should make disaster recovery planning a part of all projects that change the way in which your systems work. Examples of this would be the addition of new critical systems to your network, changes to your offsite backup storage procedures, or the implementation of new preventative measures like high-availability functionality. Each of these things will impact your disaster recovery plans and should result in a review. By including disaster recovery in project planning, you can make sure that you will be ready if disaster strikes and can force people to think about measures that they can take to minimize the risk of data loss.

Summary

This chapter covered some of the common data loss scenarios that you as a system administrator are likely to encounter. It also took a look at some preventative measures that can be taken to minimize the chance of data loss and some of the recovery methods that are available if data loss occurs. Some of the costs associated with lost data and the development of a disaster recovery plan were covered as well. This knowledge is essential and should help to ensure that you will be able to recover when the inevitable occurs.

Networking

PART
V

IN THIS PART

14 TCP/IP and Ethernet   *371*

15 Sharing Resources (Print and
   File Services)   *409*

16 Network Monitoring   *435*

17 Integrating with Windows NT Networks   *461*

18 Integrating With Other Network Operating
   Systems   *493*

TCP/IP and Ethernet

IN THIS CHAPTER

- Network Layers   *372*
- IP Addresses   *375*
- Running TCP/IP over Ethernet   *377*
- Adding an Ethernet Interface   *382*
- Routing   *383*
- Name Services   *397*

Once upon a time, computers were invariably isolated devices. Communication between them involved physically transporting bulky removable media from one system to another. The need to share data led to the development of computer networks, which began as relatively modest serial and analog telecommunications links. The Internet grew out of these modest networks, into a high-speed global set of pathways for sharing data among computers. The Internet protocols, also known as TCP/IP, are not the only networking standards in use, although as we enter the twenty-first century, they are certainly the most widely deployed. They stem from research into packet-switched networks commissioned by ARPA (the U.S. Department of Defense Advanced Research Projects Agency) in 1969. The ARPANET, the network thus developed, was switched to operational status in 1975.

Why are the Internet protocols so widely used? The most likely reason is that, whereas other networking standards were developed by individual vendors, or were defined without sufficient regard to real-world considerations, the Internet protocols were defined in terms of *working* systems. Indeed, an Internet standard (an RFC, or Request For Comment) is not officially adopted until *two* independent implementations have been developed. This approach is in some sense similar to the Free Software or Open Source ethic of "show me the source"—opinions about software design and implementation are given more weight if they are based on working programs. Similarly, proposed Internet standards are only considered if they describe working systems.

This chapter describes how to set up the fundamental requirements for networking a Red Hat Linux system with TCP/IP using Ethernet. Some of the material covered is not specific to Linux or UNIX, but a detailed knowledge of the technical background is important for achieving a comprehensive understanding of the issues. The first two sections describe Network Layers and IP Addresses, respectively, which together underpin the workings of the entire Internet. It then goes on to discuss operating-system independent considerations when using Ethernet to connect TCP/IP hosts. This chapter also discusses how to add an Ethernet interface to a Red Hat Linux system, and describes how to perform routing and provide name services under Red Hat Linux.

Network Layers

All network communications are organized as a series of layers, with the lowest layer being the physical link. A network transaction is originated by an application, and the communication moves down the layers on the system running that application. Then when the data arrives at the receiving system, the communication process is reversed: The information moves from the physical layer up to the application layer, and the transaction is then complete.

The TCP/IP protocols are described in terms of a *stack* of four such layers: the Network Access Layer, the Internet Layer, the Transport Layer, and the Application Layer. The notion of network layers is dealt with in more detail in the Open Systems Interconnect Reference Model (OSI), which describes seven layers. Although the OSI is a more complete description of the principles behind data communications, the TCP/IP model can be considered to be a practical implementation of the OSI design criteria. The breaking down of network communications into layers enables developers to deal with specific issues rather than being concerned with the global stream of communication.

Each of the four TCP/IP layers deals with data in small units; these units have different names in each layer, though they are sometimes collectively referred to by the generic term*packets*. In the highest layers of TCP/IP, there are two names for each unit, for reasons that will become clear shortly. Table 14.1 presents the data unit names for the various network layers.

TABLE 14.1 Data Unit Names in TCP/IP Network Layers

Data Unit Name Layer	TCP	UDP
Application	stream	message
Transport	segment	packet
Internet	datagram	
Network Access	frame	

The following sections discuss the layers from the bottom up.

Network Access Layer

The Network Access Layer in the TCP/IP protocol suite deals with the details of physically sending data frames across links—copper wire, fiber optic cable, or even radio or infrared for wireless networks. By far the most widespread type of link in most organizations is Ethernet, which uses copper wire; other common types include FDDI and RS232C. TCP/IP does not itself define physical networking standards, preferring to leverage existing technologies. This is possible because the Internet layer is sufficiently generic to be able to handle many different physical links.

Internet Layer

The Internet Layer encompasses IP, the Internet Protocol. IP is *connectionless* (no synchronization or handshaking is required between the source and destination systems) and *unreliable* (which means that it provides no error detection or recovery). Connection-oriented communications, as well as error handling, are provided at a higher level in the TCP/IP stack.

The current popular implementation of TCP/IP (IPv4) allows for 32-bit source and destination addresses in IP datagrams. The destination address is used by routers and gateways to determine where the datagram should be sent.

One of the crucial features of IP is that it provides for fragmentation and reassembly of datagrams. Physical networks differ in how much data can be contained in a single frame; this amount is called the MTU, or Maximum Transmission Unit. For example, FDDI has an MTU of 4500 bytes, but for Ethernet it is only 1500 bytes. When a datagram is forwarded from a network with a large MTU to one with a smaller MTU, IP splits the datagram into several fragmented datagrams, each of which will fit into a single frame on the physical network. Then, the IP implementation on the receiving system reassembles the fragmented data into a single datagram, using control information inserted into the IP headers by the forwarding system. This ability to reliably fragment datagrams is a requirement for a network protocol that, like IP, can use any of a variety of different physical links.

The Internet Layer also includes ICMP, the Internet Control Message Protocol. ICMP uses the IP datagram delivery facility to send messages that function as meta-data for the network. Perhaps the most common use of ICMP is the Echo Request/Echo Reply facility, usually accessed by the `ping` program, which essentially checks whether a given system is up and connected to the network. Other ICMP message types are Source Quench (a simple form of flow control), Destination Unreachable, and Redirect.

Transport Layer

The Transport Layer (or more properly the Host-to-Host Transport Layer) provides application-usable communication protocols. For TCP/IP, these protocols are UDP (the User Datagram Protocol) and TCP (the Transmission Control Protocol).

UDP provides applications with a connectionless, unreliable datagram-oriented protocol that has a minimum of overhead. UDP also extends the 32-bit source/destination addresses used by IP with 16-bit source and destination *port numbers*. The use of port numbers allows a system to have many UDP-based applications running on it, and still ensures that each application sees only the data intended for it.

TCP is a reliable, connection-oriented protocol that provides a straightforward byte-stream model to applications. Reliability of TCP communications is ensured by requiring the receiving system to acknowledge successful receipt of data; if the sending system doesn't get the acknowledgement, it retransmits the data. TCP communications employ a *logical connection* between a pair of systems: The application is presented with the illusion of a physical circuit existing between the two communication endpoints. This logical connection is established and maintained by an initial *three-way handshake* (so-called because the handshake needs three TCP segments to set up) and by *sequence numbers* attached to each byte of the stream in each direction. Like UDP, TCP provides a 16-bit port number for source and destination. As you might imagine, the error checking involved in tracking the connection sequence for TCP imposes an additional overhead compared to UDP. However, for many applications, a reliable data stream is a requirement, so this overhead is unavoidable.

Application Layer

The Application Layer includes the protocols normally thought of as network services. These protocols are built on top of TCP streams or UDP messages. For example, HTTP, the Hypertext Transfer Protocol which underpins the World Wide Web, is a stream-oriented protocol normally sent over TCP, and NTP, the Network Time Protocol, is a message-oriented protocol sent over UDP. Such protocols normally also specify a default port number on the server to which clients should connect. For example, HTTP defaults to TCP port 80, and NTP uses UDP port 123. Application-level services are described in more detail elsewhere in the book.

Up to this point, we have been discussing "addresses" of communication endpoints, but we have not yet mentioned the form these addresses take. Because their precise nature will be important later, the following sections describe them in detail.

IP Addresses

IPv4, the current IP standard, uses a 32-bit numerical address for each Internet host. (The next-generation standard, IPv6, uses 128-bit addresses.) These addresses are customarily written as a *dotted quad*—a series of four numbers in the range 0 to 255, separated by periods. IP addresses also encode some structured information: They are divided into a network part and a host part. These parts vary in length, and the length of the network part is determined by an address class or by a subnet mask.

Address Classes

Address classes are divisions of the IP address space into a small number of fixed-length structures. They have to some extent been obsoleted by the more general mechanism of variable-length subnet masks, but the terminology is still widely used. The three main address classes (class A, class B, and class C) are distinguished by which of several ranges the first octet in the dotted quad falls into, as shown in Table 14.2.

14

TCP/IP and Ethernet

TABLE **14.2** Address Classes in IPv4

Class	Range	Comments
A	0 to 127	<128 networks, >16 million hosts
B	128 to 191	>16000 networks, >65000 hosts
C	192 to 223	>2 million networks, 254 hosts
D	224 to 239	Multicast addresses
E	240 to 255	Reserved, unassigned addresses

Address classes D and E are rather different from the others: Class D is used for multicast (addressing multiple hosts in a single datagram) and class E is reserved for experimental use and has no assigned addresses.

Each address class provides one or more private networks, which are available for local use without needing to go through the official registration procedure. In class A, the network 10.0.0.0 is available; in class B it is all networks from 172.16.0.0 to 172.31.255.255; and in class C, the networks from 192.168.0.0 to 192.168.255.0 are available.

Two important class A networks are not allocated in the usual way. The network 127.0.0.0 is the loopback network, which allows the local host to be addressed in the same manner as remote hosts; this substantially simplifies some networking applications. The network 0.0.0.0 is not used as a network number; instead, it identifies the default route in routing tables (see the section "Routing" later in the chapter).

This scheme of address classes is not without problems. The most significant problem is that these fixed-length classes are very inflexible. Each is too large for many purposes; thus, a large part of the address space gets wasted in organizations that are unable to use all of their addresses but that have too large a network to use an address class with fewer host addresses. In some cases, an organization could use multiple smaller networks, but this would increase load on routers.

Classless IP Addresses

By the early 1990s, it had become clear that the fixed-size structures imposed by address classes were scaling poorly to a larger Internet—and indeed, there seemed to be a genuine possibility that the class B address space would soon be exhausted. The interim solution developed is called CIDR (pronounced *cider*), or Classless Inter-Domain Routing. It is considered an interim solution because in the long term, networks are expected to switch to IPv6.

The central idea of CIDR is to use variable-length network masks to distinguish the network part and host part of an IP address, rather than encoding the length of the mask in the address itself. The bit pattern of the network mask is treated as a template for interpretation of the IP address: For each bit that is set in the network mask, the corresponding bit in the IP address is treated as the network part rather than the host part. The network mask is divided into two contiguous parts: a prefix of all-bits-one and a suffix of all-bits-zero.

Network masks in isolation are usually written as dotted quads, just like IP addresses. For example, a network mask allowing eight bits for the host part would be 255.255.255.0. There is also a convenient abbreviated syntax for writing an IP address and its network mask together: The IP address is followed by a slash (/) and the number of one bits in the network mask. For example, a network mask of 255.255.0.0 could be applied to the network address 192.168.0.0; it could then be written as 192.168.0.0/16, and an individual host in that network might be 192.168.17.42/16. This process (of aggregating small networks into a network larger than the natural mask of the address class structure would indicate) is called *supernetting*.

Subnetting

Just as supernetting involves using in the host part of the address some bits that the natural mask would assign to the network part, so subnetting involves using bits from the host part within the network part. This increases the number of networks that can be addressed, at the cost of allowing fewer hosts within each network. Suppose we have the network address 172.16.0.0, whose natural mask is 255.255.0.0. Using a subnet mask of 255.255.240.0 gives us the network 172.16.0.0/20, in which there are 16 subnets that each contain more than four thousand host addresses.

We have now discussed the essentials of TCP/IP networking, though without reference to specific hardware or software implementations. The next section describes Ethernet, a very widely used standard for physical network connections.

Running TCP/IP over Ethernet

IP addresses actually denote network interfaces rather than hosts on the network; this enables a single system to be present on more than one physical network and to forward packets between them.

14

TCP/IP and
Ethernet

A typical workstation on a LAN (Local Area Network) will have two interfaces. The first is the loopback interface (though of course this is an abstract construct of the TCP/IP implementation, rather than an actual physical interface), and the second is the interface that is on the LAN itself. The common case is for the LAN interface to be on an Ethernet segment, and that is the case this chapter deals with.

Ethernet Cards and Cables

Ethernet interfaces are designed for most systems as ISA or PCI cards, although laptop computers often have PCMCIA Ethernet cards, and a few systems have Ethernet interfaces built directly onto the motherboard. Ethernet cards are often referred to as NICs, or Network Interface Cards.

There are three types of physical media commonly used for Ethernet networks: 10Base-2, 10Base-T, and 100Base-T. The "10" or "100" part of each of these designations indicates the theoretical maximum data transmission speed in megabits per second (Mbps). (Gigabit Ethernet systems have been developed, but are not yet widely available.) Many Ethernet cards support more than one of these physical media types. So-called "Combo" cards offer both 10Base-2 and 10Base-T, and there are also dual-speed cards (which can do either 10Base-T or 100Base-T).

10Base-2 Ethernet uses coaxial cable with BNC connectors. It requires a *backbone*, or *bus*, topology (see Figure 14.1): All nodes on a 10Base-2 Ethernet must connect directly to what is essentially a single length of 50-ohm thin coaxial (coax) cable. This cable must be terminated by resistors at either end, and it is broken by T-connectors. Each node is plugged into one of these T-connectors.

FIGURE 14.1
*10Base-2
networks use a
backbone
topology.*

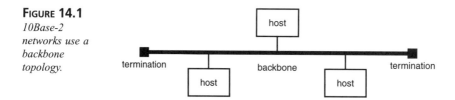

10Base-T and 100Base-T Ethernet use unshielded twisted pair (UTP) cables with RJ45 connectors (which are similar to telephone jacks). UTP cables come in various categories; Category 3 is sufficient for 10Base-T, whereas the faster data rates of 100Base-T need the higher quality provided by Category 5 cables. 10Base-T and 100Base-T networks use a different topology, known as a *star* topology, where each node connects to a central hub (see Figure 14.2). This means that when designing a 10Base-T or 100Base-T network, you must budget for a hub in each Ethernet.

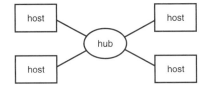

FIGURE 14.2
10Base-T networks use a star topology.

Ethernet Hubs

Ethernet hubs typically have from 4 to 24 ports for Ethernet connections. Some hubs run at only one speed (10 or 100 Mbps), whereas others are dual-speed. Cheaper dual-speed hubs will force all ports to be the same speed, so adding a 10 Mbps Ethernet interface to a network that is otherwise 100 Mbps will substantially decrease network performance. However, most modern dual-speed hubs will automatically detect the correct connection speed for each port individually; these are called *auto-sensing* hubs. Some hubs are stackable, which means that one or more ports can be used for connecting a second hub. Obviously, stackable hubs give far more opportunity for expanding a network after its original installation.

Switches

One of the distinguishing features of Ethernet rejoices in the name CSMA/CD, or Carrier Sense Multiple Access with Collision Detection. CSMA/CD is an approach for deciding what to do when more than one device on the Ethernet tries to send a frame of data simultaneously (since only one frame can be active at any given moment). Each device detects this "collision." At this point, the devices must be able to re-send their frames at different times, without communicating between themselves or using any external arbitration. The approach that Ethernet adopts is for each device to wait a random length of time before re-sending the frame.

In normal operation, this is entirely adequate. However, if a network is heavily loaded, performance degrades severely, as the Ethernet devices end up spending more and more of their time waiting for collision situations to be resolved. The network becomes saturated.

Ethernet switches get around this problem. They behave in a similar way to hubs, but where hubs create a single Ethernet out of multiple independent cables, a switch essentially puts each of its ports on a separate Ethernet, and transmits (or switches) frames between each network. You can put a network hub on each port of a switch. Alternatively, you can directly connect a single host; this would be useful for a heavily used server that many other hosts must communicate with.

14

TCP/IP and
Ethernet

Switches can also reduce a network's vulnerability to certain security problems. A host or hub on a given port of a switch is on its own Ethernet; this makes it considerably harder for would-be attackers to snoop on data being transmitted using trace tools. Such data could include passwords or other sensitive data, for example. Obviously, the advantages of this approach are limited if several hosts are placed on a switched Ethernet segment using a hub, but switches are nonetheless particularly beneficial for multi-user machines.

Using Switches

When should you use a switch? In many environments, the increased flexibility of switched Ethernet is unnecessary, and would be wasted. However, if you start seeing many collisions on a network, it is well worth examining the situation carefully. Under Linux, you can use the `ifconfig` command to check how many collisions have been detected on a network. Listing 14.1 shows some sample output.

LISTING 14.1 Using `ifconfig` to Examine Ethernet Collisions

```
$ ifconfig eth0
eth0      Link encap:Ethernet  HWaddr 00:E0:98:04:37:59
          inet addr:192.168.1.1  Bcast:192.168.1.255  Mask:255.255.255.0
          UP BROADCAST RUNNING MULTICAST  MTU:1500  Metric:1
          RX packets:455299 errors:6 dropped:0 overruns:0 frame:25
          TX packets:403376 errors:14 dropped:0 overruns:0 carrier:14
          collisions:7004 txqueuelen:100
          Interrupt:10 Base address:0x300
```

In this case, there have been 7004 collisions, out of 403,376 packets transmitted (TX), giving a collision rate of slightly under 2%. I know from experience that this rate is considerably higher than normal for this network. In this instance, it's a direct result of running several concurrent flood-pings (that is, sending ICMP Echo Request packets as fast as possible) specifically to acquire some interesting data on Ethernet collisions. In general, collision rates below 5% are nothing to worry about. If collision rates above 5% are seen consistently, and among a broad sampling of hosts on the network, it may well be time to consider splitting the network with a switch.

Choosing Ethernet Media

Which type of physical Ethernet media should you choose when setting up a new network? Each type has advantages and disadvantages.

Coax-based or UTP-based Ethernets

Coax-based Ethernets incur lower costs than the alternatives, mainly because there is no requirement to use a hub, but also because 10Base-2 NICs tend to be cheap. (Some would say that you get what you pay for with the very cheapest 10Base-2 cards, though.) Compared to UTP-based Ethernets, they use one fewer piece of cable for a given number of hosts. (Moreover, depending on the physical location of the hub in relation to the hosts, UTP-based networks may need substantially more cable overall.) Coax networks are also very simple to set up.

The biggest problem with 10Base-2 is precisely the requirement for a single backbone connecting all the nodes. If there is a failure at any point in the backbone cable, the entire network goes down. This also makes it comparatively difficult to expand them if requirements change. This makes it hard to recommend a 10Base-2 network for the majority of new installations; however, home users may find that 10Base-2 Ethernet is an ideally cheap and simple mechanism for connecting a few machines together.

10Base-T or 100Base-T UTP Ethernets

As for the UTP media types, the principal difference between 10Base-T and 100Base-T is obviously speed. Of course, this difference comes at a price: 100Base-T parts are more expensive than 10Base-T equivalents, especially for high-quality components. However, the price differential is getting smaller, and it may be cheaper in the long run to go for 100Base-T initially, rather than to start with 10Base-T only to discover at some later date that a 100 Mbps network is in fact necessary.

I would normally recommend investing in Category 5 cable even for 10Base-T networks because re-cabling a network is an expensive and time-consuming procedure. Using Category 5 for 10Base-T is unlikely to be prohibitively expensive unless you are connecting a large number of machines together. Once you have Category 5 cables in place, upgrading from 10Base-T to 100Base-T is a simple matter of installing dual-speed hubs; then individual hosts can be upgraded to 100 Mbps Ethernet cards when appropriate. Indeed, in some situations it can make sense to get dual-speed hubs initially, even if to begin with no host on the network has a NIC that can run at 100Mbps.

Now that we've described the workings of Ethernet and how it fits in with TCP/IP, the next stage is to actually get an Ethernet interface working under Red Hat Linux. The next section discusses how this is done.

14

TCP/IP and
Ethernet

Adding an Ethernet Interface

Once the hardware has been installed, configuring a new Ethernet interface can normally be divided into kernel-level (hardware driver) configuration on the one hand, and configuration of the networking software on the other. However, in Red Hat 6, the use of a fully modularized kernel build means that both of these steps can be performed from the same system administration tool—Linuxconf. Figure 14.3 shows the basic host configuration dialog in the Gnome version of Linuxconf being used to add an Ethernet interface.

FIGURE 14.3

Adding an Ethernet interface with Gnome-Linuxconf.

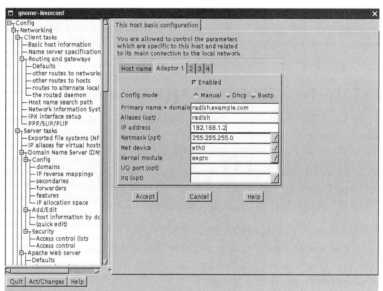

Kernel Level Configuration

The kernel-level configuration is set with the Kernel Module, I/O Port, and Irq fields. Use the Kernel-module field to select the hardware type of your Ethernet card. In this example, the card being configured is an Intel EtherExpress Pro. If you use the Gnome interface, there is a drop-down menu of Ethernet card types, but if you use the terminal-based interface, you have to know the name of the kernel module that can drive it. If you want to see a list of the available modules, you can run

```
ls /lib/modules/$(uname r)/net
```

although that directory also contains some non-Ethernet modules.

In most situations, you can let the kernel modules probe for the correct I/O port number and IRQ, but you will need to specify these values if you have one of the few types of cards that cannot be probed accurately. Also, if you have more than one card of the same type in one machine, you must configure the I/O port and IRQ for all of them in one shot. This is because the driver module is loaded only once for both cards. For example, if you have one card running on I/O port 0x300 with IRQ 10, and a second card of the same type running on I/O port 0x320 with IRQ 11, you should set the I/O port field for the first card to "0x300,0x320" and the IRQ field to "10,11".

Software Level Configuration

The other fields in this dialog relate to the software-level configuration. Perhaps the most important is the Config Mode. This determines how the other parameters are set. In Manual config mode, the administrator sets them by hand in this dialog. The other two config modes allow the interface to be configured automatically when it is brought up (usually at boot time). There are two protocols to allow this: BOOTP (the Bootstrap Protocol) and the newer DHCP (Dynamic Host Configuration Protocol), which is based on it.

If you are configuring the interface by hand, the remaining parameters are, in order: the fully-qualified name of the interface, any aliased names it may have, the IP address of the interface, and the network mask for that interface. In this instance, the eth0 interface is on the private network 192.168.1.0/24. Its name is `radish.example.com`, and it has an alias of `radish`.

Once your Red Hat Linux system has a working Ethernet interface, the next thing to consider is how it will transmit data to and from the wider Internet. This process is called *routing*, and is the subject of the following section.

Routing

IP addresses are in some sense a very abstract mechanism. Though they uniquely distinguish all directly addressable Internet interfaces, they encode no information about their location. The Internet is a network of networks, which means that it is extremely unlikely that any arbitrary pair of directly addressable hosts is on the same physical network.

How, then, is it possible to send an IP datagram from a system in one place to a remote site that is potentially many thousands of miles away? In the simplest terms, an IP datagram is transmitted from one network to another, until eventually it reaches the network that holds the destination host. Some systems, known as *gateways* or *routers*, are present on more than one network, so they can forward datagrams as necessary from one network to another. The term router is sometimes reserved for standalone devices, leaving gateway to describe a computer system performing this role, often as one of many functions. However, this usage is not applied consistently.

Although purpose-designed routing hardware will typically give better performance than co-opting a general-purpose computer, it is certainly possible to use a UNIX-like system (whether a UNIX-branded system or a clone such as Linux) to perform routing, and it may in some cases allow more flexibility. This book will talk only about using Red Hat Linux systems to perform routing.

Routing Gateways

Gateways route data between multiple networks, but individual hosts must make routing decisions as well. In the simple case, where the host has only a loopback interface and one physical interface, the routing decisions are fairly trivial. If a datagram is addressed to an interface on the loopback network, it is sent over the loopback interface. Otherwise, if it is addressed to a host on the local physical network, it is sent over the physical interface. Otherwise, it must be addressed to a host on a remote network, and it is sent to a gateway on the local physical network to be forwarded appropriately.

Configuring Routing

Routing on a given system can be configured in a wide variety of ways, but a basic distinction can be drawn between static routing and dynamic routing. The administrator must configure static routing by hand. It is useful for a network with a limited number of gateways to other TCP/IP networks—and especially for a network with only one gateway. Static routing can also help to eliminate security vulnerabilities in applications which authenticate based on IP address because it can avoid IP spoofing. Small LANs, especially those run by home users, are ideal examples of this sort of environment.

Dynamic routing, on the other hand, should be used on networks with more than one possible route to the same destination. In the general case, routing packets across multiple networks is a difficult task. This is especially true for the Internet, where issues of scale and of reliability mean that routing knowledge must be distributed: No one system or group of systems can know all the routes that exist. In addition, routers must do their best to direct datagrams over the shortest possible route. None of this can realistically be done without communication between routers. Such communication is done by the routed and gated daemons, and the information thus acquired is used automatically to configure routing decisions.

The Routing Table

On UNIX and Linux systems, information about how datagrams are to be directed is stored in a kernel structure called the routing table. It is this routing table that must be manipulated to configure routing decisions, based either on fixed information provided by the administrator (for static routing), or on reachability information acquired through the Border Gateway Protocol (for dynamic routing).

Examining the Routing Table

The routing table can be examined with the `netstat -r` command, as shown in Listing 14.2.

LISTING 14.2 Using `netstat` to Show the Routing Table

```
$ netstat -r -n
Kernel IP routing table
Destination     Gateway          Genmask          Flags   MSS Window  irtt Iface
192.168.1.2     0.0.0.0          255.255.255.255  UH       0 0           0 eth0
192.168.1.0     0.0.0.0          255.255.255.0    U        0 0           0 eth0
127.0.0.0       0.0.0.0          255.0.0.0        U        0 0           0 lo
0.0.0.0         192.168.1.1      0.0.0.0          UG       0 0           0 eth0
```

On Linux systems, you can also use `route` instead of `netstat -r`, but since other systems don't let you do this, it's probably good to get into the habit of using `netstat -r`. You can give `netstat -r` the `-e` option to make it use the same output format as `route`, or you can give `route` the `-e` option to make it use the same output format as `netstat -r`. Giving either program the `-ee` makes them use the same output format, with the combined information of the other formats; the output lines in this format are very long.

The `-n` option to `netstat` or `route` prevents them from attempting to resolve numeric IP addresses into names. As the manual points out, this switch is useful when trying to debug problems with the route to your name server—but it can also be useful in other situations. I use it here to make the network structure readily visible.

The output fields for `netstat -r -ee` have the following meanings:

- **Destination**—This identifies the destination IP addresses for which this route is considered.

- **Gateway**—This gives the IP address of the interface (if any) that will forward packets for these destinations. If no forwarding gateway is needed, an address of 0.0.0.0 appears here, or * if you omit the `-n` argument.

- **Genmask**—This is the network mask used for the destination addresses.

14

TCP/IP and Ethernet

- **Flags**—This indicates various details about the route. The most important flags are U (the route is up), G (the specified gateway should be used for this route), and H (the route is for a host, not a network). D (dynamically installed), M (modified) and R (reinstated) flags indicate that the route was created or manipulated by a routing daemon or after encountering an ICMP Redirect message. The ! flag indicates a rejecting route.

- **Metric**—This is a quality rating for the route. Normally useful only in dynamic routing.

- **Ref**—Not used by the Linux kernel, but for other systems it represents the number of references to the route.

- **Use**—Reports the number of lookups for this route.

- **MSS**—The default Maximum Segment Size for TCP connections over this route.

- **Window**—The default window size for TCP connections over this route.

- **Irtt**—Initial Round Trip Time. The kernel uses to this to select values for certain TCP parameters without having to wait for potentially slow answers from remote hosts.

The output from `netstat -r` in Listing 14.2 shows that the system has routes for the following destinations:

- 127.0.0.0—This is the route for the loopback network. For Linux kernels in the 2.2.x series or higher, this route is not actually necessary. The kernel already knows how to route to the loopback network. But even though Red Hat 6.0 ships with the 2.2.5 kernel, the boot-up procedure adds this route.

- 192.168.1.2—This IP address is actually attached to this system's own eth0 interface. Again, this route is not necessary, but it is created during the Red Hat boot-up procedure.

- 192.168.1.0—This is a route for the network that the eth0 interface is attached to. No gateway is needed.

- 0.0.0.0—This is the default route; it is used for any datagrams that aren't caught by other routes. If you omit the -n argument, the word "default" appears instead of the zeros. This route specifies that datagrams should be sent to the gateway system 192.168.1.1 for forwarding to other networks.

Adding and Deleting Static Routes

The easiest way of adding and deleting static routes under Red Hat 6 is to use Linuxconf. However, it is sometimes necessary to try to repair networks in emergency situations where complex tools are not available. This makes it worth learning to do it by hand, using the route command, and in addition it becomes obvious what happens when you use the configuration tool.

The first argument to route should be one of the words add or del to indicate that the route described by the remaining arguments is being added or deleted, respectively.

The syntax of the remaining arguments depends on the type of route being added. The simplest case is adding the default route. This command looks like

```
route add default gw gateway
```

where *gateway* is the IP address of the host that will forward packets. Note that for this route to be usable, there must already be a route (usually a static route) for *gateway*. The gateway can be specified with a hostname, but usually a numeric IP address is used. This is because static routes are usually added at boot time, when there may be no name service running.

For adding non-default routes, the second argument is normally one of the words -net or -host, to indicate whether the route is for a network or a host. However, this argument can be omitted if the route is for a host.

The argument immediately after the -net or -host is the destination IP address (either as a hostname, or as a numeric address). This should be followed by the word netmask and then the actual netmask to be used for this route. The netmask may be omitted if it matches the natural mask for the destination address.

Finally, there must be some indication of the route to take for this destination. If the destination is directly available, use the dev keyword, followed by the device that is to be used (such as eth0). If this is the last part of the command line, the dev keyword can be omitted. If routes for this destination must be forwarded by a gateway, use the gw keyword with the IP address (name or number) of the gateway system. As for the default route, there must be some existing route to the gateway system.

It is also possible to add a rejecting route. Adding the word reject to the end of the route command installs a rejecting route, which forces the route lookup to fail. It is used for masking out networks before using the default route.

Once you can add routes, deleting routes is straightforward. To delete a route, just give the command line that adds the route question, substituting the word del for the word add. Some of the parameters can be removed from the command line, but supplying all the

14

TCP/IP and
Ethernet

parameters that were set will always work. If you don't supply enough parameters, the typical response is the message `SIOCDELRT: Invalid argument`.

Example Commands for Adding Routes

The following are some examples of commands to add routes. The first two could be used to add routes that appear in the routing table in Listing 14.2, repeated here as Listing 14.3.

LISTING **14.3** A Sample Routing Table

```
$ netstat -r -n
Kernel IP routing table
Destination     Gateway         Genmask           Flags   MSS Window  irtt Iface
192.168.1.2     0.0.0.0         255.255.255.255   UH        0 0          0 eth0
192.168.1.0     0.0.0.0         255.255.255.0     U         0 0          0 eth0
127.0.0.0       0.0.0.0         255.0.0.0         U         0 0          0 lo
0.0.0.0         192.168.1.1     0.0.0.0           UG        0 0          0 eth0
```

- `route add -net 192.168.1.0 netmask 255.255.255.0 dev eth0`

   This adds a route for the 192.168.1.0/24 network over the eth0 device, which presumably has an IP address on that network.

- `route add default gw 192.168.1.1`

   This makes 192.168.1.1 the gateway for forwarding packets on the default route.

- `route add -net 127.0.0.0 netmask 255.255.255.0 lo`

   This is the correct syntax for adding a route to the loopback network. Even though this route is unnecessary under recent kernels, I include this example because the manual for `route` gets it wrong.

- `route add -net 10.0.0.0 netmask 255.0.0.0 gw 192.168.1.17`

   This adds a route to the 10.0.0.0/8 network, using the system with IP address 192.168.1.17 as the gateway. The netmask is unnecessary in this case because it matches the natural mask of the destination network.

To clarify what is happening here, Figure 14.4 shows the layout of a network for which these routes might be appropriate. The host with these routes is 192.168.1.2, on the left of the diagram.

Once you can add routes by hand like this, using Linuxconf as a front-end for adding the routes and editing the configuration files makes the process straightforward.

The first step is to set the default router, as shown in Figure 14.5.

FIGURE 14.4

Routing between two local subnets.

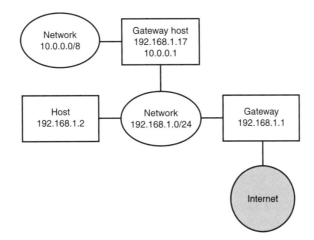

FIGURE 14.5

Setting the default route with Linuxconf.

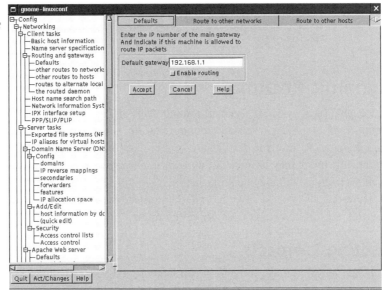

This dialog also allows the administrator to specify whether the local host can forward packets.

Routes for individual networks or hosts can be set with the Other Routes to Networks or Other Routes to Hosts dialogs. Figure 14.6 demonstrates a route to the 10.0.0.0/8 network, as in the preceding examples.

FIGURE **14.6**

*Using Linuxconf
to add a route to
another network.*

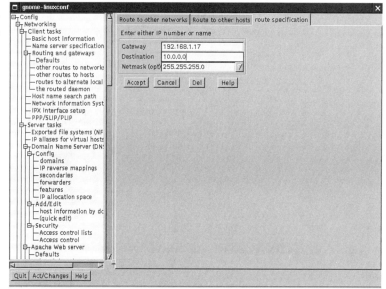

Dynamic Routing

As we have seen, systems where all routing decisions are made in advance by the
administrator are said to use static routing, but this is insufficient for networks with
multiple routes to the same destination. In such networks, routing decisions are controlled
dynamically by routing daemons. Routing daemons attempt to determine the best route to a
given destination, and they communicate with routing daemons running on other systems
to ensure that all systems have up-to-date information on which routes are best. The
protocols for this communication are called routing protocols.

Routing Protocols

There are several routing protocols in common use today, each with its own characteristics.
Routing protocols can be divided into two general groups: interior and exterior. An *interior
routing protocol* is used inside an independent network, or what TCP/IP calls an
Autonomous System (AS); an *exterior protocol* is used to transmit routing information
between multiple autonomous systems. The routing information transmitted is called
reachability information, and it quite simply describes what systems are reachable from a
given system. The following list presents the most commonly used routing protocols.

- **RIP**—The Routing Information Protocol is the interior protocol most commonly used on UNIX systems. It makes routing decisions based solely on the results of applying a distance-vector algorithm to route metrics, or hop counts. It is simple to configure, and it is adequate for most small-to-medium networks.

  RIP has some serious shortcomings for large-scale use. It limits network diameter to 15 hops. It exhibits *slow convergence*—it may take up to 180 seconds for the routing table to reflect the new situation if previously correct routes become invalid. Also, it is unaware of classless IP addresses—all RIP routes must be for addresses that use their natural mask.

- **RIP-2**—This is the Routing Information Protocol Version 2. It is a backwards-compatible version of RIP, using fields in the RIP packet that were reserved for future extensions. RIP-2 fixes most of the problems with RIP, and also adds features such as authentication for routing information.

- **OSPF**—Like RIP, Open Shortest Path First is an interior protocol, but it differs significantly in that it is a *link-state protocol*. Where RIP routers share information about the entire AS with their neighbors, OSPF routers share information about their neighbors with the entire AS. This enables them to build a model of the entire network, and to use Dijkstra's well-understood shortest-path algorithm to determine the best route.

- **BGP**—The Border Gateway Protocol is the most common exterior routing protocol in use on the Internet. BGP supports policy-based routing; that is, the use of non-technical considerations such as security, cost, and organizational matters when making routing decisions. BGP learns the entire end-to-end path of a route, to ensure that routing loops do not occur.

Miscellaneous Protocols

Other protocols have been used elsewhere, but are not common. They include the Hello protocol (which was used on the original 56 kbps NSFNET backbone) and IS-IS, the Intermediate System to Intermediate System protocol (which was used on the NSFNET T1 backbone). Both of these are interior protocols. The Exterior Gateway Protocol is an exterior protocol that was once common, but it relied on a central authority to determine the "best" routes, and it therefore scaled poorly in the face of the Internet's exponential growth. For this reason, it is seldom used nowadays.

Although there are many routing protocols, it is usually easy to select the right one in any given situation. For local area networks, RIP or RIP-2 is still the most common choice, and often its simplicity makes it a sensible one. The more complex algorithms in OSPF make it appropriate for larger networks.

14

TCP/IP and
Ethernet

Very few systems need to run exterior protocols: they are needed only when one AS must exchange routing information with another AS. Large Internet service providers are one of the few environments where exterior protocols are necessary. When an exterior protocol *is* necessary, there is rarely a choice as to the routing protocol used: If the other AS is already in operation, its administrators have almost certainly selected a routing protocol, and autonomous systems must run the same protocol to be able to exchange routing information.

Routing Daemons

There are two main routing daemons that run on UNIX-like systems: `routed` (pronounced "route-dee") and `gated` ("gate-dee"). Of these, `routed` is easier to configure, but being older, it also suffers from a lack of flexibility—it can only handle RIP. The `gated` daemon can handle RIP, RIP-2, OSPF, and BGP, as well as Hello and EGP.

To enable `routed` under Red Hat, you must first install the relevant RPM package. Then to arrange for it to be started at boot time, you can either use the Control Service Activity dialog in Linuxconf, or run the equivalent command by hand:

```
chkconfig routed on
```

To start or stop the service other than at startup or shutdown time, run one of these commands:

```
/etc/rc.d/init.d/routed start
/etc/rc.d/init.d/routed stop
```

Some configuration of `routed` can be performed with Linuxconf, as shown in Figure 14.7.

The default Red Hat configuration is for `routed` to listen to routes advertised by other systems but not to advertise routes itself; this is accomplished by starting `routed` with the -q switch. The other option in this dialog determines whether `routed` should advertise its default route (the -g switch). This is used on gateways to the Internet, or on gateways using another routing protocol whose routes are not advertised to other local routers. This setting defaults to off.

The `routed` daemon reads the `/etc/gateways` file at startup and uses the information within it to configure the routing table. It is not necessary to use this file, because the RIP messages received from other routers will be enough to let `routed` build a functioning routing table. But there are situations in which it is useful: perhaps to supplement the RIP information with an initial default route, or with information about a gateway that does not advertise its routes.

FIGURE 14.7
*Configuring
routed with
Linuxconf.*

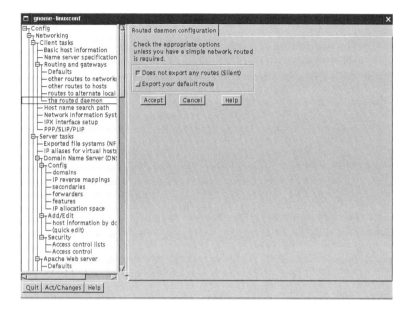

All entries in the `/etc/gateways` file have basically the same format, and that format is very similar to the command line for `route`, so it should be easy. Each entry is a single line containing the following items:

1. One of the words `net` or `host` to indicate whether the destination is to be treated as a network or a host.

2. The destination address, or 0.0.0.0 for the default route.

3. The word `gateway`.

4. The gateway's address.

5. The word `metric`.

6. The route's numeric metric value. This can be specified with route when adding a static route, but is essentially meaningless in that situation. RIP uses the metric as the cost of the route, so it prefers routes with lower metric values. For RIP, the metric should represent the number of gateways through which data must pass to reach the given destination, but it is actually an arbitrary value chosen by the administrator. If there is only one route to a given destination, that route should have a metric of 1.

7. One of the keywords `active`, `passive`, or `external`. Passive routes effectively become permanent static routes: They are not deleted by RIP, and they are not included in RIP information transmitted. Active routes, on the other hand, are advertised and updated by RIP. If no updates are received for an active route in a given period of time, it will be deleted from the routing table. External routes are

14

**TCP/IP and
Ethernet**

similar to passive routes, but `routed` will not add them to the routing table. The `external` declaration indicates that some other routing protocol will install a route for the destination in question, and that `routed` should not install alternative routes for the same destination.

Complex Routing Scenarios

More complex routing scenarios must be handled by the more flexible program `gated`. As you have already seen, `gated` can handle multiple routing protocols. It combines routing information learned from different protocols and selects the best routes available. It can advertise on exterior protocols routes whose existence was discovered by interior protocols, so reachability information announced externally can be adjusted dynamically to changing interior routes. It supports routing policies to control acceptance and advertisement of routes.

Perhaps most convenient of all for the administrator is that `gated` is configured from a single file (`/etc/gated.conf`) with a consistent syntax. There is also a group, the Gated Consortium (`http://www.gated.org`), which actively maintains it, so you can expect that bugs will be fixed and new features added.

Running `gated`

When `gated` runs, it acquires routing information from multiple protocols; if it receives routes to the same destination from different protocols, it attempts to select the best one. This is not a trivial task because metrics used by different protocols are not directly comparable. The solution adopted in gated is to use configurable preferences. The administrator can use these preferences to prefer routes from one interface over another, from one protocol over another, or from one remote gateway over another.

Enabling `gated` under Red Hat is very similar to enabling `routed`. You can enable it from the Control Service Activity dialog in Linuxconf, or you can run

```
chkconfig gated on
```

by hand (as root). To start or stop the service other than at startup or shutdown time, run one of the following:

```
/etc/rc.d/init.d/gated start
/etc/rc.d/init.d/gated stop
```

Configuring `/etc/gated.conf`

The `/etc/gated.conf` file has a number of configuration statements that are divided into several categories. Statements of each type must be grouped together, and the types must be presented in a specific order. Using a statement out of order will cause an error when `gated` parses the file.

The `gated` daemon has many configuration options—far more than this book can accommodate. If you need to understand all the possibilities provided by `gated`, you will need to read its reference manual. However, showing some sample configurations will give you an introduction to what it can do.

Host Routing Configuration

A host routing configuration for `gated` is actually quite straightforward. This is fitting, given that the work to be done is also fairly simple. Listing 14.4 gives an example.

LISTING **14.4**   A Host Routing Configuration for `gated`

```
# Enable RIP
rip yes {
     # Don't broadcast your own RIP updates
     nobroadcast ;
     interface 192.168.1.17
          # Use RIP-2
          version 2
          # Transmit updates via multicast to reduce load
          # on RIP-1 systems
          multicast ;
} ;
```

This example shows the basic structure of the configuration file, including comments introduced with a # sign, statements terminated by a semicolon, and statement grouping with braces.

Interior Gateway Configuration

An interior gateway configuration is only a little more complex. Suppose that a gateway named igw interconnects subnets 192.168.5.0 and 192.168.17.0, and that subnet 192.168.17.0 has a gateway to the Internet. The igw gateway has interfaces 192.168.5.1 and 192.168.17.3. It advertises itself to hosts on subnet 5 as the default gateway because it is the gateway to the outside world. It uses RIP-2 to advertise routes on subnet 5. On subnet 17, igw advertises itself as the gateway to subnet 5, using OSPF. Listing 14.5 shows the configuration.

14

TCP/IP and Ethernet

LISTING 14.5 An Interior Routing Configuration for gated

```
# Don't let subnet 5 time out, because this is the only path to
# that subnet.
interfaces {
     interface 192.168.5.1 passive ;
} ;


# Define an OSPF router id; we use the address of the interface
# that speaks OSPF.  The default is the address of the first
# interface encountered by gated
routerid 192.168.5.1 ;


# Enable RIP-2 and announce OSPF routes to subnet 5 with a cost
# of 5.  The cost is low because this is an internal route.
rip yes {
# Broadcast RIP-2 updates
     broadcast ;
     # The cost
     defaultmetric 5 ;
     interface 192.168.5.1
          version 2
          multicast ;
} ;


# Enable OSPF on the backbone area, subnet 17
ospf yes {
     backbone {
          interface 192.168.17.3 {
               # Use a fairly low priority to increase the
               # probability this will be elected as the
               # designated router.
               priority 5 ;
          } ;
     } ;
} ;
```

One thing to remember when configuring gated is that a syntax error in your /etc/
gated.conf will prevent it from starting properly. However, you can use the program itself
to check the syntax automatically. Suppose you are editing a copy of gated.conf in /tmp/
gated.conf.new. You can test it with the command

```
gated -c -f /tmp/gated.conf.new /tmp/gated.trace
```

This checks the syntax without actually doing any routing, and writes tracing information to `/tmp/gated.trace`. You can then examine the trace for errors before moving the new configuration file onto `/etc/gated.conf`. I recommend that you always do this when you change the configuration, no matter how small the change. You can then have a running `gated` process reload its configuration by saying

```
/etc/rc.d/init.d/gated reload
```

Name Services

From a machine's point of view, routing IP datagrams is central to the operation of the Internet. But humans find it very hard to deal with numeric IP addresses—quite simply, very few people have a good enough memory to be able to remember four three-digit numbers for every host they want to be able to use. The solution to this problem is to provide symbolic names for humans to use, but arrange for these symbolic names to be looked up and translated into numeric addresses whenever a machine must deal with them. So for example, if you want to look at the Web site for Red Hat, it's much easier to remember www.redhat.com as the correct location than 206.132.41.203—especially because this numeric address is liable to change at any time. Systems that provide lookup and translation facilities for symbolic names of this sort are called *name servers*, and this section describes how to operate and use name servers.

Historical Background

In the early days of the Internet, all host name registrations were listed in a centralized official Network Information Center (NIC) host table. Each Internet site needed to update their local copy of this host table whenever it changed. As the Internet grew, this rapidly became unfeasible, so automated solutions were sought. This search led to the creation of the Domain Name Service, the Internet's "native" name service.

Most systems still use a static host table to a limited extent. The information in the table is needed when DNS is not running, such as during system startup or if there is a serious network problem. All hosts should have a static host table containing at least an entry for that host and for `localhost`, and quite possibly for gateways and servers on the network. Very small sites where host information rarely changes might find that a static host table is sufficient, especially if supplemented for Internet host names by an offsite name server made available by the Internet service provider.

The static host table has a very simple format. Comments begin with hash signs (#). Non-comment lines contain fields separated by whitespace. The first field on each line is a numeric IP address, and the second is the usual name of that address. Subsequent fields (if any) specify aliases. Listing 14.6 shows a sample minimal /etc/hosts file, containing entries only for localhost and for the system itself.

LISTING 14.6 A Sample minimal /etc/hosts File

```
# Table of IP addresses and host names

127.0.0.1       localhost
192.168.1.2     radish.example.com radish
```

DNS

The Internet's native name server is called DNS, the Domain Name Service. It uses a distributed database of records that are automatically disseminated to those who need them. If a DNS server receives a query about a host for which it has no information, it passes the request to an authoritative server (that is, a server which is responsible for maintaining accurate information about the domain in question). The server then caches the information it receives from the authoritative server, and uses the cached version to answer equivalent queries in the future.

The DNS uses a hierarchy of hostnames similar to the hierarchy of filenames in the UNIX file system. There is a DNS *root domain* at the top of the hierarchy, served by a group of DNS domain servers called the *root servers*.

Geographic and Organizational Domains

Directly under the root domain are the top-level domains. These fall into two categories, geographic and organizational. Geographic domains exist for each country, and are named with a two-letter code that usually (but not always) corresponds to the ISO-3166 two-letter code. (For example, there is a top-level domain named UK for the United Kingdom, but the ISO-3166 code is GB.) Membership in the organizational domains is based on the type of organization to which the system belongs. The categories are shown in Table 14.3.

TABLE 14.3 Membership of DNS Organizational Domains

Domain	Description
com	Commercial organizations
edu	U.S. educational institutions
gov	U.S. government agencies
mil	U.S. military organizations
net	Network support organizations
int	International governmental or quasi-governmental organizations
org	Other types of organizations, including non-profits

The organizational domains are managed by a company called Internic. You can register a second-level domain by applying to Internic and paying an annual fee. You must also tell Internic the IP addresses of at least two hosts that will be the authoritative name servers for the new domain. When Internic approves the request, it configures its DNS servers to advertise your name servers as authoritative for the new domain. Now when the root servers receive queries for the new domain, the queries are referred to your name servers.

For the geographical domains, allocation of second-level domains is done by a national body. In many geographical domains, a further hierarchical layer is inserted, analogous to the organizational top-level domains. For example, Australia has its own second-level com, net, and edu domains within its top-level au domain.

Once a domain has been allocated to an organization, any subdomains within that domain are entirely at the discretion of the administrator of the domain. Also, note that domains are not tied to networks. A given domain can include subdomains that are in geographically disparate locations.

The domain hierarchy is reflected in domain names. Domain names are written from most specific (a hostname) to least specific (a top-level domain), with each part separated by a dot. The root domain is identified by a single dot.

Name Services on UNIX and Linux Systems

By far the most common DNS server software for UNIX in use at the moment is the Berkeley Internet Name Daemon (BIND), developed by noted programmer Paul Vixie, who was also involved in specifying DNS. Red Hat 6 uses version 8.2 of BIND; the 8.x versions are somewhat different in operation and especially in configuration from the earlier 4.9.x releases.

A new project was recently started to develop an alternative DNS server, named Dents (http://www.dents.org), licensed under the GNU General Public License. Some people consider this particularly important in the face of possible changes in the licensing terms for future versions of BIND, changes that may prevent BIND being classified as Open Source or Free Software. Dents is also designed to be modular, flexible, and secure. However, Dents has not yet been completed, let alone widely deployed, so it is hard to recommend it at the moment.

Not all systems need to run a name server. All that applications need to be able to perform name lookups is a resolver—a library that can send the right queries to a name server. A host that relies on other machines to provide a name server is called a resolver-only system.

For systems that run their own name server, the BIND server runs as a distinct process called named (pronounced "name-dee"). Name servers can be divided into three categories, depending on how they are configured.

- **Master**—The master server for a domain is the server from which all data about that domain is derived. This data is supplied by the administrator. Master servers are authoritative for their domain. Earlier versions of BIND used the term *primary* instead of master.

- **Slave**—Like a master server, a slave server possesses all the information about a domain. The difference is that where a master server gets the data directly from an administrator-supplied file, a slave server gets it from a primary server. Slave servers are also authoritative for their domain. Earlier versions of BIND used the term *secondary* instead of slave.

- **Caching-only**—A caching-only server need not hold all the information about any domain and, in fact, it rarely will. It will cache the results of queries, as do most name servers, but it has no other method of building a domain name database. Caching servers are non-authoritative: their information is second-hand and incomplete, though it is usually accurate.

Many servers will combine elements of one or more of these roles. In particular, the BIND documentation actually refers to master and slave zones rather than servers, where a server may serve any number of zones.

Resolver Library

All UNIX and Linux systems have a resolver library. The resolver has a configuration file, /etc/resolv.conf, which allows you to specify which name servers (if any) it will query. The /etc/resolv.conf may contain the following directives:

- nameserver—There may be up to three nameserver directives, each of which specifies a server to query. The server should be specified as a dotted-quad IP address. Servers after the first are queried if no response is received from earlier ones. If there is no nameserver directive (or if there is no /etc/resolv.conf file), the local host is queried. If you specify nameservers explicitly and you want the local host to be queried, you should give its official IP address rather than the loopback address. A resolver-only configuration will never need a nameserver directive that points to the local host.

- domain—The domain directive defines the default domain name. Queries for names within this domain can use short names relative to the local domain. If no domain directive is given, it is taken from the local hostname, or assumed to be the root domain if the local hostname contains no domain name.

- search—The search directive allows you to specify a series of domains that will be searched when looking up a hostname that does not contain a dot. Up to six domains may be specified, using up to 256 characters. The list defaults to the local domain name. This can generate large amounts of network traffic if the domains are not local.

Listings 14.7 and 14.8 contain sample resolver configurations.

LISTING 14.7 Sample Resolver-Only Configuration

```
# The default domain name
domain example.com
# Two name servers elsewhere on the network
nameserver 192.168.1.1
nameserver 10.0.0.42
```

LISTING 14.8 A Sample Resolver Configuration

```
# The default domain name
domain example.org
# First try this host
nameserver 192.168.1.2
# Next try the other two name servers on the network
nameserver 192.168.1.1
nameserver 10.0.0.42
```

If you do need to run a name server on a Red Hat system (rather than using a resolver-only configuration), you should install the bind and caching-nameserver packages. You can arrange for named to be started at boot time by saying

```
chkconfig named on
```

and you can launch it by saying

```
/etc/rc.d/init.d/named start
```

Configuring BIND

Like `gated`, BIND is a large and complex program, and covering all of its configuration options would take up a chapter of its own. So I will just present an overview of the most important options and some sample configurations, and direct you to the extensive documentation that comes with BIND for reference material.

Configuring BIND can be divided into two areas: the BIND configuration itself, and the zone files that contain the actual name/number mapping. The configuration is normally stored in `/etc/named.conf`. It uses a structured syntax, with statements terminated by semicolons, and braces used for grouping related items.

The first statement in most `/etc/named.conf` files will be the `options` statement, which determines global options for BIND. There may be at most one `options` statement; subsequent ones will generate a warning. The `options` statement takes a brace-delimited list of options, terminated by semicolons. The most important ones are as follows:

- `directory`—This takes a double-quoted string that names a directory to be used as the working directory of the server. Filenames without a leading slash are interpreted to be relative to this directory. The `/var/named` directory is a common choice for this.

- `forwarders`—This takes a brace-delimited list of IP addresses, terminated by semicolons. Each IP address is used as a name server for BIND to forward queries to, rather than trying to find the answer itself. Forwarders can be useful on networks with limited bandwidth to the wider Internet, but a good connection to a better-connected DNS server, such as one provided by an ISP.

- `forward`—This option is meaningless unless there is also a `forwarders` option. It takes a keyword `only` (to indicate that BIND should never try to find the answer itself—this is called a slave configuration) or `first` (to indicate that the forwarders should be checked first, but if that doesn't give the answer, then BIND should look itself).

Almost all `/etc/named.conf` files will also need to contain one or more zone statements, which actually define a zone. BIND zones come in four kinds: master, slave, stub, and hint. (Earlier releases used the terms *primary*, *secondary*, and *cache* instead of master, slave, and hint.) A hint zone specifies an initial set of root name servers. When BIND starts up, it uses the root hints (normally called `/var/named/named.ca` on Red Hat, but `/var/named/named.root` is common on some other systems) to find a root name server and get the most recent list of root name servers. A master zone contains the authoritative data for a zone; this data is stored in a zone file that is read by BIND at startup. A slave zone is a replica of a master zone, updated over the network. You may specify a zone file for a slave zone, to make BIND write a copy of the replica to the file. This will lower startup times for future instances of BIND, and will also help preserve bandwidth. A stub zone is like a slave zone, except that instead of replicating the entire master zone, it replicates only its NS (name server) records.

A zone statement consists of the word `zone`, the double-quoted name of the zone, an optional zone class, and a brace-delimited list of options. Important options for zones include the following:

- `type`—This option is required for all zones. It specifies the type of the zone, and should be followed by one of the words `master`, `slave`, `stub`, or `hint`.

- `file`—This takes a double-quoted filename, which is interpreted relative to the working directory (see the `directory` option in the preceding list). This is the zone file itself. For master and hint zones, this is required; it is optional for slave and stub zones.

- `masters`—This is required for slave and stub zones, and forbidden for master and hint zones. It is followed by a brace-delimited list of numeric IP addresses. The slave will contact each of these addresses to update its copy of the zone.

Listing 14.9 shows a sample configuration for a caching-only name server that attempts to forward requests to servers that are hopefully better connected.

LISTING **14.9** Sample `named.conf` for a Caching-Only Name Server

```
# Set basic options for named
options {
directory "/var/named";
forward first;
forwarders {
10.17.42.1;
10.17.42.2;
};
};

# Hint zone for the root name servers
zone "." {
type hint;
file "named.ca";
};

# Master zone for localhost
zone "localhost" {
type master;
file "named.local";
```

LISTING **14.9**   continued

```
}

# Master reverselookup zone for localhost
zone "127.inaddr.arpa" {
type master;
file "named.revlocal";
}
```

Red Hat provides the `named.ca` and `named.local` files in the caching-nameserver package, but it doesn't provide the `named.rev-local` file, which specifies the reverse mapping for the localhost domain. Listing 14.10 has one that you can use.

LISTING **14.10**   Sample `named.rev-local` **Reverse Mapping**

```
; Zone file for local loopback interface reverse lookups
;
@    IN    SOA    localhost. root.localhost. (
     1            ; Serial
 604800           ; Refresh
  86400           ; Retry
2419200           ; Expire
 604800 )    ; Default TTL
;
@    IN    NS    localhost.
1.0.0    IN    PTR    localhost.
```

This brings me to the subject of zone files, which store the domain database information. Zone files consist of a sequence of Resource Records (RRs) defined in RFC 1033 and others. The standard RR types are shown in Table 14.4.

TABLE **14.4**   Standard Resource Record Types for DNS Zones

Type	*Name*	*Purpose*
SOA	Start of Authority	Indicates the start of a zone's data, and defines parameters that affect the entire zone.
NS	Name Server	Lists the name of a machine that provides name service for a domain.
A	Address	Maps a hostname to an address.
PTR	Pointer	Maps an address to a hostname.
MX	Mail Exchange	Identifies a machine that will accept and relay email for the domain.
CNAME	Canonical Name	Indicates the official name for a nickname.

TABLE **14.4**   continued

Type	Name	Purpose
HINFO	Host Information	Describes a host's hardware and operating system.
WKS	Well-Known Service	Advertises which network services run on a machine.
TXT	Text	Stores arbitrary text strings.

A DNS Resource Record consists of the following items, in order.

- **Name**—This is the name of the host or domain referenced by this RR. It is treated relative to the current domain unless it ends with a dot. It may be omitted, in which case the record applies to the last named domain object. This allows several records to be specified for the same domain with a minimum of repetition.

- **Time-to-live (TTL)**—This is the length of time, in seconds, that the information in this RR should be kept in a remote cache. It is usually left blank, in which case the default TTL is used, as set in the SOA record.

- **Class**—This is usually IN, for Internet.

- **Type**—Identifies the type of RR. Normally one of the standard types listed in the table above.

- **Data**—This is the actual information stored for this record. For example, in an A record, this is the numeric IP address, and in a PTR record, this is the name corresponding to that address.

Network Information Service

The Network Information Service, or NIS, is an administrative database system developed by Sun Microsystems. It was formerly called YP (for Yellow Pages), and even though a conflicting trademark forced it to be renamed, the abbreviation YP is still visible. NIS allows important administrative files to be controlled centrally, and distributed around the local area network automatically.

NIS allows network queries to databases that contain data normally held in standard UNIX files; these databases are called NIS maps. The files for which NIS holds maps include /etc/hosts and /etc/networks. NIS is like DNS in that they both provide a means of overcoming the limitations of a network-wide static host table, but NIS is not an alternative to DNS for Internet hosts. Few systems will therefore use NIS without also using DNS for Internet name services.

14

TCP/IP and
Ethernet

NIS consists of a process `ypserv` running on a server that stores the maps. These maps can then be queried remotely by client systems, which use the `ypbind` program to locate the server.

The NIS server and its clients form a NIS domain, identified by a NIS domain name. On a network using both NIS and DNS, it is important to distinguish NIS domains and DNS domains whenever there is a chance of ambiguity. However, it is recommended practice to use the same name for a NIS domain and the equivalent DNS domain. NIS uses the domain name to create a directory within `/var/yp` to store the maps. So if we have a DNS domain name `example.com`, and we use the same name for the NIS domain, then the directory `/var/yp/example.com` will be used.

Running Red Hat as a NIS Client

It is relatively straightforward to use Red Hat as a NIS client. First, you need to install the relevant packages. These are `ypbind` to provide the client-side daemon, and `yp-tools`, to provide the user-level tools for examining and manipulating the NIS maps.

Once the packages have been installed, you need to specify the NIS domain name. This can be done by editing `/etc/sysconfig/network` to contain a setting like

```
NISDOMAIN="example.com"
```

Usually, `ypbind` can listen to network broadcasts to determine which host is the NIS server, but occasionally this must be configured explicitly. If necessary, you can set the server in `/etc/yp.conf`. Suppose `nismaster.example.com` is the NIS server in the `example.com` domain. Then `/etc/yp.conf` would contain the line

```
ypserver nismaster.example.com
```

Next, you must ensure that `ypbind` is launched at boot time:

```
chkconfig ypbind on
```

Finally, you can launch `ypbind`:

```
/etc/rc.d/init.d/ypbind start
```

These steps can be performed from Linuxconf. Setting `ypbind` to run at boot time is done with the Control Service Activity dialog, as we have seen for other services. There is also a Network Information System (NIS) dialog for configuring the NIS domain and the optional server.

You can check that things are running correctly with `ypwhich` (which tells you which NIS server is serving your client) and `ypcat` (which is the simplest command-line interface for actually obtaining data from the maps over the network.

```
$ ypwhich
nismaster.example.com
$ ypcat hosts ¦ grep nismaster
192.168.1.105   nismaster.example.com nismaster
```

You can run `ypcat -x` to find out what maps are available on the server.

Running Red Hat as a NIS Server

The NIS server is one of the few components of Red Hat 6 for which Linuxconf has no configuration modules, so it cannot be configured with Linuxconf. However, the procedure is essentially the same under Red Hat as it is under other systems.

The first step is to ensure that the system is running shadow passwords and shadow group passwords. If necessary, you can run `pwconv` to convert plain-text passwords into shadow passwords, and `grpconv` to do the same for the `/etc/group` file, though you should almost always enable shadow passwords when you install the operating system on a machine. You also need to make sure that `/etc/networks` and `/etc/netgroup` files exist.

Secondly, the `ypserv` package must be installed. This provides the `ypserv` daemon, and also the `yppasswdd` daemon that allows users on NIS clients to change their password on the server.

Third, you should configure the server to act as a client as well, in the manner described above.

The next step is to actually build the NIS maps. Go to the `/var/yp` directory, and run `make`:

```
cd /var/yp
make
```

This creates a directory for the NIS domain (`example.com` in our case) and populates it with the map files. You will need to perform this step on the server every time the data to be served by the map files changes.

The final step is to arrange for the server to be started at boot time and start it now, as usual.

```
chkconfig ypserv on
chkconfig yppasswdd on
/etc/rc.d/init.d/ypserv start
/etc/rc.d/init.d/yppasswdd start
```

Configuring Name Lookup

Because most systems using NIS will also need to run DNS, there must be some ordering applied to searching possible sources of information when looking up names. The Name Service Switch file, `/etc/nsswitch.conf`, is used to define this ordering. Despite its name,

14

TCP/IP and
Ethernet

all of the NIS databases are covered by this file. Listing 14.11 contains a sample fragment from an `nsswitch.conf` file.

LISTING 14.11   A Sample `/etc/nsswitch.conf` Fragment

```
hosts:     nis dns files
networks:  nis [NOTFOUND=return] files
```

The first entry says that a hostname lookup is first passed to NIS; if the NIS server is unable to find a match, the lookup is then passed to DNS, and finally the `/etc/hosts` file is used as a last resort. The second entry says that network names are looked up with NIS. The `[NOTFOUND=return]` indicates a fine-grained control of the lookup procedure. In this case, if the lookup worked correctly (that is, NIS is up and running) but the name wasn't found (`NOTFOUND`), then the lookup should return a failure indication immediately (`=return`). This means that the `/etc/networks` file will only be examined if NIS is down.

Summary

In this chapter, you have seen that networking is crucial to modern computer facilities, and that TCP/IP is the most widely deployed networking system. TCP/IP allows the use of a variety of physical media types, of which one of the most common is Ethernet. Switches can ease the burden on congested Ethernet networks, and can also reduce some security vulnerabilities.

TCP/IP uses 32-bit IP addresses to distinguish systems; the addresses have a variable-length network part and host part. A process called *routing* enables data to be sent to the correct address. Statically configured routing is adequate for simple networks, but large installations with redundant routes need dynamic routing. UNIX and Linux systems use a routing table to control routing. The `routed` and `gated` daemons perform dynamic routing by manipulating this routing table.

The numeric addresses used by TCP/IP are inconvenient for humans. Programs called *name servers* can translate symbolic, easily remembered names into numeric addresses. BIND (the `named` daemon) is an Internet Domain Name Server. NIS provides site-wide name lookup services, but cannot do the same for Internet hosts.

CHAPTER 15

Sharing Resources (Print and File Services)

IN THIS CHAPTER

- Networking Is About Sharing *410*
- Setting Up Print Queues *411*
- Network File Services *418*
- The Automount Daemon and Autofs *427*

Networking Is About Sharing

The primary difference between networked computers and standalone systems is that the network provides the opportunity to share common resources between all of the computers connected to it. This allows you to reduce the cost of the personal workstation by having smaller disk space requirements, sharing expensive resources such as laser printers, and reducing administrative costs by allowing application sharing and providing simple ways for users to interact with each other. This chapter looks at a couple of specific resource-sharing areas, printers, and files. It first provides an overview of the ways in which Linux and UNIX systems can share resources and also how Linux can share with other operating systems. Then it looks at some of the specifics of sharing printer and file resources.

Sharing with Linux/UNIX Hosts

Linux, just like UNIX, has long had the ability to share resources with like systems, which is one of the strengths of these operating systems. Network printers are supported under Linux by using either the Berkeley line printer daemon, `lpd`, which is included with Red Hat Linux, or with the newer and more feature-filled LPRng suite, which you can install yourself. The LPRng suite is not described here; however, if you are interested in finding out about its features, you can visit the LPRng home page at `http://www.astart.com/lprng/LPRng.html`. In addition, Linux supports file sharing with other Linux and UNIX systems via the traditional network filesystem, NFS, or with newer distributed filesystems, such as Coda and AFS. Both NFS and Coda support are included in the Linux kernel as shipped by Red Hat. The AFS system is a commercial product available for your Linux system from Transarc at `http://www.transarc.com/`.

Sharing with Other Operating Systems

One of the strengths of Linux is that it can share resources not only with other Linux and UNIX systems, but also with other operating systems including Windows, NetWare, and MacOS. This sharing can take one of two forms. The first is through packages for these other operating systems that implement the sharing protocols native to Linux. These packages allow the foreign operating systems to access NFS filesystems and to access print queues by providing a client to the printer daemons running on the Linux systems. The alternative method is for Linux to implement the protocols used by the other operating systems. An example of this is using Samba to integrate your Linux systems into a Windows network. This topic is covered in more detail in Chapter 17, "Integrating with Windows NT Networks." Another example of this is Linux emulation of a NetWare or AppleTalk server, which is also covered in Chapter 17.

Setting Up Print Queues

With the cost of laser printers, it would be a very expensive proposition to equip every workstation on a network with its own printer. This is especially true when you consider the cost of supplies, or if you have a requirement to provide color printing. It makes much more sense to share these printing resources, so that instead of spending a fortune on individual printers, you can allocate less money and still get more capabilities from your print resources.

Consider the following example. You have a network consisting of four servers and 25 user workstations. Three of the workstations are used by the marketing department, which requires color capabilities to create marketing materials. Two of the workstations are used by technical writers who need PostScript laser quality to print the masters for product manuals. The remaining 20 have normal printing requirements, ranging from laser quality to simple line printers. To satisfy these requirements, you need three color laser printers, two PostScript laser printers, and 24 standard printers for the remaining workstations and servers. At current prices, this could cost you almost twenty thousand dollars for just the printers. Fortunately, since you can share printer resources, you can reduce the requirements significantly. Sharing allows you to use one color laser for the marketing department, one high-speed PostScript printer for the technical writers, and a couple of standard printers for a cost of about five thousand dollars, which is 25% of the total if printers were not sharable. In addition, the cost of maintenance is greatly reduced as is the cost of supplies.

This section looks at the steps required to set up a printer on a local machine, how access is granted to others on the network, and how the systems without printers are configured so that they can print across the network.

Setting Up a Local Printer

Setting up a printer on your Red Hat Linux system is usually quite easy, provided you have a printer from a popular manufacturer that has a driver for GhostScript. GhostScript is a software package that implements the PostScript language that includes drivers for many popular printers. The list of available printer drivers included with your Red Hat Linux 6.0 installation is included in Table 15.1.

TABLE **15.1**   Printers Supported by GhostScript

GhostScript Driver	Printer Name
djet500	HP DeskJet 500
cdj500	HP DeskJet 400/500C/520/540C
cdj550	HP DeskJet 550C/560C/6xxC series

TABLE 15.1 continued

GhostScript Driver	Printer Name
pj	HP PaintJet
pjxl	HP PaintJet XL
pjxl300	HP PaintJet XL300 and DeskJet 1200C
declj250	DEC LJ250 (Alt)
dnj650c	HP DesignJet 650C
lj4dith	HP LaserJet 4—dithered
bjc600	Canon BJC-600 and BJC-4000
deskjet	HP DeskJet/DeskJet Plus
laserjet	HP LaserJet
laserjetplus	HP LaserJet Plus
ljet2p	HP LaserJet IId/IIp/III* with TIFF compression
ljet3	HP LaserJet III* with Delta Row Compression
ljet3d	HP LaserJet III* with duplex capability
ljet4	HP LaserJet 4/5/6 series
st800	Epson Stylus 800 & ESC/P 2 printers
ap3250	Epson AP3250 & ESC/P 2 printers
jetp3852	IBM 3853 JetPrinter
r4081	Ricoh 4081 laser printer
t4693d2	Tek 4693d color printer, 2-bit mode
t4693d4	Tek 4693d color printer, 4-bit mode
t4693d8	Tek 4693d color printer, 8-bit mode
m8510	C.Itoh M8510
appledmp	Apple Dot Matrix
iwlo	Apple Imagewriter, low-resolution
iwhi	Apple Imagewriter, high-resolution
iwlq	Apple Imagewriter, letter quality
bj10e	Canon BJ-10e
bj200	Canon BJ-100/200/210/240
cp50	Mitsubishi CP50
epsonc	Epson Color Dot Matrix, 9 pin
epsonc	Epson Color Dot Matrix, 24 pin
epson	Epson Dot Matrix, 9 pin
epson	Epson Dot Matrix, 24 pin
eps9mid	Epson Dot Matrix, 9 pin, med-res
eps9high	Epson Dot Matrix, 9 pin, hi-res
imagen	Imagen ImPress
lbp8	Canon LBP-8II
lips3	Canon LIPS III

TABLE 15.1 continued

GhostScript Driver	Printer Name
ln03	DEC LN03
la50	DEC LA50 dot matrix
la70	DEC LA70 dot matrix
la75	DEC LA75 dot matrix
la75plus	DEC LA75 Plus dot matrix
necp6	NEC P6/P6+/P60
oki182	Okidata Microline 182
lj250	DEC LJ250
sj48	StarJet 48
tek4696	Tektronics 4695/4696 inkjet plotter
xes	Xerox XES printers
POSTSCRIPT	PostScript printer
TEXT	Text-only printer
uniprint	Canon BJC-610 (UP)
uniprint	HP DeskJet 550C (UP)
uniprint	NEC Prinwriter 2X (UP)
uniprint	Epson Stylus Color (UP)

Assuming your printer is in the preceding list or is compatible with one of them, you can use the printtool utility to create the appropriate printcap entry and the configuration files used by the Red Hat print filter system. The printtool is normally invoked from the control-panel and includes dialogs that allow you to specify whether the printer is local or a network printer, the type of printer, and various other options. Figure 15.1 is a screen shot of the printtool in action, and Figure 15.2 is a screen shot of the print filter dialog, which allows you to select from a list of printers.

FIGURE 15.1

The printtool dialog.

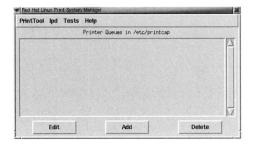

FIGURE 15.2

The print filter dialog.

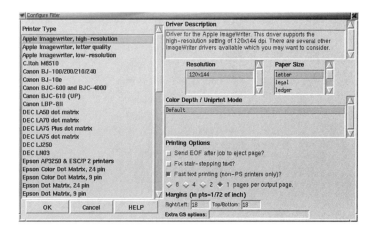

Once you have selected the appropriate printer and saved your entry, you can test your printer by selecting the test option from the printtool menu. This should print a test page on your printer that will show if your configuration is correct. Assuming that it is, you can examine the files you created by looking first at /etc/printcap. This file should contain an entry that looks something like this:

```
#
# Please don't edit this file directly unless you know what you are doing!
# Be warned that the control-panel printtool requires a very strict format!
# Look at the printcap(5) man page for more info.
#
# This file can be edited with the printtool in the control-panel.


##PRINTTOOL3## LOCAL bjc600 360x360 letter {} BJC600 24 {}
lp0:\
    :sd=/var/spool/lpd/lp0:\
    :mx#0:\
    :sh:\
    :lp=/dev/lp0:\
    :if=/var/spool/lpd/lp0/filter:
```

This entry specifies the name of the print queue, lp0, followed by other information, including the spool directory (sd), the printer device (lp), and the input filter (if). The format of the printcap file is documented in the manual pages.

In addition to the printcap entry, a number of other files are created by the printtool. The first of these is the input filter, which is located in the spool directory and is named filter. This filter is a shell script that determines the type of file being printed, converts it to PostScript and then uses the GhostScript interpreter and the specified driver to print to the defined printer device. The other files created are textonly.cfg, general.cfg, and postscript.cfg. These files contain variable definitions used by the filter script to alter the invocation of the various utilities used to convert the input into PostScript. Some of the utilities used by the filter script include

- dvips—Converts the output of TeX to PostScript

- grog—Converts nroff output to PostScript

- pnmtops—Converts pnm graphics to PostScript

- mpage—Converts ASCII to PostScript

In addition, there are several utilities for converting from other graphics formats to pnm or portable anymap format, which can then be transformed to PostScript. Here are the contents of those files associated with the printer defined in the printcap entry:

```
[tschenk@nomad lp0]$ cat general.cfg
#
# General config options for printing on this queue
# Generated by PRINTTOOL, do not modify.
#
export DESIRED_TO=ps
export PAPERSIZE=letter
export PRINTER_TYPE=LOCAL
export ASCII_TO_PS=NO

[tschenk@nomad lp0]$ cat postscript.cfg
#
# configuration related to postscript printing
# generated automatically by PRINTTOOL
# manual changes to this file may be lost
#
GSDEVICE=bjc600
RESOLUTION=360x360
COLOR=-dBitsPerPixel=24
PAPERSIZE=letter
EXTRA_GS_OPTIONS=""
REVERSE_ORDER=
PS_SEND_EOF=NO
```

```
#
# following is related to printing multiple pages per output page
#
NUP=1
RTLFTMAR=18
TOPBOTMAR=18


[tschenk@nomad lp0]$ cat textonly.cfg
#
# text-only printing options for printing on this queue
# Generated by PRINTTOOL, do not modify.
#
TEXTONLYOPTIONS=
CRLFTRANS=
TEXT_SEND_EOF=NO
```

There are, of course, alternatives to using the printtool approach to configuring printers. One such alternative would be to create the printcap entry by hand and manually create a filter script that calls your printer driver. However, unless your printer is not supported by one of the drivers that comes with Red Hat, the printtool approach is easier.

Granting Access to Others

Having defined your printer, you are now ready to grant others the right to access it via the network. This is accomplished in one of two ways. The first method is via entries in the /etc/hosts.equiv file. This file contains hostnames of the systems that are allowed to access services on the local system. This file is not only used to grant access to the local line printer daemon, so care should be taken if you decide to use this method. In fact, most security experts recommend that this method not be used at all because it is not printer specific.

The alternative method for granting access to the local line printer daemon is by making entries in the /etc/hosts.lpd file. This file is specific to the printing system and is therefore not considered the same security risk as the /etc/hosts.equiv file. Entries in this file consist of machine names that may access the line printer daemon on the local host.

Setting Up a Remote Printer

Now that you have created the print queue on the server, and created the /etc/hosts.equiv or /etc/hosts.lpd entry allowing you to access it from the client host, you can now finish up by defining the remote printer on the client. A remote printer is one that is not physically connected to your computer, but that is accessible via a network connection.

The first step in doing this is the same as when creating a local printer queue, which is running the printtool utility. The difference this time will be that you specify a remote printer instead of a local one. That is all there is to it. In fact, if you look at the printcap entry for the remote printer defined earlier, you will see little difference. Here is that entry:

```
 /etc/printcap


#
# Please don't edit this file directly unless you know what you are doing!
# Be warned that the control-panel printtool requires a very strict format!
# Look at the printcap(5) man page for more info.
#
# This file can be edited with the printtool in the control-panel.


##PRINTTOOL3## REMOTE bjc600 360x360 letter {} BJC600 24 0
lp:\
     :sd=/var/spool/lpd/lp:\
     :mx#0:\
     :sh:\
     :rm=quicksilver:\
     :rp=lp0:\
     :if=/var/spool/lpd/lp/filter:
```

As you will notice, most of the entries are exactly the same for this remote printer as they were for the local printer, with the following exceptions. First, there is an additional entry that is used to specify the host that the line printer daemon is running. This is the rm= entry and in this example, the value is quicksilver, which is the name of a host on my network. Secondly, the lp= entry from the local print queue example is replaced by an entry that specifies the name of the print queue on the remote system (rp=lp0).

Provided that the entry in the remote server's hosts.lpd file is correct and that the local printcap file accurately defines the remote printer, you should be able to print to the printer attached to the server just as easily from the client host as from the server itself. If you are using the printtool, you can test your new printer definition by printing a test page by selecting that option from the printtool menu.

As you can see, setting up printing on a Red Hat Linux system is quite simple if you use the tools provided. Problems usually arise from attempts to perform this setup by manual manipulation of the various files, like /etc/printcap and the filter scripts. If you cannot use the default printer system, you should refer to the documentation that comes with your printing software. Now we are ready to move on to the other common service provided by networks, file services.

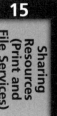

15

Sharing Resources (Print and File Services)

Network File Services

Next to printers, the most commonly shared resources on a network are filesystems and the standard method for doing this on Linux systems is with NFS. In the earlier releases of Linux, NFS was implemented using a daemon that ran in user space. This design worked but it was inefficient and prone to errors, which gained Linux the reputation of being a poor choice for an NFS server. This inefficiency led developers to look for a better solution and during the development phase of the 2.1 kernel, a team of programmers including Olaf Kirch, H.J. Lu, Rick Sladkey, Linus, and many others, implemented kernel space NFS. There were naturally a number of bumps along the way, but this implementation is changing the way that people look at NFS under Linux. The kernel space NFS support is dramatically better than the user space daemon. It is more efficient and more compliant with the NFS specification. Along with this NFS implementation, for the first time a locking daemon was implemented, which solved the biggest drawback to using Linux as an NFS server. With the 2.2 kernel, such as the one that comes with Red Hat Linux 6, Linux NFS is much improved and continues to improve all the time.

This section looks at what is required to set up Linux as an NFS server, examines the /etc/exports file, and looks at how simple it is to use Linux as an NFS client. Finally, the end of this section looks at a couple of other network filesystems, or more correctly, distributed filesystems (AFS and Coda) that are available for Linux and compares and contrasts their features with those of NFS.

NFS Server Configuration

When deciding to set up an NFS server under Linux, the first decision is whether to use the older user space NFS implementation or to use the kernel NFS support. By default, Red Hat will use the newer kernel space NFS daemon. However, if you are moving from an older version of Linux, you can continue to use the user space NFS implementation. The drawback to not using the kernel space NFS is that you will not have lockd support. If you choose to use the user space NFS method, you can refer to the NFS-Howto from the Linux Documentation Project, which has yet to be updated to cover the new NFS implementation.

Installing NFS Related Software

Assuming that you selected NFS server support during the installation of your Red Hat server, you will not have to install any software in order to set up an NFS server. But if you didn't, you will need to install the following RPM packages in order to get started:

- knfsd

- knfsd-clients

- portmap

Once these packages are installed, you will need to ensure that your kernel includes support for networking and the NFS filesystem type. There are two options associated with running the kernel space NFS server, the first being the CONFIG_NFSD. This option is not required if you are just running the user space NFS daemon, but it is an absolute must if you want to use the kernel NFS daemon support. An additional option that you may choose to set is to emulate the behavior of the Sun NFS server. This option is CONFIG_NFSD_SUN and you may set it or not depending on your requirements. An explanation of this option is available via the Help option when configuring the kernel. Once you have made the appropriate kernel configuration choices, you must rebuild and install your new kernel. Kernel configuration and building is discussed in Chapter 35, "Customizing the Linux Kernel," if you need help with this. Naturally, a new kernel means a reboot in order to activate it.

Finalizing the Setup of NFS

Now that you have the kernel configured, you are ready to proceed with the remaining steps in setting up your NFS server. The first of these steps is to decide which filesystems you want to share via the network. This may sound easy enough, but you must also make several decisions as to what capabilities users on other systems will have when accessing shared filesystems. These decisions include the following:

- Do client systems require write access to the filesystem?

- Should users be able to run setuid programs that reside on the filesystem?

- Should users be able to run any programs that reside on the shared filesystem?

- Should the root user on client systems have root privileges when accessing the filesystem?

The answers to these questions are very important because they have a significant impact on the security of your systems. This is because the NFS filesystem is inherently a security risk. Failure to consider these issues may mean that you have inadvertently opened security holes in your system. Let's take a look at a couple of examples and how we would answer these questions for each of them.

> **Note**
>
> You may be asking why I state that NFS is inherently a security risk. There are a number of reasons for this, but the primary one is that no authentication is required or supported for client interaction with the NFS server. This means that if you export a filesystem to clients on your network and do not restrict access to a specific set of systems, any system on the network with an NFS client can access the files contained on the filesystem. This is in contrast to other network filesystems such as AFS, which uses Kerberos to authenticate users before granting access.

Sharing the `/home` Filesystem

The first filesystem we want to share is the `/home` filesystem. Sharing the `/home` filesystem allows users to access their personal files from all of the machines on the network, which is a desirable feature of most networks. The answer to the first question as to whether client systems require write access to the filesystem is obviously yes because a home directory for a user without it would not be very useful. The answer to the next question should also be a no-brainer. The `/home` filesystem is an unsafe place from which to run setuid binaries, especially with the proliferation of email attachment trojans and other binaries from the Internet of unknown origin. This brings us to the third question. This question is less clear cut and is somewhat dependent on your user base. If all of your users are non-technical, you may be able to get away with not allowing the execution of programs residing on the `/home` filesystem. However, if you have a more sophisticated user base, they will invariably have favorite scripts and programs that they want to run from a personal binary directory. The final question is whether the root user on client machines should have root privileges when accessing the `/home` filesystem. The answer to this question usually depends on the role of the client system. For example, if the client system is a systems administrator's workstation, you may want to allow root on that system to equate to root on the NFS server system. If, on the other hand, the client system is used by the receptionist, you probably do not want root on this client to have root privileges on the mounted filesystem.

Sharing the `/usr/local` Filesystem

Here's a look now at another filesystem that you might want to share on the network, `/usr/local`. Unlike the `/home` directory, in which the client systems would need read and write access to the filesystem, only a limited number of systems will need this type of access in this case. The default option is for clients to mount it read-only. Because this is the case, and because the filesystem is likely to contain a significant number of binaries installed by the systems administrator, you can more safely install setuid binaries in this filesystem and the option to execute binaries is a must. The final question is answered just as before, with a limited number of client systems allowed to access the mounted filesystem with root privileges and the majority not.

The `/etc/exports` File

The next step in configuring your NFS server is to set up the `/etc/exports` file. This file defines a number of things, the first being the filesystems to make available to clients on the network. In addition to this, entries in this file define the clients that may access these shared filesystems and the type of access allowed from these clients.

To better understand the format of this file, create entries for the `/home` and `/usr/local` filesystems as previously discussed. For purposes of this example, assume that there are four clients who require access to these filesystems: gold, silver, and platinum, which are regular workstations used by non-technical users, and titanium, which is the systems administrator's workstation. Here are the entries I would make in the `/etc/exports` file for these two filesystems:

`/etc/exports`

```
/home        (rw,root_squash)  titanium(rw,no_root_squash)
/usr/local   (ro,root_squash)  titanium(rw,no_root_squash)
```

As you can see, the format is quite simple. The line containing `/home` translates to `/home` is exported to everyone (the default since no host was specified) with read-write capability, setuid binaries disallowed, and root mapped to user nobody when the client is accessing the `/home` filesystem. It is also exported to the workstation `titanium` with the same options, with the exception that root on `titanium` retains root privileges when accessing the `/home` filesystem. The next line, which defines `/usr/local` as an exported filesystem, is exported read-only to everyone and root is mapped to nobody for all systems on the network with the exception of `titanium`, which is allowed read-write access and root equivalency.

Setting Options for an Exported Filesystem

The next question that you should be asking is what options may be set on an exported filesystem that can be specified in the `/etc/exports` file. The most commonly used options and their meanings are described in Table 15.2

TABLE 15.2 /etc/exports Options

Option	Description
ro	Allows read-only access to the filesystem.
rw	Allows read-write access to the filesystem.
noaccess	Disallows access to a particular branch of an exported tree.
secure	Requires that requests originate on a secure port (one in the < 1024) range. This is the default. To disable this option, specify insecure.
map_daemon	Maps differing ids between client and server systems by using the ugidd mapping daemon.
map_static=file	Maps differing ids between client and server systems by using a text file specified as an option argument.
map_nis=nisdomain	Maps differing ids between client and server systems by doing NIS lookups.
no_root_squash	Allows root on the client system access to the filesystem with root privileges. Default is root_squash.
all_squash	Maps all ids to the anonymous user. This is opposite of the default action.
anonuid=uid	The id that user accounts are mapped to if either the root_squash or all_squash options are specified. The default is user nobody (65534).
anongid=gid	The group id that user accounts are mapped to if either the root_squash or all_squash options are set. The default is group nogroup (65534).

Now that you have an example of the format of the /etc/exports file and have a list of the available options, we can look at the syntax rules for the remainder of the file. Each entry of the file consists of three parts: the host specification, the filesystem specification, and the options list. The host specification can take one of several forms. The first form is a single hostname. This is fine for exceptions to general rules, but can become quite tedious if you need to specify every host of a large network. Another method of specifying hosts is to use NIS network group specification, given in the form @group. In this case, the host part of netgroup members is extracted and added to the access list, unless the host part consists of a single hyphen. This form can save you a lot of typing if you are running NIS. The next form is the wildcard form, in which you could specify an entire domain using an entry such as *.dejanews.com to specify all hosts in the dejanews.com domain consisting of the form host.dejanews.com. Please note that this will not include hosts in the form host.subdomain.dejanews.com. Yet another form that is accepted by the exports file is the IP network form, in which you can specify an IP/netmask pair to grant access to all systems matching that specification; for example, 192.168.50.0/255.255.255.0 to match all addresses on the class C network 192.168.50.0. These several forms are shown in the following example `/etc/exports` file:

```
/etc/exports


#
# /etc/exports
#
/home     @workstations(rw) @admins(rw,no_root_squash)
/opt    *.dejanews.com(ro) admin(rw,no_root_squash)
/opt/private (noaccess)
/vol/00    192.168.50.0/255.255.255.0(rw) 10.16.0.0/255.255.0.0(rw)
```

Now that you have ensured that the appropriate network daemons have been installed, decided which filesystem to export and with what options, and have constructed the `/etc/exports` file, you are ready to actually make the filesystems available on the network. This can be done with the `exportfs` command. This command has just a few options, as defined in Table 15.3.

TABLE 15.3 `exportfs` Options

Option	Description
`-a`	Exports or unexports all directories.
`-o options`	Specifies a list of export options like those in the `/etc/exports` file.
`-r`	Re-exports all directories and synchronizes `/etc/exports` with `/var/lib/nfs/xtab`.
`-u`	Unexports one or more directories.
`-v`	Verbose flag.

This command is new to Linux and was first included with the kernel NFS daemon implementation. Prior to this, filesystems were exported or re-exported by manually killing off and restarting the mount daemon and nfs daemon, such as happens when you run the `/etc/rc.d/init.d/nfs` script with the restart option. If you want, you can still do this, but using the `exportfs` command is much easier and less disruptive to attached clients, since it does not stop the NFS daemons like the script does. Here is an example showing the transition from a server with an exports file to a Linux NFS server:

```
[root@quicksilver /etc]# showmount -e
Export list for quicksilver.alchemy.net:

[root@quicksilver /etc]# cat /etc/exports
/mnt/cdrom 192.168.50.0/255.255.255.0(ro,root_squash)
/home    wizard(rw,no_root_squash)
/usr/local    *.alchemy.net(ro,root_squash)
```

15

Sharing Resources (Print and File Services)

```
[root@quicksilver /etc]# exportfs -a

[root@quicksilver /etc]# showmount -e
Export list for quicksilver.alchemy.net:
/usr/local *.alchemy.net
/mnt/cdrom 192.168.50.0/255.255.255.0
/home      wizard.alchemy.net
```

As you can see, the server quicksilver is now exporting the filesystems /mnt/cdrom,
/home, and /usr/local. The following section looks at setting up an NFS client system.

NFS Client Configuration

Having set up the server, you are now ready to look at what is required to set up a client to
the NFS server. This is actually quite easy. The first thing that you must do is to verify that
you have support for NFS built in to your kernel. This can be accomplished by examining
the /proc/filesystems file and finding an entry for NFS or by verifying the existence of
the nfs.o module in the modules directory for your kernel. Assuming that you have
included support for the NFS filesystem type in your kernel, you must do three things in
order to access a filesystem shared via NFS. These things are

- Ensure that you have access to the resource and request it if you do not.

- Modify the /etc/fstab file to include the information about the filesystems you
  want to mount.

- Create the appropriate mount points and mount the filesystems.

You can ensure that you have access to the resource using the same command used to
verify that the filesystems were exported in the first place—showmount. The difference this
time is that you will be passing the name of the NFS server as an argument to the
showmount command. This will look something like this:

```
[root@wizard /etc]# showmount -e quicksilver
Export list for quicksilver.alchemy.net:
/usr/local *.alchemy.net
/mnt/cdrom 192.168.50.0/255.255.255.0
/home      wizard.alchemy.net
```

From the showmount output, you can see that the client machine you are setting up,
wizard, which has an IP address of 192.168.50.20 and is part of the alchemy.net domain,
should be able to access all of the exported filesystems from quicksilver. That being the
case, you can now proceed to step two. If this had not been the case, you would have
requested access from the administrator of quicksilver, or if you administer it yourself,

simply modify the /etc/exports file on quicksilver to add wizard and re-export all of the filesystems with the command

```
exportfs -r -a
```

Step two is to modify your /etc/fstab file on wizard. The decisions you made earlier on what characteristics the mounted filesystem should have again come into play here, specifically the question regarding setuid binaries and execution of programs. The answers to these questions are used when setting the options field in the /etc/fstab file. Some of the most common options applicable to NFS filesystems are shown in Table 15.4.

TABLE 15.4 NFS mount **Options**

Options	Description
bg	If an initial attempt at mounting an NFS filesystem fails, retries in the background.
fg	If an initial attempt at mounting an NFS filesystem fails, continues to retry in the foreground. (default)
soft	A major timeout on an NFS operation results in an I/O error being returned to the application.
hard	A major timeout results in continuous retries.
rsize=n	Sets the number of bytes for NFS read operations. The default is 1024.
wsize=n	Sets the number of bytes for NFS write operations. The default is 1024.
intr	Allows file operations to be interrupted by signals. This is not the default.
nosuid	Does not allow setuid or setgid bits to take effect for binaries located on the filesystem.
noexec	Does not allow the execution of programs or scripts on the mounted filesystem.

To continue with the example, you will modify the /etc/fstab file on wizard and mount the /home and /usr/local filesystems. The /home filesystem will be mounted read-write, with setuid and setgid binaries disallowed, and root on the client system mapped to root on the server. The /usr/local filesystem will be mounted read-write, with root on the client system mapped to root on the server. These options allow wizard to act as an administrative client for these filesystems. If you wanted to make wizard a simple client, you would remove the no_root_squash options from the mount options for /home and the no_root_squash and read-write options from the mount options for /usr/local. To implement this, here are the entries from /etc/fstab for these two filesystems:

15

Sharing Resources (Print and File Services)

```
/etc/fstab
```

```
quicksilver:/home       /home      nfs bg,hard,intr,nosuid,rw,no_root_squash 1 0
quicksilver:/usr/local /usr/local nfs bg,hard,intr,rw,no_root_squash       1 0
```

As you can see, these entries differ from a normal entry in that instead of specifying a device file where the filesystem resides, you specify the server, followed by a colon and the directory that is exported. Other than this, the only other differences are the specified type of nfs, and the mount options, which for local filesystems are usually set to the keyword defaults.

Having created these entries, you must now create the directories to serve as mount points for the network filesystems. The final step is to actually mount the filesystems. This is performed by issuing the mount command as in the startup script, /etc/rc.d/init.d/ netfs. This mount command is

```
mount -a -t nfs
```

This mount command says to mount all filesystems described in the /etc/fstab file with a filesystem type of nfs.

AFS and Coda

In addition to the NFS network filesystem, there are alternatives for sharing filesystems under Linux. Two of these alternatives are AFS, a commercial filesystem from Transarc, and Coda, a freely available filesystem that supports many of the features of AFS. Both of these are distributed filesystems that differ significantly from NFS, but that share with NFS the goal of sharing data across networks.

AFS was originally developed as part of the Andrew project at MIT and was later commercialized by Transarc. Information regarding AFS for Linux is available from http://www.umlug.umd.edu/linuxafs, which is the home of the Linux AFS FAQ. This FAQ explains the status of the Linux port of AFS, discusses the terms under which you may use the Linux client, provides information on setting it up, and provides troubleshooting tips. In addition, there is a mailing list dedicated to AFS on Linux. To subscribe to this mailing list, you can issue the following command:

```
echo "subscribe linux-afs" ¦ mail linux-afs-request@mit.edu
```

The Coda filesystem, on the other hand, is a freely available distributed filesystem. Coda was developed to solve many of the same problems as AFS, and since the 2.1 kernel development tree, Linux has contained support for it. Some of the features of the Coda filesystem include support for replication between servers and disconnected operation. Details about Coda can be obtained on the web at http://www.coda.org/, including the

Coda Howto, which covers everything you need to set up Coda on your Linux system. Unfortunately, Coda is not quite ready for prime time and it is not recommended for use in production environments. Its primary use at this time is to test out the available features and improve them through testing.

Now that we have covered some of the distributed filesystem options available for Linux, let's take a look at ways to make accessing them from client systems easier.

The Automount Daemon and Autofs

One of the features of modern UNIX systems is support for the automatic mounting of filesystems as the result of attempts to access them. This capability is available in two different forms for Linux systems—through use of the BSD automounter or through use of the Linux autofs. This section takes a look at setting up both of these systems and comparing the features of each, starting with the older of the two, the BSD automount daemon.

The BSD Automount Daemon

If you have never used the automount daemon before, you may wonder what it is and why you might want to implement it on your network. In a large network environment, there are often many filesystems that need to be shared among the systems on the network. In addition, some of these filesystems are not needed all of the time or the system from which the filesystem is served is not available all of the time. To help remedy this situation, the automount daemon, or amd, was implemented to provide a mechanism by which filesystems could be mounted when someone tries to access them and unmounted when the connection becomes idle. This is a major advantage of using amd because it reduces overhead and increases performance. In addition to providing this capability for NFS filesystems, amd can also be used to automatically mount and unmount filesystems on removable media devices, such as floppies or CD-ROM drives.

Configuring the Automount Daemon

Now that you have an understanding of what the automount daemon does, let's take a look at how to configure and use it. The first step in setting up the automount daemon is to make sure that the filesystems that you want to have access to are properly exported. This is done using the procedure for exporting filesystems discussed earlier in this chapter in the section on NFS server configuration. Again, we'll use the example we have used throughout the chapter and verify that the filesystems are exported using the showmount command.

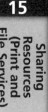

```
[tschenk@wizard chapter15]$ showmount -e quicksilver
Export list for quicksilver:
/usr/local *.alchemy.net
/mnt/cdrom 192.168.50.0/255.255.255.0
/home      wizard.alchemy.net
```

The next step is to make sure that the automount daemon software is installed. The package name for your Red Hat system is am-utils, which you must install if it is not already installed. A quick method to do this is to use the rpm command: `rpm -q am-utils`, which will return the package name if it is installed or a message indicating that it is not installed. If it is not installed, you must install it from your installation media or from a Red Hat ftp site.

Now that you have ensured that the automount daemon is installed, you must configure it. Configuration information for the automount daemon is contained in the file `/etc/amd.conf`. This is a line-oriented configuration file in which each line is a configuration parameter, a comment, or a section heading with no provisions for line continuation. Here's a look at the default `amd.conf` that comes with Red Hat:

```
/etc/amd.conf
```

```
/defaults fs:=${autodir}/${rhost}/root/${rfs};opts:=nosuid,nodev
*         rhost:=${key};type:=host;rfs:=/
```

This `amd.conf` file is quite simplistic, and allows you to automount any exported filesystem to which you have permissions by changing directory to `/net/<hostname>/exported_filesystem`. For example, given the mount points exported from `quicksilver` as shown earlier by the `showmount` command, you can access the files in `/usr/local` on `quicksilver` by simply accessing `/net/quicksilver/usr/local`. For example, if the `afio` command was installed in `/usr/local/bin` on `quicksilver`, you could run it from `wizard` by invoking the command as `/net/quicksilver/usr/local/bin/afio`. This mount would remain as long as the filesystem was being accessed and would be unmounted after some period of inactivity or until you specifically caused an unmount using the `amq` command. Having seen this simplistic `amd.conf` file, here's a more complicated one:

```
/etc/amd.conf
```

```
# Set the default mount options is not overridden by another entry.
# This entry also specifies the default path on the local machine to
# access in order to mount the remote filesystem.
```

```
/defaults    fs:=${autodir}/${rhost}/root/${rfs};opts:=nosuid,nodev

# This entry is for manual pages.  All manual pages for all architectures
# are stored on a file server, dumptruck, which stores them in a platform
# specific directory under /usr/share.

man             arch==pa-risc;fs:=/usr/share/man;type:=nfs; \
                   rhost:=dumptruck;rfs:=/usr/share/${arch} \
                arch==sunos;fs:=/usr/share/man;type:=nfs; \
                   rhost:=dumptruck;rfs:=/usr/share/${arch} \
                arch==linux;fs:=/usr/share/man;type:=nfs; \
                   rhost:=dumptruck;rfs:=/usr/share/${arch} \
                arch==freebsd;fs:=/usr/share/man;type:=nfs; \
                   rhost:=dumptruck;rfs:=/usr/share/${arch} \
                arch==solaris;fs:=/usr/share/man;type:=nfs; \
                   rhost:=dumptruck;rfs:=/usr/share/${arch}

# This final entry is for a replicated database, that is available on three
# different servers.  The database is identical on each server so that if 1
# of them is unavailable, we simply connect to one of the others.

inventory    fs:=/data/inventory;type:=nfs;rfs:=/inventory; \
             rhost:=invdb1;rhost:=invdb2;rhost:=invdb3
```

Please note that as stated earlier there is no continuation character allowed in the /etc/amd.conf file. The \ character in the preceding listing is simply used for readability. In the actual file, the entire entry would need to be entered on a single line. These examples show you some of what you can accomplish with the automount daemon. For a more complete description of the amd.conf file syntax, refer to the amd.conf manual page in section 5 of the Linux manual pages.

Starting the automount Daemon

Now that you have the /etc/amd.conf file set up to your satisfaction, you are ready to start the automount daemon. This daemon, amd, is located in /usr/sbin in a standard Red Hat installation and it is normally started by running the /etc/rc.d/init.d/amd script. This script first sources a configuration file located in /etc/sysconfig called, surprisingly enough, amd, which defines some variables used by the script. There are three variables that may be set in this file. The first is ADIR, which defines the temporary directory on which to cache mounts to remote filesystems. By default this is set to /.automount on Red Hat systems. The next variable is MOUNTPTS, which specifies the directory, /net by default on Red Hat, that serves as the root for all automounted filesystems, and the map name, which is another name for the /etc/amd.conf file. The final variable that can be set is the

AMDOPTS, in which you can specify any options to amd that you choose. An example of a good use for this variable is to specify the value of a tag used in the /etc/amd.conf file. For example, in order to make the preceding amd.conf file entry for manual pages work, you would need to set AMDOPTS to a value of -T arch=linux. Having set these variables to appropriate values for your setup, you may now start the automount daemon by issuing the following command:

```
/etc/rc.d/init.d/amd start
```

Starting the Automount Daemon at System Boot

The only remaining step is to ensure that the automount daemon is started at boot time by creating the appropriate links from the runlevel directories to start and stop amd. Please note that amd is dependent on NFS being active, so you must ensure that NFS is already started before attempting to run the automount daemon. Conversely, it is wise to first shut down the automount daemon before shutting down NFS. You can create the appropriate symlinks by hand, or if you prefer, you can use the runlevel editor that is part of the control-panel to create them for you.

Finally, before moving on to the Linux autofs, let's take a look at the amq utility previously mentioned. This utility is part of the am-utils package and is the automounter query tool. It communicates with the automount daemon and can perform a number of useful functions dependent on the command-line options provided. Table 15.5 shows a few of the more commonly used options and what they do.

TABLE 15.5 amq Options

Option	Description
-f	Asks the automounter to flush the internal caches.
-m	Prints a list of mounted filesystems and the number of references to each.
-p	Prints the pid of the locally running amd.
-s	Prints system-wide mount statistics.
-u directory	Attempts to unmount the specified directory.

There are other options to the amq utility program that are documented in the manual pages for amq.

Linux Autofs

Linux autofs includes most of the capabilities of the Berkeley automount daemon; however, it is implemented in kernel space as opposed to user space like the automount daemon. This means that support for autofs must be compiled into your kernel. In addition, you must install the automount utilities, which are contained in the am-utils-6.0 rpm package on the Red Hat installation media.

Assuming that you have autofs support compiled into your kernel and the appropriate am-utils package installed, you can begin the task of configuring autofs. The configuration files used by autofs are not as complicated as those of amd, but they are somewhat similar. The first of these configuration files to consider is the `/etc/auto.master` file, which is the main configuration file. This file consists of entries of three fields each. The first field specifies the directory root to use for filesystems specified in the map file, which is named in the second field, and the timeout value, specified in the third field, used to determine when to unmount the automounted filesystem. Here is the default `auto.master` file that comes with Red Hat:

```
/etc/auto.master
```

```
# $Id: 755915.txt,v 1.7 1999/09/23 05:35:36 tschenk Exp $
# Sample auto.master file
# Format of this file:
# mountpoint map options
# For details of the format look at autofs(8).
/misc    /etc/auto.misc    --timeout 60
```

This file specifies that a mount root of `/misc` will be used for the filesystems defined in `/etc/auto.misc` and that mounts will timeout after 60 seconds of inactivity. Here's the `auto.misc` file that comes with Red Hat Linux:

```
/etc/auto.misc
```

```
# $Id: 755915.txt,v 1.7 1999/09/23 05:35:36 tschenk Exp $
# This is an automounter map and it has the following format
# key [ -mount-options-separated-by-comma ] location
# Details may be found in the autofs(5) manpage

kernel        -ro,soft,intr        ftp.kernel.org:/pub/linux
cd          -fstype=iso9660,ro    :/dev/cdrom


# the following entries are samples to pique your imagination
#floppy        -fstype=auto        :/dev/fd0
#floppy        -fstype=ext2        :/dev/fd0
```

```
#e2floppy    -fstype=ext2        :/dev/fd0
#jaz         -fstype=ext2        :/dev/sdc1
```

The entries in these maps are made up of three fields, the first of which is referred to as the key. This key is usually also the name of the subdirectory that you would access to cause the device or filesystem specified in the third field to be mounted. As you may have guessed, the second field is a comma-separated list of options to pass to the mount program. Specifically, the line with the key kernel specifies that if a user attempts to access a directory, /misc/kernel, the automounter will attempt to mount the NFS filesystem specified by ftp.kernel.org:/pub/linux as read-only on the local mount point /misc/kernel. The next line specifies that an access attempt to /misc/cd will cause the automount program to mount the local device /dev/cdrom as filesystem type iso9660 with read-only access. The remaining lines in the file are comments, but they demonstrate how the automounter can be used to allow users to automatically mount removable devices, such as floppy drives and JAZ drives without root access, simply by accessing a specific directory.

Assuming entries as shown above, you can activate autofs support by running the autofs script found in /etc/rc.d/init.d/autofs with the start option. Having done this, you can now easily access CD-ROM drives and floppy drives as any user. The only difficulty that occurs with the setup as shown here is that the timeout value is fairly long. The timeout value specified for all filesystems defined in /etc/auto.misc was 60 seconds. This means that if you put a CD-ROM in your drive and cd to /misc/cd, you must cd out of this directory and wait 60 seconds before you can unmount the CD-ROM. That is unless you have the ability to send a signal as the root user to the automount program. Using the capabilities of sudo, you can use the killall program to send a signal USR1 to the automount program, which will cause it to attempt to immediately unmount all filesystems it has mounted.

Summary

This chapter started by discussing some of the reasons why sharing resources on the network is desirable and that the two most commonly shared resources are files and printer services. It looked at how to set up a print queue using the tools available under Red Hat, how to grant access to the printer to others on the network, and how to access these shared printer resources from client systems. It then went on to cover NFS server and client setup and configuration, using the Linux kernel NFS support. This chapter also briefly touched on two alternative network filesystems available under Linux, AFS and Coda, both distributed filesystems with a lot of interesting features not available in any other filesystem type. Finally, it took a look at the Berkeley automount daemon, and the Linux autofs capabilities that make the managing of network filesystems easier and that empower users by giving them access to local removable media such as floppies, CD-ROM drives, and JAZ drives without giving them root access.

Network Monitoring

IN THIS CHAPTER

- Why Monitor? *436*
- Monitoring Systems *437*
- Sniffers *444*
- Traffic Analyzers *451*

The Linux operating system is widely known for its high level of network integration. The Red Hat Linux distribution comes with full network support right out the box, including such software as file, mail, and Web servers. This high level of network availability comes at a price, however. Networked servers open themselves up to the outside world, greatly increasing the possibility of a successful system attack. In addition, networked computer systems can be difficult to configure properly. Configuration errors can result in network bottlenecks, loss of service, and a variety of other problems. Because networking is integrated into the Linux operating system at such a base level, diagnosing such problems can sometimes be extremely difficult.

Network monitoring allows you to peer into the low-level transactions between hosts. Such capabilities are extremely valuable to any individual planning on administering a networked Linux host. This chapter provides a look into network monitoring software and deployment techniques. You'll learn about the benefits of performing network monitoring, how to perform such activities, and how to use both network sniffers and traffic analyzers.

Why Monitor?

Today's networks are complex and dynamic entities, housing a multitude of different kinds of computer systems and embedded electronic devices. Managing these different network resources properly, ensuring good data transfer performance levels, and keeping up a good level of security among the networked devices can become quite a large task. Using a technique known as network monitoring, administrators can gain an "inside view" into the activity on their computer networks so that problems can be diagnosed quickly and properly, security issues can be fully audited, and transmission bottlenecks can be fixed.

Network monitoring is the process of capturing and examining raw data packets from a network adapter device. It bypasses the monitoring computer's protocol stack, performing all capture and analysis activities directly. Data packets are grabbed directly off the wire, before any form of packet validation or verification is done. This allows the monitoring software to perform all sorts of activities such as corrupt packet data detection, network misconfiguration problem diagnosis, and so on. These things would be impossible to do if packets were allowed to pass through the monitoring system's network stack and packet validation procedures before reaching the monitoring software.

Monitoring also provides the valuable advantage of allowing you to examine the data traffic flowing between all hosts on a network, instead of just the traffic destined specifically for the host performing the monitoring activities. This is accomplished by enabling a feature on the monitoring system's network interface device known as *promiscuous mode*. This feature allows the network device to see all traffic traveling across the network wire. Problems such as network bottlenecks and IP address conflicts can only be diagnosed if a network monitoring utility is able to capture data from a promiscuous mode interface.

The ability to see all network packet data also serves as a good tool for security auditing and system usage monitoring purposes. Using network monitoring techniques, you can detect the usage of easy-to-guess passwords, network user bandwidth utilization violations, and denial of service attacks such as SYN floods and Smurf attacks.

Monitoring Systems

In order to properly deploy and use a network monitoring system, it is important to have a solid understanding of how the systems work and the requirements of a good monitoring system. A network monitoring system is made up of several key components, as shown in Figure 16.1.

FIGURE 16.1
Layout of a network monitoring system.

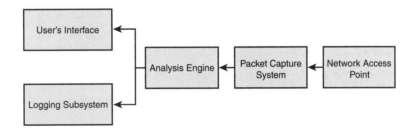

The first of these components is the network access point. The network access point provides the actual physical connection between the monitoring host and the target network. Placement of the network access point is highly dependent upon the unswitched/ switched nature of the target network. Unswitched networks differ from switched networks in that hosts residing on the network share one single communications pipe. The combined bandwidth utilization of all hosts on the network cannot exceed the limitations of the physical transport media. On switched networks, each host on the network has its own communications pipe, instead of sharing one with other hosts. This allows each host to fully utilize the limits of the physical transport media, making the overall combined bandwidth utilization of the network much higher than the limitations of the physical transport media.

For example, an 8 port 100Mbps switch would allow each port to utilize up to 100Mbps of bandwidth, making the maximum overall combined bandwidth utilization 800Mbps.

Network access point placement is also very dependent on the overall structure of the network itself. In simple single segment networks, access point placement is an easy task. However, for large segmented networks much more thought must be put into the placement of access points. The subject of network access point placement is discussed further in the "Network Monitoring System Deployment" section of this chapter.

Raw data traffic passing through the network access point is captured by the second component of a network monitoring system: the low-level data capturing mechanisms of the monitoring host. Red Hat Linux can support two different techniques for network data capture. They are the SOCK_PACKET interface and the Linux TurboPacket interface. Figure 16.2 illustrates the SOCK_PACKET interface.

FIGURE 16.2

The Linux
SOCK_PACKET
interface.

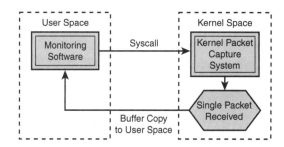

SOCK_PACKET is the simpler and less efficient of the two data capture interfaces supported under Linux. It suffers from three major drawbacks:

- A lack of in-kernel data buffering. This means that the kernel must capture network data at the instant the syscall is made, instead of allowing the kernel to buffer packet data into memory as it is received. The inability of the SOCK_PACKET interface to be able to perform in-kernel buffering can result in higher packet loss under heavy network loads.

- The ability to capture only one packet per syscall. Under Linux, syscalls are expensive in their usage of system resources. Each time a monitoring system performs a syscall, a operating system context switch from user-space into kernel-space is required. Under network conditions where large numbers of small packets are being transmitted, severe packet loss can occur.

- A kernel-space to user-space memory copy required per packet. The SOCK_PACKET interface must copy packet data received by the kernel packet capturing mechanisms from a kernel-space buffer into a user-space buffer. This extra memory copy can further degrade packet capturing performance levels.

Figure 16.3 illustrates the Linux `TurboPacket` interface.

FIGURE 16.3
The Linux
`TurboPacket`
interface.

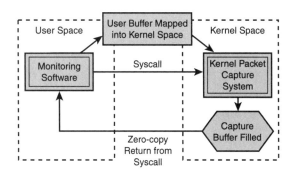

Linux TurboPacket is a new packet capture interface for 2.2.x series kernels. It addresses all of the performance limitations present in the SOCK_PACKET interface, allowing for high-speed data capture under Linux systems. The Linux TurboPacket interface has the following advantages over the SOCK_PACKET interface:

- Support for in-kernel data buffering. Linux TurboPacket is able to buffer data received from the network access point into memory, so that monitoring system processes can read network packet data more efficiently, reducing the likelihood of packet drops.

- The ability to capture multiple packets per syscall.

- A zero-copy packet capture mechanism.

The Linux TurboPacket interface is not yet a part of the official Linux kernel source tree. Instead, it must be applied as a patch and the Linux kernel must be rebuilt from source. Currently, the Linux TurboPacket patch is only available for Linux kernel v2.2.4. Source modifications may be required to allow the patch to successfully operate with a different kernel version.

To patch your Linux kernel to support the Linux TurboPacket interface, you must do the following:

1. Download the TurboPacket package from:

    ```
    ftp://ftp.inr.ac.ru/ip-routing/lbl-tools/kernel-turbopacket.dif.gz
    ```

    FTP mirror sites:

    ```
    ftp://ftp.funet.fi/pub/mirrors/ftp.inr.ac.ru/ip-routing/lbl-tools/
      ftp://ftp.src.uchicago.edu/pub/linux/ip-routing/lbl-tools/
      ftp://ftp.crc.ca/pub/systems/linux/ip-routing/lbl-tools/
    ```

2. Change your current working directory to that of the Linux kernel source tree, and apply the patch to the source tree using the following command:

```
# patch < kernel-turbopacket.dif
```

> **Note**
>
> If the kernel-turbopacket patch resides in a directory other than that of the kernel source tree, be sure to include the path of the patch file in the command line.

3. If you are not already running as root, become root using the su command so that the kernel may be properly installed.

4. Compile and install the new kernel.

5. Reboot.

Most network monitoring systems do not access the kernel packet capture mechanisms directly, but instead use a packet capture API. The API provides a monitoring system easy access to captured packet data, shielding the low-level details of the kernel packet capture mechanism. This allows network monitoring software to operate using different kernel packet capture mechanisms without requiring changes to the actual monitoring system's source code. The standard packet capture API available for Linux is libpcap, a system-independent interface for packet capture created by the Network Research Group at the Lawrence Berkeley National Laboratory.

To add libpcap support to your system you must do the following:

1. Download the libpcap package and any required patches (depending on the kernel packet capture mechanism that you want to use).

```
libpcap:
        ftp://ftp.ee.lbl.org/libpcap-0.4.tar.Z

    Patches needed for the SOCK_PACKET interface:
      None.

    Patches needed for the Linux TurboPacket interface:
      ftp://ftp.inr.ac.ru/ip-routing/lbl-tools/kernel-turbopacket.dif.gz
        ftp://ftp.inr.ac.ru/ip-routing/lbl-tools/libpcap-0.4-current.dif.gz
      mirrors:
      ftp://ftp.funet.fi/pub/mirrors/ftp.inr.ac.ru/ip-routing/lbl-tools/
```

16

```
ftp://ftp.src.uchicago.edu/pub/linux/ip-routing/lbl-tools/
    ftp://ftp.crc.ca/pub/systems/linux/ip-routing/lbl-tools/
```

2. Change your current working directory to that of the libpcap source tree, and apply any required patches to the tree using the following command:

```
# patch < patch_file
```

> **Note**
>
> If the patch file resides in a directory other than that of the libpcap source tree, be sure to include the path of the patch file in the command line.

3. If you are not already running as root, become root using the su command so that libpcap may be properly installed.

4. Compile and install the libpcap package using the following command sequence:

```
# ./configure
# make
# make install
```

The packet capture mechanisms of the monitoring host pass collected network data onto the third component of a network monitoring system: the analysis engine itself. The packet analysis engine performs network protocol decoding and, in some cases, network session reconstruction. Tasks such as statistics gathering and trend examination are also handled by the network analysis engine.

Monitoring systems perform protocol decoding so that information may be extrapolated from captured packet data. Before decoding activities occur, a packet is raw formless data. Using protocol templates, which allow raw data to be mapped into packet headers and data payloads, the previously useless packet data provides a wealth of information about network activity. Advanced monitoring systems allow for the creation of custom user-defined protocol templates, which allow a virtually unlimited number of transport protocols to be decoded and analyzed.

The analysis engine of a network monitoring system stores collected data including statistics, trend history, and actual captured packet data to disk using the fourth component of the system: the data logging mechanisms. The complexity of these mechanisms can vary from a simple text output to advanced buffered database storage techniques. Whichever data storage method is in use, speed is always considered a highly important issue. If a network monitoring system is not capable of logging data at a fast enough rate, it becomes incapable of storing captured data and statistics and becomes useless.

For a network monitoring system to be truly useful, the information that it collects must be presented in an easy to understand format. This task is handled by the fifth component of a network monitoring system: the users' interface. A good users' interface will allow different sorts of network statistics to be shown, including network utilization information, lists of active network hosts, protocol statistics, and more. Output information should be in a human readable format, with the option of writing data to a file for processing by a third party application.

A good network monitoring system must meet several key requirements in order to be used properly:

- Monitoring system hardware portability.

- Compatibility with one or more network topologies.

- Capable of monitoring at or near wire-speeds.

- Capable of storing large amounts of captured data/statistics.

- Capable of decoding network traffic on multiple protocol stack layers.

The first of these is portability. In complex segmented networks, the monitoring system must be capable of being easily moved from one segment to another. This allows for quick deployment when network problems arise and need to be diagnosed immediately.

The next requirement is that the monitoring system be capable of interfacing with all forms of physical transport media used on the target network. For example, if a network is made up of 100Mbps ethernet segments connected through an FDDI backbone, an appropriate network monitoring system would be capable of capturing data from both ethernet and FDDI interfaces. The ability to monitor packet data at or near wire-speeds is an important requirement if a network monitoring system is to be truly useful. A system that dropped a significant portion of network packets would not provide accurate data, making the system useless.

Good network monitoring systems also need to be capable of storing large amounts of captured packet data and/or network statistics quickly. This means that the system must have access to large amounts of available disk space on a storage media that supports a good write speed. For example, logging captured packet data directly to a tape backup drive or CD burner would be a bad idea, as neither media support very fast access speeds.

The last requirement of a network monitoring system is that it be able to examine captured packet data on multiple layers of the protocol stack. A protocol stack applies intelligence to network packet data, allowing messages to be exchanged with other hosts' protocol stacks in the form of datagrams and stream connections. Modern protocol stacks process data in multiple layers, allowing for different forms of communications to be sent across lower transport levels. For a network monitoring system to be truly useful in the diagnosis of network troubles and surveillance of data transactions, it must be able to decode captured packet data and examine it on each of these protocol stack layers.

Deployment of network monitoring systems must be done with careful thought and planning, otherwise the information gained from monitoring operations will be of little real-world use. This is because modern computer networks can be extremely complex, and unless a monitoring system is attached to an appropriate network access point it will be unsuccessful in capturing the data traffic that is desired for analysis. Several deployment methods currently exist, and are listed as follows:

Deployment Method	Description
Unswitched Tapping	Monitors all communications flowing through a non-switched network hub.
Port Tapping	Monitors all communications to and from a specific port on the switch.
Circuit Tapping	Monitors all communications between two specific ports on the switch.
Switch Tapping	Monitors all communications flowing through the switch.

When performing monitoring operations on a switched network segment, certain network hubs are more suited for the job than others. It is best to utilize a hub that supports the monitor port capability. A monitor port is a specialized network access port that can be configured to receive traffic destined for another port or all of the traffic traveling through the hub.

Following are a few of the switched hubs that have the monitor port capability:

3Com SuperStack LinkSwitch 2200.

3Com LANplex 2016, 2500, and 6000.

SMC EliteSwitch ES/1 and ES/1 ATX.

Bay Networks Model 28000.

Bay Networks Model 3000 with the 3328 host module.

Cisco Catalyst 5000 (software version 2.1 or greater).

Cisco Catalyst 1200 (software version 3.0 or greater).

Cisco EtherSwitch EPS-2115M.

Cisco Catalyst 1700.

Sniffers

A sniffer is a network monitoring system that captures the actual content of network sessions and datagram transmissions. Sniffers are extremely powerful entities, because they allow the protocol and application-level activity occurring on a network to be stored and analyzed. This means that sniffers are capable of monitoring both the protocol information and content of specific users' or applications' network session, exposing information such as attempted denial of service attacks, password transmissions, network or application misconfigurations, and more.

A sniffer works by capturing network packet data according to a specific filtering criteria, and extracting the payload content of the received packets. Advanced sniffers support a technique known as network session reconstruction, which allows data transmissions that span multiple packets to be reassembled into a single coherent communications stream.

Figure 16.4 illustrates tcpdump, currently the most popular network sniffer among Linux platforms. Tcpdump is shown displaying decoded data packets that were sniffed from an active network.

FIGURE 16.4

The tcpdump network sniffer.

Tcpdump is a network sniffer that can be used for network monitoring and data acquisition purposes. It decodes and prints protocol header information of captured packets, and can be used to extract the actual content of network sessions as well. Tcpdump is a product of the Network Research Group at the Lawrence Berkeley Laboratory (the same group that developed the `libpcap` packet capture API). It was originally based on the etherfind utility written by Sun Microsystems Incorporated. The tcpdump program was originally written as part of a research project by Van Jacobson. It was later rewritten, with all code fragments from the etherfind utility removed, by Steven McCanne. Clean room programming techniques were used to ensure that the rewritten version of tcpdump would be based on 100% free nonproprietary source code with no possible license conflict issues.

To install tcpdump to your system you must do the following:

1. Download the tcpdump package from:

   ```
   ftp://ftp.ee.lbl.gov/tcpdump-3.4.tar.Z
   ```

2. If you are not already running as root, become root using the `su` command so that tcpdump may be properly installed.

3. Compile and install the tcpdump package using the following command sequence:

   ```
   # ./configure
   # make
   # make install
   ```

Note

The tcpdump package is also included with the Red Hat 6.0 distribution as a pre-compiled binary RPM. You can install the tcpdump binary by executing the following command (as root):

```
rpm -Uvh /[RedHat_6.0_Mount_Point/RedHat/RPMS/tcpdump-3.4-10.i386.rpm
```

Because tcpdump requires use of kernel-level packet capture facilities that require root privileges to be accessed, it is installed setuid root. The program is also set to be executable only by the "wheel" group to prevent normal users from being able to perform network sniffing operations. Tcpdump is executed in the following manner:

```
# tcpdump command-line-options
```

Note

The tcpdump package is installed in the directory /usr/local/sbin by default. Be sure to have this directory listed in your execution path or explicitly specify the directory on the command line.

The command-line options for the tcpdump program are described in the associated manual page and in Table 16.1.

TABLE **16.1** Tcpdump Command-Line Options

Option	Description
-c count	Terminates program execution after processing count packets.
-d	Dumps any compiled packet filtering code to the stdout file descriptor and terminates program execution.
-e	For each packet that is captured and processed, prints its associated link-level header.
-f	Does not perform address resolution on foreign Internet addresses.
-F file	Uses any expressions listed in file to perform filtering on captured packets. It should be noted that using this option results in any filtering options given on the command line being ignored.
-i interface	Captures data packets from a particular network interface device. If this option is not given, tcpdump will attempt to automatically find an active network interface, using the lowest numbered device if multiple active interfaces exist.
-l	Forces program output into line buffered mode. This option is useful if you are piping output data into another running program, and want to allow the printed data to be processed line by line.
-n	Does not perform any resolution of system host addresses or port numbers into alphanumeric symbolic names.
-N	When printing resolved host names, does not print their domain qualification information.
-O	Prevents the packet filtering code optimizer from being run. This option would normally never be used unless a bug was suspected in the code optimizer routines.
-p	Does not force the network interface device into promiscuous mode upon program execution. It is important to note that using this option will not guarantee that promiscuous mode will be disabled; it simply prevents the mode from being turned on explicitly by the running instance of tcpdump.

TABLE 16.1   continued

Option	Description
-q	Outputs less detailed packet decode information per packet.
-r file	Processes packet data stored in `file`, instead of capturing data from a live network interface. If `file` is specified as '-', the stdin file descriptor is used as the input source.
-s length	Captures up to `length` bytes of data for each packet that is processed. This option allows network sniffing performance to be optimized by preventing the hosts' packet capture routines from retrieving unwanted data. Capturing only the data that is necessary for analysis tasks helps to prevent packet loss when monitoring high-speed networks. If protocol information contained in a captured packet is truncated as a result of this option a [¦proto] indicator is output, where `proto` is the protocol layer of the packet in which data truncation occurred. If this command-line option is not given, tcpdump defaults to capturing 68 bytes of data per received packet.
-S	Prints the true values of transmitted TCP sequence numbers. If this option is not set, tcpdump will attempt to keep track of sequence number state information for TCP virtual circuits, printing sequence number information relative to 0.
-t	Disables the output of time stamp information for each captured data packet.
-tt	Outputs an unformatted time stamp for each captured data packet.
-v	Outputs protocol decode information with a higher level of verbosity.
-vv	Outputs protocol decode information with the highest level of verbosity available.
-w file	Writes the captured binary packet data to file. The use of this option will prevent the output of decoded protocol information. If file is specified as "-", the binary packet information is output to stdout.
-x	Outputs received packet data in hexadecimal format, minus the link-level protocol header.
expression	Filters captured packets according to expression. Data packets will only be processed and displayed if `expression` evaluates as true. Details on how to filter incoming traffic are given in the "Analyzing Types of Traffic" section of this chapter.

Uses for Sniffers

Sniffers are extremely valuable tools for detecting network mis-configurations, performing protocol analysis, and monitoring user activity because they are doing application-level protocol analysis. Because they are capable of capturing the actual content of network sessions instead of just the protocol header information, they can provide an extremely in-depth view into network activity.

Denial of service attacks can bring network servers to their knees. Administrators can use sniffers to detect when a denial of service attack is being launched against a host on their network. Quick detection allows attacks to be recovered from faster and more efficiently. The protocol decoding abilities of tcpdump can be used to detect attacks in real-time.

The following is a list of common network denial of service attacks and how to detect them using tcpdump:

- **SYN Flood**—SYN floods are a common type of denial of service attack that involve flooding a target host with invalid connection requests. The target hosts' connection queue eventually fills, and further connection requests (including legitimate ones) are denied. SYN floods to a particular IP address may be detected using the following tcpdump command:

  ```
  # tcpdump tcp host ip-address
  ```

  Tcpdump will output the decoded tcp protocol information for the host ip_address. Extremely large numbers of TCP SYN packets (specified by the S flag in the output protocol information) can be indicative of SYN flood attacks.

- **Ping of Death**—The Ping of Death is an attack that exploits a flaw in the fragmented packet reconstruction subsystems of many hosts' TCP/IP network stacks. It involves sending an oversized fragmented packet to a vulnerable host, that when reconstructed, will result in the packet length identifier being overflowed into a negative value. Processing of such packets often results in a crash of the vulnerable machines' TCP/IP stack. Ping of Death attacks to a particular host can be detected using the following tcpdump command:

  ```
  # tcpdump dst host ip-address
  ```

  Tcpdump will output the decoded protocol information destined for the host ip-address. IP fragments that have a combined offset+length that is greater than 65,535 are indicative of Ping of Death attacks.

- **Smurf**—Smurf attacks involve sending an ICMP ping request to the broadcast address of a network. On networks that are vulnerable to the smurf attack, every active host that receives the ping request will generate a response. This can result in the generation of extremely high network load conditions. Smurf attacks can be detected using the following `tcpdump` command:

```
# tcpdump icmp dst host broadcast-address
```

Tcpdump will output decoded ICMP protocol information destined for the specified network broadcast address. Any ICMP ping requests are usually indicative of smurf attacks.

Sniffers are also extremely valuable tools for diagnosing network errors and misconfigurations. Many of these problems would be difficult or impossible to detect otherwise because they occur in the low-level network stacks of affected hosts. The tcpdump program allows network dialogs to be examined at the lowest possible level, allowing such problems to be diagnosed easily.

The following is a listing of common network problems and how to detect them using tcpdump:

- **Duplicate Ips**—If it is suspected that two hosts are using the same IP address on a network, such activity can be detected by issuing the following `tcpdump` command:

```
# tcpdump -e host ip-address
```

Tcpdump will output decoded protocol information for the specified IP address, along with the link-level headers for each captured packet. The output information must be examined to see whether or not two different MAC addresses attempt to make use of the same IP address.

- **ARP Errors**—ARP errors and misconfigurations can be detected by issuing the following `tcpdump` command:

```
# tcpdump arp
```

Tcpdump will output any decoded ARP information captured from the network. Excessive "who-has" requests can be indicative of ARP misconfiguration problems.

- **Routing Problems**—Data routing problems can be detected by using the following `tcpdump` command:

```
# tcpdump icmp
```

Tcpdump will output any decoded ICMP protocol information captured from the network. ICMP error messages such as `host unreachable` can be indicative of routing misconfigurations or other network reachability problems.

Dangers of Sniffers

Network sniffers are powerful tools, allowing network packets and sessions to be easily examined. This, like any other form of power, can be abused. Hackers and other malicious individuals can use sniffers to perform network surveillance, espionage, and protocol-level attacks. Sniffing technology can also be used to destroy personal privacy. Any network activity that a user engages in can be monitored with a sniffer; this includes electronic mail, chat sessions, Web surfing activity, and any other form of network communication.

It is important to understand that in non-switched network environments, any user is capable of the same monitoring activities as the administrator. As a result, any user with administrator-level access to a host on your non-switched network is capable of performing network surveillance. Hosts need not be high-powered UNIX workstations to perform monitoring activities because sniffing software exists for virtually all network-capable operating systems. Users capable of this sort of monitoring activity can cause a serious threat to the security and overall stability of a network. Account passwords may be captured allowing unauthorized access to network servers, sensitive information such as transmitted files and e-mail can be stolen, and captured information can be used to aid in protocol-level attacks.

The use of sniffing technology also brings with it issues related to personal privacy. Because sniffers capture the actual content of network transmissions, all user activity can be monitored and logged. Overuse of these capabilities can create a "Big Brother" type of network environment, which in many cases is quite undesirable.

It is important to understand the legal dangers related to the use of network sniffers. Using a sniffer is considered a form of wiretapping by the United States government. Unauthorized sniffing activity amounts to a serious crime, and there are also issues related to sniffing users' activity without their knowledge. The United States Department of Justice, General Litigation and Legal Advice Section, Criminal Division, advises that network administrators give all users prior notice that monitoring activities may occur. Notification of possible monitoring activity is often given through the use of text banners. An example of a possible banner is as follows:

> This system is for the use of authorized users only. Individuals using this computer system without authority, or in excess of their authority, are subject to having all of their activities on this system monitored and recorded by system personnel.

> In the course of monitoring individuals improperly using this system, or in the course of system maintenance, the activities of authorized users may also be monitored.

> Anyone using this system expressly consents to such monitoring and is advised that if such monitoring reveals possible evidence of criminal activity, system personnel may provide the evidence of such monitoring to law enforcement officials.

Administrators should tailor any banners used to suit the specifics of their network monitoring guidelines.

Because sniffers can present some very significant dangers in relation to network security and user privacy, it is important to develop strategies for protecting against them. There are currently two protection strategies most commonly in use:

- Encryption
- Switched networking

Encryption allows network traffic to be scrambled, so that only a properly authenticated receiver can view its true contents. In non-switched environments, encryption can be a quick and inexpensive solution for protecting against unauthorized sniffing. It requires no changes to network layout or equipment, and thus can be implemented solely as a software-only solution.

Switched networking can also be used as a solution to unauthorized sniffing activity. It allows only the traffic destined specifically for a network host or being broadcast to all hosts to be sent through the related network access point. This makes sniffing of other hosts' network traffic impossible.

Traffic Analyzers

Traffic analyzers are valuable tools for network problem diagnosis and resolution, and performance optimization. They provide a clear-cut view of network activity, showing exactly what is occurring and what is not occurring on a computer network. Without the aid of traffic analyzers, some network problems (such as bottlenecks and protocol level misconfigurations) would be extremely hard, if not impossible, to detect.

A traffic analyzer functions by capturing data packets traveling over a network, and subsequently performing protocol decoding and/or statistics gathering. Administrators can use the information gathered from traffic analyzers to perform baselining and trend analysis operations, so that network performance may be optimized and problems can be resolved.

Figure 16.5 illustrates ntop, a network traffic analyzer popular among Linux platforms.

Ntop is a traffic analyzer that reports network usage in a manner similar to the UNIX command top. It was written by Luca Deri of the University of Pisa, Centro SERRA. Ntop was originally based on the pcapture program but has been heavily modified and expanded from its original code-base.

Figure 16.5

The ntop network traffic analyzer.

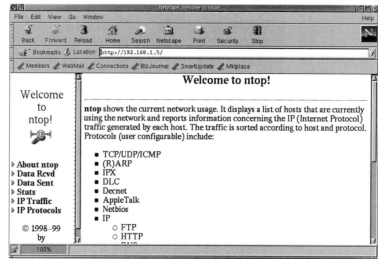

To install ntop to your system you must do the following:

1. Download the desired ntop package from:

   Source Package:

   ```
   ftp://ftp.unipi.it/pub/local/ntop/source/ntop-1.1-src.tar.gz
   ```

   Red Hat RPM Package:

   ```
   ftp://ftp.unipi.it/pub/local/ntop/package/ntop-1.1-1.rh6.i386.rpm
   ```

2. If you are not already running as root, become root using the su command so that ntop may be properly installed.

3. Compile and install the ntop package using the following command sequence:

   Source Package:

   ```
   # ./configure
   # make
   # make install
   ```

   Red Hat RPM Package:

   ```
   # rpm -Uvh ntop-1.1-1.rh6.i386.rpm
   ```

Ntop is executed in the following manner:

```
# ntop command-line-options
```

16

Note

The ntop package is installed in the directory /usr/local/sbin by default. Be sure to have this directory listed in your execution path or explicitly specify the directory on the command line.

The command-line options for the ntop program are described its associated manual page and in Table 16.2.

TABLE **16.2**   Ntop Command-Line Options

Option	Description
-r delay	Pauses for delay seconds between each ntop update. If ntop is set to output to a file, it writes data every delay seconds. If this option is not specified, the default delay period of 3 seconds will be used.
-d	Runs ntop in daemon mode. This allows ntop to detach itself from its controlling terminal so that it may continue to run in the background even after the user has logged out. This option is only available when the -w option is also specified.
-f file	Allows ntop to read from a tcpdump packet capture file instead of an active network interface.
-n	Does not perform any resolution of system host addresses into alphanumeric symbolic names.
-p proto_list	Sets the list of protocols that ntop will monitor and output statistics data for. This option also allows custom display labels to be set for monitored protocols. The format of proto_list is as follows: label=service_list,label=service_list label specifies the display label to be used by ntop to identify the protocols listed in service_list. service_list specifies a group of protocols to monitor. It is formatted in the following manner: service¦service¦service service is a text identifier matching an entry in the /etc/services file. It specifies a particular protocol that ntop should monitor.
-i interface	Captures data packets from a particular network interface device. If this option is not given, ntop will attempt to automatically find an active network interface, using the lowest numbered device if multiple active interfaces exist.
-w port	Forces ntop to output network statistics information in Web mode. Ntop uses its own integrated Web server to service client requests. This Web server will listen for client requests on port for client requests. Authentication to the ntop Web server is handled through the ~/.ntop configuration file. This file has the following format: username password

TABLE **16.2**   continued

Option	Description
-m subnet_list	Specifies the subnets that ntop should consider as local networks according to subnet_list. The format of subnet_list is as follows: network_address/subnet_mask,network_address/subnet_mask
-l log_delay	Forces ntop to log network data to the file ntop.log.
-F expr_list	Allows ntop to generate statistics information for groups of specific network traffic flows according to expr_list. These statistics are only viewable when ntop is run in Web mode. The format of expr_list is as follows: label=expression,label=expression label specifies the display label to be used by ntop to identify the traffic flow specified by expression. expression specifies the traffic filtering expression to use to identify the network flow. Information on creating filtering expressions is given in the "Analyzing Types of Traffic" section of this chapter.
expression	Filters captured packets according to expression. Data packets will only be processed and displayed if expression evaluates as true. Details on how to filter incoming traffic are given in the "Analyzing Types of Traffic" section of this chapter.

The ntop program can be run in one of two different execution modes. The first of these is interactive mode, which allows program output to be shown in a terminal window in real-time. This execution mode is illustrated in Figure 16.6.

FIGURE 16.6

Ntop interactive execution mode.

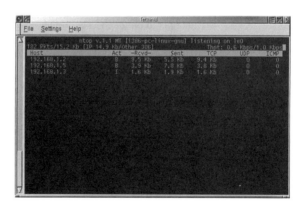

When used in interactive mode, ntop can be manipulated using the following keys:

- q—Forces ntop to quit program execution.

- n—Changes the mode in which host addresses are output. The following modes are supported:

    - **IP Address**—A numeric IP address.

    - **Symbolic Hostname**—A symbolic hostname as specified in the /etc/hosts file or resolved from a DNS server.

    - **MAC Address**—An ethernet MAC address.

    - **Board Manufacturer**—A text identifier specifying the manufacturer of the network interface hardware used by each network host.

- p—Changes the mode in which traffic information is output. The following modes are supported:

    - **Percentage**—Shows traffic information as a percentage of the total traffic sent.

    - **Absolute**—Shows traffic information as an absolute value representing the amount of data sent.

    - **Throughput**—Shows traffic information throughput information in an amount of data sent per second format.

- l—Changes the type of hosts that ntop outputs information for. The following types are supported:

    - **local**—Displays network information for hosts that are classified as inside a local network.

    - **remote**—Displays network information for hosts that are classified as inside a remote network.

- d—Sets ntop to sort hosts according to idle time or the amount of data sent/received.

- t—Sets ntop to sort hosts according to the data being sent or received.

- y—Sets ntop to sort hosts according to their associated protocol identifiers.

- <space>—Toggles showing of additional network traffic information in additional columns.

The second execution mode that is supported by ntop is Web mode; it allows program output to be monitored by multiple local or remote users through a Web browser. The ntop Web mode is illustrated in Figure 16.7.

When used in Web mode, ntop can be manipulated by selection of one of several different traffic views from the left frame of the HTML browser display window. These offer additional information not available in the ntop interactive mode. Table 16.3 lists the views available.

FIGURE 16.7

*Ntop Web
execution Mode.*

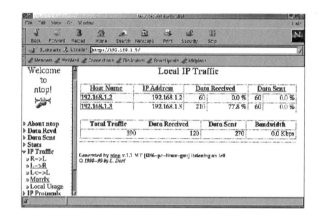

TABLE 16.3 Ntop Traffic Views

View Name	Description
Sort Traffic by Data Sent	Displays network information sorted by the amount of data sent.
Sort Traffic by Data Received	Displays network information sorted by the amount of data received.
Traffic Statistics	Displays general traffic statistics.
Active Hosts List	Displays a list of hosts that are actively sending or receiving data on the network.
Remote to Local IP Traffic	Displays network information for traffic flowing from hosts on remote networks to hosts on local networks.
Local to Remote IP Traffic	Displays network information for traffic flowing from hosts on local networks to hosts on remote networks.
Local to Local IP Traffic	Displays network information for traffic flowing from hosts on local networks to hosts on local networks.
List of Active TCP Sessions	Displays a list of TCP sessions that are currently active on the network.
IP Protocol Distribution Statistics	Displays traffic distribution statistics for the IP protocols being recognized by ntop.
IP Protocol Usage	Displays usage information for the IP protocols being recognized by ntop.
IP Traffic Matrix	Displays a traffic flow information matrix in a table format.

Determining Network Bottlenecks

A network bottleneck is a point in the path between two networked hosts at which the available bandwidth is considerably limited. Bottlenecks can often cause serious network performance degradation problems. A bottleneck can be caused by a variety of different factors, including network misconfigurations, hardware errors, and overworked servers. Traffic analyzers are valuable tools for detecting network bottlenecks because they allow traffic flow statistics to be viewed and analyzed for anomalies.

The ntop traffic analyzer is a useful tool for detecting network bottlenecks, since it makes a variety of statistical traffic flow information available to the administrator through an easy-to-use interface. It also makes tracking down the source of network bottlenecks an easier task, through the use of data flow filtering expressions. These allow statistics to be gathered for flows of packet data matching a specific user-defined filtering criteria.

When attempting to detect network bottlenecks, the ntop tool is most useful when executed in Web mode. The ntop Web mode provides many types of network statistics information not available in interactive mode. This additional information can be helpful in the analysis of network traffic and detection of bottleneck conditions.

Table 16.4 is a listing of ntop information viewing modes that can be useful when attempting to detect network bottlenecks.

TABLE **16.4**   Ntop Traffic Views Useful for Detecting Bottlenecks

View Name	*Description*
Sort Traffic by Data Received Sort Traffic by Data Sent	Allows the hosts that are sending or receiving the most data to be shown. These modes can be useful when attempting to determine if a network server is being overloaded with client requests.
Remote to Local IP Traffic Local to Remote IP Traffic Local to Local IP Traffic	Displays statistics information for traffic flowing between hosts on local networks, flowing to remote networks, or flowing from remote networks. These modes can be useful when attempting to determine if a network bottleneck is located on an internal or external network.
IP Protocol Distribution Statistics IP Protocol Usage	These modes display information regarding IP protocol usage. They can be useful when attempting to determine the protocols that are utilizing the most bandwidth on a network.
IP Traffic Matrix	Displays IP traffic flow information in a table format. Allows for side-by-side comparative analysis of flow statistics, so that anomalies may be detected.

The statistics information output by ntop can also be useful for performing baselining operations to help detect future network bottlenecks. Baselining involves the periodic capture of traffic flow statistics to generate a baseline value to which future flow samplings can be compared against. If future samplings do not fall within a reasonable range of the baseline value, they may be indicative of a bottleneck occurrence.

Analyzing Types of Traffic

Tcpdump and ntop may be used to analyze particular types of network traffic through filtering expressions. A captured data packet will only be processed and displayed if it results in a filtering expression evaluating as true.

A filtering expression is made up of one or more filtering commands, otherwise known as primitives. Groups of primitives may be evaluated through the use of logical operators to allow for complex packet filtering activity.

A primitive is made up of the following components:

```
[Qualifier Group] [Primitive ID]
```

The qualifier group is made up of one or more qualifier elements, each of which is used to restrict the type of traffic that is captured. These qualifier elements also set a context to be used with the primitive ID during filtering operations.

Table 16.5 lists the types of qualifiers that are supported.

TABLE 16.5 Network Traffic Filtering Qualifiers

Qualifier Type	Description
type	Typing qualifiers. These assign a specific data type to their associated primitive ID for use in filtering comparisons. The following type qualifiers may be used: host, net, port
direction	Data flow direction qualifiers. These allow a specific direction to be specified for use in filtering comparisons. The following direction qualifiers may be used: src, dst
protocol	Transmission protocol qualifiers. These allow captured data traffic to be restricted to a specific protocol type. The following protocol qualifiers may be used: ether, fddi, ip, arp, rarp, decnet, lat, moprc, mopdl, tcp, udp

The primitive ID is a numeric value or alphanumeric name that is used along with its associated qualifier elements to create a complete filtering statement. Primitive IDs can represent host names, IP addresses, port numbers, and other filtering values.

Complex filtering statements may be constructed through the use of primitives grouped together with logical operators and parenthesized expressions.

Logical operators allow multiple filtering primitives to be examined in a comparative fashion. Table 16.6 lists the logical operators that are supported.

TABLE 16.6 Network Traffic Filtering Operators

Operator	Description
!, not	Negation operators. These evaluate as true only if their associated primitive statement results in a false return value.
&&, and	Concatenation operators. These operators require two primitive statements, evaluating as true if both primitives result in a true return value.
‖, or	Alternation operators. These operators require two primitive statements, evaluating as true if one or both primitives result in a true return value.

Logical operators are used in the following manner:

```
[Primitive]  [Operator]  [Primitive]
```

```
Example:  port ftp && host 192.168.1.5
```

Parenthesized expressions allow groups of filtering expressions to be evaluated together as a single "virtual" primitive. This "virtual" primitive can then be used in higher-level filtering evaluations. Parenthesized expressions are used in the following manner:

```
( [Expression] )
```

```
Example: ( port ftp )
```

Primitives, logical operators, and parenthesized expressions may all be used in combination to allow for extremely complex multi-leveled packet filtering activity. Examples of these elements in combination are

```
( port ftp ¦¦ port http ) && host 192.168.1.4
( port http ) ¦¦ ( port http )
```

The use of filtering expressions make monitoring specific types of network traffic an easy task. They provide complex kernel-space packet analysis capabilities, off-loading any sort of filtering activity from having to take place in a user-space network monitoring system. This provides faster performance levels and simplifies monitoring software source code, as the monitoring system itself doesn't have to worry about any sort of packet filtering tasks.

Using the expression writing techniques outlined in this section, any type of data traffic traveling over a network may be captured and examined. These expressions provide for virtually unlimited filtering capabilities.

Summary

Network monitoring can be a powerful tool for detecting attacks against active hosts, determining network bottlenecks, and for providing a general in-depth view into the activity occurring on your network. The techniques described in this chapter will enable you to deploy and use such monitoring systems successfully on a computer network.

Integrating with Windows NT Networks

IN THIS CHAPTER

- Networking the Windows Way   *462*
- Linux and Samba in an NT Environment   *464*

With Linux making inroads into the corporate network environment, interoperability with existing network operating systems is critical and Linux does a good job of this. This chapter looks at how Linux and Windows can communicate with each other using one of the most exciting software products available for Linux today, Samba. We will first review the essentials of Windows networking and the terms used in describing them and then look at setting up Linux and Samba to act as either a client or server in a Windows network.

Networking the Windows Way

The networking support contained in Windows 98 and Windows NT is the result of years of evolution that had its beginning with the NetBIOS file-sharing protocol developed by IBM in the early days of personal computing. This simple protocol was enhanced over the years to eventually become the *Session Message Block,* or SMB, protocol and finally the *Common Internet File System,* or CIFS. To get a better understanding of the manner in which Windows networking works, let us start with some definitions and then take a look at a simple network setup using Windows NT to provide file and print services to Windows 98 clients.

Speaking the Lingo

One of the keys to understanding any technology is to understand the terminology used by practitioners of that technology. This section defines some of the terms used in describing Windows networks. The intention is not to make you fluent in the language of Windows networks, but merely to cover a few of the terms that you need to know in order to set up Samba.

A *workgroup* or *domain* refers to a group of machines on a network that query a common browsing database of shared resources. The primary difference between a workgroup and a domain is that a domain shares security information and a workgroup does not. Every Windows network consists of one or more workgroups or domains and your setup must define a domain or workgroup for Samba.

Browsing refers to the act of accessing the common database via whatever interface the operating system provides. For Windows 98 and Windows NT, this interface is usually the Windows Explorer. The browsing interface for OS/2 is the Workplace Shell and for Linux it is smbclient.

A master browser is the machine in a domain or workgroup that maintains the shared resources database that other members of the group browse. There are two types of master browser:

- The *domain master browser* holds the master browsing database for an entire domain, which may span one or more subnets.

- The *local master browser* holds the master browsing database for a local subnet and queries the domain master browser for information on resources on other subnets.

A Simple NT Network

To better understand how Linux and Samba can integrate into your network, let's first examine a simple Windows network, looking at each piece and seeing how they fit together. Our network will consist of a single domain. A Windows domain consists of the following parts:

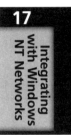

- One primary domain controller (PDC)

- One or more backup domain controllers (BDC)

- One or more resource servers

- Participating clients

For purposes of our examples, our network will be centered on a Windows NT server that acts as the *primary domain controller* (PDC). The PDC is responsible for validating user logons to the domain and maintaining the central user database. It is also the maintainer of the security policies database and is the administrative unit for the network. In addition to these roles, this system may also be a resource server, sharing filesystems, printers, or other resources with client systems on the network.

The next machine in our network is another Windows NT server that acts as the *backup domain controller* (BDC). The BDC also maintains a copy of the user database and security policies database, which it replicates from the PDC, and shares the task of authenticating users. It is intended to provide redundancy in the event that the PDC is unavailable. Again, as with the primary domain controller, the backup domain controller may also be a resource server for the network.

We have one other server in our network that is strictly a resource server. It is a file and print server, email server, and also serves as the intranet Web server. It is often desirable to separate the functions of primary and backup domain controller from the resource sharing function so that a problem with your resource server does not prevent people from logging into the network. This machine does not handle user authentication directly, but passes authentication requests to the primary domain controller. Some of the shared resources served by this machine are the two network printers. Even though these printers are not connected directly to the server, access to the printers is managed through it for accounting purposes.

The remainder of our machines on this network are client systems running Windows 98 or Windows NT Workstation, as well as a few OS/2 systems. Figure 17.1 illustrates this network layout.

FIGURE 17.1

A sample Windows network.

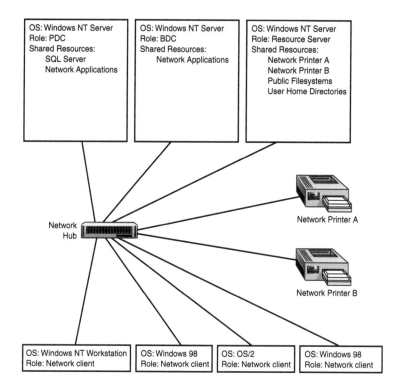

Linux and Samba in an NT Environment

Before looking at the specific roles that Samba can fill in our sample network, let's first look at an overview of what Samba is, the parts that make up the Samba package, and the syntax of the Samba configuration file. Once we have covered these topics, we will start looking at substituting Linux and Samba into our sample network and the configurations required to accomplish this task.

Samba Overview

Like most modern open source projects, including Linux, Samba grew out of a need of its developer, Andrew Tridgell. This need was to be able to share files located on his UNIX server with his DOS personal computer and although he had a solution that worked, it was not particularly stable and this led him to develop his own solution. Using a packet sniffer, Andrew set about the task of reverse-engineering the NetBIOS protocol and came up with a server-based solution that allowed his PC to access UNIX filesystems without him having to resort to setting up NFS on his machine and decreasing the stability. This initial project, which was released in 1992, solved his immediate problem, and having other things to do, he set it aside. After a hiatus of almost two years, a desire to connect a Windows PC to his Linux system revived the project, and Samba was born. Finding that the protocols he was implementing were now documented to a much greater degree than when he started, Andrew, with the help of others, began improving the product. Since that time, Samba has evolved into a multinational project involving a team of developers and is widely recognized as one of the most successful open source projects in the world today.

Now that we know a little of the history of Samba, let's take a look at what Samba does. Samba is an implementation of the four basic CIFS services for UNIX and other operating systems. These four services are

- File and print services

- Authentication and authorization

- Name resolution services

- Browsing services

These CIFS services are implemented in two key programs. The first of these is the Session Message Block daemon (smbd), which handles the file and print services and authentication and authorization portion of CIFS. The second is the NetBIOS names management daemon (nmbd), which handles the name resolution and browsing portions of CIFS. In addition to these daemons, Samba also includes several utility programs to allow you to access the services in a Windows network. The most commonly used utilities and their functions are shown in Table 17.1.

TABLE 17.1 Utilities in the SAMBA Package

Utility	Purpose
nmblookup	This utility is used to query NetBIOS names and map them to IP addresses.
smbclient	An ftp-like client that allows you to access SMB/CIFS resources on a network.

17

Integrating with Windows NT Networks

TABLE 17.1 continued

Utility	Purpose
smbmount	A specialized mount command for mounting SMB/CIFS shared filesystems on UNIX systems.
smbumount	A umount command that allows ordinary users to umount a SMB/CIFS filesystem that they have mounted.
smbpasswd	A password change client to change the local or remote SMB password.
smbprint	A stripped down smbclient that allows printing to SMB shared printer resources.
smbstatus	A utility for listing current SMB connections.
smbtar	A shell script for backing up SMB shared filesystems to a UNIX hosted tape drive.

There are additional scripts and utilities included with the Samba package and the documentation for them can be found on your Red Hat system in the /usr/doc/ samba-2.0.3 directory.

Of the utilities that come with Samba, the one likely to receive the most use is smbclient. This being the case, let's take a closer look at it, as well as the available command-line options and the interactive command set.

The smbclient program allows Linux users to access SMB resources located on the resource servers of your network. These resource servers are typically Windows machines, and if they are, you would access the files via methods including FTP, NFS, and the r-commands, such as rcp.

The smbclient utility provides an FTP-like interface that allows users to transfer files between your computer and a network share on another computer running an SMB server. This means that smbclient is an interactive interface and is meant for temporary access to a shared resource. For more permanent connections to filesystems on SMB servers, you would use the smbfs provided by the kernel and the smbmount utility from the Samba suite.

The smbclient utility provides command-line options to query a server for the shared directories available or to exchange files. Table 17.2 shows some of the most common command-line options used. For more information on all the command-line options, consult the man page for smbclient.

TABLE 17.2 Command-Line Options for smbclient

Option	Description
-N name	Uses name as the local machine's NetBIOS name. Defaults to the hostname of the local machine.
-I ipaddr	Connect to the server at IP address ipaddr.

TABLE **17.2** continued

Option	Description
-U username	Connects to the SMB service using the user account specified by username. The default is determined by value of the USER or LOGNAME environment variable if set or if neither is set, a username of GUEST is used.
-L	Lists the resources available from a server. The server may be specified by name on the command line or by IP address using the -I option.
-W workgroup	Connects to workgroup instead of the one specified in the smb.conf file.

To illustrate the use of some these command-line options, let's try a few commands with smbclient and look at the output generated.

```
[tschenk@nomad tschenk]$ smbclient -L quicksilver -U tschenk
Added interface ip=192.168.50.25 bcast=192.168.50.255 nmask=255.255.255.0
Password:
Domain=[ALCHEMY] OS=[Unix] Server=[Samba 2.0.3]

        Sharename      Type      Comment
        ---------      ----      -------
        public         Disk      Public Stuff
        IPC$           IPC       IPC Service (Samba Server)
        lp             Printer
        tschenk        Disk      Home Directories


        Server                   Comment
        ---------                -------
        QUICKSILVER              Samba Server


        Workgroup                Master
        ---------                -------
        ALCHEMY                  QUICKSILVER
```

This command shows the result of using the -L options to list the shares available on the Samba server running on the host quicksilver to SMB user tschenk.

```
[tschenk@nomad tschenk]$ smbclient //quicksilver/tschenk -U \
tschenk%passwd  -c "get MB03Q.doc"

Added interface ip=192.168.50.25 bcast=192.168.50.255 nmask=255.255.255.0
Domain=[ALCHEMY] OS=[Unix] Server=[Samba 2.0.3]
getting file MB03Q.doc of size 108544 as MB03Q.doc (602.272 kb/s)
➡(average 602.273 kb/s)
```

In the preceding example, the user connected to the server quicksilver to the share known
as tschenk as user tschenk using the password passwd and issued the command get
MB03Q.doc, which transferred the file from the server to the local machine. The following
example shows how to use smbclient interactively to accomplish the same task.

```
[tschenk@nomad tschenk]$ smbclient //quicksilver/tschenk -U tschenk
Added interface ip=192.168.50.25 bcast=192.168.50.255 nmask=255.255.255.0
Password:
Domain=[ALCHEMY] OS=[Unix] Server=[Samba 2.0.3]
smb: \> get MB03Q.doc
getting file MB03Q.doc of size 108544 as MB03Q.doc (630.952 kb/s)
➥(average 630.952 kb/s)
smb: \> quit
[tschenk@nomad tschenk]$
```

The preceding command demonstrates the ftp-like interface of smbclient. As you can see,
once the password was given, the following prompt:

```
smb: \>
```

was presented at which you could type commands. From this command line, you can issue
the commands shown in Table 17.3 to transfer and work with files.

TABLE **17.3**   Interactive Commands for smbclient

Command	Description
? or help [command]	Provides a help message on command or in general if no command is specified.
! [shell command]	Executes the specified shell command or drops the user to a shell prompt.
cd [directory]	Changes to the specified directory on the server machine (not the local machine). If no directory is specified, smbclient reports the current working directory.
lcd [directory]	Changes to the specified directory on the local machine. If no directory is specified, smbclient reports the current working directory on the local machine.
del [files]	The specified files on the server are deleted if the user has permission to do so. Files can include wildcard characters.
dir or ls [files]	Lists the indicated files. You can also use the command ls to get a list of files.
exit or quit	Exits from the smbclient program.
get [file] [local name]	Retrieves the specified file and saves the file on the local server. If local name is specified, the copied file will be saved with this filename rather than the filename on the remote server.
mget [files]	Copies all the indicated files, including those matching any wildcards, to the local machine.

TABLE 17.3 continued

Command	Description
`md` or `mkdir [directory]`	Creates the specified directory on the remote machine.
`rd` or `rmdir [directory]`	Removes the specified directory on the remote machine.
`put [file] [remotename]`	Copies the specified file from the local machine to the server renaming it to `remotename` if specified.
`mput [files]`	Copies all the specified files from the local machine to the server.
`print [file]`	Prints the specified file on the remote machine.
`queue`	Displays all the print jobs queued on the remote server.

As the table shows, the command set for the `smbclient` utility is very much like the command set for the `ftp` command and should feel quite natural to users. The major difference from the `ftp` command is the requirement that the `smb.conf` file be present in order for the client to work properly. This being the case, the next section covers the available configuration options.

Two other related utilities that can be quite useful to your users are the `smbmount` and `smbumount` commands. These utilities, if they are changed to be setuid root, can be used by non-root users to mount shared filesystems. The decision to make these utilities setuid root should not be made lightly, however, because they can represent a security risk to your systems. In addition, if a user is continuously mounting a shared resource on the network, this is probably a good candidate for adding to the system startup scripts, such as `rc.local`.

Regardless of whether you decide to give your users the ability to mount and unmount shares, it is useful to know the syntax of the `smbmount` command. This command is a stripped down version of the `smbclient` code whose sole purpose is to incorporate shared filesystems into the Linux filesystem tree. Following is an example that mounts the public share from the server `quicksilver` onto a mount point called `/win`:

```
smbmount //quicksilver/public -U tschenk -c 'mount /windows -u 500 -g 500'
```

If successful, this command results in the public share from the server called `quicksilver` being mounted at `/windows` and looking like any other part of the Linux filesystem. The `-u` and `-g` arguments of the `mount` command indicate that all files be mapped to userid 500 and groupid 500. The thing to remember at this point is that any text files created on the Linux client and stored in the mounted share area will use the end-of-line format of the client operating system. In this case, the end-of-line protocol used will be the same as for Linux, making the files difficult to read under Windows.

If you later wanted to make the shared filesystem unavailable, you would use the smbumount command. This command has a syntax much like that of the normal umount command. Here is the example to umount the previously mounted share:

```
smbumount /windows
```

In addition to the Samba suite, there is another part of Linux that enables clients running Linux to access filesystem shares on Windows networks. This part is the `smbfs` support, which you can compile into your kernel. The `smbfs` is an implementation of the SMB protocols that is based on Samba code. It allows you to mount SMB shares in a manner similar to NFS exported filesystems. To use this feature of the Linux kernel you must install the smbmount command from the Samba package; however, you are not required to run the smbd or the nmbd daemons. Red Hat goes one step further in that it provides a shell script wrapper to the smbmount program called /sbin/mount.smb that translates mount commands given in the standard mount syntax into the appropriate smbmount commands. Here is a sample of this functionality in action:

```
[root@nomad /root]# mount -t smbfs //quicksilver/public /mnt2
[root@nomad /root]# Added interface ip=192.168.50.25
bcast=192.168.50.255 nmask=255.255.255.0
Server time is Wed Jul 14 23:35:57 1999
Timezone is UTC-5.0
Password:
Domain=[ALCHEMY] OS=[Unix] Server=[Samba 2.0.3]
connected as guest security=user

[root@nomad /root]# df
Filesystem            1k-blocks      Used Available Use% Mounted on
/dev/hda2             1478572    1133273    268893  81% /
//QUICKSILVER/PUBLIC  1072672     214176    858496  20% /mnt2

[root@nomad /root]# ls -l /mnt2
total 3
-rwxr-xr-x   1 root     root          261 Jul 14 00:00 README
drwxr-xr-x   1 root     root          512 Jul 13 23:57 accounting
drwxr-xr-x   1 root     root          512 Jul 13 23:57 development
drwxr-xr-x   1 root     root          512 Jul 13 23:57 humanresources
drwxr-xr-x   1 root     root          512 Jul 14 00:00 miscellaneous
drwxr-xr-x   1 root     root          512 Jul 13 23:57 techops
```

```
[root@nomad /root]# umount /mnt2
```

```
[root@nomad /root]# ls -l /mnt2
total 0
```

The final tool available to Samba users that we will discuss is the *Samba Web Administration Tool*, known as SWAT. This is, as the name implies, a Web-based Samba administration tool. Once a separate product, SWAT is now included as part of the standard Samba package.

The purpose of SWAT is to make the management of your Samba server easier, and it accomplishes this task admirably. To get started with using SWAT, you must first ensure that your system is configured to run it. The first thing to check is the /etc/services file. In order for SWAT to work, you should have a line in this file that looks like this:

```
swat              901/tcp
```

This line indicates that SWAT uses the TCP protocol and that it listens on port 901. The next file to check is the /etc/inetd.conf file. SWAT runs as a service spawned by inetd, just like the ftpd daemon and other services. Your /etc/inetd.conf file should contain a line that looks like the following in order for swat to work correctly:

```
swat      stream  tcp     nowait.400      root /usr/sbin/swat swat
```

Assuming that these lines exist, you are ready to start using SWAT. If they do not, you must add them, uncomment them, or signal inetd to reread the inetd.conf file. To do this, you must send a HUP signal to inetd using the kill command, as shown in this command line:

```
kill -HUP ` cat /var/run/inetd.pid `
```

Alternatively, you can restart the inetd super server using the inetd script located in /etc/rc.d/init.d. To do this, you would issue the following command:

```
/etc/rc.d/init.d/inetd restart
```

Caution

As with any other service, running SWAT provides outside attackers with another potential avenue for accessing your systems. Given the configuration power of SWAT, care should be taken to ensure that systems running SWAT are protected by your firewall.

Having accomplished these steps, you can start using SWAT by invoking your browser and connecting to the URL `http://localhost:901/`. This will bring up a login dialog, which you can log in to as root. Once you do so, you will be at the SWAT home screen, which is shown in Figure 17.2.

FIGURE 17.2

The SWAT home screen.

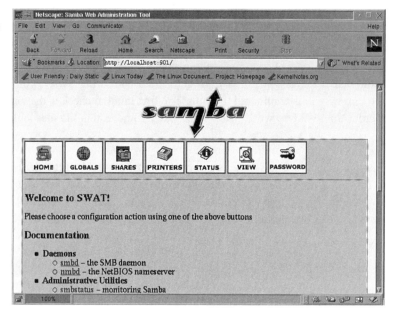

The SWAT home screen contains two main sections. The top of the screen contains several icons, which take you to the different SWAT pages. There are icons that allow you to configure the global parameters, manage shares and printers, check the status of Samba, view the Samba configuration file, and manage user passwords. The remainder of the page contains pointers to the Samba documentation and at the very end contains a pointer to the Samba mailing list. Let's take a look at the configuration screens available and the items they let you control.

The first SWAT screen icon is the Globals icon, which allows you to manipulate the `globals` special section of the `smb.conf` file. Clicking on the icon will bring up the page shown in Figure 17.3.

For each configuration parameter that belongs in the `globals` section, you can enter values, request help, and reset the value to its default. Once you are done editing, click on the Commit Changes button to write them to the `smb.conf` file.

FIGURE **17.3**
The SWAT Globals screen.

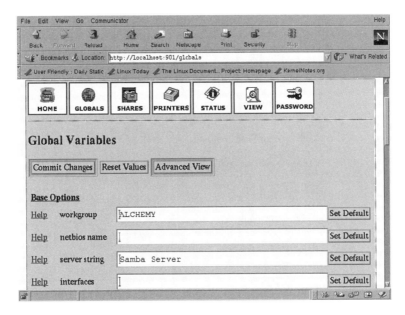

The next screen is the Shares screen, shown in Figure 17.4, which allows you to add, modify, or delete shares. The standard screen here shows the most commonly used parameters from the smb.conf file. You may also configure some of the less commonly used parameters by clicking on the Advanced View button after you have selected a share to examine.

Printers are handled in the same fashion as other shares on the Printers screen, as shown in Figure 17.5.

To check on the status of the Samba software, click on the Status icon to bring up the SWAT Status screen (see Figure 17.6). This screen not only shows you whether the software is running, but also allows you to start and stop the Samba daemons and to view active connections to your Samba server.

You can examine the contents of the smb.conf file by clicking the View icon. This will display the contents of the smb.conf files for you, as shown in Figure 17.7. It allows you to view the parameters set and their values using the Normal View as the default. If you want to see a list of all of the variables available and their values if they have one, click the Full View button.

The final screen is the Password screen, which you select by clicking the Password icon. This brings up the Password Management screen, which allows you to change both local user accounts and accounts on primary domain controller (see Figure 17.8).

FIGURE **17.4**

The SWAT Shares screen.

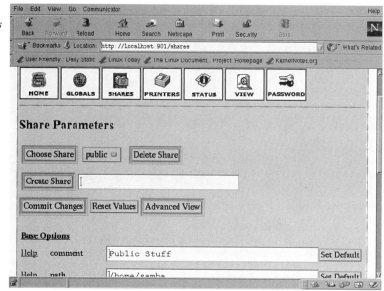

FIGURE **17.5**

The SWAT Printers screen.

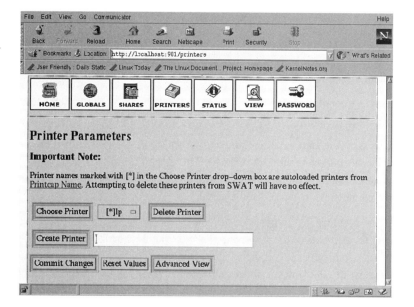

FIGURE **17.6**
The SWAT Status screen.

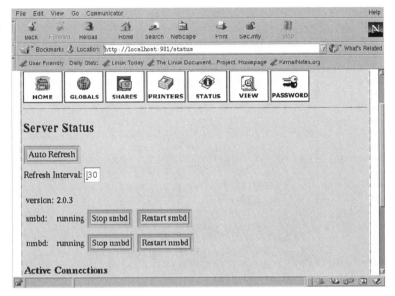

FIGURE **17.7**
The SWAT View screen.

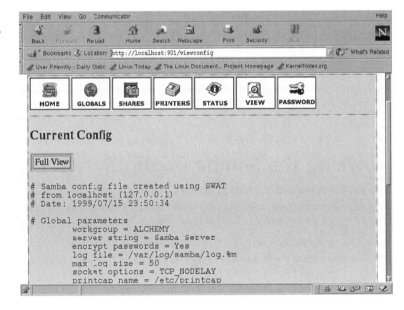

FIGURE **17.8**
*The SWAT
Password screen.*

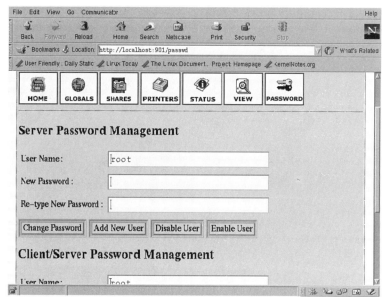

Analyzing the Samba Configuration File

Before we begin looking at Linux in specific roles in a Windows network, let's first take a look at the Samba configuration file. This file has numerous options available and complete coverage of them is beyond the scope of this book. However, we will cover the common options that someone new to Samba is likely to use and then provide some concrete examples of Linux as both a client and a server using Samba.

On Red Hat Linux systems, the default location of the Samba configuration file is in the /etc directory in a file named smb.conf. The smb.conf file that comes with Red Hat can serve as a starting point and with the exception of changing the workgroup name, it is what was used in the previous demonstration of smbclient.

Integrating with Windows NT Networks

CHAPTER 17

477

17

Integrating
with Windows
NT Networks

> **Note**
>
> Changes to the `smb.conf` file require a restart of the Samba server, `smbd`. The simplest method of accomplishing this restart is to use the `smb` script found in `/etc/rc.d/init.d`. The command to restart the Samba server is
>
> ```
> $ /etc/rc.d/init.d/smb restart
> ```

The syntax of the `smb.conf` file is quite simple. It consists of a series of named sections, denoted by a name in brackets, such as [global]. Each section contains a number of parameters, which consist of key/value pairs. Comments can be denoted by either a pound sign (#) or a semicolon (;). These comment characters are interchangeable, however it is common practice to comment out parameters using the semicolon, and to use the pound sign for ordinary comments. Here is a short example showing this syntax:

```
# This line is a comment
[section]
    key1 = value1
# The following parameter is commented out
;   key2 = value2
    key3 = value3
```

The Samba configuration file consists of three special sections and zero or more optional custom sections. The special sections are [global], [homes], and [printers].

> **Caution**
>
> It is always a good idea to make a backup of the original configuration file before making changes to it. One option for doing this is to use RCS and as you make each change, to test it before checking in the revision.

To facilitate testing, ensure that the username on the test client, whether that client be a Windows machine or a Linux client, exists on the machine running Samba. If you do not have a common user between the two systems, create one using the `adduser` and `passwd` commands.

> **Note**
>
> Samba will only work on a properly functioning network. To avoid frustration, it is a good idea to first ensure that the client and server systems you will be working on can communicate with each other. Some simple tests using ping and other network tools now will save you hours of hair pulling later.

The `[global]` Section

The `[global]` section specifies parameters for the entire SMB server. This section also provides default values for the other sections.

The first two parameters shown here specify the workgroup to which your computer belongs and how the server will identify itself when queried by clients.

In addition to specifying the workgroup to which your machine belongs, it also specifies the domain name used when the parameter `security = domain` is specified. The name specified for the workgroup parameter should be limited to no more than nine characters, should have no spaces, and should be entered in all uppercase characters.

The `server string` parameter is a human-readable string that identifies your server when queried by SMB clients.

```
[global]
    workgroup = MYGROUP
    server string = Samba Server
```

In the default configuration file that comes with Red Hat, the `hosts allow` line is commented out. If you uncomment this line, access to the Samba server will be restricted to the specified hosts or networks. In the following example, access is limited to the networks 192.168.1.0/24, 192.168.2.0/24, and to localhost. Multiple networks are separated by spaces and a shorthand syntax is allowed. Class C subnets have three numbers and three dots, class B two numbers and two dots, and class A one number and one dot.

```
    hosts allow = 192.168.1. 192.168.2. 127.
```

The next few parameters have to do with printing. The default setting in the `smb.conf` file that is included with your Red Hat Linux system will make available all of the printers defined in `/etc/printcap` as shared resources to SMB clients on the network. The printing parameter should not be required on Red Hat Linux servers.

```
# if you want to automatically load your printer list rather
# than setting them up individually then you'll need this
```

```
    printcap name = /etc/printcap
    load printers = yes


# It should not be necessary to spell out the print system type unless
# yours is non-standard. Currently supported print systems include:
# bsd, sysv, plp, lprng, aix, hpux, qnx
;    printing = bsd
```

The next entry in the `smb.conf` file is required if you want to specify a guest account for anonymous access to services on your Samba server. This is not a requirement, and by default, guest access is permitted via the `nobody` account.

```
# Uncomment this if you want a guest account, you must add this to
# /etc/passwd, otherwise the user "nobody" is used


;    guest account = pcguest
```

It is occasionally necessary to troubleshoot problems with connections by Windows clients. The following two entries specify the number of characters to compare when matching user names and passwords. The comparisons for this number of characters are case insensitive. These entries should only be uncommented while actively debugging problems.

```
# Password Level allows matching of _n_ characters of the password for
# all combinations of upper and lower case.
;    password level = 8
;    username level = 8
```

Passwords are encrypted by default with Windows 95 OSR2 and later, including of course, Windows NT. Prior to this release, passwords are passed as clear text. Encryption of passwords by the Samba server, however, is not enabled by default if using the `smb.conf` file that comes with Red Hat, as shown in the following lines:

```
# You may wish to use password encryption. Please read
# ENCRYPTION.txt, Win95.txt and WinNT.txt in the Samba documentation.
# Do not enable this option unless you have read those documents
;    encrypt passwords = yes
;    smb passwd file = /etc/smbpasswd
```

This situation means that you must make a decision on whether to support this feature. You have several options as to how to deal with this situation. Two of these are described below.

```
smbpasswd -a userid
```

17

Integrating
with Windows
NT Networks

Another option, and one involving much more effort on your part, is to disable encrypted passwords on the Windows clients. The amount of work that this will entail depends, of course, on the number of clients you must change. Additionally, this procedure is much more error prone due to the fact that the procedure involves editing the registry on each client. Following are the steps involved.

> **Caution**
>
> If you can change the setting on the Samba server, this is preferred to changing the Windows clients. Editing the registry can result in data loss or OS inoperability.

1. On your Windows client, run the registry editor, `regedit` and navigate to the entry `[HKEY_LOCAL_MACHINE\System\CurrentControlSet\Service\VxD\VNETSUP]`.

2. If there is already an object here called `EnablePlainTextPassword`, it will have a value of either 0 or 1.

3. A value of 0 means that the system is using encrypted passwords. To disable this, set the value to 1.

4. If the object does not exist, create it as a `DWORD` and set the value to 1.

5. Save your changes, exit from `regedit` and reboot the Windows system for this change to take effect.

Samba can be configured as a domain server with the following entries in the `smb.conf` file. This will allow your Linux machine to authenticate Windows clients on the network. You may also set up a per machine logon script as well as a per user login batch file. By default, these entries are commented out on your Red Hat system.

```
# Enable this if you want Samba to be a domain logon server for
# Windows95 workstations.
;    domain logons = yes


# if you enable domain logons then you may want a per-machine or
# per user logon script
# run a specific logon batch file per workstation (machine)
;    logon script = %m.bat


# run a specific logon batch file per username
;    logon script = %U.bat
```

The [homes] Section

The next special section of the smb.conf file is the [homes] section, which allows clients to access a user's home directory on your server without having to explicitly specify each one individually. When a service request is made to the Samba server, the server searches the smb.conf for a custom service with the specified name and if it is not found, a search is made for a [homes] section. If this special section exists, the requested service name is compared to user account names and if a match is found the user's home directory is shared on the network.

The following is a sample of the [homes] special section:

```
[homes]
   comment = Home Directories
   browseable = no
   read only = no
   preserve case = yes
   short preserve case = yes
   create mode = 0750
```

This differs from the default that comes with Red Hat Linux slightly. Let's take a look at each parameter and what it means.

The comment parameter is a human-readable identification string that will be displayed to clients browsing the Samba server. Note that this comment parameter is similar to the server string parameter, but the latter is only valid in the [global] special section.

The browseable parameter is set to no. This parameter specifies that the shares displayed by the server will not be called homes, but will be the names of the user directories to which the client has access.

The read only parameter controls whether a user can create and change files in the directory when shared across the network. Two alternative ways to specify this behavior is with the writable parameter, which would be set to yes or the write ok parameter, which would also be set to yes.

The preserve case and short preserve case parameters instruct the server to preserve the case of any new files written to the server. This is important because Windows filenames are not typically case sensitive, but Linux filenames are. The decision on whether to set these parameters depends on whether the filesystem is to be primarily used by Windows clients or primarily used by Linux or UNIX clients.

> **Caution**
>
> Linux and Windows use a different end-of-line sequence in text files. When editing a file through Samba, the text file protocol is determined by the OS of the client. This means that if the same file is edited by clients of both operating systems, corruption can result.

The final entry sets the default file permissions for any files created in the shared directory.

The [printers] Section

There are two ways in which Samba can make printers available to the network. One method is to create a specific share section for each printer in printcap that you want to share. The other method is to use the [printers] special section in order to share all of the printers defined in the /etc/printcap file.

> **Note**
>
> This section mentions /etc/printcap, printcap, and printcap printers several times. /etc/printcap is a file defining all the Linux system's printers. A printcap printer is a printer defined by name in /etc/printcap.
>
> It is possible to create /etc/printcap entries with a text editor, but on your Red Hat Linux system, the preferred method is to use printtool. The printtool creates both local and remote printers through an easy-to-use graphical interface.

The following is a sample [printers] special section. It shares all of the printers defined in the printcap file and permits anyone to print except the guest account.

```
[printers]
    comment = All Printers
    browseable = no
    create mode = 0700
    path = /var/spool/samba
    printable = yes
    public = no
    writable = no
```

The [printers] section defines how printing services are controlled if no specific entries are found in the smb.conf file. As with the [homes] section, if no specific entry is found for a printing service, Samba uses the [printers] section (if it's present) to allow a user to connect to any printer defined in /etc/printcap.

The comment, browseable, and create mode parameters have the same meaning here as they do in the [homes] section.

The spool directory where files are copied before printing is specified by the path parameter. The directory permissions for this spool directory is usually set to allow reading and writing just like the /tmp directory.

A new entry is the printable parameter, which is optional in the [printers] special section. If this were the definition of a specific printer, it would require this entry.

The next entry is the public parameter, which in the example is set to no. This is the line that restricts the guest account from printing. To allow printing from the guest account, change this parameter's value to yes.

The final parameter, writable, is set to no, which indicates that only print jobs are allowed to be written to the specified spool directory.

Creating Custom Sections

Custom sections are stanzas in the smb.conf file that share specific printers or directories in a non-generic manner. These sections are commonly used to share directories for specific groups of users or to create publicly shared directories writable by all. You can also use these sections to share a specific printer on a system if you do not want to share all of them.

The following is an example of a share that is available to a group. This entry defines a filesystem resource called acct, which is available to members of the accounting group acct.

```
[acct]
    comment = Accounting Department Shared Directory
    path = /home/acct
    browseable = yes
    writable = yes
    printable = no
    valid users = @acct
```

The preceding entry has the following characteristics. It creates a filesystem share from the directory /home/acct. This is browseable by SMB clients and is identified by the comment string. It is not a print service, hence the parameter printable, which is set to no. The new item in this list is the valid users parameter, which restricts access to this directory to members of the group acct.

As our next example, consider the case of a dedicated printer share. This entry is quite simple, and consists of three parameters. The first of these is the `print ok` parameter, which must be set to `yes` if you want to be able to print. The next entry specifies the printer name from the `printcap` file, and the `path` specifies the spool directory. This spool directory must be writable by whoever wants to be able to print using this service.

```
[exec_lp]
    print ok = yes
    printer name = exec_lp
    path = /var/spool/samba
```

In the dedicated print share, the `print ok` parameter (or the printable synonym) is necessary. It's also necessary to name the printer with the `printer name` line. The intent of `[printers]` is accessibility to all users with valid IDs. The intent of a special printer is typically to restrict access to a user or group, implying that it would be a good idea to add a `valid users` parameter line to the dedicated printer share. Beyond that, the `[printers]` section and dedicated print shares function pretty much the same.

Linux and Samba as a Client OS

One of the ways in which Linux and Samba can be incorporated into an existing Windows network is as a client. In this role, Samba doesn't share any resources with other systems; it merely accesses shared resources on the network's resource servers. To do this we will be looking at using the `smbclient` program, using `smbmount`, and at the `smbfs` option of the kernel and how it can be used to access SMB shared filesystems.

Setting Up the `smb.conf` File

Although you are not required to run the `smbd` or `nmbd` programs to act as a client on a Windows network, you do need to create a `smb.conf` file because it is required by Samba utilities such as `smbclient` and `smbmount`. However, since you will not be sharing any resources with the network, this file can be a minimal one. Following is a minimalist `smb.conf` file that allows our Linux client to be considered part of the domain ALCHEMY.

```
[global]
    workgroup = alchemy
```

Testing Your Configuration from Linux

Our first test of the Linux client will be to get a list of services from a server on our network. For this test, we will use the smbclient command with the -L command-line option.

```
[tschenk@nomad tschenk]$ smbclient -L quicksilver -U tschenk
Added interface ip=192.168.50.25 bcast=192.168.50.255 nmask=255.255.255.0
Password:
Domain=[ALCHEMY] OS=[Unix] Server=[Samba 2.0.3]

        Sharename      Type       Comment
        ---------      ----       -------
        public         Disk       Public Stuff
        IPC$           IPC        IPC Service (Samba Server)
        lp             Printer
        tschenk        Disk       Home Directories


        Server                    Comment
        ---------                 -------
        QUICKSILVER               Samba Server


        Workgroup                 Master
        ---------                 -------
        ALCHEMY                   QUICKSILVER
```

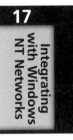

This test gives us a list of shares on the server known as quicksilver available to the user tschenk. The output shows that there is a shared public directory called public, a printer called lp, and the home directory of user tschenk.

Knowing this information, let's try to access the public directory and see what is kept there. For this we will again use the smbclient utility to browse the share.

```
[tschenk@nomad tschenk]$ smbclient //quicksilver/public -U tschenk
Added interface ip=192.168.50.25 bcast=192.168.50.255 nmask=255.255.255.0
Password:
Domain=[ALCHEMY] OS=[Unix] Server=[Samba 2.0.3]
smb: \> dir
  miscellaneous                 D        0   Wed Jul 14 00:00:52 1999
  techops                       D        0   Tue Jul 13 23:57:41 1999
  development                   D        0   Tue Jul 13 23:57:48 1999
  accounting                    D        0   Tue Jul 13 23:57:34 1999
```

```
humanresources                 D      0  Tue Jul 13 23:57:36 1999
README                               261  Wed Jul 14 00:00:45 1999

      33521 blocks of size 32768. 27022 blocks available
smb: \> quit
```

As you can see, we were able to connect to the public shared directory using the `smbclient` command and were able to view the directories and files contained there.

Now let's suppose that the user `tschenk` wants to mount his home directory on the server onto his local Linux client. To do this, he will use the `smbmount` and `smbumount` commands.

```
[tschenk@nomad tschenk]$ smbmount //quicksilver/tschenk -c 'mount samba \
-u 500 -g 500'
Added interface ip=192.168.50.25 bcast=192.168.50.255 nmask=255.255.255.0
Server time is Wed Jul 14 00:14:57 1999
Timezone is UTC-5.0
Password:
Domain=[ALCHEMY] OS=[Unix] Server=[Samba 2.0.3]
security=user

[tschenk@nomad tschenk]$ cd samba

[tschenk@nomad samba]$ ls l*
lilo-colors.tar.gz  limp_penguin_ai.zip  linux-1.3.0.tar.gz  ljf.quote
limp_penguin.ai     linux-1.0.tar.gz     linux-2.0.tar.gz    lodlin16.tgz
limp_penguin.eps    linux-1.1.0.tar.gz   linux-2.1.0.tar.gz
limp_penguin.jpg    linux-1.2.0.tar.gz   linux-2.2.0.tar.gz

[tschenk@nomad samba]$ cd ..

[tschenk@nomad tschenk]$ smbumount samba

[tschenk@nomad tschenk]$ ls samba
```

As you can see, the user `tschenk` was able to mount his shared home directory from the server onto a directory called `samba` and then unmount it again.

Caution

In order for a regular user to mount and unmount shares in this fashion, the `smbmnt` and `smbumount` commands must be made setuid root. They are not installed this way for the Red Hat RPM for Samba.

As a final test, we will attempt to print a file on the printer attached to the server. To do this, we will again be using the `smbclient` command. as shown here:

```
[tschenk@nomad tschenk]$ smbclient //quicksilver/lp -U tschenk%password \
-c 'print invite.ps'

Added interface ip=192.168.50.25 bcast=192.168.50.255 nmask=255.255.255.0
Domain=[ALCHEMY] OS=[Unix] Server=[Samba 2.0.3]
putting file invite.ps as invite.ps (383.479 kb/s) (average 383.479 kb/s)
```

As you can see, setting up Linux as a client on the Windows network is not at all difficult and if you are lucky all things will go smoothly. Of course, if you ran into trouble attempting any of the examples as shown here, you are probably asking yourself, what now? Fortunately, the Samba package includes a number of documents that can help you to diagnose problems. These documents are found on your Red Hat Linux system in `/usr/doc/samba-2.0.3/docs`. In addition, a good place to look for help is on the Web at Deja.com. Visit their Web site and use the Usenet search engine to search the newsgroups for information about Samba or post to one of the Samba newsgroups with your question.

Linux and Samba as a Server OS

A more interesting role for Linux and Samba on your Windows network is as a resource server. In our example network described earlier, a good candidate for replacement by a Linux host is the resource server that was sharing the public directory, the user home directory, and the two printers. By substituting a Linux system here, you can save considerably on the cost of your network because you will not require an NT license. In addition to sharing resources with the rest of the network, you can also use this system to handle email, run a DNS server, and set up a Web server for your intranet. You can do this all at a lower cost because the machine to be used can be much less powerful than the equivalent NT server.

Setting Up the `smb.conf` File

The `smb.conf` file required for a resource server configuration is naturally more complex than the previous one, as you may have guessed. Here is the configuration file I used while testing Samba for this book:

```
#======================= Global Settings ======================================
[global]
   workgroup = ALCHEMY
   server string = Samba Server
   hosts allow = 192.168.50. 127.
   printcap name = /etc/printcap
```

```
   load printers = yes
   print command = lpr -P %p %s ; rm %s
   log file = /var/log/samba/log.%m
   max log size = 50
   security = user
   encrypt passwords = yes
   smb passwd file = /etc/smbpasswd
   socket options = TCP_NODELAY
   dns proxy = no


#============================ Share Definitions ===============================
[homes]
   comment = Home Directories
   browseable = no
   writable = yes
   create mode = 0750


# NOTE: If you have a BSD-style print system there is no need to
# specifically define each individual printer
[printers]
   comment = All Printers
   path = /var/spool/samba
   browseable = no
   guest ok = no
   writable = no
   printable = yes


[public]
   comment = Public Stuff
   path = /home/samba
   public = yes
   writable = yes
   printable = no
   write list = @staff
```

This configuration file makes all of the printers on my Samba server available to the network as long as they are valid users. It also shares home directories and a public space for members of group staff. Once this file was created, a server restart was required and was accomplished by running the following command:

```
/etc/rc.d/init.d/smb restart
```

Testing Your Configuration from Windows

For the first test of my Samba server, I attempted to access the public directory on my Samba server from a Windows 98 client. To do this, I logged in as user `tschenk`, which also exists on the Samba server, and clicked the Network Neighborhood icon. As Figure 17.9 shows, this is where I had my first indication of success.

FIGURE 17.9

Network Neighborhood window showing my SAMBA server.

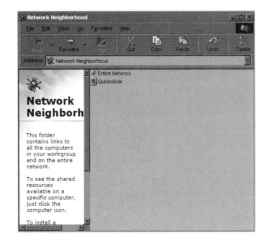

I then clicked the Entire Network icon and was presented with the screen shown in Figure 17.10, which showed that my domain of ALCHEMY was being recognized.

FIGURE 17.10

Network Neighborhood window showing the ALCHEMY Workgroup.

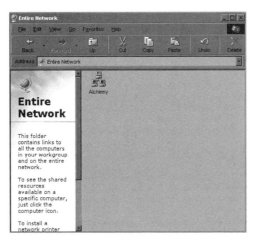

Drilling down further, I saw the hosts on my network that implemented the SMB protocol and that were visible to the network (see Figure 17.11).

FIGURE **17.11**
*Network
Neighborhood
window showing
the hosts in the
ALCHEMY
domain.*

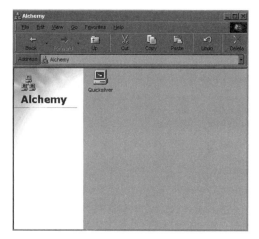

I once again drilled down by clicking the icon representing the host Quicksilver and was presented with the screen shown in Figure 17.12, which showed the resources that I was attempting to share from my Samba server.

FIGURE **17.12**
*Quicksilver
shared resources.*

A final drill down showed that I was indeed successful at sharing the resources that I specified in the smb.conf file. Figure 17.13 shows the contents of the public directory.

FIGURE **17.13**
The public shared directory.

My final test was to see if I could print to the lp printer on my Samba server. To do this, I simply clicked the lp icon, went through the configuration dialogs to configure this printer with the appropriate driver, and then printed a test page, which worked just as expected.

Naturally, it was partially luck that everything went so smoothly. But it was also due to the fact that I spent a significant amount of time reading the documentation that comes with Samba in order to understand how Windows networking behaves, as well as reviewing the manual pages for Samba.

Sources of Samba Help

If you are not so lucky in getting Samba set up, help is available and if you ask politely, you might even get help from the Samba developers. Let's take a look at a couple of sources for help with Samba.

Samba Mailing Lists

There are a number of mailing lists having to deal with all aspects of Samba, from development to support. Some of these lists are for end users as well as developers. Table 17.4 is a partial list of the mailing lists available.

TABLE **17.4**   SAMBA Mailing Lists

Listname	Focus of Discussion
samba	General discussion of the Samba software suite.
samba-announce	Announcements of new releases or other items of interest to the Samba community.
samba-docs	Discussions about Samba documentation project.
samba-technical	Developers discussion of technical issues surrounding Samba.

You can subscribe to any of these lists by sending email as shown in the following command:

```
echo "subscribe listname your full name" ¦ mail listproc@samba.org
```

You would of course, replace `listname` in the command shown with the name of the list, for example, `samba-technical`.

Samba Newsgroups

Another source of information is Usenet newsgroups, specifically the newsgroup `comp.protocols.smb`. Another resource available for looking for help is the Usenet archives at Deja.com, which allows you to search the newsgroups looking for keywords. You can read the newsgroups or search them via the Web at `http://www.deja.com/`.

The Samba Home Page

An excellent source of information about Samba is the Samba home page on the Web at `http://www.samba.org/`. This site has all of the documents that come with the source distribution, as well as pointers to other sources of information, including information on tuning the performance of Samba. Be sure to stop by there if you have any trouble getting Samba to work.

Summary

This chapter looked at what comprises a Windows network, including the requirements for setting up a domain. We also examined the Samba configuration file and tested what we learned by setting up Linux as a client system on the Windows network. We tested our connectivity and then set up Linux as a server, and tested connectivity to it from a Windows host. Finally, we looked at places where you can learn more about Samba, one of the most useful tools in the Linux arsenal.

Integrating with Other Network Operating Systems

IN THIS CHAPTER

- **Getting Along with Your Neighbors** *494*
- **Linux in a NetWare Environment** *495*
- **Linux in an AppleTalk Environment** *513*

Getting Along with Your Neighbors

As you saw with the examination of Samba, which is covered in Chapter 17, "Integrating with Windows NT Networks," one of the strengths of Linux is its ability to interact with other network operating systems. This is true not only of the various flavors of UNIX and Windows, but also with NetWare and AppleTalk networks. This chapter examines some of the tools that allow Linux to communicate with these other network operating systems and how to configure Linux so that it can share resources with them. It starts with an examination of Linux and NetWare, looking at Linux in roles as both a server and as a client, and then takes a look at the tools available that allow Linux to share resources in an AppleTalk network. In these days of heterogeneous networks, which consist of systems from multiple vendors, the ability to interoperate with other network operating systems is essential. Companies have significant investments in networks and interoperability with them means that this investment is not lost when adding Linux to them.

Using the Right Tool for the Job

One of the reasons why Linux is so often called on to work with other network operating systems is the explosive growth of the Internet. As businesses see the need to be connected, they also see that while their current network operating systems are well suited for their corporate networks, they may need to look at other options for Internet services. This is where Linux shines because a Linux server with a mail transport agent, Web serving capabilities, name services, and all of the other standard Internet features is a cost-effective way to get connected. In fact, in the small office environment, a single Linux server can provide all of the services required to get a company connected without costing an exorbitant amount of money, which explains the market for Linux-based Internet appliances, such as the Cobalt Cube.

With this opportunity for Linux to move into such environments, you may wonder why anyone would bother trying to get Linux to interoperate with these other network operating systems, when the majority of the functions that are provided by them are also provided by Linux. Why not just replace the other systems with Linux systems and go with an all Linux solution? There are many reasons why you might not want to do this. Some of these reasons are

- The cost of conversion, both in time and money is too high.

- Needed features are available only on the existing network operating system.

- Applications used in the company may not be available on Linux and no suitable replacement is available either.

- Retraining costs and time lost during retraining would be too costly.

Any or all of these are reason enough to not replace an existing system, plus the time honored maxim, "If it ain't broke, don't fix it." It may also just be the matter of using the right tool for the job, and contrary to what many Linux advocates will tell you, Linux is not always the right tool, no matter how much we wish it was.

On the other hand, there are cases where replacing the existing system may make sense. A few of these reasons are

- Maintenance of the existing systems is more expensive than implementing a new one.

- The ability to find and train people on this new system is limited.

- The features of the existing system are replicated in the new system in a more robust or secure fashion.

Replacing existing operating systems is never an easy decision and is not the focus of this chapter. This chapter covers how to make your Linux systems part of an existing NetWare or AppleTalk network, starting with NetWare.

Linux in a NetWare Environment

Red Hat Linux comes with everything you need to interoperate with NetWare networks on the installation media. The relevant packages that must be installed are

- mars-nwe-0.99pl15-3

- ncpfs-2.2.0.12-5

- ipxutils-2.2.0.12-5

The tools contained within these packages include those required for setting up your Linux system to act as a NetWare file and print server or to act as a NetWare client. Assuming that you have these installed, let's take a look at configuring them.

NetWare Interoperability Options

Although Red Hat comes with the mars_nwe package, there are other options available for Linux. One of these options is the lwared, which performs many of the same functions as mars_nwe. A full description of how to use this package, including the location of the source code and binaries, can be found in the IPX-HOWTO located in `/usr/doc/HOWTO/IPX-HOWTO` on your Red Hat system.

Another option, previously available from Caldera, was NetWare for Linux. This was a NetWare-4.1 compatible package for Linux that allowed Linux to offer all of the services that can be offered by a NetWare server. Although you can still obtain this package from the Caldera FTP site, it has not been updated since Red Hat 5.1 was released and is not recommended for use. In addition, it requires a streams implementation for Linux, which the major developers all agree will never be included in the kernel source tree, thus limiting your ability to track kernel development.

Adding IPX Protocol Support to Your Kernel

In order to allow interoperability with NetWare, you must configure your kernel to support the IPX protocol. This protocol is the protocol used by Novell and is similar in functionality to the IP protocol used in TCP/IP networking. In order to configure your kernel to act as a NetWare client or server, the option you must set is CONFIG_IPX, which you set by answering yes to the configuration prompt, "IPX networking." In addition, in order to be able to mount NetWare filesystem volumes, you must also set the CONFIG_NCP_FS option, by saying yes to the "NCP filesystem support" configuration option. For a more complete description of the kernel configuration required to support the mars_nwe and ncpfs packages, you can refer again to the IPX-HOWTO.

In order to better understand how Linux talks to NetWare, it is important to have a basic understanding of how a NetWare network works. The following description attempts to cover this, but it does not cover any of the exceptions to the rules that you are likely to find in a large Novell network.

NetWare Networking Concepts

The key concept in IPX networking is the scheme of numbered networks used. A network in this context is a collection of equipment on the same LAN segment that uses the same frame type. Frame type refers to the actual protocol used to transport the IPX datagrams over the network and is typically one of four common types. These types are Ethernet_II, 802.3, 802.2, and SNAP. Understanding the differences between these frame types is unimportant for the purposes of this discussion; however, you should know which one your network is using since you will need this information to configure mars_nwe under Linux. Different groups of equipment on the same LAN can use different frame types and are considered to be on different networks even though they are connected to the same LAN segment. Each of the networks is allocated a unique network number by which it is identified across the entire internetwork. This allocation is usually performed by a NetWare server, but if configured to do so, your Linux systems can perform this task as well. IPX clients are allocated this number at startup and this number and their frame type are all they need to know in order to access services on the network. Routing in an IPX network is performed by the server, which usually has one network card for each network that they serve. Routing information is shared between servers by means of periodic broadcasts of the routing information using the RIP protocol. Using this protocol, the servers learn the topology of the network shortly after coming up.

Linux as NetWare Client

Once you have your kernel compiled to support the IPX protocol, you are ready and able to set up your Linux system as a NetWare client. This involves the following steps:

1. Loading the ncpfs module.
2. Using the IPX tools to get your network number.
3. Finding servers on the network.
4. Mounting a NetWare volume.
5. Configuring your system to use NetWare printers.

The first step is self explanatory and simply involves issuing the `insmod` command as follows:

```
insmod ncpfs
```

Once this is done, you are ready to use the IPX tools to get your network number from the server. This is done with the `ipx_configure` command. For most installations, the command you would use is as follows:

```
ipx_configure --auto_interface=on --auto_primary=on
```

If this works, you can now query the network for a list of servers using the `slist` command. This command does a broadcast on the network and reports any responses from NetWare servers. If you know the name of your server, you can verify that it is accessible to you by issuing the `slist` command with either the complete name of the server, or a pattern that will match the name of your server. For example, if your server name is Grumpy, you could issue the following command:

```
slist G*
```

If `slist` does not find any server on the network, it will respond with a message to that effect.

Once you know the server name, and have verified with `slist` that you can see it, you can mount NetWare volumes on your Linux client. In order to do this, you will need four pieces of information. They are as follows:

- The fileserver name

- The volume name

- A login id and password on the server

- The mount point where the volume should be mounted

For example, assume that on the server Grumpy, there is a volume named ACCT01 and you want to access it as user guest who has no password. The mount point for this volume will be `/nw/acct01`. This would mean that you need to issue the following command:

```
ncpmount -S Grumpy -U guest -n -V ACCT01 /nw/acct01
```

You can now access the files on the NetWare volume just like any other filesystem on your Linux system.

Once you are configured on the network, other things that you can do include sending messages to NetWare users using the nsend command, or print to NetWare printers. Printing is normally done using the `nprint` command, but if you prefer a more persistent connection to the printer and want to use the standard print utilities, you can use the PrintTool part of the control-panel to configure the printer for you and a filter will be constructed that issues the appropriate `nprint` command. Just as with access volumes on a NetWare server, in order to do this you must know the name of the server, the queue name, a login id and password on the server with print permission, and the type of printer attached.

Linux as NetWare Server

If you choose to make Linux server in the role of a NetWare server, under Red Hat you will want to run mars_nwe or lwared. Both of these products allow Linux to provide NetWare file and print services on to a network of IPX clients. Of these two, the one covered here is the one that comes with your Red Hat distribution, mars_nwe, also known as Martin Stover's NetWare Emulator.

The mars_nwe package implements a subset of the Novell NCP protocol for file-, print-, and disk-based bindery services. This allows Linux to appear to IPX clients as a NetWare server. Assuming that you have the packages installed as noted earlier, let's take a look at the default configuration as supplied by Red Hat. The configuration file for mars_nwe is located in the `/etc` directory and is called `nwserv.conf`. As you can see, it is heavily commented. Listing 18.1 contains parts of this configuration file interspersed with explanations that are designed to help you complete the configuration of the mars_nwe package.

LISTING 18.1 Section 1 from the /etc/nwserv.conf File—Volume Configuration

```
# ==========================================================================
# Section 1: volumes (required)
#
# In this section you list all Linux-directories accessible via mars_nwe.
#
# To be more precise: a mapping from Linux-directories to mars_nwe-volumes
# is done. (Volumes are the beasts you can map to drive letters under DOS
# using map.exe ).
#
# Linux-directory                mars_nwe-volume    map.exe       DOS-Drive
# /var/local/nwe/SYS  ------->   SYS                ------------> W:
#
# More than one entry is allowed in this section.
# The maximum number of volumes is a compile-time option that must be
# specified in `config.h' before compiling mars_nwe.
#
# Please note that at least the volume SYS must be defined and it must
# contain the following sub-directories: LOGIN, PUBLIC, SYSTEM, MAIL.
# See the installation-instructions in the doc-directory for more infos.
#
#
# ------------------------------------------------------------------------
# Syntax:
#     1      VOLUMENAME     DIRECTORY              OPTIONS
#
# VOLUMENAME:  the name of the mars_nwe-volume (max. 8 characters)
# DIRECTORY:   the directory on your Linux-system associated with that
#              volume; use the special name ~ to refer to the users
#              individual home-directory
#
# OPTIONS:     none or some of the following characters (without a seperator)
#     k        allow lowercase-filenames (if you don't set this, all
#              files _must_ be upper-case)
#     m        removable volume (e.g. cd-roms)
#     r        volume is read-only and always reports "0 byte free"
#              (this is intended for copies of CD-ROMs on harddisks)
#     o        volume has only one filesystem/device/namespace
#              this is for filesystems with high inode > 0xFFFFFFFF.
```

18

LISTING **18.1** continued

```
#               because for namespace services mars_nwe normally use the
#               first 4 bit of 32 bit inode for distinguish
#               between several devices/namespaces for one volume.
#        p      "PIPE"-filesystem. All files are pipe commands.
#               See `doc/PIPE-FS'.
#
#        O      + OS/2 namespace.
#        N      + NFS  namespace.
# -------------------------------------------------------------------
#
# Examples:
#        1      SYS            /var/local/nwe/SYS      k
#        1      HOME           ~                       k
# Use /var/netware for the SYS volume, and make it read-only
     1     SYS     /var/mars_nwe/sys     rk
          1      CDROM          /mnt/cdrom                   kmr
#        1      SYS            /u3/SYS/             k
```

Section 1 of the configuration file defines the SYS volume as a read-only volume that is located on the Linux server at /var/mars_new/sys and that allows lowercase characters in filenames. It also defines a volume CDROM, which is also read-only, allows lowercase filenames, and is marked as removable media. If you wanted to define a volume HOME that corresponded to the remote user's home directory on the Linux box, you could create an entry like the example shown in Listing 18.1 containing the word HOME.

Having completed the configuration of volumes in section 1 of the configuration file, we can now move on to section 2 (see Listing 18.2). In this section, we will configure the server name to be used by the NetWare emulator running under Linux.

LISTING **18.2** Section 2 of the /etc/nwserv.conf File—Servername Configuration

```
# =========================================================================
# Section 2: servername (optional)
#
# The servername is the name under which this server will show up when
# using tools like "slist" (server-list).
#
# If you don't supply an entry for this section, the hostname of your
# Linux-machine will be converted to all-uppercase and used as the servername.
#
# -------------------------------------------------------------------
# Syntax:
```

LISTING **18.2**   continued

```
#       2       SERVERNAME
#
# SERVERNAME:  a name for this nw-server
# ------------------------------------------------------------------
#
# Example:
#       2       MARS    # name of the server would be MARS
```

As stated in the comments, since there is no name defined in this section the default name is used. This default is the name of the Linux host in all uppercase letters. For example, if I used this on a system named madmax, the NetWare server name assigned would be MADMAX. If you do not want to use this default, simply create an entry as shown in the example in Listing 18.2 and specify a name to use.

In the next section, shown in Listing 18.3, you may configure the network number to be used by your NetWare emulator. The default is to use the auto keyword, which results in the network number being automatically generated by the software.

LISTING **18.3**   Section 3 of the `/etc/nwserv.conf` File—Network Number Configuration

```
# ========================================================================
# Section 3: Number of the internal network (required)
#
# If have dealt with the TCP/IP-configuration of your Linux-Box, the term
# "ip-address" may be familiar to you. It's a number that uniquely
# identifies your machine in the internet.
# As you might already expect, even the IPX-people use a unique number to
# identify each other. Addresses in the IPX-world always consist of a
# 4-byte "network-number" plus a 6-byte "node-number" (remember the
# ip-addresses also use 4-bytes).
#
# The numbering-rule for ipx-clients is easy: their "address" is the
# external-network of the server they are connected to plus the
# hardware-address of their own ethernet-card (6 byte). As a result of this
# rule, the clients can determine their address automatically (by listening
# to the server and looking at their own ethernet-hardware) and no
# configuration-files on the clients-side have to be maintained. (It would
# really be a nasty thing if you think of very many DOS-clients [remember:
# DOS is an OS where ordinary users can screw up the configuration files].)
#
# For internal routing purposes, a netware-server has an "internal network"
#
```

LISTING 18.3 continued

```
# As there is no organisation which regulates the use of network-numbers
# in the IPX-world, you have to run "slist" (under DOS or Linux) to
# determine a number that isn't already used by another server on your
# net. You better double-check and ask the other network administrators
# before using a random value because not all servers might be on-line when
# you "listen" to the net.
#
# A reasonable choice for the internal net-number of your mars_nwe-server
# could be the ip-address of your Linux-Box. It is reasonable because
# ip-addresse are unique and if every nw-administrator uses only this uniqe
# value, potential conflicts will be minimized. Of course this choice is
# no guarantee.
#
# Please note that you have to specify the address of your "internal
# ipx-network" in hexadecimal format (the leading "0x" indicates it).
#
#
# - - - - - - - - - - - - - - - - - - - - - - - - - - - - - - - - - - - - - - - - - - - - - - - - - - - -
# Syntax:
#       3       INTERNAL_NET    [NODE]
#
# INTERNAL_NET: the hexadecimal value of your "internal ipx-network". Use
#               "0x0" or "auto" to refer to your ip-addresse (it's a kind of
#               automagically setup)
# NODE:         use 1 if you don't know what this entry is for (optional)
# - - - - - - - - - - - - - - - - - - - - - - - - - - - - - - - - - - - - - - - - - - - - - - - - - - - -
#
# Example:
#       3       auto    1       # automatic setup

        3       auto    1
```

You should have no reason to change the setting of the internal network number unless the Novell administrators on your network would prefer that you use some other internal network number.

The next section, shown in Listing 18.4, is the IPX device section. The entries here are used to set up the router built into the mars_nwe program or by the separate nwrouted program. The lines consist of a network number, frame type, network device, and the ticks parameter. Each of these is described in the comments.

LISTING 18.4 Section 4 of the `/etc/nnswerv.conf` File—IPX Devices Configuration

```
# =========================================================================
# Section 4: IPX-devices (strongly recommended)
#
# This section contains information for the ipx-router built into mars_nwe
# and/or the external program "nwrouted".
# Both processes exchange the ipx-packets between your machine and the rest
# of the world (in other words: their functionallity is essential). Of
# course, to use one of both is already sufficient.
#
# Note for people with other IPX/NCP servers on the net:
#       - choose the same frame-type as the other servers use
#       - make sure your network-number is not already in use by another
#         server (see the output of slist under Linux or DOS)
#
# Under Linux, it is possible to let the kernel detect all values
# automatically for you. This is only possible (and only makes sense then)
# if there are other IXP/NCP servers on the same net which are setup
# correctly.
#
#
# -------------------------------------------------------------------------
# Syntax:
#       4       NET_NUMBER      DEVICE FRAME    TICKS
#
# NET_NUMBER:   this number is determined by the router of the physical
#               network you're attached to. Use "0x0" to let the
#               linux-kernel determine your network number by listening
#               on the local network
# DEVICE:       the network-interface associated with the NET_NUMBER. Use
#               a "*" (star) to automatically setup all devices at once.
# FRAME:        the frame-type of the data-packets on your local network.
#               Possible values are:
#                       ethernet_ii
#                       802.2
#                       802.3   (default)
#                       snap
#                       token
#                       auto    automatic detection of the frame-type used
#                               in your ipx-environment
# TICKS:        the time data-packets need to get delivered over a
#               certain interface. If your connection goes through several
#               routers, the shortest path can be determined by summing up
```

18

Integrating with
Other Network
Operating
Systems

LISTING **18.4**   continued

```
#               all ticks for every route and compare the results.
#               (1 tick = 1/18th second)
# --------------------------------------------------------------
#
# Examples:
#    4      0x0     *       AUTO    1       # automatic setup
#    4      0x10    eth0    802.3   1       # manual setup

#       4      0x10    eth0    802.3   1
        4      0x0     *       802.3   1
```

In section 4, you define the frame type used, which as stated earlier defines which machines on your local area network segment are considered to be part of the same network. If your NetWare emulator is the only server on the network, you can allow the software to configure itself by using the automatic setup line from the examples. If it is not the only server on the network, you should consult with your NetWare administrator to determine the correct values.

Section 5 of the /etc/nwserv.conf file, shown in Listing 18.5, is a boolean flag that tells the server whether or not to save routing information between invocations of the server software.

LISTING **18.5**   Section 5 of the /etc/nwserv.conf File—Saving IPX Routes Flag

```
# ========================================================================
# Section 5: Saving of ipx-routes (required)
#
# This entry controls if the information regarding the ipx-routes should be
# saved beyond the lifetime of the server.
#
# --------------------------------------------------------------
# Syntax:
#    5      SAVE_FLAG
#
# SAVE_FLAG:
#    0      don't save routes (default)
#    1      do save routes
# --------------------------------------------------------------
#

5    0
```

Again, unless you have an especially complicated routing scheme on your NetWare network, there is probably no reason to change the value of the parameter for section 5.

Section 6 of the /etc/nswerv.conf file determines the version of NetWare that we will emulate. This section is shown in Listing 18.6.

LISTING 18.6   Section 6 of the /etc/nwserv.conf File—Version Spoofing

```
# ==========================================================================
# Section 6: version-"spoofing"
#
# Some clients work better if the server tells that it is a 3.11 Server,
# although many calls (namespace services) of a real 3.11 Server are
# missing yet.
# To test the namespace calls, this entry must be set to > 0 and ` config.h'
# must be altered before compiling "mars_nwe".
#
# -------------------------------------------------------------------------
# Syntax:
#       6          SERVER_VERSION
#
# SERVER_VERSION: the version-number reported to DOS-clients
#       0          Version 2.15 (default)
#       1          Version 3.11
#       2          Version 3.12 (not implemented yet)
# -------------------------------------------------------------------------
#

6       0
```

The value that you set in section 6 helps to define your capabilities to the client. The default value as shown in Listing 18.6 is the safest bet; however, if you follow the example in the IPX-HOWTO, you will set the value of this parameter to 1 for version 3.11.

The next section of the configuration file shown in Listing 18.7 sets the password handling policy. The syntax is the section number followed by a numeric flag that specifies how passwords will be handled for DOS clients. The comments in the listing explain the meaning of the possible numerical values.

LISTING 18.7   Section 7 of the /etc/nwserv.conf File—DOS Client Password Handling

```
# ===========================================================================
# Section 7: password handling of DOS-clients (required)
#
# When changing your "mars_nwe"-password from a DOS-client, this client
# (think of "LOGIN.EXE", "SYSCON.EXE" or "SETPASS.EXE") can encrypt your
# password before sending it to the "mars_nwe"-server (this improves
# security a little bit).
# In this section you can enforce encryption of user-passwords or allow
# not-encrypted sending of passwords over the net.
#
#
# On the Linux-side, passwords will only be stored in encrypted format.
#
#
# ----------------------------------------------------------------------
# Syntax:
#       7       FLAG
#
# FLAG:
#       0       enforce encryption of _all_ passwords by the DOS-client
#               (default)
#       1       as "0", but allow the non-encrypted version of the
#               change password-routine.
#       7       allow all non-encrypted stuff but no empty nwe passwords.
#       8       allow all non-encrypted stuff and also allow empty
#               nwe-passwords.
#       9       use all non-encryted calls + "get crypt" key will allways fail
#               so the login program will use the old unencryted calls.
#               this will *not* work with all clients !! (OS2/client)
# ----------------------------------------------------------------------

7       0
```

Again, there is a discrepancy here between the sample provided by Red Hat, shown in Listing 18.7, and the IPX-HOWTO. The HOWTO recommends a value of 1 for this parameter and the sample file specifies zero. In all experiments I have conducted, I have set this to zero and it works as it should.

The next section of interest is section 10, shown in Listing 18.8. Sections 8 and 9 are currently not used. In sections 10 and 11, you specify a non-privileged user and group, which will be used by DOS clients before they log in to the server.

LISTING **18.8** Section 10 of the `/etc/nwserv.conf` File—User and Group ids of a Non-privileged User

```
# Section 10: UID and GID with minimal rights
# ========================================================================
#
# When loading the netware-drivers in the "autoexec.bat" of your
# DOS-client, you automatically "attach" to a netware-server.
# As a result, a new drive-letter is accessible under DOS, usally
# containing the programs "login.exe" and "slist.exe".
# Because you haven't logged in, nothing else of the netware-server
# will be visible to you. All actions requested from the DOS-client
# will be done with the following UID and GID on the Linux-side in this
# case.
# To achieve some level of security, the user/group asscociated with
# the UID and GID should only have _read_ rights on the files visible,
# _nothing_ else.
#
# ----------------------------------------------------------------------
# Syntax:
#       10      GID
#       11      UID
#
# GID   numeric number of the group
# UID   numeric number of the user
# ----------------------------------------------------------------------
#
# Example:
#       10      65534
#       11      65534

        10      99
        11      99
```

The user number 99 and group number 99 correspond to the nobody user and the nobody group and in the interest of security, this is the best setting. This user account should have permission to see the files in the LOGIN directory only.

The next section, shown in Listing 18.9, defines the supervisor login for your server. This entry is required and correlates the NetWare supervisor account, which is traditionally called SUPERVISOR, with a login account on the Linux system.

LISTING **18.9**   Section 12 of the `/etc/nwserv.conf` File—Supervisor Login

```
# ==========================================================================
# Section 12: supervisor-login (required)
#
# The "supervisor" of a nw-server is much like "root" on the Linux-side.
#
# Specify a Linux-user that should be mapped to the supervisor of this
# mars_nwe-server.
# To improve security, don't use "root" for this purpose but create a
# seperate administrative account (under Linux) called "nw-adm" or similar.
#
# The nw-user defined in this section will have the mars_nwe internal UID
# "1" (remember even under Linux "root" must have the special UID "0"), so
# it is not possible to define a supervisor in section 13 (the users
# defined there will get random UIDs).
# You _can_ define a user with name "SUPERVISOR" in section 13, but he
# won't really be the "local god" on the "mars_nwe"-server.
# And of course you _can_ define a supervisor with name "GOD" or "ROOT"
# in _this_ section, which would only break the traditional naming-scheme
# of the netware-world.
#
#
# -------------------------------------------------------------------------
# Syntax:
#       12      NW_LOGIN        LINUX_LOGIN      [PASSWORD]
#
# NW_LOGIN:     the login-name for the "mars_nwe"-server (traditionally,
#               this is "SUPERVISOR")
# LINUX_LOGIN:  the account on the Linux-side associated with the NW_LOGIN
# PASSWORD:     the password for the NW_LOGIN. It must be clear-text but
#               will be encrypted and permanent stored in the
#               bindery-files, so it (the password or the whole section, at
#               your option) can be deleted after the first start of
#               "nwserv".
#
#               Make sure this file is not world-readable as long
#               as the password stands here.
#
#               If you leave this field blank when starting "mars_nwe" the
#               first time, the supervisor-login will be completely
#               disabled. In other words: there is no way to supply the
#               supervisor with no password ("null-password").
# -------------------------------------------------------------------------
```

LISTING **18.9** continued

```
#
# Example:
#      12       SUPERVISOR      nw-adm        top-secret


12  SUPERVISOR   adm    *
```

Two notes of caution on the setting in section 12: It is possible that you could map the NetWare SUPERVISOR account to the Linux root account; however, if you do you will have to expose the root password in clear text until you start the nwserv daemon for the first time. It is therefore not a recommended practice to do this. The other caution is that the entry in the configuration file that comes with Red Hat is not useful. You should define a password when you start up mars_nwe for the first time and then either remove the entry from the nwserv.conf file or change it to an asterisk as shown.

Section 13 of the configuration file is used to map NetWare user accounts with accounts on your Linux system. This section of the file is shown in Listing 18.10 and is optional. The syntax for this section is the same as for section 12.

LISTING **18.10** Section 13 of the /etc/nwserv.conf File—User Logins

```
# =========================================================================
# Section 13: user-logins (optional)
#
# You can provide mappings from the regular login-names of your Linux-Box
# to "mars_nwe"-logins here.
# Every "mars_nwe"-user _must_ have a login-name on the Linux side (even
# if he can't log in into the account associated with the login-name,
# because you locked it with a "*") in order to "own" files.
# If you specify a Linux-login that doesn't exist (one could think of a
# typo), the user will only have the minimal rights defined in
# sections 10/11.
#
# See section 12 for a description of the syntax.
#
# Unlike in section 12, you can define users with no password.
#
# Example:
#      13       MARTIN          martin
```

18

Integrating with
Other Network
Operating
Systems

In section 13, you are permitted to map NetWare usernames to Linux names, and it is highly recommended that you do so. This is because the automatic mapping options, which I will describe next, have no way of using the Linux password and if automatic mapping is enabled, you will end up with a common password for all users.

If you do opt to use automatic mapping of NetWare usernames to Linux usernames, you will need to use section 15 of the configuration file, shown in Listing 18.11.

LISTING **18.11**   Section 15 of the `/etc/nwserv.conf` File—Automatic Mapping of NetWare Users to Linux Users

```
# ============================================================================
# Section 15: automatic mapping of logins (decision required)
#
# If you have a large number of accounts on your Linux-machine, you may
# want to map all Linux-logins automatically to "mars_nwe"-logins.
#
# At this stage this section is only a quick hack to make life a bit
# easier for the administrator.
#
# WARNING: as there is no algorithm to convert the encrypted
# "Linux-passwords" into the encrypted format used by the DOS-clients (and
# therefore "mars_nwe"), you have to supply a common password for all
# automatically mapped users. This is a big security concern and you
# should never make this common password public (and, of course you
# should choose a sufficient "secure" (read: difficult) password).
# Type the common password to grant access to the users login and the
# command "setpass" instead of telling the password to the user.
#
# Only those Linux-logins will handled automatically that don't have a
# "x" or "*" as their encrypted password.
#
#
# ----------------------------------------------------------------------
# Syntax:
#       15      FLAG    DEFAULT_PASSWORD
#
# FLAG:
#       0       DON'T map the Linux-logins automatically to
#               "mars_nwe"-logins (default)
#       1       YES, DO the automatic mapping and provide every login
#               created this way with the common password given with
#               "DEFAULT_PASSWORD"
#       99      re-read the logins from /etc/passwd and overwrite even the
```

LISTING **18.11**   continued

```
#               already existing logins from the bindery (this will also
#               reset all the passwords to "DEFAULT_PASSWORD")
#
# DEFAULT_PASSWORD: the common password for all automatically created
#               logins (only needed if FLAG is not "0"); everything about
#               password in section 12 applies to this.
# .................................................................


15    99    top-secret
```

Section 15 is where you specify the automatic mapping of Linux users to NetWare users. As shipped, the Red Hat configuration file causes the user mapping to occur each time that the mars_nwe server is restarted. From the comments, you also learn that the passwords are reset each time to the supplied default password. This is far from optimal, and the flag value should probably be changed from 99 to a value of 0 as recommended in the IPX-HOWTO.

The mars_nwe server can be configured to perform a number of sanity checks when it starts. Listing 18.12 shows this section of the configuration file, and in the file as supplied by Red Hat, this flag is set.

LISTING **18.12**   Section 16 of the /etc/nwserv.conf File—Sanity Checks at Startup

```
# ===========================================================================
# Section 16: Tests on startup
#
# If you want some sanity checks at startup, set this flag to 1.
# "mars_nwe" will try to create missing directories (with the "right"
# permissions, of course) if you enable this.
#


16    1
```

Whether you enable this option is a matter of personal preference. If you are comfortable with the server creating missing directories for you on-the-fly, turn on the startup tests. If you would rather have the system fail and force you to correct the situation, set it to zero.

Section 21 is the final section of the configuration file that is of interest to most administrators. This section, which is shown in Listing 18.13, defines any printers that you want IPX clients to be able to access. The syntax is quite basic, as explained in the comments.

18

Integrating with Other Network Operating Systems

LISTING 18.13   Section 21 of the /etc/nwserv.conf File—Print Queue Definition

```
# ==========================================================================
# Section 21: print queues (optional)
#
# Which of the printers connected to your Linux-box should be accessible
# from the DOS-clients?
# Multiple entries are allowed.
#
# --------------------------------------------------------------------------
# Syntax:
#       21       QUEUE_NAME       QUEUE_DIR        PRINT_COMMAND
#
# QUEUE_NAME:   the name of the print queue on client-side (to make it
#               perfectly clear: _not_ the Linux-queue)
# QUEUE_DIR:    spooling directory for the print-jobs; this directory must
#               exist before printing (_not_ the spooling-directories of
#               the Linux-lpd)
# PRINT_COMMAND: command used for serving the print-jobs under Linux
#               (see "man lpr" and "man magicfilter" for details)
#
# Examples:
#       21       LASER         SYS:/PRINT/L    lpr -Plaser
#       21       OCTOPUSS      SYS:/PRINT/O    lpr -Php_deskjet
# --------------------------------------------------------------------------

21    LP    SYS:/PRINT/LP    lpr
```

There are a number of other sections in the configuration file, however most of them are not pertinent to this discussion. They are described in the comments of the /etc/nwserv.conf file, which I encourage you to study. These sections define paths to various files used by the software, debugging options, and other facets of server operation.

Starting the mars-nwe Server

Now that you have a configuration file, you are ready to start the server. On your Red Hat system, you can do this by using the mars-nwe script located in /etc/rc.d/init.d as follows:

```
/etc/rc.d/init.d/mars-nwe start
```

Assuming no error messages are issued, you should test your server by attempting to connect from an IPX client on your network. Assuming a successful connection, you should also create a print capture and test printing from the same IPX client. This test can be conducted in several ways. One of the simplest methods would be to use the information on using Linux as a NetWare client found earlier in this chapter to attempt to connect to your mars_nwe server. Another option, if you are using Linux as an additional NetWare server in an existing NetWare environment, is to attempt to connect from a client that is already configured with the appropriate NetWare client software. If neither of these is an option, you must configure a client from scratch. The details of doing this should be included in your client software documentation and are beyond the scope of this text.

It is important to remember that the Linux software that allows it to act as a client or server in a NetWare environment uses bindery mode only. If your NetWare environment implements services based on Novell Directory Services (NDS), which is usually the case for networks built around Novell version 4 or later, the utilities described here will not work. All is not lost, however, if you just want client services because Caldera has a NetWare client suite that supports NDS available for Linux. For more information about this client software, check the Caldera Web site at `http://www.caldera.com/`.

Having covered Linux in the NetWare environment, from both a client and server prospective, we can now move on to the other network operating environment covered in this chapter, AppleTalk.

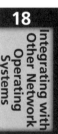

Linux in an AppleTalk Environment

Unlike the NetWare connectivity software, the packages required to share resources with an AppleTalk network are not included on the Red Hat distribution CDs, but they are available from the Red Hat contrib ftp site. The package you require is

```
ftp://contrib.redhat.com/libc6/i386/netatalk-1.4b2+asun2.1.0-5.i386.rpm
```

and you install this with the command:

```
rpm -i netatalk-1.4b2+asun2.1.0-5.i386.rpm
```

The netatalk package is an implementation of the AppleTalk protocol suite developed at the University of Michigan by the Research Systems Unix Group. It runs on a variety of UNIX systems as well as Linux. For more information, patches, and access to the developers of this package, refer to the netatalk home page at `http://www.umich.edu/~rsug/netatalk`.

This section takes a look at the requirements for sharing resources with AppleTalk clients on your network, starting with the required modifications to your kernel and then the steps involved in configuring file and print services.

Configuring Kernel AppleTalk Support

If you are running the default kernel that comes with the Red Hat 6.0 installation media, you will not have to modify your kernel at all because although Red Hat did not include the netatalk package, they did compile in support for the AppleTalk protocol. You can verify that this support is available by checking for the existence of the `appletalk.o` module under the `/lib/modules/2.2.5-15/misc` directory. If, however, you have updated your kernel, it is up to you to add support for AppleTalk.

This is done by answering yes to the configuration question, "Appletalk DDP," which causes the `CONFIG_ATALK` variable to be set in your kernel `.config` file. This code can be either integrated into your kernel or built as a module, which is the preferred method, since it allows you to load or unload support as needed. Assuming that you do build the AppleTalk support as a module, you would then load it using the `insmod` command:

```
insmod appletalk
```

This should result in a message being logged stating the version of the AppleTalk driver that was loaded.

Configuring AppleTalk Services on Linux

Having ensured that you have AppleTalk support in your kernel and having installed the netatalk rpm, you are now ready to begin configuring the services that you want to make available on your Linux system to the AppleTalk clients on your network. This will involve work in five files, four of them specific to the netatalk package and the fifth, the `/etc/services` file. Because it is the easiest one to work with, we will start with `/etc/services`.

In order for AppleTalk clients to connect to your system, you must define several services in the `/etc/services` file. By default, these already exist and you merely have to verify them. Listing 18.14 shows the steps involved in ensuring that your `/etc/services` file is set up correctly to support netatalk.

LISTING 18.14 Ensuring Support for AppleTalk Services in System Files

```
[tschenk@madmax chapter18]$ cd /etc

[tschenk@madmax /etc]$ grep ddp /etc/services
rtmp        1/ddp           # Routing Table Maintenance Protocol
nbp         2/ddp          # Name Binding Protocol
echo        4/ddp           # AppleTalk Echo Protocol
zip         6/ddp          # Zone Information Protocol

[tschenk@madmax /etc]$ grep 548 /etc/services
```

LISTING **18.14**   continued

```
afpovertcp    548/tcp        # AFP over TCP
afpovertcp    548/udp        # AFP over TCP
```

If you issue the commands as shown and do not get these six entries back, you must add them to /etc/services yourself. To do this, you can append the file /usr/doc/netatalk-1.4b2+asun2.1.3/services.atalk onto the end of your /etc/services file, or you can edit the file by hand and add the entries as shown above.

netatalk Configuration Files

With /etc/services set up properly, you can start work on the netatalk configuration files. The first of these is the atalkd.conf file, which the netatalk rpm installs in /etc/atalk. The file that is installed by the netatalk package is for all intents and purposes empty, since it contains only comments. This should be sufficient for most installs; however, if it is not, you can refer to the installed file for instructions on what to put there. This configuration file is utilized by the atalkd, which is the class AppleTalk kernel interface. This daemon serves as the link between the classic AppleTalk functions of the netatalk package and the AppleTalk module that you loaded into the kernel.

afpd.conf File

The next file we are concerned with is the afpd.conf file, which is used to set classic AppleTalk and AppleShare IP server options. In its simplest form, this file is also empty, just like the atalkd.conf file. However, this file has many more options than the atalkd.conf file and if you require a more complicated setup than the default, you can refer to the afpd manual page and the comments in the installed file to guide you in setting this up.

Sounds easy so far. The final files that we will be working with prior to attempting to turn on AppleTalk services are the AppleVolumes.default and the AppleVolumes.system files. These files define the services that are advertised to AppleTalk clients on the network. The first of these is theAppleVolumes.system file. This file is similar in function to the .mailcap file found in user home directories in that it provides information on file type to application associations. The format of the file is quite simple and includes an extension, a file type, the program associated with creating the file, and the program to run when the file is double clicked. Listing 18.15 is the AppleVolumes.system file that is included in the netatalk package. As you will see, it contains quite a few entries.

LISTING 18.15   /etc/atalk/AutoVolumes.system

```
# Last Updated July 8, 1999
# Use at your own risk.  No guarantees express or implied.
#
# Try to use MacPerl script 'ICDumpSuffixMap' included in /usr/doc
# to download file mapping list from your Internet Config Preference.
#
# inoue@ma.ns.musashi-tech.ac.jp.
#


.          "TEXT"  "ttxt"     ASCII Text               SimpleText
➥text/plain


.mf        "TEXT"  "*MF*"     Metafont                 Metafont
.sty       "TEXT"  "*TEX"     TeX Style                Textures
.psd       "8BPS"  "8BIM"     PhotoShop Document       Photoshop
.pxr       "PXR "  "8BIM"     Pixar Image              Photoshop
.sea       "APPL"  "????"     Self-Extracting Archive  Self Extracting
➥ Archive
.apd       "TEXT"  "ALD3"     Aldus Printer Description Aldus PageMaker
.pm3       "ALB3"  "ALD3"     PageMaker 3 Document     PageMaker
.pm4       "ALB4"  "ALD4"     PageMaker 4 Document     PageMaker
.pt4       "ALT4"  "ALD4"     PageMaker 4 Template     PageMaker
.pm5       "ALB5"  "ALD5"     PageMaker 5 Document     PageMaker
.pt5       "ALT5"  "ALD5"     PageMaker 5 Template     PageMaker
.pdx       "TEXT"  "ALD5"     Printer Description      PageMaker
.ppd       "TEXT"  "ALD5"     Printer Description      PageMaker
.dl        "DL  "  "AnVw"     DL Animation             MacAnim Viewer
.gl        "GL  "  "AnVw"     GL Animation             MacAnim Viewer
.url       "AURL"  "Arch"     URL Bookmark             Anarchie
message/external-body
.zoo       "Zoo "  "Booz"     Zoo Archive              MacBooz
.pdf       "PDF "  "CARO"     Portable Document Format Acrobat Reader
application/pdf
.h         "TEXT"  "CWIE"     C Include File           CodeWarrior
.hp        "TEXT"  "CWIE"     C Include File           CodeWarrior
.hpp       "TEXT"  "CWIE"     C Include File           CodeWarrior
.c         "TEXT"  "CWIE"     C Source                 CodeWarrior
.cp        "TEXT"  "CWIE"     C++ Source               CodeWarrior
.cpp       "TEXT"  "CWIE"     C++ Source               CodeWarrior
.class     "Clss"  "CWIE"     Java Class File          CodeWarrior
.java      "TEXT"  "CWIE"     Java Source File         CodeWarrior
.p         "TEXT"  "CWIE"     Pascal Source            CodeWarrior
```

LISTING 18.15 continued

.pas	"TEXT"	"CWIE"	Pascal Source	CodeWarrior
.cvs	"drw2"	"DAD2"	Canvas Drawing	Canvas
.arj	"BINA"	"DArj"	ARJ Archive	DeArj
.evy	"EVYD"	"ENVY"	Envoy Document	Envoy
.fm	"FMPR"	"FMPR"	FileMaker Pro Database	FileMaker Pro
.dbf	"COMP"	"FOX+"	DBase Document	FoxBase+
.mif	"TEXT"	"Fram"	FrameMaker MIF	FrameMaker
application/x-framemaker				
.arr	"ARR "	"GKON"	Amber ARR image	GraphicConverter
.iff	"ILBM"	"GKON"	Amiga IFF Image	GraphicConverter
.lbm	"ILBM"	"GKON"	Amiga IFF Image	GraphicConverter
.ilbm	"ILBM"	"GKON"	Amiga ILBM Image	GraphicConverter
.ani	"ANIi"	"GKON"	Animated NeoChrome	GraphicConverter
.pcs	"PICS"	"GKON"	Animated PICTs	GraphicConverter
.pc1	"Dega"	"GKON"	Atari Degas Image	GraphicConverter
.pc2	"Dega"	"GKON"	Atari Degas Image	GraphicConverter
.pc3	"Dega"	"GKON"	Atari Degas Image	GraphicConverter
.pi1	"Dega"	"GKON"	Atari Degas Image	GraphicConverter
.pi2	"Dega"	"GKON"	Atari Degas Image	GraphicConverter
.pi3	"Dega"	"GKON"	Atari Degas Image	GraphicConverter
.ic1	"IMAG"	"GKON"	Atari Image	GraphicConverter
.ic2	"IMAG"	"GKON"	Atari Image	GraphicConverter
.ic3	"IMAG"	"GKON"	Atari Image	GraphicConverter
.neo	"NeoC"	"GKON"	Atari NeoChrome	GraphicConverter
.pac	"STAD"	"GKON"	Atari STAD Image	GraphicConverter
.spc	"Spec"	"GKON"	Atari Spectrum 512	GraphicConverter
.tny	"TINY"	"GKON"	Atari TINY Bitmap	GraphicConverter
.pm	"PMpm"	"GKON"	Bitmap from xv	GraphicConverter
.scg	"RIX3"	"GKON"	ColoRIX	GraphicConverter
.sci	"RIX3"	"GKON"	ColoRIX	GraphicConverter
.scp	"RIX3"	"GKON"	ColoRIX	GraphicConverter
.scr	"RIX3"	"GKON"	ColoRIX	GraphicConverter
.scu	"RIX3"	"GKON"	ColoRIX	GraphicConverter
.cgm	"CGMm"	"GKON"	Computer Graphics Meta	GraphicConverter
.vff	"VFFf"	"GKON"	DESR VFF Greyscale Image	GraphicConverter
.cut	"Halo"	"GKON"	Dr Halo Image	GraphicConverter
.art	"ART "	"GKON"	First Publisher	GraphicConverter
.fts	"FITS"	"GKON"	Flexible Image Transport	GraphicConverter
.fit	"FITS"	"GKON"	Flexible Image Transport	GraphicConverter
➥image/x-fits				
.gem	"GEM-"	"GKON"	GEM Metafile	GraphicConverter
.img	"IMGg"	"GKON"	GEM bit image/XIMG	GraphicConverter

18

Integrating with
Other Network
Operating
Systems

LISTING **18.15**   continued

```
.grp      "GRPp"  "GKON"    GRP Image                GraphicConverter
.hpgl     "HPGL"  "GKON"    HP GL/2                  GraphicConverter
.plt      "HPGL"  "GKON"    HP GL/2                  GraphicConverter
.ief      "IEF "  "GKON"    IEF image                GraphicConverter
➥image/ief
.scc      "MSX "  "GKON"    MSX pitcure              GraphicConverter
.msp      "MSPp"  "GKON"    Microsoft Paint          GraphicConverter
.pcx      "PCXx"  "GKON"    PC PaintBrush            GraphicConverter
.pbm      "PPGM"  "GKON"    Portable Bitmap          GraphicConverter
➥image/x-portable-bitmap
.pgm      "PPGM"  "GKON"    Portable Graymap         GraphicConverter
➥image/x-portable-graymap
.ppm      "PPGM"  "GKON"    Portable Pixmap          GraphicConverter
➥image/x-portable-pixmap
.shp      "SHPp"  "GKON"    Printmaster Icon Library GraphicConverter
.qdv      "QDVf"  "GKON"    QDV image                GraphicConverter
.rif      "RIFF"  "GKON"    RIFF Graphic             GraphicConverter
.rle      "RLE"   "GKON"    RLE image                GraphicConverter
.raw      "BINA"  "GKON"    Raw Image                GraphicConverter
.bw       "SGI "  "GKON"    SGI Image                GraphicConverter
.rgb      "SGI "  "GKON"    SGI Image                GraphicConverter
➥image/x-rgb
.rgba     "SGI "  "GKON"    SGI Image                GraphicConverter
➥image/x-rgb
.six      "SIXE"  "GKON"    SIXEL image              GraphicConverter
.ct       "..CT"  "GKON"    Scitex-CT                GraphicConverter
.dcx      "DCXx"  "GKON"    Some PCX Images          GraphicConverter
.sup      "SCRN"  "GKON"    StartupScreen            GraphicConverter
.sr       "SUNn"  "GKON"    Sun Raster Image         GraphicConverter
.sun      "SUNn"  "GKON"    Sun Raster Image         GraphicConverter
.targa    "TPIC"  "GKON"    Truevision Image         GraphicConverter
.tga      "TPIC"  "GKON"    Truevision Image         GraphicConverter
.clp      "CLPp"  "GKON"    Windows Clipboard        GraphicConverter
.icn      "ICO "  "GKON"    Windows Icon             GraphicConverter
.ico      "ICO "  "GKON"    Windows Icon             GraphicConverter
.wmf      "WMF "  "GKON"    Windows Metafile         GraphicConverter
.wpg      "WPGf"  "GKON"    WordPerfect Graphic      GraphicConverter
.xbm      "XBM "  "GKON"    X-Windows Bitmap         GraphicConverter
➥image/x-xbm
.x10      "XWDd"  "GKON"    X-Windows Dump           GraphicConverter
➥image/x-xwd
.x11      "XWDd"  "GKON"    X-Windows Dump           GraphicConverter
```

LISTING 18.15   continued

```
➥image/x-xwd
.xwd      "XWDd"   "GKON"   X-Windows Dump              GraphicConverter
➥image/x-xwd
.xpm      "XPM "   "GKON"   X-Windows Pixmap            GraphicConverter
➥image/x-xpm
.m2v      "MPG2"   "MPG2"   MPEG-2 IPB videostream      MPEG2decoder
.for      "TEXT"   "MPS"    Fortran Source              MPW Shell
.htm      "TEXT"   "MSIE"   HyperText                   Internet Explorer
➥4.5      text/html
.html     "TEXT"   "MSIE"   HyperText                   Internet Explorer
➥4.5      text/html
.wri      "WDBN"   "MSWD"   MS Write/Windows            Microsoft Word
.mcw      "WDBN"   "MSWD"   Mac Word Document           Microsoft Word
.rtf      "TEXT"   "MSWD"   Rich Text Format            Microsoft Word
application/rtf
.doc      "WDBN"   "MSWD"   Word Document               Microsoft Word
application/msword
.dot      "sDBN"   "MSWD"   Word for Windows Template   Microsoft Word
.mw       "MW2D"   "MWII"   MacWrite Document           MacWrite II
application/macwriteii
.mwii     "MW2D"   "MWII"   MacWrite Document           MacWrite II
application/macwriteii
.pl       "TEXT"   "McPL"   Perl Source                 MacPerl
.asf      "ASF_"   "Ms01"   Netshow Player              Netshow Server
➥video/x-ms-asf
.asx      "ASX_"   "Ms01"   Netshow Player              Netshow Server
➥video/x-ms-asf
.oda      "ODIF"   "ODA"    ODA Document                MacODA XTND
➥Translator   application/oda
.latex    "TEXT"   "OTEX"   Latex                       OzTex
application/x-latex
.texi     "TEXT"   "OTEX"   TeX Document                OzTeX
.tex      "TEXT"   "OTEX"   TeX Document                OzTeX
application/x-tex
.texinfo  "TEXT"   "OTEX"   TeX Document                OzTeX
application/x-texinfo
.diz      "TEXT"   "R*Ch"   BBS Descriptive Text        BBEdit
.ml       "TEXT"   "R*Ch"   ML Source                   BBEdit
.mak      "TEXT"   "R*Ch"   Makefile                    BBEdit
.m2       "TEXT"   "R*Ch"   Modula 2 Source             BBEdit
.i3       "TEXT"   "R*Ch"   Modula 3 Interface          BBEdit
.m3       "TEXT"   "R*Ch"   Modula 3 Source             BBEdit
```

18

Integrating with
Other Network
Operating
Systems

LISTING **18.15**   continued

.prn	"TEXT"	"R*Ch"	Printer Output File	BBEdit
.rtx	"TEXT"	"R*Ch"	Rich Text	BBEdit
➡text/richtext				
.rpl	"FRL!"	"REP!"	Replica Document	Replica
.rib	"TEXT"	"RINI"	Renderman 3D Data	Renderman
.rsc	"rsrc"	"RSED"	Resource File	ResEdit
.rsrc	"rsrc"	"RSED"	Resource File	ResEdit
.pdb	"TEXT"	"RSML"	Brookhaven PDB file	RasMac
.mol	"TEXT"	"RSML"	MDL Molfile	RasMac
.bar	"BARF"	"S691"	Unix BAR Archive	SunTar
.aif	"AIFF"	"SCPL"	AIFF Sound	SoundApp
➡audio/x-aiff				
.aiff	"AIFF"	"SCPL"	AIFF Sound	SoundApp
➡audio/x-aiff				
.aifc	"AIFC"	"SCPL"	AIFF Sound Compressed	SoundApp
➡audio/x-aiff				
.al	"ALAW"	"SCPL"	ALAW Sound	SoundApp
.8svx	"8SVX"	"SCPL"	Amiga 8-bit sound	SoundApp
.svx	"8SVX"	"SCPL"	Amiga IFF Sound	SoundApp
.med	"STrk"	"SCPL"	Amiga MED Sound	SoundApp
.8med	"STrk"	"SCPL"	Amiga OctaMed music	SoundApp
.mod	"STrk"	"SCPL"	MOD Music	SoundApp
.nst	"STrk"	"SCPL"	MOD Music	SoundApp
.okt	"OKTA"	"SCPL"	Oktalyser MOD Music	SoundApp
.wve	"BINA"	"SCPL"	PSION sound	SoundApp
.snd	"BINA"	"SCPL"	Sound of various types	SoundApp
.hcom	"FSSD"	"SCPL"	SoundEdit Sound ex SOX	SoundApp
.voc	"VOC "	"SCPL"	VOC Sound	SoundApp
.sf	"IRCM"	"SDHK"	IRCAM Sound	SoundHack
.pkg	"HBSF"	"SITx"	AppleLink Package	StuffIt Expander
.hqx	"TEXT"	"SITx"	BinHex	StuffIt Expander[a]
application/mac-binhex40				
.sithqx	"TEXT"	"SITx"	BinHexed StuffIt Archive	StuffIt Expander
application/mac-binhex40				
.cpt	"PACT"	"SITx"	Compact Pro Archive	StuffIt Expander
.taz	"ZIVU"	"SITx"	Compressed Tape ARchive	StuffIt Expander
application/x-compress				
.gz	"SIT!"	"SITx"	Gnu ZIP Archive	StuffIt Expander
application/x-gzip				
.tgz	"Gzip"	"SITx"	Gnu ZIPed Tape ARchive	StuffIt Expander
application/x-gzip				
.lha	"LHA "	"SITx"	LHArc Archive	StuffIt Expander

LISTING 18.15   continued

```
.lzh       "LHA "   "SITx"    LHArc Archive              StuffIt Expander
.mime      "TEXT"   "SITx"    MIME Message               StuffIt Expander
message/rfc822
.bin       "SIT!"   "SITx"    MacBinary                  StuffIt Expander
application/macbinary
.arc       "mArc"   "SITx"    PC ARChive                 StuffIt Expander
.zip       "ZIP "   "SITx"    PC ZIP Archive             StuffIt Expander
application/zip
.pit       "PIT "   "SITx"    PackIt Archive             StuffIt Expander
.pf        "CSIT"   "SITx"    Private File               StuffIt Expander
.sit       "SIT!"   "SITx"    StuffIt 1.5.1 Archive      StuffIt Expander
application/x-stuffit
.uu        "TEXT"   "SITx"    UUEncode                   StuffIt Expander
.uue       "TEXT"   "SITx"    UUEncode                   StuffIt Expander
.Z         "ZIVU"   "SITx"    Unix Compress Archive      StuffIt Expander
application/x-compress
.tar       "TARF"   "SITx"    Unix Tape ARchive          StuffIt Expander
application/x-tar
.669       "6669"   "SNPL"    669 MOD Music              PlayerPro
.xm        "XM  "   "SNPL"    FastTracker MOD Music      PlayerPro
.mtm       "MTM"    "SNPL"    MultiMOD Music             PlayerPro
.s3m       "S3M "   "SNPL"    ScreamTracker 3 MOD        PlayerPro
.com       "PCFA"   "SWIN"    MS-DOS Executable          SoftWindows
.exe       "PCFA"   "SWIN"    MS-DOS Executable          SoftWindows
.obj       "PCFL"   "SWIN"    Object (DOS/Windows)       SoftWindows
.ovl       "PCFL"   "SWIN"    Overlay (DOS/Windows)      SoftWindows
.dll       "PCFL"   "SWIN"    Windows DLL                SoftWindows
.dxf       "TEXT"   "SWVL"    AutoCAD 3D Data            Swivel Pro
.avi       "VfW "   "TVOD"    AVI Movie                  QuickTime Player
➥video/avi
.fli       "FLI "   "TVOD"    FLI Animation              QuickTime Player
.flc       "FLI "   "TVOD"    FLIC Animation             QuickTime Player
.mid       "Midi"   "TVOD"    MIDI Music                 MoviePlayer
.midi      "Midi"   "TVOD"    MIDI Music                 MoviePlayer
.mpe       "MPEG"   "TVOD"    MPEG Movie of some sort    MoviePlayer
➥video/mpeg
.mpeg      "MPEG"   "TVOD"    MPEG Movie of some sort    MoviePlayer
➥video/mpeg
.mpg       "MPEG"   "TVOD"    MPEG Movie of some sort    MoviePlayer
➥video/mpeg
.m1v       "M1V "   "TVOD"    MPEG-1 IPB videostream     MoviePlayer
➥video/mpeg
```

18

Integrating with
Other Network
Operating
Systems

LISTING **18.15** continued

```
.m1a      "MPEG"   "TVOD"     MPEG-1 audiostream         MoviePlayer
➥audio/x-mpeg
.mp2      "MPEG"   "TVOD"     MPEG-1 audiostream         MoviePlayer
➥audio/x-mpeg
.mpa      "MPEG"   "TVOD"     MPEG-1 audiostream         MoviePlayer
➥audio/x-mpeg
.m1s      "MPEG"   "TVOD"     MPEG-1 systemstream        MoviePlayer
.ul       "ULAW"   "TVOD"     Mu-Law Sound               MoviePlayer
➥audio/basic
.moov     "MooV"   "TVOD"     QuickTime Movie            MoviePlayer
➥video/quicktime
.mov      "MooV"   "TVOD"     QuickTime Movie            MoviePlayer
➥video/quicktime
.qt       "MooV"   "TVOD"     QuickTime Movie            MoviePlayer
➥video/quicktime
.au       "ULAW"   "TVOD"     Sun Sound                  QuickTime Player
➥audio/basic
.wav      "WAVE"   "TVOD"     Windows WAV Sound          MoviePlayer
➥audio/x-wav
.sha      "TEXT"   "UnSh"     Unix Shell Archive         UnShar
application/x-shar
.shar     "TEXT"   "UnSh"     Unix Shell Archive         UnShar
application/x-shar
.wpm      "WPD1"   "WPC2"     WordPerfect Mac            WordPerfect
.wp4      ".WP4"   "WPC2"     WordPerfect PC 4.2 Doc     WordPerfect
.w51      ".WP5"   "WPC2"     WordPerfect PC 5.1 Doc     WordPerfect
application/wordperfect5.1
.wp       ".WP5"   "WPC2"     WordPerfect PC 5.1 Doc     WordPerfect
application/wordperfect5.1
.wp5      ".WP5"   "WPC2"     WordPerfect PC 5.x Doc     WordPerfect
application/wordperfect5.1
.wp6      ".WP6"   "WPC2"     WordPerfect PC 6.x Doc     WordPerfect
.csv      "TEXT"   "XCEL"     Comma Separated Vars       Excel
.dif      "TEXT"   "XCEL"     Data Interchange Format    Excel
.xlc      "XLC "   "XCEL"     Excel Chart                Excel
.xlm      "XLM "   "XCEL"     Excel Macro                Excel
.xl       "XLS "   "XCEL"     Excel Spreadsheet          Excel
.xls      "XLS "   "XCEL"     Excel Spreadsheet          Excel
.xlw      "XLW "   "XCEL"     Excel Workspace            Excel
.wks      "XLBN"   "XCEL"     Lotus Spreadsheet r1.x     Excel
.wk1      "XLBN"   "XCEL"     Lotus Spreadsheet r2.1     Excel
.slk      "TEXT"   "XCEL"     SYLK Spreadsheet           Excel
```

LISTING **18.15**   continued

```
.syk      "TEXT"  "XCEL"    SYLK Spreadsheet              Excel
.sylk     "TEXT"  "XCEL"    SYLK Spreadsheet              Excel
.tsv      "TEXT"  "XCEL"    Tab Separated Values          Excel
➥text/tab-separated-values
.qxd      "XDOC"  "XPR3"    QuarkXpress Document          QuarkXpress
.qxt      "XTMP"  "XPR3"    QuarkXpress Template          QuarkXpress
.image    "dImg"  "ddsk"    Apple DiskCopy Image          Disk Copy
.etx      "TEXT"  "ezVu"    SEText                        Easy View
➥text/x-setext
.out      "BINA"  "hDmp"    Output File                   HexEdit
.binary   "BINA"  "hDmp"    Untyped Binary Data           HexEdit
➥application/octet-stream
.gif      "GIFf"  "ogle"    GIF Picture                   PictureViewer
➥image/gif
.jfif     "JPEG"  "ogle"    JFIF Image                    PictureViewer
.jpe      "JPEG"  "ogle"    JPEG Picture                  PictureViewer
➥image/jpeg
.jpeg     "JPEG"  "ogle"    JPEG Picture                  PictureViewer
➥image/jpeg
.jpg      "JPEG"  "ogle"    JPEG Picture                  PictureViewer
➥image/jpeg
.pntg     "PNTG"  "ogle"    Macintosh Painting            PictureViewer
.bga      "BMPp"  "ogle"    OS/2 Bitmap                   PictureViewer
.vga      "BMPp"  "ogle"    OS/2 Bitmap                   PictureViewer
.pict     "PICT"  "ogle"    PICT Picture                  PictureViewer
➥image/x-macpict
.mac      "PICT"  "ogle"    PICT Picture                  PictureViewer
➥image/x-pict
.pct      "PICT"  "ogle"    PICT Picture                  PictureViewer
➥image/x-pict
.pic      "PICT"  "ogle"    PICT Picture                  PictureViewer
➥image/x-pict
.png      "PNG "  "ogle"    Portable Network Graphic      PictureViewer
.sgi      ".SGI"  "ogle"    SGI Image                     PictureViewer
.tif      "TIFF"  "ogle"    TIFF Picture                  PictureViewer
➥image/tiff
.tiff     "TIFF"  "ogle"    TIFF Picture                  PictureViewer
➥image/tiff
.bmp      "BMPp"  "ogle"    Windows Bitmap                PictureViewer
.tx8      "TEXT"  "ttxt"    8-bit ASCII Text              SimpleText
.asc      "TEXT"  "ttxt"    ASCII Text                    SimpleText
➥text/plain
```

18

Integrating with Other Network Operating Systems

LISTING **18.15**   continued

```
.ascii     "TEXT"   "ttxt"      ASCII Text                SimpleText
➥text/plain
.text      "TEXT"   "ttxt"      ASCII Text                SimpleText
➥text/plain
.txt       "TEXT"   "ttxt"      ASCII Text                SimpleText
➥text/plain
.faq       "TEXT"   "ttxt"      ASCII Text                SimpleText
➥text/x-usenet-faq
.a         "TEXT"   "ttxt"      Assembly Source           SimpleText
.asm       "TEXT"   "ttxt"      Assembly Source           SimpleText
.bas       "TEXT"   "ttxt"      BASIC Source              SimpleText
.boo       "TEXT"   "ttxt"      BOO encoded               SimpleText
.bib       "TEXT"   "ttxt"      BibTex Bibliography       SimpleText
.bst       "TEXT"   "ttxt"      BibTex Style              SimpleText
.nfo       "TEXT"   "ttxt"      Info Text                 SimpleText
application/text
.bat       "TEXT"   "ttxt"      MS-DOS Batch File         SimpleText
.cmd       "TEXT"   "ttxt"      OS/2 Batch File           SimpleText
.me        "TEXT"   "ttxt"      Text Readme               SimpleText
.rme       "TEXT"   "ttxt"      Text Readme               SimpleText
.1st       "TEXT"   "ttxt"      Text Readme               SimpleText
application/text
.readme    "TEXT"   "ttxt"      Text Readme               SimpleText
application/text
.ini       "TEXT"   "ttxt"      Windows INI File          SimpleText
.ps        "TEXT"   "vgrd"      PostScript                LaserWriter 8
application/postscript
.eps       "EPSF"   "vgrd"      Postscript                LaserWriter 8
application/postscript
.epsf      "EPSF"   "vgrd"      Postscript                LaserWriter 8
application/postscript
.dvi       "ODVI"   "xdvi"      TeX DVI Document          xdvi
application/x-dvi
```

As you can see, this file is quite comprehensive and you should probably not have to edit it by hand, unless you want to add support for a new file type not already included here.

AppleVolumes.default

The last file to consider is the AppleVolumes.default, which is shipped with the netatalk package and contains a single uncommented line with a tilde character on it. This tilde character indicates that user home directories should be made available to AppleTalk clients who connect to this server. Although this is quite useful, if it is not enough, you can use the information in the file itself and in the afpd manual page to make other filesystems available to AppleTalk clients.

Starting the Netatalk Server

Finally we reach the moment of truth, for now it is time to start the netatalk servers and determine if they work. In order to start the servers, you are encouraged to use the atalk script installed in /etc/rc.d/init.d by the netatalk package. This is a standard System V style script and to start the AppleTalk services, you would issue the following command:

```
/etc/rc.d/init.d/atalk start
```

Assuming no error messages, you can verify that the servers are working by going to a Mac client on your network, opening the chooser, and clicking on AppleShare. If you have everything configured correctly, you should be able to see your Linux system. Clicking on your server name should result in a password prompt and you can log in as any non-root user that has a shell and a password of eight or fewer characters.

Summary

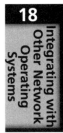

This chapter briefly covered how Linux can be used to offer services to NetWare and AppleTalk clients in a network. You also saw how Linux can be used as a NetWare client. This ability of Linux to interoperate with multiple network operating systems is a big part of the reason why Linux is so popular. And the work to allow Linux to interoperate with other network operating systems is continuing. Examples of this are projects to add protocols such as DecNET to Linux. If your favorite network protocol is not yet supported, stay tuned.

Internet Services

IN THIS PART

19 Setting Up Internet Services   *529*

20 Electronic Mail   *553*

21 FTP and Anonymous FTP   *609*

22 Web Serving   *637*

23 News Services   *671*

24 Internet Telephony and Conferencing   *713*

25 Security Principles   *739*

Setting Up
Internet Services

In This Chapter

- Choosing Services to Offer   *530*
- The Internet Server inetd   *531*
- Using TCP-Wrappers   *534*
- xinetd as an Alternative to inetd   *538*
- Standard Services: Remote Login, Execution, and File-Copy   *541*

CHAPTER

19

This chapter discusses how to set up Internet services on a Red Hat Linux system. It concentrates on the most fundamental services: remote login, remote command execution, and remote file copy facilities. It also discusses issues of access control and security relating to the provision of these services.

Choosing Services to Offer

Deciding which Internet services to offer is an important part of a system administrator's role. If users don't have access to the services they need, they won't be able to do their own jobs; yet providing more services than are necessary adds to the administrator's workload and may compromise system security.

When deciding what services to offer, it is important to draw a distinction between internal and external users, especially when external users are allowed to connect from anywhere on the Internet. In a typical organization, internal users would be those with explicit written permission to use the facilities provided, such as employees, whereas external users would be, essentially, the general public. Not all users are this easy to categorize, though; for example, different organizations might need to classify telecommuters in different ways.

It is undeniable that some external would-be users have malicious intent. It can be very hard to verify the identity of external users before granting access to a service, and it can be even harder to track down anyone who attacks the system. Internal users have a much greater degree of accountability—quite possibly including contractual terms under which unauthorized use constitutes grounds for dismissal—and therefore can be trusted with a greater degree of responsibility. (Of course, this is not to say that internal users are invariably entirely trustworthy.) In the majority of situations, external users are offered only a limited range of informational services; the services described in this chapter would typically be reserved for users known to have more responsibility.

Low-Level Services

The services that run on a machine can be broadly divided into a number of groups. The lowest-level services provide fundamentals of the actual networking system. They include the routing protocols and name services described in Chapter 14, "TCP/IP and Ethernet," and if all is well, these are invisible to users. The next step up is the services that form the infrastructure of a network—the printing and file-sharing services that were dealt with in Chapter 15, "Sharing Resources," as well as interoperability with other systems and networks (including Windows, NetWare, and AppleTalk), described in Chapters 17, "Integrating with Windows NT Networks," and 18, "Integrating with Other Network Operating Systems." The Internet services that are the subject of this chapter form the next higher level.

Internet Services

Some Internet services will be required on almost every system. One such service is email, which is a requirement at most sites, if only for local delivery of warning messages from Cron jobs and the like. Indeed, in many organizations, email will be one of the fundamental means of internal communication. Internet email using standard protocols such as SMTP, POP, and IMAP is dealt with in Chapter 20, "Electronic Mail."

Remote Login Service

Similarly, almost all sites will need some form of remote login or remote execution service. On UNIX systems, the usual choice is between Telnet, Rsh/Rlogin, and SSH; all of these services are described in detail in this chapter. I will also discuss the particularly strong security requirements of remote login and remote execution facilities.

Other Internet Services

Most of the other common Internet services can be broadly classified as information-providing. FTP, Usenet News, and World Wide Web services are among the most common, and each is covered in its own chapter in this book: see Chapter 21, "FTP and Anonymous FTP," Chapter 22, "Web Serving," and Chapter 23, "News Services." Web servers in particular are becoming ever more important for distributing static and dynamic information to both internal and external users. FTP archives and Usenet News will not be as widely needed, especially as services that must be made available to external users.

Once you have decided which services to offer, the next step is to make those services available. This is the subject of the remainder of this chapter.

The Internet Server inetd

The daemons providing many network services can be run by the so-called Internet super-server, inetd (pronounced "eye-net dee"). This daemon listens for connections on certain network ports; precisely which ports depends on how it is configured locally. When it receives connections, it invokes a program which will service that connection, again using local configuration to decide which program to run. Essentially, inetd multiplexes a number of daemons into a single one to ease configuration and reduce system load. It also makes it easier for programmers to write network daemons because it does the work of listening for and accepting connections.

Not all network services are written to use inetd. Services that normally run standalone are those that expect to accept very large numbers of connections, or to be permanently busy, or both. In these situations, the overhead of running a new process for every incoming connection is prohibitively high; having a standalone daemon service every connection itself avoids incurring this cost. For example, Web servers usually run standalone, as do mail transport agents. However, many mail transport agents have the option to be run from inetd. This may be useful for small sites that must handle relatively low volumes of email.

The `/etc/inetd.conf` File

The inetd daemon is configured with the `/etc/inetd.conf` file. Each line in this file specifies a service that will deal with an incoming connection. For example, the standard Red Hat 6 `/etc/inetd.conf` file has an entry for FTP service. (Configuring FTP services is dealt with in Chapter 21.) This entry looks like this:

```
ftp stream tcp nowait root  /usr/sbin/tcpd in.ftpd -l -a
```

Each entry consists of a number of whitespace-separated fields, as follows:

- **Name**—This is the name of a service, as listed in the `/etc/services` file. This file provides a mapping from human-readable service names to the port number and stream type used for that service. In the preceding sample entry, the service name is `ftp`. The `/etc/services` file contains the entry

  ```
  ftp  21/tcp
  ```

  so the service will use port 21.

- **Type**—This is the "socket type" or "data delivery service type" for this service. The usual types are `stream` (for the byte-stream delivery service provided by TCP), `dgram` (for the packet delivery service provided by UDP; the term `dgram` is an abbreviation for datagram, which is often used as an alternative to packet when describing UDP, though it is technically incorrect), and `raw` (for direct IP datagram service). These terms are described in more detail in Chapter 14. The preceding sample entry indicates that FTP service uses a stream socket.

- **Protocol**—This is the name of a protocol, as listed in the `/etc/protocols` file. This file translates human-readable protocol names into protocol numbers. The `/etc/inetd.conf` entry for FTP uses `tcp` because FTP uses TCP as its transport layer.

- **Wait-status**—This field should be either `wait` or `nowait`. It is usually the case that `dgram` services need `wait`, whereas `stream` services need `nowait`, but there are some exceptions. For `wait` services, inetd will wait for the server program it launches to release the network socket before beginning to listen for further connection requests on that socket. With `nowait` services, inetd continues listening for further connection requests as soon as it has launched the server program. FTP is a standard stream service, so it runs `nowait`.

You can also attach a dot and a number to this field. This indicates the maximum number of servers of this type that will be launched in 60 seconds. If no such maximum is supplied, it defaults to 40. For example, if you wanted to allow 100 FTP connections in 60 seconds, you could set this field to `nowait.100`.

- **User**—This is the username under which the server runs. Many servers are run as root, which means that because they have the ability to do anything, they must be exceptionally careful when dealing with data from potentially malicious, untrusted sources. Others may be run as an unprivileged user, such as daemon or nobody. The FTP service in the preceding sample entry runs as root.

  You can optionally specify a group by appending a dot and the group name to the username; this will then be the group id under which the server runs. For example, the Talk service usually runs as user nobody and group tty, so it has `nobody.tty` in this field. If you don't specify a group, the server will be run as the primary group of its user, as specified in `/etc/passwd`.

- **Daemon**—This is the absolute path to the program to be run for connections of this type. As described in the next section, "Using TCP-Wrappers," security considerations dictate that this should almost always be `/usr/sbin/tcpd`, as for the preceding sample entry.

  This field can also be the single word `internal`, which is used for a few simple services primarily for testing, which are built in to inetd. These services are echo (which simply echoes all the data it receives), chargen (which continuously generates a stream of characters), discard (which discards all the data it receives), daytime (which prints out a human-readable version of the current time), and time (which sends a machine-readable version of the time, in seconds elapsed since midnight on January 1, 1900). The subsequent fields may be left blank for internal services.

- **Arguments**—Any remaining fields are passed as arguments to the program launched. The first such argument is used as argv[0]—the string that the program receives as its own name—and must always be present. Subsequent fields are normal arguments. In the preceding sample, the `/usr/sbin/tcpd` daemon is given the name in.ftpd, with `-l` and `-a` as further arguments. tcpd will ultimately run this program; it looks for it in a directory specified at compile time, which for the Red Hat version is `/usr/sbin`. If the daemon you want it to run is not in that directory, you can specify an absolute path.

  If you aren't using `/usr/sbin/tcpd`, the name should be the base name of the program being run. For example, if you wanted to run FTP services without

19

Setting Up
Internet Services

/usr/sbin/tcpd, you would use /usr/sbin/in.ftpd as the daemon field, and the arguments would start with in.ftpd.

Because each line in /etc/inetd.conf corresponds to a service to be provided, you can also disable existing services by deleting or commenting out the line that corresponds to that service. Comments in /etc/inetd.conf begin with a hash sign (#) and extend to the end of line.

Similarly, if a service has an existing commented-out entry in /etc/inetd.conf, you can enable the service by removing the hash sign.

When you make changes to /etc/inetd.conf, they do not take effect until inetd restarts, or it receives a SIGHUP signal (which forces it to reread the file). You can do this by saying

```
kill -HUP $(cat /var/run/inetd.pid)
```

or you can use the init-script for inetd (which is usually preferred):

```
/etc/rc.d/init.d/inet reload
```

Using TCP-Wrappers

inetd is a very convenient way of handling Internet services, but it was not designed with security as a major goal. It offers no possibility for logging connection attempts or for controlling access to services. Many systems work around these problems with a package called TCP-Wrappers, or tcpd, written by UNIX security expert Wietse Venema. Most Linux distributions, including Red Hat 6, are configured to use tcpd out of the box.

TCP-Wrappers will log connection attempts, and it has a flexible access-control mechanism that can permit or deny connections on a per-service basis. The access-control scheme can use pattern matching on hostnames, netgroups, or IP addresses. It can also run external programs to provide more complex access-control—or for any other purpose, for that matter. Additionally, TCP-Wrappers can also do client username lookups, and it can detect hosts that pretend to have a hostname or IP address belonging to another host.

TCP-Wrappers accomplishes all this by arranging to be the program actually launched by inetd, and it performs all access-control and logging before executing the program that will actually provide the service in question. Once it has executed the real server, tcpd goes away. The advantages of this approach are that it works for any server program that might expect to be launched by inetd, and that the use of tcpd is invisible to authorized external users. The disadvantages are apparent for servers which, once launched, accept and service many client connections; in these cases, tcpd will only be aware of the connection attempt that initially caused the server process to be launched.

The remainder of this section describes in some detail how tcpd operates and how it is configured. We cover how tcpd logs connection attempts, how it decides whether to grant access, the syntax of the tcpd configuration files, and how to test a new configuration for tcpd.

Logging

TCP-Wrappers uses the syslog daemon to log all connections it handles; under Red Hat, it uses the `authlog` syslog facility, so by default its log messages go to `/var/log/secure`. Connection attempts are logged with a message of the form

```
service[pid]: connect from client
```

where `service` is the name of the service (as received in argv[0]), `pid` is the process ID of the instance of tcpd being run, and `client` is a description of the client that is attempting to connect. This is normally just the IP address of the client, but in some circumstances (described in the following section) it can include the hostname of the client and/or the name of the user requesting the connection, as reported by the remote system.

Access Control

TCP-Wrappers uses two files, `/etc/hosts.allow` and `/etc/hosts.deny`, to decide whether to grant a client access to a service. These files contain a series of entries that pattern-match connection attempts; if either does not exist, it is treated as if it exists but is empty. The pattern-match process uses the files as follows:

1. If an entry in `/etc/hosts.allow` matches the connection attempt, access is granted.
2. Otherwise, if an entry in `/etc/hosts.deny` matches the connection attempt, access is denied.
3. Otherwise, access is granted.

This scheme for handling the two files means that it is easy to use `/etc/hosts.deny` for denying access to a wide range of hosts, overriding this for smaller groups of hosts in `/etc/hosts.allow`. The reverse is not normally the case, but it can be accomplished by using the access-control language extensions that are optionally compiled into the daemon. (The Red Hat packaged version enables the language extensions.) The language extensions make it possible to use a single file to configure all access-control decisions; see the section "Configuration Language Extensions."

Configuration

The /etc/hosts.allow and /etc/hosts.deny files have the same format. They may contain comments (which begin with a hash character and continue to the end of the line) and blank lines, in addition to lines with access-control rules. Rules may be split over multiple lines if you put a backslash at the end of each incomplete line.

The allowable rules can be very complex. This section presents an overview of what can be done, but more complete information can be found in the hosts_access(5) and hosts_options(5) manual pages.

Each access-control rule has the following format:

```
daemons : clients [ : option [ : option ... ]]
```

The material between square brackets is optional. *Daemons* is a list of one or more daemon process names (from argv[0]) or wildcards. *Clients* is a list of one or more hostnames, host addresses, patterns, or wildcards to be matched against the client hostname or address. Lists are separated by whitespace and/or commas. Each *option* is a language extension, as described in the section "Configuration Language Extensions." (If tcpd is compiled without support for language extensions, only one *option* is allowed, and it is treated as a shell command.)

The host-matching patterns take one of the following forms:

- **Hostname**—A string that begins with a dot is treated as a hostname. It matches if the last components of the name match the string given. So the pattern .example.com would match the host www.example.com.

- **IP address**—A string that ends with a dot is treated as a numeric IP address. It matches if its first numeric fields match the address given. For example, the pattern 192.168.1. would match any host in the 192.168.1.0 network.

- **Network address/netmask**—A string containing four dot-separated numbers, a slash, and another four dot-separated numbers is treated as a network address and netmask. It matches hosts within the classless address given by the pair. For example, the pattern 192.168.1.0/255.255.255.0 is a more verbose equivalent of the 192.168.1. pattern.

- **Netgroup**—A string beginning with an @ sign is treated as an NIS netgroup. It matches any host within that netgroup.

The allowable daemon and client wildcards fields are as follows:

- ALL—This always matches.

- LOCAL—This matches any host whose name contains no dot.

- UNKNOWN—This matches any user whose name is unknown, or any host for which either the name or address is unknown.

- KNOWN—This matches any user whose name is known, or any host for which both the name and address are known.

- PARANOID—This matches any host whose address and name do not match, which may indicate an attempt to spoof host identity. In its default configuration, known as paranoid mode, tcpd will drop all such connections before examining the access-control rules; the Red Hat packaged version disables paranoid mode in favor of this finer-grained mechanism.

Patterns can also take the form *daemon@host* (for daemon patterns) or *user@host* (for client patterns). The *daemon@host* form is used to perform access control based on which interface is being used on a multi-homed host. The *user@host* form forces the use of the RFC931/RFC1413 (Ident) protocol to look up the name of the user on the client host. This lookup can be used to detect some forms of host address spoofing. If the client is running an Ident service and responds negatively to the lookup request, this is strong evidence that the address is being spoofed. Such attempts can be matched with the client pattern UNKNOWN@ALL.

The access control language also supports an EXCEPT operator, which excludes matches for one pattern from another. For example, you could use the daemon pattern ALL EXCEPT in.fingerd to have a rule apply to all services except finger.

Configuration Language Extensions

The language extensions provide a number of advanced facilities. The most commonly used are the ALLOW and DENY options. Only one of these may be used in any given rule, and it must appear as the last option in the rule. Using these options allows the administrator to put all access control configuration in a single file. For example, if only /etc/hosts.allow exists, you can effectively override coarse-grained "allow" rules with fine-grained denial like this:

```
ALL : .untrustworthy.domain : DENY
ALL : ALL : ALLOW
```

Information on all available options can be found in the hosts_options(5) manual page.

19

Setting Up
Internet Services

Testing tcpd Configuration

It is a good idea to test new access-control rules before enabling them for production use. The TCP-Wrappers package provides two programs, tcpdchk and tcpdmatch, to assist in this.

The tcpdchk program examines the `inetd.conf`, `hosts.allow`, and `hosts.deny` files and reports all real and potential problems it can find. Problems it finds include nonexistent pathnames, services which should not be run by the tcpd wrapper, nonexistent hostnames, invalid IP addresses, and unknown options.

The tcpdmatch program reports on how tcpd would handle a given connection attempt. It takes two arguments, a daemon and a client. The daemon can optionally have an `@host` suffix, and the client can optionally have a `user@` prefix. The client host can also be `unknown` or `paranoid` to test what tcpd would do for hosts whose name or address is unknown, or whose name and address do not match.

Both programs accept a `-d` option; this specifies that the `hosts.allow` and `hosts.deny` files to be examined should be found in the current directory rather than in `/etc`.

xinetd as an Alternative to inetd

Although it is the standard Red Hat configuration, not all administrators like the inetd+tcpd combination, and some may want to look for another super-server solution with the same advantages of logging, security, and access control. The most common alternative is called xinetd (pronounced "zy-net dee"), and it may be very useful in some circumstances, particularly if it is used on other systems at the same site. xinetd was originally written as a means of overcoming the limitations of inetd with regard to access control and logging, and although using tcpd with inetd solves most of these problems, a few areas remain where xinetd has the edge. First, it does not require that its services be listed in `/etc/services`, which means that any user may use it to start services on non-privileged ports. Second, it can perform hard reconfiguration: It can kill servers for services whose entries have been removed from the configuration, or servers controlling connections which no longer meet the access control criteria. Third, it has slightly more flexible logging options than inetd, including the ability to limit the sizes of log files created.

Red Hat does not supply xinetd as part of the operating system, so you will have to download it yourself. The source is available from `http://www.synack.net/xinetd`; this site also has source and binary RPM packages for Red Hat, though not necessarily for the latest stable release. At this writing, the latest released version is 2.1.8.7p1, and RPM packages of the 2.1.8.8pre11 pre-release are available.

Compiling xinetd locally will enable you to build it against the libwrap library which tcpd uses to perform access control. When it is built against libwrap, it will check incoming connections against /etc/hosts.allow and /etc/hosts.deny before performing its own access control. In Red Hat 6, the libwrap library is available in the tcp_wrappers package.

Configuring xinetd

xinetd is configured with its own /etc/xinetd.conf file, which uses a different syntax from that of inetd. Both the RPM package and the source provide a sample configuration file, and there is also a program itox, which can translate an existing /etc/inetd.conf file to the syntax needed by xinetd. (The Red Hat package renames this program to inetd2xinetd.) You can say

```
itox < /etc/inetd.conf > xinetd.conf.generated
```

to produce a valid xinetd.conf file of your existing configuration, ready for editing and tweaking.

The /etc/xinetd.conf file contains a series of multi-line entries. The format is as follows:

```
service service-name
{
   attribute = value ...
   ...
}
```

Each entry relates to a single service, identified by the *service-name*. A service may have a number of attributes, each of which can be adjusted with an assignment operator and a new value (or group of values). There are actually three types of assignments: "=", "-=", and "+=". Most attributes only support the simple "=" assignment operator, but those which are in fact a set of values use "-=" to remove an item from the set, and "+=" to add a new item.

The attributes that correspond to the fields in the normal /etc/inetd.conf are as follows.

- socket_type—This can take the value stream, dgram, or raw, just as the equivalent field in /etc/inetd.conf.

- protocol—The protocol name from /etc/protocols, as for /etc/inetd.conf. It may be omitted, in which case the default protocol for the service will be used.

- wait—This can be either yes or no, equivalent to wait or nowait, respectively, in /etc/inetd.conf.

- `instances`—This attribute specifies the maximum number of instances of a given server to run. In contrast to `/etc/inetd.conf`, it is not attached to the wait-status field.

- `user`—This is the user to run as, defaulting to root.

- `group`—If you need to specify a group name, it must be set in its own attribute, rather than being appended to the user name as in `/etc/inetd.conf`.

- `server`—This is the absolute path to the server to be run. Because xinetd has its own functionality equivalent to that of tcpd, it is normal to specify the server daemon itself. As with inetd, xinetd provides some services internally; for these, you should specify no server path, but instead specify `type = INTERNAL` in the entry for those services. The internal services are echo, time, daytime, chargen, and discard, just as with inetd.

- `server_args`—The arguments for the server. This should not include the server name, unlike the equivalent in `/etc/inetd.conf`.

An entry in `/etc/xinetd.conf` for the FTP service discussed in the previous section on inetd would look like this:

```
service ftp
{
    socket_type = stream
    protocol = tcp
    wait = no
    user = root
    server = /usr/sbin/in.ftpd
    server_args = -l -a
}
```

xinetd's configuration file performs access control with an `only_from` attribute. The value of this attribute is a list of IP address specifications, each of which takes one of the following forms:

- A numeric IP address in dotted-quad notation. For any trailing zeros in the address, the equivalent portions of the client's address are zeroed before comparison. For example, 192.168.1.0 matches all addresses on that class C network.

- A network name from `/etc/networks`.

- A fully qualified hostname.

- A CIDR address/netmask pair such as 192.168.1.0/24.

You may also use the no_access attribute with similar values to specify hosts for which to deny access.

Logging is configured with the log_on_success and log_on_failure attributes. The value for each is a set of items to be logged on success or failure, respectively. The following items are valid.

- HOST—Logs the address of the remote host.

- USERID—If possible, logs the user ID of the remote user, obtained by the RFC931/RFC1413 Ident protocol.

- PID—Logs the process ID of the server process launched. Only meaningful for log_on_success.

- EXIT—Logs the exit status of the server. Only meaningful for log_on_success.

- DURATION—Logs the length of time a connection was active. Only meaningful for log_on_success.

- ATTEMPT—Logs the fact that a failed connection attempt was made. Only meaningful for log_on_failure.

- RECORD—Logs information from the remote host if the server could not be started. Only meaningful for log_on_failure.

Standard Services: Remote Login, Execution, and File-Copy

This section describes the most important Internet services—those providing facilities for remote logins, remote command execution, and remote file-copying. These services are variously provided by Telnet, by a group of UNIX-derived commands collectively known as the R-commands, and by SSH, the Secure Shell service.

Telnet

Telnet is the standard Internet remote login protocol. It was originally designed in the early days of the ARPANET, and was standardized in its present form in 1983. The protocol is extremely flexible and extensible, and it has adapted well to needs that did not exist when it was designed.

This flexibility means that Telnet has acquired features that are highly desirable from a user's point of view. In particular, it interoperates well with the X Window System. A standard protocol exists to allow the client to inform the server of the user's current X display; this enables the server to arrange that X applications that are run from within the remote login use the appropriate display. There is also a standard protocol that can handle terminals whose size can change on-the-fly; obviously, this is useful in an environment where Telnet sessions are being run inside windows that the user can readily resize.

The biggest problem with Telnet is that all data is transmitted in the clear, including passwords. This means that Telnet connections are vulnerable to packet-snooping attacks—if intruders can intercept packets containing data for a Telnet connection, they are likely to be able to find a password in the data stream. This is a non-negligible security risk in many situations even when data is only traveling on internal networks. The risk is substantially higher for Telnet sessions that cross the wider Internet because the Internet's fault-tolerance means you can never know precisely what intermediate gateways will transmit data.

Telnet normally runs on port 23. Telnet services are provided by the telnetd daemon, /usr/sbin/in.telnetd. telnetd is run from inetd; the Red Hat /etc/inetd.conf file contains an entry that runs telnetd via tcpd. Once telnetd receives a connection, it sends the contents of /etc/issue.net to the client, after performing substitution on certain codes beginning with a percent character. These are shown in Table 19.1.

TABLE 19.1 Substitution Codes for /etc/issue.net

Code	Substitution
%t	Name of the current terminal
%h	Fully qualified hostname
%D	NIS domain name
%d	Current date and time
%s	Name of the operating system (Linux)
%m	CPU architecture
%r	Kernel release number
%v	Kernel compilation version
%%	A single percent character

Many sites use /etc/issue.net to display conditions on usage of the service.

Once the /etc/issue.net banner has been sent, telnetd then calls /bin/login to authenticate the remote user and provide a login service.

The R-Commands

UNIX-like systems usually include a group of commands collectively known as the R-commands, derived from the BSD systems. These commands are `rlogin` for remote login facilities; `rsh` and `rexec` for remote shell-command execution; and `rcp`for remote file copying. In that respect, they are similar to Telnet and FTP, but they differ in that even though they are now available on some other systems, they were originally UNIX-specific.

The `rexec` command uses an authentication mechanism based on user names and passwords. The `rlogin`, `rsh`, and `rcp` commands normally use an authentication mechanism based on privileged port numbers on the client side, and a comprehensive trust relationship between the client and the server. The next two sections deal with `rexec` and the trust-based R-commands, respectively.

The Rexec Service

The Rexec service normally runs on port 512 (the `exec` service) and is provided by the `rexecd` daemon, `usr/sbin/in.rexecd`. This daemon is run from inetd, but the standard Red Hat `/etc/inetd.conf` has the entry commented out. To enable it, simply un-comment the relevant line in that file and reload the inetd configuration:

```
/etc/rc.d/init.d/inet reload
```

Rexec grants or denies access on the basis of a username and password that are sent unencrypted over the network. It always denies access for root, for users with no password, and for users listed in the `/etc/ftpusers` file (see Chapter 21).

The authentication method used by Rexec is considered to be a serious security hole, to the extent that the current BSD manual page calls it "an example of how not to do things." It is not enabled by default, and there are very few situations if any in which it would be appropriate to explicitly enable it.

Trust-Based R-Commands

Rlogin normally runs on port 513 (the `login` service) and Rsh on port 514 (the `shell` or `cmd` service). The services are provided by the rlogind and rshd daemons, `/usr/sbin/in.rlogind` and `/usr/sbin/in.rshd`. These daemons are run from inetd; the Red Hat `/etc/inetd.conf` file contains entries for each. Rcp services are actually handled by Rshd: running `rcp` on a client will use the Rsh protocol to run another instance of rcp on the server, and the two instances will communicate to perform the file copy requested. Note also that since the rcp command does not know how to prompt for a password, it can only be used between hosts that have a trust relationship.

19

Setting Up
Internet Services

Rlogin has some support for interoperating with the X Window System, but it does not do quite as well as the more flexible Telnet protocol. Rlogin can communicate changes in window size from client to server, but it does not inform the server about the location of the user's X display.

Authentication for the Trust-Based R-Commands

A proper understanding of the R-commands requires knowledge of how their trust-based authentication works. Take rlogind as an example. When it is launched by inetd and tcpd, rlogind starts by checking that the TCP port used on the client is in the range 512 to 1023 (inclusive). This check is done because on UNIX systems, only processes owned by root may use those ports. Next, it determines the IP address of the client, and looks up the hostname for that IP address. If the address and hostname do not match, the connection is dropped. It then reads the name of the client-side user from the connection, followed by the username that is desired on the server.

Next it attempts to authenticate the username supplied by the client for password-free access to the named account; the details of this authentication procedure and how to configure it are described in the next section, "Configuring Trust for the R-Commands." Its final action is to launch login to actually allow the user to log in. If the authentication was successful, login is called with the -f argument; otherwise, login will prompt for a password as normal.

Clearly, the authentication scheme used by the R-commands relies on both the client machine and the communication medium being trustworthy. Note in particular that UNIX (and similar operating systems, including Linux) are unusual in restricting the use of low-numbered TCP ports; other operating systems, such as MacOS and Microsoft Windows, do not in general impose such restrictions. The R-commands are also particularly vulnerable to attacks that spoof hostnames or addresses, although running them from tcpd does help somewhat here. Also, even if users don't rely on the R-commands' willingness to permit logins without passwords, there is still the usual vulnerability of transmitting passwords in the clear.

Allowing systems to trust each other carries a definite risk; if one system is penetrated, any other system that trusts it is also vulnerable. Indeed, since there is no way to prove that other systems have not been compromised, an administrator must assume that they have been. This means that if a network uses R-commands, *any* security breach entails clean-up activity (such as re-installing the operating system) on all network hosts entering into a trust relationship.

Moreover, trust relationships are transitive. Suppose the host radish.example.com trusts cucumber.example.com but not pumpkin.example.com. The administrator of cucumber is less careful about trust relationships than the administrator of radish, so cucumber *does* trust pumpkin. Now, if `pumpkin` is penetrated, even though `radish` does not trust it directly, the attacker can also compromise `radish`, using `cucumber` as an intermediary. Obviously, large networks may have many trust relationships, which can make it harder to determine which hosts transitively trust others—especially if hosts are administrated by different people.

The R-commands were designed to operate in an environment where trust relationships between machines allow users to access network services without typing passwords. In the past, Internet usage was limited almost entirely to academic institutions, and in such contexts, it was often considered reasonable and helpful to trust users in this way. The wider use of the Internet in recent times has essentially eliminated environments of this sort, and it may well be the case now that the only situations in which it is sensible to rely on trust are those in which all the users are known, and the network is not connected to the wider Internet.

Expressing Trust Relationships for the R-Commands

Once you have decided to allow two systems to trust each other, the next question is how to configure the R-commands to express this trust. As you have seen, the R-commands grant password-free access to trusted users on trusted hosts. The system assumes that accounts with the same name on different machines are owned by a single user. For this reason, trusted hosts are also called equivalent hosts: Users with some level of access on one host should have an equivalent level of access on another.

Red Hat Linux uses Pluggable Authentication Modules (PAM) for authentication, so the details of configuration differ slightly from traditional UNIX systems. However, the essentials are the same. The R-commands use a system-wide configuration file, `/etc/hosts.equiv`, as well as per-user files stored in `$HOME/.rhosts`. PAM configuration uses files in `/etc/pam.d`; for the R-commands, the relevant files are `/etc/pam.d/rsh` and `/etc/pam.d/rlogin`. These files contain lines such as

```
auth   sufficient   /lib/security/pam_rhosts_auth.so
```

which configure authentication for the R-commands. You can add options to the end of this line to alter the way the authentication works.

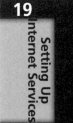

Granting Trust to Hosts and Users

The `/etc/hosts.equiv` file defines the hosts and users that are granted trusted (password-free) access to the R-commands on your system. Entries in this file contain a hostname, optionally preceded (with no intervening whitespace) by a plus sign. Naming a host grants it trusted status: Any user on that host is allowed to access a like-named account on the server. The hostname may optionally be followed by one or more trusted usernames, separated by whitespace, each of which is optionally preceded by a plus sign. Trusted users on a host are allowed password-free access to *all* accounts on the server except the root account.

Hostnames and usernames in /etc/hosts.equiv may be preceded by a minus sign instead of a plus sign, to explicitly deny trusted status. If a host is untrusted in this way, users on that host must supply a password to gain access; similarly, if a user is untrusted, that user on that host must supply a password. (See the section "Creating an .rhosts File" for more details on this.)

An entry can also consist of just a single plus sign. This allows access from any host in the world. This is clearly a significant security hole, so the PAM implementation disables this functionality by default. You can enable it by adding the option "promiscuous" to the pam_rhosts_auth module lines in /etc/pam.d/rsh and /etc/pam.d/rlogin.

Some examples will clarify the situation.

- pumpkin—Grants trusted access for any user on pumpkin to accounts of the same name.

- -pumpkin—Denies trusted access for any user on pumpkin to accounts on the server.

- pumpkin -arc—Denies trusted access to the user on pumpkin named arc.

- pumpkin arc—Grants trusted access to all non-root accounts on the server for a user on pumpkin named arc.

- + arc—Grants trusted access to all non-root accounts on the server for a user on any host in the world named arc.

Per-User .rhosts Files

Users may create an .rhosts file in their home directories. As a security measure, this file is ignored unless it is writable only by its owner, and is owned by either root or the user whose home directory it is in. Setting the privategroup option for the pam_rhosts_auth module additionally allows it to be group-writable as long as the group-owner has the same name as the user, and the user is the only member of that group.

Entries in the .rhosts file use the same format as those in /etc/hosts.equiv. They behave in almost exactly the same way, except that they grant or deny access only to that user's account. Consider the following entry:

```
pumpkin arc
```

If this entry is in the /etc/hosts.equiv file, it grants the user arc trusted access to all accounts on the server. But if it is in the .rhosts for a user named bob, it allows trusted access only to bob's account.

It is important to realize that individuals can use their .rhosts files override system-wide settings from `/etc/hosts.equiv`. For example, suppose `/etc/hosts.equiv` contains the entry

```
-pumpkin
```

to deny trusted access to users on that host. Even so, if the user `arc` has an .rhosts entry

```
pumpkin arc
```

`arc@pumpkin` will get trusted access to the account on the server. The only way to disable this is to turn off all checking based on .rhosts; this is done by adding the `no_rhosts` option to the PAM configuration. Similarly, the use of `/etc/hosts.equiv` can be disabled with the PAM option `no_hosts_equiv`.

Account-Level Equivalence with .rhosts Files

Individuals often use their .rhosts file to establish account-level equivalence between all the machines they use. There are also some situations in which the .rhosts file should be used to *deny* equivalence. Suppose that `radish` has a user named aaron, and that the individual who uses that account also has an account on `cucumber`. However, when his account was created on `cucumber`, there was an existing user named aaron, so on that machine his account is named arc. If there is machine-level equivalence between `radish` and `pumpkin`, `aaron@cucumber` can access `aaron@radish`'s account. The solution is for `aaron@radish` to put these entries in his .rhosts:

```
cucumber arc
cucumber -aaron
```

The first entry grants access for `arc@cucumber`, which is controlled by the same individual. The second entry denies trusted access for `aaron@cucumber`.

SSH, the Secure Shell Service

The facilities provided by Telnet and the R-commands are adequate, but they have a number of problems. This section discusses these problems, and presents SSH, a program that can provide a solution.

Security in Telnet and the R-Commands

Both Telnet and the R-commands are far from secure. The trust-based rhosts authentication mechanism used by the R-commands is particularly dangerous; because it relies on source IP addresses to identify users, it can easily be spoofed. Using tcpd or xinetd to detect spoofing attempts and refuse connections removes some of the risk in this approach, but they are not foolproof.

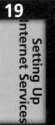

Telnet is not quite as bad in that it always requires a password before granting access, but it suffers from another flaw that is also shared by the R-commands: Because passwords, like all other data, are sent as plain text over the network, they are very susceptible to packet sniffing attacks. The risk of this approach may also be unacceptable for confidential data.

Telnet and Rlogin also have a number of problems from the user's point of view. Remote file copying is less than convenient. FTP can be seen as Telnet's file transfer mechanism, but it is rather unwieldy and difficult to script. Rcp is simple to use, but it will not work at all until the user grants account-level equivalence between machines.

Handling X11 Connections with Telnet and the R-Commands

Perhaps a bigger problem for users is the handling of X11 connections. Both Telnet and Rlogin have some support for users running in an X11 environment, but it is far from perfect. Rlogin is particularly bad: As you have seen, it cannot even inform the remote system which X11 display is in use. A bigger problem relates to X11's authentication of remote connection attempts: By default, X11 will refuse client connections from remote hosts. Many users respond to this by running xhost +—that is, by disabling all X11 authentication—which obviously results in a significant decrease in security.

Secure Shell Can Provide a Solution

The Secure Shell service, SSH, makes an excellent attempt at solving all these problems. Chief among its advantages is its use of strong encryption for data transmitted, so passwords and other data cannot be stolen even by an attacker who can listen to the data being transmitted. The use of encryption also prevents attacks where the intruder enters an existing connection and changes data in both directions. Attacks of this sort can be used to add commands to login sessions, even where the login session was authenticated by a secure one-time password. SSH uses other cryptographic techniques to perform strong authentication of hosts and clients. This means that you can have a very high degree of confidence that only authorized users are allowed to connect. SSH is also concerned with ease-of-use, and it has complete support for running X11 applications through the encrypted, authenticated channel.

The SSH Connection Process

When a client connects to an SSH server, it verifies that the server really is the machine it wanted to connect to. The client and server exchange encryption keys (doing so in a way that prevents eavesdroppers from learning the keys). The server then authenticates the client, using either the rhosts mechanism, traditional password-based authentication, or (most securely) RSA authentication. Once the client has been authenticated, the server will spawn a shell or run a command, as requested by the client.

If the $DISPLAY environment variable was set in the client, the client and server also arrange to perform X forwarding. The SSH server creates a dummy X server, and sets $DISPLAY to point to that dummy X server. X applications that are run on the SSH server connect to the dummy X server. The SSH server multiplexes the X protocol data from the dummy X server into the secure encrypted communication channel, and sends it to the SSH client. The SSH client forwards the data to the *real* X server. The SSH protocol also takes care of handling any X authorization data; but it avoids sending the real authorization data over the network.

The RSA Authentication Method

The RSA authentication method used by SSH relies on public-key cryptography, also known as asymmetric cryptography. Public-key cryptography relies on the existence of an asymmetric pair of keys: a public key and a private key. The two keys are related, but it is not possible to derive the private key from the public key without doing a brute-force search over the entire key space. The public key is used for encryption, and the private key for decryption. The private key must be kept secret, but the public key can be freely broadcast over insecure communication channels. A remote agent can use the public key to encrypt a data stream that should be private; only an agent with the correct private key will be able to read the encrypted data.

SSH also uses RSA authentication to verify the identity of both client and server hosts. This eliminates all attacks based on forging host identities by spoofing DNS, routing, or IP address.

19

Setting Up Internet Services

Arranging Secure Password-Free Access

One of the significant benefits of the R-commands over services like Telnet is that authentication does not require the user to type a password; however, the way that the R-commands provide this feature is severely detrimental to security. SSH allows users to arrange secure password-free access for themselves. The procedure is as follows, for a user arc on radish who wants secure password-free access to pumpkin:

1. Run `ssh-keygen` on `radish` to create a key pair. The private key is stored in `$HOME/.ssh/identity` and the public key is in `$HOME/.ssh/identity.pub`.

2. Connect to pumpkin with SSH: `ssh pumpkin`. If this is the first time the user has done an SSH to `pumpkin`, confirmation will be requested. The user will also have to type a password, but because the communication channel is encrypted, this is secure.

3. Use scp to copy the public key from radish: `scp radish:.ssh/identity.pub radish.id.pub`. Again, the user will have to confirm the connection, and type a password. However, no further passwords will be required. Once the public key is on the server, its contents should be added to `$HOME/.ssh/authorized_keys`, which should have permissions 0600.

4. Add an authorization entry to `$HOME/.shosts`. This file has the same format as .rhosts, so a suitable entry would be

   ```
   radish arc
   ```

At this point, the user can close all network connections, and further attempts to SSH from `radish` to `pumpkin` will not require a password to be typed. This applies to login, execution, and file-copy over SSH. The user can repeat steps 2, 3, and 4 for all hosts to which password-free access is desired.

The ability of the SSH suite to provide easy-to-use, password-free access without compromising security means that most sites should use it as a matter of course for most if not all remote login, remote execution, and remote file-copy purposes. Some administrators may feel that providing Telnet and the R-commands in addition to SSH is merely an invitation to let nave users open the system up to penetration, and that they should therefore be deleted or even disabled. I am inclined to subscribe to this point of view: SSH is known to be no less easy-to-use and no less secure than the alternatives, so there seems little reason not to use it exclusively.

The SSH daemon, sshd, is not run from inetd; instead, it is started at boot time and accepts its own connections on TCP port 22. It can be started and shut down on demand with commands such as

```
/etc/rc.d/init.d/sshd start
/etc/rc.d/init.d/sshd stop
```

Users run the command `ssh` for remote logins and remote executions; if `ssh` is given a remote hostname but no command to execute on the remote host, it performs a remote login. The `scp` command performs remote file-copy.

Installing Secure Shell

Unfortunately, SSH is not supplied with Red Hat Linux 6. This is because of current U.S. export regulations that treat cryptography software using keys longer than 40 bits as munitions. (For context, 40-bit keys can be cracked by brute force in minutes with dedicated hardware.) Since Red Hat is based in the U.S., if they included SSH with their operating system, they would not be able to export the system legally. However, it *is* legal to import cryptography software into the U.S., so a number of sites in Canada, Europe, Australasia, and elsewhere provide cryptography software for download.

ZedZ Consultants, Inc. (formerly Replay Associates) in the Netherlands has RPM packages of SSH (as well as other cryptography- and security-related software) for Red Hat Linux. They can be downloaded from `ftp://ftp.zedz.net/pub/replay/pub/linux/redhat/` `i386`. Full SSH functionality requires several packages, and this directory actually contains *two* versions of each package. This is a result of a patent claim on the RSA encryption system. The patent holder requires that the RSAREF library must be used in the U.S. to obtain fee-free licensing. (There may be other conditions on the use of RSAREF, such as a requirement for non-commercial use.) Outside the United States, RSA is not covered by a patent, and implementations other than RSAREF are considered better.

Ultimately, this means that there is a version of the packages for use only in the U.S., and another version for use anywhere else. At this writing, the files for the latest versions of the U.S. packages are

```
ssh1.2.27-7us.i386.rpm
sshclients1.2.27-7us.i386.rpm
sshextras1.2.27-7us.i386.rpm
sshserver1.2.27-7us.i386.rpm
```

The international-use packages are

```
ssh1.2.27-7i.i386.rpm
sshclients1.2.27-7i.i386.rpm
sshextras1.2.27-7i.i386.rpm
sshserver1.2.27-7i.i386.rpm
```

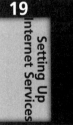

19

Setting Up
Internet Services

Normally, all four packages will be required. A minimal installation will use just the `ssh` package and either the `ssh-clients` or `ssh-server` package. Installing the base `ssh` package will generate a key pair for the host, which means that the clients or server can be used as soon as the relevant package has been installed.

Summary

Deciding what Internet services to offer is a choice that must be made in the light of local needs, and also in the light of security considerations. Many sites need to offer remote login, remote command execution, and remote file copying facilities.

Many Internet services are run from inetd, the Internet super-server. Though inetd itself cannot log connections or perform access-control for connection attempts, it can be used with tcpd, the TCP-Wrappers, to perform both these functions. The combination of inetd and tcpd can be replaced by xinetd, a super-server with logging and access-control built in.

Telnet and rlogin provide remote login services; rexec and rsh provide remote command execution, and rcp provides remote file copying. All these services are insecure to a greater or lesser degree, if only because they transmit data unencrypted. The R-commands have especially poor provision for security: They either use plaintext username/password pairs for authentication, or they rely on transitive trust relationships to grant access.

SSH provides remote login, remote execution, and remote file-copy over secure encrypted communication channels with strong cryptographic authentication of users and hosts. It also interacts well with the X Windows System.

Electronic Mail

IN THIS CHAPTER

- MTAs, MUAs, and MDAs   *554*
- POP and IMAP Services   *556*
- Configuring Mail Collection   *556*
- Choosing an MTA   *558*
- Clever Bits   *563*
- Exim   *577*
- Ancillary Programs for Mail Handling   *579*
- Fetchmail   *579*
- Supporting Multiple Email Clients   *581*
- Popular Linux Email Clients   *583*
- Aliases   *585*
- Mailing Lists with `majordomo`   *588*
- To Archive or Not to Archive   *590*
- Configuring a Digest-Only List   *591*
- Choosing and Installing an MTA   *606*
- Particular MTAs   *606*
- Anti-spam Measures   *607*

CHAPTER 20

The sending and receiving of email involves many processing steps, and quite a few programs. We need a program to accept newly composed mail and transfer it into the email system; one to display received mail; one to transfer mail between machines and networks; and a few others for general administration and to glue the bits together.

There are also other services, which are not inherently related to email, but use email as a transport mechanism. Discussion groups managed by list servers and FTP-by-email are examples.

This chapter looks at these software components and how they fit together.

MTAs, MUAs, and MDAs

The reference documentation on email is written from a point of view that uses three conceptual software elements. These elements are the *Mail Transport Agent* (MTA), the *Mail User Agent* (MUA or client), and the *Mail Distribution Agent* (MDA). All of these might not exist as separate physical pieces of software in any particular setup. In particular, the MUA, or client, will frequently take on aspects of the other two. The overall flow is as follows.

For sending mail, a user sits in front of his MUA (client) program and composes a message. When he is ready to send the message, the MUA passes it on to the MTA, which is responsible for actually transmitting the message to its destination. Under Linux, this "passing on" can happen in either of two ways: The MUA may pipe the message into the MTA, or it may write it to a spool directory from which the MTA will later extract it for transmission. Under other operating systems, such as MS Windows, only the latter method may be possible.

The MTA will then sort messages into local and remote. In this context "local" means the local machine or LAN within a privacy domain. "Remote" is anything that has to go outside the control of the local mail handlers. Those for local delivery will be written to the recipient's mailbox, possibly using a helper program such as `procmail`,`deliver`, or `mail.local`. If a message is for remote delivery, the MTA will contact the recipient's MTA over the network and pass the message on. In some cases, the MTA will be unable or will choose not to contact the destination MTA directly, but will use a *relay* MTA. The chain of relays may be arbitrarily long and you can investigate it by looking at the Received headers in any of your mail messages.

For receiving messages, the user's MUA retrieves messages from the incoming mailbox and presents them to the user for reading. How the MUA retrieves the messages depends on the MUA and where the mailbox is. If the mailbox is on the same machine that the MUA is running on, the mailbox may be read directly. If it is on a remote machine, say an ISP's server or a company's mail hub, the MUA may use an MDA such as a POP or IMAP server on the mailbox machine.

SMTP Services

Virtually all email is now carried by SMTP (Simple Mail Transfer Protocol), or ESMTP (extended SMTP). The uucp and X400 protocols are almost extinct. If you do have to deal with non-SMTP traffic, find a friendly relay host that will do all the dirty work for you and just pass the buck to it. Normally, your ISP will provide this relaying for you.

SMTP is described in RFCs 821 and 822. The protocol is layered on top of TCP/IP and was originally intended for text messages only. With the enormous growth of email traffic in recent years, and the need to transmit non-textual data such as images, the MIME (Multipurpose Internet Mail Extensions) standard has been developed. This is described in RFCs 1521, 1522, and 1523.

Although it is interesting to read these RFCs, for most purposes you will not need to know the details of the protocols. It is, however, useful to know the basic SMTP commands because you can then use telnetto test your setup by connecting manually to an MTA's listening port. Mostly, doing something like

```
telnet some.host.domain smtp
HELO  another.host.domain
QUIT
```

is enough to verify that a connection is working. Try it with localhost.

SMTP's Original Use

SMTP was originally intended for machines that are permanently connected to the Internet. However, most mail servers will store mail destined for a disconnected computer for a period of several days. So, if you are on a dial-up link, you can use SMTP for all your mail transmission and completely ignore the POP and IMAP protocols, provided that you connect to your ISP at fairly regular intervals.

That said, if you are running a mail server you may well have clients that will *only* read with POP or IMAP and will *only* send with SMTP.

For MTA to MTA communication, SMTP is all you need to concern yourself with.

POP and IMAP Services

POP and IMAP come under the heading of MDA protocols; they are for transferring mail between some reasonably local server and a client. Generally, they are only used for reading mail and SMTP is used for sending; however, both can also be used for sending.

Post Office Protocol (POP)

POP is describe in RFC 1460. It is intended for clients on dial-up, or otherwise intermittent, links. It behaves much like a post office *poste restante* service. The server's MTA delivers the client's mail to a local mailbox. So far as the MTA is concerned, it is now fully delivered. When the client comes online it can fetch the mail from the server's mailbox. There are a couple of frills, but basically all that is possible is a bulk download.

Interactive Mail Access Protocol (IMAP)

IMAP is described in RFCs 1203 and 1176. Its functions overlap somewhat with those of POP, but it is intended for a slightly different environment. The RFCs go into the details of the protocol and how client and server machines communicate. They make rather turgid reading and are of interest only to those writing mail handlers.

IMAP is intended for use on a LAN where all mail is handled by a central server. However, users may log in anywhere on the LAN and want to read and send mail. IMAP gives the MUA read/write access to the user's mailbox on the server. Its purpose is to avoid having to commit to users logging in to a particular workstation, to reduce network traffic, and to avoid file-locking problems arising from multiple access to the same mailbox.

With today's fast modems, for dial-up users, the choice between POP and IMAP depends largely on whether you have to pay connect-time charges. IMAP requires more online time than POP, but it causes less network traffic—especially if you delete some messages without actually reading them.

Although POP and IMAP are intended for clients remote from their servers, there is no prohibition on using them on a single machine setup. It may well help to avoid file locking and contention problems if you are using a carelessly coded mail client.

Configuring Mail Collection

Both IMAP and POP have daemons that can be run by `inetd`. Create a regular Linux user for each *host* or *sub-domain* that is to use these services. The user needs neither the home directory nor login shell—just an entry in the password file. Your MTA should be set up to deliver mail for these users to a regular mailbox, normally in `/var/spool/mail/username`.

All mail for the particular host or sub-domain will go into the one mailbox; it is up to the final recipient to separate out the streams. MS Exchange does this, for instance.

When the user connects to the POP or IMAP daemon with *username* and the correct password, he will be given access to his mail.

If you are handling mail for a domain other than your primary domain, you must have an MX record pointing to your server.

The only other chores are to ensure that `/etc/hosts.allow` permits access to the services, and that they are enabled in `/etc/inetd.conf`, and, of course, to check that the daemon programs are actually installed.

Dealing with Spam

Spam, named after the tinned meat sold in Britain during WWII when the real thing was not available, is something that no one wants. Another, rather more formal name, is Unsolicited Commercial Email (UCE).

There is no simple way of detecting spam automatically, although some sources of it can be eliminated quite simply.

For instance, if you register a Web site with a search engine you will receive all sorts of spam messages in reply. So, when registering, set your email reply address to an alias that discards all messages sent to it. I have the following line in my alias file:

```
registrar: /dev/null
```

and I use the rather fine sounding address `registrar@myhost.com` in my registrations.

A more sophisticated method is to have your MTA trap messages to this address and to issue a *bounce* response. It will then appear to the sender that there is no such address. For `sendmail` there is an access database that you can use. See the following section "sendmail" and `http://www.sendmail.org/m4/anti-spam.html` for more information. This is a global solution, and is possibly rather heavy-handed because it is difficult for a mail administrator to know in advance everything that his users might or might not want to receive.

There is another method for individual users. Most modern MUAs and some MTAs have *rules* that you can apply to incoming messages. The choices of how you dispose of a message are to deliver to a mailbox or folder (directory), resend to somewhere else, forward, reply, delete, or bounce (reject). If you know some pattern in either the headers or the body of the spam, you can write a rule to trap it. Care is required, however; you may let some spam through, or worse, discard genuine messages.

In really troublesome cases, try contacting the postmaster at the spammer's ISP. Be careful to get the *real* origin of the message and not to contact your own ISP or some intermediate relay—there is nothing that they can do.

See also `http://maps.vix.com/`. This site provides lists of users and sites that generate spam, and software for dealing with the problem.

Choosing an MTA

The choice and configuration of an MTA does not depend on which flavor of Linux you are running, except in one aspect: how you start the mail listener process. This is generally done from `/etc/rc.d` just after the network has been started. The MTAs will all differ somewhat in where they keep their control files and what spool directories they use. However, they must all agree on how and where they store mailboxes, otherwise the MUAs and MDAs cannot function (see "qmail" later in this chapter).

By and large, you can chop and change between MTAs without a great deal of effort, but you cannot have more than one installed and working at any one time (see the section on `qmail`): They will tread on each others' toes with respect to the `sendmail` and `mailq` binaries, and possibly the alias files as well.

Beware that some programs may make assumptions about which MTA you are running. For instance, `majordomo` assumes `sendmail`. That is not to say that `majordomo` will not work properly with other MTAs, but just watch out for problems.

A second consideration is that if you need to handle more than one local domain or do sophisticated masquerading or relay control, `sendmail` or `exim` are the only options.

> **Note**
>
> Masquerading is having one mail server pretend to be several different domains. Relaying is the forwarding of mail from one domain for another domain. These are generally issues for ISPs only.

Generational MTAs

`sendmail` may be regarded as a first generation MTA. It was originally written about 20 years ago at a time when both mail and transmission protocols were evolving rapidly. Therefore, it contains a general-purpose, pattern-matching rule processor, and in its raw form can be thoroughly intimidating.

The second generation is represented by smail, which takes as given the RFC822 specification of email messages, but still assumes that the transport is more likely to be uucp than SMTP over IP.

The third generation is represented by qmail and exim, both of which largely ignore uucp, take for granted *what* needs to be done with a message, and only require parameterization in order to do it.

The following sections look at a few MTAs in more detail.

sendmail

sendmail is the grand-daddy of all the MTAs; it predates almost all others and it set the ground rules that have developed into the standards we know today. Most other components assume that they are talking to sendmail. All other MTAs therefore implement many of the same command-line options as sendmail, and are aliased so that they can be invoked by the name sendmail.

sendmail's control files are fiendishly complex and difficult to write. Fortunately, there is a set of m4 macros that are used to generate them. Nevertheless, sendmail is still the most flexible of all the MTAs and I find that, provided you use the m4 macros, it is reasonably straightforward to configure, so there is no need to be frightened off by its fierce reputation. Fortunately, too, there is no need to know much about m4; just the ability to copy macro calls from the documentation into your own master configuration files. Make does everything else for you. The definitive reference on sendmail is the "bat book" from O'Reilly. Although this is an excellent book, it still contains gaps and I will try to fill those in by using my own working setups.

sendmail Features and Options

sendmail has more features and options than you can shake a stick at. A reasonably complete description of them runs to about 1000 pages. However, the main ones can be invoked quite simply using m4 macros, and a reasonable config file should not run to more than about 10 lines. I will consider four main configurations: a standalone computer on a dial-up line, a standalone computer on a permanent link, a workstation on a LAN, and a central mail hub. There are a myriad of ways to configure mail distribution, but I will assume that all mail is routed through and delivered to a central hub, masquerading hides outlying workstations from the outside world, and workstations use POP or IMAP to fetch their mail.

The secret of using sendmail successfully is to start from one of the canned m4 configuration files that come with the distribution and then to tweak it to suit. It is also

20

Electronic
Mail

worth looking at `http://www.sendmail.org`, which has the latest version of the code and up-to-date documentation.

All the configuration source files will live wherever you put the `sendmail` distribution, generally somewhere like `/usr/src/sendmail/cf/cf/`. Put your own tailored files there as well. Note the use of the paired backquote and forward quote in the `m4` macros and the use of `dnl` after each command.

If you have a configuration source called, for example, `hub.mc`, you then run

```
make hub.cf
```

to build the final configuration file. This may then be copied to the proper place. At one time, the `sendmail` binary lived in `/usr/lib` (it was not intended for direct execution by end users) and the control files were distributed between `/usr/lib` and `/etc`. Later, the binaries moved to `/usr/bin` and the control files to `/usr/lib` and `/etc`. Now, the standard place for the control files seems to be `/etc/mail`, but it could still be `/usr/lib` or `/etc`. If you have installed pre-built binaries, the documentation should tell you; otherwise, examine your generated `sendmail.cf` and run `strings` on the binaries to see what they expect. Best of all, build the package yourself from the source and you can control things precisely.

Setting Up `sendmail` for Various Configuration

This section looks at the four configuration types mentioned in the previous section. For each configuration there is a `.mc` file of `m4` macros that has to be converted into a `.cf` file, as described in theprevious section.

Standalone Computer with a Permanent Internet Connection

The following code snippet is indicative of a permanent Internet connection coupled to a standalone machine.

```
VERSIONID(`@(#)standalone-LAN-linux.mc  8.9 3/23/96')
OSTYPE(linux)dnl
DOMAIN(generic)dnl
MAILER(local)dnl
MAILER(smtp)dnl
```

You might prefer to route all mail through your ISP instead of contacting remote hosts directly. In this case, add:

```
define(`SMART_HOST',`my.isp.com')dnl
```

Standalone Computer on a Dial-up Line

This is much like the previous configuration, but you have to take into account that the user does not want to be dialing out more than is necessary—you want to keep down the phone costs. With this configuration you may prefer to run the mail queue from `pppd`'s `ip-up` script and use some other trigger to dial out rather than having `sendmail` be the trigger for dialing out.

```
VERSIONID(`@(#)standalone-dialup-linux.mc   8.9 3/23/96')
OSTYPE(linux)dnl
DOMAIN(generic)dnl
MAILER(local)dnl
MAILER(smtp)dnl
```

You probably also want to delay the actual delivery of mail until a time convenient to you, so add:

```
define(`confDELIVERY_MODE',`queueonly')dnl
```

It is also quicker, and cheaper, to route all mail through your ISP rather than hanging on to what might be a slow link to a remote site:

```
define(`SMART_HOST',`my.isp.com')dnl
```

If you dial-up fairly infrequently, you can add the following to change the length of time for which mail will be allowed to remain on the output queue before a warning is issued or it is rejected completely:

```
define(`confMESSAGE_TIMEOUT',`5d/2d')dnl
```

Once you have things configured, you may find that `sendmail` is timing out because your dial script takes what `sendmail` considers to be an inordinate amount of time. If this happens, look at your `sendmail.cf` file to see whether it contains a setting for `DialDelay`. It will be in a line looking something like

```
O DialDelay=10s
```

It should not have a hash at the start of the line. If there is no suitable `DialDelay` parameter, add

```
define(`confDIAL_DELAY',`10s')
```

to your `.mc` file and rebuild and reinstall the `.cf`. Adjust the 10 seconds to whatever suits you.

Workstation on a LAN

This configuration is for use with the next one, the central mail server.

```
VERSIONID(` @(#)workstation-linux.mc  8.9 3/23/96')
OSTYPE(linux)dnl
FEATURE(` null_client', ` my.mailhub.com')dnl
```

If you do not want alias processing done on the workstation but prefer to have it all done on the hub, add the line:

```
undefine(` ALIAS_FILE')dnl
```

This choice will depend on whether the workstation users will have root access. If you do implement alias processing it will probably be limited to routing root mail somewhere more convenient—like your own mailbox.

Central Mail Server

In this configuration, all mail is sent to and stored on a central server. Outgoing mail is masqueraded so that it *appears* to be from the server and not from the individual workstations. Workstations access their mailboxes by IMAP or POP.

```
VERSIONID(` @(#)hublinux.mc  8.9 3/23/96')
OSTYPE(linux)dnl
DOMAIN(generic)dnl
MAILER(local)dnl
MAILER(smtp)dnl
FEATURE(` virtusertable', ` hash /etc/mail/sendmail_virtusers')dnl
FEATURE(masquerade_entire_domain)dnl
```

If you are going to process domains other than your primary domain, you will want the following:

```
FEATURE(limited_masquerade)dnl
MASQUERADE_DOMAIN_FILE(filename)dnl
```

To alter the amount of time for which mail is permitted to remain in the output queue, use something like

```
define(` confMESSAGE_TIMEOUT', ` 5d/2d')dnl
```

You will also want one of the following two lines to deal with mail from your outlying workstations. The second line is needed if you are handling more than just your primary domain:

```
FEATURE(relay_entire_domain)dnl
FEATURE(relay_based_on_MX)dnl
```

The preceding configuration still leaves the hostname of your mail server exposed. Mail will appear to originate from that specific host and all replies will go to it. You can also hide the server's hostname and have all mail appear to originate from the domain name. To do this, you should have an MX record for your domain, not just the mail hub. This will enable mail sent to the domain name, `user@mydomain.com`, to be delivered correctly, as well as mail to `user@mailhub.mydomain.com`. If you add the line

```
MASQUERADE_AS(`mydomain.com')dnl
```

then all outgoing mail will appear to be from the domain rather than the specific mail hub.

Clever Bits

`sendmail` has a whole bunch of functions additional to the basic sending of mail between individual users and machines. Among these are the processing of mail for several domains (with or without masquerading the domain names), spam protection, and name translation with a *virtual user* table.

Multiple Domains

The first extra bit that you might want to tack on is to buffer and forward mail for some other domain, perhaps a client of yours. All you need to have is the appropriate MX records in your DNS setup and `FEATURE(relay_based_on_MX)` in your `.mc` file. All mail for the client's domain will be forwarded automatically.

If your client does not connect with SMTP, but with POP or IMAP, create a local user for him as described in the section on POP and IMAP earlier in the chapter. You will also have to create an entry in the local hosts table and the virtual users table.

The local hosts table is `/etc/mail/sendmail.cw`. It tells `sendmail` that mail for these hosts is to be processed locally and not just left in the spool directory for onward transmission. Its contents is a list of host names, one per line.

The virtual users table, which we have put into `/etc/mail/sendmail_virtusers`, tells `sendmail` what to do with mail for those extra hosts. It contains two sorts of lines: one for individual users and the other for entire hosts. A line for a single user looks like this:

```
user@client.com        localuser
```

This tells `sendmail` that mail for `user@client.com` should instead be sent to `localuser`. The destination does not have to be a local username, but it is in this example.

To route all the mail for a host, use a line like this:

```
@client.com     localuser
```

20

Electronic Mail

Again, the destination does not have to be local, but is for this example.

The two types of lines may be freely mixed; `sendmail` will try for an exact match on the username if it can, otherwise it will use the host destination if one exists. There are also more advanced uses of the virtual users table. For instance, a line of the form

```
bogus@mydomain.com    error:nouser  No such user here
```

will bounce a message completely.

You can also do a certain amount of pattern matching. For instance

```
@somedomain.com info@%1.otherdomain.com
```

will take the supplied username, `%1`, and use it to generate a hostname on the redirected message, though I am somewhat at a loss to find a real, practical use for these features.

Declaring the Virtual User Table

Now, in our sample configuration files we have declared the virtual user table to be a hashed file, so before it can be used you have to do

```
cd /etc/mail
makemap hash sendmail_virtusers < sendmail_virtusers
```

This will create `/etc/mail/sendmail_virtusers.db`.

As a Web services provider, when I set up a Web server for a client I also collect and redirect his mail to wherever his mail accounts really are. In this case, I have MX records for him, a local hosts table entry for him, and a set of virtual user entries that route his mail directly to the correct places. These destinations are not local to my machine.

A third use of the virtual user table is when you are acting as a kind of ISP. In this case, all your clients will have their mail sent to *user@client.yourdomain.com*. In this case, do *not* use `masquerade_entire_domain`: You want each client's mail to receive replies correctly addressed. You will still need an MX for each sub-domain, and entries in the local hosts table and virtual users table as before. For this kind of operation you will probably want to use two domains: one for your own mail and machines, and the other for the clients'. Your will masquerade your own domain, and the clients' domain will not be masqueraded. This is achieved by using both the `masquerade_entire_domain` and the `limited_masquerade` features.

The `access_db` feature provides a level of control over what messages you will accept, either for delivery or for relaying. It is used much like the virtual user table, in that you add a line

```
FEATURE(`access_db', `hash -o /etc/mail/access')dnl
```

to your `.mc` file and create an `/etc/mail/access` file looking much like a virtual user table. For instance, it might contain the line

```
pest@spammer.org REJECT
```

All mail from the specified sender will then be bounced. Just like the virtual user table, the access database has to be built in to a binary file by

```
cd /etc/mail
makemap hash access < access
```

Testing and Running `sendmail`

In your `/etc/rc.d/` files, just after the network is started there should be a command of the form

```
/usr/bin/sendmail -bd -q15m
```

This is the `sendmail` listener daemon. It listens for incoming mail on port 25 (the `-bd` option), and will scan the queue for work every 15 minutes (the `-q15m` option). Provided that your ISP or other upstream connection will send you mail by SMTP, this is all you need. If your upstream link will only send you mail by POP or IMAP, you must also either run a POP- or IMAP-aware MUA, or run something like `fetchmail` to download messages into your spool area.

Every time your master mail alias file changes, you also run `newaliases` manually to update the database.

You can also test the functioning of `sendmail` by running it with diagnostic command-line options.

To check where mail is going use

```
sendmail -bv user@domain.com
```

This will process the aliases, virtual user table, and other databases and tell you where `sendmail` thinks your mail is going. You can obtain more information by adding the `-v` flag:

```
sendmail -v -bv user@domain.com
```

Even more information can be obtained by adding `-d`:

```
sendmail -v -d -bv user@domain.com
```

This will give you a trace through `sendmail`'s internal rules and, while interesting, can be rather overwhelming.

20

Electronic Mail

Smail

The next MUA we consider is `smail`. This has a much simpler interface than `sendmail` because it dates from a time when mail protocols were fairly settled, but it does not offer all the functionality that `sendmail` does.

To judge by its documentation, `smail` was originally written for the uucp market. It works quite well with SMTP, but that is not the focus of its documentation. You can obtain it either as binaries or source and build it to suit yourself. The program is suitable for both workstations and mail hubs that are serving just one domain. It will not do any of the fancy masquerading and relay control that you get with `sendmail`.

The package comes with a whole raft of sample configurations that you can tailor to suit yourself. It has some fairly fancy manipulations that you can use for control of routing. This fine control is absolutely necessary for uucp mail, but for SMTP it is largely redundant.

`Smail` Transports, Directors, and Routers

`Smail` uses the concepts of transports, directors, and routers in its control mechanism.

A *transport* is a method of physically delivering a message to its destination once the MTA has decided where it is to go. Transports include SMTP, `appendfile`, and pipe.

A *director* operates on local addresses. It looks up aliases and forwarding files, applies filters, and then hands it on to the appropriate transport. Although a director is always given a local address, aliasing and forwarding may cause the generation of non-local addresses.

A *router* takes a non-local address and decides which host to send it to next. This involves DNS lookups for MX and A records. In exceptional circumstances, it may turn out that an apparently remote address is, after all, for a local domain. The transport that is invoked will generally be SMTP.

For local delivery, you have the choice of two drivers in the transports file. The `appendfile` driver will write messages directly to the user's mailbox, or the pipe driver will call `procmail` to do the work. The latter is the one of choice because it will also look at `~/.procmailrc` files and do the necessary filtering and distribution, when appropriate. Generally, though, so long as `procmail` is installed where `smail` expects it, you will not have to do anything to configure it.

`Smail` was the mailer that I originally used in preference to `sendmail` because it has a simpler configuration. However, I was forced to change over by the need to handle more than one domain. Because of having no need to route over uucp, and the availability of m4 configurations for `sendmail`, I now feel that `sendmail` is actually easier to use. However, if you have need to route FIDO or `uucp` mail, `smail` is the one for you—its maps and directors files give you just the control that you need.

For simple SMTP setups, `smail` and `sendmail` are pretty well drop-in replacements for each other. In general, for pure SMTP sites, `exim` (discussed later in this chapter) might be a better bet.

`Smail` Configuration

Most of the `smail` configuration is compiled in with the code. If you build your own version from sources, you can tailor it at the build stage. The main thing you will probably want to do is to replace all the uucp transports with SMTP. The authors of `smail` recommend that if you do not need to alter a configuration file, you should not have it at all. On the other hand, you may prefer to have everything explicitly visible in your control files rather than relying on implicit information in the binaries.

The directors, routers, and transports files are quite verbose. However, they are reasonably straightforward to create, based on the samples that come with the distribution.

The *smart path* is a "where to pass the buck" specification. On a LAN, local hosts can be addressed directly, but mail to remote hosts should go through the mail hub. Similarly, on a dial-up link all mail should just be relayed through the ISP.

`Smail` Configuration Files

The `smail` config file will contain a few tailoring parameters for your particular configuration. It should only contain your overrides and not be a complete copy of the original from the distribution in case you accidentally trample on any operating system-specific parameters. The fields you will want to look at are shown in Table 20.1.

TABLE 20.1 `Smail` Configuration Parameters

Field	Description
`smart_path`	Should point to your upstream feed
`smart_transport`	SMTP
`visible_name`	Used if you want to masquerade an entire domain

The directors file will probably need to be edited only in the aliases section. You have to choose between using a linear text file for aliases, a database, à la `sendmail`, or NIS. You must include a *complete* directors file, if you have anything at all.

Similarly, the routers file will only need to be checked to see if it uses SMTP and not uucp as its `smart_transport`. You will also have to choose between using `gethostbyname` or `bind` for resolving hostnames.

20

Electronic Mail

The transports file should only need to be edited to reflect whether you are using `bind` or `gethostbyname` for hostname resolution.

Workstation Configuration

The configuration for this is very similar regardless of whether you are on a LAN or a dial-up link. The main difference is whether you have your own visible hostname or whether you use your organization's domain name.

Configuration Files

Stand-alone Workstation with Its Own Visible Host

```
namevisible_domains = myhost.mydomain.com

# set hooks in the smartuser and smarthost drivers
smart_user = $user@myhost.mydomaincom
# default new_user for
# smartuser
smart_path = mailhub.myISP.com     # default path for
        # smarthost
smart_transport = smtp    # get to gateway using
        # smtp
        # There is no transport special
        #  transport file, so don't look for
        # one
-transport_file
```

A Workstation on a LAN with a Masqueraded Domain

```
visible_domains = mydomain.com
# set hooks in the smartuser and smarthost drivers
smart_user = $user@mydomain.com     # default new_user for smartuser
smart_path = mailhub.mydomain.com# default path for smarthost
smart_transport = smtp        # get to gateway using uusmtp
# There is no transport special transport file, so don't
# look for one
-transport_file
```

The Mail Hub's Config

```
# mode for all of the log files:
log_mode = 0644
message_log_mode = 0644
```

```
# all of our gateway names (as opposed to proper host names):
more_hostnames=mailhub.mydomain.com:mydomain.com

# If something is wrong with the aliases file, use "pat" as postmaster:
postmaster_address = pat

# Allow smail spool files to overrun into alternate filesystem:
spool_dirs = /usr/spool/smail:/u2/spool/smail

# Disallow any group or other access to spool files:
spool_mode = 0600

# mailhub is under the following domains:
visible_domains = mydomain.com

# We are the gateway for the entire domain.  We hide the network
# topology (by default) in outgoing addresses:
visible_name = mydomain.com
```

Director Files

The main function of the following file is to sort out aliases and forwarding. Workstations may use NIS (also known as YP) to get access to the master alias file, whereas the mail hub might refer directly to the master file and incidentally avoid reliance on NIS.

This file is pure boilerplate stuff. You will probably not want to alter it, other than possibly extending the "unsecure" list.

```
# the following two directors are magic for accessing mailing
# list literaladdresses supplied by the "aliasfile" driver and
# the "forwardfile" driver respectively.

# aliasinclude - expand ":include:filename" addresses produced
# by alias files
aliasinclude:
driver = aliasinclude,    # use this special-case
# driver
nobody;                   # associate nobody user
# with addresses when mild
# permission violations
        #  are encountered

copysecure,               # get permissions from
# alias director
```

```
copyowners                      # get owners from alias
# director


# forwardinclude - expand ":include:filename" addrs produced by
# forward files
forwardinclude:
driver = forwardinclude,    # use this special-
# case driver
nobody;
copysecure,                     # get perms from forwarding
# director
copyowners                      # get owners from
# forwarding director


# get aliases from /private/usr/lib/smail/aliases, which is
#   optional. This is not present on the mail hub.
private_aliases:
owner=owner-$user,
driver=aliasfile;
file=/private/usr/lib/smail/aliases,
optional,
proto=lsearch               # straight text ASCII file


# aliases - search for alias expansions stored in a database
aliases:
driver = aliasfile,         # general-purpose
# aliasing director
owner = owner-$user;        # problems go to an
# owner address
file = mail.aliases,            # use this for YP
proto = yp                  # use this for YP


# forward - search for forward expansions stored in a database
forward:
driver = aliasfile,         # general-purpose
# aliasing director
sender_okay,                # sender can be in
# the list
owner = postmaster@mydomain.com;# problems to
# forward maintainers

file = mail.forward,            # use this for YP
proto = yp                      # use this for YP
```

```
# dotforward - expand .forward files in user home directories
dotforward:
driver = forwardfile,        # general-purpose
# forwarding director
owner = Postmaster,          # problems go to the
# Postmaster
nobody,
sender_okay;                 # sender never
#removed from
# expansion
file = ~/.forward,           # .forward file in
#home directories
checkowner,                  # the user can own
# this file
owners = root,               # or root can own the
#file
modemask = 002,              # it should not be
# globally writable
caution = daemon:root,       # don't run things as
# root or daemon
# be extra careful of remotely accessible home directories
unsecure = "~ftp:~uucp:~nuucp:/tmp:/usr/tmp"


# forwardto - expand a "Forward to " in user mailbox files
#
# This emulates the V6/V7/System-V forwarding mechanism which
# uses aline of forward addresses stored at the beginning of
# user mailbox filesprefixed with the string "Forward to "
forwardto:
driver = forwardfile,
owner = real-$user, nobody, sender_okay;

file = /usr/spool/mail/${lc:user},    # point at user
# mailbox files
forwardto,                   # enable "Forward to "
#                # function
checkowner,                  # the user can own this
# file
owners = root,               # or root can own the file
modemask = 0022,             # only owner should be able
              # to write
caution = daemon:root    # don't run things as root
```

20

Electronic Mail

```
# or daemon


# user - match users on the local host with delivery to their
# mailboxes
user:    driver = user;          # driver to match usernames


transport = local          # local transport goes to mailboxes


# real_user - match usernames when prefixed with the string "real-"
#
# This is useful for allowing an address which explicitly
# delivers to a user's mailbox file.  For example, errors in a
# .forward file expansion can be delivered here, or forwarding
# loops between multiple machines can be resolved by using a
# real-username address.
real_user:
driver = user;
transport = local,
prefix = "real-"             # for example, match real-root


# let users put mailing lists on their local machines
private_lists:
caution,
owner=owner-$user,
driver=forwardfile;
file=/private/usr/lib/smail/lists/${lc:user}


# lists - expand mailing lists stored in a list directory
#
# mailing lists can be created simply by creating a file in the
# /usr/lib/smail/lists directory.
lists:    driver = forwardfile,
caution,                 # flag all addresses with
# caution
nobody,                   # and then associate the
# nobody user
owner = owner$user;


# map the name of the mailing list to lower case
file = lists/${lc:user}


# smart_user - a partially specified smartuser director
#
```

```
# If the config file attribute smart_user is defined as a string
# such as "$user@domain-gateway" then users not matched o
# therwise will be sent off to the host "domain-gateway".
#
# If the smart_user attribute is not defined, this director is
# ignored.
smart_user:
driver = smartuser;        # special-case driver


# do not match addresses which cannot be made into valid
# RFC822 local addresses without the use of double quotes.
well_formed_only
```

Router Files

The router files differ slightly between workstations and a mail hub.

Since smail assumes uucp transport by default, these router files just force everything to be SMTP over an IP link. The two files differ only in that the workstation config uses the smarthost route, but the hub expects to be able to connect to the real destinations of messages.

Workstation Routers File

```
# inet_addrs - match domain literals containing literal IP
# addresses. The library routine gethostbyaddr(3N) will be
# called to see if a reverse mapping to the cononical hostname
# is available.
inet_addrs:
driver = gethostbyaddr,        # router to match IP domain
# literals
transport = smtp;        # deliver using SMTP over
# TCP/IP

fail_if_error,        # fail malformed domain
# literal addrs
check_for_local        # see if this is really the
# local host

# paths - force some routes using the YP network path database
paths:    driver = pathalias,        # general-use paths router
transport = smtp;        # for matches, deliver over
# SMTP
```

```
file = mail.paths,       # database containing path info
proto = yp,              # look in yp database


# inet_hosts - match hostnames with gethostbyname(3N) or bind
inet_hosts:
driver = gethostbyname,       # match hosts with the
# library function
#         driver=bind,        # Alternative for DNS
transport = smtp;
domain = mydomain.com


# smart_host - a partially specified smarthost director
#
# If the config file attribute smart_path is defined as a path
# from the local host to a remote host, then hostnames not
# matched otherwise will
# be sent off to the stated remote host.  The config file
# attribute smart_transport can be used to specify a different
# transport.
#
# If the smart_path attribute is not defined, this router is
# ignored.
smart_host:
driver = smarthost,      # special-case driver
transport = smtp         # by default deliver over SMTP
```

Routers File for the Mail Hub

The routers file for the mail hub is not substantially different. The chief difference is that it may not have a smart_path defined because it expects to have access to the whole Internet, and not just to one upstream mail server. This file has all the uucp routing deleted.

```
# match-inet-addrs - match literal Internet-family addresses
#
# This director will match hostnames such as [192.2.12.200],
# which are literal addresses on a TCP/IP network.  This form
# should only be used when the actual hostname cannot be found
# in the network databases, or to get around a "forces" file
# that reroutes mail to a host listed in the databases for the
# TCP/IP network.
Match-inet-addrs:
        driver=gethostbyaddr,        # match inet domain
# literal addrs
        transport=smtp;              # delivery is over
```

```
# smtp/tcp
      fail_if_error,              # non-inet literals are
# errors
      check_for_local            # check for local host

# match-inet-hosts - match hosts in the TCP/IP network database
#
# On the mail hub we always want to use bind for host lookup
match-inet-hosts:
      driver=bind,                    # match hosts on network
transport=smtp;          # delivery is over smtp/tcp
domain = mydomain.com      # strip trailing domain
# before lookup
```

Transports File

The `smail` documentation describes the transports configuration file. However, in a pure SMTP environment it is extremely unlikely that you will ever need one.

Running `smail`

`smail` implements many of the same command-line options as `sendmail`. This is deliberate policy on the part of the authors so that other programs, such as `majordomo`, should not need to know which MTA is being run.

Qmail

Qmail is intended as a smaller, simpler replacement for sendmail+MH. Because the extra complication of running MH or `fetchmail` or something of that kind is generally unnecessary, qmail is, to a certain extent, shooting at a target that is no longer there.

`Qmail` Delivery Options

Qmail has its own way of delivering mail to local users. There are actually three different ways of dealing with it. MAILDIR format puts the mail in ~/Mail/ with each message in a separate file. This is a Good Thing from the point of view of avoiding file-locking issues, but a Bad Thing from the point of view of the MUA, which has to be patched to recognize this format. Patches are available for many popular MUAs. The second format is MAILFILE. Here the mail is all put into one file in the user's home directory, for example, ~/mbox. Many MUAs can read this format with no more than a command-line option to tell them where to look, but there are contention issues if you have two or more MUAs running at once. The contention problem clearly vanishes if your MUA uses POP or IMAP to

20

Electronic
Mail

access the messages. The third format is SPOOLDIR, which puts the mail in `/var/spool/mail/$USER`—just like traditional `sendmail`. The authors of `qmail` consider this option to be insecure, presumably because everyone's mail lives in the one directory.

`Qmail` Message Handling

Qmail's idiosyncratic way of handling messages also has the benefit that it can be run in conjunction with other MTAs and they will not tread on each others' toes. This can be useful when handling more than one domain, when running cascaded mail handlers, and in other even more obscure situations. I have only ever found one situation where it was actually useful to do so.

Like `sendmail`, `qmail` can handle virtual domains. It does not, however, have `sendmail`'s ability to do fine control over virtual users and relaying. Unless you install certain optional components, `qmail` also does not use a central alias file `/etc/alias`. In this respect also, it is rather different from other MTAs.

Qmail always delivers mail immediately. It is therefore not the best choice for dial-up users, or where all mail is routed through a hub or relay. However, it is reputed to handle high mail loads very well. It is therefore well in the running for use in conjunction with list servers such as `majordomo`. Qmail also provides a `sendmail` wrapper so that other programs need not know that they are not running real `sendmail` but only a cardboard imitation.

If you have a machine that has a very large volume of `majordomo` traffic, you might consider `sendmail` for incoming mail and `qmail` for outgoing mail. Just be careful not to create the `sendmail` wrappers when installing `qmail`.

`Qmail` User Ids and Configuration Files

Qmail uses several Linux user IDs for its processes. These are created when you install `qmail` from the rpms, as are all the necessary directories.

The configuration files live in `/var/qmail/control/`. Unlike the other MTAs, which have just one, or very few, control files, `qmail` keeps each parameter, or parameter group, in a separate file. The only essential file is `me`, which contains the fully qualified local hostname. If you want to route all outgoing mail through a mail hub or to your ISP, you will also need a `smtproutes` file. This should contain one line

```
:mailhub.myISP.net
```

which will cause all non-local mail to be relayed through the specified mail hub. For fancier routing, you can put more than one line in the control file. This may well be useful, particularly on a mail hub, if you have certain domains that you want routed over a private network.

There is a large quantity of supplementary tools and documentation that you can get from theqmail Web site at `http://www.qmail.org`.

Exim

`Exim`, the last MTA that I will consider, is also the most modern and is designed with a clear knowledge of what an MTA has to do. In contrast, the original authors of `sendmail` were very much feeling their way.

`Exim` is inspired by `smail` and is very much in the same style, but handles SMTP only. It simplifies many of the concepts of `smail` and has good, clear documentation, probably the best of any MTA that I have seen. At the same time, `exim` manages to provide many of the virtual domain and relaying functions of `sendmail` without `sendmail`'s complexity.

`Exim` also provides some queue control that is not present in any of the other MTAs.

Messages on the queue can be "frozen" and "thawed" under operator control.

Local mail can be delivered immediately, whereas remote mail can be batched up for later transmission.

There is a queue monitor utility so that the operator can keep an eye on how things are going.

Like `smail`, `exim` uses the concepts of transports,directors, and routers. It also implements many of the `sendmail` command-line options so that, for most purposes, it is a drop-in replacement.

Exim Configuration

`Exim` should run more or less out of the box on workstations. There are a few minor configuration parameters that you might want to tailor. There is just one configuration file that lives in`/usr/exim/configure`. It has several sections and, as installed, is heavily commented, so there should be no problems with editing it.

In the `local_delivery`: driver, you might want to change

```
file = /var/mail/${local_part}
```

to be

```
file = /var/spool/mail/${local_part}
```

depending on where your MUA expects user mailboxes to live.

Exim Workstations

To route all mail through your mail hub or ISP, use the `smart_route` router:

```
smart_route:
  driver = domainlist
  transport = remote_smtp
  route_list = "*  mailhub.myISP.com bydns_a"
```

This should precede the `lookuphost:` router in the default configuration.

Mail Hub

Exim has all relaying turned off by default. You will need to enable it for hosts within your own domains. To do this set

```
local_domains = mydomain.com:foobar.com
relay_domains = *.mydomain.com:*.foobar.com
```

The `local_domains` variable will treat those domains as local; that is, no relaying is involved. `relay_domains` will cause mail to those subdomains to be accepted.

Outgoing relays from your own workstations are enabled by

```
host_accept_relay = localhost:*.mydomain.com
```

Spam Protection

Exim provides user as well as system filters for incoming messages. User filters live in `~/.forward`. A filter `.forward` is distinguished from a normal `.forward` in that its first line is

```
# Exim filter
```

Capitalization and whitespace are not significant.

The simplest type of spam filter is

```
if  ${reply_address} contains "@spamsite.com" and
    ${reply_address} does not contain "postmaster@"
then
    seen finish
endif
```

This will simply discard the message.

Other variables that you can test on are `$sender_address`, `$header_from`, and `$header_subject`. As with shell variables, it is generally a good idea to enclose the actual variable name in braces as in the preceding example. Any header may be referred to by using a name of the form *$header_headername*—for instance $header_bcc or $header_reply-to.

Other actions that you can take are to resend the message elsewhere (forward it to another location), write log files, save the message to a file, and so on. The documentation in ./exim-*/doc/filter.txt is very clear and comprehensive.

The use of a system filter enables rules to be applied as soon as a message enters the system. To enable it, add the following:

```
central_filter:
  driver = forwardfile
  file = /usr/exim/filters/${local_part}
  no_check_local_user
  no_verify
  filter
  allow_system_actions
```

The setting of allow_system_actions permits the use of freeze and fail in the filter file. These commands are not available at all in user filters.

The use of $local_part in the file spec permits the system administrator to have a separate filter set for each local user. Of course, you could just have one global filter set for everyone by making the file spec a fixed string.

Ancillary Programs for Mail Handling

The rest of this chapter looks at a couple of ancillary programs. Fetchmail is a support program that helps with the collection of mail over dial-up links. Majordomo, in contrast, provides completely new functionality, discussion groups, using email as the transport medium.

Fetchmail

Fetchmail is more half an MTA than a full MTA. As its name implies, it reads mail from a server, but does not write it. This may seem strange, but such a program is sometimes necessary.

You will not need fetchmail if you have a full Internet connection. In this case, your normal mail listener on port 25 will do everything you need. You will not need fetchmail if your ISP sends you mail by SMTP and recognizes new connections so as to start the mail

20

Electronic Mail

flowing. You will also not need `fetchmail` if your MUA is POP aware, although in this case you might still like to run `fetchmail` in order to take advantage of its multiuser distribution.

You will need `fetchmail` if your ISP only sends mail by POP or IMAP, or does not automatically detect new connections to start up an SMTP send. In all cases that I know of, outgoing mail from a workstation to an ISP goes by SMTP.

`Fetchmail` reads mail from nominated servers and *forwards* it to other destinations. It does not actually deliver the mail itself. In normal use, you will ask fetchmail to forward either to port 25 on your local machine or to run `procmail` to do the actual delivery into user mailboxes.

`Fetchmail` may be run either by individual users or as a daemon.

`Fetchmail` has to be given several pieces of information in order to do its job:

- Which servers to poll
- When to poll them
- Which protocol to use
- The user ID and password, or other authentication to use
- Where to dispose of the mail it reads
- Whether to delete mail from the server

Running `Fetchmail`

The easiest way to run `fetchmail` is as a root daemon, started from `/etc/rc.d`. To do this you have to satisfy two requirements:

- Your ISP or mail hub can send mail to you by SMTP.
- You are running an SMTP listener on port 25.

To start `fetchmail`, in the appropriate place in `/etc/rc.d/`, add the following:

```
/usr/bin/fetchmail -d 3600 -f /etc/fetchmailrc
```

This will run `fetchmail` as a daemon with a polling interval of one hour and reading its commands from `/etc/fetchmailrc`. You still have to tell the program what to do.

Normally, you will only be polling one mail server, but the specification can be repeated as often as necessary.

A sample configuration would begin

```
poll mail.myISP.com protocol ETRN
```

This would download everybody's mail from the server to this workstation.

If, on the other hand, you can only use POP or IMAP for mail download, running as a root daemon is not safe. Because of the way mail from mailing lists is handled, there is a danger that your mail will never be delivered. Consequently, each user must run his own `fetchmail` daemon. In this case, the configuration is stored in each user's `~/.fetchmailrc`:

```
poll mail.myISP.net protocol POP3 username myname  password mypassword
```

This tells `fetchmail` which mail server to log in to, which protocol to use, and what user ID and password to use on the server. This user ID and password have no connection whatsoever with those on the local machine.

You also have to tell `fetchmail` which users' mail to extract from the mailbox. If you are running as a root daemon, it will probably be only root's mail that is extracted. So add

```
to myname here
```

If you receive mail by more than one name you can put

```
to myfirstname myothername here
```

Now, what is `fetchmail` to do with the mail? The two simplest answers are to deliver to one nominated user, or to deliver to the name in the To: header. To deliver to one user add

```
mda   "/usr/bin/procmail -d myname"
```

Alternatively, to deliver to the user named in the To: header add

```
mda   "/usr/bin/procmail -d '%T'"
```

You must ensure that all such users actually exist on your local machine or the mail will bounce. There are also dangers if the To: header contains more than one recipient—your mail will go all over the place and you will be very unpopular.

Supporting Multiple Email Clients

You can have as many email clients installed and running simultaneously on your system as you or your users like. The only real problem is that your users will expect you to be absolutely familiar with the ins and outs of all of them.

For instance, at one site I run two mail clients simultaneously. They collect mail from different servers, store them in different places, and display them in different windows. This way, I separate out two major groups of messages that I receive so that I can ignore the less important ones until I am ready to deal with them. Using "mail filters" in one client is another way to achieve the same thing. It just depends on what happens to be more convenient.

Inherent in the division of mail transport into an MUA and an MTA is that you have two programs trying to access the mailbox. This can clearly lead to conflict. Another conflict, though less common, is that a user may have two mail clients running simultaneously, possibly on different workstations.

Spool Access

Access to the output spool area is generally not a problem. Your MUA will either pipe its message to the MTA and pass the buck, or it will be careful to create its control files with temporary names and only rename them to what the MTA expects when everything is safely written.

Similarly, when the MTA extracts a job from the output queue, it will rename the control file before doing anything so that another instance of itself should not try to process the same job.

Locking Issues

Access to the mailbox by MTA and one or more MUAs is more problematic than access to the output spool area. In general, the MTA and the MUA come from different stables; it is important to check that they will work correctly together and use compatible locking mechanisms.

Some MUAs can also become confused if there are two instances running. I have seen problems with Sun's `mailtool` and `mail` confusing each other.

If you have the time to do so, it is best to obtain the source code of both your MTA and your chosen MUA and check that they use compatible locking. Also check the MUA for safety when multiple instances are running. Programs such as xfmail move all your messages from the input mailbox into a private work area. Because all instances of xfmail use the same private area, it is problematic as to what happens when more than one instance is running.

Use of IMAP and POP alleviates the problem of mailbox locking, but does not address that of private work areas used by MUAs.

Generally, however, problems are rare.

Popular Linux Email Clients

This section looks at three clients. One is an old fashioned command-line program that came out with the original UNIX in the dim, dark days beyond recall. The second is a character mode, full-screen, menu-driven program, and the third is X-based. Each has its uses.

Functionally, the only real difference between them is that X clients can handle attachments, or handle them more gracefully.

The choice of a mail client, like that of an editor, is very much a matter of personal taste, so if what is described here is not to your taste, try something else. There is lots to choose from.

Mail/mailx

Mail and mailx are two variants of the same program. Mail was written in the days before VDUs, and it assumes a printing terminal. Mailx is slightly more sophisticated and pipes its output through more so that it can be viewed more comfortably. If you have mailx installed, it should also be aliased to mail.

You will probably use mail mainly in scripts so that you can send messages from them. The general usage is

```
mail -s "subject" user1 user2 ...  << %%
Body of message
%%
```

To read mail with mail your mailbox must be a local file. The program knows nothing of IMAP or POP.

The program has three modes: menu, mail reading, and mail composition.

In menu mode, mail recognizes single-character commands, some of which take an argument. These are shown in Table 20.2.

TABLE 20.2 Mail Commands

Command	Description
h [number]	Displays the message headers starting from the specified message number.
x	Exits without updating the mailbox.
q	Exits and updates the mailbox by marking read messages as read, and removing deleted messages.
d [number]	Deletes the specified message, or the current one.
w file	Writes the message to a file.
p [number]	Prints (that is, displays) the specified message. Remember this program was designed for printing terminals
m user	Composes a new mail message.
r [number]	Replies to a message. There are versions of mail that do and some that do not automatically include the original message. It can, however, be controlled from the ~/.mailrc file.

In message composition mode, `mail` recognizes some tilde escapes. A message is terminated by ^D or a dot on a line by itself. The main tilde escapes are

- ~r file—Reads in a file

- ~e—Invokes the ex editor

- ~v—Invokes the vi editor

On startup, `mail` reads ~/.mailrc to obtain private aliases and set various options. Because you will probably not be using this program except in a very simple-minded way, knowledge of the .mailrc contents does not matter all that much. Man mail will tell you all you want to know.

Elm/Pine

`Elm` is a full-screen, character-mode editor that is controlled by single-letter commands. `Pine` is a development of `elm`. Although the two are now completely separate, they have a family likeness.

`Elm` presents your message headers in a scrolling area in the middle of the screen, and a reminder of the menu options at the bottom. It is easy to use, and you do not need to burden your memory with its commands. A version is also available for MS-DOS.

`Elm` and `pine` are both suitable for use over slow, dial-up links if you have to access mail on a remote machine and cannot configure a local mailer to use POP or IMAP. Simply telnet to the remote machine and fire up your mailer.

`Pine` will process and display MIME attachments. If run under X, it can even deal with graphics.

Xfmail

`Xfmail` is an X client. It provides the usual facilities that you expect from a modern, GUI-based program. Earlier versions were a little fragile, but the one that I have, 1.3, is much enhanced and quite robust. I find the 1.4 version is not as good as 1.3—the icons are not as clear and it is again a bit fragile when using copy-and-paste.

`Xfmail` will handle local mailboxes, POP, and IMAP input and it will read any number of mail sources. I have mine set up for three: a local mailbox and two POP sources. Rules enable you to filter and distribute mail to various places such as folders, other users, or discarded. Attachments can be sent and displayed. Mail can be sent either by direct SMTP, by piping to an MTA, or by POP. In short, it is a modern mail tool.

Aliases

A *mail alias* allows you to expand a mnemonic name into one or more real email addresses. Most mail systems will also permit the target of an alias to be a command pipe.

A collection of aliases is sometimes called an *address book*. Such a collection may be owned by an individual user or by the system. Generally, your MUA will look at the destinations on your outgoing messages and expand any aliases it recognizes. The system's MTA will then re-process the recipient list against its alias lists.

MTAs will also do alias expansion on incoming messages. MUAs generally do not.

Managing Aliases

Aliases are stored in two places: a global file managed by the Sysadmin and examined by the MTA, and in private files managed by each user and examined by the MUA. For the moment we are only concerned with the former.

An alias may expand into an arbitrarily long list of names, although some MTAs may place a limit on the final length. Generally, an alias expansion may also include other aliases. The MTA will handle these recursive aliases with no problems.

Alias Master File Locations

Different MTAs keep the alias master file in different places. The most common are `/etc/aliases` and `/usr/lib/aliases`, although `/etc/alias` (note: singular) and `/etc/mail/aliases` are also used. To keep your options open, just put it in the location of your choice and symlink it to the others. Generally, this file then has to be converted to some sort of binary form by a program called either `newalias` or `newaliases`, depending on your MTA. The binary database is then frozen and the MTA will not see changes to the source file unless `newaliases` is run again.

Most MTAs will also allow you to use an `include` command to read supplementary lists. There are, however, security implications in this feature that render it of limited use.

The target of an alias does not have to be an email address. Most MTAs will also permit it to be a file or a command pipe. The use of a file was illustrated earlier in the discussion on spam. The use of pipes and `include` files will appear in the discussion on majordomo.

Structuring Aliases

There are several reasons for using aliases.

Login names are generally limited to eight characters. In a large organization these login names can be highly cryptic. It is more convenient for mail to be addressed to each person's proper name, so my email address at various places has been something like `MankinR@domain.com` or `mailto:Raphael.Mankin@domain.com`.

It is frequently convenient to have a single alias associated with all the members of some project, group, or department. Large mailing lists, particularly those subject to frequent change, are better managed by majordomo.

Auto-responders, such as ftp-by-mail, list-processors, and the like require the use of command pipes as the targets of aliases.

A bit-bucket alias, such as was mentioned as an anti-spam measure, is frequently desirable.

Aliases are commonly used for job functions. Standard ones are postmaster, hostmaster, and webmaster. Other job functions, such as the configuration manager in a large software project, might be addressed by aliases. If the responsible person changes, only the alias need change; the users need not be bothered.

The format of the alias files used by the different MTAs is similar but just sufficiently different to be annoying. They all expect a sequence of lines with the alias names beginning in column 1 and the expansions following. Generally, a line beginning with whitespace is treated as a continuation of the previous line. Generally, also, a line beginning with a hash is a comment.

Now comes the annoying bit. Sometimes the alias name is separated from its expansion by a colon, sometimes by an equal sign, and sometimes by whitespace. Multiple destinations are sometimes separated by commas and sometimes by whitespace. It is no great problem to convert from one format to another, but it is a nuisance. It would have been nice if the authors of the various MTAs had all followed the same format—there is no functional difference between them.

For security reasons, alias files should be writable only by the mail administrator. The MTA usually runs as root and an alias may point to a file or a command pipe. If an outsider can capture an alias file, he can create an alias that will write to any other file in the computer, and run any arbitrary program. For this reason, include files are of limited use. They must be protected just as much as the primary alias file and so provide little possibility for the mail administrator to offload some of his work to departmental heads (see the section "Distributed Management of Alaises" later in this chapter).

Mandatory Aliases

Every alias file must contain certain entries. These are

- root—The system administrator.

- postmaster—The person responsible for mail administration, spam elimination, and all other duties to do with mail.

- hostmaster—If you run DNS, this is the DNS administrator.

- webmaster—If you run a Web server, this is the person responsible for it.

- newsmaster—If you run a news server, this is its administrator.

- nobody—This is a bit bucket. Just point it at `/dev/null`. Not strictly mandatory, but very useful.

In many organizations, of course, all these jobs are carried out by one person, so all the aliases point to the same destination. Outsiders may, however, be relying on the existence of these aliases.

Aliases Versus Mailing Lists

Every change to the alias file must be effected manually by the mail administrator. For fairly static lists, this is no great workload; for lists that change dynamically, it is better to use mailing lists under control of a list processor such as `majordomo`. That way the updating of the file happens automatically as people subscribe or unsubscribe themselves from mailing lists.

20

Electronic Mail

A good rule of thumb is that a membership list, almost any membership list, will have 25% change per annum. In a large organization, it may be worthwhile to offload departmental mailing lists to a list processor rather than maintaining them as aliases.

Another benefit of list servers is that their lists can be made *closed*. That is, only members of the list can post to the list. An alias is always public.

Distributed Management of Aliases

As mentioned, `include` files for aliases present considerable security risks. How these risks are dealt with varies between MTAs.

Provided that an include file has permission 0644 or stricter, `sendmail` will process it by changing its uid from root to that of the owner of the file. Whatever damage the aliases might do, it can be no worse than the owner of the file could do anyway. If the source file is group- or world-writable, `sendmail` will issue a diagnostic message unless you have the `dont_blame_sendmail` option set in your configuration.

Mailing Lists with `majordomo`

A mailing list, at its simplest, is a dynamic mail alias. It differs from a mail alias in that the members of the list can generally add or remove themselves from the list without any intervention from the system administrator. One of the most popular listservers is `majordomo`, and we will examine its functionality and configuration in this section.

The basic function of `majordomo` is to receive messages from individual list members and to distribute them to all the list members. Various subsidiary functions are added to this. These include list moderation, archiving, list digests, and privacy.

Every list has an owner, or moderator, who is responsible for various administrative issues on the list. Because of the rather restricted file-ownership model of Linux, this owner will generally need to be someone with root access. However, for many purposes the list owner does not need to invoke his root privilege.

A list is operated by sending messages to one of two users. Control messages, such as subscribe, unsubscribe, archive access, and approvals go to mail alias `majordomo`. Messages for distribution to the list are sent to the list name; this is an alias that pipes the message to `majordomo`'s Perl scripts.

> **Note**
>
> The program is called `majordomo`. The mail alias to which administrative requests are sent is also called `majordomo`. However, because Linux user names are restricted to eight characters, the associated user name is `majordom` (no final o) whose home directory is usually `/usr/local/majordomo`.

`Majordomo` assumes that you have `sendmail` as your MTA. If you are running something else, you may have to make adjustments to what is written in the `majordomo` documentation and at one point in the `majordomo.cf` file.

The following sections look at the functionality of `majordomo` in more detail.

Moderated Versus Unmoderated Lists

A *moderated list* is one in which all messages are referred to the moderator before they are distributed to the members. The moderator can approve the message as is, edit it and approve it, or reject it completely.

In an *unmoderated list*, all messages go straight to the members without anyone's intervention.

A list may also be *digested*. That is, periodically a digest will be created of all the messages posted since the last digest. Generally, there will be people who want to receive only the digest (fewer, but larger messages) and some who want to receive messages immediately. A digest is actually a completely separate list, although its name will generally be related to that of the main list. To set it up, you add the digest script as a target of the main list's mail alias. The digest is actually generated by sending a `mkdigest` command to majordomo. This is generally done from a crontab entry.

What the digest script does is up to you. The standard one supplied with `majordomo` just strings all the messages together into one big file. It is this big file that is mailed out as the digest.

It is also possible to create a digest-only list. In this case, everyone who asks to be subscribed to the main list is subscribed to the digest instead.

Open Versus Closed Lists

Majordomo has three subscription options. A *closed* list is one in which subscriptions have to be approved by the list owner. An *open* list is one in which subscriptions are acted on automatically without intervention. An *auto* list is one in which anyone can subscribe anyone else, in contrast to an open list in which a person can only subscribe himself.

Privacy and Security

Privacy control operates at both the list processor and the individual list level.

The posting of messages to a list can be open or restricted to members. To restrict posting to members, simply set the `restrict_post` option to point to the (already existing) list of members.

The lists command will tell the requestor what lists exist on a given installation. Whether a particular list appears in such an index is controlled by the advertise option in its configuration file.

Similarly, there are `private_index`, `private_info`, `private_which`, `private_get`, and `private_who` options to control access to the archives, to the list of subscribers, and to various bits and pieces of information about the list.

To Archive or Not to Archive

One option associated with each list is the archive. In this case, a copy of every message is saved in a nominated archive directory. Generally, a digest will be archived, but a simple list might not be. You can also put any other files you would like people to be able to retrieve in the archive directory. The archive does not have to be a single directory; it can be a whole tree. When you request a file from a `majordomo` archive, the list server emails the file to you, generally as a MIME attachment.

You access the archive by sending a get message to majordomo. The format of the message is

```
get listname pathname
```

Note that there is a space, not a slash, between the listname and the filename. Using a slash is a common mistake and list administrators get many queries of "why has my GET not worked?" because of it.

Another use of archives is to run an archive with no associated list. This is useful if you want to make certain files generally available, but cannot or do not want to open up your machine to FTP access, for instance on a dial-up link.

Archiving and FTP

You may want to make your `majordomo` archives open to anonymous FTP as well as to list-processor gets. In this case, you *must* put your archive directory in the FTP tree. It is not good enough to symlink it there because the FTP daemon does a `chroot` and will not be able to access it. The real directory must be under ~ftp and it can then be symlinked back into the ~majordom tree.

One point to note is that `majordomo` cannot serve binary files from its archives. If you need to distribute such files, for instance word-processor files or images, you must use FTP.

Configuring a Digest-Only List

The majordomo documentation is very good, and the distribution includes a sample list. To set up a normal list of your own, just copy and patch the sample. The handling of digests is not so clear, so the following is an example of a digest-only list. The name of the list is digestonly-sample.

The implementation is of two lists. The primary list, to which users actually post, is really a dummy—it receives all the incoming posts but merely stores them for the digest script to process. All the work is done in the digest list, which is called `digestonly-sample-digest`. There are therefore two sets of mail aliases and two config files.

A point to note is that there are two ways of storing passwords in `majordomo`. One is to put them literally in the config file, the other is to put them in the supplementary files mentioned in the comments in the config file. In either case, you must ensure that the files are not world readable.

First, the mail aliases; two sets, one for the list proper and one for the digest:

```
# 'digestonly-sample' uses 'resend' to validate and
# semi-moderate the messages
digestonly-sample: myuser@mydomain.com, "¦/usr/local/majordomo/wrapper resend -l
digestonly-sample -h myhost.mydomain.com -m "-odq" digestonly-sample-digestify"
# 'digestonly-sample-outgoing' is the real list membership
digestonly-sample-outgoing: digestonly-sample-digestify
owner-digestonly-sample: digestonly-sample-owner
# 'digestonly-sample-request' tells users to send to
# 'majordomo' instead.
Digestonly-sample-request: "¦/usr/local/majordomo/wrapper request-answer
```

```
digestonly-sample"
Owner-digestonly-sample-request: digestonly-sample-owner
Digestonly-sample-owner: approval@mydomain.com,
Digestonly-sample-approval: digestonly-sample-owner,


# These lines are for the digestonly-sample-digest list
digestonly-sample-digestify: "¦/usr/local/majordomo/wrapper digest -r -C -l
digestonly-sample-digest digestonly-sample-digest"
# 'digestonly-sample' uses 'resend' to validate and
# semi-moderate the messages
digestonly-sample-digest: "¦/usr/local/majordomo/wrapper  resend -l
digestonly-sample-outgoing"
# 'digestonly-sample-digest-outgoing' is the real list
# membership
digestonly-sample-digest-outgoing: :include:
 /usr/local/majordomo/lists/digestonly-sample
owner-digestonly-sample-digest: digestonly-sample-owner,
# 'digestonly-sample-request' tells users to send to
# 'majordomo' instead.
Digestonly-sample-digest-request: "¦/usr/local/majordomo/wrapper request-answer
digestonly-sample"
digestonly-sample-digest-approval:     digestonly-sample-owner,\\
```

Some of the preceding aliases are pure boilerplates for the use of majordomo itself. Some need to be set up for your configuration. Here is how they are used:

- digestonly-sample is the main list's mail alias. All messages are posted to it. Since this is not a proper list, all it does is forward the message to the digestifier with a copy to the list-owner so that he can keep an eye on things.

- digestonly-sampleoutgoing would normally be an include for the list membership. In this case it is really a dummy.

- digestonly-sample-owner and digestonlysampleapproval point to someone who will deal with administrative requests for this list.

- digestonly-sample-digestify actually builds the digest files. When, in due course, mkdigest is run, the digest will be posted to digestonly-sample-digest-outgoing.

- digestonly-sample-digest-outgoing is what actually sends out the messages. Note that the list of members it names is that for the primary list. Normally this would not be so, but this is a digest-only list.

The other aliases will probably never be used. They are included for the sake of completeness and as safety nets.

To use a digest, an extra directory must be created:

`/usr/local/majordomo/digests/listname-digest/`

In our case the directory is called `digestonly-sample-digest/`. Also, some optional files must be created in `/usr/local/majordomo/digests/`, which in our case will be called `digestonly-sample-digest.header` and `digestonly-sample-digest.trailer`. These contain texts to be prepended and appended to each digest as it is generated. All files and directories should be owned and writable by user majordom.

> **Note**
>
> The passwords for a mailing list may be given either literally in the config file or stored in a separate file. The documentation is not terribly clear about what goes where.

The following is the config file for the primary list. This is an open, unmoderated list. Its membership list is not used directly, but is picked up by the subsidiary digest list. The files are rather long and are mostly boiler plate. Probably all you will want to change are the passwords and other security and privacy items.

```
# The configuration file for a majordomo mailing list.
# Comments start with the first # on a line, and continue to the
# end of the line. There is no way to escape the # character.
# The file uses either a key = value for simple (i.e. a single)
# values, or uses a here document
#     key << END
#     value 1
#     value 2
#     [ more values 1 per line]
#     END
# for installing multiple values in array types. Note that the
# here document delimiter (END in the example above) must be the
# same at the end of the list of entries as it is after the <<
# characters.
# Within a here document, the # sign is NOT a comment character.
# A blank line is allowed only as the last line in the here
# document.
#
```

```
# The values can have multiple forms:
#
#    absolute_dir -- A root anchored (i.e begins with a /)
#    directory
#    absolute_file -- A root anchored (i.e begins with a /) file
#    bool -- choose from: yes, no, y, n
#    enum -- One of a list of possible values
#    integer -- an integer (string made up of the digits 09,
#                no decimal point)
#    float -- a floating point number with decimal point.
#    regexp -- A perl style regular expression with
#                leading and trailing /'s.
#    restrict_post -- a series of space or : separated file
#    names in which to look up the sender's address
#                (restrict-post should go away to be replaced by
#    an array of files)
#    string -- any text up until a \n stripped of
#                leading and trailing whitespace
#    word -- any text with no embedded whitespace
#
# A blank value is also accepted, and will undefine the
# corresponding keyword.
# The character Control-A may not be used in the file.
#
# A trailing _array on any of the above types means that that
# keyword will allow more than one value.
#
# Within a here document for a string_array, the '-' sign takes
# on a special significance.
#
#    To embed a blank line in the here document, put a '-' as
#    the first and ONLY character on the line.
#
#    To preserve whitespace at the beginning of a line, put a -
#     on the line before the whitespace to be preserved
#
#    To put a literal '-' at the beginning of a line, double
#    it.
#
#
# The default if the keyword is not supplied is given in ()'s
# while the  type of value is given in [], the subsystem the
# keyword is used in is listed in <>'s. (undef) as default value
```

```
# means that the keyword is notdefined or used.

# admin_passwd        [word] (digestonly-sample.admin)
#  <majordomo>
# (Default is specified in the file <listname>.passwd) The
#  password for handling administrative tasks on the list.
admin_passwd    =    mypassword

# administrivia      [bool] (yes) <resend>
# Look for administrative requests (e.g.
# subscribe/unsubscribe) and
# forward them to the list maintainer instead of the list.
administrivia    =    yes

# advertise          [regexp_array] (undef) <majordomo>
# If the requestor email address matches one of these
# regexps, then the list will be listed in the output of a
# lists command. Failure to match any regexp excludes the
# list from the output. The regexps
# under noadvertise overide these regexps.
advertise        <<   END

END

# approve_passwd      [word] (digestonly-sample.pass)
#  <resend>
# Password to be used in the approved header to allow
# posting to moderated list, or to bypass resend checks.
approve_passwd    =    digestonly-sample.passwd

# archive_dir        [absolute_dir] (undef) <majordomo>
# The directory where the mailing list archive is kept.
# This item does not currently work. Leave it blank.
archive_dir      =

# comments            [string_array] (undef) <config>
# Comment string that will be retained across config file
# rewrites.
comments          <<   END

END
```

```
# date_info         [bool] (yes) <majordomo>
# Put the last updated date for the info file at the top of
# the info file rather than having it appended with an info
# command. This is useful if the file is being looked at by
# some means other than majordomo (e.g. finger).
date_info       =   yes


# debug              [bool] (no) <resend>
# Don't actually forward message, just go though the
# motions.
debug           =   no


# description        [string] (undef) <majordomo>
# Used as description for mailing list when replying to the
# lists command. There is no quoting mechanism, and there
# is only room for 50 or so characters.
description      ="Sample digest-only list"
# digest_archive     [absolute_dir] (undef) <digest>
# The directory where the digest archive is kept. This item
# does not currently work. Leave it blank.
digest_archive   =


# digest_issue       [integer] (1) <digest>
# The issue number of the next issue
digest_issue     =   1


# digest_name        [string] (digestonly-sample) <digest>
# The subject line for the digest. This string has the
# volume  and issue appended to it.
digest_name      =   digestonly-sample


# digest_rm_footer   [word] (undef) <digest>
# The value is the name of the list that applies the header
# and footers to the messages that are received by digest.
# This allows the list supplied headers and footers to be
# stripped before the messages are included in the digest.
# This keyword is currently non operative.
digest_rm_footer =


# digest_rm_fronter  [word] (undef) <digest>
# Works just like digest_rm_footer, except it removes the
# front material. Just like digest_rm_footer, it is also
# non-operative.
```

```
digest_rm_fronter =

# digest_volume        [integer] (1) <digest>
# The current volume number
digest_volume     =    1

# digest_work_dir      [absolute_dir] (undef) <digest>
# The directory used as scratch space for digest. Don't
# change this unless you know what you are doing
digest_work_dir   =

# maxlength            [integer] (40000) <resend,digest>
# The maximum size of an unapproved message in characters.
# When used with digest, a new digest will be automatically
# generated if the size of the digest exceeds this number
# of characters.
maxlength         =    40000

# message_footer       [string_array] (undef) <resend,digest>
# Text to be appended at the end of all messages posted to
# the list. The text is expanded before being used. The
# following expansion tokens are defined: $LIST - the name
# of the current list, $SENDER  the sender as taken from
# the from line, $VERSION, the version of majordomo. If
# used in a digest, no expansion tokens are provided
message_footer    <<  END

END

# message_fronter      [string_array] (undef) <resend,digest>
# Text to be prepended to the beginning of all messages
# posted to the list. The text is expanded before being
# used. The following expansion tokens are defined: $LIST -
# the name of the current list, $SENDER - the sender as
# taken from the from line, $VERSION, the version of
# majordomo. If used in a digest, only the expansion token
# _SUBJECTS_ is available, and it expands to the list of
# message subjects in the digest
message_fronter   <<  END

END
```

```
# message_headers    [string_array] (undef) <resend,digest>
# These headers will be appended to the headers of the
# posted message. The text is expanded before being used.
# The following expansion tokens are defined: $LIST  the
# name of the current list, $SENDER - the sender as taken
# from the from line, $VERSION, the version of majordomo.
message_headers   << END

END


# moderate          [bool] (no) <resend>
# If yes, all postings to the list  must be approved by the
# moderator.
moderate          =  no


# mungedomain        [bool] (no) <majordomo>
# If set to yes, a different method is used to determine a
# matching address.  When set to yes, addresses of the form
# user@dom.ain.com are considered equivalent to addresses
# of the form user@ain.com. This allows a user to subscribe
# to a list using the domain address rather than the
# address assigned to a particular machine in the
# domain. This keyword affects the interpretation of
#  addresses for subscribe, unsubscribe, and all private
# options.
mungedomain       =  no


# noadvertise        [regexp_array] (undef) <majordomo>
# If the requestor name matches one of these regexps, then
# the list will not be listed in the output of a lists
# command. Noadvertise overrides advertise.
noadvertise       << END

END


# precedence         [word] (bulk) <resend,digest>
# Put a precedence header with value <value> into the
# outgoing message.
precedence        =  bulk


# private_get        [bool] (yes) <majordomo>
# If set to yes, then the requestor must be on the mailing
```

```
# list in order to get files.
private_get       =   yes

# private_index    [bool] (no) <majordomo>
# If set to yes, then the requestor must be on the mailing
# list in order to get a file index.
private_index     =   yes

# private_info     [bool] (no) <majordomo>
# If set to yes, then the requestor must be on the mailing
# list to use the info <list> command.
private_info      =   no
# private_which    [bool] (no) <majordomo>
# If set to yes, then the requestor must  be on the mailing
# list in order to get which info from that list.
private_which     =   no

# private_who      [bool] (no) <majordomo>
# If set to yes, then the requestor must  be on mailing the
# list in order to use the who command.
private_who       =   yes

# purge_received   [bool] (no) <resend>
# Remove all received lines before resending the message.
purge_received    =   no

# reply_to         [word] () <resend,digest>
# Put a reply-to header with value <value> into the
# outgoing message. If the token $SENDER is used, then the
# address of the sender is used as the value of the reply
# to header. This is the value of the replyto header for
# digest lists.
reply_to          =

# resend_host      [word] (undef) <resend>
# The host name that is appended to all address strings
# specified for resend.
resend_host       =
```

If you want to restrict posting, the list of file should be the membership lists of both the primary and the digest lists. In this case, the value used will be `/usr/local/majordomo/lists/`*listname*`:/usr/local/majordomo/lists/`*listname*`-digest`.

```
# restrict_post      [restrict_post] (undef) <resend>
# If defined only address listed in one of the files (colon
# or space separated) can post to the mailing list. This is
# less useful than it seems it should be since there is no
# way to create these files if you do not have access to
# the machine running resend. This mechanism will be
# replaced in a future version of majordomo/resend.
restrict_post    =


# sender            [word] (owner-digestonly-sample) <majordomo,res
# The envelope and sender address for the resent mail. This
#string has "@" and the value of resend_host appended to it
# to make a complete address. For majordomo, it provides
# the sender address for the welcome mail message generated
# as part of the subscribe command.
sender           =   owner-digestonly-sample


# strip             [bool] (yes) <majordomo>
# When adding address to the list, strip off all comments
# etc, and put just the raw address in the list file.  In
# addition to the keyword, if the file <listname>.strip
# exists, it is the same as specifying a yes value. That
# yes value is overridden by the value of this keyword.
strip            =   yes


# subject_prefix    [word] (undef) <resend>
# This word will be prefixed to the subject line, if it is
# not already in the subject. The text is expanded before
# being used. The following expansion tokens are defined:
# $LIST - the name of the current list, $SENDER - the
# sender as taken from the from line, $VERSION, the version
# of majordomo.
subject_prefix   =


# subscribe_policy   [enum] (open) <majordomo>
# /open;closed;auto/
# One of 3 possible values: open, closed, auto.  Open
# allows people to subscribe themselves to the list. Auto
# allows anybody to subscribe anybody to the list without
```

```
# maintainer approval. The existence of the file
# <listname>.auto is the same as specifying the value auto.
# Closed requires maintainer approval for all subscribe
# requests to the list. In addition to the keyword, if the
# file <listname>.closed exists, it is the same as
# specifying the value closed. The value of this keyword
# overrides the value supplied by any existent files.
subscribe_policy  =   open
```

And finally, the following is the config file for the digest. This is a closed list; in practice, no one is ever allowed to subscribe to it. It would be a pointless exercise because its membership list is never used.

Only the changes from the primary list are shown. Most of the config is identical.

```
# description      [string] (undef) <majordomo>
# Used as description for mailing list when replying to the
# lists command. There is no quoting mechanism, and there
# is only room for 50 or so characters.
description      =   "Sample digest-only list (digest)"


# digest_archive     [absolute_dir] (undef) <digest>
# The directory where the digest archive is kept. This item
# does not currently work. Leave it blank.
digest_archive    =
```

The digest issue will be updated automatically by `mkdigest`. The digest volume has to be updated manually.

```
# digest_issue       [integer] (1) <digest>
# The issue number of the next issue
digest_issue      =   23


# digest_name        [string] (digestonly-sample-digest)
# <digest>  The subject line for the digest. This string
# has the volume  and  issue appended to it.
digest_name       =   Sample Digest


# digest_volume      [integer] (1) <digest>
# The current volume number
digest_volume     =   1
```

20

Electronic
Mail

```
# digest_work_dir    [absolute_dir] (undef) <digest>
# The directory used as scratch space for digest. Don't
# change this unless you know what you are doing
digest_work_dir   =



# message_footer     [string_array] (undef) <resend,digest>
# Text to be appended at the end of all messages posted to
# the list.
message_footer    <<  END

END

# message_fronter     [string_array] (undef) <resend,digest>
# Text to be prepended to the beginning of all messages
# posted to the list. The text is expanded before being used.
# The following expansion tokens are defined: $LIST -
# the name of the current list, $SENDER - the sender as
# taken from the from line, $VERSION, the version of
# majordomo. If used in a digest, only the expansion token
# _SUBJECTS_ is available, and it expands to the list of
# message subjects in the digest
message_fronter    <<  END

END

# message_headers    [string_array] (undef) <resend,digest>
# These headers will be appended to the headers of the
# posted message. The text is expanded before being used.
# The following expansion tokens are defined: $LIST - the
# name of the current list, $SENDER  the sender as taken
# from the from line, $VERSION, the version of majordomo.
message_headers    <<  END

END\
```

Since no one should ever post to a digest list, we set it to moderated with moderate=yes in the config.

```
# moderate           [bool] (no) <resend>
# If yes, all postings to the list  must be approved by the
# moderator.
moderate          =   yes
```

```
# private_get        [bool] (yes) <majordomo>
# If set to yes, then the requestor must be on the mailing
# list in order to get files.
private_get      =   yes


# private_index      [bool] (no) <majordomo>
# If set to yes, then the requestor must be on the mailing
# list in order to get a file index.
private_index    =   yes


# private_info        [bool] (no) <majordomo>
# If set to yes, then the requestor must be on the mailing
# list to use the info <list> command.
private_info     =   no


# private_which       [bool] (no) <majordomo>
# If set to yes, then the requestor must  be on the mailing
# list in order to get which info from that list.
private_which    =   no


# private_who         [bool] (no) <majordomo>
# If set to yes, then the requestor must  be on mailing the
# list in order to use the who command.
private_who      =   yes


# purge_received      [bool] (no) <resend>
# Remove all received lines before resending the message.
purge_received   =   no]
```

Any follow-up postings should go to the main list, not to the digest list. Only messages sent to the main list will ever be passed to the digest script. Although with the way we set up the aliases, anything sent directly to the digest will simply be rerouted back to the main list automatically.

```
# reply_to            [word] (digestonly-sample)
# <resend,digest>
# Put a reply-to header with value <value> into the
# outgoing message. If the token $SENDER is used, then the
    # address of the sender is used as the value of the reply-
    # to header. This is the value of the reply-to header for
    # digest lists.
reply_to          =   Digestonly-sample@majordodomo-host.mydomain.com
```

20

Electronic
Mail

```
# resend_host        [word] (undef) <resend>
# The host name that is appended to all address strings
# specified for resend.
resend_host     =
```

Setting `restrict_post` to `/dev/null` stops anyone from posting directly to the digest.

```
# restrict_post       [restrict_post] (undef) <resend>
# If defined only address listed in one of the files (colon
# or space separated) can post to the mailing list. This is
# less useful than it seems it should be since there is no
# way to create these files if you do not have access to
# the machine running resend. This mechanism will be
# replaced in a future version of majordomo/resend.
restrict_post     = /dev/null
```

```
# sender              [word] (owner-digestonly-sample-
# digest) <majord
# The envelope and sender address for the resent mail. This
# string has "@" and the value of resend_host appended to
# it to make a complete address. For majordomo, it provides
# the sender address for the welcome mail message generated
# as part of the subscribe command.
sender          =   owner- digestonly-sample
```

```
# strip               [bool] (yes) <majordomo>
# When adding address to the list, strip off all comments
# etc, and put just the raw address in the list file.  In
# addition to the keyword, if the file <listname>.strip
# exists, it is the same as specifying a yes value. That
# yes value is overridden by the value of this keyword.
strip           =   yes
```

```
# subject_prefix      [word] (undef) <resend>
# This word will be prefixed to the subject line, if it is
# not already in the subject. The text is expanded before
# being used. The following expansion tokens are defined:
# $LIST - the name of the current list, $SENDER - the
# sender as taken from the from line, $VERSION, the version
# of majordomo.
subject_prefix   =
```

Normally, a digest list might have an open subscription policy. However, with a digest-only list, it should be closed.

```
# subscribe_policy   [enum] (open) <majordomo> /open;closed;auto/
# One of 3 possible values: open, closed, auto.  Open
# allows people to subscribe themselves to the list. Auto
# allows anybody to subscribe anybody to the list without
# maintainer approval. The existence of the file
#  <listname>.auto is the same as specifying the value
# auto. Closed requires maintainer approval for all
# subscribe requests to the list. In addition to the
# keyword, if the file <listname>.closed exists, it is the
# same as specifying the value closed. The value of
# this keyword overrides the value supplied by any existent
# files.
subscribe_policy  =   closed
```

Whenever a digest is created, it is stored in `~majordom/archives/digestonly-sample/` (that is, under the primary list name), and is mailed out to all the subscribers to the primary list.

References

The 'Bat Book': Costales B and Allman E, Sendmail; O'Reilly. Check for the latest edition.

RFCs are available from many FTP archives. A Web or archive search on for example, RFC822, should provide many locations to fetch them from.

1523 Borenstein, N. The text/enriched MIME Content-type. 1993 September; 15 p. (Format: TXT=32692 bytes)

1522 Moore, K. MIME (Multipurpose Internet Mail Extensions) Part Two: Message Header Extensions for NonASCII Text. 1993 September; 10 p. (Format: TXT=22503 bytes) (Obsoletes 1342)

1521 Borenstein, N.; Freed, N. MIME (Multipurpose Internet Mail Extensions) Part One: Mechanisms for Specifying and Describing the Format of Internet Message Bodies. 1993 September; 81 p. (Format: TXT=187425 PS=393670 bytes) (Obsoletes RFC 1341)

1460 Rose, M. Post Office Protocol - Version 3. 1993 June; 17 p. (Format: TXT=38828 bytes) (Obsoletes RFC 1225)

1203 Rice, J. Interactive Mail Access Protocol: Version 3. 1991 February; 49 p. (Format: TXT=123325 bytes) (Obsoletes RFC 1064)

20
Electronic Mail

1176 Crispin, M. Interactive Mail Access Protocol: Version 2. 1990 August; 30 p. (Format: TXT=67330 bytes) (Obsoletes RFC 1064)

1056 Lambert, M. PCMAIL: A distributed mail system for personal computers. 1988 June; 38 p. (Format: TXT=85368 bytes) (Obsoletes RFC 993)

822 Crocker, D. Standard for the format of ARPA Internet text messages. 1982 August 13; 47 p. (Format: TXT=109200 bytes) (Obsoletes RFC 733; Updated by RFC 1327, RFC 1148, RFC 1138)

821 Postel, J. Simple Mail Transfer Protocol. 1982 August; 58 p. Format: TXT=124482 bytes) (Obsoletes RFC 788)

Choosing and Installing an MTA

These sites provide information on choosing and configuring an MTA. They are part of the Linux Documentation Project (LDP).

```
http://www.linux-howto.com/LDP/HOWTO/mini/Mail-Queue.html
```

```
http://www.linux-howto.com/LDP/HOWTO/Mail-HOWTO.html
```

```
ftp://metalab.unc.edu/pub/Linux/docs/HOWTO/mini/Qmail+MH
```

Particular MTAs

These are the primary sites for downloading the source and compiled code of MTAs, and their documentation.

```
http://www.sendmail.org/
```

```
http://www.qmail.org/
```

```
http://www.exim.org/
```

```
http://www.rge.com/pub/mail/exim/
```

```
ftp://ftp.uu.net/networking/mail/smail/
```

Anti-spam Measures

From these sites you will get all sorts of information on dealing with spam: techniques, black lists, and software.

```
http://www.sendmail.org/m4/anti-spam.html
```

```
http://maps.vix.com/
```

```
http://www.imrss.org/dssl/
```

Summary

Email is generally transported by SMTP over an IP network. In the past other protocols were used, but these have largely disappeared.

Mail is handled by three software components. MUAs deal with the composition and display of message; MTAs transmit messages between machines; and MDAs (not always needed) download messages from a server to a client.

Of the MTAs, `sendmail` is the oldest and most complicated. It is also the most flexible. `Smail` is biased towards `uucp` transport, rather than SMTP, and is rather limited in its functionality. `Qmail` can handle very large volumes of mail. `Exim` is the most modern and well documented of them all.

MUAs are very much a matter of personal taste. Netscape contains a rather poor mail client. For use under X, `xfmail` is probably to be preferred. For character mode terminals, `pine` is simple to use. In scripts use `mail`.

Mailing lists and simple file archives can be administered with `majordomo`.

CHAPTER 21

FTP and Anonymous FTP

IN THIS CHAPTER

- Allowing FTP to Your Servers   *611*
- Security and Legal Issues   *621*

Networked file exchange is one of the most commonly used features of modern-day computer networks. Linux supports a variety of different file sharing facilities, each of which has various benefits and capabilities. This chapter explores how you can utilize the File Transfer Protocol (FTP) on Red Hat Linux systems. You will be shown how to configure FTP on a host, the steps that should be taken to provide anonymous FTP access to users, and the guidelines you should follow when securing an FTP server.

File Transfer Protocol (FTP) is a protocol standard used to exchange files across a network. It is one of the most widely supported network protocols for file exchange on the Internet today. FTP is a mature protocol implementation, having gone through many changes and refinements since its original implementation by the Massachusetts Institute of Technology (MIT) in 1971. Nearly thirty years after its initial release, File Transfer Protocol remains the de-facto standard for network file exchange.

The File Transfer Protocol was designed from the ground up with several key objectives in mind:

- Promote the sharing of files and other computer data.

- Promote the indirect use of remote computer resources.

- Shield end-users from the intricacies of filesystem implementations.

- Allow file data to be transferred reliably and efficiently.

FTP provides easy access to file resources on remote computer systems, allowing users to share information with one another over vast distances without concern for data transfer reliability. This capability promotes the exchange of information between users because it makes such activity a simple task to engage in. File Transfer Protocol allows computer resources to be accessed in an indirect manner through the use of software programs that make use of the FTP implementation. Such indirect usage abilities allow users to access remote resources by simply running a program on their local computer system. Users are not exposed to the internals of the File Transfer Protocol; they only interact with it in an indirect manner using such software programs.

FTP also serves to shield the intricacies of remote computer filesystem implementations from users, further simplifying the sharing of files and other information over a network. The File Transfer Protocol provides a standardized method that hosts can use to communicate file information to one another. This allows users to access file resources on remote hosts that use vastly different filesystem implementations in a unified manner. Finally, FTP allows data to be transferred between hosts reliably and efficiently. This important capability is integral to any information exchange protocol implementation because an unreliable or slow system would be virtually useless to the end user.

All FTP implementations make use of two different types of connections for relaying information between hosts. These are outlined in Table 20.1.

TABLE **20.1**   FTP Connection Types

Type	*Description*
Control FTP control connection	Used to perform basic actions on a server. These include but are not limited to logging into the FTP server navigating through remote directory trees, performing operations on files that are stored on the server, and so on. It is possible to interact with an FTP server directly by telnetting to the port that is being used for control connections, but such activities are normally done indirectly using client software packages.
Data FTP data connection	Used to transfer information between the server and client. This data directory listing information and actual file data.

The full details of the File Transfer Protocol implementation are available in its associated RFCs (Request For Comment): RFC 959 and 1579.

These RFCs may be retrieved from the following WWW locations:

- `http://www.faqs.org/rfcs/rfc959.html`

- `http://www.faqs.org/rfcs/rfc1579.html`

RFC documents are often obsoleted by newer and more updated RFCs, which contain protocol clarifications and feature extensions. FTP is not immune to such activity (the protocol was originally specified in RFC 114), and has undergone such updates numerous times over the years. Because of this, it may be desirable to see whether a newly updated RFC exists for this protocol standard. Online databases of active RFC documents can be searched if you are concerned that newer versions of a particular RFC exist. The following is a searchable Web database of RFC documents: `http://www.faqs.org/rfcs/index.html`.

Allowing FTP to Your Servers

Allowing File Transfer Protocol access to your Red Hat 6 server is a simple task. FTP access is controlled through the use of a software daemon that is installed on the host system. This daemon is normally executed in one of two different modes, as illustrated in Table 20.2.

TABLE 20.2   FTP Daemon Execution Modes

Mode	Description
Foreground	The FTP server process runs in the foreground. The stdin/stdout file descriptors are used for input/output instead of sockets. This mode is used when the server is executed via inetd.
Background	The FTP server process runs in the background as a standalone daemon. In this mode, the FTP server binds directly to the ftp control connection port, listening for connections on its own instead of relying on an external program such as inetd.

When running a FTP daemon in foreground mode, you must ensure that inetd is properly configured to listen for FTP connections. Configuration information for inetd is stored in the /etc/inetd.conf configuration file. Red Hat Linux includes a pre-configured inetd.conf file, containing the necessary entries for the FTP service. However, depending on the options specified during the Red Hat installation process, you may be required to un-comment the FTP configuration entry to enable incoming connections. Comments in the inetd.conf file are specified using leading # characters. By removing any leading # characters on the line of the FTP configuration entry, FTP will be enabled.

In situations where the inetd.conf configuration file does not contain an FTP configuration entry, you must edit the file adding a new line that contains the required configuration information. This can be done in the following manner:

```
ftp  stream  tcp  nowait  /usr/sbin/tcpd  ftp_daemon  opts
```

The preceding line specifies that connections to the ftp service via the TCP stream protocol should be routed to the tcp-wrapper tcpd, and then to the FTP daemon ftp_daemon. The command-line options opts are passed to the FTP server upon its execution.

Wuarchive-ftpd, otherwise known as wu-ftpd, is a popular file transfer protocol daemon. Brian D. O'Connor originally developed it at the University of Washington. The original author is no longer maintaining the project, however. Instead, the open source community is maintaining it.

Wu-ftpd is currently the most used ftp daemon on the Internet, supporting a wide range of hardware and software platforms and based entirely on free source code. It is licensed under the GPL (GNU Public License).

To install wu-ftpd on your system you must do the following:

1. Become root if you are not already.
2. Install the WU-FTPD RPM. You can do this during the Red Hat installation phase or with the following command (done from the RPMS directory of the Red Hat 6 CD-ROM): # rpm -Uvh wu-ftpd-2.4.2vr17-3.i386.rpm.

Wu-ftpd supports several command-line configuration options that affect its overall behavior. These options can be passed directly through the execution of the FTP daemon from a shell prompt or from the inetd process.

The command-line options for the wu-ftpd program are described in its associated man page and in Table 21.3.

TABLE **21.3** Command-Line Options

Option	Description
-a	Enables the usage of an ftpaccess configuration file. This option is disabled by default.
-A	Disables the usage of a ftpaccess configuration file. This option is enabled by default.
-d	Enables logging of debug information to syslog.
-i	Enables logging of files received by the FTP daemon. Information is written to the daemons' xferlog file. This option can be overridden through the use of an ftpaccess configuration file.
-l	Enables logging of FTP session information via syslog.
-L	Enables logging of commands sent to the FTP daemon via syslog.
-o	Enables logging of files sent by the FTP daemon. Information is written to the daemons' xferlog file. This option can be overridden through the use of an ftpaccess configuration file.
-pport	Sets the port on which the FTP daemon will accept control connections. This option is only available if the FTP server is running in the background as a standalone daemon.
-Pport	Sets the port on which the FTP daemon will spawn data connections. If this option is not specified, the ftp-data entry in the hosts' /etc/services file is used. If the ftp-data services entry is not available, the port preceding the FTP control connection port is used for data connections.
-q	Enables limiting the number of concurrent users that may access the FTP server through the use of PID files. This option is enabled by default.
-Q	Disables limiting the number of concurrent users that may access the FTP server. This option is disabled by default.

TABLE 21.3   continued

Option	Description
-r root_dir	Forces to FTP daemon to chroot to root_dir upon execution.
-s	Runs the FTP daemon in the foreground.
-S	Runs the FTP daemon in the background.
-t delay	Sets the inactivity timeout period to delay seconds. Sessions that are unresponsive for the inactivity timeout period are automatically terminated. It is important to note that FTP clients may request a different timeout period, up to the maximum allowed inactivity period. The default value the inactivity timeout period is 15 minutes.
-T max_delay	Sets the maximum allowed inactivity timeout period to delay seconds. Sessions may not request a timeout period that is larger than this value. The default for this setting is 2 hours.
-u umask	Sets the default umask that the ftp daemon will use to umask.
-v	Enables verbose logging of debug information to syslog.
-w	Enables logging of FTP user login information to the wtmp file. This option is enabled by default.
-W	Disables logging of FTP user login information to the wtmp file. This option is disabled by default.
-X	Forces any output from the -i and -o command-line options to be written to syslog instead of the xferlog file.

After installing the wu-ftpd server, it is usually desirable to customize it to match the system that it has been installed on. Such customization options include setting the email address of the FTP site administrator, banners that should be displayed, and so on. The following customization options are supported through the use of the ftpaccess configuration file:

- greeting full¦brief¦terse¦text [message]—Configures the type of greeting given to users logging into the FTP server. The full option prints the server hostname and FTP daemon version to clients. The brief option prints only the server hostname. The terse option prints the statement FTP server ready. The text option allows administrators to specify their own custom greeting. The message option is used only in conjunction with the text parameter, and thus is not supported by the full, brief, or terse parameters. The default value for this configuration setting is full.

- banner [banner-file]—Allows a banner to be shown to clients connecting to the FTP server. The banner is shown upon connection to the server, before a user logs in. The banner-file parameter specifies an absolute pathname (relative to the real root directory of the FTP server) pointing to the banner file that is to be displayed.

- `hostname [host-name]`—Specifies the default hostname that is to be used by the FTP server. The `host-name` parameter is the hostname that is to be used. This value can be overridden if you set hostnames for virtual FTP servers located on the same machine. If no `hostname` command string is used, the FTP server will default to the hostname of the machine that it is installed on.

- `email [email-address]`—Specifies the electronic mailing address of the FTP site administrator. The `email-address` parameter is the electronic mail address that is to be used.

- `alias [alias-name][directory]`—Specifies an alias to a directory on the FTP server. Aliases allow logical directories to be specified, which can be entered into from any other directory on the FTP server. Aliases may only be taken advantage of by the `CWD` (Change working directory) FTP command.

- `shutdown [shutdown-file]`—Allows a file to be defined that specifies when the FTP server should be shutdown automatically. The use of a shutdown file allows new incoming connections to be denied to the server at a specified time interval before the scheduled shutdown, and existing connections to be terminated. The shutdown file has the following format:

  `[year] [month] [day] [hour] [minute] [deny-offset]`
  `[term-offset] [message]`—The `year` parameter may be any year dated after 1970. The `month` parameter may be any month from 0 to 11. The `day` parameter may be any day from 0 to 30. The `hour` parameter may be any hour from 0 to 23. The `minute` parameter may be any minute from 0 to 59. The `deny-offset` parameter specifies the offset of time before server shutdown that new incoming connections should be denied access. It is in HHMM (2 digit hour, 2 digit minute) format. The `term-offset` parameter specifies the offset of time before server shutdown that existing FTP connections should be disconnected. It is in HHMM (2 digit hour, 2 digit minute) format. The `message` parameter specifies a message that is to be displayed to users when the FTP server is being shutdown.

The wu-ftpd package is fully capable of supporting multiple concurrent virtual FTP servers on a single host. This can be done by enabling IP aliases (extra IP addresses bound to a single network device). Red Hat Linux supports a variety of mechanisms for configuring IP aliases, the easiest of which is the Linuxconf administration tool. Using this program, you can quickly add IP aliases to a specific network device. Aliases can also be added via the command line using the `ifconfig` program. When using `ifconfig`to configure aliases, you would format commands as follows:

```
# ifconfig <interface>:<alias #> <command>
```

Example: `ifconfig eth0:1 address 192.168.1.55`

Once you have configured the desired aliased IP addresses on a host, you can configure virtual FTP servers within the wu-ftpd package by using configuration directives inside the `ftpaccess` file. These directives allow FTP daemons to support multiple virtual FTP sites, each with their own banners and directory hierarchies. The `ftpaccess` file supports the following options in relation to virtual FTP server configuration:

- `virtual [address] root [root-dir]`—Allows the root directory for a particular virtual FTP server to be specified. The `address` parameter specifies the virtual server whose root directory is being set, and the `root-dir` parameter is an absolute pathname pointing to a directory that is to be used as the virtual server's root directory.

- `virtual [address] banner [banner-file]`—Allows a banner to be shown to clients connecting to a particular virtual FTP server. The banner is shown upon connection to the server, before a user logs in. The `address` parameter specifies the virtual FTP server whose banner is being set. The `banner-file` parameter specifies an absolute pathname (relative to the actual root directory of the FTP server machine) pointing to the banner file that is to be displayed.

- `virtual [address] logfile [log-file]`—Specifies a file that is to be used for storing log data generated by a particular virtual FTP server. This allows each virtual server on a system to output its log data to a separate file. The `address` parameter specifies the virtual FTP server whose log file is being set. The `log-file` parameter specifies an absolute pathname pointing to the log file that is to be recorded to.

- `virtual [address] hostname [host-name]`—Specifies the hostname that is to be used by a particular virtual FTP server hosted on the system. The `address` parameter specifies the virtual server whose options are being modified. The `host-name` parameter is the hostname that is to be used.

- `virtual [address] email [email-address]`—Specifies the electronic mailing address of the FTP site administrator for a particular virtual FTP server hosted on the system. The `address` parameter specifies the FTP server whose options are being modified. The `email-address` parameter is the electronic mail address that is to be used.

- `virtual [address] allow [username] [..]`—Allows access to a particular virtual FTP server to be granted to individual real or guest users on the system. Ordinarily, real and guest users are denied access to virtual servers running on the system that houses their user account. This is not the case when users are considered guests and they are chroot'd to the virtual server's root directory, or when users are specifically allowed access through an `allow` directive. The `username` parameter specifies the user who is being granted virtual server access. Multiple username parameters may be given, or a username of "`*`" may be used to grant virtual server access to all users on the system.

- `virtual [address] deny [username] [..]`—Allows access to a particular virtual FTP server to be denied to individual real or guest users on the system. This statement is often used to revoke access from specific users when access was granted to all users using an `allow *` statement. The `username` parameter specifies the user who is being granted virtual server access. Multiple username parameters may be given if necessary.

- `virtual [address] private`—Allows anonymous access to a particular virtual FTP server to be disabled. Access for accounts and real users is unaffected by the use of this command string.

Several Internet resources for wu-ftpd-related information are available for use by the wu-ftpd community. These include both electronic mailing lists and WWW sites.

To subscribe to the wu-ftpd mailing list, do the following:

1. Send an electronic mail message to `listproc@mail.wustl.edu`.
2. The Subject field of this message should be blank.
3. The Body field of this message should contain the following text:

   `SUBSCRIBE WU-FTPD your-full-name`

To unsubscribe to the wu-ftpd mailing list, do the following:

1. Send an electronic mail message to `listproc@mail.wustl.edu`.
2. The Subject field of this message should be blank.
3. The Body field of this message should contain the following text:

   `UNSUBSCRIBE WU-FTPD`

To send mail to all users subscribed to the `wu-ftpd` mailing list, do the following:

1. Send an electronic mail message to `wu-ftpd@mail.wustl.edu`.
2. The Subject and Body fields of this message are set at the user's discretion.

The wu-ftpd mailing list is also available in an archived digest format through both FTP and WWW.

- WWW Archive:

   `http://landfield.com/wu-ftpd/mail-archive`

- WWW Archive Search Engine:

  ```
  http://www.landfield.com/wu-ftpd/mail-archive/search.html
  ```

- FTP Archive:

  ```
  ftp://ftp.landfield.com/wu-ftpd/mail-archive
  ```

Several additional Internet resources for wu-ftpd information also exist. They are

- Kent Landfield's wu-ftpd site:

  ```
  http://www.landfield.com/wu-ftpd/
  ```

- Academ wu-ftpd page:

  ```
  http://www.academ.com/academ/wu-ftpd/
  ```

- CERT (Computer Emergency Response Team) guidelines for systems that allow anonymous FTP access:

  ```
  ftp://ftp.cert.org/pub/tech_tips/anonymous_ftp_config
  ```

Configuring Anonymous FTP with WU-FTPD

You can allow anonymous FTP access with the wu-ftpd server on Red Hat 6 Linux through the simple process of installing a single RPM. However, it is important that any newly created anonymous FTP server be properly secured before being put into active use.

To configure your FTP server to allow anonymous access, do the following:

1. Become root if you are not already.
2. Install the anonftp RPM. This can be done during the RedHat installation phase or with the following command (done from the RPMS directory of the RedHat 6 CD-ROM):

   ```
   # rpm -Uvh anonftp-2.8-1.i386.rpm
   ```

In some situations, an incoming directory may be desired so that users can upload files to an FTP server. Such writable directories are normally not desired, because they can open the possibility for warez activity (the piracy of copyrighted computer software) and other illegal software trading activities. If it is absolutely necessary to create an incoming directory, it is advisable to set the permissions of the directory in such a manner that anonymous users cannot see the contents of the directory even though they can write to it. This helps to prevent the occurrence of illegal activities, but is not a 100 percent foolproof technique. To create an incoming directory in the manner described above, do the following:

1. Become root if you are not already.

2. Change your current working directory to that of the anonymous FTP server account. This is normally `/home/ftp`.

3. Issue following commands to create the incoming directory and set its permissions:

```
# mkdir incoming
# chmod 333 incoming
```

Caution should be taken with any site that hosts a writable incoming directory to ensure that illegal activity does not occur. More information on strategies for preventing such activity is given in the "Dealing with Warez D00dz" section of this chapter.

Alternative FTP Servers

Professional FTP Daemon, otherwise known as ProFTPD, is another popular FTP server that is publicly available. ProFTPD is based on an entirely new code-base, not using legacy code from any existing daemons such as wu-ftpd.

It was written in an attempt to create a highly configurable FTP server offering customization capabilities similar to that of the Apache Web server. ProFTPD is based entirely on free code, and is licensed under the GPL (GNU Public License).

The ProFTPD software package offers several advanced features that are not seen in many other FTP servers. These include the ability to use per-directory `.ftpaccess` configuration files and the option of using any desirable directory structure for anonymous FTP servers. ProFTPD also has several security advantages over other FTP daemons in that it can run as a non- privileged user to prevent possible root compromises, and the fact that it does not rely on any external software binaries for execution.

To install the ProFTPD software package on your system, you must do the following:

1. Download the ProFTPD RPM from the following location:

```
ftp://rhcn.redhat.com/pub/rhcn/RPMS/i386/proftpd-rhcn-1.2.0pre3-1.i386.rpm
```

2. Install the RPM with the following command:

```
# rpm -Uvh proftpd-rhcn-1.2.0pre3-1.i386.rpm
```

3. To install the ProFTPD RPM, you must first remove the wu-ftpd and anonftp packages.

4. Edit the ProFTPD configuration file to match the desired FTP server configuration. The ProFTPD configuration file is located in the following directory:

```
/etc/proftpd.conf
```

> **Note**
>
> If compiling the ProFTPD package from source code, the configuration file may be stored in a different location such as `/usr/local/etc`.

The ProFTPD configuration file supports many options in relation to general FTP server configuration, virtual FTP server setup, security/logging options, and more. All of the options supported in this file are out of the scope of this chapter, as they could warrant an entire chapter worth of discussion by themselves.

However, several Internet resources exist that offer additional information on the ProFTPD server. These include an electronic mailing list and WWW site. The mailing list exists primarily for development purposes, but also offers some limited technical support.

To subscribe to the ProFTPD mailing list, do the following:

1. Send an electronic mail message to `majordomo@evcom.net`.
2. The Subject field of this message should be blank.
3. The Body field of this message should contain the following text:

   `subscribe proftpd-l`

To unsubscribe to the ProFTPD mailing list, do the following:

1. Send an electronic mail message to `majordomo@evcom.net`.
2. The Subject field of this message should be blank.
3. The Body field of this message should contain the following text:

   `unsubscribe proftpd-l`

To send mail to all users subscribed to he ProFTPD mailing list do the following:

1. Send an electronic mail message to `proftpd-l@evcom.net`.
2. The Subject and Body fields of this message can be defined at the user's discretion.

The ProFTPD mailing list is also available in an archived digest format through the WWW Archive at `http://www.proftpd.org/proftpd-l-archive/`.

Security and Legal Issues

Because the File Transfer Protocol allows remote users to retrieve and possibly store information on your network-connected servers, it brings with it several important security and legal issues. It is necessary for all of these issues to be carefully examined before any FTP-enabled host is allowed on your network.

One extremely important issue to be aware of when setting up a File Transfer Protocol server is the legal standpoints concerning site content. United States Federal law decrees that sites are indeed responsible for their content. This means that any illegal files or data contained on an FTP server could result in possible legal ramifications for that particular site's owner. Since this can result in possible serious legal trouble for site operators depending on the type of illegal content, much planning and thought should be undertaken before setting up any FTP server. Assistance with this matter is given in the "Dealing With Warez D00dz" section of this chapter.

Administrators should also be aware of the security issues associated with operating an FTP site. File Transfer Protocol servers often run with root privileges, resulting in the possibility of a total system compromise if attackers are able to compromise a vulnerable or misconfigured server.

Security flaws are often found in many popular FTP server packages, which open sites to such vulnerabilities. Care should be taken to properly secure your FTP servers and monitor the output of the security community for vulnerabilities affecting any software packages in use.

Protecting Your FTP Servers

There are many options available that can be of assistance when securing an FTP server. This section concentrates on the options available for Red Hat 6 systems running WU-FTPD. However, it should be noted that other FTP server packages may support the same configuration methods listed here.

This is because other products may be derivatives of the WU-FTPD system or may simply share similar options and capabilities.

It may be desirable when securing an FTP server to restrict access based on remote clients' IP addresses. This can be a valuable, but not foolproof, tool for protecting a server. Address-based access control can be easily fooled using network spoofing techniques. Therefore, this method of access control should only be considered a supplemental, not primary, security measure. FTP server access may be restricted for particular user accounts according to source IP address using the `ftphosts` configuration file. This file supports the following options:

- `Allow [username] [address_list]`—Allows FTP access via the account `username` only to clients connecting from one of the host addresses in `address_list`. The `address_list` parameter is a whitespace-separated group of one or more Internet addresses, in numeric IP, numeric IP/CIDR, or numeric IP/Netmask format.

- `deny [username] [address_list]`—Denies FTP access via the `username` account to clients connecting from one of the host addresses in `address_list`. The `address_list` parameter is in the same format as in the `allow` configuration option.

The `ftpaccess` configuration file supports many options that can be useful when securing an FTP server. Using these options, administrators can enable fine-grained access control measures based on a variety of criteria, including source IP addresses, ftp account UIDs/GIDs, user classes, and time of day. The following access control capabilities are supported:

- `allow-gid [gid-range] [..]`—Allows a particular GID or range of GIDs access to an FTP server. The `gid-range` parameter may be either a single GID or a range of GIDs. GID values can be specified using their assigned names (from the `/etc/group` file), or their actual numeric values. All numeric GID values should be preceded with a "%" character to identify them as such.

- `allow-uid [uid-range] [..]`—Allows a particular UID or range of UIDs access to an FTP server. The `uid-range` parameter may be either a single UID or a range of UIDs. UID values can be specified using their assigned names (from the `/etc/passwd` file), or their actual numeric values. All numeric UID values should be preceded with a "%" character to identify them as such.

- `defaultserver allow [username] [..]`—Allows FTP access to be granted to specific user accounts. The `username` parameter may be an assigned name (from the `/etc/passwd` file) or the "*" character, which specifies that FTP access should be granted to all users by default. When access is granted to all users, you may revoke access from individual users explicitly using `defaultserver deny` command strings.

- `defaultserver deny [username] [..]`—Allows FTP access to be denied to specific user accounts. The `username` parameter may be an assigned name (from the `/etc/passwd` file) or the "*" character, which specifies that FTP access should be denied to all users by default. When access is revoked to all users, you may grant access to individual users explicitly using `defaultserver allow` command strings.

- `defaultserver private`—Allows anonymous access to the FTP server to be disabled. Access for guest accounts and real users is unaffected by the use of this command string.

- `deny [address-data] [message-file]`—Allows access to the FTP server to be denied to clients connecting from hosts matching any of the addresses specified by the `address-data` parameter. This parameter may be in the following formats:

    `[ip_address]`—A single IP address.

    `[ip_address]:[netmask]`—An IP address with a netmask.

    `[ip_address]/[cidr]`—An IP address with CIDR data.

    `!nameserved`—An identifier that specifies to deny access to any host that does not resolve via a nameserver into a valid hostname.

    `/[file-name]`—An absolute path to a text file containing more `address-data` parameters; one on each line.

    The "message-file" parameter is an absolute path to a banner file which is to be displayed to users who are denied access to the FTP server as a result of this command string.

- `deny-email [email-address]`—Allows electronic mail addresses matching the `email-address` parameter to be considered invalid by the FTP server. If the `passwd-check` option is enabled on the server, this will prevent users with matching email addresses from being able to log in to the FTP server.

- `deny-gid [gid-range] [..]`—Allows a particular GID or range of GIDs to be denied access to a FTP server. The `gid-range` parameter may be either a single GID or a range of GIDs. GID values can be specified using their assigned names (from the `/etc/group` file), or their actual numeric values. All numeric GID values should be preceded with a "%" character to identify them as such.

- `deny-uid [uid-range] [..]`—Allows a particular UID or range of UIDs to be denied access to a FTP server. The `uid-range` parameter may be either a single UID or a range of UIDs. UID values can be specified using their assigned names (from the `/etc/passwd` file), or their actual numeric values. All numeric UID values should be preceded with a "%" character to identify them as such.

- `guestserver [hostname] [..]`—Allows anonymous FTP access only to hosts listed in this command string. Multiple hostnames may be specified, allowing anonymous access to a number of hosts. If no `hostname` parameter is specified, anonymous FTP access is denied to all connecting hosts.

- `limit [class-name] [max-users] [times] [message-file]`—Allows the number of simultaneous users in a particular access class to be limited during certain times of day. The `class-name` parameter specifies the access class that is being limited. The `max-users` parameter sets the maximum number of simultaneous users for the given access class. The `times` parameter uses the same format as in the times located in the `UUCPL.sys` file. `message-file` will be displayed to users denied access to the FTP server as a result of this command string.

- `passwd-check none¦trivial¦rfc822 enforce¦warn`—Allows the level of password checking used by the FTP server to be configured. The first parameter in this command string specifies the type of password checking that should be used. The following password checking methods are supported:

  none—Disables password checking.

  trivial—Passwords are required to contain an "@" character.

  rfc822—Passwords are required to be an RFC822-compliant electronic mail address.

The second parameter in this command string specifies what action should be taken when the password checking mechanisms report an invalid password. This option may be set to either `warn`, which simply notifies the user of an invalid password use but allows them to log into the FTP server, or `enforce`, which notifies the user of the invalid password and disallows access to the server.

The `ftpaccess` file supports a number of logging mechanisms that are useful when engaging in post-mortem security auditing. The output of these logging mechanisms can also serve as input for automated host-based intrusion detection systems. The following logging capabilities are supported:

- `loginfails [count]`—Allows the threshold setting for `repeated login failures` message logging to be set to a user-definable value. The default setting for this threshold value is 5. This means that a message will be logged to the system logging facilities when an FTP client fails to log in to the FTP server more than four times during one particular session.

- `log commands [keyword-list]`—Allows the commands sent by FTP users to be logged for later analysis. The `keyword-list` parameter is a comma-separated list of keywords that allow logging to be defined for a particular type of FTP user. The `anonymous`, `guest`, and `real` keywords are supported. The `anonymous` keyword makes this command string apply only to anonymous FTP logins, the `guest` parameter applies only to guest accounts, and the `real` parameter applies to actual system users logged in to the FTP server.

- `log transfers [keyword-list] [direction-list]`—Allows the file transfers of FTP users to be logged for later analysis. The `keyword-list` parameter is a comma-separated list of keywords that allows logging to be defined for a particular type of FTP user. The `anonymous`, `guest`, and `real` keywords are supported. The `anonymous` keyword makes this command string apply only to anonymous FTP logins, the `guest` parameter applies only to guest accounts, and the `real` parameter applies to actual system users logged in to the FTP server. The direction-list parameter is a comma-separated list of direction keywords that allows this command string to be applied to incoming, outgoing, or all file transfers. Supported direction keywords are `incoming` and `outgoing`.

- `log security [keyword-list]`—Allows any violations of system security rules by FTP users to be logged for later analysis. The `keyword-list` parameter is a comma-separated list of keywords that allows logging to be defined for a particular type of FTP user. The `anonymous`, `guest`, and `real` keywords are supported. The `anonymous` keyword makes this command string apply only to anonymous FTP logins, the `guest` parameter applies only to guest accounts, and the `real` parameter applies to actual system users logged in to the FTP server.

- `log syslog`—Redirects file transfer logging messages to the syslog facilities instead of the `xferlog` file. This can be useful when attempting to do centralized log storage and when using log information as input for host-based intrusion detection systems.

User access levels and site permissions on an FTP server can be controlled using options supported by the `ftpaccess` file. These options can be used to create user classes, each with their own definable access permissions, restricted files/directories, and even restricted commands. The following permissions options are supported:

- `allowretrieve absolute¦relative class=[class-name] [..][file-name]`
  `[..]`—Allows files on the FTP server to be specified as retrievable by particular users when they would otherwise be marked as nonretrievable. This option can be used to allow users to download specific files, or all files matching the given `file-name` parameters. It overrides any earlier `noretrieve` statements that would result in the specified files being inaccessible. Multiple `file-name` parameters may be specified in this command string, in any of the following formats:

  `filename`—Specifies any files on the server with names that match `filename`.

  `/path/filename`—Specifies a particular file on the server using directory and filename specifiers.

  `/path/`—Specifies the contents of a particular directory on the server.

  The `absolute¦relative` parameter in this command string is an optional setting that can be used to specify whether pathnames specified should be treated as absolute paths, or paths relative to the chroot'd filesystem of connecting FTP clients.

The `class=` parameter in this command string is also an optional setting, which may be used to grant file download access to specific user classes instead of all users on the FTP server. Multiple `class=` parameters may be given, or none may be given at all (resulting in all users being affected by the `allowretrieve` command string).

- `anonymous-root [directory] [user-class] [..]`—Allows the root directory to be specified for a particular user class. Users matching any of the classes listed in this command string will automatically be chroot'd to `directory` upon their login to the FTP server. If a user class is not specified, the command string is used to specify the root directory for anonymous users that have not been given an explicit root directory specification.

- `autogroup [group-name] [class-name] [..]`—Allows users in any of the access classes specified in this command string to automatically have their effective group IDs set to the GID matching the `group-name` parameter. This is useful when restricting file access for anonymous users based on group IDs.

- `byte-limit raw in|out|total [max-bytes] [class-name]`—Applies a limit to the number of bytes that a user in `user-class` may transfer. This limit may be set to apply to bytes sent, received, or both. The `raw` parameter is an optional setting that allows the raw traffic instead of just the data files sent/received to be limited using this command string. If the `user-class` parameter is not specified, this setting will apply to all user classes that have not explicitly been given a byte-limit configuration setting.

- `chmod yes|no [keyword-list]`—Allows for chmod command privileges to be given to or revoked from a particular user class or group of user classes. The `keyword-list` is a comma-separated list of keywords that allows chmod access to be controlled for a particular type of FTP user. The `anonymous`, `guest`, and `real` keywords are supported. The `anonymous` keyword makes this command string apply only to anonymous FTP logins, the `guest` parameter applies only to guest accounts, and the `real` keyword applies to actual system users logged in to the FTP server.

- `class [class-name] [type-list] [address-data][..]`—Allows for a particular user class to be specified based on the type of user logging in to the FTP server and the users' source IP address. This allows for a high level of configurability when defining user access levels and permissions. The `class-name` parameter in this command string is an alphanumeric text identifier used to identify the user class so that further options may be applied to it. The `keyword-list` parameter is a comma-separated list of keywords that allows this class statement to be limited to a particular type of FTP user. The anonymous, guest, and real keywords are supported. The anonymous keyword makes this command string apply only to anonymous FTP logins, the guest parameter applies only to guest accounts, and the real parameter applies to actual system users logged in to the FTP server. The address-data parameter specifies that only users connecting from a particular source host may be considered in the given user class. Multiple address-data parameters may be given, in the following format:

[ip_address]—A single IP address.

[ip_address]:[netmask]—An IP address with a netmask.

[ip_address]/[cidr]—An IP address with CIDR data.

![address-data]—A negated identifier, which specifies that hosts not matching the given address parameter will be evaluated as true.

/[file-name]—An absolute path to a text file containing more address-data parameters; one on each line.

- compress yes¦no [class-name] [..]—Allows for file compression privileges to be given to or revoked from a particular user class or group of user classes. Multiple classes may be specified in the command string.

- delete yes¦no [keyword-list]—Allows for delete command privileges to be given to or revoked from a particular user class or group of user classes. The keyword-list is a comma-separated list of keywords that allows deletion access to be controlled for a particular type of FTP user. The anonymous, guest, and real keywords are supported. The anonymous keyword makes this command string apply only to anonymous FTP logins, the guest parameter applies only to guest accounts, and the real keyword applies to actual system users logged in to the FTP server.

- file-limit [raw] [in¦out¦total] [files-count] [class-name]—Applies a limit to the number of files that a user in class-name may transfer. This limit may be set to apply to files sent, received, or both. The raw parameter is an optional setting that allows the raw traffic instead of the number of data files sent/received to be limited using this command string. If the class-name parameter is not specified, this setting will apply to all user classes that have not explicitly been given a file-limit configuration setting.

- guestgroup [group-name] [..]—Allows any user whose group matches one of the group names specified in this command string to be authenticated as a guest user.

- `guestuser [user-name] [..]`—Allows a particular user or group of users to be classified as guest users by the FTP server, when they would otherwise be authenticated as real users.

- `limit-time *|anonymous|guest [minutes]`—Allows the amount of time that a user session may be connected to the FTP server to be limited. This option does not affect "real" users on the system. you may use this option to limit the amount of time anonymous or guest users may spend connected to an FTP server during a single session. It should be noted however, that upon any user's reconnection to the server in a new session, their full allotted time will be restored.

- `noretrieve absolute|relative class=[class-name] [..][file-name] [..]`—Allows files on the FTP server to be specified as non-retrievable by particular users. This option can prevent users from being able to download specific files, or all files matching the given `file-name` parameters. Multiple `file-name` parameters may be specified in this command string, in any of the following formats:

    `filename`—Specifies any files on the server with names that match `filename`.

    `/path/filename`—Specifies a particular file on the server using directory and filename specifiers.

    `/path/`—Specifies the contents of a particular directory on the server.

    The `absolute|relative` parameter in this command string is an optional setting that can be used to specify whether pathnames specified should be treated as absolute paths, or paths relative to the chroot'd filesystem of connecting FTP clients.

    The `class=` parameter in this command string is also an optional setting, which may be used to revoke file download access from specific user classes instead of all users on the FTP server. Multiple `class=` parameters may be given, or none may be given at all (resulting in all users being affected by the `noretrieve` command string).

- `overwrite yes|no [keyword-list]`—Allows for file overwrite privileges to be given to or revoked from a particular user class or group of user classes. The `keyword-list` is a comma-separated list of keywords that allows deletion access to be controlled for a particular type of FTP user. The anonymous, guest, and `real` keywords are supported. The anonymous keyword makes this command string apply only to anonymous FTP logins, the `guest` parameter applies only to guest accounts, and the `real` keyword applies to actual system users logged in to the FTP server.

- `realgroup [group-name] [..]`—Allows any user whose group matches one of the group names specified in this command string to be authenticated as a real user, when they would otherwise be authenticated as guest users.

- `realuser [user-name] [..]`—Allows a particular user or group of users to be classified as real users by the FTP server, when they would otherwise be authenticated as guest users.

- `restricted-gid [gid-range] [..]`—Allows for users within the given GID ranges to be restricted so that they may only access their particular home directory. The `gid-range` parameter may be either a single GID or a range of GIDs. GID values can be specified using their assigned names (from the `/etc/passwd` file), or their actual numeric values. All numeric GID values should be preceded with a "%" character to identify them as such. Multiple GID range parameters may be specified in this command string.

- `restricted-uid [uid-range] [..]`—Allows for users within the given UID ranges to be restricted so that they may only access their particular home directory. The `uid-range` parameter may be either a single UID or a range of UIDs. UID values can be specified using their assigned names (from the `/etc/passwd` file), or their actual numeric values. All numeric UID values should be preceded with a "%" character to identify them as such. Multiple UID range parameters may be specified in this command string.

- `rename yes¦no [keyword-list]`—Allows for file renaming privileges to be given to or revoked from a particular user class or group of user classes. The `keyword-list` is a comma-separated list of keywords that allows deletion access to be controlled for a particular type of FTP user. The `anonymous`, `guest`, and `real` keywords are supported. The `anonymous` keyword makes this command string apply only to anonymous FTP logins, the `guest` parameter applies only to guest accounts, and the `real` keyword applies to actual system users logged in to the FTP server.

- `tar yes¦no [class] [..]`—Allows for tar privileges to be given to or revoked from a particular user class or group of user classes. Multiple classes may be specified in this command string.

- `unrestricted-gid [gid-range] [..]`—Allows users within the given GID ranges access to areas on the FTP server that are outside their particular home directory. The `gid-range` parameter may be either a single GID or a range of GIDs. GID values can be specified using their assigned names (from the `/etc/passwd` file), or their actual numeric values. All numeric GID values should be preceded with a "%" character to identify them as such. Multiple GID range parameters may be specified in this command string.

- unrestricted-uid [uid-range] [..]—Allows users within the given UID ranges access to areas on the FTP server that are outside their particular home directory. The uid-range parameter may be either a single UID or a range of UIDs. UID values can be specified using their assigned names (from the /etc/passwd file), or their actual numeric values. All numeric UID values should be preceded with a "%" character to identify them as such. Multiple UID range parameters may be specified in this command string.

- umask yes¦no [keyword-list]—Allows for umask command privileges to be given to or revoked from a particular user class or group of user classes. The keyword-list is a comma-separated list of keywords that allows umask command access to be controlled for a particular type of FTP user. The anonymous, guest, and real keywords are supported. The anonymous keyword makes this command string apply only to anonymous FTP logins, the guest parameter applies only to guest accounts, and the real keyword applies to actual system users logged in to the FTP server.

- upload yes¦no [keyword-list]—Allows for uploading privileges to be given to or revoked from a particular user class or group of user classes. The keyword-list is a comma-separated list of keywords that allows uploading access to be controlled for a particular type of FTP user. The anonymous, guest, and real keywords are supported. The anonymous keyword makes this command string apply only to anonymous FTP logins, the guest parameter applies only to guest accounts, and the real keyword applies to actual system users logged in to the FTP server.

In addition to enabling security measures through the ftpaccess configuration file, it is advisable to properly set the permissions on all files and directories contained on your FTP server directory tree to thwart unauthorized access. It may also be wise to remove any unnecessary files from the FTP server directory tree.

You may modify the file permissions of the FTP server directory tree and its contents to ensure higher levels of system security. The following commands (executed from the root of the FTP server directory tree) may be used to secure the base anonftp directory configuration:

```
# chmod 111 bin etc lib bin/*
# chmod 444 etc/*
# chmod 555 . lib/*
```

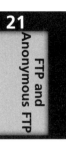

Additional files and directories added to the FTP server must have their file permissions set in the interest of security. The following file permission modification commands should be used:

Files:

```
# chmod 444 [file-name]
```

Directories:

```
# chmod 555 [directory-name]
```

The anonftp RPM on the Red Hat 6 CD-ROM also installs several files that may be unneeded depending on the FTP server configuration. It is advisable that any unneeded files be removed from the site for security purposes. The following files are often unnecessary on many FTP servers:

```
/bin/cpio
/bin/sh
/bin/zcat
/etc/ld.so.cache
```

Dealing with Warez D00dz

File Transfer Protocol sites that allow anonymous access often become victim to warez activity. Such sites are obvious targets because a valid system account is not required for FTP access. If a writable directory is available on the site, it has the potential of becoming a storehouse of pirated software, pornography, and other undesirable materials. It is important to develop strategies for detecting and preventing warez-oriented activity from occurring.

Good warez prevention strategies include plans for detection of such activity, knowing how to handle such activity when it occurs, and how to prevent future occurrences. If these plans are not developed and followed, your FTP servers could be put in jeopardy; Internet links could become clogged with pirated software transfers, and sites could be put into possible legal trouble for their content. Warez activity on Internet-connected servers is a serious matter, and should be treated as such.

There are several techniques that can be used to assist in the detection of warez activity on your FTP servers. These include

- Server traffic baselining and anomaly detection
- Disk space usage analysis
- Server content examination

All of these techniques can be of great value when attempting to detect the occurrence of warez-related activity.

Server traffic baselining allows the amount of data being sent or received from your FTP server to be examined for anomalous activity. Extraordinarily high levels of traffic flow can often be indicators of a server falling victim to warez activity. Baselining is an easy task to perform, as many network traffic analysis packages perform it automatically. One such program is the popular utility ntop, which can be used gather FTP traffic statistics so that baselining activities can be performed. Utilization of this program is illustrated in Chapter 16, "Network Monitoring."

The amount of disk space used by your anonymous FTP server can often serve as an early warning of the occurrence of illegal activity. Administrators should monitor site disk space usage on a regular basis, looking for any sort of anomalous activity. Indicators of warez-oriented activity include rapid increases in disk space usage over a short period of time. Such decreases in available free space usually occur when a site becomes used as a storehouse for pirated software. Pirated applications often take up extremely large amounts of memory. You can monitor the disk space usage of their FTP server using the popular du command, which displays disk usage information for a particular directory hierarchy. Such information should be recorded and analyzed frequently if it is to be of any use when monitoring for warez activity.

Analysis of actual server content is one of the best ways to detect whether or not warez-trading activity is taking place on your FTP servers. Most warez repositories share similar characteristics, which can be exploited to make their detection easier. These similarities include particular directory names, hierarchies, and filenames. More information on each of these is given in Table 21.4.

TABLE 21.4 Warez Repository File System Characteristics

Content Type	Description
[directory]	Warez sites often use similar directory names, or directory names that match a certain style criteria. Individuals who engage in warez trading activity often follow the "elite speak" writing style when creating directories on an FTP server. More information on "elite speak" is given later on in this section. Examples: /warez,/gamez,/utilz, /uploadz,/mp3,/gifz,/ sitez, /pr0n,/0day

TABLE **21.4**   continued

Content Type	Description
[hidden_dir]/[directory]	In an attempt to hide warez repositories from normal users and system administrators, illegal content is often hidden inside a hierarchy of hidden directories. Hidden directories are normally marked as such by prepending a leading "." character to the directory name. Directories can also be made to look like the system "." and ".." directories by appending extra spaces to the end of their filenames. Examples: /incoming/.warez/ uploadz,/pub/uploads/,/warez-site incoming/,/utilz/ pub/,/gamez
[trojan_dir]/[directory]	Trojan directory names are also used in order to hide warez repositories from users and system administrators. These directory names are fashioned in such a manner that they look like innocuous files that would normally be on the system. Examples: /incoming/index.txt/warez, /incoming/gifs/ Starscape.GIF/Filez,/pub/uploads/gcc.tar.gz/gamez
[filename]	The filenames of data stored on warez FTP sites often contain many similarities, which may be used to help in the detection of warez-related activity. Warez trading groups generally make use of standard filenaming techniques that are easy to identify. Filenames often contain actual warez group names, the names of commercial software products, and so on. Files containing several popular archive/compression extensions can also serve as indicators to warez-oriented activity. Files containing such extensions should not automatically be considered illegal content, but should simply be examined for other possible pointers to illegal activity. Examples: *.zip, *.arj, *.mp3, *.nfo

Note

As stated above, filenames containing these extensions should not automatically be considered illegal content. The above extensions are popular in both the legal and illegal software trading communities. Therefore, care must be taken to examine actual content before determinations can be made as to its legal status.

"Elite speak" refers to a method of communication popular among warez traders. Though all warez traders may not actually converse in elite speak as many consider it a childish method of communication, they often make use of it when constructing the directory structure of a warez FTP site. Elite speak may also be used in the actual filenames of pirated software stored on such sites. Elite speak can have any combination of the following characteristics:

- Slang terms are used, with words often spelled out phonetically.

    - Examples:
    - warez (pronounced "w-ay-r-z")
    - wherd (pronounced "w-er-duh")

- Vowels may be replaced with numbers that mimic their appearance.

    - Examples:
    - war3z (warez)
    - el1te (elite)

- Phrases may contain terms that are known as popular in the warez community.

    - Examples:
    - k-rad
    - elite
    - wherd
    - 0-day

Elite speak is quite easy to pick out of normal text because of its bizarre syntax. This can be to the advantage of the administrator when attempting to locate warez sites on an FTP server.

It is important to know how to deal with warez activity if it is ever detected on an FTP server. Proper strategies must be defined so that such occurrences may be dealt with swiftly and properly. At the bare minimum, your site must be sanitized of all illegal materials, and proper security measures must be put into place to prevent any future happenings. It may be advisable to take additional measures such as reporting offending parties to the proper authorities. Such authorities include law enforcement agencies, the Software Publishers Association (SPA), and security teams such as CERT. Additionally, you may want to contact the administrators of the sites from which offending parties were connecting.

The SPA investigates piracy activities and may be of assistance. They offer both Web-based incident reporting forms and telephone piracy lines. you may report incidents to the SPA at the following locations:

Web form: `http://www.spa.org/piracy/ireport.htm`

Telephone: 202-452-1600

If you want to report an incident to the Federal Bureau of Investigation, National Computer Crimes Squad, they may be reached at the following location:

FBI National Computer Crimes Squad
Washington, D.C.
202-324-9164

CERT (Computer Emergency Response Team), is an organization devoted to computer security and incident response. It may be a good idea to report any incidents that have occurred to CERT. To do so, fill out the CERT/CC Incident Reporting Form and return it. This form may be retrieved from the following location:

`ftp://info.cert.org/pub/incident_reporting_form`

CERT provides a useful guide that can be of assistance when you are attempting to contact the site administrators of machines from which software pirates were connecting. This guide is available on the Web at the following location:

`http://www.cert.org/tech_tips/finding_site_contacts.html`

After an occurrence of warez-related activity has been detected and recovered from your FTP server, it is important to ensure that such occurrences will not happen again in the future. Steps must be taken to ensure that proper site security mechanisms are in place, including examination of file permissions on site content, removal of unnecessary system binaries from the FTP server directory hierarchy, and implementing proper user access restrictions. Information on how to secure your FTP server is given in the "Protecting Your FTP Servers" section of this chapter.

Warning banners often assist in the prevention of future occurrences of warez activity on your FTP servers. If anonymous users are presented with a warning banner upon logging in to an FTP server or entrance into a particular directory, they will be made aware that the site administrator has already detected warez activity in the past. Warez traders will be less likely to attempt to use such sites again, for any of the following reasons:

- The FTP site administrator has previously detected warez activity, and will therefore be monitoring site content more closely.

- The FTP site administrator may be working in cooperation with law enforcement agencies to apprehend individuals attempting to further use the server for warez trading.

- Many anonymous FTP servers that have the potential of becoming warez sites exist on the Internet. All that is needed is a directory that allows anonymous users write and upload access. Warez traders are more likely to move on to a fresh site than attempt to salvage a site that has already been discovered.

Obviously, warning banners should not be considered as any sort of foolproof security measure. They only serve as assistance in deterring future outbreaks of illegal activity. Banners should be used in combination with proper site security measures, and not by themselves.

Summary

The File Transfer Protocol is a powerful mechanism for exchanging file resources between networked hosts. It is the most widespread form of file exchange on the Internet today, and is supported in almost every Linux distribution. The techniques outlined in this chapter will enable you to properly configure FTP on a Linux host. Information is also provided on setting up anonymous FTP services, securing your FTP server, and preventing warez attacks.

CHAPTER 22

Web Serving

IN THIS CHAPTER

- Introduction to Web Serving *638*
- Apache *638*
- Squid *665*
- Other Web Servers *667*

Introduction to Web Serving

The past few years have seen the incredible growth of the Internet. Just a decade ago, the Internet was used by only a specialized group of individuals; today it is a household name and is having a significant impact upon society as a whole. With the growth of the Internet has the come the obvious growth of Web servers. There are now a large number of Web servers available, both commercial and free.

While the Linux operating system has much merit and is the platform of choice for many computing solutions, more and more people are turning to Linux as a Web server platform. Red Hat Linux is a ready to run Web server out-of-the-box, and obviously much more. In this chapter, we will be looking at using Red Hat Linux as a Web server; in particular we will be examining the Apache Web server in detail. Apache is the default Web server that comes with Red Hat Linux 6.1. We will also be taking a quick look at other Web servers that are available for Linux, including Boa, dhttpd, fhttpd, ghttpd, Roxen, thttpd, and WN.

Apache

The default Web server that ships with Red Hat Linux 6.1, and many other Linux distributions for that matter, is Apache. Apache is currently the most popular Web server on the internet today, and runs on many different architectures besides Linux; including Solaris, HPUX, SVR4, SunOS 4.x, A/UX, the BSD family, and even Windows NT. Linux is definitely one of the more popular platforms for running Apache on due to its low cost and stability.

The Apache Project, like Linux, is another free software success story; the goal of which is to create a full-featured, robust, commercial-grade Web server. Over the years, there have been many people who have contributed code, ideas, and money to the Apache project, and have helped Apache become the success that it is. There is a core group of volunteers from all around the world known as the Apache Group; they help with the coordination and continual development of Apache. In this section, we will look in detail at how Apache came to be, how to get started using Apache, and how to tweak and configure it so that it does what you want it to.

About the Apache Project

Just a few years ago, the most popular HTTP server of the time was the NCSA httpd. In mid-1994, the main developer for the NCSA httpd left the project, leaving many Webmasters around the world to tinker with the code for httpd. Eventually, there were a number of enhancements and bug fixes that were developed for httpd; these changes where distributed in the form of source code patches. It wasn't long until the number of patches became unwieldy and the need for a standard distribution became ever more important. Around this time, a group of Webmasters began collaborating, giving birth to the Apache project. The initial group that founded the Apache project consisted of eight core members with the bandwidth of their initial project server donated by HotWired. The first official public release of the Apache server was in April 1995, and was known by the version number of 0.6.2. The version of NCSA httpd that was used as the base was 1.3, and all the known patches to httpd were applied to that version to create Apache. The name Apache comes from the fact that initially it was no more than "A PAtCHy" release of the NCSA httpd.

Throughout 1995, Apache development continued rapidly upon Apache, with many releases during the year. Finally, on December 1 of 1995 Apache version 1.0 was released on December 1, 1995. Soon after the 1.0 release, Apache became the most popular Web server on the Internet by January 1997, overtaking the NCSA's httpd as the #1 server. To this day, Apache is still the most popular Web server on the Internet due to its low cost and superior performance. Although there are some commercial Web servers that offer slight performance improvements over Apache, Apache is the fastest and most functional of all the free Web servers. Apache can also handle an incredible amount of hits without running into any problems, and it is very stable. Because of Apache's open development, it also has the benefit of very rigorous testing from developers and users around the world. When problems are found, the open development of Apache ensures that fixes are released as soon as possible.

In this section we will be looking in detail at the basics of Apache, including:

- Installing Apache
- Starting and stopping Apache
- Configuring Apache
- Various configuration techniques
- Security tips
- Apache modules
- Virtual Hosts
- Comanche
- Apache add-ons

Installing Apache

Depending upon the install time options you chose when you installed Red Hat Linux, Apache may or may not have been installed for you. If you are not sure whether Apache is installed or not, use the following rpm command to find out for sure:

```
$ rpm -q apache
package apache is not installed
$ rpm -q apache
apache-1.3.6-7
```

The preceding command will either tell you the version number of Apache that you have installed, or it will tell you that Apache is not installed. If you do not have Apache installed, then you must get the Apache rpm archive and install it using the rpm command. The Apache rpm archive will be on your Red Hat Linux 6.0 CD-ROM. After you find it, make sure you are root and then type the following command to install it:

```
# rpm -i apache-1.3.6-7.i386.rpm
```

When typing the above command, be sure you substitute the `apache-1.3.6-7.i386.rpm` filename with the exact filename for your Apache rpm because it may be a slightly different version.

If you plan on doing any Apache development, such as writing your own Apache modules, it is also a good idea to install the `apache-devel` rpm file as well.

Starting and Stopping Apache

The default rpm installation will install Apache as a standalone server, so to start and stop Apache, you can use the httpd script that is located in the `/etc/rc.d/init.d/` directory. All the system startup scripts are kept inside the `/etc/rc.d/` directory. The `init.d` directory contains the startup scripts for many Linux daemons and the contents of the `init.d` directory are executed upon system startup.

To manually start the Apache server, you can issue the following command as root:

```
# /etc/rc.d/init.d/httpd start
```

Or to manually stop the Apache server, you can issue the following command:

```
# /etc/rc.d/init.d/httpd stop
```

If you have changed some configuration parameters and you want Apache to read in the changes, you can simply restart the httpd daemon with the following command:

```
# /etc/rc.d/init.d/httpd restart
```

There are also several command-line options that you can pass to httpd when starting it. These are the more common parameters:

- *-d serverroot*—Used to set the initial value for the ServerRoot variable, which can be overridden by the value of the ServerRoot directive in the configuration files. If unspecified, the default value is /usr/local/etc/httpd.

- *-f filename*—Specifies a file that is to be read by Apache upon startup and have the contents of the file executed. You should specify the full path to the filename or else it will be taken as a path relative to the value of the ServerRoot variable. The default value for this is conf/httpd.conf.

- -x—Used to start Apache in single-process mode, this is for internal debugging purposes only and not to be used under normal Web server usage. This causes the Apache daemon to not detach itself from the terminal or to fork any children.

- -v—Prints out the version of httpd and exits.

- -h—Outputs a list of all directives along with their expected arguments. It also tells where each directive can be used.

- -l—Outputs a list of all modules that are compiled into Apache.

- -V—Displays a list of compile settings.

- -S—Displays a list of parsed settings.

- -h—Displays a list of all available configuration directives.

- -t—Runs a syntax check of all configuration files, a very useful option. This should be run after any changes to Apache's configuration files are made so that you can be sure that there are no errors.

- -?—Shows a list of all available command-line options.

Many times you won't need to make use of httpd's command-line arguments. However, they can provide very useful information and assist in the configuration of Apache, so it is a good idea to play around with them so that you understand what each argument does.

Configuring Apache

If you install Apache from the Red Hat rpm archive, then your Apache configuration files will kept in the /etc/httpd directory. There are generally several files in this directory, although there are only three main configuration files that you should know about. The three Apache configuration files are named access.conf, httpd.conf, and srm.conf. The main Apache configuration file is httpd.conf; the Apache Group's recommendation is to only use the httpd.conf file for configuring Apache, although Red Hat Linux 6.1 still uses all three files. Because Red Hat 6.1 uses all three configuration files in the default Apache rpm, we will cover how to configure Apache using all three files. To edit those configuration files, you can use any text editor, such as vi or pico.

access.conf

The `access.conf` file is where all access conditions are defined, the `httpd.conf` is the main server configuration file, and the `srm.conf` file is used to set up the server's request handling services. As you begin working with Apache, you should become very familiar with these three files. If you would like to follow the Apache group recommendation and move all directives into the `httpd.conf`, keeping both `access.conf` and `srm.conf` blank, you can do that. However, it may create problems later when you decide to upgrade your Red Hat version.

Overriding the Configuration Files

You can override the usage of each of the configuration files and tell Apache to use different files. The `httpd.conf` filename can be overridden by using the `-f` options on the command line when starting Apache. The `srm.conf` filename can be overridden by using the `ResourceConfig` directive. The `access.conf` filename can be overridden with the `AccessConfig` directive.

The main idea behind the Apache configuration files is that of configuration directives, each of which instructs the Web server to perform a specific action. Apache has quite a collection of available configuration directives; we will be taking a look at some of them later in this section. You can put comments within the configuration file as well, any line that begins with a pound sign (#) is treated as a comment by Apache. After you make changes to the file, you must restart Apache before any changes will take effect.

When editing the `httpd.conf`, keep in mind that it is divided into three main sections. The sections are as follows:

- **Global Directives**—Directives that are global to the entire Apache server process.

- **Main Directives**—Directives that define the main Apache server, all virtual hosts use these settings for their default actions.

- **Virtual Host Settings**—The settings for any virtual hosts.

When Apache is first started, it initially processes the contents of the `/etc/httpd/httpd.conf` file. Following that, the `/etc/httpd/srm.conf` file is processed, and, finally, the `/etc/httpd/access.conf` file is processed. As was mentioned earlier, Apache's configuration can be set using only the `httpd.conf` file, which is the recommended way of doing things, although under Red Hat Linux, all three of the configuration files are used.

When specifying paths within the configuration files, it is best to use the complete pathname for any files. If the filename does not begin with "/", then Apache will assume that the path is relative to the value of ServerRoot.

Configuring Apache Using Directives

Apache is configured using commands that are called *directives*. There is a huge collection of directives that are available when configuring Apache. In this section, we will go through various Apache configuration options, and we will touch upon many of the more common directives. It is recommended that you take a look at your `httpd.conf`, `access.conf`, and `srm.conf` files as you go through this section because each directive is documented within them. You can also take a look at the online documentation that came with Apache because each directive is documented in detail there.

Getting Started with Configuration

There are a few basic directives that you should know about as you go about your initial Apache configuration.

ServerAdmin

You probably should first make sure that the ServerAdmin directive is properly set. The ServerAdmin directive is used to specify the e-mail address of the administrator for the Web server and is generally found in the `httpd.conf` file. The value given to the ServerAdmin directive will be displayed on any pages that contain error messages. Here is an example of using this directive:

```
ServerAdmin webmaster@test.com
```

ServerName

Another important directive that you might want to set is the ServerName directive; this is used to specify the hostname for your server. This directive is usually commented out by default because Apache can figure out your hostname simply from the IP address of your machine.

It is also important to set up some default directories for Apache to run properly. There are two such directives to do so—DocumentRoot and ServerRoot.

DocumentRoot

The `DocumentRoot` directive is used to set the base directory from which files will be served. Thus, if your server name is www.test.com, then when anyone accesses your server at the base URL, they will access the files contained in the directory specified by

DocumentRoot. If the user accessing your server does not specify any file name, then the default file name, which is usually index.html, will be accessed.

ServerRoot

The ServerRoot directive is used to specify the directory where all the server's configuration files are kept. The default value under Red Hat Linux is /etc/httpd.

Two other important directives that you may like to configure are the User and Group directives. The User directive specifies the user id under which the server will answer requests, while the Group directive is used to specify the group id under which the server will answer requests. Both the User and Group directives will only take effect if Apache is started by root. Here is an example of using both User and Group:

```
User nobody
Group nobody
```

You can specify any valid user or group in the User and Group directives; however, nobody is used for security purposes.

With these basic directives, you can get a basic Apache server up and running. In fact, many times Apache will work immediately after you install and start it. However, the key to getting Apache to do what you want it to is to configure it properly. The directives we have covered are the bare minimum to getting a working Apache server.

Setting Up Directory-based Directives

A lot of the Apache configuration has to do with setting up access control directives for specific directories, and, thus, there is the Directory directive for doing just that. With the Directory directive, you can set up a group of directives that only apply to a particular directory. Any directives applied with the Directory directive also apply to any sub-directories of the parent directory.

The syntax for the Directory directive is as follows:

```
<Directory dir_name>
Directive
Directive
...
</Directory>
```

When specifying the *dir_name*, you can either put the full path to the directory, or you can use a wild-card string. The wild-card characters are:

- ?—Matches a single character
- *—Matches any number of characters
- []—Matches any one of the characters contained within the brackets

When using wildcards, be sure to remember that wildcards will not match the / character.

Inside of the Directory directive, you can use a number of various directives. One of the most common is the Options directive. The Options directive is used to specify which server options should be enabled in a specified directory and has the following syntax:

```
Options [+¦-]option [+¦-]option ...
```

You can specify any number of options after the Options directive, a plus symbol (+) will enable the specified option, while a minus symbol (-) will disable the specified options. There are a number of options available, including the following:

- All—Encompasses all options except for MultiViews.
- ExecCGI—Allows CGI scripts to be executed.
- FollowSymLinks—If the server encounters a symbolic link, it will follow it.
- Includes—Allows the use of server-side includes.
- IncludesNOEXEC—Allows the use of server-side includes, excluding the #exec and #include commands.
- Indexes—If a specified directory does not contain an index.html file when the client requests that directory, a directory listing will be output to the client instead.
- MultiViews—Allows the use of content negotiated MultiViews.
- SymLinksIfOwnerMatch—When the server encounters a symbolic link, it will only follow it if the link's target is owned by the same user id as the link.

If no option is specified, then the default option of All will be enabled.

Another directive that is commonly used within the Directory directive is the AllowOverride directive, and it allows you to specify what directives can be overridden from the server defaults inside the directory. This is useful when you would like to configure specific directives differently inside of various directories on the server.

Setting Up File-based Directives

You can also define access control directives based upon filenames. This works very similarly to the `Directory` directive, and is called the `Files` directive. As you know, the `Directory` directive allows you to set up directives differently based up directories; the `Files` directive works the same way except that it is based upon files, not directories. In fact, you can even nest `Files` directives with `Directory` directives to further limit the scope of your directives. The syntax for the `Files` directive is as follows:

```
<Files filename>
Directive
Directive
...
</Files>
```

The `filename` argument should consist of a filename, however it can include wildcards as well. Regular expressions are also allowed. Keep in mind that unlike `Directory` directives, the `Files` directive cannot be used inside an `.htaccess` file.

Inside the `Files` directive, you also will probably be using the `Options` and `AllowsOverride` directives.

Conditional Directives

You can have directives that only apply based upon conditional statements. This is called a conditional directive and it allows you to set up directives that will only be set if a certain parameter is true. To do so, you can use the`IfDefine` directive. A test is passed to the `IfDefine` directive, and its contents will only be processed if the test returns true. Here is the syntax:

```
<IfDefine [!]parameter_name>
Directive
Directive
...
</IfDefine>
```

The test consists of one of the two following forms:

- `parameter_name`

- `!parameter_name`

In the case of the first form, if the specified `parameter_name` is defined, the contents of the `<IfDefine>...</IfDefine>` directive are processed. The second form is the opposite: The contents are only processed if the specified `parameter_name` is not defined.

The parameter_names are defined at the httpd start by passing them on the command line with the -D option.

Setting Up Logging

A crucial part of running a Web server is logging the activity that takes place with it. Apache allows you great control over how logging takes place, starting with the LogLevel directive.

The LogLevel directive is used to specify the amount of logging you want Apache to perform, There are a number of different levels of logging at which Apache can run. This directive allows you to specify exactly how much logging you want Apache to perform. Here are the logging levels that are available:

- emerg—Only emergencies are logged.

- crit—Only critical problems are logged.

- alert—Any conditions that are alerts are logged.

- error—All errors are logged—The default level.

- warn—All errors and warnings are logged.

- notice—Any significant conditions are logged.

- info—All server information is logged.

- debug—Debugging messages are logged.

When you specify a logging level, keep in mind that it turns on logging for all levels of lesser importance as well. So specifying warn as your log level will also turn on notice, info, and debug.

You also need to specify a filename to which errors will be logged. This is done with the ErrorLog directive. For example:

```
ErrorLog logs/error_log
```

In this example, all server errors will be logged to a file called error_log that is in the logs directory.

Whenever any requests are made to your Web server, Apache will log those within the transfer log. You can specify the filename to use for the transfer log with the TransferLog directive. Here is an example:

```
TransferLog logs/access_log
```

22

Web Serving

Finally, when httpd starts, it stores the process id of its parent httpd process to the file `logs/httpd.pid`. You can change the name of the pid file with the`PidFile` directive. This is a very important file because when you want to either restart or terminate Apache, you must know the parent process id. Here is an example of setting up this file:

```
PidFile logs/httpd.pid
```

It is important to remember that when configuring a virtual host, you can specify different error logs and transfer logs for each virtual host.

Error Handling

Error handling is an important part of administering Apache. Apache has several error codes, each of which has different meanings. The following are the command error codes:

- `400`—Bad Request
- `401`—Authorization Required
- `403`—Forbidden
- `404e`—Not Found
- `500`—Internal Server Error

There are different ways of setting up Apache to handle errors. The default setting is to simply have Apache display a page with the error code that occurred, along with the corresponding error message.

Customizing Error Handling

You can, however, customize the error handling features of Apache. The simplest way to do so is to use the `ErrorDocument` directive. The `ErrorDocument` directive is used to assign an error message to a particular error code. The `ErrorDocument` directive is kept in the `srm.conf` file. The following is an example of using a customized error message:

```
ErrorDocument 403 "I'm sorry, you do not have access to this directory"
```

```
ErrorDocument 404 "I'm sorry but what you are looking for cannot be found"
```

Please note that only one quote is used after the error code, and no closing quote is needed at the end of the error message.

Another way to customize Apache's error handling is to redirect users to customize HTML error pages for various errors. Again, you use the `ErrorDocument` directive, however, this time you specify a filename instead of an error message. The following is an example of doing so:

```
ErrorDocument 403 /error_forbidden.html
```

```
ErrorDocument 404 /error_notfound.html
```

Apache looks for the filename you specify starting at the value that is given for the `DocumentRoot` directive. Or if you would like to redirect the user to an external Web site, you can also specify a URL, as shown in the following. Here is an example:

```
ErrorDocument 403 http://www.error.com
```

Finally, you can also redirect users to various scripts, such as CGIcgi or php3 scripts. This is very useful if you have scripts that can log the error code and give the user a nice message. The following is an example of using a script redirection:

```
ErrorDocument 403 /cgi-bin/forbidden.cgi
```

```
ErrorDocument 404 /cgi-bin/notfound.cgi
```

As you can see, there are many ways of handling errors under Apache. You can use all the default settings and everything will still work okay; however, with a little time and effort, you can also create scripts that will log all the different errors and allow you to analyze why those errors are occurring. With enough data, you may be able to improve your Web site so that such errors are avoided in the future.

Various Configuration Techniques

In this section, we will look at a few common tasks that are performed by Apache administrators, including password protecting directories, Server Side Includes, and CGI script configuration.

Password protecting Directories

Apache allows you to password protect any directories on your Web server. Apache uses two files to set up password protection on directories—`.htaccess` and `.htpasswd`. Any directory that contains files you want to make private needs to have both of those files created in it. Keep in mind that password protecting a directory does not apply to the contents of any subdirectories; and thus, you must also create `.htaccess` and `.htpasswd` files in every subdirectory that you want to be secure as well.

You can actually tell Apache to use a different filename besides `.htaccess`; this is done with the `AccessFileName` directive. This directive is generally used for security reasons. By storing access information in a non-standard filename, you make it more difficult for your Web server to be compromised. You can also use different filenames. All you have to do is specify them after the `AccessFileName` directive, as shown in the following example:

```
AccessFileName .htaccess .private
```

In this example, both `.htaccess` and `.private` will be searched for by Apache in any secure directory.

The `.htaccess` file contains authorization directives that limit access to the directory to all except specified users. Here is an example of an `.htaccess` file:

```
<Limit GET POST>
Require valid-user
</Limit>


AuthType       Basic
AuthName       a_protected_area
AuthUserFile /home/httpd/html/secure_stuff/.htpasswd
```

In this example, the `Limit` directive is used to set what sort of access controls will be used in the directory. In this case, we want to use the valid-user access control that will prompt for a username and password, for all GET and POST requests. We then specify the type of authorization that will be in use, which is `Basic` in this case. We also give a name to the protected directory, which is a_protected_area. Finally, we specify the file that will contain username and passwords; for this we specify `/home/httpd/html/secure_stuff/.htpasswd`.

Now you also must create an `.htpasswd` file that contains the names and passwords for all users who have access to the directory. To create an `.htpasswd` file, you can issue the following command:

```
htpasswd -c .htpasswd username
```

You will then have to type in the password for the specified username twice. The username you specified, along with an encrypted version of the password, will be stored in the `.htpasswd` file. The `-c` option is only needed when you want to create the `.htpasswd` file—if one already exists, you should not use that option.

Now, to get Apache to even process the `.htaccess` file within a directory, you must set up the `AllowOverride` directive for the specified directory. The `AllowOverride` directive tells Apache what directives in the `.htaccess` file can override the previous settings that have been loaded into the server. To set up the /home/httpd/html/secure_stuff directory to read its .htaccess file, you can use the following example:

```
<Directory /home/httpd/html/secure_stuff>
AllowOverride AuthConfig
</Directory>
```

Now, when a user accesses the /home/httpd/html/secure_stuff directory, the server should prompt for a username and password. The AllowOverride directive also takes other parameters including the following:

- None—No directives will be allowed, the server will not even read the file.

- All—All directives will be allowed.

- AuthConfig—Allows any of the authorization directives to be used.

- FileInfo—Allows any of the document-controlling directives to be used.

- Indexes—Allows any of the directory controlling directives to be used.

- Limit—Allows any of the host access controlling directives to be used.

- Options—Allows any directives that control directory settings to be used.

Disabling the Use of the .htaccess File

So, to disable the use of the .htaccess file in the /home/httpd/html/secure_stuff directory, use the following example:

```
<Directory /home/httpd/html/secure_stuff>
AllowOverride None
</Directory>
```

You should now have an idea of how to set up private areas under Apache. If you want to find out more about Apache authorization directives, take a look at the online Apache documentation.

Server-Side Includes

Server-side includes (SSI) are special directives that you can put into HTML files that are parsed by Apache at the time the file is read. HTML files that contain SSI directives are given the extension of .shtml instead of just .html.

22

Web Serving

Due to security issues, SSI is disabled by default. To enable server-side includes for your entire Apache server, you must uncomment a few lines in the Apache configuration files. In the `srm.conf` file, uncomment the two following two lines:

```
AddType text/html .shtml
AddHandler server-parsed .shtml
```

Now, in the `access.conf` file, make sure that the `Includes` option is specified for the `Options` directive that is in the `<Directory/>` section, and that the line is not commented out. For example, you should have a section in your `access.conf` file that looks like the following:

```
DocumentRoot "/home/httpd/htdocs"


<Directory />
Options Indexes FollowSymLinks Includes
AllowOverride None
</Directory>
```

Additionally, you can only enable SSI in specific directories. To do so, you must either edit or create an `.htaccess` file in the directory, and it must have the following line:

```
AddType text/x-server-parsed-html .shtml
```

Now you must also make sure that the `Includes` option has been specified on that directory. For example, if the directory to which you would like to enable SSI is `/home/httpd/htdocs/ssi_stuff`, you should add the following lines to your `access.conf` file:

```
<Directory /ssi_stuff>
    Options Indexes Includes
    AllowOverride None
</Directory>
```

Server-side includes can be very useful and provide many interesting features; however, be careful in how you use them, because they can be a security hazard and they can also degrade the performance of Apache significantly.

CGI Configuration

CGI scripting is a very popular feature of Apache. To use it, however, you must make sure that it is enabled and configured properly. The default Apache setting has CGI scripting turned off, but it is very easy to enable it.

To enable Apache to execute CGI scripts, you must set up the `ScriptAlias` directive, which is in the `srm.conf` file. The `ScriptAlias` directive is used to specify which directories contain CGI scripts and how they are accessed from the server's root URL.

Here is an example that sets up the `/home/httpd/htdocs/cgi-bin` directory to be able to execute CGI scripts, and it is accessed from the server's root URL with the subdirectory `/cgi-bin/`:

```
ScriptAlias /cgi-bin/ /home/httpd/htdocs/cgi-bin
```

Another directive that must be set up properly is the`AddHandler` directive, which must be set up to handle `.cgi` files. You should add the following line in the `srm.conf` file:

```
AddHandler cgi-script .cgi
```

The CGI script directory must also be set up with the `Directory` directive. This is done in the `access.conf` file and should look something like the following:

```
<Directory /home/httpd/htdocs/cgi-bin>
AllowOverride None
Options None
</Directory>
```

As you can see, it is not too hard to set up Apache for handling CGI scripts. Remember that you can only use CGI scripts in the directories that you set up specifically for that purpose. In the previous example, the only directory on the server from which CGI scripts can be executed is the `/home/httpd/htdocs/cgi-bin` directory.

Also remember that CGI scripts must be set to be executable in order for them to be run. Use the `chmod` command to change the permission on CGI scripts so that they are executable.

Apache Security Tips

A Linux system is only as secure as you want it to be. It can either be completely wide open for the whole world, or it can be totally closed and very secure, or it can be anywhere in between the two extremes. Obviously, it takes knowledge to properly implement security on a Linux box. Apache works in the same way. Becoming a good Apache Webmaster takes time and patience. You must be prepared to spend many hours poring over the Apache documentation and configuration files. There are, however, a few tips that you can use immediately that will help you to improve the security of Apache.

First off, take a look at what user and group your Apache server is running as. Make sure that it is not running as any administrative user such as root, daemon, bin, or lp. By default, Apache is configured to run as the nobody user and under the nobody group, this is fine. Just be careful if you ever change either of those settings. If your server happens to be running as a superuser, if someone manages to perform an exploit upon Apache they may be able to gain supcruser access to your machine, and that could be a big problem.

22

Web Serving

The key to keeping your Apache server running smoothly is to know what is going on with it. Make sure you regularly check the server logs for any strange happenings, and also be sure to keep an eye on the other system log files for your Linux system. It is especially important to take a look at the errors your server is generating; you may find some interesting things in Apache's error logs.

Server-side includes can be a security risk, as was mentioned earlier. Be sure that you use them with caution. Do not turn them on throughout your entire site—only where they are required. It is recommended that you not use any SSI on pages where the user is allowed to enter HTML tags because they may try to type in some SSI stuff.

Now, the obvious security tip is to back up regularly. This can't be stressed enough, and yet people still don't do it. If your server ever happens to be compromised, you better hope you have a recent backup because you will probably be reinstalling your entire system from scratch. Even if the system is left intact by the intruder, you never know what backdoors they have introduced for future attacks; thus, you should always reinstall your entire system after such an incident.

Apache Modules

Modules are a very powerful feature of Apache and they make it very easy to add new features. You simply need to tell Apache to load the module. Apache comes with a great number of modules by default, and it is very easy to add additional modules if you want to add more functionality into Apache. For example, it is very easy to add support for PHP to Apache by simply getting the php module and telling Apache to load it.

Adding New Modules

To add a new module to Apache, you must use two directives—the `LoadModule` directive and the `AddModule` directive. The `LoadModule` directive is used first and links the appropriate object file or library file for a specified module to a name. The following is the syntax for the `LoadModule` directive:

```
LoadModule module filename
```

You must first specify the name that the module will be known as in the Apache configuration and then specify the filename for the object or library file.

There is also the `AddModule` directive, which is used to tell Apache which modules to load upon startup. The syntax for the `AddModule` directive is as follows:

```
AddModule module1 module2 ...
```

As you can see, you can list many modules after the directive name, but generally one module is put on each line.

The following is an example of using the `LoadModule` and `AddModule` directives to add PHP3 support to Apache:

```
LoadModule php3_module         modules/libphp3.so

AddModule mod_php3.c
```

There is also a directive that will clear the list of active modules: the `ClearModuleList` directive. After clearing the modules list, you can add modules back into the list using the `AddModule` directive.

Conditional Directives Based Upon Modules

Apache has a directive that you can use when you want to execute certain directives conditionally based upon whether or not a specific module has been loaded into Apache. This is called the `IfModule` directive. A test is passed to the `IfModule` directive, and the conditional directives contained within it are only processed if the result of the test is true. Here is the syntax:

```
<IfModule [!]module_name>
Directive
Directive
...
</IfModule>
```

If the test fails, any directives contained between the `<IfModule>` and the `</IfModule>` are ignored. The format for the test can be one of two things:

- `module_name`
- `!module_name`

In the first case, the directives within the `<IfModule>` are only processed if the specified module name is loaded into Apache. In the second case, the specified directives are only processed if the specified module is not loaded into Apache.

Default Apache Modules

There are a number of modules that come with Apache by default. In this section, we will take a look at each module and briefly cover what each module does. Each module has routines that implement various features of Apache.

The following is the complete list of modules that come with the standard Apache distribution:

- Core—Contains the core Apache features.
- mod_access—Contains the access control routines.
- mod_actions—Routines for filetype/method-based script execution.
- mod_alias—Has the routines that handle aliases and redirects.
- mod_asis—Supports the handling of .asis files.
- mod_auth—Routines to authorize users based on text files.
- mod_auth_anon—Routines to authorize anonymous users.
- mod_auth_db—Routines to authorize users based upon Berkeley DB files.
- mod_auth_dbm—Routines to authorize users by using DBM files.
- mod_auth_digest—Routines to perform MD5 user authentication.
- mod_autoindex—Provides directory listing functions.
- mod_cern_meta—The routines for HTTP header metafiles.
- mod_cgi—Module used to invoke CGI scripts.
- mod_digest—Authentication using MD5.
- mod_dir—Directory handling routines.
- mod_env—Routines for passing environment settings to CGI scripts.
- mod_example—An example module demonstrating usage of the Apache API.
- mod_expires—Contains the Expiration header routines.
- mod_headers—Contains the HTTP header routines.
- mod_imap—Routines to handle imagemaps.
- mod_include—Module to handle server-parsed documents.
- mod_info—Routines for extracting server configuration information.
- mod_log_agent—User agent logging routines.
- mod_log_config—Logging configuration module.
- mod_log_referer—Logging routines for document references.
- mod_mime—Routines to determine document types based upon the file extensions.

- `mod_mime_magic`—Routines to determine document types using "magic numbers."

- `mod_mmap_static`—Routines that map files into memory, improving the speed of serving those pages.

- `mod_negotiation`—Module that performs content negotiation.

- `mod_proxy`—Routines that perform proxy caching.

- `mod_rewrite`—Maps URIs to filenames.

- `mod_setenvif`—Routines to set environment variables.

- `mod_so`—Runtime module loading routines.

- `mod_spelling`—Spelling correction routines for correcting spelling mistakes in URLs.

- `mod_status`—Routines that report on the status of the server.

- `mod_userdir`—Management of user home directories.

- `mod_unique_id`—Used to generate a unique request identifier for each request.

- `mod_usertrack`—Routines for tracking users via cookies.

- `mod_vhost_alias`—Routines for supporting dynamically configured mass virtual hosting.

There are also many more modules available for Apache that do not come with the core distribution. To find out more about what modules are available, you can take a look at the Apache module registry, which is located at `http://modules.apache.org`. I'm sure you will find some very interesting and useful modules there.

Configuring Virtual Hosts

Virtual hosts allow you to host multiple domains from a single machine. Apache supports two different types of virtual hosts: IP-based virtual hosts and name-based virtual hosts. Let's take a look at each of them now.

IP-based Virtual Hosts

IP-based virtual hosts are used when a single machine has several different IP addresses, and you want to run a virtual host on each IP address. Having multiple IP addresses for one machine is known as IP Aliasing, and you can use the `ifconfig` command to configure the IP interfaces.

Setting Up IP-based Virtual Hosts

There are two different ways to set up IP-based virtual hosts under Apache. The first way is to run a separate httpd daemon for each virtual host, and the second way is to configure a single httpd daemon to handle all the virtual hosts. The second way is the preferred method, although there are cases when the first method should be used. The main reason for running separate httpd daemons would be when you want to run each process under different User, Group, Listen, or ServerRoot settings. Unless you have a good reason to run separated httpd daemons for each virtual host, it is recommended that you stick with a single httpd daemon.

To set up virtual hosts using multiple httpd daemons, you can either install a separate copy of Apache for each virtual host or you can simply create multiple configuration files and use the `-f` option when starting Apache to tell httpd which config files to use. Inside the `httpd.conf` file for each virtual host, you can specify which IP address and port it should use with the `Listen` directive. You then can start up each Apache daemon and test your configuration. It is best to simply install a single copy of Apache and then create a new set of configuration files, server root, and doc root directories using the `-f` option when starting each instance of Apache.

To set up virtual hosts using only a single httpd daemon, you only need one install of Apache. Inside the `httpd.conf` file, you must use the `VirtualHost` directive to set up each virtual host. Inside of each `VirtualHost` directive, you can set values for the `ServerAdmin`, `ServerName`, `DocumentRoot`, `ErrorLog`, `TransferLog`, and `CustomLog` directives as they pertain to that specific virtual host. Here is an example configuration for two different virtual hosts, both on different IP addresses:

```
Port 80
ServerName www.example.com

<VirtualHost 192.168.2.50>
  ServerAdmin problems@example.com
  ServerName www.example.com
  DocumentRoot /home/example/html
  ErrorLog /home/example/logs/error_log
  CustomLog /home/example/logs/custom_log
</VirtualHost>

<VirtualHost 192.168.2.55>
  ServerAdmin problem@test.com
  ServerName www.test.com
  DocumentRoot /home/test/html
  ErrorLog /home/test/logs/error_log
```

```
    CustomLog /home/test/logs/custom_log
</VirtualHost>
```

There is also another way to set up these two virtual hosts. You can set one of the virtual hosts to be the default domain, which should be the same name as the actual server's hostname. So, if your server's hostname is www.example.com and the IP address for www.exmaple.com is 192.168.2.50, you can use the following setup:

```
Port 80
DocumentRoot /home/example/html
ServerName www.example.com

<VirtualHost 111.22.33.55>
    ServerAdmin problem@test.com
    ServerName www.test.com
    DocumentRoot /home/test/html
    ErrorLog /home/test/logs/error_log
    CustomLog /home/test/logs/custom_log
</VirtualHost>
```

Name-based Virtual Hosts

The biggest problem with IP-based virtual hosts is that you need a separate IP address for each virtual host, and as you begin hosting many domains from your machine, this can become quite cumbersome. The solution to this problem is name-based virtual hosts; they allow you to host many virtual hosts from a single IP address. Name-based virtual hosts are also easier to manage than IP-based virtual hosts—a relief for many system administrators. The only real drawback to using name-based virtual hosts is that the client's Web browser must be able to support it, a problem that is quickly fading because almost all of the Web browsers in use today support it.

Setting the Value for the `NameVirtualHost` Directive

Configuring name-based virtual hosts looks very similar to configuring IP-based virtual hosts when running a single daemon. The additional part to configuration is that you need to set the value of the `NameVirtualHost` directive, which is set to the IP address that will host the domains. Let's take a look at a sample configuration for name-based virtual hosts:

```
Port 80
ServerName www.server.com
NameVirtualHost 192.168.2.50

<VirtualHost 192.168.2.50>
    ServerAdmin problems@example.com
    ServerName www.example.com
```

22

Web Serving

```
   DocumentRoot /home/example/html
   ErrorLog /home/example/logs/error_log
   CustomLog /home/example/logs/custom_log
</VirtualHost>

<VirtualHost 192.168.2.50>
   ServerAdmin problem@test.com
   ServerName www.test.com
   DocumentRoot /home/test/html
   ErrorLog /home/test/logs/error_log
   CustomLog /home/test/logs/custom_log
</VirtualHost>
```

As you can see, not much has changed to make both the `www.example.com` and the `www.test.com` domains use the same IP address. You must remember to configure the DNS services for both domains so that they are both pointing to the same IP address. In the above setup, the `wws.server.com` is only set up to receive requests on `localhost`, while `www.example.com` takes on the duty of being the main server due to the fact that it appears first in the configuration file.

The `ServerAlias` Directive

There is another very useful directive that you can use inside the `VirtualHost` directive; it is the `ServerAlias` directive. Let's take a look at the previous example, this time using the `ServerAlias` directive as well:

```
Port 80
ServerName www.server.com
NameVirtualHost 192.168.2.50

<VirtualHost 192.168.2.50>
   ServerAdmin problems@example.com
   ServerName www.example.com
   ServerAlias *.example.com
   DocumentRoot /home/example/html
   ErrorLog /home/example/logs/error_log
   CustomLog /home/example/logs/custom_log
</VirtualHost>

<VirtualHost 192.168.2.50>
   ServerAdmin problem@test.com
   ServerName www.test.com
   ServerAlias *.test.com
   DocumentRoot /home/test/html
```

```
    ErrorLog /home/test/logs/error_log
    CustomLog /home/test/logs/custom_log
</VirtualHost>
```

Here, the `ServerAlias` directive is used to tell Apache that if it receives any requests with the domain example.com, regardless of the attached hostname, it will use the specified `VirtualHost` to respond to the requests. So, to connect to the site, I can either type in **www.example.com**, or I can just type in **example.com**. Both will resolve to the `VirtualHost` on 192.168.2.50.

You can also set up Apache to respond differently to different hosts in the same domain. For example, if you only have a single domain, you can set up various virtual hosts that all have the same domain name, yet different sub-domains. The following is an example:

```
Port 80
ServerName www.server.com
NameVirtualHost 192.168.2.50

<VirtualHost 192.168.2.50>
  ServerAdmin problems@example.com
  ServerName www.example.com
  DocumentRoot /home/example/html
</VirtualHost>

<VirtualHost 192.168.2.50>
  ServerAdmin problems@example.com
  ServerName www.dev.example.com
  DocumentRoot /home/example-dev/html
</VirtualHost>

<VirtualHost 192.168.2.50>
  ServerAdmin problems@example.com
  ServerName www.test.example.com
  DocumentRoot /home/example-test/html

</VirtualHost>
```

In addition to simply configuring Apache to respond differently to different IP addresses, you can also tell Apache to respond differently to different ports on the same IP address. For example, the following setup will send the client to the default area if he connects on the default port 80; however, if the client connects on port 443, he will be sent to the secure server area. Port 443 is the default port for handling secure HTTP connections.

```
Listen 80
Listen 443
```

```
ServerName www.server.com
NameVirtualHost 192.168.2.50

<VirtualHost 192.168.2.50:80>
  ServerAdmin problems@example.com
  ServerName www.example.com
  DocumentRoot /home/example/html
</VirtualHost>

<VirtualHost 192.168.2.50:443>
  ServerAdmin problems@example.com
  ServerName www.example.com
  DocumentRoot /home/example-ssl/html

</VirtualHost>
```

This setup will serve the user documents from the `/home/example/html` directory if they connect on port 80, or if the client connects on port 443, it will serve documents from the `/home/example-ssl/html` directory.

Hopefully, you now have an idea of how virtual hosts work, and you understand the differences between IP-based and name-based virtual hosts. Virtual hosts are a very powerful feature of Apache and give Webmasters a considerable amount of power in configuring their Web sites. Adding an additional domain to your Apache configuration is as simple as adding another `VirtualHost` entry. There is almost no limit on the number of virtual hosts that you can have.

Comanche

Red Hat 6.1 also comes with a graphical configuration tool for Apache called Comanche. Comanche is part of The Apache GUI project, the aim of which is to provide a quality cross-platform graphical tool for configuring and managing the Apache Web server and its related software. The name Comanche stands for Configuration MANager for apaCHE.

Installing Comanche

You may have installed Comanche with your default Red Hat Linux installation. If not, you can use the rpm utility to install Comanche at any time. Simply mount your Red Hat CD-ROM and find the Comanche rpm file. Then, as root, use the rpm command to install the rpm archive.

Apache Add-ons

There are many add-on programs and modules that do not come with the default Apache distribution that are really worth looking into. We will take a look at some of these enhancements to Apache in this section.

Apache-SSL

The Apache-SSL server is a secure version of Apache using SSLeay to provide the Secure Sockets Layer (SSL). Apache-SSL is distributed as a set of patches that you apply to an existing Apache source distribution. Due to the highly secure nature of Apache-SSL, you can only use it freely for non-commercial use inside the United States. Elsewhere throughout the world, you can use Apache-SSL for both commercial and non-commercial use for free. If you need to use Apache-SSL commercially in the United States, you should look into either Stronghold or Raven, which are commercial SSL implementations for Apache.

Apache Interface to OpenSSL (`mod_ssl`)

The `mod_ssl` module provides another option for setting up a secure server using Apache; it supports both the Secure Sockets Layer and the Transport Layer Security protocols. The base of `mod_ssl` comes from SSLeay, and has the advantage of being compiled as an Apache module. The same restrictions that apply to Apache-SSL also apply to `mod_ssl`.

Covalent Raven SSL Module for Apache

The Covalent Raven SSL Module for Apache is a commercial alternative to Apache-SSL and `mod_ssl`. It uses the RSA encryption engine, thus providing very strong cryptography functionality. Due to the high cryptographic capabilities of the Raven SSL module, it is only available in the United States and Canada.

mod_php

PHP is a fairly recent server-side scripting language that is embedded within HTML files. There is a module that you can compile for Apache called `mod_php` that will add PHP support to Apache. PHP is quickly becoming a very popular language for writing dynamic Web pages, and it is well known for its excellent database support.

The syntax for PHP is a mixture of C, C++, and Perl, and is very easy to learn. If you have a programming background in either of those languages, you will most likely be able to become fluent with PHP within a few days.

PHP is similar to ASP and ColdFusion in terms of functionality; however, PHP is quickly becoming the server-side scripting language of choice for many Web developers due to the fact that it is Free Software. Another strength of PHP is that it is not tied to any one platform or Web server. It runs under many UNIX versions, Linux, and even Windows NT. As far as Web servers are concerned, PHP runs under both Microsoft IIS and Netscape Enterprise Server in addition to Apache.

To find out more about this powerful Web development language, take a look at the PHP home page, which is located at `http://www.php.net`.

mod_perl

The Perl programming language is one of the most popular scripting languages that is used on the Web today. Many sites attribute their success to the power and flexibility of Perl. There is a project called the Apache/Perl integration project that is dedicated to integrating Perl with Apache.

There is a module available, called `mod_perl`, that allows Apache modules to be written in Perl. In fact, the `mod_perl` module links the Perl runtime library directly into Apache. This gives a significant speed advantage over CGI programs written in Perl and also allows programmers to get into Apache's internals using Perl. Before `mod_perl`, all Apache modules had to be written in C. Now Perl is a valid alternative as well.

The Apache/Perl integration project's home page is located at `http://perl.apache.org`. It is recommended that you visit this site to find out more.

mod_jserv

The `mod_jserv` module is a 100% pure Java servlet engine that is totally compliant with the JavaSoft Java Servlet API version 2.0 specification. The Java Servlet API is an extension to the Java platform that allows Java to be used by Web application developers for adding functionality to Web servers. The `mod_jserv` module is similar to a Java applet, except that its interface is available through the API, not through a GUI interface.

You can use `mod_jserv` with any platform that supports the version 1.1 Java Virtual Machine, which Red Hat Linux 6.0 supports. This module allows for total platform compatibility between Web servers that support the servlet API. To get further information on `mod_jserv`, take a look at The Java Apache project home page at `http://java.apache.org`.

As you can see, there are a number of add-ons that are available for Apache, each of which enhance the feature-set of Apache even further. Since Apache development is an on-going effort, be sure to look at the official Apache Web site (`www.apache.org`) to see the latest Apache additions that are available.

Squid

Squid is a proxy caching server that is available under Linux, and is known for its excellent performance and extensive feature set. Squid supports all the popular Internet protocols, including FTP, gopher, and HTTP. Squid is based upon an ARPA funded project called Harvest. The name "squid" was originally just the code name for the project, but it managed to stick around long enough to become the official name.

Squid is a free software project and is thus the culmination of a number of people's efforts. The lead developer for the project is from the National Laboratory for Applied Network Research, which is a National Science Foundation funded project.

Red Hat Linux 6.1 comes with a squid rpm that may or may not be currently installed on your system. The rpm name is `squid-2.2.STABLE1-1.i386.rpm`, so if you do not currently have it installed, you can get it from your Red Hat Linux CD-ROM and use the rpm command to install it.

22

Web Serving

Features of Squid

The main idea behind squid is the caching of Internet objects. Internet objects are made up of data that is available through the standard Internet protocols including HTTP, FTP, and gopher. The caching is done on a machine that is closer to the client than the source, thus reducing the time it takes to receive the data and also reducing bandwidth.

Squid also has many features that complement its Internet object caching, including the following:

- Caches meta data and host objects in RAM

- Caches DNS lookups

- Implements negative caching of failed requests

- Handles all requests in a single process, unlike many other caching servers

- Support for SSL

- Uses the lightweight Internet Cache Protocol

- Full request logging

As you can see, squid is an extremely powerful and full-featured caching server. The squid distribution consists of several programs, including squid, which is the main server program and dnsserver, a DNS server lookup program.

Starting Squid

The actual squid executable file is used to start and stop squid. However, you generally do not want to directly run the squid executable; instead, you will probably be running a script that calls the squid executable. You can directly call the squid executable if you want, so let's take a look at the command-line options for squid:

- `-a port`—Used to specify the HTTP port number.

- `-d`—Turns on debugging to standard error.

- `-X`—Turns on full debugging.

- `-f file`—Uses the specified file as the configuration file instead of `/etc/squid.conf`.

- `-h`—Prints a help message.

- `-N`—Disables daemon mode.

- `-V`—Enables the virtual host httpd-accelerator.

- `-k`—Sends a signal to the current squid server and exits. The available signals are reconfigure, rotate, shutdown, interrupt, kill, debug, and check.

- `-s`—Turns on syslog logging.

- `-u port`—Used to specify the ICP port number.

- `-v`—Displays the version of squid.

- `-z`—Creates directories for swap files.

- `-C`—Ignores fatal signals.

- `-D`—Turns off initial DNS checks.

- `-F`—Performs a foreground fast store rebuild.

- `-Y`—During a fast rebuild, only returns `UDP_HIT` or `UDP_MISS_NOFETCH`.

When the squid server program starts, it first spawns a configurable number of dnsserver processes. Each of the dnsserver processes can perform a single DNS lookup.

Configuring Squid

The main configuration file for squid is called `squid.conf` and is located in the `/etc` directory. The main items that you must configure for squid include the HTTP port number, the ICP request port number, the incoming and outgoing request, firewall access information, and timeout information.

If you open up the /etc/squid.conf file, you will find out that it is quite large. However, there are only a few items that you need to configure to get a working squid server.

- cache_peer—The cache_peer setting is used to specify a parent cache, if one exists. If you are using a parent cache, put the parent cache information here.

- cache_mem—Here you must put the amount of RAM you would like to use for cache.

- cache_dir—Here you put the directory you would like to devote to storing the cached files, along with the amount of hard drive space you want to use.

- acl, http_access, icp_access—These three configuration parameters are used to set up exactly what hosts are allowed to access the squid cache.

- cache_mgr—Here you put the email address of the squid manager.

- cache_effective_user—The user that squid will run as.

- visible_hostname—The hostname that the cache will have.

After you configure all these items, you must stop and restart squid for the changes to take effect. There are also other items in the /etc/squid.conf file that you may want to set up, but the previously listed options will get you a basic working cache. You should read through the entire contents of the /etc/squid.conf file to get an idea of all the available options.

Squid is a complex program and we can't cover all the configuration possibilities here, so be sure to check the documentation that comes with squid if you would like to learn more.

Other Web Servers

In this section, we will take a look at some of the other Web servers that are available under Linux. While Apache is an excellent choice, there are alternatives, and, in some situations, certain alternatives may be better choices than Apache. Apache is very much a general-purpose Web server, and under certain conditions you may find that a Web server dedicated to a specific purpose may be a better choice.

Roxen Challenger

The Roxen Challenger is a free Web server distributed under the GPL that has commercial add-ons and support available. It is developed by a company in Sweden called Idonex. The Roxen Challenger Web server boasts 128-bit and 164-bit encryption using SSL3 and has many enticing features, including platform independence, a built-in scripting language called RXML, and a graphical control center.

Several commercial add-on packages are available, including the following:

- **Roxen Sitebuilder**—A Web site creation and management tool

- **Roxen LogView**—A Web server log file analysis program

- **Roxen Intraseek**—A very capable search engine

- **Roxen database API pro**—A Web-to-database interface API

To find out more about Roxen Challenger and its related products, check out the Web site at http://www.roxen.com.

Red Hat Secure Server

Red Hat Software sells a secure version of Apache that is fully integrated with Red Hat Linux. It uses the RSA encryption schemes and is thus only available for sale within the United States or Canada.

Stronghold

The Stronghold Web server is another secure server alternative that is based upon Apache. It also uses SSL and has commercial support.

IBM HTTP Server Powered by Apache

IBM sells a secure version of Apache that supports SSL V2 and V3 and is commercially supported. IBM's HTTP Server is bundled with the IBM WebSphere Application Server.

Boa

Boa is a free Web server that is designed for high performance, and it is distributed under the GPL. The two main goals behind the development of Boa were to design a fast and secure Web server. Boa doesn't have nearly as many features as some other Web servers; for example, it does not support server-side includes. On the other hand, Boa can generally get better performance than most other Web servers. If you are looking for lots of features, you probably want to try something else besides Boa. However, if you want a very fast Web server, then Boa looks very promising.

One of the main differences of Boa from other Web servers is that Boa runs only as a single process. While most other Web servers fork for each client connection, Boa does not do this. Instead, Boa handles all of the connections internally and will only fork off CGI processes.

The boa home page is at www.boa.org.

dhttpd

Like Boa, dhttpd is designed for speed and efficiency. However, dhttpd is even more minimalistic than Boa and does not even include support for CGI programs. Thus, dhttpd is not ideal for all Web serving purposes, however it can be used for special purposes. For example, you can set up dhttpd to just serve all the graphic images for a particular Web site, thus speeding up the loading time of graphics. You can use Apache to handle all other duties.

The Web site for dhttpd is located at `http://uts.cc.utexas.edu/~foxx/dhttpd/index.html`.

fhttpd

The fhttpd Web server was designed specially to handle file transfers. The name fhttpd stands for file/hypertext transfer protocol daemon. It is a fairly full-featured Web server, supporting HTTP 0.9 and 1.0, with 1.1 support in the works. It can handle CGI scripts, server-side includes, and even virtual servers.

Although there are still some important features missing in fhttpd, such as HTTP 1.1 and posting using the PUT request, it looks very promising.

The home page for fhttpd is located at `http://www.fhttpd.org/`.

ghttpd

ghttpd is a fast and efficient HTTP server that has CGI support. ghttpd has a small memory imprint and is capable of handling thousands of simultaneous connections. It is ideal for large and small Web sites. It is very simple to configure, with only a few options to change if changing is needed at all. You easily can have ghttpd up and running within two minutes because of its very simple configuration file and installation routine. ghttpd will run on the majority of UNIX systems. ghttpd even has support for virtual hosts and inetd. The ghttpd home page is located at `http://www.gaztek.co.uk/ghttpd/index.html`.

thttpd

thttpd stands for tiny/turbo/throttling HTTP daemon. It is a very small, simple, fast, and secure Web server, while also having quite a nice feature set. thttpd supports HTTP/1.1 and handles high loads better than many of the more popular Web servers. There is also a special feature the thttpd has that no other Web server currently has called URL-traffic-based throttling. thttpd is ideal for lower-end servers because it does not use nearly as much resources as most of the other available Web servers.

To find out more information, check out the home page at `http://www.acme.com/software/thttpd/`.

WN

WN is a very full-featured Web server that is distributed for free under the GPL. It supports HTTP/1.1 and also has some very advanced features that are normally only available under CGI programs. WN was designed with the following three goals in mind: security, robustness, and flexibility.

WN has the following advanced features built in:

- **Searching**—WN has excellent navigational aids built into the server, including title searches, list searches, index searches, keyword searches, and context searches.

- **Parsed Text, Server-Side Includes and Wrappers**—WN has the ability to insert text into files being served. It also has full support for server-side includes and wrappers.

- **Filters**—You can apply filters to any files being served by WN. A filter can parse and modify a file before it's served, and can accomplish stuff like on-the-fly compression and decompression.

- **Ranges**—When accessing a file from a WN server, a range can be supplied and only the line numbers within that range will be displayed.

The WN home page is located at `http://hopf.math.nwu.edu/`.

Summary

In this chapter, we examined Web serving under Red Hat Linux. In particular, we looked at the Apache Web server, Squid, and some alternatives to Apache. You should have a good idea of how to go about configuring both Apache and Squid.

This chapter only lays the groundwork for getting started using Linux as a Web server. I trust your journey into the world of Web serving will not end here. There are many books and lots of online documentation available that will allow you to explore this topic extensively.

News Services

In This Chapter

- So You Want to Run a News Server? *672*
- INN and Friends *676*
- News Clients *705*
- Places to Ask Questions and Find Answers *711*

This chapter discusses a bit of the history of Usenet, how it works, and what it takes to run a Usenet server. We'll only discuss a few of the software packages you can use for this, but there are several ways to use any Usenet server software.

So You Want to Run a News Server?

Usenet news started when two departments on opposite sides of a college campus decided they wanted to exchange bulletin board postings. They wrote some software that exchanged posts to each others' servers, and that evolved over time into what we now know as Usenet news.

How does it work? Each message has two pieces of information that keep the message from being duplicated: the Path header and the message-id. The Path header tells you where this article has been so that you don't send it back to where it came from. That would be a waste of time and bandwidth. The message-id is a pseudo-unique message identifier. The message-id is usually based on a timestamp and the host from which the message was posted. A typical message-id would look like `<12345@hostname.domain.com>`. Each news server keeps track of the message-ids it has or has seen recently. If the server is offered a message with a duplicate message-id, the server refuses that article. A decent sized private server usually will keep between one and two million articles on hand at any given time. The size of a typical article may vary widely. In any event, you can see that a news server is going to use a lot of resources.

Capacity Planning

There are two things to consider when thinking about the capacity of a Usenet server. The disk capacity of the system that will be the server is the most obvious, but you must also consider the capacity of the Internet connection to the site at which the server will reside.

Server Storage Capacity

A full newsfeed (I hope you are sitting down) can exceed 30GB a day. Yes, that's gigabytes! That's more bandwidth than a full T1. Mind you, that includes all the binary newsgroups and all the commercial spam that nobody really wants to read. After filtering all that out, it gets down to a much more manageable number—usually less than a gigabyte a day. If you want to carry the binaries, you will need much more disk storage. We'll talk more about this in the discussion on tweaking a server, but you should consider using two or more disks for a Usenet server regardless of the size.

Now we get down to the meat of it. How much disk space do you really need? Well, that depends. That depends on how long you want to have the news around. Let's say you get a feed based on what your users will be interested in. Start with `comp.*`, `rec.*`, and `soc.*`. That should be about 100-200MB/day. Let's use 150MB as a round number for calculations. If you want to keep articles for two weeks (a reasonable time), your news spool will be 2100MB, or about 2.0GB. However, that's just for your news spool (where the articles are stored). You will also have to allocate space for your history database (so the server remembers which articles it has). A good way to figure that is to allow about 100 bytes for each article. Articles from this newsfeed (`comp.*`, `rec.*`, `soc.*`) should be about the average article size, around 3KB. You do the math and figure that a 2GB news spool will hold about 700,000 articles. So, at 100 bytes for each article, the history file would need to be about 70MB.

When planning disk usage on a Usenet server, it's always better to have too much than not enough, so for the preceding setup, I'd want a system with at least 4GB of disk space just for news use. I'd probably put 3GB toward spool, and the rest toward the news server's program storage, the history database, and the log files. Keep in mind that Usenet is growing every day, and as it does the traffic increases. This increase in traffic means something for you as well: You'll need more disk space.

I remember reading the announcement that a full newsfeed would no longer fit over a 2400-baud modem. There was some excitement among news admins when that announcement came, but nothing like the dismay felt when it was learned that a full newsfeed would no longer fit over a full T1. It was then that we all saw what kind of unpredictable beast we were trying to tame.

Bandwidth

This brings me to the second type of capacity you need to consider. How much bandwidth does your site have? I've run a limited newsfeed (similar to the one discussed) across a dual-channel ISDN line. It would use all our bandwidth at times, but not usually. If you are limited to ISDN, or a fractional T1, you might want to carry only a partial newsfeed. You definitely won't want to carry `alt.binaries.*`. The `alt.binaries` hierarchy, in my estimations, accounts for more than 60% of the Usenet bulk. There may not be as many articles posted in these groups as in the rest, but they are much larger on average because many of them include encoded binary files (pictures, fonts, sounds, and so on).

There are really two types of newsfeeds: full feeds and interest-based feeds. I'd suggest that unless you want to become a major hub in Usenet, you start with an interest-based feed. Figure out what your users want and give it to them. Start with a small feed as outlined previously and add groups as requested. A full newsfeed actually won't fit across two T1 lines anymore. One hundred percent of a T1 is about 16GB of traffic a day. You never really get 100% of your bandwidth, so if you assume 75%, you can get about 12GB of news each day. Don't forget about your outgoing newsfeeds and your user traffic. Now you're down to about 10GB each day on a T1. For a full newsfeed, you would need three T1 lines to just barely keep up. If you really want a full newsfeed, you may want to consider co-locating your server somewhere upstream from your Internet site.

Running a News Server

Usenet is very unpredictable. It might even be considered alive. It consumes (disk), it reproduces (you're thinking about starting a server, or you wouldn't still be reading this chapter), it grows (at an exponential rate), and it repairs itself (okay, you repair it when your server goes down, but then you're a part of it also). The biggest problem you are going to have with a news server is that it is very hungry. It will use a lot of disk space. Once you get a server up and running and accepting a feed from a peer, your daily maintenance consists mainly of watching disk space. To keep your available space in check, you'll find that you're constantly adjusting the amount of timebefore old articles are deleted (your expire times).You'll want to start with fairly short expire times (a few days) and expand as your disks allow. Then just when you think you've got it right, along comes a surge in traffic and you'll have to back your expire times down some.

The daily reports that come from the nightly maintenance program contain a lot of information. You should pay attention to disk space and your incoming and outgoing traffic. If you find that you are suddenly not sending any articles to any of your peers, or you aren't accepting any articles from any of them, you might have a problem. If you find that your disk space is filling up rapidly and nothing seems to be expiring, you most definitely have a problem. Disk space is your biggest worry. Other than disk space problems, your readers will bring most other problems with the news server to your attention. Things such as no new articles coming in or no outgoing posts will probably be brought to your attention before you notice them in your daily reports. Next to disk space and traffic problems, you'll have a lot of mail to read because of your Usenet server. It all gets sent to news or `usenet@your.domain`. You'll want to add those aliases to your mail configuration. Refer to Chapter 20, "Electronic Mail," for more information on that. Other problems are related to the specific news server software (which we'll discuss later), or hardware failure, which we can't do anything about.

Daily reports are generated by a cron job (see Chapter 33, "Automation," for more information on `cron`) that runs every night to do automated server maintenance. The daily reports get mailed to the news user. They contain information about who's using your server, the control message activity (group creations and deletions), disk usage, and other server usage information. In addition to the daily reports, you are going to get a lot of control messages in your mailbox. Control messages do just that—they help control the Usenet newsfeed. There are many types of control messages. The ones you will see in your mailbox are mostly going to be newsgroup and rmgroup messages. These messages will create and remove (respectively) newsgroups from your system as you choose to process them. There are ways to automate processing these messages, but those are software-specific and will be discussed later.

Outsourcing News Services

One thing you may want to consider as an alternative to running your own Usenet news server is outsourcing your news to a third party. There are a couple of ways you can do this, but they both accomplish one major goal—they reduce the maintenance tasks associated with the Usenet news server.

Port redirection, which is the simplest solution, simply does what its name implies. Connections made to a certain port are redirected to a specified port on another system (usually offsite). Responses to these redirected requests are routed through the redirector so that the client program never knows the difference between a redirection system and an actual news server. This way, you can pay someone else to run your news server for you. You won't use any more bandwidth than the articles that your users read, and you won't have any of the headaches associated with running another service for your users. Also, news outsourcing companies typically will carry a full feed, and being practiced news administrators, they can provide a higher level of service than you could as a beginning news administrator. Software to do such port redirection can be found for free. One very good example of such software is redir. A good place to look would be freshmeat at `http://www.freshmeat.net`.

Pure port redirection, however, will not be an acceptable solution if you want to have local newsgroups. In this case, you might consider running NNTPCache. This would let you have a local Usenet news server for your local groups (presumably fairly low traffic) and also redirect requests for other newsgroups to a third-party server. There are other advantages to this type of software, but we'll talk about that later when we talk about NNTPCache.

INN and Friends

There a several options, both commercial and non-commercial, when considering Usenet news server software. We'll discuss the non-commercial packages that are most widely used. The commercial packages are directed more at large servers, and if you're interested in them, I'm sure a search on your favorite search engine will turn up some info for you. This section talks about INN (pronounced eye-en-en), NNTPCache, and Diablo.

INN is the most widely used Usenet server. It has the most bells and whistles and can be more complicated to set up. INN allows you, the news administrator, more control over your newsfeed. It allows more options for filtering articles and, because it's widely used, it has many support programs and reporting scripts written for it. Although they may take more effort to configure, the extra features are, in my opinion, worth the trouble. However, they don't all have to be configured, so the installation of INN can be very simple. INN is available from `http://www.isc.org/inn.html`.

NNTPCache executes on a local system pretending to be an NNTP server. In fact, what it does is pass certain NNTP commands through to real Usenet news servers based on various pattern-matching rules. NNTPCache then takes the output from those servers and caches it. The next time the same article is read by another user, the previously cached article is sent directly from the cache without consulting the remote servers. NNTPCache is available from `http://www.nntpcache.org/`.

Diablo was originally designed as simply a large pipe transport server, usually used at the ends of a full feed. The Diablo news transit system was designed to replace INN on Usenet backbone servers. It is extremely efficient, and if all you're going to do is newsfeeds from Usenet servers to other Usenet servers, Diablo is probably what you want to use.

Installing INN

There are a couple of ways to set up INN. You can use an RPM or download the source code and compile and install it. If you're a beginning user, I'd suggest the RPM. It installs a fully functional server that is ready for your configuration.

Installing with an RPM

One major difference when using an RPM for INN is where the configuration files are located. As you can see in Figure 23.1, the RPM spreads your config files out across your system. This is not a problem as long as you know where all the files are. If you cannot find a config file with the RPM installation, `rpm -ql inn` will list all the files in the RPM for you.

FIGURE 23.1
The location of config files after an RPM install.

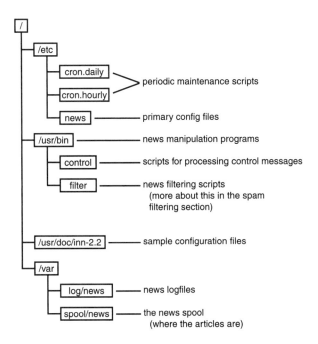

```
/
├── /etc
│     ├── cron.daily  ─┐
│     ├── cron.hourly ─┴── periodic maintenance scripts
│     └── news ──────────── primary config files
├── /usr/bin ───────────── news manipulation programs
│     ├── control ──────── scripts for processing control messages
│     └── filter ───────── news filtering scripts
│                          (more about this in the spam
│                          filtering section)
├── /usr/doc/inn-2.2 ───── sample configuration files
└── /var
      ├── log/news ─────── news logfiles
      └── spool/news ───── the news spool
                           (where the articles are)
```

After installing the RPM, there are some changes I prefer to make. I prefer to have the cron jobs executing directly out of the news user's `crontab`. The RPM installation also runs `rnews` by default. `rnews` is used for receiving a UUCP feed; however, UUCP feeds are all but gone. If you are still using a UUCP feed, the `rnews` man page and the INN FAQ (available at `http://www.blank.org/innfaq/`) should provide you with enough information on `rnews`. As rare as UUCP feeds are anymore, I won't discuss them any further except to say that the `rnews` cron job is not necessary. The file `/etc/cron.daily/inn-cron-expire` contains the following:

```
#!/bin/sh
/sbin/chkconfig innd && su - news -c "/usr/bin/news.daily delayrm"
```

Once moved to the news user's `crontab` file (refer to Chapter 33), you'll only need the part of the file that is in quotes. Thus, the news user's `crontab` file should look like this:

```
0 2 * * * /usr/bin/news.daily delayrm
```

This will run the news expire process each morning at 2 a.m. You should also add the `/etc/cron.hourly/inn-cron-nntpsend` jobs to the news user's `crontab`. Again, you'll only need the last part of the line. The file looks like this:

```
#!/bin/sh
/sbin/chkconfig innd && su - news -c /usr/bin/nntpsend
```

23

News Services

You'll only need to add /usr/bin/nntpsend to the crontab for news. Also, nntpsend should be run more often than every hour. Running nntpsend more often will send more small batches of news to your peers, instead of a few large batches. Running it too often will be wasteful.Running it every 15 minutes is about right. So, the news user's crontab file will now look like this:

```
0 2 * * * /usr/bin/news.daily delayrm
0,15,30,45 * * * * /usr/bin/nntpsend
```

This will run nntpsend once every 15 minutes. Once you've made those changes, the RPM install will be much more manageable.

The only other configuration changes will need to be made to both the RPM version and the source installed version. If you are using an RPM version, you can skip the next section.

Installing from Source

Before you even start unpacking the source for INN, you should make sure you have a couple of packages installed. Perl is required to build and install many subsystems of INN. Although Perl 4 will work for some of these scripts, Perl 5 is recommended. If you want to do spam filtering, you must have Perl 5. This shouldn't be a problem, though, because Red Hat systems have Perl 5 installed by default. If it's not installed, you'll want to install it now. It is available as an RPM with the Red Hat distribution, or you can get the source and compile it from http://www.perl.com.

Another package that you might want to install is PGP. PGP allows you to use INN's support for cryptographic authentication of control messages. PGP and information on PGP is available at http://www.cryptography.org. PGP is not required, but after you see how many control messages you'll get every day, you'll want to automate processing of them. PGP will allow you to do so securely.

First, download the source for INN from ftp.isc.org in the directory /isc/inn. Choose the latest version of the file from this directory. The files are named inn-<version>.tar.gz. As of this writing the latest version is 2.2, so the latest file is inn-2.2.tar.gz. To extract the source from the archive, execute the following:

```
gunzip -c <inn-src-file> | tar -xf -
```

This creates a directory where the INN source resides.

Before beginning installation, you should make sure that there is a user on your system named news and that this user's primary group is set to a group called news. The home directory of this user should be set to the directory under which you want to install INN (/usr/local/news is the default and is a good choice). INN will install itself as this user and group. You can change these if you want, but these are the defaults and it's easier to stick with them on a new installation.

INN 2.2 uses the GNU `configure` program to make configuration rather painless. Unless you have a very unique setup, `configure` should be able to completely configure INN for you. If you want to change the defaults, you can start the `configure` script with one or more command-line options. The most commonly used options are described in the following list.

- `--prefix=PATH`—Sets the installation prefix for INN. The default is `/usr/local/news`. All of INN's programs and support files are installed under this directory. You should set this to the home directory of your news user (it will make installation and maintenance easier). Defaults to `/usr/local/news`.

- `--with-perl`—Enables support for Perl, allowing you to install filter scripts written in Perl. Highly recommended, because many of the really good spam filters are written in Perl. You will need Perl 5.004 or later installed on your system to enable this option.

- `--disable-shared`—Does not create shared libraries.

- `--disable-static`—Does not create static libraries.

If you want to change any other parameters, such as the location of your news spool or your history file, run `./configure --help` and you will see a list of command-line options you can use with `configure`. A suggested set of options, provided you have the necessary software installed, is `./configure --with-perl`.

If the `configure` program runs successfully, you are ready to build the distribution. From the root of the INN source tree, type **make**.

At this point you can step away from the computer for a little while and have a quick snack while INN compiles. It shouldn't take too long. On a decently fast system, it should only take five or ten minutes at the most to build. On my workstation (Pentium II 266, 128MB RAM), it took about three and a half minutes. Once the build completes successfully, you are ready to install INN. To install INN, you should be logged in as `root` and then type **make install**.

This will install INN under the install directory (`/usr/local/news`) unless you specified another prefix to the configure script. You are now ready for the really fun part: configuring your copy of INN!

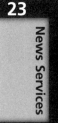

Choosing an Article Storage Format

INN supports three methods of storing articles on your system. Each method has specific advantages and disadvantages, as discussed in the following paragraphs. These storage methods are

- Traditional

- Timehash

- CNFS

Traditional—This is the storage method used by all previous versions of INN. Articles are stored as individual text files whose names are the same as the article number. The articles are divided up into directories based on the newsgroup name. For example, article 12345 in `news.software.nntp` would be stored in the article spool under the path `news/software/nntp/12345`.

> *Advantages*: Solid time-tested code, compatible with all of the third-party INN add-ons available, gives you fine control over article retention times, and is probably the easiest to understand.
>
> *Disadvantages*: Takes a fast computer with a fast I/O system to keep up with current Usenet traffic volumes due to filesystem overhead. Groups with heavy traffic tend to create a bottleneck because of inefficiencies in storing large numbers of article files in a single directory.

Timehash—Articles are stored as files as in the traditional storage method, but are divided up into directories based on the arrival time so that no directory contains enough files to cause a bottleneck.

> *Advantages*: Heavy traffic groups do not cause bottlenecks; fine control of article retention time is still possible.
>
> *Disadvantages*: Still suffers from speed degradation due to filesystem overhead.

CNFS—CNFS stores articles sequentially in preconfigured buffer files. When the end of the buffer is reached, new articles are stored from the beginning of the buffer, overwriting older articles.

> *Advantages*: Blazingly fast because no file creations or deletions are necessary to store an article. Does not require manual article expiration; old articles are deleted to make room for new ones when the buffers get too full. Also, with CNFS your server will never throttle itself due to a full spool disk, and you can restrict groups to just

certain buffer files so that they can never use more than the amount of disk space you allocate to them.

Disadvantages: Article retention times are more difficult to control because old articles are overwritten automatically.

In general, if you plan to carry a full newsfeed and want to actually have your server keep up with the traffic, you need to use CNFS. If you just want to carry a subset of newsgroups, the traditional storage method is probably what you want. Remember, you can only have one type of article storage format on a server at a time. Also, converting storage formats is a major undertaking. Take some time to choose your format now and stick with it.

Configuring INN

> **Note**
>
> Most of this section comes from the INSTALL file that comes with the INN source distribution. I've made some comments about a few gotchas and I've reworded some things that wouldn't be clear to a layperson. It's a very cookbook method of setting things up, and should be used as a guide. What you'll probably run as a news server will be configured slightly differently than what we talk about here.

One nice thing about using the source code to do your install is that the default location of everything related to news is /usr/local/news. That makes this directory a great location for the news user's home directory. When you login as the news user, you'll be in the right place by default.

All of the configuration files we'll be tweaking are in /usr/local/news/etc (~news/etc if you've set the news user's home directory as I've suggested. For the rest of the chapter, we'll assume you have). Now is the time to also mention that the wildcard pattern matching used in INN is known as the "wildmat syntax" in Usenet. These are simple wildcard matches using the asterisk (*) as the wildcard character, much like the simple wildcard expansion used by UNIX shells (but unlike UNIX shells, you cannot do full regular expressions; only the asterisk is supported).

In many cases, wildmat patterns can be specified in a comma-separated list to indicate a list of newsgroups. When used in this fashion, each pattern is checked in turn to see if it matches, and the last pattern in the line that matches the group name is used. Patterns beginning with "!" mean to exclude groups matching that pattern. For example:

```
*, !comp.*, comp.os.*
```

In this case, we're saying we match everything (*), except that we don't match anything under comp (!comp.*), unless it is actually under the comp.os hierarchy (comp.os.*). This is because non-comp groups will match only the first pattern (so we want them). comp.os groups will match all three patterns (so we want them too because the third pattern counts in this case), and all other comp groups will match the first and second patterns and will be excluded by the second pattern.

In most INN configuration files, lines beginning with a pound sign (#) are considered comments and are ignored. Any deviations from this practice should be noted in the description for that particular file.

inn.conf

The first file we'll take a look at is the inn.conf file. This file is the "mother of all config files" as far as INN is concerned. It tells where everything else is located, and some important information about the server.

Listing 23.1 is the default inn.conf that comes with the source distribution.

LISTING 23.1   Default inn.conf

```
##  $Revision: 1.24.2.1 $
##  inn.conf -- inn configuration data
##  Format:
##       <parameter>:<whitespace><value>
##
##  See the inn.conf(5) man page for a full description of each
##  of these options
##
##  Blank values are allowed for certain parameters
##  -------------------------------
# All parameters must exist
#
organization:         A poorly-installed InterNetNews site
server:               localhost
pathhost:             cartman.hackboy.com
moderatormailer:
domain:
fromhost:
pathalias:
complaints:
mta:                  /usr/sbin/sendmail -oi %s
mailcmd:              /usr/local/news/bin/innmail
checkincludedtext:    false
```

LISTING 23.1 continued

```
maxforks:              10
maxartsize:            1000000
nicekids:              4
nicenewnews:           0
verifycancels:         false
logcancelcomm:         false
wanttrash:             false
remembertrash:         true
linecountfuzz:         0
peertimeout:           3600
clienttimeout:         600
allownewnews:          true
localmaxartsize:       1000000
logartsize:            true
logipaddr:             true
logsitename:           true
maxconnections:        50
artcutoff:             14
icdsynccount:          10
hiscachesize:          0
readertrack:           false
strippostcc:           false
status:                0
timer:                 0
readerswhenstopped:    true
noreader:              false
extendeddbz:           false
nnrpdoverstats:        false
storeonxref:           true
nnrpdcheckart:         true
storemsgid:            true
usecontrolchan:        false
mergetogroups:         false
backoffauth:           false
backoffdb:             /usr/local/news/db/backoff
backoffpostfast:       0L
backoffpostslow:       1L
backofftrigger:        10000L
mimeversion:
mimecontenttype:
mimeencoding:
refusecybercancels:    false
```

23

News Services

LISTING 23.1 continued

```
activedenable:        false
activedupdate:        30
activedport:          1119
nnrpperlauth:         false
#
#
# These options are unlikely to need changing in most situations
#
chaninacttime:        600
chanretrytime:        300
pauseretrytime:       300
nntplinklog:          false
nntpactsync:          200
badiocount:           5
blockbackoff:         120
#
# ------------------------------------
# Changing these options can have an effect on the way articles are
# stored and may require recreating the spool and/or database files
#
wireformat:           false
xrefslave:            false
nnrpdposthost:
nnrpdpostport:        119
spoolfirst:           false
writelinks:           true
storageapi:           false
articlemmap:          false
overviewmmap:         true
bindaddress:          all
sourceaddress:        any
port:                 119
#
## Keywords-in-overview options
## Enabling this without stopping innd and deleting the existing overview
## database and adding  will probably confuse a lot of things. You must
## have compiled this support in too.
#
keywords:             false
keylimit:             512
keyartlimit:          100000
keymaxwords:          250
```

LISTING 23.1   continued

```
#
# Other options
innflags:
doinnwatch:             true
innwatchsleeptime:      600
pgpverify:              true
controlfailnotice:      false
logcycles:              3
innwatchpauseload:      1500
innwatchhiload:         2000
innwatchloload:         1000
innwatchspoolspace:     8000
innwatchbatchspace:     800
innwatchlibspace:       25000
innwatchspoolnodes:     200
docnfsstat:             false
#
# -------------------------------
# Paths to various aspects of the news system
#
pathnews:               /usr/local/news
pathbin:                /usr/local/news/bin
pathfilter:             /usr/local/news/bin/filter
pathcontrol:            /usr/local/news/bin/control
pathdb:                 /usr/local/news/db
pathetc:                /usr/local/news/etc
pathrun:                /usr/local/news/run
pathlog:                /usr/local/news/log
pathhttp:               /usr/local/news/log
pathtmp:                /usr/local/news/tmp
pathspool:              /usr/local/news/spool
patharticles:           /usr/local/news/spool/articles
pathoverview:           /usr/local/news/spool/overview
pathoutgoing:           /usr/local/news/spool/outgoing
pathincoming:           /usr/local/news/spool/incoming
patharchive:            /usr/local/news/spool/archive
pathuniover:            /usr/local/news/spool/uniover
overviewname:           .overview
#
# -------------------------------
```

23

News Services

It's not a small file, and that's testament to how complex a system we're dealing with here. Keep in mind that there are many config files also.

Table 23.1 shows some of the parameters in the file. You don't need to change all of them because the defaults will usually work.

TABLE 23.1 `inn.conf` **Parameters**

Parameter	Explanation
Organization	Set to the name of your organization as you want it to appear in the Organization: header of all local posts. This will be overridden by the value of the ORGANIZATION environment variable (if it exists). If neither this parameter nor the environment variable are set, no Organization: header will be added.
Pathhost	This is the name of your news server as you want it to appear in the Path header of all postings that travel through your server (this includes local posts and incoming posts that you forward out to other sites). If no pathhost is specified, the FQDN of the machine will be used instead.
Domain	Sets the domain name for your server. This is normally determined automatically by INN, but in some cases it is necessary to set it manually. For example, if you are running NIS on a SunOS system and your hostnames are not fully qualified (that is, your systems are named xxxx instead of xxxx.domain.com), you will need to use this option to set your domain name manually. If in doubt, leave this option commented out or remove it completely.
maxartsize	This is the maximum size of articles this server will accept through a newsfeed. Articles larger than this size will be rejected. GOTCHA: You might think that decreasing this setting will prevent large articles from hogging your bandwidth. However, all it will do is make the server throw articles larger than this size away after it's completed downloading them. It's not a bad idea to lower this parameter to keep large articles from taking up space.
complaints	If present, this address is used to add an X-Complaints-To: header to all local posts. The usual value would be something like abuse@your.domain or postmaster@your.domain. If not specified, the newsmaster email address will be used.
allownewnews	If set to true, INN will support the NEWNEWS command for news readers. This will really kill your server performance and it is strongly suggested that you set this to false. GOTCHA: The default is true. Change it. I don't know why it's distributed this way, but it's not a good idea.

TABLE 23.1   continued

Parameter	Explanation
localmaxartsize	This is the maximum allowed size of locally posted articles. Articles larger than this size will be rejected. GOTCHA: Unless you'll be making large posts to local newsgroups (not distributed to Usenet at large), the default parameter is too big. Large files should be made available through http or ftp access, and a link posted to Usenet. Change it. A reasonable size is 50,000-100,000 bytes.
status timer	Determines how often status and timer updates are written to the log files. The value is specified in seconds with a value of 0 disabling logging. The suggested value is 300 seconds (5 minutes).
storageapi	Set to yes if articles should be stored using the Storage Manager API. You must set this to no if you are using the traditional article storage method or yes if you are using timehash or CNFS. See the section "Choosing an Article Storage Format" for more information.
extendeddbz	This is only used if you did not configure INN for tagged hash and you are using the storage API. If set to yes, overview offset information for articles is stored in the DBZ history hash file as well as in the history text file. This will make the hash file three times larger, but should increase performance for news readers when they retrieve article overview information. If you don't mind using 200-300MB of extra space for your history database and memory, you should set this to yes.
nnrpdoverstats	If set to yes, nnrpd will log statistics about how much time was spent during the various stages of reading article overview information. Not terribly useful unless you are trying to track down news reader performance problems.
hiscachesize	The size in kilobytes to use for caching recently used history file entries. Setting this to 0 disables history caching. History caching can greatly increase the number of articles per second that your server is capable of processing. A value of 16384 (16MB) is a good choice if you can spare the RAM.
overviewmmap	Overview data is mmaped and reading overview would be faster with this.

23

News Services

TABLE 23.1   continued

Parameter	Explanation

usecontrolchan	All control messages, except cancels, will be processed in batch mode by controlchan. Otherwise, they will be processed one-by-one with forked processes from innd. To reduce excessive load when many control messages arrive in a short time, this is useful and recommended. Controlchan will log its error to syslog, if Sys::Syslog is available. Otherwise it logs to errlog. To enable Sys::Syslog, you need to do following:
	`# cd /usr/include`
	` # h2ph *`
	`  # cd /usr/include/sys`
	`  # h2ph *`
	GOTCHA: Again, this is by default not configured the recommended way. Change it. And, enabling syslog as above is a good idea too.

These are just some parameters you should look over. If you want a complete description, look in the man page for inn.conf. You can read the man page with this command:

```
man /usr/local/news/man/man5/inn.conf.5
```

> **Note**
>
> If /usr/local/news/man is in your MANPATH, you can just do man inn.conf. This is an exercise left to the reader. (I hated when my professors said that, so I take a certain pleasure in saying it to you.)

newsfeeds

The newsfeeds file determines how incoming articles are redistributed to your peers and to other INN processes. The newsfeeds file is very versatile and contains dozens of options; we will touch on just the basics here. The newsfeeds man page contains more detailed information.

The newsfeeds file is organized as a series of feed entries. Each feed entry is composed of four fields separated by colons. Entries may span multiple lines by using the backslash (\) to indicate that the next line is a continuation of the current line.

```
my-feed-site.domain.com/exclude-list\
        :newsgroup-list\
        :Tm:innfeed!
```

The first field in an entry is the name of the feed. It must be unique, and for feeds to other news servers it is usually set to the actual hostname of the remote server (this makes things easier). Optionally, a slash and an exclude list can follow the name. If the feed name or any of the names in the exclude list appear in the path line of an article, that article will not be forwarded to the feed because it is assumed that it has passed through that site once already. The exclude list is useful when a news server's hostname is not the same as what it puts in the path header of its articles, or when you don't want a feed to receive articles from a certain source.

The second field specifies a set of desired newsgroups and distribution lists, given as newsgroup-pattern/distribution-list. The distribution list is not described here; see the `newsfeeds` man page for information. The newsgroup pattern is a wildmat-style pattern list as described earlier, with one minor addition: Patterns beginning with "@" will cause any articles posted to groups matching that pattern to be dropped, even if they match patterns for groups that *are* wanted. Otherwise, articles that match both "want" and "don't want" patterns are sent.

The third field is a comma-separated list of flags that determines the type of feed entry and sets certain parameters for the entry. See the `newsfeeds(5)` man page for information on the flag settings.

The fourth field is a multi-purpose parameter. Its usage depends on the settings of the flags in the third field. Again, see the man pages for more information.

Now that you have a rough idea of the file layout, we'll begin to add the actual feed entries. First we'll set up the special ME entry. This entry is required and serves two purposes. First, the newsgroup pattern specified for this entry is prepended to the newsgroup list of all other feeds. Second, the ME entry's distribution pattern determines what distributions your server accepts from remote sites. The default ME entry in the `newsfeeds` file probably won't suit your tastes; a good starting point would be a subscription pattern of `*,!junk,!local*` and a distribution list of `!local`. This means that by default, all sites will receive all groups except the junk group and groups in the `local.*` hierarchy. It also means that you will receive all distributions except those marked as "local" (any such articles are probably being leaked out by a misconfigured server).

Next we'll set up special entries for the `overchan`, `innfeed`, `controlchan` (if you set `usecontrolchan: true` in `inn.conf`), and (if you're not using `cnfs` or `timehash`) `crosspost` programs. There are already entries for these programs in the default `newsfeeds` file; you need only uncomment them and edit the pathnames to the programs to match your setup.

23

News Services

> **Note**
>
> There are two entries for `overchan`, one for use with the Storage Manager API and one for use without it; uncomment only the one matching your setup.

Assuming you installed INN under the default path of `/usr/local/news`, the appropriate feed entries will look like the following.

For traditional storage method:

```
overview!:*:Tc,WO:/usr/local/news/bin/overchan

crosspost:*:Tc,Ap,WR:/usr/local/news/bin/crosspost

innfeed!:\
        !*\
        :Tc,Wnm*,S16384:/usr/local/news/bin/startinnfeed -y
```

For CNFS or timehash storage method:

```
overview!:*:Tc,Ao,WhR:/usr/local/news/bin/overchan

innfeed!:\
        !*\
        :Tc,Wnm*,S16384:/usr/local/news/bin/startinnfeed -y
```

If the server will not be supporting readers (a transit news server only), it's not necessary to run `overchan`. If you do that, however, and you're using CNFS or `timehash`, be sure to leave `overview.ctl` empty so that INN doesn't generate overview information either. See the section "`overview.ctl`" later in the chapter.

Finally, you need to add entries for any actual sites to which you will be feeding articles. They will all have the same general format:

```
my-feed-site.domain.com/exclude-list\
        :newsgroup-list\
        :Tm:innfeed!
```

Set the feed name to the name of the remote site, and if the site uses a name other than its hostname for path headers, put that in the exclude list (if your exclude list is empty, leave out the "/" after the site name as well). The newsgroup list can be left empty if the default newsgroup pattern from your ME entry is sufficient. Otherwise, set the newsgroup pattern appropriately. The last line should not be modified.

As for `controlchan`, this is useful and it is strongly recommended that you set it up. Processing by `controlchan` can reduce excessive load if a lot of control messages arrive in a short time. To enable `controlchan`:

```
controlchan!\
        :!*,control,control.*,!control.cancel\
        :Tc,Wnsm:/usr/local/news/bin/controlchan
```

incoming.conf

The `incoming.conf` file describes what machines are allowed to connect to your host to feed articles. This is an important file because if other servers can't connect to you to feed you news, you're going to have a very lonely news server. The `incoming.conf` file is not as complex as it seems.

The following is the example from the man page:

```
# Global value applied to all peers that have
# no value of their own.
max-connections: 5

# A peer definition.
peer uunet {
    hostname: usenet1.uu.net
}

peer vixie {
    hostname: gw.home.vix.com
    max-connections: 10 # override global value.
}

# A group of two peers who can open more
# connections than normal
group fast-sites {
    max-connections: 15

  # Another peer. The ``max-connections'' value from the
  # ``fast-sites'' group scope is used. The ``hostname'' value
  # defaults to the peer's name.
  peer data.ramona.vix.com {
  }
```

```
peer bb.home.vix.com {
    hostname: bb.home.vix.com
    max-connections: 20 # he can really cook.
}
}
```

There are three types of entries in `incoming.conf`:

- Key/value

- Peer

- Group

The key/value entries set parameters for the current peer or group entry. If the key/value pair is not in any other entry, it is a global value. In the preceding example, `max-connections: 5` is an example of a global value. This says that unless otherwise specified, peers can open at most five connections.

The uunet peer definition is a simple peer entry. This entry allows the host `usenet1.uu.net` to connect to our news server to feed us news. You can see the `vixie` entry has an override for the max-connections value. The vixie server can open 10 connections.

The group entry provides a way to simplify the file when you have more than one server with similar characteristics. The group entry acts just like an `incoming.conf` file within the `incoming.conf` file. In the `fast-sites` group, all peers can have 15 connections. This max-connections entry acts just like the global value above, but its effect runs out at the end of the group. You may notice the group `data.ramona.vix.com` doesn't have a host defined, yet the peer name looks suspiciously like a hostname. If there is no hostname value in a peer entry, the hostname defaults to the peer name.

`cycbuff.conf` (Required Only if Using the CNFS Article Storage Method)

CNFS stores articles in logical objects called *metacycbuffs*. Each of the metacycbuffs is in turn composed of one or more physical buffers called *cycbuffs*. As articles are written to the metacycbuff, each article is written to the next cycbuff in the list in a round-robin fashion. This is so that you can distribute the individual cycbuffs across multiple physical disks and balance the load between them.

Now you need to decide on the sizes of your cycbuffs and metacycbuffs. You'll probably want to separate the heavy-traffic groups (`alt.binaries.*` and maybe even the rest of `alt.*`) into their own metacycbuff so that they don't overrun the server and push out articles on the more useful groups. If you have any local groups that you want to stay around for a while, you should put them in their own metacycbuff as well.

You now need to determine how many cycbuffs will make up each metacycbuff, the size of those cycbuffs, and where they will be stored. Linux on 32-bit platforms does not support files larger than 2GB, which will force all of your cycbuffs to be less than 2GB. Also, when laying out your cycbuffs, try to arrange them across as many physical disks as possible. You shouldn't use a striped array and put them all on the same filesystem. If you do and you lose one of the disks in the array, you've just lost all your cycbuffs.

For each cycbuff you will be creating, add a line to the `cycbuff.conf` file like the following:

```
cycbuff:BUFFNAME:/path/to/buffer:SIZE
```

BUFFNAME must be unique and must be no more than eight characters in length. Something simple such as BUFF00, BUFF01, and so on is a decent choice. SIZE is the buffer size in kilobytes (1,000,000KB is approximately one GB, so if you are trying to stay under two GB, cap your sizes at 2,000,000).

Now you need to tell INN how to group your cycbuffs into metacycbuffs. This is similar to creating cycbuff entries:

```
metacycbuff:BUFFNAME:CYCBUFF,CYCBUFF,CYCBUFF
```

BUFFNAME is the name of the metacycbuff and, like cycbuff, names must be unique and no more than eight characters long. These should be a bit more meaningful than the cycbuff names because they will be used in other config files, such as `storage.conf`. Try to name them after what will be stored in them. For example, if this metacycbuff will hold `alt.binaries` postings, BINARIES would be a good choice. Finally, the last part of the name is a comma-separated list of all of the cycbuffs that should be used to build this metacycbuff. Each cycbuff should only appear in one metacycbuff line.

`storage.conf` (Required Only if Using the CNFS or Timehash Storage Methods)

The `storage.conf` file maps newsgroups into storage classes, which determine where and how the article is stored. This file has a very simple format; each line defines a storage class for articles. The first matching storage class is used to store the article; if no storage class matches, INN will reject that article.

A storage class is defined as a grouped entry consisting of size, expires, and other parameters:

```
methodname:newsgroup pattern:storage class #:minsize:maxsize:options
```

```
method <methodname> {
    newsgroups: <wildmat>
    class: <storage_class>
    size: <minsize>[,<maxsize>]
    expires: <mintime>[,<maxtime>]
    options: <options>
}
```

The group `methodname` is the name of the storage method used to store articles in this storage class. It should be set to "CNFS," "timehash," or the special storage method "trash" (which accepts the article but does not actually store it anywhere).

Note

Note that "traditional" is not a valid method name; the Storage Manager does not support traditional article storage, and if you are using the traditional method, you should skip to the next section.

The first parameter

```
newsgroups: <wildmat>
```

is a wildmat pattern in the same format used by the `newsfeeds` file, and determines what newsgroups this storage class accepts.

The second parameter

```
class: <storage_class>
```

is a unique number identifying this storage class and should be between 0 and 255. It is used primarily to control article expiration.

The third parameter

```
size: <minsize>[,<maxsize>]
```

can be used to accept only articles in a certain size range into this storage class. A maxsize of 0 means no upper limit (and of course a minsize of 0 would mean no lower limit because an article is always greater than zero bytes long).

The fourth parameter

```
expires: <mintime>[,<maxtime>]
```

can be used to accept only articles in a certain expire range into this storage class. A maxtime of 0 means no upper limit (and a mintime of non-zero would mean an article never falls in this class, if it includes an Expires header.)

The fifth parameter

```
options: <options>
```

is the options parameter. Currently, only CNFS uses this field; it should contain the name of the metacycbuff used to store articles in this storage class.

For CNFS users, create one storage class for each metacycbuff that you have defined, listing what newsgroups are to be stored in that buffer.

For timehash, the storage class IDs are used to store articles in separate directory trees so that different expiration policies can be applied to each storage class. You will need to divide up your newsgroups based on how long you want to retain articles in those groups, and create a storage class for each such collection of newsgroups. Make note of the storage class IDs you assign because they will be needed when you edit the `expire.ctl` file a bit later.

`overview.ctl` (Required Only if Using the CNFS or Timehash Storage Methods)

The `overview.ctl` file determines where article overview information is stored for each newsgroup. Overview is stored in one or more storage files identified by unique numbers between 0 and 254. Each line consists of the storage file number followed by a single colon and a wildmat pattern list of which newsgroups are to be stored in that file. As with `storage.conf`, the first matching line is used.

If your server will not be supporting any readers (if it's for news transit only), you can leave this file empty and not run an `overchan` process (see the previous section, "newsfeeds"). As a result, no overview information will be generated and reading from the server will be impossible, but the server may run faster. If you choose to do this, you won't be able to set expire times on a newsgroup-by-newsgroup basis, and if you're using timehash you'll have to use a different syntax in `expire.ctl`. See the `expire.ctl` man page for details.

The way in which you distribute articles across multiple overview storage areas is not an exact science; the goal is to spread access out across a number of smaller files rather than one large file. As a start, I suggest creating 27 storage areas; the first 26 will be for newsgroups "a*" through "z*", and the 27th will be for "*" (thus catching any groups that start with a non-letter, of which there are several). You can change the layout in the future by modifying this file and then waiting for the daily news expiration to run, at which time the overview data will be re-arranged for you during the expiration process.

23

News Services

expire.ctl

The file `expire.ctl` controls how long your articles stay on your server before they are deleted. If you're using the conventional news filesystem, this is also how you control disk usage. If your news spool gets too full, you may want to use the du utility to see what newsgroups are using up the most space, and reduce their expire times. The best way is `du -kx /usr/local/news/spool | sort -n`. This may take quite a while, so it is a good idea to background the process, and redirect the output to a file:

```
du -kx /usr/local/news/spool ¦ sort -n > /tmp/spool.du.sorted &
```

Here's a look at the default `expire.ctl` file:

```
##   $Revision: 1.1.1.1 $
##   expire.ctl - expire control file
##   Format:
##       /remember/:<keep>
##       <patterns>:<modflag>:<keep>:<default>:<purge>
##   First line gives history retention; other lines specify expiration
##   for newsgroups.  Must have a "*:A:..." line which is the default.
##       <patterns>      wildmat-style patterns for the newsgroups
##       <modflag>       Pick one of M U A -- modifies pattern to be only
##                       moderated, unmoderated, or all groups
##       <keep>          Mininum number of days to keep article
##       <default>       Default number of days to keep the article
##       <purge>         Flush article after this many days
##   <keep>, <default>, and <purge> can be floating-point numbers or the
##   word "never."  Times are based on when received unless -p is used;
##   see expire.8

##   If article expires before 14 days, we still remember it for 14 days in
##   case we get offered it again.  Depending on what you use for the innd
##   -c flag and how paranoid you are about old news, you might want to
##   make this 28, 30, etc.
/remember/:14

##   Keep for 1-10 days, allow Expires headers to work.
*:A:1:10:never

##   Some particular groups stay forever.
# Keep FAQ's for a month, so they're always available
*.answers:M:1:35:90
news.announce.*:M:1:35:90
```

```
# Some other recommendations.  Uncomment if you want
# .announce groups tend to be low-traffic, high signal.
# *.announce:M:1:30:90
# Weather forecasts
# *.weather:A:1:2:7
# test posts
# *.test:A:1:1:1

## Some particular groups stay forever.
# dc.dining*:A:never:never:never
# uunet*:A:never:never:never
```

The file is fairly well documented in the comments at the top, but you can always turn to the man page for help if you need it. The newsgroup list is the wildmat pattern we talked about earlier. Remember, the last match is used so you should start with wide matches at the top of the file and move to more specific matches as you go down.

It is worth talking about the parameters in the expire line. The first parameter is the newsgroup wildmat pattern. It determines to which groups the rest of the line applies. The second parameter tells which type of groups should be matched: Moderated (M), Unmoderated (U), or All (A) .

The third parameter is the minimum number of days to keep an article. This is useful if an article has an expire header that limits its life to less than you want. Some FAQs are posted with expire headers, and you may want to keep them around longer. The fourth parameter is the default time to keep an article. The article will be expired after this time. The last field is the purge time. Any article matching the pattern in the first field will be removed after this many days regardless of the expire time in its expire header.

These entries may not do what they appear to do:

```
comp.*:A:1:3:7
comp.os.linux.misc:A:1:30:60
comp.os*:A:1:7:14
```

What they will actually do is expire all the comp newsgroups after three days, and all of comp.os.* after seven days. However, comp.os.linux.misc articles will not expire after 30 days because the last match in the file is the comp.os*:A:1:7:14.

A little trick to immediately expire articles in removed newsgroups is to use

```
*:A:0:0:0
*:U:1:10:90
*:M:1:14:90
```

23

News Services

If you have an article in `alt.foo.bar`, and you remove that group, the article no longer belongs to any newsgroup (as far as the expire is concerned). Therefore, it doesn't belong to a moderated or unmoderated group, and it only matches the first pattern (marked for Any group). You might think that 1 would be a more appropriate number there, but remember, the article is removed if it has been on the server for greater than the number of days listed. To get all articles expired every night, you must use 0 days as your expire time.

> **Note**
>
> You can use fractional expire times (that is, `comp.*:A:0.5:2.5:10`).

Creating the Article Spool (CNFS Only)

If you are using actual files as your CNFS buffers, you will need to pre-create these files with the UNIX `dd` program. For each cycbuff in your `cycbuff.conf` file, create the buffer with the following commands as the news user:

```
dd if=/dev/zero of=/path/to/buffer bs=1k count=BUFFERSIZE
chmod 0664 /path/to/buffer
```

Substitute the buffer pathname and the buffer size (as listed in the `cycbuff.conf` file) in the appropriate spots in the commands. This will create a zero-filled file of the correct length; it may take a while to run, so be prepared to wait. The amount of time varies depending on your system and the file size. The best way to monitor progress is to use another window to watch the size of the file with `ls -l`.

Once you have created all of your cycbuffs, you are ready to continue with the next step of the installation.

Restricting Readers

The `nnrp.access` file determines which machines can connect to your system to read news. You should add a line to the default file so that users in your local domain can access your server (if you want them to, that is).

Here's the default file:

```
##   $Revision: 1.3.2.1 $
##   nnrp.access - access file for on-campus NNTP sites
##   Format:
##        <host>:<perm>:<user>:<pass>:<groups>
##        <host>:</path/file>
```

```
##  Connecting host must be found in this file; the last match found is
##  used, so put defaults first.
##      <host>          Wildcard name or IP address
##      <perm>          R to read; P to post
##      <user>          Username for authentication before posting
##      <pass>          Password, for same reason
##      <groups>        Newsgroup patterns that can be read or not read
##      </path/file>    A second file to scan in the same format as this
##  To disable posting put a space in the <user> and <pass> fields, since
##  there is no way for client to enter one.
##
## Default is no access, no way to authentication, and no groups.
*::::!*
##  Foo, Incorporated, hosts have no password, can read anything.
#*.foo.com:Read Post:::*
## Bar, Incorporated have a separate access file that they maintain
# *.bar.com:/news/etc/customers/access.bar.com
stdin:Read Post:::*
localhost:Read Post:::*
127.0.0.1:Read Post:::*
```

If you want to allow access to the rest of your domain to all your newsgroups, add the line

```
    *.your.domain.here:Read Post:::*
```

to the end of the file (substituting your domain name of course).

Creating the db Files

At this point you need to set up the news database directory (~news/db). To make things easier you should su to your news user; otherwise the files you create will be owned by root and you'll have to change the owner and group IDs on the files manually. You should also have your working directory set to the ~news/db directory, and ~news/bin should be in your PATH so that you can execute INN support commands without typing full pathnames.

To begin, you'll need current active and newsgroups files. These can be downloaded from the following location:

```
    ftp.isc.org:/pub/usenet/CONFIG
```

Download the files active and newsgroups and place them in your ~news/db directory.

Next, you need to create an empty history database. You can do this by running the following command:

```
makehistory -i
```

When it is finished, you need to move history.n* to history*. Finally, set the file permissions on all of the files you just created:

```
chmod 0664 *
```

Your news database files are now ready to go.

Setting up the News.Daily cron Job

INN requires a special cron job to be set up on your system to run the news.daily script, which performs daily server maintenance tasks such as article expiration and the processing and rotation of the server logs. Because it will slow the server down while it is running, it should be run during periods of low server usage, such as in the middle of the night. To run it at 3 a.m., for example, add the following entry to the news user's crontab file:

```
0 3 * * * /usr/local/news/bin/news.daily expireover lowmark
```

Also, a cron job should be set up to transmit to your upstream site any articles that have been posted locally and queued for transmission; for example:

```
1,11,21,31,41,51 * * * * /usr/local/news/bin/nntpsend
```

The pathnames and user ID are the installation defaults; change them to match your installation if you used something other than the defaults.

The parameters passed to news.daily in the preceding example are the most common (and usually the most efficient) ones to use. More information on what these parameters do can be found in the news.daily man page.

Starting the System

INN is normally started via the shell script rc.news. This must be run as the news user and not as root. Put the following command (or something similar) into the system boot script:

```
su news -c /usr/local/news/bin/rc.news
```

If innd gets stopped or killed and you want to restart it without rerunning rc.news, run inndstart:

```
/usr/local/news/bin/inndstart
```

If you added any values to the innflags variable in inn.conf, you'll need to add the same values to the command line of inndstart if you run it by hand.

Spam Filtering Options with INN

There are several options when choosing spam-filtering software. The three most popular are

- Cleanfeed

- NoCem (pronounced No-See-Em)

- Spamhippo

Cleanfeed is basically a very fast filter. You can customize it to reject articles from certain places, users, or servers. It can also reject articles if they have certain strings in them (also configurable). It is fairly simple to set up and the documentation that comes with it is very good. To use cleanfeed, you must have Perl enabled with the INN server. Cleanfeed is available at `http://www.exit109.com/~jeremy/news/cleanfeed.html`.

NoCem is a program that is configured to cancel articles based on other people deciding that the articles are spam. There are NoCem messages distributed through Usenet, and this program accepts them and filters the articles that are listed in them. It is configurable so that you can choose from whom, if anyone, you will accept NoCem messages. NoCem is available at `http://www.cm.org/`. There is also a version written in C, instead of Perl, that is referenced in that page.

Spamhippo filters messages based on several criteria. The most notable is repeat postings. Spamhippo must be installed before you compile INN because it patches the source code for INN. Spamhippo is available at `http://www.spamhippo.com/`.

Diablo

Diablo is the other news server you might consider running. Diablo, as mentioned before, was designed to transport large volumes of news from one place to another (usually a full feed). There are some differences between Diablo and INN. Diablo, having been designed as a transport system, doesn't have as fine control or as many tools regarding the reading of newsgroups. INN was designed to handle readers, so it has many more tools and support for dealing with readers and newsgroups.

Unless you are planning on running a full feed, I would suggest that you consider using INN as your primary news system. If you are considering a full feed, and dealing with readers, you might consider running two servers. Run a Diablo server that accepts your full feeds and feeds your INN server, which will be your reader box. The INN server will feed posts made by your readers back to your Diablo system, and it will feed those posts to the rest of Usenet through your peer feeds. Diablo is not quite as automated as INN. Although INN may be more complex to install and configure, I believe it is your best bet in the long run for supporting readers.

Using `nntpcache`

If you want to outsource most of your news, yet you would still like to have some local newsgroups, `nntpcache` is something you should look into.

Installing `nntpcache` is fairly simple. Just untar, configure, and make. The `INSTALL` file that comes with the source distribution has a cookbook configuration that is the default. If you are outsourcing your news to a third-party provider, you will want to tweak this a bit.

The `nntpcache.servers` file in Listing 23.2 is where most of your configuration will take place.

LISTING 23.2 The `nntpcache.servers` File

```
/*
# This file defines which nntp servers nntpcache uses. The reason for the
# Interface address is that if you're connecting to more than one server it
# probably means you have more than one gateway, which may well mean you
# have more than one IP address, so nntpcache allows you to configure
# which one of them you connect to each server as. A bind address of
# 0.0.0.0 or DEFAULT will select the system default address.

# A timeout of 0 means not to cache anything of that type from the
# specified server. Use this for servers on the same machine or on a
# fast local ethernet or when using nntpcache as a mere proxy.

# As in nntpcache.access, this file is parsed from the general to the
# specific, from the top to the bottom. The LAST MATCH IS DOMINANT
# over preceding matches.
#

#                              /*            timeouts           */
# host:port     Interface      Active  Act.tim Newsgrp Group   Xover   Arts

# the localhost:120 entry below is for an INN news-server running on
# localhost, port 120. We use this to serve local groups
localhost:120   localhost      30m     24h     24h     10m     0m      0m

# Change this to the name of your main NNTP news feed. We run a
```

LISTING 23.2   continued

```
# multi-homed host, and nntp.world.net won't talk to us unless the
# traffic is eminating from our 198.142.2.24 interface. Unless you are
# running multi-homed (and maybe even then) you will probably want to
# use "DEFAULT" as the interface address for your most/all of your
# servers.
nntp.world.net.   198.142.2.24   4h      24h      2d      30m     60d     60d

# This is the nntpcache.org virtual news server. you *should* have
# this in your configuration, in order to read nntpcache.*
# groups. Make sure it's one of the last entries though! Or
# news.nntpcache.org is hit with all your cache-miss <msgid> lookups!
# (and it gets a lot of traffic as it is)
news.nntpcache.org.  DEFAULT   4h      24h      2d      30m     60d     60d

# various additional servers. these are real (and mostly thanks to
# Alan Brown), but no doubt a couple of have fallen to the dark forces
# of entropy by the time you read this

news.turbopower.com.   DEFAULT   24h      4d      4d      30m     60d     60d
newsgroups.intel.com.  DEFAULT   24h      4d      4d      30m     60d     60d
nntp.net-link.net.     DEFAULT   24h      4d      4d      30m     60d     60d
publicnews.msn.com.    DEFAULT   24h      4d      4d      30m     60d     60d
secnews.netscape.com.  DEFAULT   24h      4d      4d      30m     60d     60d
service.symantec.com.  DEFAULT   24h      4d      4d      30m     60d     60d

# this line is magic. keep it.
%BeginGroups

# Understand the ordering here! The general instance should come first!

# replace the next line with your "main" server
*               nntp.world.net.

# the next line represents our local groups running on innd on port
# 120 from the same machine. you definately want to change suburbia.*
# to the name(s) of your local groups
suburbia.*      localhost:120

# nntpcache news groups. you *should* keep these here
nntpcache.*     news.nntpcache.org.

# additional groups follow
```

23

News Services

LISTING 23.2   continued

```
#
#trumpet.*      jazz.trumpet.com.au.

3dfx.*          news.3dfx.com.

#
borland.*       forums.borland.com.

#
corel.*         cnews.corel.com.

#
intel.*         newsgroups.intel.com.

#
linux.*         miriam.fuller.edu.

#
microsoft.*     msnews.microsoft.com.

# microsoft network
msn.*           publicnews.msn.com.

#
netscape.*,people.*     secnews.netscape.com.
```

The first part of the file lists servers from which nntpcache should get news. Change the
nntp.world.net line to point to your provider's news server on which you have a reader
account. You may notice the localhost:120 server in the server config file. This is the
INN server that you use to serve your local groups. Toward the bottom of that section, there
are several default servers listed. These are servers that nntpcache can fall back on if
necessary. It is not necessary to leave these in, but it shouldn't hurt anything if you do. The
last section of the file lists different newsgroup hierarchies, and which servers to fetch them
from. Notice that it lists suburbia.* as being on the localhost:120 server. This is an
example of hosting local groups. If you don't want any local groups, but still want to cache
news locally, you don't have to run an INN server at port 120. You can simply use
nntpcache to cache news articles for you.

News Clients

When it comes to reading news, you can install a news reader for your users, or you can set up a news-to-mail gateway. I do not recommend the news-to-mail gateway. Those are simply too much work to maintain, and they can cause problems with your mail system as well. Imagine that a user subscribes to a group that gets 500 posts each day, and the average size of these posts is 4KB. That user is going to get 2MB of mail each day in addition to his regular mail. That's not too bad, but now imagine that 20 of your users subscribe to this group through your news-to-mail gateway. You now have to deal with 40MB of incoming mail each day. Now you see why I don't suggest such a setup.

If you decide to install a news reader for your users, should you use a graphical news reader or a text-based one? That is going to depend on your users. We'll talk about a few news readers of each type in the upcoming sections, and then discuss news2mail, a gateway program, as well as a few situations where you might consider using it.

Text Clients

My favorite news reader is trn, probably because I cut my teeth in Usenet news with rn. The difference between rn and trn is that trn threads the articles based on subject and references to other articles. This is very useful for following discussions, and readers without this threading ability aren't of much use. As you can see in Figure 23.2, the opening screen lists the groups I'm subscribed to and the number of articles I have left to read in each of them. I haven't read news on this account in quite some time, so you can see that I'm way behind on my news.

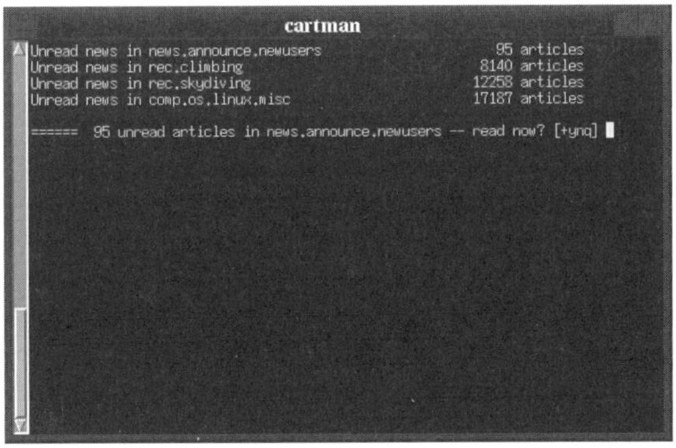

23
News Services

FIGURE 23.2
The group selection screen of trn.

Once I move into one of the groups to read, trn lists the different threads for me and shows me who's written the messages. I can select a thread by pressing the letter next to the thread subject listed. In Figure 23.3, I've selected threads on three topics. You can tell which topics are selected by the plus sign in the column next to the topic letter. There are numerous controls in trn. The best way to learn about trn is either through the online help screen (press the "h" key) or through the man page (type `man trn`).

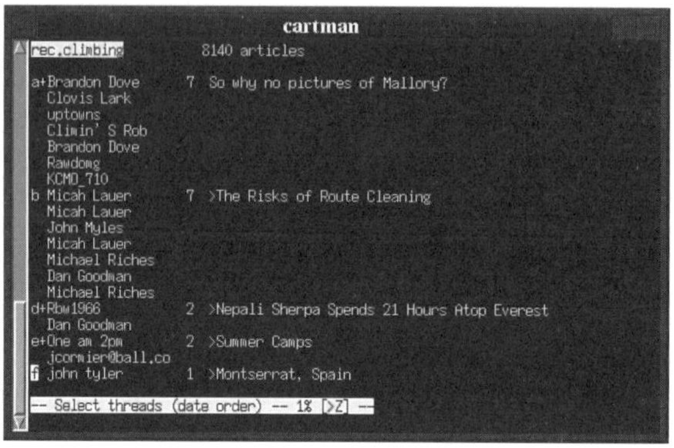

FIGURE 23.3

The thread selection screen of trn.

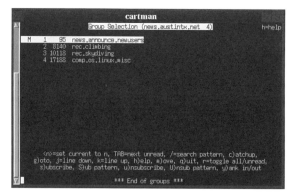

Another popular text-based client is tin. It is also a thread newsreader, and it has a few features that trn doesn't. One of the most notable is the ability to select the order in which the threads are to be read. However, tin does take a bit longer to start up than trn. Figure 23.4 shows the tin opening screen.

FIGURE 23.4

The group selection screen of tin.

There is a little better labeling of keys for major functions on this screen. One feature that you can see here is that the "M" next to the first group listed indicates that it is a moderated group. In the thread selection screen shown in Figure 23.5, you can see I've selected the same three threads. In tin, the selected thread lists the number of articles to be read instead of the + next to the topic.

FIGURE 23.5

The thread selection screen of tin.

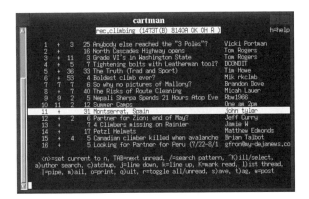

Also with tin, more help is available through the man page or by pressing "h." More information on trn and tin is available at `http://www.clari.net/~wayne/` and `http://www.tin.org/`, respectively.

Graphical Clients

Graphical clients are probably going to be simpler for your users to deal with. The downside is that they are usually slower than text-based clients and use more memory. Someone who has never used a text-based reader wouldn't notice the speed issue, and memory shouldn't be too bad because when people read news, they generally don't do anything else.

The first reader we'll discuss is xrn. It's been around the longest, and is basically an X implementation of rn (the older, non-threaded version of trn). As you can see in Figures 23.6 and 23.7, there is no thread selection dialog. You can select which group to read, and then which article to read. I think that if you try xrn, you'll quickly abandon it. I mention it only because it is installed with most Linux distributions, and it's not a bad option for a beginning news user.

FIGURE **23.6**

The group selection screen of xrn.

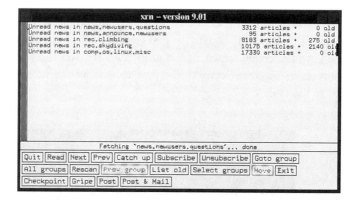

FIGURE **23.7**

The article selection screen of xrn.

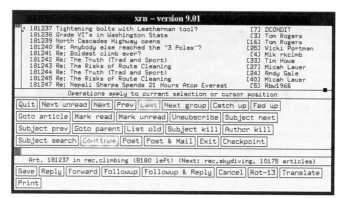

If you want to provide a threaded option to your users, knews is a good choice. It has a smaller memory footprint than Netscape, yet allows many of the threading features Netscape provides. As you've seen, most newsreaders have a similar look when it comes to group and thread selection. Knews is no exception. Knews also provides many of the features of some of the more popular text-based readers such as tin and trn. See Figures 23.8 and 23.9.

Netscape's news reader is more full-featured than the others discussed here. However, it also uses much more memory than the other selections and it tends to be slower. The upside is that most of your users will be familiar with Netscape's basic interface, which means they won't ask you as many questions about it. Netscape's interface is a little different from the norm. As you can see in Figure 23.10, the group selection dialog is the same size as the rest of the reader.

Figure 23.8

The group selection screen of knews.

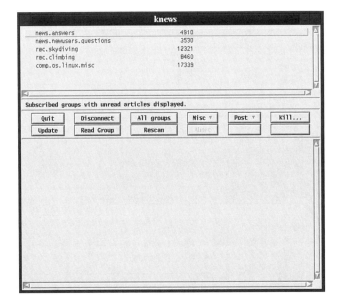

Figure 23.9

The thread selection screen of knews.

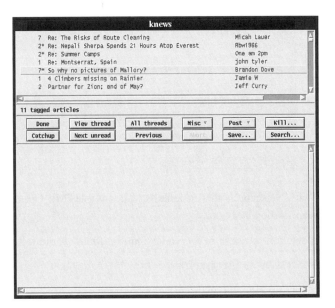

Once you get inside the group, the thread selection dialog is in the upper-right frame of the window (see Figure 23.11). You'll also notice another group selection dialog in the upper-left frame. You can switch directly to another group from there.

FIGURE **23.10**

The group selection screen of Netscape.

FIGURE **23.11**

The thread selection screen of Netscape.

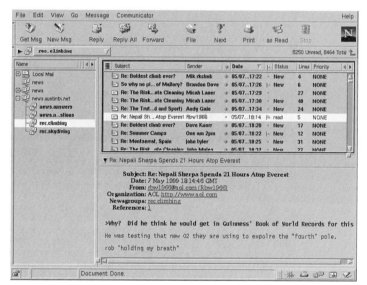

One problem with Netscape is that it defaults to posting HTML Usenet articles. Usenet articles are meant to be plain text.

Further documentation on these news readers can be found at the following Web sites.

```
http://www.matematik.su.se/users/kjj/knews.html
```

```
http://www.mit.edu/people/jik/software/xrn.html
```

```
http://www.netscape.com/
```

Alternatives for Reading News

In some cases, it's not feasible for a user to run a news reader. He may be travelling or on an external network. Whatever the reason, sometimes it is desirable to send a user the articles in the mail instead of having him connect with a news client. This is where news2mail comes in. News2mail allows articles to be sent through the mail automatically. This solution is best for various announce groups because threading and the ability to follow up are not very important in them. More information on news2mail is available at `http://members.xoom.com/alexsh/news2mail/`.

Another option is Web-based news services such as Deja.com. This service archives Usenet articles and indexes them for searching. Unless you require local groups, you may want to point your Usenet hungry users at `http://www.deja.com/` instead of running a news server.

Places to Ask Questions and Find Answers

I'm sure that after reading this chapter you still have several questions. The first thing you should do before you ask any of those questions is to read the FAQ (Frequently Asked Questions) lists posted to `news.software.nntp`. Your question has probably been answered in one of the FAQ lists.

Another thing you might do is search on Deja.com for your question. Someone else has probably posted the same question before, and by reading the answer given to them you can avoid asking the same question again. Searching Deja.com is especially useful if you are having problems with software and have an error message you can search on. If you still can't find the answer to your question, post a message to the pertinent newsgroup. If the question is about your news server software, your destination should be `news.software.nntp`. If your server isn't running yet, you'll have to go through a Web-based news service such as Deja.com to post your question. Posting your question to a non-functional server won't do much good.

Summary

Remember that the most important thing about setting up a news server is planning. Plan what groups you want to provide to your users, how much disk space you are going to use, and how much bandwidth you're going to consume. If you think about all these things ahead of time, your job will be easier. If you install your news server without planning, you should use the experiences of your first installation when planning your next one. Don't try to do more than you need to. Start small—you can always expand the server later.

Also, your users will likely ask endless questions. Have a Web page to which you can point them that has all the answers on it. You will have a FAQ list of your own. You'll also want to decide on a supported news reader—pick one you know well. Your readers will ask you questions you've never dreamed of. Look at Chapter 30, "Helping Users," for more ideas.

24

CHAPTER

Internet Telephony and Conferencing

IN THIS CHAPTER

- An Introduction to Internet Telephony *714*

- Internet Relay Chat (IRC) *721*

- ICQ and Clones *728*

- Multimedia Conferencing Tools *733*

There are very few people who haven't heard of the possibility of reducing the cost of long distance telephone calls by using the Internet—this is the basic definition of Internet telephony. Internet conferencing is just an extension of this so that three or more people (who may be geographically distant from each other) can participate in the discussion.

An Introduction to Internet Telephony

Originally, the term "Internet telephony" referred to the practice of sending voice data over the Internet to another person—exactly analogous to a regular telephone call. The current definition, however, is not so precise and depending upon who is using the term, it may refer to any form of person-to-person communication that uses the Internet as a means of transferring data. Therefore, the field of Internet telephony embraces such things as real-time text chatting, video-conferencing, and shared whiteboards as well as that old-fashioned practice of just talking to somebody.

The reduction in cost of relatively sophisticated hardware means that the experience of Internet telephony and conferencing can be enhanced by the use of real-time video so that each participant in the discussion can see all of the others—just like being there, except better!

ICQ

It isn't always required or possible to conduct real-time audio or audio-visual conversations and so we use yet another tool, ICQ, which was developed by Mirabilis Software (`http://www.icq.com`). ICQ allows real-time, text-based chat between two or more people in a similar fashion to Internet Relay Chat (IRC) except that these chats are far more private and participation is by invitation only. IRC, of course, is considered to be the original conferencing application. UNIX talk existed even before this, but is so seldom used that many people aren't even aware of its existence.

It's no great mystery as to why UNIX talk has fallen into disuse—it was originally designed only to enable text communications between two users on a single intranet. There were never any formal protocols developed for this and so, as time went by, various incompatible versions of the same program were developed.

Quite apart from the version incompatibility, talk was never intended for communication over wide area networks (such as, for example, the Internet). Lack of reliability and stability in this application has been a major contributing factor to the disuse of this program.

Although it is probably not a big issue (unless you're wanted by one the three letter agencies), it is worth noting that using the right data encryption software enables you to have conversations that are as secure as any used by the military or three letter agencies. Although current U.S. legislation prohibits the export of certain types of data encryption software, some very secure software has been developed and made available from places outside of the U.S. In addition to this, some people have illegally copied restricted export software to places outside of the U.S. This is undoubtedly a cause for concern to law enforcement agencies, but it is hard to see exactly what can be done about it. Users inside of the U.S. don't need to worry about the legality of this type of software.

Specifically at this point in time, any encryption software that implements keys having greater than 56 bits are completely banned from export, and encryption software that implements keys having greater than 40 bits are only permitted under special circumstances and with certain restrictions.

Unfortunately, a discussion of the various types of encryption software that exists is outside of the scope of this chapter but you will find that plenty of information exists on the Internet. A search for the words "encryption software" using your favorite search engine will provide many hundreds of informative links.

This chapter examines the hardware requirements for Internet telephony and conferencing, and discusses how to obtain, install, and use some of the software that is available.

The Problems That Hinder Widespread Usage of Internet Telephony

Internet telephony is still in its infancy and presents a number of problems that will need to be solved if it is to be accepted and used by large numbers of people.

The last five years have seen much effort placed into implementing widespread usage of Internet telephony and many technological hurdles have been overcome in this time. Because the problems that remain are, to one degree or another, very tightly coupled to advances in hardware technology, it isn't possible to even suggest a timeframe within which these problems will be fully overcome. My personal view is that it will take at least another five years, but somebody else would suggest double that time and somebody else again would suggest half.

The biggest problem of all is latency—the delay between one person speaking and the other person or people hearing that voice. The same problem used to exist in the early days of long-distance telephone calls and even now can still be experienced when calling some less-developed countries. A conversation carried out over a network having a high latency period will sound jerky or broken up as if the person speaking is stopping at irregular intervals (even in the middle of words), and the words themselves are often not as clear as we have come to expect.

Latency

The effect of using a network having a high degree of latency is that, although the equipment we use is capable of full duplex communications, most conversations will be essentially half duplex. Because of the delay in receiving the other person's words (or video image or drawing), we must often wait for them to stop speaking completely before responding.

Full duplex communications refers to any communication in which the participants can send and receive simultaneously. Think of your home telephone—if you want, you can speak at exactly the same time as the other person and your voice will be transmitted even though the other person is, at the same time, transmitting his own voice.

Half duplex communications is a communications system in which only one person can transmit at a time. The Citizens Band Radio system (CB) is a good example of half duplex communications. You can either transmit or receive at any given time but you cannot do both simultaneously.

Capacity and QoS

A related problem is capacity and Quality of Service (QoS). The Internet works so well for us at the moment in transferring data because most people use a Web browser to get to a certain place and then read for a while before moving on. That pause while the person is reading allows the network to service some other request. Internet telephony requires a constant stream of data—this, for a relatively lengthy period of time compared to downloading a Web page, completely monopolizes a certain percentage of the capacity of the network. At some stage, the whole of the bandwidth is going to be tied up and further telephony or more traditional uses will be impossible at certain times or between certain areas. If we keep insisting that our ISPs upgrade their equipment and connections, we are going to be faced with increased costs which, in turn, lessens the advantage of Internet telephony.

Usage and Packet Dropping

As usage increases, so does the likelihood of packet collisions and dropped packets—even with traditional uses of the Internet such as FTP, email, and Web browsing, this is becoming a greater and greater problem. Dropped packets are more likely when using Internet telephony because of the increased packet size used. There is more chance of a collision because of the transmission time and there is a greater chance of an error because of the amount of data contained in each packet. Packet dropping results in effects ranging from negligible distortion to clearly discernable "clipping" to a total loss of meaning. The Real Time Protocol (RTP) and Resource Reservation Protocol (RSVP) in combination attempt to address these issues.

Internet Telephony Protocols and Standards

Another problem with existing Internet telephony applications is the strict requirement that all of the participants use exactly the same software package (normally you must be so specific as to use the same release of the same software). Although there are a couple of Open Source packages available, most of the Internet telephony applications rely on proprietary compression algorithms. The ITU H.323 recommendation attempts to remove this problem by specifying standards for Voice Over Net (VON) applications.

H.323 specifies a highly efficient algorithm for voice transportation—a detailed discussion is beyond the scope of this chapter—and major software companies as well as private and smaller developers have already started adopting this as a standard. The effect of widespread implementation of the H.323 recommendation is to relieve users of the need to ensure that all Internet telephony participants are using the same software package. Instead, the requirement is that all participants use *any* H.323-compliant package.

In many countries, telephony services have been traditionally provided by highly regulated (and often highly profitable) monopolies. The increasing use of Internet telephony threatens this comfortable existence (for the monopolies), and so we can expect to see some backlash sooner or later. This will probably come in the form of new legislation, although it is hard to see exactly what the legislators, regulators, and operators can do at this stage.

Hardware Requirements

The minimum hardware requirement for Internet communication between two or more people is nothing more sophisticated than any old Linux box—even that 386 box that is only capable of text mode—and an Internet connection. There are a variety of text-based programs that work quite nicely on minimum configuration machines.

But why type at each other when you can actually hold real-time audio conversations? Well, the hardware requirement goes up for a start. A 486DX is considered the minimum processing power that is needed, along with 16MB RAM. Whereas text-only, real-time conversation can take place with an Internet connection speed of as little as 9600bps, audio requires a minimum of 28800bps. Of course, you have to have a sound card and a microphone as well. The good news is that you still don't need to worry a great deal about graphics—text-only display is just fine.

Of course, these are *minimum* requirements—as always, more is better. A basic machine set up as described will work, but the quality may be poor. If you are going to take Internet telephony seriously, at least 32MB of memory and a fast Pentium-class processor is going to be required. You'll also need at least a 16-bit, full-duplex sound card and a mid- to top-of-the-range microphone. You should also consider upgrading your connection to at least 33600bps.

Video and voice transmissions cannot be sent over the Internet in the form in which the computer originally receives them. The signal that the computer receives from your camera and/or your microphone needs to be converted to a digital representation before it can be sent to the receiver.

High quality video cameras and microphones ensure that the computer has the best available signal to work with. A good sound card means that more of this signal is preserved during the conversion to a digital representation, and a fast processor and more memory means that the conversion takes place faster.

Note that this is a very simplistic description of the process. For more detailed information, you should read material on digital-to-analog and analog-to-digital conversion.

Video conferencing is the ultimate in communicating, providing it is of good quality. Note that the hardware configuration described here is better performance than the absolute minimum required, but in most cases no video is better than poor video. To achieve the best results with video conferencing, you should start thinking about a Pentium II-class processor or better. You will also need a top-of-the-range video card and a nice 32-bit sound card. A high quality microphone is also required—the best quality you can afford.

A camera is required if you intend to send pictures as well as receive them. The Logitech (previously Connectix) QuickCam has been the camera of choice, primarily because it was the only one available until recently that had reliable drivers available. There have since been several others released that have Linux drivers available. The QuickCam drivers that are available only support the earlier versions of the camera. If you want or need higher quality, you may need to look elsewhere. Before making a decision about what product to purchase, it is worth visiting the Video 4 Linux Web page at `http://roadrunner.swansea.uk.linux.org/v4l.shtml`.

A connection to the Multicast Backbone (mbone) is desirable but hard to find—an increasing number of ISPs are supporting the mbone but they are still in the minority. Failing an mbone connection, a 64K ISDN connection to a well connected (T3 or better) ISP should be used. A small ISP will probably be unable to provide the bandwidth required for good quality audio-visual transmission and reception. Note that for the connection type to make a difference, all participants must be similarly connected—a chain is only as strong as its weakest link.

The Multicast Backbone (mbone)

mbone is the way of the future for Internet telephony and conferencing. Note that the discussion that follows is not meant to be an in-depth exploration of multi-casting and the mbone and is, of necessity, somewhat simplified. If you already have an idea of what multi-casting is, please feel free to skip this part.

The mbone is a part of the Internet that is reserved for streaming applications. A streaming application is one that requires a reliable and continuous flow of data—such as the live radio that many of us have listened to over the Web. If you have listened to a broadcast over the Internet, you will have noticed that the quality is somewhat variable. It is sometimes perfect, but more often speech is clipped or the volume varies. Sometimes the broadcast drops out altogether or sounds like a regular radio station that isn't tuned in properly (complete with static). This occurs because the broadcast is being sent over the "regular" Internet.

Understanding Data Flow

To understand how the mbone works, you need to understand a little bit about data flow on the Internet. When we send or receive data over the Internet, it is sent in little pieces called *packets*. The packets are sent out in order from the originator but may take any one of (probably) millions of different routes to reach their destination and may (in fact, probably will) reach the destination in a completely random order. The receiver then puts these packets back into the correct order and makes the data available to the application.

Each packet of data has extra information apart from the actual information required by the requesting application. Most importantly, each packet is individually addressed so that when it reaches the router in charge of the receiver's network, the router knows to send it to the receiver rather than sending on to another router. Packets are also given a Time To Live (TTL) to stop them from circulating forever and clogging up the system—if a packet is received by a router and its TTL is zero, the router simply discards the packet.

24

Internet Telephony and Conferencing

On a relatively frequent basis, these packets are lost or arrive damaged and the receiver has to ask the originator to retransmit that data. If you are viewing a Web page or downloading a file, this doesn't matter too much. At most, it costs a few extra seconds. But if you are trying to get a moving picture complete with lip synchronization (the picture is actually seen to be speaking the words you are hearing rather than being a little bit behind or ahead), this sort of a delay is close to intolerable.

If the originating computer is being asked to fulfil a large number of requests, it may not be able to send a continuous stream of data to the receiving computer. This is why a Web page sometimes seems to stop loading half way through or a file transfer just stops for a few seconds (or longer). There's nothing wrong with the connection or the computers, it's just that the originating machine has to service some other request. Again, this is close to intolerable in a real-time interaction.

Using the regular Internet, the receiving computer will eventually receive the packet of data that it wants—and keep it. So what if somebody else, say in a conferencing situation, wants the same data? The originating computer has to do the computations all over again and transmit the data to that person. This is analogous to a television station issuing each person a different frequency and broadcasting on that frequency as requested to do so. No television station does this because we would soon run out of available frequencies and the resources required to maintain thousands or even millions of transmitters each on a different frequency would be prohibitive. Instead, each station is allocated a single frequency on which to broadcast and those who want to receive that broadcast simply tune their receiver to that frequency.

Multi-casting

Enter multi-casting. Multi-casting is a way of ensuring that a single packet of data is distributed to every receiver that wants it and is authorized to receive it. This is exactly the same as the television station using a single transmission to reach millions of people.

Recall that each packet of data is individually addressed so that it can find the right place to go to. Well, multi-casting goes one step beyond this and adds a second address—the broadcast address (similar to the frequency of a television station)—so that when the packet is received by a router it knows to send a copy of the data to the receiver and pass the original packet onto another router. This way, every receiver that is tuned to the correct frequency gets a copy of the data. This reduces the load on the originating computer and the network itself quite substantially. To stop these packets circulating indefinitely, they also have a TTL and are sent to the bit bucket when the TTL expires. Because of this TTL, there are still occasional dropped packets but the number dropped compared to unicast is much reduced.

The mbone is nothing more than a set of IP addresses dedicated to multi-cast recipients. Unfortunately, your ISP requires a router running special software to recognize multi-cast packets, and most routers are not yet so equipped. If you want to join the mbone, the best place to start is local universities and the largest ISPs you can find.

As stated at the start of the discussion, this explanation is somewhat simplified and doesn't go into all the gory details—that would fill a very large book on its own. There are many, many resources available on the Net that do go into detail, so if you are interested in reading further, crank up your favorite search engine and search for +linux +multi-casting. You could also try spelling multi-casting without the hyphen. A good place to start reading straight away is the multi-cast FAQ at `http://andrew.triumf.ca/pub/linux/multicast-FAQ`.

You needn't save video-conferencing just for long distance communications, though. It offers a great opportunity to install full video security in your home, keep an eye on the kid's room or swimming pool, or whatever other application you can think of that requires real-time video. Although these applications are beyond the scope of this chapter, the information contained here should enable you to set up a video link to perform whatever functions you require. And obviously, if you're not going to use the Internet, all you need is a home LAN.

Now that we've spent time introducing Internet telephony, we'll go about explaining IRC and its related components.

Internet Relay Chat (IRC)

IRC is the granddaddy of Internet telephony and conferencing. It provides a medium through which many people can talk in real-time to each other but is limited to text only. This section looks at some of the IRC client software that is available for Linux.

How IRC Works

IRC works by having participants contact a server via their ISP and joining a discussion channel. Each channel is named and, supposedly, the name indicates the nature of the discussion taking place. You can't necessarily rely on the channel name, though, so if it sounds interesting just join the channel and see what's being talked about. If you don't like it, you can always leave.

If you require information about IRC or more assistance than is given here, the best place to start is `http://www.irchelp.org/`. There is more information about IRC here than you thought could possibly exist!

There's probably more IRC client software available than for any other Internet-based application. For obvious reasons of space, we can't discuss every client that exists. In fact, even if we tried there's a very good chance that someone, somewhere would be reading this and be upset because we didn't mention the client that they are using.

Where source code is available, this has been mentioned but installation of these programs from source is not discussed unless precompiled binaries are not available. In general, it is a good idea to avoid installing from source code unless you are reasonably conversant with make files. This is purely for the sake of convenience rather than security.

Having said that, you need to be aware that you should only download binaries from trusted sites. If the site you are downloading from is not well-known, it is always possible that someone could build a backdoor (security hole) into the binary and you would have no way of finding out until something out of the ordinary happens. In fact, if a person using this backdoor is sufficiently clever, you may not find out until the police come knocking on your door to discuss the latest breach of computer security at a military installation!

ircII

This is *the* IRC client. It is probably the oldest and most commonly used IRC client in the Linux/UNIX community. Unlike many other clients, though, ircII doesn't have fancy graphics and funny sounds. If you want to or have to use text only, this is the client for you.

The ircII home page is at `http://www.eterna.com.au/ircii/`.

> **Note**
>
> A note on pronunciation: Say the first three letters any way you want to—the obvious ways are I-R-C and irc (probably pronounced phonetically "erk"). But after the letters "irc," the Roman numeral is *always* pronounced as the number two. It is never I-I.

Obtaining ircII

The ircII home page provides the following:

You can FTP ircII from the following places:

Main site (Melbourne, Australia)

`ftp://ircftp.au.eterna.com.au/pub/ircII`

American `ftp://ircii.warped.com/pub/ircII`

Australia `ftp://coombs.anu.edu.au:/pub/irc/ircII`

Europe `ftp://ftp.funet.fi/pub/unix/irc/clients`

Note that the American site contains cryptography and these files should only be accessed by citizens residing in the U.S.

Copyright is similar to the GNU Public License (GPL). Note that there is one section of the source code that is copyright to The Regents of the University of California. Make sure you read the copyright file before distributing the source or binary code.

Installing ircII

First of all, you need to download the source code from one of the sites mentioned previously and then untar the package with the command `tar -xzf ircii-4_4_tar.gz`. This creates a directory underneath your current directory called ircii-4.4. Move into this directory and compile and install the code.

The file INSTALL, which is included with the package, describes the two options that are available for compiling ircII. It is recommended that you stick with the easy way using the "easyinst" script. Read the file before doing anything.

Before you start you should have the following information available (these are in the order in which installation questions are asked when using the "easyinst" script):

- You will need to know an IRC server name or IP number (there is a fairly good list at `http://central.austasia.net/info/irc.htm` and another list at `http://net.gurus.com/irc/ircservers.html`. There is also a truly massive list of servers at `http://www.geocities.com/~saintslist/`).

- Do you intend to install ircII for the system? This is a yes or no question. Unless you lack the permissions (you must have read/write/execute permissions for the installation directory tree—see the next item) or have some other good reason not to install for the system, answer yes to this question.

24

Internet
Telephony and
Conferencing

- Next you need to tell the script the parent directory for the installation. The default is /usr/local—this directory is created by default by most if not all of the distributions, so there shouldn't be a need to change it (unless, of course, your system policy specifies another place for user installed programs). Just press Enter to accept the default.

- Down to the nitty-gritty now. Where do you want to install the ircII binaries? If you used the default value in the previous question, just press Enter here to accept this default value. If you didn't use the default, enter the location specified by your system policy.

- Same as above for the next question regarding library installation.

After you have answered these questions, the script begins the installation procedure. The script prints a message suggesting you sit back and enjoy the show but you will probably have time to make a cup of your favorite beverage, catch up on some sleep, or even watch that video that you never seem to have time for.

The last thing to do is to enter the make command followed by make install. Note that these are also quite long processes.

Running ircII

The ircII executable is called "irc" and is located (if you accepted the default values as discussed above and installed for the system) in /usr/local/bin. To start running ircII, simply type **irc** at the command prompt.

If you installed just for yourself (that is, you answered no to the question "Do you intend to install ircII for the system?"), the binary is located in /home/<username>/bin/. If you installed in a non-default location, the binary is wherever you specified it should be.

In either of the preceding cases, the location is not by default searched by the shell when looking for executables, so you will have to do one of the following:

- Move to the location and type **./irc**

- Specify an absolute path to the executable and type **<absolute path>/irc**

- Specify a relative path to the executable and type **<relative path>/irc**

When ircII starts, it automatically tries to connect to the server specified during the installation process. If successful, you will see the message of the day (MOTD) from the server and ircII will sit patiently waiting for a command. If the server is not available, ircII will print an error message and again sit patiently waiting for a command.

Because most IRC client commands are common to all clients, we will discuss them further after we have looked at some other client software.

Zircon, an X-Windows Program for IRC

Zircon is a full-featured graphical client that supports just about all of the ircII commands and adds a few features of its own.

The latest version of Zircon is 1.18 and was developed using tcl version 8.0.4 and tk version 8.0.4. For obvious reasons, running Zircon requires a working X server.

The Zircon home page is located at `http://catless.ncl.ac.uk/Programs/Zircon/`.

Note that the copyright on this program is *not* GPL even though it looks similar. If you intend to distribute this program, make sure you read the copyright notice carefully.

Getting Zircon 1.18

This program is available by FTP from `ftp://catless.ncl.ac.uk/pub/zircon.tar.gz`. According to the home page, Zircon is available from several other archive sites around the world but the author neglects to mention the location of these sites.

A Red Hat source RPM is available from `ftp://catless.ncl.ac.uk/zircon.src.rpm` if you are interested in hacking it or just looking at what makes it tick. You may also need the source file if you find that the precompiled binary doesn't run on your system or if you are security-conscious.

Installing Zircon 1.18

First, you need to make sure that you have the correct versions of tcl and tk installed. Both should be version 8.0.4 or later. If you don't have these versions, Zircon just won't work—simple as that. To update, visit `http://www.scriptics.com/products/tcltk/` and get the latest version (8.2 at this writing).

The installer requires an X interface, so you start X-Windows first and then work from an x-term as required. Download the binary package and unpack it (`tar -xzfzircon.tar.gz`). This creates a directory called zircon-1.18.224, which you should cd to. Read the README file—the instructions given in this chapter may not apply to later versions.

Run the program installZircon to start the installation. As mentioned previously, this Zircon has a copyright that is not GPL, although it is similar, and now is a good time to read it. Click the Copying button to view before continuing with the installation.

To complete the installation, simply click the Install button—the default values are perfectly acceptable on a Red Hat 6.0 system.

24

Internet Telephony and Conferencing

Running Zircon 1.18

If you accepted the defaults given during the installation, the binary executable is now in `/usr/local/bin`. A small splash screen appears every time you run this program, but the first time there is also a notification window that informs you that this is a new version. Note that the splash screen mostly obscures this window, so you need to move the window so that you can click the OK button to continue. Fortunately, this only happens on the first execution after installation.

Before you try to connect to an IRC server, you need to set your Ircname and Nickname—just highlight the default values and type over them. Then select the button *above* the grayed out Server information button, select Other, and then enter the name of the IRC server that you want to connect to.

Given the large number of features that Zircon has, the best way to learn how to use it is to start it up and experiment. The display can get pretty busy while you're experimenting, but it does sort itself out in the end and you can start chatting.

X-Chat

X-Chat is the IRC client installed by default with the Red Hat 6.0 distribution. It has a nice, neat user interface and has a list of IRC servers installed by default—of course, you can add, delete, or change this list as you want.

X-Chat is a full-featured client that responds to a number of ircII commands as well as offering most command equivalents through the use of buttons on the interface. The X-Chat home page is at `http://xchat.linuxpower.org` and has additional documentation and information available. X-Chat requires X11 and GTK+ and, optionally, GNOME and Perl.

X-Chat is released under the GPL.

Getting X-Chat

As previously mentioned, X-Chat is installed by default with the Red Hat version 6.0 distribution, but for those people who want to update or who prefer to do their own installations, the RPM packaged binary can be obtained from the X-Chat download page at `http://xchat.linuxpower.org/download/`. The source code is available also from this location as a tarred and zipped archive or as an SRPM.

Installing X-Chat

At the time of this writing, the latest release is version 1.2.1. If you have an earlier version (such as is installed with Red Hat 6.0), it is well worth upgrading. X-Chat 1.2.1 offers an improved user interface as well as several other changes.

Download the RPM binary from the download page and place into an appropriate directory. Move to that directory and install using the Red Hat Package Manager,
`rpm -ivh xchat-1.2.1-1.i386.rpm`.

Note that if you have a previously installed version of X-Chat, you should use the command `rpm -Uvh xchat-1.2.1-1.i386.rpm` instead.

Running X-Chat

If you are using the GNOME interface and had a previously installed version of X-Chat, X-Chat can be run from the GNOME menu. It appears in the Internet sub-menu.

If you had no previous version of X-Chat installed and installed the latest version using RPM, the binary executable is in `/usr/bin`. This is in the default shell search path for all users.

Of course, if you installed from source, you need to read the makefile and if you installed from a tarball, the binary will usually appear in a directory of the same name as the program underneath the directory in which the tarball was placed.

Having started X-Chat, the first thing to do is to select a nickname—the default is your username—and then choose a server to connect to. X-Chat very helpfully provides a comprehensive list of servers for you to choose from so you shouldn't need to go looking on the WWW. If you know what server you require and it doesn't appear on the list, you can add it using the New Server button.

Clicking on Connect after choosing a server connects you to the server and you will normally see the message of the day. Nickname conflicts will be advised at this point.

BitchX

According the home page (`http://www.bitchx.com`), "BitchX is a modified clone of the popular ircII client, and is available for almost all UNIX OS's ...".

BitchX is another console-based IRC client that offers an alternative to ircII. Because it is console based, you don't need to worry about getting X up and running—just use that old 386 in the garage that only has a mono video card capable of 80×25 display!

Note that documentation is not installed with the program but you can find an FAQ list at`http://scripts.bitchx.com/bxfaq.html`.

Getting BitchX

BitchX is available for download at `http://www.bitchx.com/download/` in binary or source form. As usual, we recommend that you download and install the binary simply for the simplicity of it, but the download page recommends downloading the source code and compiling yourself because of the potential for security holes to be introduced.

Installing BitchX

Go to the directory into which you placed the downloaded tarball and unzip with the command `tar -xzf BitchX-75p3-Linux-glibc2-i386.tgz` to create a binary executable in the same directory. The execute bit needs to be set on this before you can run it.

Running BitchX

In the directory in which the tarball was placed (and after making sure the execute bit is set), type `./BitchX` and away you go!

BitchX connects automatically on startup to server irc.idle.net. If you want to specify a different server, you need to set the environment variable `IRCSERVER`. The bash shell command is `bash:~$export IRCSERVER "server:portserver2:port2 server3:port3"`. Note that the FAQ gives both the wrong command (`setenv`) and the wrong environment variable (`IRCSERVERS`).

ICQ and Clones

ICQ (I seek you) is a software package developed by Mirabilis (`http://www.icq.com`) to enable person-to-person and multi-party chatting in a more private environment than is available through IRC. It also has the advantages of making it easy to locate somebody and is easier to use than IRC for many people.

Clones, of course, are programs that provide the same or similar functionality as the original but are not provided or written by the authors of the original program. Under Linux, every ICQ-type program with the exception of JavaICQ as released by Miribilis is a clone.

ICQ, IP-Masquerading and Firewalls

There is a comprehensive discussion of how to configure your firewall to allow ICQ communication on the ICQ Web site at `http://www3.mirabilis.com/`.

Firewalls present a particular problem with ICQ because of the way the communication is implemented. The implementation requires that lines of communication be established between the various computers involved in the ICQ discussion. The purpose of a firewall is to stop these lines of communication being established and so separate procedures are required to bypass the firewall while minimizing the security risk.

In brief, if you don't want to access the Mirabilis site immediately, the process is quite simple.

To configure your firewall, you only need to set up rules to allow incoming socket connections through a small range of ports (for example, 5000-5020). How you do this is dependent upon the nature of your firewall. You should read and understand the information at the Mirabilis site as well as in Chapter 26, "Firewall Strategies," before implementing firewall changes.

Configuring the ICQ Client

To configure the ICQ client, you must tell the client that you are operating from behind a non-socks firewall and that the range of ports available is as specified when you modified your firewall. Finally, you need to restart the client so it is aware of the new settings and you should be all set to chat, send and receive files and messages, and so on.

JavaICQ from Mirabilis

JavaICQ is the Java implementation of ICQ. The ICQ home page is at `http://www.icq.com/`.

You need to be aware that JavaICQ has minimum requirements of 10MB hard disk space and 32MB RAM. This is a total RAM requirement, so 16MB physical RAM plus 16MB swap will satisfy that requirement (provided the whole of the swap space is available to this application).

Note that common opinion is that this application is needlessly large and is buggy. Because of this reputation, many Linux users have been put off using it but the code is under constant review by Mirabilis and improvements are gradually implemented.

The advantages of JavaICQ are that it is written and released by Miribilis and thus provides the maximum functionality that is available. The features that users of the Windows versions of ICQ have come to expect to be available are mostly available with JavaICQ, whereas the clones do not necessarily implement all of the features.

Getting JavaICQ

JavaICQ is only available as a compiled binary from the JavaICQ download page at
`http://www.icq.com/download/step-by-step-java.html`.

JavaICQ 0.98a (the latest release at this writing) requires that you have the Java
Development Kit 1.1.4 or higher (JDK 1.1.x). This is not included in the standard Red Hat
6.0 distribution, so if you have not installed it previously you will have to download this
before you can continue.

Installing JDK 1.1.x

You can obtain the JDK binaries and source from `http://www.blacktown.org/`. On the
JavaICQ download page, there is a pushbutton available to download Java that takes you
straight to this location. When you have selected a mirror site to download from, you can
download either a zipped and tarred package or a bzip2'ed package. The bzip2 packages
are smaller but require that you have bzip2 on your system.

There is also an open source version of the JDK available as part of the Kaffe package. You
can get this package from `http://www.transvirtual.com`. At the time of writing I hadn't
had the opportunity to test this package with the programs discussed here and so I cannot
comment on its suitability.

You will notice that there are two types of packages available for each release: one with the
word *native* in the title and one without. The ones with the word native in the title have
support for native threads—if you have a multi-processor machine, this is the version for
you; otherwise the other one is correct.

Download the latest stable version—you can find out which is the latest release from the
status page at `http://www.blackdown.org/java-linux/ports.html`—into the directory
`/usr/lib` and unpack it. A directory will be created with the name `jdk11x_v`*y* where the *x*
is replaced by the release number that you have chosen and the *y* is an update number. For
this chapter we chose release 7, update 3, so the directory is `/usr/lib/jdk117_v3/`.

Installing JavaICQ

Download the tarball `ICQJava_Preview.tar.gz` into your home directory and unpack it
(`tar -xzf ICQJava_Preview.tar.gz`). The tarball is unpacked into a directory called
`ICQJava`, which is created underneath the current directory.

Before proceeding with the installation, you should make sure that the environment
variable `JAVA_HOME` is set and points to the root directory of the jdk-11x package. If you
used the packages described previously, this is `/usr/lib/jdk117_v3/`. The value can be set

with the bash command `'export JAVA_HOME = "/usr/lib/jdk117_v3/"` and checked with the bash command `'echo "$JAVA_HOME"'`.

You should read the file "install" contained in the directory ICQJava to make sure that the variables are set correctly. If you have followed the directions and recommendations to this point, there shouldn't be any changes required but it always pays to check.

Start an X-Term and move into the ICQJava directory. Run the install script and ICQ will be installed onto your computer. Note that the executable has global execute permissions so if this does not suit your site, you will need to change this. When the installation has finished, you should run the ICQ program itself and register.

Running JavaICQ

The JavaICQ executable is in the same directory as the install script. If this directory is not in your shell default search path, you will have to specify an absolute or relative path. The executable is called ICQ (note the capital letters).

licq

licq is a multi-threaded ICQ. It is written in C++ and Qt. The current version, 0.76, is still in the beta stage so use accordingly.

The licq home page is at `http://www.licq.com/`, which provides additional information about the program.

At this stage, licq does not provide the facility to register a first-time user—you should use either (Java)ICQ from Mirabilis or micq (discussed later in this chapter) for this purpose.

Getting licq

licq is available for download as source or binary from the home page. There are normally rpm format packages of the latest version available at the same place. licq uses the qt shared library for some functionality and so you will also need to install the qt shared library. A link is provided to the download site from the licq home page. For this chapter we installed licq 0.70f and qt 1.44.6, which are both available as rpms.

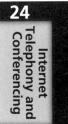

Installing licq

You need to install qt before attempting to install licq. As with other rpm packages, you only need to download to an appropriate directory and install using the rpm tool.

Running licq

The licq executable is installed into the directory `/usr/bin/licq` by default and has global execute permissions. This directory is on the default Red Hat 6.0 search path, so you shouldn't need to make any changes.

You need to make sure that you run licq from within an X session. The first time you run licq you need to issue the command `'licq -p qt-gui -s'` and afterwards you can just call the executable with no options. The `-p` option specifies a plug-in to use and `-s` tells licq to use this plug-in by default for future sessions.

There are several plug-ins and skins for licq available through pointers on the home page.

micq

micq is a text-only, console-based ICQ clone for Linux. It is a small functional replacement that doesn't require any additional libraries on your system. micq is also one of the very few ICQ clones available that lets you register a new user. Unfortunately, at this stage micq doesn't implement the chat facility, but all other functions are present.

Getting micq

The micq home page at `http://phantom.iquest.net/micq/` provides a link that allows you to download the latest version and provides additional links if you would like to download earlier versions. At the time of this writing, the latest version was 0.4.2 and the link provided only source code.

Installing micq

Download the source tarball from the micq home file and place it into an appropriate directory. Unpack it (`tar -xzf micq-0.4.2.tgz`) and it will create a directory called `micq-0.4.2/` directly underneath the current directory. You should cd into this directory and give the command `gmake` to compile the program. The executable will be in the same directory as the source code and is called `micq`.

Running micq

You must be connected to the Internet at the time you run micq. For some reason, micq attempts to connect to the ICQ network immediately when it is executed. If a connection cannot be made, program execution fails.

If you haven't put micq into a directory that is in your default path, you will have to move to the directory that it is installed in or give a relative or absolute path. The command is simply `micq`.

When micq first starts up, you are asked to enter an existing UIN or enter 0 (zero) to register a new user. Then you are asked to enter the password for that UIN, and micq attempts to make a connection to the ICQ server.

If the connection is successful, you are set to the "free for chat" mode by default.

There isn't very much configuration possible or required for micq. The README file in the source directory provides additional usage and configuration information.

Multimedia Conferencing Tools

A multimedia conferencing tool is any application-based tool that is being used to communicate utilizing different types of media, such as audio, video, and so on.

There are currently three different types of person-to-person voice communications that are available:

- PC to PC

- PC to telephone

- Telephone to telephone

PC to PC is the oldest and most commonly used form of person-to-person communications. The usual requirement is that the originator and the recipient must both be running the same software package and both must be connected to the Internet for the duration of the call. The "same software" requirement will gradually be removed as more and more developers embrace the H.323 recommendations. We will be concentrating our discussion in this chapter on PC-to-PC telephony and will look at some of the PC-to-PC voice communications software that is available for Linux.

PC-to-telephone communications is the next step up from PC-to-PC telephony and only requires that the originator of the call have an Internet connection and appropriate software. To contact somebody using PC-to-telephone communication relies on the existence of an intermediary who can link into the Public Switched Telephone Network (PSTN) at a point within local call distance of the recipient of the call. PC-to-telephone conversations are carried out as follows:

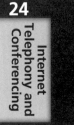

24

Internet
Telephony and
Conferencing

- The person with the Internet connection initiates a call.

- The call originator uses his or her computer to send digitized voice data to the intermediary.

- The computer that acts as the gateway between the Internet and the PSTN receives the compressed digitized data and converts it back into analog.

- The gateway then sends the analog data out onto the PSTN.

When the call recipient talks, the gateway computer simply reverses this procedure; that is, the gateway computer receives normal voice across the PSTN, which is then digitized and compressed. The digital data is again routed across the Internet until it reaches the computer of the call originator, where the communications software decompresses it and plays it back through the sound card.

The latest development in Internet telephony is telephone-to-telephone communications. In this case, it is not necessary for either party to have an Internet connection; in fact, they don't even have to have a computer! Telephone-to-telephone communications via the Internet works in a similar manner to PC to telephone except that the intermediary company has to link to the PSTN of both parties and should be within local call distance for both parties. The intermediary company is also required to do the analog -> digital / digital -> analog conversions on both sides of the conversation.

Unfortunately, Linux has been rather left behind on the video and audio-video conferencing front. As noted at the start of this chapter, the availability of drivers for the cameras is a big issue as is the matter of finding fast and reliable software.

There are a number of applications available that are specifically designed to run over the mbone, but given that many people do not have access to the mbone or the need for it, these tools are not discussed here. If you are considering an mbone connection, a good place to look for tools is `http://www-nrg.ee.lbl.gov/vic/`. This page provides information about vic (the video conferencing tool) and provides links to the other applications required to make up a full Internet conferencing suite.

Although this section serves to give you an introduction to world of multimedia conferencing, space does not permit a full discussion so we have limited our discussion mainly to the available applications for Linux. There is a comprehensive discussion of video-conferencing at `http://sunsite.utk.edu/video_cookbook/` if you want to go further.

Speak Freely

Speak Freely is an established audio-only conferencing tool for Windows that has recently become available for Linux platforms. The Speak Freely home page is at `http://www.speakfreely.org/`.

For many people, the downside of Speak Freely for Unix is that it is a console-based application at the moment. The home page states that there will be a beta X Windows version released in the near future, though.

Getting Speak Freely

Speak Freely for Unix is available from the Speak Freely for Unix home page at `http://www.fourmilab.ch/speakfree/unix/`. At the time of this writing, it was only available as source code.

Installing Speak Freely

You should have downloaded the source code into its own directory and unpacked it (`tar -xzf speak_freely-latest_tar.gz`). After unpacking you will have another directory, `speak_freely-7.1`, that contains the source code and documentation.

You must read both the README and the Makefile files before trying to compile this program. There are too many configurations of hardware available for it to be possible to create a reliable generic makefile (although the one that is supplied is pretty close). Make sure you take the advice given in the makefile and compile a simple version first before trying to take full advantage of your hardware.

The full instructions for use of this program are contained in the man pages. To obtain these, issue the command `'make manpage'` in the build directory. Note that you must have the environment variable PAGER defined before doing this.

After you have made the man pages, you should make the program itself with a simple `make` command.

Running Speak Freely

There are a number of possible invocations of Speak Freely, which are entirely dependent upon your requirements. The best place to start is with the manual pages (try `'man sflaunch'`) and the Speak Freely for Unix home page.

QSeeMe

QSeeMe is an integrated audio-visual conferencing program that also permits chatting in a manner similar to ICQ. Since Cu-SeeMe has ceased to be freely available, QSeeMe has filled that void. QSeeMe, at the time of this writing, supports sending grayscale video and receiving grayscale, M-JPEG, and H263 video as well as sending and receiving audio and chat.

Getting QSeeMe

QSeeMe is available from the home page at `http://www.pangea.org/~mavilar/qseeme/qseeme.html` as a pre-compiled binary only. Distribution is free for non-commercial purposes.

Installing QSeeMe

The tarball will unpack into its own directory called QSeeMe-0.83b and contains three files. The file `qseeme.man` should be copied or moved to an appropriate location for your manual pages (normally somewhere under the `/usr/local/man/`). No formatting of this file is required, but make sure you change the extension of the file from .man to .x where x is the man section that you decide the page belongs in—section 1 is probably a good place for it.

The file `qseeme` is the executable binary and `qseemerc` is the configuration file that is copied to the location `~/.qseemerc` when QSeeMe is executed. Again, there is very little configuration required of this program and the man page more than adequately explains the options available to you.

Running QSeeMe

QSeeMe must be started from within an X session with the command qseeme (assuming you have moved the executable to a location on your default search path). If you want to continue using the X-term that you used to start the program, you can run it as a background process without any problem.

The program is completely mouse driven and very self-explanatory.

CU-SeeMe

Originally developed by Cornell University, this was probably the most widely used video conferencing software. Unfortunately, Cornell University sold the full rights to the program to White Pine Software (`http://www.wpine.com`) in 1998 and CU-SeeMe ceased to be publicly available for the Linux platform, as did the reflector software.

White Pine has announced that it has released a version of the reflector software called MeetingPoint for Linux-based systems. Full details are available at the White Pine Software site. There is no indication at this writing when or if CU-SeeMe for Linux will be released.

CU-SeeMe and MeetingPoint offer a wide range of functions that make the conferencing process as easy and enjoyable as possible. There are complete descriptions of both of these products on the White Pine home page.

Summary

This chapter covered the topic of Internet telephony and conferencing. With Internet telephony, such topics as terminology, protocols and standards were discussed. With Internet relay chat, several different products such as Zircon and Xchat were reviewed. Moving on to multimedia conferencing tools, the concept of multimedia conferencing was discussed. In addition, such products as Speak Freely and QSeeMe were discussed, along with information on installation and configuration.

24

**Internet
Telephony and
Conferencing**

Security Principles

IN THIS CHAPTER

- Determining Your Security Needs *740*
- Securing Your Red Hat Server *743*
- Security Monitoring *772*
- Developing Security Policies *775*

Security is one of the most important things to consider when setting up a UNIX machine of any kind. Proper security considerations can save you time, grief, and depending on the contents of your system, money. At the very least, having a good security policy will give you peace of mind when you subject your system to unknown outside influences. Securing your system means knowing your system and its users well. In order for your security measures to be effective, you need to understand what you are trying to protect and what the potential threats are. You need to keep the good users in, the bad users out, and the data and services available to those who should have access. Knowing how your system is going to be used is the key to practicing good security.

For a system administrator, the word system can mean a variety of things. In a narrow sense, it could be a single computer, whereas in a much broader sense it is the entire network. It can be very difficult to police a large network. Breaking the network down into smaller modules can be the best way to get a handle on the overall system. In this manner, servers can be secured with one set of tools, while workstations can be secured with other tools. Understanding the source of potential attacks can help with your security planning.

This chapter looks at how to determine your security needs, some common types of attacks and security problems, as well as how to secure and monitor your system. It also discusses how to develop and implement a security policy that is both workable and enforceable in today's networked environment.

Determining Your Security Needs

For each system that will be exposed to security risks, you will have to determine the security measures to take and how to enforce them. You need to decide which parts of your system are most critical. This usually falls into two categories: Services and Data. If you are setting up a server that will be accessed for a particular service like http, DNS, or email, you will probably be concerned about keeping the machine running and available to your users for as much of the time as possible. If, on the other hand, your machine is going to be a development machine or a database server, although availability is still important, the contents of the machine are most likely more critical, and keeping your source code or data safe needs to be a top priority.

Some questions you should ask yourself are

- Who will be using this machine?

  Do you know the people you are going to give access to this machine, or is it going to be a public server? Do you trust them in general? Can you force them to follow the rules you outline?

- Will it be on a network?

  If so, do you trust the other machines and users on the network? The answer to this question is "No" if the network includes the Internet.

- What kind of machine is it?

  Is it a server that will live in a locked room and be accessed via network only, or is it a workstation that will have user accounts and local logins? If it is functioning as a server providing specialized remote services only, make sure general users do not have login accounts or are prevented from logging in. If the machine is a workstation, you should make sure that the users you do allow to login cannot gain more privileges than you grant them.

- What services is it going to offer to your users?

  If these services are disrupted, what will the effect be to the user population? Will it be an annoyance because your users can't do work, or will it cost your company money through loss of online sales or reputation if the machine goes down?

- How much is the data on the machine worth to you or your company?

  How much do you stand to lose in both time and money if someone hacks into the machine and reformats your drives? Your backup strategy may depend on this. If you have huge amounts of data on the system, backups and restores are not trivial tasks, and may involve significant amounts of time.

Basically, the better you understand your users and the systems and software they need, the better you can secure the environment without causing yourself or your users major headaches.

Types of Attacks

Your system can be attacked in many different ways, and knowing what they are and how to prevent them is what security is all about. Attacks on your system can be broken down into several categories, which are covered in the following sections.

Physical Attacks

Physical attacks can happen any time someone has physical access to your machine. A physical attack might be someone sitting down in front of your file server, rebooting the machine from his own floppy disk, and copying all of your source code. It might also be someone going into your server room, opening your case, and removing all your drives. These types of attacks can usually be prevented or at least minimized with a few simple procedures, which are described in the "Physical Security" section later in this chapter.

Denial of Service Attacks

A denial of service attack can range from flooding your network ports with connection requests to flooding your mail server with spam mail. In either case, the end result is usually that legitimate requests to the service are not processed either due to the sheer volume, or due to the attack causing some problem with the service itself (for example, filling up the drive where /var/spool/mail lives so no legitimate mail to your users can be received). The perpetrators of these attacks can be difficult to track down because they often use spoofed IP addresses or stolen accounts to attack your system. This discussion does not consider physical disruption of service (that is, someone walking into your server room with a sledgehammer and a pair of wire cutters) as a denial of service attack, although the end result is the same.

Privilege Attacks

A privilege attack occurs when someone tries to obtain privileges or access to privileged accounts on your system that you did not assign to him. This could be a disgruntled user attempting to gain root access to cause trouble, or it could be someone coming in over your network trying to gain access to your files. Privilege attacks can be minimized, but the security-conscious administrator must remain vigilant for obvious security holes as well as security patches for software running on the machine. Most breaches of security that happen could have been avoided by doing a few simple security audits and keeping software up-to-date.

Regardless of the source of the attack, there are a variety of simple steps that you can take to secure your systems against all but the most determined individuals. These steps are covered in the next few sections.

Securing Your Red Hat Server

Securing a network is much like securing your home or auto against theft or break-in. If someone really wants to get in, they will likely find a way. However, a few basic items can go a long way toward making a break-in attempt a difficult task. Hopefully, the attacker will give up and move on. If not, you need to capture enough information to identify the would-be attacker.

Properly setup networks are like a house with all the doors and windows locked. What you need to avoid is leaving the attacker an unlocked, or worse, open door to walk right through. System basics such as passwords, firewalls, and physical security can ensure that users need appropriate keys to unlock the doors to your network.

Passwords

Passwords are arguably the most important security feature in a Linux environment. The system always needs some way to authenticate a user, and most often in Linux it is a password. A user's Linux password and related user information is kept in a file called `/etc/passwd`. This file contains most of what the system itself knows about a user, from his numeric user ID or UID to his home directory. (See `man 5 passwd`, or Chapter 29, "Users and Groups," for full details.)

The `/etc/passwd` File

The `/etc/passwd` file is in constant use by the system. It is used by many applications to determine ownership, usually of files or processes. This means that the `/etc/passwd` file needs to be world-readable for these applications to work, or you will not be able to do things such as see the username of the person who owns files in your ls listing. However, if the file is world-readable, it is rather pointless to store plain text passwords there. To get around this small inconvenience, the passwords were hashed with a one-way encryption algorithm, and the result was stored in `/etc/passwd`. This meant that you could not regenerate someone's password just by reading the hashed text and applying a reverse algorithm to it. You could, however, pick a word at random, apply the same one-way hash to it, and compare it with what's in `/etc/passwd`. If they matched, you picked the user's password. People developed programs to take a very large dictionary of words, and apply common capitalizations and character replacements to them, hash them, and compare the results with your entire passwd file. One such program is CRACK, and it is quite good at what it does. Any password that is a dictionary word is nearly guaranteed to be found. Some systems began using better hashing algorithms (such as MD5), but that only makes CRACK work harder—it doesn't eliminate the problem of having password text in the clear.

The `/etc/shadow` File

The solution to this problem that many versions of Linux adopted was to use another file to store the hashed password text, and since most applications don't need to know about the user's password, encrypted or otherwise, this new file could be made readable by root only. The file is called `/etc/shadow`. It contains the username, the encrypted password, and some accounting fields for password expiration and the like (see man 5 `shadow`). The password field in `/etc/passwd` was replaced with a single character "x" to indicate that the password is stored elsewhere, and the authentication software was compiled to check `/etc/shadow` instead of `/etc/passwd` when it needed to compare passwords. The end result is that users can still check `/etc/passwd` to be able to associate UIDs with usernames, but they do not have access to the user's password or encrypted password string.

> **Note**
>
> Be sure that users have read-only access to `/etc/passwd` /and that only root has read access to `/etc/shadow` or your passwords will be exposed to crack attempts.

> **Tip**
>
> If you are about to install a Red Hat system, you will be asked near the end of the installation whether or not you want MD5-encrypted passwords and shadow passwords. Say yes to both of these! By saying yes at installation, all the passwords will be encrypted and placed in the correct locations. Otherwise, much of the conversion will need to be done by manually resetting each of the passwords already in the system.
>
> If you said no previously, you can convert your passwd and group files to shadow password setup with the pwconv and grpconv programs. Changing to MD5 encryption later is more problematic. It involves resetting the passwords on all user accounts and changing the PAM configuration for passwd, login, and rlogin in `/etc/pam.d`.

The `/etc/group` File

The `/etc/group` file contains information similar to `/etc/passwd`, but it pertains to user groups rather than users themselves. In the shadow configuration, `/etc/gshadow` contains the hashed group password, and `/etc/group` contains only information that other users should be able to see. You should make sure `/etc/group` and `/etc/gshadow` have the same permissions as `/etc/passwd` and `/etc/shadow`, respectively. A full explanation of `/etc/group` can be found in Chapter 29.

The `/etc/shadow` file contains fields to configure password expiration information on a user-by-user basis. This information can be changed with the `chage` function (see `man chage` for details). It is a good idea to have passwords expire to force users to change them. The longer a user uses the same password, the greater chance there is that someone else will figure it out. It is also a good idea to have accounts expire automatically if their password has expired and the account has not been accessed to change it. This can help to prevent misuse of old accounts. It is still up to you to clean up old accounts on your system frequently. Setup of password policies and defaults are covered in detail in Chapter 29.

Having the passwords hidden is a good thing, but having good passwords and keeping them that way is also extremely important. Should anyone manage to get a look at your `/etc/shadow` file, a single bad password provides a simple way for them to gain a foothold into your system. A password consisting of a word from the dictionary is totally unacceptable, and even a jumble of several random lowercase characters is not secure enough. The raw speed of modern computers combined with distributed computing techniques makes a brute-force (trying every possible combination) attack on such a password relatively easy and quick.

Making Passwords Difficult to Crack

So what should you do to make your passwords more difficult to crack? Having a minimum length is a good place to start. The longer the password is, the more character combinations are possible, and therefore the more work is required to do a brute-force attack. Another good idea is to have characters from different character groups such as uppercase letters, digits, and other symbols (!@#$%^ and so on). Having characters from different character groups greatly increases the total number of possible combinations you can have in your password, thus making a brute-force attack far more difficult. But how do you go about enforcing these rules on your users without running CRACK on your password file frequently and telling them yourself? PAM can help.

PAM

PAM (Pluggable Authentication Modules) is a set of code modules that enable the system administrator to configure the authentication methods used by programs that require authentication. It also allows the administrator to add or update authentication methods without having to rebuild the applications that use them. Red Hat comes with full PAM support, and it is preconfigured to do sanity checks on users' passwords. PAM's password-checking module does a dictionary check on the password using cracklib to make sure it

25

Security
Principles

isn't a word straight out of the dictionary. It can also make sure the password is of a certain length and contains a certain mix of different kinds of characters (letters, numbers, punctuation, and so on). In Red Hat, PAM comes pre-installed and uses /etc/pam.d to store most of its configuration files. There is one file for each service that requires authentication, with the filename being the same as the name of the service. Inside each configuration file is a list of things PAM should do when authentication is required or when changing authentication parameters. The lines form a stack of tasks for PAM to perform in order to do the required authentication for the application. Each step in a stack performs a different function. Some will affect the general pass/fail outcome of the entire stack, and some will merely log information about the state as the user proceeds through the stack. The file consists of several lines of the following format:

```
service-name module-type control-flag module-path arguments
```

The service-name is frequently the conventional name of the application such as ftpd, rlogind, and so on. There is also a special service-name reserved for defining a default authentication mechanism, it is called other.

At present there are only four possible module-types. They are

- auth—Verify that users are who they say they are (request a password).

- account—Restrict/permit access to services.

- session—Preconfiguration before granting the service to someone, or post-configuration after granting the service to someone.

- password—Update the authentication token for this user.

Like the module-type parameter, there are four possible control-flag parameters. These indicate the level of concern if a particular module succeeds or fails. The control-flag keywords are

- required—Necessary for successful authentication. Failure will not be apparent to the user until all other modules have finished.

- requisite—Similar to required, but module exits immediately on failure.

- sufficient—Meets the criteria for success for this module.

- optional—Used only in the case of an indeterminate response from other modules in the stack.

The module path in Red Hat is `/lib/security/<full modulename>`, and the following is a list of some useful modules that come preinstalled with Red Hat:

- `pam_cracklib.so`—Password strength checking
- `pam_deny.so`—Denies automatically (always fails)
- `pam_env.so`—Sets or unsets environment variables
- `pam_ftp.so`—For anonymous FTP access
- `pam_group.so`—Group settings based on `userid/tty`
- `pam_lastlog.so`—Maintains `/var/log/wtmp`
- `pam_limits.so`—Sets system resource limits
- `pam_listfile.so`—Sets service permissions based on `user/tty`
- `pam_mail.so`—Checks for existence of new mail for the user
- `pam_nologin.so`—Only root can login if `/etc/nologin` exists
- `pam_permit.so`—Always returns success for the module
- `pam_pwdb.so`—Manages `/etc/passwd`
- `pam_radius.so`—RADIUS authentication
- `pam_rhosts_auth.so`—Authenticate `rsh`, `rlogin`, `rexec`
- `pam_rootok.so`—root can login with no password
- `pam_securetty.so`—Manages `/etc/securetty` checks
- `pam_shells.so`—Manages `/etc/shells` checks
- `pam_time.so`—Restricts services based on time
- `pam_warn.so`—Extra logging
- `pam_wheel.so`—Only members of group wheel can log in

The arguments are module-specific and are described in detail in the PAM documentation. The following section describes the `pam_cracklib.so` module.

The `pam_cracklib` Module

This module allows PAM to do password strength checking. The concept is simple: We are human and tend to behave in a predictable fashion. By checking passwords against human habits, `pam_cracklib` can help prevent easy-to-crack passwords from being used. When it is present in a PAM config file, it prompts the user for a password, which is then passed through cracklib (an external password checking routine). Then, it does some checks of the following:

> A similarity check—Is the new password too similar to the old one? For example, old: testPass new: testPast
>
> A palindrome check—Are the new password and the old password palindromes of each other? For example, old: testPass new: ssaPtset
>
> A case check—Do the old and new passwords differ only by upper/lowercase? For example, old: testPass new: TestpasS
>
> A rotation check—Is the new password a rotated version of the old one? For example, old: testPass new: estPasst

The default mode of `pam_cracklib` is to ask for a single password, check the password's strength and, if it passes, verify the password by requesting it to be typed a second time. This default mode can be modified through the use of arguments. These include

- `debug`—This argument causes the module to write additional information to syslog. It will not write the actual passwords there.

- `type=<something>`—By default the user will be prompted with "New UNIX Password." With this argument, Linux will be replaced with `<something>` so that you can keep this module in context when it is being used to verify passwords other than for a UNIX account.

- `retry=n`—The number of times the user will be prompted to try again when his new password is not strong enough. (Default = 1.)

- `difok=n`—The number of characters in the new password that should not appear in the old password. (Default = 10. Note: if half of the characters in the new password are not in the old password, it will be accepted as well.)

- `minlen=n`—The minimum credits that a password must have to be accepted. Credits are granted 1 for each character, and extra for having characters of different types (lowercase alpha, uppercase alpha, numbers, and others). These credits are determined by the `lcredit`, `ucredit`, `dcredit`, and `ocredit` parameters. (Default = 9. Note: The minimum is 6 because `cracklib` demands that passwords be at least six characters long.)

- `dcredit=n`—The maximum additional credits for having digits in the password at 1 credit per digit. (Default = 1.)

- `ucredit=n`—The maximum additional credits for having uppercase characters in the password at 1 credit per uppercase character. (Default = 1.)

- `lcredit=n`—The maximum additional credits for having lowercase characters in the password at 1 credit per lowercase character. (Default = 1.)

- `ocredit=n`—The maximum additional credits for having other characters in the password at 1 credit per other character ($!#$% and so on. Default = 1.)

The following is an example for a `pam_cracklib` module line:

```
passwd password required  pam_cracklib.so difok=5 minlen=16 dcredit=2 ocredit=2
```

Using cracklib properly will guarantee that your passwords are very difficult to guess, and it is recommended that you edit the `pam_cracklib` line in `/etc/pam.d/passwd` to force users to have reasonable passwords.

Beware of Overly Strict Password Policies

Will having complex password rules help to lock down your system? So it would seem, but in fact, the security problem can move from your system to your users' workplaces, which are far more difficult to police. If the password rules are too strict and passwords become a meaningless jumble of letters and numbers, users are going to find it difficult to remember them, and instead will write them down. Now the password is committed to paper, which someone else can either read or steal. If you're lucky, the piece of paper will be kept in a safe place and not taped to the user's monitor, but I wouldn't count on it.

Although there is not much you can do to prevent users from writing down their passwords, you can at least make it possible for them to remember. Make the password rules loose enough so that the users can choose passwords that they can remember while still giving you the security you require on your system. Increasing the minimum length is a good start. If you are using MD5 (which is recommended), your password length is not limited to eight characters, and that allows your users to be a little less cryptic in choosing a password that satisfies your password rules. You may want to inform your users that they do not have to choose a pass-*word*, per se—spaces are allowed, so a pass-*phrase* is possible. A pass-phrase might be easier for your users to remember and will still provide you with the security you require. If you are going to encourage long passwords with a high minlength, make sure your difok is set accordingly. If someone enters a long password containing all the letters in the alphabet, it will be very difficult to choose a new password that has a sufficient number of different characters.

> **Note**
>
> When entering passwords on a system where MD5 is not used for password encryption, the user may enter a password of more than eight characters. However, only the first eight characters will be saved and used for the password, and the system will not log an error message or tell the user. Anything over eight characters is ignored entirely.

System Files

The vast majority of your system's security will be contained within files found on your system. Access to these files needs to be limited to the appropriate users. Obviously, programs and procedures need some level of access to these files to operate properly. Having a working knowledge of which files are used to secure the system and editing them as necessary can tighten the security on an already robust system. The next few sections examine several of the files and the modifications that can be made to improve system security.

The `/etc` directory

Systemwide configuration files are normally stored in the `/etc` directory. As many of these files are important to system security, they are covered in detail here.

at.allow/at.deny

The at command uses these files to determine which users may use at. at allows a user to queue up one or more programs to be run unattended at a later date or time. See man at for details.

As the system administrator, you will have to determine whether or not this practice should be allowed on your system. If you allow public shell access, you may want to think about limiting your users to running programs while they are physically logged into the system for tracking purposes. This can be done through the use of a shell script combined with an appropriate cron job.

at first checks at.allow to see if it exists, and if it does, only the users listed in it can use at. If at.allow doesn't exist, at.deny is checked, and if it exists, everyone but the users in at.deny can use at. If neither exists, only root may use at. Empty files are valid for both at.allow and at.deny.

As a precaution, you should add all the system users to your `at.deny` file to prevent them from being able to run at jobs.

cron.allow/cron.deny

These files operate in the same fashion as `at.allow` and `at.deny`, but they are for the cron service. Cron allows a user to set up a fixed, recurring schedule for jobs to be run.

> **Note**
>
> Since with clever use of shell scripting, cron can be made to work like at, and at can be made to work like cron, you may want to configure these two identically, allowing and denying appropriate user rights. That way, someone who has access to only one can't build a script and essentially gain access to the other.

inetd.conf

`inetd.conf` controls the services that are offered by inetd, a daemon that answers network requests on behalf of a number of other server applications. Inetd acts as a receptionist for incoming network requests on several different ports. It uses the `/etc/services` file to give a name-to-port mapping for the services it will monitor. All that inetd does is pass off connections to server programs as the requests occur. You should look through this file and disable any service that your system should not be providing. For example, if you are going to use this machine as a Web server only, you probably don't need POP-x or IMAP services, and you may want to disable telnet and ftp services as well. This will limit the number of network requests your machine will respond to—the fewer the better.

You can disable services in `inetd.conf` by inserting a # at the beginning of the line that the service appears on. The following is a list of the default entries in `inetd.conf`. You can decide whether or not to allow these services on your system. These are services implemented within inetd itself, and can safely be disabled without affecting the system. They should be disabled automatically on install.

```
#echo     stream  tcp nowait  root     internal
#echo     dgram   udp wait     root     internal
#discard    stream  tcp nowait  root     internal
#discard    dgram   udp wait     root     internal
#daytime    stream  tcp nowait  root     internal
```

```
#daytime    dgram   udp wait     root     internal
#chargen    stream  tcp nowait   root     internal
#chargen    dgram   udp wait     root     internal
#time   stream  tcp nowait   root     internal
#time   dgram   udp wait     root     internal
```

Many sites leave the next two services open, but if your machine is not an FTP server, and you are going to be doing all administration while sitting at the console, you can probably disable these and plug a number of potential holes.

```
ftp     stream  tcp     nowait  root    /usr/sbin/tcpd  in.ftpd -l -a
telnet  stream  tcp     nowait  root    /usr/sbin/tcpd  in.telnetd
```

> **Note**
>
> If you disable telnetd in `inetd.conf`, you will not be able to telnet into the machine *at all*. You will either need to sit at the machine to get shell access or install something such as SSH to provide a more secure remote shell.

Additional inetd Services

The next three services are for rsh, rlogin, and rexec respectively. There are special considerations you should think about before allowing these services on your machine. Read the `.rhosts` and `hosts.equiv` sections before enabling these services on your system.

```
#shell  stream  tcp nowait  root    /usr/sbin/tcpd  in.rshd
#login  stream  tcp nowait  root    /usr/sbin/tcpd  in.rlogind
#exec   stream  tcp nowait  root    /usr/sbin/tcpd  in.rexecd
```

The following line is for `in.comsat`, which is not installed by default in Red Hat and is left disabled in `inetd.conf`. It is associated with the biff service for mail notification. Since most modern mail packages have a notification system of their own, it is usually not necessary to install and enable comsat.

```
#comsat dgram   udp wait     root    /usr/sbin/tcpd  in.comsat
```

The three lines that follow are for communication between users on your machine or other machines. If these are enabled, you can use client software to chat with other users on your machine, or on remote machines. Disable these if you do not want to allow this service.

```
#talk   dgram   udp wait     root    /usr/sbin/tcpd  in.talkd
#ntalk  dgram   udp wait     root    /usr/sbin/tcpd  in.ntalkd
#dtalk  stream  tcp waut     nobody  /usr/sbin/tcpd  in.dtalkd
```

Mail protocols are next. If you're not running a mail server, there's no reason for inetd to be listening for mail service requests. Disable them if you're not using them.

```
#pop-2   stream  tcp     nowait  root     /usr/sbin/tcpd ipop2d
#pop-3   stream  tcp     nowait  root     /usr/sbin/tcpd ipop3d
#imap    stream  tcp     nowait  root     /usr/sbin/tcpd imapd
```

The Unix-to-Unix Copy Protocol server is not necessary in many installations, therefore there is no need to enable this service in most situations.

```
#uucp   stream  tcp nowait  uucp     /usr/sbin/tcpd/usr/lib/uucp/uucico    -l
```

The following line configures bootpd. Bootpd is used by devices that need information on bootup but have no storage media to keep it on between reboots. It is often used to serve diskless workstations and printers. If you are not serving such information, you can disable this service.

```
#bootps dgram   udp wait    root     /usr/sbin/tcpd  bootpd
```

Trivial file transfer protocol is set up with the next line. With no arguments, access is limited to the directory /tftpboot. If this directory doesn't exist, no access is granted. Any path arguments are treated as readable directories, so you should be careful to make sure there are no paths that you don't require in the argument list. It is best to disable this service unless you need it.

```
#tftp   dgram   udp wait    root     /usr/sbin/tcpd  in.tftpd
```

Using the next four services is very risky because they give outsiders information about your system. If you need a finger-type service, you should change the line in inetd.conf to use safe_finger instead of in.fingerd. safe_finger filters out data passed to in.fingerd so that a malicious user can't send arguments to in.fingerd that would break it.

```
#finger stream  tcp nowait  root     /usr/sbin/tcpd  in.fingerd
#cfinger stream tcp nowait  root     /usr/sbin/tcpd  in.cfingerd
#systat stream  tcp nowait  guest    /usr/sbin/tcpd  /bin/ps -auwwx
#netstat    stream  tcp nowait  guest    /usr/sbin/tcpd/bin/netstat     -f inet
```

The next line is for the identd service. Identd is used by external servers when someone tries to connect to them from your machine. It is supposed to return information about the user and machine attempting the connection, but some information is omitted for security purposes. The -o option tells identd not to return the operating system type. This is a good idea because a hacker learning what operating system you are running is able to tailor attacks specific to that operating system. The -l option tells identd to use the syslog utility for logging, and the -e option tells identd to return UNKNOWN_ERROR instead of more specific error messages. Many servers will not allow connections if your machine does not return some sort of ident response, so you should leave this service enabled if you expect it to be communicating with other servers.

Linuxconf is a configuration utility for Linux that can be spawned by inetd in response to connection requests on port 98. Linuxconf runs a small Web server with its own authentication and connection verification built in. By default, no hosts can connect to the linuxconf service. If you want to enable this, you can run linuxconf from either a console window or under X Windows and go to Networking, Misc, Linuxconf Network Access. There you can configure the hosts that are allowed to access linuxconf from the network. Be warned that this is usually not a good idea because the Web traffic is not secure and passwords may be snooped across the network. Unless you have a good reason to use linuxconf remotely, it is best to disable this feature. If you must enable it, use tcp wrappers to prevent unwanted access. (See the "Tcp Wrappers" section below). Here is the line for Linuxconf in inetd:

Swat is the Samba Web Administration Tool, and is also spawned by inetd. It runs a small Web server on port 901 and can be connected to by any machine on the network. Again, any packets sent to this server can be snooped, including passwords, so running this over the network is a bad idea. If you do need to use swat, connect from the local host. Adding tcp wrappers to swat is a good idea if you are going to enable it. (See the following "Tcp Wrappers" section.) Here is the line to enable/disable swat in inetd:

```
#swat     stream tcp    nowait.400     root /usr/sbin/swat swat
```

Once you have finished commenting out the services you don't require on your system, be sure to restart inetd with its new configuration using the following command:

```
killall -HUP inetd
```

Tcp Wrappers

You have pared down the services you do not want inetd to provide, but what if you want inetd to offer services to just some addresses but not others? You could use a firewall (see Chapter 26, "Firewall Strategies"), but what if you don't need the full suite of protection that a firewall offers, or you don't want to set up another machine just to protect your new server? Maybe you only want to prevent your lab workstations from accessing the news server but allow everyone else on the local network in. A quick and easy way to do this is to use tcp wrappers. Tcp wrappers act as a middleman between inetd and the services that inetd supports. Tcp wrappers work by having inetd answer incoming requests, but pass them off to tcpd to check out the originating address/userid before passing it along to the real service for processing.

The following is a sample line from `/etc/inetd.conf` for the FTP service. This particular `inetd.conf` does not use tcp wrappers for its ftp service.

```
ftp stream  tcp nowait  root  in.ftpd -l -a
```

This line will automatically pass all requests that come for FTP directly to the ftp service without any checks whatsoever.

A sample line from `/etc/inetd.conf` employing tcp wrappers is

```
ftp stream  tcp nowait  root    /usr/sbin/tcpd  in.ftpd -l -a
```

With the preceding line in `inetd.conf`, when inetd gets a connection request on the FTP port (port 21 from `/etc/services`), it calls `/usr/sbin/tcpd` and passes in as arguments the command line to run the real ftpd with the correct parameters. Tcpd logs the request using syslog, and then checks its access files—`/etc/hosts.allow` first and `/etc/hosts.deny` second (see the following section). If the host attempting the connection is permitted to use that service, ftpd is executed with the arguments that were passed to tcpd and the connection is allowed to proceed. If the host is not allowed to connect to that service, the connection request is denied in one of several ways.

hosts.allow/hosts.deny

These files are used by many inetd-related services to determine which hosts or domains on the network are trusted and which are not. The files are scanned until a match occurs—first `hosts.allow`, then `hosts.deny`. If no match is found in either file, the client is granted access.

The files follow this basic format:

```
service list : client list : action
```

The format of the files can become quite complex, however, and a more detailed explanation can be found in `man 5 hosts_access` and `man 5 hosts_options`.

> **Note**
>
> You can use the keywords `allow` and `deny` in both `hosts.allow` and `hosts.deny`, so you can specify a complete rule set in either file if you choose.

25

Security
Principles

Examples Of `hosts.deny`/`hosts.allow`

To allow people from `friendly.org` to use ftp on your server but deny everybody else, you could do the following (notice the "." before `.friendly.org`—this is interpreted as `*.friendly.org` or *any* machine from the `friendly.org` domain) :

```
in.ftpd : .friendly.org : ALLOW
ALL : ALL : DENY
```

You can also group services or locations together to give permissions on a group basis. To do this, you need to have one or more services or locations per line separated by spaces in the appropriate area.

The following lines will allow telnet and FTP connections from `friendly.com` and `niceguys.com`, but not from anybody else.

```
in.ftpd in.telnetd : .friendly.com .niceguys.com : ALLOW
in.ftpd in.telnetd : ALL : DENY
```

There is also another useful command you can put in `hosts.allow` or `hosts.deny`—the `twist` command. This allows you to run a program instead of one of your TCP services (or UDP services that do not use standard I/O) under some conditions. This is useful to print out more verbose rejection messages for people who attempt to access your machine from locations from which you have denied access.

in `/etc/hosts.allow`:

```
in.telnetd : .friendly.com .nice.com : ALLOW
in.telnetd : ALL : twist /bin/echo /etc/rejection_message
```

This will allow anyone from machines in the `.friendly.com` or `.nice.com` domains to telnet into your machine, but anyone else gets a message printed to their screen when they try to access your machine via telnet.

You can also use the `banners` command to print rejection messages for services by specifying a rejection file for each service in a separate directory:

```
in.telnetd in.ftpd : ALL : banners /etc/banners : DENY
```

In `/etc/banners`, there would be a file called `in.telnetd` and a file called `in.ftpd`, each containing a rejection message that would be printed to anyone trying to connect to the telnet or ftp ports. You do not have to deny access with the `banners` command. You can use it to print a message but still allow someone to use your service.

> **Note**
>
> The `banners` option is only useful for TCP services, not UDP.

tcpdchk and tcpmatch

Once you have configured your `inetd.conf`, `hosts.allow`, and `hosts.deny` files to your liking, you should check them over to see if you have missed any obvious holes or if you have mistyped any keywords. You can do this with the tcpdchk and tcpdmatch programs. tcpdchk will perform a sanity check on your `inetd.conf`, `hosts.allow`, and `hosts.deny` files and report on any anomalies it finds. tcpdmatch allows you to formulate a request for inetd and see how the rule sets you have defined will handle it. Using tcpdchk and tcpdmatch will help you to close any holes you have in your tcp wrapper settings.

> **Tip**
>
> If you would like to adjust your tcpd configuration on a live system without affecting the way it is currently running, you can copy your `inetd.conf`, `hosts.allow`, and `hosts.deny` files to a separate directory, modify them, and run tcpdchk and tcpdmatch on them with the `-i` and `-d` arguments (see man 5 tcpdchk and man 5tcpdmatch).

hosts.equiv

The machines listed in this file are treated as equivalent to the local host for remote access purposes. Programs such as rsh, rlogin, and rexec use this file to determine whether or not a user has permission to use them from a particular remote machine. If a remote hostname appears in this file and you have these services enabled in your `/etc/inetd.conf` file, uses can rlogin to the local machine and get a login prompt even if you have telnet disabled. They can even skip authentication if the usernames on the two machines match. A line in `hosts.equiv` looks like the following:

```
[+¦-][hostname] [+¦-][userid]
```

```
+ userid
```

This will allow the specified userid from any host to login to the system if the same userid exists on the local system.

```
hostname +
```

This will allow any user from the specified host to login to the system if the userid exists on the local system.

```
hostname -userid
```

The preceding will allow all but the named userid on the specified host to login if that userid exists locally.

This is true for all users except root. Root must have a `.rhosts` file (explained in ".rhosts" later in the chapter) in his home directory with remote users and hosts for this to work. Having entries in `hosts.equiv` can be dangerous—if any of the hosts in your `hosts.equiv` file are hacked, the hacker has an easy way to get a shell on your system. If you must use rsh/rexec/rlogin, be sure to configure `/etc/pam.d/rexec`, `etc/pam.d/rsh`, and `/etc/pam.d/rlogin` to make sure there is a line in there to add the `pam_rhosts_auth.so` module. This will perform some checks such as making sure that the user's `.rhosts` file is not writable by anyone other than the owner, and ignoring the "+" entry in `hosts.equiv` and `.rhosts` (allow all access). If you would like the system to only use `/etc/hosts.equiv` and not `.rhosts`, add the `no_rhosts` argument to the `pam_rhosts_auth.so` line.

ftpusers

`ftpusers` stores the names of local users who cannot use the ftpd service. When ftpd is invoked by inetd/tcpd in response to a network request, ftpd checks this file to make sure that the user is allowed to use FTP. At the very least you should have root in this file. Not allowing root to use FTP is a good idea because it removes yet another potential point of entry for the superuser account. You should also put all other names into this file that exist in `/etc/passwd` that should never use FTP, such as bin, sys, daemon, adm, and so on. In addition, some actual users might not have a need for ftp and they should also be included in this file.

ftphosts

This is another access control list for ftpd. It allows you to set permissions specifically for connection to the ftp service. The format is

```
allow¦deny <userid> <address, address, ...>
<userid> is any user name.
<address> is one of host.domain, IP:netmask, IP/maskbits, or netbits.*
```

ftpaccess

This file has user access and general settings for ftpd. You can configure guest groups and guest accounts in this file, as well as time, file, and byte limits for ftp transfers. If you are going to offer the ftp service on your machine, you should consider tailoring this file to protect your system as much as possible. Institute upload limits to make it difficult for a remote FTP user to crash your system by uploading massive files and filling up your hard drives.

Some important `ftpaccess` functions to use are discussed in the next sections.

noretrieve

This can be used to prevent someone from retrieving files in your ftp directory. `passwd`, `core`, and `.rhosts` are useful files to apply the `noretrieve` rule to.

upload

This is a very useful feature. It allows you to set up a directory that can be written to but not read from. This way, you can set up an incoming directory where uploads go, but those files will have to be moved to another directory before someone can download them. This gives you control over the files that are passing through your system.

loginfails <number>

Set the number of times a user can fail a login attempt. If a user repeatedly fails a login attempt, the connection will be terminated. The default value is 5.

throughput

This allows you to throttle the throughput for a connection or file list. This can be helpful when multiple users or hosts may connect simultaneously. Using `throughput`, you can prevent one or more users from using excessive bandwidth at the expense of the other users or hosts.

log commands <userlist>

This enables user commands to be logged. The `<userlist>` is a comma-separated list of one or more of the following: `real`, `guest`, and `anonymous`. `real` refers to real accounts on the system; guest and anonymous are self-explanatory. In each case, logins matching these will be logged.

log transfers <userlist> <direction>

This enables file transfer logging both to and from the server for `anonymous` and/or `real` users. The `<direction>` argument can contain either `inbound`, `outbound`, or both.

25

Security Principles

log security <userlist>

This enables the logging of security rule violations for <userlist>. The same real, guest, and anonymous list applies as above.

log syslog

This will redirect the logging operations listed above to the syslog service instead of xferlog.

These are just a few of the settings possible in the /etc/ftpaccess file. See man ftpaccess for a full explanation of all of the options that can be specified.

nologin

When this file exists, it contains a message that is printed to any user but root who tries to log into the system. Having this file in the /etc directory will effectively block everyone but root from logging into the system.

sendmail.cf

This is one of the files used to configure the sendmail package—a package to handle mail services in UNIX. The full explanation of sendmail security is beyond the scope of this chapter, but if you choose to run sendmail, you can do some things right away to make sendmail a little more secure. Disable the EXPN and VRFY commands. These commands return information about valid users on the system, and they can be used through trial and error to determine which accounts exist on your system. Once a hacker knows that, he can proceed to try those usernames with other services in an attempt to gain access to your system.

To disable EXPN and VRFY, edit /etc/sendmail.cf and add the following lines (you may want to add them in the Options section of sendmail.cf just for consistency):

```
O PrivacyOptions=noexpn
O PrivacyOptions=novrfy
```

Then restart the sendmail daemon using

```
/etc/rc.d/init.d/sendmail restart
```

In `/etc/security`

The `/etc/security` directory contains security information for the system. The information in this directory is sensitive, so it should not be world-readable. Change the permissions using

```
chmod o-rwx /etc/security.
```

access.conf

This is the configuration file for the `pam_access` module. It controls which users may log in on what devices. If login is configured with PAM to use this module, this file is checked for the first line matching the user/location combination that matches the current login attempt.

The file consists of multiple colon-delimited lines with three fields each.

The first field is a + for allow or - for disallow access.

The second field is a list of space-separated usernames, group names, and the keywords `ALL` or `EXCEPT`.

The third field is a space-separated list of locations—machines, domains, ttys, network numbers, `ALL` (anywhere), or `LOCAL` from which the users/groups are attempting a login. For example

```
-:fred:.hacker.net
```

will disallow anyone from `*.hacker.net` logging in using the userid `fred` on the local system.

```
-: ALL EXCEPT root:console
```

will disallow everyone but `root` from logging in via the console.

```
+:root:console
-: ALL: ALL
```

will disallow everyone but `root` from logging in at all, similar to having `/etc/nologin` on your system.

console.perms

This file allows you to set the permissions given to the user who logs in on the console, such as floppy devices or sound devices. This allows someone who sits down at the console to access devices they wouldn't need access to while logging in from a remote location. The file dictates which devices to give the user access to as well as which permissions to give each device. You can give or remove as many privileges as you like, but be careful about giving permission to some devices. For example, giving the console user permission to the raw hard drive device is nearly the same as giving him root access. A skilled user could open the device and write himself a new root password to login with! It's best not to give out permissions unless you fully understand how they can be used in the wrong hands.

pam_env.conf

This file contains some environment variables to be used with PAM and the pam_env.so module. This module allows users to have default environment variables set depending on their PAM authentication. (See the section on PAM earlier in this chapter.)

limits.conf

This file allows you to set system limits on a user or group basis via the pam_limits.so module. It is useful for limiting the amount of system resources that a user can grab for himself. Most of the items in this file can be exploited by a malicious user to fill up drive space, kernel memory, or process table space. Some reasonable limits might save you a headache down the road if there is potential for this type of abuse on your system. In most cases, reasonable limits are system, resource, and user dependent. For instance, a secretary doing small word-processing tasks might only need a few 10s of megabytes. However, a graphic artist or CAD designer working on large projects might need 10s of gigabytes.

> **Note**
>
> Because PAM is modular, and all modules are not loaded by default, you need to have the pam_limits.so module included in your login stack. It is the module that will implement the settings in limits.conf to take effect. Put a pam_limits.so line in /etc/pam.d/login after the last /lib/security/pam_pwdb.so line.

time.conf

This is the configuration file for the pam_time.so PAM module. It allows you to specify times when services can and cannot be used by certain users or groups. (See the previous section on PAM.) For this module to work, you will need to add a pam_time.so line to /etc/pam.d/login after the last pam_pwdb.so line.

Configuration Files In Users' Home Directories

There are some configuration files that users can have in their home directories. Because these files can contain sensitive information, it can be dangerous if anyone is able to get a copy of them or if any user but the owner is able to read them. Depending on how militant you want to be, you can either allow these files and watch them closely, or you can prevent users from making use of these files altogether. If you are going to disallow their use, you should state it in the terms of use message, and enforce it appropriately. You can take measures such as creating a root-owned non-writable version of these files in each user's home directory so that it is impossible for the user to create or modify the files, or you can regularly search for them and remove them automatically with a command like the following:

```
rm -f `find / -name "\.rhosts"`
```

.rhosts

This is the Berkeley: remote-hosts permissions file. Programs like rsh, rexec, and rlogin use this file for authentication purposes. The file maps a remote userid on a remote host to the user in whose home directory the file resides. A userid and host combination that appear in a user's .rhosts file will let the remote user log in to the local user's account. For example, in testuser's home directory on someserver.goodguys.com, there is an .rhosts file containing the following line:

```
mainserver.goodguys.com joe
```

If the user joe on mainserver.goodguys.com types rlogin aserver.goodguys.com -l testuser, he will be granted access.

Beware of entries like

```
+ joe
```

This will grant the userid joe on any other system access to this account without a password.

This is convenient if users typically have multiple accounts on different machines on your network, but it could pose problems if one of your machines is hacked. If someone were to gain control of joe's account on mainserver.goodguys.com, he could rlogin to aserver.goodguys.com without a password and wreak havoc from testuser's account. Fortunately, you have some control over this via PAM. You can have PAM use its pam_rhosts_auth.so library to make sure the .rhosts file is secure at least. It can make sure that the .rhosts being checked at the time is not writable by anybody but the owner. It also disregards the "+" entry in .rhosts, which is a wildcard let-anyone-in entry. It can also disable .rhosts lookups altogether, forcing the system to rely on /etc/hosts.equiv or nothing at all.

25

Security Principles

.netrc

This file is used by ftp and rexec to authenticate with remote machines automatically. The file contains lines of the format:

```
machine <machine name> login <name>  password <name>  {account
<account> }
```

Needless to say, having a file containing system names, usernames, and passwords is not a good idea, so this file should be treated with extreme caution. Make sure it is not group- or world-readable or anyone will be able to open the file and gain access to the machines listed within.

History Files

Any shell history file (.bash_history for example) contains a list of recently executed commands for a user. This can provide a lot of information to an outsider if the user is not careful. If the user types a password on the command line, it is logged in the user's history file. If the history file is readable by others, the user's password is also available to others. Making sure a user's history file for his particular shell is only readable by that user is a good idea.

In /etc

System-wide configuration files are normally stored on the /etc directory. These files are typically required by many programs. What follows is a brief description of some of these important files.

exports

This file tells the kernel which files are shared on the network via NFS. An exports file grants access to your filesystems across the network, so it is important to understand the configuration settings in this file. Inadvertently exporting a directory to someone you don't trust could give them access to data that they shouldn't have, or it could provide them with information about your system that could show them other parts of your system that are vulnerable. Exporting the right directory with the wrong permissions can render your system completely vulnerable to attacks.

motd

This file is displayed every time a user logs in, and for your own protection it is a good idea to put your system usage policy here. Among other things, your system policy should state that the machine is for authorized users only. If you have a succinct security or usage policy, it is a good idea to put it there. If not, put your usage rules and policies in a text file somewhere on your filesystem (/system_usage.txt) and place brief instructions on how to read the policy in motd. That way nobody who logs in has any excuse for not having read the system policy.

issue

This file is displayed along with the login prompt before anyone logs into the system. This is also a good place to put a login message informing outsiders that the system is solely for your employees/students and so on, and that unauthorized users should log off the system immediately. See Figure 25.1.

FIGURE 25.1

The /etc/issue file is displayed at the user login prompt. In this case it shows the Red Hat version running on the system.

login.defs

This file is used to set various system-wide user information. In this file you can set such things as mail directory location, password timeouts, minimum length for passwords, and whether or not you need to type in your password to change your personal information (stored in /etc/passwd). You can also prevent people from being able to change their "real name" using the chfn program.

This file also contains some useradd and groupadd default information such as minimums and maximums for the UID and GID to be used when adding new users and groups. You can also specify a special script to run when deleting a user via userdel to perform tasks such as deleting the home directory, removing cron and at jobs, and so on.

securetty

This file contains a list of TTY names on which root can login. The names are actual device names without the leading "/dev/". The login routine scans this file when a root login is attempted to make sure root is allowed to login on that device. Normally this file contains tty1 through tty8 so that root can login to all the virtual consoles. If you only want root to be able to login on the first virtual console, this file should contain one line reading tty1. You should limit the lines in this file to local tty devices and not include network login access for root. If you need to do remote administration, you should use SSH or some other secure link application and su to root from another account.

> **Note**
>
> If this file does not exist, root will be able to login on any TTY, including network TTYs. You should make sure this file exists and has at least one line in it.

usertty

Similar in purpose to `securetty`, but able to deal with multiple users, this file allows you to define CLASSES of hostnames and ttys, GROUPS from `/etc/group` and USERS from `/etc/passwd`. The file has a single section of each which starts with the word CLASSES, GROUPS, and USERS, respectively, on a line by itself.

The CLASSES section allows you to group ttys and remote host names/patterns for use in later rules.

```
CLASSES
classone      tty1 tty2 tty3 tty4 tty5 tty6
classtwo      @.niceguys.com ttyp1
```

The GROUPS section allows you to define hosts and ttys per UNIX group from `/etc/group`. This means that users in the given group will be allowed access from the ttys and hosts specified on that group's line in the GROUPS section.

```
GROUPS
ftp    ttyp1 ttyp2 ttyp3 @.ftpok.com
users classone tty7
```

The USERS section is used to define rules for particular users or classes of users. It is the default section of `usertty` if no section headings are given in the file.

```
USERS
testuser      tty1 @192.168.200.1/255.255.0.0
usertwo classtwo ttyp2 ttyp3
```

Up to this point, security has been discussed from a software point of view; in other words, setting up a secure configuration through programs and modules. An equally important aspect of security is the physical side, which is covered next.

Physical Security—Minimizing the Physical Risks

The general rule for physical security is that if someone can gain physical access to your hardware, he can gain access to all of your data, and if your machine is networked, its trusted relationships with other machines on your network can be exploited. Having said that, the only real way to be sure your machine is safe is to keep it in a locked room with the network and power cables snipped off. This brings up some availability issues, however, so you must choose a less strict policy for physical access to the machine.

If your new machine is going to be a standalone server for news, DNS, mail, Web, or the like, at least put it in a secure room so that physical access to the machine is minimized. Only allow people to login who have a legitimate reason to be on the machine. If the machine is acting as a workstation that users can log in to, or if it is a server that is not in a secure place, there is always the possibility that someone can tamper with it physically. There are, however, a few simple things you can do to make it far more difficult for people to gain inappropriate access to your machine.

Disable Booting from the Floppy Drive

If your machine has a floppy drive, you should disable booting from it in your system's BIOS settings to force the machine to boot from the hard drive every time. These days, bootable CD-ROMs are nearly as easy to create as bootable floppies, so if your BIOS supports booting from CD, disable it as well. You should also have a BIOS password so that someone can't go back into the BIOS, enable floppy boot, boot from his favorite install floppy, and mount your filesystems.

Locking Down LILO

If your machine is using LILO to boot, you should make sure nobody can pass parameters to the kernel at boot time, such as "single" to boot the system into single-user mode, thus bypassing all passwords and gaining root access. You should make sure your /etc/ lilo.conf has a few settings to minimize risks to your system.

If the user is given a LILO: prompt, he has an opportunity to pass arguments to the kernel on bootup. If your machine is not a dual-boot machine, there is really no reason to wait at the LILO: prompt for arguments. By adding

```
delay=0
```

25

Security
Principles

to the main section (or removing the `delay=` line altogether) of your `/etc/lilo.conf` file, the system will not wait for user input at all when booting. If your system is configured for dual boot, and you require a delay on bootup for input from the user about what to boot, you can still protect yourself from people passing arguments to the kernel. Adding the lines

```
restricted
password=1_good_password!   (or whatever you like)
```

to the image section of `/etc/lilo.conf` for the images you want to protect will require a user to enter the password you specified before allowing him to pass arguments to the kernel. If you decide to add a password to your `lilo.conf` file, be sure you change the permissions so that users cannot read the password you specified. Use chmod 600 `/etc/lilo.conf`.

Tip

If you want to be even more secure, you can use `chattr` with the +i flag so that no changes can be made to the `/etc/lilo.conf` file without running `chattr -i` on the file. Since only root can run `chattr` with the +/- I option, it becomes significantly more difficult for someone to disable your LILO changes.

Backup Media

One thing that is often overlooked when considering the security measures for a machine is backup media. If the system is backed up via any means, do not leave backup media where someone can get to it. Having a dump tape of your entire system is just as valuable as having the hard drives in many cases. Even if your machine is merely providing a service such as DNS or FTP, being able to pull all the configuration files off a backup tape may allow someone to gain access to your live machine. Keep your backup media in a secure place, preferably not in the same place as your machine.

Securing Services

All of us have grown used to a variety of services that are available on today's systems. Some of the services are used daily, while others might be best termed "legacy." Regardless, if these services are to be used in today's networked environments, they need to be secure. The next few sections cover ways to secure some of the more common services, such as telnet, ftp, and finger.

telnet

There is no other way to say it; telnet is insecure! Everything you type over a telnet link can be snooped by someone on the network between you and the server you're logging into, even your password! For this reason, it is not recommended to use telnet to perform any remote administration tasks. If you must administer the system from remote, use something that will encrypt your communication so that it cannot be snooped. Packages such as SSL Telnet or SSH are available for just such a purpose. SSH can be found at `http://www.ssh.fi`, and SSL Telnet can be found at `ftp://ftp.replay.com`. There is also an open source solution, OpenSSH. It can be found at `http://www.openssh.com`.

Anonymous FTP

Anonymous FTP is a handy but dangerous service to offer on your system. Handy because when the occasional legitimate outsider needs to send or retrieve a file, it provides the capability. It can be dangerous because you never know who might leave inappropriate or virus-laden files on your system. You might need to enable it, however, if you need to offer files to the public, or anyone without an account on your server for that matter. If it is not necessary to have people send you files via your anonymous FTP server, then you are relatively safe, but if you have a directory that anonymous users can write to, you run the risk of abuse by others. What often happens on the Internet is someone discovers that your system has an anonymous-writable directory on your FTP server. He tells his friends, and someone logs on and creates a directory that won't show up in a normal listing (that is, with control characters or spaces in the filename). He then puts pirated software, pornography, or other unwanted files into the directory and publishes its existence to a group of friends, if you're lucky, or a public newsgroup or Web site if you're not so lucky. Depending on the publicity this new illegitimate directory gets, your machine and your connection bandwidth can be quickly consumed by the incoming FTP traffic. At the very least, constant downloads will be a drain on your connection to the Internet. See the "ftpaccess" section earlier in the chapter for some configuration hints.

finger

The finger command displays personal information, such as name and phone number, about users that are logged in. Because of this, finger is generally disabled by system administrators, but if you feel you must have a finger service running, replace `in.fingerd` with `safe_finger` in `/etc/inetd.conf` to prevent misuse. Be aware that anyone "fingering" your machine will be able to see information about the users who are logged in, and could use it to build a list of accounts on your machine for future attacks.

sendmail

See the "sendmail.cf" section earlier in the chapter concerning disabling the EXPN and VRFY commands. Additional information about sendmail can be found in ftp://info.cert.org/pub/cert_advisories/CA-93:16.sendmail.vulnerabilities. Mail is one of the most regularly attacked services, so it would be wise to check the CERT advisories frequently and keep your sendmail package up-to-date.

DNS

DNS is the domain name system. It is a distributed database that maps machine names to IP addresses. If you have enabled the named service, you should make a few changes to make it a little more secure.

Create a New User Called named

The named service should not run as root. Therefore, we need to create a user that it can run as. For simplicity's sake the username should be named (pronounced "name-dee").

Create a New Group Called named

If you are not using private groups, you will also need to create a group called named and make the named user the only member. This is simply because every user must belong to at least one group—the group named just keeps things simple.

Modify /etc/rc.d/init.d/named

Change the line that says

```
daemon named
```

to

```
daemon named -u named -g named -t <named user's home directory>
```

Filesystem Security

Use quotas for your users!

Filesystem space may be inexpensive, but no matter how much you have, a malicious user can find a way to fill it if he wants. A simple script that creates a garbage file is enough to fill your drives and create havoc on your machine. Filesystem quotas can prevent this from happening. Using quotas, you can assign each user or group a finite amount of space on the system. There are several steps to perform when activating quota support, which are outlined in the following sections.

Modify `/etc/fstab`

You must add the quota options to the mount options field for each filesystem you would like to support quotas on. Add userquota for user-based quotas or groupquota for group-based quotas (or both!) to the end of the comma-separated list of mount options. For example, this line has user quotas enabled:

```
/dev/hda1    /    ext2    defaults,usrquota    1 1
```

Remount the Partitions You Modified in `/etc/fstab`

You can reboot to do this, or you can use `mount -o remount<partition>` to do it on-the-fly. If there are users on the system, you may want to warn them and do a nice shutdown to be safe.

Create `quota.user` and `quota.group`

For each filesystem you added quota support to in `/etc/fstab`, you will need to create a file called `quota.user` or `quota.group` depending on which kind of support you added. The file should be empty and be only readable by root. Use chmod 600 to set the file permissions.

Do the Initial Quota Check

You must populate your new `quota.user` and `quota.group` files. To do this, use `/sbin/quotacheck -av`.

Set Quotas with edquota

Use the edquota program for each user or group you would like to set a quota for and edit the quota settings to your taste. A soft quota is the maximum amount of disk space a user may use. If grace periods are in effect, the user receives a warning periodically after exceeding his soft limit until the grace period expires, after which writes will fail.

A hard quota is used when grace periods are enabled. A hard limit is the absolute block limit the user may use during his grace period before writes to the filesystem begin to fail.

To edit the grace period, use edquota with the `-t` option. The grace period will default to one week if by default.

See "Establishing Filesystem Quotas" in Chapter 7, "Filesystems," for a more complete explanation of the Red Hat Quota system.

So far, this chapter has covered a large variety of methods to secure your Red Hat system. These methods have included editing configuration files, replacing older programs with newer versions, and even preventing physical access. At this point, it can be assumed that you have a fairly secure system. Now, the trick is to keep it that way. This can be done by monitoring system activity, which is covered in the next section.

Security Monitoring

Merely taking the steps to secure your system when you set it up will not guarantee that it remains secure. After you have locked down all the loose ends you are aware of, you still need to monitor what is happening on your system. Monitoring your system is just as important as securing it in the first place. Without monitoring, you might not be aware of many failed login attempts from outside systems, or overly large file transfers to or from your system. Monitoring your system can alert you to intrusion attempts before they become successful intrusions.

Check Your Log Files

Many of the applications and packages that are security related such as PAM have the ability to save information about their status and usage. You should go through these log files regularly, either with automated assistance or by hand with grep if you need to.

Log files are sometimes kept separately for a particular application, but more often than not, logging is done through the syslog utility. Syslog provides a generic interface for applications to send log messages to a daemon (syslogd), which categorizes and saves them in a log directory for later review.

Syslogd reads its configuration from the `/etc/syslogd.conf` file. `Syslogd.conf` tells syslogd where it should be writing its log files, and how it should categorize the messages it receives. Red Hat comes preconfigured with some nice settings to split up syslog output and store the log files in the `/var/log` directory.

You should examine your log files for activity that is out of the ordinary for your system. Here are some examples of log files and the types of things to be mindful of:

- Check `/var/log/xferlog` for abnormal file transfer activity
- Check `/var/messages` for suspicious ftpd and PAM output
- Check `/var/log/secure` for sites or users you don't recognize
- Check `/var/log/maillog` for bad commands or mass-mailing
- Check `/var/log/lastlog` (using the `last` command) for any odd logins

Monitoring logs can be tedious and time-consuming. Many system administrators write scripts to check logs for suspicious activities, but there are packages available to help you monitor your log files. Psionic Logcheck (`http://www.resentment.org/abacus/logcheck`) and WOTS (`http://www.vcpc.univie.ac.at/~tc/tools`) are such tools. They are both fully configurable and they make log file monitoring much easier.

Checking Network Interfaces

Check for network interfaces that are in debug or promiscuous mode. Some legitimate network monitoring packages use these modes to gather information, but if you aren't running any of those packages, an interface in promiscuous mode can indicate someone running a packet sniffer on your network. You can use packages like ifstatus to find this out and tell you about it. ifstatus is available from `ftp://coast.cs.purdue.edu/pub/tools/unix/ifstatus/ifstatus.tar.Z`.

Check for New setuid/setgid Files

Look for new files that havethe setuid or setgid bit set. These files will actually run as the user who owns them, and if not written very carefully, can make it possible for a user to become another user at will, potentially even root. This is a common method for gaining root access on the system, so keeping track of setuid/setgid files is a good idea. You can search your filesystem for these files using

```
find / -perm 4000 -print
find / -perm 2000 -print
```

This will find all setuid/setgid files on the system owned by anyone at all, not just root or other system users, but this is a good idea anyway. If you grant some users different permissions than others, and one of the less-restricted users creates a setuid script, there is potential for one of the more-restricted users to run the script and gain privileges he shouldn't.

Check `/var/spool/cron`

Keep an eye on the jobs in `/var/spool/cron`. This is where every user's crontab is kept, and by checking these files, you can see if a hacker has left himself a backdoor script to allow him back into the system at a later time.

Check `/var/spool/atjobs`

For the same reasons as you would check for old cron jobs, you should check for old at jobs that would grant access (or do other malicious things to your system) at a later date.

Check for Altered System Files

Make sure files on your system have not been altered. If a hacker gains access to your system, he may be able to change your executables to contain trojan horses and the like. You can use programs like tripwire to take snapshots of your filesystem (even daily) and compare them to make sure nobody has altered your system files. Tripwire can be obtained from `ftp://coast.cs.purdue.edu/pub/COAST/Tripwire`.

Frequently running programs that check your system for holes is also a good idea. Nmap, SAINT, and COPS are good programs to run frequently to make sure nothing is amiss on your system.

Be Aware of the Latest Threats

CERT (Computer Emergency Response Team) provides a set of attack warnings and system bugs as they become available. The CERT Web page is an excellent place to look for advisories (`http://www.cert.org`), and the Red Hat site contains security information about Red Hat itself (`http://www.redhat.com/cgi-bin/support`). See Figure 25.2.

FIGURE 25.2

The Red Hat Web site is a good place to keep up on security issues.

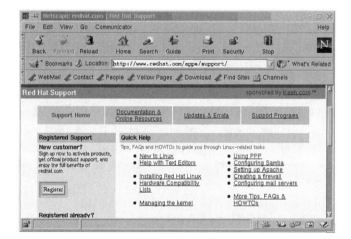

Keep Your Software Up-to-Date

Many of the security breaches you hear about in the media could have been prevented if the system administrators at the attacked sites had installed the latest versions of their server software and had applied all the vendor patches. Once a security hole has been discovered and published to the Internet, it is trivial for a hacker to apply that attack to any site fitting the target criteria, or to search for a site fitting the criteria. Your site may be targeted simply because your IP address fell within a range that the hacker specified.

Your system-checking software is also vulnerable to datedness. Once new threats are discovered, new versions of system scanning utilities are often released to properly test for the new problems. It is important to keep an eye on the versions of the checking packages you use and make sure they're the most up-to-date. Check `http://www.redhat.com/ updates` frequently for update RPMs.

Now that you know what is involved with monitoring your system's security, it is time to develop some policies to keep potential security problems to a minimum. Each installation is different, but some common themes exist. They are covered next.

Developing Security Policies

It is up to you, as the administrator, to decide on the level of security you will have on your machine. There is a three-way balance between security, convenience, and availability when deciding on a security policy for your system.

Here are some questions you should answer when you are designing your security policy:

- Who gets network access? If this is a business, do all employees need access, or only some?

- Who gets physical access? Are your systems kept in locked offices, or are they located in open cubicles?

- When do they get access? Are the users allowed access from 9 to 5 on weekdays, or is access a 24/7 proposition?

- How much access do they get? Does everyone need Internet access, or simply access to network printers?

- Which services can they use? Does anyone need access to ftp? What about telnet or finger?

- What kinds of programs can they run? Do they need access to simple office tools or sophisticated graphics and CAD programs?

25

Security
Principles

- Which other machines on the network are they allowed to reach? How many servers should they see? The Web server? How about accounting and payroll?

- How much filesystem space do users get? Do they need 100 megabytes or 10 gigabytes?

- How much kernel space do users get? Will they need more or less than 5 megabytes?

- What restrictions should there be on user passwords? Is there a minimum length? Do they need to change every week? What about every month?

- What kinds of attacks are possible? Are there modems on some systems? Do users need access from outside through the firewall?

- What kinds of attacks are most likely? Have you recently laid off or fired employees with knowledge of the system? Have there been any successful break-ins recently?

- How much down time can you afford to have to recover after a break in? Can you afford a week of downtime? What about a day? What about an hour?

- How much money will it cost? See above and add in the man hours spent returning the system to normal.

- How much is your protected data worth to someone else? Is it corporate secrets? Financial information? Customer records?

- How much will it hurt your company's reputation to suffer a publicized intrusion? What if you are a financial institution and your customers' portfolio information is compromised?

- How much will it hurt your company's sales to suffer a publicized intrusion? Do you trade on your good name and history of security? What if you provide computer security services and your systems are compromised?

Setup Policies

You should decide how your machines are going to be configured for the amount of security that makes sense at your site. Having your similar systems configured similarly will help you in initial setup, and it will help you down the road in detection by making it easy to spot a configuration that is not the same as the others.

Maintenance Policies

You should set up a schedule for system security auditing. This should include running filesystem audit software, network auditing software, and configuration auditing software. Typically cron is used to run these packages, and the output logs are scanned or mailed to the administrator on a daily basis.

You should also check periodically for vendor patches for the software you run on your system. CERT advisories are useful for this. See `http://www.cert.org`. You will need to apply patches as soon as you find them to protect your system from the latest attacks.

Reaction Policies

You should outline your reaction plan to any predictable intrusion. Identify the steps required to properly recover from an intrusion including connectivity, restoring from backups, and preventing further intrusions. Knowing what should be done to minimize the damage from an attack either in progress or after the fact will save confusion and, more importantly, time.

Making the Rules

In addition to your security policy, you should have a set of guidelines for your users to follow when they are using your system. This usage statement will outline what you expect from your users and what the consequences are for misuse of the system. Having a clearly defined usage statement also gives you a legal foothold should someone become a problem on your system. The last thing you need after having your usage policy violated is to be unable to prove that what the user was doing was against your usage policy because it wasn't posted anywhere.

A good system usage policy leaves little room for interpretation. Making sure that your users as well as others who might try to use your machine or its services know and understand the rules of the system is extremely important.

Some things to consider putting on your usage statement include

- Who owns the system. This would generally be the company or institution that is paying for the system.

- Who may use the system. This should include the words "authorized users" and consist of employees for businesses and possibly students and faculty in terms of an educational institution.

- Acceptable hours of use. These may only be from 9 to 5 for a bank or financial institution, or 24/7 for a university.

- Services that may be used. This would include programs the user is authorized to use, which is not necessarily all installed programs.

- Services that are strictly prohibited. This could include storage of unauthorized files such as pornography or pirated software, or trafficking in such.

- Software that is prohibited on the system. See above and possibly even legitimate software that is not approved by computer support.

- Penalties for misuse. This could include revocation of access and criminal penalties.

- Contact information for questions or misuse reports. Normally this would be someone in computer services or support.

- Where more information may be obtained. This might be files that are stored locally or even posted on the Internet.

You should put your usage statement where your users can read it. In /etc/issue, users will see it before logging in on the console, but you may want to add a banners section to hosts.allow (see the hosts.allow section earlier in the chapter) so that telnet users will see the message as well. You can put information that applies to anyone attempting a telnet or console login in /etc/issue or in the telnet banner message. If there is information that only valid users of your system should see, put it in /etc/motd (Message Of The Day). /etc/motd is printed to the shell after a successful login, so every user is guaranteed to see it when they log in to your system. For messages relating to FTP connections, use the banner setting in the /etc/ftpaccess file. See man ftpaccess for more information.

Enforcing Strict Compliance

The easiest and least confrontational method of enforcing compliance with your system policy is to have the system automatically enforce as much of it as possible. This will help you avoid having to personally confront users who violate your policy. If the system tells them that they are in violation, it is much more impersonal, and they will not see it as a personal attack on them. Passwords, login times, device permissions, and system resource usage limits can all be monitored and enforced by the system as discussed earlier in this chapter. This can also help to reduce your workload as an administrator.

You should keep a close watch on your system and your users. Do not allow violations of your system usage policy to go unpunished. React quickly and with the measures you dictated in your terms of use policy. Do not make exceptions to your security policy for anyone unless you are prepared to make the same exceptions for everyone. Monitor your system logs for violations on a daily basis. Keeping yourself informed about how users are using your system is an integral part of system administration.

Dealing with Infractions

People who violate your security policy should be dealt with swiftly. If the infraction is minimal and non-threatening (the user is consistently over his disk limit), issuing and documenting warnings to the user is a good first step. You can limit the user's access to resources by editing the `/etc/security/console.perms`, `/etc/security/time.conf`, and `/etc/security/limits.conf` files. If the user persists, you can increase the penalty by disabling the user's account.

Disable Account

Disabling a user's account is a very quick way to get his attention. He will have to come to you or call you to get it re-enabled, and you can use that opportunity to discuss his infractions. You can use chage or usermod to disable a user's account. With chage:

```
chage -E <yesterday's date in MM/DD/YYYY form> <userid>
```

or using the system date command:

```
chage -E `date --date '1 day ago' +%D` <userid>
( the outer ticks are back ticks )
```

With usermod:

```
usermod -e <yesterday's date in MM/DD/YYYY form> <userid>
```

When the user tries to login on the console, he will get the message

```
"Your account has expired; please contact your system
administrator"
```

and will be logged out. To re-enable the account, use

```
chage -E 0 <userid>
```

or

```
usermod -e 0 <userid>
```

Restrict Access Times

Use `/etc/security/times.conf` to restrict the times a user can log in. You may want to limit the user to times when you can actively monitor his activities.

Limit Resources

If the user has been frequently writing or running programs that hog system resources such as CPU time, memory, or space in the process table, you can change the parameters in `/etc/security/limits.conf` to keep the user below certain thresholds.

Limit Filesystem Space

If you find that some users are hogging disk space, you might want to consider installing filesystem quotas (see the section, "Filesystem Security," earlier in the chapter).

Limit Access to Devices

If a user is abusing a device, like burning too many CDs or playing loud sounds on the workstation while others are trying to work, you can edit the settings in `/etc/security/console.perms` to restrict access to these devices while the user is logged in at the console.

Limit Access to Programs

If a user is abusing his privileges by running programs that he shouldn't, or at times when he shouldn't, you can use groups to limit his access. You can make the executables for the troublesome programs group-executable (chmod g+x) and world-non-executable (chmod o-x). Then if you create a group called netapp, for example, and give netapp group ownership of the files in question, you can limit access to them based on the membership of group netapp. Only members of the netapp group will be able to use the programs.

> **Note**
>
> If your users are clever enough, when they become members of the netapp group, they could create a setgid script to run things as group netapp at a later date, even if they are no longer members. Using groups in this manner is a convenience, but is not secure. If you use this method, search for new setgid scripts frequently!

You can use this technique along with the pam_groups module to set times when users gain access to the special groups, like games and chat software after business hours. See `/etc/security/group.conf` and the section on PAM earlier in this chapter for more information.

Depending on the severity of the infraction, you can disable accounts for greater amounts of time or further limit system resources and applications. If a user is persistently violating your security policy and you have documented warnings and violations, then sometimes removing the account altogether and dismissing the user is the only option. Be sure you clean up the account thoroughly, however, as the user may become vengeful and attempt to "test" your other security policies for you. If this becomes a problem, you may want to seek legal counsel regarding the matter.

Summary

There you have it—Red Hat security in a (rather large) nutshell. This chapter looked at computer security from several different angles. It covered how to determine your security needs and offered practical examples of how to address those needs on your Red Hat system. This chapter reviewed how to monitor the system's security and verify that your security measures are working. Finally, it discussed security policies, what they are, what they should contain, and who needs to see them. Implementing these procedures takes both time and effort; however, the payoff is that when a system is broken into it probably won't be yours. But if it is, you can rest assured that the overall damage is likely to be minimal.

Security and Firewalls

PART

VII

In This Part

26 Firewall Strategies   *785*

27 The Security Administrator's Toolbox   *819*

28 I've Been Hacked: What Now?   *841*

Firewall Strategies

CHAPTER 26

IN THIS CHAPTER

- Types of Firewalls   *787*
- Firewall Options   *789*
- Linux Proxy Services   *790*
- Linux Kernel Configuration   *792*
- SOCKS Proxy Server   *795*
- Squid 2   *798*
- TIS FireWall ToolKit   *800*
- Setting Up a Firewall   *805*
- Setting Up a Firewall with ipchains   *810*
- Debugging Firewalls   *817*

In the construction trades, a firewall is an extra thick wall placed between apartments or sections of a house in order to help prevent the spread of fire. In computer security terms, a firewall is similar, but a better analogy for a network or computer firewall may be the walls surrounding a medieval castle. The walls protect the inner buildings of the castle, with access to the city through a controlled gate that is fortified to withstand assault. In essence, this is how a firewall works.

A firewall protects the computer network behind it. It is, after all, a perimeter defense. A firewall does not provide any protection once the perimeter has been breached. All access must pass through a controlled gate. An assault on a well-built firewall is expensive, time-consuming, and dangerous...just as it was to assault a walled city during medieval times. And just like the medieval walls around a city, a firewall is used to allow a network to connect to the Internet while enjoying the benefits of security the firewall provides.

A firewall provides a measure of real security for a network. It keeps the general Internet public from a network and helps ensure the integrity of proprietary or confidential data. A measure of security involves keeping undesired individuals out of your network. Although firewalls don't address the problem of someone having physical access to your system, they do deal with the problem of protecting your system from the cracker across the Net. Marcus Ranum, author of the FireWall ToolKit and president and CEO of Network Flight Recorder, notes in the firewall FAQ:

> "The internet, like any other society, is plagued with the kind of jerks who
> enjoy the electronic equivalent of writing on other people's wall with spraypaint,
> tearing their mailboxes off, or just sitting in the street blowing their car horns."

A firewall can limit your network exposure to the Internet, enforce security policy, and provide a focal point for security decisions. What a firewall cannot do is protect you from malicious insiders, viruses, or connections that do not go through it. A well-designed, well-deployed firewall can provide a great deal of security to a network. The protected network may or may not be accessible from the Internet directly depending on how the firewall is implemented.

This chapter looks at some of the different firewall models that can be used to protect your network and how to set up some of those firewalls using the Linux tools available. In many respects, a Linux system can be one of the easiest ways of setting up a firewall for your network.

Types of Firewalls

There are two basic types of firewalls: the absolute firewall and the proxy server. In the former type of firewall, no traffic is permitted to cross the firewall except through a designated access point. In this case, both sides must be able to connect to the firewall first before jumping to the other side. This model provides for a stricter control of what connection protocols may be used from one side to the other. In the latter type, a proxy machine makes the connection for the user. Here, there may or may not be restrictions on the services provided; although, to be truly effective, a proxy server does require a packet filter to be running as well as the proxy services. The services are provided by proxy agent programs running on the firewall, which permits traffic in both directions. With an absolute firewall, there may be a limited number of access points through the firewall. In order to use a service, a user may have to connect into the firewall first before crossing through. With a proxy firewall, the access may be granted on a much broader basis and may not require a distinct access point. Many variations of these architectures can be used to create firewalls. The common characteristic between all of the architectures is the use of packet filtering in order to prevent an authorized connection being made into the network.

Bastion Host System

The simplest form of an absolute firewall is that of the dual-homed bastion host system. What is a bastion host? The term *bastion host* is attributed to Marcus Ranum, who notes:

> "Bastions...overlook critical areas of defense, usually having stronger walls, room for extra troops, and the occasional use of boiling hot oil for discouraging attackers."

Ideally, a bastion host is a highly secure system exposed to the Internet, and is the main point of contact for users in the internal network as well as those out in the Internet. The emphasis in a bastion host is "host-level" security. Not only must the bastion host be hardened to attacks from the outside, but from within as well. One of the easiest ways to set up a firewall using Linux is to set up a dual-homed bastion host. It is not necessary to have two NICs in the host in order to set up a firewall. The two setups can be visualized as shown in Figures 26.1 and 26.2.

FIGURE 26.1
Dual-homed bastion host.

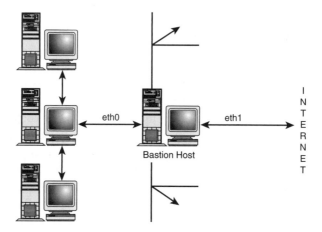

FIGURE 26.2
Screened host.

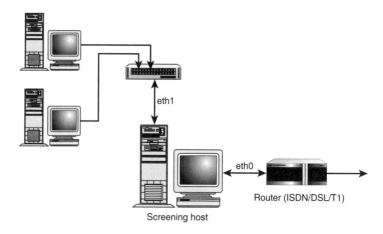

Figure 26.1 shows a network firewall where the bastion host sits outside of the network router. In this configuration, the host is the "gate" through which all contact with the Internet must pass. This is also a very good configuration for implementing IP masquerading; however, that is beyond the scope of the current discussion. In this configuration, all forwarding of packets can be turned off and provide a reasonable level of confidence in the security of the firewall. The bastion host can provide proxy services to internal programs or be a simple packet filter requiring the users to connect to it before continuing on to the internal network.

Figure 26.2 shows a screened host network firewall. In this configuration, the host providing the firewall protection is behind the router connecting the internal network to the Internet. However, all traffic is routed through this host in order to apply the firewall rules to the IP packets. A packet filter is available to selectively allow packets from within the corporate network to get out or to deny all traffic in both directions. In this configuration, the bastion host is part of the corporate network, but acts as a filter.

Figure 26.3 shows a screened subnet. This is a more complicated version of a screened host configuration. Here, the bastion host is sandwiched between two routers running packet filters. This permits more than one machine to act as a frontline host, and requires both sides of the screened subnet to connect into it in order to talk to the other side. The screened subnet is colloquially termed a "demilitarized zone," or DMZ.

FIGURE 26.3
Screened subnet.

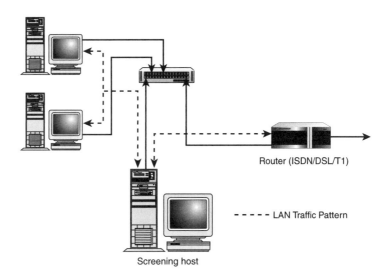

Router (ISDN/DSL/T1)

- - - - - LAN Traffic Pattern

Screening host

Each of these models has its benefits and drawbacks. However, each achieves the desired goal of protecting the internal network.

Firewall Options

Once a configuration has been chosen, the firewall policy should be considered. There are two basic models in firewalls:

1. What is not expressly prohibited is permitted.
2. What is not expressly permitted is prohibited.

Rule #2 is more restrictive than #1. With the second model, the services to be permitted are determined and everything else is turned off or denied. This model is more conservative from a security standpoint. If you've reached a point where a firewall is needed, whether this is because your site has been compromised before or you are trying to head off a potential security issue, the most conservative approach is probably the best approach to start with. Later, when a "feel" for the firewall has been developed, it may be possible to be a bit more permissive with the services provided across the firewall.

As mentioned earlier, firewalls can be broken into two main categories:

- **Packet filters**—In this case, users must connect to the firewall itself before accessing the internal network.

- **Packet filters with proxy**—Services are provided across the firewall so that the user sees little if any difference between the internal network and the firewall itself.

Packet filters without proxy services are easier to set up and maintain. Proxy servers require more configuration and may be a risk in and of themselves. However, not only must the security of the site be considered when setting up a firewall, but also the ease of use to the users. A firewall is of no value if the users within decide that it is too much of a nuisance or actually hinders the work they try to do. All it takes to expose your site is one user on the inside who finds a way to circumvent a firewall. It doesn't matter whether that method of circumvention is to install a modem on his computer so that he can dial in, or whether it is to raise a complaint about the firewall that causes management to order a relaxation of the firewall rules. The net effect is the same. Deploying a firewall requires the input of users to a degree that they do not feel as though the firewall is some administrative draconian caveat being forced upon them. Rules need to be designed.

Linux Proxy Services

One of the main questions to answer during the firewall setup is which services are to be allowed across the firewall. One of the easiest methods to provide services to users on both sides of the firewall is the proxy server initially developed at the European Institute for Particle Physics (CERN).

What is a proxy server? A proxy server is a system that resides between the Internet and a private network. Usually, a proxy server hides the private network from the Internet. It may or may not implement a firewall, although for the purposes of the examples given here, a firewall will be implemented with the proxy server. Another good use for a proxy server is the implementation of the Internet Caching Protocol (described in detail in RFCs 2186 and 2187). Regardless of how you implement a proxy server on the network, the question of which services to allow is of crucial importance.

The number of services permitted across the firewall increases the probability that someone may break through. This is a simple fact. However, it is not realistic to simply cut all traffic between the Internet and the private LAN. Users need access to the Internet while working from inside the LAN. Also, these same users may need access to their accounts while traveling. Whether it's to complete a business deal or to read email, access from the outside is necessary. This doesn't mean that the door should be left wide open. Careful consideration as to what to allow is very important.

If users need terminal access from outside, a secure connection can be established using SSH. What about access to the corporate Web server? What about FTP? These questions drive the need for proxy services. The more services provided across a firewall, the greater the possibility of a security problem. Conversely, the more services provided through a firewall, the greater the likelihood that users will be able to work with the firewall rather than against it.

Proxy Software

There are three main tools that can be used on a proxy server to provide the proxy redirect other than ipfwadm or ipchains. These are shown in Table 26.1.

TABLE 26.1 Proxy Software

Package	Latest Version	FTP Site
transproxy	0.3	`ftp://ftp.nlc.net.au/pub/linux/www`
squid	2.2	`http://squid.nlanr.net`
socks	4.2b	`ftp://metalab.unc.edu/pub/linux/system/network/misc/socks-linux-src.tgz`
TIS FWTK	2.2	`ftp.tislabs.com` (see "TIS FireWall ToolKit" later in the chapter)

Each package offers different capabilities. We will discuss each in turn and describe how to set up the package in order to implement proxy services. The first thing needing discussion, however, is kernel configuration. How the proxy server is set up depends on whether the kernel version being discussed is 2.0.X or 2.2.X. Under Linux, the firewall is an option requiring kernel configuration before the firewall can be implemented. Although kernel configuration is beyond the scope of this chapter, we will discuss the options needed in order to configure a kernel that can implement firewalls.

Linux Kernel Configuration

This section lists the configuration options necessary to compile a Linux kernel capable of running a firewall.

For Linux kernel versions prior to 2.2, the configuration for a firewalled proxy server requires the following settings:

```
Code maturity level options  --->

        [Y] Prompt for development and/or incomplete code/drivers


General Setup  --->

        [Y] Networking support


Networking options  --->

        [Y] Network firewalls
        [Y] TCP/IP networking
        [N] IP: forwarding/gatewaying
        [Y] IP: syn cookies
        [Y] IP: firewalling
        [Y] IP: firewall packet logging
        [Y] IP: masquerading
        [Y] IP: always defragment
        [Y] IP: accounting
        [Y] IP: Drop source routed frames


Network device support  --->

        [Y] Network device support
        <Y> Dummy net driver support
        [Y] Ethernet (10 or 100Mbit)
        Select your particular network card
```

Linux kernels in the 2.2.X series require these settings:

```
General Setup  --->

        [Y] Networking support
```

```
Networking options   --->

        [Y] Kernel/User netlink socket
        [Y] Network firewalls
        [Y] Socket Filtering
        [Y] TCP/IP networking
        [Y] IP: firewalling
        [Y] IP: firewall packet netlink device
        [Y] IP: always defragment (required for masquerading)
        [Y] IP: transparent proxy support
        [Y] IP: masquerading
        [Y] IP: ICMP masquerading
        [Y] IP: masquerading special modules support
        [Y] IP: aliasing support
        [Y] IP: TCP syncookie support (not enabled per default)

Network device support   --->

        [Y] Network device support
        <Y> Dummy net driver support
        [Y] Ethernet (10 or 100Mbit)
        Select your particular network card
```

Once you have finished the kernel configuration, do a

```
make clean, make dep, make zImage (or make bzImage)
```

Install the new kernel in /boot, and edit /etc/lilo.conf to reflect the new kernel. At this time, it is best not to install the new kernel as the default because it may have a problem somewhere (such as an incorrect ethernet device driver, and so on). Always test a new kernel before making it the default in lilo.

Transproxy

Transproxy is a tool that performs transparent redirection of requests from one port to another, hence the name transproxy (*trans*parent *proxy*). This tool is very useful. Transproxy provides the capability to configure a transparent proxy without having to recompile the kernel or add redirection rules to an existing firewall. In essence, this userspace program provides the same capabilities as the redirection rules in ipfwadm or the Jump chains provided in ipchains.

The first thing to do is obtain the latest version of the software. It can be found in the location shown in Table 26.1. Once the file has been downloaded, simply unpack it and build:

```
# gzip -dc transproxy_0.3.orig.tar.gz ¦ tar -xvf -
# cd transproxy-0.3
# make
# make install
```

Once installed, transproxy can be configured to run called from inetd, the network superdaemon, or as a standalone service. Either way, the following line should be added to /etc/services:

```
tproxy          tcp/81              # Transparent Proxy
```

Installing Transproxy

To install transproxy running under inetd, /etc/inetd.conf should be modified by adding the following line to it:

```
tproxy stream tcp nowait nobody /usr/sbin/tcpd in.tproxyd <destination> 8080
```

This tells inetd to accept requests on port 81 and start tproxyd, which will pass these requests to the proxy-server destination on port 8080. Say, for example, you were running a Web server called www.foo.com on the host me.foo.com, but you didn't want to run the server directly on port 80 because it is a reserved port and requires that the software be run as root. You could reconfigure your Web server software to run on port 8080, then adjust the <destination> setting to be as follows:

/etc/services:

```
tproxy          tcp/80              # Transparent Proxy
```

/etc/inetd.conf:

```
tproxy stream tcp nowait nobody /usr/sbin/tcpd in.tproxyd me.foo.com 8080
```

Thus, every time someone makes a connection to www.foo.com, the request is automatically redirected to port 8080 on me.foo.com. The user doesn't see the difference and doesn't have to know what port the server is actually running on. Of course, this is only one possible example and in fact, for a Web server, running tproxyd out of inetd is not the best configuration. The good news is that transproxy can be run as a standalone service. In this case, inetd knows nothing about the transproxy service so every time a request comes in, inetd does not have to start up another tproxyd daemon.

To configure transproxy for standalone service, the `/etc/services` file should be modified by adding the preceding example entry. Once that is done, all that needs to be accomplished is the startup of the tproxyd server. As root, type the following (the # character is the root prompt and should not be typed):

```
# /usr/sbin/in.tproxyd -s 80 -r nobody me.foo.com 8080
```

Now the tproxyd program is running on its own, listening to port 80 (`-s 80`) with the user id of nobody (`-r nobody`) and redirecting to port 8080 on the machine `me.foo.com`. To ensure that the transproxy daemon gets started every time the machine is rebooted, add the following to the Red Hat `/etc/rc.d/rc.local` file:

```
#
# Start the transproxy service to redirect port 80 to port
# 8080
#
echo  Starting transproxy service: port 80 -> port 8080
/usr/sbin/in.tproxyd -s 80 -r nobody me.foo.com 8080
```

It is possible to use firewall rules to redirect port 80 to port 81 so that you don't have to have an actual service running on port 80. You can do that if you want to be able to leave the original port 80 entries in your `/etc/services`. An example of such redirection will be given later in the chapter when we discuss ipfwadm and ipchains. Transproxy is not limited to Web server proxying—it can also be used to proxy other services such as telnet, ftp, SSH, and more.

SOCKS Proxy Server

The SOCKS proxy server package has been around for quite some time. The package comes with a SOCKS server daemon as well as some client programs (as of this writing, the latest SOCKS version is 4.2beta and supports the following client programs: ftp, telnet, whois, and finger). The SOCKS program, despite its age, can still be used effectively to provide proxying service for a network. With SOCKS, a single configuration file and a single daemon are the only things that need to be set up. The daemon handles all services.

Setting Up SOCKS

To compile SOCKS, obtain the gzipped tarfile from the FTP site listed in Table 26.1. Once the gzipped tarfile has been downloaded, untar the file as shown here and build the socks server and clients:

```
# gzip -dc socks-linux-src.tgz ¦ tar -xvf -
        # cd socks42b
```

```
edit the top-level Makefile as well as include/socks.h

# make
# make install.server (this will install the SOCKS
                       server,sockd, into the
```
destination
```
                       directory defined in the top-
                       level Makefile, as well as a
                       config file, test_sockd_conf and
                       the documentation).
# make install.clients (this will install the SOCKified
                        clients to the destination
                        directory defined in the top-
                        level Makefile
```

Note that you will need to install the clients on every machine that is being served by the SOCKS proxy server. As with any other software package that you build, be sure to read the instructions included with the package.

Once the server is installed, edit the file /etc/services and add the following line:

```
socks           1080/tcp        #SOCKS proxy service
```

Add the following to /etc/inetd.conf:

```
socks   stream  tcp   nowait  nobody  <path/to/sockd>/sockd sockd
```

Tuning SOCKS Configuration Files

There are at least two and possibly three configuration files that will need to be tuned to fit your circumstances. If you have a dual-homed host and you have disabled IP forwarding (either directly in the kernel configuration or by the command "echo 0 > /proc/sys/net/ipv4/ip_forward"), you will need to edit /etc/sockd.conf, /etc/socks.conf, and /etc/sockd.route files. A dual-homed host has more than one network interface (physical or logical). If you have a host with only one network interface or you have enabled IP forwarding (in the kernel configuration and by the command "echo 1 > /proc/sys/net/ipv4/ip_forward"), you only need /etc/sockd.conf.

The file /etc/sockd.conf determines whether a client can have access to the sockd proxy server. This file consists of two categories of entries: permit and deny. The format for the entries is

```
<Identifier Key>  <IP address>  <Netmask>
```

The identifier key is one of two values: permit or deny; the IP address refers to the source address of the requesting client; and the netmask is the modifier for that particular network. For example, say you have a private network with an assigned network range of 192.168.1.*. To permit all of the systems in the network to access the SOCKS proxy server, the following entry should be in the /etc/sockd.conf of your proxy server:

```
permit    192.168.1.0    255.255.255.0
```

This entry permits any machine whose IP address begins with 192.168.1 to connect to sockd. The best thing to do is to have the "permit" entries first and then deny everything. In essence, this causes the SOCKS server to deny everything except what was specified in the permit lines. Continuing with the preceding example, to have the sockd server only allow access from machines in the 192.168.1.* network, the sockd.conf file may consist of these entries:

```
permit    192.168.1.0    255.255.255.0
deny      0.0.0.0        0.0.0.0
```

The clients file, /etc/socks.conf, is used by SOCKS clients to determine whether to use a direct or proxied connection to a given destination. Unlike the sockd.conf file, the clients file has three entries: deny, direct, and sockd. Deny specifies which addresses the sockd server should reject. Direct specifies which IP addresses do not need to use the sockd server. Both deny and direct have the same format as in the sockd.conf file:

```
<Identifier Key> <IP address> <Netmask>
```

The sockd entry specifies which host is running the sockd server. The format for this entry is

```
sockd @=<serverlist>   <IP address>   <Netmask>
```

A simple example of a clients file would be

```
direct      127.0.0.1 255.255.255.255
direct      192.168.1.0    255.255.255.0
sockd       @=<192.168.1.1> 0.0.0.0  0.0.0.0
```

Here the loopback address is directly attached. Any system on the local network (192.168.1.0) is also considered to be directly attached since it is on the same LAN. All other addresses must use the sockd proxy server on the host 192.168.1.1 for their connections. This channels all connections from the internal network through the SOCKS proxy host.

The file /etc/sockd.route is used by a multi-homed SOCKS server to determine which of its network interfaces to use to reach a given destination address. Communication between hosts on the same side of a firewall would not need to be defined in the routing file so long as internal hosts do not use the proxy server to communicate with one another (that is, the connection is direct). The /etc/sockd.route file syntax is

```
<interface addr>    <destination addr>         <netmask>
```

The simplest /etc/sockd.route would contain one line with the interface address of the external network connection in it. For our example of an internal network of 192.168.1.0, assume that the SOCKS server has a second ethernet connection out to the Internet with the address 128.10.34.1. To route connections from within the network out to the Internet, /etc/sockd.route should contain the line

```
128.10.34.1        0.0.0.0        0.0.0.0
```

This tells the SOCKS proxy server listening on the address 192.168.1.1 that all connections with destinations to the outside net should be routed through the interface whose address is 128.10.34.1.

This brief introduction to SOCKS only begins to scratch the surface of possible configurations for the software. For a more complete discussion, it is best to read the manual pages that come with the software.

Squid 2

Squid is an acronym that stands for Source Quench Introduced Delay (SQuID). It is software that caches Internet data and provides it upon request. Squid is proxy software. The Squid software supports FTP, HTTP, GOPHER, ICP, and WAIS protocols. The software also support Secure Socket Layer (SSL), as well as caches DNS lookup requests. Some protocols that Squid does not support include RealAudio, POP, and NNTP, as well as others. Squid's strength lies in its versatility. Not only can it do caching, it can also do redirection. For more information about Squid and to download the most recent version, see the official Squid Web site at http://squid.nlanr.net.

Squid Configuration and Installation

Once you have downloaded the latest version of Squid (version 2.2 is the most recent as of this writing), you will need to configure and compile it:

```
# gzip -dc squid-2.2.STABLE3-src.tar.gz | tar -xvf -
# cd squid-2.2.STABLE3
# ./configure
# make
# make install
```

If you don't specify the installation directory during the configure process, the software and all of its attendant files will be installed in /usr/local/squid. You can also download a precompiled binary packaged in RPM format from ftp://ftp.redhat.com/redhat/current/RedHat/i386/RPMS/squid-2.2.STABLE4-8.i386.rpm.

Installing the RPM is very easy:

```
# rpm -ivh squid-2.2.STABLE4-8.i386.rpm
```

Squid will be installed from the RPM as /usr/sbin/squid, and the configuration file for Squid will be /etc/squid/squid.conf. Once installed, you will need to edit the squid.conf file. This is the only configuration file Squid uses. A complete discussion of Squid configuration can fill an entire book on its own, so we will limit our discussion to setting up Squid as an HTTP proxy (a very common use). We will not cover setting up a peer cache. We will discuss setting up Squid to cache commonly accessed Web sites in what is termed HTTP accel mode.

The Squid Configuration File

By default, the Squid configuration file defines the cache size to be 100MB located in /usr/local/squid/cache. This cache is very similar to the cache created by some Web browsers (most notably Netscape). The number of first-level directories created when Squid is run for the first time is 16; the number of second-level directories created in the cache initially is 256.

One of the most important configuration options to note about Squid is the option http_port. By default, this is set to 3128. To use Squid as a proxy server to a Web server running on your system, set this to port 80:

```
http_port 80
```

Also, uncomment httpd_accel_host, httpd_accel_port, and httpd_accel_with_proxy and set them to the following:

```
httpd_accel_host localhost
httpd_accel_port <port which your web server is listening on>
httpd_accel_with_proxy on
```

Normally, turning on the httpd_accel_host option will disable proxy caching. To reenable it, you will need to turn on httpd_accel_with_proxy.

Creating a Squid Account and Group

Once you have completed the Squid configuration, but before Squid can be run, a Squid account and group needs to be created. It is possible to use the nobody account and the nogroup group combination; however, it is best to create a separate account and group for Squid. To do this under Red Hat, either use the control-panel program and call up linuxconf or use theadduser command. When setting up the Squid account, make it a member of the group squid and assign its home directory to /usr/local/squid. The first time Squid is run, it will create the cache directories in its home directory. To do this, run Squid with the -z option:

```
# /usr/sbin/squid -z  (or /usr/local/squid/bin/squid -z)
```

To run Squid after the cache is created, use the RunCache script found in /usr/local/squid/bin:

```
#/usr/local/bin/RunCache &
```

Or, if you installed from the RPM, just use the script found in

```
/etc/rc.d/init.d:
```

```
# /etc/rc.d/init.squid start
```

For complete details on configuring Squid, consult both the configuration file, squid.conf, which contains extensive documentation on all of Squid's capabilities, as well as the documentation provided with the software. For more complete information, visit the Squid Web site at http://squid.nlanr.net. Another proxy package that can be used is the FireWall ToolKit from Trusted Information Systems (TIS).

TIS FireWall ToolKit

The Trusted Information Systems (TIS) FireWall ToolKit (hereafter referred to as FWTK) is defined by TIS as "a set of programs and configuration practices designed to facilitate the construction of network firewalls." Whereas SOCKS requires only the installation of sockd and the configuration of a few files to provide a proxy service to almost any transaction protocol, TIS's FWTK requires that one daemon be set up for each protocol. Furthermore, each daemon has its own configuration file. Once this is done and your firewall rules are in place, all other transactions are denied. With SOCKS, the client programs need to be SOCKified in order to work with the proxy server. The firewall toolkit provides a plug-in daemon that can be used to set up a daemon for a protocol not explicitly covered by the toolkit.

Obtaining FWTK

The first thing to do is to download a copy of the toolkit from TIS Labs. Unfortunately, it is not as easy as simply going to an FTP site and downloading the package. The first thing you need to do is send an email to `fwtk-request@tislabs.com` with the single word "SEND" (without double quotes) in the body. An automatic process will respond with an email message containing the hidden directory on its FTP site that contains the software. This directory is only valid for 12 hours, so once you get the email response, download the software.

Once the software has been downloaded, you will need to uncompress and untar the package:

```
# zcat fwtk2.1.tar.Z | tar -xvf -
# less README (the README file ends up in the current
               directory, not the fwtk subdirectory)
# cd fwtk
# cp Makefile.config Makefile.config.orig
# cp Makefile.config.linux Makefile.config
# edit firewall.h
# edit Makefile.config (to ensure that it matches your
                        environment)
# make
# make install
```

There is no need to run the program fixmake supplied with the kit. By default, the FWTK components are installed in `/usr/local/etc`. Once installed, the system needs to be reconfigured to make use of the software. There are three files that need to be modified:

- `/etc/services`

- `/etc/inetd.conf`

- `/usr/local/etc/netperm-table`

Configuring FWTK

The first thing that should be configured is the `/usr/local/etc/netperm-table` file. This file contains the rules that the toolkit components use to determine whether to allow a connection through the firewall. In order to configure this as securely as possible, outside users should be required to identify and authenticate themselves to the toolkit programs. In order to permit people to identify themselves, the firewall uses a database of user IDs and passwords. This database is administered through the authsrv program, which comes with the toolkit. The authsrv program reads the fields in the authsrv section of the `netperm-table` file. This section tells the authsrv program where to find the database as

well as which hosts are allowed to connect into the authsrv program running on the
database.

```
authsrv:        permit hosts 127.0.0.1
authsrv:        permit hosts 128.83.155.45
authsrv:        database /var/adm/authsrv.db


# clients using the auth server
*:              authserver 127.0.0.1 7777
```

By default, only the localhost is able to connect to the authsrv process. For this
configuration, the localhost as well as the host 128.83.155.45 are allowed to connect to the
authsrv server process. Furthermore, the database is located in /var/adm/authsrv.db. To
initialize the database, run the authsrv program as root:

```
# ./authsrv
# authsrv# adduser admin "AuthSrv_Admin"
ok - user added initially disabled
authsrv# ena admin
enabled
authsrv# proto admin pass
changed
authsrv# pass admin "r8uT%34M"
password changed
authsrv# superwiz admin
set wizard
authsrv# adduser ruser "Remote_User"
ok - user added initially disabled
authsrv# group ruser rgroup
ok - user added to group rgroup
authsrv# ena ruser
enabled
authsrv# proto ruser pass
changed
authsrv# pass ruser "L83#47!"
authsrv# list
user    group   longname          ok?    proto   last
-----   ------- ----------------   -----  ------- -----
admin           AuthSrv_Admin     ena    passw never
ruser   rgroup Remote_User        ena    passw never
authsrv# quit
#
```

Configuring the Telnet Proxy

A full discussion of the configuration of the `netperm-table` file is not possible here. Instead, we will focus on configuring the telnet proxy, tn-gw, as an example. In the default `netperm-table` file, the tn-gw software has its configuration as follows:

```
# Example telnet gateway rules:
# ---------------------------
tn-gw:        denial-msg     /usr/local/etc/tn-deny.txt
tn-gw:        welcome-msg    /usr/local/etc/tn-welcome.txt
tn-gw:        help-msg       /usr/local/etc/tn-help.txt
tn-gw:        timeout 3600
tn-gw:        permit-hosts YOURNET.* -passok -xok
# if this line is uncommented incoming traffic is permitted WITH
# authentication required
tn-gw:        permit-hosts * -auth
```

If the administrator will remotely access the firewall host running the FWTK, a special line can be added that is a bit more restrictive than for the average user:

```
 netacl-sshd: permit-hosts YOUR_ADDR -exec /usr/local/sbin/sshd
```

YOUR_ADDR is the address of the machine the administrator will be connecting from.

In the `/etc/services` file, you will need to add a port definition entry for any new service you want to enable using the toolkit's software. The core of the toolkit is the `<service>-gw` programs, which are the proxy servers for the system. Say, for example, you provide telnet access from the outside into your network. To make use of the TIS FWTK, you will need to configure the tn-gw program so that inetd starts it up anytime a telnet connection is made to the firewall. Then, depending on what is in the tn-gw section of the netperm-table, the FWTK may permit or deny the connection. The `inetd.conf` would need to reflect the use of the FWTK gateway programs. Listing 26.1 shows an example `inetd.conf` where telnet, ftp, secure shell, and identd are proxyed through the firewall.

LISTING 26.1 Example `inetd.conf` with Proxy Through TIS FireWall ToolKit

```
#
# See "man 8 inetd" for more information.
#
# If you make changes to this file, either reboot your machine or send the
# inetd a HUP signal:
# Do a "ps x" as root and look up the pid of inetd. Then do a
# "kill -HUP <pid of inetd>".
# The inetd will re-read this file whenever it gets that signal.
#
```

LISTING 26.1   continued

```
# <service_name> <sock_type> <proto> <flags> <user> <server_path> <args>
#
#
# These are standard services.
ftp   stream    tcp nowait root   /usr/local/etc/ftp-gw    /usr/local/etc/ftp-gw
telnet  stream tcp nowait root   /usr/local/etc/tn-gw     /usr/local/etc/tn-gw
ssh   stream    tcp nowait root   /usr/local/etc/plug-gw   plug-gw sshd
ssh-a    stream tcp nowait root   /usr/local/etc/netacl    sshd
#
#
# Ident service is used for net authentication
auth stream     tcp nowait root   /usr/local/etc/plug-gw      /usr/sbin/in.identd
#
# End of inetd.conf.
```

The plug-gw file is as follows:

```
#
# Secure Shell and identd gateway
#
plug-gw: -port ssh * -plug-to <ssh_server> -port ssh
plug-gw: -port 113 * -plug-to <mail_server> -port 113
```

The `plug-gw` section of `netperm-table` tells the firewall to forward connection on port 22 over to the secure shell server's ssh port (that is, port 22). For identd, any identd connections are sent over to the mail server because it is the most logical place to run identd.

Now let's take a closer look at the `ssh-a` line. This is a special port being reserved for administrative secure shell into the firewall machine. For example, sshd normally runs off of port 22. However, for this example, sshd will run on port 38. In order for inetd to understand this, the `/etc/services` file will need the entry:

```
ssh  tcp/38      ssh  # Administrative Secure Shell added.
```

Setting up a proxy server requires much more work than a simple packet filter firewall. However, a proxy server goes a very long way toward making the network more accessible and the firewall more tolerable for the users. Now that we have discussed how to set up proxy services across a firewall, we can turn our attention toward setting up the firewall itself.

Setting Up a Firewall

Before getting into the nitty-gritty of how to set up a firewall with a Linux machine, the question needs to be asked, "Do I need to set up a firewall?" If the machine that you want to set up a firewall on is continuously connected to the Internet, the answer is yes. If you have a network at home and just want to masquerade your network, the answer is probably yes. If the machine being discussed is not continuously connected to the Internet and is not playing the role of gateway to a private network, the answer may be no. Nevertheless, knowing how to set up a firewall is a necessary skill in today's Internet. The number of break-ins and attacks continues to increase every year. Knowledge of how to protect a network or even a single machine is very worthwhile.

Packet Filtering

Every firewall is basically a packet filter. The idea is to selectively control the flow of data to and/or from a network. Packet filters allow or block packets, usually while routing them, and can be implemented at the router level or the host level. When implemented in a router, the router must not only bear the burden of routing packets to their proper destinations, but also decide which packets are to be permitted and which are to be denied.

Packet Filtering with Linux

Under Linux, packet filtering is built in to the kernel. The exact implementation of the filter is dependent on whether you are running 2.2.X kernel or a 2.0.X kernel. Packet filtering was first introduced into the Linux kernel code with kernel 1.3.X, and the filter rules were set up and manipulated by a program written by Jos Vos called ipfwadm.

When the development kernel 2.1.102 was released, many people were surprised to see that their old packet filters no longer worked. With the release of kernel 2.1.103, the change was documented. A new program, called ipchains, became available that worked with the new packet filtering code. This section looks at how to set up a Linux packet filter with both ipfwadm and ipchains. As always, it is best to refer to the documentation that comes with the programs for a full discussion of their capabilities. Also, as always, if you can't find the answer to your question in the man pages, the kernel source code for packet filtering is authoritative.

Filtering Using ipfwadm

ipfwadm was originally written by Jos Vos of X/OS Systems. A built RPM can be found at `ftp://ftp.xos.nl/pub/linux/ipfwadm/ipfwadm-2.3.0-1.i386.rpm`.

To install ipfwadm:

```
# rpm -ivh ipfwadm-2.3.0-6.i386.rpm
ipfwadm                 #######################################
#
```

The program ipfwadm will be installed in /sbin. Before using ipfwadm, you will have to recompile your kernel to make sure that the firewalling code is built in. To compile the packet filtering code, the following options must be set in the kernel configuration:

```
Code maturity level options   --->

    [Y] Prompt for development and/or incomplete code/drivers

General Setup   --->

    [Y] Networking support

Networking options   --->

    [Y] Network firewalls
    [Y] TCP/IP networking
    [Y] IP: forwarding/gatewaying
    [Y] IP: syn cookies
    [Y] IP: firewalling
    [Y] IP: firewall packet logging
    [Y] IP: always defragment
    [Y] IP: accounting
    [Y] IP: Drop source routed frames

Network device support   --->

    [Y] Network device support
    <Y> Dummy net driver support
    [Y] Ethernet (10 or 100Mbit)
    Select your particular network card
```

Once you have reconfigured your kernel, do a make clean, make dep, and make zImage. Copy the new kernel to the /boot directory, edit /etc/lilo.conf to include the new kernel, and reboot.

Turning On IP Forwarding

Once the new kernel is in place and the system is back up and running, you will need to turn on IP forwarding. Although it was selected in the kernel configuration, by default it is turned off. To turn on packet forwarding, edit the file /etc/sysconfig/network and change the parameter FORWARD_IPV4 from false to true. This will turn on IP forwarding every time you reboot your system.

Next, the firewall rules need to be put into place. The filters will need to be defined at the appropriate time as the system comes up. The best place to start the firewall is just before the network devices are configured using ifconfig. Under Red Hat Linux, the interfaces are configured in the /etc/rc.d/init.d/network script. This script tends to be one of the first scripts executed in run levels 2, 3, and 5. In these run-level directories, the symbolic link for the /etc/rc.d/init.d/network shell program is S10network. One possible method of setting the packet filtering rules in place before the interfaces are configured is to create a shell script such as /etc/rc.d/init.d/firewalls. Then create the links in the run-level directories to the firewall shell program with the following command:

```
# for i in rc{2,3,5}.d ; do
# cd /etc/rc.d/$i
# ln -s ../init.d/firewalls S5firewalls
# cd ..
# done
```

This little shell loop changes directory into each of the rc2.d, rc3.d, and rc5.d run-level directories and creates a link to the firewall shell program in /etc/rc.d/init.d/ that will run before the network will be brought up. This prevents any window where a network interface may be active but not controlled by the firewall.

The shell program /etc/rc.d/init.d/firewalls is a simple bourne shell program and is shown in Listing 26.2. This script assumes the following network topology:

```
Firewall Host: fw1.fwcorp.com
Interfaces: eth0(internal), eth1(external)
Masquerade: no
eth0: 128.83.137.35
eth1: 128.83.155.44
```

LISTING 26.2   Firewall Startup Script

```
#/bin/bash
#
#  S51firewall - a simple firewall script to setup a packet filter using ipfwadm
#
#
```

LISTING 26.2   continued

```
PATH=/sbin:/usr/sbin:/bin:/usr/bin
export PATH

# flush the current rules:
ipfwadm -I -f
ipfwadm -O -f
ipfwadm -F -f
ipfwadm -A -f
# deny everything first, that way we won't have to worry about some crazed
# hacker trying to get into the system before we get a login prompt.
ipfwadm -I -p deny
ipfwadm -O -p deny
ipfwadm -F -p deny

ipfwadm -F -a deny -o -P tcp -S 0.0.0.0/0 -D 128.83.137.0.0/24
ipfwadm -F -a deny -o -P udp -S 0.0.0.0/0 -D 128.83.137.0/24

# now, allow all traffic within the local network
ipfwadm -F -a accept -P tcp -S 128.83.137.0/24 -D 0.0.0.0/0

# deny all ICMP packets coming in except for type 3, type 8 and type 11
# These rules are tricky.  The idea here is we don't want to
# allow all ICMP traffic into the network.  However, we do want to
# allow some traffic for possible debugging of firewall rules.  The way
# we want it set up is as follows
# 1. Deny ICMP packets by default
# 2. Allow ICMP type 3 (destination-unreachable), type 8 (echo-reply),
# and type 11 (used by traceroute) to come in from the outside
# 3. Deny type 8 (echo-reply) from within our own network -- no responses to
# any pings (not really necessary, but for extra insurance).
ipfwadm -I -a deny -P ICMP -S 0.0.0.0/0
ipfwadm -I -a accept -P ICMP -S 0.0.0.0/0 3
ipfwadm -I -a accept -P ICMP -S 0.0.0.0/0 8
ipfwadm -O -a deny -P ICMP -S 128.83.137.0/24 8

# allow SMTP, ftp, ftp-data, Secure Shell, DNS and WWW
ipfwadm -F -a deny -o -S 127.0.0.1/8 -D 128.83.137.0/24
ipfwadm -F -a reject -o -P tcp -S 0/0 -D 128.83.137.0/24 113
ipfwadm -F -a accept -P tcp -S 0.0.0.0/0 -D 128.83..137.0/24 20 21 22 25 53 80
ipfwadm -F -a accept -P udp -S 0.0.0.0/0 -D 172.16.37.19 53
```

Before continuing, let's take a closer look at the rules above. The first thing we do is flush (-f) the accounting (-A), forwarding (-F), input (-I), and output (-O) rules. This provides a clean slate with which to build a firewall around. Once you have set up a firewall that denies all forwarding of packets, you can start permitting the services you want to allow.

The next four commands set the default policy for all rules to deny. This prevents any packets that come in from being forwarded on to their final destinations. The particular policy of "deny" also does not provide a return response code to the originating source. So, to the other end of the connection, it appears as if the packets sent to the destination have simply disappeared. Had this policy been "reject," a response code would have been returned to the source and the user at that end would get a "connection refused" type message.

The next two commands set up the rules to allow all traffic from the internal network (128.83.155.*). The following series of rules are for control of ICMP traffic across the network. Specifically, the ICMP packet type being filtered out is the type 8 packet, also known as the ICMP "echo-request." This is the type of packet sent by the program ping. It is desirable to filter out this packet because the "ping of death" attack, a denial of service, uses this type of packet to achieve its goals. Another packet type to filter out is the "echo-reply" or type 0 ICMP packet. This is the response to a type 8 packet. This packet is filtered to prevent any possible response to a type 8 packet. When someone outside the firewall pings a machine inside the firewall, no response is received. It's as if the machine did not exist. Filtering out all ICMP packet types is not desirable because this would also prevent the ability to diagnose routing problems.

The next series of firewall rules set up the services the firewall machine will allow. These services include ftp (20), ftp-data (21), secure shell (22), smtp (25), DNS (53), and www (80).

Forwarding Connections

To forward connections from within a network out to the rest of the network, there is a simple format to the ipfwadm command:

```
ipfwadm -F -a accept -b -P <protocol> -S <source addr> -D <destination addr>
```

The reason why two rules are needed for accounting whereas only one rule is needed for forwarding is because the -b flag used in the forwarding rules is not a valid parameter for the accounting rules. It's that easy. One thing that must be handled carefully is the ICMP protocol. By denying this protocol, you will never be able to determine if there is a problem with your firewall. This is one of the weaknesses of ipfwadm: the inability to distinguish between one type of ICMP packet and another. To address this issue as well as others, ipchains was written for kernel versions later than 2.1.102.

Setting Up a Firewall with ipchains

When kernel 2.1.102 was released, those who were following the development kernels discovered that their current packet filters suddenly no longer worked. The desire was to improve the Linux packet filtering code by making it easier and more logical to set up a firewall as well as control it. ipfwadm is not very intuitive to the newcomer, and the flow control is unidirectional. To the newcomer, setting up a firewall is an error-prone process and debugging a firewall becomes difficult and time-consuming; hence, the rewriting of the packet filtering code as well as its attendant manipulation utility. With the release of the new manipulation utility, ipchains, setting up a firewall has become easier.

ipchains may be downloaded from the Red Hat site by FTP. The RPM is found in the directory `ftp://ftp.redhat.com/ pub/ current/i386/RedHat/RPMS/ipchains-1.3. 9-3.i386.rpm`.

Installing ipchains

To install ipchains, log in as root and type the command:

```
# rpm -ivh ipchains-1.3.8-3.i386.rpm
ipchains                    ######################################
#
```

This will install the main utility in `/usr/sbin` as well as the documentation in `/usr/doc` and the man pages in `/usr/man`. As always, be sure to read the man pages and any documentation that comes with the software. Also, be sure that the packet filtering code is compiled in your kernel. If there are any doubts about what needs to be selected in the kernel configuration process, see the section "Linux Kernel Configuration" earlier in the chapter. The ipchains software will work primarily with kernel version 2.1.102 and above. However, there are patches to make it work with earlier kernel versions. Making ipchains work with a kernel version prior to 2.1.102 is a non-trivial task and not recommended for the newcomer. If at all possible, use a kernel in the 2.2 series.

The packet filtering rules in a Linux 2.2.X kernel are now separated into four categories:

- IP input chain
- IP output chain
- IP forwarding chain
- User-defined chains

Contrast this to the rule categories in the older Linux packet-filtering code: IP input, IP output, IP accounting, IP forwarding, and IP masquerading. With ipfwadm, the user is restricted to using rulesets defined by someone else. ipchains provides the ability to insert custom rulesets into the packet filter.

Understanding Packet Filtering

Before continuing with how to use ipchains to set up a packet filter in the newer Linux kernels, it would be best to examine how packet filtering is now done. Figure 26.4 shows how a packet traverses a Linux 2.2 kernel running a packet filter. Each rule in the system indicates which packets match the rule and what the fate of a packet is that does match. When a packet enters the system, the kernel uses the input chain to decide its fate. Then the kernel determines where the packet is to go. Finally, before leaving the system through an interface, the kernel applies the output chain to the packet.

But, what exactly is a chain? A chain is a series of rules that say "if the packet header looks like this, then this is what you do with it." If the packet doesn't match the rule, the next rule is consulted. If the packet does not match that rule, then the following rule is consulted. This continues until either the packet matches a given rule or the rules are exhausted. If the former occurs, the packet is sent on to the next stage. If the rules are exhausted because a packet header does not match, the default chain policy is applied to the packet. In a conservative, security-conscious system, this policy should be either reject or deny.

Setting up a firewall using ipchains is not very different than setting up a firewall with ipfwadm. There are many options to ipchains, significantly more than ipfwadm. To manage whole chains, the following options are applicable:

- -F—Flush the rules out of a chain

- -N—Create a new chain

- -P—Change the policy for a built-in chain

- -X—Delete an empty chain

- -Z—Zero out the packet and byte counters in a chain

To manipulate individual rules within a chain, the following options are available:

- -A—Append a new rule to a chain

- -D—Delete a rule in the chain

- -I—Insert a new rule in the chain

- -R—Replace a rule in a chain

FIGURE 26.4
Traversal of a packet through the filters.

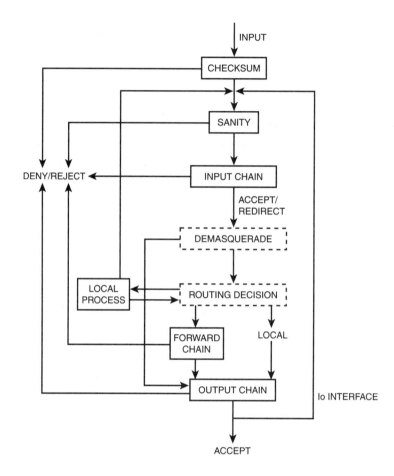

The following example shows the usefulness of manipulating individual rules within a chain:

```
# ping -c 1 127.0.0.1
PING 127.0.0.1 (127.0.0.1): 56 data bytes
64 bytes from 127.0.0.1: icmp_seq=0 ttl=255 time=0.3 ms

--- 127.0.0.1 ping statistics ---
1 packets transmitted, 1 packets received, 0% packet loss
round-trip min/avg/max = 0.3/0.3/0.3 ms
# which ipchains
/sbin/ipchains
# ipchains -A input -s 127.0.0.1 -p icmp -j DENY
# ping -c 1 127.0.0.1
PING 127.0.0.1 (127.0.0.1): 56 data bytes
```

```
--- 127.0.0.1 ping statistics ---
1 packets transmitted, 0 packets received, 100% packet loss
# ipchains -L input
Chain input (policy ACCEPT):
target prot opt    source   destination      ports
DENY   icmp ------ localhost anywhere        any -> any
```

In this example, the rule to block the ICMP packets to the localhost interface is done by appending (-A) a rule to the input chain that says that any packet whose source (-s) is 127.0.0.1 and whose protocol (-p) is icmp is sent to the target DENY.

A target is a value target that tells the kernel what to do with a packet should it match a rule in a chain. In the preceding example, the target is DENY, which has the same result as the ipfwadm policy "deny." There are six targets that ipchains uses: ACCEPT, REJECT, DENY, REDIRECT, RETURN, and user-defined. ACCEPT, REJECT, DENY, and REDIRECT are identical to the ipfwadm policies of accept, reject, deny, and redirect. RETURN causes the chain policy to automatically be applied to the packet. Finally, ipchains provides for user-defined chains. In this case, the packet jumps over to the user-defined chain and traverses the rules there. If the rules in the user-defined chain don't decide the fate of the packet, it returns to the chain from which it came and continues through that chain.

To see how ipchains can be used to create a firewall, we will re-examine the firewall setup using ipfwadm.

Traversal of a Packet Through the ipchains Filters

This section describes how an IP packet traverses the various filters set up through ipchains in the Linux kernel. Each step is described below.

1. The first step is to determine whether the packet has been corrupted in some way during transmission. A checksum is performed on the packet and if there is a problem with the packet, it is rejected.

2. Before a packet reaches a chain, it undergoes a sanity check to make sure that the packet won't confuse the rule-checking code. If it fails the sanity check, the packet is rejected.

3. Once the packet passes the sanity check, it is passed on to the input chain. If the packet meets the criteria for acceptance, it goes further on. Otherwise, it is denied.

4. After passing the input chain, the packet is de-masqueraded if it is in response to a masqueraded packet.

5. Next, the destination field is examined to decide what interface the packet should go to. This can result in one of two possible scenarios:

a. If a packet is destined for the lo (the loopback) interface, it proceeds first to the output chain and then to the input chain for the lo interface.

b. If the packet was created by a local process running on the firewall machine, then the forwarding chain is applied to the packet.

6. The forwarding chain is applied to any packets that are routed through the machine out to another machine.

7. Before leaving the machine, the packet traverses the output chain.

Examples of Firewalls

With a description in mind of the sequence of events that occur as a packet traverses the kernel, a couple of examples of firewalls are in order. To begin with, let's examine the simplest kind of firewall.

Example 1: Single-User Machine

Setup: Single-User machine

PPP connection to the Internet

No services provided except for Secure Shell on port 22

In this instance, there is no need for concern with the output rule because the desire is to simply block any unwanted packets from reaching the machine. To do this, the ipchains commands would be:

```
# ipchains -A input -s 0.0.0.0/0 -i ppp0 -j DENY
    # ipchains -A input -s 0.0.0.0/0 -d $PPP_ADDR 22 -j ACCEPT
    # ipchains -A input -i lo -j ACCEPT
```

The three commands are saying:

1. Append to the input chain a rule that any packets coming in from the outside (-s 0.0.0.0/0) on the interface ppp0 should be denied.

2. Append to the input chains a rule that any packets coming in from the outside (-s 0.0.0.0/0) whose destination is the local PPP address and for port 22 should be accepted.

3. Append to the input chain a rule to accept any packets coming in from the loopback interface to the loopback interface.

Don't worry about the fact that the PPP interface may not be up when the firewall rules are put in place. So long as the environment variable $PPP_ADDR gets defined during the interface configuration, the firewall will work. It's that simple.

Example 2: A Network Configuration

Now, let's consider a more complex network configuration. The network in the next example looks like Figure 26.5.

FIGURE 26.5

Example network interface.

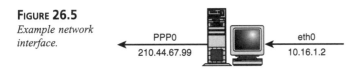

PPP0
210.44.67.99

eth0
10.16.1.2

In this example, the external interface is still a dial-up PPP link whose IP address is 210.44.67.99. There is also an internal ethernet interface, which is the gateway for a private network address space: 10.16.1.*. All incoming packets on the eth0 interface need to be masqueraded in order to traverse the Internet. Furthermore, access into the private network from the outside is available via Secure Shell. To set up such a configuration, the ipchains rules could be:

```
# ipchains -I input -s 10.0.0.0/8 -i ppp0 -l -j DENY
# ipchains -I input -s 172.16.0.0/11 -i ppp0 -l -j DENY
# ipchains -I input -s 192.168.0.0/16 -i ppp0 -l -j DENY
# ipchains -A input -s 0.0.0.0/0 -d $PPP_ADDR 22 -j ACCEPT
# ipchains -A input -i ppp0 -p ICMP -d $PPP_ADDR 0 -j ACCEPT
# ipchains -A input -i ppp0 -p ICMP -d $PPP_ADDR 3 -j ACCEPT
# ipchains -A input -i ppp0 -p ICMP -d $PPP_ADDR 11 -j ACCEPT
# ipchains -A input -i lo -j ACCEPT
# ipchains -A input -i eth0 -s ! 10.16.1.0/24 -l -j DENY
# ipchains -A forward -s 10.16.1.0/24 -d 0.0.0.0/0 -j MASQ
# ipchains -A input -s 0.0.0.0/0  -i ppp0 -j DENY
```

The rules fall into three categories: input, output, and forwarding. For the input rules, the first thing to do is deny any packets that come from private networks defined in RFC 1597. These packets should never be seen out in the "wild." If packets containing these source addresses appear on the ppp0 interface, you can assume that they are spoofed packets so you should log and drop them. The next step is to open the firewall gradually. To allow Secure Shell (on port 22), you modify the input chain by adding a rule that says that any packets from the Internet destined to the network address $PPP_ADDR port 22 should be accepted.

The next three rules have to do with ICMP traffic. You don't want to block all ICMP traffic. Although Linux is now immune to the "ping of death" attack, some of the machines on the internal network may not be. The best thing to do is to prevent any ICMP from going beyond the firewall machine. However, some ICMP packet types provide useful information. Type 0 ICMP packets are "echo-reply" packets generated in response to an ICMP "echo-request" or "ping." If you want to determine whether a machine is alive, you can ping it but you need to allow ICMP "echo-reply" back through the firewall in order to see the response. Type 3 packets are used to indicate failure to reach a destination for both the TCP and UDP protocols. Type 11 packets are used by traceroute to validate a path to a destination. It is important to allow these packets to go both in and out so that the firewall can be debugged.

Next, as was done with the previous example, the loopback interface should be allowed. The next rule deals with input from the eth0 interface. This rule is similar to its counterpart in the chain dealing with input from the ppp0 interface. In this case, all packets coming into the eth0 interface should have a 10.16.1.* source address. If they don't, something is wrong and it's best to just deny the packets but also log them.

Finally, the last rule is for the forward chain. This rule says that any traffic whose source address is 10.16.1.* and whose destination is the Internet needs to be masqueraded. This will replace the packet's source address with the ppp0 IP address.

This set of rules only begins to scratch the surface of ipchains. This tool is much more versatile and flexible than its predecessor ipfwadm. ipchains can be used to modify the type of service (TOS) fields. The TOS field is a set of four bits in the IP header that affects the way packets are handled. The four bits are "minimum cost," "minimum delay," "maximum reliability," and "maximum throughput," and only one may be set at any given time. The TOS field bits can be altered by using ipchain's -t option. This option takes two hexadecimal values as its argument. The first is ANDed with the TOS field in the IP header. The second value is then XORed with the result of the AND operation. To provide a brief example, to set ftp-data to provide maximum throughput through the packet filter, ipchains can be called as follows:

```
# ipchains -A output -p tcp -d 0/0 ftp-data -t 0x01 0x08
```

The ipchains HOWTO file provides a table with the necessary hexadecimal values for the four bits mentioned above. Once the firewall is set up, the next step is to debug it. It is a rare instance when a firewall doesn't need debugging and tuning after it has been deployed.

Debugging Firewalls

Setting up a firewall is not difficult. Debugging a firewall is where the problem lies. To begin with, ICMP can be the source of a great deal of trouble. ICMP packets are used to indicate failure for other protocols such as TCP and UDP. Blocking ICMP packets would make debugging a firewall difficult. As mentioned, however, only certain ICMP packet types need to be filtered out. These are type 0 (echo, used by ping) and type 8 (echo-reply, used by ping).

Another problem encountered when running a firewall may be encountered with FTP. Remember that in the /etc/services file there are two entries for FTP:

```
ftp-data      20/tcp
ftp            21/tcp
```

Normally, an outbound ftp connection is opened from the client to port 21 on the ftp server. When data is returned to the client, the server opens a second connection to the client on port 20. By blocking incoming connections on port 20, the results of an ls command on the ftp server or a file download will not get through. To circumvent such problems, the firewall should permit inbound connection on port 20 or the clients should be configured to run only in passive mode. With passive mode, the client opens a second connection to the ftp server, which is then used to pass data from the server back to the client.

Using DNS Servers Outside the Firewall

One last pitfall that may occur with firewalls involves the use of DNS servers outside the firewall. Modern DNS uses UDP as the transport protocol for responses to clients so long as the packets are less than 512 bytes in length. Once the packets exceed 512 bytes in length, the server will use TCP as the transport protocol to the client. By indiscriminately filtering out TCP connections, DNS will appear to sometimes work so long as the responses from the DNS server are less than or equal to 512 bytes in size.

Summary

Setting up a firewall is not a simple task. It requires a fair amount of forethought and planning. Depending on the number of services that are to be provided, the firewall rules in both ipfwadm and ipchains can be anywhere from simple and short to fairly complex and lengthy. Firewalls can be packet filters, providing only certain services through them, or they can involve proxy servers, which act on behalf of a client requesting a service. No matter how a firewall is implemented, it provides one of the best security tools you can use to protect your network.

The Security Administrator's Toolbox

IN THIS CHAPTER

- Building Your Security Administrator's Toolbox   *820*

- Security Resources on the Web   *834*

- Sources of Information Other than the Web   *836*

In order to keep up with the constant changes in the field of Linux security, every good security administrator must build up a set of tools with which to protect the systems for which he has responsibility. This toolkit should consist not only of software tools, but also of information sources where you can learn about new risks as they arise and techniques to combat them. Like the rest of systems administration, security is an ever-changing job and you have to work to keep up with system crackers and intruders. This chapter takes a look at a few of the available tools that the systems administrator can use in his role as security administrator. It starts with software, proceeds on to resources on the World Wide Web, and finally to other resources such as newsgroups and mailing lists.

Building Your Security Administrator's Toolbox

There is a plethora of software tools available to assist the systems administrator in securing systems. Some of these are replacements for standard tools with added security features. Others are designed specifically to protect systems, such as the TCP Wrappers suite, or to test for gaps in the security of your system, such as SATAN. This section looks at one tool, sudo, that should be a standard part of any security administrator's toolkit, and then looks at some sources of other security tools available on the Internet.

Granting Privileges with sudo

One of the most basic tools available to administrators that will help to improve the security of your Linux systems is the sudo command. This command allows you to grant specific privileges to users without giving them full root access. For example, if you wanted to allow users to mount a CD-ROM on their local workstations, you could configure sudo to allow them this right. The sudo command works by consulting a configuration file, which specifies the systems and commands that a user is allowed to run. If the user enters a command other than ones to which he was granted access, a warning message is sent to the systems administrator that indicates the command the user attempted. If the user is authorized to run the specified command, he is prompted to enter his own password, which when entered causes the command to be e xecuted with root privileges. You would think that a command as useful as this would be included with the Red Hat Linux distribution; however, it is not. It is available from the contributed software directory of the Red Hat FTP server and mirrors as sudo-x.x.x-x.i386.rpm, where x.x.x-x is the version number, currently at 1.6.1-1. You can also get the latest version of sudo from the sudo homepage at http://www.courtesan.com/sudo/.

This package includes not only the sudo command, but the also a starter sudoers file and visudo, a utility for editing the sudoers file. The sudoers file is the mechanism by which privileges are granted to users and should only be edited using the `visudo` command. A discussion of the syntax of this file is covered later in this chapter. To get a better grasp of what `sudo` can do for you, let's take a look first at some of the command-line options in Table 27.1.

TABLE 27.1 `sudo` **Command-Line Options**

Option	Description
-V	Prints the `sudo` version and exits.
-l	Lists the commands that a user is permitted to run and those that are explicitly forbidden.
-h	Prints a usage message and exits.
-v	Updates the user's timestamp file. The timestamp file provides a mechanism so that once you have been authenticated, you have a timeout period during which you do not have to reauthenticate.
-k	Removes a user's timestamp file. This is a good option to use in a user's `.logout` file.
-b	Runs the specified command in the background. This option is required because shell job control cannot be used to do this.
-p prompt	Overrides the default password prompt with the one specified by prompt.
-u username/#uid	Runs the specified command as the user specified by username or numeric uid.
-s	Runs the shell specified by the `SHELL` environment variable if it is set or by the shell specified in the `/etc/passwd` file.
-H	Sets the `HOME` environment variable to the home directory of the target user as specified in `/etc/passwd`.
--	Forces `sudo` to stop processing command-line arguments.

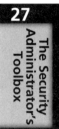

As you can probably surmise by the options list, there are any number of applications where the `sudo` command might come in handy. One immediate use that comes to mind is to create an operator menu script. A sample operator menu script is shown in Listing 27.1. This menu presents the user with options to run the backup software, add a new user, disable a user account, restart a printer, restart all printers, and exit from the menu. It is relatively crude, but with a little work it could be used to allow novice operators to perform these tasks, without giving them access to the root account. By creating a menu of commands that you want an operator to be able to run and by granting the operator access to those commands in the `sudoers` file, you can have a non-privileged account able to run a specific set of privileged commands.

LISTING 27.1   Sample Operator Menu Script `opermenu.sh`

```bash
#!/bin/bash

trap "" 1 2 3 15

function new_user {
    # Prompt for the desired username
    printf "\nEnter the desired username:  "
    read username

    EXISTS=`grep "^$username:" /etc/passwd`
    if [ "$EXISTS" != "" ]; then
        printf "\nUsername requested already exists...exiting.\n"
        sleep 1
        return
    fi

    printf "\n"

    # Prompt for primary group
    printf "\nEnter the primary group for this user (default $username):  "
    read group

    if [ "$group" = "" ]; then
      group=`echo $username`
        creategroup=1
    else
        GEXISTS=`grep "^$group" /etc/groups`
        if [ "$GEXISTS" = "" ]; then
            printf "\nGroup $group does not exist...create it (y/n): "
            read yesno

            if [ "$yesno" != "y" ]; then
                printf "\nFATAL USER CREATION ERROR...aborting.\n"
                sleep 1
                return
            else
                creategroup=1
            fi
        fi
    fi
```

LISTING 27.1   continued

```
    printf "\n"


    # Prompt for the users real name
    printf "\nEnter the users real name:  "
    read realname


    printf "\n"


    # Prompt for the users home directory
printf "\nEnter the users home directory (default /home/$username):  "
    read homedir


    if [ "$homedir" = "" ]; then
        if [ -d /home/$username ]; then
            printf "\nDirectory /home/$username exists...use anyway (y/n): "
            read yesno


            if [ "$yesno" != "y" ]; then
                printf "\nFATAL USER CREATION ERROR...aborting.\n"
                sleep 1
                return
            fi
        fi
        homedir=`echo /home/$username`
    fi


    printf "\n"


    # Prompt for the users shell
    printf "\nEnter the users shell (default /bin/bash):  "
    read shell


    if [ "$shell" = "" ]; then
        shell="/bin/bash"
    else
        if [ -x $shell ]; then
        VALIDSHELL=`grep $shell /etc/shells`
            if [ "$VALIDSHELL" = ""]; then
                printf "\nInvalid shell for user...aborting.\n"
                return
```

27

The Security
Administrator's
Toolbox

LISTING 27.1   continued

```
            fi
        fi
    fi

    printf "\n"

    # If required, create the group for the user
    if [ "$creategroup" = "1" ]; then
        /usr/sbin/groupadd $group
    fi

    # Call the useradd command with the appropriate
    # options based on the user responses
    /usr/sbin/useradd -d $homedir -g $group -s $shell \
        -c "$realname" $username

    # Invoke the passwd command to set a password for the account
    passwd $username

}

function disable_user {

    # Prompt for the user account to disable
    printf "\nEnter the user account to disable:   "
    read unlucky

    EXISTS=`grep "^$unlucky:" /etc/passwd`
    if [ "$EXISTS"' = "" ]; then
        printf "\nUser account not found...aborting.\n"
        return
    else
        /usr/sbin/usermod -p "*" $unlucky
    fi

}

function restart_queue {

    # Check for an argument of "all" and if found, restart all
    # print queues.
    if [ "$1" = "all" ]; then
```

LISTING 27.1   continued

```
            /usr/sbin/lpc restart all
    else
            # If the first argument is not all, then check the
            # number of arguments and if not zero, then restart
            # the print queues named by the arguments.  If zero,
            # then prompt for the name of a queue.
            if [ $# -ne 0 ]; then
                while [ $# -ne 0 ]; do
                    /usr/sbin/lpc restart $1
                    shift
                done
            else
                # Prompt for the queue to restart
                printf "\nEnter the name of the print queue to restart:  "
                read queue

                /usr/sbin/lpc restart $queue
            fi
    fi


}


while true; do
    # Clear the screen
    clear

    # display the menu
    printf "


            OPERATOR MENU


        1 - Start Daily Backups
        2 - Add a New User Account
        3 - Disable a User Account
        4 - Restart a Print Queue
        5 - Restart all Print Queues


        0 - Exit


    Enter your selection: "

    # read the users response
```

LISTING 27.1   continued

```
read ans

# based on their response, run the appropriate script
# from /local/sbin or the corresponding function
case $ans in

    1)  printf "\n     Executing script: /local/sbin/start_backups.sh\n"
        sleep 1
        /local/sbin/start_backups.sh &;;
    2)  printf "\n     Executing function: new_user\n"
        sleep 1
        new_user
        sleep 1;;
    3)  printf "\n     Executing function: disable_user\n"
        sleep 1
        disable_user
        sleep 1;;
    4)  printf "\n     Executing function: restart_queue\n"
        sleep 1
        restart_queue
        sleep 1;;
    5)  printf "\n     Executing function: restart_queue all\n"
        sleep 1
        restart_queue all
        sleep 1;;
    0)  exit 0;;
    *)  printf "\n         ***INVALID OPTION***\n"
        sleep 1;;

esac

done

# Exit
exit 0
```

Once the operator menu script has been created, you could add the lines shown in Listing 27.2 to the sudoers file to allow operators to perform these tasks and free up your time for doing more important tasks. These entries allow the users johnd, janed, and barneyf, which are aliased as OPERATORS, to run the opermenu.sh script in /local/sbin on the machines earth, venus, and mars, which are aliased as SERVERS.

LISTING 27.2   Entries in `/etc/sudoers` to Implement Operators Menu

```
# Define an alias for the system operators, John Doe, Jane Doe, and
# Barney Fife
User_Alias     OPERATORS=johnd,janed,barneyf


# Define an alias for the servers on our network
Host_Alias     SERVERS=earth,venus,mars


# Permit the people in the operators alias permission to run the operator
# menu on the systems defines in the Host Alias SERVERS.
OPERATORS      SERVERS=(ALL) /local/sbin/opermenu.sh
```

When the operator needs to invoke one of the functions on the operators menu, he or she would type the following command line and would be presented with a menu as shown in Figure 27.1.

```
tschenk@marcanthony:~ [768]$ sudo menushell.sh
```

FIGURE 27.1
Operator menu
`menushell.sh.`

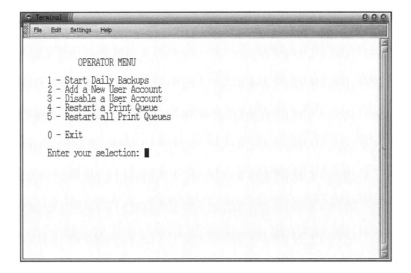

You grant privileges by editing the /etc/sudoers file, which should be done using the visudo command. This command invokes the editor specified in the EDITOR environment variable or the vi editor and on exit, performs a validity check so that changes to the file are only permitted if the syntax of the file is valid. This syntax is explained fully in the sudoers manual page, and a sample /etc/sudoers file is shown here with comments that explain the use of each line or set of lines.

/etc/sudoers

```
# sudoers file.
#
# This file MUST be edited with the 'visudo' command as root.
# See the man page for the details on how to write a sudoers file.
#
# Host alias specification.  These allow groups of machines to be
# referred to by a single name later on in the file.
Host_Alias     SERVERS=quicksilver,wizard
Host_Alias     LAPTOPS=nomad,maxmax,feralkid
Host_Alias     WRKSTNS=foolsgold,magic

# User alias specification.  Define groups of users to be referred to by
# a single alias.
User_Alias     SYSADMIN=tschenk,gregc,%wheel
User_Alias     NOMADS=eunjoung,nicholas,nia

# Runas alias specification.  Specifies users who can be specified using
# the -u option of the sudo command.
Runas_Alias    OPER=root,oracle

# Cmnd alias specification.  Specifies alias for commands to make specifying
# them later easier.
Cmnd_Alias     SHUTDOWN=/usr/bin/halt,/usr/bin/reboot,/usr/bin/shutdown

# User privilege specification.  These are the only lines required.  There
# is no requirement for host aliases, user aliases or command aliases, but
# a sudoers file without user privilege specifications does nothing.  The
# lines below specify that user tschenk can do anything anywhere, gregc is
# allowed to shutdown servers and members of the group NOMADS are allowed to
# run the shutdown commands on the group of systems aliased by LAPTOPS.
root           ALL=(ALL) ALL
tschenk        ALL=(ALL) ALL
```

```
gregc       SERVERS=(OPER) SHUTDOWN
NOMADS      LAPTOPS=(ALL) SHUTDOWN
```

You may wonder why this particular tool was chosen for coverage in this chapter on security tools. The point being made by covering the sudo command is that security measures are not black magic. They involve restricting access to sensitive parts of the system and using common-sense measures to allow only the access required for a person to do his job. This, of course, is not all there is to security, but it is a good place to start. Security also includes learning about the tools that can be used to identify weaknesses in your network and the tools that might be used to attack your system, so that you can recognize them when they appear on your system.

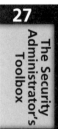

Additional Security Tools

In addition to the sudo command, which should be a part of any Linux system, there are a number of popular tools that you can obtain in order to get your security toolkit started. The following sections name a few of them along with a brief description of their functions.

Security Scanners

One of the tools that you can use to scan your system for security flaws is COPS, or Computer Oracle and Password System. This package is an internal scanner that looks for a number of well-known security holes in your system and reports any that it finds or, in some cases, automatically corrects the flaw.

Another scanner, but one that scans from the outside, is SATAN, or Security Analysis Tool for Analyzing Networks. This is one of the best known and most widely publicized tools to hit the security scene in recent years and it is controlled via a Web interface as shown in Figure 27.2. This tool is similar to COPS; however, it is designed to be run against your systems from the outside, looking for vulnerabilities in much the same way that a system cracker would. Widely publicized at its initial release, many feared the release of SATAN due to the potential for its misuse by the very people it was designed to warn you about. This has turned out not to be much of an issue, due in part to the complexity of setting SATAN up and getting it running. If you are interested in obtaining a copy of SATAN, it can be found at http://www.fish.com/~zen/satan/satan.html.

FIGURE 27.2

The SATAN main menu.

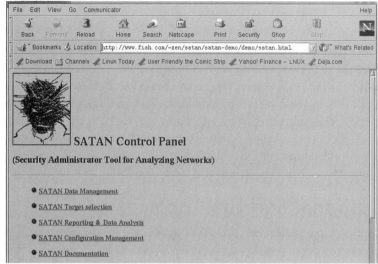

An older and less feared scanner much like SATAN is ISS, or Internet Security Scanner, which also runs against your systems to look for known problems such as sendmail exploits, NFS holes, and the like. The creators of ISS have incorporated the original ISS software into a commercial product call SAFEsuite, but if you want to look at the original free version, you can still find it at `ftp://coast.cs.purdue.edu/pub/tools/unix/iss`. The COAST homepage is shown in Figure 27.3.

> **Caution**
>
> Use of these and similar tools can provide important information regarding security flaws in your network. It is strongly recommended, however, that you do not use these tools against networks other than your own. Your actions could be taken as hostile and result in negative repercussions from the target of your scans.

Command Replacements

As previously noted, some security problems are best fi xed by replacing the program that exhibits the vulnerability. This being said, there are a number of readily available utilities and other software that can be used to replace vulnerable commands on your Linux system.

FIGURE 27.3
The COAST homepage.

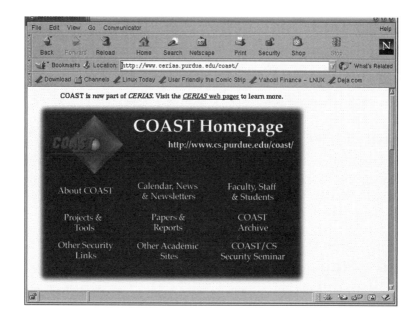

One such command is the SSH, or Secure Shell, suite of tools. This package includes the three commands `ssh`, `slogin`, `scp`, and the ssh daemon, `sshd`. This package is designed to provide a secure connection to systems via the Internet, in which all traffic between the client and the server is encrypted. The `ssh`, `slogin`, and `scp` commands can be used as direct replacements for `rsh`, `rlogin`, and `rcp`, and use much the same syntax.

Another such replacement command is `xinetd`, which serves as a replacement for the Internet super server `inetd`. It has a more robust access control mechanism that includes the concept of scheduling when services are available and provides extensive logging capabilities. If you currently use `inetd` with the TCP Wrappers package, such as comes with Red Hat, `xinetd` is a package that you may want to explore because it provides similar functionality in a single integrated package. The `xinetd` software may be obtained at `http://www.synack.net/xinetd`.

To replace the easily exploitable Berkeley FTP daemon, we have the WU-FTPD package. This package provides a more secure FTP daemon and is maintained by Washington University—St Louis. This daemon is in active development and patches for vulnerabilities in the code are quickly fi xed and released. If you are interested in using a more modern FTP daemon, another alternative is ProFTPD, which is available from `http://www.proftpd.net/`. ProFTPD is a relatively new FTP daemon that includes many of the features of the WU-FTPD plus adds many of its own.

Where Do I Find Them?

There are a number of sources for the tools we have discussed thus far, some run by government agencies, others still by the Open Source community. The next section looks at a few of these sites. The key thing to remember is to always examine the link pages that these sites maintain for additional resources and more up-to-date information.

Sources of Security Tools

You have decided to make a more concerted effort to secure your systems, and now you need to start building up your collection of tools in order to do so. This section looks at a couple of sites devoted to security and system cracking, and some of the tools available at these sites that a systems administrator can use to get started.

Computer Operations, Audit, and Security Technology Project

A good starting point for any administrator looking for security tools is the Computer Operations, Audit, and Security Technology project home page located at `http://www.cs.purdue.edu/coast`. This Web site contains a plethora of information on security resources on the Internet in addition to housing one of the largest archives of security related documents and tools available. Multiple methods are available for accessing this archive, including a subject index and an author index. For the most complete information, browse to the COAST FTP site at `ftp://coast.cs.purdue.edu/pub/` with your favorite FTP client.

ZEDZ Consultants

An equally good source of security information and tools, especially those related to cryptography and privacy, is the ZED dot NET Web site run by ZEDZ Consultants at `http://www.zedz.net`. This Web site and archive, unlike COAST, is devoted primarily to cryptography and privacy tools and is a good site if you are looking for tools like ssh, Netscape with the 128-bit encryption, and any number of other like tools. In addition, if you are concerned about privacy issues and the Internet and want to know about anonymous remailers and other tools to protect your identity while using the Internet, this is the site for you.

CIAC

Another excellent security tools site is the CIAC, or Computer Incident Advisory Capability site run by the U.S. Department of Energy. This site not only maintains links to many of the most popular and effective security tools available on the Internet, but also has sections for accessing CIAC bulletins and advisories, virus information, information on hoaxes, and a wealth of other information invaluable to the systems administrator interested in security. To paraphrase their words, CIAC aims to be the one-stop-shopping site on the Web for security information. The CIAC Web site is located at `http://ciac.llnl.gov/ciac/SecurityTools.html`.

NIST

The National Institute of Standards and Technology, or NIST, is another maintainer of security tools. Its archive home page contains an index of tools with abstracts at `http://cs-www.ncsl.nist.gov/tools/tools.htm`. A nice feature of this archive site is that like the COAST archive, the tools are categorized to make finding the right tool easier.

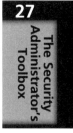

DFN-CERT

Another security tools resource located outside of the U.S. is the DFN-CERT site in Hamburg, Germany. This site is similar to some of the U.S. sites already mentioned in that it contains not only a large number of software tools, but also a wealth of other information. In addition, being outside of the U.S. means that it is not subject to the export restrictions placed on cryptographic software (which many security tools rely on) that the U.S. site is. Its URL is `http://www.cert.dfn.de/eng/` for English language pages and `http://www.cert.dfn.de/` for information in German. In addition, you can access its FTP server directly at `ftp://ftp.cert.dfn.de/pub/tools/`.

Rootshell

A final source of tools that the security administrator should be aware of is `http://www.rootshell.org/`, a Web site that chronicles exploits and vulnerabilities in various operating systems and programs. Rootshell is well known for supplying not only the information regarding what exploits are available on various systems, but also for supplying the tools and code required to exploit them. The Web site is touted as being for educational purposes only. A statement found at the bottom of each Web page states that by accessing their archives, you agree not to use any of the information gathered to crack systems or to take advantage of the exploits described there.

In addition to these repositories of security tools, there are many other resources available to the security administrator. The next section looks at some of the Web sites that can make your job as security administrator easier.

Security Resources on the Web

The explosion of the Web in recent years has included a substantial number of sites devoted to security as well as a number of sites for crackers. Both types of sites should be of interest to the security administrator—the first so that you can keep up with the latest tools for monitoring and announcements of security risks, and the second so that you can keep an eye on what the enemy is doing. This section discusses a few specific Web sites and how they can be used to help the security administrator keep ahead of the game.

The USENIX Web Site

A good place for any security administrator to begin looking for information is the USENIX Web site. USENIX is an organization of advanced computing systems professionals that is open to anyone who wants to become a member. Located at `http://www.usenix.org/`, the USENIX Web site contains a wealth of information on proceedings from the many conferences that they sponsor, including ones on security. Membership in USENIX entitles you to discounts on fees for attending these conferences, subscription to *;login:*, the official magazine of USENIX, and a number of other benefits. In addition, one of the major working groups of USENIX is SAGE, also known as the Systems Administration Guild. SAGE is focused on ensuring that systems administrators can keep up-to-date with their skills, including their skills as security administrators, and provides definitive information on the job requirements for each level of systems administrator. The USENIX and SAGE conferences are excellent and almost always include tracks on systems security for computing professionals.

Red Hat Security Information

One of the services provided by Red Hat Linux is to run the Red Hat Web site, which is not only a vendor site for its Linux distribution, but is also a general purpose Linux portal site. In addition to product information, Red Hat provides up-to-date information on security flaws discovered in its products as well as fixes. This information can be found at `http://www.redhat.com/corp/support/errata/rh60-errata-general.html` and includes descriptions of the security issues as well as the corrective action to take to eliminate the problem. An important first place to look after installing your system is the updates and general errata pages, so that you can be aware of what parts of the system you will need to replace in order for you to get up-to-date.

Linux Portal Sites

Some of the most up-to-date and timely sources of information on Linux security issues are the various Linux Portal sites. These sites monitor the Internet for announcements regarding Linux and provide pointers to this wealth of information. A few of these sites are described here.

My personal favorite resource for Linux information is the Linux Today Web site at `http://linuxtoday.com/`. This site is constantly being updated with information about Linux, including security announcements from all of the major Linux vendors as well as from many of the security monitoring agencies, such as Bugtraq. One of the most useful features of this site is the capability to search past announcements for security information, as well as the recently added Security announcement section, which filters all of the security-related information into a single page.

Another noteworthy Web site for keeping up with Linux and Linux security issues is the Linux Weekly News site at `http://www.lwn.net/`, which includes a security section in each weekly bulletin. This site contains much of the same information as the Linux Today site, however it is updated on a weekly basis instead of the minute-by-minute changes at Linux Today. One of the features that makes this a worthwhile site is the links from the Security page to various other security resources on the Web, specifically the vendor-specific pages, and the links to security archives, such as the ones already mentioned.

Linux.com, the portal site of VALinux, is also getting in on the security game with a section devoted not only to security announcements, but how-to articles and tips for the security administrator. This Web site is located at `http://linux.com/security`.

Although not Linux-specific, a significant amount of information relating to Linux and Linux security can be found at Slashdot (`http://www.slashdot.org/`) and Freshmeat (`http://www.freshmeat.net`). These sites are very popular among both the Linux and cracker communities, and information on exploits and security holes in Linux distributions often shows up here first. Additional value with both of these sites comes from the discussion forums, where new security issues are discussed in detail, often resulting in workarounds or fixes within hours of the announcements.

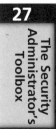

Sources of Information Other than the Web

In addition to resources on the World Wide Web, there are many other sources of information related to security on the Internet. This section takes a look at some of the more common of these that the security administrator can use to keep abreast of the latest security alerts and announcements from various monitoring agencies.

`comp.security.announce` and Other USENET Newsgroups

USENET is a system of discussion groups on just about any conceivable topic, including computer security. Some of the groups more relevant to security of Linux and UNIX systems are described here.

The `comp.security.announce` newsgroup is a moderated newsgroup devoted to security announcements, including CERT-CC advisories. This group is not intended as a discussion forum, but merely as a channel for announcements from recognized security groups.

A complementary group to the `comp.security.announce` newsgroup is the `comp.security.unix` group, which is a place for systems and security administrators to discuss security issues with UNIX and UNIX-like operating systems such as Linux.

If your interests include things other than just Linux and UNIX security issues, the `comp.security.misc` discussion group may be for you. In this newsgroup, the topics of discussion are not limited to a single operating system, but cover a wide variety of topics relating not only to systems security, but to security of networks as well.

To deal with the specific topic of firewalls, the `comp.security.firewalls` group was formed. Use this newsgroup to discuss issues related to firewall strategies, tools for building firewalls, and hardware and software solutions to the problem of keeping intruders out of your systems.

Although not directly related to security, viruses are another problem that the security administrator is often called upon to deal with, and the newsgroup `comp.virus` will keep you informed of the latest announcements on that front. This is a moderated newsgroup that allows discussions as long as the moderator feels that they remain on topic and polite. Posting guidelines are available on the Web at `http://www.ja.net/CERT/CERT-CC/virus-l/virus-l.README` and you may download them if you so desire at `ftp://corsa.ucr.edu/pub/virus-l/virus-l.README`.

Another newsgroup outside of the comp hierarchy is the `alt.security` newsgroup, which hosts discussions related to computer and network security. Unmoderated and often abused, this newsgroup may have too low of a signal-to-noise ratio to be of interest to many security administrators.

A newsgroup that might be of help while trying to develop a company security policy is `comp.admin.policy`, which along with general administrative policy discussions, also includes information that can be used to help determine a well-balanced security policy. This is an excellent resource where you can discuss administrative issues with your peers.

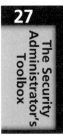

Two newsgroups not specifically devoted to security, but that often include discussion of security issues, are `comp.unix.admin` and `comp.unix.wizards`. These groups are good resources and like the `comp.admin.policy` newsgroup, you can discuss security issues with administrators from around the world.

A final, but certainly not unimportant resource is the `comp.risks` newsgroup, which is the USENET equivalent of the ACM Forum on Risks to the Public in the Use of Computers and Related Systems. This is a moderated discussion group devoted to exploring the risks to society from computers and computerization.

If you are unfamiliar with USENET, these newsgroups are normally available through your Internet service provider using any number of newsreaders, both character-based and graphical. However, if you are unable to access a news server, you may still read these newsgroups by visiting the Deja.com Web site at `http://www.deja.com` and registering for the My Deja service. This site includes a Web-based interface to the majority of USENET newsgroups, and also allows you to search these same newsgroups as far back as 1995 using their newsgroup search facility. This can prove to be an invaluable resource to system admins and to security administrators alike.

Security Mailing Lists

If you prefer electronic mailing lists to the anarchy of USENET, there are a number of options in this realm as well. Some of these are simply email to USENET gateways that turn the newsgroups into mail messages and vice versa. The problem with mailing lists is usually the volume of mail that you receive from them. It is easy to get overwhelmed with information from these lists and if you have not yet discovered mail filtering tools like procmail and mailagent, you should learn them.

This list is not intended to be comprehensive by any stretch of the imagination. It merely includes a number of lists related to security and other topics of interest to security administrators.

Bugtraq

One of the most popular mailing lists for keeping track of security announcements is Bugtraq. This list is a forum for the discussion of security flaws, how these flaws are exploited, and fi xes for them if they are available. Although not intended as such, this list is frequented by system crackers looking for new exploits of which they can take advantage. It is for this reason alone that it is to your advantage to follow this list. A word of caution is in order, however, because this is an unmoderated list and information posted to it has been proven incorrect many times in the past. Always attempt to verify through an independent source any vulnerabilities you hear about on this list. Subscription requests for Bugtraq should be sent to `bugtraq-request@fc.net` with a message body containing `subscribe bugtraq`.

> **Caution**
>
> This warning about the Bugtraq list is good advice not only for this list, but also for all security resources on the Internet. Never take news of an exploit as gospel simply because of the source, no matter how good you think that source might be. Again, always verify the information through an independent source if possible.

CERT-advisory Mailing List

Announcements of CERT-CC advisories are available via the CERT-advisory mailing list. These advisories rarely contain information on how to exploit the security defects that they are about, however they usually do contain information from vendors on workarounds or solutions to these defects. To subscribe to this list, send a message containing `subscribe cert-advisory` to `cert-advisory-request@cert.org`. In addition to the mailing list, there is an archive of past CERT-CC advisories available via anonymous FTP from the CERT FTP site at `ftp://info.cert.org/` or from the mirror site at the COAST archive, `ftp://coast.cs.purdue.edu/pub/alert/CERT`.

CIAC-notes List

Another announcement mailing list is the CIAC-notes list, which provides technical notes on workarounds and solutions to security flaws in various programs and operating systems. These notes are often more like how-to documents and, like the CERT advisories, old issues are available for anonymous FTP. The primary FTP site for these is `ftp://ciac.llnl.gov/pub/ciac/notes` and, just as with the CERT advisories, these are mirrored at the COAST archive at `ftp://coast.cs.purdue.edu/pub/alert/CIAC/notes`.

To subscribe to this list, send a message with a body of `subscribe ciac-notes [yourname]` to `ciac-listproc@llnl.gov`. Naturally, replace `[yourname]` with your real name as in this example.

```
echo "subscribe ciac-notes Thomas Schenk" | mail ciac-listproc@llnl.gov
```

The `redhat-announce` Mailing List

A Red Hat specific list that includes all security announcements from Red Hat along with fixes or workarounds is the RedHat-announce mailing list. This list is a moderated list for announcements only and is not a discussion list. To subscribe, send mail to `majordomo@redhat.com` with a message body of `subscribe redhat-announce`. A good complement to this list is the Linux-kernel list. This list is where the kernel hackers who can actually fix problems hang out. This list is, however, a very busy one, sometimes generating over one hundred messages per day. So if you do not want to subscribe by sending a message body of `subscribe linux-kernel` to `linux-kernel-request@vger.-rutgers.edu`, a good method for keeping up with what is discussed on the list is to follow `http://kt.linuxcare.com/`, which is a Web site that periodically summarizes the mailing list and provides pointers to individual messages that you can read at your leisure.

27

The Security
Administrator's
Toolbox

Miscellaneous Lists

In addition to the lists for the announcement of exploits, there are also lists about security-related topics like firewalls. Three of these are the Academic-firewall list, hosted by Texas A&M University for the discussion of firewalls in academic environments; Firewalls, which is a forum for discussions of the various types of firewalls and their strengths and weaknesses; and FWALL-users, a list specifically for users of the Trusted Information Systems Firewall Toolkit, FWTK. To subscribe to the Academic-firewall list, send mail with a body of `subscribe academic-firewalls` to `majordomo@net.tamu.edu`. To subscribe to the Firewalls list, the subscription address is `majordomo@greatcircle.com` and it likewise requires a body of `subscribe firewalls`. And finally, to subscribe to the FWALL-users list, send a message body of `subscribe fwall-users` to `fwall-users-request@tis.com`.

Each of these lists includes valuable information concerning security for your Linux systems. However, because of the volume of some of these lists, it is easy to be swamped by the incoming email. One approach to dealing with this issue is to divide the groups among a group of administrators, each of whom monitors one or more lists and forwards relevant information to the others in the group. Another alternative strategy is to create local newsgroups from the mailing lists, so that you can take advantage of the filtering and kill file features of modern newsreading software.

Summary

This chapter looked at some of the sources of information and tools that can be used to build up the repertoire of a security administrator, and demonstrated how security is largely a matter of applying common-sense rules. Security should not be considered a black art that only highly paid consultants understand. By utilizing the sites and resources described in this chapter, any systems administrator can gain useful knowledge concerning security and make great advances toward providing a secure working environment and protecting the assets of the organization for which he works.

The problem with a chapter such as this one is that the Internet is an ever-changing medium, especially the Web, which makes listing resources such as these a risky proposition. However, if just one of these links remains by the time you are reading this book, I am sure that you will find that one page will have a links page which will enable you to find current and relevant resources.

I've Been Hacked: What Now?

IN THIS CHAPTER

- Intruder Alert! *842*
- Determining the Extent of Intrusion *844*
- Reinstalling the Operating System from Scratch *855*

Intruder Alert!

You log in to your system and immediately realize that something is not right. Files that you know should exist are missing and there are things on the system that you know don't belong there, such as accounts you did not create or programs you did not install. Or you see multiple logins from a particular user over a network line, even though you know that he is not typically a remote user. What do you do? Do you shut down the system? Do you disconnect from the Internet? Do you do nothing? This chapter takes a look at the issue of a security breach on your systems, looks at a few of the things that you can do to determine what damage, if any, has been done to your system and the appropriate measures to take to remedy the situation.

Rules of Engagement

When you suspect that an intruder has gained access to your systems, it is important to follow some simple rules of engagement. The following are just general guidelines that are intended to help you deal with the intrusion effectively.

Create a Plan of Action

The first thing you should do is put your plan for dealing with a security breach into action. What plan, you say? The plan that should be a part of your security policy that outlines the actions you must take when such a breach occurs. This plan should include items such as who to notify of the intrusion; methods of determining the extent of the damage, if any; the location and status of backups and installation media if they are required; and any actions to be taken once the breach has been dealt with, such as reporting requirements to company officials or customers. Having a response plan ready will make dealing with the intrusion less painful and will let management know that you are prepared.

Don't Panic

The second thing to remember is not to panic. If you detect an intruder and immediately shut down the system and disconnect it from the network, you have stopped the intrusion but you may lose valuable evidence of what the person was doing or how they gained access. If you can remain calm, you can formulate an effective response to deal with the intrusion. Failure to remain calm can lead you to make mistakes that may be noticed by the intruder and cause him to panic, leading to a greater risk to your systems.

Keep Good Written Records

The final thing you should do is to keep a written record of everything that you find out about the suspected intrusion and what you do in response. If you look in the system logs, note that fact and if possible, make a copy of the file on another system or print them out. Use commands like the script command or record your session using emacs so that you can go back later and see exactly what you did in response to the intrusion. This record serves two purposes. First, it allows you to go back after the intrusion has been dealt with and determine where your intrusion action plan may be lacking and allows you to improve it. Second, it will help you answer the innumerable questions you will have to deal with from management and possibly from others who may want to know exactly how you responded to the crisis and what evidence is available.

Gathering Evidence of Intrusion

One of the first things you should do is determine if someone has truly broken into your system and if so, gather as much proof as possible. This may be harder than it sounds, but there are a number of signs that you can look for during this phase of gathering evidence of a break in.

Being an effective security administrator requires an extra measure of diligence on your part. You must make it your business to know what the systems under your care do and what normal activity for the users of these systems looks like. You must have a means of keeping track of configuration files and be able to easily determine if one of them has changed. And finally, you must be constantly vigilant and have the tools necessary to deal with security issues as they arise.

Fine, you say, you can do all of these things. You have monitors set up that actively monitor your system for signs of intrusion, using tools such as Tripwire. You have other monitors that scan log files for suspicious behavior, such as Swatch. And finally, you have current verified backups stored in multiple locations in the event of an emergency. What else should you be worried about?

Although all of these things are good measures to take, detecting intrusion may require still more. For example, if you have a system used primarily by administrative types whose use of the computer is to read email and run a limited set of applications, you should begin to get suspicious if one of these users suddenly starts using software development tools or scripting languages. In addition, it is a good idea to periodically scan the system logs to determine the number and frequency of failed login attempts and which accounts these are occurring against. This way, when a user starts suddenly showing dozens of failed login attempts, a red flag is raised. Other indirect indicators of a possible break-in are unexplained system sluggishness or processes running as a privileged user that you and

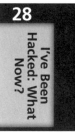

your staff did not initiate. And, of course, obvious indicators of security breaches include user accounts in /etc/passwd that you did not add or actually catching an intruder in the act. All of these things must be monitored both periodically and on a random basis to make it difficult for the mischievous or malicious system cracker to get in undetected.

Other Intrusion Indicators

In addition to all of these things, other obvious indicators of intrusion might include hacks to your Web site, email threatening a break-in, or warnings from other systems administrators about unusual activity emanating from your site.

The object of this monitoring, of course, is to be able to recognize when an intruder has gained access to your system and to gather evidence that supports your theory of a break-in when it occurs. What you do once you have determined that a break in has occurred is up to you and your security policy; however, it is important to do something. A system cracker who finds that you are not doing anything to stop him will be tempted to go even farther, and what started out as a prank may end up being a much more serious intrusion. Again, remember during the decision-making process that if you react by shutting down the system, you may lose valuable evidence. In addition, if your intruder turns out to be a script kiddie or a harmless trespasser, letting them know that you are on to them may be enough of an incentive for them to leave, especially if you gently remind them that what they are doing is illegal.

Having laid the ground rules for dealing with intruders, we can now proceed to the next step of determining what they have been up to. This is critical because the extent of the intrusion determines the appropriate response.

Determining the Extent of Intrusion

Once you have established beyond a shadow of a doubt that an intrusion has occurred, you must determine the extent of that intrusion. This process can be quite involved depending on the skill of the intruder and the strength of his tools, but with persistence, you can usually find the evidence of what the person was up to. This section examines some of the methods for determining what the intruder was up to and how much of a threat his activities posed. This information will then be used to attempt to plug the hole that let the intruder in and to determine what to do with the systems to which the intruder had access.

Analyzing System Logs

One of the first places you should look for traces of intrusion is, naturally, the system logs. Unfortunately, most crackers know this as well and will usually try to make sure that their activities are not logged and if they are, they remove them. One possible remedy to this is to use the kernel option to redirect the console to a serial port and to attach a simple line printer to this port. This, combined with changes to the `syslog.conf` file to make sure that all messages go to both the standard system logs and to the console, will result in a literal paper trail, which the system cracker cannot erase. (Assuming, of course, that they are not attacking from inside your network.) Other alternatives include logging to a centralized logging host as well as the local machine. This assumes that the intruder fails to gain root access and is not able to change the behavior of the system logger.

Assuming that there are logs available somewhere that the intruder has not been able to subvert, your next question should be, "What am I looking for?" Here is a short list of things that might indicate that someone has invaded your host:

- Logins from users at unusual hours.

- Logins by users who are on vacation or who recently left the company.

- Unexplained reboots or changes in runlevel.

- Gaps in the systems logs.

- Time changes on servers that cannot be explained.

- Unusual error messages from system daemons such as ftpd, sendmail, or other servers.

- Unauthorized or excessive use of the su command. Excessive use may indicate that someone is trying to cover his tracks by running processes as another user. Unauthorized use is self-explanatory.

- Users logging in from unfamiliar locations.

- Excessive failed logins with bad passwords.

Each of these indicators may not necessarily mean that your system has been compromised, but they are noteworthy and merit some investigation. One way to monitor the system logs for these types of activities is with programs like Swatch. Swatch is a software package that modifies the logging behavior of several system commands and then watches the log files for "important" messages and notifies the systems administrator about them. It is available from the COAST security tools archive, whose address can be found in Chapter 27, "The Security Administrator's Toolbox." If you don't like the part about modifying system commands, you can easily create your own monitoring system using a scripting language like Perl. Such a script might work something like this:

1. Create a named pipe and direct syslog messages to it.
2. Have your program attach to the named pipe and read from it one line at a time.
3. As you read each line, compare it against a list of regular expressions that define what you are looking for.
4. If you match one of your regular expressions, notify someone via e-mail or pager.

The advantage to rolling your own monitoring software is that the system cracker will not know the program name to look for and will be less likely to kill it off if he manages to gain root access.

As you examine each of these areas in the logs, make sure to document anything that you find that might indicate how the intruder gained access, what accounts were used, whether the intruder gained access to other systems on your network, and other evidence.

Intrusion Detection Tools

There are a number of intrusion detection tools that you can use to ensure that you do not overlook the warning signs of intruders on your network. One such tool, which was mentioned earlier, is Swatch. This tool monitors the system logs and looks for "important" messages and reports these to the systems administrator. Tools of this type, while useful, are not a substitute for periodically checking systems logs yourself.

Filesystem Scanner(s)

Another type of tool that can help you check for intrusion is the filesystem scanner. This type of tool includes such packages as Tripwire. Tripwire is a product that scans a filesystem and records digital signatures for the files it finds. It can then be run periodically to compare files against the recorded signatures and flag changes. Another way that you can achieve similar functionality is to store all of your system configuration files in a CVS repository and periodically do a CVS diff and note any changes that you find. The drawback to this is that CVS is best suited for text files, so it is not a good choice for finding differences in system binaries. Yet another important type of change that can be easily detected is changes in the permissions on file, especially the setuid or setgid bits. Many flavors of UNIX include scripts that are run daily to detect the addition of setuid or setgid programs, incorrect permissions on sensitive files such as .rhosts, and other anomalies. FreeBSD is one such system and the scripts used can be easily adapted to run on your Red Hat Linux system.

Standard Tools: who, top, ls, and ps

Finally, do not discount standard tools like who, top, ls, and ps. Although these tools are often subverted by system crackers, you can stay one jump ahead by keeping statically linked copies of these utilities in a nonstandard location, or better yet, on removable media, such as a CD-R disc. In addition, learn alternative methods for displaying desired information. Say, for example, you want an alternative to the ls command. A crude approximation of ls -l is shown in Listing 28.1 using echo and wc.

LISTING 28.1 Approximating ls Output Without Using ls

```
[tschenk@madmax chapter28]$ ls -al
total 34
drwxrwxr-x    3 tschenk   tschenk        1024 Sep 29 09:48 .
drwxrwxr-x   42 tschenk   tschenk        1024 Sep 11 19:13 ..
-rw-r--r--    1 tschenk   tschenk       13892 Sep 28 22:13 755928.txt
-rw-r--r--    1 tschenk   tschenk       13892 Sep 29 08:18 755928.txt.old
drwxrwxr-x    2 tschenk   tschenk        1024 Sep 28 07:54 CVS
-rw-rw-r--    1 tschenk   tschenk         304 Jul 17 15:33 toc.ch28
-rw-rw-r--    1 tschenk   tschenk           0 Sep 29 09:48 typescript

[tschenk@madmax chapter28]$ for f in .* *; do
> if [ -d $f ]; then
>     g='d'
>     s='----'
> else
>     g='-'
>   s=`wc -c $f | awk '{ print $1 }'`
> fi
> echo "$g     $s              $f"
> done
d    ----              .
d    ----              ..
-    13892             755928.txt
-    13892             755928.txt.old
d    ----              CVS
-    304               toc.ch28
-    0                 typescript

[tschenk@madmax chapter28]$
```

As you can see, I was able to determine files versus directories, display dot files, and print the size of regular files using one program external to the shell. With a little more thought, I could probably improve on this to get even more information. This is a trivial example and having an alternative to the ls command may not be of much use. However, applying the same principle to other commands, such as ps, can be very useful because it is common for system crackers to replace commands that can show their presence on the system. In the case of the ls command, application of this principal means that even if the cracker has subverted the ls command to hide directories and files from me, he would also have had to subvert my shell, awk, and the wc command as well.

Additional sources of information on security tools is included in Chapter 27, which contains a number of references to Web sites and FTP archives that are devoted to security.

The problem with dealing with any intrusion is that you don't know what has been affected on the system. Binaries may have been trojaned and their dates touched back to their original values. The tripwire binary could be trojaned, as could shutdown. I know this is rough, but I recommend that when an intrusion is discovered, you *pull the plug*. This freezes the intrusion in progress and prevents more damage. If you can afford it, have an extra disk on hand and dd a copy of the compromised disk to it to keep a clean version for you to experiment on. Now you can boot off a floppy, like Trinux as described in the next section, and inspect the system. Of course, this may be overkill, but you need to determine a security policy and stick to it. You should (if you're administering for a business) talk to lawyers and/or law enforcement officials when you're defining your security policy to make sure you don't do anything that could be considered evidence tampering!

Trinux as a Security Tool

A very useful tool that you can use in the event of a system break in is the Trinux Linux distribution. This is a floppy-based Linux distribution that uses RAM disks to provide an extensive collection of security and recovery tools in a minimal amount of space. This section takes a look at how Trinux can assist you in determining the extent of an intrusion and in preventing repeat performances.

One of the most compelling reasons for using Trinux is that you can boot the affected system using the Trinux floppies and use the included tools to diagnose the system. This allows you to investigate without affecting the state of the system and bypassing all of the tools on the system, which may have been altered by the intruder. Also, because Trinux boots from floppies, you can easily carry it with you to remote locations. The networking support in Trinux also means that you can access the network if you find a problem that cannot be dealt with by the tools included.

To get a copy of Trinux, visit its Web site at http://www.trinux.org and download the latest images and packages. These packages include tools such as packet sniffers, network monitors, network mapping and vulnerability scanners, firewall and proxies, and other utilities. With these tools, you can perform the analysis required after a security breach to determine the source of the vulnerability, while at the same time correct damage done to the system that you know was compromised.

Remedying Security Issues with Trinux

A suggested strategy that you can employ involving Trinux is to attack the problem in three phases. First, use Trinux on a laptop or other portable system attached to your network to probe the system that suffered the intrusion. You can determine how the system cracker got in and identify other possible methods of entry to the damaged system. For this phase, you can use the scanning tools on the Trinux disks, such as nmap. The nmap program is a network mapper/port scanner that identifies open ports on a system, as well as the system type and lots of other information that can be used to determine possible vulnerabilities. You can then determine if any of the services that are reported as open have security announcements regarding them and suggested fixes to remove the vulnerability, or you can simply turn off the service in question.

The second phase is to use the Trinux disks to boot the attacked system and use the utilities on the disks to look for changes to the system. This ensures that the tools you are using to check for discrepancies are not the ones that may have been compromised by the system cracker. This is very important so that you do not miss anything due to corrupted or subverted system utilities such as ls or ps.

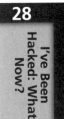

The final phase is to use the Trinux tools to scan your entire network to look for vulnerabilities on hosts other than the one that was attacked. This is best done from somewhere outside of your network so that your firewall is tested as well. One of the security tools available with Trinux that serves this purpose is SAINT, which not only scans the host that was attacked, but can also run in an exploratory mode to determine other hosts that may have vulnerabilities based on trust relations with the compromised hosts.

The following sections discuss some of the tools that are available with the Trinux distribution. The list of tools is broken down by category and each tool is briefly described.

Packet Sniffers

Packet sniffers are tools that listen on a network interface and gather information about the packets that are passing through that interface. Three such utilities that come with Trinux are

- Tcpdump
- Ipgrab
- Ngrep

Tcpdump

Tcpdump is the standard packet sniffer that comes with most flavors of UNIX and Linux. The description from the manual page states that tcpdump prints out the headers of packets that match the boolean expression supplied on the command line. This package is available by anonymous ftp from `ftp://ftp.ee.lbl.gov/tcpdump.tar.Z`.

Ipgrab

Ipgrab is another packet sniffer based on the Berkeley packet capture library. It prints out complete header information for packets at the Data Link, Network, and Transport layers. Written by Mike Borella, it is available on the Web at `http://www.xnet.com/~cathmike/MSB/Software/`.

Ngrep

The final tool in this category is ngrep. This utility is an attempt to provide GNU grep-like functionality across the Network layer. It allows you to specify a regular expression and filter expressions as understood by the Berkeley packet capture library and print out information on matching packets. This tool is available at `http://www.packetfactory.net/ngrep/`.

Network Monitors

Network monitors are used to display statistical information regarding traffic passing over a network. These types of tools can be used to determine the amount and type of traffic, including byte counts, number and types of packets, error counts, and other similar information. Here are two of tools distributed with Trinux:

- IPTraf
- Ntop

IPTraf

IPTraf is a network statistics package that displays general and detailed interface statistics showing packet counts, sizes, and a wealth of other information regarding the traffic on your network in full-screen mode. It includes a filtering mechanism that allows you to single out specific types of traffic by protocol. IPTraf is available at `http://cebu.mozcom.com/riker/iptraf/`.

Ntop

Ntop is another monitoring package that displays information in a manner similar to the top utility and, like top, shows network usage statistics in a variety of sort orders. Ntop can be used in interactive mode or Web mode. It is available from `http://www-serra.unipi.it/~ntop/`.

Network Mapping/Vulnerability Scanning

Network mapping and vulnerability scanning tools use a variety of methods to determine the layout of a network. They probe the various well-known services and use the responses to identify open ports. Or, through the use of techniques such as TCP fingerprinting, they determine the type of system it is reaching. Trinux includes several of these tools, such as

- Nmap
- Exscan
- SAINT
- QueSO
- Hping
- Firewalk
- Cgichk

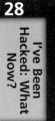

Nmap

One of the most useful tools in the Trinux tool set is nmap. This utility explores networks, identifying the types of hosts attached and possible vulnerabilities for each of them. Nmap is an excellent security auditing tool that should become part of any serious security administrator's toolset. The nmap utility is available at `http://www.insecure.org/nmap/index.html`.

Exscan

Another scanning utility is exscan. This utility, like nmap, is able to identify the operating system of the system being scanned through the use of TCP fingerprinting, a capability it gets from integrating queso. In addition to this, it captures banner information from various services on remote systems like SMTP and FTP and queries servers for information such as HTTP version and finger information. Get it at `http://exscan.netpedia.net/exscan.html`.

SAINT

SAINT is the Security Administrator's Integrated Network Tool. It probes systems looking for vulnerabilities, such as unprotected ports, and is also capable of examining vulnerabilities based on trust relationships between systems. SAINT is similar in many ways to SATAN. The SAINT home page is at `http://www.wwdsi.com/`.

QueSO

QueSO is a utility that scans a network and is able to identify the operating system of hosts connected to it through the use of TCP fingerprinting. Formerly used to scan the Internet and count operating systems, the OS counter project is now defunct and the QueSO home page is no longer available.

Hping

Hping is a utility for doing TCP/IP stack auditing, discovering firewall policy, and scanning TCP ports in various modes, among other things. Unlike the regular ping utility, hping does TCP pings instead of ICMP. You can download hping from `http://www.kyuzz.org/antirez/hping2.html`.

Firewalk

The `firewalk` utility is an analysis tool that is similar to `traceroute` and that uses the responses from systems to determine gateway access control lists. This tool can be used to determine the filter rules in effect on packet forwarding devices like routers. A complete white paper describing this technique as well as the source code is available on the Web at `http://www.packetfactory.net/firewalk/`.

Cgichk

The final tool in this category that comes with Trinux is cgichk. This is a simple scanner, available at `http://www.rootshell.com/`, that connects to a Web server and checks for known vulnerable CGI programs. The programs that this program checks for are ones that have been identified as having security flaws. Some of the CGI programs it looks for include

- phf
- Count.cgi
- test-cgi
- php.cgi
- handler
- webgais
- websendmail
- webdist.cgi
- faxsurvey
- htmlscript

- `pfdispaly.cgi`

- `perl.exe`

- `wwwboard.pl`

All of these programs have known vulnerabilities and should be removed from your system if found.

Firewalls and Proxies

The tools in this category allow you to set up packet filter-type firewalls and proxies to block unwanted intrusions into your systems. There are three of these available with Trinux:

- Ipchains

- Redir

- Tinyproxy

Ipchains

The ipchains utility is the standard packet filtering software available with Red Hat Linux 6.0 and allows you to define rule sets through which packets must be filtered before being allowed in or out of your system. There is a HOWTO that explains its use that comes with Red Hat and you can get it from your Red Hat installation media.

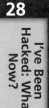

Redir

The next utility in this category is the redir port redirector. Its function is to listen on a particular port and when a connection is received, it redirects that connection to another port and passes data between them. This is the same functionality as available in the ssh utility. Redir is located on the Web at `http://users.qual.net/~sammy/hacks/`.

Tinyproxy

Lastly, we have tinyproxy, which is a small but very efficient HTTP proxy that is useful in cases where squid is too heavy or a security hazard. The tinyproxy home page is located at `http://www.flarenet.com/tinyproxy/`.

Miscellaneous

The final category of tools includes two very useful utilities. These utilities are

- Hunt

- Netcat

The hunt utility serves a number of useful purposes, one of which is the ability to attach to an active connection, such as a telnet or rlogin connection. This allows you to not only see what is going on in this session, but also to hijack the session from the user who established it. This tool is very useful if you suspect that someone is connected to your system and doing something that you do not want them to be doing. This is not the only use of hunt, however. The hunt utility can be used to automatically reset a connection, collect MAC addresses for systems on the network, and can also be used as a packet sniffer. Hunt is definitely worth the effort to learn and use, and is available on the Internet at `http://www.cfi.cz/kra/index.html`.

Another general-purpose networking utility that comes with Trinux is the `netcat` utility. Netcat is a networking utility that allows you to read and write data over a network connection using the TCP or UDP protocols. Its most basic use is to establish a connection to a network port and then simply take standard input and send it to the port to which you are connected, and to display any output received on the port on standard output. In addition to this generic client mode of operation, netcat can function as a server, listening on whatever port you like and again dumping data back and forth via the established connection.

As you can see, Trinux contains a wealth of utilities that can be useful in dealing with break-ins on your systems.

Cleaning Up After the Unwanted Visitor

If you do discover that an intruder has been on your system, you may be facing a monumental task. If you are lucky, the person restricted his intrusion to a single system. If not, you must carefully audit every system to which the intruder may have had access and make a determination as to what the person changed on your system, if anything. This is where you must be most careful, because you cannot trust anything on the system itself. Unless you found the intruder as soon as he logged in to your system and monitored every step that he made, you cannot be sure that system binaries have not been changed or replaced with Trojan horse programs. A short list of some of the things that you must check includes the following:

- System configuration files, such as `hosts.allow`, `hosts.equiv`, and other files in the `/etc` directory.

- System binaries, such as `ps`, `ls`, `login`, and `passwd`.

- New accounts that may have been added on the systems.

- Changed passwords on the existing accounts.

- Mail aliases that invoke programs.

In addition, you must determine, if possible, whether the intruder has had access to other systems on your network. The most unfortunate part of this situation is that because the system is in an unknown state, it is not safe to be used by the people who are authorized to use it, which impacts their productivity. You should also remember that the clean up phase is not complete until you can account for all discrepancies found.

Once you have determined the extent of the intrusion, you are now faced with one of the hard decisions. You must decide whether you can continue using the cleaned system or whether you need to start from scratch.

Reinstalling the Operating System from Scratch

Depending on how far the intruder went in compromising your system, you may be faced with the hard decision of whether the amount of time it would take to completely audit the system is worth it. This section takes a look at how to decide when to throw in the towel and restore your whole system from backups after a complete reinstall from media.

When to Throw in the Towel

One of the things to consider when trying to recover from an intrusion into your system is how long you can afford for the system to be offline. If it needs to be back online immediately or as soon as possible, you may be forced to just throw in the towel and start from scratch. This decision is naturally a difficult one and it is incumbent upon the administrator to make management aware of the implications. It is also important when this decision is made that the leak in security has been absolutely identified and closed, so that you do not have to repeat this process again later.

In addition to downtime considerations, another factor that may influence the decision is what the system is used for. For example, if the system is an individual workstation, reinstallation may be the quickest way to get the system back to a known good state. This, of course, assumes that anything important on the system is backed up or can be easily recovered from an alternate source. On the other hand, if the system is a workgroup server with important shared data on it that would take significant resources to recover, it may be unwise to start from scratch. In this case, the filesystem layout and partitioning scheme that you used may work to your advantage, especially if you strictly enforce separation between operating system and application files and local data. A selective reinstall over those partitions containing operating system files and application binaries, leaving the local data untouched, may be your best course.

A final factor to consider when determining whether to throw in the towel is your ability to conduct a truly thorough audit and your confidence that, once completed, all traces of the intrusion have been removed. If your confidence in this is low, you may be forced to start over whether you want to or not. Unfortunately, if this becomes the deciding factor in your decision, you may find that your position in the organization is in jeopardy due to a perceived lack of preparedness, whether it is true or not, for security events.

Trusting Your Backups

During the recovery from a security event, the question of the integrity of your backups may come up. It is for this reason that you should do everything possible to determine exactly when the intrusion occurred for the first time. If you are unable to make this determination, restoring from a backup becomes a dangerous proposition because you can't know if the files on your backup contain hacks put into place by the intruder. The correct strategy to use when recovering from backup is to restore the last full backup prior to the intrusion event and then apply incrementals up to the time of the event, so that you minimize data loss.

> **Note**
>
> Depending on the method you use to back up your systems, your backup tapes may provide a clue as to when your system was broken into. Some backup systems record the names of all files that are backed up during incremental backups. If your backup method includes this feature, you can use these logs to find out when the file changed and thus obtain a clue as to when your system was broken into.

It is a good policy to periodically test your backups by randomly selecting a tape and verifying that it can be read and that the files can be put back into place. During the recovery of your systems is not the time to verify that your backups can be read.

Reinstallation from Media

Reinstallation from the distribution media is a drastic measure to take in recovering from a system break-in, but if you are forced into taking this course of action, there are a few things that you should remember so that you do not end up wasting this effort.

Keeping Records of Changes Made to the System

The first thing to remember is that you should have a record of changes made to the system since the initial installation that indicates which packages, if any, have been updated. This is especially important for upgrades made to correct security issues, but is important for any packages updated from the vendor. This record should also note any packages that you have installed that were not on the distribution media.

Reinstalling from Clean Media

The second rule is that reinstallation should be from a medium that there is no possibility that the intruder had access to, preferably removable media that is write protected. A good example of this type of media is the Red Hat distribution CDs. This is important because if you move the installation packages from the CD to a hard drive to facilitate installs over the network, for example, you risk installing corrupted packages if the intruder was able to access your installation server.

Retrieving Fresh Copies of Updates

Next, once you have installed from the pristine media, retrieve fresh copies of any updates that you may have installed and install them. Again, do not trust previous copies that you have downloaded because the intruder may have tampered with them.

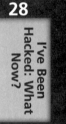

Snapshotting the System

Finally, once you have everything reinstalled, take a snapshot of the system by backing it up to tape or some other medium. If you do not have a filesystem monitoring program in place, such as Tripwire, consider installing one.

Summary

This chapter discussed a number of the issues you will face in the event of a security breach on one of your systems. If you gain nothing else from this chapter, you should remember the rules of engagement for dealing with intrusions. I also highly recommend checking out Trinux for your network analysis and disaster recover needs.

User Management and Interaction

PART

VIII

IN THIS PART

29 Users and Groups   *861*

30 Helping Users   *895*

Users and Groups

IN THIS CHAPTER

- Adding Users to the System **862**
- Granting Permissions to Users **862**
- Establishing Groups **862**
- System Files **864**
- Adding and Deleting
  User Accounts **869**
- When to Delete a User Account **882**
- Effective Use of Groups **884**
- Using Groups to Grant
  Permissions **887**
- The newgrp Command **888**
- Other System Commands Related to
  Users and Groups **888**

29

CHAPTER

Adding Users to the System

Users and groups play an important role in the overall functionality of a Red Hat system. Because they are used to determine ownership and permissions of files and devices, userids and groups can be used to grant or remove access to nearly every feature in the system. Being able to configure users and groups correctly will help you effectively manage your system and the access your users have to system resources.

If your system is going to be used by more than just you as root, you are going to need to add some users. This can be done in several different ways, usually depending on how you are accessing the system and how many accounts you want to add at a time. Red Hat comes with several tools to help you with user and group administration tasks. In this chapter, you will look at the various tasks associated with adding and deleting users, assigning them to groups, and granting permissions. In addition, you will consider the reality of users and ways to protect the system from the unhappy ones.

Granting Permissions to Users

After you have added some users to your system, you will need to give them permission to access the files and directories they require. This can be done in several ways. You can use the chown command to give the user ownership of the file or directory in question. However, this might not be the best method if there are other users that might need to use the file or directory because only one of them can have ownership of the file at a given time. Another way is to change the permission bits on the file or directory using the chmod command and give the user the needed permissions. If the user does not own the file, however, you will need to change the "others" permission setting, and any changes you make to that will apply to everyone who does not own the file. If only the user or a select few users need access to it, this method is not right either. The other way you can grant file or directory permissions to users is to use the group ownership and permission settings.

Establishing Groups

Groups are an effective tool for allocating permissions among your users without having to duplicate files or manipulate user permissions for many users and files every time you need to make a change. If several users need access to a certain file or directory, you can make them all members of a special group and then make the file or directory owned by the special group. You can then make the file or directory group readable or writable so that all group members have the access they require without granting inappropriate permissions to all the users on the system. Using groups (see Figure 29.1) is a good way to manage user permissions in a more granular way rather than having to update multiple permission settings when something changes.

FIGURE 29.1

User and group information can be accessed using the linuxconf *program.*

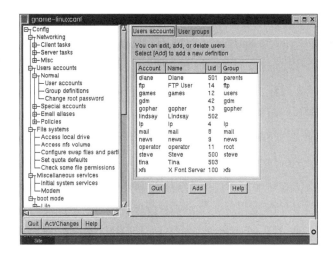

The Evils of Shared Accounts

Shared accounts are not a good idea for both manageability and security reasons. Being able to track what users do is an important facet of system administration, and being able to tell which users do what is necessary. If you have 10 people who use the same userid to log into your system, you cannot hold just one of them accountable if someone violates your system policy because you probably will not be able to tell which of the 10 it was. There is also the question of passwords—if 10 people have the password for a single account, it is more likely that an outsider will be able to find out what it is, get into your system, and use the shared account. Then there will be 11 people on your system using the same account, and determining whether 11 or 10 users are sharing a login is difficult, to say the least. This is also assuming that one of your original shared-account members is not malicious. One of the users can easily use the shared account to cause trouble for the other users if he or she is so inclined. This can be very disruptive, and also very difficult to track down.

Multiple People Working on the Same Directory

Aside from security concerns, there are other issues that arise from multiple people working in the same directory. Configuration files cannot be user-specific if everybody is logged on as the same user—everyone will have to use the same desktop layout and shell aliases. Therefore, any changes that are made could affect the working environment for the other users who share the account.

Any email addressed to the shared account can be read by anyone using the account. Hopefully, people using a shared account will realize it and not use it for email, but if they do, their emails can be read by all the people using the account.

File Editing and Overwriting

File editing and overwriting is also a problem. Two or more people can access a file at the same time, meaning that the last person to write the file out will overwrite any changes the other people might have made to the file without knowing it. This can cause a great deal of confusion and frustration if people do not realize what is going on and take measures to stay out of each other's way.

Rather than giving many people access to an account and risk all these problems, you can use groups to give people access to the same areas of the filesystem, while still maintaining separate login IDs, configuration files, and home directories. While stepping on each others' toes with file usage is still possible, at least all of the users have a place to put a copy of a file while editing it rather than having it in the same place everyone else is working.

Hopefully by now you realize the problems associated with shared user accounts. Use them at your own peril—you have been warned. Adding and deleting users is a simple matter compared to cleaning up the mess that could easily be left, either accidentally or maliciously, by a single user on a shared account. Much of the work surrounding user and group administration can be handled by editing a few critical system files. This can be done manually, automatically, or through scripts. First, let's look at the files involved.

System Files

There are two major files in Linux that are used to configure and manipulate the users and groups for the system: the /etc/passwd file and the /etc/group file. These files contain all the information the system knows about the userids. We will not discuss using NIS and having remote user information in this chapter.

The `/etc/passwd` File

`/etc/passwd` is the most important file on the system for user configuration. It contains information about the user's IDs, home directory, and which command will be run when the user logs in. The file is accessed by every user on the system to determine file and process ownership, so it must be world-readable. The file format is as follows:

`userid:password:UID:GID:GCOS:homedir:shell`

Because each of these items is important, we will cover them individually.

userid

This is the system or login name of the user. This is the name that the user will type in when logging in to the system. It is also the name that others will see when viewing file permissions for a user.

password

If you have shadow passwords enabled (you will if you answered Yes to shadow passwords when you installed the system), this field will contain an x to indicate that the password is stored somewhere else. If for some reason you aren't using shadow passwords, this field will contain the user's password after being encoded with the crypt package.

UID

This is the numeric userid for the system. It should be unique within the `/etc/passwd` file. If it is not unique, file and process ownership can become mixed up between two users. This is the number that the system will use internally for determining file and process ownership rather than the userid itself.

GID

This is the user's numeric group ID. It represents the primary group to which the user belongs. This number corresponds to an entry in `/etc/group` and does not need to be unique, though some administrators create a separate group for each user to use as their primary group.

GCOS

This field contains real text data about the user. In Red Hat Linux, the field is comma-delimited and contains the following fields: Real Name, Office Location/Number, Office Phone Number, Home Phone Number. This information is used by the `finger` service to give more information about a userid.

29

Users and Groups

homedir

This is the user's home directory. This is a directory where the user will keep his or her personal configuration and datafiles. It is owned by the user and only this user should be able to write to this directory. The default path for home directories in Red Hat is `/home/<userid>`, but you can put a home directory anywhere you can create a directory.

shell

This is the program that is executed when the user logs into the system. It is usually a shell program from the `/etc/shells` file. The shell is what allows the user to interact with the system. The default user shell in Red Hat is `bash` (the Bourne Again SHell).

The `/etc/group` File

The `/etc/group` file contains information about the groups on the system. Groups are used to offer a more granular method for granting permissions and ownership of files on the system. Users can become members of groups and gain permission to files or resources through the group permission settings. Managing file and resource permissions for a collection for users in this method is much less time-consuming than managing the permissions individually. Groups also make possible the concept of sharing files or directories with a group of users but not everyone on the system. This can be useful in a multiuser environment.

The format of the `/etc/group` file is as follows:

```
group_name:password:GID:member_list
```

Again, because of their importance, we will take a closer look at each of these parameters.

group_name

This is the actual name of the group that will appear on file ownership listings. For security reasons, system administrators often create a group for each user to use as his or her primary group rather than have the user's primary group be a global `users` group. Users are often granted membership into a global `users` group as a secondary rather than a primary group.

password

This is the password for the group. Most groups will not have a password, but you may want to assign a password to a particular group for the purposes of granting rights to certain files or areas of the system with a single password.

GID

This is the numeric ID for the group. The system will use this number internally rather than the name of the group when assigning ownership rights. This ID should be unique within the /etc/group file.

member_list

This is a comma-separated list of the userids (not UIDs) on the system who are members of this group.

If the system is using shadow passwords, two more files come into play. These are /etc/shadow and /etc/gshadow. These files are readable by root only and contain the encrypted passwords from the /etc/passwd and /etc/group files as well as some other accounting information. By moving the passwords out of /etc/passwd and /etc/group files and into a file readable only by root, system security is enhanced. Nearly all newer Linux distributions use shadow passwords because of the increased security.

The /etc/shadow File

This file is used to hide the passwords from the /etc/passwd file, which must be world-readable. It contains the encrypted password string as well as some account expiration information. The following is the format of /etc/shadow:

```
userid:password:change_days:min_change:max_change:warn_days:
➥disable_days:disable_time:reserved(leave blank)
```

userid

This is the same as the userid from the /etc/passwd field.

password

This is the encrypted password field. It is a good idea to fill this in, otherwise the account won't have a password at all. A common thing to put in is ***not set*** so that it is obvious that the password was not created with a cryptographic algorithm. If you leave this field blank, the user will be able to log in without a password, but so will anyone else who tries with that user account. If you are setting up accounts, use the passwd or chpasswd (Red Hat Only) commands to set the password to something that you can tell the user. If you also expire the password, the user will be prompted to change his password when he logs in for the first time. Just be sure that your disable_days is set for a long enough period of time that the account doesn't disable itself if the user does not attempt to log in soon enough after you expire the password.

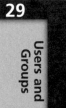

29

Users and Groups

change_days

This is the days since 01/01/1970 that the password was last modified. This should be calculated to be the current day (or less than `max_change` + `disable_days` ago if you want the account to be useful).

min_change

This is the number of days before the password may be changed. If you want the user to be able to change his or her password at any time, set this value to `0`.

max_change

This is the number of days after which the password *must* be changed. Leave this field blank if you want no password expiry.

warn_days

This is the number of days before the password expires that the user is given a warning message when he or she logs in. A good value for this field is `7`. A week should be long enough for someone to be warned about his or her password expiring.

disable_days

This is the number of days after the password expires that the account expires. If the account is not being used, it is a good idea to automatically expire it. A good indication that the account isn't being used is that nobody has logged in to change the password. This value is left to the whim of the administrator, but a few days should be good enough.

disable_time

This is the number of days since 01/01/1970 after which the account is disabled and the user cannot log in. If you want to give an account a specific lifespan, you can calculate the appropriate number of days and put the value in here. The account will be unavailable on the date you specify. This field can also be used to disable an account immediately if you need to. It is safe to leave this field blank.

The /etc/gshadow File

As with `/etc/shadow` and `/etc/passwd`, there is a file called `/etc/gshadow` that performs the same function for `/etc/group`. This file is readable to `root` only and contains the encrypted passwords for groups as well as some accounting information. The following is the format:

```
group:password:administrators:members
```

group

This is the same as in /etc/group.

password

This is the encrypted group password.

administrators

This is a comma-separated list of userids. These users can add or remove other users from the group.

members

This is a comma-separated list of userids. These are the members of the group.

The /etc/login.defs

This file contains default information for account creation and maintenance. This is where all the defaults for useradd/adduser and groupadd are kept. It also contains some settings for GID and UID ranges to use when creating new users and groups.

The /etc/skel Directory

This directory contains default configuration files to be used when creating new accounts. If you run useradd with home directory creation enabled, any files you put here will be copied into the home directory of the new account. Things to put here would be shell configuration files, window manager configuration files, or any other files or directories you think a new user should have in his or her home directory.

Now that you have a handle on the primary files that are involved, let's look at how user and group accounts can be administered on your Linux system.

Adding and Deleting User Accounts

If you are going to have users on your system, manipulating user accounts will soon become second nature to you. It does not have to be a chore. There are plenty of tools available to make life easy for the administrator. To properly understand what is happening when users and groups are added and deleted, we will take a ground-up approach to account manipulation and start with adding a user with no tools at all and work our way up to the GUI-driven tools.

Adding a User Manually

This is the most tedious and time-consuming method for adding a user, but it is good to know the steps required to add a user manually in case you are forced to do so without the use of user configuration tools.

The following sections cover the steps involved in adding a new user to your Red Hat system.

Modify /etc/group

If you are using private groups (one group for each user), you will need to create a new group for your user. Just add a line to /etc/group (see Figure 29.2) that has a unique GID and a group name that matches the new user's userid. You can also make the new userid a member of other groups by adding him or her to the comma-separated list of userids that comes at the end of each line in /etc/group. Add your new userid to any groups of which you think he or she should be a member.

FIGURE 29.2

Users can be added to groups by manually editing the /etc/group file using text editors such as vi.

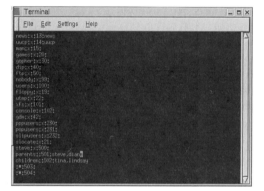

> **Note**
>
> You do not have to make a user a member of his initial group, so if you created a private group for the user, its member list should be empty. If you are making the user's primary group a common group, just use the common group's GID in the new user's /etc/passwd entry.

Create the `/etc/passwd` Entry

Next, simply add a new line to `/etc/passwd` and enter all the information you have except for the password field, which you should leave blank if you are not using shadow passwords, or use x if you are using shadow passwords. If you are not sure whether or not your system uses shadow passwords, just look at the `/etc/passwd` entry for the root user. If there is an x or a ! in the password field, your system is using shadow passwords.

If you created a private group for the user in the first step, you should use that GID for the user's initial group. Otherwise, use the GID of whichever group you want your new user to be in initially.

Modify `/etc/shadow`

If your system uses shadow passwords, you will need to create an entry in `/etc/shadow` that corresponds to the entry you just created in `/etc/passwd`. This entry will eventually contain the user's real password, as well as some accounting information. See the `/etc/shadow` section above for field details.

Modify `/etc/gshadow`

You will need to add an entry in `/etc/gshadow` to match anything you created in `/etc/group`. See the previous "Modify `/etc/shadow`" section for field details.

Create the User's Home Directory

Next, you need to create a home directory for the user. This is the directory where all the user's personal files, such as local mail folders, desktop preferences, and the like reside. It is also a general directory where the user can store his datafiles or whatever he likes. The directory `/home/<userid>` is the standard for Red Hat. Just create a directory under `/home` with the userid (not UID) as the name. The userid is the text string with which the user logs in. It is also the first field on the user's line in the `/etc/passwd` file.

Copy over Default Configuration Files

Copy the files from `/etc/skel` into the user's home directory to give your new user some default settings.

Change Ownerships

You should give the new user, and only the new user, access to his or her home directory. You need to use chown with the recursive option to give the user ownership of everything in all subdirectories from `/home/<userid>`, as shown in Figure 29.3.

```
chown -R  <userid> /home/<userid>
```

29

Users and Groups

FIGURE 29.3

The ownership of several files can be easily changed with the chown *and* chgrp *commands. The* -v *option causes the verbose mode, displaying the progress on the screen.*

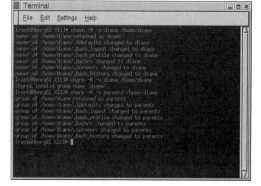

You should also set the group permissions. If you are maintaining a personal group for each user, use the following:

```
chgrp -R  <groupname> /home/<userid>
```

Even though you have set the ownership of the new user's home directory and configuration files, you still need to set file permissions so that only the user has access to the files in his or her home directory. To do this, use the chmod command with find:

```
find /home/<userid> -type d -exec chmod 0755 {} \;
find /home/<userid> ! -type d -exec chmod 0644 {} \;
```

This will allow everyone to cd to the user's home directory and read all his or her files. For better privacy, you can limit the people who can cd in and read files to the people in the user's initial group (or just the user if private groups are being used) with 0750 and 0640 respectively. If you are not using private groups and you want only the user to be able to cd and read these files, use 0700 and 0600 respectively.

Note

If you have any executable files in /etc/skel that need to remain executable, you will lose the execute bit with the previous find commands. If you do run the previous commands, when they are finished you will need to go into the user's home directory and reset the execute permissions on any files that need to be executable.

Set the Password

You created a blank password when you edited /etc/passwd, and now you should set it to something a little more secure. Use passwd <userid> to give the user a password, and have /etc/passwd and /etc/shadow updated automatically.

A Note on Editing /etc/passwd and /etc/group Manually

On a heavily used system, problems can arise if you edit /etc/passwd or /etc/group manually. For example, what would happen if you were editing the password file and someone ran the chfn command to update his personal information on the system? If you saved your copy of /etc/passwd after the user made changes, those changes would be overwritten and the old information would be in the /etc/passwd file again. This could cause much confusion. The vipw command was created to effectively lock the password file from being changed while it is being edited manually by root. The locking mechanism is the creation of /etc/ptmp as a temporary file for password edits. When the user tries to change his information and /etc/ptmp exists, he will get an error message telling him to try again later. A similar program, vigr, exists for editing the /etc/group file and uses /etc/gtmp for its lock file. You should use these two programs for all manual password edits if there is risk of someone changing the file while you have it open.

Now that you know what's involved on the back end, let's see how to do things a little differently and with much more automation.

Adding a User Using the Command-line Tools

Knowing how to add a user manually by editing the files is handy, but it's not very fast, it's prone to typos, and it's tedious if you have to do it frequently or for many users at once. Adding a user with the built-in command-line tools is much easier because it adds some automation to the process. Included with Red Hat Linux are several command-line tools to help you with user management. The following sections provide a brief synopsis of the tools for adding a user. More complete descriptions of these tools can be found in the man pages.

useradd **Red Hat**

This command is a one-line command to do all the work of setting up a new user. There is a similar command, adduser, that is a symbolic link to useradd. If you have many users to add at one time, it might be easier to write a small shell script to add them in a batch mode rather than entering them into a GUI or even typing out the useradd command line each time. The useradd arguments are as follows:

- -c *comment*   GCOS information—Full name, and so on.

- -d *home directory*   Path to home directory (defaults to /home/<userid>).

- -e *expiration date* (*YYYY/DD/MM*)   Date on which the account will be deactivated.

- -f *inactive days*   Number of days after password has expired before account is disabled.

- -g <*group*>   Initial group listing.

- -G <*group,group,...*>   Secondary group listing.

- -M   Force useradd not to create the user's home directory.

- -m   Create home directory (default).

- -k <skel *path*>   Path to use to copy setup files. (/etc/skel is the default.)

- -r   Account is a system account. No home directory will be created unless forced with -m.

- -s *shell*   Login shell.

- -u *UID*   Specify a UID. This must be unique within /etc/passwd.

- -o   Override the unique specification for -u.

- -D   Display current defaults from the /etc/login.defs file. You can modify this file if you would like to change any of these parameters. The parameters displayed are: default GID, home directory base path, inactive days, expire date, default shell, skel directory.

  If you use the -D option first, you can specify parameters after it to update the following fields:

  - -g <default GID>
  - -b <home directory base>

- -f <inactive default>   Number of days after a password expires that the account will be rendered inactive. 0 means the account will expire immediately after the password expires, and -1 means the account is never disabled after the password expires.

- -e <default expiration date>   The date on which this account will expire. You can specify this parameter as /MM/DD/YYYY or the number of days since 01/01/1970.

- -s <default shell>

Linuxconf

Linuxconf (see Figure 29.4) makes life easy for the administrator. It allows quick GUI or menu-driven configuration of most of the Red Hat system. Users and groups can be added, deleted, or modified as well using forms under X Windows or in a text console.

FIGURE 29.4

User accounts can be easily added using Linuxconf in X Windows.

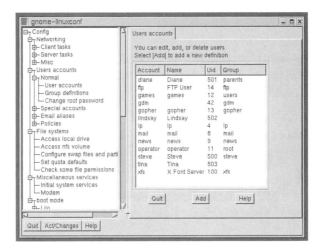

If you are running X Windows, you can either start Linuxconf from the control-panel or from a terminal window. To start the control panel, type

`/usr/bin/control-panel`

The control-panel application window should appear with several buttons for system configuration. Scroll to the bottom of the icon list and click the icon that looks like a conductor (see Figure 29.5). This is the icon for Linuxconf, and its main window should pop up shortly.

29

Users and Groups

FIGURE 29.5

Linuxconf can be started by using the System Configuration icon in the control panel.

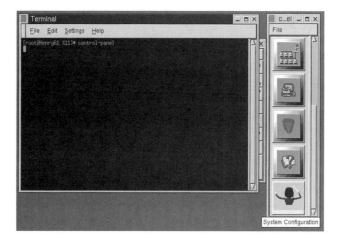

If you are in text mode, or you would like to skip going through control-panel to get to Linuxconf, you can simply type

```
linuxconf
```

at a command prompt. Linuxconf will figure out if it can pop up a new window to run in, or if it should run in the shell from which it was started. The top-level menu should look something like Figure 29.4. Linuxconf can also be started in GNOME by going to the System Menu and choosing System, LinuxConf.

Now that you have Linuxconf up and running, choose Users Accounts from the available selections. This will take you to the user and group editing window shown in Figure 29.6.

FIGURE 29.6

Linuxconf User groups screen. Behind it is the User accounts screen which can be selected by clicking on the tab.

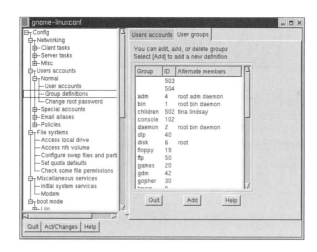

Note

You can bypass the control-panel and top-level Linuxconf screen and get to the user account configuration area by simply typing:

userconf

If you look at the tabs across the top of the screen in Figure 29.7, which appear as sections delimited by a horizontal bar in the text version, you will notice that there are three tabs from which to choose. Normal enables you to edit normal groups and accounts. Special Accounts enables you to edit POP, PPP, SLIP, and UUCP accounts. Policies enables you to set the account-related system policies. If you go into the Policies tab and choose Password & Account Policies, you will be able to edit all the default user creation information.

FIGURE 29.7

GUI interface for accessing user and group accounts. To access this interface, type userconf *on the command line.*

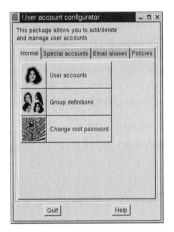

Under the Policies tab, you can choose Password & Account policies. Under this, you will find the parameters for setting password validation rules, which are as follows:

- Minimum length

- Minimum amount of non alpha char—These two features are used for systems that do not employ PAM to enforce password changing parameters. Red Hat uses PAM, so these should be ignored. For more information on configuring PAM to check the strength of passwords, see Chapter 25, "Security Principles."

29

Users and Groups

- Private Group—This setting determines whether or not new users have a private default group created when their accounts are created. This is useful for protecting users against permission problems that arise when users are put into a common default group.

- Default base directory for homes—This is the directory under which all user directories are created. It is customary to use /home, but you are free to change this at any time—it will only affect any new users created after the change. One reason for this might be a project directory for a group. If the home directory were /project, then each of the project members would have a home directory under /project. Typically, this would be done through group management, but it can be done this way if you wish.

- Creation Permissions—This is the default permission string to use on a user's files and directory when his account is created. The format is an octal number corresponding to what would be used for the chmod command to accomplish the same thing (that is, 700 is read/write/execute for the user and no permissions for group or other).

- Delete Account command—The command listed here will be executed to delete the account data, including the account's home directory and the mail inbox folder. A default command is supplied, but it can be changed if desired.

- Archive Account command—This also has a default command supplied. It will preserve the home directory and the mail inbox folder in a compressed tar file and store it in the /home/oldaccounts directory.

- Post-Create command—Each time a user account is created, this command will be executed. No default is supplied. If you use this, you must supply the absolute path of the command as well as any arguments.

- Pre-Delete command—This command is used when creating, deleting, and archiving user accounts. See the Linuxconf documentation for specific details on command-line arguments passed to this program.

The next five fields will only appear if shadow passwords are enabled on the system. They allow you to set defaults for the entries in /etc/shadow when a new account is created.

- Must Keep # days—This is the number of days a password must be kept.

- Must change after # days—This is the maximum amount of time someone can keep the same password.

- Warn # days before expiration—Users will be warned this many days in advance of their passwords expiring.

- Account Expire after # days—This is the number of days after the password expires that the account will expire.

- Standard account duration—This is the length of time (days) the account will remain active.

Note

If desired, the last five fields can be overridden on an individual basis when adding a user through the Add User window.

Choose the Normal tab to go back to the User and Group Maintenance screen. You can see that you are presented with a set of configuration options: User Accounts, Group Definitions, and Change root Password.

To add a new user, go to the User Accounts section (see Figure 29.8). You will see a form that contains information from /etc/passwd. You can scroll through the list and select a user to update if you want. If you click an entry in the list, the User Addition form will appear with the user's information filled in.

FIGURE **29.8**
The Linuxconf User account configurator menu and the User accounts menu.

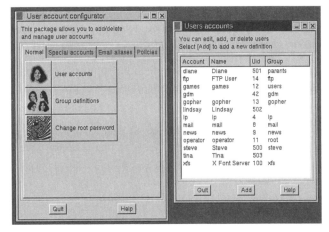

To add a new user, click the Add button on the bottom of the form. This will pull up the Linuxconf User account creation form (see Figure 29.9). This is where you will enter all the information about a user. This is also the same basic form that is used if you click a name in the User account configurator menu.

FIGURE 29.9

*The Linuxconf
User account
creation menu.*

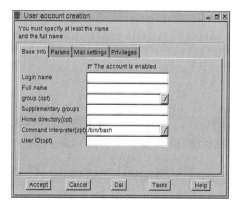

After you have the form up, you can fill in all the fields for which you have information. Any fields with (opt) beside them are optional and will be filled in with the system default values if you leave them blank.

After you have finished entering your user information, look along the top of the form—there are several other tabs you can select to configure more information about a user. Base Info, Params, and Privileges are all default fields. Other tabs, such as Mail Aliases and Disk Quota, will only be present if you have those services configured on your system.

The Params tab enables you to customize the account expiration and password changing details if you do not want to use the system defaults. These are the settings from /etc/ shadow if shadow passwords are in use.

The Privileges field enables you to allow the user to run Linuxconf to configure certain parts of the system. Use this feature with caution—it can grant a lot of power to your new user.

If you have the proper mail services enabled on your system, the Mail Aliases tab enables you to enter email aliases for this user. This is so that you can have names like *FirstName.Lastname@yourdomain.com* instead of *userid@yourdomain.com* to make mail addressing more readable.

If you have disk quotas enabled, the Disk Quota tab lets you specify disk quotas for the user for each filesystem for which user quotas are enabled. You can enter the hard limits, soft limits, and grace periods for both files and disk space.

There is a Tasks button at the bottom of the user entry screen. If you click this button, you will be prompted to enter scheduled tasks (using cron) for the new user. This can be useful if you want to have some cleanup tasks run on a schedule, such as having all temporary/ core files deleted nightly.

After you are happy with your user entry, click Accept and your new user will be created. You can now see the new user in the list. If you click the user's entry, the form pops up again and you can make any needed changes.

Manipulating User Accounts in Batch Mode

Adding users is easy with the GUI and command line tools, but if you need to set up and maintain large numbers of user accounts, the batch tools might be more efficient.

newusers

newusers is used to add new users to the system in batch mode. It reads a file that has the same format as /etc/passwd. You can generate the new user file in a text editor or by more automated means if you so desire. After the file is created, call the program as follows:

```
newusers <newusersfile>
```

The newusersfile has the same layout as /etc/passwd:

```
userid:password:UID:GID:GCOS:homedir:shell
```

The password field should contain plain text passwords for the users. These passwords will be encrypted and put into the /etc/passwd file or /etc/shadow file, depending on shadow support. The GID field will be used to map the user to a group in /etc/group. If there is no group in /etc/group with this GID, one is created with this number as its GID and the userid as the group name. The home directory will be created if it does not exist, but nothing from /etc/skel /etc/skel.d will be copied into it. The home directory ownership will be set to that of the new user.

chpasswd

chpasswd is used to update the password file in batch mode. It reads in username:password pairs from standard input and updates the password for the named user.

```
No need, removed. sje
```

If the passwords are clear text, they will be encrypted. If, however, the -e switch is used, it is assumed that the passwords on stdin are already in the proper encrypted form and should not be encrypted by the system.

29

Users and Groups

Disabling User Accounts

Being able to disable a user account is a useful administration feature. There is no better way to get a user's attention than to disable his or her account and wait for him or her to contact you. If you are using shadow passwords, you can disable a user's account with either the `chage` command

```
chage -E YYYY/MM/DD
```

or the `usermod` command

```
usermod -e YYYY/MM/DD
```

where **YYYY/MM/DD** is yesterday's date. This will prevent the user from logging in until he or she comes to you to ask it to be reset.

Disgruntled users can be a thorn in your side as a system administrator. Disabling a disgruntled user's account is the first step you should take. A disgruntled user can cause a great deal of damage to a system if he has the right permissions or access to the right files. An unhappy developer can delete all the source code he has been working on for the last year with a single command, and you will be forced to rely on whatever backup strategy you have in place to recover the data. If you disable a user's account, be sure that you remove any `cron` jobs or `at` jobs that the user has. It is possible that the user could set up programs to run using `cron` or `at` and give himself access to the system after his account has been disabled. Even if you delete his account and home directory, `cron` jobs will still run, though `at` jobs check to see if the user's ID and home directory exist before running.

Disabling an account can be a way to get a user's attention, but for a variety of reasons, there will come a time when user accounts need to be deleted. This needs to be done for security reasons as well as simple housekeeping.

When to Delete a User Account

Account cleanup is an important task for a system administrator. Old accounts can provide a hacker with a means of entry into your system and a place to store files that may not be noticed quickly. Unused accounts can also take up valuable storage space if there are files left in the user's home directory. You should delete a user account as soon as you know the user will not be using the system again within a reasonable amount of time. If the user is going to be away for an extended period of time but will eventually be back, you may want to consider backing up the user's files, deleting the user's account, and restoring the account when the user returns. For deleting accounts, `userdel` is one tool that can be quite helpful.

userdel

This command is used to remove a user from the system. It deletes entries from /etc/passwd, /etc/group, and /etc/shadow. It saves the old versions of the files as /etc/passwwd-, /etc/group-, and /etc/shadow-, respectively. userdel will run a script defined in /etc/login.defs after the userid is removed from the /etc files. The first argument passed to the script is the userid being removed. This script should perform cleanup tasks, such as removing print, at, and cron jobs from /var/spool.

To set up the delete script, add the following line to /etc/login.defs:

```
USERDEL_CMD <full path to command to run>
```

The -r flag removes the user's home directory and all its contents. However, it will not remove files owned by the user that reside in other places. Those will have to be cleaned up manually.

> **Note**
>
> If you are using private per-user groups, you will have to edit /etc/group and /etc/gshadow to delete the groups corresponding to the users you deleted. userdel does not delete groups.

Account deletion can also be an unfortunate result of dealing with abusive users. Deleting a user's account should be the final punishment for continued misbehavior.

Before you delete an account, you may want to do a search for all files owned by the user you are about to delete. You can use the find command to do this, as shown in the following:

```
find  /  -user <userid>
```

This will print out a list of every file on your system that is owned by the userid in question. You will have to change the ownerships of files that you want to keep, because they will not be removed when you remove the user from the system. What will happen is that the file will remain, but when someone tries to ls -l the file, the userid column will be replaced with the deleted user's numeric UID because the ls command can no longer find a UID-to-userid mapping in the /etc/passwd file.

29

Users and Groups

Effective Use of Groups

Groups are a helpful tool for the system administrator. They allow the administrator to manage the permissions of a set of users all at once without having to manipulate each user's account. The members of a group can share files and have common areas in which to exchange work. Groups can also be assigned permission to access system resources, including devices and executable files.

There are quite a few group management tools provided with Red Hat Linux. We will cover several of them here, including groupadd, groupdel, and groupmod.

groupadd

groupadd is a simple shell script that will add a group to /etc/group. Be warned, however, that it is not shadow-aware. If you do use shadow group passwords, you will need to run grpconv to create the /etc/gshadow file. If you have no groups with passwords, you can skip this step if you like.

The argument, -g <GID>, is not optional and must be supplied. Valid values range from 101-65535 or so and must be non-negative. The lower values are reserved for system and daemon groups, and the nouser group is 65534. The script will allow you to specify a value larger than 65535 without complaint, but the group will not be a valid group and will cause errors if you attempt to use it for anything. groupadd will create a backup of /etc/group called /etc/group-, so you can revert to your old /etc/group file if you want.

groupdel

The groupdel command is a simple shell script that deletes the named group from the /etc/group file. It is not aware of shadow support. If you are going to use groupdel with shadow support enabled, be sure to run groupconv after running groupdel to clean up the /etc/gshadow file.

groupdel <groupname>

The groupdel command will make sure that the group exists in /etc/group and simply remove the line. It creates a backup of /etc/group called /etc/group-, so you can "undelete" the group by copying /etc/group- to /etc/group if you realize you've made a mistake.

groupmod

This command is used to modify entries in /etc/group and /etc/gshadow. grpmod creates backups of /etc/group and /etc/gshadow as /etc/group- and /etc/gshadow-, respectively. Its arguments are as follows:

```
groupmod -g <new_GID> <groupname>
```

The GID of the group given as the last parameter will be changed to new_GID if it is unique within /etc/group.

> **Note**
>
> If you change the GID of a group, you will need to manually change the group ownership of any file that was owned by the original GID. You can do this with a find command:
>
> `find / -gid <old_GID> -exec chgrp <new_GID> {} \;`

This overrides the uniqueness of the -g option, so you can create multiple groups with the same GID (not usually a good idea).

```
groupmod -n <new_group_name> <groupname>
```

The name of the group will be changed to <new_group_name>.

grpck

grpck is used to perform a sanity check on your /etc/group file. You might want to run it if you modify /etc/group manually just to be sure you haven't made any typos. grpck performs the following checks on /etc/group:

Asks to delete malformed lines in /etc/group.

Asks to delete malformed lines in /etc/gshadow.

Asks to delete lines found in /etc/gshadow but not /etc/group. It does not, however, ask to delete lines found in /etc/group but not in /etc/gshadow.

Asks to delete members of groups who do not exist on the system. It seems to give up if it finds more than two errors on a line, so you may want to run it several times until it finds no errors.

grpck does not check for valid GID values, so any GID value in /etc/group or /etc/gshadow that is greater than 65535 will not result in an error message.

29

Users and Groups

Adding a Group with the GUI Tools

Adding a group through Linuxconf is very easy. Proceed as though you were adding a user, but when you get to the User Accounts window, choose Group Definitions instead of User Accounts. This will bring up a window with a list of the groups from /etc/group as shown in Figure 29.10.

FIGURE 29.10

The Linuxconf User groups menu.

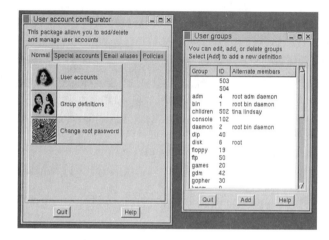

If you select an entry in this list, the group entry window will appear with that group's information, and you can edit it as you see fit.

To add a new group, click the Add button at the bottom of the Group Configuration menu and fill in the form that appears. Only the group name is required to create a new group, but you can specify a GID and some members at this time if you want. The information under the Directories tab is unused at this time. Click Accept, and your new group should appear in the list.

> **Note**
>
> When creating groups on your system, be sure you keep track of what the groups are for and who is in them. You should know exactly what each group is for and what each group should and should not be able to do. It is better to create several specialized groups rather than a greater number of general groups, because specific permissions associated with group membership can be added without granting the user too much power or can be removed without effectively disabling the account. Keep a list of the groups you need on your system and the files and directories to which each group has access.

Now that you know how to add a group, let's look at some of the things for which you can use groups. Effectively using groups can simplify your job as system administrator.

Using Groups to Grant Permissions

Granting permissions is one of the most common uses for groups. In UNIX, nearly every feature of the system is controlled by a file or a special file (directory, device, and so on). By manipulating the group ownership and group permissions on a file or device, you can grant or remove access to that file or device on a group basis. For example, you could create a group called net and make Netscape, Lynx, irc, and any other network clients owned by group net and then set the group execute bit only. That way, only members of group net will be able to run those programs.

> **Note**
>
> This is not a perfect solution. If you leave the world-readable flag set on the binaries owned by the net group, someone who is not a member of the net group could simply copy the binary to his home directory, chown the file to himself, and run it. While this will not work for all programs (some require supporting files or setuid bits to run properly), it might work for some, so care must be taken.

You can also use the pam_group module to configure which groups a user gains access to at which times. This is helpful if you only want to allow people access to the net group or the games group after business hours or on weekends.

> **Note**
>
> This is also not very secure. If a user can gain access to a group once, he can create a setgid binary to allow him to access files owned by that group at any time in the future, whether he is still a member of the group or not. Consider mounting user-writable filesystems with the nosuid option whenever possible.

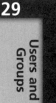

29

Users and Groups

The `newgrp` Command

Having membership in different groups is a good thing, but having to use `chgrp` to change the group ownership of your files all the time is tedious. If you are working with other users and need to share files using your common group ownership, it would be nice to be able to create files owned by the shared group by default instead of using `chgrp` constantly. You can do this with the `newgrp` and `sg` commands.

newgrp

`newgrp` allows you to temporarily change your default group to another group that you are a member of or for which you have the password. `newgrp` does not go through login or change the current directory when switching groups. You can either type **exit** to return to your previous group, or you can run the `newgrp` command with no arguments to accomplish the same thing. The syntax is:

```
newgrp <new_group_name>
```

Obviously, `<new group name>` is the group name to which to switch. If this is left blank, the user's default group from `/etc/passwd` will be used.

Other System Commands Related to Users and Groups

chage

All the date calculations for the `/etc/shadow` file can be somewhat tedious, so if you are forced to do this without the use of a menu or GUI tool, hopefully you will have the `chage` function at your disposal. The sole purpose of `chage` is to manipulate the settings in `/etc/shadow`. The `chage` command has several options:

```
-m <min_change>
```

Modify the `min_change` field.

```
-M <max_change>
```

Modify the `max_change` field.

```
-d change_days
```

Modify the `change_days` field. Can be specified as YYYY-MM-DD.

```
-I <inactive>
```

Modify the `disable_days` field.

`-E <expire_date>`

Modify the `disable_time` field. Can be specified as YYYY-MM-DD.

`-W <warn_days>`

Modify the `warn_days` field.

chfn

The `chfn` program is used to change your `finger` information. This program will let you change the GCOS field in `/etc/passwd`. This might not be very useful to you if `finger` is disabled for security reasons. Because `finger` is used to display the user's information, such as real name, office location, and office phone, those items should be kept up to date if the service is enabled. Like `chage`, `finger` has several options:

```
-f <full Name>
-o <Office Location/Number>
-p <Office Phone Number>
-h <home Phone Number>
<userid>
```

If you are `root`, you can change this information for another user.

chgrp

This command enables you to change the group ownership of a file. `chgrp` allows you to change the group ownership of a file, special file, or directory. This might be needed after a departmental reorganization or if a new project is formed through the combination of several smaller projects.

`-c`

Give more output when a change is made.

`-f`

Do not print error messages.

`--reference=<file>`

Use the ownerships of `<file>` instead of specifying them on the command line.

`-R`

Recurse subdirectories. If this argument is given on a directory name, the group changes will be applied to all files and directories below that directory in the filesystem tree.

`-v`

Verbose output.

`<new groupname>`

Change the group ownership of the file(s) to `<new groupname>`.

`<file file file ...>`

Files for which ownership is to be changed.

chown

This command changes ownership of a file. `chown` allows you to specify who owns a given file, directory, or special file. Again, as things change within an organization, people leave, new additions, and so on, file ownerships may need to be adjusted so that someone's replacement can continue to work on files that were started previously. Depending on the situation, group management might be more effective, or the management of individual files may be best. The various parameters that can be used with `chown` include the following.

- `-c` Give more output when a change is made.

- `--dereference` When called on a symbolic link, apply changes to the file it points to rather than the link itself.

- `-f` Do not print error messages.

- `--reference=<file>` Use the ownerships of `<file>` instead of specifying them on the command line.

- `-R` Recurse subdirectories. If this argument is given on a directory name, the ownership changes will be applied to all files and directories below that directory in the filesystem tree.

- `-v` Verbose output.

- `<new owner userid>` Change the ownership of the file(s) to `<new owner userid>`.

- `<new groupname>` Change the group ownership of the file(s) to `<new groupname>`.

- `<new owner userid>.<new groupname>` Change the ownership and group ownership of the file(s).

- `<filefilefile ...>` Files for which ownership is to be changed.

chsh

This command changes your login shell. With `chsh`, you can set the entry in `/etc/passwd` that specifies the program that is run when you log into the system. Although many users today may go straight to a GUI shell, many experienced users may be quite comfortable with a command line as well as a particular shell.

The `-s` switch determines which new shell to use. `chsh` will output a warning if `<shell>` does not exist in `/etc/shells` by default but can be configured through PAM to only let non-`root` users choose from `/etc/shells`. See the PAM section in Chapter 24, "Internet Telephony and Conferencing."

The `-l` switch will list shells from `/etc/shells`, and if you are `root`, you can change the shell of another user.

gpasswd

`gpasswd` is used to administer `/etc/group` and `/etc/gshadow`. It allows group administrators and `root` to add and delete users from groups, as well as changing the password for groups. Several options exist for `gpasswd`:

- `-a <user> <group>`   Add `<user>` to group `<group>`.

- `-d <user> <group>`   Delete `<user>` from `<group>`.

- `-R <group>`   This disallows logins via newgrp.

- `-A <user,user,...> <group>`   Make `<user,user,...>` into group administrators for `<group>`. These users will be able to add and remove users from this group using `gpasswd`. This does not make `<user,user,...>` members of the group, so in order for them to be able to `newgrp` to `<group>`, they will have to either add themselves with the `-a` option or `root` will have to add them.

- `-M <user,user,...> <group>`   Add `<user,user,...>` to `<group>`.

- `-r`   Remove group password.

- `<group>`   If this argument is given by itself, the system prompts for a new group password. If no password is set on a group, only group members can use the `newgrp` command to switch to this group.

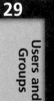

29

Users and Groups

groups

Prints the groups of which you are a member. However, it does not list the groups of which you are an administrator. When it is used with `<userid>`, it will print the groups of which another is a member.

passwd

This command changes password tokens. `passwd` is used to change your password or other passwords if you are `root`.

The `-u` switch will only change password tokens that have expired, and leave non-expired tokens alone. This is only useful with complex PAM configurations having multiple authentication tokens with different expiry times. (See Chapter 24 for discussion on PAM.)

When `passwd` is combined with `<username>`, it will change the password for `<username>`. Only `root` can do this, and authentication is performed as before.

su

`su` (switch user) is used to let one user temporarily "become" another user. The user is prompted for the new user's password and, if authentication is successful, a new shell is spawned using the shell parameter in `/etc/passwd` for the new user. If the shell parameter is not executable, `/bin/sh` is used.

A simple `-` switch will run the new user's shell-initialization scripts to re-initialize the environment. Without this, the new shell will be using the old user's environment with the new user's ID. The `-c` switch, followed by a command will cause the command to run as the new user instead of starting up an interactive shell. For `csh` and `tcsh` shells, the `-f` switch will bypass reading `.cshrc`, whereas for `bash` and `sh`, it will disable filename pattern expansion.

The `-p` switch will preserve the current environment. `HOME`, `USER`, `LOGNAME`, and `SHELL` environment variables are not touched. The shell indicated in `SHELL` is run instead of the new user's shell, unless the original user is not `root` and the old user's shell is restricted. (Not in `/etc/shells`.)

Finally, the `-s` switch followed by a shell name will run the specified shell instead of the new user's shell from `/etc/passwd`.

usermod

This command lets you modify a user's entry in `/etc/passwd` and `/etc/shadow`. You cannot change the user's name if they are logged in. There are several parameters and options available for `usermod`. They include the following:

- `-c <comment>`   Change the user's comment/GCOS field in `/etc/passwd`. Normally changed with `chfn`.

- `-h <home dir>`   Change the user's home directory to `<home dir>`.

- -e <*expire date*>   Set the date when the account will be disabled. The format for <*expire date*> is YYYY-MM-DD.

- -f <*inactive days*>   Set the number of days after the password expires that the account will be disabled. 0 disables the account immediately, and -1 never disables the account if the password expires.

- -g <*group name*/GID>   This sets the user's initial or default group.

- -G <*group,group,...*>   This sets the user's membership in addition to the user's initial group. All group memberships are removed before applying this list.

- -l <*userid*>   The userid is changed to <*userid*>. You may want to rename the user's home directory at the same time. This option will fail if the user is currently logged in. You must also change ownership of cron and at jobs this user might have running.

- -s <*shell*>   Change the user's shell to <*shell*>. A blank entry means the system will use the default shell.

- -u <UID>   Change the user's UID to <*uid*>. This value must be unique within /etc/passwd. Note that the user will no longer have access to files owned by his or her old UID. You will have to find the files with the old UID and chown them to the new UID for the user to be able to access them the same as before. Be careful to make sure that the old UID does not own any processes on the system when you change it.

- -o   This flag disables the unique check for the -u option so that more than one user can have the same UID.

Summary

In this chapter, we covered several different ways to manage users and groups. We discussed reasons why users and groups need to be managed effectively, and we touched on what can happen if users acquire more access to the system than is appropriate.

In addition to discussing user and group management, we looked at tools that are available to automate the tasks involved. These tools come in several forms. They include manually editing the files involved, command line programs, batch routines, and even the Linuxconf tool, which is available in both a text format and for the X Windows GUI.

Finally, we looked at several "utility" commands that allow user and group parameters to be adjusted quickly and easily by either the user or root if necessary.

30

CHAPTER

Effective Interaction with Your Users

IN THIS CHAPTER

- Users Are Not Lusers   *896*
- Developing a Help Desk   *903*
- Learning How to Say No   *918*

Are they the bane of your existence or the reason for your existence? This question represents the extremes of how many systems administrators feel about the users on the systems they maintain. The truth for your network is largely dependent on how you manage the inevitable interruptions from users and how you establish and enforce policies that affect their use of network resources. This chapter takes a look at ways to manage interaction with users, setting up and manning a help desk, and how and when to say no to user requests without creating an environment of you versus them. The information presented in this chapter is not specific to Linux and can be applied no matter what operating system you support. Before we get into this, however, it should be made clear that the key to applying the strategies described here is to get the backing of your management. This backing is essential because you need to be able to enforce the policies you establish. Without the support of the management of your organization, you will be powerless to do anything to make your interaction with users bearable.

Users Are Not Lusers

One of the first things that may have to change in order to make interaction with users manageable is the attitude of the systems administrator. Because the systems administrator is the resident expert on all things having to do with Linux, the questions that users ask may seem trivial or a waste of time. This can lead to an attitude that users are an annoyance and a distraction that has to be dealt with so that you can get back to your "real" work. It is often helpful at times like this to remember your introduction to Linux and the questions you had. This attitude may not be expressed verbally, but if you hold this belief, users will pick up on it and you will either alienate or intimidate them. This environment is not conducive to good user management. This section looks at ways to minimize the effects of user interruptions and how to develop a good relationship with your users.

Establishing the Ground Rules

One of the keys to managing user interaction is to establish a set of ground rules and to stick by them. These ground rules define how and when users notify you of system problems, how to request that work be done on their behalf, and how to follow up on these problem reports and requests. In addition, the first and most important ground rule that you must adhere to is to never play favorites. This may sound like an easy task, but as anyone who has had to manage a user base of more than a few people will tell you, this can be one of the hardest parts of your job as a systems administrator. This is due in large part to the rebellious nature of people and their tendency to look for the exceptions to the rules. Following are a few tips to make this chore easier and to ensure that your users know where you stand.

Word of Mouth Policy Doesn't Work

At many of the companies where I have worked, most of the systems administration policy was not published, but was passed on from sysadmin to sysadmin over the years. Unfortunately, this may work in a small company, like an Internet startup that you and your buddy are starting, but once a company begins to grow, this type of word-of-mouth policy inevitably fails.

The answer to this problem is to document every policy that you establish and to get the support of your management team. This support from management is especially important because it is often new users who are not familiar with your policies who try to challenge them. Without the backing of the your management team, you will be hard pressed to enforce them.

Posting Policy

The ideal place for any documentation of this type is on your intranet Web server. This makes the policies you create easily accessible from any desktop in the company that can access your internal Web server. If you do not like creating HTML documents, remember that you can always just create a text file and add <HTML><PRE> to the beginning and </PRE></HTML> to the end. If your business is just starting, this is an easy way to get things started and as your systems administration staff grows, you can assign new administrators to enhance their appearance while they are reviewing the policies.

Publish Rules for Granting Exceptions

Once you establish a policy, you should also publish the reason for the policy and any reasons why an exception would be granted. Consider the following example. To make it easier for you to manage the creation of user accounts, all account names are constructed by taking the user's first initial and appending the first seven characters of the user's last name. This may sound like an innocent enough policy, but consider the account names that would be constructed from real names like Samuel Crews, Patricia Hart, or David Arn. While you might find it amusing to create these account names, I doubt that the users would agree, especially if they have regular contact with people outside the company, such as sales and marketing people. Without a stated exception policy for cases such as this, you will find that users will ignore all of the good reasons why you established the policy in the first place and constantly challenge it.

30

Effective
Interaction
with Your
Users

This may sound contradictory to the previous rule about playing favorites, but if you only grant exceptions to a rule based on a published exception policy and apply this exception policy for any user who provides justification, your users will see this as just an extension to the policy. It is also a good idea to document any exception you grant under your exception policy and the reason for granting it so that if questions arise, you will have the answers.

Periodically Review and Revise Policies

Now that you have established your policies and exceptions and published them with the approval of management, what next? Well, the next step is to schedule a review period for the policy. The timetable you establish for reviewing policy should be frequent enough to ensure that policies do not become stale, but not so frequent that you end up constantly reviewing policy. My personal recommendation is to schedule an initial review for three months after the policy is established and every six months after that. The reason for the short period at the beginning is to determine the effectiveness of the policy. Three months usually is sufficient time to make this determination. The biannual reviews following that are simply to determine if the policy still needs to be maintained. You may ask why this is necessary, but consider the following example.

In the early days of automobiles, much of the traffic on city streets was horse-drawn conveyances, such as carriages or wagons The horses drawing them were often frightened by the noisy automobiles, especially at crossroads where the faster moving automobiles could suddenly appear and startle the horses. Lawmakers in several states decided that this situation needed to be addressed, with a policy or law, to protect the people travelling in these horse-drawn vehicles. They created a policy that before entering a crossroads, the car driver had to stop, fire a gun, and then launch a rocket to warn any nearby horses that they were approaching. This policy was made law and as the number of horses decreased and the number of cars increased, it was largely forgotten, but never removed from the books. Now consider a person coming to a place with such a policy on the books, who does not realize that this policy is no longer needed. The first time he comes to a crossroads, and stops to fire a gun and launch a rocket, he is likely to be arrested for violating the policy about discharging a firearm in a public place and having fireworks in the city limits. He will also be wondering why he is in trouble for following the published policy.

This doesn't have anything to do with systems administration, of course, but it does serve to illustrate the need to periodically review and revise policy as situations change. It is always important to review policies to make sure that the reasons why you put them into place still exist and to make sure that the policies do not conflict with one another. Outdated or inconsistent policies are two easy ways to ensure that all of your published policies are challenged or ignored outright.

Dealing with Interruptions

Interruptions from users are a fact of life for all systems administrators, and how you deal with these interruptions will affect how well you accomplish the multitude of tasks that you are required to perform. Interruptions in this context refer not only to people barging into your office and demanding your attention, but also to people who barrage you with email or phone calls asking questions or requesting help. There are a number of ways to minimize the effects of interruptions from users. This section looks at a few of them and discusses their merits and flaws so that you can develop a solution that works for your situation.

The "My Door Is Always Open" Strategy

One of the mistakes that some new systems administrators make, especially if they come from a customer support background, is to make it a habit to drop whatever they are doing to deal with a request from a user, no matter how trivial the request. Although this may seem like a good way to establish good relations with your users, it usually ends up causing whatever projects the sysadmin is working on to be delayed. The sysadmin is then left in the unenviable position of having to explain to his or her boss that projects were delayed so that he or she could deal with an unscheduled interruption from a user. The lesson that this type of systems administrator has to learn is how to prioritize work so that important user-generated interruptions are dealt with in a timely manner and others are dealt with within the confines of project schedules and other constraints on their time. Not learning this lesson usually results in the systems administrator either losing his job for failure to complete projects on time or not advancing in his career for the same reason.

This does not mean that you should cut yourself off from your users. A systems administrator who will take a few minutes to help out a user in distress can gain an ally for life. It is simply important to let users know that if you are working on a higher priority project, their problem may have to wait. It is important for the systems administrator to remember that even if the problem takes thirty seconds to solve, the total time involved to deal with the interruption includes the time to listen to the user's problem, formulate a solution, explain the solution to the user, implement the solution, and then resume whatever you were doing when you were interrupted.

The "Send Me an Email" Strategy

The other end of the spectrum is the systems administrator who never has time to deal with users and whose response to everything is to send them an email with the question or request. While this strategy might sound better than the previous one, it can result in a whole other set of problems. One of these problems is likely to be alienation from the system users, who start to feel that the administrator has no time for them. Just as being too accessible to users can be a problem, not being accessible enough to users can cause management to look critically at you and impair your ability to advance your career. Although you will most likely have fewer problems meeting project deadlines, your user community will not be satisfied with the level of service they are receiving from you. Another problem with this strategy is that you may become inundated with so many requests via email that you will find that you are spending more time reading email than you are dealing with the user issues. Another factor to consider is that although email is a good way to communicate, it is often easier and less time consuming to meet with a user briefly to outline the parameters of the request and then to add the request to your schedule. This avoids scenarios like the following:

> User Email 1: My mouse isn't working right.
>
> Admin Reply 1: Define not working right.
>
> User Email 2: When I start X, the middle mouse button doesn't work.
>
> Admin Reply 2: Did it work at some point in the past?
>
> User Email 3: I just received a new mouse. The old one didn't have 3 buttons.

If you demand that all interactions with your users be via email, you can see that you may spend significantly more time trying to extract information from them than would have been spent if you simply sat down with the user for a few minutes to discuss the problem.

The "Scheduled Interrupt Time" Strategy

Since minimizing the impact of user interrupts is the goal we are trying to achieve, some systems administrators try to establish a time period during which users are allowed to interrupt them. Approaches that utilize this idea may work well for a time, especially if most of your user interrupts are trivial to deal with and you have a small user community. However, as that user community grows you will often find that you have to increase the amount of scheduled interrupt time to deal with the larger number of users. Another deficit to this approach of dealing with interrupts is that every user tends to think that his problem is an emergency and seeks your help outside of the time you have set aside. This tends to be especially true of managers, who are under pressure to meet their own goals and deadlines. This can turn out to be very detrimental to your career because those people whose problems fall outside of your scheduled interrupt time may try to blame you for failure to meet their own deadlines.

Minimizing Interruptions Through Training

One of the ways to try to minimize the number of interruptions you get from users is to provide training for them. The idea is to teach the users to be self sufficient for trivial tasks and only come to you when a true crisis arises. The following sections examine a few ideas related to training your user base that can be applied to help minimize the number of trivial interruptions.

Training Your Users

Some of the most annoying users to deal with are those who come to you with questions that could have been answered with a little work on their part. An untrained user can eat up a significant portion of your time and the key to eliminating this is to get the user trained. There are many ways that you can approach the training issue, but here are some of the ways that I have found to be effective.

Making Training Enjoyable

One way to approach training is to make it as appealing as possible to the users. This can be accomplished by keeping the training informal and providing an incentive to attend. For example, if your budget allows, you might sponsor a series of lunch meetings at which a class is given on a technical topic by yourself or one of your users. If you have a room where users can sit and listen to your training while enjoying lunch, they are often more receptive to attending. It is also useful if you can videotape these lunch training sessions, so that people unable to attend can view the training at a later date. If your budget doesn't allow for buying the whole group lunch, you might provide them with soft drinks.

Start a Training Library

Another training approach that may work for you is to start a library of training books and videotapes that users can check out at their convenience. To encourage users to use these resources, you might schedule some time each week during which you make yourself available to answer questions about the materials and do some one-on-one training. This approach works best if your users are motivated to learn already.

A Systems Orientation Guide

At a minimum, it is a good idea to develop a systems orientation guide for your users. The systems orientation guide is a document that lays out for users such things as where to find items on your network and how to request new software, and describes the tools available that can make their jobs easier. A sample table of contents for a systems orientation guide might look something like this:

    I   Meet Your Servers

        A.   The Intranet Web Server

        B.   Electronic Mail

        C.   Application Servers

    II   Network Resources

        A.   Printers

        B.   Shared Filesystems

        C.   Specialized Hardware

            1.   Scanners

            2.   CD-R Burners

    III   Systems Administration Information

        A.   Acceptable Use Policy

        B.   Utilizing the Help Desk

        C.   Training Materials Available

This document does not have to be very long, but by providing a quick reference for your users that describes these items and how to make use of them, you can save yourself from having to answer these types of questions for every new employee. You could publish this information on the company intranet Web server, but for the new employee, it is often better to provide a paper copy so that they know where to look to find that Web server.

A Combination Approach to User Interaction

The approach to dealing with user interrupts that may work for many situations is to combine the three approaches already discussed. The suggested combination is to plan for some amount of interruption time when making your deadlines with a margin to deal with emergencies and to provide a communications mechanism that is a combination of email and face-to-face communications. For example, you might plan on spending a couple of hours a week training your users on Linux and on the resources available on your network. By providing this training, you will reduce the number of trivial interrupts that occur and improve the productivity of the user as well as your own. Another suggestion is to make it a habit to respond as soon as possible to user requests via email with an acknowledgement and some indication of when you will most likely be able to address their request. By giving users an estimate of when you will get to their requests, you set expectations and can manage your time more efficiently. A final suggestion is to establish a help desk with a problem-tracking system, so that users can check on the status of their requests without interrupting you. Establishing an effective help desk is not a trivial task, so the next section provides some tips for setting one up and even discusses some software that you can run on your Linux system to get you started.

Developing a Help Desk

One of the most effective ways to manage user interaction and to keep user interrupts under control is to establish a help desk for them. The help desk allows you to have a central place where users can go when they have problems instead of camping out in your office. A good help desk allows you to keep track of how much time is being spent on dealing with user issues, what actions are taken to resolve these issues, and helps you to keep track of recurring issues that may need more attention. An effective help desk solution will also help you to prioritize issues so that more important issues receive the attention that they deserve, and other issues don't become lost in the shuffle.

Developing a help desk may sound like a simple matter, but in order for a help desk to be effective, it must be used religiously and not become a dumping ground where problems are entered but are never cleared. This section looks at the qualities that make a good help desk, some help desk manning strategies, and an Open Source software package that you can use to implement your own help desk.

Qualities of a Good Help Desk

Establishing a help desk is more than just providing a mechanism for reporting problems and asking questions. A good help desk solution has a number of qualities. Among these are the following:

- An easy-to-use interface for users to enter issues
- A well-defined feedback mechanism
- Reporting capabilities
- A prioritization mechanism
- An escalation path

The following sections look at each of these qualities and why they are important to have in a help desk solution.

Easy-to-Use Interface

One of the most important qualities of any good help desk solution is an easy-to-use interface for users to enter issues. While you as a computing power user may not care how easy the interface is to work with, your users will and if the interface to your help desk is not easy to use, they will find any excuse not to use it. If your help desk also includes an expert interface or an alternative method for entering issues, so much the better. An example of this might be a help desk with a simple Web interface for your users and an email or command-line interface for experts.

A Well-Defined Feedback Mechanism

The next requirement for your help desk is a well-defined feedback mechanism. If a user enters an issue, he should be notified whenever action is taken on that issue. He should also be able to check the status of his issues whenever he chooses. The most common notification method for status changes in issues is email. It is also desirable that users be able to see the actions taken to resolve their issues, provided that seeing them will not compromise security of the systems involved.

Reporting Capabilities

The ability to extract information about the type and frequency of issues as well as how long they take to resolve is another key feature that a good help desk should have. This information is critical so that the systems administration staff can learn about problem trends or areas that might benefit from better user training. Another benefit of maintaining this type of reporting information is that you can use it to create a frequently asked questions list that can reduce your workload by allowing users to solve their own issues.

Prioritization Capabilities

Prioritization capabilities should be part of your help desk solution and the ideal system will allow both the user and the administrator to set a priority on an issue. By allowing the user to set a priority, the systems administrator can get a feel for how important the issue is to the user. The converse is also true. By allowing the systems administrator set a priority that is independent of the user set priority, the user can see what level of attention his request will receive. This ability can also point out to users the relative importance in the overall workload of the systems administration staff.

Escalation Path

A final capability required of a good help desk solution is an escalation path so that issues can go up in priority as they age. This capability ensures that issues don't stagnate on a list and that they receive the attention that they require. This is most important to users, but is also important to administrators because issues that are ignored have a bad habit of becoming chronic and often end up becoming more of a problem as they age. By raising awareness of aging issues, they can come to the attention of managers who can determine that an issue needs increased resources to resolve.

By meeting these requirements, a help desk solution can make the task of supporting users on your network manageable and keep the problem of interrupts from your users under control.

Help Desk Manning Strategies

Now that you have decided that you need a help desk and have an idea of the features that you want your help desk to support, it is time to start thinking about manning it. There are a number of approaches you can take to this problem. This section discusses a few of them as well as some of the advantages and disadvantages of each.

One option for manning your help desk is to use junior administrators so that the more senior staff members can spend time on project work. This has the advantage of freeing up the time of the more experienced administrators to do the more difficult work, while keeping your users happy. The disadvantage of this solution is that unless these junior administrators are given tasks outside of the help desk duties, they will not be developing professionally and this awareness is likely to result in job dissatisfaction and high turnover in the position.

Another option for manning your help desk is to use interns or college students whose sole purpose is to serve as dispatchers to the regular systems administration staff. If you live near a college campus, especially one with a computer science program, this can be an advantage because you will have a ready pool of potential employees. One of the disadvantages of this manning strategy is that you are likely to have to spend a significant amount of your time in hiring replacements.

If you have a small staff, another option is to work out a schedule so that each of the staff members has an assigned period during which they are responsible for dealing with user issues. This method has the advantage that you can take your scheduled time manning the help desk into account when setting deadlines and priorities and one person is not continually hampered by interruptions.

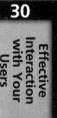

30

Effective
Interaction
with Your
Users

An Open Source Solution

Now that we have defined a desired feature set and looked at a couple of manning strategies, we can take a look at a specific help desk solution available for Linux systems. While the solution we will be looking at does not have all of the desired features, it has most of them and because it is available under the GNU Public License and comes with source code, the missing features could be added if you desire. The most noticable feature that is missing from the solution we are about to describe is an automatic escalation feature.

The solution we will look at for setting up a help desk is called WREQ and is in development at Duke University by Yunliang Yu and contributors from the user community to meet the needs of the systems administration staff there. It includes a simple Web-based interface for users as well as an email and command-line interface for expert users. It is implemented entirely in perl and is based on a similar product called REQ. The following sections take a look at how well this solution fits our desired feature set and then looks at a sample setup.

The User Interface

The first requirement is a simple user interface for users. One advantage of the WREQ help desk system is that because it is a Web-based solution, it can be accessed from any operating system or platform that supports a Web browser. The requirements for the Web browser are that it support frames and JavaScript, which is used to maintain state information. Figure 30.1 shows the WREQ issue entry screen.

A feature found in the WREQ system that makes it a better fit than some of the other systems of its type is the ability to manage multiple input queues or lists with a single installation.

In addition to this Web interface, WREQ also includes an email interface that allows you to work on issues in the absence of a Web browser. This email interface allows you to perform most of the functions of the Web interface by simply adhering to a simple syntax for the subject line. For example, if we set up WREQ and defined a list help desk, by sending email with subject lines as shown in Table 30.1 we can open, update, comment on, or resolve an issue.

FIGURE **30.1**
The WREQ issue entry screen.

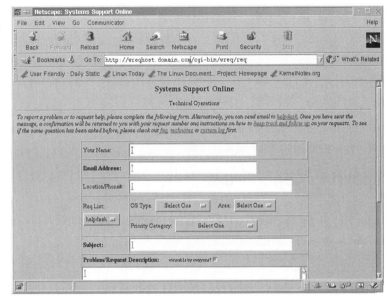

TABLE **30.1**   WREQ Email Interface Subject Line Syntax

Subject Line Syntax	Resulting Action
[helpdesk open] help me	Creates a new issue in the help desk list with a subject of help me.
[helpdesk #5 update]	Updates the actions taken on help desk issue #5 with the body of the message.
[helpdesk #5 comment]	Adds the body of the message as a comment to help desk issue #5.
[helpdesk #5 resolve]	Adds the body of the message as an action to help desk issue #5 and resolves it.
[helpdesk #6 merge]	Merges the issue whose number is specified in the body of the message with issue #6.

These are not all of the commands; however, they serve to illustrate how WREQ issues can be created, updated, or closed using email.

30

Effective
Interaction
with Your
Users

The Feedback Mechanism

The next requirement is a well-defined feedback mechanism. WREQ accomplishes this by providing automatic mail to the originator of an issue when the status of the issue changes, such as when a support person updates or makes comments to an issue. WREQ can also send this type of information to arbitrary email addresses and has a subscription mechanism that allows users to watch all of the issues related to a particular WREQ list. This feature is most useful if large ongoing projects are assigned their own list and all issues related to a particular project are tracked via that list.

Reporting Capabilities

Reporting capabilities are the next requirement and WREQ includes these with its Statistics option. The Statistics option allows you to track the number of issues created, closed, and still open as well as other information that is useful in determining the effectiveness of your help desk. Use of this part of the WREQ system requires that you download and install the GD perl module. This module is a perl interface to the GD graphics library that comes with Red Hat Linux. You can obtain the GD perl module from `http://www.genome.wi.mit.edu/ftp/pub/software/WWW/GD.html`. The statistics can be displayed as text with the option to mail them to any email address or graphically.

Setting Priority

The ability to set a priority on an issue is the next required feature. WREQ allows you to do this, but allows only a single priority as opposed to the dual prioritization that is more desirable. A nice feature of WREQ is that priorities can be defined by the systems administrator using the configuration feature of WREQ. Additionally, you may define different priorities for each list that WREQ maintains.

The Defined Escalation Path

The final desired feature is a defined escalation path. Unfortunately, this feature is not supported by WREQ, but since the package comes with full source written in perl, this feature could be added if the systems administrator determined that it was absolutely critical.

Setting Up a WREQ-Based Help Desk for Red Hat

Having determined that WREQ meets most of the stated requirements, the following sections take a look at the steps involved in setting up a WREQ-based help desk on your Red Hat Linux system, starting with retrieving the required source code.

Retrieving the WREQ Code

The code for the WREQ system is available from the Duke University Web server at `http://www.math.duke.edu/~yu/wreq`. As noted, in order to utilize the reporting features of WREQ, you must also retrieve the GD perl interface module from `http://www.genome.wi.mit.edu/ftp/pub/software/WWW/GD.html` and install it.

Installing WREQ

Once you have retrieved the code for WREQ and installed `GD.pm`, you can begin installation of WREQ. The first step of this installation is to unpack the distribution, which is contained in a file called `wreq.tar.gz`, and fix the permissions. The following session transcript demonstrates this step.

```
[root@quicksilver /root]# cd /home/httpd/cgi-bin
[root@quicksilver cgi-bin]# tar xvzf /tmp/wreq.tar.gz
wreq/index.html
wreq/req
wreq/req-common
wreq/req-config
wreq/req-convert
wreq/req-create
wreq/req-list
wreq/req-listfaq
wreq/req-login
wreq/req-mail
wreq/req-misc
wreq/req-newreq
wreq/req-null
wreq/req-search
wreq/req-show
wreq/req-showfaq
wreq/req-socket
wreq/req-status
wreq/req-time
wreq/req-tty
wreq/req-update
wreq/wreq
wreq/data/
[root@quicksilver cgi-bin]# chown -R root.root wreq
[root@quicksilver cgi-bin]# cd wreq
[root@quicksilver wreq]# ls
data        req-config   req-listfaq  req-newreq  req-showfaq  req-tty
index.html  req-convert  req-login    req-null    req-socket   req-update
```

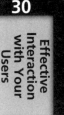

30

Effective Interaction with Your Users

```
req         req-create  req-mail     req-search  req-status  wreq
req-common  req-list     req-misc     req-show    req-time
[root@quicksilver wreq]# chown nobody.nobody data
```

The reason why the data directory is set to owner nobody and group nobody is that this is the user that the Apache Web server children run as when executing the WREQ cgi programs. Now that you have the distribution unpacked, you must perform some manual configuration by editing the following four files:

- /home/httpd/cgi-bin/wreq/req
- /home/httpd/cgi-bin/wreq/req-mail
- /home/httpd/cgi-bin/wreq/req-config
- /etc/aliases

The change required to the req script is to change line 1 to reflect the location of the perl interpreter. On a default Red Hat installation, this is /usr/bin/perl. This change is also required for the req-mail script.

An additional change to the req-mail script is required to make it work with a default Red Hat installation. This change is required so that sendmail will be able to execute the req-mail script. Comment out lines 11 and 12 from the req-mail script. These are the lines that read:

```
$rcf=$0; $rcf=~s/\-mail$/\-config/;
require "$rcf";
```

Once you have commented out these two lines, uncomment line 10 and change it so that it reads as follows:

```
require '/home/httpd/cgi-bin/wreq/req-config';
```

Once these edits have been completed, you must create a symbolic link from /etc/smrsh/req-mail to /home/httpd/cgi-bin/wreq/req-mail using the ln command as follows:

```
[root@quicksilver wreq]# cd /etc/smrsh
[root@quicksilver smrsh]# ln -sf /home/httpd/cgi-bin/wreq/req-mail .
```

This symbolic link is required if you use smrsh in order for sendmail to be allowed to invoke req-mail on your behalf. If you are not using smrsh, this step can be skipped.

WREQ stores some of its configuration variables in a file called req-config and this is the file you must change next. The minimal changes required to get WREQ working on Red Hat Linux are described in Table 30.2.

TABLE **30.2**   WREQ Configuration Variables in `req-config`

Variable	Value
`$sendmail`	For Red Hat Linux systems, set this to `/usr/sbin/sendmail` instead of `/usr/lib/sendmail`.
`$error_cc`	The userid of a person who should receive copies of error messages (usually the systems administrator).
`$wreq_host`	Set this to the name of the machine running WREQ if it is different from your mail server.
`$ph_host`	Unless you have a phonebook server running, set this to the empty string to disable this feature.

If you are following these instructions exactly, you should not have to change any other configuration variables in the `req-config` file.

The final change is to your `/etc/aliases` file. There is one alias that will be used for all lists and two additional aliases per list. For our example list, we are using the name `helpdesk` as the alias to which users send mail to create issues and `helpdesk-dist` to mail all of the people who are registered power users of the system. Here are the aliases from my `/etc/aliases` file that demonstrate how these aliases are defined:

```
# Aliases required to support the help desk
helpdesk:  wreq
wreq:   "¦/home/httpd/cgi-bin/req-mail"
helpdesk-dist:  tschenk,rgreen,bsimpson
```

You have now completed all of the initial setup required to start running WREQ. Your next step is to configure some lists, which you can do using a Web browser. In this context, a list refers to an input queue for issues entered in your help desk. For example, you could create a list that is designed to deal with user desktops only. You could also create a separate list to deal with issues concerning servers. You are limited only by your creativity in the type and number of lists to create. To get started, point a Web browser at the machine on which you installed WREQ. The URL, assuming you have installed WREQ in the directory specified, is `http://wreqhost.domain.com/cgi-bin/wreq/req` where `wreqhost.domain.com` is the hostname of your Web server. This should bring up a page as shown in Figure 30.2 asking you to configure your WREQ server.

Clicking on the word `configure` will take you to the configuration screen. At the top of this form, you may specify a department name and create a list. For our example, we will be configuring a list called `helpdesk` for the Technical Operations group (see Figure 30.3).

30

Effective
Interaction
with Your
Users

FIGURE 30.2
*The initial
screen of an
unconfigured
WREQ server.*

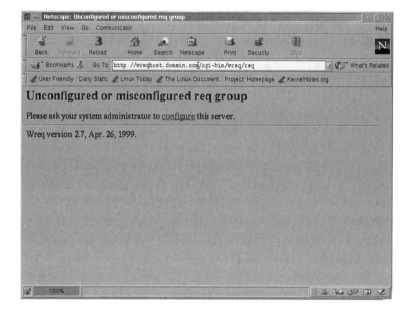

FIGURE 30.3
*The WREQ
configuration
screen.*

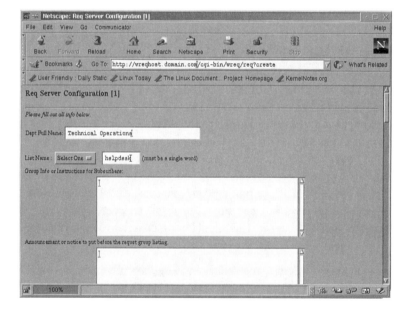

Next, since we want users to be able to track progress on their issues, we will click the radio button as shown in Figure 30.4 that makes the default visibility of the list to be viewable by all. We then define the email alias that users use to open issues and set up auto reply to submissions with the exception of some of the system users.

FIGURE 30.4
The WREQ configuration screen—setting the default visibility of issues.

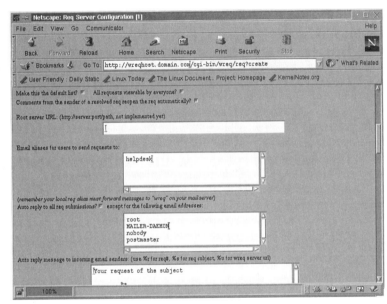

> **Caution**
>
> Always exclude the address that your mail transport agent uses when bouncing mail. This is usually `mailer-daemon@your.domain.com` or something similar. Failure to do this can result in mail loops between WREQ and sendmail.

The next two items to be configured are the distribution list for requests and the list of people who are able to work issues entered into WREQ (see Figure 30.5). The distribution list is usually an alias that includes members of your support staff and possibly others who are interested in seeing the number and types of requests that are going to your help desk.

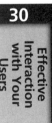

30

Effective
Interaction
with Your
Users

FIGURE 30.5

The WREQ configuration screen—defining the help desk power users.

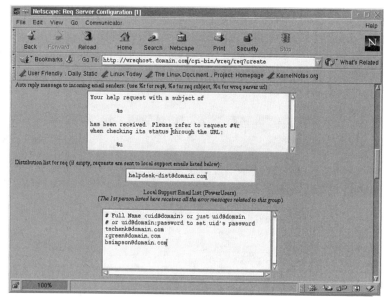

The next entries allow you to limit access to your WREQ list by IP address, to specify other hosts running WREQ FAQ servers, and the priority list. The number of priority levels and their definition is totally at the discretion of the WREQ administrator. The priorities shown in Figure 30.6 are the defaults supplied by WREQ.

The final set of entries that you can customize for your WREQ installation are the methods for categorizing problems and a template for the Web form for entering problems (see Figure 30.7). This allows you to customize the look of your problem reporting form to match your intranet design.

Once you have completed these steps, you should enter a new password and press the Send button to create your list configuration. This will result in a confirmation screen as shown in Figure 30.8.

You are now ready to start using your new help desk. Clicking on the word here will bring you into the main WREQ interface for interacting with issues, which looks like Figure 30.9.

You can now login as one of the power users you specified in the configuration phase and start working on issues. The interface is fairly straightforward, which is good because there is no real documentation for WREQ usage. To create an issue once you have logged in, you can click on the Add option, which will bring up the issue entry form or, alternatively, you can use the email interface and send mail to the help desk. Figure 30.10 shows WREQ with a few items in the help desk queue.

FIGURE 30.6
*The WREQ
configuration
screen—defining
priority levels.*

FIGURE 30.6
*The WREQ
configuration
screen—defining
priority levels.*

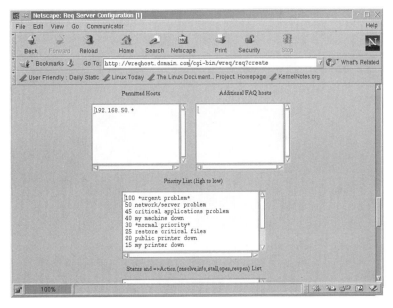

FIGURE 30.7
*The WREQ
configuration
screen—defining
problem cate-
gories and custo-
mizing the look of
WREQ screens.*

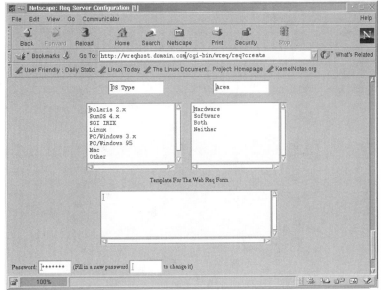

FIGURE 30.8

The WREQ configuration screen—setting the administrator password.

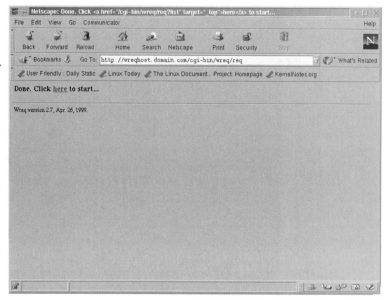

FIGURE 30.9

The configuration success screen.

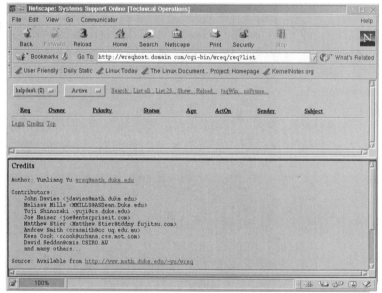

FIGURE **30.10**
A sample of WREQ with a few issues outstanding.

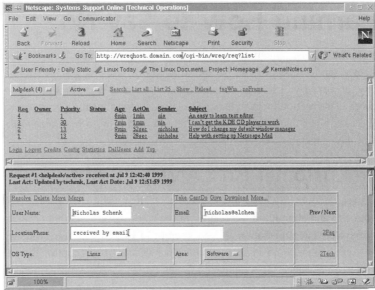

To select an issue to work on, simply click on the issue number. This will bring up the issue in the bottom frame and allow you to update, merge, take, give, resolve, or delete an issue from the queue. You can also move issues between different queues if you are using WREQ to serve multiple lists.

WREQ is but one of a number of help desk solutions available. There are others, both open source and proprietary. The important thing to remember when selecting a help desk solution is to ensure that it supports the features that are most important to you. If, for example, escalation of problems is high on your list, WREQ may not be appropriate because it currently lacks this feature. One such alternative to WREQ is Keystone, which is available at `http://www.stonekeep.com/keystone.php3`. Visit the Web page for information on pricing and features.

Now that we have covered strategies for dealing with user interruptions and how to set up a help desk, we can move on to one of the harder lessons that all systems administrators must learn, namely how to say no to users.

Learning How to Say No

One of the hardest lessons for a systems administrator, especially one who comes from a customer service background, is how to say no to user requests. Failure to develop this ability, however, will lead to constant interruptions and the loss of control over your network. This section looks at how to say no without alienating your users. It looks at some of the user types that require special attention and how to minimize their impact on your day-to-day schedule.

The Customer Isn't Always Right

You have undoubtedly heard the expression "The customer is always right" at some time in your life and although it may apply in the sales world, it certainly does not apply to the job of systems administration. If you attempt to live by this rule, you will soon find that your users have taken over and any attempts to wrest back control from them will be met with fierce resistance. This again reinforces the need to have a written policy outlining acceptable practices on your network and to have management support these policies.

The most common way that users take over control of your network is through the method they use to make requests. A user will often look at a problem, decide on a solution, and then request that you implement the solution without fully describing to you the problem. For example, a user may have a need to put HTML files on a server for display to potential customers of your firm. This will allow him to create mockups of a Web design to show the customer while making a presentation at the customer site. He knows that one way to transfer files to a server is by using an ftp client, so he requests that you open up your firewall so that he can ftp files to the Web server document directories. This may or may not be the only solution or even the best solution, but it is the solution that the user knows about. In this case, if the administrator does not go back to the problem statement, a better solution may be overlooked. Training your users to submit requests properly is the answer to this particular problem. Users should never request a specific solution, but merely state the problem that needs to be solved. If they have an idea for implementing a solution, they should by all means suggest it, but a suggested solution without a proper problem statement should always be answered with a no. A simple solution to this problem is to create a request template that outlines the information required to make a sound decision. Such a request form might look something like this:

```
             SYSTEMS ADMINISTRATION ACTION REQUEST FORM


PROBLEM STATEMENT:
```

```
        Sales people on the road need a mechanism by which they can display
        web pages created while on the road to a potential customer.

BUSINESS CASE:

        The ability to create mockups for customer that they can view on the
        web site greatly increases the chances of making the sale.

POSSIBLE SOLUTIONS:

        Provide FTP access to the web server from outside the company network.

MANAGERS COMMENTS:

        This tool will have a positive impact on our sales efforts.

WHEN REQUIRED:

        As soon as possible.

Requestor:     John Doe          Signature:
Manager:       James Williams    Signature:
```

Dealing with Troublesome Users

Most of your users are likely to give you no trouble at all. However, for every set of users, there are those that always want or need more attention. These users may be employed at any level of the company, from senior management down to the most junior of employees, and the seasoned systems administrator can usually spot them immediately. These users tend to generate the majority of your interruptions and are the ones most likely to challenge your policies. The following sections look at some of these types of users and discuss how you can deal with them.

The "I Don't Have Time to Learn That" User

Some of the most frustrating types of users to deal with are those who respond to your helpful suggestions or attempts at training with the refrain, "I don't have time to learn that." It seems that no matter how hard you work to make their interaction with the systems you administer as easy as possible, they never have time to learn. These types of users are often found in management positions and thus are very hard to deal with.

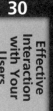

There are two strategies that you can use when dealing with these users, the first being to respond to them with the same type of answer. When this type of user makes a request of you that could be dealt with by the user after a short training session, he will invariably tell you that he does not have the time to spend learning what you have to teach. One response in this case is to outline the projects on which you are working that will suffer if you have to do his work for him. Ask him which of the projects he is willing to take responsibility for when it slips. When the user starts to realize that you are going to use his lack of cooperation as an excuse for missing deadlines, he sometimes comes around to your way of thinking. The key to this response is to immediately follow up with an email to your boss, the user's boss, and the user explaining the situation and how the user responded to your suggestion of training.

The next strategy is to respond to user requests, but to do so in such a way as to show the user and his supervisor that the user's unwillingness to learn a new skill is negatively impacting your productivity. It is usually not wise to employ this strategy with people senior in the company management hierarchy, but this response can be very effective with people who are power users. They almost always have the skills required to help themselves, but are reluctant to do so for any number of reasons. For this strategy to have the most impact, you should in your response to the request outline the steps you took to resolve the issue and be sure to send this information to the user and to the user's manager. This is important because it lets the manager know the level of effort required to resolve the issue so that if the user attempts to blame you for slowing down his work, the manager will know how easily the user could have solved the problem for himself.

The "I Can Do That Myself" User

At the opposite end of the spectrum from the user unwilling to take time to learn new skills is the user who wants to do everything himself. This is the type of user who will ask for administrator privileges on his desktop system, then come complain to you when it breaks. These users are often the ones who have enough knowledge to be a security risk on your network and bear the most watching.

The immediate response to requests for root authorities on the desktop should almost always be no. In the large network environment, consistency is the key to a manageable network. If each user is permitted to alter his system as he sees fit, it makes the task of system maintenance nearly impossible. To guard against this type of user, it is often necessary to employ measures like Tripwire or other systems for checking the consistency of systems.

In the small company environment, another key to keeping these users in check is to massage their egos by asking for their assistance in project planning or in user training. By showing them that you respect their abilities, you can get them to assist you in ways that are not threatening to your network. If they feel that you respect their opinions and will listen to their concerns, they are more likely to bend to your policies than if you try to be a hard liner with them.

The thing not to do with this type of user is to give him limited power. The power user will chafe at the restrictions you place on him, but will usually learn to live within your boundaries if all users are given the same capabilities for dealing with their systems. Once you give them privileges outside that of the normal user, they will almost always seek more, often enlisting the aid of their managers to pressure you into giving them even more control over their systems. Once this trend gets started, it is next to impossible to stop.

The "I Just Have a Quick Question" User

This type of user is one of the most troublesome to deal with because he comes to you out of genuine curiosity. The problem with these users is that many times the question and the answer are not required to accomplish their job, but is something that they stumbled across in the course of the day. They tend to initiate interruptions with phrases like, "If you are busy, I can come back later," or "I just have a quick question." You are drawn in by their lack of aggressiveness and because they were courteous enough to ask if you were busy, you tend to want to try to help them immediately. The problem with these users is that once you have answered their quick question, you realize that you have opened the door on a related subject that will take much longer to explain.

My response to these users is to try to redirect their queries to sources of information other than myself. For example, if a user is interested in what new features have been added to the latest Linux kernel, I would direct him to a Web site like Kernelnotes.Org, where he can find the information he is looking for without requiring my time.

These are just a few of the problem user types, and how you deal with them is largely dependent on how your company is organized. The key to dealing with all users is to provide a structure for interaction with them and to live by that defined structure.

Grant No Exceptions

There is an old saying that states that the exceptions prove the rule; however, in dealing with users, exceptions destroy the rules. This is true for several reasons, the most common being what I like to call the kindergarten lament, or "He has one, why can't I?" No matter how professional your user group is as individuals, as a whole, they will more often than not act like a group of spoiled children. This is why any allowed deviations from policy must be outlined as an addendum to that policy.

Take, for example, the assignment of email aliases for users. I have often seen a policy established in a company that all user names will adhere to either a first initial, last name or a first name, last initial standard. This can often lead to confusing login names that are hard to remember and when this policy is enforced, it will often generate requests for email aliases that are easier to remember. This may sound innocent enough, but consider how to deal with requests for first names as aliases. It might work if no one shared the same first name, but consider how many Mikes or Toms or Bills you are likely to have in a company of 150 people. Who gets the alias bill? What do you do if you gave the alias bill to the company mail clerk and then you hire a CEO with the same first name? As you can guess this could quickly evolve into a big problem. The solution is to make a policy that prohibits single name aliases and to grant no exceptions.

Summary

This chapter attempted to outline some of the issues that arise in dealing with the users of your systems. It talked about ways to deal with problem users and some of the ways to handle the inevitable interruptions that users generate. It looked at how a help desk can help to manage these problems, what features a help desk should be capable of supporting, and some manning strategies for your help desk. It also gave you a pointer to a tool available for Red Hat Linux to help you set up a help desk. Finally, it covered the importance of establishing policy and sticking to it. Take this information as what it was intended to be—advice—and develop your own strategies for dealing with the users of the systems you administer.

Shells, Scripting, and Automation

PART

IX

In This Part

31 Shells   *925*

32 Shell Scripting   *967*

33 Automation   *1017*

Shells

IN THIS CHAPTER

- Getting Started with Shells **926**
- bash, the Bourne Again Shell **928**
- tcsh, the Enhanced C Shell **945**
- Other Shells **964**

31

CHAPTER

This chapter looks at using Linux command-line interpreters, known as shells. It covers the two most popular shells, bash and tcsh, in detail; it also touches quickly upon some of the other shells that are available.

Getting Started with Shells

The task of administering a Red Hat Linux system involves being able to communicate with that system. Although many graphical tools are available to do this job, the true power of the administrator is only available through a shell. A shell is a program that allows you to communicate with the operating system through a series of commands. The original shell developed for the first version of UNIX was known as the Bourne shell; today the Bourne lives on in the form of bash, the Bourne Again Shell. Many different shells have been developed over the years, each having its own unique features while at the same time adhering to basic standards that allow users to move easily from one shell to another. Red Hat Linux 6.0 comes with several different shells, including ash, bash, pdksh, sash, tcsh, and zsh. Those names may look a little daunting at first glance, but don't let that fool you. Once you master one shell, you can pick up any other shell almost immediately. The default shell installed on Red Hat Linux, and also the default shell on most other Linux distributions for that matter, is called bash.

If you boot into a text mode login, you start your default shell simply by logging in. However, if your system boots directly into the X Window System (via GDM) you will have to open an xterm to start your default shell. Once you have started your shell you can find out what shell you are running by printing out the contents of the SHELL environment variable. You can use the following command to do so:

```
$ echo $SHELL
```

Unless you have modified your default shell, this command should output /bin/bash.

Differences Between the Shells

If you decide to try out some different shells during your usage of Linux, you will find that most of the shells act the same for almost all the basic commands. The main differences between the shells become apparent when you start trying out some of the more advanced features, and especially when you start trying out some shell programming. Most shells descend from either a Bourne-shell programming syntax or from a C-shell programming syntax, and there are some crucial differences. Programs written to run under the Bourne shell will probably not work under the C shell, and vice versa. It pays to learn both styles of shell programming; however, the Bourne-shell style is much more common than the C-shell syntax and many also consider it easier to learn.

Each shell has a set of built-in commands; it is through these commands that the user controls the shell. Each shell has its own unique set of commands. However, there are several commands that are common to almost every shell. Here are a few of these commands:

- echo—Displays any arguments that are passed to standard input.

- cd—Changes your current working directory to a new location in the file system.

- logout—Exits from the shell.

- set—Assigns a value to a shell variable.

You can perform many tasks in the shell using these commands. You will find many other commands that are the same in the majority of the shells. Some of the commands found in the various shells may have a slightly different syntax or have a slightly different spelling from shell to shell. Shells also have variables that help control and define the shell's environment; many variables do the same thing in different shells yet have different names.

In addition to variables, shells also have configuration files that contain all sorts of interesting settings. The names for these files are usually different for each shell. Learning a new shell usually involves just learning a few new commands, learning the shell's variable names, and finding out what the configuration files are called. Each shell has a man page that lists all the details of the shell. Additionally, the manual pages are a great place to go to see the differences between each shell. To view a manual page, simply use the man command. For example, to view bash's man page, type the following at the command prompt:

```
$ man bash
```

The manual page for bash is filled with details of bash's features and settings. After reading this chapter, be sure to consult the man pages to find out even more about using each shell.

Selecting a Shell for Interactive Use

Your default shell is specified in the /etc/passwd file. This file contains a list of users along with various bits of information about each user. Each user gets a single line in the file with each line containing fields of information about that user, and each field is separated by a colon. There are seven fields of data in all and it is in the seventh field that your default shell is specified. You can change your default shell by modifying the seventh field for your user. You can also let the passwd utility modify your entry in the /etc/passwd file for you. Simply type the following command at the prompt:

```
$ passwd -s
```

You will be prompted to enter your new shell, and whatever shell you type will be put into the /etc/passwd file. The next time you log in to the system, that shell will be started as your default.

There is also another command-line utility that allows you to change your shell. This utility is called chsh. To change your shell, type **chsh** at the command prompt:

```
$ chsh
```

You should see the following:

```
Password: [Type your password here (not shown)]
Changing the login shell for dbarber
Enter the new value, or press return for the default

    Login Shell [/bin/bash]: /bin/tcsh
```

My login shell should now be tcsh, instead of bash. Be sure that you enter in an actual shell that is installed on your system. If you enter an invalid shell, the chsh command will output an error message and your default shell will not be modified.

Interactive and Non-Interactive Modes

Most shells support two types of usage modes: interactive and non-interactive. Interactive mode is the standard mode of using the shell; the user types in one command at a time and receives any output immediately. Non-interactive mode, also called batch mode, involves writing a script that automates a series of tasks. The script is then passed to bash, and bash executes the commands in the script accordingly. Non-interactive mode may or may not require user input.

There are several differences in how the shell acts when running in interactive or non-interactive mode, although each shell handles this differently. The main difference in how the shell handles interactive and non-interactive modes is generally how it sets up the environment. The differences between both modes are covered in more detail later in this chapter.

bash, the Bourne Again Shell

The Bourne Again Shell is the default shell for Red Hat Linux and is the most commonly used shell in the Linux world. bash is derived from the Bourne shell and is totally backward-compatible to the Bourne shell while offering many advanced features, such as command-line editing. bash was developed by the Free Software Foundation as part of the GNU project and is distributed under the GNU Public License (GPL).

Features of bash

Just like many other shells under Linux, bash is controlled via the command line. The user enters commands, which bash receives and processes before sending to the operating system. Some of bash's more notable feature include

- Wildcards

- Aliases

- Command-line completion

- Pipes

- Input and output redirection

- History

- Command-line editing

- Job control

This section covers all of these features and also looks at the startup process, several built-in commands, common shell variables, and customization of bash.

Wildcards

bash has many features that help users save time when entering commands. One of the most commonly used time-savers is known as wildcards. Wildcards are special characters that allow you to generalize your commands when referring to filenames. You use wildcards to specify patterns and the shell fills in any files that match your pattern. This feature is also known as *globbing*. There are three wildcard characters that you can use in bash:

- *—Matches zero, one, or more characters.

- ?—Matches only a single character.

- [...]—Matches any one of the characters within the brackets.

A common usage of wildcards is to find files that have a common extension. If you want to get a list of every file in the current directory that ends with a .tar.gz extension, you can do so by using the expression *.tar.gz. To list out all the files that end in .tar.gz you could use that wildcard expression along with the ls command:

```
$ ls *.tar.gz
```

Wildcards can reduce several hundred commands down to one or two. For example, say you had a directory full of files and you wanted to delete every file in that directory that ended with a .old extension. You could get a listing of all the files in the directory and then one by one delete each file that ended with .old. If there were only one or two files with a .old extension, the job would be quite simple; however, if you had one hundred files that ended in .old you would be in for a lot of typing. Wildcards allow you to delete every file with a .old extension with only one command:

```
$ rm -f *.old
```

The operation of filling in all the files that match the wildcard pattern is known as *expansion*. This expansion is done by the shell before the command is executed. In the preceding example, say that the following five files with a .old extension existed in the current directory: file1.old, file2.old, file3.old, file4.old, and file5.old. The command would have then been expanded to the following before being executed:

```
$ rm -f file1.old file2.old file3.old file4.old file5.old
```

Using the wildcard saves you from typing those five filenames because the shell does that work for you. The more work you can get the shell to do for you, the more productive you will be.

The second wildcard character is the question mark. This character matches one, and only one, character. It is used to find more exact matches than the * character. For example, you could use it to find every file that ended in a three character extension. You could list those files by using the following command:

```
$ ls *.???
```

This command tells bash to find every file in the current directory that has any number of characters before the dot character and then exactly three characters after that dot character.

The third wildcard construct uses the square bracket characters and finds a match on any one character within the brackets. You can use the square brackets to find any file in the current directory that begins with either an a, b, or c character and ends with a .dat extension by using the following command:

```
$ ls [abc]*.dat
```

Ranges can also be specified within the brackets. For example, to find every file that begins with a character, has an unlimited amount of characters in the middle, and then ends with a number, use the following command:

```
$ ls [a-zA-Z]*[0-9]
```

The more you use bash, the more dependent upon wildcards you will be. In fact, after you start using them regularly, you won't know how you got by without them.

Aliases

Aliases are a very useful feature of the bash shell that saves you time while also allowing you to customize commands to your liking. Aliases allow you to create your own commands, using the existing commands as the base. There are several reasons for using aliases. You may prefer an alternative name for some commands, you may want to abbreviate a command to save keystrokes, or there may be certain parameters that you always pass to a certain command and you would like those parameters to be passed automatically.

To create an alias you must use the `alias` command. For example, to create an alias for `ls` so that the `-F` option is passed automatically, you would type the following command:

```
$ alias ls='ls -F'
```

Now whenever you invoke `ls` on the command line, `ls` will be expanded to the form `'ls -F'` and the expanded command will be executed. The concept here is very similar to the wildcard expansion concept. The expansion of the command takes place behind the scenes in both cases and is not displayed to the user. However, the expansion occurs before the command is passed on to the operating system.

Aliases last until you log out from the current shell or until they are unaliased. The `unalias` command is used to kill an alias without having to log out. To remove the `ls` alias used in the preceding command, type the following:

```
$ unalias ls
```

Now the `ls` command will go back to normal and will no longer be expanded to `'ls -F'`.

As you become more familiar with using bash, you will most likely start to use several aliases regularly. You can set up aliases to be created when you log in by adding them to the bash startup scripts. These scripts are covered later in this chapter. Some of the common aliases you might want to have set when you log in automatically are

- `alias ll='ls -l'`
- `alias la='ls -a'`
- `alias md='mkdir'`
- `alias rd='rmdir'`
- `alias rr='rm -rf'`

You can get a list of all the current aliases that are set by typing the `alias` command by itself, without passing any arguments.

Command-Line Completion

One of the most useful and commonly used features of bash is known as command-line completion. In fact, when you get used to using command-line completion on a regular basis, you won't know how you survived without it.

The main idea behind command-line completion is that bash will try to complete your current command based on what you have typed so far and what available commands start with that. The key used to perform command-line completion is the Tab key. Press the Tab key once and bash will try to complete your command. If it is unsuccessful, you can press Tab again to get a list of all the commands that can fit into what you have typed so far.

The main reasons for using command-line completion are to save some keystrokes and to find commands when you can't remember exactly how they are spelled. The following is a simple example of using command-line completion.

Say you would like to execute the `history` command in order to see all your previous commands. With command-line completion, you don't have to type in every letter. First, just type in **h** and then press Tab. Nothing should happen. That means there is more than one command in your path that begins with an h. You can press Tab again at this point to get a list of those commands. If you do so, all commands that begin with the letter h should appear. Now, continue typing in the next character in the `history` command, **i**. Then press Tab twice again. Now the search has been narrowed to all commands in your path that begin with hi. A list of those commands should be displayed. Now type the **s** and again press Tab. This time there shouldn't be any commands other than `history` that begin with his, and therefore the rest of the `history` command will be filled in for you automatically on the command line. You should now have a command line that looks like this:

```
$ history
```

To execute the command, press the Enter key. You should get a list of your most recent commands.

Pipes

One of the fundamental philosophies of UNIX was that a chain of smaller processes should solve large problems. Each of the smaller processes is performed by a single utility that was built to perform a single task, and to perform that task well. It was that philosophy that saw the creation of the small, reusable utilities that UNIX users have come to depend upon—commands like sort, less, awk, and grep. The creators of UNIX needed something to tie together all those simple commands into the chain, and thus the pipe was born.

The pipe symbol is the "¦" character and it basically means "Take the output from one command and send it as input to the next command." That way a bunch of simple commands can be strung together to perform some complicated tasks. A basic example of using a pipe is when you have a command whose output scrolls off the screen and you would like to have the output pause after every screen and continue only after a keypress. The ls command will scroll off the screen when run from a directory containing many files; however, you can get ls to display only a screenful of data at a time by piping the output of ls to the more command. You can try it by typing:

```
$ ls /dev ¦ more
```

Here, the contents of the /dev directory are displayed one screen at a time. Press the Spacebar to move down through each screen.

A more complex example of using a pipe would be to print out a sorted list of usernames from the /etc/passwd file. You would need to use several commands to accomplish this: cat, awk, and sort. cat would be needed to print the file, awk would then extract all the usernames, and finally sort would sort those names. Here is the command:

```
$ cat /etc/passwd ¦ awk -F: '{ print $1 }' ¦ sort
```

You should get a listing of all the users who have an account on your system, with one user per line.

Hopefully, you can see the power that is available through the use of pipes. Becoming familiar with using pipes requires a different way of looking at problem solving—with time and patience you will find some very innovative solutions to problems using pipes.

Input and Output Redirection

Other very useful features of bash are known as output redirection and input redirection. *Input redirection* allows you to use the contents of a file as the input for a command, whereas *output redirection* allows you to store the output of a command to a file.

The < operator is used for input redirection and the > operator is used for output redirection. For example, say you wanted to print out a sorted version of a list that was contained in a file. You would redirect that file to the sort command:

```
$ sort < inputfilename
```

Here the contents of the file would be sent to the `sort` command and the `sort` command would then display the result of the sort. Now, say you wanted to redirect the output of that sort to a different file instead of standard output. Here is the command:

```
$ sort < inputfilename > outputfilename
```

After running the command, you should not see any immediate output. Instead, you can view the output by listing the contents of the output file with the `cat` command:

```
$ cat outputfilename
```

In the case of using the > operator, anything that was previously in that file before executing the command is erased. If you would like to preserve the contents of the file and append the output onto the end of the file, you can use the >> operator instead. To append a listing of the current directory into the end of the file you just created from the `sort` command, type the following:

```
$ ls >> outputfilename
```

An example of using redirection to direct the output of a command to both standard output and standard error is

```
$ ls -1F &> filename
```

or

```
$ ls -1F >& filename
```

Executing either of these commands would cause the output of the `ls -1F` command to be put into the file specified by `filename` along with any error messages that the command generates.

History

Every command that you enter into the command prompt is saved into what is called *history*. The list of commands in your history can be of an unlimited size; however, it is usually set to a specified limit. Under bash, the shell variable HISTSIZE is used to specify the maximum number of commands to store in the history list. You can use the `history` command to search through your previous commands and execute certain commands again. The `history` command is available to get a listing of all the commands in your history file. Type the `history` command at the shell prompt:

```
$ history
```

You should get a listing of previously entered commands, and each command should also have a number associated with it. You can also pass a parameter to the `history` command to specify the number of commands to display. For example, the command

```
$ history 50
```

would display the last fifty entries in the history list. The `history` command gets its data from a file in your home directory. The default filename is `.bash_history`. The shell variable `HISTFILE` contains the name of the file to use for the history list. To use a file other than `.bash_history`, simply change the contents of the `HISTFILE` variable. Every time you execute a command in bash, that command gets added to your history list file.

In addition to viewing your previous commands, bash allows you to move through the history list. To move back one entry, use the up-arrow key; to move forward one entry, use the down-arrow key. When moving through the previous commands, you can execute them at any time by pressing the Enter key, and you can also edit the command before executing it.

You can also execute your previous command using the "bang-bang" command. This command involves typing in two exclamation marks on the command line and then pressing Enter. For example, if you just executed the `ls` command and then type in `!!` at the next prompt, bash will execute the `ls` command again. You can also execute any command in your history list simply by typing a single exclamation mark followed by the history number associated with that command. The history number is listed beside each command when you get a history listing from the `history` command. To execute the 54th command your history list, enter the following command:

```
$ !54
```

There are also a number of keystroke combinations available that allow you to move around through the history list. Here are the basics:

- Ctrl+p—Fetches the previous command from the history list.

- Ctrl+n—Fetches the next command in the history list.

- Alt+<—Moves to the first line in the history list.

- Alt+>—Moves to the last line in the history list.

You can also perform searches on your history list. Here are the commands for doing so:

- Ctrl+r—Searches backward through the history, starting at the current line and moving up through the history list.

- Ctrl+s—Searches forward through the history.

- Alt+p—Non-incremental search backward through the history.

- Alt+n—Non-incremental search forward through the history.

The commands in your history list can also be edited via the `fc` command. The `fc` command accepts the following syntax:

```
fc [-e ename] [-nlr] [first] [last]
```

The `-e` parameter allows you to specify the text editor to use when editing the history file. If you do not pass this parameter, it defaults first to the value in the `FCEDIT` shell variable, and then to the `EDITOR` variable if `FCEDIT` is not set. The `-l` parameter causes `fc` to list the lines in the history file without editing. The `-n` option just lists the history commands, this time without line numbers. The `-r` option again simply lists the history commands, this time reversing the order of the lines.

For example, to list the history commands from 50 to 100, use the command

```
$ fc -l 50 100
```

To edit command number 86 in your history file, issue the command

```
$ fc 86
```

Your default editor should open up with command 86 on the first line. You can edit the command if you want and then exit the editor when you are done. Upon exit, the command will be executed. If `fc` is started without passing any parameters, the last command you executed will be used by default.

Command-Line Editing

One of the advanced features that bash offers over the Bourne shell is command-line editing. bash makes it very easy to move around on the command line and edit your command before pressing the Enter key. You can use the left and right arrow keys to move either to the left or right by one-character increments. There are also several keystroke combinations that allow you to move around the command line. They are

- Ctrl+a—Moves to the beginning of the current line.

- Ctrl+e—Moves to the end of the current line.

- Ctrl+f—Moves forward a character.

- Ctrl+b—Moves backward a character.

- Alt+f—Moves forward a word.

- Alt+b—Moves backward to the start of the previous word (if one exists).

- Ctrl+l—Clears the screen.

- Ctrl+k—Kills the current line starting from the current cursor position.

- Ctrl+x—Kills backward to the beginning of the line.

Learning these shortcuts will help you use the command line more efficiently.

Job Control

When you execute any command under bash, that command is known to bash as a *job*. Each job is assigned a unique job id. Because Linux is a multitasking operating system, you can have many jobs running at the same time. Jobs can also have many different states associated with them: A job can be running in the foreground, in the background, or it can be suspended. When you execute a command in bash, that command normally runs in the foreground and stays in the foreground until the command exits. When a single command is running in the foreground, you cannot perform any other actions on that console until the command exits. Many commands should be run in the foreground, such as those that give immediate output or those that are interactive. However, you may want many other commands to run in the background. For commands that could possibly take a long time to finish, you are better off starting them in the background so that you can continue to use the shell as the command runs. To start a command in the background, append an ampersand onto the end of the command. For example, to run the `find` command in the background try the following:

```
$ find / -name core -print > ~/core_files &
```

This command will search your entire hard drive looking for core files and when it finds any, it will put their names into a file in your home directory called `core_file`. An operation such as this could take some time, so you can run the command in the background and continue working on other things while the command executes.

Sometimes you may start a job in the foreground but then find that it is taking a long time to process. You can move that job into the background by first suspending it and then using the `bg` command. To suspend the current running job, use the keystroke combination Ctrl+Z. If you ran the preceding command in the foreground and then suspended it, you should see a message similar to the following:

```
[2]+ Stopped    find / -name core -print >~/core_files
```

You should then get your bash prompt back. At that point, type the `bg` command at the prompt and the job will continue in the background. A message such as the following should be outputted also:

```
$ bg
[2]+ find / -name core -print > ~/core_files &
```

Ctrl+Y is another type of suspend operation that you can use. Ctrl+Y performs a delayed suspend and only stops the current job when it attempts to read input.

In addition to `bg`, which sends jobs to the background, there is also a command called `fg`, which brings jobs to the foreground. Running either command without a parameter will result in the command being executed on the current job. The current job is generally the last job that you started. In the preceding example, `bg` moved the `find` command to the background because the `find` command was the current job. Both `bg` and `fg` also accept a parameter of a job number so that you can move jobs other than the current one in and out of the foreground and background. For example, to move job 4 into the foreground, type the following command:

```
$ fg 4
```

You can get a list of all currently running processes using the `ps` command. If you execute `ps` without passing any arguments, you will get a list of all jobs that are owned by you. If you weren't doing much, you would get output similar to the following:

```
$ ps
  PID TTY          TIME CMD
  319 pts/4     00:00:00 bash
 3950 pts/4     00:00:00 ps
```

The number in the leftmost column is the job number. In this case, bash has a job id of 319, while my `ps` command has a job id of 3950. Passing a few more parameters to `ps` can get you some very interesting information. A very common operation of `ps` is to output every running process on a system. To do that, type the following:

```
$ ps aux
```

You should see quite a large list outputting from that command. There is a lot of interesting information in that output, including the job id for every process as well as the owner for each process.

Now that you know how to find the job id for each job, you can use that information to manipulate jobs. A very useful operation is the ability to kill jobs. The `kill` command is used to perform such an operation and the syntax for the command is as follows:

```
kill [-s signame ¦ -p ¦ -l] [pid ¦ job]
```

Here, the -s parameter is used to send a specific signal to the job, which is given via the signal name or the signal id number. To get a listing of all signal names and numbers, use the -l option, which outputs all the available signals. The -p option prints out only the process id for the job and will not kill it. You can pass a number to kill as -n, where n is a number between 1 and 9. The greater the number, the more powerful the kill operation will be. Finally, you must specify a job id on which to perform the kill operation.

Another way to get a listing of all the jobs you are currently running is to use the jobs command. The syntax for the jobs command is as follows:

```
jobs [-lnp] [jobspec ...]
```

If you pass the -l option, jobs will display each job's process id in addition to regular information. The -p option results in a list of only the process ids without any other information. If you pass the -n option, jobs will only display information on processes that have changed status since the last time jobs was called. You can also pass the jobspec parameter, which will cause jobs to return information only about that single job.

Another way to refer to jobs is by using the % character. Using the % character followed by either a job id or job name is similar to using the fg command on the same job. The syntax for using the % command is as follows:

```
%[id ¦ name] [&]
```

You can use wildcards when passing the job name to %. A common usage of % is to resume a stopped job in the background by appending the & at the end. For example, if you suspend job 34 you can start the job again in the foreground by typing the following command:

```
$ %34 &
```

There are also various other uses of the % command: Both %% and %+ refer to the current job, and %- refers to the previous job.

Built-In Commands

bash has a number of built-in commands that are part of the shell. Many of the commands you will be using regularly are actually not part of the shell, but instead they are executable files. For example, ls is an executable file located in /bin/ls, and is not part of bash nor any other shell.

We have already covered some of the basic built-in commands, such as alias, jobs, fg, and history. Here are some others that are also available:

- help—Gives you a list of all available bash commands or details of a single bash command that you pass to it.

- pwd—Prints out your present working directory.

- eval—Evaluates any argument that is passed to it and displays the result.

- logout—Logs you out from the current shell.

- umask—The user file-creation mask is set to MODE. If MODE is omitted, or if -S is supplied, the current value of the mask is printed. The -S option makes the output symbolic; otherwise an octal number is output. If MODE begins with a digit, it is interpreted as an octal number, otherwise it is a symbolic mode string like that accepted by chmod.

- exit—Exits the shell with a status of N. If N is omitted, the exit status is that of the last command executed.

- export—Puts any variables passed to it into the environment.

- set—Declares a variable.

- unset—Removes a variable.

There are a number of commands in addition to the these. Consult the man page for bash to find out about all of the available bash commands.

Startup for Interactive Sessions

There are several files that bash reads before giving you a command-line prompt when you begin an interactive session. These files are used to customize your bash environment. If you want to set up standard aliases or set various shell variables, the bash startup files are the place to do it. There are several files involved in the bash startup process—the first file that bash reads is /etc/profile. /etc/profile is the global bash startup script for your Linux system. Whenever any user logs in, /etc/profile will be executed if they use bash. The /etc/profile file is a great place to set up a standard bash environment.

After reading /etc/profile, bash then looks for one of several files in your home directory. It will try to locate each of the following files in order and the first one that exists gets executed. The files are

- ~/.bash_profile

- ~/.bash_login

- ~/.profile

It is within these files that individual users can customize their bash environment, including overwriting any settings that were specified in /etc/profile.

> **Note**
>
> It is possible to disable bash's startup files if you pass the `-noprofile` option to bash upon startup.

After bash starts it will read in the file `~/.bashrc`, if the file exists, and execute its contents. You can also tell bash to execute a different file by specifying the file after the `-rcfile` option. For example, to tell bash to read the file `.bash_startup` instead of `.bashrc`, start bash with the following command:

```
$ /bin/bash -rcfile ~/.bash_startup
```

You can also tell bash not to read the `.bashrc` file by passing the `--norc` option to bash upon startup.

Some other parameters that you can pass to bash upon startup include the following:

- `-version`—Displays the version number for bash upon startup.

- `-login`—Makes bash act as if it has been invoked as your login shell.

You can also start bash from within another shell or from within bash itself. This is called a *non-login interactive shell*. For non-login interactive shells, the `/etc/profile` file is ignored along with `~/.bash_profile`, `~/.bash_login`, and `~/.profile`. The only startup file that is read in this case is the `~/.bashrc` file. Again, this can also be disabled by passing the `-norc` option to bash, and you can tell bash to use a different file by passing the `-rcfile` option.

For a full listing of bash's startup parameters, see the man page for bash.

Startup for Non-Interactive Sessions

During your general use of bash, you will be using interactive mode. However, bash also has a non-interactive mode that it uses to execute shell scripts, among other things. For non-interactive mode, all the startup files that are read in interactive mode are ignored. Instead, bash simply looks for the environment variable ENV and if it contains any filename, those files will be sourced.

As with other environment variables, you can set the value for ENV within one of the interactive mode startup scripts and then that file will be executed before any of your shell scripts are executed.

Quoting

In bash, many characters and words have special meaning. To tell bash to ignore the special meaning of these characters and words you can use a technique called *quoting*. There are three ways to perform quoting:

- Escape character (\ )

- Single quotes (')

- Double quotes (")

The escape character is used when you want to preserve the literal value of only one character. To use it, simply place a non-quoted backslash (\) before the character. If you were to use quotes, it would lose its special meaning as the escape character. The only character that the escape character does not affect is the newline character. If you precede a newline character with the escape character, it will simply cause the shell to ignore the newline and no line break will occur at that place.

Using single quotes is the second method of quoting available under bash. When you place a group of characters within single quotes the literal value for all of the characters will be preserved. No additional single quotes may appear within a single quote pair, even if you precede the single quote with the escape character. This is because the escape character's special meaning is lost due to the single quotes.

The third and final method for quoting is to use double quotes around the characters you want to quote. This is similar to using single quotes except that a few of the special characters retain their special meaning even when within the double quotes. The characters $ and ` completely retain their special meaning with double quotes, so you can perform operations such as variable interpolation within the double quotes. The backslash character only partially retains its special meaning. You can only use the backslash character to escape the following characters: $, `, ", \, and the newline character. Using the backslash character you can escape the double quote character to have additional double quotes appear within the outer double quote pair.

bash Variables

Throughout this chapter you have learned about shell variables. This section examines them in a bit more detail. There are quite a few shell variables that bash uses to control its appearance, and by modifying the contents of those variables you can customize your bash environment. Additionally, you can create you own variables. A variable is simply an identifier that contains some data, and the data within variables can easily be changed at any time. To access the data within a variable, simply precede the variable name with the $

character. For example, to print out the contents of the PATH variable, type the following command:

```
$ echo $PATH
```

Here are a few of the common variables that bash uses to control its environment:

- PATH—The search path for commands. Contains a list of directories (separated by colons) in which the shell looks for commands.

- HOME—The home directory for the current user.

- PS1—The primary prompt string used by bash when displaying the command line.

- PS2—The secondary prompt string.

- HISTSIZE—The number of commands to remember in the command history. The default is 500.

- HISTFILE—The name of the file to which the command history is saved. The default is ~/.bash_history.

- HISTFILESIZE—The maximum number of lines contained the history file.

- PWD—The present working directory.

- OLDPWD—The previous working directory.

- EDITOR—The default editor for many programs and utilities.

You can change the values in any variable by typing the variable followed by an equal sign and the new value you want to put into the variable. For example, to change your history file to the file .my_history_file, type the following command:

```
$ HISFILE=".my_history_file"
```

When creating your own variables, the shell environment does not have immediate access to them; you must export them to the environment. Therefore, when creating a new variable, precede the variable name with the export command. For example, to create a new variable called MY_VARIABLE with the contents "bash is really cool", type the following command:

```
$ export MY_VARIABLE="bash is really cool"
```

To print out the contents of that variable, try the following command:

```
$ echo $MY_VARIABLE
```

The bash startup scripts are a great place to customize shell variables and also to make your own.

Modifying the Command Prompt

There are two levels to the command prompt under bash. The first level is what you see when bash is waiting for you to type in a command. This is controlled by the variable PS1. The default PS1 setting is the $ character. The second-level prompt is displayed when bash requires further input from the user to complete a command. The default PS2 setting is the > character.

To change either PS1 or PS2, use the export command, passing the variable name followed by an equal sign and then the desired prompt. To have a prompt that displays the current time followed by the current directory and finally followed by a $, try the following:

```
$ export PS1 = "\t \w\$ "
```

There are several special characters that you can use in creating your prompts:

- \!—Displays the history number of the command.
- \#—Displays the command number of the command.
- \$—Displays a $ for normal users and a # when the user is root.
- \\—Displays a backslash.
- \d—Displays the current date.
- \h—Displays the hostname of the computer on which the shell is running.
- \n—Prints out a newline character.
- \nnn—Displays the character that corresponds to the octal value of nnn.
- \s—Displays the name of the current shell.
- \t—Displays the current time.
- \u—Displays the username for the current user.
- \W—Displays the name of the current directory.
- \w—Displays the full path leading to the current directory.

The best way to create a useful and interesting command prompt is simply to experiment. Once you have a command prompt that you like, you can define it within the bash startup scripts so that you can have it set automatically when you log in.

Advantages and Disadvantages of bash

bash has quite a legacy as a shell, mostly because it's based on the Bourne shell. The Bourne shell is an extremely common shell within the UNIX world and therefore widely known. This familiarity gives bash an advantage over other shells because users who know the Bourne shell can start using bash immediately. Also, the programming interface for bash is based on the Bourne shell, and the majority of shell scripts in existence are based upon the Bourne shell syntax. In addition, bash's advanced features, such as command-line editing, command-line completion, and job control, make it a very powerful shell.

Even with all its great features, there are still some drawbacks to bash: Several other shells have extra features that bash still doesn't have, such as the ability to change key bindings, spell checking, and periodic and timed event processing. Some people also prefer the programming interface of the C shell, simply because of its similarity to the C programming language.

When it comes to picking a shell, bash more than meets most users' requirements. Generally, users stick with whatever shell they first happen to learn and for many users just learning Linux, that shell is bash.

tcsh, the Enhanced C Shell

The tcsh is an enhanced version of the Berkeley UNIX C shell, csh. tcsh has some nice additional features, such as filename completion and command-line editing. You will not notice much difference between tcsh and bash when using tcsh for basic tasks. However, there are subtle differences. The main difference between bash and tcsh is that the programming interface for tcsh is based upon the C shell, whereas the programming interface for bash is based upon the Bourne shell. Also, the shell variable names under tcsh are different than bash's variables, and many of the files used by the shell are called different names under tcsh.

Features of tcsh

tcsh has many of the same features as bash, but also a few unique features, including

- Wildcards
- Aliases
- Command-line completion
- Spelling correction
- Pipelines

- Input and output redirection

- History

- Job control

- Key bindings

- Automatic, periodic, and timed events

The unique features in tcsh are the spelling correction and key binding features. The other features are found under both bash and tcsh; however, there are differences in how each shell implements those features.

Wildcards

tcsh supports the same wildcards that bash does. Wildcards are very useful and considerably speed up many tedious tasks when working with tcsh. They allow you to specify patterns and the shell fills in any files that match your pattern. This feature is also called either globbing or expansion. The wildcards available under tcsh are the same as the wildcards available under bash. They are

- *—Matches zero, one, or more characters.

- ?—Matches only a single character.

- [...]—Matches any one of the characters within the brackets.

An example of using a wildcard would be to extract every file in the current directory that ended in the .tar.gz extension. A .tar.gz file is a compressed archive and usually contains many files. If you have fifty or so archives, it would be very tedious to extract them all one by one. Using wildcards, you can extract all of the files with a single command. The expression *.tar.gz refers to every file that ends in the .tar.gz extension, and by using it in conjunction with the tar command you can turn fifty commands into one. Here is the command that extracts all files in the current directory that end in the .tar.gz extension:

```
$ tar zxvf *.tar.gz
```

Now all those archives should be uncompressed and extracted. Unfortunately, that leaves you with a whole bunch of useless archives that you no longer need. Again, wildcards can come into play to delete all those archives. The command to delete every file in the current directory that ends in .tar.gz is

```
$ rm -f *.tar.gz
```

The interesting thing about how tcsh handles wildcards is that everything that matches the wildcard pattern is expanded in place of the wildcard, before the command is sent to the operating system. bash also treats process wildcards in the same manner. What if you had executed the preceding command and the following six files with a .tar.gz extension existed in the current directory: `file1.tar.gz`, `file2.tar.gz`, `file3.tar.gz`, `file4.tar.gz`, `file5.tar.gz`, and `file6.tar.gz`.

Well, first those six filenames would be put in place of the *.tar.gz and you would end up with the following:

```
$ rm -f file1.tar.gz file2.tar.gz file3.tar.gz file4.tar.gz file5.tar.gz
file6.tar.gz
```

After the preceding expansion takes place, the command is sent to the operating system. It is important to understand which processes the shell performs and which ones the operating system performs.

The second wildcard character is the ?. This wildcard is used when you want to match a single character. Use the ? wildcard when you need to be more specific in your matching. An example of putting the ? wildcard to use would be to list out all the files that have five characters before the dot and three after. You could list those files by using the command:

```
$ ls ?????.???
```

The output from this command should be a listing of all the files in the current directory that consist of five characters followed by a three character extension.

The third and final wildcard construct involves using the square brackets to enclose characters that you would like to match. When tcsh processes this wildcard, it matches a single character to one of the characters contained within the square brackets. An example of using the square bracket wildcard would be to find every file in the current directory that starts with either the letters a, b, or c and ends with a .dat extension. Here is the command to do so:

```
$ ls [abc]*.dat
```

tcsh also supports the use of ranges with the square brackets, just like bash.

Aliases

Aliases under tcsh work the same as aliases under bash for the most part, although there are a few subtle differences. Aliases are another reason why the shell is such a powerful tool. Every command in the shell can be renamed and tweaked using aliases. Some users may not see aliases as a useful feature; however, there are many reasons for using them. One such reason may be as simple as preferring an alternative name for some commands. Or, you may want to abbreviate a command to save keystrokes. Or maybe there are certain parameters that you always pass to a certain command and you would like those parameters to be passed automatically.

Aliases are created using the `alias` command. For example, to create an alias for `ls` so that the `-l` option is passed automatically, you would type the following command:

```
$ alias ls 'ls -l'
```

Now whenever you invoke `ls` on the command line, `ls` will be expanded to the form `'ls -l'` and the expanded command will be executed. The concept here is very similar to the wildcard expansion concept. The expansion of the command takes place behind the scenes in both cases and is not displayed to the user. You will notice a slight difference in the `alias` command under bash; the equal sign is not used when assigning aliases under the C shell. If you try to create an alias using the equal sign, it will not work.

Aliases are killed by either logging out or by using the `unalias` command. To remove the `ls` alias using the `unalias` command, type the following:

```
$ unalias ls
```

As you become more familiar with using tcsh, you will most likely start to use several aliases regularly. You can set up aliases to be created when you log in by adding them to the tcsh startup scripts. These scripts are covered later in this chapter. Some of the common aliases you might want to have set to help speed up typing when you log in automatically are

```
alias ll 'ls -l'
    alias la 'ls -a'
    alias md 'mkdir'
    alias rd 'rmdir'
    alias rr 'rm -rf'
```

You can get a list of all the current aliases that are set by typing the `alias` command by itself, without passing any arguments.

Command-Line Completion

One of the most useful and commonly used features of tcsh is known as command-line completion. Command-line completion under tcsh is similar to bash's command-line completion, with a few minor differences.

The main idea behind command-line completion is this: tcsh tries to complete your current command based on a partially typed command. The key used to perform command-line completion is the Tab key. If you type part of a command on the command line, pressing the Tab key will tell tcsh to try to complete your command based on what available commands match what you have typed so far. Under bash, if more than one command matches what you have typed, pressing the Tab key again will show you the current matches. Unfortunately, this feature is not available under tcsh.

The main reasons for using command-line completion are to save keystrokes and also to locate commands when you can't remember exactly how they are spelled. The following is a simple example of using command-line completion.

Say you would like to execute the `history` command in order to see all your previous commands. With command-line completion, you don't have type every letter. First, just type **h** and then press Tab. Nothing should happen. That means there is more than one command in your path that begins with an h, and therefore you need to give tcsh more information. Continue typing in the next character in the `history` command, **i**. Now press Tab once again. The search has been narrowed down to all commands in your path that begin with hi. If nothing happens this time, that means there is more than one command in your path that begins with hi. You need the next letter to make your command more specific. Type the **s** and again press Tab. This time there shouldn't be any commands other than `history` that begin with his, and therefore the rest of the `history` command will be filled in automatically on the command line. You should now have a command line that looks like this:

```
$ history
```

Now press the Enter key and you should get a list of your most recent commands.

Spelling Correction

Spelling correction is a very nice feature of tcsh. tcsh can usually correct the spelling mistakes for filenames, commands, and variables, as well as completing any parts and listing them.

Spelling is corrected using either the spell-word editor command or the spell-line editor command. The spell-word editor command is usually bound to Alt+S and Alt+s, although you can change the binding using the `bindkey` command. The spelling correction feature is used to correct the spelling in individual words. Key binding and using the `bindkey` command are covered later in this chapter. The spell-line editor command is usually bound to Alt+$ and it corrects the spelling of the entire input buffer.

Several shell variables help customize the spelling correction feature, including the `correct` variable and the `autocorrect` variable. The `correctshell` variable can either be set to the value of `cmd`, which tells tcsh to correct spelling mistakes in only the command name, or to `all`, which tells tcsh to correct spelling mistakes in the entire line. If the `autocorrect` shell variable is set, tcsh will attempt to correct spelling mistakes during command-line completion before each completion attempt.

Pipes

Pipes is another feature found in both bash and tcsh, and again, both shells treat pipes the same for the most part.

Input and Output Redirection

Another very useful feature of tcsh, which is also found in bash, is known as output and input redirection. Input redirection allows you to redirect where the input for a command is coming from and output redirection allows you to redirect where the output for a command is going.

The < character is used for performing input redirection. Here is an example of using input redirection to direct the input of a file to a command:

```
$ command < inputfilename
```

In the preceding case, whatever content the file `inputfilename` contains will be sent to `command` as input. The command would receive the data from the file just as it would receive data from the keyboard.

The > character is used for performing output redirection. Output redirection is often used to store the results of a command to a file. If you wanted to store the results of the preceding command to a file, you could use the following:

```
$ command < inputfilename > outputfilename
```

After running the command you should not see any immediate output. Instead, open the output file and all the output should be inside that file.

With the output redirection operator, all data within any file you direct output to is erased. There is an operator you can use instead if you want to append the output from a command to a file. It is represented by the >> character. Here is an example of using it:

```
$ command >> outputfilename
```

The output from the command would be added onto the end of the file `outputfilename`. The append operator is useful for writing log files.

History

tcsh also has a history feature, which is similar to the history feature under bash. Every command that you enter into the command prompt is saved into what is called "History." History is stored in a file in your home directory, and the default filename under tcsh is `.history`. Every time you execute a command at the prompt, that command is added to your history file. The name for your history file is stored in the shell variable `histfile`. If you want tcsh to store your history in a different file, simply change the value of the `histfile` variable. The number of commands that are stored in your history is dictated by the shell variable `savehist`; you might want to set this variable to a preferred amount in your `.login` file. History is useful for going back and seeing what commands you executed previously and also for re-executing any commands.

The `history` command can be used to get a list of all the commands in your history file. There are two different methods of calling the `history` command. The first method is with the following syntax:

```
history [-hrc] [n]
```

The `-h` option causes `history` to not output the line numbers and timestamps that are usually outputted by default. The `-r` command causes `history` to display all your history in reverse, outputting the most recent commands first. The `-c` option clears your current history, allowing you to start fresh. You can also specify exactly how many commands to display by passing the n parameter. To try out the `history` command, simply type it at the command prompt:

```
$ history
```

You should get a listing of previously entered commands. Each command should also have a number and a timestamp associated with it. Now try the `history` command with the n parameter to specify exactly how many commands to display. To tell `history` to display only the fifty most recent commands, try the following:

```
$ history 50
```

You should get the last fifty entries in the history list dumped to your screen.

The other method of invoking the `history` command is with the following syntax:

```
history -SLM [filename]
```

The `-S` option writes your history list to any file that you specify for `filename`. The `-L` option appends any history file you specify to your current history list. Finally, the `-M` option is used for merging any history file you specify with your current history list. The merge is performed based on the timestamp of each command.

In addition to viewing your previous commands, tcsh allows you to move through the history list. To move back one entry, use the up-arrow key; to move forward one entry, use the down-arrow key. When moving through the previous commands, you can execute them at any time by pressing the Enter key, and you can also edit the command before executing it.

There are also several shorthand commands that you can use to execute commands in your history list:

- !!—Causes the last command to be re-executed.

- !n—Causes the command with a history number of n to be re-executed.

- !-n—The command that is n commands from the last command in the history list gets re-executed.

- !expression—The last command that matches whatever expression you specify will be re-executed. Wildcards are allowed.

An example of using these commands would be to re-execute the 30th command in your history list. To do so, try the following:

```
$ !30
```

Also, to re-execute the last command that began with the letter a, try the following command:

```
$ !a
```

Job Control

When you execute any command under tcsh, that command is known to tcsh as a job; and just like under bash, each job is assigned a unique job id. Because Linux is a multitasking operating system, you can have many jobs running at the same time. Jobs can also have many different states associated with them: A job can be running in the foreground, in the background, or it can be suspended. When you execute a command in tcsh, normally that command runs in the foreground and stays in the foreground until the command exits. When a single command is running in the foreground, you cannot perform any other actions on that console until the command exits. Many commands should be run in the foreground, such as commands that give immediate output or commands that are interactive. However, you may want to run many other commands in the background. To start a command in the background, append an ampersand onto the end of the command. For example, to run the find command in the background try the following:

```
$ find / -name *.c -print > ~/source_files &
```

This command will search your entire hard drive looking for c source code files and when it finds them, it will put the filename into a file in your home directory called `source_files`. Such an operation could take a very long time, which is why is it smart to start the command in the background. You can now go ahead and work on other things while the command is processed behind the scenes.

Sometimes you want to start a command in the foreground but you accidentally forget to add the ampersand onto the end of the command. You can move that job into the background by first suspending it and then using the `bg` command. To suspend the current running job, use Ctrl+Z. If you ran the preceding command in the foreground and then suspended it, you should see a message similar to the following:

```
[2]+  Stopped    find / -name *.c -print >~/source_files
```

You should then get your tcsh prompt back. At that point type the `bg` command at the prompt and the job will continue in the background. A message such as the following should be outputted also:

```
$ bg
[2]+ find / -name *.c -print > ~/source_files &
```

Using the `bg` command gives you the ability to send jobs to the background. However, you can also bring jobs that are running in the background into the foreground. The command to do so is `fg`. Running either `bg` or `fg` without a parameter will result in the command being executed on the current job. tcsh's concept of the current job is the last job that was started by the user, or the last job that changed state due to user intervention. Both `bg` and `fg` also accept a parameter of a job number so that you can move other jobs other than the current job in and out of the foreground and background. For example, to move job 2 into the foreground, type the following command:

```
$ fg 2
```

You can get a list of all currently running processes using the `ps` command. If you execute `ps` without passing any arguments, you will get a list of all jobs that are owned by you. If you weren't doing much, you would get output similar to the following:

```
$ ps
 PID TTY  STAT   TIME   COMMAND
 472 p0   S     00:00   tcsh
2059 p3   S     00:00   ps
```

The number in the leftmost column is the job number. In this case, tcsh has a job id of 472, while the `ps` command has a job id of 2059. Passing a few more parameters to `ps` can get you some very interesting information. A very common operation of `ps` is to output every running process on a system. To do that, type the following:

```
$ ps aux
```

You should see quite a large list outputting from that command. There is a lot of interesting information in that output, including the job id for every process as well as the owner for each process.

Now that you know how to find the job id for each job, you can use that information to manipulate jobs. A very useful operation is the ability to kill jobs. The `kill` command is used to perform such an operation and the syntax for the command is as follows:

```
kill [-s signame ¦ -p ¦ -l] [pid ¦ job]
```

Here, the `-s` parameter is used to send a specific signal to the job, which is given via the signal name or the signal id number. To get a listing of all signal names and numbers, use the `-l` option, which outputs all the available signals. The `-p` option only prints out the process id for the job and will not kill it. You can pass a number to kill as `-n` where n is a number between 1 and 9. The greater the number, the more powerful the kill operation will be. Finally, you must specify a job id on which to perform the kill operation.

Another way to get a listing of all the jobs you are currently running is to use the `jobs` command. The syntax for the `jobs` command is as follows:

```
jobs [-lnp] [jobspec ...]
```

If you pass the `-l` option, `jobs` displays each job's process id as well as the regular information. The `-p` option results in a list of only the process id without any other information. If you pass the `-n` option, `jobs` only displays information on processes that have changed status since the last time `jobs` was called. You can also pass the `jobspec` parameter, which causes `jobs` to return information only about that single job.

Another way to refer to jobs is using the `%` character. Using the `%` character followed by either a job id or job name is similar to using the `fg` command on the same job. The syntax for using the `%` command is as follows:

```
%[id ¦ name] [&]
```

You can use wildcards when passing the job name to `%`. A common usage of `%` is to resume a stopped job in the background by appending the `&` at the end. For example, if you suspend job 34, you can start the job again in the foreground by typing the following command:

```
$ %34 &
```

There are also various other uses of the % command. Both %% and %+ refer to the current job, and %- refers to the previous job.

Another useful command available under tcsh for use in job control is the `notify` command. The `notify` command is used to tell the shell to send a message to the user whenever a change occurs to the status of any specified jobs. The syntax for the command is as follows:

```
notify [%job ...]
```

You can pass the job as a number, a string with the name of the job, or any of the shorthand commands representing jobs such as %, %%, %+, and %-. If you do not pass any job parameters, the current job is assumed.

Any jobs that are currently running can also be stopped using the `stop` command. The syntax for the `stop` command is as follows:

```
stop %job¦pid ...
```

Again, you can pass the specified job in the same way that the `notify` command accepts job specification. Also, if no job is specified, the current job is assumed.

To suspend your shell, you can use the `suspend` command. This is useful if the shell was started within another shell or with the `su` command because it will cause the current shell to stop and you will be returned to your previous shell. You can start the shell again using the `fg` command.

The last command covered here involving job control under tcsh is the `wait` command. The `wait` command causes the shell to wait for all background jobs to finish. This command is of more use when writing shell scripts and you do not want the script to end until all the jobs it spawns are finished. However, if started during an interactive shell, the user will be unable to enter any commands until all the background jobs are done. If you send an interrupt (Ctrl+Z) to the `wait` command, you will regain control of the command prompt and `wait` will print out the names and job ids of all the commands still executing in the background.

Built-In Commands

tcsh has a number of built-in commands that are part of the shell. Many of the commands you'll use regularly are actually not part of the shell, but instead are executable files. For example, `ls` is an executable file located in `/bin/ls`, and is not part of tcsh.

Some of the basic built-in commands have already been covered, such as alias, jobs, fg, and history. Here are some others that are also available:

- bindkey—Allows you to change the actions that are associated with key bindings.

- builtins—Prints out the names of all built-in commands.

- pwd—Prints out your present working directory.

- exec—Executes the specified command in place of the current shell.

- nice—Sets the scheduling for the shell to a number. The higher the number, the less cpu the process gets.

- printenv—Prints the names and values for all environment variables, or if a specific variable name is passed to it, it will only print information on that variable.

- eval—Evaluates any argument that is passed to it and displays the result.

- logout—Logs you out from the current shell.

- umask—The user file-creation mask is set to MODE. If MODE is omitted, or if -S is supplied, the current value of the mask is printed. The -S option makes the output symbolic; otherwise an octal number is output. If MODE begins with a digit, it is interpreted as an octal number, otherwise it is a symbolic mode string like that accepted by chmod.

- exit—Exits the shell with a status of N. If N is omitted, the exit status is that of the last command executed.

- set—Allows you to set the value for a shell variable.

- unset—Removes a variable.

- cd—Changes your present working directory to the directory you pass as an argument.

- source—Reads in the contents of any files passed to the command, and executes those contents.

- bg—Puts any jobs passed to it into the background, continuing any jobs that are stopped. You can pass a number of a string when referring to jobs.

- fg—Puts the job passed to it in the foreground.

- where—Prints out all known information about any command that is passed to it, including aliases, built-in commands, and executables in the path.

Key Bindings

A very nice feature of tcsh is the ability to set your own key binding and also to change any existing key bindings to your liking. tcsh allows you to bind keys to any Linux command and you can also enable either vi or emacs key bindings for command-line editing.

You can examine and set all key bindings using the `bindkey` command. To get a listing of all the current key bindings that are set under your tcsh session, simply type the `bindkey` command by itself on the command line:

```
$ bindkey
```

You should get quite an extensive list of key bindings, giving you an idea how powerful this feature is under tcsh.

There are two different syntax methods available to `bindkey`. The first form is simply used to view existing key bindings for editing or to set your editing key bindings to a specific mode:

```
bindkey [-l¦-d¦-e¦-v]
```

The `-l` option gives a listing of all editing commands along with a short description for each one. The `-d` parameter binds all keys to the bindings of your default text editor. The `-e` option binds all keys to bindings similar to GNU emacs key bindings. Finally, the `-v` option binds all keys to the vi standard key bindings.

The second method of calling `bindkey` is used for displaying and modifying the key binding for a specific key, or creating new key bindings. Here is the command-line syntax:

```
bindkey [-a] [-b] [-k] [-r] [-c] [-s] [--] key [command]
```

Passing the `-a` parameter allows you to either list or change the key bindings in the vi key-binding set. The `-b` parameter tells `bindkey` to interpret the key as a control character. The `-k` option is used to specify an arrow key; it should be followed by either `down`, `up`, `left`, or `right`. The `-r` option is used to remove a key binding. The `-c` option tells `bindkey` to treat the command as a built-in or external command rather than an editor command. There is also the `-s` option, which tells `bindkey` to take the command passed to it as a literal string so special controls characters are ignored. Finally, the `--` option tells `bindkey` to treat the next word as the key to bind, even if the next word begins with a `-` character.

When writing control characters to specify a key binding, the control character (Ctrl) is usually specified using the ^ character. So the key combination of Ctrl+A is written as ^A. The Ctrl key can also be specified using the C character, such as C+A. The Alt key is usually specified using the M character, so Alt+A is written as M+A.

Both keys and commands can also contain backslashed escape sequences, such as the following:

- \a = Bell

- \b = Backspace

- \e = Escape

- \f = Form feed

- \n = Newline

- \r = Carriage return

- \t = Horizontal tab

- \v = Vertical tab

- \nnn = The ASCII character that corresponds to the octal number nnn

As usual, an additional backslash character can be used to nullify the special significance of the backslash. So to just get one normal backslash, use two backslashes.

Here is a simple example of using the `bindkey` command:

```
$ bindkey ^C clear-screen
```

In this case, we are binding the `clear-screen` command to the key combination of Ctrl+C. Now after setting that keybinding, any time you type Ctrl+C the screen will be cleared. Here is another example:

```
$ bindkey ^U upcase-word
```

Now the key combination of Ctrl+U has been bound to the command `upcase-word`. The `upcase-word` command capitalizes any letters from your cursor to the end of the current word. You can capitalize any word your cursor is on by using the Ctrl+U key combination.

Here are some of the basic key bindings that are defined in tcsh by default:

- ^F = forward-char—Moves the cursor forward by one character.

- ^B = backward-char—Moves the cursor back by one character.

- ^A = beginning-of-line—Moves the cursor to the start of the command-prompt line.

- ^E = end-of-line—Moves the cursor to the end of the command-prompt line.

- ^H = backward-delete-char—Moves backward by one character, deleting the character.

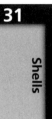

- ^K = kill-line—Deletes the contents of the entire line.

- ^L = clear-screen—Clears the entire screen.

- ^R = redisplay—Redisplays the screen.

- ^N = down-history—Moves to the next command in the history list.

- ^P = up-history—Moves to the previous command in the history list.

As you are probably starting to realize, the key-binding feature of tcsh is quite complex and very powerful.

Startup and Shutdown for Interactive Sessions

When you begin an interactive tcsh session, there are several files that tcsh reads in before giving you a command-line prompt. These files are used to customize your tcsh environment. If you want to set up standard aliases or set various shell variables, the tcsh startup files are the place to do it. There are several files involved in the tcsh startup process. The first files that tcsh reads are /etc/csh.cshrc and /etc/csh.login, which are the global tcsh startup scripts for your Linux system. Whenever any user logs in to the system, both of those files will be executed if they use tcsh. The /etc/csh.cshrc and /etc/csh.login files are a great place to set up a standard tcsh environment.

After reading the files from the etc directory, tcsh looks for one of several files in your home directory. It tries to locate each of the following files in order, and the first one that exists gets executed. The files are ~/.tcshrc and ~/.cshrc. It is within these files that individual users can customize their tcsh environment, including overwriting any settings that were specified in /etc/csh.cshrc and /etc/csh.login. After reading in one of those files, tcsh then reads in the ~/.history file, after which it reads in the ~/.login file, and then finally tcsh reads in the ~/.cshdirs file. The order of the files can be changed by compile-time options.

It is possible to tell tcsh to not read some of its startup files. Passing the -f options to tcsh causes tcsh to ignore the ~/.tcshrc file.

Some other parameters that you can pass to tcsh upon startup include the following:

- -Dname[=value]—Allows you to set up an environment variable of name and set it to value.

- -l—Makes tcsh act as if it has been invoked as your login shell.

- -v—Sets tcsh to be in verbose mode and thus all commands that are entered are echoed after history substitution.

- -x—Causes commands to be echoed to the standard output immediately before they are executed.

You can also start tcsh from within another shell or from within tcsh itself. This is called a non-login interactive shell. For non-login interactive shells, all startup files are ignored except for /etc/csh.cshrc and ~/.tcshrc or ~/.cshrc. When planning your startup files, put commands that only need to be executed once per login with your ~/.login file. Commands that should be executed at the start of all shells, even non-login shells, should go into either your ~/.tcshrc or ~/.cshrc file.

When tcsh exits from a login shell, the /etc/csh.logout file is read and executed first, followed by the ~/.logout file.

Automatic, Periodic, and Timed Events

Under tcsh, there are several ways of setting up commands to run at various times when you are using the shell. Several variables control this command automation. Here are a few:

- autologout—Sets this variable to the number of minutes that can pass without any activity before you are automatically logged out.

- mail—This variable can be set to the number of minutes between automatic mail checks.

- rmstar—If this variable is set, whenever the user types the command rm *, the shell will ask for confirmation before executing the command.

- printexitvalue—If this variable is set, it will print the exit status of any command that exits with a status other than zero.

Variables

The topic of tcsh's shell variables has come up a number of times. This section examines them in a bit more detail. There are quite a few shell variables that tcsh uses for controlling its appearance and environment. You can customize your tcsh environment by modifying the contents of those variables. Variables are represented by a name, which is called an identifier. Variables can contain a value—the set command is used to assign that value and the value can be extracted by putting a dollar sign in front of the variable name. To print out the contents of the shell variable path, simply use the echo command and add a dollar sign in front of the variable's name. For example

```
$ echo $path
```

You should get the contents of your path variable outputted to your screen, which should consist of a bunch of directories separated by colons.

tcsh has quite an extensive collection of shell variables. The tcsh man page describes all of them and you can access the man page by executing the following command:

```
$ man tcsh
```

Following are some of the more common tcsh variables, along with a brief description of each:

- argv—Contains any arguments passed to the shell; $argv[1] being the first argument, $argv[2] being the second, and so on.

- color—If it is set, this variable enables color display for the ls command.

- pathj—The search path for commands. Contains a list of directories (separated by colons) in which the shell looks for commands.

- home—The home directory for the current user.

- prompt—The primary prompt string used by bash when displaying the command line.

- prompt2—The secondary prompt string, used when the shell needs more information.

- prompt3—The third prompt string, used when confirming automatic spelling corrections.

- nobeep—If set, all beeping is completely disabled.

- noclobber—If set, the shell insures that files are not accidentally destroyed during output redirection operations and also that ">>" redirections refer to existing files.

- noglob—If set, globbing is turned off.

- histfile—The name of the file to which the command history is saved. The default is ~/.history.

- history—The maximum number of history events to save.

- cwd—The current working directory.

- edit—The default editor for many programs and utilities.

- status—The status returned by the last command.

- version—Contains the version ID stamp.

- `term`—Contains the terminal type.

- `user`—The user's login name.

The value of a variable can be changed at any time by using the `set` command. When using the `set` command, first pass the variable name followed an equal sign and then pass the new value you want to assign to that variable. For example, if you want to change the maximum number of events in your history to be 300, issue the following command:

```
$ set history=300
```

Experiment with the preceding variables—first try using the `echo` command to see the value contained in each variable. Then start changing the values of some of the variables and see how that affects your tcsh environment. You can also add data onto the existing content within variables by trying a command such as

```
$ set path="$path:/usr/local/bin"
```

Here, `path` is set to be equal to the entire contents of the current path variable plus the value `":/usr/local/sbin"`. If your previous path variable contained `"/bin:/usr/bin:/usr/local/bin"`, your new path variable will now contain the string `"/bin:/usr/bin:~/bin:/usr/local/bin"`.

Editing the Command Prompt

Just like bash, tcsh has multiple levels to the command prompt. Instead of having only two levels, however, tcsh has three levels. The first level is what you see when tcsh is waiting for you to type in a command. This is controlled by the variable `prompt`. The default value for `prompt` is simply the `%` character. The second-level prompt is displayed when tcsh requires further input from the user to complete a command. This is controlled by the variable `prompt2`. The default value for `prompt2` is `%R?`, with `%R` being a special character code that displays the status of the tcsh parser. The third-level prompt is used along with the automatic spelling feature. After an automatic spelling correction takes place the prompt changes to this. The third-level prompt is controlled by the value of the variable `prompt3`. The default value for `prompt3` is `CORRECT>%R (y¦n¦e)?`.

The `set` command can by used to customize your prompts. A simple level one prompt can be achieved with the following command:

```
$ set prompt="%/$ "
```

Your first-level prompt should now be set to your current working directory plus the dollar sign. Both `prompt2` and `prompt3` can be changed in the same manner.

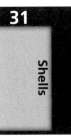

As with bash prompts, tcsh also supports special character codes that enhance your prompt and generally make your prompt more exciting. They are

- %/—Displays the current working directory.

- %n—Displays the current user's login name.

- %m—Displays the hostname you are running the shell on.

- %y—Displays the current year.

- %w—Displays the current month.

- %d—Displays the current day of the week.

- %t—Displays the current time.

- %h or %!—Displays the history number of the current command.

You can also perform simple text formatting on the contents of your prompt:

- %B...%b—Anything between the %B and the %b will be bolded.

- %U...%u—Anything between the %U and the %u will be underlined.

With a little bit of effort you can create an elegant and informative prompt. A good place to set up your prompt would be inside your startup files.

In addition to the ability to customize your prompts, tcsh also has a special feature that allows the user to specify a command to be executed before displaying each prompt. There is a special variable called precmd whose contents will be executed as a command before each prompt is displayed. Use the alias command to create and define the precmd variable. For example, to have the date command executed before every prompt try the following command:

```
$ alias precmd date
```

Now before each command prompt you should see the output of the date command.

Advantages and Disadvantages of tcsh

tcsh is a very advanced shell and has some very nice features that most other shells don't have, such as spelling correction and the ability to change key bindings. If you are a C shell user, you probably want to use tcsh as your default shell under Linux, especially if you have a collection of shell scripts that you have written under the C shell.

tcsh also has it share of disadvantages. These days, it seems that almost everyone is using bash and thus most scripts are written for bash. While it isn't a lot of work to get those scripts working under tcsh, it is work nonetheless.

Other Shells

There are many different shells available under Linux in addition to bash and tcsh. The following sections look at two of the more popular ones, zsh and pdksh.

The Z Shell

The Z shell, known as zsh, is one of the newer shells available and has many advanced features, especially as a shell scripting language. The Z shell has many original features while also incorporating the best features from many of the older shells, including bash, ksh, and tcsh. The Z shell was originally written to be compatible with the Korn shell, and in fact, it resembles the Korn shell more closely than any other shell. zsh's compatibility with the Korn shell has been gradually increasing over time. The Korn shell is one of the original UNIX shells that was very powerful for its time.

Some of zsh's features include the following:

- Command-line editing
- Advanced globbing
- Named directories
- Comprehensive integer arithmetic ability
- Array manipulation
- Spelling correction

zsh also boasts an incredibly powerful programming interface—almost every command can be customized and enhanced. No other shell is as powerful as zsh in this area.

zsh is distributed under a standard BSD-style license.

The Public Domain Korn Shell

The Public Domain Korn shell was written by David Korn. The Korn shell was the third major shell written for UNIX, after both the Bourne and the C shells, and thus it borrows features from both of its predecessors. Unfortunately, the Korn shell is a commercial shell and it is not available for free. However, a free clone was created called the Public Domain Korn Shell (pdksh).

The Public Domain Korn Shell supports many of the same features found in bash and tcsh, such as the following:

- Wildcards

- Aliases

- Command-Line completion

- Input and Output Redirection

- Command history

- Pipelines

- Job control

The pdksh is great if you are a Korn shell user and you are looking for a free replacement that is available for Linux.

Summary

This chapter looked at shells under Red Hat Linux, with emphasis on the two most popular shells, bash and tcsh. It is important for a system administrator to have a very firm grasp on using shells, and this chapter should have given you an appreciation of the power available at the command line of a Linux shell.

Shell Scripting

In This Chapter

- Introduction to Shell Scripting   *968*
- Shell Scripting Using bash   *972*
- perl Scripting   *1007*
- Other Languages   *1010*
- Programming Tools   *1014*

Introduction to Shell Scripting

Shell scripting adds a whole new dimension to the Linux shell; it gives you the ability to program your shell's interpreter. When normally working in a shell, you are using the shell's interactive mode, which involves entering a command at the shell prompt and then having the shell immediately execute that command. Shells also have another mode known as non-interactive mode, which was touched upon lightly in the last chapter. Non-interactive mode involves putting a series of commands into a text file and then telling the shell to execute the commands in that file. The text file that contains the shell commands is known as a shell script, and the process of the shell interpreter reading in the script and executing the commands in that file line-by-line is known as scripting. This chapter looks in detail at shell scripting using the bash shell, which is the most popular shell in the Linux world. It also lightly touches upon the scripting language perl, which has become an indispensable tool for many system administrators. perl combines features found in shells, various utilities such as sed and awk, and programming languages such as C into a single scripting language. This chapter also looks at the importance of shell scripting and selecting your script shell as well as offering some sample scripts.

After reading this chapter, you should be ready to tackle many system administration tasks using bash shell scripts. You will also have a firm grounding in using perl and other scripting languages such as Tcl/Tk and Python.

The Importance of Shell Scripting

The job of a Linux system administrator involves many tedious, repetitious tasks using shells. Whether you are performing backups, cleaning up the filesystem, or performing any other task that is done from the command line on a regular basis, shell scripts allow you to automate these tasks. Once you have the script written, you can run it any number of times simply by typing in the name of the script on the command line. You also have the option of automating the execution of the script using utilities such as cron and at. Scripts also have the benefit of allowing you to solve a problem once, and then utilize the results of your solution countless times. As a system administrator, learning how to write shell scripts will only benefit you and make your life easier. The initial effort of learning how to program bash will be greatly outweighed by the benefits you will receive in the long run.

The Shell Script Defined

A shell script is just a regular text file into which you put commands that you would normally type at the command prompt. In addition, most shells have many standard programming constructs built in that allow you perform conditional execution of statements, multi-branched program execution, all types of loops, and the modularization of statements into subroutines or functions. If you have a programming background in any language such as C/C++, Lisp, or Fortran, you will find that your knowledge of program design and construction will benefit you greatly. Learning shell programming is then simply a matter of learning the syntax of the shell, and can normally be done in a few hours. If you are new to programming, do not feel intimidated by the idea of learning a programming language. The best way for you to learn is to try all the examples that are given in this chapter and play with them—add new features and modify the programs to your liking. Before you know it, you will be an expert at writing shell scripts.

Traditionally, there are two main flavors of shell scripting syntax available: the syntax descended from the Bourne shell and the syntax descended from the C-Shell. Many modern shells, such as bash, adopt the Bourne shell type syntax because of the Bourne shell's popularity and widespread usage. This chapter focuses on the bash shell for all of our scripts because it is the most commonly used shell in the Linux world. Many of the shell scripts that you will find throughout the Linux community are written for bash. Once you have mastered shell scripting under bash, moving to another shell is simply a matter of taking a glance at the man page for the new shell and seeing what is different. Chances are that very few things will be different between different shells, although this does vary considerably.

The C-Shell scripting syntax still lives on to this day in the tcsh shell. The scripts written in this chapter will not generally work under tcsh. However, modifying the scripts to run under tcsh is not a very difficult task. If you are up for a challenge, try out the scripts in this chapter using tcsh and see if you can get them running error-free. The main difference between scripts written for bash and scripts written for tcsh will be the built-in commands that are available and the syntax of the programming constructs that are available. For instance, although both bash and tcsh have an `if` statement, the syntax for the `if` statement will be different under each shell.

Interpreted Versus Compiled

When a shell executes a shell script, it does so by reading in the file one line at a time and immediately executing that line before going on to the next. This is known as interpreted program execution because each line is interpreted immediately before it is executed. If a syntax error occurs on line 10 in your shell script, you will not discover that error until you reach that line. Interpreted programs have the benefit of quick development time because you do not have to compile the program before you execute it, a process that can be time-consuming especially when you are debugging programs. Also, when you have a program that you want to add features to, an interpreted language usually makes it very quick and easy to do so.

A compiled programming language uses a different approach: Before you execute your program you must run it through a compiler. The compiler checks the syntax of your entire program and then converts it into a native binary format that is executed independently of any interpreter. For a program written in a compiled language, such as C++, the syntax must be correct before it can be executed. This is a benefit because you know that you will not run into any syntax errors halfway through your program. Also, because they are converted to a native binary format before execution, compiled programs run significantly faster. Although compiled programs can eliminate syntax errors, they are still prone to logic errors, which are the bane of many a programmer.

There are benefits to both methods of program execution. Generally, which method you pick is dependent upon the job. For larger applications that need fast program execution, using a compiled language is usually the best approach. When it comes to small utilities and the like, an interpreted language is usually used. For small programs and utilities, you want a quick development time and runtime speed is usually not critical.

Many of the more recent languages that have been developed include features from interpreted languages and features from compiled languages. With these languages, the programmers get the best of both worlds, although there are other weaknesses in such an approach. An example of such a language is perl, which performs a byte-compile on every script before executing it. The byte-compile does a syntax check and compiles the program into a native perl format, which speeds up the program execution. The byte-compile syntax check ensures that there are no syntax errors in your program before executing the first line, and so program execution should be syntax error-free.

Selecting Your Scripting Shell

Because a shell script is just a plain text file with some commands in it, you must be able to specify which scripting language to use for that script file. There are two ways to specify the scripting interpreter to use: You can either pass your script to the interpreter as a command-line parameter or you can specify the path to the interpreter on the first line of your script. If you had a script file written for bash that was called `myscript`, to pass it to bash you could enter the command:

```
$ /bin/bash myscript
```

bash will then take the contents of the file `myscript` and execute them line-by-line. This method can be a little cumbersome because you must remember what interpreter the script was written for. As your library of scripts grows, this can be quite a challenge. The second method is to put the full path to the bash executable as the first line in your script. For example, if the first line of `myscript` was

```
#!/bin/bash
```

you could then execute the script `myscript` without passing it to bash. Notice the two characters before `/bin/bash`—they are absolutely necessary; the# symbol is a comment symbol and it tells bash that this first line is a comment. It is important to put the comment there; otherwise bash will try to execute the line and will only end up starting another instance of bash. The second character, `!`, is also a special character; this tells bash that the line contains the path to the interpreter. bash will use whatever you put after the `!` as the interpreter for the script. Be sure to remember to put the full path to the interpreter on the line because it may not be in your path. You can also pass any command-line parameters to the interpreter on this line.

Making Scripts Executable

Before you can actually execute your script on the command line, you must tell the shell you are using that the file is executable. To do so, use the `chmod` command:

```
$ chmod +x myscript
```

Here, you are changing the attribute of the file myscript to be executable by the owner. The `chmod` command is quite a complex command. To learn more about it, check out the `chmod` man page. After the file is executable, it is a simple matter to execute it—simply type in the filename:

```
$ ./myscript
```

By typing in the filename, your shell will first check if the file is executable. If it is, it will start trying to execute it. Notice the two characters before the script name, `./`. This tells your shell that the script is in the current directory. Normally your current directory is not in your path due to security reasons, and if you do not specify that the script is in the current directory, your shell will not be able to find it.

Executing the Script

When the execution of the script begins, the shell will read in the first line, where it will find the path to the interpreter that will be used to execute the rest of the script. It will then fire up that interpreter and pass along the rest of the file's contents to that interpreter. It is important to keep in mind that your normal login shell plays no role in which shell is used to execute your scripts. You can use tcsh as your normal shell and write scripts for bash under tcsh. bash shell scripts can also be executed under tcsh, or any other shell for that matter.

Standardizing Scripts

An important aspect of any type of programming is standardization. Due to the fact that many shells are available under Linux, there are bound to be differences between the scripting capabilities and features of each shell. It is a good idea to standardize all your shell programming to run using only one single shell. It is up to you to choose your shell; however, the recommended shell is bash. bash is the most widely used shell in the Linux world and is found on virtually every Linux system. Writing your scripts for bash will guarantee that they will run on all of those systems; you cannot be sure that every system has zsh or pdksh.

Also, because you can run bash shell scripts under tcsh or any other shell, programming bash does not require you to change your regular interactive shell to bash. With that said, let's look at scripting for the bash shell.

Shell Scripting Using bash

bash (Bourne Again Shell) is based upon the Bourne shell, and thus it is completely backward-compatible with the Bourne shell. Any scripts written for the Bourne shell will work under bash, which is the default shell for Red Hat. This section examines programming under the bash shell in detail. It looks at bash syntax, variable creation and use, expressions, and control structures, as well as several other topics.

After reading this section you should be familiar with all the main features of bash shell programming and be able to write your own bash scripts. To find out even more about bash you should read the man page for bash, where all of bash's features are described in detail.

bash Syntax

Anything that you can do regularly under bash, you can put into a shell script and tell bash to execute the script. The script is read in line-by-line and every line that is read in gets executed immediately. bash scripts do not have a main function, like more advanced programming languages have, but bash does support capabilities such as control structures, pipelines, and aliasing.

Commenting Your Scripts

A key to writing good code is to comment appropriately. Any programming language, no matter how simple, should include a facility for commenting your code. bash supports comments using the pound character (#), and allows comments to appear anywhere in your program. Placing a comment symbol on a line in your program tells bash to ignore everything else that appears on that line. Here is an example of a bash script with comments:

```
#!/bin/bash
# This is a bash script written to demonstrate comments
echo This program does nothing     # You can start a comment
# anywhere on a line
# this is the end of the program
```

When you run the preceding script, all it does is output the following line:

```
This program does nothing
```

All of the text that follows the pound symbol is ignored by bash, and as you can see, the pound symbols can start anywhere on a line. You should definitely get in the habit of using comments regularly in your bash scripts.

Including Text Blocks

You can include blocks of text in your bash shell scripts by using the << operator followed by an identifier. The identifier signals the start of the text block and the end of the text block. This can be used to include a multiline comment in a shell script. Here is an example of a multiline comment:

```
#!/bin/bash
<< COMMENT
Bash ignores this:
COMMENT
```

You can also output blocks of text using the same method by including the `cat` command before you put the << symbol. For example, the following code outputs a welcome message:

```
#!/bin/bash
cat << MESSAGE
Welcome to my program
Thank you for running it!
MESSAGE
```

Running the preceding program will give you the following output:

```
Welcome to my program
Thank you for running it!
```

This method is useful when you have a lot of text to output because you do not have to put an `echo` command at the start of every line.

bash Exit Codes

A very important aspect of any sort of programming is handling the exit codes of commands and routines. In bash, every command you execute has an exit status and your script also returns an exit status when it terminates. Under bash, an exit status of zero indicates success and a non-zero exit status indicates failure.

If a command is terminated with a fatal signal, an exit value of the signal number plus 128 is generated. If bash tries to execute a command, but that command is not found, an exit value of 127 is returned. If bash tries to execute a command but that command is non-executable, an exit value of 126 is returned.

When a bash script exits, the return value of the script is the exit status of the last command that was executed. If the script runs into a syntax error during execution, it will execute with a non-zero value, indicating the error code.

Creating and Using Variables

Creating your own variables in a bash shell script is identical to creating them on the command line. You simply type a name for your variable followed by the equal sign (=), and then the value you want to assign to your variable. The general syntax is as follows:

```
name=value
```

Here, the name of the variable is represented by `name` and the value is represented by `value`. To assign a value of 10 to a variable called years, you would enter the following:

```
years=10
```

During your shell script, you can manipulate and change the value contained within any variable you create. After assigning a value to a variable, you can access that value simply by putting a dollar sign in front of the variable name. For example, to print out the value of years, use the following statement:

```
echo years = $years
```

When that statement is executed, the value contained within the variable years will put printed out in place of `$years`. If the value of years is 10, executing the preceding statement will generate the following:

```
years = 10
```

bash also has commands that allow you to declare and manipulate variables. The following few sections take a look at those commands.

The `declare` Command

The `declare` command is used to declare variables or to change the attributes of existing variables. Simply calling `declare` without passing a variable name to it will cause `declare` to list all the variables currently declared. `declare` also takes various arguments that allow you to specify which types of variables you would like to see outputted.

Here is the syntax for the `declare` command:

```
declare [-fix] [name[=value]]
```

As you can see, `declare` takes several arguments. They are

- `-f`—Shows only function names.

- `-I`—Changes the variable to be an integer. Any values assigned to the variable will be evaluated arithmetically before being assigned to the variable.

- `-r`—Changes any variable passed to `declare` as read-only. The values contained within those variables will now be fixed until the read-only attribute is removed.

- `-x`—Changes any variable passed to be exported to the environment.

All these options also can be passed using the plus sign (+) instead of the minus sign (-). The plus sign will turn off any of the passed attributes instead of turning them on. The `declare` command will return a value of 0 upon successful execution. Problems can occur if an unknown option is passed, a value is assigned to a read-only variable, or the variable name is illegal or unknown according to the shell.

The `unset` Command

After a variable is declared, it can be used throughout your shell script. However, there is a command available under bash that will remove variables called the `unset` command. This is helpful when you need to disable a function, or, in a long script, when you no longer need a certain variable.

The syntax for the `unset` command is as follows:

```
unset [-f] [name ...]
```

The `unset` command takes a single option, followed by a list of variable names to remove. The `-f` option tells `unset` that the following names refer to functions, not variables. Therefore, you can disable functions using the `unset` command. There are certain special variables that cannot be unset; they are PATH, PPID, PS1, PS2, IFS, EUID, and UID. If any other special variables are unset, they will lose any special properties that they have, even if they are assigned values at a later part in your script.

The return value of unset will be true if the variable exists and is not a special non-unsettable variable.

The `readonly` Command

The readonly command is used to turn regular variables into constant variables whose values cannot be modified. The syntax for the readonly command is as follows:

```
readonly [-f] [name ...]
```

Passing the -f option to readonly tells readonly to treat any names that are passed as function names. If readonly is invoked without any arguments, a list of all variables that are readonly will be printed. If readonly is successful in its execution, it will return a value of 0; if an error occurs it will return a non-zero error code.

Accessing Variables

There are several other methods to access the value of a variable. These might be used to update the variable or perform a simple test on the variable's status. Table 32.1 lists all the methods available for accessing variables under bash.

TABLE 32.1 Alternative Methods of Accessing Variables in bash

Method	Description
$variable	Replaces $variable with the value of variable.
${variable}	Replaces ${variable} with the value of variable. This method is used when there are other characters that immediately follow the variable name and would otherwise be interpreted as part of the variable name.
${variable-word}	Replaces ${variable-word} with the value of variable if variable is set. If variable is not set, the value of word will be used.
${variable+word}	Replaces ${variable+word} with the value of word if variable is set. If variable is not set, the statement is ignored.
${variable=word}	Assigns the value of word to variable if variable is not set. ${variable=word} will then be replaced by the resulting value of variable.
${variable?word}	Replaces ${variable?word} with the value of variable if variable is set. If variable is not set, the value of word will be outputted to standard error.
${#variable}	Replaces ${#variable} with the length in characters of the value inside variable.
${variable#word}	The value of word is expanded to generate a pattern. That pattern is then compared to the beginning portion in variable. If a match occurs, ${variable#word} is replaced with the value inside variable with the shortest matching pattern removed.

TABLE 32.1   continued

Method	Description
${variable##word}	The value of word is expanded to generate a pattern. That pattern is then compared to the beginning portion in variable. If a match occurs, ${variable##word} is replaced with the value inside variable with the longest matching pattern removed.
${variable%word}	The value of word is expanded to generate a pattern. That pattern is then compared to the trailing portion of the value inside variable. If a match occurs, ${variable%word} is replaced with the value inside variable with the shortest matching pattern removed.
${variable%%word}	The value of word is expanded to generate a pattern. That pattern is then compared to the trailing portion of the value inside variable. If a match occurs, ${variable%%word} is replaced with the value inside variable with the longest matching pattern removed.

32

Shell Scripting

Special bash Variables

There are many special variables built in to the shell scripting functionality of bash. Table 32.2 lists some of them in detail. These special variables can be used to pass parameters between the script and the shell.

TABLE 32.2   Special Variables in bash

Variable	Description
$1-$9	These variables are called the positional parameters and each one contains any arguments passed to the shell script. The first argument is passed in the variable $1, the second argument is passed in the variable $2, and so on up to $9.
$0	This variable contains the command that was used to execute the script.
$#	This variable contains the number of positional arguments that were passed to the script. It basically contains the number of position parameters that have a value inside them. If $# contains a 3, that means that $1, $2, and $3 all contain values that were passed to the script on the command line.
$?	This variable contains the exit value of the last command that was executed. If the command was successful, the $? variable will contain a value of 0. If the command was not successful, the $? variable will contain a non-zero value.
$$	This variable contains the process id number of the current shell within which the script is executing. This value is useful for unique logging of data.

TABLE 32.2 continued

Variable	Description
$!	This variable contains the process id number of the last command that was run from the script in the background.
$-	This variable contains all the options that were passed to the current shell upon invocation.
$*	This variable contains every argument that was passed to the shell, separated by spaces.
$@	This variable contains every argument that was passed to the shell, just like $* does. There is a slight difference between the two variables, however. It occurs when the arguments passed to the script contain quotes. In such a case, $@ will keep the arguments exactly as they are passed to the script, whereas $* will strip off any quotes.

Expressions

Expressions are a core concept in shell scripting. Simply put, an *expression* is a statement that has a value associated with it. That value can be used to control program flow. An expression can have two types of values: a true value or a false value. An example of an expression under bash is simply the value of a variable. A variable that has not been set will have a value of false when evaluated, whereas if that variable contains anything, it will have a value of true. Within a system administration environment, you probably want to track things like the number of files and the amount of disk space in use by some or all of your users. You could then warn them when they approach preset limits.

Testing the values of expressions and combinations of expressions is a common operation in shell scripts. The test utility is provided to determine the value of expressions, and bash provides operators for use in performing tests on files and strings.

The test Utility

The test utility allows you to test the value of any expression. It has the following syntax:

```
$ test expression
```

test will return a zero if the expression evaluates to true, or it will return a non-zero value if the expression evaluates to false. The return value of test is generally used in control structures for branching purposes.

When passing several expressions to `test`, you can combine them using logical operators. The available logical operators are

- `!`—The not operator. Returns the opposite value of the expression.
- `&&`—The and operator. Returns true if both expressions are true.
- `||`—The or operator. Returns true if either expression is true.

There are various ways of passing expressions to `test`. This is needed because program logic may require specific answers such as a false when the expression evaluates as true, or when a single answer is based on two or more expressions. Here are some common arguments:

- `( expression )`—Returns the value of the expression. The brackets override any normal operator precedence rules.
- `! expression`—Returns the value opposite of expression. If expression is true, false will be returned.
- `( expression1 ) && ( expression2 )`—Returns true if the value of both `expression1` and `expression2` are true. It is important to note that if `expression1` evaluates to false, `expression2` is ignored completely because its value would not affect the final result.
- `( expression1 ) || ( expression2 )`—Returns true if the value of either `expression1` or `expression2` is true; it returns false otherwise. It is important to note that if `expression1` evaluates to true, `expression2` is ignored completely and a value of true will be returned.
- `!(expression1 && expression2)`—Returns false if the values of both `expression1` and `expression2` are true.
- `expression1 -a expression2`—Returns true if both `expression1` and `expression2` are true.
- `expression1 -o expression2`—Returns true if either `expression1` or `expression2` is true.

Those are some basic combinations of expressions, and you can combine as many expressions as you want. In the end, you will be returned a single value that will be either true or false.

32

Shell Scripting

File Test Operators

One of the command tasks performed under shell scripts is file manipulation. There are many operations available under bash to find out information about files and to perform basic tests on them. As a system administrator, much of your work may be concerned with files stored on the systems you administrate. Using scripts, as well as the following operators, can make it easy to track important files. For instance, you might write a script that notifies you whenever a system configuration file is changed. Table 32.3 lists the tests available under bash. Each test requires a filename upon which the test is performed.

TABLE 32.3 bash File Test Operators and Results

File Test Operator	Result
-a filename	Returns true if a file called filename exists
-b filename	Returns true if a file called filename exists and is a block special file.
-c filename	Returns true if a file called filename exists and is a character special file.
-d filename	Returns true if a file called filename exists and is a directory. (Remember, under Linux directories are really just a type of file.)
-e filename	Returns true if a file called filename exists.
-f filename	Returns true if a file called filename exists and is a regular file.
-g filename	Returns true if a file called filename exists and is set-group-id.
-k filename	Returns true if a file called filename exists and its "sticky" bit is set.
-p filename	Returns true if a file called filename exists and is a named pipe (FIFO).
-r filename	Returns true if a file called filename exists and is readable.
-s filename	Returns true if a file called filename exists and has a size greater than zero.
-t filename	Returns true if a filename refers to an open file descriptor for a terminal.
-u filename	Returns true if a file called filename exists and its set-user-id bit is set.
-w filename	Returns true if a file called filename exists and is writable.
-x filename	Returns true if a file called filename exists and is executable.
-O filename	Returns true if a file called filename exists and is owned by the effective user id.
-G filename	Returns true if a file called filename exists and is owned by the effective group id.
-L filename	Returns true if a file called filename exists and is a symbolic link.

TABLE **32.3**   continued

File Test Operator	Result
-S filename	Returns true if a file called filename exists and is a socket.
-N filename	Returns true if a file called filename exists and has been modified since the last read.
filename1 -nt filename2	Returns true if the file filename1 is newer than the file filename2 (specified by the modification date).
filename1 -ot filename2	Returns true if filename1 is older than filename2.
filename1 -ef filename2	Returns true if both files have the same device and inode numbers.

The file test operators are very useful and really come in handy when you need to find out information about files, or to manipulate certain types of files.

String Test Operators

Manipulating strings is another common task performed using shell scripts. bash has a number of operators for testing strings. Each one takes a string as an argument and tests that string, returning either true or false. Table 32.4 lists the operators available under bash.

TABLE **32.4**   bash String Test Operators and Results

String Test Operator	Result
-z string	Returns true if the string length is zero.
-n string	Returns true if the string length is non-zero.
string	Returns true if the string length is non-zero.
string1 == string2	Returns true if both strings are equal.
string1 = string2	Returns true if both strings are equal.
string1 != string2	Returns true if both strings are not equal.
string1 < string2	Returns true if string1 sorts before string2.
string1 > string2	Returns true if string2 sorts before string1.

Arithmetic Operators

Number crunching is not one of bash's strong points; however, basic number tests are available for testing integers. Each operator takes two integer arguments, one on each side of the operator, and returns the result of the test. These are useful when counting the number of files a user has, or looking at disk usage. Table 32.5 lists the available arithmetic operators.

32

Shell Scripting

TABLE **32.5**   bash Arithmetic Operators

Arithmetic Operator	Results
integer1 -eq integer2	Returns true if both integers are equal.
integer1 -ne integer2	Returns true if both integers are not equal.
integer1 -lt integer2	Returns true if integer1 is less than integer2.
integer1 -le integer2	Returns true if integer1 is less than or equal to integer2.
integer1 -gt integer2	Returns true if integer1 is greater than integer2.
integer1 -ge integer2	Returns true if integer1 is greater than or equal to integer2.

When arithmetic expressions are evaluated by bash, all evaluation is performed using long integers without any overflow checking. Any shell variable upon which arithmetic operations occur will be forced into long integers. If division by zero occurs, the error is trapped by the shell and flagged appropriately. The following operator precedence rules are implemented by bash; the operators are executed according to the precedence rules. Parentheses can be used to override the built-in operator precedence rules. This listing is from greatest to least precedence:

- - +—Unary minus and plus

- ! ~—Logical and bitwise negation

- * / %—Multiplication, division, remainder

- + -—Addition, subtraction

- << >>—Left and right bitwise shifts

- <= >= < >—Comparison

- == !=—Equality and inequality

- &—Bitwise AND

- ^—Bitwise exclusive OR

- ¦—Bitwise OR

bash also supports all types of number bases, including octal, hexadecimal, and binary. Octal numbers are written with a leading 0, and hexadecimal numbers are written with either a leading 0x or 0X. Other number bases are written as follows:

```
[base#]number
```

The word base is written first, followed by a number representing the base. The number can be from 2 to 36. You then must put the actual number that is going to be put into the specified base. Although you can use all types of bases, doing so is not a common operation of shell scripts.

Control Structures

Controlling the flow of a program is crucial to writing complex shell scripts. All the standard control structures that are available in common procedural languages are also available under bash. These are needed because you may want to do different things based on various parameters. For instance, if a user is close to their allotted disk space, you may want to warn them or increase their allotment. This section examines all the control structures that are available under bash, giving an example for each one.

The `for` Statement

The `for` statement is used to loop through a list of values. The loop will iterate once for each value in the list. The syntax for the `for` loop is as follows:

```
for name [ in list ]
do
  command list;
done
```

Here, each value in the list variable is placed into the variable name and then the command list is executed. If the list is not provided, bash uses $@ instead. A useful example of using this statement is as follows:

```
#!/bin/bash
for name in name1 name2 name3
do
  echo $name;
done
```

When executed, this program should output:

```
name1
name2
name3
```

The program loops three times, once for each item in the list. Upon each iteration of the loop, the value for one of the items in the loop is placed into the variable name and then the body of the loop is executed. In this case, the body of the loop is the `echo` command, which prints out the contents of the name variable. Therefore, the purpose of the program is simply to print out each item in the list.

The `case` Statement

The case statement is used when multi-way branching based on the value of a single string is needed. The syntax for the `case` statement is as follows:

```
case expression in
  pattern1 [¦ pattern2 ])
    command list
    ;;
  pattern3)
    command list
    ;;
  *)
esac
```

The case statement takes an expression that evaluates to a string and then compares it to the specified patterns. If a matching pattern is found, the command list under that pattern is executed, after which the shell jumps to the `esac` command. Multiple patterns can be specified for a single command list by separating the patterns with the pipe symbol (¦). Wildcards are allowed in the patterns as well.

Listing 32.1 shows an example of using the `case` statement.

LISTING 32.1   Example of Using the `case` Statement Within a Script

```
#!/bin/bash
echo Bash Menu System
option=0
while test $option -ne 6
do
  cat << MENUHEADER

  Menu Options

  1    => print the name of the current shell
  2    => print out your path
  3,4  => print out your home directory
  5    => print out your present working directory
=> quit the menu

MENUHEADER
echo -n 'Option: '
read option
echo
case $option in
```

LISTING 32.1 continued

```
"1")
  echo $SHELL
  ;;
"2")
  echo $PATH
  ;;
"3"|"4")
  echo $HOME
  ;;
"5")
  echo $PWD
  ;;
"6")
  echo Thanks for using the Bash Menu System!
  ;;

*)
  echo Sorry, invalid option
  ;;
esac
done
```

Here is the output from executing the preceding script:

```
Bash Menu System

    Menu Options

  1    => print the name of the current shell
  2    => print out your path
  3,4  => print out your home directory
  5    => print out your present working directory
  6 => quit the menu


Option: 1

/bin/bash

    Menu Options

  1    => print the name of the current shell
  2    => print out your path
```

```
3,4  => print out your home directory
5    => print out your present working directory
6 => quit the menu

Option: 3

/home/dbarber

    Menu Options

1    => print the name of the current shell
2    => print out your path
3,4  => print out your home directory
5    => print out your present working directory
6 => quit the menu

Option: 6

Thanks for using the Bash Menu System
```

As you can see, the case statement is ideal for parsing a single value and having a multi-way branching structure based upon that single value.

The `if` Statement

The `if` statement is used for conditional branching. The `if` statement takes several forms, based upon complexity. The simplest form of the `if` statement has the following syntax:

```
if list;
then
  command list;
fi
```

Here, the commands in list are executed. If the last command in list succeeds, the commands in command list are executed. If the last command in list fails, nothing is executed. Here is an example of using the `if` statement:

```
#!/bin/bash
secretname=John
echo -n 'Please enter your name: '
read name
```

```
if test $name = $secretname
then
  echo "John!  You made it!"
fi
```

Here is the output from running the preceding script:

```
$ ./secretname
Please enter your name: Derek
$ ./secretname
Please enter your name: John
John!  You made it!
$ ./test2
Please enter your name: john
```

As you can see, only if the user enters in the name "John" will the line inside the `if` statement be executed. The `if` statement can also become much more complex. Here is the full syntax for the `if` statement:

```
if list1;
then
  command list
elif list2;
then
  command list;
else
  list;
fi
```

In this case, the evaluation is performed exactly the same; however, if `list1` evaluates to be false, the shell will then go on to test `list2`. If `list2` is true, its command list will be executed. However, if it is false, the command list under the `else` statement will be executed by default. Here's an example:

```
#!/bin/bash
secretname1=John
secretname2=john
echo -n 'Please enter your name: '
read name

if test $name = $secretname1
then
  echo "John!  You made it!"
elif test $name = $secretname2
then
```

```
  echo "john!  You made it!"
else
  echo "Sorry...I don't know you!"
fi
```

Now, here is the output from the preceding program:

```
$ ./secretname2
Please enter your name: Derek
Sorry...I don't know you!
$ ./secretname2
Please enter your name: John
John!  You made it!
$ ./secretname2
Please enter your name: john
john!  You made it!
```

As you can see, a variety of possibilities exist with the if-then-else constructions. Variables can be tested and program flow can be changed easily based on the lists used and the construction of the `if` statements.

The `while` Statement

The `while` statement is used for repeating a series of commands numerous times. This might occur if you wanted to move the contents of a directory from one server to another. Anytime the script would run, it would check for files in the source directory and move them to the destination. Here is the syntax for the while statement:

```
while list;
do
  command list;
done
```

First, the `while` loop executes the commands contained within `list`. If those commands succeed, the body of the `while` statement is executed. If the commands in `list` fail, the body is not executed and the program execution continues at the first line after the `done` statement.

Let's look at an example of using the `while` statement. The following program continues to ask for a password until the password is entered correctly.

```
#!/bin/bash
password="openup"
guess=0
while test $password != $guess
do
```

```
   echo -n "Please enter the password to continue: "
   read guess
done
```

Running the preceding program gives the following output:

```
Please enter the password to continue: help
Please enter the password to continue: letmein
Please enter the password to continue: openup
```

The while statement will continue to loop until the word "openup" is entered. When openup is finally entered, the script exits immediately.

The `until` Statement

The `until` command is similar to the `while` statement except that `until` will continue to loop until the series of commands in `list` succeed. As long as the commands in `list` fail, the body of the loop will continue to execute. Here is the syntax for the `until` statement:

```
until list;
do
  command list;
done
```

Here is an example of using the `until` statement:

```
#!/bin/bash
number=0
until test $number -gt 0
do
  echo -n "Enter a positive number: "
  read number
  if test $number -lt 0 || test $number -eq 0
  then
    echo "You did not enter a positive number!"
    echo;
  fi
done
```

When you run the program, you should get output similar to the following:

```
You did not enter a positive number!

Enter a positive number: -4
You did not enter a positive number!

Enter a positive number: 20
```

The `until` loop, in this case, will continue to loop until a number that is greater than zero is entered. As soon as a positive number is entered, the script exits.

Built-in Commands

The preceding section looked at the control constructs that are available under bash. They work well for controlling program flow, but provide limited support for accessing and manipulating data. To do that, you can use the built-in commands in the bash shell, which are examined in this section. The bash shell has many built-in commands that can be used in creating your shell programs. This section examines the most useful commands that are available.

The `source` Command

The `source` command is used when you would like to read in and execute the contents of another file. This command is useful when creating large shell scripts because it allows you to break up your program into separate files. It also allows you to put generic routines that you use in many shell scripts into their own files, so that any program that needs access to those routines can simply call the `source` command to use them.

Here is the syntax for the `source` command:

```
source filename [arguments]
```

As you can see, the `source` command takes a filename as an argument. You can also pass additional arguments that will be used as arguments to the file being sourced. If the filename contains a slash, bash will try to find the file based on the exact filename you pass. If the filename does not contain a slash, the file that is passed to source will first be searched for all the directories in your PATH variable. If it is not found there, source will then look for the file in the current directory. After the file is found, it will be read in and executed and the exit value of the last command will be returned. If the file is not found, an exit value of false will be returned. Any arguments that are supplied after `filename` become positional parameters that are passed to `filename`.

The `dirs` Command

The `dirs` command displays a list of directories found on the system. Directories are added to the list using the `pushd` command, and removed using the `popd` command. The `dirs` command works like a stack—items added using the `pushd` command are placed on the top of the stack, and items removed using the `popd` command are taken off the top of the stack. This can be useful to a system administrator especially if new and/or unauthorized directories are being created.

The syntax for the `dirs` command is as follows:

```
dirs [-l] [+/-n]
```

The `dirs` command will return a value of 0 if it executes successfully, otherwise it will return a non-zero value. Passing an illegal option or an invalid n value will cause `dirs` to fail. The `dirs` command also takes a few arguments. They are

- -l—Generates an extended listing with the full path to the home directory. The default list displays the home directory using the tilde character.
- +n—Shows only the nth item in the stack starting from the bottom of the stack and counting up.
- -n—Shows the nth item in the stack starting from the top of the stack and moving down to the bottom.

The `popd` Command

The `popd` command is used to remove directories from the top of the directory stack. The syntax for `popd` is as follows:

```
popd [+/-n]
```

If `popd` is called without any arguments, the top directory on the stack is removed and the command changes the current directory to the new top directory on the stack. Passing the +n parameter will remove the nth directory from the stack, with n calculated from the bottom of the stack counting toward to top. Passing the -n parameter will remove the nth directory from the stack, with n being calculated from the top of the stack counting toward the bottom.

If `popd` is executed successfully, it will return a value of 0, otherwise it will return a non-zero value. Passing an invalid parameter or passing a value for n that is out of range will cause `popd` to fail. If the directory stack is empty when it is called, that will also cause `popd` to fail.

An example of removing the bottom directory from the stack follows:

```
popd +0
```

To remove the directory that is second from the bottom, use the following command:

```
popd +1
```

To remove the third directory from the top of the stack, use the following command:

```
popd -2
```

32

Shell Scripting

Both popd and pushd could be used within a script while searching through directories and checking the files within each directory. These checks might include integrity checks for security reasons, or simply checking the age of files for backup purposes.

The pushd Command

The pushd command is used to add a specified directory to the top of the directory stack, to rotate the directories in the stack, or to add the current working directory to the stack. The syntax for pushd is as follows:

```
pushd [+/-n] [dir]
```

Invoking pushd without any arguments will cause the top two directories in the stack to be exchanged with one another, as long as there are at least two entries in the directory stack. Passing the +n option will cause the directory stack to be rotated, making the nth item from the bottom of the stack to now be the top item. Passing the -n option will also cause the directory stack to be rotated, with the nth item from the top of the stack being moved to the top. Passing a directory to the pushd command will cause that directory to be added to the top of the stack and the shell will change the current working directory to be that directory.

If pushd completes successfully, it will cause the dirs command to be executed as well. If any error occurs, pushd will return a non-zero value, otherwise it returns a 0, indicating success.

The break Command

The break command is used to prematurely exit out of any loop structure, including the for, while, and until loops. The syntax for the break command is as follows:

```
break [n]
```

The break command takes an option argument, which is to specify the number of levels to break out of. This argument is useful when you have nested loops and want to break out of more than just the current loop. If the break command executes successfully, it returns a value of 0.

Here is an example of using the break command:

```
#!/bin/bash
for fruit in apple orange pear grape banana
do
  if test $fruit = grape
  then
    break
```

```
    else
       echo $fruit
    fi
done
```

Here when the program is executed, the following output occurs:

```
apple
orange
pear
```

You will notice that `grape` and `banana` are not printed out, the output stops after `pear`. This is due to the `break` command, which is executed when the fruit variable contains the word `grape`. When the break occurs, the program jumps to the `done` keyword and exits.

The `continue` Command

The `continue` command is similar to the `break` command. The main difference is that whereas the `break` command completely exits the loop, the `continue` command only skips over the current loop iteration. The next loop iteration continues on as normal. This is useful for skipping over parts of code that are within the body of a loop. Here is the syntax for the `continue` command:

```
continue [n]
```

The `continue` command also takes an argument that specifies how many levels of nested loops to skip over and resume program execution. The `continue` command will return a value of 0 if it is successful.

Following is an example of using the `continue` command:

```
#!/bin/bash
for fruit in apple orange pear banana grape apricot
do
  if test $fruit = banana
  then
    continue
  fi

  echo $fruit
done
```

Here is the output from the preceding program:

```
apple
orange
pear
```

```
grape
apricot
```

You will notice that banana is not printed out. This is because when the fruit variable contains the word banana, the continue command is executed and the program jumps up to the for keyword and continues the loop iteration with the next item in the list.

The echo Command

The echo command does exactly what you would think it does. It takes anything passed to it and prints it out, essentially echoing your input.

Here is the syntax for the echo command:

```
echo [-neE] [arg....]
```

There are several parameters you can pass to echo that modify its behavior. These could be used to format the output, making it more readable to the operator. They are

- -n—Does not print a newline character at the end of output.
- -e—Turns on the interpretation of the backslash escape sequences.
- -E—Turns off the interpretation of the backslash escape sequences.

The following backslash escape sequences are recognized by the echo command:

- \a—Alert (usually sounds the bell)
- \b—Backspace
- \c—Suppresses any trailing newline characters
- \f—Form feed
- \n—New line
- \r—Carriage return
- \t—Horizontal tab
- \v—Vertical tab
- \\—Backslash
- \nnn—The character whose ASCII code is nnn (octal)

The value returned from echo is always 0, which is success.

The `eval` Command

The `eval` command forces bash to evaluate any arguments that are passed to it, returning the exit value of the evaluation. If multiple arguments are passed to `eval`, it will concatenate them together into a single command.

The syntax for `eval` is as follows:

```
eval [arg...]
```

`eval` takes no options and if it is invoked with either null arguments or without any arguments, it will always return a value of true.

The `exec` Command

The `exec` command is used to execute external commands without creating any new processes. The syntax for `exec` is as follows:

```
exec [[-] command [arguments]]
```

The `exec` command only takes a single command to execute and any other arguments provided are passed as arguments to that command. A single - character can be passed as well, which causes bash to make the `$0` variable passed to the command to be simply a dash instead of the name of the command.

If the command cannot be executed or is not found, exec will return a status of failure. Otherwise, a value of success will be returned.

The `hash` Command

The `hash` command is used to determine and remember the full pathname of any command that is passed to it. The syntax for the `hash` command is as follows:

```
hash [-r] [name]
```

If the `hash` command is called without any arguments, it prints out all the command paths that are in its list. Passing the `-r` option will cause the command path list to be erased. When any command is passed to `hash`, hash searches all the directories in the `PATH` variable and if it finds the command, it will add it along with its full path to the list.

To add a command to `hash`, try the following command:

```
$ hash gawk
```

The full path to the `gawk` command will now be in the hash list. To view the list, simply type the `hash` command by itself:

```
$ hash
hits    command
```

```
4    /bin/chmod
1    /bin/mkdir
2    /usr/bin/man
3    /usr/bin/pico
0    /bin/gawk
4    /bin/ls
1    /bin/mv
2    /usr/bin/pine
1    /bin/rm
1    /bin/vi
```

Passing two dashes (--) as an argument will turn off any further option checking for all other arguments. If hash is successful it will return a value of 0, otherwise it will return a non-zero value.

The `let` Command

The let command is used to evaluate arithmetic expressions. The syntax is as follows:

```
let arg [arg ...]
```

For every argument that is passed to let, it evaluates it arithmetically and then it returns 1 if the value of the last argument evaluated to 0, otherwise it returns a value of 0.

The `trap` Command

The trap command takes a command as an argument along with a signal. It will then cause the command to be executed whenever the signal is received. Here is the syntax for trap:

```
trap [-l] [command] [sigspec...]
```

You can pass several signals to trap, then whenever any of those signals are received, the specified command will be executed. If a signal value of 0 is specified, the command will be executed when the shell script ends. By omitting the command, any traps set on the specified signals are reset to their original values. If the command is passed as an empty string, the signals are ignored when encountered. By executing trap without any arguments, a listing of all signals and their trap settings is outputted. Passing the -l option to trap will cause trap to list out all signal names with their corresponding numbers.

Signals can be passed by either their name or by their number. All available signals are defined in the file signal.h.

The `exit` Command

The exit command causes the shell script to exit immediately upon encountering the command. The syntax for exit is as follows:

```
exit [n]
```

The n parameter allows you to specify the exit status of the script. If n is not provided, the exit value of the last command that was executed is returned. If a trap has been set to execute upon exit, that command will be executed before the shell exits.

The read Command

The read command is used to read a single line of data from standard input and assign that data to variables. Every word in the input line is put into a different variable; the first word is assigned to the first variable name, the second word is assigned to the second variable name, and so on. Any extra words on the input line are assigned to the last variable name.

Here is the syntax for the read command:

```
read [-r] [name ...]
```

The -r option tells read to process any backslash-newline pairs and to treat the backslash as part of the current line. If no arguments are passed to read, the value of the line is placed into the REPLY variable automatically. The return value for read will always be zero unless it encounters an end-of-file character, which will generate a non-zero error value.

The printf Command

Programmers coming from a C background will be familiar with the printf command. The printf command allows formatting to take place upon the arguments that are passed to it before they are printed out. The syntax for the printf command is as follows:

```
printf format [arguments]
```

Any arguments passed to the printf command are formatted according to the format argument and then they are written to standard output. The format string can contain three types of items: plain characters, which are copied to standard output exactly as they are; character escape sequences, which are processed and sent to standard output; and format specifications. Every format specification grabs the next argument from the argument list and prints out the value of that argument based upon the format specification. The bash printf command accepts all the standard printf formats that exist in C, including some extra format specifications. Here is a list of many of the format specifications available under the bash printf function:

- %d—Displays argument as a signed decimal integer.

- %o—Displays argument as an unsigned octal integer.

- %u—Displays argument as an unsigned decimal integer.

- %x—Displays argument as an unsigned hexadecimal integer using lowercase letters.

- %X—Displays argument as an unsigned hexadecimal integer using uppercase letters.

- %s—Displays the argument as a string.

- -—Left justifies output within the specified field.

- +—Displays a plus sign before positive values and a minus sign before negative values.

- 0 (zero)—Pads a field with leading zeros.

- %b—Expands any backslash escape sequences that are in the corresponding argument.

- %q—Displays the argument in a format that can be reused as shell input.

- %%—Displays an actual percent symbol.

Here's an example of using the `printf` command:

```
#!/bin/bash
printf "%05d\n" 34
printf "Hello my name is %s\n" Derek
printf "%+d %+d\n" 14 -12
printf "%x %X\n" 250 250
```

Now here is the output from the preceding script:

```
00034
Hello my name is Derek
+14 -12
fa FA
```

Because you can embed formatting info, including symbols such as percent signs, nearly all the work of formatting an output string can be built into the `printf` command line, making it very powerful in formatting data. To find out more, type **man printf** at the command line.

The `wait` Command

The `wait` command is used when you want your script to pause until a specified process has finished executing. The syntax for `wait` is as follows:

```
wait [n]
```

The `wait` command takes a parameter of n, which can be a process ID or a job specification. The `wait` command will halt all script execution until the specified process ID or job spec has terminated, and it will then return the status value for that process. If `wait` is invoked without any arguments, it will simply wait until all active child processes of the current process are completed and then return a status value of zero. If an unknown process or job is passed to `wait`, it will return a value of 127.

The suspend Command

The suspend command is used to suspend the execution of the shell script until it receives a SIGCONT signal. Here is the syntax for the command:

```
suspend [-f]
```

You can pass the -f option to suspend, which tells suspend to complain if the calling shell is not a login shell and just to suspend the shell anyway. suspend will return a value of 0 if it executes successfully, or a non-zero error code otherwise. suspend can fail if called from a login shell and the -f option is not passed.

Parsing Command-Line Parameters

You can pass command-line parameters to shell scripts. The arguments will come into your shell script as a number of variables. The variable name of each argument will simply be the number of the argument. The name of your shell script is actually the first argument, so it will be passed in the variable $0. Any other arguments will be passed in the variables $1, $2, and so on. There is also a special variable called $#, which contains the number of command-line parameters passed to your script.

Here is a sample program that outputs any parameters that have been passed to your script:

```
#!/bin/bash

echo The first argument you passed was $1
echo The total number of arguments you passed was $#
echo All of the arguments you passed were:
for param in $*
do
  echo $param
done
```

When you run the program, you should get output similar to the following:

```
$ ./arg how are you doing today?
The first argument you passed was how
The total number of arguments you passed was 5
All of the arguments you passed were:
how
are
you
doing
today?
```

Arguments are a very useful feature of shell scripting under bash. They allow you to pass parameters such as filenames, switches, or numeric values to your scripts. There are several commands that aid in manipulating the arguments passed in to your program. The following sections take a look at those commands.

The `shift` Command

Using `shift` will move the values of the command-line arguments left one position. What that means is that if three command-line arguments were passed to your shell script—$1, $2, and $3—after calling `shift` the value of $3 would be put into $2, the value of $2 would be put into $1, and the value in $1 would be lost.

The syntax for the `shift` command is:

```
shift [n]
```

Passing n to `shift` causes `shift` to move the position parameter of n+1 to $1. If a zero is passed to `shift`, nothing happens. When passing n, it must be a non-negative integer that is less than or equal to $#. If a value greater than $# is passed to `shift`, then no positional parameters are changed. If `shift` executes successfully it returns an return value of 0.

The `getops` Command

The `getops` command provides an interface for processing the positional parameters and arguments that were passed to the script. The syntax for the `getopts` command is as follows:

```
getopts optionstring name [args]
```

The optionstring parameter contains letters for any options that can be passed to the script. If any of the letters in optionstring are followed by a colon, that means the option has an argument that should be passed after the letter, separated from the letter by a space. The specified name parameter is the name for the variable in which to place the current option that is being parsed. If the variable does not exist, it is first initialized, and then filled with the current parameter. Every time `getopts` is executed, it gets the next option from the command line and puts it into the variable specified by name and then puts the index of the next argument in the OPTIND variable. The OPTIND variable is automatically initialized to 1 at the beginning of every shell script. For options that have an argument (specified by the colon), the argument for that option is put into the OPTARG variable.

The `getopts` command also makes use of the OPTERR variable, which determines whether or not to display error messages. If OPTERR is set to 0, error messages are suppressed, otherwise a diagnostic message is printed.

By default, `getopts` parses the values within the positional parameters; however, passing extra arguments with the `args` parameter will cause `getopts` to parse those instead.

Using Functions

You can create your own functions under bash. You could use a function, or a series of functions, to automate the task of creating a new user or deleting an old or expired user. A function definition looks like the following:

```
[ function ] name () { list; }
```

The function is called `name`, and the body of the function is represented by the list of commands between the`{` and `}` characters. Whenever the function is called by its name, the body of the function will be executed. The exit value returned from the function will be the exit value of the last command executed from the body of the function.

Functions allow you to modularize your shell programs. As your scripts get larger, you will find that breaking up your programs into functions produces code that is easier to develop and maintain. Functions also lead to the production of reusable routines that can be used again in other shell scripts. When a function is executed, your shell program jumps to the first line of code in the body of the function and begins execution. It then goes through the body of the function, executing the code line-by-line until the body ends or until it encounters a return statement. It is important to note that the execution of functions do not create any new processes.

Functions can also have arguments passed to them; when calling a function you can pass arguments by putting them after the name of the function. Inside the function the arguments can be accessed using the positional parameters $1-$9, which are local to the function (local variables are covered later). The variable $#, which contains the number of arguments passed to the script, is updated within the function to contain the number of arguments passed to the function. Outside of the function, these values remain unchanged. However within the function, those variables contain new values.

Naming Functions

When creating your functions, it is important to give them meaningful names. When someone looks at your code, he or she should be able to see exactly what your program is doing just by looking at the names of your functions. If you have a function that prints out a string, call that function `print_string`, not `abc`.

The bash shell also supports the recursive calling of functions. A function can call itself any number of times because bash has no limit on how deep recursion can go. Recursion is another topic completely; however, if you know how to use it, feel free to implement it in your bash shell programs.

32

Shell Scripting

Here's an example of using a function:

```
#!/bin/bash

# declare the print_hello function, it prints out a message
function print_hello () {
  echo "Hello...I'm inside a function!"
}

echo "Welcome to this program"
print_hello
echo "Goodbye!"
```

When you run the preceding program, you should get the following output:

```
Welcome to this program
Hello...I'm inside a function!
Goodbye!
```

As you can see, the program begins by executing the 8th line in the program. It then calls the function, which causes it to jump up to the 5th line and execute that. Following that, the program jumps back down to the 10th line and executes that.

The following sections take a look at the `return` and `local` commands, which are both very useful when writing your own functions.

The `return` Command

The `return` command is used with functions to cause a function to exit with a specific return value. The syntax for return is:

```
return [n]
```

The n parameter is optional and represents the return value that the function will exit with if provided. If the n value is not provided, the return value of the last command executed will be sent as the function's return value.

The `return` command can also be used outside of a function. It can be used in conjunction with the `source` command, and if it exists with a script that is called by the `source` command, it will cause `source` to stop executing the file when it encounters the `return` command. In such a case, the value of the `return` command will be sent as the return value for the `source` command.

If the `return` command is used in a regular script within the main body of the script, it will simply return a value of false.

The `local` Command

The `local` command is used to create local variables within functions. A local variable is specific to that function's scope and does not exist outside of that function. A local variable can have the same name as other variables within your script and yet be completely different. Local variables are also accessible to functions that are called from within the function where the local variable was declared.

The syntax of the `local` command is as follows:

```
local [name[=value] ...]
```

If no options are passed to `local`, it simply outputs a list of all the current local variables. If `local` is used outside of a function definition or if an invalid name is passed, it returns a non-zero value indicating failure. If local succeeds in creating the variable, it returns a return value of 0.

That wraps up our look at commands and capabilities that are available within bash scripts. You have seen how to control program flow, use variables, and create functions. Next, we will look at some samples that put these capabilities to use within a system environment.

Some Sample bash Scripts

This section examines a few shell scripts in detail. This should help to give you the bigger picture of programming your own shell scripts. The majority of this chapter has looked at pieces of bash programming; now it is time to put the pieces together and write a few programs that actually do something.

Converting Filenames to Lowercase

Here is a very useful script that converts all filenames in a specified directory to lowercase. If you ever have to work with files that come from a DOS/Windows environment, you will find that many of those filenames are completely uppercase. This program will help in dealing with such files. Here is the code:

```
1  #!/bin/bash
2  # this script converts all file names in a specified directory
3  # to lower case.
4  # When invoking this script pass the directory in which to
5  # perform the upper->lower case routine on.
6  dir=$1
7
8  for oldname in `ls $dir `
9  do
10  newname=`echo $a | tr A-Z a-z `
```

```
11    mv $dir/$oldname $dir/$newname
12 done
13 exit 0
```

Now let's step though the script, line-by-line. The first line tells your shell to use /bin/ bash as the interpreter for this script. Lines 2-5 consist of comments that describe what the program does and how to invoke the program. Line 6 takes the first argument that was passed to your program and assigns it to the dir variable. Line 8 begins a for loop which loops through all the filenames in the directory that were passed to the script. For each loop iteration, the current filename is assigned to the oldname variable. Lines 9-12 consist of the body for the loop and they first define a variable called newname, which is set to the value of oldname after all the letters in oldname have been converted to lowercase using the tr utility. Finally, the filename contained in the oldname variable is moved to the filename contained in the newname variable.

Finding a Specific Word Inside a File

This script takes two arguments: a filename and a word to search for. It then searches the specified file for the word. If the word is found, it prints a message of success, otherwise it prints a message of failure.

```
1  #!/bin/bash
2  # this script searches a file for a specific word
3  # you need to pass two arguments to this script, the first is the
4  # name of the file to search, the other is the word to search for
5  if test $# -ne 2
6  then
7    echo "Invalid arguments!"
8  else
9    filename=$1
10   word=$2
11
12   if grep $word $filename > /dev/null
13     then
14     echo "The word was found!"
15   else
16     echo "The word was not found."
17   fi
18 fi
19 exit 0
```

Now let's examine this script line-by-line. The first line specifies the location of the bash interpreter, and lines 2-4 are comments that tell the user what the program does and how to invoke it. Line 5 tests to make sure two arguments have been passed to the script. If the test is a success the program execution continues, otherwise an error message is printed on line 7. The program then continues on line 9, assigning the variables `filename` and `word` to the first and second arguments, respectively. Line 12 then executes `grep` to search for the word in the specified filename, redirecting all output from grep to `/dev/null`. If the `grep` command is successful, the message on line 14 is outputted, otherwise the message on line 16 is outputted.

Debugging Shell Scripts

When you have a shell script that contains errors, it can be a very time-consuming process to find and eliminate those errors. Luckily, bash has a few features that help with debugging your shell scripts. There is an argument that you can pass to bash that prints out each command and any arguments as they are executed. It is the `-x` option. To use it in your shell scripts, change the first line of your scripts to the following:

```
#!/bin/bash -x
```

The `-x` option will show you the exact point at which any errors occur in your program.

Another useful option is the `-e` option, which puts the shell into non-interactive mode causing it to exit immediately if any command fails. Passing the `-v` option to bash will cause it to print out all shell input lines as they are read. Again, this option helps you track down exactly where the error is occurring in your program. bash also has a `-n` option that tells it to only read in commands without executing them.

Here is a script that has an error in it:

```
#!/bin/bash
var1=testvar1
var2=testvar2
if [ $var1 = "testvar1" ]
then
 echo var1 is equal to $var1
fi
if [ $var2 = "testvar2" ]
then
```

```
  echo var2 is equal to $var2
fi
if [ $var3 = "testvar3" ]
then
  echo var3 is equal to $var3
fi
exit 0
```

When this script is run, it will give the following output:

```
var1 is equal to testvar1
var2 is equal to testvar2
./debug: [: =: unary operator expected
```

This output doesn't really tell you that much; by changing the first line of the program to #!/bin/bash -x, you can get a lot more information out of bash. Here is the output from the program when the -x option is added:

```
+ [ -f /etc/bashrc ]
+ . /etc/bashrc
++ PS1=[\u@\h \W]\$
+ var1=testvar1
+ var2=testvar2
+ [ testvar1 = testvar1 ]
+ echo var1 is equal to testvar1
var1 is equal to testvar1
+ [ testvar2 = testvar2 ]
+ echo var2 is equal to testvar2
var2 is equal to testvar2
+ [ = testvar3 ]
./debug: [: =: unary operator expected
+ exit 0
```

Now you can see exactly where the problem is. It is with the variable testvar3—it is not defined before the test takes place and thus it returns an error.

As you can see, the -x option can aid greatly in debugging shell scripts, especially when your scripts get large. When you are in the process of debugging your scripts, it never hurts to pass the -x option to bash.

Once you have mastered shell scripting, you may want to move on to other types of scripting/programming. One language that is commonly used with Linux systems is perl, which is covered in the next section.

perl Scripting

perl, like Linux, is another free software success story. perl stands for Practical Extraction and Reporting Language, although its creator, Larry Wall, has been known to also call it the "Pathologically Eclectic Rubbish Lister." Larry Wall created perl a number of years ago when he found that he couldn't accomplish what he wanted with shell scripting and the various UNIX utilities. He decided to create a general-purpose scripting language whose specialty was originally text and file manipulation. Larry released perl to the Internet community under an open license and very soon he had people all around the world improving and enhancing perl. As of today, perl has evolved into an extremely powerful and flexible language used by many programmers worldwide. Due to perl's strong text-processing ability, it has also become a language core to the development of many Internet sites. For systems administrators, perl's text and file manipulation capabilities can be quite helpful.

Features of perl

perl combines features found in shells, various utilities such as sed and awk, and programming languages such as C into a single scripting language. Thus, perl is able to perform many complex tasks by itself, which previously had to be solved using a combination of tools. By lumping so many features into a single tool, perl ignores the traditional UNIX philosophy of having every tool perform a single task.

perl is best suited for the following tasks:

- Rapid prototyping
- Building software development tools
- Building system administration tools
- Building system utilities
- Database access
- Network programming
- Internet programming

This section takes a quick look at how to get started programming in perl and where you should look next for more information.

Getting Started with perl

perl is an interpreted language, just like bash, so you create your perl scripts the same way. The main difference in creating your perl scripts is that you must change the first line to refer to the perl executable instead of the bash executable. The first line of every perl program should look like this:

```
#!/usr/bin/perl
```

You can also pass command-line arguments to the perl executable. A commonly passed argument is -w, which turns on warnings. If you pass -w, your first line will look like this:

```
#!/usr/bin/perl -w
```

As with shell scripts, you must also make your scripts executable before you can run them. Again, you use the chmod command:

```
chmod +x scriptname
```

perl borrows the comment symbol from the shell scripting syntax and uses the pound symbol (#). perl also uses the same structure as shell scripts; there is no "main" function like C. perl takes the entire script as simply a collection of statements to execute.

Although perl is an interpreted language, it actually completely reads in your script, performs a syntax check, and compiles it into an internal format before execution takes place. This feature of perl is very enticing because it combines the syntax checking of compilation with the rapid deployment of interpreted languages.

So, exactly what does a perl program look like? Here is the standard hello world program:

```
#!/usr/bin/perl -w
print "Hello, world!\n";
```

To run the program, don't forget to make it executable using the chmod command. When you run it you should get the following output:

```
Hello, world!
```

In the preceding program, the print function is used to output data to the screen. In this case, the output is simply a string. The control character \n tells print to output a newline character.

Here is a slightly more complicated program that uses variables and also gets input from the user:

```
#!/usr/bin/perl -w
print "Enter your name: ";
$name = <STDIN>;
```

```
chomp($name);
print "Enter your age: ";
$age = <STDIN>;
chomp($age);
print "Well $name, it seems you are $age years old.\n";
```

Executing this program will give output similar to the following:

```
Enter your name: Joe Nobody
Enter your age: 25
Well Joe Nobody, it seems you are 25 years old.
```

The program first prints out a message, asking for your name. It then uses the <STDIN> construct to grab a line of data from standard input and puts that data into the variable name. The chomp function that follows removes the end-of-line character from name. The program then asks for your age, and puts your response into the variable age. Finally, the program prints out a message with your name and age as part of the message.

perl Control Structures

perl supports all the standard control structures, including if..else, while, and until loops, for statements and many other structures.

Here's a program that uses some of these control structures:

```
#!/usr/bin/perl -w
$age = 0;   # initialize the age variable
until (($age > 0) && ($age < 150)) {
  print "Please enter your age: ";
  chomp($age = <STDIN>);
  if (($age <= 0) || ($age >= 150)) {
    print "Invalid age!\n";
  }
}
if ($age < 20) {
  print "You are young!\n";
} elsif ($age < 60) {
  print "You are getting old!\n";
} else {
  print "You are old!\n";
}
```

If this program is saved to a file called age, the output is as follows:

```
$ ./age
Please enter your age: 500
```

```
Invalid age!
Please enter your age: 20
You are getting old!
$ ./age
Please enter your age: 5
You are young!
```

The preceding program uses both the until and the if constructs to control the flow of the program. The purpose of the program is to get you to enter your age and then print a message out that depends upon your age range. The until loop is there for error checking. It makes sure that the user does not enter an age that is less that 1 or is greater than 149. If the user enters an invalid age, an error message is printed and the loop continues. After a valid age is entered, a message is printed and then the program exits.

Additional perl Resources

You should now have an idea of what perl is and what perl code looks like. There are many books available on perl that you should read if you are interested in learning perl. After learning perl, you will find that you will be spending more and more time writing perl scripts and less time writing shell scripts. perl is much more flexible and powerful than any shell scripting language.

There are also many Internet resources that aid in learning perl. The best place to start is www.perl.com, which has an extensive collection of documentation about perl including all the best links to other perl sites.

Other Languages

There are also many other languages available under Red Hat Linux that can greatly aid in system administration tasks. This section looks at three of the more popular languages: Tcl/Tk, Python, and Eiffel.

Tcl/Tk

Tcl (pronounced tickle) stands for the Tool Command Language and it is a scripting language that borrows features from C and csh, while also incorporating its own. Tk is a graphical library, originally written for the X Window System, that provides a toolkit for creating graphical user interfaces. Almost from the beginning, both Tcl and Tk were written to support each other, although today you can write Tk-based applications using many other languages such as perl and Python. In addition, Tcl/Tk has been ported to both Windows and Mac platforms providing a platform-independent development environment.

A Tcl/Tk program can be written on Linux and then you can take that program and run it on any platform that has a Tcl/Tk interpreter, including the Windows and Macintosh platforms. The program will also retain the native look and feel for the platform it is running under, so the same program running under Windows will look like a Windows application, and if run under Linux, it will have a Motif look.

John Ousterhout originally developed Tcl/Tk while he was a professor at the University of California at Berkeley. Today, John has formed his own start-up company called Scriptics and continues to develop the free core language while providing value-added commercial products and services.

Tcl/Tk has many advantages as a scripting language including

- It is an easy-to-learn language.
- It is freely available.
- It is very flexible.
- Many extensions are freely available.
- Commercial support is available.
- It is cross-platform.

It is very easy to create very powerful applications with only a few lines of code using Tcl/Tk. System administration tasks can be easily scripted within a GUI environment with Tcl/Tk, which can simplify their use by inexperienced staff. For example, here is a program that displays the text "Hello, world!" in a graphical window:

```
button .b -text "Hello, World!" -command exit
pack .b
```

Tcl/Tk is also widely used. Of all the scripting languages currently available, Tcl/Tk seems to be making the biggest impact in the Windows developer market. Many Windows developers seem to be attracted to Tcl/Tk due to its support for GUI application development.

Another very attractive feature of Tcl/Tk is its extendibility. It allows you to extend the language's functionality without having to learn any of the internals of the language. Today, many extensions are available, so chances are there is a Tcl/Tk extension available for almost every common problem. Before writing any Tcl/Tk code, check to see if there is an extension available that provides many of the features you wanted to implement.

Python

Python is a newer language and was developed originally by Guido van Rossum as part of the Amoeba operating system at CWI in the Netherlands. Python was first released on the Internet under an open license in 1991, and the number of supporters has grown rapidly ever since.

Just like many other scripting languages, Python is an interpreted language. Its strong point, however, is its object-oriented features, which were incorporated into the language from the beginning. Python also has many other features, including the following:

- Modules

- Exceptions

- Dynamic typing

- Very high level dynamic data types

- Cross-platform

- Classes

- Very clear syntax

- Interfaces to many system calls and libraries

- Various GUI toolkits

Python is known as a very extensible and flexible language—it is easily incorporated into other programs that require a scripting language. It is also very easy to add components onto Python, and such components can be loaded into the interpreter dynamically, upon demand.

Python also has several drawbacks. Just like any other language, it is not for use in every situation. Here are some of Python's weaker points:

- Unsuitable for writing device drivers

- Slow for floating point operations

- Slow for data compression algorithms

- Unsuitable for writing very large, monolithic applications

Python is currently being used extensively as an Internet programming language. Python is especially known for its ability to process and format HTML, and is an excellent CGI programming language. In addition, python's network protocol implementations are very easy to use and extremely powerful and flexible. Python's text manipulation ability is extremely powerful and is very fast.

Python has been used for several significant projects including a Web browser called Grail, a multimedia teleconferencing tool, and a virtual reality engine. The entire student administration system, called TELE-Vision, at the University of California, Irvine, was written in Python. Also, the Melbourne Cricket Ground in Australia wrote its scoreboard system in Python.

Many people are moving from perl to Python due to Python's greater support of object-oriented programming and it's cleaner syntax, which produces code that is generally easier to maintain than perl.

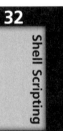

Eiffel

Eiffel is an advanced object-oriented programming language and is very pure in its implementation of object-oriented principles and concepts. Eiffel focuses upon high-quality software design and construction and also the reusability of components. Eiffel goes beyond the standard object-oriented language by providing not only a syntax to follow, but also an entire software development methodology to follow. The practicality of Eiffel has yet to be demonstrated fully, although it is an excellent teaching language and it is also an excellent language with which to learn object-oriented programming.

Eiffel was first developed by Bertrand Meyer in 1985 at his company, Interactive Software Engineering (ISE), in Goleta, CA. Much of Eiffel descends from Dr. Meyer's research into object-oriented programming, and his experience with Simula, an object-oriented language that supports linked lists and discrete process simulation.

Eiffel has the following advantages:

- It is a pure object-oriented language.
- It is very modular.
- It stresses reliability.
- It is easy to learn.
- It facilitates design by contract.
- It has an elegant design and programming style.

- It brings design and programming closer together.

- It encourages the reuse of software components.

Eiffel also has many advanced features not found in many other languages, including the following:

- Classes

- Multiple inheritance

- Polymorphism

- Static typing and dynamic binding

- Constrained and unconstrained genericity

- A disciplined exception mechanism

- Systematic use of assertions to promote programming by contract

- Deferred classes for high-level design and analysis

There are many Eiffel compilers available, however many are commercial. The GNU project has an Eiffel compiler that is available under the GPL called SmallEiffel. SmallEiffel is a very fast and small Eiffel compiler that is available for many platforms including Red Hat Linux. It is the recommended compiler for any Eiffel development under Linux.

Programming Tools

There are many programming tools that come with your Red Hat Linux distribution. This section looks at three of those tools: make, RCS, and CVS.

Make

Make is a very powerful tool for managing software projects that have multiple source code files. Make is a standard GNU utility that is available under the GPL and its main purpose is to keep track of how to make your program. To use make, you need to create a Makefile, which is a text file that tells make what instructions to use in compiling and linking your program. Make also tracks dependencies between your source files so when you change any of the files, only the necessary files are recompiled—a time-saving feature that becomes especially apparent for larger projects. If you are working on a program that has multiple source code files, you will definitely want to look into learning and using make.

Make is language-independent, although it is generally used for compiled languages because it gives instructions on how to compile your program. However, you can use make for many other things besides compiling programs. It is a great tool for automating various tasks that are regularly performed during software development. To use make for a project, you need to create a Makefile that contains instructions for the make utility. Here is a sample Makefile that is meant to be used with the GNU C++ compiler, g++ (proper indentions and spacing are very important within a Makefile, and are necessary for proper operation):

```
main : main.o support.o
        g++ -o main main.o support.o

main.o : main.cc
        g++ -c main.cc

support.o : support.cc
        g++ -c support.cc

clean :
        rm main main.o support.o
```

To find out more about make, head over to the GNU project's Web site at www.gnu.org and there you can read the make manual. Since Red Hat Linux also comes with make, you can also type **man make** at the command prompt to read the manual page for make.

RCS

RCS stands for Revision Control System and is used to control software revisions within a software creation project. RCS is managed with a series of files called RCS files, and an RCS file contains multiple revisions of the source file, a change log, descriptive text, an access list, and some control attributes. For a user to be able to use RCS he must be on the access list. RCS also has source-file locking, which helps when several people are working on the same project.

CVS

CVS stands for version control system and it keeps track of source file versions and also keeps a log of any changes made to that source file. It tracks the details of any changes including who changed the file, when the file was changed, and why the changes took place. The main difference between CVS and RCS is that CVS controls files under a hierarchical structure, called a repository. A CVS repository allows the creation of subdirectories with the repository, and files can be put in any subdirectory within the repository tree. CVS is especially useful when multiple people are working on a single source code tree because it handles the concurrent editing of source files among multiple authors and logs any changes to files. If errors are introduced to certain source files, previous versions can be retrieved to eliminate the errors.

Generally, any time you are working on a large software project that involves single or multiple developers, you should implement some form of version control. CVS is generally accepted as one of the best version control systems available under Linux.

Summary

This chapter looked in detail at shell scripting, especially at scripting using the bash shell. It covered all the main features of programming the bash shell and then looked at a few practical examples. In addition to shell scripting, it also took a look at a few other scripting languages such as perl, Tcl/Tk, and Python. Finally, the chapter looked a few programming tools including make, RCS, and CVS.

Automation

IN THIS CHAPTER

- Managing Chaos   *1018*
- Using at for One Time Tasks   *1021*
- Using cron   *1031*
- Debugging cron Jobs   *1040*

Managing Chaos

Red Hat Linux is an incredibly powerful operating system, and all the little details that a system administrator must keep track of can sometimes be a little intimidating. Being a multitasking operating system, there can be any number of jobs running in the background at a given time. In fact, you can take a look at all the processes running on your system at a given time by using the ps aux command. The following is a sample output from executing that command under Red Hat Linux 6.0:

```
$ ps aux
```

USER	PID	%CPU	%MEM	VSZ	RSS	TTY	STAT	START	TIME	COMMAND
root	1	0.0	0.0	1096	52	?	S	Jul09	5:21	init [3]
root	2	0.0	0.0	0	0	?	SW	Jul09	0:00	[kflushd]
root	3	0.0	0.0	0	0	?	SW	Jul09	0:00	[kpiod]
root	4	0.0	0.0	0	0	?	SW	Jul09	0:01	[kswapd]
root	289	0.0	0.1	1272	372	?	S	Jul09	0:57	syslogd -m 0
root	300	0.0	0.0	1120	0	?	SW	Jul09	0:00	[klogd]
daemon	314	0.0	0.0	1112	104	?	S	Jul09	0:00	/usr/sbin/atd
root	328	0.0	0.0	1284	112	?	S	Jul09	0:00	crond
root	342	0.0	0.0	1244	68	?	S	Jul09	0:07	inetd
root	382	0.0	0.0	1060	0	tty1	SW	Jul09	0:00	[mingetty]
root	383	0.0	0.0	1060	0	tty2	SW	Jul09	0:00	[mingetty]
root	384	0.0	0.0	1060	0	tty3	SW	Jul09	0:00	[mingetty]
root	385	0.0	0.0	1060	0	tty4	SW	Jul09	0:00	[mingetty]
root	386	0.0	0.0	1060	0	tty5	SW	Jul09	0:00	[mingetty]
root	387	0.0	0.0	1060	0	tty6	SW	Jul09	0:00	[mingetty]
root	396	0.0	0.0	1052	36	?	S	Jul09	0:09	update (bdflush)
root	1010	0.0	0.0	1664	0	?	SW	Jul09	0:00	[safe_mysqld]
mysql	1027	0.0	1.2	12748	3204	?	SN	Jul09	2:58	/usr/sbin/mysqld
mysql	1029	0.0	1.2	12748	3204	?	SN	Jul09	2:39	/usr/sbin/mysqld
mysql	1030	0.0	1.2	12748	3204	?	SN	Jul09	5:51	/usr/sbin/mysqld
root	4235	0.0	0.0	1056	52	?	S	Jul10	4:50	supervise /var/su
root	4238	0.0	0.0	1056	52	?	S	Jul10	2:20	supervise /var/su
root	25107	0.0	1.1	5500	3060	?	S	Jul23	0:05	/usr/local/apache
nobody	17265	0.1	1.5	6180	4044	?	S	11:53	0:00	/usr/local/apache
nobody	17696	0.1	1.6	6296	4200	?	S	11:53	0:00	/usr/local/apache
nobody	18997	0.0	1.6	6308	4132	?	S	11:56	0:00	/usr/local/apache
nobody	19006	0.2	1.6	6540	4360	?	S	11:56	0:01	/usr/local/apache
nobody	20067	0.0	1.5	6048	3900	?	S	11:58	0:00	/usr/local/apache
nobody	21113	0.0	1.4	5812	3616	?	S	12:00	0:00	/usr/local/apache
nobody	21125	0.1	1.5	6044	3932	?	S	12:00	0:00	/usr/local/apache

```
nobody    21126  0.3  1.5  5992 3892 ?       S    12:00   0:00 /usr/local/apache
nobody    21135  0.0  1.3  5724 3576 ?       S    12:00   0:00 /usr/local/apache
nobody    22874  0.0  1.2  5512 3104 ?       S    12:04   0:00 /usr/local/apache
mysql     23007 11.0  1.2 12748 3204 ?       SN   12:04   0:00 /usr/sbin/mysqld
mysql     23008  0.0  1.2 12748 3204 ?       SN   12:04   0:00 /usr/sbin/mysqld
```

As you can see from the output, there are a number of processes running, and you will notice that each job lists a process id (the PID column). Take a look at PID 314, it is the process for the at daemon (/usr/sbin/atd), which we will be examining later in this chapter. Another process to note is PID 328, the cron daemon (crond), another topic we will be looking at in this chapter.

Many of the processes that are running on your machine are *daemons*, background processes that wait around until they are needed. Many of these daemons are started by the init files on system startup. However, you can have processes that start up automatically at any given time, as if by magic, and go about their duties. Well, there actually is no magic involved in getting process to start up automatically. Rather, there are two utilities available that allow you to schedule jobs to execute at predefined times or at predefined intervals. The two utilities are known as at and cron. The at utility is used to schedule one-time tasks and works on the idea of a job queue. The cron utility is more powerful than at and is used to schedule jobs that are to be executed on a regular basis at predefined intervals.

By default, Red Hat Linux comes with a number of predefined cron jobs that execute regularly, taking care of various housecleaning jobs. These tasks can be found in the usual places where cron files are kept. We will explore those places in detail later in this chapter.

After reading this chapter, you should understand why job automation is important and under what circumstances it should be used. You will also explore the at and cron utilities in detail. You should become intimately familiar with those tools, and this chapter will help get you started with using them. The last section of the chapter deals with debugging cron jobs, a very important section that helps you figure out where problems are occurring in your cron jobs.

Automating Tasks

The last chapter took a look at shell scripting as a way to solve problems one time because, as a system administrator, you do not want to reinvent the wheel. You have enough work on your hands; you do not need to be wasting your time on repetitious tasks that can easily be automated. This chapter takes the concept of problem solving one step further with an introduction to job automation.

33

Automation

If you solve a problem once, obviously you want to utilize your solution as many times as needed. The shell scripting covered in the last chapter was great because it allowed you to take a number of commands that you normally type in on the command line and put those commands into a file. All those commands you put in the file turn into a single command; all you have to do is type the name of the file and all the commands in it will be executed. This shell scripting ability turns many tedious tasks into one-line commands.

What if you could take this one step further and not even have to type in the name of the shell scripts? Well, with job automation using at and cron, you can do just that by simply telling either at or cron to execute the command at a specific time. Then you don't even have to be logged in to the system, and your commands will be executed. You must remember, of course, that the system must be powered on for cron and at to do their jobs.

Automating Regular Tasks

You may be wondering exactly what sorts of tasks are useful to automate, because not everything lends itself to automation. There still are things you need to do on the system that cannot be automated and probably never will.

There are, however, many tasks that can and should be automated. In fact, if you find that there is any task you do on a regular basis, you should think about automating that job to make your life easier. The following are a number of tasks that can easily be automated:

- *Fetching email from a remote server*—You can schedule cron to fetch your email from your mail server using the `fetchmail` command every few minutes.

- *Updating newsgroups*—If you read newsgroups regularly, you can get cron to update all the newsgroups you subscribe to regularly.

- *Removing core files*—Through regular system use, core files do tend to build up, especially if you have a number of developers on your system. It is a simple matter to set up a cron job that periodically removes all core files from your filesystem.

- *Cleaning up temporary files and logs*—Both the temporary file area and your log files can get cluttered with useless information and can waste precious disk space. You can write a script that will clean up those files and then you can get cron to execute that script regularly.

- *Doing backups*—Backing up your files is the most important job on your system. You must do this regularly, and cron is the tool to automate this task. It is recommended that you perform any backups when the system load is low, and a good time to do that is early in the morning.

As a system administrator, it is crucial to be in control of your system. A game plan is needed to keep tasks in check. When you are juggling a number of different duties, you do not want to forget to execute crucial jobs. You can set up job automation so that jobs will execute at a specified time, freeing you from remembering to execute the job yourself. That is where at comes in handy. If you have a job you know you need to execute later in the day, give it to at and you will not have to worry about it.

The thought of automating jobs may seem a little daunting if you have never heard of at or cron before. However, as you will see, it is a simple matter to schedule jobs to be executed automatically and can usually be done in a matter of minutes. More complex jobs may take more time, of course, but if you already have a script written that you want to automate, all it takes to automate it is to add a single line to a text file. We will go over all the details of doing so in this chapter, so please read on and you will become a master of job automation before you know it.

Using at for One-Time Tasks

The at utility is really a batching tool and is only useful for scheduling one-time tasks. cron should be used for tasks that you want to be executed regularly. We will cover cron in the next section.

The main idea behind at is that of job queues—you put jobs into a specific queue and then the jobs in the queue are executed at their specified times. There are a number of different queues you can use with at, and different queues have different scheduling priorities. All the queues under at consist of a single letter and encompass all the letters in the alphabet, with upper- and lowercase letters referring to different queues.

Many times, you will use at for a task that you want performed within either the current day or the next day, such as an unscheduled backup of a special project that will be completed by the end of the day. Or, you may need to set up accounts for a large group of new hires that will be starting the next day. When you have a job that you need to perform in a few hours, but you will not be at your computer at that time, you can queue the job using at. It will then be executed automatically, even if you are not logged in to your computer.

This section looks at the following topics:

- The at utility
- Examples of using at
- The batch utility
- The atq utility

- The atrm utility

- The atrun utility

- The at daemon atd

- Specifying which users can use at

By the end of this section, you should be familiar with using at and be able to batch and manipulate your own jobs easily.

The at Utility

at is a very useful tool for queueing jobs that are to be processed at a later time, such as adding new users or deleting old users. There are several other utilities that work with at: batch, atq, and atrm. We will look at each of these tools in this section.

There are two different syntax forms that you can use when calling at. The first form is used to add new jobs to the queue, while the second form is used to list out the details of specific jobs. The following is the syntax for the first form:

```
at [-V] [-q queue] [-f file] [-mldbv] TIME
```

As you can see, there are several options you can pass to the at command. The following is an overview of what each option does:

- -V   Outputs the version number of at to standard error.

- -q   Allows you to specify which queue to use. The queue is a single letter and can be from a to z or from A to Z. The default queue for at is a and is used when no queue specification is given. The higher the letter given for the queue, the greater niceness will be given to that job. The *niceness* of a job determines the scheduling priority of a job—a job with a greater niceness will be given a higher scheduling priority. There is also a special queue called "=". It contains any jobs that are currently running. You cannot directly add jobs to the "=" queue—at will put them there when they start executing.

- -m   Tells at to send mail to the user when the specified job has been completed.

- -f   File reads the job commands from the specified file instead of reading them from standard input.

- -l   Performs the same function as atq, which is to list the status of any pending jobs for the current user. If executed as root, all pending jobs for all users will be listed.

- -d   Allows you to delete specific jobs, performing the same functionality as atrm.

- -v   Displays when the job is scheduled to be executed immediately after the at utility is executed before any commands are read from standard input.

- TIME   The time that the job is to be executed. We will examine the allowable time specifications you can pass to at in the "at Time Specifications" section.

As you can see, you have a high level of control over queuing jobs with at. When you pass commands to at, the commands can be in a file or you can pass them on standard input. As you saw, the -f option is used to specify a file from which to read commands. If the -f option is not given, at will read your commands from standard input by default. When reading your commands from standard input, at will put the cursor at the beginning of the next blank line and then display a prompt that looks like "at>". You can then proceed to type in the commands you want executed after the prompt, pressing the Enter key at the end of each command. When you are finished typing in your commands, put an end-of-file character on a blank line to tell at that you are done. The keystroke combination of Ctrl+D will generate an EOF character.

When specifying the time that the job is to be executed, at allows for a great deal of flexibility in how you represent your time. at conforms to the POSIX.2 standard for time specification, accepting many different forms of time specifications. For a detailed outline of all the possible time representations that you can use, take a look at the /usr/doc/ at-3.1.7/timespec file.

at Time Specifications

Let's take a look at a few of the possible time specifications that at accepts. To schedule a job for the current day, specify the hours and minutes that the job is to be executed using the form HH:MM. If you specify a time that has already passed, the job will be run at the time specified on the following day. You can also append to HH:MM either an AM or PM if you prefer to work in the 12-hour time format, but at takes times in the 24-hour format by default. You can also tell at to execute jobs using words. There are three different words that at knows, which represent specific times during a day: midnight, noon, and teatime (4:00 p.m.). So, instead of putting your time as 00:00, you can use the word midnight; instead of using the time 12:00, you can use the word noon.

You can also tell at to execute a job on any day in the future by specifying the date using one of the following forms: MMDDYY, MM/DD/YY, or DD.MM.YY. You must put the date specification after the time specification. For example, to tell at to execute a command at 15:30 on January 4th, 1999, use the following time specification: 15:30 010499. You can also use the other forms; either 15:30 01/04/99 or 15:30 01.04.99.

You can also give at relative time specifications. Using the word now, you can tell at to execute commands in a specific amount of minutes, hours, days, or weeks into the future.

By passing the word now as your time specification followed by a plus symbol and then a count followed by the time-units for the count, you can give at a relative time. The time units that at knows about are minutes, hours, days, and weeks. However, at also accepts the words today and tomorrow placed after the time unit to specify whether the job should be executed today or tomorrow. For example, to execute a job tomorrow, five hours ahead of the current time, use the following time specification: now + 5 hours tomorrow. To execute a job five minutes into the future, you can use the time specification: now + 5 minutes.

The Second Form of at

Now that you have examined the first form of syntax for at, take a look at the second form. As mentioned earlier, the second form is not used to schedule any new jobs. Instead, it is used to list the details regarding specific jobs. The main difference with the second form of at is that you pass the -c option followed by any number of job IDs. You do not need to pass any time specifications—the second form is only used to see exactly what commands will be executed by a job that is awaiting execution. The following is the syntax for the second form of at:

```
at -c job [job...]
```

This form of at has only two types of parameters that you can pass to it. The following provides an explanation for both:

- -c   Tells at to output all the listed jobs to standard output.

- job   You can pass any number of jobs to at on the command line. The details of any job you pass will be displayed on standard output. This is very useful when you want to get the information for a specific job. The complete script that is to be executed for each job is displayed for each job you pass to at.

As you can see, the at command is very powerful for scheduling one-time jobs. The following section shows a few examples of using at.

Examples of Using at

The first example schedules a job to be executed at 7:00 a.m. exactly one week in the future. The following is the command used to schedule the job:

```
$ at 7am + 1 week
at> echo "Hello"
at> <EOT>
warning: commands will be executed using /bin/sh
job 2 at 1999-08-20 07:00
```

As you can see, the -f option was not used so at displayed its prompt and I typed in the echo command. I then pressed Enter and pressed the keystroke combination of Ctrl+D on the next line to specify the end of input. I was then told that the shell /bin/sh would be used to execute the command, and that the job number for my command was job 2.

Specifying the -c option will cause at to display the full script that will be executed for job 2, as shown in the following:

```
$ at -c 2

#!/bin/sh
# atrun uid=511 gid=511
# mail  dbarber 0
umask 2
USERNAME=; export USERNAME
HISTSIZE=1000; export HISTSIZE
HOSTNAME=medullas.com; export HOSTNAME
LOGNAME=dbarber; export LOGNAME
HISTFILESIZE=1000; export HISTFILESIZE
MAIL=/var/spool/mail/dbarber; export MAIL
HOSTTYPE=i386; export HOSTTYPE
PATH=/usr/local/bin:/bin:/usr/bin:/usr/X11R6/bin:/home/dbarber/bin; export PATH
HOME=/home/dbarber; export HOME
INPUTRC=/etc/inputrc; export INPUTRC
PS1=[\\u@\\h\ \\W]\\\$\ ; export PS1
USER=dbarber; export USER
BASH_ENV=/home/dbarber/.bashrc; export BASH_ENV
OSTYPE=Linux; export OSTYPE
SHLVL=1; export SHLVL
cd /var/log ¦¦ {
        echo 'Execution directory inaccessible' >&2
        exit 1
}
echo Hello
```

As you can see, at generates a lot of code around that simple echo statement. It does this to preserve the settings of your environment that were in place when you queued the command.

Now queue another job for the same time as the first:

```
$ at 7am + 1 week
at> echo "Goodbye"
at> <EOT>
```

```
warning: commands will be executed using /bin/sh
job 3 at 1999-08-20 07:00
```

This job is given a job number of 3 and will be executed at 7:00 a.m. on August 20, 1999.

To delete job 2, use the following the command:

```
$ at -d 2
```

No output is displayed from this command, which means that the operation was successful. Many times, Linux only displays messages from commands when something goes wrong, as is the case with at.

Now try a slightly different time specification and use a different queue. This job will be scheduled to execute on September 3 at 2:00 p.m. The command is as follows:

```
$ at -q b 2pm Sep 3
at> echo "Looking for core files"
at> find / -name core -print
at> <EOT>
warning: commands will be executed using /bin/sh
job 5 at 1999-09-03 14:00
```

This time, I used a two-line command, searching for all core files on my filesystem. Notice how I specified that queue b was to be used. This job is given an ID of 5.

Now try another time specification. Use a file containing some commands this time instead of typing them in on standard input. The command is as follows:

```
$ at -f mycommands 5pm tomorrow
warning: commands will be executed using /bin/sh
job 6 at 1999-08-14 17:00
```

Now that you have queued job 6, take a look at all the jobs you've just queued. To do so, pass the -l option to at, as shown in the following:

```
$ at -l
5        1999-09-03 14:00 b
3        1999-08-22 07:00 b
4        1999-08-22 07:00 a
6        1999-08-16 17:00 a
```

As you can see, you have four jobs currently queued for execution. The times they will be executed are displayed, along with their queues.

Just a note about how at displays time formats. By default, the time displayed will be in the format "YYYY-MM-DD HH:MM". However, if you set the environment variable POSIXLY_CORRECT, the time will be displayed in the format "Fri Mar 11 12:25:00 1999". All of the previous examples were displayed using the default format.

The batch Utility

The batch utility is very similar to at, but it only executes jobs when the system load is less than a specified amount. The default system load level at which batch executes commands is under 0.8, but you can specify a different value using the atrun command (covered in "The atrun Utility" section later in this chapter). You might want to specify a different number because your system is rather busy and might not reach the default system load, or your batch jobs might require considerable system resources and you do not want to load the system unless there is sufficient overhead available. The syntax for batch is as follows:

```
batch [-V] [-q queue] [-f file] [-mv] [TIME]
```

- -V   Prints the version number of at out to standard error.

- -q   Allows you to specify which queue to use. The queue syntax that batch accepts is the same as the queue syntax for at. Take a look at the at command section for more details on queues.

- -f file   Tells batch to the read the job commands from the specified file instead of reading them from standard input.

- -v   Displays when the job is scheduled to be executed.

- -m   Tells batch to send mail to the user when the specified job has been completed.

When passing the time specification to batch, you can use all the same formats as at (refer to the discussion on at time formats earlier in this chapter). As mentioned earlier in the "at Time Specifications" section, the allowable formats are specified in the /usr/doc/at-3.1.7/timespec file.

For examples using batch, take a look at the examples for at that were listed previously, because batch takes the same options as at. All examples that work with at should also work with batch, but with batch, you do not need to specify a time. If you do not specify a time, the commands will be executed whenever the system load is under the specified amount.

The atq Utility

The atq utility is used to output the status of any pending jobs for the current user. If executed as `root`, all pending jobs for all users are displayed. When jobs are displayed, there are four columns of information for each job: the job number, date, hour, and job class. The syntax for atq is as follows:

```
atq [-V] [-q queue]
```

- -V   Prints the version number of at out to standard error.

- -q   Allows you to specify the exact queue for which to display the status of pending jobs. If -q is not passed, all jobs, regardless of queue, will be displayed.

The following is an example of calling atq:

```
$ atq -q a
4        1999-08-22 07:00 a
6        1999-08-16 17:00 a
1999-08-16 00:00 a
```

As you can see, this command lists out all pending jobs that are in the queue.

The atrm Utility

The atrm utility is used to delete pending jobs from the queue. Its syntax is

```
atrm [-V] job [job...]
```

- -V   Prints the version number of at out to standard error.

- job   You can pass any number of jobs to atrm. Every job passed will be deleted from the queue, as long as it exists.

The following is an example of using the atrm utility:

```
$ atrm 2
```

As long as job 2 exists, no output should appear, meaning that the command completed successfully. Job 2 will be dequeued after executing the command and will no longer execute as scheduled.

The atrun Utility

The atrun utility can be used to change the default load average under which jobs submitted via batch will be executed. The `atrun` command is actually a shell script that invokes the at daemon (located at /usr/sbin/atd) passing the -s option. The -s option tells the at daemon to process the at/batch queue only once, running only the next job in the queue.

The `atrun` command is supplied only for backward compatibility because some older programs may invoke it. You should avoid using atrun and call atd directly instead. The syntax for the `atrun` command is as follows:

```
atrun [-l load_avg]
```

- `-l`   Allows you to change to the load average at which `batch` commands are executed. The default load average at which `batch` commands are executed is 0.8 percent.

The following is an example of using the `atrun` command:

```
$ atrun -l 2
```

After executing this command, the load average at which `batch` commands are executed at will be 2 percent, not 0.8 percent. This might be needed on busy systems that never reach the 0.8 percent load.

The at Daemon

The actual program that controls the behavior of at is known as the at daemon. The at daemon is located at `/usr/sbin/atd`. The actual purpose of atd is to run the jobs that have been queued by at. This is done in the background without user intervention. However, you can directly execute atd to change various parameters of atd's behavior. The following is the syntax for the at daemon:

```
atd [-l load_avg] [-b batch_interval] [-d] [-s]
```

As you can see, there are several parameters that you can pass to atd; the following is a description of each one:

- `-l`   Allows you to specify the maximum load factor at which jobs queued by the `batch` command can be run. As mentioned earlier, the default option for this is 0.8. The current load of the system is determined by the `/proc/loadavg` file, and so a working `/proc` filesystem is necessary to make use of this feature.

- `-b`   Allows you to specify the minimum time interval (in seconds) between which two `batch` jobs can be started. The default time interval is 60 seconds.

- `-d`   Turns on the verbose debugging feature that outputs all error messages to standard error as opposed to logging all errors using syslog.

- `-s`   Tells the at daemon to process the job queue one time. This feature is generally only used by the atrun script and is not particularly useful. Like atrun, the `-s` parameter is primarily provided only for backward compatibility.

33

Automation

When jobs are queued by either at or batch, they are stored in the /var/spool/at directory. This directory should be mode 700 and owned by the daemon user. To view the contents of the directory, you must log in as root, or you will be denied. Within the /var/spool/at directory is a subdirectory spool where all output is stored. This directory is useful when examining the results of at jobs and is also of mode 700 and owned by the daemon user.

When invoking either at or batch, you must pass the commands that are to be executed on standard input or specify a file that contains the commands. To specify a file, pass the -f option to either at or batch. When passing the commands to at or batch on standard input, you can end your input with the EOF character (Ctrl+D).

When at or batch is invoked, it has access to all the current environment variables except for TERM, DISPLAY, and _. It also retains the current working directory and the umask of the user invoking at. If a user invokes at or batch from an su shell, the real userid of the user is kept.

When atd executes any commands in the at queue, any results sent to either standard error or standard output are mailed to the user who originally queued the commands. The command used to send the mail is the standard /usr/sbin/sendmail. If you choose to install an MTA other than the Red Hat default of sendmail, be sure to keep /usr/sbin/ sendmail as a symbolic link to your new MTA, or you will break that mail feature of atd. If a user invokes at or batch while in an su shell, because the actual userid of that user is retained, when the commands are executed, mail will be sent to the actual user, not root.

Specifying Which Users Can Use at

You can have complete control over which users on your system can use the at utility. System security is the primary reason to limit access to at. Allowing users to start jobs when they are not logged in can be a potential security hole, however this is a matter best left to the system administrator. There are two files located in the /etc directory that allow you to limit which users are allowed to use the at utility. The /etc/at.deny file allows you specify users that are not allowed to use the at utility. Usernames are listed one per line.

The /etc/at.allow file allows you to specify exactly which users are allowed to use at. Again, usernames are listed one per line. If /etc/at.allow does not exist but /etc/ at.deny does exist, all users are allowed to use at, except the users listed in /etc/at.deny. If /etc/at.allow does exist but the /etc/at.deny file does not exist, only the users listed in /etc/at.allow are allowed to use at. If neither file exists, only the superuser account can be used to invoke at.

The default Red Hat 6.0 configuration for at comes with a blank /etc/at.deny, so all users can use at and batch out-of-the-box.

We have covered all the features of at, examined exactly how to use it, and have seen how at works. We will now move on to cron, which can be used to run commands at regular intervals.

Using cron

Unlike the at utility, which is great for scheduling one-time tasks, cron is ideal for setting up jobs that execute regularly at specified times or intervals. The main idea behind cron is that of crontab files. A *crontab file* is a file that contains commands for cron, setting up and configuring cron jobs. This section explores all the following topics regarding cron:

- cron startup
- Using crontab effectively
- The anatomy of a crontab entry
- Global cron files
- Specifying which users can use cron
- Examples of using cron

By the end of this section, you should know about configuring and using cron.

cron Startup

The cron daemon is invoked upon system startup from the /etc/rc.d/rnN.d/S40crond (where N = 2,3, 4 or 5) script. On startup, the cron daemon immediately examines the /var/spool/cron directory for any crontab files. Crontab files are named after user accounts in the /etc/passwd file, so each user can have his or her own separate crontab file. Any crontab files that are found are processed by cron and then loaded into memory. In addition to /var/spool/cron, the files in /etc/cron.d are also loaded by cron at this time. cron then looks for the /etc/crontab file and loads the contents of that file. The following is the default content of the /etc/crontab file:

```
SHELL=/bin/bash
PATH=/sbin:/bin:/usr/sbin:/usr/bin
MAILTO=root
HOME=/
# run-parts
01 * * * * root run-parts /etc/cron.hourly
02 4 * * * root run-parts /etc/cron.daily
22 4 * * 0 root run-parts /etc/cron.weekly
42 4 1 * * root run-parts /etc/cron.monthly
```

As you can see, it is within the /etc/crontab file that the directories /etc/cron.hourly, /etc/cron.daily, /etc/cron.weekly, and /etc/cron.monthly are set up. The following is the breakdown on what the /etc/crontab file sets up for those four directories:

- The contents of the /etc/cron.hourly directory are set to be run every hour on the first minute of the hour.

- The contents of the /etc/cron.daily directory are set to be run every day at the second minute of the fourth hour.

- The contents of the /etc/cron.weekly directory are set to be run every Sunday on the 22nd minute of the fourth hour.

- The contents of the /etc/cron.monthly directory are set to be run on the first day of every month on the 42nd minute of the fourth hour.

How I got all those details from the /etc/crontab file will be covered shortly when we examine exactly what makes up a crontab file. All the contents of those directories are run as the root user, so you must be careful what sort of scripts you put in those directories. It is possible to put scripts in those directories that will do damage to your system.

As I mentioned, the contents of the files in the /etc/cron.d directory are read in by cron upon startup. By default, Red Hat Linux comes with a single file in the /etc/cron.d directory called kmod. The following are the contents of the kmod file:

```
# rmmod -a is a two-hand sweep module cleaner
*/10 * * * *    root    /sbin/rmmod -as
```

Again, you can see the crontab syntax in this file. You can put any number of scripts in the /etc/cron.d directory, and all their contents will be read in by cron when it starts.

After cron starts and finishes reading in all the crontab files, it sleeps, waking up every minute and checking if any of the stored crontabs have any commands that are to be executed in the current minute. The owner of each crontab is determined by either the ownership of the crontab file or by the value contained in the MAILTO environment variable, if one exists in the crontab.

cron also checks if any of the files in /var/spool/cron, /etc/cron.d, or the /etc/crontab files have changed or if any new files have been added. If any changes have occurred, the affected files are reloaded. cron determines if any changes have occurred by checking the modtime of all the directories and files. This feature ensures that the cron daemon does not need to be restarted every time crontabs are updated or new crontabs are added. Thus, users can add new crontabs or update their crontabs without needing superuser privileges to restart cron.

Using `crontab` Effectively

The `crontab` command is used to add and edit crontab files. Each user can use the `crontab` command to maintain his or her individual crontab files. The crontab files should not be edited directly because this can cause problems if, for example, the file is open when the cron daemon attempts to read it. Rather, the `crontab` command should be used to perform any changes to the crontab files. The crontab files give instructions to the cron daemon for scheduling any cron jobs. The `crontab` command that comes with Red Hat Linux conforms to the current POSIX standard and differs from the classic SVR4 syntax with which you may be familiar.

There are four main actions that can be performed on crontab files using the `crontab` command: add a new crontab file, edit a crontab file, remove an existing crontab file, and list the contents of an existing crontab file. The crontab files are kept under the `/var/spool/cron` directory, and the `crontab` command allows you to manage the crontab files kept there.

There are two different ways to invoke the `crontab` command. The first form of `crontab` is used when you want to install a new crontab file. The syntax is as follows:

```
crontab [ -u user ] file
```

- `-u user`   Allows you to specify a username to add a new crontab for a specific user. If the `-u` option is not supplied, the username of the user invoking the `crontab` command is used. When executing `crontab` from within an su shell, you should always use the `-u` option because not doing so can confuse the `crontab` command, and you can end up with some unpredictable results.

- `file`   The name of the file that contains the commands that you want to be put into the new crontab. If you simply pass the `-` character as the filename, `crontab` will read the contents of the new crontab from standard input. When using standard input to specify the contents of your crontab file, use the EOF (Ctrl+D) character to stop editing.

When using this first form of the `crontab` command, keep in mind that each user can only have one crontab file. So, by installing a new crontab file, you will replace your old crontab file with the new one. Anything that is in your old crontab file will be overwritten by the new one.

The Second Form of `crontab`

The second form of the `crontab` command is used to perform operations on an existing crontab file. The following is the syntax for the second form:

```
crontab [ -u user ] { -l ¦ -r ¦ -e }
```

The syntax on this form of `crontab` varies slightly from the previous version. It is

- `-u user`   Just as in the first form of `crontab`, the `-u` option allows you to specify a username whose crontab file you want to modify. If the `-u` option is not supplied, the username of the user invoking the `crontab` command is used. Keep in mind that you should always use the `-u` option when invoking `crontab` from an su shell for reasons listed earlier.

- `-l`   This option gets `crontab` to list the contents of the crontab file to standard output.

- `-r`   This option removes the crontab file for the specified user.

- `-e`   This option is used to edit an existing crontab file for the specified user, or to install an initial crontab file if one does not exist. A text editor is used for this operation. `crontab` will invoke a specific editor based on the values in either the VISUAL or EDITOR environment variables. If you save the modified crontab file in the editor, the modified crontab file is installed immediately.

The Anatomy of a crontab Entry

When you create entries in a crontab file, each entry consists of a single command and a specific time and date at which the command is to be executed. cron ignores any blank lines or leading spaces in crontab files, and you can add comments in a crontab file by using the pound character (#). As opposed to shell scripts, where comments can appear on the same line as commands, the first non-space character of a comment line in crontab files must be a pound character. Thus, comments must be on lines by themselves; you cannot have comments on the same line as cron commands or any environment variable assignments.

Crontab files can contain either comments, environment variable assignments, or cron commands.

Environment variable assignment in crontab files is the same as it is under shell scripting. The following is the general form:

`name = value`

The spaces around the equal sign (=) are optional and do not affect the variable assignment. The contents of `value` can contain spaces, however trailing spaces are ignored unless quotation marks are put around `value`, in which case any leading or trailing spaces are preserved.

When the cron daemon starts, it sets up a number of environment variables by default. The following are the variables it sets up:

- SHELL   Set to /bin/sh

- LOGNAME   Set to the name of the user, taken from the user's entry in the /etc/passwd file

- HOME   Set to the user's home directory, also taken from the user's entry in the /etc/ passwd file

You can override the values in SHELL and HOME within your crontab file, but you cannot override the value in LOGNAME. You might want to change your shell if your scripts are for a different shell, or if you need access to specific shell features. Also, overriding the home directory might be useful for keeping the results of cron jobs separate from other items.

cron also uses the value of the environment variable MAILTO to get the email address of the user to whom to send mail. Any output from commands that are run from a user's crontab file will be sent to the user specified in the MAILTO variable for that particular user. If MAILTO is set but is empty (MAILTO=""), the mail feature is disabled and no mail is sent. If MAILTO is not set, mail will be sent to the owner of the crontab from which the commands were executed.

As mentioned earlier, the third thing that you can have in a crontab file is cron commands. There are two different forms of the possible crontab commands you can use; user crontab files have a different syntax than the global crontab files contained under the /etc directory. The following section examines both formats of cron commands.

cron Commands for User crontab Files

cron commands are used to set up cron jobs. They are essentially a list of what to do, and when. The format of cron commands under Red Hat Linux 6.0 is very similar to the V7 standard, with a few new features that are upward-compatible. The user crontab files are kept in the /var/spool/cron directory. Each command in the user crontab files occurs on a single line and consists of six fields. The following is the general format:

minute   hour   dayofmonth   month   dayofweek   command

The allowable values for the above fields are as follows:

- minute   Value from 0 to 59.

- hour   Value from 0 to 23.

- dayofmonth   Value from 1 to 31.

- month   Value from 1 to 12 or a name from jan to dec.

- `dayofweek` Value from 0 to 6 (where 0 is Sunday) or a name from sun to sat.

- `command` The command to execute at the specified time; it can be made up of single or multiple words. cron will simply execute everything on the line after the `dayofweek` field until the newline character as a command. In addition to being able to use the newline character to specify the end of the command, you can also use a non-escaped percent sign (%). If any data is on the line after the percent sign, it will be sent as arguments to the command. The command will think those arguments were passed in by standard input.

Any of these date and time fields can also include an asterisk (*), which will cause that field to be `true` for all possible values.

For all the date and time fields, in addition to being able to specify a single value, you can also specify a value range. A value range is made up of two values separated by a hyphen. All values that occur between those two values, including those two values, are `true` for that field. For example, if the range 4-6 is specified in the month field, the command will be executed when the month is 4, 5, or 6, which would cause these jobs to only happen in the second quarter. A similar situation might be to have jobs only execute on weekdays or weekends.

A list is also allowed in time and date fields. A *list* is a set of values separated by commas; ranges are also acceptable list values. An example of a list is `3, 5, 7-9, 15`. If that list was given as the value for a `dayofmonth` field, the specified command would have only been executed on the 3rd, 5th, 7th, 8th, 9th, and 15th days of the month. In addition to simple values and ranges of values, you can use what is called "step values" in your lists. Step values are put after ranges and are of the format /*number*. A *step value* is a range for which only values of specific increments are `true`. An example of a step value is `0-20/2`. For this range, only every second value in the range will be `true`. You can also use the asterisk with a step value. For example, to get a command to execute once every two hours, use the `*/2` step value.

Specifying Values

When specifying values for either the `dayofweek` field or the `month` field, you can also use the first three characters of the name of the day or month instead of a number. For example, instead of putting a `0` in the `dayofweek` field, you can put the three characters `sun` to specify Sunday. There is one drawback when using words instead of numbers—you cannot use ranges or lists in such a context.

For each `cron` command in a crontab file, the specified command is executed whenever the specified minute, hour, and month match the current system values, and either `dayofmonth` or `dayofweek` matches the current system day value.

Problems can occur with cron during Daylight Saving Time (DST) conversions, which will cause supposed matches to fail or to occur twice. This can be avoided by not scheduling jobs on Sundays from 1 a.m. to 3 a.m., as DST occurs at 2 a.m. Hourly jobs should be scheduled for a few minutes after the hour for the same reason. Finally, setting the hardware clock to Universal Time avoids the problem, because DST only affects local time, not Universal Time.

As mentioned earlier, cron checks all the values of its `crontab` commands every minute on the minute.

`cron` Commands for System `crontab` Files

The format of `cron` commands for system crontab files are slightly different than their user crontab file counterparts. The system crontab files are kept in the `/etc/cron.d/` directory and `/etc/crontab` file. There is an extra field for the `cron` commands in these files that allows you to specify under which user account the command should be run. The following is the general format for `cron` commands in system crontab files:

```
minute hour day month dayofweek username command
```

The allowable values for these fields are as follows:

- `minute`   Value from 0 to 59.

- `hour`   Value from 0 to 23.

- `dayofmonth`   Value from 1 to 31.

- `month`—Value from 1 to 12 or a name from jan to dec.

- `dayofweek`   Value from 0 to 7 (where both 0 and 7 are Sunday) or a name from sun to sat.

- `username`   The username under which the command will be executed.

- `command`   The command to execute at the specified time. It can be multiple words.

All of the other features that are available in the user crontab files are also available under the system crontab files.

As with user-defined crontable files, for each `cron` command in a system crontab file, the specified command is executed whenever the specified minute, hour, and month match the current system values and either `dayofmonth` or `dayofweek` matches the current system day value. The only difference is that the command is now executed under the specified username, rather than under the username of the file's owner.

Global cron Files

As mentioned earlier, the /etc/crontab file sets up several directories under the /etc directory, where you can put files that will be executed periodically by cron. There are four such directories: /etc/cron.hourly/, /etc/cron.daily/, /etc/cron.weekly/, and /etc/cron.monthly/. You can put any number of scripts in those directories, and they can be any type of script. Just remember to make sure they are executable.

As mentioned earlier, any scripts that you put into the /etc/cron.hourly directory will be executed by cron every hour on the first minute of the hour. If you put any scripts into the /etc/cron.daily directory, they will be executed once a day on the second minute of the fourth hour. Any scripts that are in the /etc/cron.weekly directory are executed once a week, on Sunday, at the 22nd minute of the fourth hour. Finally, any scripts that are in the /etc/cron.monthly directory will be run on the first day of every month on the 42nd minute of the fourth hour.

The type of scripts you want to put into the cron subdirectories are periodic scripts over which you don't need a great deal of control. You get far more control using commands that are set up as crontab files; however, there are certain tasks that you just want to be executed regularly, say once a day. In such a case, it is easier to simply create the script and then copy it into the /etc/cron.daily directory. You don't even have to worry about creating a crontab entry—it is almost too easy. An example might be to sync the system clock with universal time (this needs to be done with care) or search the system for certain types of files (viruses, pornography, and so on).

Specifying Which Users Can Use cron

You can specify exactly which users on your system can use cron and add their own crontab entries. There are two files in the /etc directory that allow you to control the access privileges to cron; they are /etc/cron.allow and /etc/cron.deny.

If the /etc/cron.allow file exists and /etc/cron.deny does not exist, only the users listed in that file are allowed to run cron, and each username must be on a separate line in the file. If the /etc/cron.allow exists and the /etc/cron.deny file also exists, the same rules are in effect as if the /etc/cron.deny file did not exist. If the /etc/cron.deny file exists but the /etc/cron.allow file does not exist, all users can use cron except for the users listed in the /etc/cron.deny file.

If neither of the /etc/cron.allow or /etc/cron.deny files exist, only the superuser will be able to use cron and have crontab files, under normal circumstances.

Examples of Using cron

Now you'll take a look at some sample crontab file entries and figure out exactly what each one is doing.

The following crontab command will cause the string "It is 1 am" to be outputted everyday at 1:00 a.m. This will result in the owner of the crontab file receiving an email every day at 1:00 a.m. with the words "It is 1 am" in the email body.

```
0 1 * * * echo "It is 1 am"
```

The following is a slightly more complex example:

```
1 5 10 jul * echo "It is July 10th"
```

This crontab command is similar to the first example, but this time the string outputted reads "It is July 10th" instead of "It is 1 am". In addition, this time the command is executed only once a year on July 10th at 5:01 in the morning.

Take a look at an example that uses a list value:

```
* 2,5,15 4,20 * * find / -name core -print
```

This example will send you an email with a list of every core file on your system and will be executed at 2:00, 5:00, and 15:00 on the 4th and 20th days of each month. Here the list values allow you to specify more than one value for a single field.

The following is an example using range values with a cron command:

```
* 5 4-10 0-3 * find / -name core -print
```

This example does the same things as the last example, but this time it is executed at 5:00 on the 4th, 5th, 6th, 7th, 8th, 9th, and 10th days of the months of January, February, March, and April. Range values are very useful when you want to match a span of values.

The following is another example, making use of the step value notation:

```
* */2 * * sat rm -rf /tmp/*
```

In this case, the command rm -rf /tmp/* is executed every other hour on every Saturday. The value */2 is true every second hour of the day and is equivalent to using the list 0,2,4,6,8,10,12,14,16,18,20,22.

We have covered all the standard features and usage of the cron utility. You should have a solid understanding of how to use cron and be able to implement automated jobs using cron. The next section takes a look at the process of debugging cron jobs and covers a few techniques for ensuring that all cron jobs run as expected.

Debugging cron Jobs

There are a number of techniques you can use to debug your cron jobs. If you are not careful, your cron jobs can have unintentional results, such as deleting files unexpectedly. This could happen if you search for `*.tmp`, not realizing that a music composition program uses `.tmp` extensions for timpani files. Because of this, it is very useful to learn a few tips and tricks for debugging cron jobs. This section explores exactly that, covering the following topics:

- Capturing output

- Using `printf` and `echo` as debugging tools

- Examining the log files

Capturing Output

You can redirect the output of cron jobs to specific files using the standard output redirection syntax. This is very useful because it will create files after each cron job is run that you can examine for errors and debug if necessary. The following is an example of a `crontab` command that will output all errors from the specified command to a file:

```
0 1 * * * rm -rf /tmp/* 2>/home/dbarber/del_tmp.cron
```

Using this command, if any errors occur when cron is trying to execute the `rm -rf /tmp/*` command, they will be put into the `/home/dbarber/del_tmp.cron` file. Every time the cron job runs, it overwrites the contents of the `/home/dbarber/del_tmp.cron` file with the errors from the latest cron job.

Redirecting the output of a command can also be very useful because it will cause all output from that command to go to a file, instead of having an email sent to you. If you find that you are getting a number of useless emails from a specific cron job, you may want to change the crontab entry for that job, redirecting the output to a file.

Using `printf` and `echo` as Debugging Tools

You can use both the `printf` and `echo` commands in your crontab files to print out exactly what the commands in your crontab entry are doing. When `printf` or `echo` displays any output, that output will be mailed to the user of the crontab file so that he or she can examine exactly what his or her cron job is doing.

For example, say you have the following shell script that you want to execute every day at a specific time:

```
#/bin/sh
rm -rf /home/dbarber/backup/*
cp -r /home/dbarber/files/* /home/dbarber/backup/
```

If something goes wrong with this script, you will be emailed any error messages that are outputted from the commands in the script. However, if you have a number of these types of scripts running daily, the error messages by themselves may actually be confusing, and you may not know exactly what command is causing the error. It is a very good idea to print out each command before you execute it so that when the output is emailed to you, you will have a listing of each command executed. If any errors occur, they will appear directly after the command. You will immediately be able to figure out what command caused the error.

The following is the same script, this time with some echo commands outputting some extra information:

```
#/bin/sh
echo Backing up files in /home/dbarber/files to /home/dbarber/backup
echo rm -rf /home/dbarber/backup/*
rm -rf /home/dbarber/backup/*
echo cp -r /home/dbarber/files/* /home/dbarber/backup/
cp -r /home/dbarber/files/* /home/dbarber/backup/
echo end of backup script
```

To get cron to execute that script once a day at 2:00 a.m., add the following file to your crontab file (assuming you saved the previous script as backup.sh):

```
0 2 * * * /home/dbarber/backup.sh
```

When adding lots of output to your cron scripts, be careful to use caution if the cron script executes several times each day, because it will be sending you an email each time that script executes. If each email has a number of lines of output, you will find that your disk space may start to disappear if you do not delete the emails regularly. This is especially true for scripts run as root, because you may not log in as root for several days and the amount of email sent from cron can grow quite rapidly.

Of course, you can also use the printf command instead of echo if you want to specifically format the output. This might be needed if the files are imported into a database of spreadsheet. For many situations however, the echo command is more than sufficient.

Examining the Log Files

There are several files that are under the `/var/log` directory where cron logs all of commands it runs. The files are called `cron`, `cron.1`, `cron.2`, `cron.3`, and `cron.4`, and you must have superuser privileges to view their contents. The following is a listing of the contents of the `/var/log/cron` file:

```
# cat /var/log/cron

root (08/15-04:22:00-3862) CMD (run-parts /etc/cron.weekly)
root (08/15-05:01:00-3974) CMD (run-parts /etc/cron.hourly)
root (08/15-06:01:00-4003) CMD (run-parts /etc/cron.hourly)
root (08/15-07:01:00-4015) CMD (run-parts /etc/cron.hourly)
root (08/15-08:01:00-4041) CMD (run-parts /etc/cron.hourly)
root (08/15-09:01:00-4069) CMD (run-parts /etc/cron.hourly)
root (08/15-10:01:00-4122) CMD (run-parts /etc/cron.hourly)
root (08/15-11:01:00-4154) CMD (run-parts /etc/cron.hourly)
root (08/15-12:01:00-4338) CMD (run-parts /etc/cron.hourly)
root (08/15-13:01:00-4677) CMD (run-parts /etc/cron.hourly)
root (08/15-14:01:00-4797) CMD (run-parts /etc/cron.hourly)
root (08/15-15:01:00-4957) CMD (run-parts /etc/cron.hourly)
root (08/15-16:01:00-4977) CMD (run-parts /etc/cron.hourly)
root (08/15-17:01:00-5118) CMD (run-parts /etc/cron.hourly)
```

In the `/var/log/cron` file, you have all the times that cron has been run in the past day. As you can see, the contents of the `/etc/cron.weekly` directory was executed at 4:22 a.m., and the contents of the `/etc/cron.hourly` directory was executed every hour on the first minute of the hour.

The files `cron.1`, `cron.2`, and `cron.3` contain similar information, although slightly older than cron. The cron log files are great to check on whether your cron jobs are executing at the correct time or whether they are even executing at all. If you have many cron jobs set up on your system, it is wise to check the cron log files every few days just to make sure that all the cron jobs are executing properly.

Summary

This chapter examined job automation in detail, specifically covering the reason for automating jobs as well as exactly how to go about scheduling jobs to be automated. You should have a solid understanding of the concept of job automation and how to employ it in your system administration duties.

The two utilities that allow you to perform job automation under Red Hat Linux were covered in detail; they are the at and cron utilities. You should be able to use either of those utilities to automate jobs, using at for one-time tasks and cron for regular tasks. I believe that you will find both utilities to be very helpful in your system administration duties.

Finally, this chapter looked at debugging cron jobs, a useful skill for any Red Hat Linux system administrator to master. Things can go wrong with cron jobs and because they execute automatically, it can be difficult to isolate problems.

In closing, I hope you have gained some useful knowledge and skills from this chapter and that you can find new and interesting way of automating your system administration tasks.

System Tuning and Kernel Building

PART
X

IN THIS PART

34 Tuning Your Linux System   *1047*

35 Customizing the Linux Kernel   *1081*

36 Centennial School District, Portland, Oregon   *1135*

34

Tuning Your Linux System

IN THIS CHAPTER

- General Areas of Tuning *1049*
- Weighing Costs and Benefits *1052*
- Understanding Performance Measurement Techniques *1055*
- Understanding Network Performance *1067*
- Memory and Swap Space *1068*
- Swap Space Priorities *1071*
- Swap Partitions Versus Swap Files *1074*
- Tunable Parameters in /proc *1075*
- Using echo to Alter System Behavior *1078*

CHAPTER

Linux Systems require a great deal of maintenance and care. Performance tuning is the art of making a Linux system operate at its best possible level. This chapter focuses on performance considerations including techniques, costs and benefits, memory, swap space and priorities, swap partitions, and manipulating the /proc filesystem (the interface to the Linux Kernel).

Among the many chores and tasks a systems administrator must perform, tuning is definitely one of the most rewarding (perhaps second to installation activities). Tuning means that the administrator has taken the time and effort to make sure the system operates at a level of acceptable performance. Most often this can be measured by the user's experience. For example, a terminal user who is on the local network expects immediate response from listing files, whereas a programmer expects a certain time to elapse while compiling a project he is working on. Over time, the administrator will develop an affinity for how the system should perform at different time intervals and periods.

All systems, including Linux, require some degree of performance tuning. Perhaps not immediately, but it is rare that a system's tasks do not grow to the point where the system's performance must be examined. As the system's functions become more complex, require more processor time, and put more demand on memory and disk I/O, tuning becomes an important factor in the growth and well-being of the system.

Users are what ultimately matter. Linux provides a strong base to operate from (as do HURD and many commercial versions of UNIX). However, no system will ever operate at the level users expect it to. What users expect and what they receive is very important. Of all people, a systems administrator should expect (and sympathize with) what the user wants. Just because you like Linux does not mean the average user does; you must forget how you perceive the system and see how the users perceive it. Many users outright dislike UNIXish systems. This is where tuning takes its shape, beating what is expected by delivering what is real and giving your system as much power as it can have. This is the essence of performance tuning.

Tuning a system sounds great, but what are some of the aspects of tuning, or perhaps more appropriately, where are the aspects of tuning and what does a systems administrator have to take into account when approaching bottlenecks and other performance issues? Let's take that two-part question and address the first half, general areas of tuning.

General Areas of Tuning

Problems come in three major areas, two of which (I/O and CPU) are nearly directly related (it is important to note that all three are related in one way or another). The three general areas are

- CPU

- I/O (disk writes and reads)

- Memory (excessive paging—related to disk I/O)

Initially, these seem relatively simple. If it is the CPU, how can better load balancing be achieved? Perhaps with another CPU or faster chipset? If it is excessive paging, the answer may be more memory or a change in how swapping is done. If it is I/O, a change in how disks are arranged and formatted may be required. What if it is a specific user or process that is causing performance issues? How do you ascertain whether an I/O problem is in the disks or swapping? Note the use of *perhaps*, *maybe*, and *if* in this paragraph thus far. That is how performance monitoring is—a great deal of "ifs" until the problem is eventually found and rectified.

Specific Tuning Aspects and Questions

Well, it gets worse. Along with the aforementioned rudimentary questions you have to take into account when attacking a performance issue, there are a handful of more complex (yet succinctly related) questions that come into play as well.

What Is a Bottleneck?

Aside from the more obvious portion of a beer bottle, in system's terms a bottleneck is anything that slows down the system to a point where it is readily apparent (or not so readily apparent).

A readily apparent bottleneck might be something like users saying they listed a directory and it took two minutes to list ten entries.

A not so readily apparent bottleneck (or as I like call them, "creeping death") are those that are potential bottlenecks. A case in point might be the gradual increase of use on an ftp server. Although it is still running fast now, after a certain point in time it will become quite apparent that it is too slow.

Frequency of Bottlenecks

How often does a particular bottleneck occur? This is a very big question that pertains mostly to user inquiries. More often than not, you may discover later that there was no cause for alarm because the user was doing something that was not routine or that was a one-time, isolated incident. Some good examples of this are when a user improperly invokes a command or application, when a user is trying a new way of performing some task, or when a user is trying something completely new. This can happen a great deal in very progressive environments where change is the norm. Such an environment, for example, is one in which new systems and methods are being developed and brought online rapidly. Sometimes, users may not even be aware of them until they start wondering why a job is taking so long.

Bottleneck Location

Where exactly is the bottleneck occurring? This will be examined later in this chapter in the section "Performance Measurement Techniques," but it is worth glancing at now. Is the bottleneck staring at you right now? If so, you may want to investigate it as soon as possible. Prolonged, easily identifiable bottlenecks should at least be made known so that users and/or managers might better understand that there is a problem, that you know what it is, and that you will identify a recourse. Sometimes bottlenecks can mask other bottlenecks or are a result of another bottleneck. Figuring which is happening can be puzzling, especially when you consider it can be only one of three general areas. Where this is seen most often is between paging and disk I/O.

Bottleneck Duration

Is the bottleneck sustained? This is a very important and often overlooked factor about performance—a "take it with a grain of salt" issue. When a user complains that the system is sluggish or perhaps you look at a quick snapshot of the CPU and notice high usage, how long does it really last? Is it long enough to become apparent to other users? A prime example of this might be a user compiling a program. Of course, to the user and even to the system it will appear to be very resource-intensive—but how long does it take to finish and what sort of system-level impact is it having?

General Bottleneck Focal Point Location

Is it within the box? This is one of the most important questions to ask yourself and to determine quickly. Is it within the box or a network issue? It is also one of the most confusing when network file transfers, system-to-system database transactions, or multinode intranets come into play. Network issues can often cloud the perception of where a bottleneck may be. It may not even be on the system you are examining at all, or it may be on the network or another host altogether.

What other processes that do not appear to be intensive are running? As an example, let's say that when job X on Linux server Larry runs, there are normally only 100 users logged in. For some reason, on this particular day there are 200 users logged in. When you scanned the top monitor (mentioned later in this chapter), you didn't notice the other users or maybe it looked like they were not individually eating up resources. This can happen and you might be surprised if it does.

Relative Importance of Tuning

Is it even worth it? The next section, "Weighing Costs and Benefits," discusses this in greater detail, but it also deserves mention in the "Considerations" context. Can the users live with it? Can you? Perhaps even more important, can the system?

Is there any risk involved? Number one question: Will you endanger the system by changing a kernel parameter or changing swap priority? Will an improvement here cause a detriment there? This is a very important, and tough, decision to make.

> **Note**
>
> Always try to keep a "basher box" or test system lying around to see how a change may affect a live system. Even though the systems may be radically different, at least you get a "warm fuzzy" for what changes you might expect to see. Most of the time, changes on a test system do accurately reflect how they would affect a live system.

34

Tuning Your
Linux System

No system is ever running at peak efficiency out of the box, even if the person who installed it was very specific about what the system would be doing, what services it would be running, and its general configuration. Chances are there is something, somewhere, that could be better or (as is more often the case) just isn't needed.

> **Note**
>
> Unrequired services rarely put a load on a Linux system; however, some of them can actually cause a system to become somewhat unstable.

Unrequired services should be a no-brainer. Always look for unrequired services that were started or installed that you don't need. Aside from the obvious possible load they may put on the system, running unused (and subsequently unmonitored) services is a security risk. Coupled with the security issues is another very important issue: startup and/or recovery time. In a multiuser environment (in my own case, nearly 500 users at peak times) startup and recovery time is crucial. Unrequired services should be eliminated for the sole purpose of speed at boot time. A prime example of this is the Apache Web Server. Many distributions have Apache turned on by default; however, what if you never plan to use it? It is wasting processor cycles regardless of how lightweight the Apache processes may be. This also relates to the troubles of micro-examining a system and changing configurations, as discussed in the following section.

Weighing Costs and Benefits

There is a wide variety of different costs with a common benefit—better performance. The costs come in the form of money and time. They include money required for more hardware, the time (which ends up costing money) a system must be down, or the time in man-hours required to increase a system's level of performance.

Many performance issues (especially memory-related ones) can only be solved by purchasing newer or additional hardware. Granted, this is less often the case with Linux systems and more so with other operating systems, but it certainly does happen. Sometimes the question arises as to whether is it worth the expense. Not only does the hardware cost issue arise, but man-hours are also a pertinent cost. Is it really worth the headache to spend hours, days, or sometimes weeks to find a better solution? Is it worth the cost in your or your department's man-hours? Piled on top of both of these is the ultimate cost-weighted (and most loaded) question: Is the whole system a bottleneck? Is it time for more than just more memory or more cache?

Ultimately, the question is when do you have to buy hardware and when can you get away with not buying it? The best way to answer this is through an example. One time that more hardware must be bought is when meeting minimum specifications. To install a certain database product, you may have to have a minimum of 512MB of memory and 1GB of swap space. Sometimes to scale that appropriately you may have to have a TB of memory and swap, whatever the case may be. If you do not have the required amount, chances are you will need it or you face a potentially crippling bottleneck. In other cases, a tape drive may not be finishing backups on time or requires multiple tapes, which then makes the backup run too long and slows down the system. You will most likely have to find a faster and higher density device.

Hardware Costs

Hardware costs can become a complicated matter. At what point does it become prohibitive to continue to add hardware to a particular architecture? On RISC-based systems, this is usually a very easy question (consult the hardware documentation guides) but on x86-based systems, this can be very hard to determine. The reason for this is the incredible scalability of Linux systems. Many times, you can increase performance on other cost-versus-benefit weights such as using a less resource-intensive Window Manager (or not using one at all). In such a case, the loss is Window Manager eye candy and the gain is out-and-out performance. Another cost might be the time it takes to perform a full backup of data and repartition the system for better disk I/O performance. It does, however, often come down to more or newer hardware. There is a point that can be reached where the system is the bottleneck—you have reached the limit of upgradability and simply have to purchase a new system (again, a rarity in Linux).

> **Note**
>
> One practice a systems administrator may find useful is "musical servers." How this works is relatively simple. Say you have three Linux systems, Larry, Curly, and Moe. Larry is the Web and FTP server. Curly is the mSQL database and Moe is your basher box. You buy a new server because Larry is under stress and you have used up its hardware scalability. But, it is more powerful than Curly, which is more powerful than Moe. Simply transfer Larry to the new system, and then Curly to Larry and now you either have two basher boxes or Moe has been freed up for some other purpose (your personal workstation?).

34

Tuning Your Linux System

System Requirements and Needs

Combining all of the elements of symptoms and cost ultimately leads to the big question, which is how much of a real need is this? Sometimes you will discover that the need is exaggerated or not as important as you were led (or led yourself) to believe.

Perhaps one of the biggest costs may be running the risk of damaging the system or facing major downtime to make enhancements. This cost issue is rare in Linux but can happen. You must also take into account when you are not sure what (if any) side effects will result in a change in how the system operates. Being prepared for a disaster is very important when deciding to make system-level changes. Sometimes things can (and seem more often to) go awry. This should be the number one factor when approaching critical problems such as filesystem and memory/cache issues. The cost may be more than you bargained for. Where this really comes into play is modifying the kernel and system parameters for better performance. Sometimes side effects may happen, and they may be worth it. Some processes within an organization do (and should) take priority over others and, as a result, you may be forced to cause some detriment to others to gain better performance for a given service or process. An example of this might be weighing the priority of a real-time process that collects data versus someone simply viewing files leisurely. The real-time data collection would be a higher priority. The key here is to ensure that you do not accidentally inflict system-wide detriment by "enhancing" a particular aspect of the system. Although this is rare, it most certainly can happen.

> **Note**
>
> As will be noted in later chapters, always keep a backup kernel and snapshot of the system handy in case you are making critical changes to enhance performance.

Performance Enhancements

Luckily, most performance enhancements do not require running the risk of blasting the system into oblivion. Shutting down unrequired services means that if someone was actually using one, it can be restarted. Many caching parameters can be enlarged or shrunken without affecting the system's overall operation. It is important to note, however, what you are changing and how to undo it.

All of these factors must come into play when deciding on how to best serve the system's performance needs. The system's performance is ranked nearly beside stability and uptime. What good is a system if it is so slow no one is getting anything done? Not much, but with practice and patience, a system that appears to be slow can be tuned for optimum performance, which leads to how you determine where a problem is and how to tackle it.

Understanding Performance Measurement Techniques

We have discussed performance considerations, costs, and benefits, but how does it actually get done? There is always a bottleneck somewhere. But there is a point that can be reached where the bottleneck is not apparent to the user because it is actually small compared to one you may have just gotten rid of. Here is a good example: The Linux server Larry has some sort of obvious memory bottleneck. Larry needs more memory and complimentary swap space. Being the wise administrator you are, you planned for this. You add memory to Larry and summarily increase swap space. Larry now appears to be running just fine. In your day-to-day monitoring of Larry, you notice that the disk I/O is now the bottleneck, but the system appears to be running just fine. This is where bottleneck masking comes into play. In this case it is acceptable, but sometimes you may discover that there is another problematic (or soon to be) bottleneck that was hidden because of a more urgent and pressing performance issue.

There are a wide variety of tools both inherent and off-the-shelf for performance monitoring. For the sake of simplicity (and perhaps reality), this section focuses on tools that come with Linux systems. First, we will examine console-based tools, then move onto some X-tools that are available with most distributions of Linux. Finally, we will look at tools that may or may not be included with common distributions but are easily downloaded and usable under a variety of X Windows environments.

Console-Based Tools

On most UNIX systems (Linux being no exception), an administrator's most common performance monitoring tools are console-based tools, or rather tools that operate from the command line. The main reason for this is remote access. An administrator can telnet in from home or across a network and quickly assess what is happening and how to fix it. Another reason for this is that console-based tools tend not to create as much of a load on a system as X Windows–based tools.

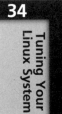

Process Monitoring with `top`

Arguably one of the most-used console performance monitoring tools to date is `top`, which, by definition, displays the top CPU-intensive processes in real time. The `top` display is refreshed every five seconds by default, but can be modified with the `-s` option for longer or shorter intervals. Top also provides an interactive interface for modifying processes. Following is the syntax for starting `top` in default mode:

```
$ top
```

Figure 34.1 shows an example of top output as seen from an xiterm window.

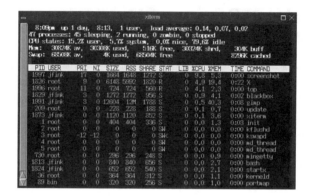

Table 34.1 explains the monitor fields in top.

TABLE **34.1** top Monitor Fields

Field	Description
up	How long the system has been up and the three load averages.
processes	Total number of processes running as of the last update including a count of running, waiting, sleeping, stopped, and zombied tasks.
CPU States	The average in percentage of CPU time in system, user, idle, and niced (negative values only) tasks. *Note:* Niced tasks are also counted in system and user time so the total can be more than 100%.
Mem	Memory statistics such as total, available, free, used, shared, and buffered.
Swap	Swap statistics including total allocated swap space, available swap space, and used swap space. *Note:* Swap and Mem are similar to the output of free, which is discussed later in the text.

Table 34.2 explains the process fields in top.

TABLE **34.2** top Process Fields

Field	Description
PID	Process ID of each task.
USER	The username of a task's owner.
PRI	The priority of a task.
NI	The nice value of a task.

TABLE **34.2** continued

Field	Description
SIZE	The total size of a task including code, data, plus stack space in kbytes.
RSS	Amount of physical memory used by a task.
SHARE	Amount of shared memory used by a task.
STATE	Current CPU state of a task. The states can be S for sleeping, D for uninterrupted, R for running, T for stopped/traced, and Z for zombied.
TIME	The CPU time a task has used since it was started.
%CPU	The CPU time a task has used since the last update.
%MEM	A task's share of physical memory.
COMMAND	The task's command name.

Note

A task's command name is truncated if the tasks only have the program name in parentheses.

As noted earlier, top does have interactive commands that can be invoked while top is running. Table 34.3 shows the output of the interactive help option (invoked by pressing h while top is running).

TABLE **34.3** Interactive top Commands

Key	Function
space	Update display
^L	Redraw the screen
fF	Add and remove fields
oO	Change order of displayed fields
h or ?	Print this list
S	Toggle CPU cumulative mode
i	Toggle display of idle processes
c	Toggel display of command name/line
l	Toggle display of load average
m	Toggle display of memory information

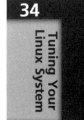

TABLE **34.3**   continued

Key	Function
t	Toggle display of summary information
k	Kill a task (with any signal)
r	Renice a task
P	Sort by CPU usage

top also has some command-line options to modify its default behavior prior to starting it up. They are as follows:

- d—Changes the delay between screen updates
- q—Causes top to refresh without any delay

Note

If run as superuser, top takes the highest possible priority.

- S—Specifies CPU cumulative mode
- s—Tells top to run in secure mode

Note

The s command disables potentially dangerous interactive commands.

- i—Starts top ignoring idle or zombie processes
- c—Displays command line instead of the command name only

vmstat

Another good monitoring utility is vmstat. The vmstat command gives you a great deal of information concerning the system's condition—it measures CPU, memory, swap, and I/O usage. The vmstat command's syntax is as follows:

```
$ vmstat interval [count]
```

A sample syntax with an interval of five seconds and five counts would look like this:

```
$ vmstat 5 5
   procs                    memory      swap        io     system          cpu
 r  b  w   swpd   free  buff cache   si  so   bi   bo    in   cs   us  sy  id
 1  0  0     68   5416  2724 25796    0   0    1    0   113   57    1   0  99
 0  0  0     68   5424  2724 25796    0   0    0    2   108   28    1   0  99
 0  0  0     68   5424  2724 25796    0   0    0    1   106   25    0   1  99
 0  0  0     68   5424  2724 25796    0   0    0    0   105   25    0   1  99
 0  0  0     68   5424  2724 25796    0   0    0    0   102   25    0   0  99
```

The very first line output by vmstat is the average values for statistic since boot time (so don't be alarmed).

vmstat is actually broken up into five sections: procs, memory, swap, io, and cpu.

Each section is outlined in the following tables.

The procs section:

Procs	*Description*
r	Number of processes waiting for run time
b	Number of interrupted sleep processes
w	Number of swapped out processes, but able to run

The memory section:

Memory	*Description*
Swpd	Amount of virtual memory used in kbytes
Free	Amount of idle memory used in kbytes
Buff	Amount of memory used by buffers in kbytes
Cache	Amount of memory left in cache in kbytes

The swap section:

Swap	*Description*
si	Amount of memory swapped in from disk in kbytes
so	Amount of memory swapped to disk

34

Tuning Your Linux System

The io section:

IO	Description
bi	Blocks sent to a block device in `blocks/s`
bo	Blocks received from a block device in `blocks/s`
cs	Number of context switches per second

The cpu section:

CPU	Description
us	A percentage of CPU cycles spent on user tasks
sy	A percentage of CPU cycles spent on total system tasks
id	A percentage of unused CPU cycles or idle time

uptime

There are also a few short and quick console commands that display useful information about the system load. Although not as useful as `top` or `vmstat` for long-term analysis, they provide a fleeting glance at aspects of system performance.

The first of these is `uptime`. When invoked (or monitored with `top`), `uptime` displays three load averages. They are the average number of processes ready to run during the last 1, 5, and 15 minutes.

The `uptime` command is invoked like so:

```
$ uptime
```

Here is some sample output from a machine that has been up for some time:

```
 4:29pm  up  120:48,  1 user,  load average: 0.00, 0.00, 0.00
```

The fields of `uptime` are the current time, how long the system has been running, how many users are currently logged on, and the three system load averages mentioned earlier.

free

The next command is `free`. With `free`, an administrator can look at memory that is free and used. The default syntax for `free` is pretty straightforward:

```
$ free
```

Following is an example of `free`'s output without any options:

```
               total       used       free     shared    buffers     cached
Mem:           55064      48480       6584      44520       3352      25832
-/+ buffers/cache:        19296      35768
Swap:         137016         68     136948
```

The first line of output shows the physical memory and the last line shows similar information for swapped spaces. Table 34.4 shows a description of each of the fields in the output of `free`.

TABLE 34.4 `free` Command Output Fields

Field	Description
total	Total amount of user available memory (excluding the kernel memory, which is normally around 1MB)
used	The total amount of used memory
free	The total amount of free memory
shared	The total amount of process shared memory
buffers	The current size of disk buffer cache
cached	Amount of memory that has been cached off onto disk

The `free` command does have some options that can be specified when it is invoked. Table 34.5 explains the different options.

TABLE 34.5 `free` Command Options

Option	Description
-b	Displays the amount of memory in bytes
-k	Displays the amount of memory in kilobytes (default)
-m	Displays the amount of memory in megabytes
-t	Displays a line containing the totals
-o	Disables the display of a "buffer adjusted line"
-s	Activates continuous polling in <delay> apart

34

Tuning Your Linux System

time

Finally, one very simple and interesting way to figure out how long a given command takes to run is `time`. `time` returns a string value with information about a process and is launched with the process like so:

```
$ time <command_name> [options]
```

Here is an example:

```
$ time ls -all /usr/bin
```

The output from that syntax looks like this (after the command specified after `time` runs):

```
0.22user 0.92system 0:02.00elapsed 50%CPU (0avgtest+avgdata 0maxresident)k
0inouts+0outputs (117major+122minore)pagefaults 0swaps
```

Although this is very low level, the `time` command can give very enlightening information about a particular command or program.

When the opportunity presents itself, command-line tools can most certainly be pushed aside for the easy-to-follow (and visually digest) GUI tools.

Graphical Utilities

In addition to console-based utilities, there are several default graphical utilities that come with a Linux system. The differences between console-based and GUI tools (aside from the obvious appearance, of course) are the speed at which they can disseminate the information they see and how much of a load the tool places on the system. For example, running a long `vmstat` may be difficult to read, but it is much less intense than xload. The following sections detail each GUI tool.

Xosview

Xosview is a relatively low-overhead (as in almost none) graphical monitoring tool that you can run all of the time. If your Window Manager has an entry for xosview, you can start it from X or simply start up any terminal window and type

```
$ xosview &
```

It should look something like Figure 34.2.

FIGURE 34.2

An example of xosview.

There are six fields in xosview, which are explained in detail in the following list.

- Load—The load has two colors; the first color is the load average of processes and the second color is the background. If the average goes above 1.0, the bar will change color.

- CPU—The CPU field has four color indicators; usr, nice, sys, and free.

- `Mem`—In this section, the full amount of real memory in use is being shown. There are four colors in this section, all of which have meaning. Starting from the left, used+shar is how much the user is using; buff shows the amount in buffer; cache is the amount being cached; and the remainder is what is left. It is important to note that the entire bar is used and the rightmost section is not the background.

- `Swap`—The swap section displays information about swap space. More specifically, how much data is being swapped out onto disk. The used memory is one color and the other color is free memory. Once again the entire bar is used.

- `Page`—The page section indicates how much data is being swapped in and out of memory. There are three colors: paging in, paging out, and idle.

> **Note**
>
> Occasional spikes in paging and swap should not cause alarm. That means the system is working correctly. Seeing either (usually both) peaked for prolonged periods could mean a problem.

- `Ints`—The ints display shows interrupts as they are being used (by IRQ). For example, moving a mouse will cause the corresponding interrupt to light up momentarily.

The xosview utility is pretty nice (no pun intended). Leaving it running on the desktop of a system will do no harm whatsoever—it is a great way to just sit and watch how the system performs.

Xload

The next common graphical utility is xload. Xload is a simple system-wide (as in all resources) load average display utility. To start xload without an X Window menu option, simply start a terminal up and type

```
$ xload &
```

The window should look something like Figure 34.3.

FIGURE 34.3
An example xload session.

Some X Windows Managers have xload built in to them, such as the AfterStep load monitor asload shown in Figure 34.4.

FIGURE 34.4
The AfterStep load monitor.

> **Note**
>
> Many of these can run under different Window Managers, such as xosview and xload.

Real Time Versus Gathered Performance Data

All graphical utilities such as xosview and xload are "real time" and difficult to capture for later use. Tools such as xview or the GIMP can be used, but these hardly seem appropriate or efficient for capturing data at a specific time. Unlike graphical tools, the console-based utilities mentioned earlier in this section can be used to captured specific measurements at specific times.

An Example of Monitoring Over Time

As an example, let's say that Linux system Larry is running an Apache Web server on your intranet and users have been complaining that between noon and 12:30 p.m. the server seems slow and sluggish. You know for a fact that it isn't the network. You do not want to be at the server during your lunch. The answer is simple—write a short shell script to capture data and schedule it to run several times between noon and 12:30 p.m. in cron. You can use several commands, but for simplicity, vmstat will be used here. The shell script (gather_vmstats) might look like this:

```
#!/usr/bin/sh
date >> /root/reports/lunch_bog.txt
vmstat 5 5 >> /root/reports/lunch_bog.txt
```

Then make the script executable with chmod:

```
$ chmod /root/scripts/gather_vmstats
```

Next, for posterity, empty the file the utility will append to by using NULL before scheduling it in cron:

```
$ >/root/reports/lunch_bog.txt
```

Finally, schedule the script to run at five-minute intervals. The cron entry would look like this:

```
# temporary cronjob so I can eat out instead of at the vending machine
00 12 * * * /root/scripts/gather_vmstats 2&>1
05 12 * * * /root/scripts/gather_vmstats 2&>1
10 12 * * * /root/scripts/gather_vmstats 2&>1
15 12 * * * /root/scripts/gather_vmstats 2&>1
20 12 * * * /root/scripts/gather_vmstats 2&>1
25 12 * * * /root/scripts/gather_vmstats 2&>1
30 12 * * * /root/scripts/gather_vmstats 2&>1
```

With a Perl script, you could also have told `vmstat` to run at five minute intervals in a loop for a half hour instead of scheduling it for every five minutes in crontab. There are many ways to do this, but you should be seeing the possibilities here. You can easily make a set of nicely formatted performance reports using languages such as Perl. If you wanted to go a step further, you could easily build a historical reference of reports to keep handy using the enhanced parsing and formatting capabilities of Perl.

Another scenario you may have is a wide range of times that the system is being bogged down. One way to track down those times and further identify the problem would be to run a script once an hour for 24 hours. Identify the hours that are showing high usage and then run it several times within that hour, then half hour, and so forth. This method is very similar to the hardware troubleshooting method of half splitting, in which you eliminate one half of a circuit and focus next on eliminating half of the remaining half until the problem is localized.

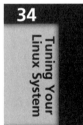

Process Management

Although process management via the `top` utility was mentioned earlier, it was never fully explained. This section provides an overview of single process management on a Linux operating system.

Nice and Renice

The nice value indicates how "nice" a program or process is to other programs. The nicer (or higher) the nice priority, the slower a program will be to use resources; the lower the nice priority (which in reality is a higher process priority) the "less nice" a program will be to other programs, and it will use resources at an increased rate.

The `nice` and `renice` commands are used to modify the priority of a program. The `nice` command is used in conjunction with the program's invocation to set it to a priority other than the default (which on Red Hat Linux is 0). The syntax looks like this:

```
$ nice -n (priority) command [command_options]
```

For example, if I were compiling a program and I wanted to increase its nice value to 5, the syntax would look like this:

```
$ nice -n 5 gcc myprog.c
```

This gives the task `gcc myprog.c` a nice value of 5. The valid range on Red Hat Linux is -20 to 20.

There are times in which you have a running job that probably needs a higher priority, but you do not want to stop it and restart it with a higher priority. Enter `renice`. With `renice`, you can raise the priority of a process on-the-fly. The syntax of the `renice` command is as follows:

```
renice priority [[-p] pid . . . ] [[-g] pgrp . . . ] [[-u] user . . . ]
```

In the following example, a process's nice priority is changed:

```
$ renice 10 5123
5123: old priority 0, new priority 10
```

Note

The owner of a process may raise its priority; however, only root may lower a nice priority (in effect raising its system priority) for any process.

Okay, so what exactly does changing a process's priority have to do with performance measurement? It can be used, mainly by the systems administrator, as a benchmark tool for certain processes or as a holdover measure until a better resolution for a performance issue can be found.

There are other measures and steps to be taken when monitoring systems. The following section looks at some of those.

Understanding Network Performance

The next aspect of performance is networking. Finding out if a Linux system's network interface is getting bottlenecked is relatively simple. It becomes difficult when other systems peruse a Linux system or they pass data back and forth over the network. What appears to be a "box" problem may in fact be overall network bandwidth, or it may be another box. When there appears to be a problem, say in a database upload from your server to another, attempt to isolate the problem quickly or you may find yourself spinning your wheels. Although this chapter does not go into detail about solving network issues (see Chapter 16, "Network Monitoring"), it is important to be aware of the possibility.

Benchmarking and Testing the Network

One of the best ways to prevent a bottleneck is to benchmark and test. Not all bottlenecks that occur on a system are random. Most of the time, just the opposite is true. Benchmarking new processes, methods, and applications is very important before deployment. This falls into the category of preventative measurement techniques. A good example of this is implementing new filesharing systems. For the sake of argument, assume that Linux server Larry is also going to need to share files with Win32 PC systems via some mechanism. The first and most obvious choice is SAMBA's SMB/CIFS services. Instead of simply dumping SMB/CIFS onto the network and making it available to everyone, test it first. See what kind of stress a couple of users put the system under. Finding ways to enhance its performance, then deploying, benchmarking, and testing—especially filesharing services—is both very important and rewarding. It can save a lot of headaches in the long run.

Overall system performance is not as difficult as it might seem. Almost every time there is a real bottleneck it will be readily apparent. However, there are occasions when bottlenecks are difficult to find or are masked altogether. Perseverance and patience are your greatest attributes when hunting the part of the system that is causing problems. With a little ingenuity and crafty scripting, an administrator can easily track down and identify bottlenecks.

34

Tuning Your Linux System

Memory and Swap Space

One of the jobs of being a systems administrator is purchasing additional or new hardware for a Linux system, and that can be a difficult and mysterious process. Within the context of performance, one of the most important decisions about getting hardware is RAM (Random Access Memory). RAM is where system operations, processes, and tasks are stored until called upon by the CPU. RAM also uses swap space (discussed later in this section) as virtual memory in case there is not enough physical RAM or it is convenient to swap information out of RAM and onto the disk. The first part of this section deals with initially deciding how much RAM is needed and the second part deals with determining how much RAM may need to be added to an existing system.

Deciding How Much RAM Is Needed

The best method of determining how much RAM you need to purchase is to go by some general guidelines per platform type and applications. What that means is certain Linux systems simply may not need nearly as much as others. The best way to illustrate this is to separate the types into single user and multi-user. We all know that Linux systems by default are multi-user. The question is how many users will actually be using the Linux system you are installing? If it is only one, one at a time, or a handful, looking at RAM from a single-user point of view is practical. The multi-user system, as we all know with a free operating system is pretty much limitless, but for the sake of argument let's say there are 200 simultaneous users.

Single-User System

The single-user system is obviously the easiest to purchase RAM for (all things being equal). If a console environment is acceptable, 16MB of RAM on a single-user system will easily suffice. Otherwise, if X Windows will be used, 32MB and up is advisable for smooth operation. It is worth mentioning that three Window Managers—FVWM, FVWM2, and Blackbox—are all very light (the lightest of the three being Blackbox) and operate well between 16MB and 32MB of RAM. The next consideration on a single-user system is what type of applications will be running on it. Will the GIMP be used for a great deal of image manipulation? If so, consider slapping even more RAM (8-16MB more) on top of the base estimate of 16 or 32MB. Will there be constant compiling or program testing? Once again, use roughly the same amount of RAM as the GIMP. All in all, on a single- or few-user system, 32-64MB is a safe bet. On a completely single-user system running a light Window Manager, 32MB will suffice.

Multi-User System

The larger multi-user system is a completely different situation. Easily estimating user memory space, although not impossible, can seem improbable. The best bet is to always err on the high side. Filesharing systems such as NFS and SAMBA require extra RAM for general overhead but not a great deal more than the base on a larger multi-user system, which should be at least 64MB for nominal tasks and 128MB-5GB for file and print sharing for a lot of users (say around 200 or so). Being the "err on the high side" type, I would go for .75 to 1 full GB for large capacity filesharing systems.

On the flip side, Web servers alone with static HTML pages rarely need a lot of RAM. Whereas 128MB should be enough for a simple Web server, up to 1GB may be required for Web servers that are expected to perform a lot of server side tasks such as cgi-bin invoked Perl programs or continuous dynamic content updates.

With Linux's growing acceptance in the mainstream commercial market, there is a new beast to grapple with insofar as capacity planning—the database. Databases require an immense amount of RAM, disk, and CPU power to operate normally. Most commercial databases have grown into monolithic systems all their own (as a matter of fact, some are emerging with their own filesystems). The current corporate standard for databases such as Oracle 8i is 1GB per processor in addition to your base RAM estimate. Smaller databases such as mSQL do not require nearly as much, even with a lot of users—a safe bet is .5GB of RAM in addition to the base memory.

Figuring Actual RAM Requirements

So how does it all add up? Simple. Let's say you need to purchase RAM for a maximum of 200 simultaneous users on a system that will be running the following services/ applications:

- NFS
- SAMBA
- mSQL
- Apache Web Server
- A Perl front end connecting the Web server to mSQL db

First you decide to use FVWM as the Window Manager at the system console. So your initial base RAM is 32MB (because we always err on the high side). Next, you want to pick up an additional .5GB of RAM for NFS and SAMBA servers, and another .5GB for mSQL transactions. Now you are up around 1.032GB of RAM. To make life simple, bump it up to 1.5GB of RAM—a pretty accurate measurement, actually.

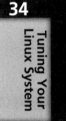

There are (as always) exceptions. Power users, programmers, and systems administrators fall outside of both the high-end server range and home hacking system low-end range. They all have special needs that vary. More often than not, however, all of those three have a pretty fair idea based on experience of what they need. For a systems administrator, a machine powerful enough to at least prototype some of the software that will be on servers is desirable. Usually about half of the RAM the servers have will suffice for testing (since you will be doing the testing). Power users may opt for fancier graphics and different X Window Managers, so a healthy 64MB may be in order. Linux programmers usually require about 32–64MB of RAM to run and compile programs.

Additional RAM

Getting additional RAM is an altogether different situation. It really depends on how bottlenecked the memory currently is on a system. If it is nearly swap thrashing all of the time, buy at least twice as much RAM just get out of an obviously bad situation. Otherwise, take a backward incremental approach to buying additional RAM. If excessive swapping is happening at certain times, make sure it is indeed the RAM that is causing it and buy close to twice as much. If the system is marginally swapping it is probably alright, but if you discover it is constantly paging at around 50% or so, it wouldn't hurt to pick up 20%–30% more RAM just to be on the safe side.

Purchasing RAM for a New System

The good thing about buying additional RAM is that you have a base to go from. When buying RAM for a new and unused system, it is unclear as to how much you should get. Always err on the high side with systems that are going to be used in an organizational setting. On a final note, when transferring a system, the normal capacity plan is to double the current system and add roughly 20% to the result of doubling. Although that formula is normally used for disk capacity, I have found it works well with RAM also.

To summarize, single-user or few-user systems with basic Web server processes running need 64MB of RAM. Above that, look at .5 to 1GB of memory. A strange gap, yes, but not unrealistic. It draws parallel to previous UNIX systems and should be no surprise to the seasoned systems administrator. The great thing about Linux is that user processes are not directly proportionate to RAM. If you as a single user need 32MB of RAM, that does not mean that two users on a multi-user system require 64MB of RAM; as a matter of fact, in that instance no change would be required.

As a disclaimer, it should be noted that there are systems out there that operate in the terabyte range for memory, such as large On Line Transaction Processing Systems. Linux has not yet reached that level; however, one day it will. The measurement techniques for such systems are vastly different than those for small to mid-range systems.

Once the amount of RAM is determined, the next obvious step is swap space, which is covered in the next section.

Swap Space Priorities

RAM is obviously not the only consideration when piecing together or adding to a Linux system. Swap space is also another great priority. While many UNIX pundits will advise using the following formula:

```
2 * RAM = swap space
```

there are many alternatives to help you preserve disk space and use a practical amount of swap space.

Calculating Swap Space

Following is a method I have heard of that many Linux administrators use, and it is quite practical:

1. Estimate your total memory needs. Consider the largest amount of space you will need at any given time. Consider what programs you will be running simultaneously. The easiest way to do this is to set up bogus swap space and load up all of the programs you will be using at once. Then see how much memory is being used.

2. Add a couple of megabytes as a buffer for programs you may have missed or think may in fact be used.

3. Subtract the amount of physical memory you have from this total. The amount left over will be the amount required to run your system while it is in full use.

4. If the total in step 3 is three times the amount of physical memory you have, you will have problems. Consider getting more RAM.

If using this method shows you use less than the amount of physical memory, you might assume that you do not need any swap space. You should add some swap space anyway because the system will use it on a convenience basis by swapping out any data that is not in use. In this case, create about the same amount of swap space as you have physical memory (or a little lower).

Of course, swap space, like all other performance issues in Linux, becomes much more complicated when large groups of users come into play. When dealing with large groups of users for whom the betterment of your system is beholden to err on the high side, provide physical RAM times two in swap space (the default method mentioned above).

34

Tuning Your
Linux System

While Pitt's method can be used for determining how much swap space is needed on larger systems, within the context of large systems it is a much more prudent practice to use the maximum recommended swap space to ensure users will not run into any problems.

Assigning Swap Space

Once you have decided how much swap is actually going to be used, the task of assigning it comes into play. Most Linux distributions (and Red Hat is no exception) provide a means to set up swap during the installation. It is also a good practice to try to actually create most of the swap space on the first portion of the first drive within the system. This means that the drive heads will have a smaller distance to travel while paging data in and out of RAM. Another practice is to divide up swap to reduce I/O contention. Again, keeping the swap space near the beginning of each physical drive is recommended to keep the distance traveled by the heads to a minimum. When using multiple disks, try to keep the swap space assigned as equal as possible. For instance, say you have three 8GB disks and 128MB of RAM. You have determined that you will actually require 256MB of swap space. The first swap area should be 86MB, the second 85MB, and the last one 85MB.

> **Note**
>
> There may be instances that take exception to equally distributing swap space. For example, you can apply the first method and set up the first (and highest priority) swap area to match "expected" use, then divide up the rest into other lower priority swap areas.

Swapon/Swapoff

Let's take a quick glance at the `swapon/swapoff` commands. By definition, `swapon` and `swapoff` are used to specify devices on which paging and swapping are to take place or be disabled. At boot time, `swapon` is used in `/etc/rc` to specify the system's swap areas. `swapon` is interesting in that you can look at paging activity with it as well assign priority and space. The syntax for looking at activity is:

```
$ swapon -s device_name
```

To allocate swap space, let us again use the aforementioned example of 86MB for our first swap partition running at default priority (changing or starting with a different priority will be discussed a little later).

First, using either the fdisk utility, disk druid, or some other utility, we create the swap partition at:

```
/dev/hda6 with a size of 86MB
```

> **Note**
>
> The command `mkswap` can also be used to set up swap space. The syntax is:
> ```
> $ mkswap -c device_filename blocksize
> ```

Next, we tell the system to use it:

```
$ swapon /dev/hda6
```

> **Note**
>
> For a swap file versus partition, we would simply allocate the filename:
> ```
> $ swapon /my_swap_file
> ```

Once the actual swap areas have been allocated, you may want to peruse swap prioritization. For instance, with the preceding example, you probably would like the first swap area to have the highs and the other two some lower priority value. For the example, let's say our swap has already been built and allocated according to this list:

```
/dev/hda6    86MB
/dev/hda7    85MB
/dev/hda8    85MB
```

And we want our general priorities to look like this:

```
/dev/hda6    highest
/dev/hda7    second highest
/dev/hda8    third highest
```

The basic premise is that /dev/hda6 must be exhausted before using /dev/hda7, and so on. Since there are only three swap areas, it makes sense to set the highest priority to 2, and not set a priority for /dev/hda8 (leaving it at the low default priority of 0). Here is the syntax for changing the priority for /dev/hda6 and 7:

```
$ swapon -p 2 /dev/hda6
$ swapon -p 1 /dev/hda7
```

Where this does not make sense is if you want paging responsibilities to be equally shared by all three physical drives. If all three drives are the same model and on the same bus, there is not much point in assigning a swap priority any different than the default. If, however, you know the average amount of swap being used by the system, it wouldn't hurt to give the fastest drive an amount of swap space equivalent to and a little larger than that value and giving it the highest value.

Finally, to make a swap partition or file available permanently, entries like the following would be required in `/etc/fstab`:

```
/dev/hda8 none swap 0 0 # example of a swap partition
/my_swap_file none swap 0 0 # example of a swap file
```

As you can see, swap priorities and swap space assignment can be tricky, but if given great consideration, micromanaging swap space can reward serious performance benefits.

Swap partitions are not the only way to setup swap. The next section looks at swap partitions and swap files.

Swap Partitions Versus Swap Files

Linux is an extremely scalable and advanced system. One of its more powerful abilities is to use the filesystem for swapping instead of using a dedicated swap partition.

The matter of using swap partitions over swap files or vice versa is again usage dependent. On smaller and simplistic single-user systems, perusing a swap file or set of swap files is perfectly acceptable. On larger systems that require high performance, dedicated, fast SCSI partitions are better because they are safer and yield better performance.

Swap Files

To simplify the matter, let's look at both and weigh the benefits and costs of each one. First we will discuss swap files. A swap file should be employed on lower-end systems where I/O contention is not a concern. It is also wise (but not necessary) to put a few swap files on different partitions in case one of them accidentally fills up or to keep them from filling up. In a sense, you can make a pseudo swap partition by creating a partition, mounting it somewhere, and creating a swap file on it and nothing else. However, this kind of defeats the purpose of having swap partitions at all. Another case for the swap file is if you want to "flat install" a system; that is, having one partition with everything on it including all of the swap (a practice I do not advocate). This practice should be avoided because it is very dangerous and will yield lesser performance. Without a doubt, the best implementation of swap files is a temporary one. If you are rapidly running out of swap space and the system is thrashing, you can quickly add a swap file to stem off a potentially dangerous system lockup.

Swap Partitions

The case for swap partitions has two drawbacks: they are a little (but not much) harder to manage than swap files and they are finite to the partition. A swap file is also finite to the partition, but you can always create newer filesystem partitions and in general play "musical swap files" a lot more easily than you can with swap partitions. The advantage of swap partitions is primarily performance. The system can read and write to them in raw format and when set up very discriminatingly, their performance can yield better results than swap files.

Memory and swap are not difficult to set up, maintain, and modify. Skillfully applying location, priorities, and differing sizes can help a system perform better and last longer. RAM and swap space, not unlike many other factors of Linux, are relative to the system's usage. Applying the right level for the amount of users and programs can make the difference between high performance and boggish throughput.

Tunable Kernel Parameters in /proc

Kernel tuning is not exactly the easiest of pastimes. On older UNIX variants, it was next to impossible (not to mention not fun in the least). Linux has managed, after its own fashion, to turn kernel and system tuning into something that is actually enjoyable. Older UNIX systems would have you run through a million and one calls, commands, and functions just to change the tiniest of parameters, whereas more modern ones implement a system somewhat similar to xconfig (see Chapter 35, "Customizing the Linux Kernel"). Kernel recompiling is not the only way to tune kernel parameters. In reality, the 2.2 kernel suggests that *not* using the make utilities (at least initially) may in fact be better. While this is largely a matter of preference and/or skill, this section discusses ways to alter system behavior using the /proc filesystem. First we will examine what the /proc filesystem is by examining some parts of it, then we will highlight two tunable parameters in /proc, and finally see how we can use console echos to modify those parameters.

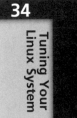

34

Tuning Your
Linux System

Why Alter the Kernel?

The main reason a kernel would need to be altered is to change a value that affects the way a system operates. For example, you can increase the number of available inodes on the system to allow for more free inodes to be used for files.

Understanding /proc

One of the more interesting FAQs out on the Internet about Linux has a heading that looks something like this: "What is this file /proc/kcore and why is it so big?"

That particular file is an image of the system's memory. The rest of the /proc filesystem is pretty much a running snapshot of the entire Linux system. Each numbered directory contains process information, whereas other more obviously labeled directories such as /proc/net contain very specific system information (/proc/net contains networking information). /proc is also not a "real" filesystem in that it is not stored on disk, but rather is all in memory. So when you do see unusual file sizes, don't be alarmed. The /proc filesystem serves as a place to see what is happening on the system and it provides an interface to the kernel. This is what makes it so unlike many versions of UNIX (although many versions of UNIX have and do use a /proc filesystem, just as many do not). Certain commands also make use of /proc, such as the ps command. Instead of directly querying the kernel, ps can simply descend /proc looking for the appropriate information.

Table 34.6 describes each directory and some of the more important files in the /proc directory.

TABLE 34.6 The /proc Directory

Directory/Filename	Description
loadavg	Values of the average system load for the last 1, 5, and 15 minutes (directly read by uptime and top) are in this file.
uptime	This file indicates the time in seconds since the system start and time used by idle processes.
meminfo	This file contains the number of total, free, and used main memory and swap areas.
kmsg	This file supplies kernel messages that have not been read by syslog.
version	This file holds version information about the system (from the kernel parameter linux_banner).
cpuinfo	This file contains parameters recognized by the system at boot time pertaining to the CPU.
pci	This file contains PCI slot location and general information.
self/	This directory contains information about the processes accessing the /proc/ filesystem.
net/	This directory has information about the Linux network layer.
scsi/	This directory contains individual files about each SCSI device.
malloc	This file is for monitoring the kmalloc and kfree operations.
kcore	This file is a core dump of the kernel (size = main memory plus one page size).

TABLE **34.6** continued

Directory/Filename	Description
modules	This file contains information on single loaded modules in use by the system.
stat	This file contains general Linux kernel statistics.
devices	This file contains information about known (registered) device drivers (for example, mem, pty, and ttyp).
interrupts	This file contains IRQ assignments.
filesystems	This file contains existing filesystem implementations.
ksyms	This file contains kernel symbols that have been exported.
dma	This file contains all occupied DMA channels.
ioports	This file contains I/O ports currently occupied.
smp	This file contains information on single or multiple CPU configurations.
cmdline	This file contains any command-line parameters passed to the kernel at startup.
sys/	This directory is very important. It contains information about the kernel itself including algorithms, limits, and networking information.
mtab	This file contains currently mounted filesystems.
md	This file contains usage statistics for multiple device driver support.
rc	This file contains Real Time Clock (RTC) values.

The /proc filesystem provides many places where system tunable parameters may be altered. Although we will not look at every single one, they are usually easy to find and for the most part pretty intuitive. The examples we will look at are very intuitive in that it makes complete sense to be able to manipulate them via /proc; however, not all parameters can be modified in /proc. Many /proc files are not even writable to, whereas others are strictly snapshots. For example, the file /proc/sys/kernel/hostname is set to the following permissions: -rw-r--r--. This indicates that it is readable and writable to by root. It is not, however, permanent. If you edit this file, your hostname will actually be altered until your next reboot.

As you can see, /proc provides a powerful and flexible means of tuning a system with a very significant price—you must be careful not to do any harm. If you are unsure of how changing a parameter can affect the system, try to find out first or use a test box if you have one available. If there is an easier interface to information stored within /proc, as was the case with /proc/sys/kernel/hostname where you can simply use either linuxconf or the command hostname to change the hostname, use it. Otherwise, peruse /proc for fine tuning and/or testing the changing of certain values in the kernel.

Now that we have covered /proc, the next section will look at some simple ways to alter files in /proc.

Using echo to Alter System Behavior

Previously we examined /proc and what it is, and introduced the concept of changing system values within /proc to alter how the system operates. What we have not done is examine exactly how this can be accomplished with relative ease. We will look at two examples of passing information to the system using terminal echoing.

> **Note**
>
> All of the examples discussed may or may not work depending on the revision of the kernel. For example, some parameter locations may be different or they may not even exist.

> **Note**
>
> These examples are taken directly from http://www.linux.com/tuneup/ database.phtml/Kernel/ and http://www.nl.linux.org/linuxperf/.

Understanding the Anti-Ping Setting

The first example is the anti-ping setting. For the sake of an example, let's say that on your corporate intranet, someone keeps pinging the Linux server Larry to see if it is alive instead of just browsing to the Web server. Although you would like to tell the user how you appreciate his ingenuity, you would prefer he just browsed to Larry's server and you will let him know if there are any problems. Of course, he doesn't listen. As a matter of fact, he has taken to running ping for hours on end. As a temporary measure, you would like to shut off the inbound ping requests without altering any other protocols. There is a long way to do this, which we will not get into, but the easiest way is to simply try this:

```
$ echo 1 > /proc/sys/net/ipv4/icmp_echo_ignore_all
```

This will cause the system to ignore all ping requests.

Not only can certain running conditions or values be altered, but some system limits can be changed as well. Here is an example that shows how to use echo to change the maximum file and maximum inode count:

```
$ echo NEWVALUE > /proc/sys/fs/file-max
$ echo NEWVALUE > /proc/sys/fs/inode-max
```

For example, changing the maximum inodes to 65536 (a very popular value for some reason) would look like:

```
$ echo 65536 > /proc/sys/fs/inode-max
```

Once again, you should see the possible dangers here. Although changes such as file-max and inode-max are not too dangerous, there are plenty of ways to get your system into hot water by fooling around in /proc.

Summary

Performance monitoring and tuning is not a lightweight topic. This chapter provided a brief look at both actions on Linux systems; however, there is much more to it when you have multiple systems and ever-growing systems. This should be enough to get you started in monitoring and tuning a Linux system after a little practice with the utilities and methods we discussed.

34

Tuning Your
Linux System

CHAPTER 35

Customizing the Linux Kernel

IN THIS CHAPTER

- Use the Source   *1082*
- Patching the Kernel Source   *1091*
- Kernel Loadable Modules   *1094*
- Kernel Building   *1100*

When speaking to people unfamiliar with Linux, one of the misconceptions often heard is that rebuilding the Linux kernel is difficult and that only expert users should attempt this operation. This chapter attempts to dispel this myth. It begins by looking at reasons why you might want to compile the kernel source code. It then covers where to obtain the kernel source code and official patches to update from one kernel version to the next. Next, this chapter covers the issue of patches to the kernel source and the use of unofficial patches in the default Red Hat kernel. It then takes a look at the layout of the kernel source tree, explaining what is found in each directory. Once the layout is described, the discussion moves to a description of how to patch the Linux kernel source. A short section is devoted to examining the modules system, and the final part of the chapter is devoted to explaining the configuration options available when compiling the kernel and how to actually build a kernel using make.

Use the Source

One of the primary reasons for the explosive growth that Linux has seen is the availability of the source code for just about any part of the system, including the operating system kernel. This freedom allows people from all over the Internet to modify or extend the functionality of the system as their programming talent allows. This freedom has attracted the attention of some of the brightest minds on the Internet and they contribute to making Linux a flexible and stable operating system.

For the systems administrator, having the source code means that the Linux kernel can be streamlined to suit the machines on which it will run, eliminating unused functionality, adding processor specific optimizations, or adding new functionality.

This section covers why you would want to recompile the kernel source code, where to obtain it, and how the kernel distributed by Red Hat differs from the kernel source distributed by Linus.

Why Recompile? Reasons for Recompiling

If you examine the configuration of the kernel that comes with your Red Hat Linux system, you will see that it is as generic as possible and that support for as much hardware as possible is included through modules. By generic, I mean that it contains support for most common hardware and is not specifically tuned for the machine on which it will be running. Because it is likely that this kernel will run on any machine you install it on, you may ask why you should recompile the kernel. There are several reasons. Here are a few of them:

- Removing unused or unwanted drivers and modules.

- Adding missing functionality.

- Upgrading to a later kernel release.

A common reason for recompiling your kernel is to remove unused or unwanted drivers from the kernel. This allows your kernel to use up less space on the hard drive, and possibly to load faster, because checks for hardware that you do not have are eliminated. Considering the fact that large capacity hard drives are now standard on most systems and are relatively inexpensive, the space issue may seem inconsequential, but if you are building boot floppies, every byte used can make a difference.

Adding missing functionality is another reason why you might want to recompile your Linux kernel. There are numerous options available for the Linux kernel and not all of them are included with the default kernel installed by Red Hat. In addition, patches are available independent of the kernel source that add functionality. For example, there is a driver available for SCSI changer devices such as those used in tape libraries or CD changers. The driver for this functionality is distributed as a kernel patch that you can add to your kernel. Another example of this is the PCMCIA drivers, which come with your Red Hat install media that add support for PCMCIA cards used in most laptop computers.

Probably the most common reason for recompiling your kernel source is to upgrade to a new kernel version. The open source development model ensures that kernel development proceeds at a fairly rapid pace. Between the time that the Red Hat install media was created and the time that you are reading this book, there may have been dozens of upgrades to the kernel source and these upgrades may include new functionality or important security fixes.

You may be wondering how often you should upgrade to a new kernel version. The answer is highly dependent on the purpose of the system in question. If the system is a corporate Web server that needs to be up and running twenty-four hours a day, you will probably only want to upgrade to add a significant new feature or to eliminate a specific defect. Another reason for upgrading is to plug a security hole. In general, you should only upgrade to achieve some tangible benefit. As the old adage goes, "If it ain't broke, don't fix it."

Obtaining the Source

Since the beginning, the release of the Linux kernel source code has been controlled by Linus Torvalds. Linus serves as the chief architect of the Linux kernel, and the kernel released by him is considered the official kernel. The primary FTP site for the kernel source code is `ftp.kernel.org` and its mirror sites. The official mirror sites use a standard naming convention of `ftp.XX.kernel.org`, where *XX* is the two digit country code for the country in which the mirror is located. For example, the United States mirror site is `ftp.us.kernel.org`, the United Kingdom mirror site is `ftp.uk.kernel.org`, and so on. A complete list of mirror sites can be found at the `kernel.org` Web site at `http://www.kernel.org`.

The directory layout for these mirrors differs slightly from site to site, but once you reach the kernel directory the layout is well defined. For each kernel version, where kernel version is defined by a major and a minor release number, there is a directory whose name is vM.N; M being the major release number and N being the minor release number. For example, for the current stable release at the time that this book was written, this directory would be v2.2. All of the various kernel releases and patches for this release are in this directory.

> **Note**
>
> Beginning with the release of the 1.0 Linux kernel, a kernel numbering scheme was devised to differentiate between stable kernel tracks and development tracks. This numbering scheme states that kernels with an even minor number are considered to be on the stable track and that patches to this kernel should only be made to correct deficiencies. On the other hand, the development track kernels are given an odd minor number, may include new features, and allow for the evolution of the kernel from one stable release to the next.

The most recent release is indicated by a file in that directory named LATEST-IS-M.N.P, where M is the major release number, N is the minor release number, and P is the patch level. For example, when the 2.2.5 version of the kernel was released, this file was updated and was named LATEST-IS-2.2.5. Listing 35.1 is an example of an FTP session showing this directory structure.

LISTING 35.1   FTP Session Transcript to `ftp.us.kernel.org`

```
[tschenk@quicksilver tschenk]$ ftp ftp.us.kernel.org
Connected to ftp.us.kernel.org.
```

LISTING 35.1 continued

```
220 freeamp.org FTP server (Version wu-2.4.2-academ[BETA-16](1) Thu May 7
 23:18:05 EDT 1998) ready.
Name (ftp.us.kernel.org:tschenk): anonymous
331 Guest login ok, send your complete e-mail address as password.
Password:
230 Guest login ok, access restrictions apply.
Remote system type is UNIX.
Using binary mode to transfer files.
ftp> cd pub/linux/kernel
250-Please read the file README
250-  it was last modified on Mon Dec 21 00:41:37 1998 - 209 days ago
250 CWD command successful.
ftp> dir
200 PORT command successful.
150 Opening ASCII mode data connection for /bin/ls.
total 141
drwxrwsr-x  14 500      100          1024 May 11 20:01 .
drwxrwxr-x   9 root     100          1024 Dec 31  1998 ..
-r--r--r--   1 500      100         18458 Dec 21  1998 COPYING
-r--r--r--   1 500      100         36981 Dec 21  1998 CREDITS
drwxrwsr-x   4 500      100          1024 Dec 17  1998 Historic
-r--r--r--   1 500      100         12056 Dec 21  1998 README
drwxrwsr-x   2 500      100          1024 Feb 10  1997 SillySounds
lrwxrwxrwx   1 500      100            11 Mar 18 21:23 alan -> people/alan
lrwxrwxrwx   1 500      100            12 Dec 29  1998 davem -> people/davem
lrwxrwxrwx   1 500      100            10 Dec 29  1998 hpa -> people/hpa
drwxrwsr-x   7 500      100          1024 Apr 11 00:45 people
drwxrwsr-x   3 500      100         13312 Jul 16 01:14 testing
drwxrwsr-x   2 500      100          1024 Dec 17  1998 v1.0
drwxrwsr-x   2 500      100          7168 Dec 17  1998 v1.1
drwxrwsr-x   2 500      100          2048 Dec 17  1998 v1.2
drwxrwsr-x   2 500      100         14336 Dec 17  1998 v1.3
drwxrwsr-x   2 500      100          5120 Jun 14 05:18 v2.0
drwxrwsr-x   2 500      100         17408 Jan 26 01:43 v2.1
drwxrwsr-x   2 500      100          2048 Jun 21 02:08 v2.2
drwxrwsr-x   2 500      100          2048 Jul  8 22:56 v2.3
lrwxrwxrwx   1 500      100            13 Dec 29  1998 whawes -> people/whawes
226 Transfer complete.
ftp> cd v2.2
250-Please read the file README
250-  it was last modified on Tue Jan 26 01:43:01 1999 - 173 days ago
250 CWD command successful.
```

35
Customizing the Linux Kernel

LISTING 35.1   continued

```
ftp> dir
200 PORT command successful.
150 Opening ASCII mode data connection for /bin/ls.
total 148145
drwxrwsr-x   2 500      100          2048 Jun 21 02:08 .
drwxrwsr-x  14 500      100          1024 May 11 20:01 ..
-rw-r--r--   1 500      100             0 Jun 14 05:33 LATEST-IS-2.2.10
-rw-rw-r--   1 500      100            27 Jan 26 01:43 README
-rw-r--r--   1 500      100      13080195 Jan 26 01:41 linux-2.2.0.tar.gz
-rw-r--r--   1 500      100           344 Jan 26 01:41 linux-2.2.0.tar.gz.sign
-rw-r--r--   1 500      100      13098205 Jan 28 20:56 linux-2.2.1.tar.gz
-rw-r--r--   1 500      100           344 Jan 28 20:56 linux-2.2.1.tar.gz.sign
-rw-r--r--   1 500      100      13902979 Jun 14 05:33 linux-2.2.10.tar.gz
-rw-r--r--   1 500      100           344 Jun 14 05:33 linux-2.2.10.tar.gz.sign
-rw-r--r--   1 500      100      13112203 Feb 23 02:58 linux-2.2.2.tar.gz
-rw-r--r--   1 500      100           344 Feb 23 02:58 linux-2.2.2.tar.gz.sign
-rw-r--r--   1 500      100      13228966 Mar  9 00:42 linux-2.2.3.tar.gz
-rw-r--r--   1 500      100           344 Mar  9 00:42 linux-2.2.3.tar.gz.sign
-rw-r--r--   1 500      100      13403132 Mar 23 22:33 linux-2.2.4.tar.gz
-rw-r--r--   1 500      100           344 Mar 23 22:33 linux-2.2.4.tar.gz.sign
-rw-r--r--   1 500      100      13497506 Mar 29 06:54 linux-2.2.5.tar.gz
-rw-r--r--   1 500      100           344 Mar 29 06:54 linux-2.2.5.tar.gz.sign
-rw-r--r--   1 500      100      13588897 Apr 16 21:46 linux-2.2.6.tar.gz
-rw-r--r--   1 500      100           344 Apr 16 21:46 linux-2.2.6.tar.gz.sign
-rw-r--r--   1 500      100      13677325 Apr 28 18:42 linux-2.2.7.tar.gz
-rw-r--r--   1 500      100           344 Apr 28 18:42 linux-2.2.7.tar.gz.sign
-rw-r--r--   1 500      100      13808890 May 11 19:59 linux-2.2.8.tar.gz
-rw-r--r--   1 500      100           344 May 11 19:59 linux-2.2.8.tar.gz.sign
-rw-r--r--   1 500      100      13827947 May 13 23:54 linux-2.2.9.tar.gz
-rw-r--r--   1 500      100           344 May 13 23:54 linux-2.2.9.tar.gz.sign
-rw-r--r--   1 500      100         24433 Jan 28 20:56 patch-2.2.1.gz
-rw-r--r--   1 500      100           344 Jan 28 20:56 patch-2.2.1.gz.sign
-rw-r--r--   1 500      100        317718 Jun 14 05:33 patch-2.2.10.gz
-rw-r--r--   1 500      100           344 Jun 14 05:33 patch-2.2.10.gz.sign
-rw-r--r--   1 500      100         95815 Feb 23 02:58 patch-2.2.2.gz
-rw-r--r--   1 500      100           344 Feb 23 02:58 patch-2.2.2.gz.sign
-rw-r--r--   1 500      100        331290 Mar  9 00:42 patch-2.2.3.gz
-rw-r--r--   1 500      100           344 Mar  9 00:42 patch-2.2.3.gz.sign
-rw-r--r--   1 500      100        684886 Mar 23 22:33 patch-2.2.4.gz
-rw-r--r--   1 500      100           344 Mar 23 22:33 patch-2.2.4.gz.sign
-rw-r--r--   1 500      100         98116 Mar 29 06:54 patch-2.2.5.gz
-rw-r--r--   1 500      100           344 Mar 29 06:54 patch-2.2.5.gz.sign
```

LISTING 35.1   continued

```
-rw-r--r--   1 500     100        443593 Apr 16 21:46 patch-2.2.6.gz
-rw-r--r--   1 500     100           344 Apr 16 21:46 patch-2.2.6.gz.sign
-rw-r--r--   1 500     100        303097 Apr 28 18:42 patch-2.2.7.gz
-rw-r--r--   1 500     100           344 Apr 28 18:42 patch-2.2.7.gz.sign
-rw-r--r--   1 500     100        489541 May 11 19:59 patch-2.2.8.gz
-rw-r--r--   1 500     100           344 May 11 19:59 patch-2.2.8.gz.sign
-rw-r--r--   1 500     100         32992 May 13 23:54 patch-2.2.9.gz
-rw-r--r--   1 500     100           344 May 13 23:54 patch-2.2.9.gz.sign
226 Transfer complete.
ftp> quit
221 Goodbye.
```

As you can see, in the current version directory, there are files for each patch level that contain a full source code tree as well as patch files that you can apply to existing source trees. It is sometimes easier to grab the entire source archive instead of the patches, especially if you want to move up several patch levels or if you have a large number of custom patches in addition to the version patches.

In addition to the official mirror sites, there are many other sites that mirror the Linux kernel sources. Often these sites are mirrors of the mirror sites or are mirrors of the large Linux archives.

Kernel Sources and Patches Provided by Red Hat

All Linux distributions come with the Linux kernel source, and Red Hat is no exception. Unfortunately, the source code is not installed by default. You have to specifically request that it be installed, or you will only get the header files for the kernel. To correct this, select the kernel source RPMs as part of the installation, or add them later from the Red Hat media or the Red Hat FTP site. The Red Hat 6.0 distribution comes with the 2.2.5 kernel plus a number of patches.

In order to provide extra functionality over what is provided by the standard kernel, the Red Hat Linux 6.0 distribution includes a number of kernel patches. The patches have been applied to the stock kernels that the install procedure installs, so if you want to recompile your kernel on a Red Hat system, it is a good idea to know where to look to determine which patches have been applied.

The first thing to do to find out what patches have been applied to the standard Linux kernel is to install the Linux kernel source RPM. By this I mean the SRPM from the second install CD for the Linux kernel source that contains the spec file. This file also contains the configuration file used to build the default kernels that can be installed by the Red Hat

installer. Once you have this file installed, change directory to /usr/src/redhat/SPECS
and take a look at the file called kernel-2.2.spec (see Listing 35.2). In this file, you will
find the list of patches applied to the standard source code tree before building the kernel
used by Red Hat.

LISTING 35.2   Excerpt from Kernel-2.2. Spec File

```
Patch0:  linux-2.2.5-sparc.patch
Patch1:  aic7xxx-5.1.15-2.2.5.patch.gz
Patch2:  i386-2.2.3-compression.patch
Patch3:  linux-2.2.5-ramdisk.patch
Patch4:  linux-2.2.4-DAC960.patch
Patch5:  linux-2.2.5-accessSuSv2.patch
Patch6:  smart2-0.9.9-for-2.2.3.patch
Patch7:  fdset-2.2.4.diff
Patch8:  nfsd-2.2.5-file.patch
Patch9:  nfsd-2.2.5-1.patch
Patch10: linux-2.2.3-tlan.patch
Patch11: linux-2.2.5-defrag.patch
Patch14: linux-2.2.5-alpha-smp.patch
Patch15: linux-2.2.5-nohang.patch
Patch16: linux-2.2.5-pci2000.patch
Patch17: linux-2.2.5-alan.patch
Patch18: linux-2.2.5-sparc64-aic.patch
Patch19: linux-2.2.5-raid-0.90-B.patch
Patch20: linux-2.2.5-alan2.patch
Patch21: linux-2.2.5-aarp.patch
Patch23: linux-2.2.5-dac960include.patch
Patch24: linux-2.2.5-tokenring.patch
Patch25: kernel-2.2.6-alpha.patch
Patch26: kernel-2.2.6-ftruncate.patch
Patch27: kernel-2.2.6-mmap.patch
Patch28: kernel-2.2.6-shm.patch
Patch29: kernel-2.2.6-x86.patch
Patch30: linux-2.2.5-networking.patch
Patch31: linux-2.2.5-silly.patch
Patch40: ibcs-2.1-rh.patch
Patch41: pcmcia-cs-%{pcmciaver}-script.patch
```

As you can see, this list is quite long, including a total of thirty-one patches. Some of these update drivers for various devices include Mylex RAID controllers and Thunderlan network interface cards. Others update the software RAID drivers, add support for dynamically allocated file descriptor sets, and add support for PCMCIA devices. A glaring omission on the part of Red Hat is that each of these patches and their purpose is not described in a README file along with their origin. This makes it difficult to track them down again if you want to upgrade your kernel.

Kernel Source Code Layout

The kernel source code, if installed, can be found in `/usr/src/linux` on your Red Hat system. This is usually a symbolic link to the real directory, which points to a directory called linux-M.N.P, where M is the major release number, N is the minor release, and P is the patch level. This directory contains the following files and subdirectories:

```
COPYING         README                  drivers/  ipc/     net/
CREDITS         README.kernel-sources   fs/       kernel/  pcmcia-cs-3.0.9/
Documentation/  REPORTING-BUGS          ibcs/     lib/     scripts/
MAINTAINERS     Rules.make              include/  mm/
Makefile        arch/                   init/     modules/
```

Let's take a look at what is contained in each of the subdirectories, starting with Documentation. The Documentation directory was created in an attempt to collect into one place the bulk of the documentation written by contributors to the kernel source code. This differs from the original kernel source layout, in which documentation for features was scattered throughout. If you are new to Linux, it is highly recommended that you take some time to look over the information found in the Documentation directory. Even if you are not new to Linux, you should always look to this directory for new files so that you can keep up with the latest kernel developments.

In the beginning, Linux supported only the Intel ix86 platform. Now it is available for a number of different platforms, including PowerPC, Sparc, Alpha, Motorola 68000 series, ARM, and Sparc64. The architecture-specific files used to build the kernel are found in the`/usr/src/linux/arch` directory. It is under this hierarchy that the actual kernel image will end up once the compilation is completed.

Device Drivers

Device drivers for the plethora of devices supported by the Linux kernel are found in the `/usr/src/linux/drivers` subdirectory, which is subdivided into further subdirectories containing things like sound drivers, SCSI drivers, block drivers, and others.

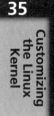

35

Customizing the Linux Kernel

Filesystem Code

The code to support the various filesystems available under Linux is contained in the `/usr/src/linux/fs` subdirectory. This subdirectory contains the code to implement the virtual filesystem layer, or VFS, the binary format support code, and various subdirectories that implement specific filesystem types, such as nfs, msdos, minix, and ext2.

IBCS Support Code

The next subdirectory is the `ibcs` subdirectory. This contains code that supports the Intel Binary Compatibility Standard. This support allows you to run binaries from other operating systems that adhere to this standard, such as SCO UNIX, Solaris for ix86, and others. This code is primarily of interest if you own one of these systems and would like to run commercial software that you purchased for it on your Linux system. This code is not part of the kernel distributed from the kernel FTP sites, but is included with your Red Hat distribution.

The `include` Subdirectory

Another top-level subdirectory is the `include` subdirectory, which contains the header files required to build the kernel. It contains several architecture-specific directories prefixed with `asm-`. These directories define kernel structures in the native assembly of these architectures. In addition, there are directories for network specific headers, SCSI headers, and other kernel header files in the `linux` subdirectory.

The `init`, `ipc`, `kernel`, `lib`, and `mm` Subdirectories

The next five subdirectories, `init`, `ipc`, `kernel`, `lib`, and `mm`, contain source code for the kernel main function, System V style interprocess communication, low-level kernel interfaces, the scheduler, and memory management routines that are not architecture specific. These form the heart of the kernel and anyone interested in understanding the specific algorithms implemented in the Linux kernel for these functions should spend some time studying them.

The `modules` Subdirectory

The `modules` subdirectory is empty until you build your kernel, at which time it is populated by symbolic links to the various parts of the kernel source that you have requested to be built as modules. There will also be some files that indicate where these modules will be installed.

The `net` Subdirectory

Another large subtree of the kernel source code is the `net` subdirectory. It contains the network protocol stack for the kernel, including implementations of IP version 4, IP version 6, IPX, X.25, and others. This code is a must read for those interested in network protocol stacks.

The `scripts` Subdirectory

The final top-level subdirectory is called `scripts`. This subdirectory contains code for presenting the configuration dialogs, both the text-based ones and the GUI interface. It also contains an OOPs decoder called `ksymoops`. This program allows you to decode a kernel OOPs to make it easier to debug.

At first glance, the kernel source tree can seem intimidating. However, as you can see it is divided into sections by functionality. This division makes it relatively easy to find your way around in the source tree. For serious study of the kernel source code, you may want to obtain and install the Linux Cross Reference package available at http://lxr.linux.no/. This package allows you to index the kernel source code and make it browsable via a Web interface. This can be especially useful in debugging problems or locating where a specific function or variable is defined.

Now that you have a basic understanding of the layout of the kernel source tree, we can move on to the topic of patching the kernel source. This section will be of interest if you want to add functionality to your kernel or upgrade to a later version.

Patching the Kernel Source

Some purists believe that patching your kernel with patches other than the version patches from the kernel mirror sites is a bad idea because they have not been approved by Linus and there is no guarantee that they ever will be. Others argue that if no one uses patches other than the version patches, new functionality will never be added to the kernel because there will be no pool of tested candidate patches.

This section is devoted to examining both sides of this issue. It looks at the arguments for and against using unofficial patches, some of the sources of patches, and how to minimize the effects of using unofficial patches on your production systems.

Official Versus Unofficial Patches

For purposes of our discussion, it is useful to make a distinction between official patches and unofficial patches. By official patches, I refer to two specific types of patches. These are the version patches, which take your kernel from one version to another and are released at the kernel FTP sites. Other patches that can be considered official are driver updates from the driver authors, such as new network driver releases from Donald Becker. On the other hand, by unofficial patches, I refer to new functionality patches that add features not yet adopted by Linus into the kernel source tree or drivers for new hardware not previously supported by the kernel.

Differences Regarding Patch Source

You may ask what difference the source of the patch makes or why it hasn't been incorporated into the standard kernel. The real difference is that with unofficial patches, you run the risk of patch abandonment. This term refers to what happens when a patch author stops maintaining the patch and no new maintainer steps forward to continue it. Given the open nature of Linux kernel development, this scenario is a real issue. Consider, for example, if you were a software development firm that builds a product that relies on the functionality of an unofficial kernel patch. If you do not maintain the patch yourself, you run the risk that the person who did develop the patch will stop maintaining it. Because it is not a part of the standard kernel releases, you would be forced to either start maintaining the patch or rewrite your product to not use it. Either of these options can become quite an expensive proposition. To reduce the risks in this case, it is useful to consider the following issues:

- Who wrote the patch?

- Where was the patch announced?

- Is the patch generally useful?

Let's examine why these issues are important and how their answers can help you to decide whether to use a given patch.

Patch Author

One of the first things to consider is the author of the patch. It is usually a safer bet to use a patch that comes from one of the well-known kernel developers, such as Alan Cox, Stephen Tweedie, or Dave Miller. These core Linux developers have contributed significant amounts of code to the Linux kernel and usually have an idea when they write the patch whether Linus will accept it for inclusion in the kernel source tree. It is often these patches that are incorporated into the development branch of the kernel to become the basis for the next stable branch.

Patch Announcement

Another thing to consider is where the patch was announced and indeed whether it was widely announced at all. A good place to watch for patch announcements is the linux-kernel mailing list. This list is frequented by many of the key Linux developers and it is on this list that many patches to the kernel are discussed to determine their merit. By following this list and seeing the responses, if any, to patch announcements, you can often gauge whether it is likely to become part of the kernel proper. You should also not be afraid to directly raise the question of whether this patch has a chance for inclusion into a future kernel. The kernel developers are not the least bit shy about voicing their opinions on the merits or flaws of a patch. Patches that are never discussed on the linux-kernel mailing list are usually not likely to become part of the kernel, but it never hurts to ask the author of a patch whether he plans on submitting it to Linus or to the mailing list. The answers to these questions are a good indication of whether the author will likely be around for awhile or if the patch is destined for patch abandonment.

Patches that make it into the kernel proper and eventually become part of the official patches are those that are generally useful. If the patch addresses a problem that affects only a tiny subset of installations, or if it implements a driver for a highly specialized piece of hardware, it becomes less likely to make it into the kernel. It fails to meet the generally useful criteria. An example of this might be a driver to support connecting a floppy drive from an Apple II+ to a PC. This is opposed to patches that add support for new hardware that is likely to be found in many systems, such as a driver for a DVD decoder board. In the case of patches that are highly specialized and not generally useful, it is very important to try to establish whether the author is likely to remain committed to keeping the patch up to date with newer kernels. If the answer to this question is no, I would question the wisdom of relying on it for your production systems.

In order to minimize the effect of using unofficial patches, you should consider all of these factors and based on your answers to these questions make the decision to use or not to use the patch.

Where to Obtain Patches

You may be asking where all of these patches come from. There are many sources for patches to the kernel, and this section takes a look at some of the more popular ones.

The linux-kernel Mailing List

A good place to begin looking for kernel patches is in the archives of the linux-kernel mailing list. This mailing list is where the majority of kernel patches that make it into the final kernels can be found and discussed. Any person who is serious about tracking the development of the kernel and seeing what features are coming in future releases should follow this mailing list. Unfortunately, this mailing list is a very high-traffic list and what often turns out to be a useful patch can be lost in the noise. To combat this problem and as an alternative to subscribing to the list, you can follow the discussion by checking the Kernel Threads Web site. The maintainers of this Web site summarize the various discussion threads that occur on the mailing list and archive the original posts. You select the threads of interest based on the summary and can then read the original posts. This Web site is located at `http://www.kernelthreads.org`.

KernelNotes

Another excellent place to begin looking for kernel patches is the KernelNotes Web site at `http://www.kernelnotes.org/`. This site contains a plethora of information related to kernel releases and patches available for the Linux kernel. Of special note here are the links to patch archives, which are sites that collect patches from all over the Internet, categorize them, and keep track of maintainers and other information related to these patches.

ac Patches

A set of patches that deserves special mention are the "ac" patches, named for their maintainer, Alan Cox. In order to help Linus manage the amount of interaction with potential developers, Alan Cox collects many of the patches and after some cleanup and testing, integrates them into a single patch. He then submits them to Linus for merging with the official kernel source. These patches often contain features ported from the development branch or functionality and it is a relatively safe bet that these patches will become part of the official kernels. These patches are available at all kernel source FTP sites. For a pointer to their location, you can refer to the KernelNotes Web site.

There are, of course, many other sources of patches, but these three sources give you a good starting point. If you are looking for specific functionality, and you do not find anything at one of these locations, you can always refer to Deja.com and search the newsgroup archives there to see if anyone else has heard of or is developing a patch that meets your needs.

Now that we have covered kernel patches, both official and unofficial, we are ready to move on to our next topic, kernel loadable modules.

Kernel Loadable Modules

Beginning with the 1.1 development track, support for loadable kernel modules was added to Linux. Loadable kernel modules are pieces of kernel code that are loaded into a running kernel to implement new features or provide a driver for a specific piece of hardware. Loadable kernel modules are usually referred to simply as modules. The two terms are interchangable and both are used in this chapter. This allows for a great deal of flexibility at the expense of some extra setup work. Although most modern kernels utilize this functionality, it is not required. You may choose to include all of the drivers and features that you use for your kernel and not use any modules at all. This type of kernel is sometimes referred to as a *monolithic* kernel. This being said, however, it would be hard to imagine a modern Linux system that did not use modules.

This section looks at the advantages of using modules versus including everything in the kernel. It also looks at the utilities for loading, querying, and unloading modules and discusses the parts of the kernel that you might not want to compile as a module.

Advantages of Modular Kernels

Prior to the advent of loadable kernel modules, all drivers and features that were selected during the kernel configuration were made part of the kernel at compile time. This means that if you forgot to add support for a piece of hardware in your system or changed a piece of hardware, you were required to recompile your kernel. The module system means that you no longer have to do this. If your shop is anything like ours, you probably have a wide variety of ethernet cards, sound cards, SCSI controllers, and other hardware in the systems on your network. Now suppose that you have to upgrade the kernel on all of these machines to the next level. You have two options. The first is to go to each machine and build a customized kernel that supports the hardware found in that particular machine. Your second option is to build a generic kernel with modular support for all of the various pieces that differ from machine to machine and load the modules appropriate to each machine.

Another advantage to using kernel modules is that it can help you minimize the kernel memory footprint. Consider this scenario: You have a system that has a SCSI tape drive, a SCSI CD-R drive, and two ethernet cards in it. During normal daily usage, you use a single network interface and none of the other devices described. One day per week, you configure the second ethernet interface, load the SCSI tape and SCSI CD-ROM modules, and do backups. If you didn't use modules, the tape, CD-ROM, and the second ethernet card, drivers would always be loaded and taking up memory. On the other hand, if you made your kernel such that support for these devices was through modules, you would be able to remove them from memory when not in use.

These are just a couple of the advantages to using modules with your kernel. Others include the fact that modules can be configured to automatically load and unload themselves as required, thus ensuring that the maximum amount of memory is always available to run applications on your systems.

35

Customizing
the Linux
Kernel

Enabling Module Support

Now that you have heard some of the advantages of using a modular kernel, let's take a look at what you need to take advantage of them. The first thing, of course, is to have a kernel configured. This involves selecting one or more of the following three kernel configuration options:

- CONFIG_MODULES

- CONFIG_MODVERSIONS

- CONFIG_KMOD

The first of these options is mandatory. If you do not set the CONFIG_MODULES variable to Y (for yes), you will not be able to utilize modules.

The next option, CONFIG_MODVERSIONS, if defined, means that you may be able to use the same modules with different kernel versions. Depending on whether you want this flexibility, you may answer Y or N to this question. The safe bet for this configuration option is to say N, meaning that the modules you build will only work with the kernel with which they were compiled. One reason you might want to answer Y to this option is if you are using modules built by someone else, such as a hardware vendor who supplies a modular driver in binary form.

The final configuration option in this set is CONFIG_KMOD, which if set to Y means that the kernel will be able to load and unload modules automatically as needed. Whether or not you select this, modules will work. But if you do not say Y to this option, you lose one of the advantages of using modules, namely having the kernel load and unload modules as needed. You will almost always want to say Y here. Figure 35.1 shows these options set to support loadable kernel modules from the make xconfig dialog.

FIGURE 35.1

Enabling kernel module support.

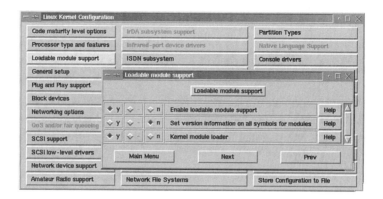

Having set these configuration options, you can then specify that drivers and features that have been written with this capability be built as modules instead of being compiled into the kernel.

The Module Utilities

Having enabled module support and having selected drivers and features to be built as modules, the next requirement is to configure the module utilities. These utilities are contained in the RPM package called `modutils-2.1.121-14.i386.rpm` and are a standard part of every installation. The module utilities and their functions are detailed later in this chapter. The Red Hat 6.0 distribution comes with the correct module utilities for the default kernel, but if you change kernels, you should always check the Changes file in the kernel Documentation directory to find out which version of module utilities is required to support the kernel you are building. Listing 35.3 is an excerpt from this file that shows this information.

LISTING 35.3 Changes File Excerpt

```
Excerpt from /usr/src/linux/Documentation/Changes

Current Minimal Requirements
Upgrade to at least these software revisions before thinking you've encountered a bug!
If you're unsure what version you're currently running, the suggested command should
tell you.
- Kernel modutils      2.1.121        ; insmod -V
- Gnu C                 2.7.2.3        ; gcc --version
- Binutils              2.8.1.0.23     ; ld -v
- Linux libc5 C Library 5.4.46         ; ls -l /lib/libc*
- Linux libc6 C Library 2.0.7pre6      ; ls -l /lib/libc*
- Dynamic Linker (ld.so) 1.9.9         ; ldd --version or ldd -v
- Linux C++ Library     2.7.2.8        ; ls -l /usr/lib/libg++.so.*
- Procps                1.2.9          ; ps --version
- Procinfo              16             ; procinfo -v
- Psmisc                17             ; pstree -V
- Net-tools             1.50           ; hostname -V
- Loadlin               1.6a
- Sh-utils              1.16           ; basename --v
- Autofs                3.1.1          ; automount --version
- NFS                   2.2beta40      ; showmount --version
- Bash                  1.14.7         ; bash -version
- Ncpfs                 2.2.0          ; ncpmount -v
- Pcmcia-cs             3.0.7          ; cardmgr -V
```

LISTING **35.3**   continued

- PPP	2.3.5	; pppd --version
- Util-linux	2.9i	; chsh -v

If you need to obtain a new version of the module utilities, they are distributed in the kernel source directories of the kernel FTP sites. For example, the module utilities noted in the Changes file, version 2.1.121, are found at the following URL:

```
ftp://ftp.us.kernel.org/pub/linux/kernel/v2.1/modutils-2.1.121.tar.gz
```

The version number of the module utilities matches the version number of the kernel that was current at the time of their release. This does not mean that you must upgrade immediately to this version. Always check the Changes file to determine the version required to support the kernel you are building.

The module utilities consist of several programs. Table 35.1 lists those utilities and describes their function. For usage information about these utilities, refer to the manual pages.

TABLE **35.1**   Module Utilities and Descriptions

Utility	Description
lsmod	Lists the modules currently loaded by the kernel and whether they are in use.
insmod	Loads a module into the running kernel.
rmmod	Removes a module from the running kernel.
modprobe	Loads module(s) and can be used to handle dependencies through its configuration file.
depmod	Generates the dependency information required by the modprobe utility.
kerneld	The kernel daemon, used to automatically load and unload modules as required.
genksyms	Generates version information for module symbols. It is run during the kernel make process if the config variable CONFIG_MODVERSIONS is set.
ksyms	Shows module symbols.
modinfo	Displays information about a module.

When Not to Use Modules

There are parts of your kernel that should usually not be built as modules. These parts include the filesystem driver used by your root partition, normal hard drive support, network support, and TCP/IP support. In addition, if you do not want to rely on the initial RAM disk feature of the kernel, you should not compile the driver for your boot disk SCSI controller (if you boot from a SCSI drive). All of these items are required to boot the kernel.

You can opt to build some of these items as modules provided that you include support for an initial RAM disk in your kernel. The initial RAM disk is loaded by the boot loader and loads modules required to continue booting the system. The Red Hat distributed kernel includes this support and uses the initial RAM disk to load SCSI drivers required to boot the system. The initial RAM disk alters the manner in which the kernel is booted, causing system startup to occur in two phases. The initial phase brings up the kernel with a minimal set of compiled in drivers, loads the initial RAM disk as the root filesystem, and then executes commands to load additional modules required to complete the boot process.

Booting the System Utilizing Initial RAM Disk Support

These are the steps in booting the system when utilizing the initial RAM disk support:

1. The boot loader loads the kernel and creates the initial RAM disk.
2. The initial RAM disk is converted to a normal RAM disk and the memory used by the initial RAM disk is freed.
3. This new RAM disk is mounted read/write as the root filesystem.
4. An executable (program or script) called /linuxrc is executed. This script normally is used to load modules required to complete booting the system.
5. Upon termination of the /linuxrc script or program, the root filesystem is mounted. The root filesystem in this case is the one built in to the kernel.
6. If a directory called /initrd exists on the root filesystem, the initial RAM disk is moved to it, otherwise it is unmounted.
7. The normal boot sequence then commences with the invocation of the init process, using the new root filesystem.

With this basic knowledge of what modules are, when to use them, and why they are useful, we are ready now to proceed with configuring the Linux kernel.

35

Customizing the Linux Kernel

Kernel Building

Now we come to the part that many new users of Linux consider black magic or high art—building the kernel from source. There are many reasons for building a customized kernel. As discussed at the beginning of this chapter, three of the most common are

- Removing unused or unwanted drivers and modules.

- Adding missing functionality.

- Upgrading to a later kernel release.

This section looks at the various configuration options, discusses the kernel makefile, looks at ways to manage having multiple configurations of the same kernel version, and takes a look at the support in the source tree for customized installation scripts. To finish out the chapter, we will look at the make process and the sequence of events for building your kernel.

Configuring the Linux Kernel

Before beginning the configuration of your customized kernel, it is important to consider a few things. For example, do you have enough space in the filesystem where the kernel source lives to build the new kernel? Do you know how to modify the `lilo.conf` file to add your new kernel? Do you have a set of rescue disks handy if something goes wrong? These are important questions to consider before beginning to modify your operating system kernel. In these cases, always apply the Boy Scout motto, "Be Prepared."

Once you have considered these issues, you are almost ready to actually run one of the four available configuration programs. Before you do this, however, you should check the Changes file in `/usr/src/linux/Documentation` to ensure that you have the required versions of the system utilities. Once you have done so, you can start configuring your kernel. The four methods to this include the old style configuration script, a text menu-based configuration program, a GUI program using tcl/tk, and a semiautomated update method that builds a configuration based on an old configuration file. These configuration methods are selected using make targets:

`make config`	To use the old configure script
`make menuconfig`	To use the menu-based program
`make xconfig`	To use the GUI kernel configurator
`make oldconfig`	To use the old configuration file method

You may ask yourself why you would need four different configuration methods and which one is best. Unfortunately, there is no answer to which one is best, but the reason for having four methods is to accommodate the needs of different users. Consider the fact that not all Linux systems have fancy color monitors and the capability to run a GUI. This eliminates the xconfig option. Some do not have addressable text consoles that allow the use of the curses library, thus eliminating the menuconfig option, and sometimes, you don't have the time or desire to interactively configure your new kernel, thereby eliminating the make config option. Having these four targets makes it possible to deal with all of these cases.

All that being said, however, I find that the most useful and the easiest to understand configuration method is the GUI one. This method requires that you are running X Windows, that you have your DISPLAY environment variable set, and that you have permission to connect to the running X server. If you do not meet these requirements, my next recommendation is the menuconfig option, which requires ncurses.

Getting Started

To begin configuring your kernel, you must first change directory to the top level of your kernel source tree. This default location for the kernel source code in Red Hat Linux systems is/usr/src/linux, which is a symbolic link to /usr/src/linux-M.N.P-XX, where M.N.P is the kernel version. For Red Hat 6.0, this would be linux-2.2.5. Once in this directory, you type one of the make commands shown in the preceding section to start the configurator.

When selecting either the GUI configurator or the menu-based configurator, there will be a brief period of activity while the config programs are built, followed by either the appearance of the GUI or the menu-based interface. The initial screens for these two methods are shown in Figure 35.2 and Figure 35.3.

FIGURE 35.2

The GUI kernel configurator.

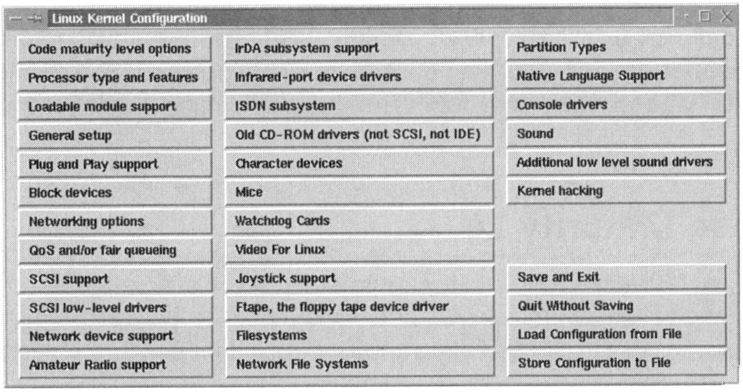

Code maturity level options	IrDA subsystem support	Partition Types
Processor type and features	Infrared-port device drivers	Native Language Support
Loadable module support	ISDN subsystem	Console drivers
General setup	Old CD-ROM drivers (not SCSI, not IDE)	Sound
Plug and Play support	Character devices	Additional low level sound drivers
Block devices	Mice	Kernel hacking
Networking options	Watchdog Cards	
QoS and/or fair queueing	Video For Linux	
SCSI support	Joystick support	Save and Exit
SCSI low-level drivers	Ftape, the floppy tape device driver	Quit Without Saving
Network device support	Filesystems	Load Configuration from File
Amateur Radio support	Network File Systems	Store Configuration to File

35

Customizing the Linux Kernel

FIGURE 35.3

The menu-based kernel configurator.

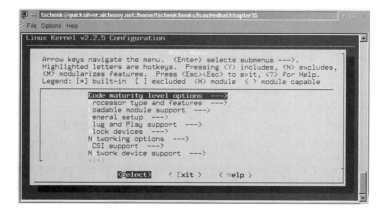

Choosing Configuration Options

Now you can begin examining the various options that you can configure on your Linux kernel. We will not be examining all of the options, (there are currently over 400 of them), but will take a look at those that you are more likely to want to change. If you see an option not covered here, your first step should always be to read the help text for the option. It explains the options and gives you suggestions on if and when you would want to change it.

Tip

In order to answer some of the questions about various kernel options, you will need to know about the various parts of your computer. You'll need to know the chipset used on the motherboard, whether your parallel port is a standard port or supports the newer extensions, the type of network card you have, and many more details about the inner workings of your PC. If you are converting your computer from a Windows system to a Linux system, you can get a lot of this type of information by printing out the hardware profile of your computer. You might also want to have your hardware manuals on hand to look things up.

Code Maturity Level

The 2.2 series kernel distributed with Red Hat Linux 6.0 is part of what is considered the stable or production release kernel branch; however, there are some features that are deemed experimental. This experimental designation may mean that they represent a feature for which a standard is evolving. It may be a driver that is considered essential enough to include in the release, but is not tested enough to be considered rock solid.

> **Caution**
>
> Experimental features are so designated because they are not heavily tested or are subject to change or removal. Using these features may make your system unstable. This instability may result in your system crashing. If you are building a system that requires high availability, you should carefully consider whether the experimental features should be included in your configuration.

All of the features in the kernel that are of this nature are clearly marked and you should use them only if they meet a need. Please be aware, however, that if your system becomes unstable, you should first remove any experimental options from your kernel before filing a bug report, especially if you think that the bug exists in a non-experimental feature or driver.

It is your decision as to whether you want to be presented with these experimental features. If you are not interested in taking risks, say no to this option. I usually say yes and may try one or two of the experimental options so that by real-world testing, they can move beyond the experimental stage.

Processor Type and Features

One part of the kernel sources that you will most likely want to change is the selection of the processor type and features, due to the fact that the kernel distributed with some Linux distributions is compiled for the lowest common denominator, an Intel 386 with no math coprocessor.

By specifying the proper processor type, your kernel will be built with optimizations for that specific processor turned on, which is intended to increase performance. It is important to remember, however, that a kernel built for an advanced CPU may fail to run on an older machine, so if you build all of the kernels for your network on a single host, you should select the processor type with this in mind.

The following excerpt from the `/usr/src/linux/Documentation/Configure.help` file describes the proper setting of this option.

Here are the settings recommended for greatest speed:

- "386" for the AMD/Cyrix/Intel 386DX/DXL/SL/SLC/SX, Cyrix/TI
  486DLC/DLC2 and UMC 486SX-S. Only "386" kernels will run on a 386
  class machine.
- "486" for the AMD/Cyrix/IBM/Intel DX4 or 486DX/DX2/SL/SX/SX2,
  AMD/Cyrix 5x86, NexGen Nx586 and UMC U5D or U5S.
- "586" for generic Pentium CPUs, possibly lacking the TSC

```
(time stamp counter) register.
- "Pentium" for the Intel Pentium/Pentium MMX, AMD K5, K6 and
  K6-3D.
- "PPro" for the Cyrix/IBM/National Semiconductor 6x86MX, MII and
  Intel Pentium II/Pentium Pro.
```

Memory type range register (MTRR) support may optionally be included on Pentium II and Pentium Pro systems. These registers are typically used to control processor access to memory ranges. Saying yes to this option enables write-combining, allowing bus write transfers to be combined into larger transfers before bursting over the PCI/AGP bus. This can increase performance of the video image writes substantially. You should set this option if you have a Pentium Pro or faster system, especially if you also enable SMP support, since setting this options also fixes a problem with some SMP BIOSes.

Another processor feature that you may now set through the configurator is support for multiple CPUs or SMP. With the 2.2 kernel, Linux is capable of supporting up to 16 processors on Intel systems. This limitation may soon change, however, and by the time you read this, support for up to 64 processors may be available.

The SMP support in the 2.2 kernels is not considered experimental and is the result of a significant development effort that began with the 1.3 development branch of the kernel. This support continues to improve with each kernel revision and now that the Intel SMP support has reached this level of stability, the other architectures supported by Linux are adding support for SMP systems as well. The maturest support among the other architectures is for the Sparc and Sparc64 architectures.

Tip

If you enable SMP support, you will also need to enable the Enhanced Real Time Clock Support option. This is required so that the Real Time Clock in your system is read and set in an SMP safe manner. Please also note that by specifying support for SMP, you disable support for Advanced Power Management features.

Although kernels compiled with SMP support may run on a single processor system, it will usually be at the cost of performance. It is therefore best to not run SMP kernels on single processor systems. Also note that enabling SMP support in your kernel may require that you change your BIOS settings. It is highly recommended that you read and follow the advice given in the SMP FAQ, which can be found on your Red Hat system in /usr/doc/FAQ/txt/SMP-FAQ.

Loadable Module Support

As discussed earlier in this chapter, kernel module support allows your systems to be made more generic, adds flexibility in supporting various hardware configurations, and makes the kernel footprint smaller by unloading unused modules dynamically. It is difficult to imagine a modern kernel that does not include support for modules.

General Setup

General setup includes options for various binary formats, advanced power management, PCI options, and parallel port options. This is also the place where you enable networking support, support for System V style interprocess communication (IPC), process accounting, and sysctl support.

Networking Support

Networking support is a must for most Linux systems, even those that are not connected to a network, due to the fact that some programs require this support even on non-networked machines. Unless you know that your system does not include any software of this nature, you should always enable networking support.

BSD Process Accounting Support

BSD process accounting support is generally considered a good idea. This support allows you to track system usage by creating a log of system activity, including processes created, their owner, and other information. A user-level utility is available to parse this information. This option is of special interest to ISPs and other organizations that want to track system utilization for billing or other accounting purposes.

System V Interprocess Communications (IPC)

System V Interprocess Communications (IPC) is a protocol for synchronizing and exchanging data between separate programs that uses the System V UNIX model of providing shared memory segments, message queues, and semaphores. This support is required for many database programs, including Oracle, and for the DOS emulator, DOSEMU, as well. You should probably enable this support, either by compiling the support into your kernel or as a loadable module.

Adding sysctl Support

Adding sysctl support provides a means for modifying the behavior of a kernel that is already running, either through system calls or, if the /proc system is enabled, by writing to pseudo-files in the /proc/sys directory. It also allows you to query the current settings of a number of kernel parameters. This directory is divided into several subdirectories that govern different aspects of the running kernel as described in Table 35.2.

35

Customizing
the Linux
Kernel

TABLE 35.2 Subdirectories of /proc/sys and Their Purposes

Subdirectory	Description
dev/	Device-specific information (dev/cdrom/info).
fs/	Entries that allow you to query and set kernel parameters, such as the maximum number of file descriptors, and that allow you to configure support for miscellaneous binaries.
kernel/	Sets kernel tuning parameters or queries kernel status.
net/	Networking parameters.
sunrpc/	SUN Remote Procedure Call (NFS).
vm/	Virtual memory, and buffer and cache management.

These services provide flexibility and are quite powerful. They are also very dangerous if you don't know what you are doing. Setting kernel parameters to inappropriate values can result in your system becoming unusable or crashing. Please be sure to read the information in /usr/src/linux/Documentation/sysctl for details on using this interface. It is usually a good idea to support this option.

Miscellaneous Binary Support

One of the most interesting features that you can enable in this section is the option for miscellaneous binary support. This option is a generalized version of the older option that supported Java binaries. By enabling this option, you can make the execution of Java, MS-DOS executables, Windows programs, or other non-native executable formats as simple as executing an ELF binary or shell script.

Registering a New Binary Type with the Kernel

Once you have enabled this support in your kernel, the first step is to register a magic cookie for your new binary type with the kernel. A magic cookie is a means to uniquely identify the executable and could be the first few bytes of a binary file or the extension. For example, the magic cookie for an ELF binary is the presence of the following four hex values in the first four bytes of the file:

```
7f 45 4c 46
```

which in ASCII is a DEL character followed by the letters E, L, and F. You register your magic cookie by echoing a string to a file in the /proc filesystem called /proc/sys/fs/binfmt_misc/register. The format of this string is:

```
:name:type:offset:magic:mask:interpreter:
```

The following is a thorough description of the preceding string:

- Name is an arbitrary identifier for this type of executable.

- Type is either M for mask if your magic cookie is a byte sequence or E for extension if your magic cookie is based on the filename.

- Offset is the count in bytes from the beginning of the file to start looking for your cookie. If the type is E or if the byte sequence is at the beginning of the file, leave this blank.

- Magic is the sequence of bytes to match or the file extension to match. You may specify hex values as \xDD where DD is the hex value.

- Mask is an optional bit mask that must be the same length as the magic value. This bitmask is applied to the contents of the file before comparison to the magic cookie sequence.

- Interpreter is the program that is used to run the executable.

Enabling Support For Your Binary Format at Boot Time

To enable the support for your binary format at boot time, you could create a control script in `/etc/rc.d/init.d` that loads the `binfmt_misc` module (if you opted for this support as a module) and then echoes the string for the binary format into `/proc/sys/fs/binfmt_misc/register`. You could also just add the echo statement to `rc.local`.

Examples of binary formats that you might want to support in this manner are Java programs, Java applets in html files, and Windows executables that can be run using WINE. Once you have registered them, you need only set the permissions so that the execute bit is set and invoke them on the command line just like you would for any other binary on your system.

To check the status of this support on your system, you can cat the contents of the file `/proc/sys/fs/binfmt_misc/`*Name*, where *Name* is the name specified in your string used to register the binary format.

More documentation for this feature, including a pointer to the Web site of the author, can be found in the kernel source Documentation directory in the files `binfmt_misc.txt` and `java.txt`.

Parallel Port Support

Parallel port support has been changed significantly in the 2.2 kernel with the introduction of the parport module. This module abstracts the representation of the parallel ports and allows for support of a wide range of devices other than printers, such as Zip drives and other devices.

35

Customizing
the Linux
Kernel

Probing of parallel ports is a dangerous proposition and may result in the system locking up. It is much safer to specify port settings, such as addresses and IRQ settings, by specifying these parameters on the boot command line, in `lilo.conf`, or when loading the parport modules.

The parport module divides the control of the parallel port into two modules, one of which manages the port sharing that is architecture independent and an architecture-dependent module. One or both of these may be compiled as modules.

Again, more documentation of this feature is found in the Documentation directory in the files `parport.txt` and `paride.txt`.

Many modern systems, especially laptops and other portables, include support for Advanced Power Management, also known as APM. APM-capable systems have the ability to conserve power by shutting down monitors during periods of inactivity, spinning down and parking hard drives, or suspending the system completely. Unfortunately, each vendor's implementation of APM differs, making it difficult to support in the kernel. These differences also mean that if you are having problems with your kernel, you should first turn off support for APM and then attempt to reproduce the problem.

There are options in two different places for watchdog systems whose function is to take action in the event the system crashes. Hardware-based watchdog systems are set later on, but in the general options section, you may set support for software-based watchdog systems. With this option set, the kernel will monitor and periodically update `/dev/watchdog` and if the update fails to occur on schedule, a reboot of the system will be forced. This support is useful if you have systems that are remotely administered and that must be rebooted in the event of a crash.

More information on software and hardware watchdogs can be found in the kernel Documentation tree in the file `watchdog.txt`.

Plug-and-Play Support

With recent kernels, some support for plug-and-play devices has been added and in this section of the kernel configuration, you can select whether or not to include it. Read the help information for these options and set them according to your needs.

Block Devices

The next major subdivision of the kernel configuration contains options to support various block devices. These options include support for IDE/ATAPI devices, parallel port IDE device support, various PCI chipsets, and support for Linux software RAID, which is discussed in detail in Chapter 9, "Linux and RAID." Let's take a closer look at a few of these options.

One of the most configurable drivers among the block devices is the floppy disk driver. This driver has the capability to control not only floppy drives, but backup devices as well and it is also capable of running multiple disk controllers. There are a number of command-line arguments that can be passed to the floppy driver either on the kernel command line or via the `/etc/lilo.conf` file using the append command. Table 35.3 describes a few of these options.

TABLE 35.3 Floppy Driver Option

Option	Description
`floppy=daring`	Usable on most modern Pentium systems, this option allows for optimizations that can speed up floppy access, but is not compatible.
`floppy=one_fdc`	This options tells the driver that there is only one controller available.
`floppy=two_fdc` or `floppy=<address>, two_fdc`	Uses two controllers with the second located at the specified address.
`floppy=thinkpad`	Required for some ThinkPad laptops that invert the convention for the disk change line.
`floppy=omnibook` or `floppy=nodma`	Prevents the use of DMA for data transfers. Required for some HP Omnibook systems.
`floppy=yesdma`	Used to force DMA mode. This option is the default setting.
`floppy=nofifo`	Use this setting if you receive "Bus master arbitration" errors from the Ethernet card or other devices while using your floppy.
`floppy=<threshold>, fifo_depth`	Sets the FIFO depth for DMA mode. Compiling as a module allows experimentation with this parameter to find optimal settings.
`floppy=<drive>, <type>,cmos`	Sets the CMOS type for the specified drive to the given type. This option is required if you have more than two floppy drives.
`floppy=broken_dcl`	Avoids using the disk change line and assumes that the disk has been changed whenever the device is reopened. Useful for some laptops and older PCs.
`floppy=L40SX`	Prevents printing of messages when unexpected interrupts are received. Required on IBM L40SX laptops to prevent a conflict between the video and floppy disk controllers.
`floppy=<nr>,irq` and `floppy=<nr>,dma`	Sets the IRQ or DMA channel for thespecified device.
`floppy=slow`	Required for some PS/2 machines that have a slower step rate.

The complete list of floppy module options can be found in `README.fd` in the `/usr/src/linux/drivers/block` directory and the fdutils package. A set of floppy driver utility programs, including an enhanced mtools kit, can be downloaded from `ftp://metalab.unc.edu/pub/Linux/system/Misc/`.

> **Tip**
>
> The floppy driver options are specified as shown in the preceding table, but unlike many other kernel and module options, you are allowed to make only one such declaration. Therefore, to set multiple options, you must specify them all at one time. For example, to specify the `daring` and `two_fdc` to the floppy module, you would issue the following command:
>
> ```
> insmod floppy 'floppy="daring two_fdc"'
> ```
>
> You may also pass options to the floppy driver using the append line in the LILO configuration file `/etc/lilo.conf`, on the kernel command line, or through the older environment variable syntax.

Enhanced IDE Support under Linux is also selected under the block devices option, and in addition to supporting up to eight IDE drives, there is also support for IDE/ATAPI CD-ROM, tape drive, and floppy drives. The new driver in the 2.2 kernel also includes support for the PIO modes on OPTi chipsets, SCSI host emulation, as well as support for a large number of chipsets.

Tuning of the IDE drives is accomplished using the `hdparm` utility. Additional details on options and tuning is available in the Documentation directory in the `ide.txt` file.

> **Caution**
>
> If you are required to pass options to the IDE driver while loading it as a module, you must replace any commas with semicolons in the command line.
>
> ```
> insmod ide.o options="ide0=serialize ide2=0x1e8;0x3ee;11"
> ```

Loopback Devices

Loopback devices allow you to create files and then treat them as a filesystem. For example, you can create an image of a floppy disk or create a CD-ROM image from a filesystem and then use the loopback device to mount it as a regular filesystem and make changes before committing the image to a disk or CD-R. The loopback device is also used in some of the available schemes for encrypting filesystems as outlined in the Loopback Encrypted Filesystem HOWTO, which can be found at `http://www.linux.com/ Loopback-Encrypted-Filesystem-HOWTO.html`. In order to take advantage of the loopback device, you must have an up-to-date util-linux package. To determine the correct version to support your kernel, refer to the Changes file in the `/usr/src/linux/ Documentation` directory.

Support for Network Block Devices

An experimental option that can be selected under block devices is support for network block devices. Network block devices allow the client system to access a block device on a remove system transparently over TCP/IP. This is different from NFS or Coda in that the block devices accessed in this manner can be used for any type of filesystem, including swap devices.

Linux Software RAID

One of the major features you can select under block devices is support for software RAID. This software RAID is fully described in Chapter 9 along with utilities required to manipulate RAID arrays under Linux.

Parallel Port IDE Devices

Support for parallel port IDE devices is included here as well. This option allows you to use devices such as external hard drives and other IDE/ATAPI devices that connect to your computer via the parallel port. One caveat is that if you compile this option as a module, you must also compile the parport option as a module.

Networking Options

Just like UNIX, Linux is a network operating system and the Linux system that stands alone is rare. Even the workstation in the home office is typically connected to the Internet via the PPP network protocol. A Linux workstation without network services is like a car on blocks. It has a powerful engine and lot's of cool buttons and knobs, but...

35

Customizing
the Linux
Kernel

For most systems that just want to be able to participate in a TCP/IP network, setting up networking is merely a matter of choosing TCP/IP network support, selecting support for a network interface device, and then configuring them. You could also add support for SMB protocols to interoperate with Windows networks, IPX/SPX support for talking to Novell networks, or Appletalk support for talking to Macintosh networks, but these are all optional.

On the other hand, with the guidance of an experienced network administrator, the options presented here provide a plethora of choices for providing services and supporting protocols. These options allow Linux to serve as the glue that binds your multi-OS, multiprotocol network together. Linux is like a master translator at the United Nations, able to speak the native protocol of NetWare, Appletalk, TCP/IP, and SMB networks and translate between them for the mutual benefit of all.

Other optional features include support for network filesystems such as NFS and Coda that allow your system to share files with other systems either as a client or as a server. There are also options to add packet filtering and masquerading capabilities that can transform a system into a powerful and flexible firewall, and options that can turn your Linux system into an inexpensive yet powerful router.

Kernel netlink socket support is an option that provides a communication channel between kernel services, such as routing and packet filtering, and user programs through a character device in the /dev directory. You should enable this option if you want to be able to log network behavior related to routing or to record information from the IP firewall code about possible attacks. It is also required if you want to use the arpd daemon to manage the ARP cache or if you want to use the ethertap support, which allows user space programs to read and write raw Ethernet frames.

As the systems administrator for a large network connected to the Internet, you are undoubtedly concerned with the possibility of an attack against your computing resources, and the Linux kernel provides help in this regard. One of the options available under the Network Options tab is network firewall support. The Linux kernel includes a packet-based protection option that allows you to accept or deny incoming or outbound packets based on the protocol, port, source, and destination addresses. This feature was changed for the 2.2 kernel to be much more robust than the protection provided by the 2.0 kernels. Used in combination with other firewall solutions, such as proxy-based systems, Linux with firewall support can be a very effective deterrent to people trying to gain access to your systems. For additional information on utilizing this feature, refer to Chapter 26, "Firewall Strategies."

Implementing A TCP/IP Packet-Based Firewall

To implement a TCP/IP packet-based firewall, you should include both the network firewall option as well as the IP firewalling option. You may also want to include the IP masquerading options and transparent proxy support. These options allow you to provide access to the outside world through a gateway system that hides the identity of the machines on your internal network.

IP Masquerading, Tunneling, and Aliasing

The IP masquerading option deserves a little more attention. This options allows you to do some interesting things. For example, if you have a small network at home, like I do, it is not practical to give every system its own phone line and modem. However, if you don't, you end up having to take turns using a single phone line, meaning that only one system can access the Internet at a time. An alternative is to get a single connection for your Linux system and to set up IP masquerading. In this setup, all of the systems on your network use the Linux system as a gateway, and to the outside world, all of your systems appear to be a single system. This means that you can use private network numbers for all of your systems except the Linux system. For a more complete description of this feature, you can refer to the IP Masquerading mini-HOWTO found on your Red Hat system in `/usr/doc/HOWTO/ mini/IP-Masquerade`.

If you plan on using your Linux system as a router, then you should select the IP: optimize as router not host option, which will turn off some of the checksums calculated on incoming TCP/IP packets.

IP tunneling is a technique that encapsulates IP packets within IP packets. This may not sound very useful, but it is the basis of such technologies as mobile IP for laptops or virtual private networks.

Another form of tunneling that Linux supports is GRE or Generic Routing Encapsulation over IP. This option allows for the creation of broadcast WANs when combined with the Broadcast GRE over IP option and the IP multicast routing option. This means that you can have a network using the same LAN IP numbers that appear to all be within the local LAN, but that are physically located all over the Internet.

A feature of interest to Webmasters who need multi-homing capabilities is IP aliasing. IP aliasing allows you to specify multiple IP addresses for a single network interface card. This feature can also be useful if you have machines that act as spares. Say, for example, that you have a large Web site with fifteen Web servers that all answer to the name `www.yoursite.org` through DNS rotation. If you lose one machine due to faulty hardware or any other reason, until you replace the machine you will be losing one fifteenth of your traffic. To avoid this, you could IP alias the address of the crashed machine to another machine, allowing one machine to answer to two different addresses. You could also assign several names to a system using IP aliasing and have Web servers listen for any traffic to that address.

One of the common denial of service attacks used by system crackers and malcontents is to use TCP SYN cookies to tie up your machines' resources and prevent legitimate users from utilizing them. Turning on the IP: TCP syncookie support option will help detect and defend against this type of attack. To use this option, you must also enable the /proc filesystem and sysctl support mentioned later on.

> **Tip**
>
> Selecting this option in the kernel configuration does not turn on the feature, it only allows you to turn it on. This is done by issuing the following command:
>
> ```
> echo 1 >/proc/sys/net/ipv4/tcp_syncookies
> ```
>
> This is why you must enable support for the /proc filesystem and the sysctl support in order to use this feature.

IPX and Appletalk

Two of the options available for Linux that make is so well suited in mixed networks are the options to support IPX and Appletalk protocols. These protocols allow Linux to participate in Netware and Apple networks using the native protocols. Linux can be configured to look like a Netware file and print server to Netware clients. By using the netatalk program, you can do the same for networks of Mac systems. Details on setting up this support can be found in Chapter 18, "Integrating with Other Network Operating Systems."

For the enterprise network administrator, Linux includes support for the X.25 protocol, which is a mechanism for running multiple virtual circuits via a single physical line. This support does not include support for dedicated X.25 network cards, but does provide for X.25 services or ordinary modems and Ethernet networks using the 802.2 LLC or LAPB protocols.

Another option of interest to the enterprise network administrator is the WAN option, which allows you to turn your Linux system into a WAN router. You can also add encryption to your WAN, using software from the FreeS/WAN project in Toronto, which offers a free encryption layer, using 1,024-bit keys and 168-bit Triple-DES technology. This software also implements IPSEC, or Internet Protocol Security. This software is free from U.S. import restrictions because it was developed outside of the country.

Related to this option is the option to support frame-relay under Linux. This will be discussed more when we get to the discussion of network devices in the section "Network Device Support" later in this chapter.

Because Linux is not as resource intensive as some other operating systems, it can be used to allow older hardware to have a longer useful life. This can lead to problems, however, because many of these older machines can be overrun by a busy 10Mb/sec Ethernet connection. If you experience problems with network overruns, try turning on the CPU is too slow to handle full bandwidth option.

Another option to allow you to tune the performance of the TCP/IP protocol stack is the one that allows you to adjust the scheduling algorithm used in this part of the kernel. You can turn on support for changing the scheduler by selecting the *QOS and/or fair queuing* option. This allows you to specify the algorithm used to schedule packets.

SCSI Support

Although IDE drives are more common for desktop PCs, on servers the need for higher performance and reliability dictates the use of SCSI devices. SCSI support is also needed to support some types of external devices connected to the parallel port, such as the Iomega Zip drive. Linux SCSI support includes drivers for SCSI disks, CD drives (both read-only and read-write), tape drives, and other devices through the SCSI generic option. These other devices include scanners, SCSI changers, and synthesizers.

Once you have selected the types of devices to support, you will then need to select the driver for the particular SCSI controller used in your systems. This will require that you know your hardware. It is highly recommended that you have your controller manual handy or that you be intimately familiar with the details of its configuration. The number of supported adapters is quite large and there are more being added all the time.

Network Device Support

In this section of the kernel configuration, you select the types of network devices to support. These devices include not only ethernet cards, but other types of network adapters, such as token ring and arcnet as well. Additionally, this section includes options for other devices and networking features of the Linux kernel. If you will be connecting to a network, even if it is only via PPP or SLIP, you will need to enable network device support.

One of the features that you can enable is called dummy network device support. A dummy network device is not a real device, but is used as a placeholder for a real device. For example, the demand dialing program, `diald`, uses the dummy network device as a place to queue up packets until the Internet connection is established, at which time they are rerouted to the real device.

35

Customizing
the Linux
Kernel

Although it is unlikely to be of interest to an enterprise network, the EQL load balancing support allows you to bind together several modems as the same IP interface and effectively multiply the bandwidth. This option could be used to provide bandwidth on demand by adding connections as required, thus providing bandwidth equivalent to ISDN or xDSL lines. This can be useful in cases where you have higher bandwidth requirements than a single dialup line can provide, but where high-speed lines are unavailable or too expensive. One drawback to this option is that support for EQL is required at both ends of the connection.

Networking with Serial Devices and Parallel Ports

In addition to the traditional TCP/IP support used with ethernet devices, Linux also supports networking via serial devices and parallel ports, using the PLIP, SLIP, and PPP options. PLIP is a means to network two systems via a null printer cable, such as those used to support Laplink, and provides four or eight parallel data channels. This option is often useful for installing Linux on laptops that don't have a CD-ROM drive and that do not have an available PCMCIA slot for a networking card. It might also be used to synchronize your laptop with a desktop. If you don't have access to a Laplink cable, the pinout for the required cable is documented in the Documentation directory of the kernel source in the `PLIP.txt` file in the networking subdirectory.

SLIP is a protocol that allows IP packets to be transported via a serial line, such as over a modem. Although SLIP is not as widely supported as it used to be, it still has uses and is required if you want to use the diald demand dialer or if you want to use SliRP.

A newer protocol for IP over serial lines that is in common use today is PPP. The kernel that comes with your Red Hat Linux 6.0 distribution includes PPP support by default.

Wireless Networking Options

For those of you who must be connected no matter how remote the location, Linux supports IP over short-wave radio with the Amateur Radio Support. A description of this can be found on the Web at the Wireless Papers home page at `http://www.ictp.trieste.it/~radionet/papers`. You can also visit the Packet Radio Home-page at `http://www.tapr.org/tapr/html/pkthome.html`.

A related option is the support in the Linux kernel for Wireless LAN and the AT&T WaveLAN. This is documented in the network subdirectory of the Documentation directory in a file named `wavelan.txt`. There is also support for the MosquitoNet StarMode RadioIP systems that are used by some laptop owners. This is described on the Web at `http://mosquitonet.stanford.edu/`.

New to Linux 2.2 is support for the protocols of the Infrared Data Association, commonly referred to as the IrDA. These protocols provide for infrared communications between laptops and PDAs at speeds up to 4Mbps. With this option selected, these devices are transparent to the networking system. For more information on these devices and on the utility programs required to use them, check the IR-HOWTO in the `/usr/docs/HOWTO` directory on your Red Hat system.

ISDN Subsystem Support

There are two ways in which you can use ISDN service with your Linux system. The first is through the use of an ISDN card in your PC, which is what this section of the kernel configuration is concerned with. The other is to use a router capable of managing the ISDN line itself. If you are using the router option, you do not need to enable ISDN support in your kernel. If you are using an internal ISDN card, you must select the ISDN support option as well as support for your particular brand of ISDN card. The big difference here is the cost and the ease of administration. For more information on ISDN support, refer to the isdn subdirectory of the Documentation directory. There you will find README files for the various supported ISDN modem cards.

> **Tip**
>
> If your system is already connected to a network via an ethernet card, it is probably easier to use the router option to connect to an ISDN line because you will not have to recompile your kernel or worry about configuring the ISDN modem card under Linux. This method also has the advantage that if you upgrade your service to T-1 or greater service, the Linux systems do not have to change.

Old CD-ROM Drivers

Before the advent of the IDE CD-ROM drive, many CD manufacturers required a special interface card to use their drives. This is true of many of the CD drives created prior to 1994. If your CD-ROM drive connects to a sound card or to a dedicated card, you will most likely have to include support for it here. If you have a modern PC, you will most likely have either an IDE/ATAPI CD-ROM drive or a SCSI drive and you will not require the support of any of the options found in this section.

Character Devices

In this section, you will select support for devices that communicate with the kernel via a stream of characters. These devices include terminals, serial ports, printers, and others. For most server applications, you will need, at a minimum, support for terminal devices, parallel printer support, and a new option for the 2.2 series of kernels, Unix98 PTY support.

This section also allows you to select support for multiport serial cards, such as Stallion cards or Rocketport cards that support multiple serial devices.

Under this section, the minimum support normally required is to configure console support on a virtual terminal and virtual terminal support. Optional support for the console on a serial terminal is also included here, which is often useful in situations where it is inconvenient to have a monitor attached to the system.

Caution

Enabling the console on a serial terminal option is not sufficient to get this feature to work properly. In addition, you must specify the device to which you want kernel messages to be sent. This is done by passing the kernel command-line option `console =/dev/ttyNN` at the LILO prompt or by adding this option to the append line in your `lilo.conf` file.

Serial port support under Linux includes support for not only the standard four ports supported by the BIOS of most modern PCs, but also support for many multiport serial boards, such as those needed to support a modem pool. This support is also important for serial-based data acquisition systems. Support is also available for IRQ sharing among serial ports that have such support in the hardware.

If you have ever experienced the problem of running out of PTYs on your multiuser systems, the support of Unix98 PTYs will be important to you. Unlike systems based on the Linux 2.0 kernel, which were limited to support for 256 pseudo terminals, the Linux 2.2 kernel can support up to 2048. The Unix98 support works differently than the old BSD-style support. If this options is selected, a program opens a pseudo terminal multiplexer device, `/dev/ptmx`, which dynamically creates an associated slave tty using the `/dev/pts` filesystem. As you might surmise, this requires that you include support for this filesystem later on in the configuration.

Another character device you will likely want to support is a parallel printer. This device requires support for the parport device described earlier. In addition, if your system has more than one parallel port and you want to use a device other than a printer on one of them, you must specify this when you load the module, or use the append keyword in the LILO configuration file.

Mice

Linux supports a number of different types of mice, both serial and bus. The bus mouse support includes support for PS/2 style mice, including the touch pads, track points, and other mice found on laptops. This support can be built in to the kernel or as modules.

Watchdog, NVRAM, and Real-Time Clock Devices

For systems such as servers, where uptime is more important, Linux supports a watchdog timer device. This driver requires the creation of a device, which is created using the following command:

```
mknod /dev/watchdog c 10 130
```

This device is opened by a watchdog daemon and if a write does not occur within a given interval, the system is rebooted. There are both software and hardware watchdogs available for Linux. The advantage of using a hardware watchdog is that some of these devices provide not only the /dev/watchdog interface, but temperature monitoring as well. A description of some of the watchdog hardware devices can be found in the file watchdog.txt in the kernel Documentation directory.

A new character device available for Linux is the NVRAM device, which provides read/write access to the 50-byte CMOS memory. The device required to support this options is created with the following command:

```
mknod /dev/nvram c 10 144
```

All computers have a real-time clock, but unlike many operating systems, Linux allows you to use it. By enabling the real-time clock option under Linux, you can generate a reliable signal from 2Hz to 8kHz. This clock can also be programmed as a 24-hour alarm that will raise IRQ 8 when the alarm goes off. The character device required to support this options is created using the following command:

```
mknod /dev/rtc c 10 135
```

A description of this option along with sample code for using the real-time clock module is in/usr/src/linux/Documentation/rtc.txt.

DoubleTalk Speech Synthesizer

The name of this option says it all. This option provides support for a speech synthesizer under Linux. If you have users who are visually impaired, you might be interested in checking out the Blinux distribution and Emacspeak. Linux is one of a very limited number of operating systems that can grant blind users access to all of the functions of their computers and to services on the Internet.

Video4Linux

The video4linux support grew out of the support previously provided for a plethora of different radio and video devices. This option provides a common programming interface for audio/video capture or overlay cards, radio tuning cards, and other devices. This support is required if you plan on using any of the current TV/FM tuner cards or video conferencing cameras, such as the Connectix Quickcam. Further information on support devices and tools for manipulating them can be found on the Web at `http://roadrunner.swansea.linux.org/v4l.shtml` and a collection of applications that are video4linux aware can be found at `ftp://ftp.uk.linux.org/pub/linux/video4linux`.

Joystick Support

With the release of the 2.2 kernel, the support for joysticks under Linux is much improved and this support is growing to include digital, serial, and USB joysticks. In addition, the developers of these drivers are working on including support for force feedback joysticks. This is similar to the rumble pack feature of popular game systems such as Nintendo 64. For a list of supported devices and applications that are compatible with the 2.2 kernel, take a look on the Web at `http://atrey.karlin.mff.cuni.cz/~vojtech/joystick/`.

Floppy Tape Device Driver

If you need to support tape devices that connect to the floppy controller or specialized cards that use compatible chipsets, such as the Ditto controller, you can enable that support using this dialog.

Filesystems

Just as with networking support, Linux supports a wide variety of native and foreign filesystems. Among the Linux native filesystems supported by the 2.2 kernel are the extended, xiafs, and extended 2 filesystems. Of these, the most commonly used is the extended 2 filesystem. You must include support for this filesystem in your kernel configuration. Another filesystem that you will most likely want to support is the ISO9660 filesystem, used on CD-ROM drives.

Linux also supports a number of filesystems from other operating systems. This support includes UNIX filesystems, such as Minix, System V, Xenix, and UFS. Support is also available for the filesystems native to Microsoft operating systems such as DOS and Windows. This support includes FAT-16, FAT-32, VFAT, and read-only support for NTFS. There is also support for filesystems from Macintosh, Amiga, and OS/2. These are primarily of support on dual boot systems so that you may share information between the different operating systems installed.

The filesystem dialog, shown in Figure 35.4, also includes the options for supporting filesystem quotas, kernel automounter support, and support for specialized filesystems including the /proc filesystem and the /dev/pts filesystem. You should definitely turn on support for the /proc filesystem and if you said yes to the Unix98 PTY support, you must also include support for the /dev/pts filesystem. The kernel automounter is an alternative to the BSD automount daemon.

One type of filesystem not yet officially supported by the Linux kernel is the UDF filesystem type. This is the filesystem used on DVD drives. Although Linux does support the ISO9660 filesystem standard for CD-ROMs as well as the Microsoft Joliet extensions for Unicode filesystems, if you want support for DVD drives, you must patch your kernel. The driver for DVD and other UDF peripherals is available on the Web from http://www.trylinux.com/projects/udf/.

Network Filesystems

A common feature of all network filesystems is the ability to share the disk resources of server systems with other systems on the network. UNIX and Linux systems typically do this with the NFS filesystem originally developed by Sun Microsystems. The network filesystems dialog allows you to add this support to your Linux system.

NFS is the current standard for distributed filesystems under Linux and UNIX systems. NFS is available under Linux in two flavors: the older one implemented in user space, and the newer, kernel based one. The choice of which to run depends on several factors, such as code maturity, level of support from the developers, and so on. For example, the kernel-based nfsd is faster, however it is not as mature as the user-space nfsd. Also, all new NFS enhancements are being created for the kernel-based nfsd, while development of the user-space nfsd has all but stopped.

FIGURE 35.4

The Kernel Configuration Filesystem dialog box.

Network filesystem support in Linux is not limited to NFS. Linux also supports the Coda filesystem. The Coda filesystem is similar to the older Andrew Filesystem, or AFS. It is a distributed filesystem that includes authentication and encryption features, disk replication, caching, and support for discontinuous connections for mobile computer users and telecommuters. Details of the Coda implementation, including client programs and other information, are available at the Coda Homepage at `http://www.code.cs.cmu.edu/`.

Another network filesystem type supported by Linux is the SMB filesystem type, which allows your Linux system to mount Windows shares. This support is not required if you want to share filesystems with Windows systems. Support for this is provided by the Samba, which is described in detail in Chapter 17.

Linux also supports the Netware Core Protocol, or NCP, which allows Linux systems to mount shared filesystems on Novell Netware servers. Just as with SMB support, this filesystem support is not required for Linux to serve as a Netware server.

Due to the Linux support for all of these filesystems, Linux is well suited to serve as the glue system for heterogeneous networks that include one or more network operating systems. Descriptions of how your Linux system can be incorporated into Windows, Netware, and Appletalk networks can be found in Chapters 17 and 18.

Partition Types

Not only does Linux support filesystems of other operating systems, it also supports their partitioning schemes as well. Currently, Linux supports the partition formats of BSD UNIX, SunOS, Solaris, and Macintosh. This support is primarily useful for exchanging information with other operating systems on dual-boot systems or for exchanging removable media such as optical disks or Zip disks.

Native Language Support

This section of the kernel configuration is something of a misnomer. These options support different cultural languages, but only for reading and displaying of these character sets on Microsoft filesystems.

For this support on MS-DOS and Windows filesystems, you should select one or more of the available code page options. For the same support on VFAT or Joliet CD-ROM filesystems, select one or more of the NLS options.

All of the code pages and NLS options can be compiled as modules and loaded and unloaded on demand. If you are not sure if you will need a code page or NLS option, compiling as a module is always a safe bet.

Console Drivers

In the Console Drivers dialog, the first two options are pretty much self explanatory. The first enables support for the standard VGA graphics card in text mode. Unless your system is headless (that is to say it has no monitor attached), you probably want to enable this option. The second option is required if you want to set the vga mode using LILO.

The remaining options in this dialog are not as straightforward as these two. For example, the third option can be selected to support a dual-headed system where one of the displays is an X capable display on a VGA monitor and the other is a monochrome display adapter, possibly only capable of displaying text. This option is not for use on systems where the monochrome display adapter is the primary display.

During the 2.1 kernel development cycle, support was added to the Linux kernel for a graphical console device supported by a hardware-specific frame buffer.

In order to take advantage of this support, you need an X server that is aware of frame buffers. This is available in the version of XFree86 that comes with your Red Hat distribution. Documentation of this feature can be found in the `framebuffer.txt` file under the Documentation directory of the Linux source tree.

Sound

Although of minor importance on most server systems, the Linux sound drivers are next on the list of items to configure. The sound driver was derived from the OSS/Free driver by Hannu Savolainen, which is the freely available version of the OSS drivers available from `http://www.opensound.com/`. Work is underway to change the sound driver layer to one where this is not the case, however, and the current driver in the kernel is the result of work funded by Red Hat. Although a large number of sound cards are supported by the kernel sound drivers, you may find that if your sound hardware is obscure or very new, you will need to purchase the commercial OSS drivers if you want to use that hardware under Linux.

The first option in the sound configuration dialog is a simple switch to indicate whether or not you want any sound support in the kernel. If you do not answer this question in the affirmative, you will not get sound support. If you want support for sound, answer yes or indicate that you want sound built as a module.

The remaining options are about specific sound cards and are relatively straightforward. You will need to have information regarding IRQ numbers, DMA channels, and port addresses for your particular sound card, but if you choose to build sound support as modules, you can pass the majority of this information on to the module when it is loaded. If you are looking to build generic sound support, it is usually best to build the various drivers as modules. This has the additional advantage of making it easier to configure sound with the soundcfg tool provided by Red Hat.

If your sound hardware is of the plug-and-play variety, you may be required to obtain the isapnp tools and experiment with them to get your sound card working properly. If this is the case, be sure to build your sound card driver as a module, or you will not be able to properly configure the sound hardware with isapnp before the driver is loaded.

If you do not find a feature of your particular sound card listed in the sound configuration dialog, all is not lost. The next section of the kernel configuration is an extension of the sound configuration dialog with additional drivers for audio hardware subsystems, such as support for Soundblaster AWE and Audio Excel DSP.

Kernel Hacking

Unlike previous versions of the Linux kernel, the 2.2 kernel has removed the profiling support from the kernel hacking dialog and the only option that remains is one to enable the SysRQ interrupt keys. These keys provide a method to get information about a running system or to shut down a system in the event of an emergency, such as being unable to login to the system because of a system crash. This is especially useful if you are experimenting with a development kernel and find that you are unable to log in to the machine for some reason. Table 35.4 includes a list of the keybindings and what action or information is obtained from using them. To use any of these key commands, you would press Alt+SysRq+<command key>.

TABLE 35.4 SysRQ Command Keys and Their Functions

Command Key	Description
r	Turns off keyboard raw mode and sets it to XLATE. This is useful if the X server or a program that uses `svgalib` hangs or crashes.
k	Kills all programs on the current virtual console. Also of use when X hangs or crashes.
b	Causes your system to reboot immediately without syncing or unmounting your disks. This may lead to disk corruption and should only be used as a last resort.
o	Shuts your system off via APM, provided that you have built your kernel with APM support.
s	Attempts to sync all mounted filesystems.
u	Attempts to remount all mounted filesystems as read-only.
p	Dumps the current registers and flags to the console. Useful in debugging a system crash.
t	Dumps a list of current tasks and their information to your console. This is also useful in debugging system crashes.
m	Dumps current memory info to your console.
0-9	Sets the console log level, controlling which kernel messages will be printed to your console. Setting this to 0, for example would result in only emergency messages like PANICs or OOPSes being displayed on the console.
e	Sends a `SIGTERM` to all processes, except for `init`.
i	Sends a `SIGKILL` to all processes, except for `init`.
l	Sends a `SIGKILL` to all processes, including `init`.

As you can see, a number of these options can be used to bring down a system and you should carefully consider whether you would want to enable this on systems where users have physical access to the machine, such as with desktop or workstation machines.

Load/Save Configuration

The remaining four options on the kernel configurator require no explanation. The first saves your configuration as `.config` in `/usr/src/linux` and exits the program after telling you what to do next to build your kernel. Conversely, the quit without saving option does just that, after prompting you to make sure that this is really what you want to do.

The remaining two options are useful if you need to build several differently configured kernels. The first allows you to load a configuration from a file. For example, if you install the source RPM for the kernel source, you will find a number of files in `/usr/src/redhat/SOURCES` with names ending in `.config`. You can load one of these to get your new kernel to match the one originally installed with your Red Hat CD. The final option allows you to save your configuration to a file and prompts you for a filename to save it with.

Tweaking the Makefile

There are a number of tweaks that can be made to the top-level kernel makefile to affect the building and installation of your Linux kernel. These tweaks are accomplished by defining various variables in the makefile that result in modifications to the built kernel or that change where the kernel is installed. The first of these is the `EXTRAVERSION` variable. This variable can be used to differentiate between different configurations of the same kernel and becomes part of the kernel version reported by the `uname` command. This can be problematic if you have scripts that depend on the kernel version output by `uname` being made up of just the version, patchlevel, and sublevel, but these are usually easy enough to work around.

The next variable that you might want to change is the `CROSS_COMPILE` variable, which you would define to a string to be prepended to the various compilation commands, such as `gcc`, `ld`, and `as`. If you are not cross compiling your kernel, don't touch this variable.

If you want, you can specify the device containing the root filesystem for your system. This defaults to `CURRENT`, but it can be changed to a specific device. This is not the only method to specify this and, in fact, it is not likely that you would want to change it, but you may if you so desire. If you find that you have incorrectly set this variable, the `rdev` command can be used to set this to the correct device.

The `INSTALL_PATH` variable specifies where to place the update kernel and system map when you issue the make install, make zlilo, or any of the other make targets to install your newly built kernel. If you use a single machine to build kernels for many machines on, you may want to set this as well as the `INSTALL_MOD_PATH` to a path where they will not interfere with the kernel on the build system.

A final variable that you might want to set in the makefile is the SVGA_MODE. By default this is set to NORMAL_VGA, which usually translates to 80 characters by 25 lines, but if you prefer, you can set this to the same number that you would ordinarily press at bootup if you had specified vga=ask in /etc/lilo.conf.

You have noticed that unlike the 2.0 series of kernels, you do not specify SMP support in the makefile any longer. This option has been folded into the configuration scripts of the kernel under general options, as described earlier in this chapter.

Handling Multiple Versions of the Kernel

Unless you have a very small shop, it is likely that you will have a variety of different machines with different hardware configurations. There are any number of ways in which you can manage this, but here are two that you might consider:

- Build a generic kernel with modules for everything.
- Create clone trees, one for each hardware configuration.

Let's take a look at these two methods and discuss the advantages and disadvantages of each.

Building a Generic Kernel

The obvious advantage of this approach to dealing with different hardware configurations is that you only have to build a single kernel, meaning that you will spend a lot less time compiling. The tradeoff is that you will most likely spend more time configuring each individual system. This is the similar to the approach that Linux distributions take, although Red Hat does come with a number of different kernels and the one that is installed is one that is built for your processor type. Another advantage of this method is that if a piece of hardware in the system changes, say an ethernet card for example, it is likely that you will already have the module built to support it. On the flip side, it is likely that your generic kernel will not be as efficient as one that contains only those drivers required for a particular machine.

Note

Even if you choose to use a single configuration for all systems on your site, you will need to maintain two kernels if you have a mix of SMP and uniprocessor systems. This is because an SMP kernel will not always run on a uniprocessor system and even if it does, you will be giving up performance.

35

Customizing the Linux Kernel

Creating Clone Trees

If you decide to build multiple configurations that are better tuned to the individual hardware configurations of systems at your site, creating clone trees may be the way to go. A clone tree in this context refers to a directory structure that matches the kernel source tree, with the exception that all of the source files are actually symbolic links to the original source code. This approach is one that I have used for some time and how it works is quite simple. The first step in this approach is to unpack your kernel source tree into a directory. I usually do not choose /usr/src/linux for this directory, so that the kernel on the build machine is not affected by my work. The next step is to create a cloning script that creates a build tree from the original source. Listing 35.3 shows the one that I use.

LISTING 35.3 clone_tree.pl script

```perl
#!/usr/bin/perl

# Modules
use POSIX;
use Getopt::Std;
use strict;

use vars qw($opt_s $opt_t $opt_h);

my $scriptdir = "/usr/local/buildkernel/bin";

# Parse the command line arguments
getopts("s:t:h");

if (defined $opt_h) {
    &print_usage;
    exit 0;
}

my $source = (defined $opt_s) ? $opt_s : "linux";
my $target = (defined $opt_t) ? $opt_t : undef;
my $extraver = undef;

# First, collect the directory structure of the kernel source tree.
open(FPROC, "find $source -type d -print |");
my @dirtree = <FPROC>;
close(FPROC);

# Now reproduce it, changing the top level directory to a different
```

LISTING 35.3   continued

```perl
# name supplied on the command line, (defaults to linux.N where N is
# an integer value starting at 0).
 if (!defined $target) {
    my $i = 0;
    while ( -d "linux.$i" ) { $i++ }
    $target = "linux.$i";
    $extraver = "$i";
}

foreach my $dir (@dirtree) {
    chomp $dir;
    $dir =~ s/$source/$target/;
    `mkdir -p $dir`;
}

# Now collect the names of all files in the source tree that are not
# directories and create symbolic links from the clone tree into the
# original source tree.
open(FPROC, "find $source -type f -print |");
my @srcfiles = <FPROC>;
close(FPROC);

my $wd = `pwd`;
chomp $wd;
foreach my $file (@srcfiles) {
    chomp $file;
    my $sfile = "$wd/$file";
    $file =~ s/$source/$target/;
    `ln -sf $sfile $file`;
}

# Make copies of a few special files that we will always be modifying.
# These include the top level Makefile and the install script.
unlink "$target/Makefile";
 `cp $source/Makefile $target/Makefile.src`;
unlink "$target/arch/i386/boot/install.sh";
 `cp $source/arch/i386/boot/install.sh $target/arch/i386/boot/install.sh.src`;

# Modify the Makefile, setting the INSTALL_PATH and the INSTALL_MOD_PATH.
open(MFILESRC, "<$target/Makefile.src");
open(MFILE, ">$target/Makefile");
```

LISTING 35.3   continued

```perl
while (<MFILESRC>) {
    if ($_ =~ /^\#INSTALL_PATH/) {
        print MFILE "INSTALL_PATH=$wd/dist/$target/boot\n";
        print MFILE "INSTALL_MOD_PATH=$wd/dist/$target\n";
    } elsif ($_ =~ /^EXTRAVERSION/ ) {
        if (defined $extraver) {
            print MFILE "EXTRAVERSION = -$extraver\n";
        } else {
            print MFILE "EXTRAVERSION = -$target\n";
        }
    } else {
        print MFILE "$_";
    }
}
close(MFILE);
close(MFILESRC);
unlink "$target/Makefile.src";

open(IFILESRC, "<$target/arch/i386/boot/install.sh.src");
open(IFILE, ">$target/arch/i386/boot/install.sh");
while (<IFILESRC>) {
    if ($_ =~ /installkernel/) {
        my $newline = "if [ -x $scriptdir/installkernel ]; then exec"
                    . "$scriptdir/installkernel \"\$@\"; fi";

        print IFILE "$newline\n";
    } else {
        print IFILE "$_";
    }
}
close(IFILE);
close(IFILESRC);
unlink "$target/arch/i386/boot/install.sh.src";

# Create the dist directories for this kernel
if ( -d "$wd/dist/$target" ) {
    rename "$wd/dist/$target", "$wd/dist/$target.old";
}
`mkdir -p $wd/dist/$target/{boot,lib/modules}`;

# Exit.
exit 0;
```

LISTING 35.3   continued

```
# Subroutines
sub print_usage {
    my $usage = "Usage:  clone_tree -s srcdir -t targetdir\n";

    print $usage;
}
```

This script that I call `clone_tree` runs through the kernel directory specified as the `-s` argument and creates a clone directory with the name specified as the `-t` argument. This clone directory is simply a symbolic link farm that points to the actual files in the source directory, with the exception of the top-level Makefile and the `install.sh` script in the directory `arch/i386/boot`. The nice thing about this is that it takes up much less space than a real source tree and patching does the right thing. By this I mean that if you apply a patch to the clone tree, the symbolic link is renamed and a new version of the file is created in the clone tree so that the original source is unchanged. The script also takes the target name and uses this to set the `EXTRAVERSION` variable in the kernel Makefile.

Now that you have your clone tree created, you can CD to it and perform a normal kernel build, starting with configuring your kernel. You would then proceed to the make process, where you run `make` as follows:

```
make dep; make clean; make bzImage; make modules; make modules_install
```

Your next step is to create a customized installation script, which is described in the next section. Once you have done this, you can do a make install and have the kernel image, system map, and associated modules all in a directory where they can be packaged and moved to the target systems.

Custom Installation Scripts

Most networks are made up of many different types of systems. Some might be single-processor workstations without SCSI devices, whereas others have multiple processors and all SCSI drives. This usually means that you will have to maintain multiple versions of the kernel. If you have to maintain several kernel versions or just want to customize the installation of your kernel to match your distribution, you will probably want to create a custom installation script. The Linux kernel source code has provisions for this that are relatively straightforward. You must simply create a script called `installkernel` and place it in the `/sbin/directory`. This script is passed four arguments, as follows:

- $1—Kernel version

35

Customizing
the Linux
Kernel

- $2—Kernel image file

- $3—Kernel map file

- $4—Default install path (blank if root directory)

Here is a simple `installkernel` script that works with the cloning trees method described previously:

```
#!/bin/bash

if [ -f $4/vmlinuz-$1 ]; then
    mv $4/vmlinuz-$1 $4/vmlinuz-$1.old
fi

if [ -f $4/System.map-$1 ]; then
    mv $4/System.map-$1 $4/System.map-$1.old
fi

cat $2 > $4/vmlinuz-$1
cp $3 $4/System.map-$1
```

As you can see, this script is quite simple. Your script can be as simple or as complicated as you desire.

Running `make`

To actually build your kernel, you must run a series of `make` commands to turn the kernel source code into a kernel image file that you can install on your system. There are several make targets that you should be familiar with, which are run in a specific order to accomplish the build, and this section covers the essential ones.

The first make target that we are concerned with is the one to update the dependency information needed to build the kernel. To accomplish this, we run `make` with a target of `dep`, as shown here:

```
make dep
```

This will check all of the dependencies and update the `.depend` files accordingly. The next target that you should use is the `clean` target, which will clean up any object files created and remove old copies of the kernel image that may be lying around from a previous build. This step is performed as follows:

```
make clean
```

The next step is to build the kernel image. The target used here depends on how big your kernel image will be once compiled. If you configured a minimalist kernel with very few options, you can usually use the `zImage` target, but if you included a large number of drivers or lots of modules, you will probably need to use the `bzImage` target. Here is a shortcut that tries to build using the `zImage` target and only if that fails, builds a `bzImage`.

```
make zImage || make bzImage
```

The next two targets you would use build the modules you elected to build and installs them. This command looks like:

```
make modules; make modules_install
```

> **Caution**
>
> If you build a kernel with the same version number as one currently installed on your system, be careful that you do not overwrite your old modules directory in `/lib/modules/<version>`. There is no provision for moving the old modules out of the way in the standard kernel source files.

So putting it all together, you could issue the following commands following configuration to build and install your new kernel:

```
make dep; make clean; make zImage || make bzImage ; make modules ; make
modules_install ; make install
```

Summary

This chapter has attempted to take some of the mystery out of the kernel building process. Although you will have to know a good deal about your hardware in order to customize your kernel, it is not black magic or high art, just a matter of knowing where to look to find the appropriate information. Building a Linux kernel is no more difficult than building any other complex software package and should be no cause for trepidation. By taking a few simple precautions, you can safely modify your kernel to obtain the best performance for your particular needs.

Centennial School District, Portland, Oregon

IN THIS CHAPTER

- Background on Centennial *1136*
- Red Hat 6.0 and the Internet *1144*
- Web Server *1147*
- Network Authentication, Access, and User Administration with Samba *1148*
- Networking Macintosh Computers in the Linux Environment *1152*
- Limited Administrative Control and Access to the Network *1153*
- Using IP Masquerading *1155*
- Electronic Mail *1156*
- System Administration *1158*
- Managing Users and Groups *1159*
- Content Management Using TCP Wrappers *1161*

This case study involves Centennial School District's migration from a Novell 4.11 domain to a Linux Enterprise. The District's computer resources encompass a heterogeneous platform environment of various Macintosh computers, Microsoft Windows 95/98 computers, and Novell NetWare. The District decided to migrate to Linux after Michael Richards joined the IT department and convinced David Pierce to visit a production Linux implementation at the University of Portland.

At the university, Kent Thompson, the senior systems administrator, provided ample evidence that Linux was a stable, versatile, and easily managed network solution. He first demonstrated the topology he deployed and the interoperability between Solaris, Windows, Macintosh, and DOS platforms. Next, he showed the Centennial engineers the power, reliability, security, remote access, and remote administration lacking in Centennial's network. When Kent demonstrated rapid business continuity by replacing a down workstation with a standby Linux machine, David and Michael could visualize Linux in their enterprise.

David and Michael brought back information on what they had learned to Mike Caron, the network systems manager, and Connie Freeman, the media and technology supervisor. During this initial conference, Michael and David presented a compelling business case for Linux as a migration path.

While continuing to verify their findings for the Linux business case with additional studies and analysts' reports, David and Michael visited Paul Nelson of the Riverdale School District. Paul showed them that all the Riverdale services ran from two Linux servers. He also discussed problems he had with his NetWare and NT servers while showing how his Linux boxes performed. He showed them that his Linux servers had run continuously for 18 months without rebooting. David and Michael left convinced.

Connie Freeman took the department's business case to the assistant superintendent, who approved the move. Centennial's IT department had the go-ahead to migrate to Linux. Now, they needed the know-how.

Background on Centennial

Centennial District was formed in 1976 by the merger of the old Lynch District and Centennial High School, which was formerly part of the neighboring Gresham District. In 1993, the District added the Centennial Learning Center, an alternative high school.

The number of computers in the District grew from a handful of Apple IIs to around 1,600 Macs and PCs in 1998. In 1995, the District set up a Novell Domain using generic servers. Mike Caron tells us that since then, all of the old servers have been replaced with Compaqs.

Centennial School District, Portland, Oregon
CHAPTER 36 | 1137

36
Centennial
School District,
Portland,
Oregon

The technology department resulted from the efforts of a few volunteer teachers who began using Apple and IBM personal computers in the early 1980s. As the District grew and began buying additional equipment, the need arose to begin sharing resources.

How Bynari Got Involved

In July, before Mike first contacted us, the District sent three of its technical staff to a week of boot camp training on Linux in Utah. The attendees included Mike Caron, David Pierce, and Michael Richards. Over the course of a week, the staff got a taste of what Linux could do, but they didn't feel they had enough experience to make the switch from Novell to Linux.

The previous summer, David Pierce, the senior technology supervisor and a CNE, led a project to upgrade all of the servers in the District from Novell 3.11 to version 4.11 so the District could take advantage of several features used on the new servers. He knew the amount of effort involved in migrating platforms and he wanted help.

During the next year, the technology center became stressed and pressured from having to manage new services and a different set of problems than it had in previous years. Convinced by their visits to the University of Portland and Riverdale, Mike Caron decided the time had come to migrate.

Mike Caron began looking for consultants to help with the District's migration. He placed a level I service call to Bynari's support center and asked about additional services.

Bynari's technology director found Mike Caron a pleasant person, but didn't feel as if he could assuage Mike's frustrations and anxieties about moving to a new system, especially one that was so radically different than the Novell world to which he was accustomed. So, both parties spent a lot of time and several calls answering questions about migrating to Linux and how to manage the project.

After approximately five hours of discussion, Mike asked if Bynari had anyone who could come to Portland to help set up a Linux test domain and train his staff. Bynari's technology manager felt uneasy sending a trainer to Portland when he knew the client needed Professional Project Management assistance.

From Dallas to Portland

The request for assistance came in late August, when Mike called in a state of frustration. He had presented a business case on Linux two months prior, his supervisor went up the chain of command to get approval, and he now needed to demonstrate results.

Bynari's technology manager volunteered to personally supervise the project and asked Nicholas Donovan, one of the senior partners of Bynari, to go with him. No time seemed good to go. Nick had commitments that stretched far into the future. Still, he knew that if he didn't make time in his schedule, he would never free up, and Mike needed his help.

Connie Freeman arranged travel and lodging for the Bynari consultants. She also scheduled the trip to work through a weekend, which helped Bynari's consultants. Several of the Bynari associates took on extra responsibilities until the team returned from Portland.

Written Requirements from Connie

Connie Freeman included a list of requirements. She wrote:

"Issues we hope to work through include:

- Configuration file types, purposes, locations

- Install Red Hat 6.0; apply updates and patches

- Discuss concepts related to Compaq RAID configuration

- Build two Compaq servers (One completed prior to your arrival)

- Configure off-line WAN between two servers; discuss routing issues

- Configure two Win95 clients

- Configure DHCP & discuss related issues

- Configure IP Masquerading services and related issues

- Discuss e-mail administration; security options—FTP, etc.

- Discuss Macintosh issues"

Concerns of the Project Team

The Centennial School District implementation team consisted of Mike Caron, the network services manager; Dave Pierce, the technology manager; Michael Richards, assistant systems administrator; and Connie Freeman acting as management liaison. The Bynari team consisted of Tom Adelstein and Nicholas Donovan.

Centennial School District, Portland, Oregon

CHAPTER 36

1139

36

Centennial
School District,
Portland,
Oregon

The Centennial Independent School District exhibited most elements we find in any larger-size enterprise. The chief technology officer had built an excellent enterprise networking facility while facing the kinds of deployment hurdles businesses see daily. David Pierce felt concern about changing operating systems after his experience upgrading Novell the previous summer.

Michael Richards felt concern about how much training the staff would need on a new platform. He expressed concern about support calls and an increased workload.

After the Bynari team arrived, the Centennial team met with them in a "brown paper" session. Using butcher paper taped on the wall of a conference room, Bynari's project manager walked everyone through a project plan. Within an hour, the team had a direction, time line, tasks, deliverables, and a migration path. Table 36.1 depicts the notes from the "brown paper" session.

TABLE 36.1 Work Breakdown Structure

Steps	As-is	To-be	Requirements	Scope
Requirements	Novell 4.11 (NDS)	Linux	Authentication	Production System
Constraints	Local servers		Home Directories	User profiles (skel)
Specifications	Routers	Mail	Mail groups & users	Client access, Windows, Mac, Linux
Scope Document	T-1 access/ Frame	Messaging	POP3 IMAP SMTP LDAP	Mail
Project Plan	10 mbps hubs	Scheduling		Backup
Task List	Groupwise	Network Printing		User Administration
Milestones	Compaq Proliants	Backup		Kick starting
Time Lines	Admin tools	DHCP	Web services	Firewalling

Summarizing Centennial's Resources

In an email sent to Bynari, Mike Caron provided the following information:

"The Centennial School District consists of 1 high school, 1 middle school, 6 elementary, 1 alternative, an admin building, a maintenance/transportation/food service building, and a technology center (housing Mike Caron and assoc.).

"Each building has a LAN supported by an internal fibre backbone, CAT 5, and at least 2 hub racks (the high school has 7).

"The high school and middle school each have a building fileserver and a library server. The elementary schools run the library system on their building fileserver. The maintenance building and technology center each have their own servers.

"The district also has a mail server (Novell Groupwise) and a web server running Novell's web server software.

"All servers (typically Compaqs with RAID) are running Novell 4.11 with the exception of the 2 dedicated library servers (IBM's with multiple CD drives) which are still on 3.12.

"Workstations are Pentium class PC's for office and admin, and Macs of all flavors for teachers, classrooms and student labs. Elementary labs are Localtalk to a lab AppleShare server running an Ethernet gateway to the building LAN.

"Microsoft Office 97 is the office standard suite.

"Each building has a Bay Networks multi-protocol router, Kentrox CSU and a T1 link to our Educ. Service District. The service district provides all Internet, accounting, student record and WAN services including firewall.

"Our goal is to reduce the high cost and high maintenance of Novell products.

"We want to replace all Novell OS with Linux, GroupWise with POP3 and Novell's Web Server with Apache. Minimal change for users when accessing shared apps and data.

"We plan to start with the server in technology center, and work out to nearest buildings and beyond. Systematically retrofit one building at a time.

"Centennial is also planning to implement PVC's with US West for our own frame cloud to better manage traffic on our WAN.

"We have the following server inventory [shown in Table 36.2]:

TABLE 36.2   Existing Equipment

Qty	Type
2	ProLiant 800—128mb RAM, Smart 2 SL controller, (3) 4gb HD, 4/8gb HP DAT tape.
3	ProLiant 1200—256mb RAM, Smart 2 SL RAID controller, (3) 4gb HD, 12/24gb Compaq DAT tape
8	ProLiant 1600—256mb RAM, Smart 2 SL RAID controller, (3) 4gb HD, 12/24gb Compaq DAT tape
2	ProLiant 2500—256mb RAM, Smart 2 SL RAID controller, (3) 9gb HD, 12/24gb HP DAT tape Other than a few tape drives, all components are "pure Compaq." LAN/WAN backup:Seagate Backup Exec, single and enterprise licenses."

Organizational Initiatives

During an interview with Connie Freeman, Bynari's consultants learned that "The Centennial Independent School District's primary initiative focuses on improved learning and real world experience which involves communication, research and tapping real world resources. The ability to find real professionals and real world challenges interests us.

"When technology can further the accomplishment of that initiative, the District uses technology for staff and students. Today, the District sees the deployment of interoperability and communication as the most effective and efficient way to facilitate its initiative."

Centennial Chooses Red Hat

After numerous tests of various distributions, the technology team narrowed their selections to Red Hat 6.0 and Mandrake 6.0. They felt Red Hat was the best way to implement their network. While Mandrake provided compatibility with Red Hat 6.0, David chose to install Red Hat on his Compaq servers.

Red Hat installed easily on the Compaq servers, created bootable partitions on their Smart 2 RAIDs, and striped with little problem. Michael chose to use Mandrake since it worked similarly to Red Hat and provided him with the KDE office desktop.

The Challenge

Bynari Systems got involved with the District in July of 1999 when Mike Caron surveyed the market for support and professional services. To test the various firms in the Linux industry, he made support calls and asked for someone to contact him.

Mike objected to several practices in the support industry. First, he couldn't present a case for long-term bundles of support incidents. Secondly, he needed immediate response when using call support. Finally, he wanted first-hand experience working with support technicians before he made any commitments.

In many ways, Bynari's structure fit his situation. Bynari began helping him with support calls right away. Bynari charged by the incident and guaranteed its work. In other words, he didn't pay unless a fix of the problem on the phone occurred within a few minutes.

Secondly, Bynari accepted open invoices, which meant it only billed clients when they used a service. Finally, Bynari's support group didn't require a commitment beyond the most current support call.

Enter Linux and Red Hat's 6.0

The unspoken theme at Centennial continued to ring through each effort of work accomplished.

Technology exists for the benefit of the instructors and their students. If technology can facilitate improvements in competencies, then it is welcome. Dave and Mike say that they meet with little resistance and great support among students, faculty, and administrators when they provide best-of-class service.

The technology budget objective for the 1999-2000 school year at Centennial concentrated on distributing more reliable support logistics on a timely basis. In that context, networking with its improved communications, intranet tools, and print sharing, Internet access had value only if it facilitated better education.

In looking at Centennial's project in the educational context, the requirements became clear. If a process didn't add value, it didn't belong.

The team asked, "What will the Media and Technology Department need to accomplish the district's objective?"

First, the technology department had to get a productivity suite to replace Novell's Groupwise. The replacement application needed to reach each faculty and administrative member. Each teacher had to use his or her productivity suite to efficiently help drive students to an improved educational structure.

Once a teacher determined his or her class' needs, he or she had to find and use appropriate teaching materials. Each teacher could then devise his or her own lesson plan.

The Internet for Curriculum

The faculty found that the Internet provided an efficient and effective medium to meet their needs. Centennial determined they could use high-speed access to the Internet for technology to help meet their main initiatives.

Centennial's technology administrators saw a need to filter content and provide security measures for student users. The teaching community objected to restrictions.

The technology department found enterprise-level firewalls and filtering software costly, especially if the schools teaching administration demanded free access to the Internet. Linux firewalls presented a true alternative in situations where cost would become a barrier.

Red Hat 6.0 Helps Centennial Meet Requirements

Dave liked Red Hat 6.0 because of its capabilities and ease of installation. The Compaq servers as well as the least expensive computers bought by the District turned out to have hardware compatible with Red Hat. Red Hat provided video drivers that allowed the latest computer acquisitions to work with Linux.

Once Red Hat was installed, the performance of the slower computers exceeded everyone's expectations. This provided potential systems for students who otherwise wouldn't have had access to a computer course.

Academically, learning to use Linux, a UNIX-style operating system, had more value to the graduates than learning to use word processing and spreadsheet programs provided by the network base of Microsoft and Novell proprietary domains.

Red Hat 6.0 and the Internet

One key feature of Linux provides for an inexpensive solution to manage content and network access via firewalls. The term *firewall* comes from the firewall used in cars. The firewall protects occupants in the cabin from a fire in the engine compartment.

A firewall on a network protects both users and data located behind it on the local network from unauthorized intrusion. It can also be used to prevent users on the local network from connecting to prohibited sites.

Two kinds of firewalls exist in Linux. Each of these types has two subtypes. The two basic types include "packet filters" and "proxy" firewalls.

Packet filter firewalls can be one the following types:

- **Forwarding**—With this kind of packet filter, firewall decisions relate to whether or not to forward packets to the Internet.

- **Masquerading**—These firewalls can rewrite the source and destination addresses in the packet headers to keep outsiders from learning the addresses and topology of the internal network.

Proxy firewalls can be one of the following types:

- **Standard**—With this type of proxy firewall, a workstation on the private network connects to a server. The workstation's packets go through a special port or opening and are then redirected out through another port.

- **Transparent**—With this firewall, the workstation does not use a special port. The firewall software proxies, or acts for the workstation, sending and returning data packets through the connection transparently.

The Linux kernel that ships with Red Hat 6.0 comes precompiled with everything the District needed to utilize packet filtering. Network administrators accomplish firewalling through the capabilities of modern Linux kernels. Centennial chose to enable IP Chains to masquerade their private network behind the firewall. They also chose to use a proxy server to limit access to and from the private network.

Defining Other Requirements

Centennial became acutely aware of the need for centralized management, scalability, separation of local networks, and business continuity.

Summarizing, the technology department's requirements included

1. Deployment of distributed applications
2. Internet connectivity
3. Increased security and content management
4. Centralized management

Constraints

Centennial worked under many constraints, not all budgetary. Some had to do with the facilities, and computer literacy in the student and faculty population and among other school employees. Centennial, like all districts, faced budget constraints from funding issues and fiscal management. The issue of access to Internet content, while unresolved, kept technology management from making decisions on content management.

Technical Expertise and Knowledgeable Management

Centennial confronted a lack of computer-literate talent within the faculty, and among the administration and the student population. The technology department consisted primarily of Dave Pierce, Mike Caron, and Michael Richards.

The team had to provide planning, network administration, application support, and application development. Administrators of the District also expected them to provide deskside support, identify needs, find outside resources, submit purchase requests that require heavy justification, and maintain the physical plant.

Project Specifications

Combining Centennial's technology requirements with their constraints, Mike could begin to develop a specifications document. For example, requirement #1 said that Centennial had to deploy distributed applications. When Mike added the constraints of stable and reliable, low maintenance, and scarce resources, the specifications became

1. Deploy a stable and reliable, low-maintenance application over a network using a distributed user interface.
2. Provide stable and reliable, low-maintenance Internet connectivity using a local area network.

3. Provide stable and reliable, low-maintenance content management and security.

4. Provide centralized network management with ease of use.

At this point, Centennial could only see the initiative from a macro view. A complete specifications document requires that someone identify available platforms such as hardware and operating systems, applications, resources, and user interfaces.

When the specifications of an enterprise initiative are defined, a project plan can figuratively "fall-out" of the document into a task list. In the case of Centennial, the technology department needed to address so many areas that just a list of incomplete items already started served as a task list.

Short- and Long-Term Objectives

Dave defined Linux as his operating system of choice after experimenting with many operating systems. He wanted to take the next step and invigorate his network.

The District's long-term objectives include bringing advanced computer science into their classrooms. Many school districts in Oregon have taught computer science courses for several years. The first courses taught at Centennial were word processing and spreadsheets.

The District has aspirations of providing system administration, networking, and programming into the curriculum. The technology department, however, has concerns about opening its resources to students who might breach security and resources.

The resolution of the conflict of interests between the academic community and the network administrators will be resolved by bringing higher levels of curriculum into the classrooms while allowing the technical department to manage enterprise resources.

The Project Plan

The District defined its project for the current school year as deployment of a manageable network platform. Dave called it the Linux Project for short.

To complete Dave's productivity application and distribute it to the faculty, he needed a platform-neutral graphical interface. With a working Web-enabled application, Centennial would need to provide secure access via a Web server to each faculty member.

Using Internet technologies to deliver an application to a user base internally meant that Dave needed an intranet.

Centennial School District, Portland, Oregon
CHAPTER **36** | 1147

36
Centennial
School District,
Portland,
Oregon

Web Server

Red Hat distributes Red Hat 6.0 with an Apache Web server. The server comes installed and configured by default. This Web server is used for processing online help requests and online documentation within Red Hat 6.0 at the desktop level. Users can also deploy their Apache server to share documents or Web applications with local network users.

HTML documents can be accessed from an Apache Web server by local users. They specify the IP address of the host computer or the URL of the local Web site in their Web browser to access documents.

One of the most basic, yet important, services available for use in Red Hat 6.0 is the Web servers. Apache has many different features that you can configure. The numerous modifications and extensions that you can make to the basic Web server provide a surprisingly flexible mechanism.

Securing Access to the Applications

The configuration modifications options available to Centennial on Apache included

- **Authorization**—The process of determining if a client is allowed to access a specific Web site.

- **Access Control**—The process of allowing or preventing access to specific Web site objects, based on the authorization of a client or user.

- **Host-based Authorization**—Controlling access to a Web site or part of the site based on the hostname or IP address of the client.

- **User-based Authorization**—Controlling access to the Web application based on the identity of the user.

- **Authentication**—The process of determining the identity of a remote user. In Red Hat 6.0, this involves having the user provide a name and password, which only an authorized user will know.

Host-based authorization provides an attractive aspect. Users and administrators find it simple and non-intrusive. With host-based authorization, the process of authorizing clients doesn't affect the user at all.

User-based authorization requires the user to enter a name and password to access the Web site or directory. User-based authorization provides the most secure and reliable security. Unfortunately, it requires additional work on the part of the system administrator.

Centennial made the trade-off because of the sensitive nature of the data involved in the productivity suite. The application integrity of the productivity suite facility required the best security possible. This insured that the data would not be compromised.

Centennial reduced administrative duties by defining groups of users as well as users themselves. By managing sets of users, the system administrator defined a group file for use with Apache. This eliminated defining individual access rights by placing users in a group definition.

Network Authentication, Access, and User Administration with Samba

For authentication services and network management, Centennial needed to use smb protocol. Samba is an Open Source software package available for Linux that provides support for the protocols used by Windows 95/98 and Windows NT.

Samba allows Windows clients to access the file and print capabilities of the Linux system in a manner similar to how those clients would access a Windows NT server.

Choosing the Samba package included with Red Hat 6.0 allowed Centennial to save money. The District did not have to pay license fees based on users or seats to provide basic NT services. Advantages of using Samba include

- A stable and reliable solution. Samba running on Linux provided the District with the default services it would have deployed with Windows NT. Again, the Linux solution does not require user license fees.

- Less administrative time.

On Centennial's main authentication server, the technical department installed the Samba and sambas rpms from Red Hat 6.0. Under version 2.05, Samba can act as a domain controller. In previous versions, Samba did not authenticate users as a domain controller. Red Hat improved Red Hat 6.0's functionality by adding this application to Red Hat 6.0.

Centennial School District, Portland, Oregon

CHAPTER 36   1149

36

Centennial
School District,
Portland,
Oregon

Samba in Centennial's Heterogeneous Environment

The developers of Samba created a set of programs that allows UNIX and UNIX-like operating systems like Linux to communicate with Microsoft hosts. Microsoft uses a protocol known as NetBEUI, which implements server message blocks for network communication. Since many of Centennial's workstations ran Windows 95/98, implementing Samba became necessary in order to use Linux.

Training the Centennial Team

To provide an example of how Bynari coached the Centennial team, we'll use the Samba configuration to demonstrate Bynari's methodology. Mike Caron explains:

"We began the samba install initially without setting up the server as an NT domain server. We learned how to create Linux users, and how to make samba users from existing Linux users. We then edited the /etc/hosts file to include the ip numbers of our samba client boxes. This was done because we were not ready to implement DNS services in our test lan. The smb.conf was then edited to set up disk shares.

"The following steps are a general guideline we used for installing Samba and creating an NT Domain on a Linux Server.

- The very first step is to download the most current stable RPM for Samba and then install it. rpm -Uvh <rpm name> (The "U" is for "upgrade")

- Next create a public directory, and use chmod to give all users full access.

- We mkdir /home/pub and then chmod /home/pub 777.

- We edited /etc/hosts and created a public share for the /home/pub directory.

- We copied a template smb.conf file to the /etc directory and edited it to the specific server, domain name and any other specific settings.

- Now run linuxconf to edit some specific network settings for the server.

- Select Browse Master=yes, Local Master=yes, os level=65 (Later Domain Master=yes, os level=255)

- Select Synchronize Linux from SMB passwords (yes)

- Create Linux user, adduser if necessary and then create the Samba user smbadduser for any users that want access to this samba server.

"Now configure the Windows workstation. Change Network Neighborhood properties to the following:

- Identification Tab to the new workgroup (csd28)

- Access Control to Share level access control

- Client for Microsoft Networks properties to new workgroup (csd28)

- TCP/IP properties

    IP Number: 192.168.3.10 (Initially, any static number)

    DNS Configuration:

    Domain: mtc.net

    Host:

    DNS Search Order: Initially Disabled Later added 192.168.3.15 (MTC proxy server, it was the ESD server)

    Gateway: 198.236.3.1

- Turn on File & print sharing

- Add to the end of the c:/Windows/LM Hosts file 192.168.3.15 CSD28 (ip & workgroup)

- Reboot"

The Bynari approach uses gradients to teach the administrators how to configure any service. In the beginning of the samba process, the Centennial team only performed one function. They created a user called "guest" and added the user to both the Linux password file and the smbpasswd file. They also configured a Windows 98 system to log on to the Samba server. They added the Windows information to the Linux "hosts" file and made entries to the smb.conf.

Once the team experienced success with a simple guest share, they added functionality until the test LAN had domain authentication, Dynamic Host Configuration Protocol (DHCP), mail, and the ability to browse the Internet through a Linux firewall.

Back to Samba

Samba 2.0 introduced a program to assist in setting up and administering Samba via a Web browser. People know the program as SWAT, for Samba Web Administration Tool. With Centennial's scarce resources, the technical department needed a simple way to provide administration for Microsoft workstations. Red Hat 6.0 provides SWAT on its distribution.

Centennial School District, Portland, Oregon

CHAPTER 36 | 1151

36

Centennial
School District,
Portland,
Oregon

To enable SWAT in Red Hat 6.0, the technology department used the "inetd" method, which doesn't require a Web server. Under this method, the various components of Samba can be configured and maintained via a Web browser. Though Red Hat 6.0 provides Samba and SWAT, the system administrator must configure it.

The Samba Web Administration Tool provided considerable challenges to the relatively new Linux network managers. When installing Samba 2.05, the installation program automatically puts an entry in the system's `inetd.conf` file.

When configuring Samba, the administrator must open the configuration file and remove the comment symbol (#) in front of the SWAT entry in this file. Removing the comment allows Samba to be called during the system initiation process.

Next, the administrator must enter `swat` as a service in the system services file. The name of this file is simply `services` and it lives in the `/etc` directory. Using a text editor, the administrator opens the files and locates a section where the port numbers allow for a "900" series entry. The entry that SWAT requires in this configuration file is `swat 901/tcp #swat`.

Once the entry is made, the administrators must restart the services for the changes to take effect. By using the command `/etc/rc.d/inet.d/inet restart` the system enables SWAT for use. On execution of this command at the root user's command-line prompt, he or she will see a series of entries similar to those seen on booting the computer. Then the administrator can open his Web browser and access the SWAT interface.

The administrators typed `http://localhost:901` and the SWAT interface opened in the browser. A sense of astonishment usually accompanies the first site of the SWAT interface and in Centennial's case, this occurred.

Suddenly, light could be seen at the end of the proverbial tunnel. The small group consisting of Dave and his team became even more intrigued with the remote administration possibilities when they went to a workstation in another room and accessed SWAT from a remote browser.

Once the administrators configured Samba on Centennial's Compaq server, they enabled printing services for their Windows workstations.

Global Printing Services Using Samba

The Linux administrator configured a Public directory on the Samba server. The administrator created a public share and private shares on a per-user basis, and gave all users access to a shared printer controlled by the Samba server. This allowed one computer with the Linux operating system to provide shared Samba printing along with other services, such as secure Web services and user authentication to access the network.

Using Samba to Access the Red Hat 6.0 System from a Windows PC

The administrators had to provide deskside support to each of the Windows workstations. Each PC had to have its network properties configured by hand. By verifying that Windows Networking and TCP/IP were installed and running, they could begin the process of connectivity with the Linux server.

The administrators logged into the Windows PC using the same username that was granted access using a Samba username during Samba configuration. They then opened the Network Neighborhood on the Windows Desktop.

The Linux system appeared in the list and looked to the Windows user like another Windows computer on the network. On right-clicking the Linux Samba server icon in the Windows 95/98 network neighborhood and choosing Properties, the caption reads Windows Print and File Services.

The administrator then double-clicked on the Linux system and entered the Linux user password when prompted. The administrator and the user could browse within the Linux file system as needed.

Now, the user could map a drive to a particular Linux directory, right-click on that item, and choose from the pop-up menu. By mapping a network drive from a Windows 95/98 system, the Windows username would be the same as the username on the Red Hat 6.0 machine. The user, if granted permission by the directory owner, could view those files.

Networking Macintosh Computers in the Linux Environment

Centennial used the AppleTalk internetworking stack, which allowed a peer-to-peer network model for functionality such as file and printer sharing for its Macintosh computers. Each machine could simultaneously act as a client and a server, and the software and hardware necessary were included with every Apple computer.

Centennial used the AppleTalk networking system and TCP/IP available on all Apple Macintosh computers and a variety of printers. The AppleTalk protocol suite encompasses high-level file sharing using AppleShare, LaserWriter printing services, and print spoolers along with lower-level data streams and simple datagram delivery.

Although the term AppleTalk was originally used for both the protocol and connecting cables, it became available on different media, so LocalTalk was used to describe the simple shielded twisted-pair cable used to connect Macs to other Macs or printers.

Centennial School District, Portland, Oregon

CHAPTER 36   1153

36
Centennial
School District,
Portland,
Oregon

Centennial used EtherTalk over ethernet so AppleTalk data can be carried within different protocols, both SNAP and TCP/IP, for encapsulation.

Linux provides full AppleTalk networking. Netatalk, the kernel-level implementation of the AppleTalk Protocol Suite originally for BSD-derived systems, includes support for routing AppleTalk, serving UNIX and AFS filesystems over AFP (AppleShare), serving UNIX printers, and accessing AppleTalk printers over PAP.

The District system administrators wanted access to Mac printers like a LaserWriter sitting with its EtherTalk adapter on the network. The Mac user wanted to get access to any printer accessible from Linux. To set up such a service under Linux, the administrators used the same procedure in both cases.

After having compiled and installed the AppleTalk software netatalk, Dave started all the daemons using rc.atalk in the /etc directory. We made sure the AppleTalk service was working before trying to configure a printer.

Using the command /usr/local/atalk/bin/getzones enabled the administrators to see whether all the AppleTalk zones were visible to the main Linux server.

"With the command line option we found out which zone we were in:

```
root# /usr/local/atalk/bin/getzones -m
Admin
root#
```

"The local zone was Admin. The complete list of all local zones was obtained using the -l option.

"We also found the name of the printers to make the Linux printers available to AppleShare clients."

Now, the Linux network accommodated Windows 95/98 clients, Macintosh and UNIX computers both used as clients, learning tools, and for administration. All protocols and services existed on a single system.

Limited Administrative Control and Access to the Network

The system administrators could also access a Windows PC from Red Hat 6.0. When the Windows user provides resources for sharing, the Linux user can access those resources by entering a Red Hat 6.0 command:

```
$ smbclient //windowshost/resourcename
For example:  $ smbclient //usernameC_drive
```

The Linux user would need the Windows password for this service when prompted.

The `smb:\>` prompt appears when using the Samba client service to access the Windows workstation. The `smb:\>` prompt is an FTP-like interface. Linux users can use commands such as `put` and `get` to exchange files with the Windows PC.

When first attempting to use the smbclient, we discovered that program, smbclient, had not been installed using the default Red Hat 6.0 program. By using the Internet, we went to a site referred to as RPMfind.net.

We entered the Web site at `http://www.rpmfind.net/Linux/RPM` and found a repository of rpm files housed by the W3C organization. They have the largest repository of RPMs in the world. W3C dedicates approximately a terabyte of space for these programs.

We found the latest version of samba client as an rpm (Red Hat Package Manager) and installed it. We then used the Kpackage manager and by right-clicking the link, installed the program directly off the ftp site in Kfilemanager.

The administrators found using a command-line utility tedious and time-consuming. Once we asked the administrator to transfer a file from a Windows share to the Linux server, he made server typing errors and discovered that he didn't have the flexibility of bash. This gave us an opportunity to demonstrate the flexibility of Linux.

We asked the administrator to access the Windows share through the kvt terminal window. Once he made the connection, we asked him to do a listing of the files in the share. We then asked him to highlight the text of the file he wanted to transfer.

To his surprise, by clicking the middle mouse button (or both mouse buttons simultaneously as in emulating a three button mouse), the file displayed on the Linux server command line.

By typing "get" in front of the text and pressing the Enter key, the file transferred from the Windows box immediately. The administrators commented that they felt as if this process would speed their administrative tasks and provide ftp-like access to Windows workstations, which by design do not have ftp services by default.

Progress for Centennial

By using Linux and Samba, the technology department could provide a centralized print, file, and application server so that the various local area networks could communicate with each other.

Centennial School District, Portland, Oregon
CHAPTER 36 | 1155

36
Centennial
School District,
Portland,
Oregon

In addition to Samba, Linux also implements Apple Computer's network protocol called AppleTalk. The Linux server has the capability to provide full network services to Centennial's Macintosh computers simultaneously with its services to Microsoft computers.

Internet Access

The next task in the project plan involved providing Internet access to the private network inside the school while preventing unchallenged access from the Internet into the school. This required a firewall and a proxy solution.

Using IP Masquerading

To allow multiple computers to use a single connection to the Internet through a firewall server, an administrator needs to enable IP Masquerading in Red Hat 6.0. If a Linux host is connected to the Internet with IP Masquerading enabled, then computers connecting to it usually on the same LAN can reach the Internet invisibly as well, even though they have no officially assigned IP addresses.

Advantages of Using IP Masquerading

Centennial installed Red Hat 6.0 on a Pentium II computer, with a configuration of 96 megabytes of RAM and a 6.5 GB hard drive. This Linux host connected to the Internet and established a connection through the existing network. Other computers running TCP/IP connected to a Linux box on a local network to reach the Internet as long as the server maintained its connection.

Linux 2.2.x Kernels

The technical department at Centennial attempted to establish a firewalling scheme using IPFWADM, which worked on previous Linux kernels. Using the documentation for IP Masquerading in Red Hat 6.0's online documentation, the Centennial administrators discovered how to implement their firewall.

They also discovered IPFWADM was no longer the firewall tool for manipulating IP Masquerading rules for both the 2.1.x and 6.0.x kernels. Thus, they became familiar with Red Hat's 6.0 kernel using the IPCHAINS tool.

The administrators set reserved IP addresses (192.168.x.x) for each internal MASQed computer they wanted to provide with Internet access. The administrators now needed to point each internal client machine to the Linux server providing the Masquerading services, using this server as the default gateway.

The process simply involved the administrators entering the address of the Linux host as the machine's gateway address. The server's networking hardware included two Intel Pro 100 network interface cards. In setting up the network interface card, the administrators assigned an IP address to it. They obtained an IP address for the outside network interface card via DHCP (Dynamic Host Control Protocol) from their Internet service provider.

Client machines connected to the server required name resolution services in order to navigate the Web. By running either the ROUTED protocol (on smaller networks), or configuring DNS, the client machines could use the same DNS servers that the Linux server used.

Distributing the Productivity Application

As stated before, Centennial utilized the features and capabilities of the Apache Web server to distribute their productivity application. In addition, the District needed mail, file transfer capabilities, and multi-user access to applications.

Electronic Mail

Red Hat 6.0 includes the sendmail Mail Transfer Agent (MTA). Sendmail allows a Red Hat 6.0 system to complete mail services such as the following:

- **SMTP**—Simple Mail Transport Protocol. This service allows users to send email over the Internet. When someone configures a mail client on the PC or MAC, he specifies an SMTP server on his ISP's network to provide mail transport. This service is the "send" part of the email process.

- **POP3**—The POP3 server in sendmail allows users to retrieve their mail from the Internet. So, the sending agent and the receiving agent function on the same server and in the same mail program—sendmail.

- **Internal Mail**—On the local area networks, clients specify the Linux computer as both their internal and external mail transport agent. This allows seamless mail access internally and externally. Using the Linux computer, the administrator creates an alias in the configuration file that refers to the sendmail server as mail.domain-name.com.

Centennial School District, Portland, Oregon

CHAPTER 36 | 1157

36

Centennial
School District,
Portland,
Oregon

The mail user agents on the local desktop specify the alias as their mail server, which provides all their email services. The user must have a mail client on his desktop that can send and receive standard Internet protocol mail.

Sendmail provided on the Red Hat distribution is a complete mail server and can reside on the same computer as the authentication server and the Samba application.

People have found configuring sendmail challenging. Red Hat provides excellent documentation on configuring sendmail.

Two initial configuration files Centennial used as a guide were provided in the Red Hat 6.0 distribution. These included the /etc/sendmail.cw file and the /etc/sendmail.cf file.

It should be noted as well that there exists a facility called m4, which makes the configuration of sendmail's cryptic configuration files a more manageable task. M4 allows the administrator to produce sendmail configuration files much more easily by converting these simpler text files into actual Sendmail.cf files.

The sendmail configuration Centennial used had a single machine act as a mail gateway for all the machines on the network. For example, the authentication server handled internal mail and acted as the main gateway to the Internet gateway. The Pentium II server handled all Internet mail accounts.

When the administrators added the hostnames of other machines in the District to the configuration file, mail sent to those machines were captured by the main mail server.

Then on the other machines, they edited the /etc/sendmail.cf file to "masquerade" as the main server when sending mail, and to forward any local mail processing to the Samba server. To do this, the administrators found the DH and DM lines in /etc/sendmail.cf and edited them.

Example: `sendmail.cf` File

```
# who gets all local e-mail traffic ($R has precedence for unqualified

# whoImasquerade as (null for no masquerading) Centennial.com.
```

With this type of configuration, all mail sent appeared as if it were sent from the main server and any mail sent to the efa Pentium II server or the other hosts was delivered to the Dell authentication server.

System Administration

Administration tasks on Centennial's Red Hat 6.0 system appeared overwhelming when Dave Pierce began planning for resources. As chief technology supervisor, Dave felt relief to discover the many administration tools available for Linux. For example, Nick Donovan introduced the Centennial team to Cheops—a graphical scanning program that provides a means to see all computers on the network, their operating system, IP address, the tables in routers, and statistics on each machine on the network.

One of the responsibilities of a network administrator is to have an in-depth understanding of how the operating system works. A fundamental building block of that understanding is knowing how the system boots up and initializes itself. This is something we breezed through when assisting the District administrators in understanding their tasks.

The startup process for Red Hat 6.0 is based on the UNIX SystemV initialization system. After the Linux kernel is started by the LILO boot manager or Master Boot program located in the Master Boot Record, the following steps occur, under the control of the Linux kernel:

1. The kernel initializes its own internal systems.

2. The init program is started.

3. The init program reads the `/etc/inittab` file and prepares for the run level defined in that file.

4. The `/etc/rc.d/rc.modules` script is executed by init. This loads all auto-loaded kernel modules.

5. The `/etc/rc.d/rc.boot` script is executed by init. This processes other system information.

6. Depending on the mode of operation (run level) indicated by the inittab file, one of the run-level directories is examined and all of the services listed in that directory are started or stopped. Services that start with an S are started. Services that start with a K are stopped and their associated parent processes killed.

   For example, if run level 3 is specified, the services in directory `/etc/rc.d/rc3.d` are processed.

7. The getty program (terminal startup manager) is started on each of the virtual consoles defined by the inittab file.

Among the programs generally started by the run-level scripts is the initd super-server, which watches for traffic on the network ports defined by `/etc/services` and starts server programs when a request is received, according to the server specified in `/etc/inetd.conf`.

Centennial School District, Portland, Oregon

CHAPTER 36

1159

36

Centennial
School District,
Portland,
Oregon

The virtual consoles defined by /etc/inittab are accessed on Alt+F1 through Alt+F6. These consoles each provide a character-based login, as if you were working from a dumb terminal. You can log in from these consoles using any valid user account, then switch between the consoles using the Alt+F1 through F6 key combinations.

If you are in the graphical system, you can switch to the other virtual consoles by pressing Ctrl+Alt+Fx (Fx is one of the keyboard function keys from F1 to F6, inclusive). Once you are in the character-mode consoles, the user can use Alt+Fx. To switch back to the graphical system, press Ctrl+Alt+F7.

Managing Users and Groups

As mentioned previously, Linux is a multi-user operating system. OS multi-usability refers to many requirements that an OS must possess. Among these characteristics are the ability to run applications at the server itself, the underlying object model of request handling, and that multiple users can simultaneously access and use Linux.

Multi-usability is an important requirement for any OS in the enterprise. Not all OS's are multi-user (DOS and Windows are examples of single-user operating systems). Managing users on a multi-user OS such as Open Linux is a critical task for the system administrator.

This section illustrates how to set up and manage multiple user accounts.

To create a new user account on their system, Centennial had a choice of methods:

- Use the command adduser new_user_name

- Use the command useradd new_user_name

- Use the Linuxconf administration tools by selecting Linuxconf, System, Accounts on the KDE main menu

- Use the character-mode lisa tool by entering the command lisa\useradd

In each case, the administrators could follow the onscreen prompts to enter information about the user account they wanted to create.

Different User Account Management Scenarios

When setting up the main server, the tasks become very data entry intensive. In this case, the administrators chose to use Linuxconf because of its simplicity. The less technical members of Dave's staff could enter the user information and allow the other members to attend to the many technical challenges ahead of them.

The utilities passwd and usermod can be used to manage user accounts after they are created. The District can alter passwords, expiration dates of passwords, default shells, and more. Red Hat 6.0 provides manual (internal documentation or help files) pages of each command for more information. If the administrator wants quick help, he or she can simply type the following at the command prompt:

```
#adduser -h
```

(For example) The result should output something similar to the following:

```
usage: adduser [-u uid][-g group] [-G group,...]
               [ -d home] [ -s shell] [-c comment]
```

The -u in this example, which you will see continuously in Linux documents, means that after you issue a command, the command needs an argument. The minus sign tells the system that an argument has been specified. (Sometimes arguments have two dashes as well.)

The -u argument tells the system that the administrator will be adding a user identification number rather than having the system increment the number for him or her.

Linuxconf doesn't require the administrator to specify a typical UNIX argument because it provides visual text boxes to enter the data. This is one of the advantages the District had by using the administrative tools included in the Red Hat 6.0 distribution.

The other command-line options for user administration in the quick help (-h) are:

> The -g in the preceding example refers to the administrator specifying the default group that the user will belong to rather than accepting the system default assignment. Linuxconf allows the administrator to easily specify a group or groups that a user will belong to.

> The -G in the preceding example refers to the administrator specifying the supplementary groups that a user will belong to. Again, optional group specifications are easily done in Linuxconf.

> The -d option refers to the directory specification by the administrator rather than accepting the system default for users (that is, /home/username).

> The -s option refers to the default user shell (command environment) that will be issued to the user by the administrator.

The command-line scenario provided remote administration ability by allowing the administrator at Centennial to use the telnet program to log in to a remote computer.

Centennial School District, Portland, Oregon

CHAPTER 36   1161

36
Centennial
School District,
Portland,
Oregon

For example, the administrator could telnet to a user's machine in another building. The administrator would enter his or her user identification and password and become a remote user on that machine. He would then obtain administrative privileges and use the command line to issue user administration commands and parameters.

The administrators also had the ability to create a new user account, using the information in the /etc/skel directory. They could copy the contents of skel into the new users home directory. The skel directory contains information such as basic startup scripts and configuration information. This allows the system administrators to enforce various rights and privileges when a new user account is created or modified.

Content Management Using TCP Wrappers

As a security measure, Red Hat 6.0 network services are managed by a protective program called a TCP Wrapper. The protected services are those listed in the /etc/inetd.conf file that use the /usr/sbin/tcpd program. These services include, for example, FTP and Telnet access.

A sample line from the /etc/inetd.conf file is shown here:

```
ftp stream tcp nowait root /usr/sbin/tcpd in.ftpd -l \a
```

This line shows that the FTP service is maintained by the inetd program.

Whenever a request for FTP service arrives on the computer named for FTP in the /etc/services file, the tcpd program starts with in.ftpd, the FTP server program, as a parameter.

By encapsulating (wrapping) network services using tcpd, the District could control access to the service by configuring and maintaining the hosts.allow and hosts.deny files in the /etc directory.

The District found this feature of Red Hat 6.0 invaluable for content management. One concern expressed continually by faculty and administration of the District when discussing Internet Services focused on content management.

The rules contained in the hosts.allow and hosts.deny files included security based on which service was requested, such as

- The IP address of the requesting client
- The domain name of the requesting client

A sample `etc/hosts.allow` file, when edited to allow access to services, might look like this:

```
ALL: Centennial.edu

in.talkd: ALL

in.ntalkd: ALL

in.fingerd: ALL

in.ftpd: ALL
```

This configuration allows all connections from Centennial and Centennial.edu machines to use the services. It also allows the services talk, finger, and ftp to accept requests from all machines.

The tcpd program allows much more sophisticated access control, using a combination of the files `/etc/hosts.allow` and `/etc/hosts.deny`. The administrators of Centennial learned to use this technique to enable content management.

Using an FTP Server to Download Files

An FTP server is configured and running after a standard Red Hat 6.0 installation. Users can use anonymous FTP to exchange files on Red Hat 6.0 system via any FTP client, including a Web browser. To demonstrate this capability, the administrators allowed several users to try this by entering their URL from any client that could access the Linux system over a network:

```
ftp://linux_system_name/
```

When using this command, users accessed the directory `/home/ftp` on the Red Hat 6.0 system. Any files that were placed in the directory `/home/ftp/pub` were accessible by default to anonymous users who logged in to the system using FTP.

FTP can also be used to access regular user accounts with a URL like this one:

```
ftp://username@linux_system_name/
```

The user gets prompted for a password before he or she can see the files on the Linux system. Several files located in the `/etc` directory define the configuration of the FTP server running on Red Hat 6.0. Although the default configuration is fairly secure, many

Centennial School District, Portland, Oregon
CHAPTER 36 | 1163

36
Centennial
School District,
Portland,
Oregon

system administrators review the configuration files carefully before using FTP openly on an Internet-connected Red Hat 6.0 server.

The following files are relevant to an FTP server:

/etc/inetd.conf: Defines how FTP connection requests are processed by the TCP Wrapper program.

/etc/hosts.allow and /etc/hosts.deny: Define who can access the FTP server.

/etc/ftpusers: Defines regular users on the Red Hat 6.0 system who cannot use FTP (this is intended as a security protection).

/etc/ftpaccess: Defines access rules for all user accounts, including the anonymous user.

/var/log/xferlog: Logs all transfers between FTP clients and the FTP server, both for regular and anonymous users.

Network users find the File Transfer Protocol useful for disseminating information to their public. In this case, Centennial decided to allow incoming and outgoing ftp service to a group of users. In addition to dissemination of materials in electronic format, many users find personal ftp services useful for backing up important files from their workstations to more stable servers.

Summary

The Centennial Independent School District, like many school districts around the country, exhibited most elements found in medium-size enterprises. Centennial had to deal with a variety of computer platforms and self-generated enterprise applications.

Utilizing Internet protocols such as the Hypertext Transfer Protocol used on the World Wide Web, the District enabled applications that could be used by any computer host with a Web browser.

Dave Pierce, the chief technology officer, built an excellent enterprise solution while facing the kinds of deployment hurdles businesses see daily. In this study, we examined how Red Hat 6.0 helped the District meet and face its challenges.

First, Red Hat 6.0 provided Centennial with file, print, and application services. Using Samba, for example, the District was able to emulate an NT enterprise providing authentication services. Using Netatalk, the administration of AppleTalk print and file services quickly became available.

Secondly, Red Hat 6.0 provided the District with Web services such as intranet, telnet, and ftp. Dave was able to distribute the productivity application he developed using a Web-enabled interface. This enabled him to quickly provide a front-end to his database and productivity application while making it platform neutral.

Red Hat 6.0 also provided the District with security in the form of firewalling and IP Masquerading. This gave Centennial the ability to manage content and access to its network. It also allowed the District to provide user-level authentication so that the productivity application could remain free from compromise.

Red Hat 6.0 gave the enterprise additional benefits that had longer-term effects. By allowing users to dual boot a computer from Microsoft Windows into Linux, students had a development environment to learn higher levels of computer science. The development environment of Red Hat 6.0 provides the GNU utilities for learning programming, system administration, and Web mastering.

Red Hat 6.0 also provides glue to bring diverse computer platforms together. The heterogeneous environment of Intel PCs, Apple Macintosh, and UNIX systems that existed in the Centennial Independent School District could communicate with each. They could share files, printers, and other resources. This allowed an enterprise to truly behave as an enterprise.

INDEX

Symbols

& (and operator), 979
\ (backslash), 688
!! command, 935, 952
% command, 939, 954
\\ command prompt, 944
\! command prompt, 944
\$ command prompt, 944
\# command prompt, 944
%! command prompt, 963
%/ command prompt, 963
- command-line option
  (su command), 892
– command-line option
  bindkey command, 957
  hash command, 996
  sudo command, 821
-? command-line option
  (httpd script), 641
-? –help command-line
  option (sfdisk utility), 184
(comment symbol), 971
{} (curly braces), 1001
= (equal sign), 974
\ (escape character), 942
\\ escape sequence (echo
  command), 994
! (interpreter path line
  symbol), 971
! (not operator), 979
> operator, 933, 950
>> operator, 934, 950
|| (or) operator, 979
| (pipe character), 932-933,
  950
(pound symbol)
  bash comments, 972
  Perl comments, 1008
(') (single quotes), 942
$! variable, 978
$# variable, 977
$$ variable, 977
$* variable, 978
$- variable, 978

$? variable, 977
$@@ variable, 978
$0 variable, 977
* (wildcard character),
  929-930, 946
... (wildcard character), 929
? (wildcard character),
  929-930, 946
3Com LANplex 2016, 443
3Com LANplex 2500, 443
3Com LANplex 6000, 443
3Com SuperStack
  LinkSwitch 2200, 443
4mm DDS (Digital Data
  Storage) tapes, 337
8mm tapes, 338
8mm/AITs (Advanced
  Intelligent Tapes), 339
10Base-2 Ethernet, 378, 381
10Base-T Ethernet, 378, 381
100Base-T Ethernet, 378, 381

A

\a escape sequence, 958, 994
-a command-line option
  bindkey command, 957
  cfdisk utility, 182
  exportfs command, 423
  fsck utility, 188-189
  gpasswd command, 891
  ipchains utility, 811
  implementing quotas, 207
  mount command, 194
-A number command-line
  option (sfdisk utility), 184
-a port command-line option
  (Squid), 666
absolute firewalls, 787-789
AC (Alan Cox) patches, 1094
Academ wu-ftpd Web page,
  618
Academic-firewall mailing
  list, 839

access. *See also* security
  Apache, 642
  Centennial School District
    case study, 1147-1148
  /etc/passwd files, 744
  /etc/xinetd.files, 540
  external users, 530
  filesystems
    mount command, 194-195
    unmount command, 195
  internal users, 530
  Internet, IP masquerading,
    1155
  R-commands
    /etc/hosts.equiv files,
    545-546
    .rhosts files, 545-547
  removable media device, 289
    automatic mounting,
    294-295
    combinations, 296
    mounting, 292-294
    mtools package, 289-292
  shared printers, 416
  spools, 582
  SSH, 549-550
  systems, 358
  TCP-Wrappers, 534
    access-control rules,
    536-537
    configuration language
    extensions, 537
    configuring, 536-537
    etc/hosts.allow files, 535
    etc/hosts.deny files, 535
    logging, 535
    process, 534
    testing, 538
  Usenet servers, 698-699
  users, 780-781
  Windows PCs, 1153-1154
access time, 779

access.conf file
Apache access, 642
/etc/security directory, 761
AccessFileName directive, 650
accessing
Red Hat from Windows PCs, 1152
variables, 976-977
account module-type, 746
accounts (user)
archiving, 878
deleting, 882-883
disabling, 779, 882
shared, 863
squid, 800
active terminators, 222-223
Adaptec controllers, 219
AddHandler directive, 653
adding
Apache modules, 654-655
directories, 992
Ethernet interface, 382-383
kernel-level configuration, 382-383
software-level configuration, 383
groups
/etc/group file, 884
GUI tools, 886-887
system, 862
IPX protocol support, 496
missing functionality, 1083
parallel port storage device kernel support, 286-287
quota support, 771
RAM, 1070
static routes, 387-389
users manually, 870
default configuration files, 871
/etc/group file, 870
/etc/gshadow file, 871
/etc/passwd file, 871
/etc/shadow file, 871
groups, 891

ownership, 871-872
passwords, 873
system, 862
user home directories, creating, 871
users with command-line tools, 873
batch mode, 881
linuxconf, 875-881
useradd command, 874-875
AddModule directive, 654
address books, 585
address classes, 375-376
addresses (IP), 375
address classes, 375-376
aliases, 615
classless, 376-377
detecting duplicates, 449
subnetting, 377
supernetting, 377
translating numbers to symbolic names. *See* name servers
writing, 377
adduser command (squid accounts), 800
ADIR variable, 429
administrative networks
administration server install customizations, 76
administrative workstation install customizations, 76
development server install customizations, 76
development workstation install customizations, 76
install customization, 75-76
install templates, 75
machine classes, 69
administrators parameter (etc/gshadow file), 869
Advanced Power Management. *See* APM
afio utility, 56
afpd.conf file, 515-524

AFS
filesystem sharing, 426-427
mailing list, 426
Web site, 410, 426
Alan Cox (AC) patches, 1094
alias command, 931, 948
aliases
bash, 931-932
killing, 931, 948
tcsh, 947-948
user errors, preventing, 350-351
aliases (mail), 585
bit-bucket, 586
digest-only mailing lists, 591-592
distributed management, 588
mailing lists, 587-588
managing, 585
mandatory, 587
master file locations, 586
security, 587
separating, 587
structuring, 586-587
All parameter
AllowOverride directive, 651
Options directive, 645
all squash option (etc/exports file), 422
allownewnews parameter (inn.conf file), 686
AllowOverride directive, 650-651
alt.security newsgroup, 837
altered system files, 774
am-utils package, 428
Amateur Radio Support, 1116
amd configuration file, 428-429
AMDOPTS variable, 429
AMI MegaRAID RAID controller driver, 268
amq command, 428-430

analyzing
  network traffic, 458-460
  system logs, 160-163
and operator (&), 979
announcements, 1093
anongid option
(/etc/exports file), 422
anonuid option
(/etc/exports file), 422
anonymous FTP
  configuring, 618-619
  security, 769
anti-ping settings,
1078-1079
Apache, 638
  add-ons, 663
    Apache-SSL server, 663
    Covalent Raven SSL
    Module, 663
    Java Servlets, 664
    mod ssl module, 663
    Perl scripting , 664
    PHP server-side , 663
  Comanche, 662
  configuring, 641
    access, 642
    CGI scripting, 652-653
    conditional directives,
    646-647
    directives, 643-644
    directory-based directives,
    644-645
    error handling, 648-649
    file-based directives, 646
    logging, 647-648
    overriding configuration
    files, 642-643
    password protecting
    directories, 649-651
    SSI (Server-Side Includes),
    651-652
  development history, 638-639
  error codes, 648
  /etc/httpd directory, 90
  installing, 640
  module registry Web site, 657

  modules, 654
    adding, 654-655
    conditional directive based,
    655
    default, 655-657
  security, 653-654
  starting, 640-641
  stopping, 640
  virtual hosts, 657-662
    IP-based, 657-659
    name-based, 659-662
Apache Group, 638
Apache-SSL server, 663
Apache/Perl integration
project Web site, 664
APIs, libpcap, 440-441
APM (Advanced Power
Management), kernel
support, 1108
AppleTalk, 1152
  kernel support, 1114-1115
  netatalk server, starting, 525
appletalk.o module, 514
AppletTalk, 513
  kernel support, 514
  services
    afpd.conf file, 515-524
    AppleVolumes.default file,
    524
    configuring, 514-525
    netatalk configuration files,
    515
    system files support,
    514-515
AppleVolumes.default file,
524
AppleVolumes.system file,
515-524
Application Layer, 375
applications. *See also*
commands; utilities
  backing up after install, 311
  Centennial School District case
  study, 1147-1148
archives, mailing lists,
590-591

archiving
  files, cpio program, 326
  user accounts, 878
arguments. *See* options;
parameters
argv variable, 961
arithmetic operators
(expressions), 981-982
ARP errors, detecting, 449
ARPA (U.S. Department of
Defense Advanced
Research Projects Agency),
372
article spools, 698
articles (news), 680-681
assigning swap space,
1072-1074
asymmetric cryptography,
549
asterisk (*) wildcard,
929-930, 946
async option, mount
command, 195
AT Attachment Packet
Interface. *See* ATAPI drives
at utility, 1021-1023
  at daemon, 1029-1030
  examples, 1024-1027
  options, 1022-1023
  syntax, 1022, 1024
  time specifications, 1023-1024
  users, 1030-1031
AT&T WaveLAN, 1116
at.allow file, 750
at.deny file, 750
atalkd.conf file, 515
ATAPI (AT Attachment
Packet Interface) drives,
288-289, 340
atd (at daemon), 1029-1030
atq utility, 1028
atrm utility, 1028
atrun utility, 1028-1029

attacks
  denial of service attacks, 742
    detecting, 448-449
    Ping of Death, 448
    smurf attacks, 448-449
    SYN floods, 448
  physical, 742
  privilege attacks, 742
  warez D00dz, 631-636
**-audio command-line
  option (cdrecord
  command), 282**
auth module-type, 746
authconfig command, 36
**AuthConfig parameter
  (AllowOverride
  directive), 651**
authentication
  Centennial School District
    case study, 1148
  INN, 678
  PAM, 545
  passwords, 746
  R-commands, 543
    rexec, 543
    trust-based, 544-545
  RSA, 549
authors, 1092
authsrv program, 801-802
**-auto option (mount
  command), 195**
auto-sensing hubs, 379
auto.master file, 431
auto.misc file, 431-432
autocorrect variable, 950
autofs, 294, 431-432
**autoloading mechanisms,
  335-336**
autologout variable, 960
**automating tasks,
  1019-1020**
  atq utility, 1028
  atrm utility, 1028
  atrun utility, 1028-1029
  batch utility, 1027
  cron. *See* cron jobs

  one-time tasks. *See* at utility
  regular tasks, 1020-1021
automount daemon, 427
  configuring, 427-429
  starting, 429-430
awk command, 29-30

B

%b command prompt, 963
**\b escape sequence, 958,
  994**
-b command-line option
  atd, 1029
  bindkey command, 957
  free utility, 1061
  sudo command, 821
**-b block size option
  (mkfs utility), 188**
**-b boot image command-
  line option (mkisofs
  command), 275**
backslash (\), 688
**Backup Central Web site,
  334**
**backup domain controller
  (BDC), 463**
backups, 311
  archiving (quick), 326
  automating, 1020
  case study, 321
  categories, 300
  commands, 300
  configuration files, 301
  costs, 362
  daily operations, 312
    *graphical tool changes,
      312*
    site strategies, 313
    text editor changes, 312
  data recovery, 360

  dedicated software, 327
    compatibility, 329
    *evaluation example,
      329-330*
    evaluations, 328-329
    kdat program, 330
    obtainability, 329
    open source, 328
    proprietary, 328
    reliability, 328
  devices, 300, 304-305
  file restoration, 320-321,
    324-326
  filesystem contents, 300-301
  full, 306-307, 313-314
    disadvantages, 308
    dump command, 324-326
    *remote machines,
      307-308*
  incremental, 314
    levels, 314-315
    storing, 319
  media, 768
    *autoloading mechanisms,
      335-336*
    *data storage capacity,
      335*
    *device/software
      compatibility, 335*
    floppies, 322
    *information resources,
      334*
    kernel support, 335
    multiple copies, 342
    offsite storage, 342
    onsite storage, 341
    *rewritable CD-ROMs,
      322*
    selecting, 334-335
    storing, 341
    *tape escrow services,
      342-343*
    tapes. See tape backups
    transfer rates, 335
    writable CD-ROMs, 321
    Zip/Jaz drives, 322

operating systems, 310-311
partial, 309, 314
personal, 353
problems, 327
Red Hat Linux box online, 310
   application backups, 311
   daily operations backups,
    312
   operating system backups,
    310-311
   site strategies, 313
rotation schedule, 315
   casual home user,
    315-318
   workstations, 318-321
scripts,
   creating, 323
   personal, 353
security breaches, 856
set capacity, 319-320
site policy, 300
strategies, 305-306, 313
tar command, 323-324
task-oriented files, 302
user files, 301
user errors, preventing, 353
**backward-char command,
958**
**backward-delete-char
command, 958**
**bandwidth, Usenet
servers, 673-674**
**bang-bang command, 935,
952**
banners command, 756
**bash (Bourne Again Shell),
926, 972**
advantages/disadvantages, 945
aliases, 931-932
another file's contents,
  reading/executing, 990
built-in commands, 939-940,
  990
   break, 992-993
   continue, 993-994
   dirs, 990-991

echo, 994
eval, 995
exec, 995
executing on signals, 996
exit, 996
hash, 995-996
let, 996
popd, 991-992
printf, 997-998
pushd, 992
read, 997
source, 990
suspend, 999
trap, 996
wait, 998
command pathnames,
  995-996
command prompt
  customizations, 944
command-line completion, 932
command-line editing,
  936-937
command-line parameters,
  parsing, 999-1001
comments, 972-973
control structures, 983
   case statement, 984-986
   for statement, 983
   if statement, 986-988
   until statement, 989-990
   while statement, 988-989
data, reading/assigning
  variables, 997
debugging scripts, 1005-1006
directory lists
   adding directories, 992
   deleting directories from,
    991-992
   viewing, 990-991
exit codes, 974
exiting, 996
expressions, 978
   defined, 978
   file test operators, 980-981
   math operators, 981-982

   string test operators, 981
   testing values, 978-979
external command executions,
  995
features, 929
filenames, converting to
  lowercase, 1003-1004
formatting before printing,
  997-998
functions, 1001
   exiting with specific return
    values, 1002
   local variables, 1003
   names, 1001-1002
globbing, 22
history list, 934-936
   commands, 936
   navigating, 935
   searches, 935
input/output redirection,
  933-934
interactive session startup,
  940-941
job control, 937-939
   % command, 939
   jobs running (list of),
    938-939
   killing jobs, 938
   moving jobs to background,
    937
   moving jobs to foreground,
    938
   starting commands in
    background, 937
   suspending jobs, 937
loops
   exiting, 992-993
   skipping iterations,
    993-994
math expressions,
  evaluating, 996
non-interactive session startup,
  941
option evaluations, 995
pausing, 998
pipes, 932-933

printing, 994

quoting, 942

specific words in files,
    finding, 1004-1005

suspend execution, 999

syntax, 972-974

text blocks, 973

variables, 942-943, 974

    accessing, 976-977

    contents, printing, 943

    creating, 943, 974

    declaring, 975

    deleting, 975-976

    read only, 976

    special, 977-978

    values, 974

wildcards, 929-931

basher boxes, 1051

bashrc file, 941

bastion hosts, 787-789

batch utility, 881, 1027

Bay Networks Model 3000, 444

Bay Networks Model 28000, 444

BDC (backup domain controller), 463

beginning-of-line command, 958

benchmarking, 1067

Berkeley Internet Name Daemon. *See* **BIND**

Berkeley line printer daemon. *See* **lpd**

bg command

    moving jobs to background, 937, 953

    NFS mounting, 425

    tcsh, 956

BGP (Border Gateway Protocol), 391

/bin directory, 85-87

binary kernel support, 1106-1107

    boot time support, 1107

    new binary types registration, 1106-1107

BIND (Berkeley Internet Name Daemon), configuring, 402-405

    caching-only name server configuration sample, 403-404

    DNS zone RRs (Resource Records), 404-405

    global options, 402

    reverse mapping sample, 404

    zones, 402-403

binding keys. *See* **key bindings**

bindkey command, 956-957

binfmt misc.txt file, 1107

BIOS hardware errors, 145

bit-bucket aliases, 586

BitchX, 727-728

    download Web site, 728

    FAQ Web site, 727

    finding, 728

    installing, 728

    running, 728

    Web site, 727

blank=type command-line option (cdrecord command), 281

block devices, 1108-1110

Boa, 668

/boot directory, 85

boot floppies

    CD-ROM Red Hat installs, 51

    cloning installs, 56-57

    hard drive Red Hat installs, 51

    rawrite utility, 53

    setup function, 57, 59-60

    YARD, 56

boot loaders, 112

    bootactv, 128

    CHOS, 128

    GRUB, 128

    LILO (LInux LOader), 113-114

        /sbin/lilo map installer, 113, 116, 121

        alternatives, 127-128

        booting up multiple operating systems, 122-127

        command-line options, 121

        installing, 114

        lilo.conf file, 115-127

        patches for color screens and line drawing characters, 125

    LOADLIN, 127

    operation of, 112-113

    SYSLINUX, 128

    System Commander Deluxe, 128

bootactv program, 128

booterd system initialization script, 130

booting

    binary format support, 1107

    boot loaders. *See* boot leaders

    boot floppies

        CD-ROM Red Hat installs, 51

        cloning installs, 56-57

        hard drive Red Hat installs, 51

        rawrite utility, 53

        setup function, 57, 59-60

        YARD, 56

    from RAID devices, 265-266

    physical security, disabling, 767

    system, 430

Border Gateway Protocol (BGP), 391

bottlenecks, 457-458, 1049
  duration, 1050
    focal point location, 1051
    tuning importance,
      1051-1052
  frequency, 1050
  location, 1050
Bourne Again Shell.
  See bash
Bourne shell, 926, 807-809
bracket expressions, 21
breaches (security), 842
  action plan, 842
  backups, 856
  cleaning up, 854-855
  evidence, finding, 843-844
  extent, 844
  indicators, 843-844
  intrusion detection tools, 846
    filesystem scanners, 846
    who/top/ls/ps commands,
      847-848
  reinstallation (media),
    856-857
  remain calm, 842
  system log analysis, 845-846
  Trinux, 848-849
    firewalls/proxies, 853
    hunt utility, 854
    netcat utility, 854
    network mapping/
      vulnerability scanning,
      851-853
    network monitors,
      850-851
    packet sniffers, 849-850
  when to start from scratch,
    855-856
  written records, 843
break command, 992-993
browsing interface, 462
BSD automount daemon,
  427
  configuring, 427-429
  starting, 429-430

BSD processes accounting,
  1105
Bugtraq mailing list, 838
built-in bash commands,
  939-940, 990
  break, 992-993
  continue, 993-994
  dirs, 990-991
  echo, 994
  eval, 995
  exec, 995
  exit, 996
  hash, 995-996
  let, 996
  popd, 991-992
  printf, 997-998
  pushd, 992
  read, 997
  source, 990
  suspend, 999
  trap, 996
  wait, 998
built-in tcsh commands,
  955-956

C

-c option (usermod
  command), 892
\c escape sequence
  (echo command), 994
-C command-line option
  (Squid), 666
-c option
  at utility, 1024
  bindkey command, 957
  chgrp command, 889
  chown command, 890
  history command, 951
  mkfs utility, 187
  su command, 892
  top utility, 1058
  useradd command, 874

C (programming language),
  191-194
-c –id number command-line
  option (sfdisk utility), 184
-c boot catalog command-
  line option (mkisofs
  command), 275
-c cylinders command-line
  option
  cfdisk utility, 182
  sfdisk utility, 185
-c filename operator, 980
-C last sess start command-
  line option (mkisofs
  command), 275
-C next sess start command-
  line option (mkisofs
  command), 275
C-Shell scripting syntax, 969
cables
  Ethernet, 378
  SCSI devices, 221-222
caching-only servers, 400
Caldera Web site, 513
capacity, Internet
  telephony, 716
cards, Ethernet, 378
Carrier Sense Multiple
  Access with Collision
  Detection. *See* CSMA/CD
case statements, 984-986
case study (Centennial
  School District), 1136
  application access, 1147-1148
  authentication, 1148
  background, 1136-1137
  Bynari involvement, 1137
  Centennial team training,
    1149-1150
  challenge, 1142
  constraints, 1145
  content management,
    1161-1162
  email, 1156-1157
  firewalls, 1144

FTP server file downloads,
  1162-1163
initiatives, 1141
Internet access, 1155
Internet for curriculum, 1143
knowledgeable management,
  1145
Linux 2.2.x kernels,
  1155-1156
Macintosh networking,
  1152-1153
network management, 1148
objectives, 1146
plan, 1146
productivity application,
  1156
project specifications,
  1145-1146
project team concerns,
  1138-1139
Red Hat access from
  Windows PCs, 1152
Red Hat benefits, 1142-1143
Red Hat selection, 1141
requirements, 1138, 1144
resources, 1140-1141
Samba, 1149-1151
server inventory, 1141
SWAT, 1151
system administration,
  1158-1159
technical expertise, 1145
user account management
  scenarios, 1159-1161
users/groups management,
  1159
Web server, 1147
Windows PCs access from
  Red Hat, 1153-1154
**casual home user backup
  rotation schedule, 315**
  dump program configuration
    for installation level,
    317-318
  rationale, 316
cat command, 973

cd command
  shells, 927
  tcsh, 956
CD-R drives, 274-285
CD-ROM drives, 273-274
  created before 1994, 1117
  Red Hat installs, 51
CD-ROMs
  rewritable, 322
  writable, 321
CD-RW drives, 274-285
**-cdi command-line option
  (cdrecord command), 282**
cdrecord command
  command-line options,
    281-282
  transferring ISO9660
    filesystem images to
    CD-R/CD-RW media, 280
  writing/mounting/verifying
    ISO9660 filesystem images
    to disks, 282-284
CDs, creating, 274-285
cdwrite command, 280
**Centennial School District
  case study, 1136**
  application access, 1147-1148
  authentication, 1148
  background, 1136-1137
  Bynari involvement, 1137
  Centennial team training,
    1149-1150
  challenge, 1142
  constraints, 1145
  content management,
    1161-1162
  email, 1156-1157
  firewalls, 1144
  FTP server file downloads,
    1162-1163
  initiatives, 1141
  Internet access, 1155
  Internet for curriculum, 1143
  knowledgeable management,
    1145

Linux 2.2.x kernels,
  1155-1156
Macintosh networking,
  1152-1153
network management, 1148
objectives, 1146
plan, 1146
productivity application,
  1156
project specifications,
  1145-1146
project team concerns,
  1138-1139
Red Hat access from
  Windows PCs, 1152
Red Hat benefits, 1142-1143
Red Hat selection, 1141
requirements, 1138, 1144
resources, 1140-1141
Samba, 1149-1151
Samba printing services,
  1151
server inventory, 1141
SWAT, 1151
system administration,
  1158-1159
technical expertise, 1145
user account management
  scenarios, 1159-1161
users/groups management,
  1159
Web server, 1147
Windows PC access from
  Red Hat, 1153-1154
**CERT (Computer Emer-
  gency Response Team)**
  FTP, 618
  security, 774
  warez activity, 635, 774
**CERT-advisory mailing list,
  838**
cfdisk utility, 181-182
CGI scripting, 652-653
cgichk utility, 852-853
chains, 811

change command
   /etc/shadow file
      customizations, 888
   user accounts, disabling, 882
Changes file, 1097-1098
change_ days parameter
   (/etc/shadow file), 868
character devices,
   1118-1119
character-mode consoles,
   1159
chargen, 533
chatting. *See* Internet
   telephony
-checkdrive command-line
   option (cdrecord
   command), 281
checking
   altered system files, 774
   devices, 101-107
   log files, 772-773
   network interfaces, 773
   quotas, 771
   setgid files, 773
   setuid files, 773
   /var/spool/atjobs files, 773
   /var/spool/cron files, 773
checkspace script, 199-204
chfn command, 889
chgrp command
   group ownerships, 889
   users/groups, 890
chmod command
   executable scripts, 971, 1008
   user permissions, 862
CHOS, 128
chown command
   file ownership, 890
   user permissions, 862
   users/groups, 890
chpasswd command, 881
chsh command, 891, 928
CIAC (Computer Incident
   Advisory Capability)
   Web site, 832
CIAC-notes mailing list, 838

CIDR (Classless Inter-Domain
   Routing),
   376-377
CIFS (Common Internet File
   System), 462
Cisco Catalyst 1200, 444
Cisco Catalyst 1700, 444
Cisco Catalyst 5000, 444
Cisco EtherSwitch EPS-
   2115M, 444
ckraid command, 237
classes (address), 375-376
Classless Inter-Domain
   Routing (CIDR), 376-377
cleanfeed (spam filter), 701
clear-screen command, 959
ClearModuleList directive,
   655
clients
   ICQ, 729
   IRC
      BitchX, 727-728
      ircII, 722-725
      X-Chat, 726-727
      Zircon, 725-726
   Linux NetWare, 497-498
   NFS, 424-426
clocks, real-time clock, 1119
clone trees, 1128-1131
clones, 728, 732-733
cloning installs, 56
   boot floppies, 56-57
   customizing OS image, 68
   installing OS image, 65-67
   kickstart, 68
   lilo, 68
   procedure, 56
   remote partitioning, 61-65
   setup function, 57-60
cloning script (clone trees),
   1128-1131
closed mailing lists, 590
cmdline file, 1077
CNFS article storage
   article spools, 698
   cycbuff.conf file, 692-693

   INN, 680
   newsfeeds file configuration,
      690
   overview.ctl file, 695
   storage.conf file, 693-695
COAST FTP site, 832
COAST Web site, 832
coax-based Ethernets, 381
Coda,
   filesystem sharing, 426-427,
      1122
   Web site, 426, 1122
color variable (tcsh), 961
com domain, 398
Comanche, 662
COMMAND process field
   (top utility), 1057
command prompt
   customizing
      bash, 944
      tcsh, 962-963
   special characters
      bash, 944
      tcsh, 963
command-line completion
   bash, 932
   tcsh, 948-949
command-line editing,
   936-937
command-line options.
   ***See* specific options and**
   commands
command-line utilities
   ***See also* tools**
   !!, 935, 952
   !-n, 952
   !expression, 952
   !n, 952
   %, 939, 954
   adduser, 800
   afio, 56
   alias, 931, 948
   amq, 428-430
   at, 1021-1023
      at daemon, 1029-1030
      examples, 1024-1027

options, 1022-1023
syntax, 1022, 1024
time specifications,
    1023-1024
users, specifying,
    1030-1031
atq, 1028
atrm, 1028
atrun, 1028-1029
authconfig, 36
awk, 29-30
backup, 300
backward-char, 958
backward-delete-char, 958
bang-bang, 935, 952
batch, 1027
beginning of line, 958
bg
    moving jobs to back-
        ground, 937, 953
    tcsh, 956
bindkey, 956-957
built-in bash commands,
    939-940, 990
    break, 992-993
    continue, 993-994
    dirs, 990-991
    echo, 994
    eval, 995
    exec, 995
    exit, 996
    hash, 995-996
    let, 996
    popd, 991-992
    printf, 997-998
    pushd, 992
    read, 997
    source, 990
    suspend, 999
    trap, 996
    wait, 998
built-in shell, 927
built-in tcsh commands,
    955-956
cat, 973
cd, 927, 956

cdrecord, 280-284
cdwrite, 280
cfdisk, 181-182
cgichk, 852-853
chage, 882, 888
chfn, 889
chgrp, 889-890
chmod
    executable scripts,
        creating, 971, 1008
    user permissions, 862
chown, 890
chpasswd, 881
chsh, 891, 928
ckraid, 237
clear screen, 959
configure, 679
cpio, 56, 326
cron
    system crontab files, 1037
    user crontab files,
        1035-1037
crontab, 1033-1034
dd
    preventing data loss,
        360-361
    recovering data, 360-361
declare, 975
depmod, 1098
diald, 1115
dirs, 991
down-history, 959
dump
    full backups, 306,
        324-326
    configuring for installa-
        tion level, 317-318
dvips, 415
e2fsprogs, 160
echo, 927
edquota, 205, 208
elm, 584-585
end-of-line, 958
eval
    bash, 940
    tcsh, 956

exec, 956
executing before displaying
    prompts, 963
executing on signals (bash),
    996
exim, 559, 577
    configuration, 577
    mail hub, 578
    spam protection, 578-579
    workstations, 578
exit
    bash, 940
    tcsh, 956
export, 940
exportfs, 423
exscan, 851
fc, 936
fdisk, 177-181
fg
    moving jobs to
        foreground, 938, 953
    tcsh, 956
find command, 25-26
    command-line options,
        26-27
    tests, 27-28
    warning about, 29
finger, 769, 889
forward-char, 958
fsck
    command-line options,
        188-189
    maintaining/repairing
        filesystems, 188-194
    return code handling,
        189-190
    return code interpreta-
        tions, 190-194
genksyms, 1098
getops, 1000
gpasswd, 891
grog, 415
groupadd, 884
groupdel, 884
groupmod, 885
groups, 891

grpck, 885
halt, 139
hdparm, 1110
help, 939
history, 934, 951
history list
    bash, 934-936
    editing, 936
    navigating, 935
    searches, 935
    tcsh, 951-952
ifconfig
    Ethernet collision
        examinations, 380
    system failure diagnosis,
        149-150
insmod, 497, 1098
ipfwadm
    forwarding connections,
        809
    installing, 806
    packet filtering, 805-806
ipchains, 853
    chain management, 811
    chain rules, 811
    filters, packet traversal,
        813-814
    firewall configuration, 810
    installing, 810-811
    targets, 813
ipgrab, 850
IPTraf, 850
isapnp, 148-149
ipx configure, 497
jobs, 939, 954
kbdconfig, 36
kdat, 330
kerneld, 1098
kill, 938, 954
kill-line, 959
ksymoops, 165-168, 1091
ksyms, 1098
linuxconf, 31-33, 875-879
    groups, adding, 886-887
    GUI interface, 877

password validation rules,
    877-879
starting, 876
User and Group
    Maintenance screen, 879
users, adding, 879-881
logout
    bash, 940
    shells, 927
    tcsh, 956
logrotate, 161
ls, 847-848
lsmod, 1098
m user, 584
mail/mailx, 583-584
make, 1132-1133
    make bzImage, 1133
    make clean, 1132
    make dep, 1132
    make modules, 1133
    make modules install, 1133
    make zImage, 1133
mattrib, 289
mbadblocks, 289
mcd, 289
mcopy, 290
mdel, 290
mdeltree, 290
mdir, 290
mdu, 290
mformat, 290
mkdigest, 589
mkfs, 187-188
mkisofs
    command-line options, 275
    ISO9660 filesystem image,
        creating,
        276-280
mkraid, 235-236
mkswap, 1073
mlabel, 290
mmd, 290
mmove, 290
modinfo, 1098
modprobe, 1098
module, 1097-1098

mount, 194-195, 426
mouseconfig, 36
mpage, 415
mrd, 290
mren, 290
mtools package, 289-290
mtx, 336
mtype, 290
mzip, 290
netstat, 385-386
newgrp, 888
newusers, 881
ngrep, 850
nice
    process management, 1066
    tcsh, 956
nmap, 849, 851
notify, 955
nprint, 498
nsend, 498
Ntop, 850
passwd, 892, 927
pathnames, 995-996
pause, 191-194
pci-config, 151
Perl, 30
pfdisk package, 128
pine, 584-585
pnmtops, 415
post-create, 878
poweroff, 139
pre-delete, 878
printenv, 956
ps
    intrusion detection,
        847-848
    jobs running (list of), 938,
        953
pwd
    bash, 940
    tcsh, 956
quotacheck, 205
quotaoff, 205
quotaon, 205

R-commands, 543
 authentication, 543-545
 etc/hosts.equiv files,
  545-546
 rcp, 543
 rexec, 543
 .rhosts files, 545-547
 rlogin, 543-544
 rsh, 543
 security, 547-548
 X11 connections, 548
raidadd, 238
raidhotadd, 235-238
raidhotremove, 235-238
raidrun, 238
raidstart, 235-238
raidstop, 235-238
rawrite, 53
rdev, 1126
readonly, 976
reboot, 139
redir, 675, 853
redisplay, 959
renice, 1066
repquota, 205
restore, 324-326
return, 1002
rmmod, 1098
rpm, 356, 428
sed, 30-31
set
 bash, 940
 command prompt
  customizations, 962
 shells, 927
 tcsh, 956
 variable values, 960
setup function, 60
sfdisk
 command-line options,
  184-185
 input fields, 183-184
 partitioning, 182-185
sndconfig, 36
sfdisk, 61-64
shift, 1000

showmount, 424
shutdown, 139
slist, 497
sndconfig, 36
source, 956
starting in background, 937,
 952
stop, 955
su, 892
sudo, 820-829
 command-line options,
  821
 operator menu imple-
  mentation example,
  826-827
 operator menu script
  example, 822-826
 Web site, 820
suspend, 955
swapoff, 1072-1074
swapon, 1072-1074
taper, 329-330
tar
 backups, 323-324
 full backups, 307
 operating system back-
  ups, 311
tcpdump, 850
tcpdchk, 538, 757
tcpdmatch, 538
tcpmatche, 757
tcsh automation, 960
timeconfig, 36
tinyproxy, 853
tomsrtbt, 158
top
 command-line options,
  1058
 interactive commands,
  1057-1058
 intrusion detection,
  847-848
 monitor fields, 1056
 performance monitoring,
  1055-1058

 process fields, 1056-1057
 starting, 1055
transproxy, 793
 FTP site, 791
 installing, 794-795
 standalone service
  configuration, 795
twist, 756
umask
 bash, 940
 tcsh, 956
unalias, 931, 948
unmount, 195
uptime, 1060
unset
 bash, 940, 975-976
 tcsh, 956
up-history, 959
upcase-word, 958
user permissions, 862
useradd, 874-875
userdel, 883
usermod, 882, 892-893
users/groups
 chage, 888
 chfn, 889
 chgrp, 889-890
 chown, 890
 chsh, 891
 gpasswd, 891
 groups, 891
 passwd, 892
 su, 892
 usermod, 892-893
visudo, 820
vmstat, 1058-1060
wait, 955
where, 956
who, 847-848
comment symbol (#), 971
comments
 bash, 972-973
 etc/inetd.conf files, 534
 Perl, 1008
Common Internet File Sys-
  tem (CIFS), 462

communications (Internet) .
    See Internet telephony
comp.admin.policy
    newsgroup, 837
comp.os.linux.hardware
    newsgroup, 334
comp.periphs.scsi
    newsgroup, 334
comp.risks newsgroup, 837
comp.security.announce
    newsgroup, 836
comp.security.firewalls
    newsgroup, 836
comp.security.misc
    newsgroup, 836
comp.security.unix
    newsgroup, 836
comp.unix.admin
    newsgroup, 837
comp.unix.wizards
    newsgroup, 837
comp.virus newsgroup, 836
compatibility, backup
    software, 329
compiled programs, shell
    scripting, 970
compiling
    kernel source code,
        1082-1083
    xinetd, 539
complaints parameter
    (inn.conf file), 686
compliance with system
    policies, enforcing, 778
Computer Emergency
    Response Team (CERT)
    FTP, 618
    warez activity, 635
conditional directives,
    646-647, 655
conferencing
    multimedia tools, 733-734
        CU-SeeMe, 736
        MeetingPoint, 736
        QSeeMe, 735-736

Speak Freely, 734-735
Web site, 734
video, 718, 734
**CONFIG KMOD variable,
    1096**
**CONFIG MODULES
    variable, 1096**
**CONFIG MODVERSIONS
    variable, 1096**
**configuration dialog boxes,
    1091**
configuration files
    Apache, 642-643
    automatic mounting
        support, 294
    backing up, 301
    /etc directory, 764-766
        /etc/hosts.equiv, 545-546
        /etc/inetd.conf, 532-534
        etc/xinetd.conf, 539-541
    INN
        cycbuff.conf, 692-693, 698
        expire.ctl, 696-698
        incoming.conf, 691-692
        inn.conf, 682-688
        newsfeeds, 688-691
        nnrp.access, 698-699
        overview.ctl, 695
        storage.conf, 693-695
    raidtab configuration file,
        236-237
    rewriting, 156
    shells, 927
    smb.conf, 476-478
        custom sections, 483-484
        [global] section, 478-480
        [homes] section, 481-482
        *[printers] section,
            482-483*
        setting up, 484, 487-488
        testing, 485-489
    users home directories,
        763-764
configuration tools
    authconfig, 36
    kbdconfig, 36

Linuxconf, 32-33
mouseconfig, 36
sndconfig, 36
timeconfig, 36
configure program, 679
**configuring. See also
    customizing**
    anonymous FTP, with wu-ftpd,
        618-619
    Apache, 641
        access, 642
        CGI scripting, 652-653
        *conditional directives,
            646-647*
        *configuration files,
            overriding, 642-643*
        directives, 643-644
        *directory-based directives,
            644-645*
        error handling, 648-649
        file-based directives, 646
        logging, 647-648
        *password protecting
            directories, 649-651*
        *SSI (Server-Side Includes),
            651-652*
        virtual hosts, 657-662
    AppleTalk
        kernel support, 514
        services, 514-525
    automount daemon, 427-429
    BIND, 402-405
        *caching-only name server
            configuration sample,
            403-404*
        *DNS zone RRs (Resource
            Records), 404-405*
        global options, 402
        *reverse mapping sample,
            404*
        zones, 402-403
    digest-only mailing lists,
        591-605
        aliases, 591-592
        digest config file, 601-605
        directory, 593

follow-up postings, 603
posting restrictions, 600
primary list config file,
593-601
/etc/exports file, 421-424
exim, 577
gated daemon, 395-397
host routing, 395
interior gateway, 395-396
ICQ client, 729
INN, 681-682
access restrictions,
698-699
article spool, creating,
698
cycbuff.conf file, 692-693
daily maintenance tasks
script, 700
expire.ctl file, 696-698
incoming.conf file,
691-692
inn.conf file, 682-688
news database directory,
699-700
newsfeeds file, 688-691
overview.ctl file, 695
storage.conf file, 693-695
IP aliases, 615
IP-based virtual hosts,
658-659
IPX devices, 502, 504
kernel, 1100-1101
APM (Advanced Power
Management) support,
1108
binary support,
1106-1107
block devices, 1108-1110
BSD processes account-
ing support, 1105
CD-ROM drives (created
before 1994) support,
1117
character devices
support, 1118-1119

code maturity level,
1102-1103
console drivers support,
1123-1124
doubletalk speech
synthesizer, 1120
filesystems support,
1120-1121
firewalls, 792-793
floppy tape device
drivers, 1120
hacking, 1125
ISDN support, 1117
joysticks, 1120
loading, 1126
loopback devices, 1111
makefile, 1126-1127
mice support, 1119
module support, 1105
native language support,
1123
network block devices,
1111
network devices support,
1115-1117
network filesystems
support, 1121, 1123
networking options,
1111-1115
networking support, 1105
NVRAM devices support,
1119
options, 1102
parallel port IDE devices,
1111
parallel port support,
1107-1108
parallel printer support,
1119
partitions support, 1123
plug-and-play support,
1108
processor types,
1103-1104
real-time clock support,
1119

saving, 1126
SCSI support, 1115
serial port support, 1118
software RAID, 1111
sound support, 1124
sysctl support, 1105-1106
System V Interprocess
Communications
support, 1105
terminal support, 1118
video4linux, 1120
watchdog devices
support, 1119
local printers, 411-416
logging, 647-648
mail collection, 556-557
name lookups (NIS), 407-408
NetWare printers, 498
network numbers, 501-502
NFS clients, 424-426
NFS servers, 418-419
/etc/exports file
configuration, 421-424
software installations,
418-419
print queues, 411
access, granting, 416
local printers, 411-416
remote printers, 416-417
printers, 416-417, 511-512
routing, 384
sendmail
central mail server,
562-563
LAN workstation, 562
standalone computer with
dial-up connection, 561
standalone computer with
permanent Internet
connection, 560
servernames, 500-501
smail, 567
configuration files,
567-568
workstation, 568-569

SOCKS, 795-796
Squid, 666-667
   accounts, 800
   configuration file, 799
   groups, 800
system parts, 880
TCP-Wrappers, 536-537
   access-control rules,
     536-537
   configuration language
     extensions, 537
telnet proxies, 803-804
TIS FWTK, 801-802
volumes, 499-500
Windows workstation, 1150
WREQ help desk, 910-911
   etc/aliases files, 911
   list configuration,
     911-914
   req script, 910
   req-config file, 910-911
   req-mail script, 910
connections
forwarding, firewalls, 809
INN, 691-692
network
   production network install
     templates, 70
   setup function, 57-60
SSH, 549
X11, 548
console drivers, 1123-1124
Console Drivers dialog box,
  1123
console-based utilities,
  performance monitoring,
  1055
free, 1060-1061
time, 1061-1062
top, 1055-1058
uptime, 1060
vmstat, 1058-1060
console.perms file, 761-762
consoles, 1159
consulting, Linuxcare, 39

continue command,
  993-994
control characters, 957
control messages, 675
control structures
bash, 983
   case statement, 984-986
   for statement, 983
   if statement, 986-988
   until statement, 989-990
   while statement, 988-989
Perl scripts, 1009-1010
control-flag parameters
  (PAM), 746
control-panel, 31-33
controlchan entry
  (newsfeeds file
  configuration), 691
controllers
RAID
   AMI MegaRAID, 268
   DAC960, 267
   EATA/DMA, 268
SCSI, 218-219
cookies, 1114
COPS (Computer Oracle and
  Password System), 829
copying
cloning installs, 56
   boot floppies, 56-57
   customizing OS image, 68
   installing OS image,
     65-67
   kickstart, 68
   lilo, 68
   procedure, 56
   remote partitioning,
     61-65
   setup function, 57-60
files, 157-159
core files, deleting
  automatically, 1020
correct variable, 950

costs
data recovery, 362
   backup costs, 362
   hardware replacement, 362
   project delays, 363
   sysadmin, 363
   system downtime, 363-364
disaster recovery plans,
  365-366
Covalent Raven SSL Module,
  663
cpio command, 307
cpio program, 56, 326
%CPU process field (top
  utility), 1057
cpu section (vmstat utility),
  1060
CPU States monitor field
  (top utility), 1056
crackers, 357
cracking passwords, 745-749
cron commands
system crontab files, 1037
user crontab files, 1035-1037
cron jobs, 1019, 1031
cron commands
   system crontab files, 1037
   user crontab files,
     1035-1037
crontab command, 1033-1034
crontab entries, 1034-1035
debugging, 1040
   echo command, 1040-1041
   log files, 1042
   output, redirecting, 1040
   printf command, 1040-1041
examples, 1039
global cron files, 1038
INN daily maintenance tasks,
  700
startup, 1031-1032
user specifications, 1038
cron.allow file, 751
cron.deny file, 751
crontab command,
  1033-1034

crontab file, 1031
  entries, 1034-1035
  examples, 1039
  system 1037
  user, 1035-1037
CROSS_ COMPILE variable, 1126
CSMA/CD (Carrier Sense Multiple Access with Collision Detection), 379
CU-SeeMe, 736
curly braces ({}), 1001
custom installation scripts, 1131-1132
custom installations, 50, 55
customizing. *See also* configuring
  Apache error handling, 648-649
  command prompt
    bash, 944
    tcsh, 962-963
  /etc/group, 885
  /etc/passwd, 892
  /etc/shadow file, 888
  install templates
    administrative network templates, 75-76
    production network templates, 77
  login shells, 891
  OS images (cloning installs), 68
  ownerships (users), 871-872
  password tokens, 892
  users accounts in batch mode, 881
CVS (Concurrent Versions System), 351-352, 1015-1016
cwd variable, tcsh, 961
cycbuff.conf file, 692-693, 698
cycbuffs, 692

D

\d command prompt, 944
%d command prompt, 963
-d command-line option
  httpd script, 641
  sendmail, 565
  Squid, 666
  user administration, 1160
-d option
  at utility, 1022
  atd, 1029
  bindkey command, 957
  gpasswd command, 891
  sfdisk utility, 184
  top utility, 1058
  useradd command, 874
-D option (ipchains utility), 811
-D –DOS command-line option (sfdisk utility), 185
-d change days option (change command), 888
-d home directory option (useradd command), 874
d [number] command (mail utility), 584
DAC960 RAID controller driver, 267
daemons, 1019
  at, 1029-1030
  automount, 427
    configuring, 427-429
    starting, 429-430
  gated, 392-397
    host routing configuration, 395
    interior gateway configuration, 395-396
    running, 394
  inetd
    chargen, 533
    daytime, 533
    discard, 533

    echo, 533
    etc/inetd.conf files, 532-534
    process, 531
    time, 533
  klogd, 164
  lpd, 410
  routed, 392-394
  routing, 392-394
    gated, 394
    routed, 392-394
  xinetd
    benefits, 538
    compiling, 539
    downloading, 538
    /etc/xinetd.conf files, 539-541
daily maintenance tasks (INN), 700
daily operations, backing up, 312
  graphical tool changes, 312
  site strategies, 313
  text editor changes, 312
daily reports, 674-675
-data command-line option (cdrecord command), 282
data flow (Internet), 719-720
data loss
  disaster scenarios, 361
  loss scenarios, 346
    destructive software, 355
    disaster recovery plans, 365-366
    hard drive failures, 359
    malcontents, 357
    memory errors, 359
    mistyped commands, 347-348
    output redirection and piping errors, 348-349
    root access users, 349
    system crackers, 357
    trojan horses, 354

user errors, *347*
viruses, *354*
worms, *354*
malcontents, preventing, *358*
preventing
RAID, *359*
system log watchers, *360*
RCS, preventing, *351-352*
recovery
costs, *362-364*
data recovery companies,
361
dd command, *360-361*
plans, *364-367*
tape backups, *360*
system crackers, preventing,
358
data recovery
companies, 361
costs, 362
backup costs, *362*
hardware replacement, *362*
project delays, *363*
sysadmin, *363*
system downtime,
363-364
databases
firewall user IDs/passwords,
801-802
RAM requirements, 1069
daytime, 533
dd command, 360-361
-debug command-line
option
cdrecord command, 281
pam_cracklib module, 748
debugfs program, 160
debugging. *See also*
troubleshooting
cron jobs, 1040
echo command,
1040-1041
log files, *1042*
output, redirecting, *1040*
printf command,
1040-1041

firewalls, 817
shell scripts, 1005-1006
declare command, 975
decoding kernel errors,
165-168
decompressing. *See*
unpacking
dedicated backup
software, 327
compatibility, 329
evaluation example, 329-330
evaluations, 328-329
kdat program, 330
obtainability, 329
open source, 328
proprietary, 328
reliability, 328
default Apache modules,
655-657
default home directories,
878
default installations, 50
defaults option (mount
command), 195
Deja.com, 711, 837
delays (project), 363
deleted files, recovering,
160
deleting
core files automatically, 1020
directories, 991-992
drivers, 1083
groups, 884
static routes, 387-388
user accounts, 882-883
users, 878, 891
variables, 975-976
denial of service attacks, 742
detecting, 448-449
Ping of Death, 448
smurf attacks, 448-449
SYN floods, 448
Dents, 399
deploying network moni-
toring systems, 443
depmod utility, 1098

–dereference option
(chown command), 890
detecting
ARP errors, 449
bottlenecks, 457-458
denial of service attacks,
448-449
duplicate IPs, 449
routing problems, 449
warez activity on FTP servers,
631-636
determining security needs,
740-741
/dev directory, 85-86
-dev option (mount
command), 195
-dev=target command-line
option (cdrecord
command), 281
developing
disaster recovery plans, 364
help desks, 903
feedback, *904*
good help desk qualities,
903-905
interfaces, *904*
Keystone, *917*
prioritization capabilities,
904
priority escalation paths,
905
report capabilities, *904*
selecting personnel, *905*
WREQ, *906-908*
security policies, 775-776
device access, 780
device drivers, 1089
device supported
filesystems, 198
devices
checking, 101-107, 304-305
/dev directory, 85-86
IDE (Integrated Drive
Electronics), 212
interface, *212-214*
interface filenames, *213*

interface filenames for
partitions, 213
names, 212-214
naming schemes, 107
alternatives, 108-109
assigned major and
minor numbers,
107-108
SCSI (Small Computer
System Interface), 217
active/passive termina-
tors, 222-223
benefits, 217
cabling requirements,
221-222
controller selection,
218-219
IDs, 222-223
naming, 223-225
SCSI chains, 217-218
supported, 219-221
technologies/capabilities,
218
terminating, 222-223
devices file, 1077
devices.txt file, 107-108
DFN-CERT Web site, 833
dhttpd, 669
Diablo, 676, 701-704
diagnostic tools
DOS diagnostics, 151-152
ifconfig utility, 149-150
isapnp program, 148-149
NIC diagnostic programs,
150-151
proc filesystem, 147-148
diald program, 1115
dialog boxes
Console Drivers, 1123
Kernel Configuration
Filesystem, 1121
kernel configuration, 1091
**difok=n argument (pam_
cracklib module), 748**
digest config file, 601-605

**digest-only mailing lists,
589-605**
aliases, 591-592
digest config file, 601-605
directory, 593
follow-up postings, 603
posting restrictions, 600
primary list config file,
593-601
**Digital Linear Tapes (DLTs),
338-339**
directives
AccessFileName, 650
AddHandler, 653
AddModule, 654
AllowOverride, 650-651
Apache configuration,
643-644
ClearModuleList, 655
conditional
Apache configuration,
646-647
module based, 655
Directory, 644
directory-based, 644-645
DocumentRoot, 643
ErrorDocument, 648
ErrorLog, 647
file-based, 646
Files, 646
IfDefine, 646
IfModule, 655
Limit, 650
LoadModule, 654
LogLevel, 647
NameVirtualHost, 659-660
Options, 645
PidFile, 648
ScriptAlias, 652
ServerAdmin, 643
ServerAlias, 660-662
ServerName, 643
ServerRoot, 644
SSI (Server-Side Includes),
651-652

TransferLog, 647
VirtualHost, 658
**director files (smail),
569-573**
directories
adding to directory lists, 992
Apache, password protection,
649-651
default home, 878
deleting from directory lists,
991-992
digest-only mailing lists, 593
directory hierarchy (install
template implementation),
77, 79
Documentation, 1089
/etc, 750
aliases file, 586
at.allow file, 750
at.deny file, 750
configuration files,
764-766
cron.allow file, 751
cron.deny file, 751
crontab file, 1032
exports file, 764
httpd file, 90
inetd.conf file, 751-760
issue file, 765
login.defs file, 765
motf file, 765
rc.d directory, 89
security directory,
761-762
skel directory, 869
sysconfig directory, 89
usertty file, 766
/home, 545-547, 878
/isc/inn, 678
linux-M.N.P, 1089
lists
adding directories, 992
deleting directories from,
991-992
viewing, 990-991

mail spool, 175
majordom/archives/
    digestonly-sample, 605
multiple users on, 864
/net, 1076
/news/db, 699-700
/proc, 91-98, 1076-1077, 1106
/root directory, 84-85
    /bin directory, 85-87
    /boot directory, 85
    /dev directory, 85-86
    /etc directory, 85-86
    /home directory, 86
    /lib directory, 86
    /mnt directory, 86
    /opt directory, 86
    /root directory, 86
    /sbin directory, 85
    /tmp directory, 86
    /usr directory, 87-88
    /var directory, 88-89
/scsi, 1076
/self, 1076
/sys, 1077
user homes, 763-764
    creating, 871
    /etc/passwd file, 866
/usr
    /usr/exim/configure, 577
    /usr/lib/aliases, 586
    /usr/local/majordomo, 589
    /usr/local/news, INN
        installation, 681
    /usr/src/linux, 1089-1091
    /usr/src/linux/arch, 1089
    /usr/src/linux/
        Documentation/rtc.txt,
        1119
    /usr/src/linux/drivers, 1089
    /usr/src/linux/drivers/block,
        1110
    /usr/src/linux/fs, 1090
    /usr/src/linux/ibcs, 1090
    /usr/src/linux/include, 1090
    /usr/src/linux/init, 1090
    /usr/src/linux/ipc, 1090

/usr/src/linux/kernel, 1090
/usr/src/linux/lib, 1090
/usr/src/linux/mm, 1090
/usr/src/linux/modules,
    1090
/usr/src/linux/net, 1091
/usr/src/linux/scripts, 1091/
    var
/var/log, 160
/var/log/messages, 160
/var/qmail/control, 576
/var/spool/mail/username, 556
directors (email), 566
Directory directive, 644
directory-based directives,
    644-645
dirs command, 990-991
–disable-shared option
    (configure program), 679
-disable-static option
    (configure program), 679
disable_ days parameter
    (/etc/shadow file), 868
disable_ time parameter
    (/etc/shadow file), 868
disabling
    floppy drive booting,
        physical security, 767
    services, etc/inetd.conf files,
        534
    user accounts, 779, 882
disaster recovery plans, 364
    data loss scenarios
        fire example, 365
        fire example cost
            analysis, 365
        fire example preventative
            measures, 366
        outlining, 365
    developing, 364
    maintaining, 367
    preventative measures,
        outlining, 366
    publishing, 367
    recovery costs, estimating,
        365-366

reviews, maintaining, 367
updates, maintaining, 367
discard, inetd, 533
Disk Druid, partitioning,
    185-186
disk quotas, users, 880
disks
    floppy, 322
    Jaz, 322
    partitioning, 175
        cfdisk utility, 181-182
        Disk Druid, 185-186
        fdisk utility, 177-181
        minimizing, 176-177
        partitions each filesystem,
            175-176
        sfdisk utility, 182-185
    RAM, 1099
    rescue, 152-153
        creating, 153-154
        emergency file copying,
            157-159
        image, 153
        rebuilding LILO, 155-156
        recovering deleted files,
            160
        repairing partitions,
            156-157
        rescue sessions, 154
        rewriting configuration
            files, 156
        toolkit, 155
    single/multiple, compared,
        174-175
    Zip, 322
DLTs (Digital Linear Tapes),
    338-339
DMA channel assignments,
    148
dma file, 1077
-Dname option
    (tcsh startup), 959

DNS (Domain Name Service), 398
  BIND, 399
    caching-only name server configuration sample, 403-404
    configuring, 402-405
    global options, 402
    reverse mapping sample, 404
    zones, 402-403
  Dents, 399
  geographic/organizational domains, 398-399
  group named, securing, 770
  hierarchy, 398
  securing, 770
  servers, 817
  username named, securing, 770
  zone RRs (Resource Records), 404-405
documentation
  documenting policies
    exceptions, 897-898, 922
    intranet posting, 897
    written documentation, 897
  FTP archives, 43
  Linux Documentation Project, 36
  location of, 90
  systems orientation guides, 902
Documentation directory, 1089
DocumentRoot directive, 643
domain directive, 401
Domain Name Service. *See* DNS
Domain parameter (inn.conf file), 686
domains, 462
  caching-only servers, 400
  com, 398

  edu, 398
  geographic, 398-399
  gov, 398
  int, 398
  master servers, 400
  mil, 398
  net, 398
  org, 398
  organizational, 398-399
  root, 398
  slave servers, 400
Donald Becker's Linux at CESDIS Web site, 150
DOS
  creating rescue disks, 153
  diagnostics, 151-152
  filesystems, 289-292
dotted quad, 375
Doubletalk speech synthesizer, 1120
down-history command, 959
downloading
  files, FTP servers, 1162-1163
  GD perl module, 908-909
  Keystone help desk, 917
  SSH, 551
  TIS FWTK, 801
  xinetd, 538
drgram sockets, 532
drivers
  console, 1123-1124
  deleting, 1083
  DVD/UDF peripherals Web site, 1121
  floppy, 1109-1110, 1120
  ftape, 339
  imm (Iomega Matchmaker), 286
  paride, 286
  ppa, 286
  RAID controller drivers, 267
    AMI MegaRAID, 268
    DAC960, 267
    EATA/DMA, 268
  SCSI changer device, 336

drives
  4mm DDS, 337
  8mm, 338
  ATAPI (AT Attachment Packet Interface), 340
  CD-R, 274-285
  CD-ROM, 273-274, 1117
  CD-RW, 274-285
  floppy, 272-273
  floppy tape, 339-340
  IDE, 1110
  Jaz, 322
  SCSI (Small Computer System Interface), 340-341
  tape, 304
  Zip, 287-288, 322
dual-homed bastion hosts, 788
dual-homed hosts, 796
-dummy command-line option (cdrecord command), 281
dump command, 306, 317-318, 324-326
DVD/UDF peripherals drivers Web site, 1121
dvips utility, 415
dynamic routes, 384
dynamic routing, 390
  daemons, 392-394
    gated, 394
    routed, 392-394
  gated daemon configuration, 395-397
    host routing, 395
    interior gateway, 395-396
  protocols, 390-392

E

-E option (change command), 889
-e option (usermod command), 893

\e escape sequence, 958
-e option
  bindkey command, 957
  chpasswd command, 881
  crontab command, 1034
  debugging scripts, 1005
  echo command, 994
  fc command, 936
-e expiration date option
  (useradd command), 874
-e filename operator, 980
e2fsprogs utilities, 160
EATA/DMA RAID
  controller driver, 268
ECC (error-correcting code),
  231
echo command, 533, 994
  anti-ping settings, 1078-1079
  escape sequences, 994
  options, 994
  shells, 927
edit variable, 961
editing
  command-line editing,
    936-937
  /etc/group file, 873
  /etc/inetd.conf files, 534
  /etc/passwd file, 873
  grace period, 771
  history list commands, 936
  system initialization scripts,
    137
EDITOR variable, 943
edquota, 205, 208, 771
edu domain, 398
educational resources,
  Linuxcare, 39
Eiffel, 1013-1014
elite speak, 634
elm, 584-585
email
  aliases, 585
    bit-bucket, 586
    distributed management,
      588
    mailing lists, 587-588

    managing, 585
    mandatory, 587
    master file locations, 586
    security, 587
    separating, 587
    structuring, 586-587
  Centennial School District case
    study, 1156-1157
  directors, 566
  elm, 584-585
  exim, 559, 577
    configuration, 577
    mail hub, 578
    spam protection, 578-579
    workstations, 578
  fetchmail, 579-581
  IMAP (Interactive Mail Access
    Protocol), 556
  mail collection, configuring,
    556-557
  mail/mailx, 583-584
  MDA (Mail Distribution
    Agent), 554-555
  MTA (Mail Transport Agent),
    554-555
    generational, 558
    resources, 606
    selecting, 558-559
  MUA (Mail User Agent),
    554-555
  multiple client support,
    581-582
    locking, 582-583
    spool access, 582
  pine, 584-585
  POP (Post Office Protocol),
    556
  qmail, 559, 575
    configuration files, 576
    delivery options, 575-576
    message handling, 576
    user IDs, 576
    Web site, 577
  retrieving from remote servers,
    1020
  routers, 566

  sendmail, 558-559
    central mail server
      configuration, 562-563
    features/options, 559-560
    LAN workstation
      configuration, 562
    m4 macros, 559
    multiple domains, 563-564
    standalone computer with
      dial-up connection
      configuration, 561
    standalone computer with
      permanent Internet
      connection configuration,
      560
    testing, 565
    virtual user tables, 564-565
    Web site, 560
  services, 531
  smail, 559, 566
    configuration, 567
    configuration files, 567-568
    director files, 569-573
    router files, 573-575
    running, 575
    transports file, 575
    transports/directors/
      routers, 566-567
    workstation configuration,
      568-569
  smart paths, 567
  SMTP (Simple Mail Transfer
    Protocol), 555
  spam, 557-558, 607
  user requests, managing, 900
  xfmail, 585
email aliases, 880
email interface (WREQ help
  desk), 906-907
enabling services, 534
encryption, 451
  MD5-encrypted passwords,
    744
  shadow passwords, 744
  SSH, 548

end-of-line command, 958

enforcing system policies, 778

enhanced IDE support, 1110

enhancements (performance), 1054

environment variables, 1035

epoch, 317

equivalent hosts, 545

error-correcting code (ECC), 231

ErrorDocument directive, 648

ErrorLog directive, 647

errors. *See also* **trouble-shooting**

    Apache, 648-649

    ARP errors, detecting, 449

    BIOS, 145

    hardware, 144

        BIOS errors, 145

        identifying at startup, 144-145

        last change syndrome, 145

        PCI devices, 146-147

        PnP devices, 145-146

    kernel, 163-164

        decoding, 165-168

        kernel oops, 163-164

        system.map file, 168-169

    memory, data loss scenarios, 359

    PCI devices, 146-147

    piping, data loss scenarios, 348-349

    piping and redirection, 348-349

    PnP devices, 145-146

    redirection, data loss scenarios, 348-349

    users

        data loss scenarios, 347

        preventing, 349-353

escalation paths (help desk priorities), 905, 908

escape character (\), 942

ESMTP (Extended SMTP), 555

establishing

    administrative network machine classes, 69

    install templates, 69

        administrative network templates, 75

        creating directory hierarchies, 77-79

        implementation plans, 77-79

        production network templates, 69-74

    production network machine classes, 69

estimating recovery costs, disaster recovery plans, 365-366

/etc directory, 85-86

    aliases directory, 586, 911

    at.allow file, 750

    at.deny file, 750

    configuration files, 764-766

    cron.allow file, 751

    cron.deny file, 751

    crontab directories, 1032

    csh.login files, 959

    exports file, 421-424, 764

    fstab file, 293-294, 425, 771

    group file

        editing, 873

        entries, customizing, 885

        users, adding, 870

        users/groups, 866-867

    gshadow file

        users, adding, 871

        users/groups, 868-869

    gtmp file, 873

    hosts.allow files (TCP-Wrappers), 535

    hosts.deny files (TCP-Wrappers), 535

    hosts.equiv files, 545-546

    httpd directory, 90

    inetd.conf file, 532-534, 751-754

        ftpaccess file, 759-760

        ftphosts file, 758

        ftpusers file, 758

        hosts.allow/hosts.deny files, 755-756

        hosts.equiv file, 757-758

        nologin file, 760

        sendmail.cf file, 760

        tcp wrappers, 754-755

        tcpdchk/tcpdmatch programs, 757

    issue file, 765

    login.defs file, 765, 869

    mail files

        mail/sendmail virtusers, 563-564

        mail/sendmail.cw, 563

    motf file, 765

    passwd file

        access, 744

        editing, 873

        entries, customizing, 892

        users, adding, 871

        users/groups, 865-866

    profile file, 940

    ptmp file, 873

    rc.d directory, 89

    rc.d/init.d/amd script, 429

    services file, 514-515

    shadow file

        customizing, chage command, 888

        entries, customizing, 885, 892

        passwords, 745

        users, adding, 871

        users/groups, 867-868

    skel directory, 869

    sysconfig directory, 89

    usertty file, 766

xinetd.conf files, 539-541
  access control, 540
  fields, 539-540
  logging, 541
etherfind utility, 445
Ethernet
  10Base-2, 378, 381
  10Base-T, 378, 381
  100Base-T, 378, 381
  cards/cables, 378
  coax-based, 381
  collisions, 380
  CSMA/CD (Carrier Sense
    Multiple Access with
    Collision Detection), 379
  hubs, 379
  interface
    adding, 382-383
    kernel-level
      configuration, 382-383
    software-level
      configuration, 383
  media selections, 380-381
  switches, 379-380
eval command, 995
  bash, 940
  tcsh, 956
evaluating backup
  software, 328-330
Exabyte Corporation Web
  site, 334
exceptions (policies),
  897-898, 922
exchanging files. *See*
  sharing files
exec command, 956, 995
ExecCGI parameter (Options
  directive), 645
executable scripts, creating,
  971, 1008
exim, 559, 577
  configuration, 577
  mail hub, 578
  spam protection, 578-579
  workstations, 578
exit codes, 974

exit command, 996
  bash, 940
  tcsh, 956
exiting
  bash scripts, 996
  functions with specific return
    values, 1002
  loops, 992-993
expansion, 930
expire.ctl file, 696-698
export command, 940
exportfs command, 423
exports file, 764
!expression command, 952
expressions, 978
  defined, 978
  file test operators, 980-981
  math, 981-982, 996
  string test operators, 981
  values, testing, 978-979
exscan utility, 851
extended 2 filesystem, 198
Extended SMTP (ESMTP),
  555
extended type 2
  filesystem, 188
extendeddbz parameter
  (inn.conf file), 687
extensions, configuration
  language extensions
  (TCP-Wrappers), 537
Exterior Gateway protocol,
  391
external commands (bash),
  executing, 995
external routing protocols,
  390
external users, 530
EXTRAVERSION variable,
  1126

F

-f option (finger command),
  889
-f option (usermod
  command), 893
\f escape sequence, 958, 994
-f command-line option
  amq utility, 430
  at utility, 1022
  batch utility, 1027
  chgrp command, 889
  chown command, 890
  declare command, 975
  httpd script, 641
  mkisofs command, 275
  mount command, 194
  readonly command, 976
  Squid, 666
  suspend command, 999
  tcsh startup, 959
  unset command, 975
-F option (ipchains utility),
  811
-f –force command-line
  option (sfdisk utility), 185
-f file command-line option
  (Squid), 666
-f filename operator, 980
-f inactive days option
  (useradd command), 874
failures (system), 142
  diagnostic tools, 147
    DOS diagnostics, 151-152
    ifconfig utility, 149-150
    isapnp program, 148-149
    NIC diagnostic programs,
      150-151
    proc filesystem, 147-148
  hardware errors, 144
    BIOS errors, 145
    identifying at startup,
      144-145
    last change syndrome, 145

PCI devices, 146-147
PnP devices, 145-146
kernel errors, 163-164
decoding, 165-168
kernel oops, 163-164
system.map file, 168-169
kernel oops, 142
kernel panic, 143
newsgroup resources, 169
rescue disks, 152-153
creating, 153-154
emergency file copying,
157-159
image, 153
rebuilding LILO, 155-156
recovering deleted files,
160
repairing partitions,
156-157
rescue sessions, starting,
154
rewriting configuration
files, 156
toolkit, 155
resources, 169
system log analysis, 160-163
Father (media groups), 319
favoritism, 896
**FBI, National Computer
Crimes Squad, 635**
fc command, 936
fdisk utility
command-line options, 178
partitioning, 177-181
fdutils package, 1110
**Federal Bureau of Investi-
gation, National Compu-
ter Crimes Squad, 635**
**feedback mechanisms
(help desks), 904, 908**
fetchmail, 579-581
fg command
moving jobs to foreground,
938, 953
tcsh, 956

**FHS (Filesystem Hierarchy
Standard), 82**
root directory, 84-85
/bin directory, 85-87
/boot directory, 85
/dev directory, 85-86
/etc directory, 85-86
/home directory, 86
/lib directory, 86
/mnt directory, 86
/opt directory, 86
/root directory, 86
/sbin directory, 85
/tmp directory, 86
/usr directory, 87-88
/var directory, 88-89
Web site, 209
fhttpd, 669
Fibre Channel storage, 225
**-file option (crontab
command), 1033**
file sharing (FTP), 610
connection types, 611
daemon execution modes,
612
inetd.conf file, 612
legal issues, 621
ProFTPD, 619-620
RFCs, 611
security, 621-631
warez D00dz, 631-636
wu-ftpd, 612-619
**File System Standard
(FSSTND), 82**
**file test operators
(expressions), 980-981**
**File Transfer Protocol.
See FTP**
file-based directives, 646
**FileInfo parameter
(AllowOverride
directive), 651**
**filename parameter (Files
directive), 646**
**filename substitution, 18,
22**

demonstration of, 22-24
meta characters, 22
**filename1 -ef filename2
operator, 981**
**filename1 -nt filename2
operator, 981**
**filename1 -ot filename2
operator, 981**
filenames
converting to lowercase
script, 1003-1004
IDE device interface, 213
IDE device interface for IDE
partitions, 213
files. See also specific files
added since install, finding,
303-304
alias master file, 586
altered system files, checking,
774
Apache configuration,
overriding, 642-643
archiving, 326
backing up. See backups
common beginning letters,
finding, 930
common extension, finding,
929
core, deleting automatically,
1020
deleted, recovering, 160
digest configuration, 601-605
downloading, FTP servers,
1162-1163
editing, 864
emergency copying, 157-159
extracting with same
extensions, 946
File System Standard
(FSSTND), 82
Filesystem Hierarchy
Standard, 82-83, 84-89
filesystems, 1077
Name Service Switch, 408
overwriting, 864
ownership, 890

ranges, finding, 930
restoring, 320-321, 324-326
specific extensions,
    finding, 930
specific words, finding,
    1004-1005
task-oriented, backing up, 302
temporary, cleaning up
    automatically, 1020
Files directive, 646
**Filesystem Configuration
File, 215-217**
**Filesystem Hierarchy
Standard. *See* FHS**
filesystem layout, 89
filesystem scanners, 846
**filesystem spaces, users,
limiting, 780**
filesystems
accessing
    *mount command,
    194-195*
    unmount command, 195
adding quota support, 771
AFS
    *filesystem sharing,
    426-427*
    mailing list, 426
    Web site, 410, 426
automatic mounting, 427
    autofs, 431-432
    *automount daemon,
    427-430*
checking quotas, securing, 771
Coda, 1122
    *filesystem sharing,
    426-427*
    Web site, 426
contents, backing up,
    300-301
    configuration files, 301
    task-oriented files, 302
    user files, 301
creating, 187-188
DOS, 289-292
extended type 2, 188

growth estimations, 196-197
kernel source code layout, 1090
kernel support, 1120-1121
local, 204
maintaining/repairing,
    188-194
mounting, 426
Netware Core Protocol, 1123
NFS. *See* NFS
partitions for each, 175-176
proc. *See* proc filesystem
remounting partitions, 771
securing, 770
setting quotas, 771-772
sharing, 204, 418-421
    AFS, 426-427
    Coda, 426-427
    *NFS client configuration,
    424-426*
    *NFS server configuration,
    418-424*
SMB, 1122
space allocation, 196
space management, 198
    *local/shared filesystems,
    204*
    quotas, 206-209
    space usage, 199-204
types, 197
    extended 2, 198
    kernel supported, 198
    Minix, 197
    network, 198
    original extended, 198
    *special device supported,
    198*
    xia, 198
UDF, 1121
filesystems file, 1077
filter script utilities, 415
filters
ipchains, packet traversal,
    813-814
spam, 578

find command, 25-26
command-line options, 26-27
tests, 27-28
warning about, 29
finding
BitchX, 728
files
    *common beginning letters,
    930*
    common extension, 929
    ranges, 930
    specific extension, 930
ircII, 723
JavaICQ, 730
kernel patches, 1093-1094
kernel source code, 1084-1087
licq, 731
micq, 732
new files, 303-304
QSeeMe, 736
security breach evidence,
    843-844
security tools, 832
servers, 497
Speak Freely, 735
specific words in files script,
    1004-1005
X-Chat, 726
Zircon, 725
finger command, 769, 889
firewalk utility, 852
firewalls, 786
absolute, 787-789
Centennial School District
    case study, 1144
debugging, 817
DNS servers, debugging, 817
examples
    *network configuration,
    815-816*
    single-user machine, 814
ICQ, 728-729
ipchains utility, 810
    chain management, 811
    chain rules, 811
    filters, 813-814

installing, 810-811
targets, 813
kernel configuration, 792-793
mailing lists, 839
options, 789-790
packet filtering, 790, 805,
811-813, 1144
chains, 811
connections, 809
IP forwarding, 807-809
*ipfwadm program,
805-806*
Linux, 805
*packet traversal through
ipchains filters,
813-814*
proxy services, 790
proxy servers, 787, 790-791,
1144
programs, 791
SOCKS, 795-798
squid, 798-800
*TIS FWTK (Trusted
Information Systems
FireWall ToolKit),
800-804*
transproxy, 793-795
startup script, 807-809
system crackers,
preventing, 358
TCP/IP packet-based, 1113
Trinux tools, 853
user IDs/passwords database,
801-802
Firewalls mailing list, 839
firewalls newsgroup, 836
**-fix command-line option
(cdrecord command), 281**
floppy disks,
backup media, 322
boot floppies
*CD-ROM Red Hat
installs, 51*
cloning installs, 56-57
*hard drive Red Hat
installs, 51*

rawrite utility, 53
setup function, 57, 59-60
YARD, 56
**floppy driver utility
programs Web site, 1110**
**floppy drives, 272-273,
339-340, 1120**
**follow-up postings
(digest-only mailing
lists), 603**
**FollowSymLinks parameter
(Options directive), 645**
for statements, 983
format, fstab file, 214-217
**forms, user request forms,
918-919**
**forward chain rule
(ipchains), 816**
**forward-char command,
958**
**frame types (NetWare
networking), 496**
framebuffer.txt file, 1124
free utility, 98, 1060-1061
FreeS/Wan project, 1114
**freshmeat Web site, 41, 56,
675, 835**
fsck utility
command-line options,
188-189
maintaining/repairing
filesystems, 188-194
return code handling,
189-190
return code interpretations,
190-194
fstab file, 214
format, 214-215
line-by-line dissection,
215-217
mount options, 214-215
ftape driver, 339
**FTP (File Transfer Protocol),
610**
anonymous, 769
archives, 43

contrib.redhat.com, 43
developer.redhat.com, 43
ftp..kernel.org, 43*
ftp.redhat.com, 43
metalab.unc.edu, 43
tsx-11.mit.edu, 43
updates.redhat.com, 43
connection types, 611
daemon execution modes,
612
firewall debugging, 817
FTP installs, 54
inetd.conf file, 612
ircII sites, 723
legal issues, 621
mailing list archives, 591
ProFTPD
installing, 619-620
mailing list, 620
RFCs, 611
security, 621-631
servers, 1162-1163
services, 531
sites
ipfwadm program, 805
kernel source code, 1084
socks, 791
squid, 791
TIS FWTK, 791
transproxy, 791
warez D00dz, 631-636
wu-ftpd, 612
anonymous FTP, 618-619
*command-line options,
613-614*
*customization options,
614-615*
ftpaccess file, 616-617
installing, 613
Internet resources, 618
IP aliases, 615
mailing list, 617-618
Zircon site, 725
ftpaccess file, 759
ftphosts file, 758
ftpusers file, 758

full backups, 306-307, 313-314
disadvantages, 308
dump command, 324-326
remote machines, 307-308
full duplex communications, 716
full feeds, 674
fully compliant implementations, 83-84
functions
{} (curly braces), 1001
bash, 1001
exiting with specific return values, 1002
ftpaccess file
log commands, 759
log security, 760
log syslog, 760
log transfers, 759
loginfails, 759
noretrieve, 759
throughput, 759
upload, 759
local variables, bash, 1003
names, bash, 1001-1002
setup
cloning installs, 57, 59-60
required utilities, 60
FWALL-users mailing list, 839
FWTK (FireWall ToolKit). See TIS FWTK

G

-g option,
useradd command, 874
usermod command, 893
-G option,
useradd command, 874
usermod command, 893

-g command-line option,
edquota command, 208
routed daemon, 392
user administration, 1160
-g –show-geometry command-line option (sfdisk utility), 184
-g filename operator, 980
Gated Consortium Web site, 394
gated daemon, 392-394
configuring, 395-397
host routing, 395
interior gateway, 395-396
running, 394
gated.conf file, configuring, 395-397
host routing, 395
interior gateway, 395-396
gateways, 383
interior, configuring, 395-396
routing, 384
gathered performance data, 1064-1065
GCOS parameter (/etc/passwd file), 865
GD perl module, downloading, 908-909
general.cfg file, 415
generational MTAs, 558
generic kernel, creating, 1127
Generic Routing Encapsulation (GRE), 1113
genksyms utility, 1098
geographic domains, 398-399
getops command, 1000
getty processes, 132
-gfilename option (GNU tar program), 327
GFS Project Web site, 225
GhostScript, 411-413
ghttpd, 669

GID paramete r
/etc/group file, 867
/etc/passwd file, 865
global cron files, 1038
globbing, 18, 22. See also wildcards
demonstration of, 22-24
meta characters, 22
GNOME environment, 99
gov domain, 398
gpasswd command, 891
grace period, 771
Grandfather (media groups), 319
graphical news readers, 707-708, 710
graphical utilities, performance monitoring, 1062
Xload, 1063
Xosview, 1062-1063
GRE (Generic Routing Encapsulation), 1113
greater than operator (>), 933, 950
grog utility, 415
group ids
/etc/passwd file, 865
non-privileged users, NetWare, 506-507
group named, 770
group parameter (/etc/gshadow file), 869
option (gpasswd command), 891
groupadd command, 884
groupdel command, 884
groupmod command, 885
groups, 862
adding
/etc/group file, 884
GUI tools, 886-887
system, 862
Centennial School District case study, 1159

commands
  chage, 888
  chfn, 889
  chgrp, 889-890
  chown, 890
  chsh, 891
  gpasswd, 891
  groups, 891
  passwd, 892
  su, 892
  usermod, 892-893
deleting, 884
/etc/inetd.conf files, 533
/etc/skel directory, 869
file editing/overwriting, 864
ids, 867
management tools
  groupadd command, 884
  groupdel command, 884
  groupmod command, 885
  grpck command, 885
multiple users on same
  directory, 864
names, 866
ownerships, 889
passwords
  /etc/group file, 866
  /etc/shadow file, 867
permissions, granting, 887
printing, 891
private, 878
shared accounts, 863
shared files, 888
squid, 800
system files, 864
  /etc/group, 866-867
  /etc/gshadow, 868-869
  /etc/login.defs, 869
  /etc/passwd, 865-866
  /etc/shadow, 867-868
users, adding/deleting, 891
groups command, 891
**group_ name parameter
  (/etc/group file), 866**
**growth estimations
  (filesystems), 196-197**

grpck command, 885
GRUB, 128
gtop, 99
**GUI interface, linuxconf,
  877**
GUI tools, 886-887

H

**-h option (usermod
  command), 892**
**h option (finger com-
  mand), 889**
\h command prompt, 944
%h command prompt, 963
-h command-line option
  history command, 951
  httpd script, 641
  mount command, 194
  Squid, 666
  sudo command, 821
**-h heads command-line
  option,**
  cfdisk utility, 182
  sfdisk utility, 185
**h [number] command
  (mail utility), 584**
**hackers. *See* security,
  breaches**
**half duplex
  communications, 716**
halt command, 139
handling
  errors. *See* error handling
  multiple kernel versions,
    1127
    clone trees, 1128-1131
    generic kernel, 1127
hard drive, 112
  boot sector, 112
  failures, 359
  master boot record (MBR),
    112-113

partitions, 61-65, 112
Red Hat installs, 51-52
hard limits (quotas), 206
hard quotas, 771
hardware
  errors, 144
    BIOS errors, 145
    identifying at startup,
    144-145
    last change syndrome,
    145
    PCI devices, 146-147
    PnP devices, 145-146
  Internet telephony
    requirements, 717-719
  performance costs, 1053
  removable media devices. *See*
    removable media devices
hardware RAID, 266-267
**hardware replacement,
  362**
hash command, 995-996
hdparm utility, 1110
header files, 1090
Hello protocol, 391
help. *See also* help desks
  help command, 939
  systems orientation guides,
    902
  Usenet server resources, 711
help desks. *See also* help
  feedback mechanisms, 904
  good help desk qualities,
    903-905
  interfaces, 904
  Keystone, 917
  prioritization capabilities, 904
  priority escalation paths, 905
  reporting capabilities, 904
  selecting personnel, 905
  WREQ, 906
    adding requests, 914, 917
    configuring, 910-911
    downloading WREQ
    code, 909
    email interface, 906-907

escalation paths, 908
feedback feature, 908
list configuration,
911-914
prioritization, 908
setting, 908, 910-914
Statistics option, 908
unpacking WREQ
distribution, 909-910
Web interface, 906
here-documents, 183
hierarchy, DNS, 398
High-Availability (RAID)
  HOWTO Web site, 306
hint zones (BIND), 402
hiscachesize parameter
  (inn.conf file), 687
HISTFILE variable, 935, 951
  bash, 943
  tcsh, 961
history command, 934, 951
history files, 764
history lists
  bash, 934-936
  commands
    editing, 936
    executing, 952
    navigating, 952
  searches, 935
  tcsh, 951-952
history variable, 961
HISTSIZE variable
  bash, 943
  history lists, 934
/home directory, 86, 878
  .rhosts files, 545-547
  users
    creating, 871
    /etc/passwd file, 866
HOME variable
  bash, 943
  cron daemon, 1035
  tcsh, 961
host routing (gated
  daemon), 395
host specifications, 422

Host-to-Host Transport
  Layer. *See* **Transport Layer**
host.equiv, 758
hostmasters, 587
hosts
  equivalent, 545
  trusted, 545
  victim, 356
hosts.allow file, 755-756
hosts.deny file, 755-756
hosts.equiv file
  inetd.conf file, 757-758
  shared printer access, 416
hosts.lpd file, 416
hot-swapping, 229
hping utility, 852
htaccess file
  disabling, 651
  processing, 650
HTML files, SSI (Server-Side
  Includes), 651
htpasswd file, 650
HTTP installs, 54
httpd script
  command-line options, 641
  starting/stopping Apache,
    640-641
httpd.conf file, 642
httpd.pid file, 648
hubs
  auto-sensing, 379
  Ethernet, 379
hunt utility, 854

I

-I option (change
  command), 889
-l option
  declare command, 975
  dump command, 325
  ipchains utility, 811

sfdisk utility, 185
top utility, 1058
-i –increment command-line
  option (sfdisk utility), 184
IBCS (Intel Binary Compat-
  ibility Standard), 1090
-IBM –leave-last command-
  line option (sfdisk utility),
  185
IBM HTTP Server, 668
ICMP (Internet Control Mes-
  sage Protocol) packets, 374
  firewall debugging, 817
  firewall network
    configuration, 815
ICQ, 714-715, 728
  client configuration, 729
  firewalls/IP-masquerading,
    728-729
  JavaICQ, 729
    download Web site, 730
    finding, 730
    installing, 730-731
    JDK installation, 730
    running, 731
  licq, 731
    finding, 731
    installing, 731
    running, 732
    Web site, 731
  micq, 732
    finding, 732
    installing, 732
    running, 732-733
    Web site, 732
  Web site, 714, 728-729
IDE (Integrated Drive Elec-
  tronics) devices, 175, 212,
  288-289
  drives, tuning, 1110
  interface, 212-214
  names, 212-214
ids
  non-privileged users/groups,
    506-507
  SCSI devices, 222-223

if statements, 986-988
ifconfig, 149-150, 380, 615
IfDefine directive, 646
IfModule directive, 655
images
   ISO9660
     creating, 275-280
     transferring to CD-R/
      CD-RW media, 280
     writing/mounting/verify-
      ing to disks, 282-284
   kernel, 1133
   OS. *See* cloning installs
   rescue disks, 153
IMAP (Interactive Mail
  Access Protocol), 556
imm (Iomega MatchMaker)
  driver, 286
Includes parameter
  (Options directive), 645
IncludesNOEXEC para-
  meter (Options direc-
  tive), 645
incoming.conf file, 691-692
incremental backups, 314
   levels, 314-315
   storing, 319
Indexes parameter
   AllowOverride directive, 651
   Options directive, 645
inetd
   chargen, 533
   daytime, 533
   discard, 533
   echo, 533
   /etc/inetd.conf files, 532-533
     arguments entries, 533
     comments, 534
     disabling services, 534
     editing, 534
     enabling services, 534
     ftpaccess file, 759-760
     ftphosts file, 758
     ftpusers file, 758
     hosts.allow/hosts.deny
      files, 755-756

     hosts.equiv file, 757-758
     name field, 532-533
     protocol field, 532
     sendmail.cf file, 760
     system security, 751-754
     tcp wrappers, 754-755
     tcpdchk/tcpdmatch
      programs, 757
     type field, 532
     user field, 533
     wait-status field, 533
   process, 531
   time, 533
inetd.conf file
   arguments entries, 533
   comments, 534
   disabling services, 534
   editing, 534
   enabling services, 534
   ftpaccess file, 759-760
     log commands function,
      759
     log security function, 760
     log syslog function, 760
     log transfers function,
      759
     loginfails function, 759
     noretrieve function, 759
     throughput function, 759
     upload function, 759
   ftphosts file, 758
   ftpusers file, 758
   hosts.allow/hosts.deny files,
     755-756
   hosts.equiv file, 757-758
   name field, 532-533
   protocol field, 532
   sendmail.cf file, 760
   system security, 751-754
   tcp wrappers, 754-755
   tcpdchk/tcpdmatch programs,
     757
   type field, 532
   user field, 533
   wait-status field, 533

   InformationWeek Research
     1999 National IT Salary
     Survey, 8-9
init system initialization
  script, 129-132, 134
initialization scripts. *See*
  system initialization
  scripts
INN, 676
   article storage format,
     680-681
   configuring, 681-682
     access restrictions,
      698-699
     article spool, 698
     cycbuff.conf file, 692-693
     daily maintenance tasks
      script, 700
     expire.ctl file, 696-698
     incoming.conf file,
      691-692
     inn.conf file, 682-688
     news database direc-
      tories, 699-700
     newsfeeds file, 688-691
     overview.ctl file, 695
     storage.conf file, 693-695
   FAQ Web site, 677
   installing, 676
     authentication, 678
     RPM, 676-678
     source, 678-679
   spam filtering, 701
   starting, 700
   Web site, 676
inn.conf file, 682-688
   listing, 682-686
   parameters, 686-688
input fields (sfdisk utility),
  183-184
input redirection
   bash, 933-934
   tcsh, 950
input rules (ipchains rules),
  815

-inq command-line option
(cdrecord command), 281
insmod command, 497, 1098
installing
    Apache, 640
    automount daemon, 428
    BitchX, 728
    CD-ROM Red Hat installs, 51
    cloning installs, 56
        boot floppies, 56-57
        customizing OS image, 68
        installing OS image,
            65-67
        kickstart, 68
        lilo, 68
        procedure, 56
        remote partitioning,
            61-65
        setup function, 57, 59-60
    Comanche, 662
    custom installations, 50, 55
    default installations, 50
    FTP installs, 54
    hard drive Red Hat installs,
        51-52
    HTTP installs, 54
    INN, 676
        authentication, 678
        RPM, 676-678
        source, 678-679
    install templates, 69
        administrative network
            templates, 75-76
        creating directory
            hierarchies, 77, 79
        implementation plans,
            77-79
        production network
            templates, 69-74, 77
    ipchains utility, 810-811
    ipfwadm program, 806
    ircII, 723-724
    JavaICQ, 730-731
    JDK, 730
    licq, 731
    LILO (LInux LOader), 114

    micq, 732
    ncpfs module, 497
    NFS installs, 52-53
        network boot floppies, 53
        related software, 418-419
        requirements, 52
    nntpcache, 702
    ntop, 452-453
    ProFTPD, 619-620
    QSeeMe, 736
    Samba, 1149
    Speak Freely, 735
    squid, 798-799
    SRPM, 235
    SSH, 551
        international
            packages, 551
        U.S. packages, 551
    tcpdump, 445-446
    transproxy, 794-795
    wu-ftpd, 613
    X-Chat, 727
    Zircon, 725
INSTALL_ MOD_PATH
    variable, 1126
INSTALL_ PATH variable,
    1126
int domain, 398
integer1 -eq integer2
    operator, 982
integer1 -ge integer2
    operator, 982
integer1 -gt integer2
    operator, 982
integer1 -le integer2
    operator, 982
integer1 -lt integer2
    operator, 982
integer1 -ne integer2
    operator, 982
integrating Linux with
    Windows, 462
    Samba, 465-492
    smbfs, 470-471
integrity checkers, 356

Intel Binary Compatibility
    Standard (IBCS), 1090
interactive bash sessions,
    940-941
Interactive Mail Access
    Protocol (IMAP), 556
interactive modes, 928
interactive tcsh sessions,
    959-960
interfaces
    Ethernet
        adding, 382-383
        kernel-level configuration,
            382-383
        software-level
            configuration, 383
    help desks, 904-907
    IDE, 212-214
    libpcap interface, 440-441
    network, checking, 773
    SOCK PACKET interface, 438
    TurboPacket interface, 438-440
interior gateway (gated
    daemon), 395-396
interior routing protocols,
    390
Intermediate System to
    Intermediate System
    protocol, 391
internal users, 530
Internet
    access, IP masquerading, 1155
    data flow, 719-720
    DNS
        geographic/organizational
            domains, 398-399
        hierarchy, 398
    name servers
        BIND configuration,
            402-405
        categories, 400
        development history,
            397-398
        NIS (Network Information
            Service), 405-408

resolver libraries,
  400-401
UNIX/Linux systems,
  399-405
protocols, *372*
services
  email, 531
  FTP, 531
  information-providing,
    531
  low-level, 530
  newsgroups, 531
  remote login, 531
  selecting, 530-531
  WWW, 531
telephony. *See* Internet
** telephony**
Internet Control Message
** Protocol (ICMP), 374**
Internet Layer, 373-374
Internet Relay Chat. *See*
** IRC**
Internet Security Scanner
** (ISS), 830**
Internet telephony, 714
  clones, *728*
  full duplex communications,
    716
  half duplex communications,
    716
  hardware requirements,
    717-719
  ICQ, *714-715, 728*
    client configuration, 729
    firewalls/IP-masquerad-
      ing, 728-729
    JavaICQ, 729-731
    licq, 731-732
    micq, 732-733
    Web site, 714, 728-729
  IRC (Internet Relay Chat),
    721
    BitchX client, 727-728
    ircII client, 722-725
    server names/IP numbers
      lists Web sites, 723

Web site, 721
X-Chat client, 726-727
Zircon client, 725-726
mbone (multicast backbone),
  719
  data flow, 719-720
  multi-casting, 720-721
multimedia conferencing
  tools, *733-734*
  CU-SeeMe, 736
  MeetingPoint, 736
  QSeeMe, 735-736
  Speak Freely, 734-735
problems, *715-716*
  capacity, 716
  latency, 716
  packet dropping, 717
  protocols, 717
  QoS (Quality of Service),
    716
  standards, 717
  video conferencing, *718, 734*
Internic, 399
interpreted programs
** (shell scripts), 969-970**
interpreter path line
** symbol (!), 971**
interrupt conflicts, 147
interruptions. *See*
** requests (users)**
intr option, NFS mounting,
** 425**
intranets, 897
intrusion detection tools,
** 846**
  filesystem scanners, *846*
  who/top/ls/ps commands,
    847-848
intrusions. *See* security,
** breaches**
io section (vmstat utility),
** 1060**
Iomega MatchMaker
** driver, 286**
ioports file, 1077

IP
  addresses, *375*
    address classes, 375-376
    aliases, 615
    classless, 376-377
    detecting duplicates, 449
    subnetting, 377
    supernetting, 377
    translating numbers to
      symbolic names. See
      name servers
    writing, 377
  aliasing, *1113*
  forwarding, *807-809*
  masquerading, *728-729, 1155*
  tunneling, *1113*
  virtual hosts, *657-659*
ipchains utility, 853
  chain management, *811*
  chain rules, *811*
  filters, packet traversal,
    813-814
  firewall configuration, *810*
  installing, *810-811*
  targets, *813*
ipfwadm program
  connections, forwarding, *809*
  installing, *806*
  packet filtering (firewalls),
    805-806
ipgrab utility, 850
IPTraf utility, 850
ipx configure command,
** 497**
IPX
  devices, *502, 504*
  kernel support, *1114-1115*
  networks, *496-497*
  support, adding, *496*
  route flags, saving, *504-505*
IRC (Internet Relay Chat),
** 714, 721**
  BitchX, *727-728*
    download Web site, 728
    FAQ Web site, 727
    finding, 728

installing, 728
running, 728
Web site, 727
ircII (client), 722
finding, 723
installing, 723-724
running, 724-725
Web site, 722
server names/IP numbers lists
Web sites, 723
Web site, 721
X-Chat, 726-727
download Web site, 726
finding, 726
installing, 727
running, 727
Web site, 726
Zircon, 725
finding, 725
installing, 725
running, 726
Web site, 725
ircII, 722
finding, 723
installing, 723-724
running, 724-725
Web site, 722
**IS-IS (Intermediate System
to Intermediate System)
protocol, 391**
isapnp program, 148-149
/isc/inn directory, 678
ISDN lines, 1117
ISO9660 images
creating, 275-280
transferring to CD-R/CD-RW
media, 280
writing/mounting/verifying to
disks, 282-284
**-isosize command-line
option (cdrecord
command), 282**
**ISS (Internet Security
Scanner), 830**
issue file, 765

iterations (loops),
skipping, 993-994

J

**-J command-line option
(mkisofs command), 275**
**Java Apache project Web
site, 664**
Java Servlets, 664
**Java status page Web site,
730**
JavaICQ, 729
download Web site, 730
finding, 730
installing, 730-731
JDK installation, 730
running, 731
Jaz drives, 322
JDK
installing, 730
open source version Web site,
730
JDK binaries Web site, 730
job control
bash, 937-939
% command, 939
*jobs running (list of),
938-939*
killing jobs, 938
*moving jobs to
background, 937*
*moving jobs to
foreground, 938*
*starting commands in
background, 937*
suspending jobs, 937
tcsh, 952-955
% command, 954
*jobs running (list of),
953-954*
killing jobs, 954
*moving jobs to
background, 953*

*moving jobs to
foreground, 953*
notify command, 955
*starting commands in
background, 952*
stopping jobs, 955
suspending jobs, 953, 955
*waiting for all background
jobs to finish, 955*
-job option
at utility, 1024
atrm utility, 1028
jobs
% command, 939, 954
bash, 937
killing, 938, 954
moving to background, 937,
953
moving to foreground, 938, 953
notify command, 955
running (list of), 938-939,
953-954
stopping, 955
suspending, 937, 953-955
tcsh, 952
waiting on all background jobs
to finish, 955
jobs command, 939, 954
joysticks, 1120

K

**-k option (useradd
command), 874**
-k command-line option
bindkey command, 957
free utility, 1061
Squid, 666
sudo command, 821
-k filename operator, 980
kbdconfig command, 36
kcore file, 1076
kdat program, 330
KDE environment, 99

**Kent Landfield's wu-ftpd
Web site, 618**
kernel
APM (Advanced Power
Management) support,
1108
AppleTalk support, 514
backup media support, 335
binary support, 1106-1107
block devices, 1108-1110
BSD processes accounting
support, 1105
CD-ROM drives (created
before 1994) support, 1117
character devices support,
1118-1119
code maturity level,
1102-1103
configuration, 1100-1101
loading, 1126
saving, 1126
configuration options, 1102
console drivers support,
1123-1124
console sound support, 1124
custom installation scripts,
1131-1132
doubletalk speech synthesizer
support, 1120
drivers, deleting, 1083
errors, 163-164
decoding, 165-168
kernel oops, 163-164
system.map file, 168-169
filesystems support,
1120-1121
firewall configurations,
792-793
floppy tape device drivers
support, 1120
FTP session directory layout
example, 1084-1087
hacking, 1125
image, 1133
ISDN support, 1117
joysticks support, 1120

loopback devices, 1111
make commands, 1132-1133
make targets, 1132
makcfilc, tweaking,
1126-1127
mice support, 1119
missing functionality, 1083
modules, 1094-1095, 1105
advantages, 1095
*support, enabling,
1096-1097*
utilities, 1097-1098
when not to use, 1099
monolithic, 1095
multiple version handling,
1127
clone trees, 1128-1131
generic kernel, 1127
native language support, 1123
network devices support,
1111, 1115-1117
*serial devices/parallel
ports, 1116*
wireless networking, 1116
network filesystems support,
1121, 1123
networking options,
1111-1112
IP aliasing, 1113
IP masquerading, 1113
IP tunneling, 1113
*IPX/Appletalk protocols,
1114-1115*
*TCP/IP packet-based
firewalls, 1113*
*TCP/IP protocol stack,
1115*
WAN routers, 1114
networking support, 1105
new binary types, registering,
1106-1107
NFS support verification, 424
numbering scheme, 1084
NVRAM devices support,
1119

parallel port IDE devices,
1111
parallel port storage device
support, 286-287
parallel port support,
1107-1108
parallel printer support, 1119
partitions support, 1123
patches, 1091
*ac (Alan Cox) patches,
1094*
announcements, 1093
*applied to standard
source code tree
(list of), 1088*
authors, 1092
finding, 1093-1094
*official/unofficial,
compared, 1092-1093*
Red Hat, 1087-1089
sources, 1092
version, 1092
plug-and-play support, 1108
processor types, 1103-1104
real-time clock support, 1119
SCSI support, 1115
serial port support, 1118
software RAID, 1111
source code, 1082
*compiling reasons,
1082-1083*
*configuration dialog
boxes, 1091*
default location, 1101
device drivers, 1089
filesystems, 1090
finding, 1084-1085, 1087
header files, 1090
IBCS support, 1090
layout, 1089-1091
modules, 1090
*network protocol stack,
1091*
Red Hat, 1087-1089
sysctl support, 1105-1106

System V Interprocess
Communications support,
1105
terminal support, 1118
tuning, 1075-1078
upgrading, 1083
video4linux support, 1120
watchdog timer devices
support, 1119
**Kernel Configuration File-
system dialog box, 1121**
kernel oops, 142, 163-164
kernel panic, 143
kernel space NFS, 418
**kernel supported
filesystem, 198**
**Kernel Threads Web site,
1094**
kernel updates
Kernelnotes, 38
Linux Kernel Archives, 37
kernel-2.2.spec file, 1088
kernel.org Web site, 1084
kerneld utility, 1098
Kernelnotes, 38, 1094
key bindings, 957-959
control characters, 957
default, 958-959
escape sequences, 958
listing of, viewing, 957
Keystone (help desk), 917
keywords
LILO
*global section keywords,
118-125*
for Linux kernels, 120
*per-image keywords,
119-120, 125-127*
raidtab configuration file,
236-237
kickstart, 68
kill command, jobs, 938, 954
kill-line command, 959
killing
aliases, 931, 948
jobs, 938, 954

klogd daemon, 164
kmsg file, 1076
knews news reader, 708
kpm, 99
**ksymoops utility, 165-168,
1091**
ksyms file, 1077
ksyms utility, 1098
ktop, 99

L

**-l option (usermod
command), 893**
-l command-line option
at utility, 1022
atd, 1029
atrun utility, 1029
bindkey command, 957
chsh command, 891
crontab command, 1034
dirs command, 991
fc command, 936
fdisk utility, 178
history command, 951
httpd script, 641
jobs command, 939, 954
kill command, 939, 954
sudo command, 821
tcsh startup, 959
trap command, 996
**-L –Linux command-line
option (sfdisk utility), 185**
**-l –list command-line option
(sfdisk utility), 184**
-L filename operator, 980
**-l filename option
(mkfs utility), 187**
**-L label command-line
option (mount command),
194**

languages
Eiffel, 1013-1014
native, kernel support, 1123
Perl. *See* Perl scripting
Python, 1012-1013
Tcl/Tk, 1010-1011
**last change syndrome
(hardware errors), 145**
**latency, Internet telephony,
716**
**Lawrence Berkeley
Laboratory,**
libpcap, 440
tcpdump, 445
**layers, TCP/IP network
layers, 372-373**
Application Layer, 375
data unit names, 373
Internet Layer, 373-374
Network Access Layer, 373
Transport Layer, 374-375
**layout, kernel source code,
1089-1091**
configuration dialog boxes,
1091
device drivers, 1089
filesystems, 1090
header files, 1090
IBCS support, 1090
modules, 1090
network protocol stack, 1091
**lcredit=n argument
(pam_ cracklib module),
749**
**LDP (Linux Documentation
Project) Web site, 606**
legal issues, FTP, 621
length of passwords, 877
**less than operator (>), 933,
950**
let command, 996
/lib directory, 86
libpcap interface, 440-441
**libraries, training libraries,
901**
licq, 731-732

LILO (LInux LOader),
113-114
alternatives, 127-128
booting up multiple operating
systems, 122-127
cloning installs, 68
command-line options, 121
installing, 114
keywords
for Linux kernels, 120
global section keywords,
118-119, 122-125
per-image keywords,
119-120, 125-127
lilo.conf file, 115, 120
global keywords section,
118-119, 122-125
per-image keywords
section, 119-120,
125-127
patches for color screens and
line drawing characters,
125
physical security, 767-768
rebuilding, 155-156
/sbin/lilo map installer, 113,
116, 121
securing, 768
Limit directive, 650
Limit parameter
(AllowOverride direc-
tive), 651
limiting
device access, 780
filesystem spaces, 780
program access, 780-781
limits.conf file, 762
Linux
distribution on the Internet,
36
networking advantages,
494-495
Linux Applications and
Utilities Web site, 327
Linux Cross Reference
package Web site, 1091

Linux Documentation
Project, 36
Linux Kernel Archives, 37
Linux Links Web site, 327
LInux LOader. *See* **LILO**
Linux Portal Web sites, 835
Linux Today, 40, 835
Linux Web site, 41
Linux Weekly News Web
site, 835
linux-kernel mailing list,
169, 1093-1094
linux-M.N.P. directory,
1089
Linux.com web site, 835
LinuxApps Web site,
YARD, 56
LinuxBerg Web site, 327
Linuxcare, 39
linuxconf program, 31-33,
875-879
groups, adding, 886-887
GUI interface, 877
password validation rules,
877-879
starting, 876
User and Group Maintenance
screen, 879
users, adding, 879-881
LinuxHQ, 38
listings
AppleTalk services, system
files support, 514-515
AppleVolumes.system file,
515-524
caching-only name server
configuration sample,
403-404
case statement example,
984-985
Changes file excerpt,
1097-1098
clone tree cloning script,
1128-1131

directory hierarchy example
(install template implementation), 77-79
Ethernet collision examination, 380
firewall startup script,
807-809
FTP session kernel source
code directory layout
example, 1084-1087
host routing configuration
(gated daemon), 395
hosts file sample, 398
inetd.conf with proxy through
TIS FWTK, 803-804
inn.conf file, 682-686
installing OS images
(cloning installs), 65-67
interior routing configuration
(gated daemon), 395-396
kernel-2.2.spec file, 1088
LILO (LInux LOader),
/etc/lilo.conf file, 122-127
ls command, intrusion
detection, 847
misplaced wildcard character,
347-348
nntpcache.servers file,
702-704
nsswitch.conf file sample,
408
nwserv.conf file
automatically mapping
NetWare/Linux
usernames, 510-511
DOS client password
handling, 505-506
IPX device configuration,
502-504
IPX route flags, saving,
504-505
network number
configuration, 501-502
non-privileged user/group
ids, 506-507

printer configuration,
511-512
servername configuration,
500-501
startup sanity checks, 511
supervisor logins,
507-509
user logins, 509-510
version spoofing, 505
volume configuration,
499-500
operator menu
implementation, 826-827
operator menu script,
822-826
pause program, 191-194
personal backup scripts with
tar, 353
piping and redirection errors,
348-349
production network install
template packages, 70-74
RCS preventing data loss,
351-352
resolver library configuration
sample, 401
reverse mapping sample, 404
rm aliases preventing data loss,
350
routing table sample, 388
routing tables, viewing,
385-386
setup function, 57-60
sfdisk command, remotely
partitioning hard drives,
61-63
space usage monitoring script,
199-204
listservers, majordomo,
588-589
archives, 590-591
digest-only lists, 591-605
digested lists, 589
moderated/unmoderated lists,
589
open/closed lists, 590

password storage, 591
privacy, 590
security, 590
loadable kernel modules.
See **modules**
loadable modules,
checking if loaded, 148
loadavg file, 1076
loading kernel
configuration, 1126
LOADLIN, 127
LoadModule directive, 654
local command, 1003
local filesystems, 204
local hosts table, 563
local printers, 411-416
local variables, 1003
localmaxartsize parameter
(inn.conf file), 687
locating bottlenecks, 1050
locking multiple email
clients, 582-583
log commands function, 759
log files
checking, 772-773
cleaning up automatically, 1020
cron jobs, viewing, 1042
system. *See* system logs
log security function, 760
log syslog function, 760
log transfers function, 759
log watchers, 360
-log-file command-line
option (mkisofs
command), 275
logical connections, 374
logging
Apache, 647-648
/etc/xinetd.files, 541
levels, 647
TCP-Wrappers, 535
logical operators, 979
login magazine, 834
-login option (bash startup),
941
login.defs file, 765

loginfails function, 759
logins
login names, character length,
586
login shells, 891
NetWare supervisors,
507-509
NetWare users, 509-510
Logitech QuickCam, 718
LogLevel directive, 647
LOGNAME variable, 1035
logout command
bash, 940
shells, 927
tcsh, 956
logrotate program, 161
logs. *See* **log files**
loopback devices, 1111
Loopback Encrypted
Filesystem HOWTO
Web site, 1111
loops
exiting, 992-993
for, 983
iterations, skipping, 993-994
until, 989-990
while, 988-989
loss scenarios, 346
destructive software, 355
hard drive failures, 359
malcontents, 357
memory errors, 359
mistyped commands, 347-348
output redirection and piping
errors, 348-349
root access users, 349
system crackers, 357
trojan horses, 354
user errors, 347
viruses, 354
worms, 354
low-level services, 530
lpd daemon, 410
LPRng suite, 410
ls command, 847-848
lsmod utility, 1098

M

%m character (command prompt), tcsh, 963

-m option

  amq utility, 430

  batch utility, 1027

  free utility, 1061

  gpasswd command, 891

  history command, 951

  useradd command, 874

-M device option (mkisofs command), 275

-m glob option (mkisofs command), 275

-m integer option (mkfs utility), 188

-M path option (mkisofs command), 275

m user command (mail utility), 584

m4 macros, 559

Macintosh networking, 1152-1153

macros, m4, 559

magic cookies, 1106

mail aliases. *See* aliases (mail)

Mail Distribution Agent (MDA), 554-555

mail hubs, 568, 578

mail spool directories, mounting, 175

Mail Transport Agents. *See* MTAs

Mail User Agent (MUA), 554-555

mail variable, 960

mail/mailx, 583-584

mailing lists, 42-43, 588-589

  AFS, 426

  aliases, 587-588

  archives, 590-591

  digest-only, 591-605

    aliases, 591-592

    digest config file, 601-605

    directory, 593

    follow-up postings, 603

    posting restrictions, 600

    primary list config file, 593-601

  digested, 589

  kernel patches, 1093-1094

  linux-kernel, 1093-1094

  linux-raid mailing list, 269

  moderated/unmoderated, 589

  open/closed, 590

  password storage, 591

  privacy, 590

  ProFTPD mailing list, 620

  Red Hat, 169

  Samba mailing lists, 491-492

  security, 590, 837-839

    Bugtraq, 838

    CERT-advisory, 838

    CIAC-notes, 838

    firewalls, 839

    Red Hat, 839

  wu-ftpd mailing list, 617-618

MAILTO environment variable, 1035

maintaining disaster recovery plans, 367

maintenance policies, 777

maintenance reports, 674-675

majordom/archives/digest only-sample directory, 605

majordomo listserver, 588-589

  archives, 590-591

  digest-only lists, 591-605

    aliases, 591-592

    digest config file, 601-605

    directory, 593

    follow-up postings, 603

    posting restrictions, 600

    primary list config file, 593-601

  digested lists, 589

  moderated/unmoderated lists, 589

  open/closed lists, 590

  password storage, 591

  privacy, 590

  security, 590

make bzImage command, 1133

make clean command, 1132

make commands, 1132-1133

make dep command, 1132

make modules command, 1133

make modules install command, 1133

make targets, 1132

make tool, 1014-1015

make zImage command, 1133

makefile, 1126-1127

malloc file, 1076

management tools

  groupadd command, 884

  groupdel command, 884

  groupmod command, 885

  grpck command, 885

managing

  chains, ipchains utility, 811

  filesystem space, 198

    local/shared filesystems, 204

    quota hard/soft limits, 206

    quotas, 206-209

    space usage, monitoring, 199-204

  user requests

    email strategy, 900

    help desks. See help desks

    open door strategy, 899

*planning user
management approach,
902-903*
*scheduled user request
times, 900-901*
*setting request forms,
918-919*
WREQ help desks, 914, 917
users, 918
attitude issues, 896
documenting policies, 897
favoritism, 896
intranet policy posting, 897
*overly independent users,
920-921*
*policy exceptions,
897-898, 922*
*policy review/revision,
898-899*
setting policies, 896
user questions, 921
*users who resist training,
919-920*
mandatory aliases, 587
manning help desks, 905
map daemon option
(/etc/exports file,) 422
map nis option (/etc/exports
file), 422
map static option
(/etc/exports file), 422
mapping NetWare/Linux
usernames automatically,
510-511
mars-nwe server, starting,
512-513
mars_ nwe package,
nwserv.conf file
automatically mapping
NetWare/Linux usernames,
510-511
DOS client password
handling, 505-506
IPX device configuration, 502,
504

IPX route flags, saving,
504-505
network number
configuration, 501-502
non-privileged user/group ids,
506-507
printer configuration,
511-512
servername configuration,
500-501
startup sanity checks, 511
supervisor login, 507, 509
user logins, 509-510
version spoofing, 505
volume configuration,
499-500
Martin Stover's NetWare
Emulator. *See* mars_ nwe
package
masks, 377
masquerading, 558
master boot record (MBR),
112-113
master browsers, 462-463
master servers, 400
master zones (BIND), 402
math expressions, 996
math operators
(expressions), 981-982
mattrib command, 289
maxartsize parameter
(inn.conf file), 686
max_ change parameter
(/etc/shadow file), 868
mbadblocks command, 289
mbone (multicast back-
bone), 719
data flow, 719-720
multi-casting, 720-721
MBR (master boot record),
112-113
mcd command, 289
mcopy command, 290
md driver, 234
md file, 1077

MD5-encrypted passwords,
encrypting, 744
MDA (Mail Distribution
Agent), 554-555
mdel command, 290
mdeltree command, 290
mdir command, 290
mdu command, 290
ME entry, newsfeeds file,
689
media (backup)
autoloading mechanisms,
335-336
data storage capacity, 335
device/software compatibility,
335
floppies, 322
information resources, 334
kernel support, 335
rewritable CD-ROMs, 322
selecting, 334-335
storing, 341
multiple copies, 342
offsite, 342
onsite, 341
*tape escrow services,
342-343*
tapes, 322
*4mm DDS (Digital Data
Storage), 337*
*8mm/AITs (Advanced
Intelligent Tapes),
338-339*
*ATAPI (AT Attachment
Packet Interface) drives,
340*
autoloaders, 335-336
*DLTs (Digital Linear
Tapes), 338-339*
floppy tape drives, 339-340
information resources, 334
*SCSI (Small Computer
System Interface) drives,
340-341*
selecting, 334-337

transfer rates, 335

writable CD-ROMs, 321

Zip/Jaz drives, 322

MeetingPoint, 736

%MEM process field (top utility), 1057

Mem monitor field (top utility), 1056

members parameter (/etc/gshadow file), 869

member_ list parameter (/etc/group file), 867

meminfo file, 1076

memory errors, 359

memory section (vmstat utility), 1059

Memory type range register (MTRR), 1104

memory. See RAM

message-ids, 672

messages

logs, interpreting, 161-163

startup, viewing, 144

metacycbuffs, 692

methods, 90

proc filesystem, 91

checking devices, 101-107

numbered directories, 91-98

process status tools, 98-99

mformat command, 290

micq, 732-733

microphones, Internet telephony, 718

mil domain, 398

minimizing partitioning, 176-177

Minix filesystem, 197

minlen=n argument (pam_ cracklib module), 748

min_ change parameter (/etc/shadow file), 868

mirroring (RAID), 230

N-way mirrors, 241-242

with multiple striped arrays, 243-244

misplacing wild card characters, 347-348

mistyping commands, 347-348

mkdigest command, 589

mkfs utility, 187-188

mkisofs command, 275-280

mkraid command, 235-236

mkswap command, 1073

mlabel command, 290

mmd command, 290

mmove command, 290

/mnt directory, 86

mod jserv module, 664

mod perl module, 664

mod php module, 663

mod ssl module, 663

-mode2 command-line option (cdrecord command), 282

moderated mailing lists, 589

modinfo utility, 1098

modprobe utility, 1098

modules, 1094-1095

advantages, 1095

Apache, 654

adding, 654-655

conditional directive based, 655

default, 655-657

registry Web site, 657

applettalk.o, 514

Covalent Raven SSL, 663

GD perl module, downloading, 908-909

kernel source code layout, 1090

loadable, checking if loaded, 148

mod jserv, 664

mod perl, 664

mod php, 663

mod ssl, 663

ncpfs, installing, 497

PAM, 747-749

parport, 1108

support, 1105-1097

utilities, 1097-1098

when not to use, 1099

modules file, 1077

modutilities-2.1.121-14.i386.rpm package, 1097

monitor fields (top utility), 1056

monitor ports, 443

monitoring

networks, 436-437

network monitoring systems, 437-458

network monitoring systems, 437

promiscuous mode, 436

performance. *See performance monitoring*

security, 772

space usage (filesystems), 199-204

monolithic kernel, 1095

motf file, 765

mount command, 194-195, 426

mount options, fstab file, 214-215

mount points

creating, 292-293

fstab file, 214

mounting

filesystems, 426-427

autofs, 431-432

automount daemon, 427-430

ISO9660 images to disks, 282-284

mail spool directory, 175

NetWare volumes, 498

NFS options, 425
removable media devices,
  292-294
  automatically, 294-295
  /etc/fstab filesystem table
    modifications, 293-294
  mount points, creating,
    292-293
MOUNTPTS variable, 429
mouseconfig command, 36
moving jobs
  background, 937, 953
  foreground, 938, 953
mpage utility, 415
mrd command, 290
mren command, 290
-msinfo command-line
  option (cdrecord
  command), 281
mtab file, 1077
MTAs (Mail Transport
  Agents), 554-555
  exim, 559, 577
    configuration, 577
    mail hub, 578
    spam protection, 578-579
    workstations, 578
  generational, 558
  qmail, 559, 575
    configuration files, 576
    delivery options, 575-576
    message handling, 576
    user IDs, 576
    Web site, 577
  resources, 606
  selecting, 558-559
  sendmail, 558-559
    central mail server
      configuration, 562-563
    features/options, 559-560
    LAN workstation
      configuration, 562
    m4 macros, 559
    multiple domains,
      563-564

  standalone computer with
    dial-up connection
    configuration, 561
  standalone computer with
    permanent Internet
    connection
    configuration, 560
  testing, 565
  virtual user tables,
    564-565
  Web site, 560
  smail, 559, 566
    configuration, 567-568
    director files, 569-573
    router files, 573-575
    running, 575
    transports file, 575
    transports/directors/
      routers, 566-567
    workstation
      configuration, 568-569
mtools package, 289-290
mtools.conf file, 290-292
MTRR (memory type range
  register), 1104
mtx command, 336
mtype command, 290
MUA (Mail User Agent),
  554-555
-multi command-line option
  (cdrecord
  command), 281
multi-cast FAQ Web site, 721
multi-casting (mbone),
  720-721
multi-user systems, 1069
multicast backbone. *See*
  mbone
multimedia conferencing
  tools, 733-734
  CU-SeeMe, 736
  MeetingPoint, 736
  QSeeMe, 735-736
  Speak Freely, 734-735
  Web site, 734

multiple disks, 174-175
multiple email clients,
  581-582
  locking, 582-583
  spool access, 582
multiple installations. *See*
  cloning installs
multiple kernel versions,
  handling, 1127
  clone trees, 1128-1131
  generic kernel, 1127
MultiViews parameter
  (Options directive), 645
musical servers, 1053
Mylex controllers, 218
mzip command, 290

N

!-n command, 952
!n command, 952
\n character (command
  prompt), 944
\n escape sequence, 958, 994
%n character (command
  prompt), 963
-N command-line option
  fsck utility, 188
  ipchains utility, 811
  mount command, 194
  Squid, 666
-n option
  debugging scripts, 1005
  dirs command, 991
  echo command, 994
  fc command, 936
  history command, 951
  jobs command, 939, 954
  kill command, 939, 954
  popd command, 991
  sfdisk utility, 185
-N –number command-line
  option (sfdisk utility), 184
-N filename operator, 981

-n string operator, 981
N-way mirrors, 241-242
name servers, 397
   categories, 400
   development history, 397-398
   DNS. *See* DNS
   NIS (Network Information
     Service), 405-406
     name lookup configura-
      tion, 407-408
     running as NIS client,
      406-407
     running as NIS server,
      407
   UNIX/Linux systems,
     399-405
     BIND configuration,
      402-405
     resolver libraries,
      400-401
Name Service Switch file,
  408
name-based virtual hosts,
  659-662
   NameVirtualHost directive,
     659-660
   ServerAlias directive,
     660-662
names devices, 107
   alternatives, 108-109
   assigned major and
     minor numbers,
     107-108
   floppy drives, 273
   functions, 1001-1002
   groups
     /etc/group file, 866
     /etc/inetd.conf files, 533
   httpd.pid file, changing, 648
   IDE devices, 212-214
   login, 586
   SCSI devices, 223-225
   servers, 500-501
   tasks, 1057
   usernames, 533, 865

nameserver directive, 400
NameVirtualHost directive,
  659-660
NASA sunspot activity
  Web site, 300
National IT Salary Survey,
  8-9
native languages, kernel
  support for, 1123
navigating
   command line, 936
   history list, 935, 952
NCP (Netware Core
  Protocol), 1123
ncpfs module, installing,
  497
net domain, 398
/net directory, 1076
Netatalk, 1153
   configuration files, 515
   package, 513
   server, starting, 525
   Web site, 513
netcat utility, 854
netperm-table file, 801
.netrc file, 764
Netscape news reader, 708
netstat command, 385-386
NetWare, 495
   interoperability options,
     495-496
   IPX protocol support, adding,
     496
   Linux client, 497-498
   Linux server, 498, 500-512
     automatically mapping
      NetWare/Linux
      usernames, 510-511
     DOS client password
      handling, 505-506
     IPX device configuration,
      502-504
     IPX route flags, saving,
      504-505
     network number
      configuration, 501-502

     non-privileged user/group
      ids, 506-507
     printer configuration,
      511-512
     servername configura-
      tion, 500-501
     startup sanity checks, 511
     supervisor login, 507-509
     user logins, 509-510
     version spoofing, 505
     volume configuration,
      499-500
   mars-nwe server, starting,
     512-513
   networking concepts,
     496-497
   printer configuration, 498,
     511-512
   sanity checks, 511
   supervisor logins, 507-509
   user logins, 509-510
   usernames, automatically
     mapping to Linux user-
     names, 510-511
   versions, spoofing, 505
Netware Core Protocol
  (NCP), 1123
NetWare volumes,
  mounting, 498
Network Access Layer, 373
network filesystems, 198
Network Information
  Center (NIC), 397
Network Information
  Service. *See* NIS
network installs
   FTP installs, 54
   HTTP installs, 54
   NFS installs, 52-53
     network boot floppies, 53
     requirements, 52
network integration, 436
network interface cards
  (NICs), 149-150
network interfaces, 773

**network mapping (Trinux),
851-853**
network masks, 377
**network monitoring,
436-437**
  network monitoring systems,
  437
    access point, 437-438
    analysis engine, 441-442
    data capture, 438-441
    deployment, 443
    requirements of, 442-443
    sniffers, 444-451
    traffic analyzers, 451-458
    user interfaces, 442
  promiscuous mode, 436
  Trinux, 850-851
Network Research Group
  libpcap, 440
  tcpdump, 445
networks   *See also* sharing
  access point, 437-438
  administrative
    *administration server
      install customizations, 76*
    *administrative
      workstation install
      customizations, 76*
    *development server install
      customizations, 76*
    *development workstation
      install customizations, 76*
    *establishing machine
      classes, 69*
    *install customization,
      75-76*
    install templates, 75
  analysis engines, 441-442
  AppletTalk, 513, 525
    kernel support, 514
    *services, configuring,
      514-525*
  block devices, 1111
  complexity of, 436

connections
  *production network install
    templates, 70*
  setup function, 57, 59-60
data capture, 438-441
devices, 1115-1117
filesystems, 1121-1123
firewall example, 815-816
firewalls, 786
  absolute, 787
  *bastion host system,
    787-789*
  debugging, 817
  DNS servers, 817
  ipchains utility, 810-814
  *kernel configuration,
    792-793*
  *network configuration
    example, 815-816*
  options, 789-790
  *packet filtering, 790,
    805-809, 811, 813*
  *packet traversal through
    ipchains filters,
    813-814*
  *proxy servers, 787,
    790-791*
  *single-user machine
    example, 814*
  startup script, 807-809
  *user IDs/passwords
    database, 801-802*
frame types, 496
IPX, 496-497
kernel options, 1111-1112
  IP aliasing, 1113
  IP masquerading, 1113
  IP tunneling, 1113
  *IPX/Appletalk protocols,
    1114-1115*
  *TCP/IP packet-based
    firewalls, 1113*
  *TCP/IP protocol stack,
    1115*
  WAN routers, 1114

kernel support, 1105
NetWare, 495-497
  *interoperability options,
    495-496*
  IPX protocol support, 496
  Linux client, 497-498
  Linux server, 498-512
  mars-nwe server, 512-513
numbers
  configuring, 501-502
  retrieving from servers, 497
performance, 1067
printers, 482-483
production
  *establishing machine
    classes, 69*
  install customization, 77
  install templates, 69-74
protocol stack, 1091
servers, 497
switched networks, 451
TCP/IP network layers,
  372-373
  Application Layer, 375
  data unit names, 373
  Internet Layer, 373-374
  Network Access Layer, 373
  Transport Layer, 374-375
traffic, 436
  analyzing, 458-460
  bottlenecks, 457-458
user interfaces, 442
Windows networks
  *backup domain controller
    (BDC), 463*
  browsing interface, 462
  clients, 464
  domains, 462
  example of, 463-464
  master browsers, 462-463
  *primary domain controller
    (PDC), 463*
  resource servers, 463
  workgroups, 462
wireless, 1116

new files, finding, 303-304
option (chown command),
890
newgrp command, 888
news database directory,
699-700
news readers, 705
  alternatives, 711
  graphical clients, 707-710
  text clients, 705-707
news servers. *See* Usenet
servers
news.daily script, 700
/news/db directory,
699-700
news2mail, 711
newsfeeds, 674, 688-691
  CNFS storage, 690
  controlchan entry, 691
  ME entry, 689
  site entries, 690
  timehash storage, 690
  traditional storage, 690
newsgroups, 43-44
  alt.security, 837
  backup media information,
    334
  comp.admin.policy, 837
  comp.os.linux.hardware, 334
  comp.periphs.scsi, 334
  comp.risks, 837
  comp.security.announce, 836
  comp.security.firewalls, 836
  comp.security.misc, 836
  comp.security.unix, 836
  comp.unix.admin, 837
  comp.unix.wizards, 837
  comp.virus, 836
  mapping into storage classes,
    693-695
  Samba newsgroups, 492
  security, 836-837
  services, 531

  system failures, 169
  updating automatically, 1020
newsmasters, 587
newusers command, 881
NFS, 1121
  client configuration, 424-426
  installs, 52-53
    network boot floppies, 53
    requirements, 52
  kernel space, 418
  kernel support verification,
    424
  mounting options, 425
  security, 420
  server configuration, 418-419
    /etc/exports file
    configuration, 421-424
    software installations,
    418-419
  software, installing, 418-419
ngrep utility, 850
NI process field (top utility), 1056
NIC (Network Information
Center), 150-151, 397
nice command
  process management, 1066
  tcsh, 956
NICs (network interface
cards), 149-150
NIS (Network Information
Service), 405-406
  name lookup configuration,
    407-408
  running as NIS client,
    406-407
  running as NIS server, 407
NIST (National Institute of
Standards and Technol-
ogy) Web site, 833
nmap program, 849-851
nmblookup utility, 465
\nnn character (command
prompt), 944
\nnn escape sequence,
958, 994

nnrp.access file, 698-699
nnrpdoverstats parameter
(inn.conf file), 687
NNTPCache, 675-676,
702-704
  installing, 702
  nntpcache.servers file listing,
    702-704
  Web site, 676
no root squash option
(/etc/exports file), 422
–no-reread command-line
option (sfdisk utility),
185
noaccess option (/etc/
exports file), 422
noatime option, 175, 195
noauto option, 195, 293
nobeep variable, 961
nobody alias, 587
NoCem (spam filter), 701
noclobber variable, 961
nodev option (mount
command), 195
noexec option
  mount command, 195
  NFS mounting, 425
-nofix command-line
option (cdrecord
command), 281
noglob variable, 961
nologin file, 760
non alpha characters, 877
non-interactive bash
sessions, 941
non-interactive modes,
928
non-login interactive
shells, 941
None parameter
(AllowOverride
directive), 651
-norc option (bash
startup), 941
noretrieve function, 759

NORMAL_ VGA variable, 1127

-nosuid option

mount command, 195

mounting removable media devices, 293

NFS mounting, 425

not operator (!), 979

notebooks, APM (Advanced Power Management), 1108

notify command, 955

nowait services, 532

nprint command, 498

nsend command, 498

nsswitch.conf file, 408

NT Domains, creating on Linux servers, 1149

ntop, 451, 850

command-line options, 453-454

demonstration, 457-458

execution modes, 454

installing, 452-453

traffic views, 456-458

NVRAM devices, 1119

nwserv.conf file

DOS client password handling, 505-506

IPX device configuration, 502-504

IPX route flags, saving, 504-505

network number configuration, 501-502

non-privileged user/group ids, 506-507

printer configuration, 511-512

servername configuration, 500-501

startup sanity checks, 511

supervisor login, 507, 509

user logins, 509-511

version spoofing, 505

volume configuration, 499-500

O

o option (finger command), 889

-o option

free utility, 1061

mount command, 195

useradd command, 874

usermod command, 893

-O file command-line option (sfdisk utility), 185

-o filename command-line option (mkisofs command), 275

-O filename operator, 980

-o options option (exportfs command), 423

ocredit=n argument (pam_ cracklib module), 749

official kernel patches, 1092-1093

offsite backup media storage, 342

OLDPWD variable, 943

onsite backup media storage, 341

open mailing lists, 590

Open Shortest Path First protocol (OSPF), 391

open source backup software, 328

open source development

Freshmeat, 41

Linuxcare, 39

OpenSSH Web site, 769

operating systems, backing up, 310-311

operator menu script, 822, 824-826

operators, 973

file test, 980-981

logical, 979

math, 981-982

precedence, 982

string test, 981

/opt directory, 86

option control-flag parameters (PAM), 746

Options directive, 645

Options parameter (AllowOverride directive), 651

or operator (||), 979

org domain, 398

Organization parameter (inn.conf file), 686

organizational domains, 398-399

original extended filesystem, 198

OS images. *See* cloning installs

OSPF (Open Shortest Path First) protocol, 391

OSS drivers Web site, 1124

output fields (free utility), 1061

output redirection

bash, 933-934

piping errors, 348-349

tcsh, 950

outsourcing Usenet servers, 675, 702-704

overview.ctl file, 695

overviewmmap parameter (inn.conf file), 687

overwriting files, 864

ownership

customizing, 871-872

files, 890

groups, 889

P

p option (finger command), 889
-p option
   amq utility, 430
   fsck utility, 188
   jobs command, 939, 954
   kill command, 939, 954
   su command, 892
-P option (ipchains utility), 811
-p filename operator, 980
-P opt command-line option (cfdisk utility), 182
-p prompt command-line option (sudo command), 821
-p prototype user option (edquota command), 208
p [number] command (mail utility), 584
packages
   am-utils, 428
   fdutils, 1110
   Linux Cross Reference, 1091
   mars_ nwe, 498-499
   modutilities-2.1.121-14.i386.rpm, 1097
   mtools
      commands, 289-290
      removable media device access, 289-292
   netatalk, 513
   PGP, 678
   RPM, NFS server, 418
   SSH (Secure Shell), 831
   system, upgrading, 196
   WU-FTPD, 831
   xinetd, 831
   ypbind, 406
packet dropping, 717
packet filtering
   chains, 811

firewalls, 790, 805, 811-813, 1144
   connections, forwarding, 809
   IP forwarding, 807-809
   ipfwadm program, 805-806
   Linux, 805
   with proxy services, 790
   traversal through ipchains filters, 813-814
Packet Radio Web site, 1116
packet sniffers (Trinux), 849-850
packets, 373, 719
PAM (Pluggable Authentication Modules), 545, 746-749
pam env.conf file, etc/security directory, 762
pam_ cracklib module
   arguments
      debug, 748
      difok=n, 748
      lcredit=n, 749
      minlen=n, 748
      ocredit=n, 749
      retry=, 748
      type=(something), 748
      ucredit=n, 748
   PAM, 545, 747-749
parallel port IDE devices, 1111
parallel ports
   kernel support, 1107-1108
   serial device combination networking, 1116
   storage devices, 285
      ATAPI/IDE devices, 288-289
      kernel support, adding, 286-287
      Zip drives, 287-288

parallel printers, 1119
parameters. *See* specific parameter names
paride driver, 286
parport module, 1108
partial backups, 309, 314
partially compatible implementations, 84
partially compliant implementations, 84
partitioning, 175
   cfdisk utility, 181-182
   Disk Druid, 185-186
   fdisk utility, 177-181
   minimizing, 176-177
   partitions each filesystem, 175-176
   sfdisk utility, 182-185
partitions
   cloning installs, 61-62, 64-65
   hard drive Red Hat installs, 51-52
   kernel support, 1123
   remounting, securing filesystems, 771
   repairing, rescue disks, 156-157
   swap, 1073-1075
passive terminators, 222-223
passwd command, 892, 927
password module-type, 746
password parameter
   /etc/group file, 866
   /etc/passwd file, 865
   /etc/shadow file, 867
password-free access (SSH), 549-550
passwords
   Apache directory protection, 649-651
   authentication, PAM, 746
   etc/group file, 745
   etc/gshadow file, 869

etc/passwd file, 743, 865
etc/shadow, 744-745, 867
expiration details, 880
files, updating in batch mode,
  881
groups, 866
length, 877
majordomo listserver, 591
MD5-encrypted, 744
NetWare Linux servers,
  505-506
non alpha characters 877
policies, 749
preventing cracking, 745-749
shadow, 744
users, setting, 873
validation rules, 877-879
**passwords parameter
(/etc/gshadow file), 869**
patches
  kernel, 1091
    ac (Alan Cox) patches,
      1094
    announcements, 1093
    applied to standard source
      code tree
      (list of), 1088
    authors, 1092
    finding, 1093-1094
    official/unofficial,
      compared, 1092-1093
    Red Hat, 1087-1089
    sources, 1092
    version, 1092
  LILO (LInux LOader), 125
  for original Linux source tree,
    235
**Path headers (Usenet
servers), 672**
PATH variable, 943
**Pathhost parameter
(inn.conf file), 686**
pathj variable, 961
**pathnames (bash
commands), 995-996**

paths
  escalation
    help desk priorities, 905
    WREQ help desk, 908
  /etc/inetd.conf files, 533
pause program, 191-194
pausing bash scripts, 998
**PC-to-PC communications,
733**
**PC-to-telephone
communications, 733**
PCI device errors, 146-147
pci file, 1076
pci-config utility, 151
**PDC (primary domain
controller), 463**
**peer entry, incoming.conf
file, 692**
performance
  bottlenecks, 1049
    duration, 1050
    focal point location, 1051
    frequency, 1050
    location, 1050
    tuning importance,
      1051-1052
  costs/benefits, 1052-1053
  enhancements, 1054
  hardware costs, 1053
  musical servers, 1053
  monitoring. *See* performance
    monitoring
  networks, 1067
  RAM
    additional, 1070
    amount needed,
      1068-1069
    buying, 1070
    requirements, calculating,
      1069-1070
  swap space, 1071
    assigning, 1072-1074
    calculating, 1071-1072
    prioritization, 1073

    swap files, 1074-1075
    swap partitions,
      1073-1075
  system requirements/needs,
    1053-1054
  tuning, 1048-1049
  unrequired services, 1052
**performance monitoring,
1055**
  console-based utilities, 1055
    free, 1060-1061
    time, 1061-1062
    top, 1055-1058
    uptime, 1060
    vmstat, 1058-1060
  graphical utilities, 1062
    Xload, 1063
    Xosview, 1062-1063
  over time example,
    1064-1065
  process management,
    1065-1066
  real time/gathered
    performance data
    compared, 1064-1065
**Perl (practical extraction and
reporting language), 1007**
  GD Perl module,
    downloading, 908-909
  INN source installation, 678
  scripting, 664, 1007
    command-line
      parameters, 1008
    comments, 1008
    control structures,
      1009-1010
    executable scripts,
      creating, 1008
    features, 1007
    printing, 1008
    resources, 1010
    scripts, creating,
      1008-1009
  Web site, 1010

perl command, 30
Perl/Apache integration project Web site, 664
permissions
    groups, 887
    users, 862, 878
person-to-person voice communications, 733-734
personal backup scripts, 353
personnel, help desks, 905
pfdisk package, 128
PGP package, 678
PHP server-side scripting, 663
PHP Web site, 664
physical security, 767
    backup media, 768
    floppy drive booting, disabling, 767
    LILO settings, 767-768
physical system attacks, 742
PID process field (top utility),1056
PidFile directive, 648
pine, 584-585
ping, 1078-1079
Ping of Death, 448
pipes
    bash, 932-933
    tcsh, 950
piping and redirection errors, 348-349
piping errors, 348-349
planning
    disaster recovery, 364
        developing, 364
        estimating recovery costs, 365-366
        fire example, 365
        fire example cost analysis, 365
        fire example preventative measures, 366
        maintaining, 367

outlining data loss scenarios, 365
outlining preventative measures, 366
publishing, 367
install template implementation, 78-79
    creating directory hierarchies, 77-79
    sample procedure, 77
user management strategy, 902-903
plug-and-play devices, 145-146, 1108
Pluggable Authentication Modules. *See* PAM
pnmtops utility, 415
policies
    documenting, 897
    exceptions, 897-898, 922
    intranet posting, 897
    maintenance, 777
    reaction, 777
    reviewing/revising, 898-899
    security, developing, 775-776
    setup, 776
    system
        enforcing compliance, 778
        infractions, 779
        security, 777-778
    user management issues, 896
pools (backup media), 319
POP (Post Office Protocol), 556
popd command, 991-992
port redirection, 675
positional parameters, 977
post-create command, 878
postmasters, 587
postscript.cfg file, 415
pound symbol (#), 972
power supply, 132
poweroff command, 139
ppa driver, 286
PPP protocol, 1116

practical extraction and reporting language. *See* Perl
-prcap command-line option (cdrecord command), 282
pre-delete command (user accounts), 878
precedence (operators), 982
precmd variable, 963
predefined cron jobs, 1019
–prefix=PATH option (configure program), 679
preventing
    data loss
        data recovery companies, 361
        dd command, 360-361
        malcontents, 358
        RAID, 359
        RCS, 351-352
        system crackers, 358
        system log watchers, 360
        tape backups, 360
    destructive software
        environment settings, 356
        software integrity checkers, 356
        victim hosts, 356
        virus scanning software, 355-356
    password cracking, 745-749
    system access, 358
    user errors, 349
        backups, 353
        revision control systems, 351-352
    user errors with aliases, 350-351
PRI process field (top utility), 1056
primary domain controller (PDC), 463
primary lists (digest-only mailing lists), 593-601

print queues, configuring, 411
  access, granting, 416
  local printer, 411-416
  remote printers, 416-417
printcap file, 414
printenv command, 956
printers
  GhostScript supported, 411-413
  local, 411-416
  NetWare configuration, 498, 511-512
  networking, 482-483
  parallel, 1119
  remote, 416-417
  sharing, 411
    access, granting, 416
    local printer configuration, 411-416
    remote printer configuration, 416-417
printexitvalue variable, 960
printf command, 997-998
printing
  bash, 943, 994, 997-998
  groups, 891
  Perl, 1008
  Samba services, 1151
  variable path contents, 960
printtool utility
  local printers, 413
  remote printers, 417
priorities, help desks
  escalation paths, 905
  setting prioritization capabilities, 904
  WREQ, 908
privacy, mailing lists, 590
private groups, 878
private keys (RSA authentication), 549
privilege system attacks, 742

privileges
  granting, 820-829
  operator menu implementation example, 826-827
  operator menu script example, 822-826
proc directory, 1076-1077
proc filesystem, 91, 1076-1078
  checking devices, 101-107
  numbered directories, 91-98
  system failure diagnosis, 147-148
/proc/filesystems file, 424
/proc/interrupts file, 147
/proc/modules file, 148
/proc/pci file, 146
/proc/sys directory, 1106
process fields (top utility), 1056-1057
process management, 1065-1066
process status tools, 98
  gtop, 99
  kpm, 99
  ktop, 99
  procinfo, 99
processes monitor field (top utility), 1056
processors, kernel configuration options, 1103-1104
procinfo, 99
procps package, 98-99
procs section (vmstat utility), 1059
production networks
  establishing machine classes, 69
  install customization, 77
  install templates, 69-74
    network connectivity support, 70
    packages, 70-74
    runtime support, 70
    utilities, 70

ProFTPD, 619, 831
  installing, 619-620
  mailing list, 620
program access, 780-781
programming tool
  CVS (Concurrent Versions System), 1015-1016
  make, 1014-1015
  RCS (Revision Control System), 1015
programs. *See* command-line utilities; software; tools
project delays, data recovery costs, 363
promiscuous mode, 436
prompt variable, 961
prompt2 variable, 961
prompt3 variable, 961
proprietary backup software, 328
protocols
  Appletalk, 1114-1115
  BGP, 391
  /etc/inetd.conf files, 532
  Exterior Gateway, 391
  FTP, 54
  Hello, 391
  HTTP, 54
  ICMP, 374
  IMAP, 556
  Internet, 372
  Internet telephony, 717
  IPX, 496, 1114-1115
  IS-IS, 391
  OSP, 391
  POP, 556
  PPP, 1116
  RIP, 391
  RIP-2, 391
  routing, 390-392
  SLIP, 1116
  SMTP, 555
  TCP, 374
  TCP/IP. *See* TCP/IP
  Telnet

benefits, 541
drawbacks, 542
process, 542
security, 547-548
substitution codes, 542
X11 connections, 548
UDP, 374
X.25, 1114
proxies, Trinux tools, 853
proxy servers, 790
firewalls, 787, 790-791, 1144
programs, 791
SOCKS, 795-798
squid, 798-800
TIS FWTK (Trusted
Information Systems
FireWall ToolKit),
800-804
transproxy, 793-795
ps command, 98
intrusion detection, 847-848
jobs running (list of), 938,
953
PS1 variable, 943
PS2 variable, 943
PSTN (Public Switched
Telephone), 733
Public Domain Korn shell,
964-965
public keys (RSA
authentication), 549
Public Switched Telephone
(PSTN), 733
public-key cryptography,
549
publishing disaster
recovery plans, 367
pushd command, 992
pwd command
bash, 940
tcsh, 956
PWD variable, 943
Python, 1012-1013

Q

-q option,
at utility, 1022
atq utility, 1028
batch utility, 1027
mkfs utility, 188
routed daemon, 392
top utility, 1058
-q –quiet command-line
option (sfdisk utility),
185
q command (mail utility),
584
qmail, 559, 575
configuration files, 576
delivery options, 575-576
message handling, 576
user IDs, 576
Web site, 577
QoS (Quality of Service),
716
QSeeMe, 735-736
QueSO utility, 852
question mark (?), 929-930,
946
queues (print), configur-
ing, 411
access, granting, 416
local printer, 411-416
remote printers, 416-417
quick archives, 326
Quota Mini-Howto Web
site, 209
quota tools Web site, 205
quotacheck utility, 205
quotaoff utility, 205
quotaon utility, 205
quotas
checkings, 771
creating, 205
hard/soft limits, 206, 771
implementing, 206-208
option examples, 208-209

setting, securing filesystems,
771-772
support, adding, securing
filesystems, 771
quoting, 942

R

\r escape sequence, 958,
994
-r option
bindkey command, 957
exportfs command, 423
fc command, 936
fsck utility, 189
history command, 951
mkisofs command, 275
-R option
chgrp command, 890
chown command, 890
crontab command, 1034
declare command, 975
fsck utility, 188
gpasswd command, 891
hash command, 995
implementing quotas, 207
ipchains utility, 811
mkisofs command, 275
mount command, 194
read command, 997
sfdisk utility, 185
useradd command, 874
userdel command, 883
-r filename operator, 980
r [number] command
(mail utility), 584
R-commands, 543
authentication, 543
rexec, 543
trust-based, 544-545
/etc/hosts.equiv files,
545-546
rcp, 543

rexec, 543

.rhosts files, 545

    account-level
       equivalence, 547

    entries, 546-547

rlogin, 543-544

rsh, 543

security, 547-548

X11 connections, 548

RAID (Redundant Array of Inexpensive Disks), 228, 305

    array types

       linear arrays, 239-240

       RAID level 0 arrays, 240-241

       RAID level 1 arrays, 241-242

       RAID level 4 arrays, 242-243

       RAID level 5 arrays, 242-243

    Case for RAID paper, 228

    commands, 235

       ckraid, 237

       mkraid, 235-236

       raidadd, 238

       raidhotadd, 235-238

       raidhotremove, 235-238

       raidrun, 238

       raidstart, 235-238

       raidstop, 235-238

    controller drivers, 267

       AMI MegaRAID, 268

       DAC960, 267

       EATA/DMA, 268

    data loss, preventing, 359

    devices

       adding, 238

       booting from, 265-266

       configuring, 238

       creating, 237

       external RAID devices, 268

       removing, 238

hardware RAID, 266-267

history of Linux support, 228

hot reconstruction, 239

hot-swapping, 229

implementing, 244-265

levels, 230

    RAID level 0, 233-234

    RAID level 0/1, 234

    RAID level 1, 230

    RAID level 2, 231

    RAID level 3, 231

    RAID level 4, 231

    RAID level 5, 232

    RAID level 10, 234

mailing list, 269

md driver, 234

mirroring, 230

    with multiple striped arrays, 243-244

    N-way mirrors, 241-242

objectives of, 228

    performance, 229-230

    reduced cost, 228-229

    reliability, 229

raidtab configuration file, 236-237

software, 1111

striping, 233-234

raidadd command, 238

raidhotadd command, 235-238

raidhotremove command, 235-238

raidrun command, 238

raidstart command, 235-238

raidstop command, 235-238

raidtab configuration file, 236-237

RAM (Random Access Memory), 1068

    adding, 1070

    amount needed, 1068

       multi-user systems, 1069

       single-user systems, 1068

    buying, 1070

    disk, 1099

    requirements, calculating, 1069-1070

raw sockets, 532

rawrite utility, 53

rc file, 1077

rc scripts, 130-131

rc.news script, 700

-rcfile option (bash startup), 941

rcp command, 543

RCS (Revision Control System), 351-352, 1015

rdev command, 1126

reachability information, 390

reaction policies, 777

read-only variables, 976

reading news, 705

    graphical clients, 707-710

    news reader alternatives, 711

    text clients, 705-707

readonly command, 976

real-time performance monitoring, 1064-1065

real-time clocks, 1119

reboot command, 139

rebuilding LILO, 155-156

recovering data
   costs, 362-366
   data recovery companies, 361
   dd command, 360-361
   deleted files, 160
   plans, 364-367
      developing, 364
      estimating recovery costs,
      365-366
      fire example, 365
      fire example cost
      analysis, 365
      fire example preventative
      measures, 366
      maintaining, 367
      outlining data loss
      scenarios, 365
      outlining preventative
      measures, 366
      publishing, 367
   tape backups, 360
**Red Hat Installation Guide
Web site, 186**
**Red Hat Linux box online,
310**
   application backups,
   after install, 311
   daily operations backups, 312
      graphical tool changes,
      312
      site strategies, 313
      text editor changes, 312
   operating system backups,
   310-311
**Red Hat mailing list, 169,
839**
Red Hat Secure Server, 668
**Red Hat Web site, 397, 775,
834**
redir port redirector, 853
redir program, 675
**redirection and piping
errors, 348-349**
redisplay command, 959

**Redundant Array of
Inexpensive Disks.
See RAID**
**–reference option
(chown command), 890**
**registering new binary
types, 1106-1107**
regular expressions, 18, 21
   bracket expressions, 21
   demonstration of, 19-21
   meta characters, 18-19
**regular tasks, automating,
1020-1021**
**reinstalling, system,
856-857**
relaying, 558
**reliability of backup
software, 328**
**remembering passwords,
749**
remote login services, 531
**remote machines, full
backups to, 307-308**
**remote printers,
configuring, 416-417**
**remote servers, automated
email retrieval, 1020**
**remount option (mount
command), 195**
remounting partitions, 771
**removable media devices,
272**
   access, 289
      combinations, 296
      mtools package, 289-292
   CD-R drives, 274-285
   CD-ROM drives, 273-274
   CD-RW drives, 274-285
   floppy drives, 272-273
   mounting, 292-294
      automatically, 294-295
      /etc/fstab filesystem table
      modifications, 293-294
      mount points, creating,
      292-293

   parallel port storage devices,
   285
      ATAPI/IDE devices,
      288-289
      kernel support, adding,
      286-287
      Zip drives, 287-288
renice command, 1066
repairing
   filesystems, 188-194
   partitions, rescue disks,
   156-157
**replies, help desk feedback
mechanisms, 904, 908**
**reports, help desk, 904,
908**
repquota utility, 205
requests (users)
   managing
      email strategy, 900
      help desks. See help desks
      open door strategy, 899
      planning user manage-
      ment approach,
      902-903
      scheduled user request
      times, 900-901
   open door strategy, 899
   setting request forms,
   918-919
**required control-flag
parameters (PAM), 746**
**requisite control-flag
parameters (PAM), 746**
rescue disks, 152-153
   creating, 153-154
   deleted file recovery, 160
   emergency file copying,
   157-159
   image, 153
   rebuilding LILO, 155-156
   repairing partitions, 156-157
   rescue sessions, starting, 154
   rewriting configuration files,
   156
   toolkit, 155

rescue sessions, starting, 154
resolver libraries, 400-401
Resource Records (RRs), 404-405
resource servers, 463
resources
backup media information, 334
MTAs, 606
Perl, 1010
security, 834-836
Linux Portal Web sites, 835
mailing lists, 837-839
Red Hat Web site, 834
Usenet newsgroups, 836-837
USENIX Web site, 834
security tools, 832-833
spam, 607
system failures, 169
Usenet servers, 711
users, limiting, 780
restore command, 324-326
restoring files, 320-321, 324-326
restricting access time, 779
retry=n argument (pam_ cracklib module), 748
return codes, fsck utility
handling, 189-190
interpreting, 190-194
return command, 1002
reviewing policies, 898-899
revising policies, 898-899
Revision Control System (RCS), 351-352, 1015
rewritable CD-ROMs, 322
rewriting configuration files, 156
rexec command, 543
.rhosts file, 545, 763
account-level equivalence, 547
entries, 546-547
RIP (Routing Information Protocol), 391

RIP-2 (Routing Information Protocol Version 2), 391
rlogin command, 543-544
rm aliases, 350
rmmod utility, 1098
rmstar variable, 960
ro option
/etc/exports file, 422
mount command, 195
root access users, 349
/root directory, 84-85
/bin directory, 85-87
/boot directory, 85
/dev directory, 85-86
/etc directory, 85-86
/home directory, 86
/lib directory, 86
/mnt directory, 86
/opt directory, 86
/root directory, 86
/sbin directory, 85
/tmp directory, 86
/usr directory, 87-88
/var directory, 88-89
root domains (DNS), 398
root servers (DNS), 398
root user, 587
Rootshell Web site, 833
rotation schedule (backups), 315
casual home users, 315
dump program configuration for installation level, 317-318
rationale, 316
workstations, 318
files, restoring, 320-321
incremental backup storage, 319
rationale, 318
set capacity, 319-320
route flags (IPX), saving, 504-505
routed daemon, 392-394

router files, 573-575
mail hub, 574-575
workstation, 573-574
routers, 384, 566
routing, 383-384
configuring, 384
daemons, 392-394
gated, 394
routed, 392-394
dynamic, 384, 390
daemons, 392-394
gated daemon, 394
gated daemon configuration, 395-397
protocols, 390-392
routed daemon, 392-394
gated.conf file configuration, 395-397
host routing, 395
interior gateway, 395-396
gateways, 384
protocols, 390-392
routing tables, 385
sample, 388
viewing, 385-386
static routes, 384
adding, 387-389
adding/deleting, 388
deleting, 387
Routing Information Protocol (RIP), 391
Routing Information Protocol Version 2 (RIP-2), 391
routing problems, detecting, 449
routing tables, 385
sample, 388
viewing, 385-386
Roxen Challenger, 667-668
rpm command, 428
RPM packages, 418, 676-678
rpm utility, 356
RRs (Resource Records), 404-405

RSA authentication
  public-key cryptography, 549
  SSH, 549
rsh command, 543
rsize option, NFS
  mounting, 425
RSS process field
  (top utility), 1057
rules. *See* policies
runlevel editor, 136
runlevels, 134-139
running
  BitchX, 728
  fetchmail, 580-581
  gated daemon, 394
  ircII, 724-725
  JavaICQ, 731
  licq, 732
  micq, 732-733
  QSeeMe, 736
  smail, 575
  Speak Freely, 735
  system as NIS client, 406-407
  system as NIS server, 407
  TCP/IP over Ethernet, 377
    Ethernet cards/cables,
      378
    Ethernet collision
      examination, 380
    Ethernet hubs, 379
    Ethernet media selec-
      tions, 380-381
    Ethernet switches,
      379-380
  Usenet servers, 674-675
  X-Chat, 727
  Zircon, 726
runtime support, 70
rw option
  /etc/exports file, 422
  mount command, 195

S

\s character (command
  prompt), 944
-s command-line option
  amq utility, 430
  atd, 1029
  bindkey command, 957
  chsh command, 891
  free utility, 1061
  fsck utility, 188
  history command, 951
  httpd script, 641
  kill command, 939, 954
  mount command, 194
  Squid, 666
  su command, 892
  sudo command, 821
  top utility, 1058
  user administration, 1160
-s filename operator,
  980-981
-s partition command-line
  option (fdisk utility), 178
-s sectors command-line
  option
  cfdisk utility, 182
  sfdisk utility, 185
-s option
  useradd command, 874
  usermod command, 893
-s –show-size command-
  line option (sfdisk uti-
  lity), 184
SAGE (Systems Adminis-
  tration Guild), 9-11
SAINT (Security Adminis-
  trator's Integrated
  Network Tool), 851
salaries of systems
  administrators, 8-9
Samba, 462, 465
  Centennial School District
    case study, 1148-1151
  as client OS, 484-487

  installing, 1149
  mailing lists, 491-492
  newsgroups, 492
  printing services, 1151
  Red Hat access from
    Windows PCs, 1152
  as server OS, 487
  shares, accessing, 468
  smb.conf configuration file,
    476-478
    custom sections, 483-484
    [global] section, 478-480
    [homes] section, 481-482
    [printers] section,
      482-483
    setting up, 484, 487-488
    testing, 485-489
  utilities, 465-466
    Samba Web Administra-
      tion Tool (SWAT),
      471-473, 476
    smbclient, 466-469
    smbmount, 469
    smbumount, 469-470
  Web address, 492
Samba Web Administra-
  tion Tool (SWAT),
  471-473, 476
  Globals screen, 472
  home screen, 472
  Password screen, 473
  Printers screen, 473
  Shares screen, 473
  Status screen, 473
  View screen, 473
sanity checks (NetWare),
  511
SATAN (Security Analysis
  Tool for Analyzing
  Networks), 829
savehist variable, 951
saving
  IPX route flags, 504-505
  kernel configuration, 1126
scalability issues, 55

-scanbus command-line option (cdrecord command), 281
scanners (security), 829-830
scenarios, data loss, 346
    destructive software, 355
    disasters, 361
    fire example, 365-366
    hard drive failures, 359
    malcontents, 357
    memory errors, 359
    mistyped commands, 347-348
    outlining, 365
    output redirection and piping
        errors, 348-349
    root access users, 349
    system crackers, 357
    trojan horses, 354
    user errors, 347
    viruses, 354
    worms, 354
scheduled tasks, 880
scheduling user request time, 900-901
screened hosts, 789
screened subnets, 789
ScriptAlias directive, 652
scripting interpreters, 970-971
scripting languages
    Eiffel, 1013-1014
    Perl. *See* Perl scripting
    Python, 1012-1013
    Tcl/Tk, 1010-1011
scripting shells. *See* shell scripting
scripts
    autofs, 294
    backup, creating, 323
        full backups/file restoration, 324-326
        quick archiving, 326
        tar command, 323-324

bash
    filenames, converting to lowercase, 1003-1004
    specific words in files, finding, 1004-1005
CGI scripting, 652-653
checkspace, 199-204
cloning (clone trees), 1128-1131
custom installation, 1131-1132
debugging, 1005-1006
etc/rc.d/init.d/amd, 429
executable, 971
executing, 971
here-documents, 183
httpd
    command-line options, 641
    starting/stopping Apache, 640-641
news.daily, 700
Perl, 664
    creating, 1008-1009
    executable, 1008
PHP server-side scripting, 663
rc.news, starting INN, 700
standardizing, 972
system initialization scripts, 112, 128-129
    booterd, 130
    editing, 137
    init, 129-134
    rc scripts, 130-131
    runlevels, 134
SCSI (Small Computer System Interface)
    chains, 217-218
    changer device driver, 336
    devices, 217, 340-341
        active/passive terminators, 222-223
        benefits, 217
        cabling requirements, 221-222

        controller selection, 218-219
        IDs, 222-223
        naming, 223-225
        SCSI chains, 217-218
        supported, 219-221
        technologies/capabilities, 218
        terminating, 222-223
    kernel support, 1115
/scsi directory, 1076
search directive, 401
search-and-replace, 30-31
secure option (/etc/exports file), 422
Secure Shell service. *See* SSH
securing
    DNS, 770
    filesystems, 770-772
    finger command, 769
    LILO, 768
    sendmail, 770
security. *See also* access; firewalls
    admin tx, 820
        command replacements, 830-831
        operator menu implementation example, 826-827
        operator menu script example, 822-826
        security scanners, 829-830
        sudo command, 820-829
        sudoers file example, 828-829
        tool resources, 832-833
        tools, finding, 832
    aliases (mail), 587
    altered system files, checking, 774
    anonymous FTP, 769
    Apache, 653-654

breaches, 842
  action plan, 842
  backups, 856
  cleaning up, 854-855
  evidence, 843-844
  extent, 844
  indicators, 843-844
  intrusion detection tools,
    846-848
  reinstallation (media),
    856-857
  remain calm, 842
  system log analysis,
    845-846
  Trinux, 848-854
  when to start from
    scratch, 855-856
  written records, 843
CERT, 774
determining security needs,
  740-741
FTP, 621-631
kernel hacking, 1125
log files, checking, 772-773
mailing lists, 590
maintenance policies, 777
monitoring, 772
network interfaces, 773
NFS, 420
physical, 767
  disabling floppy drive
    booting, 767
  LILO settings, 767-768
policies, 775-776
privileges
  granting, 820-829
  operator menu imple-
    mentation example,
    826-827
  operator menu script
    example, 822-826
R-commands, 547-548
reaction policies, 777

resources, 836
  mailing lists, 837-839
  Usenet newsgroups,
    836-837
security scanners, 829-830
security shared accounts, 863
servers, 743
setgid files, 773
setuid files, 773
setup policies, 776
software, updating, 775
SSH
  benefits, 548
  connection process, 549
  downloading, 551
  encryption, 548
  installing, 551
  international packages,
    551
  RSA authentication, 549
  setting secure password-
    free access, 549-550
  U.S. packages, 551
system
  /etc directory, 750-760
  /etc/security directory,
    761-762
system attacks, 742
system crackers, 358
system policies, 777-778
TCP-Wrappers, 534
  access-control rules,
    536-537
  configuration language
    extensions, 537
  configuring, 536-537
  /etc/hosts.allow files, 535
  /etc/hosts.deny files, 535
  logging, 535
  process, 534
  testing, 538
Telnet, 542, 547-548, 769
trust-based authentication
  (R-commands), 544-545
/var/spool/atjobs files, 773

/var/spool/cron files, 773
Web resources, 834-835
Security Administrator's
Integrated Network Tool
(SAINT), 851
Security Analysis Tool for
Analyzing Networks
(SATAN), 829
sed command, 30-31
selecting
  backup media, 334-335
  backup site strategies, 313
  default shells, 927
  Ethernet media, 380-381
  help desk personnel, 905
  Internet services, 530-531
  kernel configuration options,
    1102
  APM (Advanced Power
    Management) support,
    1108
  binary support,
    1106-1107
  block devices, 1108-1110
  BSD processes account-
    ing support, 1105
  CD-ROM drives (created
    before 1994) support,
    1117
  character devices
    support, 1118-1119
  code maturity level,
    1102-1103
  console drivers,
    1123-1124
  doubletalk speech
    synthesizer, 1120
  filesystems, 1120-1121
  floppy tape device
    drivers, 1120
  hacking, 1125
  ISDN support, 1117
  joysticks, 1120
  loading, 1126
  loopback devices, 1111
  mice support, 1119

module support, 1105
native languages, 1123
network block devices, 1111
network devices support, 1115-1117
network filesystems, 1121, 1123
networking support, 1105
NVRAM devices support, 1119
parallel port IDE devices, 1111
parallel port support, 1107-1108
parallel printer support, 1119
partitions, 1123
plug-and-play support, 1108
processor types, 1103-1104
real-time clock support, 1119
saving, 1126
SCSI support, 1115
serial port support, 1118
software RAID, 1111
sound, 1124
sysctl support, 1105-1106
System V Interprocess Communications support, 1105
terminal support, 1118
video4linux, 1120
watchdog timer devices support, 1119
kernel networking options, 1111-1112
IP aliasing, 1113
IP masquerading, 1113
IP tunneling, 1113
IPX/Appletalk protocols, 1114-1115
TCP/IP packet-based firewalls, 1113

TCP/IP protocol stack, 1115
WAN routers, 1114
MTA, 558-559
scripting interpreters, 970-971
SCSI controller, 218-219
shells, 927-928
tape backups, 334-337
4mm DDS, 337
8mm, 338
8mm/AITs (Advanced Intelligent Tapes), 339
DLTs (Digital Linear Tapes), 338-339
variable values, 960
/self directory, 1076
sendmail, 558-559
configuring
central mail server, 562-563
LAN workstation, 562
standalone computer with dial-up connection, 561
standalone computer with permanent Internet connection, 560
features/options, 559-560
m4 macros, 559
multiple domains, 563-564
securing, 770
testing, 565
virtual user tables, 564-565
Web site, 560
sendmail spam Web site, 557
sendmail.cf file, 760
sequence numbers, 374
serial devices.
parallel port combination networking, 1116
serial ports, 1118
Server-Side Includes. See SSI
ServerAdmin directive, 643
ServerAlias directive, 660-662

ServerName directive, 643
ServerRoot directive, 644
servers
Apache. *See* Apache
backup domain controller (BDC), 463
caching-only servers, 400
finding on networks, 497
FTP, file downloads, 1162-1163
inetd
chargen, 533
daytime, 533
discard, 533
echo, 533
/etc/inetd.conf files, 532-534
process, 531
time, 533
Linux NetWare, 498-512
automatically mapping NetWare/Linux usernames, 510-511
DOS client password handling, 505-506
IPX device configuration, 502, 504
IPX route flags, 504-505
network number configuration, 501-502
non-privileged user/group IDs, 506-507
printer configuration, 511-512
servername configuration, 500-501
startup sanity checks, 511
supervisor login, 507, 509
user logins, 509-510
version spoofing, 505
volume configuration, 499-500
mars-nwe, 512-513
master servers, 400
musical servers, 1053

name servers, 397
  BIND configuration,
    402-405
  categories, 400
  development history,
    397-398
  DNS. See DNS
  NIS (Network Information
    Service), 405-408
  resolver libraries,
    400-401
  UNIX/Linux systems,
    399-405
names, configuring, 500-501
netatalk, starting, 525
network numbers, retrieving,
  497
news. See Usenet servers
NFS, 418-424
passwords, 743
  cracking, preventing, 745
  cracking, preventing with
    PAM, 745-749
  /etc/group file, 745
  /etc/passwd file, 743
  /etc/shadow file, 744
  policies, 749
primary domain controller
  (PDC), 463
proxy. See proxy servers
resource servers, 463
root, DNS, 398
security, 743
slave servers, 400
thin, 70-74
Usenet, 672
  bandwidth, 673-674
  control messages, 675
  daily reports, 674-675
  Diablo, 676
  INN. See INN
  message id, 672
  NNTPCache, 676
  outsourcing, 675
  Path header, 672
  port redirection, 675

running, 674-675
server storage capacity,
  672-673
software, 676
Web. See Web servers
xinetd
  benefits, 538
  compiling, 539
  downloading, 538
  etc/xinetd.conf files,
    539-541

services
Appletalk
  afpd.conf file, 515-524
  AppleVolumes.default file,
    524
  configuring, 514-525
  netatalk configuration
    files, 515
  system files support,
    514-515
disabling, 534
enabling, 534
Internet, 530-531
nowait, 532
R-commands, 543
  authentication, 543-545
  /etc/hosts.equiv files,
    545-546
  rcp, 543
  rexec, 543
  .rhosts files, 545-547
  rlogin, 543-544
  rsh, 543
  security, 547-548
  X11 connections, 548
SSH
  benefits, 548
  connection process, 549
  downloading, 551
  encryption, 548
  installing, 551
  international packages,
    551
  RSA authentication, 549

setting secure password-
    free access, 549-550
  U.S. packages, 551
Telnet
  benefits, 541
  drawbacks, 542
  process, 542
  security, 547-548
  substitution codes, 542
  X11 connections, 548
  unrequired, performance
    tweaking, 1052
  wait, 532
**Session Message Block
(SMB), 462**
**session module-type, PAM,
746**
**set capacity (backups),
319-320**
set command
  bash, 940
  command prompt
    customizations, 962
  shells, 927
  tcsh, 956
  variable values, 960
setgid files, 773
**setting. *See also*
configuring**
  LILO, physical security,
    767-768
  policies
    documenting, 897
    exceptions, 897-898, 922
    intranet posting, 897
    reviewing/revising,
      898-899
    user management issues,
      896
  priorities
    help desks, 904-905
    WREQ help desk, 908
  quotas, 771-772
  SSH, secure password-free
    access, 549-550
  user request forms, 918-919

WREQ help desk, 908-914
  configuration, 910-911
  downloading WREQ code,
    909
  list configuration, 911-914
  unpacking WREQ
    distribution, 909-910
setuid files, 773
setup function
  cloning installs, 57-60
  required utilities, 60
setup policies, 776
sfdisk command, 61-64
  command-line options,
    184-185
  input fields, 183-184
  partitioning, 182-185
shadow passwords,
  encrypting, 744
SHARE process field
  (top utility), 1057
shares, accessing Samba,
  468
sharing, 410
  accounts, 863
  files (FTP), 610
    connection types, 611
    daemon execution modes,
      612
    inetd.conf file, 612
    legal issues, 621
    ProFTPD, 619-620
    RFCs, 611
    security, 621-631
    warez D00dz, 631-636
    wu-ftpd, 612-619
  filesystems, 204, 418
    AFS, 426-427
    Coda, 426-427
    /home filesystem, 420
    NFS client configuration,
      424-426
    NFS server configuration,
      418-424
    /usr/local filesystem,
      420-421

/home filesystem, 420
with Linux/UNIX hosts, 410
with other operating systems,
  410
printers, 411
  access, granting, 416
  local printer
    configuration, 411-416
  remote printer
    configuration, 416-417
shell programs
  /etc/passwd file, 866
  firewall startup script,
    807-809
shell scripting, 968-969
  bash (Bourne Again Shell), 972
    another file's contents,
      reading/executing, 990
    break command, 992-993
    built-in commands, 990
    case statement, 984-986
    command pathnames,
      995-996
    command-line parameters,
      parsing,
      999-1001
    comments, 972-973
    continue command,
      993-994
    control structures, 983
    data, reading/assigning
      variables, 997
    directory lists, 990-992
    dirs command, 990-991
    echo command, 994
    eval command, 995
    exec command, 995
    executing commands on
      signals, 996
    exit codes, 974
    exit command, 996
    exiting, 996
    external command
      executions, 995
    filenames, converting to
      lowercase, 1003-1004

    for statement, 983
    formatting before
      printing, 997-998
    functions, 1001-1003
    hash command, 995-996
    if statement, 986-988
    let command, 996
    loops, 992-994
    math expressions, 996
    option evaluations, 995
    pausing, 998
    popd command, 991-992
    printf command, 997-998
    printing, 994
    pushd command, 992
    read command, 997
    source command, 990
    specific words in files,
      finding, 1004-1005
    suspend command, 999
    suspend execution, 999
    syntax, 972-974
    text blocks, 973
    trap command, 996
    until statement, 989-990
    variables. See variables
    wait command, 998
    while statement, 988-989
  Bourne shells, 969
  C-Shell syntax, 969
  compiled programs, 970
  debugging, 1005-1006
  defined, 968
  importance, 968
  interpreted programs,
    969-970
  scripting interpreter, 970-971
  scripts
    executable, 971
    executing, 971
    standardizing, 972
shell scripts, 700
SHELL variable, 1035

shells, 926
  bash (Bourne Again Shell),
     22, 926-928
     advantages/
        disadvantages, 945
     aliases, 931-932
     built-in commands,
        939-940
     command prompt
        customizations, 944
     command-line comple-
        tion, 932
     command-line editing,
        936-937
     features, 929
     history list, 934-936
     input/output redirection,
        933-934
     interactive session
        startup, 940-941
     job control, 937-939
     non-interactive session
        startup, 941
     pipes, 932-933
     quoting, 942
     variables, 942-943
     wildcards, 929-931
  Bourne, 926, 969
  built-in commands, 927
  configuration files, 927
  default, selecting, 927
  differences between, 926-927
  filename substitution, 18, 22
     demonstration of, 22-24
     meta characters, 22
  globbing, 18, 22
     demonstration of, 22-24
     meta characters, 22
  interactive/non-interactive
     modes, 928
  logins, customizing, 891
  non-login interactive, 941
  Public Domain Korn,
     964-965
  selecting, 927-928
  tcsh, 22, 945

     advantages/disadvan-
        tages, 963
     aliases, 947-948
     built-in commands,
        955-956
     command automation,
        960
     command prompt
        customizations,
        962-963
     command-line comple-
        tion, 948-949
     features, 945-946
     history list, 951-952
     input/output redirection,
        950
     interactive sessions
        startup/shutdown,
        959-960
     job control, 952-955
     key bindings, 957-959
     pipes, 950
     spelling correction,
        949-950
     variables, 960-962
     wildcards, 946-947
  variables, 927
  zsh, 964
shift command, 1000
showmount command,
  424
shutdown command, 139
shutting down, 112, 137
  commands, 139
  Ctrl+Alt+Del key sequence,
     139
  runlevels, 138-139
  tcsh interactive sessions,
     959-960
Simple Mail Transfer
  Protocol. *See* SMTP
single disks, comparing to
  multiple disks, 174-175
single quotes ('), 942
Single, Large, and Expen-
  sive Disks (SLEDs), 228

single-user machine
  firewall example, 814
single-user systems, 1068
site policy, 300
sites (Web). *See* Web sites
SIZE process field
  (top utility), 1057
Slashdot, 41, 835
slave servers, 400
slave zones (BIND), 402
SLEDs (Single, Large, and
  Expensive Disks), 228
SLIP protocol, 1116
slist command, 497
smail, 559, 566
  configuration files, 567-568
  director files, 569-573
  router files, 573-575
     mail hub, 574-575
     workstation, 573-574
  running, 575
  transports file, 575
  transports/directors/routers,
     566-567
  workstation configuration,
     568-569
     LAN with masqueraded
        domain, 568
     mail hub, 568
     stand-alone workstation
        with visible host, 568
Small Computer System
  Interface. *See* SCSI
smart paths, 567
SMB (Session Message
  Block), 462, 1122
smbclient browsing
  interface, 462
smbclient program,
  465-469
smbfs, 470-471
smbmount utility, 466, 469
smbpasswd utility, 466
smbprint utility, 466
smbstatus utility, 466
smbtar utility, 466

smbumount utility, 466,
   469-470
SMC EliteSwitch ES/1, 444
SMC EliteSwitch ES/1 ATX,
   444
smp file, 1077
SMTP (Simple Mail Transfer
   Protocol), 555
smurf attacks, 448-449
snapshots (system), 857
sndconfig command, 36
sniffers, 444
   dangers of, 450-451
   protection against, 451
   tcpdump, 444-445
      command-line options,
         446-447
      demonstration, 448-449
      installing, 445-446
   uses for, 448-449
SOCK PACKET interface, 438
sockd.conf file, 796
sockd.route file, 797
sockets
   dgram, 532
   /etc/inetd.conf files, 532
   raw, 532
   stream, 532
SOCKS, 795
   configuring, 795-798
   FTP site, 791
socks.conf file, 797
soft limits (quotas), 206
soft option, NFS mounting,
   425
software. *See also* tools
   administrative network install
      templates, 75
   dedicated backup, 327
      compatibility, 329
      evaluation example,
         329-330
      evaluations, 328-329
      kdat program, 330
      obtainability, 329
      open source, 328

proprietary, 328
reliability, 328
destructive
   data loss scenario, 355
   preventing, 355-356
NFS related, installing,
   418-419
production network install
   template packages, 70-74
security, updating, 775
Usenet servers, 676
virus scanning, 355-356
software integrity
   checkers, 356
Software Publishers Asso-
   ciation (SPA), 634-635
software RAID. *See* RAID
   (Redundant Array of
   Inexpensive Disks)
Son (media groups), 319
sound, kernel support for,
   1124
sound cards, 718
source code (kernel). *See
   also* listings
   compiling reasons,
      1082-1083
   configuration dialog boxes,
      1091
   default location, 1101
   device drivers, 1089
   filesystems, 1090
   finding, 1084-1085, 1087
   header files, 1090
   IBCS support, 1090
   layout, 1089-1091
   modules, 1090
   network protocol stack, 1091
   Red Hat, 1087-1089
source command, 956, 990
source INN installation,
   678-679
Source Quench Introduced
   Delay. *See* Squid
source RPM, installing, 235

SPA (Software Publishers
   Association), 634-635
space allocation
   (filesystems), 196
space management
   (filesystems), 198
   local/shared filesystems, 204
   quotas, 205-206
      hard/soft limits, 206
      implementing, 206-208
      option examples, 208-209
   space usage, monitoring,
      199-204
spam, 557-558
   exim protection, 578-579
   filtering, INN, 701
   Web sites, 558, 607
spamhippo (spam filter), 701
Speak Freely, 734-735
special bash variables,
   977-978
special characters
   (command prompt)
   bash, 944
   tcsh, 963
speech synthesizers, 1120
speed=# command-line
   option (cdrecord com-
   mand), 281
spelling correction (tcsh),
   949-950
spools, 582
spuinfo file, 1076
square brackets ([]),
   929-930
Squid (Source Quench Introduced Delay), 665, 798
   accounts, 800
   command-line options, 666
   configuration file, 799
   configuring, 666-667
   FTP site, 791
   groups, 800
   installing, 798-799
   starting, 666

Squid Web site, 798
squid.conf file, 666
SRPM, installing, 235
SSH (Secure Shell service), 548, 831
benefits, 548
connection process, 549
downloading, 551
encryption, 548
full backups to remote machines, 307-308
installing, 551
international packages, 551
RSA authentication, 549
setting secure password-free access, 549-550
U.S. packages, 551
Web site, 307, 769
SSI (Server-Side Includes), 651-652
SSL Telnet Web site, 769
standalone services, 795
standards
File System Standard (FSSTND), 82
Filesystem Hierarchy Standard, 82-89
Internet telephony, 717
starting
Apache, 640-641
automount daemon, 429-430
bash interactive session, 940-941
bash non-interactive session, 941
CD-ROM Red Hat installs, 51
commands, background, 937, 952
cron jobs, 1031-1032
INN, 700
ircII, 724
linuxconf, 876
mars-nwe server, 512-513
netatalk server, 525
rescue sessions, 154

Squid, 666
tcsh interactive sessions, 959-960
top utility, 1055
Xload, 1063
Xosview, 1062
startup
boot loaders, 112
bootactv, 128
CHOS, 128
GRUB, 128
LILO (LInux LOader), 113-127
LOADLIN, 127
operation of, 112-113
SYSLINUX, 128
System Commander Deluxe, 128
hard drive, 112
boot sector, 112
master boot record (MBR), 112-113
partitions, 112
hardware problem identification, 144-145
messages, viewing, 144
from RAID devices, 265-266
sanity checks, 511
system initialization scripts, 112, 128-129
booterd, 130
editing, 137
init, 129-134
rc scripts, 130-131
runlevels, 134
UPS, 132
stat file, 1077
STATE process field (top utility), 1057
statements (bash)
case, 984-986
for, 983
if, 986-988
until, 989-990
while, 988-989

static host table, 398
static routes, 384
adding, 387-389
deleting, 387-388
Statistics option (WREQ help desk), 908
status timer parameter (inn.conf file), 687
status variable, 961
stop command, 955
stopping
Apache, 640
jobs, 955
storage
article formats, 680-681
article information, 695
Fibre Channel, 225
IDE devices, 212
filenames for IDE partitions, 213
interface, 212-214
names, 212-214
SCSI devices, 217
benefits, 217
cabling, 221-222
controller selection, 218-219
IDs, 222-223
naming, 223-225
SCSI chains, 217-218
supported, 219-221
terminating, 222-223
Ultra3 SCSI standard, 225
Ultra160/m, 225
Usenet server capacity
bandwidth, 673-674
servers, 672-673
storage.conf file, 693-695
storageapi parameter (inn.conf file), 687
storing
backup media, 341
multiple copies, 342
offsite, 342

onsite, *341*

tape escrow services,
342-343

incremental backups, 319

strategies (backup), 305-306

full backups, 306-307

disadvantages, 308

remote machines, 307-308

partial backups, 309

site, selecting, 313

stream sockets, 532

string operator, 981

**string test operators
(expressions), 981**

**string1 != string2
operator, 981**

**string1 string1 > string2
operator, 981**

**string1 = string2
operator, 981**

**string1 == string2
operator, 981**

striping, 233-234

Stronghold, 668

stub zones (BIND), 403

su command, 892

subnetting, 377

sudo command, 820-829

command-line options, 821

operator menu implementation
example, 826-827

operator menu script example,
822-826

Web site, 820

sudoers file, 820, 828-829

**sufficient control-flag para-
meters, 746**

**Sun Microsystems, etherfind
utility, 445**

supernetting, 377

suspend command, 955, 999

**suspend execution
(bash scripts), 999**

**suspending, jobs, 937,
953-955**

SVGA_ MODE variable, 1127

**-swab command-line option
(cdrecord
command), 282**

swap files, 1074-1075

**Swap monitor field
(top utility), 1056**

swap partitions, 1075

**swap section (vmstat
utility), 1059**

swap space, 1071

assigning, 1072-1074

calculating, 1071-1072

prioritization, 1073

swap files, 1074-1075

swap partitions, 1073-1075

**swapoff command,
1072-1074**

**swapon command,
1072-1074**

**SWAT (Samba Web Admin-
istration Tool), 471-472,
476**

Centennial School District case
study, 1151

Globals screen, 472

home screen, 472

Password screen, 473

Printers screen, 473

Shares screen, 473

Status screen, 473

View screen, 473

Swatch, 845

system log watcher, 360

Web site, 360

switched hubs, 443

switched networking, 451

**SymLinksIfOwnerMatch
parameter (Options
directive), 645**

SYN floods, 448

**Synack Corporation
Web site, 538**

**-sync option (mount
command), 195**

/sys directory, 1077

**sysadmin (system adminis-
tration) time, data
recovery costs, 363**

sysctl, 1105-1106

SYSLINUX, 128

SysRQ interrupt keys, 1125

system administrators

duties and responsibilities, 13

*hardware and software
maintenance, 14*

*network administration,
14-15*

user management, 13

job descriptions, 9-11

required background and skills,
11-12

roles of, 8

SAGE, 9-11

salaries, 8-9

systems binaries, /sbin
directory, 86-87

system attacks, 742

**System Commander Deluxe,
128**

system crackers

data loss, preventing, 358

data loss scenario, 357

system access, preventing, 358

**system downtime, data
recovery costs, 363-364**

system failures, 142

diagnostic tools, 147

*DOS diagnostics,
151-152*

ifconfig utility, 149-150

isapnp program, 148-149

*NIC diagnostic programs,
150-151*

proc filesystem, 147-148

hardware errors, 144

BIOS errors, 145

*identifying at startup,
144-145*

last change syndrome, 145

PCI devices, 146-147

PnP devices, 145-146

kernel errors, 163-164
    decoding, 165-168
    kernel oops, 163-164
    system.map file, 168-169
kernel oops, 142, 163-164
kernel panic, 143
newsgroup resources, 169
rescue disks, 152-153
    creating, 153-154
    emergency file copying,
        157-159
    image, 153
    rebuilding LILO, 155-156
    recovering deleted files,
        160
    repairing partitions,
        156-157
    rescue sessions, 154
    rewriting configuration
        files, 156
    toolkit, 155
resources, 169
system log analysis, 160-163
system initialization
scripts, 112, 128-129
    booterd, 130
    editing, 137
    init, 129-134
    rc scripts, 130-131
    runlevels, 134
system log watchers, 360
system logs
    analysis, 160-161
    analyzing after security
        breaches, 845-846
    message interpretation,
        161-163
system packages,
    upgrading, 196-197
system policies
    compliance, enforcing, 778
    infractions, 779
    security, 777-778
system processes, viewing,
    1018-1019

system security.
    See security
System V Interprocess
    Communications, 1105
system.map file, 168-169
Systems Administration
    Guild (SAGE), 9-11
systems administrators
    duties and responsibilities, 13
        hardware and software
            maintenance, 14
        network administration,
            14-15
        user management, 13
    job descriptions, 9-11
    required background and
        skills, 11-12
    roles of, 8
    SAGE, 9-11
    salaries, 8-9
    systems binaries, 86-87

T

\t
    character (command prompt),
        944
    escape sequence, 958, 994
%t character (command
    prompt), 963
-T command-line option
    fsck utility, 188
    httpd script, 641
    mkisofs command, 275
-t option
    edquota command, 208
    free utility, 1061
    taper program, 329
-T –list-types command-
    line option (sfdisk
    utility), 184
-t filename operator, 980

-t fstype command-line
    option
    fsck utility, 189
    mkfs utility, 187
-t vfstype command-line
    option (mount
    command), 194
tables, routing, 385
    sample, 388
    viewing, 385-386
tape backups
    4mm DDS (Digital Data
        Storage), 337
    8mm/AITs (Advanced
        Intelligent Tapes), 338-339
    ATAPI (AT Attachment
        Packet Interface) drives,
        340
    autoloaders, 335-336
    data, recovering, 360
    data loss, preventing, 360
    DLTs (Digital Linear Tapes),
        338-339
    floppy tape drives, 339-340
    information resources, 334
    SCSI (Small Computer
        System Interface) drives,
        340-341
    selecting, 334-337
tape drives, 304
tape escrow services,
    342-343
taper program
    backup software evaluation
        example, 329-330
    Web site, 329
tar command
    backups, 323-324
    full backups, 307
    personal backup scripts, 353
    operating system backups,
        311
targets, ipchains utility,
    813
task-oriented files, backing
    up, 302

tasks
automating, 1019-1020. *See also* cron jobs
   atq utility, 1028
   atrm utility, 1028
   atrun utility, 1028-1029
   batch utility, 1027
command names, 1057
daily maintenance, 700
one-time, automating. *See* at utility
regular, automating, 1020-1021
scheduled, 880
Tcl/Tk (Tool Command Language), 1010-1011
tcl/tk Web site, 725
TCP (Transmission Control Protocol), 374
TCP SYN cookies, 1114
tcp wrappers
   Centennial School District case study, 1161-1162
   inetd.conf file, 754-755
TCP-Wrappers (tcpd), 534
   access-control rules, 536-537
   configuration language extensions, 537
   configuring, 536-537
   /etc/hosts.allow files, 535
   /etc/hosts.deny files, 535
   logging, 535
   process, 534
   testing, 538
TCP/IP
   Ethernet interface
     adding, 382-383
     kernel-level configuration, 382-383
     software-level configuration, 383
   IP addresses, 375
     address classes, 375-376
     classless, 376-377
     subnetting, 377
     supernetting, 377
     writing, 377

name servers, 397
   BIND configuration, 402-405
   categories, 400
   development history, 397-398
   DNS (Domain Name Service). See DNS
   NIS (Network Information Service), 405-408
   resolver libraries, 400-401
   UNIX/Linux systems, 399-405
network layers, 373
   Application Layer, 375
   data unit names, 373
   Internet Layer, 373-374
   Network Access Layer, 373
   Transport Layer, 374-375
packet-based firewalls, 1113
routing, 383-384
   configuring, 384
   daemons, 392-394
   dynamic. See dynamic routing
   external protocols, 390
   gated daemon, 394-397
   gateways, 384
   interior protocols, 390
   protocols, 390-392
   routed daemon, 392-394
   routing tables, 385-386
   static routes, 387-389
running over Ethernet, 377
   Ethernet cards/cables, 378
   Ethernet collision examination, 380
   Ethernet hubs, 379
   Ethernet media selections, 380-381
   Ethernet switches, 379-380
tcpd. See TCP-Wrappers
tcpdchk program, 538, 757
tcpdmatch program, 538

tcpdump sniffer, 444-445, 850
   command-line options, 446-447
   demonstration, 448-449
   installing, 445-446
tcpmatch program, 757
tcsh, 945
   advantages/disadvantages, 963
   aliases, 947-948
   built-in commands, 955-956
   command automation, 960
   command prompt customizations, 962-963
   command-line completion, 948-949
   features, 945-946
   globbing, 22
   history list, 951-952
   input/output redirection, 950
   interactive sessions startup/ shutdown, 959-960
   job control, 952-955
     % command, 954
     jobs running (list of), 953-954
     killing jobs, 954
     moving jobs to background, 953
     moving jobs to foreground, 953
     notify command, 955
     starting commands in background, 952
     stopping jobs, 955
     suspending jobs, 953-955
     waiting for all background jobs to finish, 955
   key bindings, 957-959
     control characters, 957
     default, 958-959
     escape sequences, 958
     listing of, viewing, 957
   pipes, 950
   spelling correction, 949-950

variables, 960-962
wildcards, 946-947
technical support, Linuxcare, 39
telephone-to-telephone communications, 734
Telnet
benefits, 541
drawbacks, 542
OpenSSH, 769
process, 542
security, 547-548, 769
SSH, 769
SSL, 769
substitution codes, 542
X11 connections, 548
telnet proxies, 803-804
templates
install, 69
administrative network templates, 75-76
creating directory hierarchies, 77-79
implementation plans, 77-79
production network templates, 69-74, 77
user request forms, 918-919
temporary files, cleaning up automatically, 1020
term variable, 962
terminals, 1118
test systems, 1051
test utility, 978-979
testing
expression values, 978-979
local printer configuration, 414
network performance, 1067
sendmail, 565
TCP-Wrappers, 538
text blocks, 973
text editors, 312
text news readers, 705-707
textonly.cfg file, 415
thin servers, 70-74

three-way handshake, 374
throughput function, 759
thttpd (tiny/turbo/throttling HTTP daemon), 669
time
access, restricting, 779
at utility specifications, 1023-1024
inetd, 533
real-time clocks, 1119
TIME option (at utility), 1023
TIME process field (top utility), 1057
Time To Live (TTL), 719
time utility, 1061-1062
time.conf file, 762
timeconfig command, 36
timehash article storage
INN, 680
newsfeeds file configuration, 690
overview.ctl file, 695
storage.conf file, 693-695
tin news reader, 706-707
tinyproxy utility, 853
TIS FWTK (Trusted Information Systems FireWall ToolKit), 800
configuring, 801-802
downloading, 801
FTP site, 791
inetd.conf with proxy example, 803-804
telnet proxy, 803-804
uncompressing, 801
tk/tcl Web site, 725
-toc command-line option (cdrecord command), 281
tokens (password), customizing, 892
tomsrtbt tool, 158
Tool command Language (Tcl/Tk), 1010-1011

tools. *See also* **command-line utilities**
authconfig, 36
control-panel, 31, 33
COPS (Computer Oracle and Password System), 829
diagnostic. *See* diagnostic tools
group management
groupadd script, 884
groupdel command, 884
groupmod command, 885
grpck command, 885
GUI, 312, 886-887
intrusion detection, 846
filesystem scanners, 846
who/top/ls/ps commands, 847-848
ISS (Internet Security Scanner), 830
kbdconfig, 36
Linuxconf, 31-33
mouseconfig, 36
multimedia conferencing, 733-734
CU-SeeMe, 736
MeetingPoint, 736
QSeeMe, 735-736
Speak Freely, 734-735
Web site, 734
pfdisk package, 128
process status tools, 98-99
programming
CVS (Concurrent Versions System), 1015-1016
make, 1014-1015
RCS (Revision Control System), 1015
quotas, 205
rescue disk toolkit, 155
sa toolbox, 820

command replacements,
  830-831
operator menu implemen-
  tation example, 826-827
operator menu script
  example, 822, 824-826
security scanners, 829-830
sudo command, 820-829
sudoers file example,
  828-829
tool resources, 832-833
tools, finding, 832
Samba, 465-466
  Samba Web Administration
    Tool (SWAT), 471
  smbclient, 466-469
  smbmount, 469
  smbumount, 469-470
SATAN (Security Analysis
  Tool for Analyzing
  Networks), 829
security
  finding, 832
  resources, 832-833
sniffers
  dangers of, 450-451
  protection against, 451
  tcpdump, 444-449
  uses for, 448-449
traffic analyzers, 451-458
Trinux, 848-849
  firewalls/proxies, 853
  network mapping/vulner-
    ability scanning, 851-853
  network monitors, 850-851
  packet sniffers, 849-850
  Web site, 848
top utility, 98
command-line options, 1058
interactive commands,
  1057-1058
intrusion detection, 847-848
monitor fields, 1056
performance monitoring,
  1055-1058

process fields, 1056-1057
starting, 1055
Torvalds, Linus, 1084
**TOS (Type of Service) fields,
816**
tracking files, 351-352
traditional article storage
INN, 680
newsfeeds file configuration,
  690
traffic analyzers, ntop, 451
  command-line options,
    453-454
  demonstration, 457-458
  execution modes, 454
  installing, 452-453
  traffic views, 456-458
training users, 901
enjoyment level, 901
overly independent users,
  920-921
systems orientation guides, 902
training libraries, 901
training resources, 39
users who resist training,
  919-920
transfer rates, 335
TransferLog directive, 647
**Transmission Control
  Protocol (TCP), 374**
Transport Layer, 374-375
transports (email), 566
transports file, 575
transproxy, 793
FTP site, 791
installing, 794-795
standalone service
  configuration, 795
trap command, 996
Trinux, 848-849
firewalls/proxies, 853
hunt utility, 854
netcat utility, 854
network mapping/vulnerability
  scanning, 851-853
network monitors, 850-851

packet sniffers, 849-850
Web site, 848
Tripwire, 356, 846
trn news reader, 705-706
trojan horses, 354
**troubleshooting. *See also*
debugging; errors**
Apache, 648
backups, 327
cronjobs, 1040
  echo command,
    1040-1041
  log files, 1042
  output, redirecting, 1040
  printf command,
    1040-1041
hardware errors, 144
**trust-based authentication,
544-545**
trusted hosts, 545
**Trusted Information
  Systems FireWall ToolKit.
  See TIS FWTK**
**TTL (Time To Live), packets,
719**
tulip-diag utility, 150
tuning performance, 1048
bottlenecks, 1049-1052
costs/benefits, weighing,
  1052-1053
enhancements, 1054
general areas, 1049
hardware costs, 1053
IDE drives, 1110
kernel, 1075-1078
system requirements/needs,
  1053-1054
unrequired services, 1052
**TurboPacket interface,
438-440**
**tweaking kernel makefile,
1126-1127**
twist command, 756
**Type of Service (TOS) fields,
816**

type=(something)
argument (pam_ cracklib
module), 748

U

-u option (usermod
command), 893
\u character (command
prompt), 944
-u option
  edquota command, 208
  exportfs command, 423
  fdisk utility, 178
  passwd command, 892
  user management, 1160
-u directory option
  (amq utility), 430
-u filename operator, 980
-u port command-line
  option (Squid), 666
-u UID option (useradd
  command), 874
-u username/#uid
  command-line option
  (sudo command), 821
-U uuid command-line
  option (mount
  command), 194
%U...%u character
  (command prompt), 963
U.S. Department of
  Defense Advanced
  Research Projects Agency
  (ARPA), 372
-uB command-line option
  (sfdisk utility), 184
-uC command-line option
  (sfdisk utility), 184
ucredit=n argument
  (pam_ cracklib module),
  748
UDF filesystem, 1121

UDF/DVD peripherals
  drivers Web site, 1121
UDP (User Datagram
  Protocol), 374
UID parameter (/etc/
  passwd file), 865
Ultra3 SCSI standard, 225
Ultra160/m storage, 225
-uM command-line option
  (sfdisk utility), 184
umask command
  bash, 940
  tcsh, 956
unalias command, 931, 948
uncompressing TIS FWTK,
  801
uninterruptible power
  supply (UPS), 132
UNIX
  commands
    awk, 29-30
    find, 25-29
    Perl, 30
    regular expressions,
      18-21
    sed, 30-31
  name services, 399-405
  resolver libraries, 400-401
unmoderated mailing lists,
  589
unmount command, 195
unofficial kernel paths,
  1092-1093
unpacking WREQ
  distribution, 909-910
unrequired services,
  performance tweaking,
  1052
unset command
  bash, 940
  bash variables, 975-976
  tcsh, 956
Unsolicited Commercial
  Email (UCE). *See* spam
untaring, TIS FWTK, 801
until statements, 989-990

up monitor field (top
  utility), 1056
up-history command, 959
upcase-word command,
  958
updating
  newsgroups automatically,
    1020
  password files in batch mode,
    881
  software, security, 775
upgrading
  kernel, 1083
  system packages, 196-197
upload function, 759
UPS, 132
uptime, 98, 1060, 1076
-uS command-line option
  (sfdisk utility), 184
useccntrolchan parameter
  (inn.conf file), 688
Usenet newsgroups,
  836-837
Usenet servers, 672
  bandwidth, 673-674
  control messages, 675
  daily reports, 674-675
  Diablo, 676, 701-704
  INN. *See* INN
  message-id, 672
  news readers, 705
    alternatives, 711
    graphical clients,
      707-710
    text clients, 705-707
  NNTPCache, 676
  outsourcing, 675
  Path header, 672
  port redirection, 675
  resources, 711
  running, 674-675
  server storage capacity,
    672-673
  software, 676

USENIX
SAGE, 9-11
Web site, 9, 834
user accounts, disabling, 779
User Datagram Protocol
(UDP), 374
user errors
aliases, 350-351
backups, 353
data loss scenario, 347
preventing, 349
revision control systems,
351-352
user files, backing up, 301
user ids
non-privileged users, NetWare,
506-507
qmail, 576
-user option
mount command, 195
mounting removable media
devices, 293
USER process field
(top utility), 1056
user variable, 962
useradd command, 874-875
userdel command, 883
userids, 865
/etc/passwd file, 865
/etc/shadow file, 867
usermod command, 882,
892-893
username named, 770
usernames
/etc/inetd.conf files, 533
NetWare/Linux, automatically
mapping, 510-511
users
accounts
archiving, 878
Centennial School District
case study, 1159-1161
customizations in batch
mode, 881
deleting, 882-883
disabling, 882

adding manually, 870
batch mode, 881
default configuration files,
copying, 871
/etc/group file, 870
/etc/gshadow file, 871
/etc/passwd file, 871
/etc/shadow file, 871
ownerships, 871-872
passwords, 873
user home directories, 871
adding with command-line
tools, 873
linuxconf, 875-881
useradd command,
874-875
adding/deleting from groups,
891
commands
chage, 888
chfn, 889
chgrp, 889-890
chown, 890
chsh, 891
gpasswd, 891
groups, 891
passwd, 892
su, 892
usermod, 892-893
cron specifications, 1038
deleting, 878
device access, limiting, 780
disk quotas, 880
email aliases, 880
/etc/skel directory, 869
external, access, 530
filesystem spaces, limiting, 780
home directories, 866, 871
information, viewing, 889
internal, access, 530
managing, 918
attitude issues, 896
Centennial School District
case study, 1159
documenting policies, 897
favoritism, 896

intranet policy posting, 897
overly independent users,
920-921
policy exceptions,
897-898, 922
policy review/revision,
898-899
setting policies, 896
user questions, 921
users who resist training,
919-920
NetWare logins, 509-510
non-privileged, 506-507
passwords
/etc/passwd file, 865
/etc/shadow file, 867
setting, 873
permissions, 862, 878
program access, limiting,
780-781
request management
email strategy, 900
help desks. See help desks
open door strategy, 899
planning user management
approach,
902-903
scheduled user request
times, 900-901
setting request forms,
918-919
WREQ help desks, 914, 917
resources, limiting, 780
root, 349, 587
training, 901
enjoyment level, 901
systems orientation guides,
902
training libraries, 901
usertty file, 766
/usr directory
/usr/exim/configure directory,
577
/usr/lib/aliases directory, 586
/usr/local filesystem, sharing,
420-421

/usr/local/majordomo directory, 589

/usr/local/news directory, INN installation, 681

/usr/src/linux directory, 1089

  drivers subdirectory, 1089

  fs subdirectory, 1090

  ibcs subdirectory, 1090

  include subdirectory, 1090

  init/ipc/kernel/lib/mm subdirectories, 1090

  modules subdirectory, 1090

  net subdirectory, 1091

  scripts subdirectory, 1091

/usr/src/linux/arch directory, 1089

/usr/src/linux/Documentation/ rtc.txt directory, 1119

/usr/src/linux/drivers directory, 1089

/usr/src/linux/drivers/ block directory, 1110

/usr/src/linux/fs directory, 1090

/usr/src/linux/ibcs directory, 1090

/usr/src/linux/include directory, 1090

/usr/src/linux/init directory, 1090

/usr/src/linux/ipc directory, 1090

/usr/src/linux/kernel directory, 1090

/usr/src/linux/lib directory, 1090

/usr/src/linux/mm directory, 1090

/usr/src/linux/modules directory, 1090

/usr/src/linux/net directory, 1091

/usr/src/linux/scripts directory, 1091

utilities. *See* tools; command-line utilities

-u_ user option (crontab command), 1033-1034

V

\v escape sequence, 958, 994

-v –verify command-line option (sfdisk utility), 184

-v –version command-line option (sfdisk utility), 184

-v option

  bindkey command, 957

  cfdisk utility, 182

  cdrecord command, 281

  exportfs command, 423

  fdisk utility, 178

  fsck utility, 188

  httpd script, 641

  mkfs utility, 188

  mkisofs command, 275

  mount command, 194

  sendmail, 565

  Squid, 666

  sudo command, 821

  tcsh startup, 960

-V option

  at utility, 1022-1023

  atq utility, 1028

  atrm utility, 1028

  batch utility, 1027

  chgrp command, 890

  chown command, 890

  debugging scripts, 1005

  mkfs utility, 187

-V volid command-line option (mkisofs command), 275

V Communications, System Commander Deluxe, 128

/var directory

  /var/log, 160

  /var/log/messages, 160-161

  /var/qmail/control, 576

  /var/spool/mail/username, 556

variables

  ADIR, 429

  AMDOPTS, 429

  argv, 961

  autocorrectn, 950

  autologout, 960

  bash, 942-943, 974

    accessing, 976-977

    contents, printing, 943

    creating, 943, 974

    declaring, 975

    deleting, 975-976

    read only, 976

    special, 977-978

    values, 974

  color, 961

  CONFIG KMOD, 1096

  CONFIG MODULES, 1096

  CONFIG MODVERSIONS, 1096

  correct, 950

  CROSS_ COMPILE, 1126

  cwd, 961

  edit, 961

  EDITOR, 943

  environment, 1035

  EXTRAVERSION, 1126

  HISTFILE, 935

    bash, 943

    history lists, 951

    tcsh, 961

HISTFILESIZE, 943
history, 961
HISTSIZE
    bash, 943
    history lists, 934
HOME
    bash, 943
    cron daemon, 1035
    tcsh, 961
INSTALL_ MOD_PATH, 1126
INSTALL_ PATH, 1126
local, 1003
LOGNAME, 1035
mail, 960
MOUNTPTS, 429
nobeep, 961
noclobber, 961
noglob, 961
NORMAL_ VGA, 1127
OLDPWD, 943
PATH, 943
path contents, printing, 960
pathj, 961
precmd, 963
printexitvalue, 960
prompt, 961
prompt2, 961
prompt3, 961
PS1, 943
PS2, 943
PWD, 943
rmstar, 960
savehist, 951
SHELL, 1035
shells, 927
status, 961
SVGA_ MODE, 1127
tcsh, 960-962
term, 962
user, 962
values, selecting, 960
version, 961
verifying
    ISO9660 images, 282-284
    NFS kernel support, 424

-version option
    bash startup, 941
    cdrecord command, 281
version control system *See*
    CVS (Concurrent Versions
    System)
version file, 1076
version patches, 1092
version variable, 961
versions
    module utilities, 1098
    multiple kernel, 1127
        clone trees, 1128-1131
        generic kernel, 1127
    NetWare, spoofing, 505
victim hosts, 356
Video 4 Linux Web site, 718
video cameras, 718
video conferencing, 718, 734
video4linux, 1120
viewing
    aliases (list of), 932
    command history. See history
        lists
    cron job log files, 1042
    directories (list of), 990-991
    jobs running (list of),
        938-939, 953-954
    kernel patches applied to stan-
        dard source code tree, 1088
    key bindings list, 957
    routing tables, 385-386
    startup messages, 144
    system processes, 1018-1019
    user information, 889
virtual consoles, 1159
virtual hosts
    Apache configuration,
        657-662
    IP-based, 657-659
    name-based, 659-662
        NameVirtualHost
        directive, 659-660
        ServerAlias directive, 660-
        662

virtual user tables, 563-565
VirtualHost directive, 658
virus scanning software,
    355-356
viruses, 354
viruses newsgroup, 836
visudo command, 820
vmstat, 98, 1058-1060
volumes
    configuring, 499-500
    NetWare, mounting, 498
vulnerability scanning tools
    (Trinux), 851-853

W

\W character (command
    prompt), 944
%w character (command
    prompt), 963
-w command-line option
    mount command, 194
    Perl scripting, 1008
-W option (change
    command), 889
w file command
    (mail
    utility), 584
-w filename operator, 980
wait command, 955, 998
wait services, 532
WAN routers, 1114
warez D00dz, 631-636
warn_ days parameter
    (/etc/shadow file), 868
watchdog timer devices,
    1119
watchdog.txt file, 1119
Web interface (WREQ help
    desk), 906
Web servers, 638
    Apache, 638
        access, 642
        add-ons, 663-664

CGI scripting, 652-653
Comanche, 662
conditional directives,
  646-647
conditional directives
  based on modules, 655
configuration files,
  overriding, 642-643
configuring, 641
default modules, 655-657
development history,
  638-639
directives, 643-644
directory-based direc-
  tives, 644-645
error handling, 648-649
file-based directives, 646
installing, 640
IP-based virtual hosts,
  657-659
logging, 647-648
modules, 654-655
name-based virtual hosts,
  659-662
password protecting
  directories, 649-651
security, 653-654
SSI (Server-Side
  Includes), 651-652
starting, 640-641
stopping, 640
virtual hosts, 657-662
Boa, 668
Centennial School District
  case study, 1147
dhttpd, 669
fhttpd, 669
ghttpd, 669
IBM HTTP, 668
RAM requirements, 1069
Red Hat Secure, 668
Roxen Challenger, 667-669
Squid, 665-667
Stronghold, 668
WN, 670

Web sites
Academ wu-ftpd page, 618
AFS, 410, 426
Apache module registry, 657
Apache/Perl integration
  project, 664
Backup Central, 334
BitchX, 727
BitchX download, 728
Caldera, 513
CERT, 774
cgichk utility, 852
CIAC (Computer Incident
  Advisory Capability), 832
cleanfeed, 701
COAST, 832
Coda, 1122
Code, 426
Deja.com, 711, 837
Dents, 399
DFN-CERT, 833
dhttpd, 669
Donald Becker's Linux at
  CESDIS, 150
DVD/UDF peripherals
  drivers, 1121
e2fsprogs utilities, 160
Exabyte Corporation, 334
exscan utility, 851
fhttpd, 669
Filesystem Hierarchy
  Standard, 209
firewalk utility, 852
floppy driver utility
  programs, 1110
Freshmeat, 41, 56, 675, 835
Gated Consortium, 394
GD perl module download,
  908-909
GFS Project, 225
ghttpd, 669
High-Availability (RAID)
  HOWTO, 306
hping utility, 852
hunt utility, 854
ICQ, 714, 728-729

INN, 676
INN FAQ, 677
ipgrab packet sniffer, 850
IPTraf, 850
IRC information, 721
IRC server names/IP numbers
  lists, 723
ircII, 722
ISS, 830
Java Apache project, 664
Java status, 730
JavaICQ download, 730
JDK binaries, 730
JDK open source version,
  730
joysticks 2.2 kernel
  compatibility, 1120
Kent Landfield's wu-ftpd
  site, 618
Kernel Threads, 1094
kernel.org, 1084
Kernelnotes, 38, 1094
Keystone help desk
  downloading, 917
knews, 710
LDP, MTA information, 606
licq, 731
Linux, 41
Linux Applications and
  Utilities, 327
Linux Cross Reference
  package, 1091
Linux Documentation
  Project, 36
Linux Kernel Archives, 37
Linux Links, 327
Linux Portal, 835
Linux Today, 40, 835
Linux Weekly News, 835
linux-kernel mailing list
  FAQ, 169
Linux.com, 835
LinuxApps, YARD, 56
LinuxBerg, 327
Linuxcare, 39
LinuxHQ, 38

Loopback Encrypted
   Filesystem HOWTO, 1111
LPRng, 410
micq, 732
module utilities, 1098
MTA information, 606
mtx command, 336
multi-cast FAQ, 721
multimedia conferencing
   tools, 734
NASA sunspot activity, 300
netatalk, 513
Netscape, 710
news2mail, 711
ngrep, 850
NIST (National Institute of
   Standards and Technology),
   833
nmap utility, 851
NNTPCache, 676
NoCem, 701
Ntop, 851
OpenSSH, 769
OSS drivers, 1124
Packet Radio, 1116
Perl, 1010
PGP package, 678
PHP, 664
ProFTPD, 831
qmail, 577
QSeeMe, 736
Quota Mini-Howto, 209
quota tools, 205
Red Hat, 397, 775, 834
Red Hat Installation Guide, 186
Red Hat mailing list, 169
redir port redirector, 853
Rootshell, 833
Roxen Challenger, 668
SAINT, 851
Samba, 492
SATAN, 829
SCSI changer device
   driver, 336
sendmail, 560
sendmail spam, 557

Slashdot, 41, 835
Software Publishers
   Association, 635
spam lists, 558
spamhippo, 701
Speak Freely, 734-735
Squid, 798
ssh, 307
SSH Telnet, 769
SSL Telnet, 769
sudo command, 820
Swatch, 360
taper, 329
tcl/tk, 725
thttpd, 670
tin, 707
tinyproxy utility, 853
tomsrtbt tool, 158
Trinux, 848
TripWire, 356
USENIX, 9, 834
V Communications, 128
video conferencing, 734
video4linux, 718, 1120
White Pine Software, 736
Wireless Papers, 1116
WN Web server, 670
X-Chat, 726
xinetd downloads, 538, 831
xrn, 710
ZedZ Consultants, Inc., 551,
   832
Zircon, 725
**Web-based news services,
   711**
webmasters, 587
where command, 956
while statements, 988-989
**White Pine Software Web
   site, 736**
who command, 847-848
wildcards, 929
   *, 929-930, 946
   ?, 929-930, 946
   bash, 929-931

tcsh, 946-947
..., 930
Windows networks
   backup domain controller
      (BDC), 463
   browsing interface, 462
   clients, 464
   Common Internet File
      System (CIFS), 462
   domains, 462
   example of, 463-464
   integration with, 462
      Samba, 465-492
      smbfs, 470-471
   master browsers, 462-463
   primary domain
      controller (PDC), 463
   resource servers, 463
   Session Message Block (SMB),
      462
   workgroups, 462
Windows PCs
   accessing from Red Hat,
      1153-1154
   Red Hat access, 1152
   workstation configuration,
      1150
Wireless LAN, 1116
wireless networks, 1116
**Wireless Papers Web site,
   1116**
**–with-perl option (configure
   program), 679**
WN Web server, 670
workgroups, 462
**Workplace Shell browsing
   interface, 462**
workstations
   backup rotation schedule, 318
      files, restoring, 320-321
      *incremental backup
         storage, 319*
      rationale, 318
      set capacity, 319-320
   exim, 578
   sendmail, 562

smail, 568
   LAN with masqueraded
     domain, 568
   stand-alone with visible
     host, 568
World Wide Web (WWW),
531. *See also* Web
servers; Web sites
worms, 354
WREQ (help desk), 906
   adding user requests, 914,
     917
   email interface, 906-907
   escalation paths, 908
   feedback feature, 908
   prioritization, 908
   setting, 908-914
     configuration, 910-911
     downloading WREQ
      code, 909
     list configuration,
      911-914
   Statistics option, 908
   unpacking WREQ
     distribution, 909-910
   Web interface, 906
writable CD-ROMs, 321
writing
   IP addresses, 377
   ISO9660 images to disks,
     282-284
   network masks, 377
written policies, 897
wsize option, NFS
mounting, 425
wu-ftpd, 612, 831
   command-line options,
     613-614
   customization options,
     614-615
   ftpaccess file, 616-617
   installing, 613
   Internet resources, 618
   IP aliases, 615
   mailing list, 617-618

wuarchive-ftpd, 612
   anonymous FTP, 618-619
   command-line options,
     613-614
   customization options,
     614-615
   ftpaccess file, 616-617
   installing, 613
   Internet resources, 618
   IP aliases, 615
   mailing lists, 617-618
WWW (World Wide Web),
531. *See also* Web
servers; Web sites

X

-x option
   debugging scripts, 1005
   declare command, 975
   httpd script, 641
   Squid, 666
   tcsh startup, 960
-X option (ipchains utility),
811
-x –show-extended option
(sfdisk utility), 184
x command (mail utility),
584
-x filename operator, 980
X-Chat, 726-727
   download Web site, 726
   finding, 726
   installing, 727
   running, 727
   Web site, 726
X.25 protocol, 1114
X11 connections, 548
-xa2 command-line option
(cdrecord command), 282
-xal command-line option
(cdrecord command), 282
xfmail, 585
xia filesystem, 198
xinetd
   benefits, 538

   compiling, 539
   downloading, 538
   /etc/xinetd.conf files, 539-541
     access control, 540
     fields, 539-540
     logging, 541
xinetd package, 831
Xload utility, 1063
Xosview utility, 1062-1063
xrn news reader, 707

Y

%y character
(command prompt), 963
-Y command-line option
(Squid), 666
YARD (Yet Another Rescue
Disk), 56
YP (Yellow Pages). *See* NIS
ypbind package, 406

Z

-z option
   cfdisk utility, 182
   Squid, 666
-Z option (ipchains utility),
811
Z shell, 964
-z string operator, 981
ZedZ Consultants, Inc.
   FTP download site, 551
   Web site, 832
Zip drives, 287-288, 322
Zircon, 725
   finding, 725
   installing, 725
   running, 726
   Web site, 725
zones
   BIND, 402-403
   DNS RRs (Resource
     Records), 404-405
zsh, 964

Linux and UNIX Installation Instructions

These installation instructions assume that you have a passing familiarity with UNIX commands and the basic setup of your machine. As UNIX has many flavors, only generic commands are used. If you have any problems with the commands, please consult the appropriate man page or your system administrator.

Insert the CD-ROM in CD drive.

If you have a volume manager, mounting of the CD-ROM will be automatic. If you don't have a volume manager, you can mount the CD-ROM by typing

```
mount   -tiso9660   /dev/cdrom   /mnt/cdrom
```

NOTE: /mnt/cdrom is just a mount point, but it must exist when you issue the mount command. You may also use any empty directory for a mount point if you don't want to use /mnt/cdrom.

Navigate to the root directory of your CD-ROM. If your mount point matches the example listed above, type

```
cd  /mnt/cdrom
```

Open the file software.htm with your Web browser or kfm to find out what's on the CD-ROM.

WELCOME TO THE REVOLUTION

LINUX
MAGAZINE
THE CHRONICLE OF THE REVOLUTION

DON'T MISS AN ISSUE!

Linux Magazine is the monthly information source for the whole Linux community. Whether you are a system administrator developer, or simply a Linux enthusiast, *Linux Magazine* delivers the information and insight you need month after month.

Our feature stories, in-depth interviews, and reviews will help you navigate and thrive in the ever-changing world of Linux and Open Source Software. What does Microsoft really think of Linux? What's the best way to build a Linux machine from scratch? How can you integrate Linux into a Windows-based network? Whatever you are looking for, *Linux Magazine* is where you will find it.

With regular columns from such Open Source luminaries as Alan Cox, Paul 'Rusty' Russell, Randal Schwartz, and Larry Augustin you know you can't go wrong...

So don't miss an issue — Subscribe today to *Linux Magazine,* "The Chronicle of the Revolution."

Check out our website at www.linux-mag.com